英汉双解词典

Oxford
Elementary Learner's
English-Chinese
Dictionary

Third edition
第三版

英语原文版
编辑：Alison Waters

Victoria Bull

英汉双解版
翻译：高永伟
审订：黄勉之

商務印書館
THE COMMERCIAL PRESS

OXFORD
UNIVERSITY PRESS
牛津大学出版社

OXFORD
UNIVERSITY PRESS

牛津大学出版社隶属牛津大学，出版业务遍布全球，致力弘扬牛津大学推动优质研究、学术和教育的宗旨。

牛津　纽约
奥克兰　开普敦　达累斯萨拉姆　香港
卡拉奇　吉隆坡　马德里　墨尔本
墨西哥城　内罗毕　新德里　上海
台北　多伦多

OXFORD 是牛津大学出版社的商标
牛津初阶英汉双解词典（第三版）
英语原版 Oxford Essential Dictionary
© Oxford University Press 2006
英汉版（繁体字本）© Oxford University Press 2010
英汉版（简体字本）© Oxford University Press 2011

The Commercial Press has made some changes to the original work in order to make this edition more appropriate for Chinese readers.
商务印书馆对原书进行了个别修改，使其更符合中国读者的需要。

ISBN 978-7-100-07582-4（标准本）

请注意识别
此扉页用含有商务印书馆注册商标的特制防伪纸印制，有这种扉页的《牛津初阶英汉双解词典》（第三版）是正版图书。

出版：商务印书馆
　　　北京王府井大街36号
　　　（邮政编码100710）
　　　牛津大学出版社（中国）有限公司
　　　香港鲗鱼涌英皇道979号太古坊
　　　和域大厦东翼18楼

ACKNOWLEDGEMENTS

We would like to thank the following for their permission to reproduce photographs: Bananastock P4 (girl's face); Corel A–Z illustrations, P1 (ferry, helicopter, lorry, plane, ship, train), P2 (cow, budgie, cat, dog, donkey, goose, horse, parrot, peacock, sheep, turkey), P3 (elephant, jaguar, koala, lion, polar bear, rhinoceros, tiger), P6 (milk, milkshake, orange juice, water), P7 (chicken, pizza, beef, soup, stew), P8 (apple, bananas, grapes, orange), P9 (celery, lettuce, peppers), P14 (baseball, canoe, cricket, football, rugby, skating, surfing, swimming, windsurfing), P15 (cycling, judo, horse riding, snooker, snowboarding, working out); *Corbis* A–Z illustrations, P3 (bear), P15 (sunset); *Getty Images* A–Z illustrations, P1 (underground), P2 (chicken, hamster, guinea pigs, pig), P5 (leotard, shorts), P6 (biscuits, herbs, olives, salt and pepper), P7 (fast food, pasta), P8 (coconut, half-lemon, melon, pineapple, strawberry), P9 (beans, sprouts), P11 (classroom), P12 (doctor, farmer, judge, plumber, policeman, vet, waiter), P13 (all images), P14 (basketball, waterskiing), P15 (bowling, hiking, skateboarding, yoga), P16 (flood, fog, icicles); *Hemera Technologies Inc.* A–Z illustrations, P5 (pyjamas, skirt, suit), P6 (coffee, tea), P7 (cereal, ice cream, kebab, pancakes, quiche, salad, spaghetti), P8 (pear), P11 (bin, computer), P12 (dentist); *Ingram Publishing* A–Z illustrations, P3 (crocodile, giraffe, hippopotamus, leopard, wolf), P6 (cake), P7 (hotdog), P8 (plum), P9 (beetroot, cucumber), P11 (calculator); *iStockphoto.com* P6 (butter), P7 (fish, rice), P9 (garlic); *John Foxx* P6 (jam); *Peter Burgess* P11 (exercise book); *Punchstock* P12 (carpenter, chef, nurse, painter, teacher), P16 (wind); *Rubberball* P4 (boy, girl standing), P5 (dress); *Stockbyte* A–Z illustrations, P6 (cracker, doughnut, eggs, noodles, vinegar), P7 (curry, fish and chips), P8 (blackcurrants, dates, gooseberries), P9 (tomato).

Illustrations: Lorna Barnard, Jeremy Bays, David Burroughs, Martin Cox, Mark Dunn, David Eaton, Gay Galsworthy, Karen Hiscock, Margaret Jones, Richard Lewington, Martin Lonsdale/Hardlines, Vanessa Luff, Kevin Maddison, Martin Shovel, Technical Graphics Department OUP, Harry Venning, Graham White, Michael Woods.

Maps © Oxford University Press

印刷：中国
中国大陆地区总发行：商务印书馆
中国香港、澳门、台湾地区以及世界其他地区总发行：
牛津大学出版社（中国）有限公司

《牛津初阶英汉双解词典》

（第 3 版）

（简体汉字本）

出版说明

　　本词典与《牛津高阶英汉双解词典》和《牛津中阶英汉双解词典》构成了完整的英语学习词典系列。该词典系列问世以来，深受我国广大英语教师和学生的喜爱。

　　本词典收录的单词、短语和词义切合初学者水准，词义的解释通俗易懂，例句浅显生动并能充分显示词的典型用法，汉语译文贴切传神，特别适合初阶英语学习者的需要。

　　本词典在继承第二版优点的基础上，做了如下改动：增收词目 4 000 个，跟进英语发展的步伐；新增 120 余个发音框，提示读者注意容易读错的单词；同义词和反义词参见增至 1100 个，扩大了信息量；2 000 个核心词标注清晰，提示读者掌握最重要词汇；调整了插图和彩色插页，更有助读者理解词义；去掉了美式英语读音，更符合初学者需求；改为双色印刷，更便于读者查考。

　　现经牛津大学出版社惠允，我馆在内地出版发行该词典的简体汉字本。出版前，我们对原书进行了必要的编辑加工和技术处理，以便更适合内地读者的需要。疏漏错讹之处，敬望广大读者批评指正。

商务印书馆辞书研究中心

2011 年 6 月

Contents 目录

Study pages 研习专页

出版说明

1981 年，牛津大学出版社编订了查考便捷的 *Oxford Basic English Dictionary*（后易名 *Oxford Elementary Learner's Dictionary of Current English*），收录 10 000 个单词，对象为初学英语的非英语为母语人士，将深具时代意义的学习词典（Learner's Dictionary）推广至英语的初级学习者。1994 年重新修订，易名为 *Oxford Elementary Learner's Dictionary*，收词增至 15 000 条，并增加专项说明辨析难字，采用彩色插页介绍专题项目。

1988 年，本社据 *Oxford Elementary Learner's Dictionary of Current English* 翻译出版《牛津初阶英汉双解词典》。1997 年推出第二版；2000 年加入英语发音光碟；2004 年增修补编，收录逾千个新词，与时俱进。

2006 年，根据大量教学研究成果，并使用庞大的语料库搜集真实例子，牛津大学出版社推出了富革新意的 *Oxford Essential Dictionary* —— 按最新的语言发展趋势，增修新词，对原有条目去芜存菁，增设多项语法标签和说明，词条结构进一步跟随《高阶》和《中阶》词典。新版的书名改用 essential 一词，正好呼应推出初版时的目标：编订最切合初学英语的非英语为母语人士需要的词典。

继 2008、2009 年分别推出新版的《牛津高阶英汉双解词典》和《牛津中阶英汉双解词典》后，本社在 2010 年按 *Oxford Essential Dictionary* 翻译出版全新第三版的《牛津初阶英汉双解词典》，内容有以下特色：

（一）收词 19 000 条，涵盖英美词汇，包括 2 000 个经专家审定必须学习的英语核心词（在正文条目中以 ⟃ 钥匙符号标示）

（二）释义简明翔实，全使用核心词编写

（三）例句逾 13 000 条，摘自语料库，以真实例子示范正确用法

（四）图解词语 400 项，帮助理解和记忆

（五）列明动词、形容词、名词复数等变化模式，让初学英语人士更容易掌握常见的词形变化

（六）620 项用法说明，辨析难字，解释语法，教授读音，介绍文化知识

（七）附彩色插页，以专题形式介绍日常生活用语

（八）新编研习专页，附练习和参考答案

本词典（繁体字本）继续配备发音光碟，由英语专家示范词目的英美读音，并设示范短片和多元练习，教授国际音标的标准发音，强化听读能力。

词典编辑工作繁复琐碎，疏漏之处在所难免，尚祈广大读者不吝指正为感。

牛津大学出版社（中国）有限公司
二〇一〇年六月

Advisory Board and Editorial Team
顾问及编辑人员名单

vi

Guide to the dictionary 本词典用法说明

Finding words and phrases 查找词和短语

The **2 000 keywords** (= the most important words to learn) are clearly marked and there is a list of them at the back of the dictionary. 应学会的 2 000 个核心词标示清晰，并列于词典末的核心词表。

easy ⁰ᵆ /'iːzi/ *adjective* 形容词 (easier, easiest)
1 not difficult to do or understand 容易的；不费劲的：*The homework was very easy.* 作业很容易做。◇ *English isn't an easy language to learn.* 英语不是一种容易学的语言。◆ OPPOSITE **difficult**, **hard** 反义词为 difficult 和 hard
2 without problems or pain 舒适的；安逸的：*He has had an easy life.* 他一直过着舒适的生活。◆ OPPOSITE **difficult**, **hard** 反义词为 difficult 和 hard
take it easy, take things easy to relax and not worry or work too much 放松点；别急；别太担心：*After my exams I'm going to take it easy for a few days.* 我考试之后要放松几天。

Idioms and **phrasal verbs** (which have a special meaning) are shown below the main words. 有特定含义的习语和短语动词列在词目之下。

Words with the **same spelling**, but different parts of speech, have different numbers. 拼法相同但词性不同的词目以不同的号码列出。

smoke¹ ⁰ᵆ /sməʊk/ *noun* 名词 (*no plural* 不用复数形式)
the grey, white or black gas that you see in the air when something is burning 烟：*The room was full of smoke.* 房间里都是烟。◇ *cigarette smoke* 香烟的烟

smoke² ⁰ᵆ /sməʊk/ *verb* 动词 (smokes, smoking, smoked /sməʊkt/)
to breathe in smoke through a cigarette, etc. and let it out again; to use cigarettes, etc. in this way, as a habit 吸烟；抽烟：*He was smoking a cigar.* 他抽着雪茄。◇ *Do you smoke?* 你吸烟吗？
▶ **smoker** /'sməʊkə(r)/ *noun* 名词：*Her parents are both heavy smokers* (= they smoke a lot). 她父母烟瘾很大。

Related words are given below the main word. 相关的词列在词目之下。

Grammar 语法

To make the plural of most nouns, you add –s (for example girl, girl**s**). For all other nouns, we give you full information. Some nouns have a completely different **plural form**, or there is a change to the spelling. 大多数名词的复数加 -s（如 girl 的复数形式为 girls），其余所有的名词均附详细信息。有些名词的复数形式完全不同，或拼法有所改变。

speak ⁰ᵆ /spiːk/ *verb* 动词 (speaks, speaking, spoke /spəʊk/, has spoken /'spəʊkən/)
1 to say things; to talk to somebody 说话；谈话；讲话：*Please speak more slowly.* 请说得慢一点。◇ *Can I speak to John Smith, please?* (= words that you say on the telephone) 请叫约翰·史密斯来听电话好吗？◇ *The head teacher spoke for over an hour.* 校长讲了一个多小时。

knife ⁰ᵆ /naɪf/ *noun* 名词 (*plural* 複數形式 knives /naɪvz/)
a sharp metal thing with a handle that you use to cut things or to fight 刀：*a knife and fork* 一副刀叉

the **forms of a verb** 动词形式
We show the *he/she* form, the *–ing* form, the *past tense* (and the *past participle* of irregular verbs). 列出 he/she 用的形式、-ing 形式、过去式（以及不规则动词的过去分词）。

clothes 0️⃣ /kləʊðz/ *noun* 名词 (*plural* 用复数形式)

things like trousers, shirts and coats that you wear to cover your body 衣服；服装： *She was **wearing new clothes**.* 她穿着新衣服。 ◇ *Take off those wet clothes.* 把那些湿衣服脱下来吧。

> Some nouns are always **plural**. We give you extra help with these. 有些名词只用复数形式，会有附加说明。

information 0️⃣ /ˌɪnfə'meɪʃn/ *noun* 名词 (*no plural* 不用复数形式)

facts about people or things 信息；资讯；资料： *Can you give me some **information** about trains to London?* 你能不能给我一些往伦敦列车的信息？

> Nouns with no plural form often have notes giving extra information about grammar. 不用复数形式的名词常提供额外的语法说明。

> the **part of speech** (for example *noun*, *verb* or *adjective*) 词性（如名词、动词或形容词）

🔎 **GRAMMAR** 语法说明

Be careful! You cannot say 'an information'. You say **some information** or **a piece of information**. 注意：不说 an information，要说 some information 或 a piece of information： *She gave me an interesting piece of information.* 她向我提供了一则有趣的信息。

> Comparative and superlative forms are given, unless they are formed with *more* or *most* (for example beautiful, more beautiful). 比较级和最高级形式除了加 more 和 most 构成之外（如 beautiful、more beautiful），其余逐一列出。

> Sometimes a noun has **no plural** form and it cannot be used with *a* or *an*. 有时名词不用复数形式，不能与 a 或 an 连用。

busy 0️⃣ /'bɪzi/ *adjective* 形容词 (busier, busiest)

1 with a lot of things that you must do; working or not free 忙的；忙碌的： *Mr Jones can't see you now – he's busy.* 琼斯先生现在不能见你，他在忙。

Understanding and using words 词语理解和运用

> Both **British English** and **American English** are given. 提供英式英语和美式英语用词。

anticlockwise /ˌænti'klɒkwaɪz/ (*British* 英式英语) (*American* 美式英语 counterclockwise) *adjective*, *adverb* 形容词，副词

in the opposite direction to the hands of a clock 逆时针方向（的）： *Turn the handle anticlockwise.* 逆时针转动把手。

> **Example sentences** help you to understand a word and show you how it is used. 示例有助于理解词义，同时显示用法。

> **pronunciation** and **stress** 读音和重音

best man /ˌbest 'mæn/ *noun* 名词 (*no plural* 不用复数形式)

a man at a wedding who helps the man who is getting married (the bridegroom) 伴郎；男傧相

> **Related words** help you to build your vocabulary. 相关的词有助于扩充词汇。

clever 0️⃣ /'klevə(r)/ *adjective* 形容词 (cleverer, cleverest)

quick at learning and understanding things 聪明的；聪颖的 ⊃ SAME MEANING **intelligent** 同义词为 intelligent： *a clever student* 聪明的学生 ⊃ OPPOSITE **stupid** 反义词为 stupid

> **meaning** (or **definition**) 词义（或释义）

> Many **opposites** and **synonyms** (= words with the same meaning) are given. 多个词条均列出反义词和同义词。

WORD BUILDING notes show you related words and help build your vocabulary. "词汇扩充"列出相关词语，有助于学习词汇。

cat 0╍ /kæt/ *noun* 名词
1 a small animal with soft fur that people keep as a pet 猫

> **WORD BUILDING** 词汇扩充
> A young cat is called a **kitten**. 小猫叫做 kitten。
> A cat **purrs** when it is happy. When it makes a loud noise, it **miaows**. 猫惬意时发出呼噜声称作 purr，大声喵喵叫称作 miaow: *My cat miaows when she's hungry.* 我的猫饿了就喵喵叫。

SPEAKING Some words are used only in **formal** situations and there may be a word that is used more often, especially in **speech**. "表达方式说明"指出有些词仅用于正式场合，可能有较常用的口语词。

assist /ə'sɪst/ *verb* 动词 (assists, assisting, assisted) (*formal* 正式)
to help somebody 帮助；援助: *The driver assisted her with her suitcases.* 司机帮她拿行李箱。

> **SPEAKING** 表达方式说明
> **Help** is the word that we usually use.
> * help 是常用词。

SPELLING and **PRONUNCIATION** notes help you remember how to spell a word and tell you how to pronounce difficult words. "拼写说明"和"读音说明"有助于记住词语的拼法和难拼词语的读音。

piece 0╍ /piːs/ *noun* 名词

> **SPELLING** 拼写说明
> Remember! I comes before E in **piece**. 记住：piece 中的 i 在 e 前面。
> Use the phrase **a piece of pie** to help you remember. 可用词组 a piece of pie 来帮助记忆。

daughter 0╍ /'dɔːtə(r)/ *noun* 名词

> **PRONUNCIATION** 读音说明
> The word **daughter** sounds like **water**, because we don't say the letters **gh** in this word. * daughter 读音像 water，因为 gh 在这里不发音。

WHICH WORD? notes show you the difference between words that you might confuse. "词语辨析"阐明容易混淆的词。

pile[1] 0╍ /paɪl/ *noun* 名词

> **WHICH WORD?** 词语辨析
> **Pile** or **heap**? 用 pile 还是 heap?
> A **pile** may be tidy or untidy. A **heap** is untidy. * pile 可指整齐或不整齐的一堆，而 heap 指不整齐的一堆。

CULTURE notes tell you about life in Britain and the US. "文化资料补充"讲解有关英美生活的信息。

English /'ɪŋglɪʃ/ *noun* 名词

> **CULTURE** 文化资料补充
> Be careful! The people of **Scotland** (the **Scots**) and the people of **Wales** (the **Welsh**) are **British**, not **English**. 注意：称苏格兰人（the Scots）和威尔士人（the Welsh）为英国人时要用 British，而不能用 English。

Dictionary Quiz 词典知识小测验

This quiz shows how your **Oxford dictionary** can help you.
这个测验让你知道牛津词典如何帮助学习。
You will find the answers to all these questions in the dictionary.
下列问题的答案均可在本词典中找到。

Meanings 词义

The dictionary explains the meanings of words in simple language. The example sentences also help you to understand words and use them correctly. Words marked with a key are important words for you to learn. There is a list of the 2 000 keywords at the back of the dictionary. 本词典使用浅显的文字解释词义。示例亦有助于理解词义和学习正确的用法。标有钥匙的词语是应该学会的重要词语。词典末列有 2 000 个核心词。

1 On which part of your body do you wear **wellingtons**?

2 When is **Boxing Day**?

Vocabulary 词汇

There are hundreds of notes that give useful extra vocabulary or show the differences between words. 数百个用法说明额外提供有用的词语或说明词语之间的分别。

The dictionary has a lot of photos and pictures that help you understand words and build your vocabulary. As well as the pictures in the main part of the dictionary, there is a 16-page Picture Dictionary section in the middle with colour pictures of things like clothes, food and drink, and the weather. 词典中有很多照片和插图，有助于理解词义和扩充词汇。除正文中的插图外，词典中间还有 16 页关于服装、食物和饮料、天气等的彩图。

3 What is a young **goat** called?

4 What is the opposite of **wide**?

5 *I bought this book in the **library**.* In this sentence, the word **library** is wrong. What is the right word?

6 What is the name of the central part of a **tree**, that grows up from the ground?

7 What is the name of this fruit?

8 Is the word **lung** a noun, a verb or an adjective?

9 Is it correct to say:
*Can you give me some **advices**?*

10 What is the past tense of the verb **break**?

11 What is the *-ing* form of the verb **hit**?

12 How do you spell the plural of **party**?

13 Do the words **son** and **sun** have the same sound?

14 Does **enough** sound like **though** or **tough**?

Grammar 语法

You can check if a new word is a noun, a verb, an adjective, etc. by looking in the dictionary. 翻阅本词典可查检生词的词性是名词、动词或形容词等。

The dictionary gives you extra help with some nouns. For example, it gives irregular and difficult noun plurals and tells you if a word cannot be used in the plural. 本词典为一些名词提供附加说明，例如列出不规则和难拼的名词复数形式，并注明某词可否用复数形式。

The important verb forms are listed for each verb, and there is a list of irregular verbs with their past tenses and past participles on pages 688–689. 每个动词均列出重要词形，第 688–689 页另附不规则动词表，列出过去式和过去分词。

Spelling 拼写

You can use the dictionary to check how to spell a word, and it also shows changes in the spelling of other forms of the word, for example the plurals of nouns and the *-ing* forms of verbs. 使用本词典可查检词语的拼写，以及同一词不同形式的拼写变化，例如名词的复数形式和动词的 -ing 形式。

Pronunciation 读音

The dictionary gives the pronunciation of words, and on page xiii you will find help with reading the phonetic symbols. There are also notes to help you with words that have the same sound or words that are difficult to pronounce. 本词典标示词语的读音，第 xiii 页说明如何识读音标。另外正文还有同音词和难读词语的说明。

15 How do you *say* this **date**: 4 July, 2010?

16 What is the name of the exam that all British pupils must take in secondary school?

17 Is **Yours faithfully** the correct ending to a formal or an informal letter?

18 Name three young farm animals.

19 On which part of your body is your **nostril**?

20 What is the word for a person who comes from **Spain**?

Extra information 额外信息

The blue Study Pages in the middle give useful information on topics like dates, education and writing letters and emails. The colourful Picture Dictionary section shows you groups of related words in topic areas such as animals and the body. At the end of the dictionary you will find helpful lists of words such as geographical names and irregular verbs. 词典中间蓝色的研习专页包含各类有用的信息，例如日期、教育、写信和写电邮等。彩页部分按主题分类列出相关词语，如动物、人体等。词典末则附有地名表、不规则动词表等有用的资料。

Answers 答案

1 your feet
2 26 December
3 a kid
4 narrow
5 bookshop/bookstore
6 the trunk
7 a pineapple
8 a noun
9 No. (The word 'advice' does not have a plural form.)
10 broke
11 hitting
12 parties
13 yes
14 tough
15 the fourth of July (or July the fourth), two thousand and ten
16 General Certificate of Secondary Education (GCSE)
17 formal
18 lamb, foal, calf
19 nose, face
20 a Spaniard

xii

Phonetic symbols 音标

Vowels 元音

iː	see	/siː/	ʌ	cup	/kʌp/
i	happy	/'hæpi/	ɜː	bird	/bɜːd/
ɪ	sit	/sɪt/	ə	about	/ə'baʊt/
e	ten	/ten/	eɪ	say	/seɪ/
æ	cat	/kæt/	əʊ	go	/gəʊ/
ɑː	father	/'fɑːðə(r)/	aɪ	five	/faɪv/
ɒ	got	/gɒt/	aʊ	now	/naʊ/
ɔː	saw	/sɔː/	ɔɪ	boy	/bɔɪ/
ʊ	put	/pʊt/	ɪə	near	/nɪə(r)/
u	situation	/ˌsɪtʃu'eɪʃn/	eə	hair	/heə(r)/
uː	too	/tuː/	ʊə	pure	/pjʊə(r)/

Consonants 辅音

p	pen	/pen/	s	so	/səʊ/
b	bad	/bæd/	z	zoo	/zuː/
t	tea	/tiː/	ʃ	shoe	/ʃuː/
d	did	/dɪd/	ʒ	vision	/'vɪʒn/
k	cat	/kæt/	h	hat	/hæt/
g	got	/gɒt/	m	man	/mæn/
tʃ	chain	/tʃeɪn/	n	no	/nəʊ/
dʒ	jam	/dʒæm/	ŋ	sing	/sɪŋ/
f	fall	/fɔːl/	l	leg	/leg/
v	van	/væn/	r	red	/red/
θ	thin	/θɪn/	j	yes	/jes/
ð	this	/ðɪs/	w	wet	/wet/

(ˈ) shows the strong stress: it is in front of the part of the word that you say most strongly, for example **because** /bɪ'kɒz/. (ˈ) 表示主重音，标示在一词最重读的音节之前，例如 because /bɪ'kɒz/。

(ˌ) shows a weaker stress. Some words have a part that is said with a weaker stress as well as a strong stress, for example **OK** /ˌəʊ'keɪ/. (ˌ) 表示次重音，有些词既有主重音又有次重音，例如 OK /ˌəʊ'keɪ/。

(r) at the end of a word means that in British English you say this sound only when the next word begins with a vowel sound. In American English, you always pronounce this 'r'. (r) 在词尾时，表示在英式英语中若随后的词以元音开头才发 r 音，美式英语则在任何情况下均发 r 音。

Some words, for example **at** and **must**, have two pronunciations. We give the usual pronunciation first. The second pronunciation must be used when the word is stressed, and is also often used when the word is at the end of a sentence. 有些词有两种读音，例如 at 和 must。常用的读音放在前面，另一种读音在重读该词时用，或在句末时也常用。

For example 例如: *This book is for /fə(r)/ Lisa.*
Who is this book for /fɔː(r)/?

A a

A, a /eɪ/ *noun* 名词 (*plural* 复数形式 A's, a's /eɪz/)
the first letter of the English alphabet 英语字母表的第 1 个字母: *'Apple' begins with an 'A'.* * apple 一词以字母 a 开头。

a ⚖ /ə; eɪ/ (*also* 亦作 **an** /ən; æn/) *article* 冠词
1 one or any 一个；任何一个: *Would you like a drink?* 你想喝点东西吗? ◇ *A dog has four legs.* 狗有四条腿。 ◇ *He's a teacher.* 他是教师。
2 each, or for each 每一: *She phones her mother three times a week.* 她每星期给母亲三次电话。 ◇ *Calls cost 16p a minute.* 电话每分钟收费 16 便士。

> 🔎 **WHICH WORD?** 词语辨析
> **A** or **an**? 用 a 还是 an?
> You use **an** in front of words that start with a vowel sound. Be careful! It is the sound that is important, not the spelling. For example, words like *euro* and *university* take **a** instead of **an**, and words that begin with a silent 'h', like *hour*, take **an** instead of **a**. 在元音开头的词之前用 an。注意: 重要的是发音，而不是拼写。例如，像 euro 和 university 等词用 a 而不是 an，以不发音的 h 开头的词如 hour 用 an 而不是 a。
> Look at these examples 请看下例:
> *a box* 一个盒子 ◇ *an apple* 一个苹果 ◇
> *a singer* 一名歌手 ◇ *an hour* 一个小时 ◇
> *a university* 一所大学 ◇ *an MP* 一位议员
> ◇ *a euro* 一欧元 ◇ *an umbrella* 一把伞

abandon /ə'bændən/ *verb* 动词 (**abandons, abandoning, abandoned** /ə'bændənd/)
1 to leave somebody or something completely 离弃；遗弃；抛弃；舍弃: *He abandoned his car in the snow.* 他在雪中弃车而行。
2 to stop doing something before it is finished 中止: *When the rain started, we abandoned our game.* 一下雨，我们就中止了比赛。

abbey /'æbi/ *noun* 名词 (*plural* 复数形式 **abbeys**)
a building where religious men or women (called **monks** and **nuns**) live or lived 修道院

abbreviate /ə'bri:vieɪt/ *verb* 动词 (**abbreviates, abbreviating, abbreviated**)
to make a word shorter by not saying or writing some of the letters 简称作: *The word 'telephone' is often abbreviated to 'phone'.* * telephone 常缩写为 phone。

abbreviation /ə,bri:vi'eɪʃn/ *noun* 名词
a short form of a word 缩写词；缩略语: *TV is an abbreviation for 'television'.* * TV 是 television 的缩略形式。

abdomen /'æbdəmən/ *noun* 名词 (*formal* 正式)
the front middle part of your body, which contains your stomach 腹；腹部

ability ⚖ /ə'bɪləti/ *noun* 名词 (*plural* 复数形式 **abilities**)
the power and knowledge to do something 能力；本领: *She has the ability to pass the exam, but she must work harder.* 她有能力通过考试，不过得更用功才行。

able ⚖ /'eɪbl/ *adjective* 形容词
be able to do something to have the power and knowledge to do something 能够；有能力做某事: *Will you be able to come to the party?* 你能来参加聚会吗? ◇ *Is Simon able to swim?* 西蒙会游泳吗?
➲ OPPOSITE **unable** 反义词为 unable
➲ Look at **can**[1] (2). 见 can[1] 第 2 义。

abnormal /æb'nɔ:ml/ *adjective* 形容词
different from what is normal or usual, in a way that worries you or that is unpleasant 不正常的；反常的；畸形的: *They thought the boy's behaviour was abnormal.* 他们认为那个男孩行为异常。

aboard /ə'bɔ:d/ *adverb, preposition* 副词，介词
on or onto a ship, train, bus or plane 在船（或火车、公共汽车、飞机）上；上船（或火车、公共汽车、飞机）: *Are all the passengers aboard the ship?* 所有乘客都上船了吗? ◇ *Welcome aboard flight 603 to Nairobi.* 欢迎乘坐前往内罗毕的 603 号航班。

abolish /ə'bɒlɪʃ/ *verb* 动词 (**abolishes, abolishing, abolished** /ə'bɒlɪʃt/)
to stop or end something by law 废除;

A
B
C
D
E
F
G
H
I
J
K
L
M
N
O
P
Q
R
S
T
U
V
W
X
Y
Z

废止: *The Americans abolished slavery in 1863.* 美国在 1863 年废除了奴隶制。
▶ **abolition** /ˌæbə'lɪʃn/ *noun* 名词 (*no plural* 不用复数形式): *the abolition of hunting* 狩猎活动的废除

about 0ᴛ /ə'baʊt/ *preposition, adverb* 介词, 副词
1 a little more or less than; a little before or after 大约; 左右: *She's about 30 years old.* 她 30 岁上下。◇ *There were about 2,000 people at the concert.* 大约 2 000 人参加了音乐会。◇ *I got there at about two o'clock.* 我在两点前后到了那儿。
2 of; on the subject of 有关; 关于: *a book about cats* 关于猫的书 ◇ *We talked about the problem.* 我们谈了这个问题。◇ *What are you thinking about?* 你在想什么?
3 (*also* 亦作 around) in a lot of different directions or places 到处; 在各处: *The children were running about in the garden.* 孩子们在园子里四处跑。◇ *There were books lying about on the floor.* 地上到处都是书。
4 almost; nearly 将近; 几乎: *Dinner is just about ready.* 晚餐快做好了。
5 (*also* 亦作 around) in a place; here 在某处; 在这里: *It was late and there weren't many people about.* 时间不早, 那里人不多了。
be about to do something to be going to do something very soon 即将做某事: *The film is about to start.* 电影就要开始了。

above 0ᴛ /ə'bʌv/ *preposition, adverb* 介词, 副词
1 in or to a higher place; higher than somebody or something 在⋯上面; 向⋯上面; 比⋯高: *I looked up at the sky above.* 我抬头仰望天空。◇ *My bedroom is above the kitchen.* 我的卧室在厨房上面。◇ *There is a picture on the wall above the fireplace.* 壁炉上方的墙上挂着一幅画。
⊃ OPPOSITE **below** 反义词为 below
2 more than a number or price 大于; 多于: *children aged ten and above* 十岁或以上的儿童 ⊃ OPPOSITE **below, under** 反义词为 below 和 under
above all more than any other thing; what is most important 最重要的; 首要的: *He's handsome and intelligent and, above all, he's kind!* 他既英俊又聪明, 最要紧的是他人很好!

abroad 0ᴛ /ə'brɔːd/ *adverb* 副词
in or to another country 在国外; 去国外: *She lives abroad.* 她住在国外。◇ *Are you going abroad this summer?* 你今年夏天出国吗?

abrupt /ə'brʌpt/ *adjective* 形容词
1 sudden and unexpected 突然的; 意外的: *an abrupt change of plan* 计划的突然改变
2 seeming rude and unfriendly 莽撞的; 唐突的: *I'm sorry for being so abrupt with you.* 我这么唐突, 实在不好意思。
▶ **abruptly** /ə'brʌptli/ *adverb* 副词: *The conversation ended abruptly.* 谈话突然终止了。

absence /'æbsəns/ *noun* 名词 (*no plural* 不用复数形式)
a time when a person or thing is not there 缺席; 不在: *I am doing Julie's job in her absence.* 朱莉不在, 我正在做她的工作。

absent /'æbsənt/ *adjective* 形容词
not there 缺席的; 不在的 ⊃ SAME MEANING **away** 同义词为 away: *He was absent from work yesterday because he was ill.* 他昨天病了, 所以没上班。

absent-minded /ˌæbsənt 'maɪndɪd/ *adjective* 形容词
often forgetting or not noticing things, perhaps because you are thinking about something else 健忘的; 心不在焉的 ⊃ SAME MEANING **forgetful** 同义词为 forgetful: *Grandma is getting more absent-minded as she gets older.* 奶奶越老越健忘了。

absolute /'æbsəluːt/ *adjective* 形容词
complete 完全的; 绝对的: *I've never played chess before. I'm an absolute beginner.* 我没下过国际象棋, 完全是个新手。◇ *The whole trip was an absolute disaster.* 整个旅程糟糕透顶。

absolutely 0ᴛ *adverb* 副词
1 /'æbsəluːtli/ completely 完全地; 绝对地: *It's absolutely freezing outside!* 外面冷得要命!
2 /ˌæbsə'luːtli/ (used when you are strongly agreeing with somebody) yes; certainly (强调同意)当然, 对极了: *'It is a good idea, isn't it?' 'Oh, absolutely!'* "这个主意不错, 不是吗?""哦, 当然是的。"

absorb /əb'sɔːb; əb'zɔːb/ *verb* 动词
(**absorbs, absorbing, absorbed** /əb'sɔːbd; əb'zɔːbd/)
to take in something like liquid or heat, and hold it 吸收: *The dry ground absorbed all the rain.* 干燥的地面把雨水都吸收了。

absorbent /əb'sɔːbənt; əb'zɔːbənt/ *adjective* 形容词
able to take in and hold something,

especially liquid 能吸收（液体等）的：
an absorbent cloth 吸水布

absorbing /əbˈsɔːbɪŋ; əbˈzɔːbɪŋ/ *adjective* 形容词
very interesting 十分吸引人的：
an absorbing book 一本引人入胜的书

abstract /ˈæbstrækt/ *adjective* 形容词
1 about an idea, not a real thing 抽象的：*abstract thought* 抽象思维
2 not like a real thing 不像实物的：*an abstract painting* 抽象画

absurd /əbˈsɜːd/ *adjective* 形容词
so silly that it makes you laugh 荒谬的；荒唐的：*The guards look absurd in that new uniform.* 警卫穿着那套新制服，看上去很可笑。◇ *Don't be absurd! I can't possibly do all this work in one day.* 别犯傻了！我不可能在一天之内全部做完。
⊃ SAME MEANING **ridiculous** 同义词为 ridiculous

abuse¹ /əˈbjuːz/ *verb* 动词 (abuses, abusing, abused /əˈbjuːzd/)
1 to use something in a wrong or bad way 滥用：*The manager often abuses her power.* 经理常常滥用她的职权。
2 to say rude things to somebody 辱骂：*The player got a red card for abusing the referee.* 那名球员因辱骂裁判而吃了红牌。
3 to be cruel or unkind to somebody 虐待：*The children were abused by their father.* 孩子们遭到了父亲虐待。

abuse² /əˈbjuːs/ *noun* 名词 (*no plural* 不用复数形式)
1 using something in a wrong or bad way 滥用：*the dangers of drug abuse* 滥用药物的危险
2 rude words 辱骂；恶语：*The lorry driver shouted abuse at the cyclist.* 卡车司机对那个骑车的人破口大骂。◇ *racial abuse* 种族虐骂
3 being cruel or unkind to somebody 虐待：*The child had suffered verbal and physical abuse.* 这孩子受到了辱骂和肉体摧残。

abusive /əˈbjuːsɪv/ *adjective* 形容词
using rude words to insult somebody 辱骂的；恶语的：*an abusive remark* 恶言谩骂

academic /ˌækəˈdemɪk/ *adjective* 形容词
connected with education, especially in schools and universities 学业的；学术的：*Our academic year begins in September.* 我们的学年九月份开始。

accelerator /əkˈseləreɪtə(r)/ *noun* 名词
the part of a vehicle that you press with your foot when you want it to go faster

加速踏板；油门：*She put her foot down on the accelerator and overtook the bus.* 她踩下油门，超过了公共汽车。

accent /ˈæksent/ *noun* 名词
1 the way a person from a certain place or country speaks a language 口音；腔调：*She speaks English with an American accent.* 她说英语带有美国口音。
2 saying one word or part of a word more strongly than another 重音：*In the word 'because', the accent is on the second part of the word.* because 这个词的重音放在第二个音节。
3 (in writing) a mark, usually above a letter, that changes the sound of the letter 读音符号：*Fiancé has an accent on the 'e'.* fiancé 在 e 上标有变音符号。

accept 0ᵤ /əkˈsept/ *verb* 动词 (accepts, accepting, accepted)

> ♪ SPELLING 拼写说明
> Remember! Don't confuse **accept** with **except**, which sounds nearly the same. 记住：不要混淆读音相近的 accept 和 except。

1 to say 'yes' when somebody asks you to have or do something 接受：*Please accept this present.* 请收下这份礼物。◇ *I accepted the invitation to his party.* 我接受了参加他聚会的邀请。
2 to believe that something is true 相信；接受（事实）：*She can't accept that her son is dead.* 她不能接受儿子已经去世。

acceptable 0ᵤ /əkˈseptəbl/ *adjective* 形容词
allowed by most people; good enough 认可的；合意的；尚可的：*It's not acceptable to make so many mistakes.* 犯这么多的错误是不能接受的。

acceptance /əkˈseptəns/ *noun* 名词 (*no plural* 不用复数形式)
taking something that somebody offers you or asks you to have 接受：*Her quick acceptance of the offer surprised me.* 她很快接受了建议，让我感到很意外。

access¹ /ˈækses/ *noun* 名词 (*no plural* 不用复数形式)
a way to go into a place or to use something 通道；通路；使用的途径：*We don't have access to the garden from our flat.* 从我们的公寓没有路直通花园。◇ *Do you have access to a computer at home?* 你在家能用电脑吗？

access² /ˈækses/ *verb* 动词 (accesses, accessing, accessed /ˈæksest/)
(*computing* 电脑) to find information on

B
C
D
E
F
G
H
I
J
K
L
M
N
O
P
Q
R
S
T
U
V
W
X
Y
Z

a computer 存取： *Click on the icon to access a file.* 点击图标来存取文件。

accident 0︎ /ˈæksɪdənt/ *noun* 名词
something bad that happens by chance 事故；意外： *I had an accident when I was driving to work – my car hit a tree.* 我开车上班时出了事故 —— 车撞到树了。 ◊ *I'm sorry I broke your watch – it was an accident.* 对不起，把你的手表弄坏了，这是个意外。

by accident by chance; not because you planned it 偶然；意外地： *I took Jane's book by accident. I thought it was mine.* 我无意中拿了简的书，我还以为是自己的呢。

accidental /ˌæksɪˈdentl/ *adjective* 形容词
If something is **accidental**, it happens by chance and is not planned. 偶然的；意外的： *Police do not know if the plane crash was accidental or caused by a bomb.* 警方不清楚坠机事件是意外还是由炸弹造成的。

▶ **accidentally** /ˌæksɪˈdentəli/ *adverb* 副词： *He accidentally broke the window.* 他不小心打破了窗户。

accommodation /əˌkɒməˈdeɪʃn/ *noun* 名词 (*no plural* 不用复数形式)

> 🔍 SPELLING 拼写说明
>
> Remember! You spell **accommodation** with **CC** and **MM**.
> 记住：accommodation 拼写中有 cc 和 mm。

a place to stay or live 停留处；住处： *It's difficult to find cheap accommodation in London.* 在伦敦很难找到便宜的住宿。

> 🔍 GRAMMAR 语法说明
>
> **Accommodation** has no plural. We cannot say 'I will help you find an accommodation.' * accommodation 没有复数形式，不说 I will help you find an accommodation。
> Sometimes it is better to use a different phrase instead. In this case we could say, 'I will help you to find somewhere to live.' 有时最好换成其他的表达方式，比如 I will help you to find somewhere to live。

accompany /əˈkʌmpəni/ *verb* 动词
(accompanies, accompanying, accompanied /əˈkʌmpənid/)
1 (*formal* 正式) to go with somebody to a place 陪同；陪伴： *Four teachers accompanied the class on their school trip.* 四名教师陪同全班学生参加了学校旅行。

2 to happen at the same time as something else 伴随；与⋯同时发生： *Thunder is usually accompanied by lightning.* 打雷时通常伴随着闪电。
3 to play music while somebody sings or plays another instrument 伴奏： *You sing and I'll accompany you on the guitar.* 你唱歌，我用吉他给你伴奏。

accomplish /əˈkʌmplɪʃ/ *verb* 动词
(accomplishes, accomplishing, accomplished /əˈkʌmplɪʃt/)
to succeed in doing something difficult that you planned to do 完成（困难的事） ⊃ SAME MEANING **achieve** 同义词为 achieve： *The first part of the plan has been safely accomplished.* 计划的第一部分已经顺利完成。

accord /əˈkɔːd/ *noun* 名词 (*no plural* 不用复数形式)

of your own accord because you want to, not because somebody has asked you 主动地；自愿地： *She left the job of her own accord.* 她主动离职了。

according to 0︎ /əˈkɔːdɪŋ tə/ *before a, e, i, o or u* 在 a、e、i、o、u 之前读 /əˈkɔːdɪŋ tuː/ *or* 或 /tu/ *preposition* 介词
as somebody or something says 根据： *According to Mike, this film is really good.* 据迈克说，这部电影真的很好看。 ◊ *The church was built in 1395, according to this book.* 据此书所载，这座教堂建于1395年。

account¹ 0︎ /əˈkaʊnt/ *noun* 名词
1 words that somebody says or writes about something that happened 叙述；描述；报告： *She gave the police a full account of the robbery.* 她向警方详尽地叙述了抢劫的经过。
2 an arrangement with a bank which lets you keep your money there 账户： *I paid the money into my account.* 我把钱存进了我的银行账户。 ◊ *to open an account* 开户
3 accounts (*plural* 用复数形式) lists of all the money that a person or business receives and pays 账目： *Who keeps* (= writes) *the accounts for your business?* 你的公司谁管账？

on account of something because of something 由于；因为： *Our school was closed on account of bad weather.* 由于天气恶劣，我们学校停课了。

on no account, not on any account for not any reason 决不；绝对不： *On no account should you walk home on your own.* 你绝对不能一个人走回家。

take account of something, take something into account to remember something when you are thinking about other things 考虑到: *John is always last, but you must take his age into account – he is much younger than the other children.* 约翰总是最后一名，但要考虑到他的年龄，毕竟他比其他孩子小得多。

account² /ə'kaʊnt/ *verb* 动词
account for something
1 to explain or give a reason for something 解释；说明: *How can you account for the missing pieces?* 你如何解释丢失的几件东西呢?
2 to make the amount that is mentioned （数量上）占: *Sales to Africa accounted for 60% of our total sales last year.* 去年非洲的销量占我们总销量的 60%。

accountant /ə'kaʊntənt/ *noun* 名词
a person whose job is to make lists of all the money that people or businesses receive and pay 会计；会计师: *Nicky is an accountant.* 尼基是会计。

accuracy /'ækjərəsi/ *noun* 名词 (*no plural* 不用复数形式)
the quality of being exactly right, with no mistakes 准确；精确

accurate /'ækjərət/ *adjective* 形容词
exactly right; with no mistakes 正确无误的；准确的；精确的: *He gave an accurate description of the thief.* 他对小偷的描述很准确。 ⊃ OPPOSITE **inaccurate** 反义词为 inaccurate
▸ **accurately** /'ækjərətli/ *adverb* 副词: *The map was accurately drawn.* 这张地图绘制得很精确。

accuse 0— /ə'kjuːz/ *verb* 动词 (accuses, accusing, accused /ə'kjuːzd/)
to say that somebody has done something wrong or broken the law 指责；控告: *His classmates accused him of cheating in the exam.* 他的同学指责他考试作弊。 ◇ *She was accused of murder.* 她被控谋杀。
▸ **accusation** /ˌækjuˈzeɪʃn/ *noun* 名词: *The accusations were not true.* 这些指控都不成立。

accustomed /ə'kʌstəmd/ *adjective* 形容词
familiar with something and accepting it as normal or usual 习惯于 ⊃ SAME MEANING **used to** 同义词为 used to: *My eyes slowly grew accustomed to the dark.* 我的眼睛慢慢适应了黑暗。

ace /eɪs/ *noun* 名词
a PLAYING CARD (= one of 52 cards used for playing games) which has only one shape on it. An **ace** has either the lowest or the highest value in a game of cards. * A 纸牌；爱司: *the ace of hearts* 红桃爱司

ache¹ /eɪk/ *verb* 动词 (aches, aching, ached /eɪkt/)
to hurt; to give you pain 引起疼痛: *She was aching all over.* 她浑身疼痛。 ◇ *My legs ached after the long walk.* 走了长长的一段路后，我双腿发疼。

ache² /eɪk/ *noun* 名词 (*no plural* 不用复数形式)
a pain that lasts for a long time （持续的）疼痛: *If you eat all those sweets, you'll get stomach ache.* 要是吃下所有的糖果，你会肚子疼的。 ◇ *She's got earache.* 她耳朵疼。

> 🔍 GRAMMAR 语法说明
> We often use **ache** with a part of the body. * ache 常与指称身体部位的词连用。
> In British English, we usually use **ache** without 'a' or 'an'. 在英式英语中，ache 通常不加 a 或 an: *I've got backache.* 我背痛。 But we always say 'a headache'. 但说 a headache: *I've got a terrible headache.* 我头痛得要命。
> In American English, we usually use **ache** with 'a' or 'an', especially when talking about a particular attack of pain. 在美式英语中，ache 通常加 a 或 an，尤其用于指一阵疼痛时: *I have an awful toothache.* 我牙疼得厉害。

achieve 0— /ə'tʃiːv/ *verb* 动词 (achieves, achieving, achieved /ə'tʃiːvd/)
to do or finish something well after trying hard 达到；实现；努力取得: *He worked hard and achieved his aim of becoming a doctor.* 他很努力，实现了当医生的理想。

achievement /ə'tʃiːvmənt/ *noun* 名词
something that somebody has done after trying hard 成就；成绩: *Climbing Mount Everest was his greatest achievement.* 登上珠穆朗玛峰是他最大的成就。

acid 0— /'æsɪd/ *noun* 名词
(in chemistry) a liquid substance that burns things or makes holes in metal （化学）酸

acid rain /ˌæsɪd 'reɪn/ *noun* 名词
(*no plural* 不用复数形式)
rain that has chemicals in it from factories, for example. It causes damage to trees, rivers and buildings. 酸雨

acknowledge /ək'nɒlɪdʒ/ *verb* 动词
(acknowledges, acknowledging, acknowledged /ək'nɒlɪdʒd/)
1 to agree or accept that something is true 承认: *He acknowledged that he had made a mistake.* 他承认犯了错误。

A
B
C
D
E
F
G
H
I
J
K
L
M
N
O
P
Q
R
S
T
U
V
W
X
Y
Z

B
C
D
E
F
G
H
I
J
K
L
M
N
O
P
Q
R
S
T
U
V
W
X
Y
Z

2 to write to somebody who has sent you a letter, etc. to say that you have received it 告知收悉: *She never acknowledged my letter.* 她从来没说过收到我的信。

▶ **acknowledgement** /əkˈnɒlɪdʒmənt/ *noun* 名词: *I didn't receive an acknowledgement of my application.* 我没有收到申请的确认函。

acne /ˈækni/ *noun* 名词 (*no plural* 不用复数形式)
a skin problem, common among young people, that causes red spots, especially on the face 痤疮；粉刺

acorns 橡实

acorn /ˈeɪkɔːn/ *noun* 名词
a small nut with a base like a cup. **Acorns** grow on large trees (called oak trees). 橡子；橡实

acquaintance /əˈkweɪntəns/ *noun* 名词
a person that you know a little but who is not a close friend 认识的人；泛泛之交

acquire /əˈkwaɪə(r)/ *verb* 动词 (acquires, acquiring, acquired /əˈkwaɪəd/) (*formal* 正式)
to get or buy something 获得；得到；购得: *He acquired some English from listening to pop songs.* 他听流行歌曲学到了些英语。

acre /ˈeɪkə(r)/ *noun* 名词
a unit for measuring an area of land; about 4 050 square metres 英亩（约4 050 平方米）: *a farm of 40 acres* 一座40英亩的农场

acrobat /ˈækrəbæt/ *noun* 名词
a person who performs difficult acts such as walking on high ropes, especially in a CIRCUS (= a show that travels to different towns) 杂技演员

across /əˈkrɒs/ *adverb, preposition* 副词，介词
1 from one side to the other side of something 从一边到另一边；横过: *We walked across the field.* 我们走过田地。◇ *A smile spread across her face.* 她脸上泛出笑容。◇ *The river was about twenty metres across.* 那条河宽约二十米。
2 on the other side of something 在…的另一边: *There is a bank just across the road.* 马路对面就有家银行。

Across or **over**? 用 across 还是 over?
We can use **across** or **over** to mean 'on or to the other side'. * across 或 over 都可用以表示"在（或向）另一边": *I ran across the road.* 我跑过马路。◇ *I ran over the road.* 我跑过马路。
We usually use **over** to talk about crossing something high. 越过高处通常用 over: *Adam climbed over the wall.* 亚当爬过了墙。
With 'room' we usually use **across**. 与 room 搭配通常用 across: *I walked across the room.* 我穿过房间。

act¹ /ækt/ *verb* 动词 (acts, acting, acted)
1 to do something, or to behave in a certain way 做事；行动: *Doctors acted quickly to save the boy's life after the accident.* 事故发生后，医生迅速行动，抢救男孩的生命。◇ *Stop acting like a child!* 行为别像个孩子!
2 to pretend to be somebody else in a play, film or television programme 扮演
⊃ SAME MEANING **perform** 同义词为 perform

act as something to do the job of another person, usually for a short time 代职；暂时代理职务: *He acted as manager while his boss was ill.* 老板生病时，他代行经理职务。

act² /ækt/ *noun* 名词
1 a thing that you do 行为；行动: *an act of kindness* 善行

Act, action or **activity**? 用 act、action 还是 activity?
Act and **action** can have the same meaning. * act 和 action 有着相同的意思: *It was a brave act.* 那是勇敢的行为。◇ *It was a brave action.* 那是勇敢的行为。
Act, but not **action**, can be followed by **of**. * act 后可跟 of，action 则不可: *It was an act of bravery.* 那是勇敢的行为。
We say **activity** for something that is done regularly. * activity 指经常进行的活动: *I like outdoor activities such as walking and cycling.* 我喜欢户外活动，诸如散步和骑自行车。

2 one of the main parts of a play or an OPERA (= a musical play)（戏剧或歌剧的）一幕: *This play has five acts.* 这出戏共有五幕。

3 a law that a government makes 法案；法令： *an act of Parliament* 议会法案
4 behaviour that hides your true feelings 假装： *She seems very happy, but she's just putting on an act.* 她看上去很开心，但其实是装出来的罢了。
in the act (of doing something) while doing something wrong 正在（做坏事）；当场： *I caught him in the act of stealing the money.* 他偷钱时被我逮个正着。

acting /ˈæktɪŋ/ *noun* 名词 (*no plural* 不用复数形式)
being in plays or films 演戏；电影演出： *Have you ever done any acting?* 你演过戏吗？

action 0̄ /ˈækʃn/ *noun* 名词
1 (*no plural* 不用复数形式) doing things, especially for a particular purpose 行动： *Now is the time for action!* 现在该行动了！◇ *If we don't take action quickly, it'll be too late!* 我们若不赶快采取行动就来不及了！
2 (*plural* 复数形式 actions) something that you do 行为： *The little girl copied her mother's actions.* 这个小女孩模仿她母亲的一举一动。
3 (*no plural* 不用复数形式) exciting things that happen 激动人心的事： *I like films with a lot of action in them.* 我喜欢有许多刺激场面的影片。◇ *an action-packed film* 精彩纷呈的影片
in action doing something; working 在工作中；在运行： *We watched the machine in action.* 我们看着机器在运转。

active 0̄ /ˈæktɪv/ *adjective* 形容词
1 If you are **active**, you are always busy and able to do a lot of things. 活跃的；闲不住的： *My grandmother is 75 but she's still very active.* 我祖母75岁了，可是仍然十分活跃。
2 (*grammar* 语法) when the person or thing doing the action is the subject of a sentence or verb 主动语态的： *In the sentence 'The dog bit him', the verb is active.* 在 The dog bit him 一句中，动词是主动语态。◇ You can also say 'The verb is in the active'. 也可以说 The verb is in the active。◇ OPPOSITE **passive** 反义词为 passive

activity 0̄ /ækˈtɪvəti/ *noun* 名词
1 (*no plural* 不用复数形式) a lot of things happening and people doing things 热闹场面： *On the day of the festival there was a lot of activity in the streets.* 节日里街上很热闹。

2 (*plural* 复数形式 activities) something that you do, usually regularly and because you enjoy it 活动： *The hotel offers a range of leisure activities.* 这家旅馆提供一系列的休闲娱乐活动。

actor 0̄ /ˈæktə(r)/ *noun* 名词
a man or woman who acts in plays, films or television programmes 演员

actress 0̄ /ˈæktrəs/ *noun* 名词 (*plural* 复数形式 actresses)
a woman who acts in plays, films or television programmes 女演员

actual 0̄ /ˈæktʃuəl/ *adjective* 形容词
that really happened; real 实际的；真实的： *The actual damage to the car was not as bad as we'd feared.* 汽车的实际损坏没有我们担心得那么严重。◇ *They seemed to be good friends but in actual fact they hated each other.* 他俩看似是好朋友，实际上却彼此憎恨。

actually 0̄ /ˈæktʃuəli/ *adverb* 副词
1 really; in fact 实际上；事实上： *You don't actually believe her, do you?* 你其实并不相信她，是不是？◇ *I can't believe I'm actually going to Australia!* 我简直无法相信我真的要去澳大利亚了！
2 a word that you use to disagree politely or when you say something new（婉转表示不同意或转换话题）说实在的： *I don't agree. I thought the film was very good, actually.* 我可不这么想。说实话，我认为这部电影很不错。◇ *'Let's go out tonight.' 'Actually, I'd like to stay in and watch a film.'* "今晚我们出去玩吧。""说实在的，我想待在家里，看部电影。"

🔎 **WHICH WORD?** 词语辨析
Be careful! **Actually** does **not** mean 'now'. 注意：actually 没有"现在"的意思。
We can say **currently**, **at present** or **at the moment** instead. 表示"现在"可以用 currently、at present 或 at the moment： *He's currently working in China.* 他现时在中国工作。◇ *I'm studying for my exams at the moment.* 我正在温习功课，准备考试。

acute /əˈkjuːt/ *adjective* 形容词
very serious; very great 十分严重的： *an acute shortage of food* 食物的严重短缺

acute angle /əˌkjuːt ˈæŋgl/ *noun* 名词
(*maths* 数学) an angle of less than 90° 锐角 ◇ Look also at **obtuse angle** and

A
B
C
D
E
F
G
H
I
J
K
L
M
N
O
P
Q
R
S
T
U
V
W
X
Y
Z

right angle. 亦见 obtuse angle 和 right angle。

AD /ˌeɪ 'diː/ *abbreviation* 缩略式
AD in a date shows that it was after Christ was born. 公元: *1066 AD* 公元 1066 年 ⊃ Look at **BC**. 见 BC。

ad 0➔ /æd/ *noun* 名词 (*informal* 非正式) **short for** ADVERTISEMENT * advertisement 的缩略式

adapt /ə'dæpt/ *verb* 动词 (**adapts**, **adapting**, **adapted**)
1 to change the way that you do things because you are in a new situation 适应: *He has adapted very well to being at a new school.* 他已经很适应新学校的生活。
2 to change something so that you can use it in a different way 修改; 改造: *The car was adapted for use as a taxi.* 这辆汽车经过改装用作出租车了。

adaptable /ə'dæptəbl/ *adjective* 形容词 able to change in a new situation 能适应的; 适应能力强的: *He'll soon get used to his new school. Children are very adaptable.* 他很快会适应新学校，因为孩子的适应能力很强。

add 0➔ /æd/ *verb* 动词 (**adds**, **adding**, **added**)
1 to put something with something else 增加; 添加: *Mix the flour with the milk and then add the eggs.* 把面粉和牛奶搅拌好再加上鸡蛋。 ◇ *Add your name to the list.* 把你的名字加进名单里。
2 to put numbers together so that you get a total 加: *If you add 2 and 5 together, you get 7.* * 5 加 2 等于 7。 ◇ *Add $10 to the total, to cover postage and packing.* 总额上再加 10 元，作为邮资和包装费。 ⊃ OPPOSITE **subtract** 反义词为 subtract
3 to say something more 补充说: *'Go away – and don't come back again,' she added.* "走开——别再回来。" 她又加上一句。

add up to find the total of several numbers 把…加起来: *The waiter hadn't added up the bill correctly.* 服务员没算对账。

add up to something to have as a total 总计为: *How much does all the shopping add up to?* 买的东西加起来总共多少钱?

addict /'ædɪkt/ *noun* 名词 a person who cannot stop wanting something that is bad for them 成瘾的人; 嗜…成性的人: *a drug addict* 吸毒成瘾的人

addicted /ə'dɪktɪd/ *adjective* 形容词 not able to stop wanting something that is bad for you 上瘾的; 成瘾的: *He is addicted to heroin.* 他吸海洛因成瘾。

addition /ə'dɪʃn/ *noun* 名词
1 (*no plural* 不用复数形式) putting numbers together 加; 加法: *We learnt addition and subtraction at primary school.* 我们在小学学了加减法。
2 (*plural* 复数形式 **additions**) a thing or person that is added to something 增加物; 增加的人: *They have a new addition to their family* (= a new baby). 他们家添了一口人。

in addition, in addition to something as well as 除…以外 (还): *He speaks five languages in addition to English.* 他除英语之外还会说五种语言。

address¹ 0➔ /ə'dres/ *noun* 名词 (*plural* 复数形式 **addresses**)

> 🔎 SPELLING 拼写说明
> Remember! You spell **address** with **DD** and **SS**. 记住: address 拼写中有 dd 和 ss。

1 the number of the building and the name of the street and town where somebody lives or works 住址; 地址: *Her address is 18 Wilton Street, London NW10.* 她的地址是伦敦 NW10 威尔顿街 18 号。 ◇ *Are you still living at that address?* 你还住在那个地方吗?
2 (*computing* 电脑) a group of words and symbols that tells you where you can find somebody or something using a computer 地址: *What's your email address?* 你的电邮地址是什么?

address² /ə'dres/ *verb* 动词 (**addresses**, **addressing**, **addressed** /ə'drest/)
1 to write on a letter or package the name and address of the person you are sending it to 写 (收信人) 姓名地址: *The letter was addressed to Alison Waters.* 这封信是寄给艾莉森·沃特斯的。
2 to make a formal speech to a group of people 向…发表演说: *The President will address the assembly.* 总统将在集会发表演说。

adequate /'ædɪkwət/ *adjective* 形容词 enough for what you need 足够的; 充足的: *They are very poor and do not have adequate food or clothing.* 他们很穷，缺吃少穿。 ⊃ OPPOSITE **inadequate** 反义词为 inadequate

adjective /'ædʒɪktɪv/ *noun* 名词 (*grammar* 语法) a word that you use with

a noun, that tells you more about it
形容词： *In the sentence 'This soup is hot',
'hot' is an adjective.* 在 This soup is hot
一句中，hot 是形容词。

adjust /ə'dʒʌst/ *verb* 动词 (adjusts,
adjusting, adjusted)
to make a small change to something, to
make it better 调整；调节： *You can
adjust the height of this chair.* 你可以调节
这把椅子的高度。

administration /əd,mɪnɪ'streɪʃn/ *noun*
名词 (*no plural* 不用复数形式)
controlling or managing something, for
example a business, an office or a school
管理；行政

admiral /'ædmərəl/ *noun* 名词
a very important officer in the navy 海军
将官

admire 0== /əd'maɪə(r)/ *verb* 动词
(admires, admiring, admired /əd'maɪəd/)
to think or say that somebody or
something is very good 钦佩；仰慕；
欣赏： *I really admire you for doing
such a difficult job.* 我真佩服你能做这么
难的工作。◇ *They were admiring the
view from the top of the tower.* 他们在
塔顶上欣赏景色。
▶ **admiration** /,ædmə'reɪʃn/ *noun* 名词
(*no plural* 不用复数形式)： *I have great
admiration for her work.* 我十分钦佩她的
工作。

admission /əd'mɪʃn/ *noun* 名词
1 (*no plural* 不用复数形式) allowing
somebody to go into a school, club,
public place, etc. 准许进入： *There is no
admission to the park after 8 p.m.* 晚上
8 时以后不准进入公园。◇ *All those who
were not wearing a tie were refused
admission to the club.* 没戴领带者不准
进入俱乐部。
2 (*no plural* 不用复数形式) the amount of
money that you have to pay to go into a
place 入场费；门票费： *Admission to the
zoo is €10.* 动物园的门票是 10 欧元。
3 when you agree that you did something
wrong or bad 承认；招认： *an admission
of guilt* 认罪

admit 0== /əd'mɪt/ *verb* 动词 (admits,
admitting, admitted)
1 to say that you have done something
wrong or that something bad is true
承认；招认： *He admitted stealing the
money.* 他承认偷了钱。◇ *I admit that
I made a mistake.* 我承认犯了错误。
◯ OPPOSITE **deny** 反义词为 deny
2 to allow somebody or something to go

into a place 准许进入： *This ticket admits
one person to the museum.* 这张票准许
一人进入博物馆。

adolescence /,ædə'lesns/ *noun* 名词
(*no plural* 不用复数形式)
the period of a person's life between
being a child and becoming an adult
青春期

adolescent /,ædə'lesnt/ *noun* 名词
a young person who is developing from
a child into an adult 青少年 ◯ SAME
MEANING **teenager** 同义词为 teenager

adopt /ə'dɒpt/ *verb* 动词 (adopts,
adopting, adopted)
to take the child of another person into
your family and treat them as your own
child by law 收养；领养： *They adopted
Micky after his parents died.* 他们在米基
父母死后收养了他。

adore /ə'dɔː(r)/ *verb* 动词 (adores,
adoring, adored /ə'dɔːd/)
to love somebody or something very
much 爱慕；热爱： *She adores her
grandchildren.* 她非常疼爱孙辈们。

adult 0== /'ædʌlt; ə'dʌlt/ *noun* 名词
a person or an animal that has grown to
the full size; not a child 成年人；成年
动物： *Adults as well as children will enjoy
this film.* 这部电影老少咸宜。
▶ **adult** *adjective* 形容词： *an adult
ticket* 成人票 ◇ *adult education* 成人教育

advance¹ /əd'vɑːns/ *noun* 名词
progress or a new development in
something 进步；进展： *major advances
in computer technology* 电脑技术的重大
进步
in advance before something happens
预先；事先： *You should book tickets for
the concert well in advance.* 你应该早早
预订音乐会的票。

advance² /əd'vɑːns/ *verb* 动词 (advances,
advancing, advanced /əd'vɑːnst/)
1 to move forward 前进；行进： *The
army advanced towards the city.* 军队向那
座城市开进。◯ OPPOSITE **retreat** 反义词
为 retreat
2 If technology, etc. **advances**, it develops
and gets better. 发展；进步

advanced /əd'vɑːnst/ *adjective* 形容词
of or for somebody who is already good
at something; difficult 高级程度的；高等
的： *an advanced English class* 英语高级班

advantage 0== /əd'vɑːntɪdʒ/ *noun*
名词
something that helps you or that is useful

A
B
C
D
E
F
G
H
I
J
K
L
M
N
O
P
Q
R
S
T
U
V
W
X
Y
Z

有利条件；优点： *One advantage of camping is that it's cheap.* 露营的一大优点是花钱少。 ⊃ OPPOSITE **disadvantage** 反义词为 disadvantage

take advantage of something to make good use of something to help yourself 利用…（使自己得益）： *Buy now and take advantage of these special prices!* 特价优惠，把握机会，即刻购买！

adventure /əd'ventʃə(r)/ *noun* 名词 something exciting that you do or that happens to you 冒险活动；奇遇： *She wrote a book about her adventures in Africa.* 她写了一部书，讲述她在非洲的冒险经历。

adventurous /əd'ventʃərəs/ *adjective* 形容词 An **adventurous** person likes to do exciting, dangerous things. 有冒险精神的；爱冒险的

adverb /'ædvɜ:b/ *noun* 名词 (*grammar* 语法) a word that tells you how, when or where something happens 副词： *In the sentence 'Please speak slowly', 'slowly' is an adverb.* 在 Please speak slowly 一句中，slowly 是副词。

advert /'ædvɜ:t/ *noun* 名词 short for ADVERTISEMENT * advertisement 的缩略式

advertise /'ædvətaɪz/ *verb* 动词 (**advertises, advertising advertised** /'ædvətaɪzd/) to put information in a newspaper, on television, on a wall, etc., to make people want to buy something or do something 做广告；登广告： *I saw those trainers advertised in a magazine.* 我在杂志广告上看到了那些运动鞋。 ◇ *It's very expensive to advertise on television.* 在电视上做广告非常昂贵。

advertisement 0ᵣ /əd'vɜ:tɪsmənt/ (*also informal* 非正式亦作 **ad advert**) *noun* 名词 information in a newspaper, on television, on the Internet, on a wall, etc. that makes people want to buy something or do something 广告： *an advertisement for a new kind of chocolate bar* 新品巧克力棒的一则广告

advertising /'ædvətaɪzɪŋ/ *noun* 名词 (*no plural* 不用复数形式) telling people about things to buy 广告活动；做广告： *He works in advertising.* 他从事广告业。 ◇ *The magazine gets a lot of money from advertising.* 这份杂志通过刊登广告赚到很多钱。

advice 0ᵣ /əd'vaɪs/ *noun* 名词 (*no plural* 不用复数形式) words that you say to help somebody decide what to do 建议；忠告： *The book gives some good advice on travelling abroad.* 这本书提供了出国旅游的一些好建议。 ◇ *I took the doctor's advice* (= I did what the doctor told me to do) *and stayed in bed.* 我听从医嘱，卧床休息。

🔎 GRAMMAR 语法说明
Be careful! You cannot say 'an advice'. 注意：不说 an advice。
You can say **some advice** or **a piece of advice**. 可以说 some advice 或 a piece of advice： *I need some advice.* 我需要些建议。 ◇ *Let me give you a piece of advice.* 让我给你一个忠告吧。

advise 0ᵣ /əd'vaɪz/ *verb* 动词 (**advises, advising, advised** /əd'vaɪzd/)

🔎 SPELLING 拼写说明
Remember! Don't confuse **advise**, which is a verb, with **advice**, which is a noun. 记住：不要混淆动词 advise 和名词 advice： *He gave me some useful advice.* 他给我提了些有用的建议。 ◇ *He advised me to tell the police.* 他建议我报警。

to tell somebody what you think they should do 建议；忠告；劝告： *The doctor advised him to lose weight.* 医生建议他减肥。

▸ **adviser** (*British* 英式英语) (*American* 美式英语 **advisor**) /əd'vaɪzə(r)/ *noun* 名词 a person who gives advice to a company, government, etc. 顾问

aerials 天线

aerial 天线

aerial /'eəriəl/ *noun* 名词 (*British* 英式英语) (*American* 美式英语 **antenna**) a long metal stick on a building, car, etc. that receives radio or television signals 天线

aerobics /eə'rəʊbɪks/ *noun* 名词 (*no plural* 不用复数形式)

physical exercises that people often do in classes, with music 有氧运动；健美操

aeroplane /'eərəpleɪn/ *noun* 名词 (*American* 美式英语 **airplane**) (*British and American also* 英式和美式英语亦作 **plane**) a vehicle with wings that can fly through the air 飞机 ⊃ Look at the note at **plane**. 见 plane 条的注释。

aerosol /'eərəsɒl/ *noun* 名词 a container with liquid in it. You press a button to make the liquid come out in a lot of very small drops. 喷雾器

affair /ə'feə(r)/ *noun* 名词
1 (*plural* 复数形式 affairs) something that happens; an event 事情：*The wedding was a very quiet affair.* 婚礼不事铺张。
2 affairs (*plural* 用复数形式) important events and situations 事务；大事：*the minister for foreign affairs* 外交部长 ◊ *We talked about current affairs* (= the political and social events that are happening at the present time). 我们讨论了时事。
3 (*no plural* 不用复数形式) something private that you do not want other people to know about 私事：*What happened between us is my affair. I don't want to talk about it.* 我们之间发生的是我的私事，我不想谈。
4 (*plural* 复数形式 affairs) a sexual relationship between two people, usually one that is secret 私通；风流韵事：*Her husband was having an affair.* 她丈夫那时有外遇。

affect ⊙ /ə'fekt/ *verb* 动词 (affects, affecting, affected)

> 🔍 SPELLING 拼写说明
> Be careful! Don't confuse **affect**, which is a verb, with **effect**, which is a noun. If you **affect** something then you have an **effect** on it. 注意：不要混淆动词 affect 和名词 effect。一般用 affect something 和 have an effect on something。

to make something or somebody change in a particular way, especially a bad way 影响：*Smoking can affect your health.* 吸烟影响健康。◊ *His parents' divorce affected the child deeply.* 父母离异对这孩子影响很深。

affection /ə'fekʃn/ *noun* 名词 (*no plural* 不用复数形式) the feeling of loving or liking somebody 爱；喜爱：*She has great affection for her aunt.* 她很爱她的姨妈。

affectionate /ə'fekʃənət/ *adjective* 形容词 showing that you love or like somebody very much 充满爱的；充满感情的：*a very affectionate child* 充满爱心的孩子
▸ **affectionately** /ə'fekʃənətli/ *adverb* 副词：*He smiled at his son affectionately.* 他对儿子慈爱地微笑。

afford ⊙ /ə'fɔːd/ *verb* 动词 (affords, affording, afforded)
can afford something If you **can afford something**, you have enough money to pay for it. 消费得起；负担得起：*I can't afford a holiday this year.* 我今年没钱度假。

afraid ⊙ /ə'freɪd/ *adjective* 形容词 If you are **afraid** of something, it makes you feel fear. 害怕；畏惧：*Some people are afraid of snakes.* 有些人怕蛇。◊ *I was afraid to open the door.* 我不敢去开门。
I'm afraid ... a polite way of saying that you are sorry 恐怕；对不起：*I'm afraid I've broken your calculator.* 对不起，我把你的计算器弄坏了。◊ *I'm afraid that I can't come to your party.* 恐怕我不能参加你的聚会了。

after¹ ⊙ /'ɑːftə(r)/ *preposition* 介词
1 later than somebody or something （时间）在…之后：*Jane arrived after dinner.* 简是在饭后来的。◊ *After doing my homework, I went out.* 我做完作业后出去了。
2 behind or following somebody or something 在…后面；跟随：*Ten comes after nine.* 十在九的后面。◊ *Close the door after you.* 随手关门。
3 trying to get or catch somebody or something 追赶；追捕：*The police officer ran after her.* 警察追捕她。
after all
1 used when you thought something different would happen 毕竟；终究：*I was worried about the exam, but it wasn't difficult after all.* 我很担心这次考试，却原来并不难。
2 used to mean 'do not forget' 别忘了；说到底：*She doesn't understand. After all, she's only two.* 她不明白的。说到底，她只有两岁。
be after something to be trying to get or find something 寻找：*What kind of work are you after?* 你在找什么样的工作？

after² /'ɑːftə(r)/ *conjunction, adverb* 连词，副词 at a time later than somebody or something （时间）在…之后：*We arrived after the film had started.* 我们在

A
B
C
D
E
F
G
H
I
J
K
L
M
N
O
P
Q
R
S
T
U
V
W
X
Y
Z

电影开始后才到。◇ *Jane left at ten o'clock and I left soon after.* 简在十点钟离开，不久以后我也走了。

afternoon 0☞ /ˌɑːftəˈnuːn/ *noun* 名词
the part of a day between midday (= 12 o'clock) and the evening 下午: *We had lunch and in the afternoon we went for a walk.* 我们吃过午饭，下午出去散步了。◇ *I saw Jane this afternoon.* 我今天下午见到简了。◇ *Yesterday afternoon I went shopping.* 昨天下午我买东西去了。◇ *I'll see you on Monday afternoon.* 星期一下午见。

> 🔎 GRAMMAR 语法说明
> We usually say **in the afternoon**. 通常说 in the afternoon: *We went to Windsor Castle in the afternoon.* 下午我们去了温莎城堡。
> If we include a day or date then we use **on**. 具体地说某一天用 on: *We went shopping on Monday afternoon.* 星期一下午我们去购物了。

aftershave /ˈɑːftəʃeɪv/ *noun* 名词
(*no plural* 不用复数形式)
a liquid with a nice smell that men sometimes put on their faces after they SHAVE (= cut the hair off their face) 须后水；胡后水

afterwards 0☞ /ˈɑːftəwədz/ *adverb* 副词
later; after another thing has happened 后来；以后: *We had dinner and went to see a film afterwards.* 我们吃完饭后去看了场电影。

again 0☞ /əˈgen/ *adverb* 副词
1 one more time; once more 再一次；又一次: *Could you say that again, please?* 请再说一遍好吗？◇ *I will never see him again.* 我再也不会见他了。
2 in the way that somebody or something was before 复原；恢复原样: *You'll soon feel well again.* 你很快就会康复的。
again and again many times 一再；再三: *I've told you again and again not to do that!* 我已经再三跟你说不要做那件事！

against 0☞ /əˈgenst/ *preposition* 介词
1 on the other side in a game, fight, etc. 与…竞争；对垒: *They played against a football team from another village.* 他们和另一个村的足球队比赛。
2 If you are **against** something, you do not agree with it. 反对: *Many people are against the plan.* 很多人反对这项计划。
3 touching somebody or something for

support 靠；倚: *I put the ladder against the wall.* 我把梯子靠墙放着。
4 to stop something 防止；预防: *Have you had an injection against the disease?* 你打过这种病的预防针吗？

age 0☞ /eɪdʒ/ *noun* 名词
1 (*plural* 复数形式 **ages**) the amount of time that somebody or something has been in the world 年龄；年纪: *She is seven years of age.* 她七岁。◇ *I started work at the age of 16.* 我 16 岁开始工作。

> 🔎 SPEAKING 表达方式说明
> When we want to ask someone's **age**, we say **How old are you?** 询问年龄时通常说 How old are you?
> To say your age, you say **I am 10** or **I'm 10 years old** (but NOT 'I am 10 years'). 表示自己的年龄说 I am 10 或 I'm 10 years old（而不说 I am 10 years）。

2 (*no plural* 不用复数形式) being old 老年；陈年: *Her hair was grey with age.* 她年纪大了，头发也白了。
3 (*plural* 复数形式 **ages**) a certain time in history 时代: *the computer age* 电脑时代 ◇ *the history of art through the ages* 各个时代的艺术史 ◇ *the Stone Age* (= when people used stone tools) 石器时代
4 **ages** (*plural* 用复数形式) (*informal* 非正式) a very long time 很长时间；很久: *We waited ages for a bus.* 我们等公共汽车等了很久。◇ *She's lived here for ages.* 她在这儿住很久了。

aged 0☞ /eɪdʒd/ *adjective* 形容词
of the age mentioned …岁: *They have two children, aged three and five.* 他们有两个孩子，一个三岁一个五岁。

agency /ˈeɪdʒənsi/ *noun* 名词 (*plural* 复数形式 **agencies**)
the work or office of somebody who does business for others 代理；代理机构: *A travel agency plans holidays for people.* 旅行社专门给人安排度假活动。

agenda /əˈdʒendə/ *noun* 名词
a list of all the things to be talked about in a meeting 议程；议事日程: *The next item on the agenda is the school sports day.* 议程的下一项是校运会。

agent /ˈeɪdʒənt/ *noun* 名词
a person who does business for another person or for a company 代理人；经纪人: *An actor's agent tries to find work for actors and actresses.* 演员的经纪人尽力为演员寻找工作机会。◇ *a travel agent* 旅行代理商

aggressive /ə'gresɪv/ *adjective* 形容词
If you are **aggressive**, you are ready to
argue or fight. 好争吵的；好斗的：*He
often gets aggressive after drinking alcohol.*
他喝酒后常常爱生事。

ago 0ᵣ /ə'gəʊ/ *adverb* 副词
before now; in the past （一段时间）
之前，以前：*His wife died five years ago.*
他妻子在五年前去世了。◇ *I learned to
drive a long time ago.* 我很久以前就学会
开车了。
long ago a very long time in the past
很久以前：*Long ago there were no cars
or aeroplanes.* 很久以前没有汽车也没有
飞机。

agony /'ægəni/ *noun* 名词 (*plural* 复数
形式 agonies)
very great pain 巨痛；极大的痛苦：*He
screamed in agony.* 他痛得尖声高叫。

agree 0ᵣ /ə'griː/ *verb* 动词 (agrees,
agreeing, agreed /ə'griːd/)
1 to have the same opinion as another
person about something 持相同观点；
赞同：*Martin thinks we should go by train
but I don't agree.* 马丁认为我们应该乘火车
去，但我不同意。◇ *I agree with you.*
我同意你的意见。➋ OPPOSITE **disagree**
反义词为 disagree
2 to say 'yes' when somebody asks you to
do something 答应；同意：*Amy agreed
to give me the money.* 埃米同意给我那笔
钱。➋ OPPOSITE **refuse** 反义词为 refuse
3 to decide something with another
person 约定；商定：*We agreed to meet
on March 3rd.* 我们约好 3 月 3 日见面。◇
Liz and I agreed on a price. 利兹和我谈好
了价格。

agreement 0ᵣ /ə'griːmənt/ *noun* 名词
1 (*no plural* 不用复数形式) having the
same opinion as somebody or something
意见一致：*She nodded her head in
agreement.* 她点头表示同意。➋ OPPOSITE
disagreement 反义词为 disagreement
2 (*plural* 复数形式 agreements) a plan or
decision that two or more people have
made together 协定；协议：*The leaders
reached an agreement after five days of
talks.* 经过五天的谈判之后，领导人达成了
协议。

agriculture /'ægrɪkʌltʃə(r)/ *noun* 名词
(*no plural* 不用复数形式)
keeping animals and growing plants for
food 农业 ➋ SAME MEANING **farming**
同义词为 farming
▸ **agricultural** /ˌægrɪ'kʌltʃərəl/ *adjective*
形容词：*agricultural workers* 农工

ahead 0ᵣ /ə'hed/ *adverb* 副词
1 in front of somebody or something
在前面：*We could see a light ahead of us.*
我们看见前面有灯。
2 before or more advanced than
somebody or something 早于；领先：
*Inga and Nils arrived a few minutes ahead
of us.* 英格和尼尔斯比我们早到几分钟。
◇ *London is about five hours ahead of
New York.* 伦敦比纽约早大约五个小时。
3 into the future 到将来：*He's got a
difficult time ahead of him.* 他以后的
日子不好过。◇ *We must think ahead
and make a plan.* 我们得向前看并制订
计划。
4 winning in a game, competition, etc.
领先：*Italy were one goal ahead at half
time.* 意大利队半场以一球领先。
go ahead used to give somebody
permission to do something 可以做
某事：*'Can I borrow your bike?' 'Sure,
go ahead.'* "我能借你的自行车吗？"
"行，用吧。"

aid /eɪd/ *noun* 名词 (*no plural* 不用复数
形式)
1 help, or something that gives help
帮助：*He walks with the aid of a stick.*
他拄拐杖走路。◇ *She wears a hearing aid*
(= a small thing that you put in your ear
so you can hear better). 她戴助听器。
2 money, food, etc. that is sent to a
country or to people in order to help
them 援助；救援物资：*We sent aid to
the earthquake victims.* 我们给地震灾民
送去救援物资。
in aid of somebody or 或 **something**
for somebody or something, especially for
a charity 为了帮助…：*a concert in aid of
Children in Need* 为慈善组织"儿童求助"
筹款的音乐会

AIDS (*British also* 英式英语亦作 Aids) /eɪdz/
noun 名词 (*no plural* 不用复数形式)
a very serious illness which destroys the
body's ability to fight other illnesses
艾滋病：*the AIDS virus* 艾滋病病毒

aim¹ 0ᵣ /eɪm/ *noun* 名词
something that you want and plan to do;
a purpose 目标；目的：*Kate's aim is to
find a good job.* 凯特的目标是找份好
工作。

aim² 0ᵣ /eɪm/ *verb* 动词 (aims, aiming,
aimed /eɪmd/)
1 to try or plan to do something 力求
做到；计划做：*He's aiming to leave at
nine o'clock.* 他打算九点钟离开。
2 to plan something for a certain person
or group 针对；对象是：*This book is*

A

B
C
D
E
F
G
H
I
J
K
L
M
N
O
P
Q
R
S
T
U
V
W
X
Y
Z

aimed at teenagers. 这本书的对象是
青少年。

3 to point something, for example a gun,
at somebody or something that you want
to hit 瞄准: *The farmer **aimed** his gun **at**
the rabbit and fired.* 农夫把枪对准了兔子，
然后开了枪。

air[1] ⚪━ /eə(r)/ *noun* 名词 (*no plural* 不用
复数形式)

1 the mixture of gases that surrounds the
earth and that you take in through your
nose and mouth when you breathe
空气: *Please open a window – I need
some fresh air*. 请打开窗，我需要吸点
新鲜空气。

2 the space around and above things
空中；天空: *He threw the ball up **into**
the air*. 他把球抛到空中。

3 travel or transport in an aircraft 空中
旅行；空运: *It's more expensive to travel
by air than by train.* 坐飞机比坐火车贵。

◇ *an air ticket* 飞机票

on air, on the air on the radio or on
television 播出（广播、电视）节目: *This
radio station is on the air 24 hours a day.*
这个广播电台一天 24 小时播音。

air[2] /eə(r)/ *verb* 动词 (airs, airing, aired
/eəd/)

1 to make a room, etc. fresh by letting air
from outside into it 使（房间等）通风

2 to tell people what you think about
something 发表: *The discussion gave
people a chance to air their views*. 这次
讨论给了大家发表意见的机会。

air conditioning /'eə kəndɪʃnɪŋ/ *noun*
名词 (*no plural* 不用复数形式)
a system that keeps the air in a room,
building, car, etc. cool and dry 空气调节
系统

▶ **air-conditioned** /'eə kəndɪʃnd/
adjective 形容词: *air-conditioned offices*
有空调的办公室

aircraft ⚪━ /'eəkrɑːft/ *noun* 名词 (*plural*
复数形式 aircraft)
any vehicle that can fly in the air, for
example a plane 飞行器（如飞机等）

air force /'eə fɔːs/ *noun* 名词
the aircraft that a country uses for
fighting, and the people who fly them
空军

air hostess /'eə həʊstəs/ *noun* 名词
(*plural* 复数形式 air hostesses)
a woman whose job is to look after people
on a plane（客机上的）女乘务员；空中
小姐: *Alison is an air hostess.* 艾莉森是

空姐。 ⚡ SAME MEANING **stewardess**
同义词为 stewardess

airline /'eəlaɪn/ *noun* 名词
a company that takes people or things to
different places by plane 航空公司:
Which airline are you flying with? 你乘坐
哪家航空公司的飞机?

airmail /'eəmeɪl/ *noun* 名词 (*no plural*
不用复数形式)
the system of sending letters, packages,
etc. by plane 航空邮递: *I sent the parcel
by airmail.* 我用空邮把包裹寄出了。 ◇
I sent it airmail. 我用空邮把它寄出了。

airplane /'eəpleɪn/ *American English for*
AEROPLANE 美式英语，即 aeroplane

airport ⚪━ /'eəpɔːt/ *noun* 名词
a place where people get on and off
planes, with buildings where passengers
can wait 机场: *I'll meet you at the airport.*
我会在机场跟你会合。

aisle /aɪl/ *noun* 名词
a way between lines of seats in a church,
plane, etc.（教堂、飞机等座位之间的）
走道

alarm[1] /ə'lɑːm/ *noun* 名词
1 (*no plural* 不用复数形式) a sudden
feeling of fear 惊恐；惊慌: *He heard a
noise, and jumped out of bed in alarm.*
他听到声响，吓得跳下了床。

2 (*plural* 复数形式 alarms) something that
tells you about danger, for example by
making a loud noise 报警器: *Does your
car have an alarm?* 你的汽车有报警器吗?
◇ *a burglar alarm* 防盗报警器 ◇ *a fire
alarm* 防火报警器

3 = ALARM CLOCK

⚡ Look also at **false alarm** at **false**.
亦见 false 条的 false alarm。

alarm[2] /ə'lɑːm/ *verb* 动词 (alarms,
alarming, alarmed /ə'lɑːmd/)
to make somebody or something feel
suddenly frightened or worried 使惊恐;
使担心: *The noise alarmed the bird and
it flew away.* 那阵声响把鸟吓飞了。 ◇ *She
was alarmed to hear that Peter was ill.*
她听说彼得病了，马上就很担心。

alarm clock /ə'lɑːm klɒk/ (*also* 亦作
alarm) *noun* 名词
a clock that makes a noise to wake you
up 闹钟: *She set the alarm clock for half
past six.* 她把闹钟定在六点半。

album /'ælbəm/ *noun* 名词
1 a collection of songs on one CD, tape,
etc. 音乐专辑: *The band are about to
release their third album.* 这个乐队即将

推出第三张专辑。 ⊃ Look at **single**² (2).
见 single² 第 2 义。
2 a book in which you can keep stamps,
photographs, etc. that you have collected
集邮簿；相册；影集：*a photograph
album* 相册

alcohol ⊶ /ˈælkəhɒl/ *noun* 名词
(*no plural* 不用复数形式)
1 the clear liquid in drinks such as beer
and wine that can make people drunk
酒精
2 drinks like wine, beer, etc. that contain
alcohol 含酒精饮料；酒

alcoholic ⊶ /ˌælkəˈhɒlɪk/ *adjective*
形容词
containing alcohol 含酒精的：
an alcoholic drink 含酒精的饮料

> 🔍 WORD BUILDING 词汇扩充
>
> Drinks without alcohol are called
> **soft drinks**. 不含酒精的饮料叫做 soft
> drink。

alert¹ /əˈlɜːt/ *adjective* 形容词
watching, listening, etc. for something
with all your attention 警觉的；留神的：
A good driver is always alert. 好的驾驶员
时刻保持警觉。

alert² /əˈlɜːt/ *noun* 名词
a warning of danger 警报
on the alert (for something) ready or
prepared for danger or an attack 警戒
着；戒备着

A level /ˈeɪ levl/ *noun* 名词
an exam that students in Britain take
when they are about eighteen. You
usually take **A levels** in two, three or four
subjects and you need good results (called
grades) if you want to go to university. **A
level** is short for **Advanced level**. (英国)
高级证书考试 (A level 是 Advanced level
的缩略式) ⊃ Look at **GCSE**. 见 GCSE。

alarm clock 闹钟

hand 指针

algebra /ˈældʒɪbrə/ *noun* 名词 (*no plural*
不用复数形式)
a type of mathematics in which letters
and symbols are used to represent
numbers 代数

alien /ˈeɪliən/ *noun* 名词
1 (*formal* 正式) a person who comes from
another country 外国人；外侨：*an illegal
alien* 非法外侨
2 a person or an animal that comes from
another planet 外星人；外星动物：*aliens
from outer space* 外星人

alight /əˈlaɪt/ *adjective* 形容词
on fire; burning 着火；燃烧：*A cigarette
set the petrol alight.* 香烟引燃了汽油。

alike /əˈlaɪk/ *adjective, adverb* 形容词，
副词
1 very similar 相像；十分相似：*The two
sisters are very alike.* 这对姐妹长得很像。
2 in the same way 同样地：*The book is
popular with adults and children alike.*
这本书大人小孩都爱看。

alive ⊶ /əˈlaɪv/ *adjective* 形容词
living; not dead 活着：*Are your
grandparents alive?* 你的祖父母还健在吗?

all¹ ⊶ /ɔːl/ *adjective, pronoun* 形容词，
代词
1 every part of something; the whole of
something 全部；整体：*She's eaten all
the bread.* 她把面包吃光了。◊ *It rained all
day.* 雨下了一整天。
2 every one of a group 所有；全体：*All
cats are animals but not all animals are
cats.* 所有的猫都是动物，但并非所有的动
物都是猫。◊ *I invited thirty people to the
party, but not all of them came.* 我邀请了
三十人参加聚会，但并不是所有人都来
了。◊ *Are you all listening?* 你们都在
听吗?
3 everything that; the only thing that
全部；唯一：*All I've eaten today is one
banana.* 我今天只吃了一根香蕉。
(not) at all in any way 一点也 (不)；
完全 (不)：*I didn't enjoy it at all.* 我一点
也不喜欢。

all² ⊶ /ɔːl/ *adverb* 副词
completely 完全：*She lives all alone.*
她独自一人生活。◊ *He was dressed all in
black.* 他穿着一身黑衣服。
all along from the beginning 从一开始：
I knew all along that she was lying. 我一
开始就知道她在撒谎。
all over everywhere 到处；处处：*We've
looked all over for that ring.* 我们到处找
那枚戒指。

A
B
C
D
E
F
G
H
I
J
K
L
M
N
O
P
Q
R
S
T
U
V
W
X
Y
Z

allergic /ə'lɜːdʒɪk/ *adjective* 形容词
having an ALLERGY 过敏的: *He's allergic
to cow's milk.* 他对牛奶过敏。

allergy /'ælədʒi/ *noun* 名词 (*plural* 复数
形式 allergies)
a medical condition that makes you ill
when you eat, touch or breathe
something that does not normally make
other people ill 过敏反应: *She has an
allergy to cats.* 她对猫过敏。

alley /'æli/ *noun* 名词 (*plural* 复数形式
alleys)
a narrow path between buildings 小巷;
胡同

alliance /ə'laɪəns/ *noun* 名词
an agreement between countries or
groups of people to work together and
help each other 联盟; 同盟

alligator /'ælɪgeɪtə(r)/ *noun* 名词
a big long animal with sharp teeth.
Alligators live in the lakes and rivers of
the US and China. 钝吻鳄

allow ⚪ /ə'laʊ/ *verb* 动词 (allows,
allowing, allowed /ə'laʊd/)
to say that somebody can have or do
something 允许; 准许: *My parents allow
me to stay out late at weekends.* 我父母
允许我周末晚点回家。◇ *Smoking is not
allowed in most cinemas.* 大部分电影院都
不准吸烟。◇ *You're not allowed to park
your car here.* 此处不准停车。

> 🔍 **WHICH WORD?** 词语辨析
> **Allow** or **let**? 用 allow 还是 let?
> **Allow** is used in both formal and
> informal English. * allow 可用于正式和
> 非正式场合。
> **Let** is very common in spoken English.
> * let 在英语口语中很常用。
> You **allow somebody to do something**,
> but you **let somebody do something**
> (without 'to'). 一般用 allow somebody
> to do something 和 let somebody do
> something（不跟 to）: *Jenny was
> allowed to stay up late last night.* 珍妮
> 昨晚获准晚些睡觉。◇ *Her parents let
> her stay up late last night.* 她父母昨晚
> 准许她晚些睡觉。
> In written English you can use **permit**.
> 书面英语可用 permit: *Smoking is not
> permitted in this building.* 这栋大楼内
> 禁止吸烟。

allowance /ə'laʊəns/ *noun* 名词
an amount of money that you receive
regularly to help you pay for something
that you need 津贴; 补贴: *All employees

receive a travel allowance.* 员工都可以拿
到交通补贴。

all right ⚪ /ɔːl 'raɪt/ (*also informal
非正式亦作* alright) *adjective, adverb,
exclamation* 形容词, 副词, 感叹词
1 good, or good enough 好的; 还不错:
Is everything all right? 一切都好吗?
2 well; not hurt 安然无恙; 没受伤:
I was ill, but I'm all right now. 我病了,
但现在好了。
3 used to say 'yes, I agree' when
somebody asks you to do something
（表示同意）好, 行, 可以: *'Can you get
me some stamps?' 'All right.'* "你能帮我买
几张邮票吗?""行, 没问题。"

ally /'ælaɪ/ *noun* 名词 (*plural* 复数形式
allies)
a person or country that agrees to help
another person or country, for example
in a war 盟友; 盟国

almond /'ɑːmənd/ *noun* 名词
a flat pale nut that you can eat 杏仁
➲ Look at the picture at **nut**. 见 nut 的
插图。

almost ⚪ /'ɔːlməʊst/ *adverb* 副词
nearly; not quite 几乎; 差不多: *It's
almost three o'clock.* 快三点钟了。◇
I almost fell into the river! 我差一点就掉进
河里!

alone ⚪ /ə'ləʊn/ *adjective, adverb* 形容
词, 副词
1 without any other person 独自; 单独
➲ SAME MEANING **on your own, by
yourself** 同义词为 on your own 和 by
yourself: *I don't like being alone in the
house.* 我不喜欢一个人待在家里。◇
My grandmother lives alone. 我祖母独自
生活。
2 only 只有 *You alone can help me.*
只有你能帮助我。

> 🔍 **WHICH WORD?** 词语辨析
> **Alone** or **lonely**? 用 alone 还是 lonely?
> **Alone** means that you are not with
> other people. * alone 表示独自: *She
> lived alone in a flat near the city centre.*
> 她一个人住在市中心附近的公寓里。
> **Lonely** means that you are unhappy
> because you are not with other people.
> * lonely 表示孤独: *He felt lonely at the
> new school without his old friends.* 他在
> 新学校没有老朋友, 感到很孤独。

along¹ ⚪ /ə'lɒŋ/ *preposition* 介词
1 from one end of something towards the
other end 沿着; 顺着: *We walked along
the road.* 我们沿着那条路走。

2 in a line next to something long 靠着…的边; 沿着: *There are trees along the river bank.* 沿河长着树。

along² ⊶ /əˈlɒŋ/ *adverb* 副词
1 forward 向前; 往前: *He drove along very slowly.* 他驱车缓慢地前进。
2 (*informal* 非正式) with somebody （和某人）一道, 一起: *We're going for a walk. Why don't you come along too?* 我们要去散步, 你干吗不一块去?

alongside /əˌlɒŋˈsaɪd/ *preposition, adverb* 介词, 副词
next to something 在…旁边; 在旁边: *Put your bike alongside mine.* 把你的自行车放在我的自行车旁边。◇ *Nick caught up with me and rode alongside.* 尼克追上了我, 和我并排往前骑。

aloud /əˈlaʊd/ *adverb* 副词
in a normal speaking voice that other people can hear 高声地; 大声地: *I read the story aloud to my sister.* 我给妹妹大声朗读这个故事。

alphabet ⊶ /ˈælfəbet/ *noun* 名词
all the letters of a language 字母表: *The English alphabet starts with A and ends with Z.* 英语字母表从 A 开始到 Z 结束。

alphabetical /ˌælfəˈbetɪkl/ *adjective* 形容词
in the order of the alphabet 按字母顺序的: *Put these words in alphabetical order* (= with words beginning with A first, then B, then C, etc.). 把这些词按字母顺序排列。
▶ **alphabetically** /ˌælfəˈbetɪkli/ *adverb* 副词: *The books are listed alphabetically.* 这些书是按字母顺序排列的。

already ⊶ /ɔːlˈredi/ *adverb* 副词
before now or before then 已经; 早已: *'Would you like some lunch?' 'No, thank you – I've already eaten.'* "吃午饭吗?" "不, 谢谢, 我已经吃了。" ◇ *We ran to the station but the train had already left.* 我们跑到车站, 但火车已经开走了。

> 🔍 **WHICH WORD?** 词语辨析
> **Already** or **yet**? 用 already 还是 yet?
> **Yet** means the same as **already**, but you only use **yet** in negative sentences and questions. * yet 的意思与 already 一样, 但只用于否定句和疑问句: *I have finished this book already.* 我已经看完这本书了。◇ *I haven't finished this book yet.* 我还没看完这本书呢。◇ *Have you finished the book yet?* 你看完这本书了吗?

alright /ɔːlˈraɪt/ (*informal* 非正式) = ALL RIGHT

also ⊶ /ˈɔːlsəʊ/ *adverb* 副词
as well; too 也; 而且: *He plays several instruments and also writes music.* 他会演奏好几种乐器, 还会谱曲。◇ *The food is wonderful, and also very cheap.* 食物相当好, 而且很便宜。

> 🔍 **WHICH WORD?** 词语辨析
> **Also**, **too** or **as well**? 用 also、too 还是 as well?
> You use **also** in writing, but you usually use **too** or **as well** in spoken English. * also 用于书面语, too 和 as well 则通常用于口语。
> **Also** usually goes before a main verb or after 'is', 'are', 'were', etc. * also 通常用于主动词之前或 is、are、were 等词之后: *He also enjoys reading.* 他也喜欢阅读。◇ *He has also been to Australia.* 他也去过澳大利亚。
> **Too** and **as well** usually go at the end of a phrase or sentence. * too 和 as well 通常用于短语或句子的结尾: *We're going to the cinema tomorrow. Would you like to come too?* 我们想明天去看电影, 你也想去吗? ◇ *I really love this song, and I liked the first one as well.* 我真的喜欢这首歌, 也喜欢第一首歌。

alter /ˈɔːltə(r)/ *verb* 动词 (alters, altering, altered /ˈɔːltəd/)
to make something different in some way; to change 改变; 更改: *We've altered our plans and will now stay for a week instead of ten days.* 我们改变了计划, 将逗留一个星期, 而不是十天。◇ *He had altered so much I hardly recognized him.* 他变化太大, 我几乎认不出来了。

alteration /ˌɔːltəˈreɪʃn/ *noun* 名词
a small change （小的）改变, 变化: *We want to make a few alterations to the house before we move in.* 我们想对房子作几处改动再搬进去。

alternate¹ /ɔːlˈtɜːnət/ *adjective* 形容词
1 with first one thing, then the other, then the first thing again, etc. 交替的; 轮流的: *The cake had alternate layers of fruit and cream.* 这个蛋糕的水果层和奶油层相间。
2 one out of every two 间隔的: *He works alternate weeks* (= he works the first week, he doesn't work the second week, he works again the third week, etc.). 他隔周工作。
3 (*American* 美式英语) (*British* 英式英语

A
B
C
D
E
F
G
H
I
J
K
L
M
N
O
P
Q
R
S
T
U
V
W
X
Y
Z

alternative) that you can use, do, etc. instead of something else 可供替代的: *an alternate plan* 一替代计划

alternate² /ˈɔːltəneɪt/ *verb* 动词
If two things **alternate**, first one thing happens and then the other and then the first thing happens again, etc. 交替; 轮流: *She seemed to **alternate** between loving him and hating him.* 她好像对他又爱又恨。

alternative¹ /ɔːlˈtɜːnətɪv/ *adjective* 形容词
that you can use, do, etc. instead of something else 可供替代的: *The road was closed so we had to find an alternative route.* 这条路封闭了，我们得找另一路线。

alternative² /ɔːlˈtɜːnətɪv/ *noun* 名词
a thing that you can choose instead of another thing 可供选择的事物: *We could go by train – the alternative is to take the car.* 我们可以坐火车去，坐汽车去也行。

alternatively /ɔːlˈtɜːnətɪvli/ *adverb* 副词
used to talk about a second possible thing you can do 要不; 或者: *We can go by bus. Alternatively, I could take the car.* 我们可以乘公共汽车去，或者我开车去。

although 0→ /ɔːlˈðəʊ/ *conjunction* 连词

> 🔊 PRONUNCIATION 读音说明
> The word **although** ends with the same sound as **go**. * although 末段的发音和 go 相同。

1 in spite of something 虽然; 尽管; 即使: *Although she was ill, she went to work.* 她虽然病了，但还是上班去了。
2 but 但是; 然而: *I love dogs, although I wouldn't have one as a pet.* 我喜欢狗，尽管我不会把它当作宠物来养。 ⮑ SAME MEANING **though** 同义词为 though

altogether /ˌɔːltəˈɡeðə(r)/ *adverb* 副词
1 completely 完全: *I don't altogether agree with you.* 我不完全同意你的看法。
2 counting everything or everybody 总共; 一共: *There were ten of us altogether.* 我们总共十个人。

always 0→ /ˈɔːlweɪz/ *adverb* 副词
1 at all times; every time 总是; 每次都是: *I have always lived in London.* 我一直住在伦敦。 ◇ *The train is always late.* 火车老是晚点。
2 for ever 永远: *I will always remember that day.* 我会永远记住那一天。
3 again and again 老是; 一再: *My sister is always borrowing my clothes!* 我妹妹老是借我的衣服穿!

> 🔊 GRAMMAR 语法说明
> **Always** usually goes before the main verb or after 'is', 'are', 'were', etc. * always 通常用于主动词之前或 is、are、were 等词之后: *He always wears those shoes.* 他总是穿那双鞋。 ◇ *Fiona is always late.* 菲奥娜老是迟到。
> **Always** can go at the beginning of a sentence when you are telling somebody to do something. 叫某人做某事时，always 可用在句首: *Always stop and look before you cross the road.* 过马路前先要停下来看看。

am *form of* BE * be 的不同形式

a.m. (*American also* 美式英语亦作 A.M.) /ˌeɪ ˈem/ *abbreviation* 缩略式
You use **a.m.** after a time to show that it is between midnight and midday. 上午: *I start work at 9 a.m.* 我上午 9 点钟上班。 ⮑ You use **p.m.** for times between midday and midnight. 用 p.m. 表示下午。

amateur /ˈæmətə(r)/ *noun* 名词
a person who does a sport or an activity because they enjoy it, but not for money as a job 业余爱好者; 业余运动员: *Only amateurs can take part in the tournament.* 只有业余选手才能参加这次锦标赛。 ⮑ OPPOSITE **professional** 反义词为 professional
▶ **amateur** *adjective* 形容词: *an amateur photographer* 业余摄影师

amaze /əˈmeɪz/ *verb* 动词 (**amazes, amazing, amazed** /əˈmeɪzd/)
to surprise somebody very much; to be difficult for somebody to believe 使惊奇; 使难以置信: *It amazes me that anyone could be so stupid!* 竟有这么笨的人，真让我惊讶!

amazed /əˈmeɪzd/ *adjective* 形容词
very surprised 大为惊奇: *She was amazed to discover the truth about her father.* 她发现关于父亲的真相后大为吃惊。 ◇ *I was amazed at her knowledge of French literature.* 她的法国文学知识如此丰富使我大为惊奇。

amazement /əˈmeɪzmənt/ *noun* 名词 (*no plural* 不用复数形式)
great surprise 惊奇; 惊诧: *She looked at me in amazement.* 她惊诧地看着我。

amazing /əˈmeɪzɪŋ/ *adjective* 形容词
If something is **amazing**, it surprises you very much and is difficult to believe. 令人惊奇的; 难以置信的 ⮑ SAME MEANING **incredible** 同义词为 incredible: *He has*

shown amazing courage. 他表现出了惊人的勇气。◇ *I've got an amazing story to tell you.* 我有一件令人难以置信的事要告诉你们。

▶ **amazingly** /ə'meɪzɪŋli/ *adverb* 副词: *Jo plays the violin amazingly well.* 乔拉小提琴拉得出奇的好。

ambassador /æm'bæsədə(r)/ *noun* 名词
an important person who represents his or her country in a foreign country 大使；使节: *the British Ambassador to Italy* 英国驻意大利大使

> 🔍 **WORD BUILDING** 词汇扩充
>
> An ambassador works in an **embassy**. 大使工作的地方叫做 embassy（大使馆）。

ambition /æm'bɪʃn/ *noun* 名词
1 something that you really want to do 追求的目标: *My ambition is to become a doctor.* 我的志愿是当医生。
2 (*no plural* 不用复数形式) a very strong wish to be successful, to have power, etc. 野心；抱负；志向: *Louise is intelligent, but she has no ambition.* 路易丝很聪明，可是她胸无大志。

ambitious /æm'bɪʃəs/ *adjective* 形容词
A person who is **ambitious** wants to be successful, to have power, etc. 有雄心的；有野心的

ambulance /'æmbjələns/ *noun* 名词
a vehicle that takes people who are ill or hurt to hospital 救护车

American football /ə,merɪkən 'fʊtbɔːl/ (*British* 英式英语) (*American* 美式英语 **football**) *noun* 名词 (*no plural* 不用复数形式)
a game that is played by two teams of eleven players who kick, throw or carry the ball to the end of the field. The players wear special clothing to protect their heads and bodies. 美式足球

ammunition /,æmju'nɪʃn/ *noun* 名词
(*no plural* 不用复数形式)
things that you throw or fire from a gun to hurt people or damage things 弹药: *They had no more ammunition.* 他们没有弹药了。

among 0━ /ə'mʌŋ/ (*also* 亦作 **amongst** /ə'mʌŋst/) *preposition* 介词
1 in the middle of a group of people or things 在…中间: *I often feel nervous when I'm among strangers.* 我在陌生人中间常常感到紧张。
2 in a particular group of people or things 在（群体）中间: *There is a lot of*

anger among students about the new law. 学生对新法大为愤怒。
3 for or by more than two things or people 在…中（分配或选择）: *He divided the money among his six children.* 他把钱分给了六个子女。

> 🔍 **WHICH WORD?** 词语辨析
>
> **Among** or **between**? 用 among 还是 between?
> We use **among** when we are talking about more than two people or things. 谈到两个以上的人或事物时用 among: *You're among friends here.* 这里都是你的朋友。
> If there are only two people or things, we use **between**. 要是只有两个人或两件事物就要用 between: *Sarah and I divided the cake between us.* 我和萨拉把蛋糕分了。◇ *I was standing between Alice and Cathy.* 我站在艾丽斯和凯茜中间。

among 在…中间

| a house **among** some trees 树丛中的房子 | a small house **between** two large ones 两所大房子之间的小房子 |

amount¹ 0━ /ə'maʊnt/ *noun* 名词
how much there is of something 数量；数额: *He spent a large amount of money.* 他花了很大一笔钱。

amount² /ə'maʊnt/ *verb* 动词 (**amounts, amounting, amounted**)
amount to something to make a certain amount when you add everything together 总计；共计: *The cost of the repairs amounted to £500.* 修理费共计 500 英镑。

amp /æmp/ *noun* 名词
a measure of electricity 安，安培（电流单位）

amplifier /'æmplɪfaɪə(r)/ *noun* 名词
an electrical machine that makes sounds louder 扩音器；扬声器

A
B
C
D
E
F
G
H
I
J
K
L
M
N
O
P
Q
R
S
T
U
V
W
X
Y
Z

amuse 0̶ⁿ /əˈmjuːz/ *verb* 动词 (amuses, amusing, amused /əˈmjuːzd/)
1 to make somebody smile or laugh 使发笑；逗乐：*Rick's joke did not amuse his mother.* 里克讲的笑话并没有把母亲逗乐。
2 to keep somebody happy and busy 使娱乐；消遣：*We played games to amuse ourselves on the long journey.* 我们在长途旅程中玩游戏自娱。

amused /əˈmjuːzd/ *adjective* 形容词
thinking that something is funny and wanting to laugh or smile 觉得好笑的：*He was amused to see how seriously she took the game.* 看见她玩游戏那么认真的样子，他觉得好笑。

amusement /əˈmjuːzmənt/ *noun* 名词 (*no plural* 不用复数形式)
the feeling that you have when something makes you laugh or smile 好笑；愉悦：*We watched in amusement as the dog chased its tail.* 那条狗追着自己的尾巴，我们看得大乐。

amusement park /əˈmjuːzmənt pɑːk/ *noun* 名词
a large park which has a lot of things that you can ride and play on and many different activities to enjoy 游乐场；游乐园

amusing 0̶ⁿ /əˈmjuːzɪŋ/ *adjective* 形容词
Something or somebody that is **amusing** makes you smile or laugh. 好笑的；有趣的：*an amusing story* 有趣的故事 ⊃ SAME MEANING **funny** 同义词为 funny

an 0̶ⁿ /ən; æn/ *article* 冠词
1 one or any 一个；任何一个：*I ate an apple.* 我吃了一个苹果。
2 each, or for each 每一：*It costs £2 an hour to park your car here.* 在这里停车每小时两英镑。 ⊃ Look at the note at **a**. 见 a 条的注释。

anaesthetic (*British* 英式英语) (*American* 美式英语 **anesthetic**) /ˌænəsˈθetɪk/ *noun* 名词
a drug that a doctor gives you so that you will not feel any pain during an operation 麻醉药：*The patient will be under anaesthetic for about an hour.* 病人要被麻醉大约一小时。

analyse (*British* 英式英语) (*American* 美式英语 **analyze**) /ˈænəlaɪz/ *verb* 动词 (analyses, analysing, analysed /ˈænəlaɪzd/)
to look at or think about the different parts of something carefully so that you can understand it 分析：*They will*

analyse the statistics. 他们将分析这些统计数据。

analysis /əˈnæləsɪs/ *noun* 名词 (*plural* 复数形式 **analyses** /əˈnæləsiːz/)
the process of carefully examining the different parts of something 分析：*Some samples of the water were sent to a laboratory for analysis.* 一些水样送到了实验室做分析。

ancestor /ˈænsestə(r)/ *noun* 名词
Your **ancestors** are the people in your family who lived a long time before you. 祖宗；祖先：*My ancestors came from Norway.* 我的祖先来自挪威。

anchor 锚

anchor /ˈæŋkə(r)/ *noun* 名词
a heavy metal thing that you drop into the water from a boat to stop the boat moving away 锚

ancient 0̶ⁿ /ˈeɪnʃənt/ *adjective* 形容词
very old; from a time long ago 很老的；古老的；古代的：*ancient buildings* 古老的建筑物

and 0̶ⁿ /ənd; ænd/ *conjunction* 连词
a word that joins words or parts of sentences together 和；与；跟；同：*fish and chips* 炸鱼薯条 ◊ *The cat was black and white.* 那是只黑白花猫。 ◊ *They sang and danced all evening.* 他们整晚又唱又跳。

anesthetic *American English for* ANAESTHETIC 美式英语，即 anaesthetic

angel /ˈeɪndʒl/ *noun* 名词
a spirit who carries messages from God. In pictures, **angels** are usually dressed in white and they have wings. 天使

anger 0̶ⁿ /ˈæŋɡə(r)/ *noun* 名词 (*no plural* 不用复数形式)
the strong feeling that you have when something has happened or somebody has done something that you do not like 怒火；怒气：*She was shaking with anger.* 她气得直发抖。

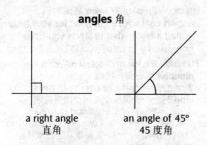

angles 角

a right angle   an angle of 45°
直角   45 度角

angle 🔑 /'æŋgl/ *noun* 名词

> 🔍 SPELLING 拼写说明
>
> Remember! You spell **angle** with L
> before E. You spell **angel** with E before
> L. 记住：angle 中的 l 在 e 之前，而
> angel 中的 l 在 e 之后。

the space between two lines that meet.
Angles are measured in degrees. 角：
*an angle of 40° * 40 度角

> 🔍 WORD BUILDING 词汇扩充
>
> A **right angle** measures exactly 90°.
> 直角（right angle）是 90 度。
> An **acute angle** measures less than 90°
> and an **obtuse angle** measures more
> than 90°. 锐角（acute angle）小于
> 90 度，钝角（obtuse angle）则大于
> 90 度。

angry 🔑 /'æŋgri/ *adjective* 形容词
(**angrier, angriest**)
If you are **angry**, you feel or show anger.
生气的；愤怒的：*My father was angry
with me when I got home late.* 我回家晚
了，爸爸很生气。

▸ **angrily** /'æŋgrəli/ *adverb* 副词:
*'Somebody has taken my book!' she
shouted angrily.* "有人把我的书拿走了！"
她生气地喊道。

animal 🔑 /'ænɪml/ *noun* 名词
1 any living thing that can move and feel
but is not a person, a bird, a fish or an
insect 兽；牲畜；动物（不包括人、鸟、
鱼或昆虫）： *Cats, horses and rats are
animals.* 猫、马、老鼠都是动物。 ⊃ Look
at Picture Dictionary pages **P2-P3**. 见彩页
P2-P3。
2 any living thing that can move and feel,
including people, birds, etc. 动物（包括
人、鸟等）： *Humans are social animals.*
人是群居的动物。

animated /'ænɪmeɪtɪd/ *adjective* 形容词
1 full of interest and energy 兴致勃勃的；

活跃的： *an animated discussion* 热烈的
讨论 ⊃ SAME MEANING **lively** 同义词为 lively
2 If a film is **animated**, drawings or
models of people and animals are made
to look as if they can really move and
talk. 动画的： *animated cartoons* 动画片

animation /ˌænɪ'meɪʃn/ *noun* 名词
(*no plural* 不用复数形式)
the process of making films, videos and
computer games in which drawings or
models of people and animals seem to
move 动画制作： *computer animation*
电脑动画制作

ankle /'æŋkl/ *noun* 名词
the part of your leg where it joins your
foot 踝 ⊃ Look at Picture Dictionary page
P4. 见彩页 P4。

anniversary /ˌænɪ'vɜːsəri/ *noun* 名词
(*plural* 复数形式 **anniversaries**)
a day that is exactly a year or a number
of years after a special or important event
周年纪念日： *Today is their 25th wedding
anniversary.* 今天是他们结婚 25 周年纪念
日。 ◇ *It happened on the anniversary of
her husband's death.* 这事发生在她丈夫的
忌日。 ⊃ Look at the note at **birthday**.
见 birthday 条的注释。

announce 🔑 /ə'naʊns/ *verb* 动词
(**announces, announcing, announced**
/ə'naʊnst/)
to tell a lot of people something
important 宣布；发布： *The teacher
announced the winner of the competition.*
老师宣布了比赛的优胜者。 ◇ *She
announced that she was going to have a
baby.* 她告诉大家她快要生孩子了。

announcement /ə'naʊnsmənt/ *noun*
名词
important information that somebody
tells a lot of people 公告；通告： *Ladies
and gentlemen, I'd like to **make an
announcement**.* 各位，我要宣布一件事。

announcer /ə'naʊnsə(r)/ *noun* 名词
a person whose job is to tell us about
programmes on radio or television
（电台、电视台的）广播员，播音员

annoy 🔑 /ə'nɔɪ/ *verb* 动词 (**annoys,
annoying, annoyed** /ə'nɔɪd/)
to make somebody a little angry 使气恼；
使生气： *It really annoys me when my
brother leaves his clothes all over the floor.*
弟弟把衣服扔得满地都是，真叫我生气。 ◇
Close the door if the noise is annoying you.
这声响让你烦的话，就关上门。

annoyance /ə'nɔɪəns/ *noun* 名词
(*no plural* 不用复数形式)

A
B
C
D
E
F
G
H
I
J
K
L
M
N
O
P
Q
R
S
T
U
V
W
X
Y
Z

the feeling of being a little angry 气恼；
生气: *She could not hide her annoyance
when I arrived late.* 我来晚了，看得出她
生气了。

annoyed 0➔ /əˈnɔɪd/ *adjective* 形容词
a little angry 恼怒的；恼火的: *I was
annoyed when he forgot to phone me.*
他忘了给我打电话，我很不高兴。◇ *My
dad is annoyed with me.* 我爸爸正在生我
的气呢。

annoying 0➔ /əˈnɔɪɪŋ/ *adjective* 形容词
If a person or thing is **annoying**, they
make you a little angry. 气人的；使人
恼火的: *It's annoying when people don't
listen to you.* 说话时别人不注意听很叫人
生气。

annual /ˈænjuəl/ *adjective* 形容词
1 that happens or comes once every year
每年的；一年一次的: *There is an annual
meeting in June.* 六月开年会。
2 for a period of one year 一年的: *Their
annual income* (= the money they earn in
a year) *is less than $20 000.* 他们的年收入
不到 20 000 元。
▶ **annually** /ˈænjuəli/ *adverb* 副词:
Payment will be made annually. 每年付费
一次。

anonymous /əˈnɒnɪməs/ *adjective*
形容词
1 If a person is **anonymous**, other people
do not know their name. （人）匿名的；
不透露姓名的: *An anonymous caller told
the police about the bomb.* 有人打匿名电
话把炸弹的事告诉了警方。
2 If something is **anonymous**, you do not
know who did, gave or made it. （物）
匿名的；不具名的: *She received an
anonymous letter.* 她收到了一封匿名信。

anorak 带帽防寒短上衣

anorak /ˈænəræk/ *noun* 名词
a short coat with a covering for your head
(called a **hood**) that protects you from
rain, wind and cold 带帽防寒短上衣

another 0➔ /əˈnʌðə(r)/ *adjective,
pronoun* 形容词，代词
1 one more thing or person of the same
kind 另一个，又一个（同类的事物或
人）: *Would you like another drink?*
你要再喝一杯吗？◇ *I like these cakes – can
I have another one?* 我很喜欢这些蛋糕，
能再来一块吗？
2 a different thing or person 又一，另一
（不同的事物或人）: *I can't see you
tomorrow – can we meet another day?*
我明天不能见你，改天行吗？◇ *If you've
already seen that film, we can go and see
another.* 假如你已经看过那部电影，我们
可以去看另外一部。

answer[1] 0➔ /ˈɑːnsə(r)/ *noun* 名词

🔎 **PRONUNCIATION** 读音说明
The word **answer** sounds like **dancer**
because we don't say the letter w in
this word. * answer 读音像 dancer，
因为 w 在这里不发音。

1 something that you say or write when
you answer somebody or something
回答；答复: *Thanks for the offer but the
answer is still no.* 谢谢你的建议，但答案
仍然是否定的。◇ *Have you had an
answer to your letter?* 你收到回信了吗？
2 when somebody opens the door or
picks up the telephone because
somebody has knocked or rung 应门；接
电话: *I knocked on the door and waited
but there was no answer.* 我敲了门，等了
一下，但没人应门。
3 a way of stopping a problem 解决办
法: *I didn't have any money so the only
answer was to borrow some.* 我没钱，因此
唯一的办法就是去借一点。
4 the correct reply to a question in a test
or an exam 答案: *What was the answer
to question 4?* 第 4 题的答案是什么？◇ *All
the answers are at the back of the book.*
所有的答案都附在书本后面。

answer[2] 0➔ /ˈɑːnsə(r)/ *verb* 动词
(answers, answering, answered /ˈɑːnsəd/)
1 to say or write something back when
somebody has asked you something or
written to you 回答；答复: *I asked him if
he was hungry but he didn't answer.* 我问
他饿不饿，他没回答。◇ *I couldn't answer
all the exam questions.* 我不是所有的考题
都会答。
2 to write a letter to somebody who has

written to you 回信：*She didn't answer my letter.* 她没回我的信。 ⊃ SAME MEANING **reply** 同义词为 reply

answer the door to open the door when somebody knocks or rings 应门：*Can you answer the door, please?* 请你去应门好吗？

answer the telephone to pick up the telephone when it rings, and speak 接电话

answering machine /ˈɑːnsərɪŋ məˌʃiːn/ (*British also* 英式英语亦作 **answerphone** /ˈɑːnsəfəʊn/) *noun* 名词
a machine that answers the telephone for you and keeps messages so that you can listen to them later 电话答录机：*He wasn't at home, so I left a message on his answering machine.* 他没在家，我在他的电话答录机上留了言。

ant /ænt/ *noun* 名词
a very small insect that lives in big groups in the ground and works very hard 蚂蚁

the Antarctic /ði ænˈtɑːktɪk/ *noun* 名词
(*no plural* 不用复数形式)
the very cold lands in the most southern part of the world 南极地区 ⊃ Look at **Arctic**. 见 Arctic。⊃ Look at the picture at **earth**. 见 earth 的插图。

antelope 羚

antelope /ˈæntɪləʊp/ *noun* 名词
a wild animal with long horns and long thin legs, that can run fast 羚

antennae 触角；触须

antenna wing
触角 翅膀

shell antenna
壳 触须

bee 蜜蜂   **snail** 蜗牛

antenna /ænˈtenə/ *noun* 名词 (*plural* 复数形式 **antennae** /ænˈteniː/)
1 one of the two long thin parts on the heads of some insects, and of some animals that live in shells, which they use to feel and touch things 触角；触须
2 *American English for* AERIAL 美式英语，即 aerial

anti- /ˈænti/ *prefix* 前缀
against; not 反；反对：*an anti-smoking campaign* 禁烟运动

antibiotic /ˌæntibaɪˈɒtɪk/ *noun* 名词
a medicine which fights illness in a person's body 抗生素；抗菌素：*The doctor gave me some antibiotics for a chest infection.* 医生给我开了些治疗胸部感染的抗生素。

anticipate /ænˈtɪsɪpeɪt/ *verb* 动词
(**anticipates, anticipating, anticipated**)
to think that something will happen and be ready for it 预料；预计：*We didn't anticipate so many problems.* 我们没有预料到会有这么多问题。

anticipation /ænˌtɪsɪˈpeɪʃn/ *noun* 名词
(*no plural* 不用复数形式)
excited feelings about something that is going to happen 期盼；期待：*They queued outside the stadium in excited anticipation.* 他们满怀期待的心情在体育馆外排队。

anticlockwise /ˌæntiˈklɒkwaɪz/ (*British* 英式英语) (*American* 美式英语 **counterclockwise**) *adjective, adverb* 形容词，副词
in the opposite direction to the hands of a clock 逆时针方向（的）：*Turn the handle anticlockwise.* 逆时针转动把手。
⊃ OPPOSITE **clockwise** 反义词为 clockwise

antique /ænˈtiːk/ *noun* 名词
an old thing that is worth a lot of money 古董；古玩：*These chairs are antiques.* 这些椅子是古董。
▶ **antique** *adjective* 形容词：*an antique vase* 古董花瓶

anxiety /æŋˈzaɪəti/ *noun* 名词 (*plural* 复数形式 **anxieties**)
a feeling of worry and fear 焦虑；忧虑；担忧

anxious /ˈæŋkʃəs/ *adjective* 形容词
1 worried and afraid 焦虑的；担心的：*She's anxious because her daughter hasn't arrived yet.* 女儿还没到到，她很着急。
2 If you are **anxious** to do something, you want to do it very much. 急切；渴望：*My family are anxious to meet you.* 我的家人都非常想见你。

A
B
C
D
E
F
G
H
I
J
K
L
M
N
O
P
Q
R
S
T
U
V
W
X
Y
Z

A
B
C
D
E
F
G
H
I
J
K
L
M
N
O
P
Q
R
S
T
U
V
W
X
Y
Z

▶ **anxiously** /'æŋkʃəsli/ *adverb* 副词:
We waited anxiously. 我们焦急地等待着。

any[1] ⃞ /'eni/ *adjective, pronoun*
形容词，代词
1 a word that you use instead of 'some' in
questions and after 'not' and 'if' （用于疑
问句，或用于 not 和 if 后）任何: *Have
you got any money?* 你有钱吗？◇ *I don't
speak any Spanish.* 我不会说西班牙语。◇
She asked if I had any milk. 她问我有没有
牛奶。◇ *I want some chocolate but there
isn't any.* 我想要些巧克力，但没有了。
つ Look at the note at **some**. 见 some
条的注释。
2 used for saying that it does not matter
which thing or person you choose 任一:
Come any day next week. 下周随便哪一天
来吧。◇ *Take any book you want.* 你想要
哪本书就拿哪本书。

any[2] ⃞ /'eni/ *adverb* 副词
used in negative sentences or questions
to make an adjective or an adverb
stronger （用于否定句和疑问句，强调形容
词或副词的语气）一点儿: *I can't walk
any faster.* 我无法走得更快了。◇ *Is your
dad feeling any better?* 你爸爸好些了吗？
◇ *I don't want any more.* 我不再要了。

anybody ⃞ /'enibɒdi/ *another word
for* ANYONE * anyone 的另一种说法

anyhow /'enihaʊ/ *another word for*
ANYWAY * anyway 的另一种说法

any more /ˌeni 'mɔː(r)/ (*British* 英式英语)
(*British and American also* 英式和美式英语
亦作 **anymore**) *adverb* 副词
used at the end of negative sentences and
questions to mean 'any longer' 再也
（不）；（不）再: *She doesn't live here
any more.* 她不再住这里了。◇ *Why
doesn't he speak to me any more?* 为什么
他不再跟我说话了？

anyone ⃞ /'eniwʌn/ (*also* 亦作
anybody) *pronoun* 代词
1 used in questions and negative
sentences to mean 'any person' 任何人:
There wasn't anyone there. 那里一个人都
没有。◇ *Did you see anyone you know?*
你见到任何熟人了吗？◇ *Would anyone
like more to eat?* 有人想再多吃一点吗？
2 any person; it does not matter who
无论谁: *Anyone can learn to swim.* 谁都
可以学会游泳。

anyplace /'enipleɪs/ *American English for*
ANYWHERE 美式英语，即 anywhere

anything ⃞ /'eniθɪŋ/ *pronoun* 代词
1 used in questions and negative
sentences to mean 'a thing of any kind'

任何事物: *Is there anything in that box?*
那个盒子里有东西吗？◇ *I can't see
anything.* 我什么都看不见。◇ *'Would you
like anything else?' asked the waitress.*
"您还需要其他东西吗？"女服务员问道。
2 any thing or things; it does not matter
what （无论）任何事物，任何东西: *I'm
so hungry, I could eat anything!* 我太饿
了，吃什么都行！◇ *I'll do anything you
say.* 你说什么我都会照办。

not anything like somebody or 或
something not the same as somebody
or something in any way 一点也不像:
She isn't anything like her sister. 她一点也
不像她姐姐。

anyway ⃞ /'eniweɪ/ (*also* 亦作
anyhow) *adverb* 副词
1 a word that you use when you give a
second, more important reason for
something 再说；况且: *I don't want to
go out tonight and anyway I haven't got
any money.* 我今晚不想出去，再说我也
没钱。
2 in spite of something else 即使如此；
尽管: *It was very expensive but she
bought it anyway.* 尽管那东西很贵，她还
是买了。◇ *I'm afraid I'm busy tonight,
but thanks for the invitation anyway.*
恐怕今天晚上我很忙，但还是要谢谢你的
邀请。
3 a word that you use when you start to
talk about something different or when
you go back to something you talked
about earlier （转换或回到原来话题时说）
无论如何，好了: *That's what John told
me. Anyway, how are you?* 那是约翰告诉
我的。对了，你身体好吗？

anywhere ⃞ /'eniweə(r)/ (*British*
英式英语) (*American* 美式英语 **anyplace**)
adverb 副词
1 used in negative sentences and in
questions instead of 'somewhere' 在任何
地方: *I can't find my pen anywhere.*
我哪儿都找不到我的笔。◇ *Are you going
anywhere this summer?* 你今年夏天会去
什么地方吗？
2 in, at or to any place, when it does not
matter where 无论什么地方: *Just put
the box down anywhere.* 把箱子放到哪里
都行。

apart ⃞ /ə'pɑːt/ *adverb* 副词
1 away from the others; away from each
other 相隔；分开: *The two houses are
500 metres apart.* 两所房子相距 500 米。
◇ *My mother and father live apart now.*
我母亲和父亲现在分开居住。
2 into parts 成碎件；成各部分: *He took*

my radio apart to repair it. 他把他的收音机拆开修理。

apart from somebody or 或 **something** except for 除了…外: *There's nobody here, apart from me.* 这里只有我，没有别人。◇ *I like all vegetables apart from carrots.* 除了胡萝卜之外，我什么蔬菜都爱吃。

apartment 0= /ə'pɑːtmənt/ *American English for* FLAT² 美式英语，即 flat²

ape /eɪp/ *noun* 名词
an animal like a big MONKEY (= an animal that lives in hot countries and can climb trees), with no tail and with long arms. There are different types of **ape**. 类人猿: *Gorillas and chimpanzees are apes.* 大猩猩和黑猩猩都是类人猿。◇ Look at the pictures at **chimpanzee** and **gorilla**. 见 chimpanzee 和 gorilla 的插图。

apologize /ə'pɒlədʒaɪz/ *verb* 动词 (apologizes, apologizing, apologized /ə'pɒlədʒaɪzd/)
to say that you are sorry about something that you have done 道歉；致歉: *I apologized to John for losing his book.* 我把约翰的书弄丢了，向他赔了不是。

apology /ə'pɒlədʒi/ *noun* 名词 (*plural* 复数形式 apologies)
words that you say or write to show that you are sorry about something you have done 道歉: *Please accept my apologies.* 请接受我的道歉。

apostrophe /ə'pɒstrəfi/ *noun* 名词
the sign (') that you use in writing 撇号；省字号；省略符号

> 🔍 GRAMMAR 语法说明
>
> You use an **apostrophe** to show that you have left a letter out of a word or that a number is missing, for example in *I'm* (= I am) and *'05* (= 2005). 撇号用以表示单词中省略了字母或数字，如 I'm（I am）和 '05（= 2005）。
> You also use it to show that something belongs to somebody or something. 撇号还用以表示某物属于某人或某物: *the boy's room* 那个男孩的房间
> If the **apostrophe** comes after the letter *s*, it shows that there is more than one person. 撇号用在 s 之后，表示该物所属多于一人: *the boys' room* (= a room which is shared by two or more boys) 那些男孩的房间

appalling /ə'pɔːlɪŋ/ *adjective* 形容词
very bad; terrible 极坏的；糟糕的: *appalling cruelty* 极度残忍

apparent /ə'pærənt/ *adjective* 形容词
easy to see or understand; clear 显而易见的；明显的: *It was apparent that she didn't like him.* 她显然不喜欢他。◇ SAME MEANING **obvious** 同义词为 obvious

apparently /ə'pærəntli/ *adverb* 副词
You use **apparently** to talk about what people say, or how something appears, when you do not know if it is true or not. 据说；看来；似乎: *Apparently, he's already been married twice.* 据说他结过两次婚。◇ *He was apparently undisturbed by the news.* 看来他对这个消息无动于衷。

appeal¹ /ə'piːl/ *noun* 名词
1 (*no plural* 不用复数形式) a quality that makes somebody or something attractive or interesting 吸引力；魅力: *I can't understand the appeal of stamp collecting.* 我无法理解集邮的乐趣。
2 asking a lot of people for money, help or information 呼吁；恳求: *The police made an appeal for witnesses to come forward.* 警方呼吁目击者提供线索。

appeal² /ə'piːl/ *verb* 动词 (appeals, appealing, appealed /ə'piːld/)
1 to ask in a serious way for something that you want very much 呼吁；吁求: *Aid workers in the disaster area appealed for food and clothing.* 灾区的救援人员呼吁捐献食物和衣物。
2 to be attractive or interesting to somebody 吸引: *Living in a big city doesn't appeal to me.* 我对在大城市生活并不感兴趣。

appear 0= /ə'pɪə(r)/ *verb* 动词 (appears, appearing, appeared /ə'pɪəd/)
1 to seem 看来；似乎；好像: *She appears to be very happy at her new school.* 她在新学校显得很开心。◇ *It appears that I was wrong.* 看来是我错了。
2 to suddenly be seen; to come into sight 出现；显现: *The sun suddenly appeared from behind a cloud.* 太阳突然从云后露出脸来了。◇ *We waited for an hour but he didn't appear.* 我们等了一个小时，可是他没有露面。◇ OPPOSITE **disappear** 反义词为 disappear

appearance 0= /ə'pɪərəns/ *noun* 名词
1 the way that somebody or something looks or seems 外貌；外表；外观: *A new hairstyle can completely change your appearance.* 新发型可以彻底改变人的外表。
2 the coming of somebody or something; when somebody or something is seen 到来；出现: *Jane's appearance at the*

A B C D E F G H I J K L M N O P Q R S T U V W X Y Z

party surprised everybody. 简来参加聚会，大家都很惊奇。◇ *Is this your first appearance on television?* 这是你第一次上电视吗?

appetite /ˈæpɪtaɪt/ *noun* 名词
the feeling that you want to eat 食欲; 胃口: *Swimming always gives me an appetite* (= makes me hungry). 我一游泳就容易饿。

appetizer /ˈæpɪtaɪzə(r)/ *noun* 名词
American English for STARTER 美式英语，即 starter

applaud /əˈplɔːd/ *verb* 动词 (applauds, applauding, applauded)
to make a noise by hitting your hands together to show that you like something 鼓掌; 拍手: *We all applauded loudly at the end of the song.* 那首歌唱完后我们都热烈地鼓掌。

applause /əˈplɔːz/ *noun* 名词 (no plural 不用复数形式)
when a lot of people hit their hands together to show that they like something 鼓掌: *There was loud applause from the audience.* 观众中响起了热烈的掌声。

apple 0— /ˈæpl/ *noun* 名词
a hard round fruit with green or red skin 苹果 ⊃ Look at Picture Dictionary page P8. 见彩页 P8。

appliance /əˈplaɪəns/ *noun* 名词
a useful machine for doing something in the house（家用）器具: *Washing machines and irons are electrical appliances.* 洗衣机和熨斗是家用电器。

applicant /ˈæplɪkənt/ *noun* 名词
a person who APPLIES (= asks) for a job or a place at university, for example 申请人: *There were six applicants for the job.* 有六个人申请这份工作。

application /ˌæplɪˈkeɪʃn/ *noun* 名词
1 writing to ask for something, for example a job 申请: *Applications for the job should be made to the Personnel Manager.* 求职申请应交人事经理。
2 (computing 电脑) a computer program that is designed to do a particular job 应用程序; 应用软件

application form /ˌæplɪˈkeɪʃn fɔːm/ *noun* 名词
a special piece of paper that you write on when you are trying to get something, for example a job 申请表; 申请书: *Please fill in the application form.* 请填写申请表。

apply 0— /əˈplaɪ/ *verb* 动词 (applies, applying, applied /əˈplaɪd/)

1 to write to ask for something 申请: *Simon has applied for a place at university.* 西蒙已向大学递交入学申请。
2 to be about somebody or something; to be important to somebody or something 有关; 适用于: *This law applies to all children over the age of sixteen.* 这条法律适用于所有十六岁以上的孩子。

appoint /əˈpɔɪnt/ *verb* 动词 (appoints, appointing, appointed)
to choose somebody for a job or position 任命; 委任: *The bank has appointed a new manager.* 银行已经委任了一位新经理。

appointment /əˈpɔɪntmənt/ *noun* 名词
1 an arrangement to see somebody at a particular time 约会; 预约: *I've got an appointment with the doctor at ten o'clock.* 我约好十点看医生。◇ *You can telephone to make an appointment.* 你可以打电话预约。
2 (formal 正式) a job 工作

> 🔎 SPEAKING 表达方式说明
> **Job** is the word that we usually use.
> * job 是常用词。

appreciate /əˈpriːʃieɪt/ *verb* 动词 (appreciates, appreciating, appreciated)
1 to enjoy something or understand how good somebody or something is 欣赏; 赏识: *Van Gogh's paintings were only appreciated after his death.* 凡•高的画在他死后才为人所赏识。◇ *My boss doesn't appreciate me.* 我老板并不赏识我。
2 to understand that a situation is difficult 了解（困境）: *I appreciate your problem, but I can't help you.* 我理解你的难处，但我没法帮助你。
3 to be grateful for something that somebody has done for you 感激; 感谢: *Thank you for your help. I appreciate it.* 谢谢你的帮助，我十分感激。

appreciation /əˌpriːʃiˈeɪʃn/ *noun* 名词 (no plural 不用复数形式)
1 understanding and enjoyment of how good somebody or something is 欣赏: *She shows little appreciation of good music.* 她不太会欣赏好的音乐。
2 the feeling of being grateful for something that somebody has done for you 感激; 感谢: *We gave her some flowers to show our appreciation for her hard work.* 我们给她送花，对她的辛勤工作表示感谢。

apprentice /əˈprentɪs/ *noun* 名词
a young person who is learning to do a

job 学徒；徒弟：*an apprentice electrician* 电工学徒

approach¹ /ə'prəʊtʃ/ ***verb*** 动词
(**approaches**, **approaching**, **approached** /ə'prəʊtʃt/)
to come near to somebody or something in distance or time 接近；靠近；临近：*As you approach the village, you'll see a church on your right.* 快到村子时，会看到右边有个教堂。◇ *The exams were approaching.* 快要考试了。

approach² /ə'prəʊtʃ/ ***noun*** 名词
1 (*plural* 复数形式 **approaches**) a way of doing something 方法；方式：*This is a new approach to learning languages.* 这是学习语言的新方法。
2 (*no plural* 不用复数形式) coming near or nearer to somebody or something 接近；靠近；临近：*the approach of winter* 冬天的来临

appropriate 0-ㅠ /ə'prəʊpriət/ ***adjective*** 形容词
suitable or right for a particular situation, person, etc. 适当的；合适的：*Jeans and T-shirts are not **appropriate for** a job interview.* 求职面试时不宜穿牛仔裤和T恤衫。➲ OPPOSITE **inappropriate** 反义词为 inappropriate
▸ **appropriately** /ə'prəʊpriətli/ ***adverb*** 副词：*Please come appropriately dressed.* 请穿着得体前来。

approval 0-ㅠ /ə'pru:vl/ ***noun*** 名词
(*no plural* 不用复数形式)
feeling, showing or saying that something or somebody is good or right 赞成；同意；认可：*Tania's parents **gave** the marriage **their approval**.* 塔妮娅的父母同意了她的婚事。➲ OPPOSITE **disapproval** 反义词为 disapproval

approve 0-ㅠ /ə'pru:v/ ***verb*** 动词
(**approves**, **approving**, **approved** /ə'pru:vd/)
to think or say that something or somebody is good or right 赞成；同意：*My parents don't **approve of** my friends.* 我父母不喜欢我的朋友。◇ *She doesn't approve of smoking.* 她不赞成吸烟。
➲ OPPOSITE **disapprove** 反义词为 disapprove

approximate /ə'prɒksɪmət/ ***adjective*** 形容词
almost correct but not exact 近似的；大约的：*The approximate time of arrival is three o'clock.* 到达时间大约是三点钟。

approximately /ə'prɒksɪmətli/ ***adverb*** 副词
about; more or less 大约；大概：*I live approximately two miles from the station.* 我住的地方离车站大约两英里。➲ SAME MEANING **roughly** 同义词为 roughly

apricot /'eɪprɪkɒt/ ***noun*** 名词
a small soft yellow or orange fruit with a large stone inside 杏

April 0-ㅠ /'eɪprəl/ ***noun*** 名词
the fourth month of the year 四月

apron 围裙

apron /'eɪprən/ ***noun*** 名词
a thing that you wear over the front of your clothes to keep them clean, especially when you are cooking 围裙

aquarium /ə'kweəriəm/ ***noun*** 名词
1 a large glass container filled with water, in which fish are kept 水族缸；养鱼缸
2 a building where people can go to see fish and other water animals 水族馆

arches 拱

arch /ɑ:tʃ/ ***noun*** 名词 (*plural* 复数形式 **arches**)
a part of a bridge, building or wall that is in the shape of a half circle 拱（弧形的建筑结构）

A
B
C
D
E
F
G
H
I
J
K
L
M
N
O
P
Q
R
S
T
U
V
W
X
Y
Z

archaeologist (*British* 英式英语)
(*American* 美式英语 **archeologist**)
/ˌɑːkiˈɒlədʒɪst/ *noun* 名词
a person who studies or knows a lot
about ARCHAEOLOGY 考古学家；考古学者

archaeology (*British* 英式英语)
(*American* 美式英语 **archeology**)
/ˌɑːkiˈɒlədʒi/ *noun* 名词 (*no plural* 不用
复数形式)
the study of the past by looking at objects
or parts of old buildings that are found in
the ground 考古学

archbishop /ˌɑːtʃˈbɪʃəp/ *noun* 名词
a very important priest in the Christian
church 大主教： *the Archbishop of
Canterbury* 坎特伯雷大主教

architect /ˈɑːkɪtekt/ *noun* 名词
a person whose job is to design and plan
buildings 建筑师

architecture /ˈɑːkɪtektʃə(r)/ *noun* 名词
(*no plural* 不用复数形式)
1 the study of designing and making
buildings 建筑学： *He has a degree in
architecture.* 他拥有建筑学的学位。
2 the design or style of a building or
buildings 建筑设计；建筑风格： *Do you
like modern architecture?* 你喜欢现代建筑
风格吗？

the Arctic /ði ˈɑːktɪk/ *noun* 名词
(*no plural* 不用复数形式)
the very cold land and countries in the
most northern part of the world 北极地区
⊃ Look at **Antarctic**. 见 Antarctic。⊃ Look
at the picture at **earth**. 见 earth 的插图。

are *form of* BE * be 的不同形式

area /ˈeəriə/ *noun* 名词
1 a part of a town, country or the world
地区；区域： *Do you live in this area?*
你住在这一带吗？ ◇ *the desert areas of
North Africa* 北非的沙漠地区
2 the size of a flat place. If a room is
three metres wide and four metres long,
it has an **area** of twelve square metres.
面积
3 a space that you use for a particular
activity 地方；场地： *The restaurant has
a non-smoking area* (= a part where you
must not smoke). 这家餐馆设有无烟区。

arena /əˈriːnə/ *noun* 名词 (*plural* 复数形式
arenas)
a place with seats around it where you
can watch sports or concerts 圆形运动
场；圆形剧场

aren't /ɑːnt/ *short for* ARE NOT * are not 的
缩略式

argue ᴏ⃝ /ˈɑːgjuː/ *verb* 动词 (**argues,
arguing, argued** /ˈɑːgjuːd/)
1 to talk angrily with somebody because
you do not agree 争论；争吵；争辩： *My
parents **argue** a lot **about** money.* 我父母
经常因为钱的事情吵架。 ◇ *I often **argue**
with my brother.* 我常跟弟弟吵架。
2 to say why you think something is right
or wrong 论证；说理： *Billy **argued** that
war is not the answer.* 比利认为战争不是
解决问题的办法。

argument ᴏ⃝ /ˈɑːgjumənt/ *noun* 名词
an angry discussion between people who
do not agree with each other 争论；争
吵；争执： *They **had** an **argument** about
where to go on holiday.* 他们为到哪里去
度假争论了一番。 ◇ *I **had** an **argument**
with my father.* 我和父亲争执起来。

arise /əˈraɪz/ *verb* 动词 (**arises, arising,
arose** /əˈrəʊz/, **has arisen** /əˈrɪzn/) (*formal*
正式)
If a problem or difficult situation **arises**,
it happens or starts to exist. 产生；发生；
出现

aristocracy /ˌærɪˈstɒkrəsi/ *noun* 名词
(*no plural* 不用复数形式)
the people of the highest social class who
often have special titles 贵族

arithmetic /əˈrɪθmətɪk/ *noun* 名词
(*no plural* 不用复数形式)
(*maths* 数学) working with numbers, for
example by adding or multiplying, to find
the answer to a sum 算术： *I'm not very
good at **mental arithmetic**.* 我不太擅长
心算。

arm ᴏ⃝ /ɑːm/ *noun* 名词
the part of your body from your shoulder
to your hand 胳膊；上肢： *Put your arms
in the air.* 把手臂举起来。 ◇ *He was
carrying a book under his arm.* 他腋下夹
着一本书。 ⊃ Look at Picture Dictionary
page **P4**. 见彩页 P4。
arm in arm with your arm holding
another person's arm 臂挽着臂；挎着
胳膊： *The two friends walked arm in arm.*
两个朋友挽臂而行。

armchair 扶手椅

armchair /ˈɑːmtʃeə(r)/ *noun* 名词
a soft comfortable chair with side parts
where you can put your arms 扶手椅:
She was asleep in an armchair. 她在扶手
椅上睡着了。

armed /ɑːmd/ *adjective* 形容词
carrying a gun or other weapon 携带武器
的；武装的: *an armed robber* 持械劫匪
◇ *Are the police armed in your country?*
你们国家的警察携带武器吗？

the armed forces /ðiˌɑːmd ˈfɔːsɪz/
noun 名词 (*plural* 用复数形式)
a country's soldiers who fight on land, at
sea or in the air 武装部队；武装力量

armour (*British* 英式英语) (*American*
美式英语 **armor**) /ˈɑːmə(r)/ *noun* 名词
(*no plural* 不用复数形式)
metal clothes that men wore long ago
to cover their bodies when they were
fighting 盔甲；甲胄: *a suit of armour*
一副盔甲

armpit /ˈɑːmpɪt/ *noun* 名词
the part of your body under your arm,
where your arm joins your body 腋窝;
胳肢窝 ➡ Look at Picture Dictionary page
P4. 见彩页 P4。

arms /ɑːmz/ *noun* 名词 (*plural* 用复数形式)
guns, bombs and other weapons for
fighting 兵器；武器

army ০┅ /ˈɑːmi/ *noun* 名词 (*plural* 复数
形式 **armies**)
a large group of soldiers who fight on
land in a war 陆军: *He joined the army
when he was 17.* 他 17 岁参军。◇ *the
British Army* 英国陆军

> ♫ WORD BUILDING 词汇扩充
>
> A soldier who fights on land is **in the
> army**, one who fights at sea is **in the
> navy** and a soldier who fights in the air
> is **in the air force**. 在陆军服役说 in the
> army；在海军服役说 in the navy；在
> 空军服役说 in the air force。
> The **army**, the **navy** and the **air force**
> together are called **the armed forces**.
> 海陆空军统称武装部队（the armed
> forces）。

arose *form of* ARISE * arise 的不同形式

around ০┅ /əˈraʊnd/ *preposition,
adverb* 介词，副词
1 (*also* 亦作 round) in or to different
places or in different directions 在各处;
到处: *Her clothes were lying around the
room.* 她的衣服四散在房间里。◇ *We
walked around for an hour looking for a*

restaurant. 我们为找餐馆四处走了一个小
时。◇ *The children were running around
the house.* 孩子们在屋里到处跑。
2 (*also* 亦作 round) in the opposite
direction or in another direction 朝着相
反（或另一）方向: *Turn around and go
back the way you came.* 转身沿着你来的
路走回去。
3 (*also* 亦作 round) on or to all sides of
something, often in a circle 在周围;
围绕: *We sat around the table.* 我们围着
桌子坐。◇ *He ran around the track.* 他绕
着跑道跑。◇ *There is a wall around the
garden.* 花园四周有围墙。
4 in a place; near here 在某处；在附近:
Is there a bank around here? 这儿附近有
银行吗？◇ *Is Helen around? I want to
speak to her.* 海伦在这儿吗？我想跟她
说话。
5 (*also* 亦作 about) a little more or less
than; a little before or after 大约: *I'll see
you around seven* (= at about 7 o'clock).
我们七点左右见。

arrange ০┅ /əˈreɪndʒ/ *verb* 动词
(**arranges, arranging, arranged** /əˈreɪndʒd/)
1 to make a plan for the future 安排:
I have arranged to meet Tim at six o'clock.
我安排好六点钟与蒂姆见面。◇ *We
arranged a big party for Debbie's birthday.*
我们为戴比的生日举行了一个大型派对。
2 to put things in a certain order or place
整理；排列；布置: *Arrange the chairs in
a circle.* 把椅子围成一圈。

arrangement ০┅ /əˈreɪndʒmənt/
noun 名词
1 a plan or preparation that you make so
that something can happen in the future
安排；筹划: *They are **making the
arrangements** for their wedding.* 他们正在
筹备婚礼。
2 a group of things put together so that
they look nice 整理好的东西: *a flower
arrangement* 插花

arrest¹ ০┅ /əˈrest/ *verb* 动词 (**arrests,
arresting, arrested**)
When the police **arrest** somebody, they
take that person away to ask them
questions about a crime. 逮捕；拘捕:
*The man was **arrested for** carrying a
weapon.* 那名男子因携带武器被逮捕了。

arrest² /əˈrest/ *noun* 名词
the act of arresting somebody 逮捕;
拘捕: *The police **made** five **arrests**.* 警方
抓了五个人。◇ *The wanted man is now
under arrest* (= has been arrested). 通缉
犯已经落网。

A
B
C
D
E
F
G
H
I
J
K
L
M
N
O
P
Q
R
S
T
U
V
W
X
Y
Z

A
B
C
D
E
F
G
H
I
J
K
L
M
N
O
P
Q
R
S
T
U
V
W
X
Y
Z

arrival /ə'raɪvl/ *noun* 名词
coming to a place 到达；抵达： *My brother met me at the airport on my arrival*. 我到达的时候，哥哥在机场接我。 ⊃ OPPOSITE **departure** 反义词为 departure

arrive ⊶ /ə'raɪv/ *verb* 动词 (arrives, arriving, arrived /ə'raɪvd/)
1 to come to a place 到达；抵达： *What time did you arrive home?* 你几点到家的？ ◇ *What time does the train arrive in Paris?* 火车什么时候到达巴黎？ ◇ *They arrived at the station ten minutes late*. 他们晚了十分钟到达车站。 ⊃ OPPOSITE **leave**, **depart** 反义词为 leave 和 depart

> 🔍 GRAMMAR 语法说明
> Be careful! We use **arrive in** with the name of a town or country and **arrive at** with a building such as a station, an airport or a school. 注意：到达城镇或国家用 arrive in，到达车站、机场或学校用 arrive at。

2 to come or happen 到来；发生： *Summer has arrived!* 夏天到了!

arrogant /'ærəgənt/ *adjective* 形容词
A person who is **arrogant** thinks that they are better and more important than other people. 傲慢的；自大的

arrows 箭；箭头

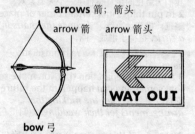

arrow 箭   arrow 箭头

WAY OUT

bow 弓

arrow ⊶ /'ærəʊ/ *noun* 名词
1 a long thin piece of wood or metal with a point at one end 箭

> 🔍 WORD BUILDING 词汇扩充
> You shoot an **arrow** by pulling back the string on a curved piece of wood called a **bow** and then letting go. You try to hit a **target**. 射箭时拉弓（bow）后放手把箭（arrow）射向靶子（target）。

2 the sign (→) that shows where something is or where you should go 箭号；箭头： *The arrow is pointing left*. 箭头指向左边。

art ⊶ /ɑːt/ *noun* 名词
1 (*no plural* 不用复数形式) making beautiful things, like paintings and drawings 美术： *He's studying art at college*. 他在大学学美术。
2 (*no plural* 不用复数形式) beautiful things like paintings and drawings that somebody has made 美术作品： *modern art* 现代美术作品 ◇ *an art gallery* 美术馆
3 the arts (*plural* 用复数形式) things like films, plays and literature 艺术： *How much money does the government spend on the arts?* 政府在艺术方面投入多少钱？
4 (*no plural* 不用复数形式) a skill, or something that needs skill 技巧： *the art of letter writing* 书信写作技巧
5 arts (*plural* 用复数形式) the subjects you can study at school or university which are not science subjects, for example history or languages 文科： *She has an arts degree*. 她拥有一个文科学位。

artery /'ɑːtəri/ *noun* 名词 (*plural* 复数形式 **arteries**)
one of the tubes in your body that carry blood away from your heart to other parts of your body 动脉 ⊃ Look at **vein**. 见 vein。

arthritis /ɑː'θraɪtɪs/ *noun* 名词 (*no plural* 不用复数形式)
a disease which causes pain when you bend your arms, fingers, etc. 关节炎

artichoke /'ɑːtɪtʃəʊk/ *noun* 名词
a green vegetable with a lot of thick pointed leaves that looks like a flower. You eat the bottom part of the leaves and its centre when it is cooked. 洋蓟（绿色厚叶基部和茎中心均可食用） ⊃ Look at Picture Dictionary page P9. 见彩页 P9。

article ⊶ /'ɑːtɪkl/ *noun* 名词
1 a piece of writing in a newspaper or magazine 报刊文章： *Did you read the article about young fashion designers?* 你读过那篇有关青年时装设计师的文章吗？
2 a thing 物件；物品： *Many of the articles in the shop are half-price*. 这家商店很多物品半价出售。 ◇ *articles of clothing* (= things like skirts, coats and trousers) 衣物
3 (*grammar* 语法) the words *a* and *an* (called the indefinite article) or *the* (called the definite article) 冠词（即不定冠词 a、an 和定冠词 the）

artificial ⊶ /ˌɑːtɪ'fɪʃl/ *adjective* 形容词
not natural or real, but made by people 人造的；人工的： *artificial flowers* 假花

A
B
C
D
E
F
G
H
I
J
K
L
M
N
O
P
Q
R
S
T
U
V
W
X
Y
Z

artificial intelligence /ˌɑːtɪfɪʃl
mˈtelɪdʒəns/ *noun* 名词 (*no plural* 不用
复数形式) (*abbr.* 缩略式 AI)
(*computing* 电脑) the study of the way
in which computers can copy the way
humans think 人工智能（学）；人工智慧

artist ⊶ /ˈɑːtɪst/ *noun* 名词
a person who paints or draws pictures
艺术家；画家： *Monet was a famous
French artist.* 莫奈是著名的法国画家。

artistic ⊶ /ɑːˈtɪstɪk/ *adjective* 形容词
good at painting, drawing or making
beautiful things 有艺术天赋的；善于绘画
的： *He's very artistic – his drawings are
excellent.* 他很有艺术天分，画画很不错。

as ⊶ /əz; æz/ *conjunction*, *preposition*
连词，介词
1 while something else is happening 当…
的时候；随着： *Just as I was leaving the
house, the phone rang.* 我正要出去，电话
就响了。
2 as … as words that you use to compare
people or things; the same amount 像…
一样；如同： *Paul is as tall as his father.*
保罗跟他父亲一样高。◇ *I haven't got as
many clothes as you have.* 我的衣服没有
你的多。◇ *I'd like it done as soon as
possible.* 我想尽快把它做完。
3 used to say that somebody or
something has a particular job or purpose
作为；当做： *She works as a secretary for
a big company.* 她在一家大公司当秘书。
◇ *I used my shoe as a hammer.* 我把我的
鞋子当锤子用。
4 in the same way 照…方式： *Please do
as I tell you!* 请照我告诉你的去做吧！
5 because 因为： *As she was ill, she didn't
go to school.* 她因病没去上学。

asap /ˌeɪ es eɪ ˈpiː/ *abbreviation* 缩略式
(*informal* 非正式)
as soon as possible 尽快： *I'd like the
report on my desk asap.* 尽快把报告放在
我桌子上。

ash /æʃ/ *noun* 名词 (*no plural* 不用复数
形式)
the grey powder that is left after
something has burned 灰；灰烬：
cigarette ash 烟灰

ashamed ⊶ /əˈʃeɪmd/ *adjective*
形容词
feeling sorry and unhappy because you
have done something wrong, or because
you are not as good as other people
惭愧，羞愧；愧疚： *I was ashamed about
lying to my parents.* 我向父母撒了谎，感

到羞愧。◇ *She was ashamed of her old
clothes.* 她对自己的旧衣服感到难为情。

ashore /əˈʃɔː(r)/ *adverb* 副词
onto the land from the sea or a river
到岸上；上岸： *We left the boat and went
ashore.* 我们下了船，上了岸。

ashtray /ˈæʃtreɪ/ *noun* 名词
a small dish for cigarette ASH and the
ends of cigarettes 烟灰缸

aside /əˈsaɪd/ *adverb* 副词
on or to one side; away 在一边；向一边：
*He put the letter aside while he did his
homework.* 他做作业的时候，把信放在一
边了。

ask ⊶ /ɑːsk/ *verb* 动词 (asks, asking,
asked /ɑːskt/)
1 to try to get an answer by using a
question 问；提问： *I asked him what the
time was.* 我问他几点了。◇ *'What's your
name?' she asked.* "你叫什么名字？"她
问道。◇ *Liz asked the teacher a question.*
利兹向老师问了个问题。
2 to say that you would like somebody
to do something for you 要求；请求：
I asked Sara to drive me to the station.
我让萨拉开车送我到车站去。
3 to try to get permission to do
something 请求允许： *I asked my teacher
if I could go home.* 我问老师我可不可以
回家。◇ *I asked if I could go home early.*
我问了我能不能早点回家。
4 to invite somebody to go somewhere
with you 邀请： *Mark has asked me to a
party on Saturday.* 马克邀请我星期六参加
派对。

ask for somebody to say that you want
to speak to somebody 说要找某人：
Phone this number and ask for Mrs Green.
打这个电话号码找格林太太。

ask for something to say that you want
somebody to give you something 请求给
予某物： *He asked for a new bike for his
birthday.* 他说他生日要一辆新自行车。

asleep ⊶ /əˈsliːp/ *adjective* 形容词
sleeping 睡着： *The baby is asleep in the
bedroom.* 婴儿在卧室里睡觉。◇ *He fell
asleep* (= started sleeping) *in front of the
fire.* 他在炉火前睡着了。➲ OPPOSITE
awake 反义词为 awake

🔎 WHICH WORD? 词语辨析
Asleep or **sleeping**? 用 asleep 还是
sleeping?
We usually say someone is **asleep**, not
sleeping. 说某人睡着了通常用 asleep，
不用 sleeping。

A
B
C
D
E
F
G
H
I
J
K
L
M
N
O
P
Q
R
S
T
U
V
W
X
Y
Z

We use **go to sleep** or **fall asleep** to talk about starting to sleep. 开始睡觉用 go to sleep 或 fall asleep: *Laura fell asleep as soon as she got into bed.* 劳拉一上床就睡着了。◇ *Tom read for half an hour before he went to sleep.* 汤姆睡觉前看了半小时的书。
You use **sleeping**, not **asleep**, before a noun. 名词前用 sleeping，不用 asleep: *She put the sleeping child in his cot.* 她把睡着的孩子放到婴儿床上。

asparagus /əˈspærəgəs/ *noun* 名词
(*no plural* 不用复数形式)
thin green plants with pointed ends that are eaten as a vegetable 芦笋 ○ Look at Picture Dictionary page **P9**. 见彩页 P9。

aspect /ˈæspekt/ *noun* 名词
one of the qualities or parts of a situation, idea, problem, etc. 方面；层面: *Spelling is one of the most difficult aspects of learning English.* 拼写是学习英语最困难的地方之一。

aspirin /ˈæsprɪn/ *noun* 名词
a medicine that stops pain 阿司匹林（镇痛的药物）: *I took an aspirin for my headache.* 我头疼，吃了一片阿司匹林。

assassinate /əˈsæsmeɪt/ *verb* 动词
(assassinates, assassinating, assassinated)
to kill an important or famous person 暗杀；行刺: *John F. Kennedy was assassinated in 1963.* 约翰·肯尼迪在 1963 年遭暗杀。
▸ **assassination** /əˌsæsɪˈneɪʃn/ *noun* 名词: *an assassination attempt* 企图暗杀

assault /əˈsɔːlt/ *verb* 动词 (assaults, assaulting, assaulted)
to attack or hurt somebody 攻击；袭击: *He assaulted a policeman.* 他袭击了一名警察。
▸ **assault** *noun* 名词: *an assault on an old lady* 对一个老太太的人身侵犯

assembly /əˈsembli/ *noun* 名词 (*plural* 复数形式 assemblies)
a meeting of a big group of people for a special reason 集会: *Our school assembly is at 9.30 in the morning.* 我们全校集会在上午 9 时 30 分进行。

assess /əˈses/ *verb* 动词 (assesses, assessing, assessed /əˈsest/)
to judge how good, bad or important something is 评定；评估: *It's difficult to assess the effects of the price rises.* 价格上涨的影响难以估计。
▸ **assessment** /əˈsesmənt/ *noun* 名词:

I made a careful assessment of the risks involved. 我对涉及的风险作了仔细评估。

assignment /əˈsaɪnmənt/ *noun* 名词
a job or piece of work that somebody is given to do 工作；任务: *You have to complete three written assignments each term.* 每学期要完成三次书面作业。

assist /əˈsɪst/ *verb* 动词 (assists, assisting, assisted) (*formal* 正式)
to help somebody 帮助；援助: *The driver assisted her with her suitcases.* 司机帮她拿行李箱。

🔊 **SPEAKING** 表达方式说明
Help is the word that we usually use. * help 是常用词。

assistance /əˈsɪstəns/ *noun* 名词
(*no plural* 不用复数形式) (*formal* 正式)
help 帮助；援助: *I can't move this piano without your assistance.* 没有你帮忙，我可挪不动这架钢琴。

assistant /əˈsɪstənt/ *noun* 名词
a person who helps somebody in a more important position 助手；助理: *Ms Dixon is not here today. Would you like to speak to her assistant?* 狄克逊女士今天不在，您想跟她的助手谈吗？ ○ Look also at **shop assistant**. 亦见 shop assistant。

associate /əˈsəʊʃieɪt/ *verb* 动词
(associates, associating, associated)
to make a connection between things or people in your mind 将⋯联系起来: *Most people associate Austria with snow and skiing.* 提起奥地利，大多数人联想到雪和滑雪运动。◇ *These illnesses are associated with smoking.* 这些疾病与吸烟有关。

association /əˌsəʊʃiˈeɪʃn/ *noun* 名词
a group of people who join or work together for a special reason 协会；社团；联盟: *the Football Association* 足球联盟

assume /əˈsjuːm/ *verb* 动词 (assumes, assuming, assumed /əˈsjuːmd/)
to think that something is true although you are not really sure 假设；假定: *Jo is not here today, so I assume that she is ill.* 乔今天不在，我看她是病了。

assumption /əˈsʌmpʃn/ *noun* 名词
something that you think is true, although you are not really sure 假设；假定: *It's unfair to make assumptions about a person before you get to know them.* 认识之前就对他人妄加臆断是不公平的。

assure /əˈʃʊə(r)/ *verb* 动词 (assures, assuring, assured /əˈʃʊəd/)
to tell somebody what is true or certain so that they feel less worried 使确信；向…保证: *I assure you that the dog isn't dangerous.* 我向你保证这狗不危险。

asterisk /ˈæstərɪsk/ *noun* 名词
the symbol (*) that you use to make people notice something in a piece of writing 星号

asthma /ˈæsmə/ *noun* 名词 (*no plural* 不用复数形式)
an illness which makes breathing difficult 哮喘: *He had an asthma attack.* 他哮喘发作。

astonish /əˈstɒnɪʃ/ *verb* 动词 (astonishes, astonishing, astonished /əˈstɒnɪʃt/)
to surprise somebody very much 使十分惊讶: *The news astonished everyone.* 大家对这个消息都感到震惊。

astonished /əˈstɒnɪʃt/ *adjective* 形容词
very surprised 十分惊讶的: *I was astonished to hear that he was getting married.* 听到他即将结婚的消息，我惊讶不已。

astonishing /əˈstɒnɪʃɪŋ/ *adjective* 形容词
If something is **astonishing**, it surprises you very much. 令人震惊的: *an astonishing story* 令人惊异的故事

astonishment /əˈstɒnɪʃmənt/ *noun* 名词 (*no plural* 不用复数形式)
a feeling of great surprise 震惊；惊愕: *He looked at me in astonishment when I told him the news.* 我告诉他那个消息的时候，他吃惊地看着我。

astrologer /əˈstrɒlədʒə(r)/ *noun* 名词
a person who studies or knows a lot about ASTROLOGY 占星家

astrology /əˈstrɒlədʒi/ *noun* 名词 (*no plural* 不用复数形式)
the study of the positions and movements of the stars and planets and the way that some people believe they affect people and events 占星术；占星学

astronaut /ˈæstrənɔːt/ *noun* 名词
a person who works and travels in space 宇航员；航天员；太空人

astronomer /əˈstrɒnəmə(r)/ *noun* 名词
a person who studies or knows a lot about ASTRONOMY 天文学家

astronomy /əˈstrɒnəmi/ *noun* 名词 (*no plural* 不用复数形式)
the study of the sun, moon, planets and stars 天文学

at ⁰⁻ /ət; æt/ *preposition* 介词
1 a word that shows where 在（某处）: *They are at school.* 他们在学校。◇ *Jane is at home.* 简在家。◇ *The answer is at the back of the book.* 答案在书的后面。
2 a word that shows when 在（某时间）: *I go to bed at eleven o'clock.* 我十一点睡觉。◇ *At night you can see the stars.* 晚上你看得到星星。
3 towards somebody or something 向；朝: *Look at the picture.* 看这幅图。◇ *I smiled at her.* 我朝她笑笑。◇ *Somebody threw an egg at the President.* 有人向总统扔鸡蛋。
4 a word that shows what somebody is doing or what is happening 正在: *The two countries are at war.* 两国正在交战。◇ *We were hard at work.* 我们在努力工作。
5 a word that shows how much, how fast, how old, etc. （表示价格、速度、年龄等）以: *We were travelling at about 50 miles per hour.* 我们以每小时约 50 英里的速度行进。◇ *He left school at sixteen* (= when he was sixteen years old). 他十六岁离开了学校。
6 a word that shows how well somebody or something does something 在…方面: *I'm not very good at maths.* 我的数学不怎么样。
7 because of something 因为；由于: *We laughed at his jokes.* 听了他的笑话，我们大笑起来。
8 (*computing* 电脑) the symbol @ which is used in email addresses after a person's name （用于电邮地址的符号 @）➜ Look at the note at **dot**. 见 dot 条的注释。

ate *form of* EAT * eat 的不同形式

athlete /ˈæθliːt/ *noun* 名词
a person who is good at sports like running or jumping, especially one who takes part in sports competitions 运动员: *Athletes from all over the world go to the Olympic Games.* 来自世界各地的运动员参加奥运会。

athletic /æθˈletɪk/ *adjective* 形容词
having a fit, strong and healthy body 健壮的

athletics /æθˈletɪks/ *noun* 名词 (*plural* 用复数形式)
sports like running, jumping and throwing 田径运动

atlas /ˈætləs/ *noun* 名词 (*plural* 复数形式 atlases)
a book of maps 地图册；地图集: *an atlas of the world* 世界地图集

A

B
C
D
E
F
G
H
I
J
K
L
M
N
O
P
Q
R
S
T
U
V
W
X
Y
Z

ATM /ˌeɪ tiː ˈem/ *American English for* CASH MACHINE 美式英语，即 cash machine

atmosphere 0﹍ /ˈætməsfɪə(r)/ *noun* 名词 (*no plural* 不用复数形式)
1 the atmosphere the mixture of gases around the earth 大气；大气层: *pollution of the atmosphere* 大气污染
2 the air in a place（某处的）空气: *a smoky atmosphere* 烟雾缭绕的空气
3 the feeling that places or people give you 气氛；氛围: *The atmosphere in the office was very friendly.* 办公室的气氛很融洽。

atom /ˈætəm/ *noun* 名词
one of the very small things that everything is made of 原子: *Water is made of atoms of hydrogen and oxygen.* 水是由氢原子和氧原子构成的。 ➜ Look also at **molecule**. 亦见 molecule。

atomic /əˈtɒmɪk/ *adjective* 形容词
1 of or about ATOMS 原子的；与原子有关的: *atomic physics* 原子物理学
2 using the great power that is made by breaking ATOMS 原子能的: *an atomic bomb* 原子弹 ◇ *atomic energy* 原子能

attach /əˈtætʃ/ *verb* 动词 (attaches, attaching, attached /əˈtætʃt/)
to join or fix one thing to another thing 附上…；把…固定在…: *I attached the photo to the letter.* 我把照片附在信里了。

attached /əˈtætʃt/ *adjective* 形容词
liking somebody or something very much 非常喜欢: *We've grown very attached to this house.* 我们渐渐喜欢上了这座房子。

attachment /əˈtætʃmənt/ *noun* 名词
1 a strong feeling of love or liking for somebody or something 依恋；爱慕: *a child's strong attachment to its parents* 孩子对父母的深深依恋
2 (*computing* 电脑) a document that you send to somebody using email 附件

attack¹ 0﹍ /əˈtæk/ *noun* 名词
1 a violent act which is done in order to hurt somebody or damage something 袭击；攻击: *There was a terrorist attack on the city.* 这座城市遭到了恐怖袭击。
2 a time when you are ill（疾病的）发作，侵袭: *an attack of flu* 流感的侵袭

attack² 0﹍ /əˈtæk/ *verb* 动词 (attacks, attacking, attacked /əˈtækt/)
to start fighting or hurting somebody or something 袭击；攻击: *The army attacked the town.* 军队袭击市镇。 ◇ *The old man was attacked and his money was stolen.* 那个老先生遇袭，钱也让人偷走了。

attacker /əˈtækə(r)/ *noun* 名词
a person who tries to hurt somebody by using force 袭击者；攻击者: *The victim of the assault didn't recognize his attackers.* 遇袭者认不出袭击他的人。

attempt /əˈtempt/ *verb* 动词 (attempts, attempting, attempted)
to try to do something that is difficult 尝试 ➜ SAME MEANING **try** 同义词为 try: *He attempted to sail round the world.* 他想驾船环游世界。
▸ **attempt** *noun* 名词: *She made no attempt to help me.* 她没有尝试帮助我。 ◇ *a brave attempt at breaking the world record* 为打破世界纪录的勇敢尝试

attend /əˈtend/ *verb* 动词 (attends, attending, attended)
to go to or be present at a place where something is happening 参加；出席: *Did you attend the meeting?* 你参加了那次会议吗？

attendance /əˈtendəns/ *noun* 名词
1 (*no plural* 不用复数形式) being present at a place, for example at school 出席；到场: *Attendance at these lectures is compulsory.* 这些课必须要出席听讲。
2 (*plural* 复数形式 attendances) the number of people who go to an organized event 出席人数；到场人数: *Cinema attendances have risen again recently.* 上电影院的人近来又增加了。

attendant /əˈtendənt/ *noun* 名词
a person whose job is to serve or help people in a public place 服务员；接待员: *a car park attendant* 停车场管理员

attention 0﹍ /əˈtenʃn/ *noun* 名词 (*no plural* 不用复数形式)
looking or listening carefully and with interest 专心；注意: *I shouted in order to attract her attention* (= make her notice me). 我大声叫喊以引起她的注意。 ◇ *Can I have your attention, please?* (= please listen to me) 请听我讲话好吗？
pay attention look or listen carefully 注意；留心: *Please pay attention to what I'm saying.* 请注意我要讲的话。

attic /ˈætɪk/ *noun* 名词
the room or space under the roof of a house 屋顶间；阁楼 ➜ SAME MEANING **loft** 同义词为 loft: *My old clothes are in a box in the attic.* 我的旧衣服都放在阁楼的箱子里。 ➜ Look at Picture Dictionary page **P10**. 见彩页 P10。

attitude /ˈætɪtjuːd/ *noun* 名词
the way you think or feel about something 态度；看法: *What's your*

attitude to marriage? 你对婚姻有什么看法?

attorney /əˈtɜːni/ *American English for* LAWYER 美式英语，即 lawyer

attract 0̄ /əˈtrækt/ *verb* 动词 (attracts, attracting, attracted)
1 to make somebody like somebody or something 使喜欢；吸引: *He was attracted to her.* 他很喜欢她。◊ *I had always been attracted by the idea of working abroad.* 我以前总是向往去国外工作。
2 to make somebody or something come somewhere 吸引；招引: *Moths are attracted to light.* 飞蛾趋光。◊ *The new film has attracted a lot of publicity.* 新影片引起了媒体的广泛报道。

attraction /əˈtrækʃn/ *noun* 名词
1 (*no plural* 不用复数形式) a feeling of liking somebody or something very much 爱慕；喜爱；吸引: *I can't understand his attraction to her.* 我不明白他怎么看上了她。
2 (*plural* 复数形式 **attractions**) something that makes people come to a place 吸引人的事物: *Buckingham Palace is a major tourist attraction.* 白金汉宫是主要的旅游胜地。

attractive 0̄ /əˈtræktɪv/ *adjective* 形容词
1 A person who is **attractive** is nice to look at. 好看的；漂亮的: *He's very attractive.* 他很英俊。 ➋ Look at the note at **beautiful**. 见 beautiful 条的注释。
2 Something that is **attractive** pleases you or interests you. 诱人的；讨人喜爱的: *That's an attractive offer.* 那是个诱人的提议。 ➋ OPPOSITE **unattractive** 反义词为 unattractive

aubergine /ˈəʊbəʒiːn/ *noun* 名词 (*British* 英式英语) (*American* 美式英语 **eggplant**)
a large purple vegetable that is white inside 茄子 ➋ Look at Picture Dictionary page **P9**. 见彩页 P9。

auction /ˈɔːkʃn/ *noun* 名词
a sale where each thing is sold to the person who will give the most money for it 拍卖
▸ **auction** *verb* 动词 (auctions, auctioning, auctioned /ˈɔːkʃnd/) to sell something at an AUCTION 拍卖

audience /ˈɔːdiəns/ *noun* 名词
the people who are watching or listening to a film, play, concert, programme, etc. 观众；听众

audio /ˈɔːdiəʊ/ *adjective* 形容词
connected with the recording of sound 录音的: *audio tapes* 录音带

audio-visual /ˌɔːdiəʊ ˈvɪʒuəl/ *adjective* 形容词
using both sound and pictures 视听的: *audio-visual aids for the classroom* 课堂视听教具

August 0̄ /ˈɔːɡəst/ *noun* 名词
the eighth month of the year 八月

aunt 0̄ /ɑːnt/ *noun* 名词 (*also informal* 非正式亦作 **auntie**, **aunty** /ˈɑːnti/)

> 🔍 PRONUNCIATION 读音说明
> The word **aunt** sounds like **plant**.
> * aunt 读音像 plant。

the sister of your mother or father, or the wife of your uncle 姨妈；姑妈；舅妈；婶母；伯母: *Aunt Mary* 玛丽姨妈

auntie /ˈɑːnti/ *noun* 名词
aunt 姨妈；姑妈；舅妈；婶母；伯母

au pair /ˌəʊ ˈpeə(r)/ *noun* 名词 (*British* 英式英语)
a young person who lives with a family in a foreign country in order to learn the language. An **au pair** looks after the children and helps in the house. 换工 (在国外家庭住宿，帮做家务，照看小孩以学习语言)

authentic /ɔːˈθentɪk/ *adjective* 形容词
real and true 真实的；真正的: *That's not an authentic Van Gogh painting – it's just a copy.* 那幅画不是凡·高的真迹，只是复制品而已。

author /ˈɔːθə(r)/ *noun* 名词
a person who writes books or stories 作者；作家: *Who is your favourite author?* 你特别喜欢哪个作家?

authority /ɔːˈθɒrəti/ *noun* 名词
1 (*no plural* 不用复数形式) the power to tell people what they must do 权力；权威: *The police have the authority to stop cars.* 警察有权截停车辆。
2 (*plural* 复数形式 **authorities**) a group of people that tell other people what they must do 当局；当权者: *the city authorities* 市政当局

autobiography /ˌɔːtəbaɪˈɒɡrəfi/ *noun* 名词 (*plural* 复数形式 **autobiographies**)
a book that a person has written about their life 自传

autograph /ˈɔːtəɡrɑːf/ *noun* 名词
a famous person's name, which they themselves have written (名人的) 亲笔

I
J
K
L
M
N
O
P
Q
R
S
T
U
V
W
X
Y
Z

A
B
C
D
E
F
G
H
I
J
K
L
M
N
O
P
Q
R
S
T
U
V
W
X
Y
Z

签名: *He asked Madonna for her autograph.* 他请麦当娜给他签名。

automatic /ˌɔːtəˈmætɪk/ *adjective* 形容词
1 If a machine is **automatic**, it can work by itself, without people controlling it. （机器）自动的: *automatic doors* 自动门
2 that you do without thinking 不假思索的; 无意识的: *Breathing is automatic.* 呼吸是无意识的。
▶ **automatically** /ˌɔːtəˈmætɪkli/ *adverb* 副词: *This light comes on automatically at five o'clock.* 这盏灯一到五点就自动亮起来。

automobile /ˈɔːtəməbiːl/ *American English for* CAR 美式英语, 即 car

autumn 0-ᴡ /ˈɔːtəm/ *noun* 名词 (*British* 英式英语) (*American* 美式英语 **fall**)
the part of the year between summer and winter 秋天; 秋季: *In autumn, the leaves begin to fall from the trees.* 秋天, 树木开始落叶。 ᴐ Look at Picture Dictionary page **P16**. 见彩页 P16。

available 0-ᴡ /əˈveɪləbl/ *adjective* 形容词
ready for you to use, have or see 可使用（或得到、看到）的: *I phoned the hotel to ask if there were any rooms available.* 我打了电话到旅馆询问有没有空房间。 ◇ *I'm sorry – the manager is not available this afternoon.* 很抱歉, 经理今天下午没空。

avalanche /ˈævəlɑːnʃ/ *noun* 名词
a very large amount of snow that falls quickly down the side of a mountain 雪崩

avenue /ˈævənjuː/ (*abbr.* 缩略式 Ave.) *noun* 名词
a wide road or street 大街: *I live in Connaught Avenue.* 我住在康诺特大道。 ◇ *Burnham Ave.* 伯纳姆道

average¹ /ˈævərɪdʒ/ *noun* 名词
1 (*plural* 复数形式 averages) the result you get when you add two or more amounts together and then divide the total by the number of amounts you added 平均数: *The average of 2, 3 and 7 is 4 (2 + 3 + 7 = 12, and 12 ÷ 3 = 4).* * 2、3、7 的平均数是 4。
2 (*no plural* 不用复数形式) the normal amount, quality, etc. 正常标准; 平均水平; 一般情况: *On average, I buy a newspaper about twice a week.* 我平均一周大约买两次报纸。

average² /ˈævərɪdʒ/ *adjective* 形容词
1 (used about a number) found by

calculating the AVERAGE¹ (1) （数字）平均的: *The average age of the students is 19.* 这些学生的平均年龄是 19 岁。
2 normal or usual 正常的; 平常的: *The average student gets around 5 hours of homework a week.* 一般学生每周要做 5 小时左右的家庭作业。

avoid 0-ᴡ /əˈvɔɪd/ *verb* 动词 (avoids, avoiding, avoided)
1 to stop something happening; to try not to do something 防止; 避免: *He always tried to avoid an argument if possible.* 他总是尽可能避免与人争执。 ◇ *She has to avoid eating too much chocolate.* 她得尽量少吃巧克力。
2 to stay away from somebody or something 避开; 躲避: *We crossed the road to avoid our teacher.* 我们走过马路以躲开老师。

await /əˈweɪt/ *verb* 动词 (*formal* 正式) (awaits, awaiting, awaited)
to wait for something 等候; 等待: *We sat down to await the arrival of the guests.* 我们坐下等宾客到来。

awake 0-ᴡ /əˈweɪk/ *adjective* 形容词
not sleeping 醒着: *The children are still awake.* 孩子们还没睡着。 ᴐ OPPOSITE **asleep** 反义词为 asleep

award¹ /əˈwɔːd/ *noun* 名词
a prize or money that you give to somebody who has done something very well 奖项; 奖品; 奖金: *She won the award for best actress.* 她获颁最佳女演员奖。

award² /əˈwɔːd/ *verb* 动词 (awards, awarding, awarded)
to officially give a prize to somebody 授予; 颁发: *He was awarded first prize in the writing competition.* 他获得写作比赛一等奖。

aware 0-ᴡ /əˈweə(r)/ *adjective* 形容词
If you are **aware** of something, you know about it. 明白; 意识到: *He's not aware of the problem.* 他还没意识到这个问题。 ◇ *I was aware that somebody was watching me.* 我知道有人在注视着我。 ᴐ OPPOSITE **unaware** 反义词为 unaware

away 0-ᴡ /əˈweɪ/ *adverb* 副词
1 to or in another place 向另一处; 在另一处: *She ran away from him.* 她从他身边跑开了。 ◇ *He put his books away.* 他把书放在一边。
2 from a place 从某处: *The sea is two miles away.* 大海离这里有两英里。
3 not here 不在 ᴐ SAME MEANING **absent** 同义词为 absent: *Tim is away from*

school today because he is ill. 蒂姆今天
因病没上学。
4 in the future 在将来；距今：*Our
holiday is only three weeks away.* 还有
三个星期我们就放假了。

awesome /ˈɔːsəm/ *adjective* 形容词
1 very impressive and perhaps rather
frightening 令人惊叹的；使人敬畏的：
an awesome sight 令人赞叹的景象
2 (*American* 美式英语) (*informal* 非正式)
very good, enjoyable, etc. 很棒的；极好
玩的 ⊃ SAME MEANING **great** 同义词为
great：*I just bought this awesome new
CD!* 我刚买了这张棒极了的新激光唱片！
◇ *Wow! That's totally awesome!* 哇！真是
了不起！

awful /ˈɔːfl/ *adjective* 形容词
very bad 极坏的；糟糕透顶的：*The pain
was awful.* 疼得很厉害。◇ *What awful
weather!* 多么糟糕的天气！⊃ Look at the
note at **bad**. 见 bad 条的注释。

awfully /ˈɔːfli/ *adverb* 副词
very 极；非常 ⊃ SAME MEANING **terribly**
同义词为 terribly：*It was awfully hot.*
热死了。◇ *I'm awfully sorry!* 我万分抱歉！

awkward /ˈɔːkwəd/ *adjective* 形容词
1 difficult or causing problems 难对付
的；难处理的：*This big box will be
awkward to carry.* 这个大箱子很不好搬。
◇ *an awkward question* 棘手的问题
2 not comfortable; embarrassing 不舒服
的；令人尴尬的：*I felt awkward at the
party because I didn't know anybody.*
我在派对上感到很不自在，因为我谁都不
认识。
3 not able to move your body in an easy
way 动作笨拙的：*He's very awkward
when he dances.* 他跳舞时很笨拙。

axe (*British* 英式英语) (*American* 美式英语
ax) /æks/ *noun* 名词
a tool for cutting wood 斧：*He chopped
down the tree with an axe.* 他用斧子把树
砍倒了。

A
B
C
D
E
F
G
H
I
J
K
L
M
N
O
P
Q
R
S
T
U
V
W
X
Y
Z

B b

B, b /biː/ *noun* 名词 (*plural* 复数形式 B's, b's /biːz/)

the second letter of the English alphabet 英语字母表的第 2 个字母: *'Ball' begins with a 'B'.* * ball 一词以字母 b 开头。

BA /ˌbiː ˈeɪ/ *noun* 名词

the certificate that you receive when you complete a university or college course in an ARTS subject (= a subject that is not a science subject). **BA** is short for 'Bachelor of Arts'. 文学士（修完大学文科课程后获得的学位，BA 是 Bachelor of Arts 的缩略式） ➜ Look also at **BSc**. 亦见 BSc。

baby 婴儿

baby /ˈbeɪbi/ *noun* 名词 (*plural* 复数形式 babies)

a very young child 婴儿: *She's going to have a baby.* 她快生孩子了。◇ *a baby boy* 男婴 ◇ *a baby girl* 女婴

baby carriage /ˌbeɪbi ˈkærɪdʒ/ *American English for* PRAM 美式英语，即 pram

babysit /ˈbeɪbisɪt/ *verb* 动词 (babysits, babysitting, babysat /ˈbeɪbisæt/, has babysat)

to look after a child while the parents are not at home 代人临时照看孩子；当临时保姆

babysitter /ˈbeɪbisɪtə(r)/ *noun* 名词

a person who looks after a child while the parents are not at home 代人临时照看孩子的人；临时保姆

bachelor /ˈbætʃələ(r)/ *noun* 名词

1 a man who has never married 未婚男子；单身汉

2 Bachelor a person who has a university

degree (= they have finished the course and passed all their exams) 学士: *a Bachelor of Science* 理学士

back 后面

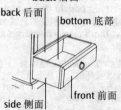

back[1] /bæk/ *noun* 名词

1 the part of a person or an animal that is between the neck and the bottom 背；背部: *He lay on his back and looked up at the sky.* 他仰卧着看天空。◇ *She was standing with her back to me so I couldn't see her face.* 她背对我站着，所以我看不到她的脸。➜ Look at Picture Dictionary page **P4**. 见彩页 P4。

2 the part of something that is behind or furthest from the front 后部；后面: *The answers are at the back of the book.* 答案在书的末尾。◇ *Write your address on the back of the cheque.* 把你的地址写在支票的背面。◇ *We sat in the back of the car.* 我们坐在汽车的后排座上。

back to front 前后颠倒

back to front with the back part where the front should be 前后颠倒: *You've got* *your sweater on back to front.* 你把毛衣前后穿反了。

behind somebody's back when somebody is not there, so that they do not know about it 背着某人；暗中：*Don't talk about Kate behind her back.* 不要在背后说凯特。

back² 0━ /bæk/ *adjective* 形容词
furthest from the front 后部的；后面的：*the back door* 后门 ◇ *back teeth* 白齿

back³ 0━ /bæk/ *adverb* 副词
1 in or to the place where somebody or something was before 在原处；回到原处；恢复原状：*I'll be back* (= I will return) *at six o'clock.* 我六点钟回来。◇ *Go back to sleep.* 回去睡觉吧。◇ *We walked to the shops and back.* 我们走到商店，然后又走了回来。
2 away from the front 向后；在后面：*I looked back to see if she was coming.* 我向后瞧了瞧，看她有没有来。◇ *Could everyone move back a bit, please?* 请大家往后移一下，好吗？⊃ OPPOSITE **forward** 反义词为 forward
3 as a way of returning or answering something 回应；回答；归还：*He paid me the money back.* 他把钱还给了我。◇ *I wrote her a letter, but she didn't write back.* 我给她写了封信，可是她没回信。◇ *I was out when she rang, so I phoned her back.* 她来电话的时候我出去了，我就给回了个电话。

back and forth from one place to another and back again, many times 反复来回：*She travels back and forth between London and Glasgow.* 她往返于伦敦和格拉斯哥之间。

back⁴ /bæk/ *verb* 动词 (backs，backing，backed /bækt/)
1 to move backwards or to make something move backwards （使）后退，倒退：*She backed the car out of the garage.* 她把车倒出车库。
2 to give help or support to somebody or something 帮助；支持：*They're backing their school team.* 他们支持自己的校队。

back away to move away backwards 向后退；退避：*Sally backed away from the big dog.* 萨莉看到那条大狗就往后退。

back out to not do something that you promised or agreed to do 退出；反悔：*You promised you would come with me. You can't back out of it now!* 你答应过会和我一起去的，现在你可不能说话不算数！

back something up
1 to say or show that something is true 支持；证实：*All the evidence backed up*

what the woman had said. 所有的证据都证明了那个女人所说属实。
2 (*computing* 电脑) to make a copy of information in your computer that you do not want to lose 做备份

backbone /ˈbækbəʊn/ *noun* 名词
the line of bones down the back of your body 脊柱；脊椎 ⊃ SAME MEANING **spine** 同义词为 spine

background /ˈbækɡraʊnd/ *noun* 名词
1 the things at the back in a picture（图片的）背景：*This is a photo of my house with the mountains in the background.* 这是我房子的照片，背景是山。⊃ OPPOSITE **foreground** 反义词为 foreground
2 the type of family that a person comes from and the education and experience that they have 出身背景：*She's from a poor background.* 她出身贫寒。

backpack 背包

backpack
(*British also* 英式英语亦作 **rucksack**) 背包

backpack¹ /ˈbækpæk/ *noun* 名词
a large bag that you carry on your back when you are travelling 背包 ⊃ SAME MEANING **rucksack** 同义词为 rucksack

backpack² /ˈbækpæk/ *verb* 动词
(backpacks，backpacking，backpacked)
to go walking or travelling with your clothes, etc. in a BACKPACK 背包旅行

⌕ SPEAKING 表达方式说明
You say **go backpacking** when you talk about spending time backpacking. 表示背包旅行说 go backpacking：*We went backpacking round Europe last summer.* 我们去年夏天背着背包在欧洲各地旅行。

backside /ˈbæksaɪd/ *noun* 名词 (*informal* 非正式)
the part of your body that you sit on 屁股 ⊃ SAME MEANING **bottom** 同义词为 bottom

A

B

C

D

E

F

G

H

I

J

K

L

M

N

O

P

Q

R

S

T

U

V

W

X

Y

Z

backstroke /'bækstrəʊk/ *noun* 名词
(*no plural* 不用复数形式)
a way of swimming on your back 仰泳

backup /'bækʌp/ *noun* 名词
1 extra help or support that you can get if
necessary 增援；后援： *The police had
backup from the army.* 警方得到了军队的
增援。
2 (*computing* 电脑) a copy of information
that you have put in your computer and
which you do not want to lose 备份

backward /'bækwəd/ *adjective* 形容词
1 in the direction behind you 向后的：
a backward step 后退的一步
2 slow to learn or change 落后的： *Our
teaching methods are backward compared
to some countries.* 与一些国家相比，我们
的教学方法比较落后。

backwards ⊶ /'bækwədz/ (*also* 亦作
backward /'bækwəd/) *adverb* 副词
1 towards a place or a position that is
behind 向后： *Could everybody take a
step backwards?* 大家能往后退一步吗？
⊃ OPPOSITE **forwards** 反义词为 forwards
2 with the back or the end first 朝反方
向；倒着： *If you say the alphabet
backwards, you start with 'Z'.* 要是倒念
字母表，就从 Z 开始。

backwards and forwards first in one
direction and then in the other, many
times 来来回回： *The dog ran backwards
and forwards, fetching sticks.* 那条狗跑来
跑去捡棍子。

backyard /ˌbæk'jɑːd/ *noun* 名词
(*American* 美式英语)
the area behind and around a house,
including the garden 后院

bacon /'beɪkən/ *noun* 名词 (*no plural*
不用复数形式)
long thin pieces of meat from a pig 咸猪
肉；熏猪肉： *We had bacon and eggs for
breakfast.* 我们早餐吃了咸猪肉和鸡蛋。

bacteria /bæk'tɪəriə/ *noun* 名词 (*plural*
用复数形式)
very small things that live in air, water,
earth, plants and animals. Some **bacteria**
can make us ill. 细菌

bad ⊶ /bæd/ *adjective* 形容词 (worse,
worst)
1 not good or nice 不好的；令人不快的：
The weather was very bad. 天气很糟糕。
◇ *He's had some bad news – his uncle has
died.* 他收到了一个坏消息——他舅舅死
了。◇ *a bad smell* 臭味
2 serious 严重的： *She had a bad
accident.* 她出了严重的意外。

3 not done or made well 做得不好的；
劣质的： *bad driving* 糟糕的驾驶技术
4 not able to work or do something well
能力差的；不能胜任的： *My eyesight is
bad.* 我视力很差。◇ *He's a bad teacher.*
他是个不称职的教师。
5 too old to eat; not fresh 不新鲜的：
bad eggs 坏鸡蛋

> 🔎 **WORD BUILDING** 词汇扩充
>
> If something is very bad, you can say
> **awful**, **dreadful** or **terrible**. 表示非常
> 糟糕可用 awful、dreadful 或 terrible：
> *I've had a dreadful day.* 我这天过得很
> 糟糕。
> Something that is unpleasant or
> somebody who is unkind is **horrible**.
> 描述讨厌的事或不友善的人可用
> horrible： *He's always saying horrible
> things to me.* 他总是对我说刻薄的话。

bad at something If you are **bad at
something**, you cannot do it well. 不擅长
某事： *I'm very bad at sports.* 我非常不擅
长体育运动。
bad for you If something is **bad for you**,
it can make you ill. 对身体有害： *Smoking
is bad for you.* 吸烟有损身体健康。
go bad to become too old to eat 腐烂；
变质： *This fish has gone bad.* 这条鱼已经
腐烂。
not bad (*informal* 非正式) quite good
挺好；不错： *'What was the film like?'
'Not bad.'* "电影怎么样？" "还不错。"
too bad (*informal* 非正式) words that
you use to say that you cannot change
something 可惜；不幸： *'I want to go out.'
'Too bad – you can't!'* "我想出去。"
"太不幸了，你不能出去！"

badges 徽章；名牌

badge 缀饰

badge /bædʒ/ *noun* 名词
a small piece of metal, cloth or plastic

with a design or words on it that you wear on your clothes 徽章： *All employees must wear a name badge.* 所有员工均须佩戴名牌。

badger 獾

badger /'bædʒə(r)/ *noun* 名词
an animal with black and white lines on its head that lives in holes in the ground and comes out at night 獾（头上有黑白线条，居于洞穴，夜间活动）

badly ⚬ /'bædli/ *adverb* 副词 (worse, worst)
1 in a way that is not good enough; not well 拙劣地；糟糕地；差： *She played badly.* 她表现得很糟糕。◇ *These clothes are badly made.* 这些衣服做工粗糙。
2 very much 非常；很： *I badly need a holiday.* 我急需休假。◇ *He was badly hurt in the accident.* 他在事故中受了重伤。

badminton 羽毛球运动

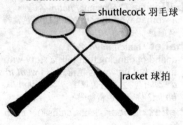
shuttlecock 羽毛球
racket 球拍

badminton /'bædmɪntən/ *noun* 名词 (no plural 不用复数形式)
a game for two or four players who try to hit a kind of light ball with feathers on it (called a shuttlecock) over a high net, using a RACKET (= a piece of equipment which you hold in your hand) 羽毛球运动： *Do you want to play badminton?* 你想打羽毛球吗？

bad-tempered ⚬ /,bæd 'tempəd/ *adjective* 形容词
often angry or impatient 脾气坏的；易怒的；没有耐性的： *Her neighbour was a*

bad-tempered old man. 她的邻居是个爱发脾气的老头。

bag ⚬ /bæg/ *noun* 名词
a thing made of cloth, paper, leather, etc., for holding and carrying things 袋；包： *He put the apples in a paper bag.* 他把苹果放进了纸袋。◇ *a plastic shopping bag* 塑料购物袋 ⊃ Look also at **carrier bag** and **handbag**. 亦见 carrier bag 和 handbag。

bagel 百吉圈

bagel /'beɪgl/ *noun* 名词
a type of bread roll in the shape of a ring 百吉圈（面包）

baggage /'bægɪdʒ/ *noun* 名词 (no plural 不用复数形式)
bags and suitcases that you take with you when you travel 行李： *We put all our baggage in the car.* 我们把行李都放在汽车里了。 ⊃ SAME MEANING **luggage** 同义词为 luggage ⊃ Look at the note at **luggage**. 见 luggage 条的注释。

baggy /'bægi/ *adjective* 形容词
If clothes are **baggy**, they are big and loose. （衣服）肥大的，宽松的： *He was wearing baggy trousers.* 他穿着宽松的裤子。

bagpipes /'bægpaɪps/ *noun* 名词 (plural 用复数形式)
a musical instrument that is often played in Scotland （苏格兰）风笛

bait /beɪt/ *noun* 名词 (no plural 不用复数形式)
food that is used to catch animals or fish with 鱼饵；诱饵

bake /beɪk/ *verb* 动词 (bakes, baking, baked /beɪkt/)
to cook food, for example bread or cakes, in an oven 烘烤： *My brother baked a cake for my birthday.* 我哥哥为我过生日烤了个蛋糕。

baked beans /,beɪkt 'biːnz/ *noun* 名词 (plural 用复数形式)
white BEANS cooked in tomato sauce, that

A

B

C

D

E

F

G

H

I

J

K

L

M

N

O

P

Q

R

S

T

U

V

W

X

Y

Z

you buy in a tin 番茄酱烘豆 ⊃ Look at Picture Dictionary page **P7**. 见彩页 **P7**。

baked potato /ˌbeɪkt pəˈteɪtəʊ/ (*plural* 复数形式 **baked potatoes**) (*also* 亦作 **jacket potato**) *noun* 名词
a whole potato cooked in its skin in an oven（带皮）烤土豆: *a baked potato and beans* 一份烤土豆加烘豆 ⊃ Look at Picture Dictionary page **P7**. 见彩页 **P7**。

baker /ˈbeɪkə(r)/ *noun* 名词
1 a person who makes and sells bread and cakes 面包师傅；糕饼师傅；面包店老板
2 baker's a shop that sells bread and cakes 面包店: *I went to the baker's to buy some bread.* 我去面包店买了些面包。⊃ Look at Picture Dictionary page **P13**. 见彩页 **P13**。

bakery /ˈbeɪkəri/ *noun* 名词 (*plural* 复数形式 **bakeries**)
a place where bread and cakes are baked to be sold in shops 面包烘房；糕饼烘房

balance¹ 0━ /ˈbæləns/ *noun* 名词
1 (*no plural* 不用复数形式) when two things are the same, so that one is not bigger or more important, for example 平衡；均衡: *You need a balance between work and play.* 你需要在工作和娱乐之间保持平衡。
2 (*no plural* 不用复数形式) the ability to keep steady with an equal amount of weight on each side of the body 平衡能力: *I struggled to keep my balance on my new skates.* 我穿着新溜冰鞋，吃力地保持平衡。◇ *She cycled round the corner, lost her balance and fell off.* 她骑自行车到拐角处时失去平衡，摔了下来。
3 (*plural* 复数形式 **balances**) the amount of money that is left after you have used some money 余额: *I must check my bank balance* (= find out how much I have in my account). 我得查一下我的银行账户余额。

balance² /ˈbæləns/ *verb* 动词 (**balances, balancing, balanced** /ˈbælənst/)
to put your body or something else into a position where it is steady and does not fall（使）保持平衡: *He balanced the bag on his head.* 他把袋子在头顶上放稳。◇ *She balanced on one leg.* 她以单脚稳站着。

balcony /ˈbælkəni/ *noun* 名词 (*plural* 复数形式 **balconies**)
a small platform on the outside wall of a building, above the ground, where you can stand or sit 阳台

balcony 阳台

bald /bɔːld/ *adjective* 形容词
with no hair or not much hair 秃顶的；秃头的: *My dad is going bald* (= losing his hair). 我爸爸快秃顶了。⊃ Look at the picture at **hair**. 见 hair 的插图。

ball 0━ /bɔːl/ *noun* 名词
1 a round thing that you use in games and sports 球: *Throw the ball to me.* 把球扔给我。◇ *a football* 足球 ◇ *a tennis ball* 网球
2 any round thing 球状物: *a ball of string* 一团绳子 ◇ *a snowball* 雪球
3 a big formal party where people dance 大型舞会

ballerina /ˌbæləˈriːnə/ *noun* 名词
a woman who dances in BALLETS 芭蕾舞女演员

ballet /ˈbæleɪ/ *noun* 名词
a kind of dancing that tells a story with music but no words 芭蕾舞: *I went to see a ballet.* 我去看芭蕾舞了。◇ *Do you like ballet?* 你喜欢芭蕾舞吗？

ballet dancer /ˈbæleɪ dɑːnsə(r)/ *noun* 名词
a person who dances in BALLETS 芭蕾舞演员

balloon /bəˈluːn/ *noun* 名词
1 a small coloured rubber thing that you blow air into and use as a toy or for decoration 气球: *We are going to hang balloons around the room for the party.* 我们会在联欢会的房间里挂满气球。
2 (*also* 亦作 **hot-air balloon**) a big thing like a **balloon** that flies in the sky, carrying people in a container (called a **basket**) underneath 热气球: *I would like to go up in a balloon.* 我想坐热气球升空。⊃ Look at Picture Dictionary page **P1**. 见彩页 **P1**。

ballot /'bælət/ *noun* 名词
when people choose somebody or
something by writing secretly on a piece
of paper 无记名投票： *We held a ballot
to choose a new president.* 我们投票选举
新主席。

ballpoint /'bɔːlpɔɪnt/ (*also* 亦作 **ballpoint
pen** /ˌbɔːlpɔɪnt 'pen/) *noun* 名词
a pen that has a very small ball at the end
that rolls the ink onto the paper 圆珠
笔；原子笔 ⊃ SAME MEANING **Biro** 同义词
为 Biro ⊃ Look at Picture Dictionary page
P11. 见彩页 P11。

bamboo /ˌbæm'buː/ *noun* 名词 (*plural*
复数形式 **bamboos**)
a tall plant that grows in hot countries
and is often used for making furniture
竹；竹子： *a bamboo chair* 竹椅 ◇
bamboo shoots (= young bamboo plants
that can be eaten) 竹笋

ban /bæn/ *verb* 动词 (**bans, banning,
banned** /bænd/)
to say that something must not happen;
to not allow something 禁止： *The film
was banned.* 这部电影遭禁映了。
▸ **ban** *noun* 名词： *There is a ban on
smoking in restaurants.* 餐馆里禁止吸烟。

banana /bə'nɑːnə/ *noun* 名词
a long curved yellow fruit 香蕉 ⊃ Look at
Picture Dictionary page **P8**. 见彩页 P8。

band 0━ /bænd/ *noun* 名词
1 a group of people who play music
together 乐队： *a rock band* 摇滚乐队 ◇
a jazz band 爵士乐队
2 a thin flat piece of material that you
put around something 带；箍： *I put an
elastic band round the letters to keep
them together.* 我用橡皮筋把信捆在一起。
◇ *The hat had a red band round it.* 帽子上
饰有一圈红带。
3 a line of colour or material on
something that is different from the rest
of it 条纹；条饰： *She wore a red jumper
with a green band across the middle.* 她穿
着一件红色套头毛衣，中间有一道绿色
条纹。

bandage[1] /'bændɪdʒ/ *noun* 名词
a long piece of white cloth that you tie
around a part of the body that is hurt
绷带

bandage[2] /'bændɪdʒ/ *verb* 动词
(**bandages, bandaging, bandaged**
/'bændɪdʒd/)
to put a BANDAGE around a part of the
body 用绷带包扎： *The nurse bandaged
my foot.* 护士用绷带把我的脚包扎好。

Band-Aid™ /'bænd eɪd/ *American English
for* PLASTER[1] (3) 美式英语，即 plaster[1]
第 3 义

bandit /'bændɪt/ *noun* 名词
a person who attacks and robs people
who are travelling 土匪；强盗： *They
were killed by bandits in the mountains.*
他们在山里遭土匪杀害了。

bang[1] /bæŋ/ *verb* 动词 (**bangs, banging,
banged** /bæŋd/)
to make a loud noise by hitting
something hard or by closing something
猛撞；砰地关上： *He banged his head on
the ceiling.* 他脑袋砰的一声撞到天花板上
了。◇ *Don't bang the door!* 不要砰地
关门!

bang[2] /bæŋ/ *noun* 名词
1 a sudden very loud noise 突然的巨响：
He shut the door with a bang. 他砰的一声
把门关上了。
2 a short, strong knock or hit, especially
one that causes pain and injury 猛撞：
He fell and got a bang on the head. 他摔
倒了，脑袋狠狠地磕了一下。
3 bangs (*plural* 用复数形式) *American
English for* FRINGE (1) 美式英语，即 fringe
第 1 义

banish /'bænɪʃ/ *verb* 动词 (**banishes,
banishing, banished** /'bænɪʃt/) (*formal
正式*)
to send somebody away from a place as
a punishment 放逐；流放

banister /'bænɪstə(r)/ *noun* 名词
a long piece of wood or metal that you
hold on to when you go up or down stairs
楼梯扶手 ⊃ Look at the picture at
staircase. 见 staircase 的插图。

bandage 绷带

bandage 绷带

bank¹ 0— /bæŋk/ *noun* 名词
1 a place that keeps money safe for people 银行: *I've got £500 in the bank.* 我在银行里存了 500 英镑。
2 the land along the side of a river 河岸: *People were fishing along the banks of the river.* 沿河两岸有人垂钓。

bank² /bæŋk/ *verb* 动词 (banks, banking, banked /bæŋkt/)
to keep your money in a particular bank 存款: *Who do you bank with?* 你把钱存在哪家银行?
bank on someone or 或 **something** to expect and trust someone to do something, or something to happen 依靠; 指望; 期待: *The boss might give you the day off but I wouldn't bank on it.* 老板那天可能会让你休息, 不过我可不敢打包票。

bank account /bæŋk əkaʊnt/ *noun* 名词
an arrangement that you have with a bank that lets you keep your money there 银行账户: *I'd like to open a bank account.* 我想开个银行账户。

> 🔍 WORD BUILDING 词汇扩充
>
> If you have a **bank account** you can **deposit** money (**pay it in**) or **withdraw** it (**take it out**). 开立银行账户 (bank account) 后, 可以存入 (deposit) 或提取 (withdraw) 款项: *I'd like to withdraw £50, please.* 请给我提取 50 英镑。
> If you don't want to **spend** your money, you can **save** it (keep it in the bank). 不想花费 (spend) 的钱可以储蓄 (save) 起来。

banker /'bæŋkə(r)/ *noun* 名词
a person who owns a bank or who has an important job in a bank 银行老板 (或要员); 银行家

bank holiday /ˌbæŋk 'hɒlədeɪ/ *noun* 名词 (*British* 英式英语)
a public holiday, for example Christmas Day, New Year's Day, etc. 银行假日; 公共假日

banking /'bæŋkɪŋ/ *noun* 名词 (*no plural* 不用复数形式)
the type of business done by banks 银行业: *She chose a career in banking.* 她选择从事银行业。

banknote /'bæŋknəʊt/ *noun* 名词
a piece of paper money 纸币; 钞票: *These are German banknotes.* 这些是德国钞票。

bankrupt /'bæŋkrʌpt/ *adjective* 形容词
not able to continue in business because you cannot pay the money that you owe 破产: *His business went bankrupt after a year.* 一年后他的公司破产了。

banner /'bænə(r)/ *noun* 名词
a long piece of cloth with words on it. People carry **banners** to show what they think. 横幅: *The banner said 'Stop the war'.* 横幅上写着"停止战争"。

baptism /'bæptɪzəm/ *noun* 名词
a religious ceremony when somebody is BAPTIZED 洗礼; 浸礼

baptize /bæp'taɪz/ *verb* 动词 (baptizes, baptizing, baptized /bæp'taɪzd/)
to put water on somebody and give them a name, to show that they belong to the Christian Church 授洗; 施洗

bars 条; 柜台

bar code 条形码

bar of soap 一块肥皂

bar stool 酒吧高脚凳

bar 酒吧柜台

bar of chocolate 一条巧克力

bar 窗条

window 窗

bar¹ 0— /bɑ:(r)/ *noun* 名词
1 a place where people can go and buy drinks, especially alcoholic drinks 酒吧: *There's a bar in the hotel.* 旅馆里有个酒吧。
2 a long, high table where you buy drinks in a bar or pub (酒吧或酒馆里提供饮料的) 柜台: *We stood at the bar.* 我们站在酒吧柜台处。
3 a place where you can get a particular kind of food or drink (专售某类饮食的) 小吃店, 柜台: *a coffee bar* 咖啡馆 ◇ *a sandwich bar* 三明治柜台 ➋ Look at the note at **restaurant**. 见 restaurant 条的注释。
4 a small block of something hard 条形

硬物： *a bar of soap* 一块肥皂 ◇ *a bar of chocolate* 一条巧克力
5 a long thin piece of metal 长条金属: *There were iron bars on the windows.* 窗户上装有铁栅栏。

bar² /bɑː(r)/ *verb* 动词 (**bars, barring, barred** /bɑːd/)
1 to put something across a place so that people cannot pass 阻挡；拦住: *A line of police barred the road.* 一排警察封锁了道路。
2 to say officially that somebody must not do something or go somewhere 禁止: *He was barred from the club for fighting.* 他因打架而被禁止进入俱乐部。

barbecue /'bɑːbɪkjuː/ *noun* 名词 (*abbr.* 缩略式 **BBQ**)
a party where you cook food on a fire outside 户外烧烤聚会: *We had a barbecue on the beach.* 我们在海滩上烧烤野餐。

barbed wire 带刺铁丝

barbed wire /ˌbɑːbd 'waɪə(r)/ *noun* 名词 (*no plural* 不用复数形式)
wire with a lot of sharp points on it. Some fences are made of **barbed wire**. 带刺铁丝

barber /'bɑːbə(r)/ *noun* 名词
1 a person whose job is to cut men's hair （为男子服务的）理发师
2 barber's a shop where men go to get their hair cut （男子）理发店

bar code /bɑː kəʊd/ *noun* 名词
a pattern of black lines that is printed on things you buy. It contains information that a computer reads to find the price. 条码，条形码（印在商品上，电脑可读的信息代码）

bare /beə(r)/ *adjective* 形容词
1 (used about a part of the body) with no clothes covering it （身体部位）裸露的，光着的: *He had bare feet* (= he wasn't wearing shoes or socks). 他光着脚。
2 without anything covering it or in it 无遮盖的；光秃秃的: *They had taken the paintings down, so the walls were all bare.* 他们把画都取了下来，墙上就光秃秃的了。

barefoot /'beəfʊt/ *adjective, adverb* 形容词，副词
with no shoes or socks on your feet 赤脚（的）: *The children ran barefoot along the beach.* 孩子们光着脚在海滩上跑。

barely /'beəli/ *adverb* 副词
almost not; only just 几乎没有；仅仅；勉强 ⊃ SAME MEANING **hardly** 同义词为 hardly: *She barely ate anything.* 她几乎没吃东西。

bargain¹ /'bɑːɡən/ *noun* 名词
something that is cheaper than usual 减价品；便宜货: *At just £10, the dress was a real bargain!* 这件连衣裙只要10英镑，真便宜！

bargain² /'bɑːɡən/ *verb* 动词 (**bargains, bargaining, bargained** /'bɑːɡənd/)
to try to agree on the right price for something 议价；讨价还价: *I think she'll sell the car for less if you bargain with her.* 我看你要是跟她讲讲价，她那辆汽车会卖得便宜点。

barge /bɑːdʒ/ *noun* 名词
a long boat with a flat bottom for carrying things or people on rivers or CANALS (= artificial rivers) 驳船

bark 树皮

bark 树皮

bark¹ /bɑːk/ *noun* 名词
1 (*no plural* 不用复数形式) the hard surface of a tree 树皮
2 (*plural* 复数形式 **barks**) the short loud sound that a dog makes 吠声

bark² /bɑːk/ *verb* 动词 (**barks, barking, barked** /bɑːkt/)
If a dog **barks**, it makes short loud sounds. 吠: *The dog always barks at people it doesn't know.* 这条狗总是冲着陌生人叫。

barley /'bɑːli/ *noun* 名词 (*no plural* 不用复数形式)
a plant that we use for food and for making beer and some other drinks 大麦

barmaid /'bɑːmeɪd/ *noun* 名词 (*British* 英式英语) (*American* 美式英语 **bartender**)
a woman who serves drinks in a bar or pub 酒吧女招待

A

B

C

D

E

F

G

H

I

J

K

L

M

N

O

P

Q

R

S

T

U

V

W

X

Y

Z

barman /'bɑːmən/ *noun* 名词 (*plural* 复数形式 **barmen** /'bɑːmən/) (*American also* 美式英语亦作 **bartender**)
a man who serves drinks in a bar or pub 吧台服务员；酒吧男招待

barn /bɑːn/ *noun* 名词
a large building on a farm for keeping crops or animals in 谷仓；畜棚

barometer /bə'rɒmɪtə(r)/ *noun* 名词
an instrument that helps us to know what the weather will be 气压计；晴雨表

barracks /'bærəks/ *noun* 名词 (*plural* 用复数形式)
a building or group of buildings where soldiers live 兵营；营房： *an army barracks* 陆军营房

barrel /'bærəl/ *noun* 名词
1 a big container for liquids, with round sides and flat ends 桶： *a beer barrel* 啤酒桶 ◇ *a barrel of oil* 一桶石油
2 the long metal part of a gun that a bullet goes through 枪管

barricade /ˌbærɪ'keɪd/ *noun* 名词
a line of things arranged across a road, etc. to stop people from getting past 路障；街垒
▶ **barricade** *verb* 动词 (**barricades**, **barricading**, **barricaded**): *He barricaded the door to keep the police out.* 他封住了门不让警察进去。

barrier /'bæriə(r)/ *noun* 名词
a wall or fence that stops you going somewhere 障碍物；屏障： *You must show your ticket at the barrier before you get on the train.* 必须在检票处出示车票才能上火车。

bartender /'bɑːtendə(r)/ *American English for* BARMAID *or* BARMAN 美式英语，即 barmaid 或 barman

base¹ 0➔ /beɪs/ *noun* 名词
1 the bottom part of something; the part that something stands on 底部；底座： *The lamp has a heavy base.* 这个灯底座很沉。 ◇ *the base of a column* 柱基
2 a person's or a company's main home or office 总部；大本营： *She travels all over the world but London is her base.* 她周游世界各地，但主要还是住在伦敦。
3 a place where soldiers in the army, navy, etc. live and work 军事基地： *an army base* 陆军基地

base² 0➔ /beɪs/ *verb* 动词 (**bases**, **basing**, **based** /beɪst/)
be based somewhere If a person or a company **is based in** a place, that is where they have their main home or office. 总部设在…；以…为大本营
base something on something to make or develop something, using another thing as a starting point 以…为基础： *The film is based on a true story.* 这部电影是根据真实故事拍摄的。

baseball /'beɪsbɔːl/ *noun* 名词
1 (*no plural* 不用复数形式) a game in which two teams hit a ball with a wooden stick (called a **bat**) and then score points by running round four fixed points (called **bases**) on a large field 棒球运动： *We played baseball in the park.* 我们在公园打了棒球。 ➔ Look at Picture Dictionary page **P14**. 见彩页 P14。
2 (*plural* 复数形式 **baseballs**) a ball for playing this game 棒球

basement /'beɪsmənt/ *noun* 名词
part of a building that is under the level of the ground 地下室： *a basement flat* 地下室套房

bases¹ /'beɪsɪz/ *plural of* BASE¹ * base¹ 的复数形式

bases² /'beɪsiːz/ *plural of* BASIS * basis 的复数形式

bash /bæʃ/ *verb* 动词 (**bashes**, **bashing**, **bashed** /bæʃt/) (*informal* 非正式)
to hit somebody or something very hard 猛击；猛撞： *I fell and bashed my knee.* 我摔倒了，把膝盖磕了。

basic 0➔ /'beɪsɪk/ *adjective* 形容词
1 most important and necessary 基本的；基础的： *A person's basic needs are food, clothes and a place to live.* 人最基本的需要就是吃穿住。
2 simple; including only what is necessary 简单的；初级的： *This course teaches basic computer skills.* 这门课教授基础的电脑技能。

basically /'beɪsɪkli/ *adverb* 副词
in the most important ways 基本上；大体上： *She's a little strange but basically a very nice person.* 她有点怪，但总体来说人很不错。

basin /'beɪsn/ *noun* 名词
1 = WASHBASIN
2 a round bowl for cooking or mixing food（烹饪用的）盆

basis 0➔ /'beɪsɪs/ *noun* 名词 (*plural* 复数形式 **bases** /'beɪsiːz/)

1 the most important part or idea, from which something grows 基础；要素：*Her notes formed the **basis** of a book.* 她的笔记成了一本书的基础。
2 the way something is done or organized 方式；准则：*We meet **on a regular basis*** (= often). 我们经常见面。

basket 篮子

basket /ˈbɑːskɪt/ *noun* 名词
a container made of thin sticks or thin pieces of plastic or metal, that you use for holding or carrying things 篮；篓；筐：*a shopping basket* 购物篮 ◇ *a bread basket* 面包筐 ⊃ Look also at **waste-paper basket**. 亦见 waste-paper basket。

basketball /ˈbɑːskɪtbɔːl/ *noun* 名词
1 (*no plural* 不用复数形式) a game for two teams of five players who try to throw a ball into a high net 篮球运动 ⊃ Look at Picture Dictionary page **P14**. 见彩页 P14。
2 (*plural* 复数形式 **basketballs**) a ball for playing this game 篮球

bass /beɪs/ *adjective* 形容词
with a deep sound 低音的：*She plays the bass guitar.* 她弹低音吉他。 ◇ *a bass drum* 低音鼓

bat¹ /bæt/ *noun* 名词
1 a piece of wood for hitting the ball in a game like BASEBALL or TABLE TENNIS 球棒；球板

> 🔎 **WHICH WORD?** 词语辨析
> The thing that you use to hit the ball has different names in different sports. 击球所用之物在不同运动项目中有不同的名称。
> You use a **bat** in baseball, cricket and table tennis. 棒球、板球、乒乓球用球棒或球板（bat）。
> You use a **racket** to play badminton, squash and tennis. 羽毛球、壁球、网球用球拍（racket）。
> To play golf, you use a **club** and to play

hockey, you use a **stick**. 高尔夫球棒叫做 club，曲棍球的棍叫做 stick。
2 an animal like a mouse with wings. **Bats** come out and fly at night. 蝙蝠

bat² /bæt/ *verb* 动词 (**bats, batting, batted**)
to try to hit a ball in games like BASEBALL or CRICKET 用球棒（或球板等）击球：*He bats very well.* 他擅长击球。

batch /bætʃ/ *noun* 名词 (*plural* 复数形式 **batches**)
a group of things 一批：*She made a batch of cakes.* 她做了一批蛋糕。

bath¹ 0━ /bɑːθ/ *noun* 名词 (*plural* 复数形式 **baths** /bɑːðz/)
1 (*British* 英式英语) (*American* 美式英语 **bathtub**) a large container that you fill with water and sit in to wash your body 浴缸；浴盆 ⊃ Look at Picture Dictionary page **P10**. 见彩页 P10。
2 washing your body in a bath 洗澡：*I had a bath this morning.* 我今天早上洗了个澡。

bath² /bɑːθ/ *verb* 动词 (**baths, bathing, bathed**) (*British* 英式英语)
to give a BATH¹ (2) to somebody 给⋯洗澡：*It's your turn to bath the baby.* 轮到你给宝宝洗澡了。

bathe /beɪð/ *verb* 动词 (**bathes, bathing, bathed** /beɪðd/)
1 to wash a part of your body carefully 清洗（身体部位）：*He bathed the cut on his finger.* 他清洗了手指上的伤口。
2 to swim in the sea or in a lake or river （在海、湖、河中）游泳：*On hot days we often bathe in the lake.* 天热的时候，我们常在湖里游泳。

> 🔎 **SPEAKING** 表达方式说明
> It is more usual nowadays to say **go swimming**. 现在较常用 go swimming。

bathrobe /ˈbɑːθrəʊb/ *noun* 名词
a piece of clothing, like a loose soft coat, that you put on after having a bath or shower 浴衣；浴袍

bathroom 0━ /ˈbɑːθruːm/ *noun* 名词
1 (*British* 英式英语) a room where you can wash and have a bath or shower 浴室 ⊃ Look at Picture Dictionary page **P10**. 见彩页 P10。
2 (*American* 美式英语) a room with a toilet in it 厕所；卫生间；洗手间：*Can I go to the bathroom* (= use the toilet)?

A B C D E F G H I J K L M N O P Q R S T U V W X Y Z

A
B
C
D
E
F
G
H
I
J
K
L
M
N
O
P
Q
R
S
T
U
V
W
X
Y
Z

我能上洗手间吗？ ⊃ Look at the note at **toilet**. 见 toilet 条的注释。

bathtub /'bɑːθtʌb/ *American English for* BATH¹ (1) 美式英语，即 bath¹ 第 1 义

batter /'bætə(r)/ *verb* 动词 (batters, battering, battered /'bætəd/)
to hit someone or something hard many times 连续猛击；殴打

batteries 电池

battery /'bætri/ *noun* 名词 (*plural* 复数 形式 batteries)
a thing that gives electricity. You put **batteries** inside things like toys, radios and cars to make them work. 电池

battle¹ /'bætl/ *noun* 名词
1 a fight between armies in a war 战斗；战役：*the battle of Waterloo* 滑铁卢战役
2 trying very hard to do something difficult 奋斗；斗争：*After three years, she lost her battle against cancer.* 与癌症抗争三年之后，她去世了。

battle² /'bætl/ *verb* 动词 (battles, battling, battled /'bætld/)
to try very hard to do something difficult

奋斗；斗争；搏斗：*The doctors battled to save her life.* 医生奋力抢救她。

bay /beɪ/ *noun* 名词 (*plural* 复数形式 bays)
a part of the coast where the land goes in to form a curve 海湾：*There was a ship in the bay.* 海湾里有一艘船。◇ *the Bay of Bengal* 孟加拉湾

bazaar /bə'zɑː(r)/ *noun* 名词
a market in Asia or Africa （亚洲或非洲 地方的）集市

BC /ˌbiː 'siː/ *abbreviation* 缩略式
'BC' in a date shows it was before Christ was born. 公元前：*Julius Caesar died in 44 BC.* 尤里乌斯·凯撒死于公元前 44 年。 ⊃ Look at **AD**. 见 AD。

be 0ᵐ /bi; biː/ *verb* 动词
1 there is/there are to exist or be present in a place 有；存在：*There are a lot of trees in our garden.* 我们的花园里种着 许多树。◇ *I tried phoning them but there was no answer.* 我试着给他们打过电话， 但没人接。◇ *Is there a post office near here?* 这里附近有邮局吗？
2 a word that you use to give the position of somebody or something or the place where they are 位于；在（某 处）：*Jen's* (= Jen is) *in her office.* 珍在 她的办公室里。◇ *Where are the scissors?* 剪刀放哪里了？
3 a word that you use when you are giving the name of people or things, describing them or giving more information about them （提供名称或信 息时用）：*I'm* (= I am) *Ben.* 我叫本。◇ *The film was excellent.* 这部电影非常棒。◇ *John is a doctor.* 约翰是医生。◇ *Roberta's Italian.* 罗伯塔是意大利人。◇ *'What colour is your car?' 'It's red.'* "你的车子是

be

present tense 现在式		short forms 缩写	negative short forms 缩写否定式
I	**am** /æm/	**I'm**	**I'm not**
you	**are** /ɑː(r)/	**you're**	**you aren't**
he/she/it	**is** /ɪz/	**he's/she's/it's**	**he/she/it isn't**
we	**are**	**we're**	**we aren't**
you	**are**	**you're**	**you aren't**
they	**are**	**they're**	**they aren't**

past tense 过去式		present participle 现在分词	past participle 过去分词
I	**was** /wɒz/		
you	**were** /wɜː(r)/	**being**	**been**
he/she/it	**was**		
we	**were**		
you	**were**		
they	**were**		

什么颜色的？" "红色。" ◇ *Today is Friday*. 今天是星期五。
4 a word that you use to talk about the age of somebody or something or to talk about time（表示年龄或时间）：*'How old is she?' 'She's twelve.'* "她多大了？" "十二岁了。" ◇ *Her birthday was in May*. 她的生日在五月。◇ *It's six o'clock*. 六点了。
5 a word that you use with another verb（与动词现在分词连用）：*'What are you doing?' 'I'm (= I am) reading.'* "你在干什么？" "我在看书。"
6 a word that you use with part of another verb to show that something happens to somebody or something（与动词过去分词连用）：*This cheese is made in France*. 这种乳酪产于法国。◇ *The house was built in 1910*. 这所房子建于1910年。
7 a word that shows that something must or will happen（表示必定或即将发生的事）：*You are to go to bed immediately!* 你得马上去睡觉!

beach¹ /biːtʃ/ *noun* 名词 (*plural* 复数形式 **beaches**)
a piece of land next to the sea that is covered with sand or stones 海滩：*a sandy beach* 沙滩 ◇ *We lay on the beach in the sun*. 我们躺在海滩上晒太阳。

bead /biːd/ *noun* 名词
a small ball of wood, glass or plastic with a hole in the middle. **Beads** are put on a string to make jewellery.（有孔的）珠子

beak /biːk/ *noun* 名词
the hard pointed part of a bird's mouth（鸟的）嘴；鸟喙 ◆ Look at the picture at **bird**. 见 bird 的插图。

beam¹ /biːm/ *noun* 名词
1 a line of light 光束：*a laser beam* 激光束
2 a long heavy piece of wood that holds up a roof or ceiling（支撑屋顶或天花板的）梁

beam² /biːm/ *verb* 动词 (**beams, beaming, beamed** /biːmd/)
to have a big happy smile on your face 开颜地笑

bean /biːn/ *noun* 名词
a seed, or a seed container, that we use as food 豆；豆荚：*green beans* 青刀豆 ◇ *coffee beans* 咖啡豆 ◆ Look at Picture Dictionary page **P9**. 见彩页 P9。

bear¹ /beə(r)/ *verb* 动词 (**bears, bearing, bore** /bɔː(r)/, **has borne** /bɔːn/)
1 to be able to accept something unpleasant without complaining 承受；

忍受：*The pain was difficult to bear.* 疼痛难忍。
2 to hold somebody or something up so that they do not fall 支撑：*The ice is too thin to bear your weight.* 冰太薄，承受不了你的重量。
can't bear somebody or 或 **something** to hate somebody or something 忍无可忍；讨厌：*I can't bear this music.* 我讨厌这音乐。◇ *He can't bear having nothing to do.* 无所事事，他可受不了。

bear² /beə(r)/ *noun* 名词
a big wild animal with thick fur 熊 ◆ Look at Picture Dictionary page **P3**. 见彩页 P3。

beard 胡须

beard 络腮胡子

beard /bɪəd/ *noun* 名词
the hair on a man's chin 胡须；络腮胡子：*He has got a beard.* 他蓄着胡子。

beast /biːst/ *noun* 名词
1 (*formal* 正式) a wild animal 野兽

> 🔊 SPEAKING 表达方式说明
> **Animal** is the word that we usually use. * animal 是常用词。

2 an unkind or cruel person 凶残的人

beat¹ /biːt/ *verb* 动词 (**beats, beating, beat, has beaten** /ˈbiːtn/)
1 to win a fight or game against a person or group of people 打败；战胜：*Daniel always beats me at tennis.* 丹尼尔跟我打网球总赢我。◇ *Our team was beaten 2-1.* 我们队 1 比 2 输了。
2 to hit somebody or something very hard many times 猛击；敲打：*She beats her dog with a stick.* 她用棍子打她的狗。◇ *The rain was beating on the roof.* 雨点敲打着屋顶。
3 to make the same sound or movement

A
B
C
D
E
F
G
H
I
J
K
L
M
N
O
P
Q
R
S
T
U
V
W
X
Y
Z

many times 有节奏地动: *His heart was beating fast.* 他的心脏跳得很快。
4 to mix food quickly with a fork, for example 快速搅拌: *Beat the eggs and sugar together.* 把鸡蛋和糖搅拌在一起。
beat somebody up to hit or kick somebody hard, many times 痛殴；毒打: *He was badly beaten up by a gang of youths.* 他被一帮年轻人打得遍体鳞伤。

beat² /biːt/ *noun* 名词
a sound that comes again and again 反复的声音: *We heard the beat of the drums.* 我们听到了鼓声。 ⊃ Look at **heartbeat**. 见 heartbeat。

beautician /bjuːˈtɪʃn/ *noun* 名词
a person whose job is to give special treatments to your face and body to make you look good 美容师

beautiful ⊶ /ˈbjuːtɪfl/ *adjective* 形容词
1 very pretty or attractive 美丽的；漂亮的: *a beautiful woman* 漂亮的女人

> 🔎 **WORD BUILDING** 词汇扩充
> When we talk about people, we usually say **beautiful** and **pretty** for women and girls, and **handsome** and **good-looking** for men and boys. 形容女性通常用 beautiful 和 pretty；形容男性通常用 handsome 和 good-looking。
> **Attractive** can be used for both. * attractive 形容男性和女性均可。

2 very nice to see, hear or smell 美好的；美妙的 ⊃ SAME MEANING **lovely** 同义词为 lovely: *Those flowers are beautiful.* 那些花真漂亮。 ◇ *What a beautiful song!* 多动听的歌啊!
▸ **beautifully** /ˈbjuːtɪfli/ *adverb* 副词: *Louis sang beautifully.* 路易斯唱得动听极了。

beauty ⊶ /ˈbjuːti/ *noun* 名词 (*no plural* 不用复数形式)
the quality of being beautiful 美；美丽: *She was a woman of great beauty.* 她是个大美人。 ◇ *the beauty of the mountains* 群山之美

because ⊶ /bɪˈkɒz/ *conjunction* 连词
for the reason that 因为: *He was angry because I was late.* 因为我迟到了，所以他很生气。
because of something or 或 **somebody** as a result of something or someone 由于（某事或某人）: *We stayed at home because of the rain.* 由于下雨，我们待在家里。

beckon /ˈbekən/ *verb* 动词 (**beckons**, **beckoning**, **beckoned** /ˈbekənd/)

to move your finger to show that you want somebody to come nearer 招手示意；挥手召唤

become ⊶ /bɪˈkʌm/ *verb* 动词
(**becomes**, **becoming**, **became** /bɪˈkeɪm/, **has become**)
to begin to be something 开始变得；变成；成为: *She became a doctor in 1982.* 她在 1982 年成了医生。 ◇ *The weather is becoming colder.* 天气变冷了。

> 🔎 **SPEAKING** 表达方式说明
> In conversation, we usually say **get** instead of **become** with adjectives. It is less formal. 人们在说话时通常将 get 与形容词连用，而不用 become。此用法较非正式: *The weather is getting colder.* 天气开始冷了。 ◇ *She got nervous as the exam date came closer.* 随着考试日期的临近，她变得紧张起来。

what became of ... ? used to ask what has happened to somebody or something（结果）怎么样?: *What became of that student who used to live with you?* 以前和你一起住的那个学生后来怎么样了?

bed ⊶ /bed/ *noun* 名词
1 a thing that you sleep on 床: *It was time to go to bed.* 该上床睡觉了。 ◇ *The children are in bed.* 孩子们都上床了。 ◇ *to make the bed* (= to make it ready for somebody to sleep in) 铺床

> 🔎 **WORD BUILDING** 词汇扩充
> A bed for one person is called a **single bed** and a bed for two people is called a **double bed**. 单人床叫做 single bed，双人床叫做 double bed。
> Children often sleep in **bunk beds**, which are two single beds built with one above the other. 儿童常睡的双层床叫做 bunk bed。

2 the bottom of a river or the sea 河床；海底

bed and breakfast /ˌbed ən ˈbrekfəst/ (*abbr.* 缩略式 **B and B** or 或 **B & B**) /ˌbiː ən ˈbiː/ *noun* 名词 (*British* 英式英语)
a private house or small hotel where you pay for a room to sleep in and a meal the next morning 提供住宿和早餐的小旅馆: *I stayed in a bed and breakfast.* 我住在一家提供早餐的小旅馆里。

bedclothes /ˈbedkləʊðz/ *noun* 名词 (*plural* 用复数形式)
the sheets and covers that you use on a bed 床单和枕被套

beds 床

bedspread
床罩

duvet 羽绒被

mattress
床垫

pillow 枕头

blanket 毯子

sheet 床单

bunk beds 双层床　　　　**double bed 双人床**　　　　**single bed 单人床**

bedding /'bedɪŋ/ *noun* 名词 (*no plural* 不用复数形式)
everything that you put on a bed and need for sleeping 卧具；床上用品；寝具

bedroom ०ᆏ /'bedruːm/ *noun* 名词
a room where you sleep 卧室 ⊃ Look at Picture Dictionary page P10. 见彩页 P10。

bedside /'bedsaɪd/ *noun* 名词 (*no plural* 不用复数形式)
the area that is next to a bed 床边: *She sat at his bedside all night long.* 她整夜守候在他的床边。 ◇ *A book lay open on the bedside table.* 床头柜上摊放着一本书。

bedsit /'bedsɪt/ (*also* 亦作 bedsitter /ˌbed'sɪtə(r)/) *noun* 名词
one room that you live and sleep in 卧室兼起居室

bedspread /'bedspred/ *noun* 名词
an attractive cover for a bed that you put on top of the sheets and other covers 床罩 ⊃ Look at the picture at **bed**. 见 bed 的插图。

bedtime /'bedtaɪm/ *noun* 名词
the time when somebody usually goes to bed 就寝时间

bee /biː/ *noun* 名词
a black and yellow insect that flies and makes a sweet food that we eat (called **honey**) 蜜蜂

bee 蜜蜂

beef /biːf/ *noun* 名词 (*no plural* 不用复数形式)
meat from a cow 牛肉: *roast beef* 烤牛肉 ⊃ Look at the note at **cow**. 见 cow 条的注释。 ⊃ Look at Picture Dictionary page **P7**. 见彩页 P7。

beefburger /'biːfbɜːɡə(r)/ *noun* 名词
(*British* 英式英语) *another word for* HAMBURGER * hamburger 的另一种说法

beehive /'biːhaɪv/ *noun* 名词
a thing that BEES live in 蜂房；蜂箱

been ०ᆏ /biːn; bɪn/
1 *form of* BE * be 的不同形式
2 *form of* GO[1] * go[1] 的不同形式
have been to to have gone to a place and come back again 曾经去过: *Have you ever been to Scotland?* 你去过苏格兰吗?

> 🔎 **WHICH WORD?** 词语辨析
> **Been** or **gone**? 用 been 还是 gone?
> If somebody has **been** to a place, they have travelled there and returned. * have been 表示去过某处并已经返回: *I've been to Scotland three times.* 我去过苏格兰三次。 ◇ *You were a long time. Where have you been?* 好久没见你了。你去哪里了?
> If somebody has **gone** to a place, they have travelled there and they are still there now. * have gone 表示去了某处并仍待在那里: *Judy isn't here. She's gone to Scotland.* 朱迪不在，她去苏格兰了。 ◇ *Mum's gone out, but she'll be back soon.* 妈妈出去了，但她很快会回来。

beer ०ᆏ /bɪə(r)/ *noun* 名词
1 (*no plural* 不用复数形式) an alcoholic drink made from grain 啤酒: *a pint of beer* 一品脱啤酒
2 (*plural* 复数形式 beers) a glass, bottle or can of beer 一杯（或一瓶、一罐）啤酒: *Three beers, please.* 请来三杯啤酒。

A
B
C
D
E
F
G
H
I
J
K
L
M
N
O
P
Q
R
S
T
U
V
W
X
Y
Z

beetle /ˈbiːtl/ ***noun*** 名词
an insect with hard wings and a shiny body 甲虫

beetroot /ˈbiːtruːt/ ***noun*** 名词 (*British* 英式英语) (*American* 美式英语 **beet** /biːt/)
a round dark red vegetable that you cook before you eat it 甜菜根 ➲ Look at Picture Dictionary page **P9**. 见彩页 P9。

before[1] /bɪˈfɔː(r)/ ***preposition, conjunction*** 介词，连词
1 earlier than somebody or something; earlier than the time that 比…早；在…以前： *He arrived before me.* 他比我先到。◇ *I said goodbye before I left.* 我临走前说了声再见。◇ *Ellen worked in a hospital before getting this job.* 在得到这份工作之前，埃伦在医院上班。◇ *They should be here **before long*** (= soon). 他们应该很快就来到这里。
2 in front of somebody or something 在…前面： *B comes before C in the alphabet.* 在字母表中，B 排在 C 前面。
➲ OPPOSITE **after** 反义词为 after

before[2] /bɪˈfɔː(r)/ ***adverb*** 副词
at an earlier time; in the past 以前；过去： *I've never met them before.* 我以前从来没见过他们。◇ *I've seen this film before.* 我以前看过这部电影。

beforehand /bɪˈfɔːhænd/ ***adverb*** 副词
at an earlier time than something 提前；事先： *Tell me beforehand if you are going to be late.* 要是你会晚来就事先告诉我一声。

beg /beɡ/ ***verb*** 动词 (**begs, begging, begged** /beɡd/)
1 to ask somebody for something especially in an anxious way because you want or need it very much 恳求；乞求： *She **begged** me **to** stay with her.* 她恳求我留下来和她在一起。◇ *He **begged for** help.* 他求人帮忙。
2 to ask for money or food because you are very poor 乞讨；行乞： *There are a lot of people begging in the streets.* 街上有很多人在行乞。
I beg your pardon (*formal* 正式) I am sorry 对不起；请原谅： *I beg your pardon, could you say that again?* 对不起，你能再说一遍吗？

beggar /ˈbeɡə(r)/ ***noun*** 名词
a person who asks other people for money or food 乞丐

begin /bɪˈɡɪn/ ***verb*** 动词 (**begins, beginning, began** /bɪˈɡæn/, **has begun** /bɪˈɡʌn/)
1 to start to do something or start to happen 开始 ➲ SAME MEANING **start** 同义词为 start： *I'm **beginning to** feel cold.* 我开始感到寒冷。◇ *The film begins at 7.30.* 电影 7 点 30 分开始。
2 to start in a particular way 以…开头： *The name John **begins with** a 'J'.* * John 这个名字以字母 J 开头。 ➲ OPPOSITE **end** 反义词为 end
to begin with at first; at the beginning 起初；一开始： *To begin with they were very happy.* 一开始他们很幸福。

> **WHICH WORD?** 词语辨析
> **Begin** or **start**? 用 begin 还是 start？
> **Begin** and **start** both mean the same thing, but **start** is more often used in speaking. * begin 和 start 表示相同的意思，但 start 在口语中更为常用：
> *Shall we eat now? I'm starting to feel hungry.* 我们现在吃饭好吗？我开始感到饿了。

beginner /bɪˈɡɪnə(r)/ ***noun*** 名词
a person who is starting to do or learn something 新手；初学者

beginning /bɪˈɡɪnɪŋ/ ***noun*** 名词
the time or place where something starts; the first part of something 开头；开端；开始部分： *I didn't see the **beginning of** the film.* 我没看到电影的开头。
➲ OPPOSITE **end** 反义词为 end

begun *form of* BEGIN * begin 的不同形式

behalf /bɪˈhɑːf/ ***noun*** 名词
on behalf of somebody, on somebody's behalf for somebody; in the place of somebody 为某人；代表某人： *Mr Smith is away, so I am writing to you on his behalf.* 史密斯先生不在，所以我代他给你写信。

behave /bɪˈheɪv/ ***verb*** 动词 (**behaves, behaving, behaved** /bɪˈheɪvd/)
to do and say things in a certain way 表现： *They behaved very kindly towards me.* 他们对我很友善。◇ *The children behaved badly all day.* 孩子们整天都调皮捣蛋。
behave yourself to be good; to do and say the right things 表现得体；守规矩： *Did the children behave themselves?* 孩子们乖吗？

behavior *American English for* BEHAVIOUR 美式英语，即 behaviour

behaviour (*British* 英式英语) (*American* 美式英语 **behavior**) /bɪˈheɪvjə(r)/ ***noun*** 名词 (*no plural* 不用复数形式)
the way you are; the way that you do and say things 行为；举止： *He was sent out*

of the class for bad behaviour. 他因调皮捣蛋而被赶出了教室。

behind ⊶ /bɪˈhaɪnd/ *preposition, adverb* 介词，副词
1 at or to the back of somebody or something 在（或向）…后面: *I hid behind the wall.* 我躲在墙的后面。◇ *I drove off and Jim followed behind.* 我开车离去，吉姆跟在后面。
2 slower or less good than somebody or something; slower or less good than you should be 落后于（某人、某事物或自己本身的进度或水平）: *She is behind with her work because she is often ill.* 她因为经常生病而工作落后了。
3 in the place where somebody or something was before 在原来的地方: *I got off the train and left my bag behind* (= on the train). 我下火车时忘了拿包。

beige /beɪʒ/ *adjective* 形容词
with a light brown colour 浅褐色的；米黄色的

being¹ *form of* BE * be 的不同形式

being² /ˈbiːŋ/ *noun* 名词
a person or living thing 人；生物: *a being from another planet* 来自另一星球的生物

belief ⊶ /bɪˈliːf/ *noun* 名词
a sure feeling that something is true or real 信仰；信念: *his belief in God* 他对上帝的信仰 ◇ *Divorce is contrary to their religious beliefs.* 离婚违背他们的宗教信仰。

believable /bɪˈliːvəbl/ *adjective* 形容词
that you can believe 可相信的 ⊃ OPPOSITE **unbelievable** 反义词为 unbelievable

believe ⊶ /bɪˈliːv/ *verb* 动词 (believes, believing, believed /bɪˈliːvd/)
1 to feel sure that something is true; to feel sure that what somebody says is true 相信；认为…真实: *Long ago, people believed that the earth was flat.* 很久以前，人们认为地球是平的。◇ *She says she didn't take the money. Do you believe her?* 她说她没有拿那些钱。你相信她吗？
2 to think that something is true or possible, although you are not certain 认为…有可能: *'Does Mick still work here?' 'I believe so.'* "米克还在这儿工作吗？" "我想是的。"
believe in somebody or 或 **something** to feel sure that somebody or something exists 相信…的存在: *Do you believe in ghosts?* 你相信有鬼吗？

bell ⊶ /bel/ *noun* 名词
a metal thing that makes a sound when something hits or touches it 铃；钟: *The church bells were ringing.* 教堂的钟声响了起来。◇ *I rang the bell and he answered the door.* 我按了门铃后他来开门了。

bell 铃

belly /ˈbeli/ *noun* 名词 (plural 复数形式 bellies)
the part of your body between your chest and your legs 腹部；肚子 ⊃ SAME MEANING **stomach** 同义词为 stomach

belong ⊶ /bɪˈlɒŋ/ *verb* 动词 (belongs, belonging, belonged /bɪˈlɒŋd/)
1 to be somebody's 属于（某人）: *'Who does this pen belong to?' 'It belongs to me.'* "这支笔是谁的？" "是我的。"
2 to be a member of a group or an organization 是…的成员: *Do you belong to any political party?* 你加入了什么政党吗？
3 to have its right or usual place 应在（某处）: *That chair belongs in my room.* 那把椅子是我房间的。

belongings /bɪˈlɒŋɪŋz/ *noun* 名词 (plural 用复数形式)
the things that you own 个人财物: *They lost all their belongings in the fire.* 他们的财产在那场大火中损失殆尽。

below ⊶ /bɪˈləʊ/ *preposition, adverb* 介词，副词
1 in or to a lower place than somebody or something 在（或到）…下面: *From the plane we could see the mountains below.* 我们从飞机上能看到下面的山脉。◇ *He dived below the surface of the water.* 他潜入水中。◇ *Do not write below this line.* 不要在这条线下写字。⊃ OPPOSITE **above** 反义词为 above
2 less than a number or price 少于；低于: *The temperature was below zero.* 温度在零度以下。

belt ⊶ /belt/ *noun* 名词
a long piece of cloth or leather that you wear around the middle of your body 腰带；皮带 ⊃ Look also at **safety belt** and **seat belt**. 亦见 safety belt 和 seat belt。

A
B
C
D
E
F
G
H
I
J
K
L
M
N
O
P
Q
R
S
T
U
V
W
X
Y
Z

bench 长椅

bench /bentʃ/ *noun* 名词 (*plural* 复数形式 **benches**)

a long seat for two or more people, usually made of wood 长椅，长凳（通常为木制的）: *They sat on a park bench.* 他们坐在公园的长椅上。

bend 弯曲

He is **bending** down. 他弯下身来。
(*also* 亦作 **bending** over)

She is **bending** a spoon.
她把调羹弄弯。

bend¹ ⊶ /bend/ *verb* 动词 (bends, bending, bent /bent/, has bent)

1 to make something that was straight into a curved shape 把…弄弯: *Bend your legs!* 屈腿!
2 to be or become curved 变曲；拐弯: *The road bends to the left.* 路向左转弯。
bend down, bend over to move your body forward and down 弯腰；弯身: *She bent down to put on her shoes.* 她弯下腰来穿鞋。

bend² /bend/ *noun* 名词
a part of a road or river that is not straight 转弯处: *Drive slowly – there's a bend in the road.* 开慢些——路上有个弯。

beneath ⊶ /bɪˈniːθ/ *preposition, adverb* 介词，副词
in or to a lower place than somebody or something 在（或向）…下面 ⊃ SAME

MEANING **below, underneath** 同义词为 below 和 underneath: *From the tower, they looked down on the city beneath.* 他们从塔上俯视下面的城市。◇ *The boat sank beneath the waves.* 小船被大浪吞没了。⊃ OPPOSITE **above** 反义词为 above

benefit¹ ⊶ /ˈbenɪfɪt/ *noun* 名词
1 (*plural* 复数形式 **benefits**) something that is good or helpful 好处；益处: *What are the benefits of having a computer?* 有台电脑有什么好处？◇ *I did it for your benefit* (= to help you). 我那样做是为你好。
2 (*no plural* 不用复数形式) (*British* 英式英语) money that the government gives to people who are ill or poor or who do not have a job 补助金；救济金: *housing benefit* 住房补助

benefit² /ˈbenɪfɪt/ *verb* 动词 (benefits, benefiting, benefited or 或 benefitting, benefitted)
to be good or helpful for somebody 对…有益；使受益: *The new law will benefit families with children.* 新法规让有孩子的家庭受惠。
benefit from something to get something good or useful from something 得益于；受益于: *She will benefit from a holiday.* 度假对她有好处。

bent¹ *form of* BEND¹ * bend¹ 的不同形式

bent² /bent/ *adjective* 形容词
not straight; curved 弯曲的: *Do this exercise with your knees bent.* 做此动作时要屈膝。◇ *This knife is bent.* 这把刀弯了。⊃ OPPOSITE **straight** 反义词为 straight

beret /ˈbereɪ/ *noun* 名词
a soft flat round hat 贝雷帽

berry /ˈberi/ *noun* 名词 (*plural* 复数形式 **berries**)
a small soft fruit with seeds in it 浆果；莓: *Those berries are poisonous.* 那些浆果有毒。◇ *raspberries* 悬钩子

beside ⊶ /bɪˈsaɪd/ *preposition* 介词
at the side of somebody or something 在…旁边（或附近）⊃ SAME MEANING **next to** 同义词为 next to: *Come and sit beside me.* 过来坐在我旁边。

besides¹ /bɪˈsaɪdz/ *preposition* 介词
as well as somebody or something; if you do not count somebody or something 除…之外（还）: *We have lots of things in common besides music.* 除了音乐外，我们还有很多共通点。

besides² /bɪˈsaɪdz/ *adverb* 副词
also 而且；再说: *I don't really want to*

go. Besides, it's too late now. 我真的不想走，再说，现在天也太晚了。

best¹ 0━ /best/ *adjective* 形容词 (**good**, **better**, **best**)

better than all others 最好的；最出色的：*This is the best ice cream I have ever eaten!* 这是我吃过的最好的冰激凌！◇ *Tom is my best friend.* 汤姆是我最好的朋友。◇ *Jo's the best player on the team.* 乔是队中最出色的球员。 ⊃ OPPOSITE **worst** 反义词为 worst

best² 0━ /best/ *adverb* 副词

1 most well 最好地：*I work best in the morning.* 我早上工作效率最高。
2 more than all others 最 ⊃ SAME MEANING **most** 同义词为 most：*Which picture do you like best?* 你最喜欢哪幅画？ ⊃ OPPOSITE **least** 反义词为 least

best³ 0━ /best/ *noun* 名词 (*no plural* 不用复数形式)

the person or thing that is better than all others 最好的人（或事物）：*Mike and Ian are good at tennis but Paul is the best.* 迈克和伊恩都很会打网球，可是保罗打得最好。

all the best words that you use when you say goodbye to somebody, to wish them success（告别用语）祝一切顺利
do your best to do all that you can 竭尽全力：*I don't know if I can finish the work today, but I'll do my best.* 我不知道今天能否把工作做完，但会尽力而为。

best man /ˌbest ˈmæn/ *noun* 名词 (*no plural* 不用复数形式)

a man at a wedding who helps the man who is getting married (the **bridegroom**) 伴郎；男傧相

best-seller /ˌbest ˈselə(r)/ *noun* 名词

a book or other product that is bought by large numbers of people 畅销书；畅销产品

bet /bet/ *verb* 动词 (**bets**, **betting**, **bet**, has **bet**)

to risk money on a race or a game by saying what the result will be. If you are right, you win money. 打赌；下赌注：*I bet you £5 that our team will win.* 我和你赌 5 英镑，我们队会获胜。
I bet (*informal* 非正式) I am sure 我敢肯定：*I bet it will rain tomorrow.* 我管保明天会下雨。◇ *I bet you can't climb that tree.* 我谅你爬不上那棵树。
▶ **bet** *noun* 名词：*I lost the bet.* 我赌输了。

betray /bɪˈtreɪ/ *verb* 动词 (**betrays**, **betraying**, **betrayed** /bɪˈtreɪd/)

to harm your friends or your country by giving information to an enemy 出卖；背叛：*She betrayed the whole group to the secret police.* 她向秘密警察出卖了整队人。

better¹ 0━ /ˈbetə(r)/ *adjective* 形容词 (**good**, **better**, **best**)

1 of a higher standard or quality; not as bad as something else 较好的：*This book is better than that one.* 这本书比那本好。
2 less ill（病势）好转：*I was ill yesterday, but I feel better now.* 我昨天病了，但现在好多了。 ⊃ OPPOSITE **worse** 反义词为 worse

better² 0━ /ˈbetə(r)/ *adverb* 副词

in a more excellent or pleasant way; not as badly 更好；较好：*You speak French better than I do.* 你法语说得比我好。
be better off to be happier, richer, etc. 情况更好：*I'm better off now that I've got a new job.* 因为我有了新工作，手头宽松多了。◇ *You look ill – you'd be better off in bed.* 你气色不好——卧床会好一些。
had better ought to; should 应该；最好：*You'd better go now if you want to catch the train.* 要想赶上火车，你最好现在就走。

between 0━ /bɪˈtwiːn/ *preposition*, *adverb* 介词，副词

1 in the space in the middle of two things or people 在…之间：*The letter B comes between A and C.* 字母 B 在 A 和 C 之间。◇ *I sat between Sylvie and Bruno.* 我坐在西尔维和布鲁诺之间。◇ *I see her most weekends but not very often in between.* 我大多数周末能见到她，但平时不常见到。 ⊃ Look at the note at **among**. 见 among 条的注释。
2 to and from two places 往返于：*The boat sails between Dover and Calais.* 这艘船来往于多佛尔和加来之间。
3 more than one thing but less than another thing（两数目）之间：*The meal will cost between £20 and £25.* 这一餐要花 20 到 25 英镑。
4 after one time and before the next time 在（两个时间）之间：*I'll meet you between 4 and 4.30.* 我会在 4 点到 4 点 30 分见你。
5 for or by two or more people or things 合用；分享：*We shared the cake between us* (= each of us had some cake). 我们把蛋糕分了。
6 a word that you use when you compare two people or things（用于比较两个人或事物）：*What is the difference between 'some' and 'any'?* * some 和 any 有什么区别？

A
B
C
D
E
F
G
H
I
J
K
L
M
N
O
P
Q
R
S
T
U
V
W
X
Y
Z

beware /bɪ'weə(r)/ *verb* 动词
beware of somebody or 或
something to be careful because
somebody or something is dangerous
当心；小心；提防：*Beware of the dog!*
(= words written on a sign) 小心有狗!

bewildered /bɪ'wɪldəd/ *adjective* 形容词
If you are **bewildered**, you do not
understand something or you do not
know what to do. 困惑的 ⊃ SAME MEANING
confused 同义词为 confused：*I was
completely bewildered by his sudden
change of mood.* 他情绪突变，让我大惑
不解。

beyond ⊶ /bɪ'jɒnd/ *preposition, adverb*
介词，副词
on the other side of something; further
than something 在…的另一边；比…远：
*The road continues beyond the village up
into the hills.* 那条路经过村后往上通到
群山中。◇ *We could see the lake and the
mountains beyond.* 我们看到湖泊和后面的
山脉。

bib /bɪb/ *noun* 名词
a piece of cloth or plastic that a baby
wears under its chin when it is eating
围嘴儿；围兜

the Bible /ðə 'baɪbl/ *noun* 名词
the book of great religious importance to
Christian and Jewish people《圣经》

bicycle 自行车

handlebars 车把
saddle 车座
spoke 辐条
wheel 车轮
tyre (*British* 英式英语)
tire (*American* 美式英语) 轮胎
pedal 脚蹬
chain 链条

bicycle ⊶ /'baɪsɪkl/ (*also informal*
非正式亦作 **bike**) *noun* 名词
a vehicle with two wheels. You sit on a
bicycle and move your legs to make the
wheels turn. 自行车；脚踏车：*Can you
ride a bicycle?* 你会骑自行车吗?

bid¹ /bɪd/ *verb* 动词 (bids, bidding, bid,
has bid)
to offer some money because you want to
buy something 出价：*He bid $10 000 for
the painting.* 他出价 10 000 元买那幅画。

bid² /bɪd/ *noun* 名词
an offer of money for something that you
want to buy（买方的）出价：*She made
a bid of £250 for the vase.* 她出 250 英镑
买那个花瓶。

big ⊶ /bɪg/ *adjective* 形容词 (bigger,
biggest)
1 not small; large 大的：*Milan is a big
city.* 米兰是个大城市。◇ *This shirt is too
big for me.* 这件衬衫我穿太大了。◇ *How
big is your flat?* 你的公寓有多大?
⊃ OPPOSITE **small** 反义词为 small
2 great or important 重大的；重要的：
a big problem 一个大难题
3 older 年龄较大的：*Amy is my big sister.*
埃米是我姐姐。⊃ OPPOSITE **little** 反义词
为 little

bike /baɪk/ *noun* 名词 (*informal* 非正式)
a bicycle or a motorbike 自行车；
摩托车：*I go to school by bike.* 我骑自行
车上学。

bikini /bɪ'ki:ni/ *noun* 名词
a piece of clothing in two pieces that
women wear for swimming 比基尼（女子
泳装）

bilingual /ˌbaɪ'lɪŋgwəl/ *adjective* 形容词
1 able to speak two languages equally
well 会说两种语言的：*Their children are
bilingual.* 他们的孩子会说两种语言。
2 having or using two languages 有两种
语言的；使用两种语言的：*a bilingual
dictionary* 双语词典

bill ⊶ /bɪl/ *noun* 名词
1 (*British* 英式英语) (*American* 美式英语
check) a piece of paper that shows how
much money you must pay for something
账单：*Can I have the bill, please?* (= in a
restaurant) 请给我结账好吗?
2 *American English for* NOTE¹ (3) 美式
英语，即 note¹ 第 3 义：*a ten-dollar bill*
一张十元钞票

billfold /'bɪlfəʊld/ *American English for*
WALLET 美式英语，即 wallet

billion ⊶ /'bɪljən/ *number* 数词
1 000 000 000; one thousand million
十亿：*five billion pounds* 五十亿英镑 ◇
The company is worth billions of dollars.
这家公司值数十亿元。

bird 鸟

beak 喙
wing 翅膀
claw 爪

the study of the life of animals and plants 生物学: *Biology is my favourite subject.* 生物学是我最喜欢的科目。
▶ **biologist** /baɪˈɒlədʒɪst/ *noun* 名词
a person who studies **biology** 生物学家

bird ⊶ /bɜːd/ *noun* 名词
an animal with feathers and wings 鸟: *Gulls and sparrows are birds.* 海鸥和麻雀都是鸟。

🔍 **WORD BUILDING** 词汇扩充
Most birds can **fly** and **sing**. They build **nests** and **lay eggs**. 鸟类大多数会飞 (fly) 和鸣叫 (sing) , 还会筑巢 (nest) 和下蛋 (lay eggs) 。
There are many different types of **bird**. Here are some of them: chicken, eagle, ostrich, parrot, pigeon, seagull. * bird 的种类很多, 如: chicken (鸡) 、eagle (雕) 、ostrich (鸵鸟) 、parrot (鹦鹉) 、pigeon (鸽子) 、seagull (海鸥) 。

🔍 **GRAMMAR** 语法说明
We say **five billion dollars** (without 's'), but **billions of** dollars. 要说 five billion dollars (billion 不加 s) , 但形容数量大时要说 billions of dollars。

bin /bɪn/ *noun* 名词
a thing that you put rubbish in 垃圾箱: *Put your rubbish in the bin.* 把垃圾投进垃圾箱。 ⊃ Look also at **dustbin**. 亦见 dustbin。

bind /baɪnd/ *verb* 动词 (binds, binding, bound /baʊnd/, has bound)
to tie string or rope round something to hold it firmly 捆绑: *They bound the prisoner's arms and legs together.* 他们把那个囚犯的胳膊和腿绑在一起。

bingo /ˈbɪŋɡəʊ/ *noun* 名词 (no plural 不用复数形式)
a game where each player has a card with numbers on it. When the person who controls the game says all the numbers on your card, you win the game. 宾戈游戏 (玩者各持一张数字卡, 首先凑齐庄家喊出的数字者胜出)

binoculars 双筒望远镜

binoculars /bɪˈnɒkjələz/ *noun* 名词 (plural 用复数形式)
special glasses that you use to see things that are far away 双筒望远镜 ⊃ Look at **telescope**. 见 telescope。

biodegradable /ˌbaɪəʊdɪˈɡreɪdəbl/ *adjective* 形容词
Biodegradable substances can go back into the earth and so do not damage the environment. 可生物降解的

biography /baɪˈɒɡrəfi/ *noun* 名词 (plural 复数形式 biographies)
the story of a person's life, that another person writes 传记: *a biography of Nelson Mandela* 纳尔逊·曼德拉的传记 ⊃ Look at **autobiography**. 见 autobiography。

biology ⊶ /baɪˈɒlədʒi/ *noun* 名词 (no plural 不用复数形式)

bird flu /ˈbɜːd fluː/ *noun* 名词 (no plural 不用复数形式)
a serious illness that birds, especially chickens, can catch and which can be spread from birds to humans and can cause death 禽流感 (鸟类传染病, 可感染人类并导致死亡)

bird of prey /ˌbɜːd əv ˈpreɪ/ *noun* 名词
a bird that catches and eats other birds and small animals 猛禽 (捕食其他鸟和小动物的鸟): *Eagles are birds of prey.* 雕是猛禽。

Biro™ /ˈbaɪrəʊ/ *noun* 名词 (plural 复数形式 Biros)
a pen with a very small ball at the end that rolls ink onto the paper 伯罗圆珠笔 ⊃ SAME MEANING **ballpoint** 同义词为 ballpoint

A
B
C
D
E
F
G
H
I
J
K
L
M
N
O
P
Q
R
S
T
U
V
W
X
Y
Z

birth ⊶ /bɜːθ/ *noun* 名词

🔍 **PRONUNCIATION** 读音说明
The word **birth** sounds like **earth**.
* birth 读音像 earth。

the time when a baby comes out of its
mother; being born 出生；诞生：*the
birth of a baby* 婴儿的出生 ◊ *What's your
date of birth* (= the date when you were
born)? 你的出生日期是哪天？
give birth to have a baby 生孩子：*My
sister gave birth to her second child last
week.* 我姐姐上周生下了第二个孩子。

birthday ⊶ /ˈbɜːθdeɪ/ *noun* 名词
(*plural* 复数形式 birthdays)
the day each year that is the same as the
date when you were born 生日：*My
birthday is on May 2nd.* 我的生日是 5 月
2 日。◊ *a birthday present* 生日礼物 ◊
Happy Birthday! 生日快乐！

🔍 **CULTURE** 文化资料补充
On your birthday people say **Happy
Birthday!** 有人过生日时，人们会说
Happy Birthday（生日快乐）！
Family and friends give you cards and
presents. You can have a **birthday
party**, and a **birthday cake** with
candles. 家人和朋友送上生日贺卡和礼
物。过生日的人举行生日聚会（birthday
party），吃插上蜡烛的生日蛋糕
（birthday cake）。
Your **18th birthday** is important
because that is when you legally
become an adult. * 18 岁的生日（18th
birthday）很重要，因为在法律上从那天
起是成人了。
An **anniversary** is not the same as a
birthday. It is the day in each year
which is the same date as an
important event that happened in the
past. * anniversary 跟 birthday 不同，
它指的是过去发生重大事件的周年纪念
日：*We celebrated our tenth wedding
anniversary.* 我们庆祝了结婚十周年。

biscuit ⊶ /ˈbɪskɪt/ (*British* 英式英语)
(*American* 美式英语 cookie) *noun* 名词
a kind of small thin hard cake that is
usually sweet 饼干：*a packet of biscuits*
一包饼干 ◊ *a chocolate biscuit* 一块巧克力
饼干 ⟳ Look at Picture Dictionary page
P6. 见彩页 P6。

bishop /ˈbɪʃəp/ *noun* 名词
an important priest in the Christian
church, who looks after all the churches
in a large area（基督教的）主教

bit ⊶ /bɪt/ *noun* 名词
1 a small piece or amount of something
小块；少量：*Would you like a bit of
cake?* 你要一小块蛋糕吗？ ◊ *Some bits of
the film were very funny.* 这部电影有几个
片段很有趣。
2 a bit a little 一点：*You look a bit tired.*
你看上去有点累了。
3 a bit a short time 一会儿：*Let's wait a
bit.* 我们等一会儿吧。
4 (*computing* 电脑) a unit of information
that is stored in a computer's memory
比特，二进制位，位（电脑的最小信息
单位）
a bit of a … (*informal* 非正式) used when
talking about unpleasant things to mean
'rather a' 相当；有点儿：*It's a bit of a
long way to the station.* 到车站可够远的。
bit by bit slowly or a little at a time
慢慢地；一点一点地：*Bit by bit, I started
to feel better.* 我觉得一点一点好起来了。
quite a bit (*informal* 非正式) a lot
很多的：*It must have rained quite a bit
in the night.* 那晚肯定下了很大的雨。

bite¹ ⊶ /baɪt/ *verb* 动词 (bites, biting,
bit /bɪt/, has bitten /ˈbɪtn/)
1 to cut something with your teeth 咬：
That dog bit my leg! 那条狗咬了我的腿！
2 If an insect or snake **bites** you, it hurts
you by pushing a small sharp part into
your skin. 叮；螫；咬：*I've been bitten
by mosquitoes.* 我被蚊子叮了。

bite² /baɪt/ *noun* 名词
1 a piece of food that you can put in your
mouth 一口（食物）：*He took a bite of
his sandwich.* 他咬了一口三明治。
2 a painful place on your skin made by
an insect or an animal 虫咬处；咬伤：
a snake bite 蛇咬的伤口

bitter ⊶ /ˈbɪtə(r)/ *adjective* 形容词
1 angry and sad about something that
has happened 气愤的；难过的：*He felt
very bitter about losing his job.* 他丢了
工作，心里很难过。
2 Bitter food has a sharp unpleasant
taste. 味苦的：*The coffee was bitter.*
咖啡有点苦。
3 very cold 严寒的：*a bitter wind* 刺骨的
寒风
▶ **bitterness** /ˈbɪtənəs/ *noun* 名词 (*no
plural* 不用复数形式)：*The strike caused
great bitterness.* 罢工引起了极大愤恨。

bizarre /bɪˈzɑː(r)/ *adjective* 形容词
very strange 非常奇怪的；怪诞的 ⟳ SAME
MEANING **weird** 同义词为 weird：*He has
a bizarre sense of humour.* 他的幽默感很
奇怪。

▶ **bizarrely** /bɪˈzɑːli/ *adverb* 副词:
bizarrely dressed teenagers 穿着奇装异服的青少年

black¹ 0️⃣ /blæk/ *adjective* 形容词
(**blacker, blackest**)
1 with the colour of the sky at night 黑色的: *a black dog* 一条黑狗
2 belonging to a race of people with dark skins 黑人的;黑皮肤的: *Martin Luther King was a famous black leader.* 马丁·路德·金是著名的黑人领袖。
3 without milk 不加奶的: *black coffee* 不加奶的咖啡

black² /blæk/ *noun* 名词
1 the colour of the sky at night 黑色: *She was dressed in black.* 她穿着一身黑色衣服。
2 a person who belongs to a race of people with dark skins 黑人
black and white with the colours black, white and grey only 黑白的: *We watched a black and white film on TV.* 我们在电视上看了部黑白片。

blackberry /ˈblækbəri/ *noun* 名词 (*plural* 复数形式 **blackberries**)
a small soft black fruit that grows on a bush 黑莓

blackbird /ˈblækbɜːd/ *noun* 名词
a bird with black feathers 乌鸫

blackboard /ˈblækbɔːd/ *noun* 名词
a dark board that a teacher writes on with a white substance (called chalk) 黑板: *Look at the blackboard.* 看黑板。
➜ Look at Picture Dictionary page **P11**. 见彩页 P11。

blackcurrant /ˌblækˈkʌrənt/ *noun* 名词
a small round black fruit that grows on a bush 黑醋栗;黑加仑子 ➜ Look at Picture Dictionary page **P8**. 见彩页 P8。

black eye /ˌblæk ˈaɪ/ *noun* 名词
a dark area of skin around a person's eye where somebody or something has hit them (被打成的)青肿眼眶: *He got a black eye in a fight.* 他打架时眼睛被打青了。

blackmail /ˈblækmeɪl/ *noun* 名词
(*no plural* 不用复数形式)
saying that you will tell something bad about somebody if they do not give you money or do something for you 勒索;敲诈
▶ **blackmail** *verb* 动词
(**blackmails, blackmailing, blackmailed** /ˈblækmeɪld/): *She blackmailed him into giving her thousands of pounds.* 她勒索了他几千英镑。

blacksmith /ˈblæksmɪθ/ *noun* 名词
a person whose job is to make and repair things made of iron 铁匠

blade /bleɪd/ *noun* 名词
1 the flat sharp part of something such as a knife or a tool (刀等的)刃、锋 ➜ Look at the picture at **knife**. 见 knife 的插图。
2 a long thin leaf of a plant such as grass 叶片: *a blade of grass* 一片草叶

blame 0️⃣ /bleɪm/ *verb* 动词 (**blames, blaming, blamed** /bleɪmd/)
to say that a certain person or thing made something bad happen 归咎;责怪: *The other driver blamed me for the accident.* 另外的那个司机怪我酿成了事故。
▶ **blame** *noun* 名词 (*no plural* 不用复数形式): *Eve took the blame for the mistake.* 伊夫为这次失误承担了责任。

bland /blænd/ *adjective* 形容词
1 ordinary and not very interesting 平淡的;乏味的: *I find her songs rather bland.* 我觉得她的歌平淡无味。
2 Bland food does not have a strong taste. 味道清淡的: *a bland diet of rice and fish* 淡而无味的米饭和鱼

blank /blæŋk/ *adjective* 形容词
1 with no writing, pictures or anything else on it 空白的: *a blank piece of paper* 一张白纸
2 If your face is **blank**, it shows no feelings or understanding. 没表情的: *I asked her a question, but she just gave me a blank look.* 我问她一个问题,她却木然地看了我一眼。

blanket /ˈblæŋkɪt/ *noun* 名词
a thick cover that you put on a bed 毯子
➜ Look at the picture at **bed**. 见 bed 的插图。

blast¹ /blɑːst/ *noun* 名词
1 when a bomb explodes 爆炸: *Two people were killed in the blast.* 有两人在爆炸中丧生。
2 a sudden movement of air 突如其来的气流: *a blast of cold air* 一股寒流
3 a sudden loud noise 响声: *The driver gave a few blasts on his horn.* 司机按了几下汽车喇叭。

blast² /blɑːst/ *verb* 动词 (**blasts, blasting, blasted**)
to make a hole in something with an explosion 炸开;炸出(洞等): *They blasted through the mountain to make a tunnel.* 他们把山炸穿,修建隧道。

A

B

C

D

E

F

G

H

I

J

K

L

M

N

O

P

Q

R

S

T

U

V

W

X

Y

Z

blast-off /ˈblɑːst ɒf/ *noun* 名词 (*no plural* 不用复数形式)
the time when a SPACECRAFT (= a vehicle that travels into space) leaves the ground （航天器的）发射，升空

blaze¹ /bleɪz/ *verb* 动词 (blazes, blazing, blazed /bleɪzd/)
to burn strongly and brightly 熊熊燃烧：*a blazing fire* 熊熊烈火

blaze² /bleɪz/ *noun* 名词
a large and often dangerous fire 大火；烈火：*It took firefighters four hours to put out the blaze.* 消防队员花了四小时才把大火扑灭。

blazer /ˈbleɪzə(r)/ *noun* 名词
a jacket. **Blazers** sometimes show which school or club you belong to. （有时候带有学校或俱乐部标记的）夹克

bleak /bliːk/ *adjective* 形容词 (bleaker, bleakest)
1 A **bleak** situation is not hopeful or encouraging. 没有希望的；令人沮丧的：*The country's future looks bleak.* 这个国家的前景暗淡。
2 cold and grey 寒冷灰沉的：*It was a bleak winter's day.* 那是一个阴冷的冬日。

bleed /bliːd/ *verb* 动词 (bleeds, bleeding, bled /bled/, has bled)
to lose blood 流血：*I've cut my hand and it's bleeding.* 我把手割破流血了。

blend /blend/ *verb* 动词 (blends, blending, blended)
1 to mix 混合；掺和：*Blend the sugar and the butter together.* 把糖和黄油混在一起。
2 to look or sound good together 协调；配合得当：*These colours blend very well.* 这些颜色搭配得很协调。
▸ **blend** *noun* 名词：*This is a blend of two different kinds of coffee.* 这是由两种咖啡混合起来的。

bless /bles/ *verb* 动词 (blesses, blessing, blessed /blest/)
to ask for God's help for somebody or something 求上帝降福；祝福：*The priest blessed the young couple.* 神父祝福了这对年轻夫妇。
Bless you! words that you say to somebody when they SNEEZE (= make a loud noise through their nose) （别人打喷嚏时说）长命百岁

blew *form of* BLOW¹ * blow¹ 的不同形式

blind¹ /blaɪnd/ *adjective* 形容词
not able to see 瞎的；失明的：*My grandad is going blind.* 我的爷爷快瞎了。
◇ *He trains guide dogs for the blind*

(= people who are not able to see). 他为盲人训练导盲犬。
▸ **blindness** /ˈblaɪndnəs/ *noun* 名词 (*no plural* 不用复数形式)：*The disease can cause blindness.* 这种病能导致失明。

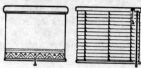

blinds （卷式）窗帘

blind² /blaɪnd/ *noun* 名词
a piece of cloth or other material that you pull down to cover a window （卷式）卷帘

blindfold /ˈblaɪndfəʊld/ *noun* 名词
a piece of cloth that you put over somebody's eyes so that they cannot see 遮眼布；眼罩
▸ **blindfold** /ˈblaɪndfəʊld/ *verb* 动词 (blindfolds, blindfolding, blindfolded)：*The prisoners were blindfolded and pushed into vans.* 囚犯被蒙上了眼睛，推进了囚车。

blink /blɪŋk/ *verb* 动词 (blinks, blinking, blinked /blɪŋkt/)
to shut and open your eyes very quickly 眨眼
▸ **blink** *noun* 名词 ⊃ Look at **wink**. 见 wink.

blister /ˈblɪstə(r)/ *noun* 名词
a small painful place on your skin, that is full of liquid. Rubbing or burning can cause **blisters**. （皮肤上摩擦或烫起的）疱，水疱：*My new shoes gave me blisters.* 我的新鞋把脚磨出水疱来了。

blizzard /ˈblɪzəd/ *noun* 名词
a very bad storm with snow and strong winds 暴风雪

blob /blɒb/ *noun* 名词
a small amount of a thick liquid 一点，一滴（黏稠液体）：*There are blobs of paint on the floor.* 地板上有几点油漆。

block¹ 0━ /blɒk/ *noun* 名词
1 a big heavy piece of something, with flat sides 一大块：*a block of wood* 一块木头 ◇ *The bridge is made of concrete blocks.* 这座桥是混凝土块砌成的。
2 a big building with a lot of offices or flats inside 办公楼；公寓楼：*an office block* 一栋办公楼 ◇ *a block of flats* 一栋公寓楼

3 a group of buildings with streets all round it 街区: *We drove round the block looking for the hotel.* 我们开车绕着街区找那家酒店。

4 a thing that stops somebody or something from moving forward 障碍物: *The police have put road blocks around the town.* 警方在全城周围设置了路障。

block² /blɒk/ *verb* 动词 (blocks, blocking, blocked /blɒkt/)
to stop somebody or something from moving forward 阻挡: *A fallen tree blocked the road.* 有棵树倒下挡住了路。

block capitals /ˌblɒk ˈkæpɪtlz/ *noun* 名词
big letters such as 'ABC' rather than 'abc' 正楷大写字母: *Please write your name in block capitals.* 请用正楷大写字母填写姓名。

blog /blɒg/ *noun* 名词
a personal record that somebody puts on their website saying what they do every day and what they think about things 网志; 博客
▶ **blogger** /ˈblɒgə(r)/ *noun* 名词 a person who writes a BLOG 写网志的人; 写博客的人

bloke /bləʊk/ *noun* 名词 (*British* 英式英语) (*informal* 非正式)
a man 家伙; 伙计: *He's a really nice bloke.* 他这人挺不错的。

blonde /blɒnd/ (*also* 亦作 blond) *adjective* 形容词
with light-coloured hair 金黄色头发的: *She is tall and blonde.* 她个子高, 金黄色头发。◇ *He's got blond hair.* 他一头金发。
▶ **blonde** *noun* 名词 a woman who has **blonde** hair 金发女郎: *She's a natural blonde.* 她天生就是金发。

blood 0ᴍ /blʌd/ *noun* 名词 (*no plural* 不用复数形式)
the red liquid inside your body 血; 血液

blob 一滴

soap 肥皂

blob 一滴

blood vessel /ˈblʌd vesl/ *noun* 名词
one of the tubes in your body that blood flows through 血管

bloody /ˈblʌdi/ *adjective* 形容词 (bloodier, bloodiest)
1 covered with blood 血淋淋的; 流血的: *a bloody nose* 流血的鼻子
2 with a lot of killing 血腥的; 嗜杀的: *It was a bloody war.* 那是场血腥的战争。

bloom /bluːm/ *verb* 动词 (blooms, blooming, bloomed /bluːmd/)
to produce flowers 开花: *Roses bloom in the summer.* 玫瑰在夏天开花。

blossom /ˈblɒsəm/ *noun* 名词 (*no plural* 不用复数形式)
the flowers on a tree, especially a fruit tree (果树等的) 花: *The apple tree is covered in blossom.* 苹果树上开满了花。
▶ **blossom** *verb* 动词 (blossoms, blossoming, blossomed /ˈblɒsəmd/): *The cherry trees are blossoming.* 樱桃树正在开花。

blouse /blaʊz/ *noun* 名词
a piece of clothing like a shirt that a woman or girl wears on the top part of her body (女装) 短上衣, 衬衫

blow¹ 0ᴍ /bləʊ/ *verb* 动词 (blows, blowing, blew /bluː/, has blown /bləʊn/)

> ♪ PRONUNCIATION 读音说明
> The word **blow** sounds like **go**. * blow 读音像 go。

1 When air or wind **blows**, it moves. (空气或风) 吹: *The wind was blowing from the sea.* 风从海上吹来。
2 to move something through the air 吹动: *The wind blew my hat off.* 风吹掉了我的帽子。
3 to send air out from your mouth 吹; 吹气: *Please blow into this tube.* 请向管内吹气。
4 to send air out from your mouth into a musical instrument, for example, to make a noise 吹响, 吹奏 (乐器等): *The referee blew his whistle.* 裁判吹响了哨子。

blow up, blow something up
1 to explode or make something explode, for example with a bomb (使) 爆炸: *The plane blew up.* 飞机爆炸了。◇ *They blew up the station.* 他们把车站炸了。
2 to fill something with air 给…充气: *We blew up some balloons for the party.* 我们为聚会吹了一些气球。

blow your nose to clear your nose by **blowing** strongly through it onto a piece of cloth or paper (called a handkerchief) 擤鼻涕

blow² /bləʊ/ *noun* 名词

1 a hard hit from somebody's hand or a weapon 猛击；狠打：*He felt a blow on the back of his head.* 他感到后脑勺被猛打了一下。

2 something that happens suddenly and that makes you very unhappy 打击；挫折：*Her father's death was a terrible blow.* 她父亲的去世对她是个沉重的打击。

blue ⬤▪ /bluː/ *adjective* 形容词 (**bluer, bluest**)

having the colour of a clear sky when the sun shines 蓝色的：*He wore a blue shirt.* 他穿了一件蓝衬衫。◊ *dark blue curtains* 深蓝色窗帘 ◊ *Her eyes are bright blue.* 她的眼睛是碧蓝色的。

▸ **blue** *noun* 名词：*She was dressed in blue.* 她穿着一身蓝色衣服。

blunt /blʌnt/ *adjective* 形容词

1 with an edge or point that is not sharp 不锋利的；钝的：*This pencil is blunt.* 这支铅笔不尖了。➔ OPPOSITE **sharp** 反义词为 sharp

2 If you are **blunt**, you say what you think in a way that is not polite. 嘴直的；直言的

blur /blɜː(r)/ *verb* 动词 (**blurs, blurring, blurred** /blɜːd/)

to make something less clear 使模糊不清：*If you move while you are taking the photo, it will be blurred.* 拍照时若移动，照片就会模糊不清。

blush /blʌʃ/ *verb* 动词 (**blushes, blushing, blushed** /blʌʃt/)

If you **blush**, your face suddenly becomes red, for example because you are shy. 脸红：*She blushed when he looked at her.* 他看她的时候，她脸红了。

boar /bɔː(r)/ (*also* 亦作 **wild boar**) *noun* 名词

a wild pig 野猪

board¹ ⬤▪ /bɔːd/ *noun* 名词

1 a long thin flat piece of wood 木板：*I nailed a board across the broken window.* 我在破窗上钉上了一块木板。◊ *floorboards* 木质地板条

2 a flat piece of wood, for example, that you use for a special purpose（作特定用途的）板：*There is a list of names on the noticeboard.* 布告栏上有个名单。◊ *a chessboard* 棋盘 ◊ *an ironing board* 熨衣板 ➔ Look at **blackboard**. 见 blackboard。

3 a group of people who have a special job, for example controlling a company

董事会；委员会；理事会：*the board of directors* 董事会

on board on a ship or a plane 在轮船（或飞机）上：*How many passengers are on board?* 飞机上有多少乘客？

board² /bɔːd/ *verb* 动词 (**boards, boarding, boarded**)

to get on a ship, bus, train or plane 登上（交通工具）：*We boarded the plane at Gatwick.* 我们在盖特威克登机。◊ *Flight BA 193 to Lisbon is now boarding* (= is ready for passengers to get on). 飞往里斯本的 BA193 号航班现在开始登机。

boarding card /'bɔːdɪŋ kɑːd/ *noun* 名词

a card that you must show when you get on a plane or a ship 登机卡；登船卡

boarding school /'bɔːdɪŋ skuːl/ *noun* 名词

a school where the pupils live 寄宿学校

boast /bəʊst/ *verb* 动词 (**boasts, boasting, boasted**)

to talk in a way that shows you are too proud of something that you have or something that you can do 吹嘘；自吹自擂：*He's always boasting about what a good footballer he is.* 他老是吹嘘自己是多么出色的足球员。

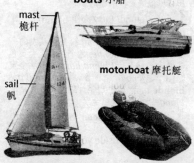

boats 小船

mast 桅杆

motorboat 摩托艇

sail 帆

yacht 帆船

dinghy 小艇

boat ⬤▪ /bəʊt/ *noun* 名词

a small vehicle for travelling on water 小船：*a fishing boat* 渔船 ◊ *We travelled by boat.* 我们乘船去。➔ Look at **ship**. 见 ship。

bob /bɒb/ *verb* 动词 (**bobs, bobbing, bobbed** /bɒbd/)

to move quickly up and down（快速地）上下移动：*The boats in the harbour were*

bobbing up and down in the water. 港口
的船只在水面上颠簸不停。

body ⚬ᴙ /ˈbɒdi/ *noun* 名词 (*plural* 复数
形式 **bodies**)
1 the whole physical form of a person or
an animal 身体; 身躯: *the human body*
人体 ⊃ Look at Picture Dictionary page **P4**.
见彩页 P4。
2 all of a person or animal except the
legs, arms and head 躯干: *The baby
mice have thin bodies and big heads.*
幼鼠身小头大。
3 a dead person （人的）尸体，死尸:
The police found a body in the river.
警方在河里发现了一具尸体。

bodybuilding /ˈbɒdibɪldɪŋ/ *noun* 名词
(*no plural* 不用复数形式)
making the muscles of your body bigger
and stronger by exercise 健身

bodyguard /ˈbɒdigɑːd/ *noun* 名词
a person or group of people whose job is
to keep an important person safe 保镖:
The President's bodyguards all carry guns.
总统保镖都佩枪。

boil ⚬ᴙ /bɔɪl/ *verb* 动词 (**boils, boiling,
boiled** /bɔɪld/)
1 When a liquid **boils**, it becomes very
hot and makes steam and bubbles.
沸腾: *Water boils at 100° C.* 水在 100
摄氏度时沸腾。
2 to heat a liquid until it **boils** 煮沸;
烧开: *I boiled some water for the pasta.*
我烧了点水来煮意大利面。
3 to cook something in **boiling** water
用沸水煮: *Boil the rice in a pan.* 把米
放在锅里煮。◇ *a boiled egg* 水煮蛋
boil over to boil and flow over the sides
of a pan 煮溢: *Don't let the milk boil over.*
别让牛奶溢出来。

boiler /ˈbɔɪlə(r)/ *noun* 名词
a big metal container that heats water for
a building 锅炉

boiling /ˈbɔɪlɪŋ/ (*also* 亦作 **boiling hot**)
adjective 形容词
very hot 很热的: *I'm boiling.* 我热死了。
◇ *It's boiling hot in here.* 这里很热。

bold /bəʊld/ *adjective* 形容词 (**bolder,
boldest**)
brave and not afraid 大胆的; 不畏惧
的: *It was very bold of you to ask for
more money.* 你还想要更多钱，胆子可
真大。
▶ **boldly** /ˈbəʊldli/ *adverb* 副词: *He
boldly said that he disagreed.* 他大胆地说
他不同意。

bolt 螺栓

bolt 螺栓

nut 螺帽

bolt /bəʊlt/ *noun* 名词
1 a piece of metal that you move across a
door to lock it 门闩; 插销
2 a thick metal pin that you use with
another piece of metal (called a **nut**) to
fix things together 螺栓
▶ **bolt** *verb* 动词 (**bolts, bolting, bolted**)
to lock a door by putting a **bolt** across it
用插销闩上

bomb¹ ⚬ᴙ /bɒm/ *noun* 名词
a thing that explodes and hurts or
damages people or things 炸弹: *Aircraft
dropped bombs on the city.* 飞机向这座
城市投下了炸弹。◇ *A bomb went off*
(= exploded) *at the station.* 有枚炸弹在
车站爆炸了。

bomb² /bɒm/ *verb* 动词 (**bombs,
bombing, bombed** /bɒmd/)
to attack people or a place with **bombs**
投炸弹; 轰炸: *The city was bombed in
the war.* 该城在战争中遭到了轰炸。

bone ⚬ᴙ /bəʊn/ *noun* 名词
one of the hard white parts inside the
body of a person or an animal 骨; 骨头:
She broke a bone in her foot. 她的脚骨折
了。◇ *This fish has a lot of bones in it.*
这条鱼有很多刺。

bonfire /ˈbɒnfaɪə(r)/ *noun* 名词
a big fire that you make outside （在室外
生起的）大火堆，篝火

Bonfire Night /ˈbɒnfaɪə naɪt/ *noun* 名词
(*no plural* 不用复数形式)
In Britain, **Bonfire Night** is the evening of
5 November, when people have a party
outside with a BONFIRE and FIREWORKS
(= things that explode in the sky with
coloured lights and loud noises). 篝火之夜
（11 月 5 日夜晚，英国人会在室外燃起
篝火和放烟火）

bonnet /ˈbɒnɪt/ *noun* 名词
1 (*British* 英式英语) (*American* 美式英语
hood) the front part of a car that covers
the engine （汽车的）发动机罩，引擎盖
⊃ Look at Picture Dictionary page **P1**.
见彩页 P1。

A B C D E F G H I J K L M N O P Q R S T U V W X Y Z

A
B
C
D
E
F
G
H
I
J
K
L
M
N
O
P
Q
R
S
T
U
V
W
X
Y
Z

2 a soft hat that you tie under your chin
（系带）软帽

book¹ ⁰╍ /bʊk/ *noun* 名词
a thing that you read or write in, that has
a lot of pieces of paper joined together
inside a cover 书；本子： *I'm reading
a **book** by George Orwell.* 我正在读一本
乔治·奥威尔的著作。◇ *an exercise book*
(= a book that you write in at school)
练习本

book² /bʊk/ *verb* 动词 (books, booking,
booked /bʊkt/)
to arrange to have or do something later
预订；预约： *We **booked** a table for six at
the restaurant.* 我们在餐馆预订了一张六人
餐桌。◇ *The hotel is **fully booked** (= all
the rooms are full).* 酒店房间已经预订
一空。

bookcase 书柜

bookcase /'bʊkkeɪs/ *noun* 名词
a piece of furniture that you put books in
书架；书柜

booking /'bʊkɪŋ/ *noun* 名词 (British 英式
英语)
an arrangement that you make to travel
somewhere, go to the theatre, etc. in the
future 预订： *When did you **make** your
booking?* 你什么时候预订的？

booking office /'bʊkɪŋ ɒfɪs/ *noun* 名词
a place where you buy tickets 售票处

booklet /'bʊklət/ *noun* 名词
a small thin book that gives information
about something 小册子

bookshop /'bʊkʃɒp/ *noun* 名词
a shop that sells books 书店 ⊃ Look at
Picture Dictionary page **P13**. 见彩页
P13。

boom¹ /buːm/ *noun* 名词
(*business* 商业) a period in which

something increases or develops very
quickly 繁荣；兴盛；激增： *a boom in
car sales* 汽车销售量的巨增

boom² /buːm/ *verb* 动词 (booms,
booming, boomed /buːmd/)
to make a loud deep sound 轰鸣： *We
heard the guns booming in the distance.*
我们听到远处炮声隆隆。

boost /buːst/ *verb* 动词 (boosts, boosting,
boosted)
to make something increase in number,
value, or strength 使增长；促进： *Lower
prices have boosted sales.* 降价促进了销
售。◇ *What can we do to **boost her
confidence** (= make her feel more
confident)?* 我们能做些什么来增强她的
信心呢？

boot ⁰╍ /buːt/ *noun* 名词
1 a shoe that covers your foot and ankle
and sometimes part of your leg 靴子；长
靴 ⊃ Look at the pictures at **shoe** and **ski**.
见 shoe 和 ski 的插图。
2 (*British* 英式英语) (*American* 美式英语
trunk) the part of a car where you can
put bags and boxes, usually at the back
（汽车）行李箱 ⊃ Look at Picture
Dictionary page **P1**. 见彩页 P1。

border ⁰╍ /'bɔːdə(r)/ *noun* 名词
1 a line between two countries 国界；
边界： *You need a passport to cross the
border.* 过境要持护照。 ⊃ Look at
boundary. 见 boundary。
2 a line along the edge of something
包边；镶边： *a white tablecloth with a
blue border* 带蓝色边的白桌布

bore¹ *form of* BEAR¹ ＊ bear¹ 的不同形式

bore² /bɔː(r)/ *verb* 动词 (bores, boring,
bored /bɔːd/)
1 to make somebody feel bored,
especially by talking too much（尤指因
啰唆）使厌烦： *He bores everyone with his
long stories.* 他讲的长篇故事让所有人都感
到厌烦。
2 to make a thin round hole in
something 钻；挖： *These insects bore
holes in wood.* 这些虫在木头上蛀洞。

bore³ /bɔː(r)/ *noun* 名词
a person who talks a lot in a way that is
not interesting（因为话多）令人厌烦的人

bored ⁰╍ /bɔːd/ *adjective* 形容词
not interested; unhappy because you
have nothing interesting to do 不感兴趣
的；感到厌烦的： *I'm **bored with** this
book.* 我对这本书感到厌倦。◇ *The
children were **bored stiff** (= extremely
bored).* 孩子们个个感到闷透了。

🔍 **WHICH WORD?** 词语辨析
Bored or **boring**? 用 bored 还是 boring?
If you have nothing to do, or if what you are doing does not interest you, then you are **bored**. * bored 表示没事可做或对所做的事不感兴趣而感到无聊: *Grace was so bored that she went home.* 格雷丝觉得很无聊，就回家去了。
The person or thing that makes you feel like this is **boring**. * boring 表示某人或某物让人觉得无聊: *The film was very boring.* 那部电影真没劲。

▸ **boredom** /ˈbɔːdəm/ *noun* 名词 (*no plural* 不用复数形式): *I started to eat too much out of boredom.* 我感到无聊，开始无节制地大吃起来。

boring 0┅ /ˈbɔːrɪŋ/ *adjective* 形容词
not interesting 没趣的；令人厌烦的: *That lesson was so boring!* 那堂课真没劲!

born 0┅ /bɔːn/ *adjective* 形容词
be born to start your life 出生: *He was born in 1990.* 他生于 1990 年。◇ *Where were you born?* 你是在哪儿出生的?

borne *form of* BEAR[1] * bear[1] 的不同形式

borrow/lend 借入/借出

He's **borrowing**
some money from
his mother.
他向母亲借一些钱。

She's **lending**
her son
some money.
她借给儿子一些钱。

borrow 0┅ /ˈbɒrəʊ/ *verb* 动词 (borrows, borrowing, borrowed /ˈbɒrəʊd/)
to take and use something that you will give back after a short time 借；借用: *I borrowed some books from the library.* 我从图书馆借了一些书。◇ *Can I borrow your pen?* 能借你的笔用一下吗?

🔍 **WHICH WORD?** 词语辨析
Borrow or **lend**? 用 borrow 还是 lend?
If you **borrow** something, you have it for a short time and you must give it back. * borrow 表示从别人处借用一段时间后归还: *I borrowed a CD from Alexi for the weekend.* 我跟亚历克西借来了一张激光唱片在周末听听。
If you **lend** something, you give it to someone for a short time. * lend 表示借东西给别人使用一段时间: *Alexi lent me a CD for the weekend.* 亚历克西借我一张激光唱片，让我在周末听听。

boss[1] /bɒs/ *noun* 名词 (*plural* 复数形式 **bosses**) (*informal* 非正式)
a person who controls a place where people work and tells people what they must do 老板；领班: *I asked my boss for a holiday.* 我向老板申请休假。

boss[2] /bɒs/ *verb* 动词 (bosses, bossing, bossed /bɒst/)
boss somebody about, boss somebody around to tell somebody what to do, in a way that annoys them 使唤；支使: *I wish you'd stop bossing me about.* 我希望你不要再使唤我。

bossy /ˈbɒsi/ *adjective* 形容词 (bossier, bossiest)
A **bossy** person likes to tell other people what to do. 爱使唤人的；爱支使人的: *My sister is very bossy.* 我妹妹很爱支使人。

both 0┅ /bəʊθ/ *adjective, pronoun* 形容词，代词
the two; not only one but also the other 两个；两个都: *Hold it in both hands.* 用双手拿着。◇ *Both her brothers are doctors.* 她两个弟弟都是医生。◇ *Both of us like dancing.* 我们俩都喜欢跳舞。◇ *We both like dancing.* 我们俩都喜欢跳舞。
both … and not only … but also 不仅…而且…；…和…都: *She is both rich and intelligent.* 她不仅富有而且聪明。

bother[1] /ˈbɒðə(r)/ *verb* 动词 (bothers, bothering, bothered /ˈbɒðəd/)
1 to spend extra time or energy doing something 花费时间精力，费心（做某事）: *Don't bother about the washing-up – I'll do it later.* 别管洗碗的事了，我等会儿洗。◇ *He didn't even bother to say goodbye.* 他连再见也没说一声。
2 to annoy or worry somebody, especially when they are doing something else 烦扰；打扰: *Don't bother me now – I'm busy!* 别打扰我，我正忙着! ◇ *Is this*

A B C D E F G H I J K L M N O P Q R S T U V W X Y Z

music bothering you? 这音乐烦到你吗？ ◇ ***I'm sorry to bother you**, but there's someone on the phone for you.* 对不起，打扰你了，有你的电话。

can't be bothered If you **can't be bothered** to do something, you do not want to do it because it is too much work. 懒得（做某事）： *I can't be bothered to do my homework now.* 我现在懒得做作业。

bother² /ˈbɒðə(r)/ ***noun*** 名词 (*no plural* 不用复数形式)
something that causes you difficulty 麻烦；困难 ➲ SAME MEANING **trouble** 同义词为 trouble： *'Thanks for your help!' 'It was **no bother**.'* "多谢你的帮助！" "没什么。"

bottle 瓶子

bottle 🔑 /ˈbɒtl/ ***noun*** 名词
a glass or plastic container for liquids, with a thin part at the top 瓶子： *a beer bottle* 啤酒瓶 ◇ *They drank two **bottles of** water.* 他们喝了两瓶水。

bottle bank /ˈbɒtl bæŋk/ ***noun*** 名词
a large container in a public place where people can leave old empty bottles so that the glass can be used again (**recycled**) 玻璃瓶回收箱

bottom¹ 🔑 /ˈbɒtəm/ ***noun*** 名词
1 the lowest part of something 底部： *They live **at the bottom of** the hill.* 他们住在山脚下。 ◇ *The book was at the bottom of my bag.* 那本书放在我包的最下面。 ◇ *Look at the picture at the bottom of the page.* 请看这一页下边的图。 ➲ OPPOSITE **top** 反义词为 top ➲ Look at the picture at **back¹**. 见 back¹ 的插图。
2 the last part of something; the end 末端；尽头： *The bank is at the bottom of the road.* 银行在路的尽头。 ➲ OPPOSITE **top** 反义词为 top
3 the lowest position compared to other people or groups 最末位置： *I was always at the bottom of the class in maths.* 我的数学成绩在班上总是排最后。 ➲ OPPOSITE **top** 反义词为 top
4 the part of your body that you sit on 臀部；屁股 ➲ Look at Picture Dictionary page **P4**. 见彩页 P4。

bottom² /ˈbɒtəm/ ***adjective*** 形容词
lowest 最底部的： *Put the book on the bottom shelf.* 把书放在架子的最底层。 ➲ OPPOSITE **top** 反义词为 top

bought *form of* BUY * buy 的不同形式

boulder /ˈbəʊldə(r)/ ***noun*** 名词
a very big rock 巨石

bounce 弹起

bounce /baʊns/ ***verb*** 动词 (**bounces, bouncing, bounced** /ˈbaʊnst/)
1 (used about a ball) to move away quickly after hitting something hard; to make a ball do this（球）弹起；使（球）弹起： *The ball **bounced off** the wall.* 球碰到墙后弹开了。 ◇ *The boy was bouncing a basketball.* 那个男孩拍着篮球。
2 to jump up and down many times 跳动；蹦： *The children were bouncing on their beds.* 孩子们在床上又蹦又跳。

bound¹ *form of* BIND * bind 的不同形式

bound² /baʊnd/ ***adjective*** 形容词
bound to certain to do something 一定会（做某事）： *She works very hard, so she is bound to pass the exam.* 她很用功，所以一定能通过考试。
bound for going to a place 前往： *This ship is bound for Hong Kong.* 这艘船开往香港。

bound³ /baʊnd/ ***verb*** 动词 (**bounds, bounding, bounded**)
to run with long steps 跳跃着跑： *The dog bounded up the steps.* 那条狗连蹦带跳跑上了台阶。

boundary /ˈbaʊndri/ ***noun*** 名词 (*plural* 复数形式 **boundaries**)
a line between two places 边界；分界线：

This fence is the **boundary between** the two gardens. 这道篱笆是两个花园的分界线。 ⊃ Look at **border**. 见 border。

bouquet /buˈkeɪ/ *noun* 名词
a group of flowers that is arranged in an attractive way 花束： *He gave her a bouquet of roses.* 他送了她一束玫瑰。

bow¹ /baʊ/ *verb* 动词 (bows, bowing, bowed /baʊd/)

> 🔊 PRONUNCIATION 读音说明
> With this meaning, the word **bow** sounds like **now**. 作此义时 bow 读音像 now。

to bend your head or body forward to show respect 鞠躬；点头： *The actors bowed at the end of the play.* 演员在戏演完后鞠躬谢幕。
▸ **bow** *noun* 名词： *He gave a bow and left the room.* 他鞠了个躬就离开了房间。

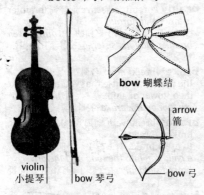

bows 琴弓；蝴蝶结；弓

violin 小提琴 | bow 琴弓 | bow 蝴蝶结 | arrow 箭 | bow 弓

bow² /bəʊ/ *noun* 名词

> 🔊 PRONUNCIATION 读音说明
> With these meanings, the word **bow** sounds like **go**. 作这些含义时 bow 读音像 go。

1 a curved piece of wood with a string between the two ends. You use a **bow** to send arrows through the air. 弓
2 a knot with two loose round parts and two loose ends that you use when you are tying shoes, etc. 蝴蝶结
3 a long thin piece of wood with hair stretched across that you use for

playing some musical instruments （乐器的）弓；琴弓： *a violin bow* 小提琴琴弓

bowl 碗

bowl¹ 0🔑 /bəʊl/ *noun* 名词
a deep round dish that is used for holding food or liquids 碗；钵： *a sugar bowl* 糖钵 ◇ *a bowl of soup* 一碗汤

bowl² /bəʊl/ *verb* 动词 (bowls, bowling, bowled /bəʊld/)
(in games such as CRICKET) to throw a ball so that somebody can hit it （板球运动等）投（球）

bowling /ˈbəʊlɪŋ/ *noun* 名词 (*no plural* 不用复数形式)
a game in which you roll a heavy ball down a special track towards a group of wooden objects shaped like bottles and try to knock them all down 保龄球运动： *We go bowling every Friday night.* 我们每周五晚上打保龄球。 ⊃ Look at Picture Dictionary page **P15**. 见彩页 P15。

bow tie /ˌbəʊ ˈtaɪ/ *noun* 名词
a tie in the shape of a BOW² (2) that some men wear on formal occasions 蝶形领结

box¹ 0🔑 /bɒks/ *noun* 名词 (*plural* 复数形式 boxes)
a container with straight sides. A box often has a lid. 箱子；盒子： *Put the books in a cardboard box.* 把书放在纸箱里。 ◇ *a box of chocolates* 一盒巧克力 ◇ *a box of matches* 一盒火柴 ⊃ Look at the picture at **container**. 见 container 的插图。

box² /bɒks/ *verb* 动词 (boxes, boxing, boxed /bɒkst/)
to fight with your hands, wearing thick gloves, as a sport 拳击

boxer /ˈbɒksə(r)/ *noun* 名词
a person who BOXES as a sport 拳击运动员： *Muhammad Ali was a famous boxer.* 穆罕默德・阿里是著名的拳击手。

boxer shorts /ˈbɒksə ʃɔːts/ (*also* 亦作 **boxers** /ˈbɒksəz/) *noun* 名词 (*plural* 用复数形式)

A
B
C
D
E
F
G
H
I
J
K
L
M
N
O
P
Q
R
S
T
U
V
W
X
Y
Z

men's underwear that looks like a pair of short trousers （男式）平角短内裤

boxing /'bɒksɪŋ/ *noun* 名词 (*no plural* 不用复数形式)
the sport of fighting with your hands, wearing thick gloves 拳击运动

Boxing Day /'bɒksɪŋ deɪ/ *noun* 名词
the day after Christmas Day; 26 December 节礼日（圣诞节的次日，即 12 月 26 日）

> 🔎 CULTURE 文化资料补充
> In Britain, **Boxing Day** is a holiday. 节礼日在英国是假日。

box office /'bɒks ɒfɪs/ *noun* 名词
a place where you buy tickets in a theatre or cinema 售票处；票房

boy 0─┅ /bɔɪ/ *noun* 名词 (*plural* 复数形式 **boys**)
a male child; a young man 男孩；小伙子：*They have three children, two boys and a girl.* 他们有三个孩子，两个男孩，一个女孩。◇ *The older boys at school used to tease him.* 学校里大一些的男生过去常常取笑他。

boyfriend 0─┅ /'bɔɪfrend/ *noun* 名词
a boy or man who somebody has a romantic relationship with 男朋友：*She has had a lot of boyfriends.* 她交过很多男友。

Boy Scout /,bɔɪ 'skaʊt/ *American English for* SCOUT (2) 美式英语，即 Scout 第 2 义

bra /brɑ:/ *noun* 名词 (*plural* 复数形式 **bras**)
a thing that a woman wears under her other clothes to cover and support her breasts 胸罩；文胸

bracelet 手镯

bracelet /'breɪslət/ *noun* 名词
a pretty piece of metal, wood or plastic that you wear around your arm 手镯

brackets /'brækɪts/ *noun* 名词 (*plural* 用复数形式)
two marks, ( ) or [ ], that you put round extra information in a piece of writing

括号：(*This sentence is written in brackets.*)（本句子放在括号内。）

brag /bræg/ *verb* 动词 (**brags, bragging, bragged** /brægd/)
to talk in a way that shows you are too proud of something that you have or something that you can do 吹嘘；自吹自擂 ⊃ SAME MEANING **boast** 同义词为 boast：*She's always bragging about how clever she is.* 她总是吹嘘说自己有多么聪明。

braid /breɪd/ *American English for* PLAIT 美式英语，即 plait

Braille (*also* 亦作 **braille**) /breɪl/ *noun* 名词 (*no plural* 不用复数形式)
a system of printing using little round marks that blind people can read by touching the page 布拉耶盲文（失明者用手触摸阅读）

brain 0─┅ /breɪn/ *noun* 名词
the part inside the head of a person or an animal that thinks and feels 脑：*The brain controls the rest of the body.* 大脑控制整个身体。

brainy /'breɪni/ *adjective* 形容词 (**brainier, brainiest**) (*informal* 非正式)
clever 聪明的；脑子好使的：*Laura's even brainier than her sister.* 劳拉甚至比她姐姐还聪明。

brake¹ /breɪk/ *noun* 名词
the part of a vehicle that you use to make it go slower or stop 刹车；制动器：*I put my foot on the brake.* 我踩了刹车。

brake² /breɪk/ *verb* 动词 (**brakes, braking, braked** /breɪkt/)
to use a **brake** 刹（车）；用制动器减速：*A child ran into the road and the driver braked suddenly.* 有个孩子跑到路上，司机猛地刹了车。

branch 0─┅ /brɑ:ntʃ/ *noun* 名词 (*plural* 复数形式 **branches**)
1 one of the parts of a tree that grow out from the thick main part (called the trunk) 树枝
2 an office or a shop that is part of a big company 处；公司；分店；分行：*This bank has branches all over the country.* 这家银行在全国各地都有分行。

brand /brænd/ *noun* 名词
the name of a product that a certain company makes 品牌：*Which brand of coffee do you buy?* 你买什么牌子的咖啡？

brand new /,brænd 'nju:/ *adjective* 形容词
completely new 全新的；簇新的；

崭新的：*a brand new car* 一辆全新的
汽车

brandy /'brændi/ *noun* 名词
1 (*no plural* 不用复数形式) a strong
alcoholic drink made from wine 白兰地
（酒）
2 (*plural* 复数形式 **brandies**) a glass of
brandy 一杯白兰地

brass /brɑːs/ *noun* 名词 (*no plural* 不用
复数形式)
a yellow metal 黄铜：*brass buttons* 黄铜
纽扣

brave ०━ /breɪv/ *adjective* 形容词
(**braver, bravest**)
ready to do dangerous or difficult things
without fear 勇敢的；无畏的：*brave
soldiers* 勇敢的士兵 ◇ *Try to be brave.*
勇敢一些吧。
▶ **bravely** *adverb* 副词：*He fought
bravely in the war.* 他英勇作战。
▶ **bravery** /'breɪvəri/ *noun* 名词 (*no
plural* 不用复数形式)：*He won a medal
for bravery.* 他赢得了英勇奖章。

bread 面包

slice 面包片
crust 面包皮

a loaf of bread 一条面包

bread ०━ /bred/ *noun* 名词 (*no plural*
不用复数形式)

> 🔊 PRONUNCIATION 读音说明
> The word **bread** sounds like **red**.
> * bread 读音像 red。

food made from flour and baked in an
oven 面包：*I bought a loaf of bread.*
我买了一条面包。◇ *a slice of bread and
butter* 一片涂黄油的面包

breadth /bredθ/ *noun* 名词
how far it is from one side of something
to the other 宽度 ⊃ SAME MEANING **width**
同义词为 width ⊃ The adjective is **broad**.
形容词为 broad。

break¹ ०━ /breɪk/ *verb* 动词 (**breaks,
breaking, broke** /brəʊk/, **has broken**
/'brəʊkən/)
1 to make something go into smaller

pieces, for example by dropping it or
hitting it 弄破；弄裂；弄碎：*He broke the
window.* 他打破了窗户。◇ *She has broken
her arm.* 她把胳膊弄断了。
2 to go into smaller pieces, for example
by falling or hitting 摔破；砸碎：
I dropped the cup and it broke. 我把杯子
摔碎了。
3 to stop working; to damage a machine
so that it stops working 坏掉；损坏：
You've broken my watch. 你把我的手表
弄坏了。
4 to do something that is against the law
or against what has been agreed or
promised 违反（法律）；违背（协议或
诺言）：*People who break the law must
be punished.* 违法者必定受到惩罚。◇
I never break my promises. 我从不食言。

break down
1 If a machine or car **breaks down**, it
stops working. 出故障；坏掉：*We were
late because our car broke down.* 我们
来晚了，因为我们的汽车抛锚了。
2 If a person **breaks down**, they start to
cry. 哭起来：*He broke down when he
heard the news.* 他一听到这个消息就哭了
起来。

break in, break into something to go
into a place by breaking a door or
window so that you can steal something
强行进入；破门（窗）而入：*Thieves
broke into the house. They broke in
through a window.* 小偷光顾了那所房子。
他们是破窗而入的。

break off to take away a piece of
something by breaking it 折断；掰断：
He broke off a piece of chocolate for me.
他掰下一块巧克力给我。

break out
1 to start suddenly 突然开始；爆发：*A
fire broke out last night.* 昨晚突然失火了。
2 to get free from a place like a prison
（从监狱等）逃脱：*Four prisoners broke
out of the jail last night.* 昨晚有四名囚犯
越狱了。

break up (*British* 英式英语) to start the
school holidays （学校）开始放假：*We
break up at the end of July.* 我们七月底
放假。

break up with somebody to end a
relationship with somebody 结束关系；
分手：*Susy broke up with her boyfriend
last week.* 苏茜上星期和男友分手了。

break² /breɪk/ *noun* 名词
1 a short time when you stop doing
something 小休：*We worked all day
without a break.* 我们歇都没歇地工作了
一整天。

A B C D E F G H I J K L M N O P Q R S T U V W X Y Z

2 a place where something opens or has broken 间隙；空间: *The sun shone through a break in the clouds.* 太阳从云隙中露了出来。

breakdown /'breɪkdaʊn/ *noun* 名词
a time when a machine, car, etc. stops working 故障: *We had a breakdown on the motorway.* 我们在高速公路上抛锚了。

breakfast ⭕ /'brekfəst/ *noun* 名词
the first meal of the day 早餐；早饭: *I had breakfast at seven o'clock.* 我七点钟吃早餐。

breast /brest/ *noun* 名词

> 🔎 PRONUNCIATION 读音说明
> The word **breast** sounds like **test**.
> * breast 读音像 test。

1 one of the two soft round parts of a woman's body that can give milk 乳房
2 the front part of a bird's body （鸟的）胸部

breaststroke 蛙泳

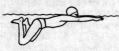

breaststroke /'breststrəʊk/ *noun* 名词
(*no plural* 不用复数形式)
a way of swimming on your front 蛙泳:
Can you do breaststroke? 你会游蛙泳吗?
↪ Look also at crawl². 亦见 crawl²。

breath ⭕ /breθ/ *noun* 名词
taking in or letting out air through your nose and mouth 呼吸: *Take a deep breath.* 深吸一口气。

hold your breath to stop breathing for a short time 屏住呼吸: *We all held our breath as the winner was announced.* 宣布获胜者时，我们都屏住了呼吸。

out of breath breathing very quickly 气喘吁吁: *She was out of breath after climbing the stairs.* 她爬上楼梯后气喘吁吁。

breathe ⭕ /briːð/ *verb* 动词 (breathes, breathing, breathed /briːðd/)
to take in and let out air through your nose and mouth 呼吸: *The doctor told me to breathe in and then breathe out again slowly.* 医生叫我吸一口气然后再慢慢呼出来。

breathless /'breθləs/ *adjective* 形容词
breathing quickly or with difficulty 气喘吁吁的；上气不接下气的: *Running made them hot and breathless.* 跑步使他们浑身发热，上气不接下气。

breed¹ /briːd/ *verb* 动词 (breeds, breeding, bred /bred/, has bred)
1 When animals **breed**, they produce young animals. 繁殖: *Birds breed in the spring.* 鸟类在春天繁殖。
2 to keep animals so that they will produce baby animals 饲养；培育: *They breed horses on their farm.* 他们在农场养马。

breed² /briːd/ *noun* 名词
a kind of animal （动物的）品种: *There are many different breeds of dog.* 狗有很多不同的品种。

breeze /briːz/ *noun* 名词
a light wind 微风

brewery /'bruːəri/ *noun* 名词 (*plural* 复数形式 breweries)
a place where beer is made 啤酒厂

bribe /braɪb/ *noun* 名词
money or a present that you give to somebody to make them do something for you, especially something dishonest 贿赂

▶ **bribe** *verb* 动词 (bribes, bribing, bribed /braɪbd/): *The prisoner bribed the guard to let him go free.* 囚犯买通了看守，让他逃走。

brick ⭕ /brɪk/ *noun* 名词
a small block of CLAY (= a type of earth) that has been baked until it is hard. **Bricks** are used for building. 砖: *a brick wall* 砖墙

bricklayer /'brɪkleɪə(r)/ *noun* 名词
a person whose job is to build things with bricks 砌砖工；泥瓦匠

bride /braɪd/ *noun* 名词
a woman on the day of her wedding 新娘

bridegroom /'braɪdɡruːm/ (*also* 亦作 groom) *noun* 名词
a man on the day of his wedding 新郎

bridesmaid /'braɪdzmeɪd/ *noun* 名词
a girl or woman who helps a BRIDE at her wedding 伴娘；女傧相

bridge ⭕ /brɪdʒ/ *noun* 名词
a thing that is built over a road, railway or river so that people, trains or cars can cross it 桥: *We walked over the bridge.* 我们走过了桥。

bridge 桥

brief 0┳ /briːf/ ***adjective*** 形容词 (**briefer**, **briefest**)
short or quick 短时间的；短暂的： *a brief telephone call* 简短的电话通话 ◇ *Please be brief.* 请简明扼要。
in brief in a few words 简言之： *Here is the news in brief* (= words said on a radio or television programme). 现在是新闻简报。
▸ **briefly** /ˈbriːfli/ ***adverb*** 副词： *He had spoken to Emma only briefly.* 他和埃玛只讲了短短的几句话。

briefcase 公事包

briefcase /ˈbriːfkeɪs/ ***noun*** 名词
a flat case that you use for carrying papers, especially when you go to work 公文包；公事包

bright 0┳ /braɪt/ ***adjective*** 形容词 (**brighter**, **brightest**)
1 with a lot of light 光线充足的；明亮的： *It was a bright sunny day.* 那天阳光灿烂。◇ *That lamp is very bright.* 那灯很亮。
2 with a strong colour 鲜艳的： *a bright yellow shirt* 鲜黄色的衬衫
3 clever 聪明的： *She is the brightest child in the class.* 她是班上最聪明的孩子。
▸ **brightly** /ˈbraɪtli/ ***adverb*** 副词： *brightly coloured clothes* 色彩鲜艳的衣服
▸ **brightness** /ˈbraɪtnəs/ ***noun*** 名词 (*no plural* 不用复数形式)： *the brightness of the sun* 太阳的光辉

brighten /ˈbraɪtn/ ***verb*** 动词 (**brightens**, **brightening**, **brightened** /ˈbraɪtnd/) (*also* 亦作 **brighten up**)
to become brighter or happier; to make something brighter （使）快活起来；（使）更加明亮（或鲜艳等）： *Her face brightened when she saw him.* 她看到他时面露喜色。◇ *These flowers will brighten the room up.* 这些花使房间亮丽生色。

brilliant /ˈbrɪliənt/ ***adjective*** 形容词
1 with a lot of light; very bright 耀眼的；灿烂的： *brilliant sunshine* 耀目的阳光
2 very intelligent 聪颖的： *a brilliant student* 才华横溢的学生
3 (*British* 英式英语) (*informal* 非正式) very good 极好的；非常棒的： *The film was brilliant!* 这部电影很不错!
▸ **brilliance** /ˈbrɪliəns/ ***noun*** 名词 (*no plural* 不用复数形式)： *the brilliance of the light* 那道光的灿烂夺目
▸ **brilliantly** /ˈbrɪliəntli/ ***adverb*** 副词： *She played brilliantly.* 她表现得很出色。

brim /brɪm/ ***noun*** 名词
1 the edge around the top of something like a cup, bowl or glass （杯或碗等的）口，边，沿： *The glass was **full to the brim**.* 杯子斟得满满的。
2 the wide part around the bottom of a hat 帽檐

bring 0┳ /brɪŋ/ ***verb*** 动词 (**brings**, **bringing**, **brought** /brɔːt/, **has brought**)
1 to take something or somebody with you to a place 带；取： *Could you bring me a glass of water?* 你能给我拿杯水吗？◇ *Can I bring a friend to the party?* 我能带个朋友来参加聚会吗？
2 to make something happen 使发生： *Money doesn't always bring happiness.* 金钱未必能带来幸福。
bring something back
1 to return something 归还： *I've brought back the book you lent me.* 我把你借给我的书带来了。
2 to make you remember something 使回忆起： *These old photographs bring back a lot of happy memories.* 这些老照片带来许多愉快的回忆。
bring somebody up to look after a child until they are grown up 抚养；养育： *He was brought up by his aunt after his parents died.* 父母死后，他由姑妈抚养成人。
bring something up
1 to be sick, so that food comes up from your stomach and out of your mouth 呕吐
2 to start to talk about something 提出：

A

B

C

D

E

F

G

H

I

J

K

L

M

N

O

P

Q

R

S

T

U

V

W

X

Y

Z

Can you bring up this problem at the next meeting? 你能不能在下次会议上提出这个问题?

bring 拿来

Bring the newspaper. 把报纸拿来。

Fetch the newspaper. 去把报纸拿来。

Take the newspaper. 把报纸拿走。

brisk /brɪsk/ *adjective* 形容词 (**brisker, briskest**)
quick and using a lot of energy 轻快的:
We went for a brisk walk. 我们轻快地散了步。

bristle /ˈbrɪsl/ *noun* 名词
a short thick hair like the hair on a brush 短而硬的毛发;刚毛

brittle /ˈbrɪtl/ *adjective* 形容词
Something that is **brittle** is hard but breaks easily. 硬而易碎的;脆的: *This glass is very brittle.* 这个玻璃杯很容易碎。

broad /brɔːd/ *adjective* 形容词 (**broader, broadest**)
large from one side to the other 宽的;宽阔的 ➋ SAME MEANING **wide** 同义词为 wide: *a broad river* 宽阔的河 ➋ The noun is **breadth**. 名词为 breadth。
➋ OPPOSITE **narrow** 反义词为 narrow

broadband /ˈbrɔːdbænd/ *noun* 名词 (*no plural* 不用复数形式)
(*computing* 电脑) (used about an Internet connection) able to send and receive a lot of information quickly(用于互联网连接的)宽带,宽频: *Have you got broadband?* 你装了宽带了吗?

broadcast /ˈbrɔːdkɑːst/ *verb* 动词 (**broadcasts, broadcasting, broadcast, has broadcast**)
to send out sound or pictures by radio or television 广播,播送(电台或电视节目): *The Olympics are broadcast live around the world.* 奥运会赛事在全球各地直播。
▶ **broadcast** *noun* 名词: *a news broadcast* 新闻广播
▶ **broadcaster** /ˈbrɔːdkɑːstə(r)/ *noun* 名词
a person whose job is to talk on radio or television 播音员

broad-minded /ˌbrɔːd ˈmaɪndɪd/ *adjective* 形容词
happy to accept ways of life and beliefs that are different from your own 胸怀宽阔的;气量大的 ➋ OPPOSITE **narrow-minded** 反义词为 narrow-minded

broccoli /ˈbrɒkəli/ *noun* 名词 (*no plural* 不用复数形式)
a vegetable with green or purple flowers that you eat 绿菜花;西兰花 ➋ Look at Picture Dictionary page P9. 见彩页 P9。

brochure /ˈbrəʊʃə(r)/ *noun* 名词
a thin book with pictures of things you can buy or places you can go on holiday 资料手册;小册子: *a travel brochure* 旅游指南

broke (*also* 还有 broken) *forms of* BREAK¹
* break¹ 的不同形式

broken ⚬┭ /'brəʊkən/ *adjective* 形容词
in pieces or not working 破碎的；损坏的：*a broken window* 破窗 ◇ '*What's the time?' 'I don't know – my watch is broken.*'
"几点了？""我不知道，我的手表坏了。" ◇ *The TV is broken.* 电视机坏了。
Ⴢ The verb is **break**. 动词为 break。

bronze /brɒnz/ *noun* 名词 (*no plural* 不用复数形式)
a dark red-brown metal 青铜：*a bronze medal* 铜牌

brooch /brəʊtʃ/ *noun* 名词 (*plural* 复数形式 **brooches**)
a piece of jewellery with a pin at the back that you wear on your clothes 饰针；胸针

broom /bruːm/ *noun* 名词
a brush with a long handle that you use for cleaning the floor 扫帚 Ⴢ Look at the picture at **brush¹**. 见 brush¹ 的插图。

brother ⚬┭ /'brʌðə(r)/ *noun* 名词
a man or boy who has the same parents as you（同父母的）哥哥，弟弟：*My younger brother is called Mark.* 我弟弟叫马克。◇ *Gavin and Nick are brothers.*
加文和尼克是亲兄弟。◇ *Have you got any brothers and sisters?* 你有兄弟姐妹吗？

brother-in-law /'brʌðər ɪn lɔː/ *noun* 名词 (*plural* 复数形式 **brothers-in-law**)
1 the brother of your wife or husband 大伯子；小叔子；大舅子；小舅子
2 the husband of your sister 姐夫；妹夫
Ⴢ Look at **sister-in-law**. 见 sister-in-law。

brought *form of* BRING * bring 的不同形式

brow /braʊ/ *noun* 名词 (*formal* 正式)
the part of your face above your eyes 额头 Ⴢ SAME MEANING **forehead** 同义词为 forehead

brown ⚬┭ /braʊn/ *adjective* 形容词 (**browner, brownest**)
having the colour of earth or wood 棕色的；褐色的：*brown eyes* 褐色的眼睛 ◇ *I go brown* (= my skin becomes brown) *as soon as I sit in the sun.* 我一坐在太阳底下皮肤就会晒黑。
▸ **brown** *noun* 名词：*Brown suits you* (= makes you look good). 棕色很适合你。

browser /'braʊzə(r)/ *noun* 名词 (*computing* 电脑) a program that lets you look at pages on the Internet（网络）浏览程序，浏览器：*a Web browser* 互联网浏览器

bruise /bruːz/ *noun* 名词
a dark mark on your skin that comes after something hits it 淤伤；青肿
▸ **bruise** *verb* 动词 (**bruises, bruising, bruised** /bruːzd/): *He fell and bruised his leg.* 他摔倒并把腿给撞淤了。

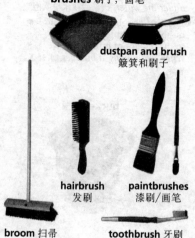

brushes 刷子；画笔

dustpan and brush 簸箕和刷子

hairbrush 发刷

paintbrushes 漆刷/画笔

broom 扫帚

toothbrush 牙刷

brush¹ ⚬┭ /brʌʃ/ *noun* 名词 (*plural* 复数形式 **brushes**)
a thing that you use for cleaning, painting or making your hair tidy 刷子；画笔；梳子：*a clothes brush* 衣刷

brush² ⚬┭ /brʌʃ/ *verb* 动词 (**brushes, brushing, brushed** /brʌʃt/)
to clean or tidy something with a brush（用刷子）刷，梳：*I **brush** my teeth twice a day.* 我一天刷两次牙。◇ ***Brush** your hair!* 梳梳你的头发吧！

Brussels sprout /,brʌslz 'spraʊt/ (*also* 亦作 **sprout**) *noun* 名词
a very small round green vegetable consisting of a tight ball of leaves 汤菜；抱子甘蓝 Ⴢ Look at Picture Dictionary page **P9**. 见彩页 P9。

brutal /'bruːtl/ *adjective* 形容词
very cruel 残忍的；兽性的：*a brutal murder* 残暴的谋杀
▸ **brutally** /'bruːtəli/ *adverb* 副词：*She was brutally attacked.* 她遭到了残忍的暴力伤害。

BSc /,biː es 'siː/ *noun* 名词
the certificate that you receive when you complete a university or college course

A
B
C
D
E
F
G
H
I
J
K
L
M
N
O
P
Q
R
S
T
U
V
W
X
Y
Z

in a science subject. **BSc** is short for
'Bachelor of Science'. 理学士（修完大学
理科课程后获得的学位，BSc 是 Bachelor
of Science 的缩略式） ⊃ Look also at **BA**.
亦见 BA。

bubble¹ ⊶ /'bʌbl/ *noun* 名词
a small ball of air or gas inside a liquid
泡；气泡：*The children **blew bubbles**
under the water.* 孩子们在水里吹泡泡。

bubble² /'bʌbl/ *verb* 动词 (bubbles,
bubbling, bubbled /'bʌbld/)
to make a lot of **bubbles** 起泡；冒泡：
When water boils, it bubbles. 水开了会
冒泡。

bucket 提桶

bucket /'bʌkɪt/ *noun* 名词
a round metal or plastic container with
a handle. You use a **bucket** for carrying
water, for example. 提桶

buckle /'bʌkl/ *noun* 名词
a metal or plastic thing on the end of a
belt or on a shoe that you use for
fastening it （皮带或鞋的）搭扣，锁扣
⊃ Look at the picture at **shoe**. 见 shoe 的
插图。

bud /bʌd/ *noun* 名词
a leaf or flower before it opens 芽；苞；
花蕾：*The trees are covered in buds.* 这些
树长满了花蕾。 ⊃ Look at the picture at
plant¹. 见 plant¹ 的插图。

Buddhism /'bʊdɪzəm/ *noun* 名词 (*no
plural* 不用复数形式)
the religion that is based on the teaching
of Buddha 佛教

Buddhist /'bʊdɪst/ *noun* 名词
a person who follows the religion of
BUDDHISM 佛教徒
▶ **Buddhist** *adjective* 形容词：*a Buddhist
temple* 一座佛寺

budge /bʌdʒ/ *verb* 动词 (budges, budging,
budged /bʌdʒd/)
to move a little or to make something
move a little （使）轻微移动：*I tried*

to move the rock but it wouldn't budge.
我尝试挪这块石头，可是它就是纹丝不动。

budgerigar /'bʌdʒərigɑ:(r)/ (*also
informal* 非正式亦作 budgie /'bʌdʒi/) *noun*
名词
a small blue or green bird that people
often keep as a pet 虎皮鹦鹉 ⊃ Look at
Picture Dictionary page **P2**. 见彩页 P2。

budget /'bʌdʒɪt/ *noun* 名词
a plan of how much money you will have
and how you will spend it 预算：*We have
a weekly budget for food.* 我们每周都有购
买食物的预算。
▶ **budget** *verb* 动词 (budgets, budgeting,
budgeted)：*I am budgeting very carefully
because I want to buy a new car.* 我现在
精打细算，因为想买辆新车。

buffalo /'bʌfələʊ/ *noun* 名词 (*plural* 复数
形式 buffalo)
a large wild animal that looks like a cow
with long curved horns 水牛 ⊃ Look at
Picture Dictionary page **P3**. 见彩页 P3。

buffet /'bʊfeɪ/ *noun* 名词
a meal when all the food is on a big table
and you take what you want 自助餐：
a buffet lunch 自助午餐

bug /bʌg/ *noun* 名词
1 a small insect 小昆虫；虫子
2 an illness that is not serious 小病：
I've caught a bug. 我生病了。
3 a fault in a machine, especially a
computer system or program （机器，
尤指电脑的）缺陷，漏洞，程序错误

buggy /'bʌgi/ *noun* 名词 (*plural* 复数形式
buggies) (*British* 英式英语) (*American*
美式英语 stroller)
a chair on wheels in which a young child
is pushed along 婴儿车；童车 ⊃ SAME
MEANING **pushchair** 同义词为 pushchair
⊃ Look at the picture at **pushchair**.
见 pushchair 的插图。

build ⊶ /bɪld/ *verb* 动词 (builds,
building, built /bɪlt/, has built)
to make something by putting parts
together 建筑；建造：*He built a wall in
front of the house.* 他在屋前修了一道墙。
◊ *The bridge is built of stone.* 这座桥是用
石头砌成的。

builder /'bɪldə(r)/ *noun* 名词
a person whose job is to make buildings
建筑商；建筑工人

building ⊶ /'bɪldɪŋ/ *noun* 名词
a structure with a roof and walls. Houses,
schools, churches and shops are all
buildings. 建筑物；楼房

building society /ˈbɪldɪŋ səsaɪəti/ *noun* 名词 (*British* 英式英语) (*plural* 复数形式 **building societies**)
a kind of bank that lends you money when you want to buy a house or flat 房屋互助会（提供购房贷款等服务）

built *form of* BUILD * build 的不同形式

bulb /bʌlb/ *noun* 名词
1 (*also* 亦作 **light bulb**) the glass part of an electric lamp that gives light 电灯泡
2 a round thing that some plants grow from（植物）鳞茎: *a tulip bulb* 郁金香鳞茎 ➷ Look at the picture at **plant¹**. 见 plant¹ 的插图。

bulge /bʌldʒ/ *verb* 动词 (**bulges**, **bulging**, **bulged** /bʌldʒd/)
to go out in a round shape from something that is usually flat 鼓起; 凸起: *My stomach is bulging – I have to get some exercise.* 我的肚子发福了，我得锻炼锻炼了。
▶ **bulge** *noun* 名词: *a bulge in the wall* 墙上的鼓包

bulky /ˈbʌlki/ *adjective* 形容词 (**bulkier**, **bulkiest**)
big, heavy and difficult to carry 庞大的; 笨重的: *a bulky parcel* 大件包裹

bull /bʊl/ *noun* 名词
the male of the cow and of some other animals 公牛; 雄兽 ➷ Look at the picture at **cow**. 见 cow 的插图。

bulldog /ˈbʊldɒg/ *noun* 名词
a strong dog with short legs and a large head 斗牛狗; 牛头犬

bulldozer 推土机

bulldozer /ˈbʊldəʊzə(r)/ *noun* 名词
a big heavy machine that moves earth and makes land flat 推土机

bullet ०━ /ˈbʊlɪt/ *noun* 名词
a small piece of metal that comes out of a gun 子弹: *The bullet hit him in the leg.* 子弹打中了他的腿。

bulletin board /ˈbʊlətɪn bɔːd/ *American English for* NOTICEBOARD 美式英语，即 noticeboard

bully /ˈbʊli/ *noun* 名词 (*plural* 复数形式 **bullies**)
a person who hurts or frightens a weaker person 恃强凌弱者
▶ **bully** *verb* 动词 (**bullies**, **bullying**, **bullied** /ˈbʊlid/): *She was bullied by the older girls at school.* 她在学校里遭年纪较大的女生欺负。

bum /bʌm/ *noun* 名词 (*informal* 非正式)
1 (*British* 英式英语) the part of your body that you sit on 屁股

> 🔎 SPEAKING 表达方式说明
> Some people think this word is quite rude. **Bottom** is the more usual word. 有些人认为这词颇粗俗。bottom 更常用。

2 (*American* 美式英语) a person who has no home or job and who asks other people for money or food 流浪乞丐

bump¹ /bʌmp/ *verb* 动词 (**bumps**, **bumping**, **bumped** /bʌmpt/)
1 to hit somebody or something when you are moving 碰; 撞: *She bumped into a chair.* 她撞到了一把椅子。
2 to hit a part of your body against something hard 碰上; 撞上: *I bumped my knee on the table.* 我的膝盖撞到了桌子。
bump into somebody to meet somebody by chance 偶然遇见: *I bumped into David today.* 我今天碰见了戴维。

bump² /bʌmp/ *noun* 名词
1 the action or sound of something hitting a hard surface 碰撞（声）: *He fell and hit the ground with a bump.* 他砰的一声摔倒在地上。
2 a round raised area on your body where you have hit it 肿块; 疙瘩: *I've got a bump on my head.* 我头上起了个疙瘩。
3 a small part on something flat that is higher than the rest 隆起处: *The car hit a bump in the road.* 汽车撞到了路上的隆起处。

bumper /ˈbʌmpə(r)/ *noun* 名词
a bar on the front and back of a car which helps to protect the car if it hits something（汽车头尾的）保险杠
➷ Look at Picture Dictionary page **P1**. 见彩页 P1。

A
B
C
D
E
F
G
H
I
J
K
L
M
N
O
P
Q
R
S
T
U
V
W
X
Y
Z

A B C D E F G H I J K L M N O P Q R S T U V W X Y Z

bumpy /ˈbʌmpi/ ***adjective*** 形容词 (**bumpier, bumpiest**)
not flat or smooth 崎岖不平的；不平稳的：*We had a bumpy flight.* 我们的飞行旅途很颠簸。◇ *The road was very bumpy.* 道路十分崎岖不平。 ➲ OPPOSITE **smooth** 反义词为 smooth

bun /bʌn/ ***noun*** 名词
a small round cake or piece of bread 小圆蛋糕；小圆面包

bunch /bʌntʃ/ ***noun*** 名词 (*plural* 复数形式 **bunches**)
a group of things that grow together or that you tie or hold together 串；束；捆：*a **bunch of** grapes* 一串葡萄 ◇ *two bunches of flowers* 两束花

bundle /ˈbʌndl/ ***noun*** 名词
a group of things that you tie or wrap together 捆；束：*a **bundle of** old newspapers* 一捆旧报纸

bungalow /ˈbʌŋgələʊ/ ***noun*** 名词 (*British* 英式英语)
a house that has only one floor, with no upstairs rooms 平房

bunk /bʌŋk/ ***noun*** 名词
1 a narrow bed that is fixed to a wall, for example on a ship or train （轮船或火车等的）卧铺
2 (*also* 亦作 **bunk bed**) one of a pair of single beds built one on top of the other （双层单人床的）床铺；上铺；下铺
➲ Look at the picture at **bed**. 见 bed 的插图。

bunny /ˈbʌni/ ***noun*** 名词 (*plural* 复数形式 **bunnies**)
a child's word for RABBIT (= a small animal with long ears) （儿语）兔子

buoy /bɔɪ/ ***noun*** 名词 (*plural* 复数形式 **buoys**)
a thing that floats in the sea to show ships where there are dangerous places 浮标

burden /ˈbɜːdn/ ***noun*** 名词
something that you have to do that causes worry, difficulty or hard work 重担；负担：*I don't want to be a **burden** to my children when I'm old.* 我不想在年老的时候成为子女的累赘。

burger /ˈbɜːgə(r)/ ***noun*** 名词
meat cut into very small pieces and made into a flat round shape, that you eat between two pieces of bread 汉堡牛肉饼；汉堡包 ➲ SAME MEANING **hamburger** 同义词为 hamburger：*a burger and chips* 一份汉堡包和薯条

burger 汉堡包

burglar /ˈbɜːglə(r)/ ***noun*** 名词
a person who goes into a building to steal things 入室盗贼

burglarize /ˈbɜːgləraɪz/ *American English for* BURGLE 美式英语，即 burgle

burglary /ˈbɜːgləri/ ***noun*** 名词 (*plural* 复数形式 **burglaries**)
the crime of going into a house to steal things 入室盗窃（罪）：*He was arrested for burglary.* 他因入室盗窃而被捕。

burgle /ˈbɜːgl/ ***verb*** 动词 (**burgles, burgling, burgled** /ˈbɜːgld/) (*American* 美式英语 **burglarize**)
to go into a building illegally, usually using force, and steal from it 入室盗窃：*Our house was burgled.* 我们家失窃了。

burial /ˈberiəl/ ***noun*** 名词
the time when a dead body is put in the ground 埋葬 ➲ The verb is **bury**. 动词为 bury。

buried (*also* 还有 **buries**) *forms of* BURY
* bury 的不同形式

burn[1] 0━ /bɜːn/ ***verb*** 动词 (**burns, burning, burnt** /bɜːnt/ or 或 **burned** /bɜːnd/, **has burnt** or 或 **has burned**)
1 to make flames and heat; to be on fire 燃烧；着火：*Paper burns easily.* 纸很容易烧着。◇ *She escaped from the burning building.* 她从失火的大楼中逃了出来。
2 to harm or destroy somebody or something with fire or heat 烧毁；烧伤；烫伤：*I burnt my fingers on a match.* 我的手指被火柴烧伤了。◇ *We burned the wood on the fire.* 我们在炉火上烧木头。
burn down, burn something down
to burn, or to make a building burn, until there is nothing left 烧毁；焚毁：*Their house burnt down.* 他们的房子焚毁了。

burn[2] /bɜːn/ ***noun*** 名词
a place on your body where fire or heat has hurt it 烧伤；烫伤：*I've got a burn on my arm.* 我胳膊上有处烫伤。

burnt /bɜːnt/ ***adjective*** 形容词
damaged by burning 烧坏的；烧伤的：

A
B
C
D
E
F
G
H
I
J
K
L
M
N
O
P
Q
R
S
T
U
V
W
X
Y
Z

burnt food 烤焦的食物 ◇ *Her hand was badly burnt.* 她的手严重烧伤了。

burp /bɜːp/ *verb* 动词 (burps, burping, burped /bɜːpt/)
to make a noise from your mouth when air suddenly comes up from your stomach 打嗝: *He burped loudly.* 他大声打嗝。
▶ **burp** *noun* 名词: *I heard a loud burp.* 我听到很响的打嗝声。

burrow /ˈbʌrəʊ/ *noun* 名词
a hole in the ground where some animals, for example RABBITS (= small animals with long ears), live （动物的）洞穴

burst¹ 0- /bɜːst/ *verb* 动词 (bursts, bursting, burst, has burst)
1 to break open suddenly or to make something do this （使）爆裂；（使）胀开: *The bag was so full that it burst.* 袋子给撑破了。◇ *He burst the balloon.* 他弄炸了气球。
2 to go or come suddenly 闯入: *Steve burst into the room.* 史蒂夫闯进了房间。
burst into something to start doing something suddenly 突然做某事: *She read the letter and burst into tears* (= started to cry). 她读着读着信就哭了起来。
◇ *The car burst into flames* (= started to burn). 汽车突然着火了。
burst out laughing to suddenly start to laugh 突然笑起来: *When she saw my hat, she burst out laughing.* 她一看到我的帽子就大笑起来。

burst² /bɜːst/ *noun* 名词
something that happens suddenly and quickly 突发: *a burst of laughter* 一阵大笑

bury 0- /ˈberi/ *verb* 动词 (buries, burying, buried /ˈberid/, has buried)

1 to put a dead body in the ground 埋葬 ⊃ The noun is **burial**. 名词为 burial。
2 to put something in the ground or under something 掩藏在地下；埋藏: *The dog buried the bone in the garden.* 狗把骨头埋在花园里了。

bus 0- /bʌs/ *noun* 名词 (plural 复数形式 buses)
a large vehicle that carries a lot of people along the road and stops often so they can get on and off 公共汽车；巴士: *We went to town by bus.* 我们乘公共汽车进了

城。◇ *Where do you get off the bus?* 你在哪儿下公交车?

buses 公共汽车

bus 公共汽车

double-decker bus 双层公共汽车

bush 0- /bʊʃ/ *noun* 名词
1 (*plural* 复数形式 bushes) a plant like a small tree with a lot of branches 灌木: *a rose bush* 玫瑰丛
2 the bush (*no plural* 不用复数形式) wild country with a lot of small trees in Africa or Australia （非洲或澳大利亚的）荒野

business 0- /ˈbɪznəs/ *noun* 名词
1 (*no plural* 不用复数形式) buying and selling things 买卖；生意；商业: *I want to go into business when I leave school.*

A
B
C
D
E
F
G
H
I
J
K
L
M
N
O
P
Q
R
S
T
U
V
W
X
Y
Z

我打算毕业后从商。◇ *Business is not very good this year.* 今年生意不太好。
2 (*plural* 复数形式 businesses) a place where people sell or make things, for example a shop or factory 商业机构；公司；商店；工厂
3 the work that you do as your job 公事；差事；业务： *The manager will be away* **on business** *next week.* 经理下星期要出差。◇ *a business trip* 出差
it's none of your business, mind your own business words that you use to tell somebody rudely that you do not want to tell them about something private 与你无关；少管闲事： *'Where are you going?' 'Mind your own business!'* "你去哪里？" "你管不着！"

businessman /ˈbɪznəsmæn; ˈbɪznəsmən/ *noun* 名词 (*plural* 复数形式 businessmen /ˈbɪznəsmen/)
a man who works in business, especially in a top position（尤指上层）商界人员

businesswoman /ˈbɪznəswʊmən/ *noun* 名词 (*plural* 复数形式 businesswomen /ˈbɪznəswɪmɪn/)
a woman who works in business, especially in a top position（尤指上层）商界女性人员 ➲ Look at Picture Dictionary page **P12**. 见彩页 P12。

bus stop /ˈbʌs stɒp/ *noun* 名词
a place where buses stop and people get on and off 公共汽车停靠站

busy ০━ /ˈbɪzi/ *adjective* 形容词 (busier, busiest)
1 with a lot of things that you must do; working or not free 忙的；忙碌的： *Mr Jones can't see you now – he's busy.* 琼斯先生现在不能见你，他在忙。
2 with a lot of things happening 事情多的；工作忙的： *I had a busy morning.* 我忙了一个上午。◇ *The shops are always busy at Christmas.* 商店在圣诞节总是很忙。
3 (used about a telephone) being used（电话）占线的 ➲ SAME MEANING **engaged** 同义词为 engaged： *The line is busy – I'll try again later.* 电话占线，我稍后再打。
▶ **busily** /ˈbɪzɪli/ *adverb* 副词： *He was busily writing a letter.* 他正忙着写信。

but¹ ০━ /bət; bʌt/ *conjunction* 连词
a word that you use to show something different 但是；可是： *My sister speaks French but I don't.* 我姐姐会说法语，我却不会。◇ *He worked hard but he didn't pass the exam.* 他很用功，但是考试没及格。◇ *The weather was sunny but cold.* 天气晴朗，可是却很冷。

but² /bət; bʌt/ *preposition* 介词
except 除…外： *She eats nothing but chocolate.* 她除了巧克力什么都不吃。

butcher /ˈbʊtʃə(r)/ *noun* 名词
1 a person who sells meat 肉贩
2 **butcher's** a shop that sells meat 肉店；肉铺： *She went to the butcher's for some lamb chops.* 她去肉店买了羊排。➲ Look at Picture Dictionary page **P13**. 见彩页 P13。

butter ০━ /ˈbʌtə(r)/ *noun* 名词 (*no plural* 不用复数形式)
a soft yellow food that is made from milk. You put it on bread or use it in cooking. 黄油： *She spread butter on the bread.* 她把黄油涂在面包上。➲ Look at Picture Dictionary page **P6**. 见彩页 P6。
▶ **butter** *verb* 动词 (butters, buttering, buttered /ˈbʌtəd/) to put butter on bread 把黄油涂在…上： *I buttered the toast.* 我把黄油涂在烤面包片上了。

butterfly 蝴蝶
antenna 触须
wing 翅膀

butterfly /ˈbʌtəflaɪ/ *noun* 名词 (*plural* 复数形式 butterflies)
an insect with big coloured wings 蝴蝶

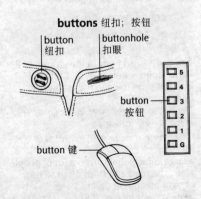

buttons 纽扣；按钮
button 纽扣
buttonhole 扣眼
button 按钮
button 键

buttock /ˈbʌtək/ ***noun*** 名词
one of the two parts of your body that you sit on 屁股的一边

button 🗝 /ˈbʌtn/ ***noun*** 名词
1 a small round thing on clothes that holds them together. You push it through a small hole (called a **buttonhole**). 纽扣；扣子
2 a small thing on a machine, that you push 按钮；按键： *Press this* ***button*** *to ring the bell.* 按这个键，电铃就响了。

buy 🗝 /baɪ/ ***verb*** 动词 (**buys**, **buying**, **bought** /bɔːt/, **has bought**)

> **PRONUNCIATION** 读音说明
> The word **buy** sounds like **my**.
> * buy 读音像 my。

to give money to get something 买；购买： *I bought a new watch.* 我买了块新手表。◇ *He* ***bought*** *the car* ***from*** *a friend.* 他从朋友那里买了这辆车。 ➲ Look at **sell**. 见 sell。

buzz /bʌz/ ***verb*** 动词 (**buzzes**, **buzzing**, **buzzed** /bʌzd/)
to make the sound that a flying insect such as a BEE (= a black and yellow insect) makes 发出嗡嗡声： *A fly was buzzing against the window.* 一只苍蝇在窗边嗡嗡作响。
▶ **buzz** ***noun*** 名词 (*plural* 复数形式 **buzzes**): *the buzz of insects* 昆虫的嗡嗡声

by[1] 🗝 /baɪ/ ***preposition*** 介词
1 very near 靠近；在旁边 ➲ SAME MEANING **beside** 同义词为 beside: *The telephone is by the door.* 电话在门的旁边。◇ *They live by the sea.* 他们住在海边。
2 a word that shows who or what did something 由；被： *a painting by Matisse* 马蒂斯的画作 ◇ *She was caught by the police.* 她被警察抓了。
3 using or doing something 通过；使用： *I go to work* ***by train***. 我坐火车上班。◇ *He paid* ***by cheque***. 他用支票付款。◇ *You turn the computer on by pressing this button.* 按这个键启动电脑。
4 as a result of something 由于；因为： *I got on the wrong bus* ***by mistake***. 我不小心上错了公共汽车。◇ *We met* ***by chance***. 我们偶然相遇了。
5 not later than 不迟于 ➲ SAME MEANING **before** 同义词为 before: *I must finish this work by six o'clock.* 我六点钟前得把这工作做完。
6 from one side of somebody or something to the other 经过 ➲ SAME MEANING **past** 同义词为 past: *He walked by me without speaking.* 他没说一句话就从我身旁走过。
7 used for showing the measurements of an area（表示尺寸时用）： *The table is six feet by three feet* (= six feet long and three feet wide). 桌子长六英尺，宽三英尺。

by[2] /baɪ/ ***adverb*** 副词
past 经过： *She drove by without stopping.* 她开车经过时没停车。

bye 🗝 /baɪ/ (*also* 亦作 **bye-bye** /ˌbaɪ ˈbaɪ/) ***exclamation*** 感叹词
goodbye 再见： *Bye! See you tomorrow.* 再见！明天见。

byte /baɪt/ ***noun*** 名词
(*computing* 电脑) a unit of information in a computer 字节；位组；位元组

C c

C, c /siː/ *noun* 名词

1 (*plural* 复数形式 **C's, c's** /siːz/) the third letter of the English alphabet 英语字母表中的第 3 个字母: *'Car' begins with a 'C'.* * car 一词以字母 c 开头。

2 C *short way of writing* CELSIUS, CENTIGRADE * Celsius、centigrade 的缩写形式

cab /kæb/ *noun* 名词

1 *another word for* TAXI * taxi 的另一种说法

2 the part of a lorry, train or bus where the driver sits（卡车、火车或公共汽车的）驾驶室

cabbage /'kæbɪdʒ/ *noun* 名词

a large round vegetable with thick green or white leaves 卷心菜；洋白菜 ⊃ Look at Picture Dictionary page **P9**. 见彩页 P9。

cabin /'kæbɪn/ *noun* 名词

1 a small bedroom on a ship 船舱

2 the part of a plane where people sit 机舱: *the passengers in the first-class cabin* 头等舱的乘客

3 a small simple house made of wood 小木屋: *a log cabin at the edge of the lake* 湖边的原木小屋

cabinet /'kæbɪnət/ *noun* 名词

1 (*plural* 复数形式 **cabinets**) a piece of furniture that you can keep things in 贮藏柜: *a bathroom cabinet* 浴室橱柜 ◇ *a filing cabinet* (= one that you use in an office to keep documents in) 文件柜 ⊃ Look at Picture Dictionary page **P10**. 见彩页 P10。

2 the Cabinet (*no plural* 不用复数形式) a group of the most important people in the government 政府内阁

cable /'keɪbl/ *noun* 名词

1 a strong thick metal rope 金属缆绳；钢索

2 a wire that carries electricity or messages 电缆

3 (*also* 亦作 **cable television** /,keɪbl 'telɪvɪʒn/) (*also* 亦作 **cable TV** /,keɪbl tiː'viː/) (*no plural* 不用复数形式) a way of sending television programmes along wires in the ground 有线电视

cactus /'kæktəs/ *noun* 名词 (*plural* 复数形式 **cactuses** or 或 **cacti** /'kæktaɪ/)

a plant with a lot of sharp points that grows in hot dry places 仙人掌

cactus 仙人掌

cafe (*also* 亦作 **café**) /'kæfeɪ/ *noun* 名词

a place where you can buy a drink and something to eat 咖啡馆；小餐馆

cafeteria /,kæfə'tɪəriə/ *noun* 名词

a restaurant where you choose and pay for your meal and then carry it to a table. Places like factories, colleges and hospitals often have **cafeterias**. 自助食堂；自助餐厅

caffeine /'kæfiːn/ *noun* 名词 (*no plural* 不用复数形式)

the substance in coffee and tea that makes you feel more active and awake 咖啡因 ⊃ Look at **decaffeinated**. 见 decaffeinated。

cage /keɪdʒ/ *noun* 名词

a place with bars round it where animals or birds are kept so that they cannot escape 笼子

cake 0━ /keɪk/ *noun* 名词

a sweet food that you make from flour, eggs, sugar and butter and bake in the oven 蛋糕；糕饼: *a chocolate cake* 巧克力蛋糕 ◇ *Would you like a piece of cake?* 你要一块蛋糕吗？ ⊃ Look at Picture Dictionary page **P6**. 见彩页 P6。

calculate 0━ /'kælkjuleɪt/ *verb* 动词 (**calculates, calculating, calculated**)

to find an amount or a number by using mathematics 计算: *Can you calculate how much the holiday will cost?* 你能不能算一下这次度假要花多少钱？

calculation /,kælkju'leɪʃn/ *noun* 名词

finding an answer by using mathematics 计算

calculator /'kælkjuleɪtə(r)/ *noun* 名词
a small electronic instrument that you use for CALCULATING numbers 计算器
⊃ Look at Picture Dictionary page **P11**. 见彩页 P11。

calendar /'kælɪndə(r)/ *noun* 名词
a list of the days, weeks and months of one year 日历

calf /kɑːf/ *noun* 名词 (*plural* 复数形式 **calves** /kɑːvz/)
1 the back of your leg, below your knee 腓；腿肚子
2 a young cow 小牛；牛犊 ⊃ Look at the note and the picture at **cow**. 见 cow 的注释和插图。

call[1] 0̄ᵣ /kɔːl/ *verb* 动词 (**calls, calling, called** /kɔːld/)
1 to give a name to somebody or something 起名字；称呼：*They called the baby Sophie.* 他们给孩子取名索菲。
2 to speak loudly and clearly so that somebody who is far away can hear you 大声叫；喊：*'Breakfast is ready,' she called.* "吃早餐了。"她大声喊道。◇ *She called out the names of the winners.* 她大声宣读了获胜者的名字。
3 to telephone somebody 打电话：*I'll call you later.* 我稍后给你打电话。◇ *Who's calling, please?* 请问是哪位？
4 to ask somebody to come 叫（某人）来；召唤：*He was so ill that we had to call the doctor.* 他病得很重，我们只好请医生来。
5 to make a short visit 短暂到访：*I'll call in to see you this evening.* 我今晚去探望你。◇ *Can you call round later? I've got something for you.* 你待会儿过来好吗？我有些东西给你。
be called to have as a name 名字叫做；名为：*'What is your teacher called?' 'She's called Mrs Gray.'* "你们老师怎么称呼？""她叫格雷夫人。"
call somebody back to telephone somebody again 给某人回电话：*I can't talk now – I'll call you back later.* 我现在说话不方便，待会儿再给你回电话吧。
call collect *American English for* REVERSE THE CHARGES 美式英语，即 reverse the charges
call for somebody (*British* 英式英语) to go to somebody's house on your way to a place so that they can come with you 接某人（一起去某处）：*Rosie usually calls for me in the morning and we walk to school together.* 罗茜早上常常找我一起走路上学。
call something off to say that a

planned activity or event will not happen 取消：*The football match was called off because of the bad weather.* 足球比赛因天气差而取消了。⊃ SAME MEANING **cancel** 同义词为 cancel

call[2] 0̄ᵣ /kɔːl/ *noun* 名词
1 an act of using the telephone or a conversation on the telephone 电话；通话：*I got a call from James.* 詹姆斯给我打了个电话。◇ *I haven't got time to talk now – I'll give you a call later.* 我现在没空谈话，过一会儿给你打电话。
2 a loud cry or shout 呼喊；喊叫声：*a call for help* 呼救声
3 a short visit to somebody 短暂到访：*The doctor has several calls to make this morning.* 医生今天早上要出诊几次。

call box /'kɔːl bɒks/ *noun* 名词 (*plural* 复数形式 **call boxes**) *another word for* PHONE BOX * phone box 的另一种说法

calm[1] 0̄ᵣ /kɑːm/ *adjective* 形容词 (**calmer, calmest**)

> **PRONUNCIATION** 读音说明
> The word **calm** sounds like **arm**, because we don't say the letter l in this word. * calm 读音像 arm，因为 l 在这里不发音。

1 quiet, and not excited or afraid 冷静的；镇定的：*Try to keep calm – there's no danger.* 尽量保持镇静，没有什么危险。
2 without big waves 风平浪静的：*a calm sea* 平静的大海
3 without much wind 风力微弱的：*calm weather* 平和无风的天气
▶ **calmly** /'kɑːmli/ *adverb* 副词：*He spoke calmly about the accident.* 他平静地讲述了那起事故。

calm[2] /kɑːm/ *verb* 动词 (**calms, calming, calmed** /kɑːmd/)
calm down to become less afraid or excited; to make somebody less afraid or excited （使）平静；（使）镇定：*Calm down and tell me what happened.* 镇定一些，告诉我怎么回事。

calorie /'kæləri/ *noun* 名词
a unit for measuring the energy value of food. Food that has a lot of **calories** in it can make you fat. 大卡，千卡（食物的热量单位）：*a low-calorie drink* 低热量饮料

calves *plural of* CALF * calf 的复数形式

camcorder /'kæmkɔːdə(r)/ *noun* 名词
a camera that you can carry around and use for recording moving pictures and sound 便携式摄像机

A
B
C
D
E
F
G
H
I
J
K
L
M
N
O
P
Q
R
S
T
U
V
W
X
Y
Z

came *form of* COME * come 的不同形式

camel /ˈkæml/ *noun* 名词
a large animal with one or two round parts (called **humps**) on its back. **Camels** carry people and things in hot dry places. 骆驼

camel 骆驼
| hump 驼峰

camera ⊶ /ˈkæmərə/ *noun* 名词
a thing that you use for taking photographs or moving pictures 照相机；摄像机： *I need a new film for my camera.* 我的相机要换新胶卷了。

camp¹ ⊶ /kæmp/ *noun* 名词
a place where people live in tents for a short time 营地

camp² ⊶ /kæmp/ *verb* 动词 (camps, camping, camped /kæmpt/)
to live in a tent for a short time 露营： *The children camped in the garden overnight.* 孩子们在花园里露营过夜。

> 🔎 SPEAKING 表达方式说明
>
> It is more usual to say **go camping** when you mean that you are living in a tent on holiday. 度假时露营较常说 go camping： *We went camping last summer.* 去年夏天我们去露营了。

campaign¹ /kæmˈpeɪn/ *noun* 名词
a plan to do a number of things in order to get a special result（为实现某目标的）运动： *a campaign to stop people smoking* 禁烟运动

campaign² /kæmˈpeɪn/ *verb* 动词 (campaigns, campaigning, campaigned)
to take part in planned activities in order to get a special result（为实现某目标）参加运动： *The school is campaigning for new computer equipment.* 学校正展开一场运动，争取新的电脑设备。

camping ⊶ /ˈkæmpɪŋ/ *noun* 名词 (*no plural* 不用复数形式)
sleeping or spending a holiday in a tent

露营： *Camping is no fun when it rains.* 露营时碰到下雨就没意思了。

campsite /ˈkæmpsaɪt/ *noun* 名词
a place where you can stay in a tent 野营地；露营地

campus /ˈkæmpəs/ *noun* 名词 (*plural* 复数形式 **campuses**)
the area where the buildings of a college or university are（学院或大学的）校园： *the college campus* 学院校园

can¹ ⊶ /kən; kæn/ *modal verb* 情态动词

> 🔎 GRAMMAR 语法说明
>
> The negative form of **can** is **cannot** or **can't**. * can 的否定式为 cannot 或 can't： *She can't swim.* 她不会游泳。
> The past tense of **can** is **could**. * can 的过去时为 could： *We could see the sea from our hotel room.* 我们从旅馆房间可以看到大海。
> The future tense of **can** is **will be able to**. * can 的将来时为 will be able to： *You will be able to see it if you stand on this chair.* 你要是站在这张椅子上就能看到了。

1 to be able to do something; to be strong enough, clever enough, etc. to do something 能够；会： *She can speak three languages.* 她会说三种语言。◇ *Can you ski?* 你会滑雪吗？
2 to be possible or likely to happen 可能： *It can be very cold in the mountains in winter.* 冬天山里会非常冷。
3 a word that you use with verbs like 'see', 'hear', 'smell' and 'taste'（与 see、hear、smell、taste 等动词连用）： *I can smell something burning.* 我闻到有东西烧煳了。◇ *'What's that noise?' 'I can't hear anything.'* "那是什么声音？" "我什么也没听到。"
4 to be allowed to do something（表示允许）可以： *You can go now.* 你现在可以走了。◇ *Can I have some more soup, please?* 我可以再要点汤吗？◇ *The doctor says she can't go back to school yet.* 医生说她还不能回校上课。
5 a word that you use when you ask somebody to do something（提出请求）可以： *Can you tell me the time, please?* 请问现在几点了？⊃ Look at the note at **modal verb**. 见 modal verb 条的注释。

can² ⊶ /kæn/ *noun* 名词
a metal container for food or drink that keeps it fresh 金属罐： *a can of lemonade* 一罐柠檬味汽水

🔎 WHICH WORD? 词语辨析

Can or tin? 用 can 还是 tin?
In British English we usually use the
word **tin** when it contains food. 在英式
英语中，通常用 tin 表示食品罐:
a tin of soup 一罐汤
Can is used for drinks. * can 用来表示
饮料罐: *Two cans of lemonade, please.*
请来两罐柠檬味汽水。
In American English **can** is used for
both food and drink. 在美式英语中,
can 表示装食品和饮料的: *a can of
beans* 一罐豆

⮑ Look at the picture at **container**.
见 container 的插图。

canal /kəˈnæl/ *noun* 名词
a path that is made through the land and
filled with water so that boats can travel
on it 运河: *the Suez Canal* 苏伊士运河

canary /kəˈneəri/ *noun* 名词 (*plural* 复数
形式 **canaries**)
a small yellow bird that people often
keep as a pet 金丝雀

cancel /ˈkænsl/ *verb* 动词 (*British* 英式
英语 **cancels, cancelling, cancelled**
/ˈkænsld/) (*American* 美式英语 **canceling,
canceled**)
to say that a planned activity or event will
not happen 取消；撤销: *The singer was
ill, so the concert was cancelled.* 歌手病
了，所以演唱会取消了。

cancellation /ˌkænsəˈleɪʃn/ *noun* 名词
a decision that a planned activity or event
will not happen 取消: *the cancellation of
the President's visit* 总统访问的取消

cancer /ˈkænsə(r)/ *noun* 名词
a very dangerous illness that makes some
very small parts in the body (called **cells**)
grow too fast 癌症: *Smoking can cause
cancer.* 吸烟可以致癌。

candidate /ˈkændɪdət/ *noun* 名词
1 a person who wants to be chosen for
something 候选人；申请人: *There were
a lot of candidates for the job.* 有很多人
申请这个职位。
2 (*British* 英式英语) a person who is taking
an exam 考生；应试者

candle /ˈkændl/ *noun* 名词
a round stick of WAX (= solid oil or fat)
with a piece of string in the middle
(called a **wick**) that burns to give light
蜡烛

candlestick /ˈkændlstɪk/ *noun* 名词
a thing that holds a CANDLE 蜡烛台

candle 蜡烛

candle 蜡烛 —

candlestick
蜡烛台

candy 0ᴍ /ˈkændi/ *American English for*
SWEET² (1) 美式英语，即 sweet² 第 1 义

cane /keɪn/ *noun* 名词
the long central part of some plants, for
example BAMBOO (= a tall tropical plant),
that can be used for making furniture
（竹子等的）茎: *sugar cane* 甘蔗 ◇
a cane chair 藤椅

canned /kænd/ *adjective* 形容词
in a can 金属罐装的: *canned drinks*
罐装饮料

cannibal /ˈkænɪbl/ *noun* 名词
a person who eats other people 食人者

cannon /ˈkænən/ *noun* 名词
an old type of big gun that fires big stone
or metal balls （旧式）大炮

cannot 0ᴍ /ˈkænɒt/ *form of* CAN¹ * can¹
的不同形式

canoe 独木舟

canoe /kəˈnuː/ *noun* 名词
a light narrow boat for one or two people
that you move through the water using
a flat piece of wood (called a **paddle**)
独木舟；小划子

🔎 SPEAKING 表达方式说明

When you talk about using a canoe,
you often say **go canoeing**. 划独木舟常

A
B
C
D
E
F
G
H
I
J
K
L
M
N
O
P
Q
R
S
T
U
V
W
X
Y
Z

说 go canoeing: *We went canoeing on the river.* 我们到河里划独木舟了。

➲ Look at Picture Dictionary page **P14**. 见彩页 P14。

can't /kɑːnt/ *short for* CANNOT * cannot 的缩略式

canteen /kæn'tiːn/ *noun* 名词
the place like a restaurant where people eat when they are at school or work 食堂

canvas /'kænvəs/ *noun* 名词 (*no plural* 不用复数形式)
a strong heavy cloth, used for making tents, bags and sails, and for painting pictures on 帆布；画布

canyon /'kænjən/ *noun* 名词
a deep valley with steep sides of rock 峡谷

cap /kæp/ *noun* 名词
1 a soft hat with a hard curved part at the front 鸭舌帽：*a baseball cap* 棒球帽
➲ Look at Picture Dictionary page **P5**. 见彩页 P5。
2 a thing that covers the top of a bottle or tube 盖子：*Put the cap back on the bottle.* 把瓶盖盖好。

capable ⊶ /'keɪpəbl/ *adjective* 形容词
1 able to do something 有能力：*You are capable of passing the exam if you work harder.* 你只要再用功一点，考试就能及格。
2 able to do things well 能干的：*a capable student* 能力高的学生 ➲ OPPOSITE **incapable** 反义词为 incapable

capacity /kə'pæsəti/ *noun* 名词 (*plural* 复数形式 **capacities**)
how much a container or space can hold 容量；容积：*a tank with a capacity of 1 000 litres* 容量为 1 000 升的箱

cape /keɪp/ *noun* 名词
1 a piece of clothing that covers your body and your arms, but does not have separate sleeves 披肩；短斗篷
2 a high part of the land that goes out into the sea 海角；岬：*the Cape of Good Hope* 好望角

capital ⊶ /'kæpɪtl/ *noun* 名词
1 the most important city in a country, where the government is 首都：*Tokyo is the capital of Japan.* 东京是日本的首都。
2 (*no plural* 不用复数形式) (*business* 商业) a large amount of money that you use to start a business, etc. 资本；资金：*When she had enough capital, she bought a shop.* 她凑足资金后便买下了一家商店。
3 (*also* 亦作 **capital letter**) a big letter of

the alphabet, used at the beginning of sentences 大写字母：*Please fill in the form in capitals.* 请用大写字母填写表格。
◇ *Names of people and places begin with a capital letter.* 人名和地名的开头用大写字母。

capital punishment /ˌkæpɪtl 'pʌnɪʃmənt/ *noun* 名词 (*no plural* 不用复数形式)
punishment by death for serious crimes 死刑；极刑

capsize /kæp'saɪz/ *verb* 动词 (**capsizes**, **capsizing**, **capsized** /kæp'saɪzd/)
If a boat **capsizes**, it turns over in the water. 翻船；倾覆：*During the storm, the boat capsized.* 船在暴风雨中翻了。

captain /'kæptɪn/ *noun* 名词
1 the person who is in charge of a ship or an aircraft 船长；机长：*The captain sent a message by radio for help.* 船长用无线电发出求救信号。
2 the leader of a group of people 队长；首领：*He's the captain of the school basketball team.* 他是学校篮球队队长。

caption /'kæpʃn/ *noun* 名词
the words above or below a picture in a book or newspaper, that tell you about it（图片）说明文字

captive /'kæptɪv/ *noun* 名词
a person who is not free 俘房；囚徒
➲ SAME MEANING **prisoner** 同义词为 prisoner

captivity /kæp'tɪvəti/ *noun* 名词 (*no plural* 不用复数形式)
being kept in a place that you cannot leave 囚禁；关押：*Wild animals are often unhappy in captivity.* 野生动物关起来后常常闷闷不乐。

capture /'kæptʃə(r)/ *verb* 动词 (**captures**, **capturing**, **captured** /'kæptʃəd/)
to catch somebody and keep them somewhere so that they cannot leave 俘房；捕获：*The police captured the criminals.* 警方捉拿了那些罪犯。
▸ **capture** *noun* 名词 (*no plural* 不用复数形式): *the capture of the escaped prisoners* 逃犯的捕获

car ⊶ /kɑː(r)/ *noun* 名词
1 (*British* 英式英语) (*American also* 美式英语亦作 **automobile**) a vehicle with four wheels, usually with enough space for four or five people 汽车；轿车：*She travels to work by car.* 她开车上班。
➲ Look at Picture Dictionary page **P1**. 见彩页 P1。

2 *American English for* CARRIAGE (1) 美式英语，即 carriage 第 1 义

caravan 旅行拖车

caravan /ˈkærəvæn/ (*British* 英式英语) (*American* 美式英语 **trailer**) *noun* 名词
a large vehicle that is pulled by a car. You can sleep, cook, etc. in a **caravan** when you are travelling or on holiday. 旅行拖车

carbohydrate /ˌkɑːbəʊˈhaɪdreɪt/ *noun* 名词
one of the substances in food, for example sugar, that gives your body energy 碳水化合物: *Bread and rice contain carbohydrates.* 面包和米饭含有碳水化合物。

carbon /ˈkɑːbən/ *noun* 名词 (*no plural* 不用复数形式)
the chemical that coal and diamonds are made of and that is in all living things 碳

carbon dioxide /ˌkɑːbən daɪˈɒksaɪd/ *noun* 名词 (*no plural* 不用复数形式)
a gas that has no colour or smell that people and animals breathe out 二氧化碳

card 0̈ /kɑːd/ *noun* 名词
1 a piece of thick paper with writing or pictures on it 卡；卡片；贺卡: *We send birthday cards and postcards to our friends.* 我们给朋友寄生日贺卡和明信片。 ⊃ Look also at **credit card** and **phonecard**. 亦见 credit card 和 phonecard。
2 (*also* 亦作 **playing card**) one of a set of 52 cards (called a **pack of cards**) that you use to play games 纸牌；扑克牌: *Let's have a game of cards.* 我们玩纸牌吧。 ◇ *They often play cards in the evening.* 他们晚上经常打扑克。

> 🔎 WORD BUILDING 词汇扩充
>
> A pack of cards has four groups of thirteen cards, called **suits**. 一副纸牌有四种花色（suit），每种花色有十三张牌。
> Two suits are red (**hearts and diamonds**) and two are black (**clubs and spades**). 两种花色是红色的，即红桃（hearts）和方块（diamonds）；

两种是黑色的，即梅花（clubs）和黑桃（spades）。

⊃ Look at the picture at **playing card**. 见 playing card 的插图。

cardboard 0̈ /ˈkɑːdbɔːd/ *noun* 名词 (*no plural* 不用复数形式)
very thick paper that is used for making boxes, etc. 硬纸板

cardigan /ˈkɑːdɪɡən/ *noun* 名词
a piece of clothing which fastens at the front like a jacket and is usually made of wool 开襟毛衣 ⊃ Look at the note at **sweater**. 见 sweater 条的注释。

cardinal /ˈkɑːdɪnl/ *noun* 名词
an important priest in the Roman Catholic church （罗马天主教的）枢机，枢机主教

care¹ 0̈ /keə(r)/ *noun* 名词 (*no plural* 不用复数形式)
thinking about what you are doing so that you do not make a mistake or break something 小心；谨慎: *Wash these glasses with care!* 洗这些玻璃杯时要小心！
care of somebody = C/O
take care
1 to be careful 小心；当心: *Take care when you cross the road.* 过马路时要当心。
2 (*informal* 非正式) used when you are saying 'goodbye' to somebody 保重: *Bye now! Take care!* 再见！多保重！
take care of somebody or 或 **something** to look after somebody or something; to do what is necessary 照顾；照料；处理: *She is taking care of her sister's baby today.* 今天她给她姐姐看孩子。 ◇ *Don't worry about cooking the dinner – I'll take care of it.* 做饭你不用操心了，我会搞定的。

care² 0̈ /keə(r)/ *verb* 动词 (**cares**, **caring**, **cared** /keəd/)
to think that somebody or something is important 关心；关注；在乎: *The only thing he cares about is money.* 他只在乎钱。 ◇ *I don't care who wins – I'm not interested in football.* 我不在乎谁胜出。我对足球不感兴趣。

> 🔎 SPEAKING 表达方式说明
>
> It is not polite to say **I don't care**, **Who cares?** or **I couldn't care less**. 说 I don't care、Who cares? 或 I couldn't care less 是不礼貌的。
> You can say **I don't mind** instead. 可改用 I don't mind: *Would you like*

A
B
C
D
E
F
G
H
I
J
K
L
M
N
O
P
Q
R
S
T
U
V
W
X
Y
Z

tea or coffee? – I don't mind. 你想喝茶还是咖啡？——什么都行。

care for somebody to do the things for somebody that they need 照顾；照料：*After the accident, her parents cared for her until she was better.* 出了事故后，她父母照料她，直到她好些为止。

career 0ㅌ /kəˈrɪə(r)/ *noun* 名词
a job that you learn to do and then do for many years 职业；事业：*He is considering a career in teaching.* 他在考虑从事教学工作。◇ *His career was always more important to him than his family.* 以往他总认为事业比家庭重要。

careful 0ㅌ /ˈkeəfl/ *adjective* 形容词
thinking about what you are doing so that you do not make a mistake or have an accident 小心的；谨慎的：*Careful! The plate is very hot.* 小心！这盘子很烫。◇ *Be careful! There's a car coming.* 当心！有车来。◇ *He's a careful driver.* 他开车很谨慎。
▶ **carefully** /ˈkeəfəli/ *adverb* 副词：*Please listen carefully.* 请留心听。

careless 0ㅌ /ˈkeələs/ *adjective* 形容词
not thinking enough about what you are doing so that you make mistakes 粗心的；马虎的：*Careless drivers can cause accidents.* 粗心大意的司机可能导致事故。
▶ **carelessly** /ˈkeələsli/ *adverb* 副词：*She threw her coat carelessly on the floor.* 她随手把大衣扔在地上。
▶ **carelessness** /ˈkeələsnəs/ *noun* 名词 (*no plural* 不用复数形式)

caretaker /ˈkeəteɪkə(r)/ (*British* 英式英语) (*American* 美式英语 **janitor**) *noun* 名词
a person whose job is to look after a large building like a school or a block of flats 管理员；看门人

cargo /ˈkɑːɡəʊ/ *noun* 名词 (*plural* 复数形式 **cargoes**)
the things that a ship or plane carries （船运或空运的）货物：*a cargo of wheat* 一船托运的小麦

carnation /kɑːˈneɪʃn/ *noun* 名词
a pink, white or red flower with a nice smell 康乃馨

carnival /ˈkɑːnɪvl/ *noun* 名词
a public festival that takes place in the streets with music and dancing 狂欢节；嘉年华：*the Rio carnival* 里约热内卢狂欢节

carol /ˈkærəl/ *noun* 名词
a Christian song that people sing at Christmas 圣诞颂歌

carousel /ˌkærəˈsel/ *American English for* MERRY-GO-ROUND 美式英语，即 merry-go-round ➭ Look at the picture at **merry-go-round**. 见 merry-go-round 的插图。

car park /ˈkɑː pɑːk/ (*British* 英式英语) (*American* 美式英语 **parking lot**) *noun* 名词
an area or a building where you can leave your car for a time 停车场

carpenter /ˈkɑːpəntə(r)/ *noun* 名词
a person whose job is to make things from wood 木工；木匠 ➭ Look at Picture Dictionary page **P12**. 见彩页 P12。
▶ **carpentry** /ˈkɑːpəntri/ *noun* 名词 (*no plural* 不用复数形式) making things from wood 木工手艺；木工活

carpet 0ㅌ /ˈkɑːpɪt/ *noun* 名词
a soft covering for a floor that is often made of wool and is usually the same size as the floor 地毯 ➭ Look at Picture Dictionary page **P10**. 见彩页 P10。

carriage /ˈkærɪdʒ/ *noun* 名词
1 (*British* 英式英语) (*American* 美式英语 **car**) one of the parts of a train where people sit （火车的）客车厢：*The carriages at the back of the train were empty.* 火车后面的车厢都是空的。 ➭ Look at the picture at **train¹**. 见 train¹ 的插图。
2 a road vehicle, usually with four wheels, that is pulled by horses and was used in the past to carry people 马车：*The Queen rode in a carriage through the streets of the city.* 女王坐着马车穿过了市区街道。

carried *form of* CARRY ＊ carry 的不同形式

carrier bag /ˈkærɪə bæɡ/ (*also* 亦作 **carrier**) *noun* 名词
a bag made from plastic or paper that you use for carrying shopping 购物袋

carrot /ˈkærət/ *noun* 名词
a long thin orange vegetable 胡萝卜 ➭ Look at Picture Dictionary page **P9**. 见彩页 P9。

carry 0ㅌ /ˈkæri/ *verb* 动词 (**carries, carrying, carried** /ˈkærid/, **has carried**)
1 to hold something and take it to another place or keep it with you 拿；提；扛；背；携带：*He carried the suitcase to my room.* 他把行李箱拿到我的房间去。◇ *I can't carry this box – it's too heavy.* 我搬不动这个箱子，它太重了。◇ *Do the police carry guns in your country?* 你们国家的警察带枪吗？

> 🔎 **WHICH WORD?** 词语辨析
>
> **Carry** or **wear**? 用 carry 还是 wear?
> You use **wear**, not **carry**, to talk about
> having clothes on your body. 穿衣服用
> wear, 不用 carry: *She is wearing a*
> *red dress and carrying a black bag.*
> 她穿着红色连衣裙，提着黑色的包。

2 to move people or things 运送: *Special*
fast trains carry people to the city centre.
特快列车载客至市中心。
carry on to continue 继续: *Carry on*
with your work. 继续做你的工作。◇ *If you*
carry on to the end of this road, you'll see
the post office on the right. 你沿着这条路
走到尽头，就会看到邮局在右边。
carry out something to do or finish
what you have planned 实施；执行:
The bridge was closed while they
carried out the repairs. 桥于维修期间
封闭了。

cart /kɑːt/ *noun* 名词
1 (*American* 美式英语) = TROLLEY
2 a wooden vehicle with wheels that a
horse usually pulls 木制马车

carton /'kɑːtn/ *noun* 名词
a container made of very thick paper
(called **cardboard**) or plastic 硬纸盒；塑
料盒: *a carton of milk* 一盒牛奶 ◯ Look
at the picture at **container**. 见 container
的插图。

cartoon /kɑːˈtuːn/ *noun* 名词
1 a funny drawing, for example in a
newspaper 卡通；漫画
2 a film that tells a story by using moving
drawings instead of real people and
places 动画片；卡通片: *a Mickey Mouse*
cartoon 米老鼠动画片

carve /kɑːv/ *verb* 动词 (carves, carving,
carved /kɑːvd/)
1 to cut wood or stone to make a picture
or shape 雕刻；刻: *Her father carved a*
little horse for her out of wood. 她父亲用
木头给她雕了一匹小马。
2 to cut meat into thin pieces after you
have cooked it 把（熟肉）切片

case 0━ /keɪs/ *noun* 名词
1 a situation or an example of something
事例；情况: *In some cases, students had*
to wait six months for their exam results.
在某些情况下，学生得等上六个月才知道
考试结果。◇ *There were four cases of this*
disease in the school last month. 这种病上
个月在该校发生过四例。
2 a crime that the police must find an
answer to 案件: *a murder case* 谋杀案

3 a question that people in a court of law
must decide about 诉讼案: *a divorce*
case 离婚案
4 a container or cover for keeping
something in 箱子；盒子；套子: *Put the*
camera back in its case. 把照相机放回套
里。◇ *a pencil case* 铅笔盒 ◯ Look at
Picture Dictionary page **P11**. 见彩页
P11。◯ Look also at **briefcase** and
suitcase. 亦见 briefcase 和 suitcase。
in any case words that you use when
you give a second reason for something
无论如何；不管怎样 ◯ SAME MEANING
anyway 同义词为 anyway: *I don't want to*
see the film, and in any case I'm too busy.
我不想看这部电影，再说我也太忙了。
in case because something might
happen 以防；以防万一: *Take an*
umbrella in case it rains. 带把伞以防下雨。
in that case if that is the situation 既然
那样: *'There's no coffee.' 'Well, in that*
case we'll have tea.' "没咖啡了。" "哦，
那样的话，我们喝茶吧。"

cash¹ 0━ /kæʃ/ *noun* 名词 (*no plural*
不用复数形式)
money in coins and notes 现金: *Are you*
paying in cash or by cheque? 你付现金还
是支票? ◯ Look at the note at **money**.
见 money 条的注释。

cash² /kæʃ/ *verb* 动词 (cashes, cashing,
cashed /kæʃt/)
to give somebody a cheque and get
money for it 兑现（支票）: *I'd like to*
cash some traveller's cheques, please. 请给
我把旅行支票兑换成现金。

cash desk /'kæʃ desk/ *noun* 名词 (*British*
英式英语)
the place in a shop where you pay for
things 收款处；收银台

cashier /kæˈʃɪə(r)/ *noun* 名词
the person whose job is to take or give
out money in a bank, shop or hotel
出纳员；收银员

cash machine /'kæʃ məʃiːn/ (*British*
英式英语) (*British also* 英式英语亦作
Cashpoint™ /'kæʃpɔɪnt/) (*American* 美式
英语 **ATM**) *noun* 名词
a machine that you can get money from
by using a special plastic card 自动取款机

cassette /kəˈset/ *noun* 名词

> 🔎 **SPELLING** 拼写说明
>
> Remember! You spell **cassette** with **SS**
> and **TT**. 记住: cassette 拼写中有 ss 和
> tt。

a plastic box with special tape inside for

recording and playing sound or pictures
盒式磁带；卡式磁带：*a video cassette*
录像带

cassette player /kəˈset pleɪə(r)/ (*also*
亦作 **cassette recorder** /kəˈset rɪˌkɔːdə(r)/)
noun 名词
a machine that can record sound or
music on tape and play it again later
盒式磁带播放机；盒式磁带录音机

cast¹ /kɑːst/ *verb* 动词 (**casts**, **casting**, **cast**,
has cast)
to choose an actor for a particular part
in a film or a play 选派演员；分派角色：
*She always seems to be cast in the same
sort of role.* 她似乎总是被派演同一类型的
角色。
cast a spell to use magic words that
have the power to change somebody or
something 施魔法；施咒：*The witch cast
a spell on the handsome prince.* 女巫在
英俊的王子身上施了魔法。

cast² /kɑːst/ *noun* 名词
all the actors in a film, play, etc. 全体
演员：*The whole cast was excellent.* 全体
演员都很出色。

castle o─ /ˈkɑːsl/ *noun* 名词
a large old building that was built in the
past to keep people safe from attack
城堡；堡垒：*Windsor Castle* 温莎城堡

casual /ˈkæʒuəl/ *adjective* 形容词
1 showing that you are not worried about
something; relaxed 轻松的；漫不经心的：
She gave us a casual wave as she passed.
她走过时向我们轻松地挥了挥手。
2 (used about clothes) not formal（衣服）
休闲的，随便的：*I wear casual clothes
like jeans and T-shirts when I'm not at
work.* 我不上班的时候穿得比较随便，
像牛仔裤、T 恤衫之类的。
▶ **casually** /ˈkæʒuəli/ *adverb* 副词：*They
chatted casually on the phone.* 他们在电话
上闲聊。

casualty /ˈkæʒuəlti/ *noun* 名词
1 (*plural* 复数形式 **casualties**) a person
who is hurt or killed in an accident or a
war（事故或战争中的）死伤者
2 (*no plural* 不用复数形式) (*British also*
英式英语亦作 **casualty department**
/ˈkæʒuəlti dɪpɑːtmənt/) (*American* 美式
英语 **ER**, **emergency room**) the place in
a hospital where you go if you have been
hurt in an accident or if you have
suddenly become ill 急诊室：*The victims
were rushed to casualty.* 受害者被迅速送往
急诊室了。

cat 猫
whiskers 须 | tail 尾巴
claw 爪子
paw 爪
cat 猫   **kitten** 小猫

cat o─ /kæt/ *noun* 名词
1 a small animal with soft fur that people
keep as a pet 猫

> **WORD BUILDING** 词汇扩充
> A young cat is called a **kitten**. 小猫叫做
> kitten。
> A cat **purrs** when it is happy. When it
> makes a loud noise, it **miaows**. 猫惬意
> 时发出呼噜声称作 purr，大声喵喵叫称
> 作 miaow：*My cat miaows when she's
> hungry.* 我的猫饿了就喵喵叫。

2 a wild animal of the cat family 猫科
动物：*the big cats, such as tigers and lions*
像老虎、狮子等大型猫科动物

catalogue (*British* 英式英语) (*American*
美式英语 **catalog**) /ˈkætəlɒg/ *noun* 名词
a complete list of all the things that you
can buy or see somewhere 商品目录；
阅览目录：*an online catalogue* 网上商品
目录

catastrophe /kəˈtæstrəfi/ *noun* 名词
a sudden disaster that causes great
suffering or damage 灾难；灾祸：*major
catastrophes such as floods and
earthquakes* 诸如洪水、地震等大灾难

catch o─ /kætʃ/ *verb* 动词 (**catches**,
catching, **caught** /kɔːt/, **has caught**)
1 to take and hold something that is
moving 接住：*He threw the ball to
me and I caught it.* 他把球扔给我，我接
住了。
2 to find and hold somebody or
something 捕获；逮住：*They caught a
fish in the river.* 他们从河里抓到一尾鱼。
◇ *The man ran so fast that the police
couldn't catch him.* 那个人跑得太快，警察
没能抓住他。
3 to see somebody when they are doing
something wrong 当场发现：*They caught
the thief stealing the painting.* 他们撞见贼
在偷画。

4 to be early enough for a bus, train, etc. that is going to leave 赶上： *You should run if you want to catch the bus.* 你想赶上这班公共汽车就得跑了。 ➲ OPPOSITE **miss** 反义词为 miss
5 to get an illness 患上： *She caught a cold.* 她感冒了。
6 to let something be held tightly 卡住： *I caught my fingers in the door.* 我的手指被门夹住了。

catch fire to start to burn 着火；起火： *The house caught fire.* 房子着火了。

catch up, catch somebody up to do something quickly so that you are not behind others 赶上；追上： *If you miss a lesson, you can do some work at home to catch up.* 要是缺了课，在家中用点功就能赶上。 ◇ *Quick! Run after the others and catch them up.* 快！追上去，赶上大家。

category /ˈkætəɡəri/ *noun* 名词 (*plural* 复数形式 **categories**)
a group of people or things that are similar to each other 类别；种类： *The results can be divided into three main categories.* 结果可分为三大类。

caterpillar /ˈkætəpɪlə(r)/ *noun* 名词
a small animal with a long body and a lot of legs. A **caterpillar** later becomes an insect with large coloured wings (called a **butterfly**). 毛虫（蝴蝶的幼虫）

cathedral /kəˈθiːdrəl/ *noun* 名词
a big important church 大教堂；主教座堂

Catholic /ˈkæθlɪk/ = ROMAN CATHOLIC

cattle /ˈkætl/ *noun* 名词 (*plural* 用复数形式)
cows that are kept for their milk or meat（产奶或供食用的）牛： *a herd* (= a group) *of cattle* 一群牛

caught *form of* CATCH * catch 的不同形式

cauliflower /ˈkɒliflaʊə(r)/ *noun* 名词
a large vegetable with green leaves outside and a round white part in the middle 花椰菜；菜花 ➲ Look at Picture Dictionary page **P9**. 见彩页 P9。

cause¹ 0━ /kɔːz/ *noun* 名词

🔊 PRONUNCIATION 读音说明
The word **cause** sounds like **doors**.
* cause 读音像 doors。

1 a thing or person that makes something happen 原因；起因： *Bad driving is the cause of most road accidents.* 驾驶不当是造成大多数交通事故的原因。
2 something that people care about and want to help（慈善）事业，目标： *They*

gave the money to a good cause – it was used to build a new hospital. 他们为慈善事业捐款，款项用于兴建一所新医院。

cause² 0━ /kɔːz/ *verb* 动词 (**causes, causing, caused** /kɔːzd/)
to be the reason why something happens 导致；引起： *What caused the accident?* 是什么造成这起事故的？ ◇ *The fire was caused by a cigarette.* 火灾是由一根香烟引起的。

caution /ˈkɔːʃn/ *noun* 名词 (*no plural* 不用复数形式)
great care, because of possible danger 谨慎；慎重： *Caution! Wet floor.* 当心！地面湿滑。

cautious /ˈkɔːʃəs/ *adjective* 形容词
careful because there may be danger 谨慎的；慎重的： *He has always been cautious about driving at night.* 他晚上开车一直都很小心。

▶ **cautiously** /ˈkɔːʃəsli/ *adverb* 副词： *He cautiously pushed open the door and looked into the room.* 他小心翼翼地推开门，往房间里看。

cave /keɪv/ *noun* 名词
a large hole in the side of a mountain or under the ground 山洞；地洞： *Thousands of years ago, people lived in caves.* 上万年前，人类住在山洞里。

CD 0━ /ˌsiː ˈdiː/ *noun* 名词 (*also* 亦作 **disc**)
a small, round piece of hard plastic on which you can record sound or store information 光盘；光碟；激光唱片

CD player /ˌsiː ˈdiː pleɪə(r)/ *noun* 名词
a machine that you use to play CDs 激光唱片播放机

CD-ROM /ˌsiː diː ˈrɒm/ *noun* 名词
a CD on which you can store large amounts of information, sound and pictures, to use on a computer 只读光盘 ➲ CD-ROM is short for 'compact disc read-only memory'. * CD-ROM 是 compact disc read-only memory 的缩略式。

cease /siːs/ *verb* 动词 (**ceases, ceasing, ceased** /siːst/) (*formal* 正式)
to stop 停止；终止： *Fighting in the area has now ceased.* 该地区的战斗现已停止。

ceiling 0━ /ˈsiːlɪŋ/ *noun* 名词

🔊 PRONUNCIATION 读音说明
The word **ceiling** sounds like **feeling**.
* ceiling 读音像 feeling。

the top part of the inside of a room 天花板

🔍 SPELLING 拼写说明

IE or EI? 是 ie 还是 ei?
When the sound is /iː/ (which rhymes with 'be'), the rule is **I before E, except after C**, so **ceiling** is spelled with **EI**.
当读音为 /iː/（与 be 押韵）时，拼写规则是："i 在 e 前面，除非 c 在前"。因此，ceiling 拼写中作 ei。

celebrate ⇌ /ˈselɪbreɪt/ *verb* 动词 (**celebrates, celebrating, celebrated**)
to do something to show that you are happy for a special reason or because it is a special day 庆祝；庆贺： *If you pass your exams, we'll have a party to celebrate.* 你要是考试及格，我们开个派对庆祝一下。◊ *Grandma celebrated her 90th birthday last week.* 奶奶上周庆祝了 90 大寿。

celebration ⇌ /ˌselɪˈbreɪʃn/ *noun* 名词
a time when you enjoy yourself because you have a special reason to be happy 庆祝活动；庆典： *birthday celebrations* 生日的庆祝活动

celery /ˈseləri/ *noun* 名词 (*no plural* 不用复数形式)
a vegetable with long green and white sticks that can be eaten without being cooked 芹菜： *a stick of celery* 一根芹菜 ⊃ Look at Picture Dictionary page **P9**. 见彩页 P9。

cell ⇌ /sel/ *noun* 名词
1 a small room for one or more prisoners in a prison or police station 牢房
2 the smallest part of any living thing. All plants and animals are made up of **cells**. 细胞： *red blood cells* 红细胞

cellar /ˈselə(r)/ *noun* 名词
a room in the part of a building that is under the ground 地窖；地下室 ⊃ Look at Picture Dictionary page **P10**. 见彩页 P10。

cello 大提琴

cello /ˈtʃeləʊ/ *noun* 名词 (*plural* 复数形式 **cellos**)
a large wooden musical instrument with strings. You sit down to play it and hold it between your knees. 大提琴

cellphone /ˈselfəʊn/ *American English for* MOBILE PHONE 美式英语，即 mobile phone

Celsius /ˈselsiəs/ (*also* 亦作 **centigrade**) *noun* 名词 (*no plural* 不用复数形式) (*abbr.* 缩略式 C)
a way of measuring temperature. Water freezes at 0° **Celsius** and boils at 100° **Celsius**. 摄氏度： *The temperature tonight will fall to 2°C* (= We say 'two degrees Celsius'). 今晚的气温将降至 2 摄氏度。⊃ Look also at **Fahrenheit**. 亦见 Fahrenheit。

cement /sɪˈment/ *noun* 名词 (*no plural* 不用复数形式)
a grey powder that becomes hard like stone when you mix it with water and leave it to dry. **Cement** is used in building for sticking bricks or stones together or for making very hard surfaces. 水泥

cemetery /ˈsemətri/ *noun* 名词 (*plural* 复数形式 **cemeteries**)
an area of ground where dead people are put under the earth 墓地；公墓

cent ⇌ /sent/ *noun* 名词
a small coin that people use in many countries around the world. There are 100 **cents** in a dollar or a euro. 分（货币单位）

center *American English for* CENTRE 美式英语，即 centre

centigrade /ˈsentɪɡreɪd/ *another word for* CELSIUS * Celsius 的另一种说法

centiliter *American English for* CENTILITRE 美式英语，即 centilitre

centilitre (*British* 英式英语) (*American* 美式英语 **centiliter**) /ˈsentiliːtə(r)/ *noun* 名词 (*abbr.* 缩略式 cl)
a measure of liquid. There are 100 **centilitres** in a litre. 厘升，公勺（容量单位；100 厘升等于 1 升）： *250 cl* * 250 厘升

centimeter *American English for* CENTIMETRE 美式英语，即 centimetre

centimetre ⇌ (*British* 英式英语) (*American* 美式英语 **centimeter**) /ˈsentimiːtə(r)/ *noun* 名词 (*abbr.* 缩略式 cm)
a measure of length. There are 100 **centimetres** in a metre. 厘米；公分

central 0— /ˈsentrəl/ *adjective* 形容词
in the middle part of something 在中心
的; 中央的: *central London* 伦敦市中心

central heating /ˌsentrəl ˈhiːtɪŋ/ *noun*
名词 (*no plural* 不用复数形式)
a system for heating a building from one
main point. Air or water is heated and
carried by pipes to all parts of the
building. 中央供暖系统

centre 0— (*British* 英式英语) (*American*
美式英语 **center**) /ˈsentə(r)/ *noun* 名词
1 the part in the middle of something
中心; 中央; 中部: *the city centre* 市中心
◇ *The flower has a yellow centre with white
petals.* 这种花中间是黄的, 花瓣是白的。
2 a place where people come to do a
particular activity 中心（进行特定活动的
地方）: *a shopping centre* 购物中心 ◇
Our town has a new sports centre. 我们
镇上有个新的体育中心。

century 0— /ˈsentʃəri/ *noun* 名词
(*plural* 复数形式 **centuries**)
a period of 100 years 世纪: *People have
been making wine in this area for
centuries.* 几百年来, 人们一直在这地区
酿制葡萄酒。 ◇ *We are living at the
beginning of the twenty-first century.*
我们生活在 21 世纪初。

cereal /ˈsɪəriəl/ *noun* 名词
1 (*plural* 复数形式 **cereals**) a plant that
farmers grow so that we can eat the grain
(= the seed) 谷物: *Wheat and oats are
cereals.* 小麦和燕麦都是谷物。
2 (*no plural* 不用复数形式) a food made
from grain, that you can eat for breakfast
with milk 谷类食物: *a bowl of cereal
with milk* 一碗加奶的麦片粥 ➾ Look at
Picture Dictionary page **P7**. 见彩页 P7。

ceremony 0— /ˈserəməni/ *noun* 名词
(*plural* 复数形式 **ceremonies**)
a formal public or religious event 典礼;
仪式: *the opening ceremony of the
Olympic Games* 奥运会开幕式 ◇ *a wedding
ceremony* 婚礼

certain 0— /ˈsɜːtn/ *adjective* 形容词
1 sure about something; without any
doubt 确定; 肯定: *I'm certain that I've
seen her before.* 我肯定以前见过她。 ◇ *Are
you certain about that?* 你对那件事确定
吗? ➾ OPPOSITE **uncertain** 反义词为
uncertain
2 used for talking about a particular thing
or person without saying what or who
they are（不指明人或事物）某个, 某些:
*Do you want the work to be finished by a
certain date?* 你想这项工作在某个日期之

前完成吗? ◇ *It's cheaper to telephone at
certain times of the day.* 在一天的某些
时段打电话比较便宜。

for certain without any doubt 肯定;
无疑: *I don't know for certain where she
is.* 我说不准她在哪里。

make certain to check something so
that you are sure about it 确保; 弄清楚:
*Please make certain that the window is
closed before you leave.* 走前请务必把窗户
关好。

certainly 0— /ˈsɜːtnli/ *adverb* 副词
1 without any doubt 肯定; 无疑 ➾ SAME
MEANING **definitely** 同义词为 definitely:
*She is certainly the best swimmer in the
team.* 她肯定是队最好的游泳选手。
2 used when answering questions to
mean 'of course'（用于回答问题）当然:
*'Will you open the door for me, please?'
'Certainly.'* "你可以帮我开开门吗?"
"当然可以。" ◇ *'Are you going to
apologize?' 'Certainly not!'* "你会
道歉吗?" "当然不会!"

certificate 0— /səˈtɪfɪkət/ *noun* 名词
an important piece of paper that shows
that something is true 证书; 证明: *Your
birth certificate shows when and where
you were born.* 出生证明上写着出生日期
和地点。

chains 链

link 链节
clasp 扣环
chain 链子

chain 链条

chain¹ 0— /tʃeɪn/ *noun* 名词
a line of metal rings that are joined
together 链子; 链条: *Round her neck she
wore a gold chain.* 她脖子上戴了条金链
子。 ◇ *My bicycle chain is broken.* 我自行车
的链条断了。 ➾ Look at the picture at
bicycle. 见 bicycle 的插图。

chain² /tʃeɪn/ *verb* 动词 (**chains, chaining,
chained** /tʃeɪnd/)
to attach somebody or something to a
place with a **chain** 用链子拴住: *The dog*

*was **chained to** a tree.* 狗被链子拴到了树上。

chair 0ᵐ /tʃeə(r)/ *noun* 名词
1 a piece of furniture for one person to sit on, with four legs, a seat and a back 椅子: *a table and four chairs* 一张桌子和四把椅子 ⊃ Look at Picture Dictionary page **P10**. 见彩页 **P10**。
2 = CHAIRPERSON

chairperson /'tʃeəpɜːsn/ *noun* 名词 (*also* 亦作 **chair, chairman** /'tʃeəmən/, **chairwoman** /'tʃeəwʊmən/)
a person who controls a meeting（会议的）主持人，主席

chalk /tʃɔːk/ *noun* 名词 (*no plural* 不用复数形式)
1 a type of soft white rock 白垩
2 a white or coloured stick of **chalk** that you use for writing or drawing 粉笔: *The teacher picked up a piece of chalk.* 老师捡起了一支粉笔。

challenge¹ 0ᵐ /'tʃælɪndʒ/ *noun* 名词
1 a new or difficult thing that makes you try hard 挑战；艰巨任务: *Climbing the mountain will be a real challenge.* 登这座山可真是个挑战。
2 an invitation to fight or play a game against somebody 挑战书；参赛邀请

challenge² /'tʃælɪndʒ/ *verb* 动词 (**challenges, challenging, challenged** /'tʃælɪndʒd/)
1 to refuse to accept a set of rules; to say that you think somebody or something is wrong 拒绝接受；提出质疑；挑战: *She does not like anyone challenging her authority.* 她不喜欢任何人挑战她的权威。
2 to ask somebody to play a game with you or fight with you to see who wins 发出挑战: *The boxer **challenged** the world champion **to** a fight.* 这名拳击手向世界冠军下了战书，要求决一高下。

champagne /ʃæm'peɪn/ *noun* 名词 (*no plural* 不用复数形式)
a French white wine with a lot of bubbles 香槟酒

champion /'tʃæmpiən/ *noun* 名词
a person who is the best at a sport or game 冠军: *a chess champion* 国际象棋冠军 ◇ *the world champion* 世界冠军

championship /'tʃæmpiənʃɪp/ *noun* 名词
a competition to find the best player or team in a sport or game 锦标赛: *Our team won the championship this year.* 我们队赢得了今年的锦标赛。

chance 0ᵐ /tʃɑːns/ *noun* 名词
1 (*no plural* 不用复数形式) a possibility that something may happen 可能性: *There's no chance that she'll come now.* 现在她不可能来了。 ◇ *She has a good **chance of** becoming team captain.* 她很有可能成为队长。 ◇ *He doesn't **stand** (= have) a chance of passing the exam.* 他不可能通过考试。
2 (*plural* 复数形式 **chances**) a time when you can do something 机会；机遇 ⊃ SAME MEANING **opportunity** 同义词为 opportunity: *It was their last **chance to** escape.* 那是他们逃走的最后机会。 ◇ *Be quiet and give her **a chance** to explain.* 安静些，给她一个解释的机会吧。
3 (*no plural* 不用复数形式) when something happens that you cannot control or that you have not planned 偶然 ⊃ SAME MEANING **luck** 同义词为 luck: *We must plan this carefully. I don't want to **leave** anything **to chance**.* 我们必须周密地策划这件事，我不想有任何意外。 ◇ *We met **by chance** at the station.* 我们在车站偶然相遇。

no chance (*informal* 非正式) used to say that there is no possibility of something happening 不可能: *'Perhaps your mum will give you the money.' 'No chance!'* "或许你妈妈会给你钱。""不可能！"

take a chance to do something when it is possible that something bad may happen because of it 冒险: *We may lose money but we'll just have to take that chance.* 我们可能会损失金钱，但也得碰碰运气。

change¹ 0ᵐ /tʃeɪndʒ/ *verb* 动词 (**changes, changing, changed** /tʃeɪndʒd/)
1 to become different 起变化: *She has changed a lot since the last time I saw her – she looks much older.* 自从我上次见到她以来，她变了很多，看上去老了许多。 ◇ *Water **changes into** ice when it gets very cold.* 天气很冷时水会结冰。
2 to make something different 改变: *At this restaurant they change the menu every week.* 这家餐馆每周换菜单。
3 to put or take something in place of another thing 替换；换成: *My new watch didn't work, so I took it back to the shop and changed it.* 我的新手表坏了，便拿回商店去换了一只。 ◇ *I went to the bank to change my euros into dollars.* 我到银行把欧元换成美元。 ◇ *Can you change a £5 note please? I need some pound coins.* 请你换开 5 英镑的钞票好吗？我需要一些英镑硬币。

4 (*also* 亦作 get changed) to put on different clothes 换衣服: *I need to change before I go out.* 我出门前得换换衣服。◇ *You need to get changed for football.* 去踢足球你得换衣服。

5 to get off a train or bus and get on another one 换乘；转乘: *I have to change trains at Kings Cross.* 我得在国王十字车站换车。

change² 0━/tʃeɪndʒ/ *noun* 名词
1 (*plural* 复数形式 changes) when something becomes different 改变；变化: *The new government has made a lot of changes.* 新政府进行了很多改革。◇ *There has been a change in the weather.* 天气变了。
2 (*no plural* 不用复数形式) the money that you get back if you pay more than the amount something costs 找头；找零: *If a newspaper costs 60p and you pay with a pound coin, you will get 40p change.* 假如一份报纸 60 便士，你付一英镑，应找回 40 便士。
3 (*no plural* 不用复数形式) small pieces of money; coins 零钱；硬币: *I haven't got any change.* 我没有零钱。

for a change because you want something different 变化一下: *Today we had lunch in a restaurant for a change.* 今天我们换换口味，在餐馆吃了午餐。

channel /'tʃænl/ *noun* 名词
1 a TV station 电视台；频道: *Which channel is the film on?* 这部电影在哪个频道播出？
2 a long narrow place where water can go 水道；海峡: *the English Channel* (= the sea between England and France) 英吉利海峡

chaos /'keɪɒs/ *noun* 名词 (*no plural* 不用复数形式)
when everything is confused and nothing is organized 混乱；杂乱: *The house was in chaos after the party.* 聚会后，房子里乱七八糟的。

chapel /'tʃæpl/ *noun* 名词
a room or a small church where Christians go to speak to God (to pray) 小教堂

chapter /'tʃæptə(r)/ *noun* 名词
one of the parts of a book （书的）章，回: *Turn to Chapter 4.* 翻到第四章。

character 0━/'kærəktə(r)/ *noun* 名词
1 (*no plural* 不用复数形式) the qualities that make somebody or something different from other people or things 性格；特质: *He has a strong character.* 他个性很强。◇ *The new factory will*

change the character of the village. 新工厂将改变村子的风貌。
2 (*plural* 复数形式 characters) a person in a book, play or film 人物；角色: *Homer Simpson is a famous cartoon character.* 霍默·辛普森是很有名的卡通人物。

characteristic 0━/ˌkærəktə'rɪstɪk/ *noun* 名词
a quality that somebody or something has 特征；特点: *personal characteristics such as age, height and weight* 诸如年龄、身高、体重等个人特征

charge¹ 0━/tʃɑːdʒ/ *noun* 名词
1 the money that you must pay for something 收费；要价: *There is a charge of £50 for the use of the hall.* 使用礼堂的收费是 50 英镑。◇ *We deliver free of charge.* 我们免费送货。⊃ Look at the note at **price**. 见 price 条的注释。
2 when the police say that somebody has done something wrong 指控；控告: *a murder charge* 谋杀指控

be in charge of somebody or 或 **something** to take care of or be responsible for somebody or something 照管；负责: *Tim is in charge of his baby brother while his mother is out.* 蒂姆在母亲外出时负责照看幼小的弟弟。

charge² 0━/tʃɑːdʒ/ *verb* 动词 (**charges**, **charging**, **charged** /tʃɑːdʒd/)
1 to ask somebody to pay a certain price for something 收取费用: *The garage charged me £200 for the repairs.* 汽车修理厂收了我 200 英镑修理费。
2 to say that somebody has done something wrong 控告；起诉: *The police have charged him with murder.* 警方控告他犯谋杀罪。
3 to run quickly and with a lot of force 猛冲；冲锋: *The bull charged.* 公牛向前猛冲。◇ *The children charged into the room.* 孩子们冲进了房间。

charity 0━/'tʃærəti/ *noun* 名词
1 (*plural* 复数形式 charities) an organization that collects money to help people who need it 慈善组织: *The Red Cross is a charity.* 红十字会是慈善机构。◇ *They give a lot of money to charity.* 他们向慈善机构捐很多钱。
2 (*no plural* 不用复数形式) being kind and helping other people 仁爱；善心

charm¹ /tʃɑːm/ *noun* 名词
1 (*no plural* 不用复数形式) a quality that makes people like you 魅力；吸引力: *He was a man of great charm.* 他是个魅力非凡的男人。
2 (*plural* 复数形式 charms) a small thing

that you wear because you think it will bring good luck 吉祥小饰物: *She wears a chain with a lucky charm on it.* 她戴的链子上挂着个吉祥小饰物。

charm² /tʃɑːm/ *verb* 动词 (charms, charming, charmed /tʃɑːmd/)
to make somebody like you 吸引; 迷住: *The baby charmed everybody with her smile.* 宝宝以她的微笑迷倒了所有人。

charming /ˈtʃɑːmɪŋ/ *adjective* 形容词
very pleasant or attractive 有吸引力的; 迷人的: *a charming little village* 令人着迷的小村庄

chart /tʃɑːt/ *noun* 名词
1 a drawing that gives information about something 图表: *a temperature chart* 温度图
2 a map of the sea or the sky 航海图; 星象图

chase ⊶ /tʃeɪs/ *verb* 动词 (chases, chasing, chased /tʃeɪst/)
to run behind somebody or something and try to catch them 追赶; 追逐; 追捕: *The dog chased the cat around the garden.* 狗在花园里四处追着猫。◇ *The police **chased after** the thief but he escaped.* 警方追捕那名窃贼, 但最后还是让他跑了。
▶ **chase** *noun* 名词: *The film includes an exciting car chase.* 这部电影有一场刺激的汽车追逐。

chat¹ /tʃæt/ *verb* 动词 (chats, chatting, chatted)
to talk in a friendly, informal way to somebody 闲聊; 聊天: *We chatted on the phone for a few minutes.* 我们在电话上聊了几分钟。

chat² /tʃæt/ *noun* 名词
a friendly talk 闲聊; 聊天: *Let's have a chat about it later.* 我们稍后聊一聊这件事吧。

chat room /ˈtʃæt ruːm/ *noun* 名词
an area on the Internet where you can join in a discussion with other people 网络聊天室

chatter /ˈtʃætə(r)/ *verb* 动词 (chatters, chattering, chattered /ˈtʃætəd/)
to talk quickly about things that are not very important 叽里呱啦地说话; 喋喋不休; 唠叨: *Stop chattering and finish your work.* 别唠叨了, 把工作做完吧。

cheap ⊶ /tʃiːp/ *adjective* 形容词 (cheaper, cheapest)
costing little money 便宜的; 廉价的: *That restaurant is very good and quite*

cheap. 那家餐馆价廉物美。◇ *Computers are getting cheaper all the time.* 电脑一向越来越便宜。 ⊃ OPPOSITE **expensive** 反义词为 expensive

cheat ⊶ /tʃiːt/ *verb* 动词 (cheats, cheating, cheated)
to do something that is not honest or fair 欺骗: *She cheated in the exam – she copied her friend's work.* 她考试作弊, 抄了朋友的卷子。
▶ **cheat** *noun* 名词 a person who **cheats** 骗子: *That man's a liar and a cheat.* 那人谎话连篇, 是个骗子。

check¹ ⊶ /tʃek/ *verb* 动词 (checks, checking, checked /tʃekt/)
1 to look at something to see that it is right, good or safe 检查; 核查; 核对; 核实: *Do the sums and then use a calculator to check your answers.* 先算一算, 再用计算器核对答案。◇ *Before driving off, I checked the oil and water.* 在驾车离开之前, 我检查了汽油和水。◇ *Check that all the windows are closed before you leave.* 离开前检查一下所有的窗户是否都关好。
2 American English for TICK¹ (2) 美式英语, 即 tick¹ 第 2 义
check in to tell the person at the desk in a hotel or an airport that you have arrived 登记入住旅馆; 办理登机手续: *I have to check in an hour before my flight.* 我要在飞机起飞前一小时办理登机手续。
check out to pay your bill and leave a hotel 结账离开旅馆

check² ⊶ /tʃek/ *noun* 名词
1 a look to see that everything is right, good or safe 检查; 核查; 核对; 核实: *They do regular safety **checks** on all their products.* 他们定期给所有产品做安全检查。◇ *a security check* 安全检查
2 a pattern of squares; one of the squares in a pattern 方格图案; 格子: *a shirt with blue and red checks* 蓝红格子衬衫
3 American English for CHEQUE 美式英语, 即 cheque
4 American English for BILL (1) 美式英语, 即 bill 第 1 义
5 (also 亦作 **check mark** /ˈtʃek mɑːk/) American English for TICK² (1) 美式英语, 即 tick² 第 1 义

checkbook American English for CHEQUEBOOK 美式英语, 即 chequebook

checked /tʃekt/ *adjective* 形容词
with a pattern of squares 有格子图案的: *a checked shirt* 格子衬衫

checked 格子图案的

checkers /'tʃekəz/ *American English for* DRAUGHTS 美式英语，即 draughts

checkout /'tʃekaʊt/ *noun* 名词
the place in a large shop where you pay for things 付款处；收款台：*a supermarket checkout* 超市付款处

check-up /'tʃek ʌp/ *noun* 名词
a general examination by a doctor to make sure that you are healthy 体格检查；体检：*You should visit your dentist for a check-up twice a year.* 你应该每年去牙医那里检查两次。

cheek 0̄ /tʃiːk/ *noun* 名词
1 (*plural* 复数形式 cheeks) one of the two soft parts of your face below your eyes 面颊；脸颊 ⊃ Look at Picture Dictionary page **P4**. 见彩页 **P4**。
2 (*no plural* 不用复数形式) (*British* 英式英语) talk or behaviour that people think is annoying, rude or not showing respect 放肆；恬不知耻：*What a cheek! Somebody has eaten my sandwiches.* 太讨厌了！有人竟把我的三明治给吃了。

cheeky /'tʃiːki/ *adjective* 形容词 (cheekier, cheekiest) (*British* 英式英语)
not polite and not showing respect 放肆的；无礼的 ⊃ SAME MEANING **rude** 同义词为 rude：*Don't be so cheeky!* 别这样放肆！◇ *She was punished for being cheeky to a teacher.* 她对老师无礼，因而受到了惩罚。

cheer¹ /tʃɪə(r)/ *noun* 名词
a loud shout that shows that you are pleased 欢呼声；喝彩声：*The crowd gave a loud cheer as the singer came onto the stage.* 歌手一上台，观众就大声欢呼起来。

cheer² /tʃɪə(r)/ *verb* 动词 (cheers, cheering, cheered /tʃɪəd/)
to shout to show that you like something or to encourage somebody 欢呼；喝彩：*The crowd cheered loudly when the players*

ran onto the pitch. 球员跑上球场时，观众高声欢呼。

cheer up, cheer somebody up to become or to make somebody happier（使）高兴起来；（使）振奋起来：*Cheer up! You'll feel better soon.* 振作点！你很快会好起来的。◇ *We gave Julie some flowers to cheer her up.* 我们给朱莉送花，想让她开心点。

cheerful /'tʃɪəfl/ *adjective* 形容词
happy 快乐的；高兴的：*a cheerful smile* 愉快的微笑 ◇ *You don't look very cheerful today. What's the matter?* 你今天看上去不很高兴，怎么了？

cheers /tʃɪəz/ *exclamation* 感叹词 (*informal* 非正式)
1 a word that people say to each other as they hold up their glasses to drink（用于祝酒）干杯：*'Cheers,' she said, raising her glass.* "干杯！"她举起酒杯说道。
2 (*British* 英式英语) goodbye 再见
3 (*British* 英式英语) thank you 谢谢

cheese 0̄ /tʃiːz/ *noun* 名词
a yellow or white food made from milk 奶酪；干酪：*bread and cheese* 面包和奶酪 ⊃ Look at Picture Dictionary page **P6**. 见彩页 **P6**。

cheeseburger /'tʃiːzbɜːgə(r)/ *noun* 名词
a HAMBURGER with cheese in it 干酪汉堡包

chef /ʃef/ *noun* 名词
a professional cook, especially the head cook in a hotel or restaurant 职业厨师；主厨 ⊃ Look at Picture Dictionary page **P12**. 见彩页 **P12**。

chemical¹ 0̄ /'kemɪkl/ *adjective* 形容词
connected with chemistry or chemicals 化学的；化学品的：*a chemical experiment* 化学实验

chemical² 0̄ /'kemɪkl/ *noun* 名词
a solid or liquid substance that is used or produced in a chemical process 化学品；化学制品

chemist /'kemɪst/ *noun* 名词
1 (*British* 英式英语) (*British and American also* 英式和美式英语亦作 pharmacist) a person who prepares and sells medicines 药剂师
2 chemist's (*British* 英式英语) (*American* 美式英语 drugstore) a shop that sells medicines, soap and other personal goods 药房；药店：*I'm just going to the chemist's to get my tablets.* 我正要去药店买药片。◇ Look at Picture Dictionary page **P13**. 见彩页 **P13**。
3 a person who studies chemistry 化学家

chemistry /'kemɪstri/ *noun* 名词
(*no plural* 不用复数形式)
the science that studies gases, liquids and solids to find out what they are and how they behave 化学

cheque (*British* 英式英语) (*American* 美式英语 **check**) /tʃek/ *noun* 名词

🔑 **PRONUNCIATION** 读音说明
The word **cheque** sounds like **neck**.
* cheque 读音像 neck。

a piece of paper from a bank that you can write on and use to pay for things 支票: *I gave him a cheque for £50.* 我给了他一张 50 英镑的支票。◇ *Can I pay by cheque?* 我付支票行吗?

chequebook (*British* 英式英语) (*American* 美式英语 **checkbook**) /'tʃekbʊk/ *noun* 名词
a book of CHEQUES 支票簿 ⊃ Look at the picture at **money**. 见 money 的插图。

cherry /'tʃeri/ *noun* 名词 (*plural* 复数形式 **cherries**)
a small round red or black fruit that has a large seed inside it (called a **stone**) 樱桃 ⊃ Look at Picture Dictionary page **P8**. 见彩页 P8。

chess /tʃes/ *noun* 名词 (*no plural* 不用复数形式)
a game that two people play on a board with black and white squares on it (called a **chessboard**). Each player has sixteen pieces that can be moved around the board in different ways. 国际象棋；西洋棋

chest /tʃest/ *noun* 名词
1 the top part of the front of your body 胸部 ⊃ Look at Picture Dictionary page **P4**. 见彩页 P4。
2 a large strong box with a lid that you use for storing or carrying things 大箱子

chest of drawers /ˌtʃest əv 'drɔːz/ *noun* 名词 (*plural* 复数形式 **chests of drawers**)
a large piece of furniture with parts that you can pull out (called **drawers**). A **chest of drawers** is usually used for keeping clothes in. 抽屉式衣橱；五斗橱 ⊃ Look at Picture Dictionary page **P10**. 见彩页 P10。

chew /tʃuː/ *verb* 动词 (**chews**, **chewing**, **chewed** /tʃuːd/)
to use your teeth to break up food in your mouth when you are eating 咀嚼: *You should chew your food thoroughly.* 食物应充分咀嚼。

chewing gum /'tʃuːɪŋ ɡʌm/ *noun* 名词
(*no plural* 不用复数形式)
a sweet sticky substance that you can CHEW for a long time 口香糖

chick /tʃɪk/ *noun* 名词
a baby bird, especially a baby chicken 雏鸟；小鸡: *a hen with her chicks* 母鸡和它的小鸡 ⊃ Look at the picture at **shell**. 见 shell 的插图。

chicken /'tʃɪkɪn/ *noun* 名词
1 (*plural* 复数形式 **chickens**) a bird that people often keep for its eggs and its meat 鸡 ⊃ Look at Picture Dictionary page **P2**. 见彩页 P2。

🔑 **WORD BUILDING** 词汇扩充
A female **chicken** is called a **hen** and a male chicken is called a **cock**. A young chicken is a **chick**. 母鸡叫做 hen，公鸡叫做 cock，小鸡叫做 chick。

2 (*no plural* 不用复数形式) the meat from this bird 鸡肉: *roast chicken* 烤鸡 ⊃ Look at Picture Dictionary page **P7**. 见彩页 P7。

chickenpox /'tʃɪkɪnpɒks/ *noun* 名词
(*no plural* 不用复数形式)
a disease, especially of children. When you have **chickenpox** you feel very hot and get red spots on your skin that make you want to scratch. 水痘

chief¹ /tʃiːf/ *adjective* 形容词
most important 最重要的；主要的；首要的: *Bad driving is one of the chief causes of road accidents.* 驾驶不当是造成道路交通事故的主要原因之一。

chief² /tʃiːf/ *noun* 名词
the leader or ruler of a group of people 首领；领导人: *the chief of an African tribe* 非洲一个部落的首领 ◇ *police chiefs* 警察局长

chiefly /'tʃiːfli/ *adverb* 副词
not completely, but mostly 主要地；首要地 ⊃ SAME MEANING **mainly** 同义词为 mainly: *His success was due chiefly to hard work.* 他的成功主要是由于勤奋。

child /tʃaɪld/ *noun* 名词 (*plural* 复数形式 **children** /'tʃɪldrən/)
1 a young boy or girl 儿童；孩子: *There are 30 children in the class.* 班上有 30 个孩子。
2 a daughter or son 女儿；儿子: *Have you got any children?* 你有孩子吗? ◇ *One of her children got married last year.* 她的一个孩子去年结婚了。

childhood /'tʃaɪldhʊd/ *noun* 名词
(*no plural* 不用复数形式)
the time when you are a child 童年；

孩童时期: *She had a happy childhood.* 她的童年很快乐。

childish /'tʃaɪldɪʃ/ *adjective* 形容词
like a child 幼稚的；孩子气的 ➲ SAME MEANING **immature** 同义词为 immature: *Don't be so childish! It's only a game.* 别那么幼稚！这只是游戏。

childminder /'tʃaɪldmaɪndə(r)/ *noun* 名词 (*British* 英式英语)
a person whose job is to look after a child while his or her parents are at work （孩子父母上班时）受雇照看孩子的保姆

chilli (*British* 英式英语) (*American* 美式英语 chili) /'tʃɪli/ *noun* 名词 (*plural* 复数形式 **chillies** or 或 **chilies**)
a small green or red vegetable that has a very strong hot taste 辣椒 *chilli powder* 辣椒粉

chilly /'tʃɪli/ *adjective* 形容词 (**chillier**, **chilliest**)
cold 寒冷的: *a chilly morning* 寒冷的早晨

chime /tʃaɪm/ *verb* 动词 (**chimes**, **chiming**, **chimed** /tʃaɪmd/)
to make the sound that a bell makes 鸣响；敲响: *The clock chimed midnight.* 时钟响过午夜十二点。

chimney /'tʃɪmni/ *noun* 名词 (*plural* 复数形式 **chimneys**)
a large pipe over a fire that lets smoke go outside into the air 烟囱 ➲ Look at Picture Dictionary page **P10**. 见彩页 P10。

chimpanzee 黑猩猩

chimpanzee /ˌtʃɪmpæn'ziː/ *noun* 名词
an African animal like a large MONKEY with no tail 黑猩猩

chin o╾ /tʃɪn/ *noun* 名词
the part of your face below your mouth 颏；下巴 ➲ Look at Picture Dictionary page **P4**. 见彩页 P4。

china /'tʃaɪnə/ *noun* 名词 (*no plural* 不用复数形式)
a hard white material made from earth, or things like plates and cups that are made from this 瓷；瓷器: *a china cup* 瓷杯

chip¹ /tʃɪp/ *noun* 名词
1 (*British* 英式英语) (*British and American also* 英式和美式英语亦作 **French fry, fry**)
a thin piece of potato cooked in hot oil 炸薯条: *We had fish and chips for lunch.* 我们午餐吃了炸鱼薯条。 ➲ Look at Picture Dictionary page **P7**. 见彩页 P7。
2 *American English for* CRISP² 美式英语，即 crisp²
3 the place where a small piece of wood, stone or other material has broken off a larger piece （小块木头、石头等的）缺口，碴口，豁口: *This dish has a chip in it.* 这碟子有个缺口。
4 a very small thing inside a computer that makes it work 芯片 ➲ SAME MEANING **microchip** 同义词为 microchip

chip² /tʃɪp/ *verb* 动词 (**chips**, **chipping**, **chipped** /tʃɪpt/)
to break a small piece off something hard 碰掉；弄缺: *I chipped a cup.* 我把茶杯碰了个缺口。

chirp¹ /tʃɜːp/ *verb* 动词 (**chirps**, **chirping**, **chirped** /tʃɜːpt/)
to make the short high sound that small birds make （小鸟）吱喳叫，叽叽叫

chirp² /tʃɜːp/ *noun* 名词
the short high sound that a small bird makes 吱喳的鸟叫声；叽叽的鸟叫声

chocolate 巧克力

chocolate o╾ /'tʃɒklət/ *noun* 名词
1 (*no plural* 不用复数形式) a dark brown sweet food that is made from the seeds (called **cocoa beans**) that grow on trees in hot countries 巧克力: *Do you like chocolate?* 你喜欢巧克力吗？ ◇ *a bar of chocolate* 一条巧克力 ◇ *a chocolate cake* 巧克力蛋糕
2 (*plural* 复数形式 **chocolates**) a sweet

A
B
C
D
E
F
G
H
I
J
K
L
M
N
O
P
Q
R
S
T
U
V
W
X
Y
Z

made of **chocolate** 巧克力糖： *a box of chocolates* 一盒巧克力

choice ☞/tʃɔɪs/ *noun* 名词
1 (*plural* 复数形式 choices) the act of choosing between two or more people or things 选择；抉择： *You **made** the right **choice**.* 你作出了正确的选择。
2 (*no plural* 不用复数形式) the right or chance to choose 选择权；选择机会： *We **have** no **choice**. We have to leave.* 我们别无选择，只好离开。
3 (*plural* 复数形式 choices) the things that you can choose from 供选择的东西： *The cinema has **a choice** of six different films.* 这家影院有六部不同的影片可供选择。

choir /ˈkwaɪə(r)/ *noun* 名词
a group of people who sing together 合唱团；唱诗班： *a school choir* 学校合唱团

choke /tʃəʊk/ *verb* 动词 (chokes, choking, choked /tʃəʊkt/)
to not be able to breathe because something is in your throat 哽噎；窒息： *He was **choking on** a fish bone.* 他让鱼刺卡住了。

choose ☞/tʃuːz/ *verb* 动词 (chooses, choosing, chose/tʃəʊz/, has chosen /ˈtʃəʊzn/)
to decide which thing or person you want 挑选；选择： *She chose the chocolate cake.* 她挑了巧克力蛋糕。 ◇ *Mike had to choose between getting a job or going to college.* 迈克得在找工作和上大学之间作出选择。 ⊃ The noun is **choice**. 名词为 choice。

chop 切

chop[1] /tʃɒp/ *verb* 动词 (chops, chopping, chopped /tʃɒpt/)
to cut something into pieces with a knife, etc. 砍；切；剁： *Chop the meat up into small pieces.* 把肉切碎。 ◇ *We chopped*

some wood for the fire. 我们砍了些柴生火。

chop[2] /tʃɒp/ *noun* 名词
a thick slice of meat with a piece of bone in it（有骨的）肉排： *a lamb chop* 羊排

chopsticks /ˈtʃɒpstɪks/ *noun* 名词 (*plural* 用复数形式)
a pair of thin sticks that are used for eating with, especially in some Asian countries 筷子

chord /kɔːd/ *noun* 名词
two or more musical notes that are played at the same time 和弦

chorus /ˈkɔːrəs/ *noun* 名词 (*plural* 复数形式 choruses)
a part of a song that you repeat 副歌

chose *form of* CHOOSE * choose 的不同形式

chosen *form of* CHOOSE * choose 的不同形式

Christ /kraɪst/ = JESUS

christen /ˈkrɪsn/ *verb* 动词 (christens, christening, christened /ˈkrɪsnd/)
to give a name to a baby and make him or her a member of the Christian church in a special ceremony（基督教）施洗时起名字，施洗 ⊃ Look also at **baptize**. 亦见 baptize。

christening /ˈkrɪsnɪŋ/ *noun* 名词
the ceremony when a baby is CHRISTENED（基督教）洗礼

Christian /ˈkrɪstʃən/ *noun* 名词
a person who believes in Jesus Christ and what He taught 基督徒
▶ **Christian** *adjective* 形容词： *the Christian church* 基督教教会

Christianity /ˌkrɪstiˈænəti/ *noun* 名词 (*no plural* 不用复数形式)
the religion that follows what Jesus Christ taught 基督教

Christian name /ˈkrɪstʃən neɪm/ *noun* 名词 (*plural* 复数形式 Christian names) (*British* 英式英语)
a person's first name, not their family name（人的）名字；圣名；教名： *Her family name is Baker and her Christian name is Anna.* 她姓贝克，名安娜。

Christmas /ˈkrɪsməs/ *noun* 名词
the period of time around and including 25 December, when Christians remember the birth of Christ 圣诞节期间；圣诞节： *Merry Christmas!* 圣诞快乐！ ◇ *Where are you spending Christmas this year?* 今年你们在哪儿过圣诞？

🔍 **CULTURE** 文化资料补充

Christmas is a very important festival in Britain and the US. 圣诞节是英国和美国一个非常重要的节日。
The day before **Christmas Day** is called **Christmas Eve**, and the day after is called **Boxing Day**. 圣诞节（Christmas Day）前一天叫做 Christmas Eve，后一天叫做 Boxing Day。
Many children believe that **Father Christmas** (also called **Santa Claus**) visits them at Christmas to bring presents. 很多孩子相信圣诞老人（Father Christmas 或 Santa Claus）在圣诞节会到访并送礼物。
People send **Christmas cards** and give presents to their friends and family. Many people go to church at Christmas and sing **carols**. 人们会给亲友寄圣诞贺卡（Christmas card）和送礼物，也有很多人在圣诞节去教堂唱圣诞颂歌（carol）。
We put special trees (called **Christmas trees**) in our homes and decorate them with coloured lights and other pretty things. 我们会在家里摆放圣诞树（Christmas tree），挂上彩灯和其他漂亮的饰物来装饰。
On **Christmas Day** we eat **Christmas dinner**, a special meal with roast turkey (= a large bird) and **Christmas pudding** (= a kind of cake made with dried fruit). 在圣诞节当天我们会吃圣诞大餐（Christmas dinner），通常有烤火鸡和圣诞布丁（Christmas pudding）。
Christmas is sometimes written informally as **Xmas**. 有时 Christmas 用非正式的写法 Xmas。

chubby /'tʃʌbi/ *adjective* 形容词
slightly fat in a pleasant way 胖乎乎的；圆圆胖胖的：*a baby with chubby cheeks* 脸蛋胖乎乎的宝宝

chunk /tʃʌŋk/ *noun* 名词
a large piece of something 大块；厚块：*a chunk of cheese* 一大块奶酪

church ⚬₋ /tʃɜːtʃ/ *noun* 名词 (*plural* 复数形式 **churches**)
a building where Christians go to speak to God (to **pray**) 教堂：*They **go to church** every Sunday.* 他们每个星期天都到教堂做礼拜。

🔍 **GRAMMAR** 语法说明

When we talk about going to a ceremony (a **service**) in a church we

say **in church**, **to church** or **at church** without 'a' or 'the'. 表示去教堂做礼拜（service）用 in church、to church 或 at church，church 前不加 a 或 the：*Was Mr Poole at church today?* 普尔先生今天去教堂做礼拜了吗?
We use **a** or **the** to talk about the building. 表示教堂本身时，church 前加 a 或 the：*the church where we got married* 我们结婚的教堂 ◇ *a historic church* 有历史意义的教堂

churchyard /'tʃɜːtʃjɑːd/ *noun* 名词
a piece of land around a church, often used for burying dead people in 教堂庭院；教堂墓地 ⊃ Look also at **cemetery** and **graveyard**. 亦见 cemetery 和 graveyard。

cigar /sɪ'gɑː(r)/ *noun* 名词
a thick roll of dried leaves (called tobacco) that some people smoke. **Cigars** are larger than cigarettes. 雪茄烟

cigarette ⚬₋ /ˌsɪgə'ret/ *noun* 名词
a thin tube of white paper filled with dried leaves (called tobacco), that some people smoke 香烟：*He smokes two packets of cigarettes a day.* 他一天抽两包烟。

cinema ⚬₋ /'sɪnəmə/ (*British* 英式英语) (*American* 美式英语 **movie theater**) *noun* 名词
a place where you go to see a film 电影院：*Let's go to the cinema tonight.* 咱们今晚去看电影吧。

🔍 **CULTURE** 文化资料补充

In American English, you use **movie theater** to talk about the building where you see a film but **the movies** when you are talking about going to see a film there. 在美式英语中，movie theater 表示去看电影，用 the movies 则表示去看电影：*There are five movie theaters in this town.* 这个镇上有五家电影院。◇ *Let's go to the movies this evening.* 咱们今晚去看电影吧。

circle ⚬₋ /'sɜːkl/ *noun* 名词
a round shape; a ring 圆形；圆圈：*There are 360 degrees in a circle.* 一个圆有 360 度。⊃ Look at the picture on the next page. 见下页的插图。

circular /'sɜːkjələ(r)/ *adjective* 形容词
with the shape of a circle 圆形的 ⊃ SAME MEANING **round** 同义词为 round：*a circular table* 圆桌

A
B
C
D
E
F
G
H
I
J
K
L
M
N
O
P
Q
R
S
T
U
V
W
X
Y
Z

circle 圆

|semicircle 半圆

diameter 直径 — circumference 圆周

radius 半径

circulate /'sɜːkjəleɪt/ *verb* 动词
(circulates, circulating, circulated)
to move around 循环；环流： *Blood
circulates round the body.* 血液在体内
循环。

circulation /ˌsɜːkjə'leɪʃn/ *noun* 名词
(*no plural* 不用复数形式)
the movement of blood around the body
血液循环

circumference /sə'kʌmfərəns/ *noun*
名词
the distance around a circle 圆周；周长
⊃ Look at the picture at **circle**. 见 circle 的
插图。

circumstances /'sɜːkəmstənsɪz/ *noun*
名词 (*plural* 用复数形式)
the facts that are true in a particular
situation 情况；情形；环境
in or 或 **under no circumstances**
never; not for any reason 无论如何都不；
不论怎样都不： *Under no circumstances
should you go out alone at night.* 无论如何
你都不要晚上一个人出去。
in or 或 **under the circumstances** as
the result of a particular situation 在这种
情况下： *It's not an ideal solution, but it's
the best we can do in the circumstances.*
这并非最理想的解决办法，但在目前这种情
况下我们也只能这么做了。

circus /'sɜːkəs/ *noun* 名词 (*plural* 复数形式
circuses)
a show in a big tent, with a performance
by a group of people and trained animals
马戏表演

citizen /'sɪtɪzn/ *noun* 名词
a person who belongs to a country or
a city 公民；市民： *She became an
American citizen in 1995.* 她在 1995 年
成了美国公民。

citrus fruit /'sɪtrəs fruːt/ *noun* 名词
a fruit such as an orange or a lemon 柑橘
类果实

city ০⃥ /'sɪti/ *noun* 名词 (*plural* 复数形式
cities)
a big and important town 城市： *the city
of Rome* 罗马市 ◇ *the city centre* 市中心

civil /'sɪvl/ *adjective* 形容词
1 connected with the people who live in
a country 国民的；平民的： *civil disorder*
(= involving groups of people within the
same country) 民众骚乱
2 connected with the state, not with the
army or the Church 政府的，国家的（非
军事或宗教的）： *a civil wedding* (= not
a religious one) 非宗教仪式的婚礼

civilian /sə'vɪliən/ *noun* 名词
a person who does not belong to a
military organization or the police 平民；
老百姓

civilization /ˌsɪvəlaɪ'zeɪʃn/ *noun* 名词
the way people live together in a society
with laws, education and a government
文明： *the ancient civilizations of Greece
and Rome* 希腊和罗马的古代文明

civilized /'sɪvəlaɪzd/ *adjective* 形容词
(used about a society) well-organized and
having a high level of social and cultural
development （社会）文明的，开化的

civil rights /ˌsɪvl 'raɪts/ *noun* 名词 (*plural*
用复数形式)
a person's legal rights to freedom and to
equal treatment in society 民权；公民权

civil servant /ˌsɪvl 'sɜːvənt/ *noun* 名词
a person who works in THE CIVIL SERVICE
公务员

the civil service /ðə ˌsɪvl 'sɜːvɪs/ *noun*
名词 (*no plural* 不用复数形式)
the government departments in a
country, and the people who work for
them 政府部门；（统称）公务员

civil war /ˌsɪvl 'wɔː(r)/ *noun* 名词
a war between groups of people who live
in the same country 内战

cl *short way of writing* CENTILITRE
* centilitre 的缩写形式

claim¹ /kleɪm/ *verb* 动词 (claims,
claiming, claimed /kleɪmd/)
1 to say that something is true 宣称；
声称： *He claims that he did the work
without help.* 他声称是他独自一人完成了
这项工作。
2 to ask for something because it is yours
索要；认领： *If nobody claims the camera
you found, you can have it.* 你拾到的相机
要是没人认领，你就可以拿去。

claim² /kleɪm/ *noun* 名词
1 saying that something is true 宣称；
声明： *Nobody believed his claim that
he had found the money on the street.*

他说那些钱是在街上捡到的，但没有人相信他的话。

2 something that you ask for because you think you have a right to it 要求应得的东西：*The workers are **making a claim** for better pay.* 工人要求加薪。

clang /klæŋ/ *verb* 动词 (**clangs, clanging, clanged** /klæŋd/)
to make a loud sound, like metal when you hit it with something 哐当作响；叮当作响：*The iron gates **clanged shut**.* 铁门哐的一声关上了。

clap[1] /klæp/ *verb* 动词 (**claps, clapping, clapped** /klæpt/)
to hit your hands together to make a noise, usually to show that you like something 拍手；鼓掌：*At the end of the concert the audience clapped loudly.* 音乐会结束时，观众热烈鼓掌。

clap[2] *noun* 名词
the sound that you make when you hit your hands together 拍手声；掌声

clarinet 单簧管

clarinet /ˌklærəˈnet/ *noun* 名词
a musical instrument made of wood with holes in it. You play it by blowing into it. 单簧管；黑管

clash[1] /klæʃ/ *noun* 名词 (*plural* 复数形式 **clashes**)
1 a fight or a serious argument 打斗；争执；冲突：*a clash between police and demonstrators* 警方与示威者之间的冲突
2 a loud noise that you make by hitting two metal objects together （金属）撞击声

clash[2] /klæʃ/ *verb* 动词 (**clashes, clashing, clashed** /klæʃt/)
1 to fight or argue about something 打斗；争执；起冲突：*Police **clashed with** demonstrators outside the Town Hall.* 警方与示威者在市政厅外发生了冲突。

2 to happen at the same time 时间上互相抵触；时间上相冲突：*The match **clashed with** my swimming lesson, so I couldn't watch it.* 那场比赛和我的游泳课时间有冲突，所以我没看成。
3 If colours **clash**, they do not look nice together. （颜色）不协调，不搭配：*That red tie **clashes with** your shirt.* 那条红领带与你的衬衫不相配。

clasp[1] /klɑːsp/ *verb* 动词 (**clasps, clasping, clasped** /klɑːspt/)
to hold somebody or something tightly 抱紧；握紧；抓紧 ➡ SAME MEANING **grip** 同义词为 grip：*He clasped the child in his arms.* 他把孩子紧紧地抱在怀里。

clasp[2] /klɑːsp/ *noun* 名词
a metal object that fastens or holds something together （金属）扣子，搭扣：*the clasp on a necklace* 项链扣环 ➡ Look at the picture at **chain**[1]. 见 chain[1] 的插图。

class 0→ /klɑːs/ *noun* 名词 (*plural* 复数形式 **classes**)
1 a group of children or students who learn together 班；班级：*There is a new girl in my class.* 我们班新来了个女生。 ◇ *The whole class passed the exam.* 全班同学都通过考试了。
2 the time when you learn something with a teacher 课；上课 ➡ SAME MEANING **lesson** 同义词为 lesson：*Classes begin at nine o'clock.* 九点钟开始上课。 ◇ *You mustn't eat **in class** (= during the lesson).* 上课时不能吃东西。
3 a group of people or things that are the same in some way 种类；类别：*There are many different classes of animals.* 动物有很多不同的种类。
4 how good, comfortable, etc. something is 等级；级别：*It costs more to travel **first class**.* 头等舱票价较高。

classic /ˈklæsɪk/ *noun* 名词
a book, film or piece of music that is so good that it is still popular many years after it was written or made 经典作品；名著：*'Alice in Wonderland' is a children's classic.* 《艾丽丝漫游奇境记》是儿童文学名著。

classical /ˈklæsɪkl/ *adjective* 形容词
1 in a style that people have used for a long time because they think it is good 古典的；传统的；经典的 ➡ SAME MEANING **traditional** 同义词为 traditional：*classical dance* 传统舞蹈 ➡ OPPOSITE **modern** 反义词为 modern
2 connected with ancient Greece or Rome 古希腊的；古罗马的：*classical Greek architecture* 古希腊式建筑

3 Classical music is serious and important. （音乐）古典的: *I prefer pop music to classical music.* 我喜欢流行音乐胜于古典音乐。

classmate /'klɑːsmeɪt/ *noun* 名词
a person who is in the same class as you at school or college 同班同学

classroom /'klɑːsruːm/ *noun* 名词
a room where you have lessons in a school or college 教室 ● Look at Picture Dictionary page **P11.** 见彩页 P11。

clatter /'klætə(r)/ *verb* 动词 (**clatters, clattering, clattered** /'klætəd/)
to make the loud noise of hard things hitting each other （硬物相碰）发出响亮的撞击声: *The knives and forks clattered to the floor.* 刀叉掉在地上当啷作响。
▶ **clatter** *noun* 名词 (*no plural* 不用复数形式): *the clatter of horses' hoofs* 嗒嗒的马蹄声

clause /klɔːz/ *noun* 名词
(*grammar* 语法) a part of a sentence that has a verb in it 从句；分句: *The sentence 'After we had finished eating, we went out.' contains two clauses.* * After we had finished eating, we went out 这个句子中有两个分句。

claw /klɔː/ *noun* 名词
one of the hard pointed parts on the feet of some animals and birds 爪；脚爪: *Cats have sharp claws.* 猫有尖爪。 ● Look at the pictures at **bird, cat, crab** and **lion.** 见 bird、cat、crab 和 lion 的插图。

clay /kleɪ/ *noun* 名词 (*no plural* 不用复数形式)
a kind of heavy earth that becomes hard when it is dry 黏土；陶土: *clay pots* 陶罐

clean¹ ⊶ /kliːn/ *adjective* 形容词
(**cleaner, cleanest**)
not dirty 清洁的；干净的: *clean clothes* 干净的衣服 ◇ *Are your hands clean?* 你的手干净吗? ● OPPOSITE **dirty** 反义词为 dirty

clean² ⊶ /kliːn/ *verb* 动词 (**cleans, cleaning, cleaned** /kliːnd/)
to remove the dirt or marks from something; to make something clean 清洁；打扫；弄干净: *Sam helped his mother to clean the kitchen.* 萨姆帮母亲把厨房打扫干净了。 ◇ *Don't forget to clean your teeth before you go to bed.* 别忘了睡前刷牙。
▶ **clean** *noun* 名词 (*no plural* 不用复数形式): *The car needs a clean.* 汽车该清洗了。

---

cleaner /'kliːnə(r)/ *noun* 名词
a person whose job is to clean people's houses or other buildings 清洁工: *an office cleaner* 办公室清洁工

clear¹ ⊶ /klɪə(r)/ *adjective* 形容词
(**clearer, clearest**)
1 easy to see, hear or understand 清晰的；清楚的: *She spoke in a loud, clear voice.* 她以嘹亮而清楚的声音说话。 ◇ *These instructions aren't very clear.* 这些指示不太清晰。 ◇ *It's clear that he's not happy.* 他显然不开心。 ◇ *I made it clear to him that he was not welcome here any more.* 我给他讲清楚了，他在这里不再受欢迎。
2 easy to see through 透明的；清澈的: *clear glass* 透明的玻璃
3 free from marks 无痕的；无斑的: *a clear sky* (= without clouds) 晴朗的天空 ◇ *clear skin* (= without spots) 光洁的皮肤
4 with nothing blocking the way 无障碍的；畅通无阻的: *Most roads are now clear of snow.* 大多数路上的积雪已经清除。

clear² ⊶ /klɪə(r)/ *verb* 动词 (**clears, clearing, cleared** /klɪəd/)
1 to remove things from a place because you do not want or need them there 清除；清理: *They cleared the snow from the path.* 他们清扫了路上的积雪。 ◇ *When you have finished your meal, clear the table* (= take away the dirty plates). 吃完饭后把桌子收拾干净。
2 to become **clear** 变得清楚（或清澈、晴朗等）: *It rained in the morning, but in the afternoon the sky cleared.* 早上下过雨，但下午天就放晴了。

clear off (*informal* 非正式) to go away 走开；滚开: *He got angry and told them to clear off.* 他很生气，叫他们都走开。

clear something out to make something empty and clean by removing things or throwing things away that you do not want 把⋯清空；清理

clear up, clear something up to make a place clean and tidy 清理；整理： *She helped me to clear up after the party.* 聚会结束后，她帮我一起收拾。◇ *Clear up your own mess!* 你搞得一团糟，你自己来收拾！

clearly 0➔ /'klɪəli/ *adverb* 副词
1 in a way that is easy to see, hear or understand 清楚地；清晰地： *Please speak louder – I can't hear you very clearly.* 请说话大声点——我听不大清楚。◇ *The notes explain very clearly what you have to do.* 你要做什么，笔记上写得很清楚。
2 without any doubt 毫无疑问地；显然 ⊃ SAME MEANING **obviously** 同义词为 obviously： *She is clearly very intelligent.* 她显然很聪明。

clerk /klɑːk/ *noun* 名词
1 a person whose job is to do written work or look after accounts in an office, a bank or shop 文书；文员
2 *American English* for SHOP ASSISTANT 美式英语，即 shop assistant

clever 0➔ /'klevə(r)/ *adjective* 形容词 (**cleverer, cleverest**)
quick at learning and understanding things 聪明的；聪颖的 ⊃ SAME MEANING **intelligent** 同义词为 intelligent： *a clever student* 聪明的学生 ⊃ OPPOSITE **stupid** 反义词为 stupid
▸ **cleverly** /'klevəli/ *adverb* 副词： *The book is cleverly written.* 这本书写得很好。

click¹ /klɪk/ *verb* 动词 (**clicks, clicking, clicked** /klɪkt/)
1 to make a short sharp sound 发出咔嗒声： *The door clicked shut.* 门咔嗒一声关上了。
2 (*computing* 电脑) to press one of the buttons on a computer mouse 点击（鼠标）： *To open a file, click on the menu.* 要打开文件，点击选单。◇ *Click the OK button to start.* 点击 OK 来启动。⊃ Look at **double-click**. 见 double-click。

click² /klɪk/ *noun* 名词
1 a short sharp sound 咔嗒声： *the click of a switch* 开关的咔嗒声
2 (*computing* 电脑) the act of pressing a button on a computer mouse （鼠标的）点击： *You can do this with a click of the mouse.* 可以点击鼠标来完成。

client /'klaɪənt/ *noun* 名词
a person who pays another person, for example a lawyer, for help or advice 客户；委托人

cliff 悬崖

cliff /klɪf/ *noun* 名词
the high steep side of a hill by the sea （濒海的）悬崖，峭壁

climate 0➔ /'klaɪmət/ *noun* 名词
the normal weather conditions of a place 气候： *Coffee will not grow in a cold climate.* 咖啡不能在寒冷的地方生长。

climax /'klaɪmæks/ *noun* 名词 (*plural* 复数形式 **climaxes**)
the most important part of something or of a period of time 高潮；顶点： *Winning an Oscar was the climax of his career.* 赢得奥斯卡奖是他事业的顶峰。

climb 0➔ /klaɪm/ *verb* 动词 (**climbs, climbing, climbed** /klaɪmd/)

🔍 PRONUNCIATION 读音说明
The word **climb** sounds like **time**.
* climb 读音像 time。

1 to go up towards the top of something 爬；攀登： *They climbed the mountain.* 他们爬那座山了。◇ *The cat climbed to the top of the tree.* 猫爬上了树顶。
2 to move to or from a place when it is not easy to do it 吃力地移动： *The boys climbed through a hole in the fence.* 那些男孩从篱笆上的洞爬了过去。
3 to move to a higher place 爬升；上升： *The road climbs steeply.* 这条路陡直而上。
▸ **climb** *noun* 名词 (*no plural* 不用复数形式)： *It was a long climb to the top of the mountain.* 攀到山顶要很长时间。

climber /'klaɪmə(r)/ *noun* 名词
a person who climbs mountains or rocks as a sport 登山者；登山运动员： *a rock climber* 攀岩者

climbing /'klaɪmɪŋ/ *noun* 名词 (*no plural* 不用复数形式)
the sport of climbing mountains or rocks 登山运动；攀岩运动： *They usually go*

A
B
C
D
E
F
G
H
I
J
K
L
M
N
O
P
Q
R
S
T
U
V
W
X
Y
Z

climbing in their holidays. 他们通常在假日时去登山。

cling /klɪŋ/ *verb* 动词 (clings, clinging, clung /klʌŋ/, has clung)
to hold tightly or stick to somebody or something 抓紧；紧握；粘住：*The girl was crying and clinging to her mother.* 那个女孩哭喊着，紧紧搂住她母亲。◇ *His wet clothes clung to his body.* 他一身湿透的衣服紧贴着身体。

clinic /'klɪnɪk/ *noun* 名词
a place where you can go to get special help from a doctor 诊所；门诊部

clip¹ /klɪp/ *noun* 名词
a small piece of metal or plastic for holding things together or in place 夹子；回形针：*a hair clip* 发夹 ⇨ Look at **paper clip**. 见 paper clip。

clip² /klɪp/ *verb* 动词 (clips, clipping, clipped /klɪpt/)
to join something to another thing with a CLIP（用夹子）夹住；（用别针）别住：*Clip the photo to the letter.* 把照片别在信上。◇ *Do your earrings clip on?* 你的耳环是夹式的吗？

cloak /kləʊk/ *noun* 名词
a long loose coat that does not have separate sleeves 披风；斗篷

cloakroom /'kləʊkruːm/ *noun* 名词
a room in a public building where you can leave your coat or bag 衣帽间

clock ⊶ /klɒk/ *noun* 名词
a thing that shows you what time it is 钟；时钟：*an alarm clock* 闹钟

> 🔎 **WORD BUILDING** 词汇扩充
> A small clock that you wear on your wrist is called a **watch**. 手表叫做 watch。
> You say that a clock or watch is **fast** if it shows a time that is later than the real time. You say that it is **slow** if it shows a time that is earlier than the real time. 钟表走快了说 fast，走慢了说 slow。

⇨ Look at the picture at **watch²**. 见 watch² 的插图。

clockwise /'klɒkwaɪz/ *adjective, adverb* 形容词，副词
in the direction that the hands of a clock move 顺时针方向（的）：*Turn the handle clockwise.* 沿顺时针方向转动把手。⇨ OPPOSITE **anticlockwise** (*British*), **counterclockwise** (*American*) 反义词为 anticlockwise（英式英语）和 counterclockwise（美式英语）

close¹ ⊶ /kləʊz/ *verb* 动词 (closes, closing, closed /kləʊzd/)

> 🔎 **PRONUNCIATION** 读音说明
> When the word **close** is a verb, it has a /z/ sound as in **grows** or **nose**. * close 作动词时尾音是 /z/，发音像 grows 或 nose。
> When the word **close** is an adjective, it has an /s/ sound as in **dose**. * close 作形容词时尾音是 /s/，发音像 dose。

1 to shut 关；关闭；合上：*Please close the window.* 请把窗户关上。◇ *Close your eyes!* 闭上眼睛！◇ *The door closed quietly.* 门轻轻地关上了。
2 to stop being open, so that people cannot go there 关门；停止开放：*What time does the bank close?* 银行什么时候关门？⇨ OPPOSITE **open** 反义词为 open

close down, close something down
to stop all business at a shop, factory, etc. 倒闭；（使）停业：*The shop closed down when the owner died.* 店主死后商店就停业了。◇ *Health inspectors have closed the restaurant down.* 卫生检查人员已经让这家餐馆停业。

close² ⊶ /kləʊs/ *adjective, adverb* 形容词，副词 (closer, closest)
1 near 接近；靠近：*We live close to the station.* 我们住的地方离车站很近。◇ *The photographer asked us to stand closer together* (= with less space between us). 摄影师叫我们靠拢点站。
2 If people are **close**, they know each other well and like each other very much. 亲密的；密切的：*I'm very close to my sister.* 我和我妹妹很近。◇ *John and I are close friends.* 我和约翰是亲密的朋友。
3 (used about a competition or race) only won by a small amount（竞赛或赛跑）实力相当的，以微弱优势获胜的：*a close match* 难分高下的比赛
4 careful 仔细的；细致的：*Take a close look at this picture.* 仔细看看这张照片。
▶ **closely** /'kləʊsli/ *adverb* 副词：*Paul entered, closely followed by Mike.* 保罗走了进来，后面紧跟着迈克。◇ *We watched her closely* (= carefully). 我们密切注视她。

closed ⊶ /kləʊzd/ *adjective* 形容词
not open 关闭；不开放 ⇨ SAME MEANING **shut** 同义词为 shut：*The shops are closed on Sundays.* 商店星期天都不开门。◇ *Keep your eyes closed.* 闭着眼睛。⇨ OPPOSITE **open** 反义词为 open

closet /'klɒzɪt/ *noun* 名词 (*American* 美式英语)
a space in a wall with a door that reaches

the ground, used for storing clothes, shoes, etc. 贮藏室；壁橱: *a walk-in closet* 步入式衣帽间

cloth /klɒθ/ *noun* 名词
1 (*no plural* 不用复数形式) material made of wool, cotton, etc. that you use for making clothes and other things 布；布料

> *SPEAKING* 表达方式说明
> **Material** is the word we usually use. * material 是常用词: *Gloria bought some material to make a dress.* 格洛丽亚买了些布来做连衣裙。

2 a piece of **cloth** that you use for a special job（有特定用途的）布: *Do you have a cloth I can use to wipe the floor with?* 你有没有布可以让我擦地板? ⊃ Look at **tablecloth**. 见 tablecloth。

clothes /kləʊðz/ *noun* 名词 (*plural* 用复数形式)
things like trousers, shirts and coats that you wear to cover your body 衣服；服装: *She was wearing new clothes.* 她穿着新衣服。 ◊ *Take off those wet clothes.* 把那些湿衣服脱下来吧。

> *SPEAKING* 表达方式说明
> If you want to describe one thing that you wear, you call it **an item of clothing** or **a piece of clothing**. 指一件衣服用 an item of clothing 或 a piece of clothing: *A kilt is an item of clothing worn in Scotland.* 格呢短褶裙是苏格兰的一种服装。

⊃ Look at Picture Dictionary page **P5**. 见彩页 P5。

clothing /ˈkləʊðɪŋ/ *noun* 名词 (*no plural* 不用复数形式)
clothes, especially a particular type of clothes 衣服；（尤指某种）服装: *You will need waterproof clothing.* 你将需要穿防水服。

> *WHICH WORD?* 词语辨析
> **Clothing** is more formal than **clothes**. * clothing 比 clothes 正式。

cloud /klaʊd/ *noun* 名词
1 a white or grey shape in the sky that is made of small drops of water 云；云朵: *Look at those dark clouds. It's going to rain.* 看那些乌云，要下雨了。 ⊃ Look at Picture Dictionary page **P16**. 见彩页 P16。
2 a large collection of dust or smoke that looks like a **cloud**（灰尘或烟形成的）云状物: *clouds of smoke* 一团团的烟

cloudy /ˈklaʊdi/ *adjective* 形容词 (**cloudier, cloudiest**)
If the weather is **cloudy**, the sky is full of clouds. 多云的: *a cloudy day* 阴天

clove /kləʊv/ *noun* 名词
1 the small dried flower of a tree that grows in hot countries, used as a spice in cooking. **Cloves** look like small nails. 丁香（热带树木的干花，形似小钉子，用作调味品）
2 one of the small separate sections of GARLIC (= a vegetable of the onion family with a strong taste and smell, used in cooking) 蒜瓣: *Crush two cloves of garlic.* 捣碎两瓣蒜。

clown /klaʊn/ *noun* 名词
a person who wears funny clothes and a big red nose and does silly things to make people laugh 小丑

club¹ /klʌb/ *noun* 名词
1 a group of people who do something together, or the place where they meet 俱乐部: *I belong to the golf club.* 我是高尔夫球俱乐部的。
2 (*also* 亦作 **nightclub**) a place where people, especially young people, go and listen to music, dance, etc. 夜总会
3 a heavy stick with one thick end, used as a weapon 击棍（一头粗一头细，用作武器）
4 a long thin stick that is used for hitting a ball when playing GOLF (= a game played on grass in which you hit a small ball into a number of holes) 高尔夫球棒 ⊃ Look at the note at **bat¹**. 见 bat¹ 条的注释。
5 clubs (*plural* 用复数形式) the group of playing cards (called a **suit**) that have the shape ♣ on them（纸牌）梅花: *the three of clubs* 梅花三 ⊃ Look at the picture at **playing card**. 见 playing card 的插图。

club² /klʌb/ *verb* 动词 (**clubs, clubbing, clubbed** /klʌbd/)
club together to give money so that a group of people can buy something 凑份子；分摊费用: *We all clubbed together to buy him a leaving present.* 我们大家凑份子给他买了份赠别礼。

go clubbing (*British* 英式英语) (*informal* 非正式) to go out to places where there is music and dancing (called **nightclubs**) 去夜总会消遣: *They go clubbing every Saturday night.* 他们每周六晚上都去泡夜总会。

clue /kluː/ *noun* 名词
something that helps to find the answer

A
B
C
D
E
F
G
H
I
J
K
L
M
N
O
P
Q
R
S
T
U
V
W
X
Y
Z

to a problem, or to know the truth 线索; 提示: *The police are looking for clues to help them find the missing man.* 警方正在寻找能帮助他们找到失踪者的线索。 ⊃ Look at the picture at **crossword**. 见 crossword 的插图。

not have a clue (*informal* 非正式) to know nothing about something 一无所知: *'What's his name?' 'I haven't a clue.'* "他叫什么名字？" "我完全不知道。"

clumsy /ˈklʌmzi/ *adjective* 形容词 (**clumsier, clumsiest**) If you are **clumsy**, you often drop things or do things badly because you do not move in an easy or careful way. 笨拙的; 笨手笨脚的: *I'm so clumsy! I've just broken a glass.* 我真是笨手笨脚! 我刚打碎一个玻璃杯。

▸ **clumsily** /ˈklʌmzəli/ *adverb* 副词: *He clumsily knocked the cup off the table.* 他笨手笨脚地把桌子上的杯子碰跌了。

clung *form of* CLING * cling 的不同形式

clutch¹ /klʌtʃ/ *verb* 动词 (**clutches, clutching, clutched** /klʌtʃt/) to hold something tightly 紧握; 抱紧 ⊃ SAME MEANING **grip** 同义词为 grip: *The child clutched his mother's hand.* 那个孩子紧紧抓住母亲的手。

clutch² /klʌtʃ/ *noun* 名词 (in a vehicle) the part that your foot presses while your hand moves the stick that changes the engine speed (车辆的) 离合器踏板

cm *short way of writing* CENTIMETRE * centimetre 的缩写形式

Co. /kəʊ/ *short for* COMPANY (1) * company 第 1 义的缩略式

c/o /ˌsiː ˈəʊ/ *abbreviation* 缩略式 You use **c/o** (short for **care of**) when you are writing to somebody who is staying at another person's house. (用于投递给寄居人的信件上) 由…转交 (care of 的缩略式): *Ms S Garcia, c/o Mr Michael Nolan* 迈克尔·诺兰先生转 S·加西亚女士收

coach¹ /kəʊtʃ/ *noun* 名词 (*plural* 复数形式 **coaches**) **1** a person who trains a person or team in a sport (体育) 教练: *a baseball coach* 棒球教练 **2** (*British* 英式英语) a comfortable bus for taking people on long journeys 长途汽车; 长途客车: *It's cheaper to travel by coach than by train.* 坐长途汽车要比坐火车便宜。 **3** (*British* 英式英语) one of the parts of

a train where people sit (火车) 客车厢 ⊃ SAME MEANING **carriage** 同义词为 carriage **4** a vehicle with four wheels that is pulled by horses 四轮马车 ⊃ SAME MEANING **carriage** 同义词为 carriage: *The Queen travelled to the wedding in the royal coach.* 女王乘坐王室马车出席婚礼。

coach² /kəʊtʃ/ *verb* 动词 (**coaches, coaching, coached** /kəʊtʃt/) to teach somebody to play a sport or do something better 训练; 指导: *She is coaching the team for the Olympics.* 她正在训练这个队备战奥运。

coal /kəʊl/ *noun* 名词 (no plural 不用复数形式) a hard black substance that comes from under the ground and gives out heat when you burn it (煤) *Put some more coal on the fire.* 往炉火上再加点煤。 ⊃ Look at the picture at **fireplace**. 见 fireplace 的插图。

coarse /kɔːs/ *adjective* 形容词 (**coarser, coarsest**) made of thick pieces so that it is not smooth 大颗粒的; 粗糙的: *coarse sand* 粗沙 ◇ *coarse material* 粗糙的材料 ⊃ OPPOSITE **fine** 反义词为 fine

coast /kəʊst/ *noun* 名词 the part of the land that is next to the sea 海岸: *Their house is near the coast.* 他们的房子靠海。 ◇ *The city is on the west coast of France.* 该城位于法国的西海岸。

coastguard /ˈkəʊstɡɑːd/ *noun* 名词 a person whose job is to watch the sea and ships and help people who are in danger 海岸警卫队队员

coastline /ˈkəʊstlaɪn/ *noun* 名词 the edge of the land next to the sea 海岸线: *a rocky coastline* 多岩石的海岸线

coat¹ /kəʊt/ *noun* 名词 **1** a piece of clothing that you wear over your other clothes when you are outside 外套; 大衣: *Put your coat on – it's cold today.* 把大衣穿上吧 —— 今天很冷。 ⊃ Look at Picture Dictionary page **P5**. 见彩页 P5。 **2** the hair or fur that covers an animal 动物皮毛: *a dog with a smooth coat* 毛皮光滑的狗 ⊃ Look at the picture at **lion**. 见 lion 的插图。

coat² /kəʊt/ *verb* 动词 (**coats, coating, coated**) to put a thin covering of something over another thing 给…涂上一层: *Their shoes* *were **coated with** mud.* 他们的鞋子粘上了一层泥。

coat hanger 衣架

coat hanger /ˈkəʊt hæŋə(r)/ (*also* 亦作 **hanger**) *noun* 名词
a curved piece of wood, plastic or wire, with a hook at the top, that you hang clothes on 衣架

cobweb /ˈkɒbweb/ *noun* 名词
a net that a spider makes to catch insects 蜘蛛网

Coca-Cola™ /ˌkəʊkə ˈkəʊlə/ *noun* 名词
1 (*no plural* 不用复数形式) a sweet brown drink with bubbles in it 可口可乐
2 (*plural* 复数形式 **Coca-Colas**) a glass, bottle or can of **Coca-Cola** 一杯（或一瓶、一罐）可口可乐

cock /kɒk/ *noun* 名词 (*British* 英式英语) (*American* 美式英语 **rooster**)
an adult male chicken 公鸡；雄鸡
➪ Look at the note at **chicken**. 见 chicken 条的注释。

cockerel /ˈkɒkərəl/ *noun* 名词
a young male chicken 小公鸡

cockpit /ˈkɒkpɪt/ *noun* 名词
the part of a plane where the pilot sits （飞机）驾驶舱

cockroach /ˈkɒkrəʊtʃ/ *noun* 名词 (*plural* 复数形式 **cockroaches**)
a large brown insect that you find in houses, especially dirty ones 蟑螂

cocktail /ˈkɒkteɪl/ *noun* 名词
a drink usually made of alcohol and fruit juices mixed together. It can also be made without alcohol. 鸡尾酒：*a cocktail bar* 鸡尾酒酒吧

cocoa /ˈkəʊkəʊ/ *noun* 名词 (*no plural* 不用复数形式)
1 a dark brown powder made from the seeds (called **cocoa beans**) of a tree that grows in hot countries. **Cocoa** is used in making chocolate. 可可粉（用于制作巧克力）
2 a drink of hot milk mixed with this powder 可可热饮：*a cup of cocoa* 一杯可可热饮

coconut /ˈkəʊkənʌt/ *noun* 名词
a large fruit that grows on trees in hot countries. **Coconuts** are brown and hard on the outside, and they have sweet white food and liquid inside. 椰子 ➪ Look at Picture Dictionary page **P8**. 见彩页 P8。

cod /kɒd/ *noun* 名词 (*plural* 复数形式 **cod**)
a large fish that lives in the sea and that you can eat 鳕鱼

code /kəʊd/ *noun* 名词
1 a way of writing secret messages, using letters, numbers or special signs 密码；暗码：*The list of names was written **in code**.* 名单是用密码写的。
2 a group of numbers or letters that helps you find something 代码；代号：*What's **the code** (= the telephone number) for Paris?* 巴黎的电话区号是多少?
3 a set of rules for a group of people 守则；法规；法典：*the Highway Code* (= the rules for driving on the roads) 公用通道法规

coffee ☞ /ˈkɒfi/ *noun* 名词
1 (*no plural* 不用复数形式) a brown powder made from the seeds (called **coffee beans**) of a tree that grows in hot countries. You use it for making a drink. 咖啡粉
2 (*no plural* 不用复数形式) a drink made by adding hot water to this powder 咖啡（热饮料）：*Would you like coffee or tea?* 你要咖啡还是茶? ◇ *a cup of coffee* 一杯咖啡 ➪ Look at Picture Dictionary page **P6**. 见彩页 P6。
3 (*plural* 复数形式 **coffees**) a cup of this drink 一杯咖啡：*Two coffees, please.* 请来两杯咖啡。

> 🔎 **WORD BUILDING** 词汇扩充
> **White** coffee has milk in it and **black** coffee has no milk. 白咖啡（white coffee）指加牛奶的咖啡，黑咖啡（black coffee）指不加牛奶的咖啡。

coffee table /ˈkɒfi teɪbl/ *noun* 名词
a small low table that you put magazines, cups or other similar things on 咖啡茶几 ➪ Look at Picture Dictionary page **P10**. 见彩页 P10。

coffin /ˈkɒfɪn/ *noun* 名词
a box that a dead person's body is put in 棺材

coil[1] /kɔɪl/ *verb* 动词 (**coils**, **coiling**, **coiled** /kɔɪld/)
to make something into a lot of circles

A B C D E F G H I J K L M N O P Q R S T U V W X Y Z

that are joined together （使）缠绕，
盘绕：*The snake coiled itself round a
branch.* 蛇把身体缠绕在树枝上。

coil² /kɔɪl/ *noun* 名词
a long piece of rope or wire that goes
round in circles （绳索或金属线的）圈，
卷，盘：*a coil of rope* 一卷绳子 ➔ Look
at the picture at **rope**. 见 rope 的插图。

coin ०━ /kɔɪn/ *noun* 名词
a piece of money made of metal 硬币：
a pound coin 一英镑的硬币 ➔ Look at the
picture and the note at **money**. 见 money
的插图和注释。

coincidence /kəʊˈɪnsɪdəns/ *noun* 名词
two or more similar things happening at
the same time or in the same place by
chance, in a surprising way 巧合：*What
a coincidence! I was thinking about you
when you phoned!* 太巧了！我正想着你呢
你就把电话打来了！

coincidental /kəʊˌɪnsɪˈdentl/ *adjective*
形容词
happening by chance; not planned 巧合
的；碰巧的

Coke™ /kəʊk/ *(informal 非正式)* *short for*
COCA-COLA * Coca-Cola 的缩略式

cola /ˈkəʊlə/ *noun* 名词
1 *(no plural 不用复数形式)* a sweet brown
drink with bubbles in it 可乐
2 *(plural 复数形式 colas)* a glass, bottle or
can of **cola** 一杯（或一瓶、一罐）可乐

cold¹ ०━ /kəʊld/ *adjective* 形容词 (**colder,
coldest**)
1 not hot or warm; with a low
temperature 冷的；寒冷的：*Put your coat
on – it's cold outside.* 把大衣穿上——外面
很冷。◇ *I'm cold. Will you put the heater
on?* 我觉得冷，你把暖气打开好吗？◇ *hot
and cold water* 热水和冷水 ➔ OPPOSITE **hot**
反义词为 hot

🔎 WHICH WORD? 词语辨析
Cool, cold or **freezing?** 用 cool、cold
还是 freezing？
Cool means quite cold, especially in a
pleasant way. * cool 表示凉快：*It's hot
outside but it's nice and cool in here.*
外面很热，但这里舒适而凉爽。
Freezing means extremely cold, often
in an unpleasant way. * freezing 表示
极冷：*It's absolutely freezing outside.*
外面冷死了。

2 not friendly or kind 冷淡的；不友善的：
She gave him a cold, hard look. 她冷冷地
瞪了他一眼。

▸ **coldly** /ˈkəʊldli/ *adverb* 副词：*She
looked at me coldly.* 她冷冷地看着我。

cold² ०━ /kəʊld/ *noun* 名词
1 *(no plural 不用复数形式)* cold weather
冷；寒冷：*Don't go out in the cold.* 天气
冷，别出去。
2 *(plural 复数形式 colds)* a common
illness of the nose and throat. When you
have a **cold**, you often cannot breathe
through your nose and your throat hurts.
感冒；伤风：*I've got a cold.* 我感冒了。
◇ *Come in out of the rain, or you'll catch
a cold.* 快进来避雨吧，不然你会感冒的。

collapse /kəˈlæps/ *verb* 动词 (**collapses,
collapsing, collapsed** /kəˈlæpst/)
to fall down suddenly （突然）倒塌，
倒下：*The building collapsed in the
earthquake.* 那栋楼在地震中倒塌了。◇
*She collapsed in the street and was rushed
to hospital.* 她晕倒在街上，被赶紧送进
医院去了。
▸ **collapse** *noun* 名词：*the collapse of
the bridge* 桥的倒塌

collar /ˈkɒlə(r)/ *noun* 名词
1 the part of your clothes that goes round
your neck 衣领；领子 ➔ Look at the
pictures at **lace** and **shirt**. 见 lace 和 shirt
的插图。
2 a band that you put round the neck of
a dog or cat （狗或猫的）颈圈

colleague /ˈkɒliːɡ/ *noun* 名词
a person who works with you 同事

collect ०━ /kəˈlekt/ *verb* 动词 (**collects,
collecting, collected**)
1 to take things from different people or
places and put them together 收集：*The
waiter collected the dirty glasses.* 服务员
收走了脏杯子。
2 to bring together things that are the
same in some way, to study or enjoy
them 搜集；收藏：*My son collects
stamps.* 我儿子集邮。
3 *(British 英式英语)* to go and bring
somebody or something from a place
领走；接走：*She collects her children
from school at 3.30.* 她 3 点 30 分去学校
接孩子

collection ०━ /kəˈlekʃn/ *noun* 名词
1 a group of similar things that somebody
has brought together 收集物；收藏品：
*The Tate Gallery has a large collection
of modern paintings.* 泰特美术馆收藏了
大量现代绘画作品。◇ *a CD collection*
* CD 收藏品
2 taking something from a place or from

people 收集；收取： *rubbish collections*
垃圾收集

collector /kə'lektə(r)/ *noun* 名词
a person who collects things as a hobby
or as a job 收集者；收藏家： *a stamp
collector* 集邮者 ◇ *a ticket collector at
a railway station* 火车站的收票员

college 0ㅋ /'kɒlɪdʒ/ *noun* 名词
1 a place where you can go to study after
you have left school 学院；大学；职业
学校： *She's going to college next year.*
她明年上大学。◇ *My brother is at college.*
我弟弟在读大学。
2 a part of a university （大学的）学院：
King's College, London 伦敦大学国王学院
⊃ Look at the note at **school**. 见 school 条
的注释。

collide /kə'laɪd/ *verb* 动词 (**collides,
colliding, collided**)
to move fast towards somebody or
something and hit them hard 碰撞；相撞
⊃ SAME MEANING **crash** 同义词为 crash:
The two trucks collided. 两辆卡车相撞了。
◇ *He ran along the corridor and collided
with his teacher.* 他在走廊上跑，撞上了
老师。

collision /kə'lɪʒn/ *noun* 名词
when things or people **collide** 碰撞；相撞
⊃ SAME MEANING **crash** 同义词为 crash:
*The driver of the car was killed in the
collision.* 汽车司机撞车死了。

colon /'kəʊlən/ *noun* 名词
the mark (:) that you use in writing, for
example before a list 冒号

colonel /'kɜːnl/ *noun* 名词
an officer of a high level in the army
（陆军）上校

colony /'kɒləni/ *noun* 名词 (*plural* 复数
形式 **colonies**)
a country or an area that is ruled by
another country 殖民地： *Kenya was
once a British colony.* 肯尼亚曾经是英国的
殖民地。

color, colored, colorful *American
English for* COLOUR, COLOURED, COLOURFUL
美式英语，即 colour、coloured、
colourful

colour¹ 0ㅋ (*British* 英式英语) (*American
美式英语 color*) /'kʌlə(r)/ *noun* 名词
Red, blue, yellow and green are all
colours. 颜色： *'What colour are your
new shoes?' 'Black.'* "你的新鞋是什么颜色
的？""黑色。" ◇ *The leaves change
colour in autumn.* 树叶到秋天会变色。

colour² (*British* 英式英语) (*American* 美式
英语 color) /'kʌlə(r)/ *verb* 动词 (**colours,
colouring, coloured** /'kʌləd/)
to put colour on something, for example
by painting it 给…着色： *The children
coloured their pictures with crayons.* 孩子
用蜡笔在图画上涂颜色。

coloured 0ㅋ (*British* 英式英语)
(*American* 美式英语 colored) /'kʌləd/
adjective 形容词
having a particular colour or different
colours …色的；彩色的： *She was wearing
a brightly coloured jumper.* 她穿着一件
鲜艳的针织套衫。◇ *coloured paper* 色纸

colourful (*British* 英式英语) (*American* 美
式英语 colorful) /'kʌləfl/ *adjective* 形容词
with a lot of bright colours 颜色鲜艳的；
五彩缤纷的： *The garden is very colourful
in summer.* 花园在夏天五彩缤纷。

column 0ㅋ /'kɒləm/ *noun* 名词
1 a tall solid piece of stone that supports
part of a building 柱子；石柱
2 a long thin section of writing on one
side or part of a page （页面上的）栏：
*Each page of this dictionary has two
columns.* 这本词典每页有两栏。

comb 梳子

comb¹ /kəʊm/ *noun* 名词
a flat piece of metal or plastic with thin
parts like teeth. You use it to make your
hair tidy. 梳子

comb² /kəʊm/ *verb* 动词 (**combs,
combing, combed** /kəʊmd/)
to make your hair tidy with a COMB 梳，
梳理（头发）： *Have you combed your
hair?* 你梳过头发了吗？

combination 0ㅋ /ˌkɒmbɪ'neɪʃn/
noun 名词
two or more things joined together

A
B
C
D
E
F
G
H
I
J
K
L
M
N
O
P
Q
R
S
T
U
V
W
X
Y
Z

结合；联合；混合 ⊃ SAME MEANING
mixture 同义词为 mixture: *The building is a combination of new and old styles.* 这栋楼是新旧风格的结合体。

combine 0━ /kəm'baɪn/ *verb* 动词 (combines, combining, combined /kəm'baɪmd/)
to join; to mix two or more things together （使）结合，联合，混合: *The two schools combined and moved to a larger building.* 两所学校合并后迁往更大的校舍了。

come 0━ /kʌm/ *verb* 动词 (comes, coming, came /keɪm/, has come)
1 to move towards the person who is speaking or the place that you are talking about 来: *Come here, please.* 请到这儿来。◇ *The dog came when I called him.* 我一叫，这只狗就来。◇ *Here comes Colin* (= Colin is coming). 科林来了。◇ *I'm sorry, but I can't come to your party.* 很抱歉，我不能来参加你的聚会。
2 to arrive at or reach a place 到达；抵达: *If you go along that road, you will come to the river.* 顺着那条路走，就会到河边了。◇ *A letter came for you this morning.* 今天上午有你的一封信。
3 to go somewhere with the person who is speaking 与⋯同行: *I'm going to a party tonight. Do you want to come with me?* 今晚我会参加一个聚会。你想跟我一起去吗？
4 to be in a particular position 位于；处于: *June comes after May.* 六月在五月之后。

come about to happen 发生: *How did this situation come about?* 这情况是怎么回事？
come across something to find something when you are not looking for it 偶然遇到；碰见: *I came across these old photos yesterday.* 我昨天偶然发现了这些旧照片。
come apart to break into pieces 破碎；破裂: *This old coat is coming apart.* 这件旧大衣有点破烂了。
come back to return 回来；返回: *What time will you be coming back?* 你什么时候回来？
come down to fall or become lower 下降；降低: *The price of oil is coming down.* 油价在下跌。
come from somewhere or 或 **something**
1 The place that you **come from** is where you were born or where you live. 出生于；来自: *I come from Japan.* 我是日本

人。◇ *Where do you come from?* 你是哪儿的人？
2 to be made from something or produced somewhere 产自: *Wool comes from sheep.* 羊毛出自绵羊。
come in to enter a place 进入；进去: *Come in and sit down.* 进来坐吧。
come off something to become removed from something 从⋯掉下；与⋯分离: *The handle has come off this cup.* 这个杯子的手柄脱落了。
come on!, come along! words that you use for telling somebody to hurry or to try harder（用于催促或鼓励）快，加油: *Come on! We'll be late!* 快点！我们要迟到了！
come out to appear 出现: *The rain stopped and the sun came out.* 雨停了，太阳出来了。◇ *His first novel came out in 2004.* 他的第一部小说于 2004 年出版。
come round to visit a person at their house not very far away（到近处）探访: *Come round for lunch on Saturday.* 周六过来吃午饭吧。
how come … ? (*informal* 非正式) why or how … ? 怎么会；怎么回事: *How come you're here so early?* 你怎么来得这么早？
to come in the future 未来；今后: *You'll regret it in years to come.* 将来你会后悔的。

comedian /kə'miːdiən/ *noun* 名词
a person whose job is to make people laugh 喜剧演员；滑稽演员

comedy /'kɒmədi/ *noun* 名词 (*plural* 复数形式 comedies)
a funny play or film 喜剧；喜剧片

comet /'kɒmɪt/ *noun* 名词
a thing in the sky that moves around the sun. A **comet** looks like a bright star with a tail. 彗星

comfort¹ /'kʌmfət/ *noun* 名词
1 (*no plural* 不用复数形式) having everything your body needs; being without pain or problems 舒适；安逸: *They have enough money to live in comfort.* 他们有足够的钱过安逸的生活。
2 (*plural* 复数形式 comforts) a person or thing that helps you or makes life better 令人感到安慰的人（或事）；使生活舒适的东西: *Her children were a comfort to her when she was ill.* 她生病的时候，她的孩子对她是个安慰。

comfort² /'kʌmfət/ *verb* 动词 (comforts, comforting, comforted)
to make somebody feel less unhappy or worried 安慰；抚慰: *A mother was*

comforting her crying child. 一名母亲哄着
啼哭的孩子。

comfortable 0→ /ˈkʌmftəbl/
adjective 形容词
1 nice to sit in, to be in, or to wear 使人
舒服的；舒适的： *This is a very
comfortable bed.* 这是张非常舒适的床。
◇ *comfortable shoes* 舒适的鞋
2 physically relaxed; with no pain or
worry 放松的；安逸的： *Sit down and
make yourself comfortable.* 请坐，你自便
吧。 ⊃ OPPOSITE **uncomfortable** 反义词为
uncomfortable
▶ **comfortably** /ˈkʌmftəbli/ *adverb*
副词： *If you're all sitting comfortably,
then I'll begin.* 要是你们都舒舒服服地坐
好了，我就开始。

comic¹ /ˈkɒmɪk/ (*also* 亦作 **comical**
/ˈkɒmɪkl/) *adjective* 形容词
funny 滑稽的；好笑的： *a comic scene in
a play* 剧中的滑稽场面

comic² /ˈkɒmɪk/ *noun* 名词
a magazine for children, with pictures
that tell a story（儿童）连环画杂志

comma /ˈkɒmə/ *noun* 名词 (*plural* 复数
形式 **commas**)
a mark (,) that you use in writing to
separate parts of a sentence or things in
a list 逗号

command¹ 0→ /kəˈmɑːnd/ *noun* 名词
1 (*plural* 复数形式 **commands**) words that
tell you that you must do something 命令
⊃ SAME MEANING **order** 同义词为 order：
*The soldiers must obey their general's
commands.* 士兵必须服从将军的命令。
2 (*plural* 复数形式 **commands**)
an instruction to a computer to do
something（电脑）指令： *Use the Find
command to look for a word in the file.*
用"搜索"指令来查找文档里的文字。
3 (*no plural* 不用复数形式) the power to
tell people what to do 指挥；控制 ⊃ SAME
MEANING **control** 同义词为 control： *Who
is in command of this ship?* 这艘船由谁
指挥？

command² /kəˈmɑːnd/ *verb* 动词
(**commands, commanding, commanded**)
to tell somebody that they must do
something 命令 ⊃ SAME MEANING **order**
同义词为 order： *He commanded us to
leave immediately.* 他命令我们立刻离开。

comment¹ 0→ /ˈkɒment/ *noun* 名词
something that you say that shows what
you think about something 评论；意见：
She made some interesting comments

about the film. 她对这部电影提出了一些
有趣的见解。

comment² 0→ /ˈkɒment/ *verb* 动词
(**comments, commenting, commented**)
to say what you think about something
评论；表达意见： *A lot of people at school
commented on my new watch.* 学校里
很多人都评论我的新手表。

commentary /ˈkɒməntri/ *noun* 名词
(*plural* 复数形式 **commentaries**)
when somebody describes an event while
it is happening, especially on the radio or
television（尤指电台或电视的）实况
报道，现场解说： *a sports commentary*
体育比赛的实况报道

commentator /ˈkɒmənteɪtə(r)/ *noun*
名词
a person who gives a COMMENTARY on the
radio or television（电台或电视的）评论
员，解说员

commerce /ˈkɒmɜːs/ *noun* 名词 (*no
plural* 不用复数形式)
the business of buying and selling things
商业；商务

commercial¹ /kəˈmɜːʃl/ *adjective* 形容词
connected with buying and selling things
商业的： *commercial law* 商业法

commercial² /kəˈmɜːʃl/ *noun* 名词
an advertisement on the television or
radio（电视或电台的）广告

commit /kəˈmɪt/ *verb* 动词 (**commits,
committing, committed**)
to do something bad 做（坏事）；
犯（罪）： *This man has committed
a very serious crime.* 这名男子犯了非常
严重的罪。

commitment /kəˈmɪtmənt/ *noun* 名词
1 (*plural* 复数形式 **commitments**)
a promise to do something 承诺，许诺：
*When I make a commitment, I always
stick to it.* 我向来信守承诺。
2 (*no plural* 不用复数形式) being prepared
to give a lot of your time and attention to
something 奉献；投入： *I admire his
commitment to his work.* 我敬佩他对工作
的投入。

committed /kəˈmɪtɪd/ *adjective* 形容词
prepared to give a lot of your time and
attention to something 尽心尽力的；
投入的： *We are committed to raising
standards in schools.* 我们致力提高学校的
水平。

A
B
C
D
E
F
G
H
I
J
K
L
M
N
O
P
Q
R
S
T
U
V
W
X
Y
Z

committee /kə'mɪti/ *noun* 名词

> 🔍 SPELLING 拼写说明
>
> Remember! You spell **committee** with **MM**, **TT** and **EE**. 记住：committee 拼写中有 mm、tt 和 ee。

a group of people that other people choose to discuss or decide something 委员会：*She's on the planning committee.* 她是规划委员会的成员。

common¹ 0☞ /'kɒmən/ *adjective* 形容词 (**commoner**, **commonest**)
1 happening often or found in many places 常见的；普遍的：*Jackson is a common English name.* * Jackson 是常见的英文名。 ◗ OPPOSITE **rare** 反义词为 rare
2 shared by two or more people or by everybody in a group 共同的；共有的：*They share a common interest in photography.* 他们都爱好摄影。

common² /'kɒmən/ *noun* 名词
a piece of land that everybody can use 公共用地：*We went for a walk on the common.* 我们到公地上散步去了。

have something in common to be like somebody in a certain way, or to have the same interests as somebody 有共通点；有共同之处：*Paul and I are good friends. We have a lot in common.* 我和保罗是好朋友。我们有很多共同之处。

common sense /,kɒmən 'sens/ *noun* 名词 (*no plural* 不用复数形式)
the ability to think about things and do the right thing and not make stupid mistakes 常识；常理：*Jane's got no common sense. She lay in the sun all day and got sunburnt.* 简一点儿常识都没有。她晒了一整天太阳，皮肤都晒伤了。

communicate 0☞ /kə'mju:nɪkeɪt/ *verb* 动词 (**communicates**, **communicating**, **communicated**)
to share and exchange information, ideas or feelings with somebody 交流；沟通：*Parents often find it difficult to communicate with their children.* 父母往往觉得很难与子女沟通。

communication 0☞
/kə,mju:nɪ'keɪʃn/ *noun* 名词
1 (*no plural* 不用复数形式) sharing or exchanging information, feelings or ideas with somebody 交流；沟通：*Communication is difficult when two people don't speak the same language.* 没有共同语言很难交流。
2 **communications** (*plural* 用复数形式) ways of sending or receiving information,

especially telephones, radio, computers, etc. 通信；通讯；联系：*a communications satellite* 通信卫星

community 0☞ /kə'mju:nəti/ *noun* 名词 (*plural* 复数形式 **communities**)
1 all the people who live in a place; the place where they live 社区：*Life in a small fishing community is very different from life in a big city.* 渔业小社区的生活与大城市的截然不同。
2 a group of people who join together, for example because they have the same interests or religion 团体；界：*the Asian community in Britain* 英国的亚裔团体

commute /kə'mju:t/ *verb* 动词 (**commutes**, **commuting**, **commuted**)
to travel a long way from home to work every day（远距离）上下班往返；通勤：*She lives in the country and commutes to London.* 她住在乡村，每天乘车到伦敦上班。
▸ **commuter** /kə'mju:tə(r)/ *noun* 名词
a person who **commutes**（远距离）上下班往返的人；通勤者

compact disc /,kɒmpækt 'dɪsk/ *noun* 名词 = CD

companion /kəm'pæniən/ *noun* 名词
a person who travels with you or spends time with you 同伴；旅伴

company 0☞ /'kʌmpəni/ *noun* 名词
1 (*plural* 复数形式 **companies**) a group of people who work together to make or sell things 公司：*an advertising company* 广告公司

> 🔍 WHICH WORD? 词语辨析
>
> In names, **company** is written with a capital letter. The abbreviation is **Co.** * company 用于名称时首字母大写，缩略式为 Co.：*the Walt Disney Company* 沃尔特·迪斯尼公司 ◇ *Milton and Co.* 米尔顿公司

2 (*no plural* 不用复数形式) being with a person or people 陪伴；陪同：*I always enjoy Mark's company.* 我总是喜欢和马克在一起。

keep somebody company to be or go with somebody 陪伴某人；给人做伴：*Please stay and keep me company for a while.* 请留下陪我一会儿吧。

comparable /'kɒmpərəbl/ *adjective* 形容词
similar in size or quality to something else 类似的：*Salaries here are comparable to salaries paid by other companies.* 这儿的工资与其他公司的差不多。

comparative /kəmˈpærətɪv/ *noun* 名词
(*grammar* 语法) the form of an adjective
or adverb that shows more of something
（形容词或副词的）比较级: *The
comparative of 'bad' is 'worse'.* * bad 的
比较级是 worse。
▶ **comparative** *adjective* 形容词:
'Longer' is the comparative form of 'long'.
* longer 是 long 的比较级形式。➔ Look
at **superlative**. 见 **superlative**.

compare ⊶ /kəmˈpeə(r)/ *verb* 动词
(**compares**, **comparing**, **compared**
/kəmˈpeəd/)
to think about or look at people or things
together so that you can see how they are
different 比较；对比: *Compared to the
place where I grew up, this town is exciting.*
与我长大的地方相比，这个城镇充满乐
趣。◇ *Steve is quite tall, compared with
his friends.* 史蒂夫与他的朋友相比算长得
挺高的。◇ *Compare your answers with
your neighbour's.* 把你的答案和你邻座的
对照一下。

comparison ⊶ /kəmˈpærɪsn/ *noun*
名词
looking at or understanding how things
are different or the same 比较；对比:
*It's hard to make comparisons between
athletes from different sports.* 很难对不同
体育项目的运动员进行比较。
by or 或 **in comparison with
somebody** or 或 **something** when you
compare two or more people or things
与…相比: *In comparison with many
other people, they're quite rich.* 与其他
许多人相比，他们挺有钱的。

compartment /kəmˈpɑːtmənt/ *noun*
名词
1 one of the sections which a part of
a train (called a **carriage**) is divided into
（火车车厢的）隔间: *He found an empty
first-class compartment.* 他找到一个空的
头等车厢隔间。
2 a separate part inside a box, bag or
other container（容器的）格子，隔层:
*The suitcase had a secret compartment at
the back.* 行李箱背面有个秘密夹层。

compass /ˈkʌmpəs/ *noun* 名词 (*plural*
复数形式 **compasses**)
1 a thing for finding direction, with a
needle that always points north 指南针；
罗盘: *You need a map and a compass.*
你需要地图和指南针。
2 (*also* 亦作 **compasses**) (*plural* 用复数
形式) an instrument with two long thin
parts joined together at the top that is

used for drawing circles 圆规: *Use a pair
of compasses.* 使用圆规。

compasses 指南针；圆规
north 北
north-west 西北　　north-east 东北
west 西　　　　　　　east 东
south-west 西南　　　south-east 东南
south 南
compass 指南针

compass 圆规 or 或
a pair of compasses
一副圆规

compete /kəmˈpiːt/ *verb* 动词 (**competes**,
competing, **competed**)
to try to win a race or a competition
竞争；比赛；较量: *The world's best
athletes compete in the Olympic
Games.* 世界上最优秀的运动员在奥运
会竞技。

competition ⊶ /ˌkɒmpəˈtɪʃn/ *noun*
名词
1 (*plural* 复数形式 **competitions**) a game
or test that people try to win 比赛；
竞赛: *I entered the painting competition
and won first prize.* 我参加绘画比赛赢得了
一等奖。
2 (*no plural* 不用复数形式) trying to win or
be better than somebody else 竞争；
角逐: *We were in competition with a
team from another school.* 我们同另一所
学校的队伍角逐。

competitive /kəmˈpetətɪv/ *adjective*
形容词
1 in which people or organizations
COMPETE against each other 竞争的:
competitive sports 竞技性体育运动
2 wanting to win or be better than other
people 喜欢竞争的；一心求胜的: *She's
very competitive.* 她好胜心很强。

competitor /kəmˈpetɪtə(r)/ *noun* 名词
a person who is trying to win a
competition 竞争者；对手

A
B
C
D
E
F
G
H
I
J
K
L
M
N
O
P
Q
R
S
T
U
V
W
X
Y
Z

complain ⚬╼ /kəm'pleɪn/ *verb* 动词
(complains, complaining, complained
/kəm'pleɪnd/)
to say that you do not like something or
that you are unhappy about something
抱怨；投诉: *She is always complaining
about the weather.* 她总是在抱怨天气。◇
*He complained to the waiter that his soup
was cold.* 他向服务员投诉，说汤是凉的。

complaint ⚬╼ /kəm'pleɪnt/ *noun* 名词
when you say that you do not like
something 抱怨；投诉: *We made a
complaint to the hotel manager about
the dirty rooms.* 我们向酒店经理投诉房间
太脏。

complete¹ ⚬╼ /kəm'pliːt/ *adjective*
形容词
1 in every way 完全的；彻底的 ⇒ SAME
MEANING **total** 同义词为 total: *Their visit
was a complete surprise.* 他们的来访完全
出人意料。
2 with none of its parts missing 完整的；
全部的 ⇒ SAME MEANING **whole** 同义词为
whole: *I've got a complete set of
Shakespeare's plays.* 我有全套的莎士比亚
戏剧作品。⇒ OPPOSITE **incomplete**
反义词为 incomplete
3 finished 完成；结束: *The work is
complete.* 工作已经完成。⇒ OPPOSITE
incomplete 反义词为 incomplete

complete² ⚬╼ /kəm'pliːt/ *verb* 动词
(completes, completing, completed)
to finish doing or making something
完成: *She was at university for two years
but she did not complete her studies.* 她上
了两年大学，但是没有完成学习。◇ *When
will the new building be completed?* 新楼
什么时候建成?

completely ⚬╼ /kəm'pliːtli/ *adverb*
副词
in every way 完全地；彻底地 ⇒ SAME
MEANING **totally** 同义词为 totally: *The
money has completely disappeared.* 钱全
不见了。◇ *I completely forgot that it was
your birthday!* 那天是你的生日，但我忘得
一干二净!

complex¹ /'kɒmpleks/ *adjective* 形容词
difficult to understand because it has
a lot of different parts 复杂的；难懂的
⇒ SAME MEANING **complicated** 同义词为
complicated: *a complex problem* 复杂的
问题 ⇒ OPPOSITE **simple** 反义词为 simple

complex² /'kɒmpleks/ *noun* 名词 (*plural*
复数形式 complexes)
a group of buildings 建筑群: *a sports
complex* 体育中心

complicated ⚬╼ /'kɒmplɪkeɪtɪd/
adjective 形容词
difficult to understand because it has
a lot of different parts 复杂的；难懂的:
*I can't explain how to play the game.
It's too complicated.* 我无法解释怎样玩这
个游戏，太复杂了。⇒ OPPOSITE **simple**
反义词为 simple

complication /ˌkɒmplɪ'keɪʃn/ *noun* 名词
something that makes a situation more
difficult 使情况变复杂的因素

compliment /'kɒmplɪmənt/ *noun* 名词
something nice that you say about
somebody 赞扬；称赞: *People often pay
her compliments on her piano playing.*
人们经常夸奖她钢琴弹得好。
▶ **compliment** /'kɒmplɪment/ *verb* 动词
(compliments, complimenting,
complimented): *They complimented
Frank on his cooking.* 他们称赞弗兰克烹调
手艺高。

compose /kəm'pəʊz/ *verb* 动词
(composes, composing, composed
/kəm'pəʊzd/)
to write something, especially music
写作；(尤指)作曲: *Verdi composed
many operas.* 威尔地创作了很多歌剧。
be composed of something or 或
somebody to be made or formed from
different parts or people 由…构成；
由…组成: *Water is composed of oxygen
and hydrogen.* 水由氧和氢结合而成。

composer /kəm'pəʊzə(r)/ *noun* 名词
a person who writes music 作曲家:
My favourite composer is Mozart. 我最
喜爱的作曲家是莫扎特。

composition /ˌkɒmpə'zɪʃn/ *noun* 名词
a piece of writing or music 作文；音乐
作品

compound /'kɒmpaʊnd/ *noun* 名词
1 something that is made of two or more
parts 复合物；混合物: *Salt is a chemical
compound.* 盐是化合物。
2 (*grammar* 语法) a word that is made
from two or more other words 复合词:
'Hairdryer' and 'car park' are compounds.
* hairdryer 和 car park 是复合词。

comprehension /ˌkɒmprɪ'henʃn/ *noun*
名词 (*no plural* 不用复数形式)
understanding something that you hear
or read 理解 (力): *a test in listening
comprehension* 听力测验

comprehensive school
/ˌkɒmprɪ'hensɪv skuːl/ (*also* 亦作
comprehensive) *noun* 名词
(in Britain) a school for pupils of all levels

of ability between the ages of 11 and 18
（在英国接收各种资质学生的）综合中学

compromise /ˈkɒmprəmaɪz/ **noun** 名词
an agreement between people when each person gets part, but not all, of what they wanted 妥协；折衷：*After long talks, the workers and management reached a compromise.* 经过长时间谈判，劳资双方达成了妥协。

compulsory /kəmˈpʌlsəri/ **adjective** 形容词
If something is **compulsory**, you must do it. 必须做的；强制的：*School is compulsory for all children between the ages of five and sixteen.* 五岁到十六岁的所有孩子必须上学。 **⊃** OPPOSITE **optional** 反义词为 optional

computer ⊶ /kəmˈpjuːtə(r)/ **noun** 名词
a machine that can store and find information, calculate amounts and control other machines 电脑；计算机：*All the work is done by computer.* 所有的工作由电脑完成。 ◇ *He spends a lot of time on the computer, sending emails.* 他把很多时间花在电脑上，发送电子邮件。 ◇ *a computer program* (= information that tells a computer what to do) 电脑程序 ◇ *They play computer games every evening.* 他们每天晚上玩电脑游戏。 **⊃** Look at Picture Dictionary page **P11**. 见彩页 P11。

computer programmer /kəmˌpjuːtə ˈprəʊɡræmə(r)/ **noun** 名词
a person who writes computer programs 电脑程序设计员

computing /kəmˈpjuːtɪŋ/ **noun** 名词
(*no plural* 不用复数形式)
using computers to do work 电脑技术；信息处理技术：*She is studying computing at college.* 她正在大学学习电脑技术。

conceal /kənˈsiːl/ **verb** 动词 (conceals, concealing, concealed /kənˈsiːld/) (*formal* 正式)
to hide something 隐藏；隐瞒：*They concealed the bomb in a suitcase.* 他们把炸弹藏在了行李箱里。

🔎 SPEAKING 表达方式说明
Hide is the word that we usually use. * hide 是常用词。

conceited /kənˈsiːtɪd/ **adjective** 形容词
too proud of yourself and what you can do 自负的；骄傲自大的

concentrate ⊶ /ˈkɒnsntreɪt/ **verb** 动词 (concentrates, concentrating, concentrated)
to give all your attention to something 集中注意力；聚精会神：*Stop looking out of the window and concentrate on your work!* 别看窗外了，专心干活！ ◇ *Be quiet and let him concentrate.* 安静点，让他集中精神。

concentration /ˌkɒnsnˈtreɪʃn/ **noun** 名词 (*no plural* 不用复数形式)
the ability to give all your attention to something 专心；专注：*You need total concentration for this type of work.* 做这种工作你得全神贯注。

concern[1] /kənˈsɜːn/ **verb** 动词 (concerns, concerning, concerned /kənˈsɜːnd/)
1 to be important or interesting to somebody 影响；涉及；关系到 **⊃** SAME MEANING **affect** 同义词为 affect：*Please pay attention because this information concerns all of you.* 请注意，这则消息跟你们所有人都有关系。
2 to be about something 与…有关：*The story concerns the prince's efforts to rescue Pamina.* 这个故事讲的是王子奋力营救帕米娜。
3 to worry somebody 使担心；使操心：*It concerns me that she is always late.* 让我担心的是她老是迟到。

concern[2] /kənˈsɜːn/ **noun** 名词
1 (*no plural* 不用复数形式) worry 担心；忧虑：*There is a lot of concern about this problem.* 这个问题着实让人担心。
2 (*plural* 复数形式 concerns) something that is important or interesting to somebody 重要的事；关注的事：*Her problems are not my concern.* 她的问题跟我毫不相干。

concerned /kənˈsɜːnd/ **adjective** 形容词
worried about something 担心的；忧虑的：*They are very concerned about their son's health.* 他们非常担心儿子的健康。

concerning /kənˈsɜːnɪŋ/ **preposition** 介词 (*formal* 正式)
about something 有关；关于：*He asked several questions concerning the future of the company.* 他问了几个有关公司前景的问题。

concert ⊶ /ˈkɒnsət/ **noun** 名词
a public performance of music 音乐会；演唱会：*a rock concert* 摇滚音乐会

conclude /kənˈkluːd/ **verb** 动词 (concludes, concluding, concluded)
1 to decide something, after you have

studied or thought about it 推断出；得出结论：*The report **concluded that** the working conditions were unsafe.* 这份报告认为工作环境不安全。

2 (*formal* 正式) to end or make something end 结束；终止：*The Prince **concluded** his tour with a visit to a local hospital.* 王子最后访问了当地的一家医院，由此结束他的行程。◇ *May I **conclude by** thanking our guest speaker.* 最后我要感谢我们的演讲嘉宾。

conclusion 0━ /kən'kluːʒn/ *noun* 名词 what you believe or decide after thinking carefully about something 结论；推断：*We came to the **conclusion** that you were right all along.* 我们断定你一直是对的。

concrete /'kɒŋkriːt/ *noun* 名词 (*no plural* 不用复数形式) a hard grey material used for building things 混凝土：*a concrete wall* 混凝土墙

condemn /kən'dem/ *verb* 动词 (**condemns, condemning, condemned** /kən'demd/)
1 to say strongly that somebody or something is very bad or wrong 谴责；指责：*Many people **condemned** the government's decision.* 许多人谴责政府的决定。
2 to say that somebody must be punished in a certain way 宣判；判处 ⊃ SAME MEANING **sentence** 同义词为 sentence：*The murderer **was condemned** to death.* 杀人犯被判处死刑。

condition 0━ /kən'dɪʃn/ *noun* 名词
1 (*no plural* 不用复数形式) the state that somebody or something is in 状态；状况：*The car was cheap and **in good condition**, so I bought it.* 这辆车便宜，车况也不错，所以我买下了。
2 conditions (*plural* 用复数形式) the situation in which people live, work or do things（居住、工作或做事的）环境，条件：*The prisoners lived in terrible **conditions**.* 囚犯的生活环境恶劣。
3 (*plural* 复数形式 **conditions**) something that must happen before another thing can happen（影响某事发生的）条件：*One of the **conditions** of the job is that you agree to work on Saturdays.* 这份工作的一个前提条件是得同意星期六上班。
on condition that ... only if 在⋯条件下；只有：*You can go to the party **on condition that** you come home before midnight.* 你可以去参加聚会，条件是午夜前回来。

conduct¹ /kən'dʌkt/ *verb* 动词 (**conducts, conducting, conducted**)

1 to organize or do an activity 组织；从事：*They are going to **conduct** an experiment.* 他们将进行一项实验。
2 to stand in front of a group of musicians and control what they do 指挥（乐团）：*The orchestra was **conducted** by Peter Jones.* 管弦乐团由彼得•琼斯指挥。
3 to show somebody where to go 领路；引路：*She **conducted** us on a tour of the museum.* 她带领我们参观了博物馆。

conduct² /'kɒndʌkt/ *noun* 名词 (*no plural* 不用复数形式) (*formal* 正式) the way somebody behaves 行为；举止 ⊃ SAME MEANING **behaviour** 同义词为 behaviour

conductor /kən'dʌktə(r)/ *noun* 名词
1 a person who stands in front of a group of musicians and controls what they do（乐团的）指挥
2 (*British* 英式英语) a person who sells or checks people's tickets on a bus or train（公共汽车或火车的）售票员，查票员

cones 球果；圆锥

cone 球果   **ice cream**   **traffic cone**
(*British also*   **cone**   锥形警告路标
英式英语亦作   蛋卷冰激凌
fir cone)

cone /kəʊn/ *noun* 名词
1 a shape with one flat round end and one pointed end 圆锥形；圆锥体
2 the hard fruit of some trees (called **pine** and **fir**) 球果：*a pine **cone*** 松果

conference /'kɒnfərəns/ *noun* 名词 a large meeting, where many people with the same job or interests come together to discuss their views（大型）会议，研讨会：*an international **conference** on climate change* 有关气候变化的国际会议

confess /kən'fes/ *verb* 动词 (**confesses, confessing, confessed** /kən'fest/) to say that you have done something wrong 供认；坦白 ⊃ SAME MEANING **admit** 同义词为 admit：*She **confessed** that she had stolen the money.* 她承认偷了那笔钱。

◇ He *confessed to the crime.* 他认罪了。
⊃ OPPOSITE **deny** 反义词为 deny

confession /kən'feʃn/ *noun* 名词
when you say that you have done
something wrong 承认错误；供认：
She made a full confession to the police.
她向警方坦白交代了一切。

confidence ⊶ /'kɒnfɪdəns/ *noun*
名词 (*no plural* 不用复数形式)
the feeling that you can do something
well 信心；自信： *She answered the
questions with confidence.* 她信心十足地
回答了问题。◇ *I'm sure you'll pass the
exam. I have great confidence in you.*
我肯定你会通过考试，我对你充满信心。
in confidence If somebody tells you
something **in confidence**, it is a secret.
秘密地；不公开

confident ⊶ /'kɒnfɪdənt/ *adjective*
形容词
sure that you can do something well, or
that something will happen 有信心的；
自信的： *I'm confident that our team will
win.* 我深信我们队会赢。

confidential /ˌkɒnfɪ'denʃl/ *adjective*
形容词
If somebody tells you something that is
confidential, you should keep it a secret
and not tell other people. 机密的；保密
的： *confidential information* 机密情报

confirm /kən'fɜːm/ *verb* 动词 (confirms,
confirming, confirmed /kən'fɜːmd/)
to say that something is true or that
something will happen 确认；证实：
*Please write and confirm the date of
your arrival.* 请写明并确认你到达的
日期。

confirmation /ˌkɒnfə'meɪʃn/ *noun*
(*no plural* 不用复数形式)
saying that something is true or will
definitely happen 确认；证实

conflict¹ /'kɒnflɪkt/ *noun* 名词
a fight or an argument 冲突；争执

conflict² /kən'flɪkt/ *verb* 动词 (conflicts,
conflicting, conflicted)
to disagree or be different 互相矛盾；
抵触： *These results conflict with earlier
research results.* 这些结果与之前的研究
结果不相符。

confuse ⊶ /kən'fjuːz/ *verb* 动词
(confuses, confusing, confused
/kən'fjuːzd/)
1 to mix somebody's ideas, so that they
cannot think clearly or understand
使困惑；使迷惘： *They confused me by

asking so many questions.* 他们提了一大堆
问题，把我都弄糊涂了。
2 to think that one thing or person is
another thing or person 混淆： *I often
confuse Lee with his brother. They look so
similar.* 我经常把李和他弟弟搞错。他们
长得太像了。
▶ **confusing** /kən'fjuːzɪŋ/ *adjective* 形容词
difficult to understand 令人困惑的；费解
的： *This map is very confusing.* 这张地图
真让人看不明白。

confused ⊶ /kən'fjuːzd/ *adjective*
形容词
not able to think clearly 糊涂的；迷惑的：
*The waiter got confused and brought
everybody the wrong drink!* 那名服务员糊
里糊涂的，把大家点的饮料都上错了。

confusion /kən'fjuːʒn/ *noun* 名词 (*no
plural* 不用复数形式)
not being able to think clearly or
understand something 困惑；不解： *He
looked at me in confusion when I asked
him a question.* 我向他提了个问题，他迷
惘地看看我。

congratulate /kən'grætʃuleɪt/ *verb* 动词
(congratulates, congratulating,
congratulated)
to tell somebody that you are pleased
about something that they have done
祝贺；道贺： *I congratulated Sue on
passing her exam.* 我祝贺苏考试及格了。

congratulations /kən,grætʃu'leɪʃnz/
noun 名词 (*plural* 用复数形式)
something you say to somebody when
you are pleased about something they
have done 恭喜；祝贺： *Congratulations
on your new job!* 恭喜你找到新工作了！

congress /'kɒŋgres/ *noun* 名词
1 (*plural* 复数形式 congresses) a large
formal meeting of many people to talk
about important things 代表大会；大型
会议
2 Congress (*no plural* 不用复数形式)
a group of people who make the laws in
some countries, for example in the US
国会（美国等国家的立法机关）

🔎 CULTURE 文化资料补充
The US **Congress** is made up of two
groups: the **Senate** and the **House
of Representatives**. 美国国会
（Congress）由参议院（Senate）和
众议院（House of Representatives）
组成。

conjunction /kən'dʒʌŋkʃn/ *noun* 名词
(*grammar* 语法) a word that joins other

A
B
C
D
E
F
G
H
I
J
K
L
M
N
O
P
Q
R
S
T
U
V
W
X
Y
Z

words or parts of a sentence 连词;
连接词: *'And', 'or' and 'but' are
conjunctions.* * and、or 和 but 是连词。

conjuror /ˈkʌndʒərə(r)/ *noun* 名词
a person who does clever tricks that seem
to be magic 变戏法的人; 魔术师 ⊃ SAME
MEANING **magician** 同义词为 magician:
The conjuror pulled a rabbit out of a hat.
魔术师从帽子里掏出一只兔子来。

connect ०᠆ /kəˈnekt/ *verb* 动词
(connects, connecting, connected)
to join one thing to another thing 连接;
联结: *This wire connects the DVD player
to the television.* 这根电线把 DVD 播放机
与电视机连接起来。◇ *The two cities are
connected by a motorway.* 两个城市之间
由一条高速公路连接起来。

connection ०᠆ /kəˈnekʃn/ *noun* 名词
1 the way that one thing is joined or
related to another 连接; 联结; 联系:
*We had a bad connection on the phone so
I couldn't hear him very well.* 电话线路
不好，我听不太清楚他的声音。◇ *Is there
a connection between violence on TV and
crime?* 电视上的暴力与犯罪有关联吗?
2 a train, plane or bus that leaves a place
soon after another arrives, so that people
can change from one to the other 转乘的
火车（或飞机、公共汽车等）: *The train
was late, so I missed my connection.*
火车误点了，所以我没赶上要转乘的车。
in connection with something
(*formal* 正式) about something 与…有关:
*A man has been arrested in connection
with the murder of the teenager.* 一名男子
因与这起谋杀少年案有关而被捕。

conscience /ˈkɒnʃəns/ *noun* 名词
the feeling inside you about what is right
and wrong 良心; 良知: *He has a guilty
conscience* (= he feels that he has done
something wrong). 他问心有愧。

conscientious /ˌkɒnʃiˈenʃəs/ *adjective*
形容词
careful to do things correctly and well
认真负责的; 一丝不苟的: *She's a very
conscientious student.* 她是个一丝不苟的
学生。

conscious ०᠆ /ˈkɒnʃəs/ *adjective*
形容词
1 If you are **conscious** of something, you
know about it. 意识到; 注意到 ⊃ SAME
MEANING **aware** 同义词为 aware: *I was
conscious that somebody was watching
me.* 我意识到有人在注意我。
2 awake and able to see, hear, feel and
think 有知觉的; 有意识的; 清醒的:

*The patient was conscious during the
operation.* 手术进行时病人是清醒的。
⊃ OPPOSITE **unconscious** 反义词为
unconscious

consciousness /ˈkɒnʃəsnəs/ *noun* 名词
(*no plural* 不用复数形式)
the state of being able to see, hear, feel
and think 清醒状态; 知觉: *As she fell,
she hit her head and lost consciousness.*
她跌倒时撞到头部，失去了知觉。

consent[1] /kənˈsent/ *noun* 名词 (*no plural*
不用复数形式)
agreeing to let somebody do something
同意; 许可 ⊃ SAME MEANING **permission**
同义词为 permission: *Her parents gave
their consent to the marriage.* 她父母同意
了婚事。

consent[2] /kənˈsent/ *verb* 动词 (consents,
consenting, consented) (*formal* 正式)
to agree to something 同意; 允许:
*He finally consented to his daughter's
marriage.* 他最后应允了女儿的婚事。

consequence /ˈkɒnsɪkwəns/ *noun* 名词
a result of something that has happened
后果; 结果: *Their actions had terrible
consequences.* 他们的行动造成了严重
后果。◇ *I've just bought a car and, as a
consequence, I've got no money.* 我刚买了
辆汽车，这样一来我就没钱了。

consequently /ˈkɒnsɪkwəntli/ *adverb*
副词
because of that 因此; 所以 ⊃ SAME
MEANING **therefore** 同义词为 therefore:
*He didn't do any work, and consequently
failed the exam.* 他没做一点功课，所以
考试不及格。

conservation /ˌkɒnsəˈveɪʃn/ *noun* 名词
(*no plural* 不用复数形式)
taking good care of the world and its
forests, lakes, plants, and animals（对
自然环境的）保护: *the conservation of
the rainforests* 对雨林的保护

conservative /kənˈsɜːvətɪv/ *adjective*
形容词
1 not liking change or new ideas 保守
的; 守旧的 ⊃ SAME MEANING **traditional**
同义词为 traditional: *the conservative
opinions of his parents* 他父母的保守观念
2 Conservative (*politics* 政治) belonging to
or connected with THE CONSERVATIVE
PARTY 保守党的

the Conservative Party
/ðə kənˈsɜːvətɪv pɑːti/ *noun* 名词 (*also* 亦作
the Tory Party)
(*politics* 政治) one of the important
political parties in Britain（英国）保守党

⊃ Look at **Labour Party** and **Liberal
Democrats**. 见 Labour Party 和 Liberal
Democrats。

consider ⊶/kən'sɪdə(r)/ *verb* 动词
(considers, considering considered
/kən'sɪdəd/)
1 to think carefully about something
考虑；细想：*I'm considering applying for
another job.* 我在考虑申请另一份工作。
◇ *We must consider what to do next.* 我们
得考虑下一步怎么办。
2 to think that something is true 认为；
觉得：*I consider her to be a good teacher.*
我认为她是个好老师。
3 to think about the feelings of other
people when you do something 考虑到，
顾及（某人的感受）：*I can't move to
Australia! I have to consider my family.*
我不能搬到澳大利亚去！我得替我的家人
着想。

considerable /kən'sɪdərəbl/ *adjective*
形容词 (formal 正式)
great or large 相当多的；相当大的：*The
car cost a considerable amount of money.*
这辆汽车价值不菲。
▶ **considerably** /kən'sɪdərəbli/ *adverb*
副词：*My flat is considerably smaller than
yours.* 我的公寓比你的小多了。

considerate /kən'sɪdərət/ *adjective*
形容词
A person who is **considerate** is kind, and
thinks and cares about other people.
顾及他人的；体贴的；周到的：*Please
be more considerate and don't play loud
music late at night.* 请为别人着想，别在
深夜时大声播放音乐。 ⊃ OPPOSITE
inconsiderate 反义词为 inconsiderate

consideration /kən,sɪdə'reɪʃn/ *noun*
名词 (no plural 无复数形式)
1 (formal 正式) thinking carefully about
something 仔细考虑；深思 ⊃ SAME
MEANING **thought** 同义词为 thought：
*After a lot of consideration, I decided not
to accept the job.* 经过再三考虑，我决定
不接受这份工作。
2 being kind, and caring about other
people's feelings 体贴；体谅：*He shows
no **consideration** for anybody else.* 他对谁
都毫不关心。
take something into consideration
to think carefully about something when
you are deciding 考虑到；顾及：*We must
take the cost into consideration when
planning our holiday.* 我们在计划度假时
必须考虑费用问题。

consist ⊶/kən'sɪst/ *verb* 动词 (consists,
consisting, consisted)

consist of something to be made
from two or more things; to have things
as parts 由…构成（或组成）：*Jam
consists of fruit and sugar.* 果酱由水果和
糖制成。

consistent /kən'sɪstənt/ *adjective* 形容词
always the same 一致的；始终如一的：
His work isn't very consistent. 他的工作
表现不太稳定。 ⊃ OPPOSITE **inconsistent**
反义词为 inconsistent
▶ **consistently** /kən'sɪstəntli/ *adverb*
副词：*We must try to keep a consistently
high standard.* 我们必须努力保持一贯的
高标准。

console[1] /kən'səʊl/ *verb* 动词 (consoles,
consoling, consoled /kən'səʊld/)
to make somebody happier when they
are sad or disappointed 安慰；抚慰
⊃ SAME MEANING **comfort** 同义词为
comfort

console[2] /'kɒnsəʊl/ *noun* 名词
a piece of equipment with buttons and
switches on it which you connect to a
computer to play games（电脑游戏的）
控制台

consonant /'kɒnsənənt/ *noun* 名词
any letter of the alphabet except *a, e, i, o*
and *u* 辅音字母；子音字母：*The letters
't', 'm', 's' and 'b' are all consonants.* 字母
t、m、s 和 b 都是辅音字母。 ⊃ Look at
vowel. 见 vowel。

constable /'kʌnstəbl/ *noun* 名词
an ordinary police officer 警察；警员

constant /'kɒnstənt/ *adjective* 形容词
happening all the time 不断的；重复的：
the constant noise of traffic 车辆不断发出
的噪音
▶ **constantly** *adverb* 副词：*The situation
is constantly changing.* 形势一直在变。

constituency /kən'stɪtjuənsi/ *noun* 名词
(plural 复数形式 constituencies) (British
英式英语)
a town or an area and the people who
live in it. Each **constituency** chooses one
person in the government (called a
Member of Parliament). 选区；选区选民

constitution /,kɒnstɪ'tjuːʃn/ *noun* 名词
the laws of a country, a state or an
organization 宪法；章程

construct /kən'strʌkt/ *verb* 动词
(constructs, constructing, constructed)
to build something 建筑；建造：*The
bridge was constructed out of stone.* 这座
桥是用石头修筑的。

A
B
C
D
E
F
G
H
I
J
K
L
M
N
O
P
Q
R
S
T
U
V
W
X
Y
Z

🔎 SPEAKING 表达方式说明

Build is the word that we usually use. * build 是常用词。

construction /kənˈstrʌkʃn/ *noun* 名词
1 (*no plural* 不用复数形式) building something 建筑；建造：*the construction of a new airport* 新机场的施工
2 (*plural* 复数形式 **constructions**) (*formal* 正式) something that people have built 建筑物

consul /ˈkɒnsl/ *noun* 名词
a person who works in a foreign city and helps people from his or her country who are living or visiting there 领事

consult /kənˈsʌlt/ *verb* 动词 (consults, consulting, consulted)
to ask somebody or to look in a book when you want to know something 咨询；请教；查阅：*If the pain doesn't go away, you should consult a doctor.* 要是疼痛不止，你就得去看医生。

consultant /kənˈsʌltənt/ *noun* 名词
a person who knows a lot about a subject and gives advice to other people about it 顾问：*a firm of management consultants* 管理顾问公司

consume /kənˈsjuːm/ *verb* 动词 (consumes, consuming, consumed /kənˈsjuːmd/) (*formal* 正式)
to eat, drink or use something 吃；喝；消耗：*This car consumes a lot of fuel.* 这辆车很耗油。

consumer /kənˈsjuːmə(r)/ *noun* 名词
a person who buys or uses something 消费者；顾客：*Consumers want more information about the food they buy.* 消费者想要更多有关他们所买食物的信息。

consumption /kənˈsʌmpʃn/ *noun* 名词 (*no plural* 不用复数形式)
eating, drinking or using something 消费；消耗：*This car has a high fuel consumption* (= it uses a lot of fuel). 这辆车很耗油。

contact¹ 0🔜 /ˈkɒntækt/ *noun* 名词 (*no plural* 不用复数形式)
meeting, talking to or writing to somebody 联系；联络：*Until Jane went to school, she had little contact with other children.* 简在上学之前与别的孩子没什么来往。◇ *Are you still **in contact** with the people you met on holiday?* 你跟度假时认识的那些人还有联系吗？ ◇ *Doctors **come into contact with** (= meet) a lot of people.* 医生接触很多人。

containers 容器

can 金属罐

tin (*British* 英式英语)
can (*American* 美式英语) 罐

bottles 瓶子

bags 袋

tube 软管

boxes 盒子

carton 硬纸盒

jars 玻璃罐

contact² 0┳ /ˈkɒntækt/ *verb* 动词 (**contacts, contacting, contacted**)
to telephone or write to somebody, or go to see them 联系；联络： *If you see this man, please contact the police.* 要是看见这个男子，请与警方联系。

contact lens /ˈkɒntækt lenz/ *noun* 名词 (*plural* 复数形式 **contact lenses**)
a small round piece of thin plastic that you wear in your eye so that you can see better 隐形眼镜 ➲ Look at **glasses**. 见 glasses。

contagious /kənˈteɪdʒəs/ *adjective* 形容词
A **contagious** disease passes from one person to another person if they touch each other. 接触传染的 ➲ Look at **infectious**. 见 infectious。

contain 0┳ /kənˈteɪn/ *verb* 动词 (**contains, containing, contained** /kənˈteɪnd/)
to have something inside 包含；含有： *This box contains pens and pencils.* 这个盒子里放了钢笔和铅笔。 ◇ *Chocolate contains a lot of sugar.* 巧克力含有很多糖分。

container 0┳ /kənˈteɪnə(r)/ *noun* 名词
a thing that you can put other things in. Boxes, bottles and packets are all **containers**. 容器

contemporary¹ /kənˈtemprəri/ *adjective* 形容词
1 belonging to the same time as somebody or something else 同时代的；同时期的
2 belonging to the present time 当代的；现代的 ➲ SAME MEANING **modern** 同义词为 modern： *contemporary art* 当代艺术

contemporary² /kənˈtemprəri/ *noun* 名词 (*plural* 复数形式 **contemporaries**)
a person who lives or does something at the same time as somebody else 同代人；同辈人

content /kənˈtent/ *adjective* 形容词
happy or satisfied with what you have 满意；满足： *She is not **content with** the money she has – she wants more.* 她不满足于自己现有的钱，她还想要更多。

contented /kənˈtentɪd/ *adjective* 形容词
happy or satisfied, especially because your life is good（尤指因生活好而）满意的，满足的： *a contented smile* 惬意的微笑

contents /ˈkɒntents/ *noun* 名词 (*plural* 用复数形式)
what is inside something 所含之物；内容： *I poured **the contents of** the bottle into a bowl.* 我把瓶子里的东西倒进碗里了。 ◇ *The **contents page** of a book tells you what is in it.* 书本的目录页列出书中的内容。

contest /ˈkɒntest/ *noun* 名词
a game or competition that people try to win 比赛；竞赛： *a boxing contest* 拳击赛

contestant /kənˈtestənt/ *noun* 名词
a person who tries to win a CONTEST 参赛者；竞争者： *There are six contestants in the race.* 这项赛跑有六个参赛者。

context /ˈkɒntekst/ *noun* 名词
the words that come before and after another word or sentence 上下文；语境： *You can often understand the meaning of a word by looking at its context.* 看看上下文往往可以理解一个词的含义。

continent /ˈkɒntɪnənt/ *noun* 名词
one of the seven main areas of land in the world, for example Africa, Asia or Europe 大陆；洲
▸ **continental** /ˌkɒntɪˈnentl/ *adjective* 形容词： *a continental climate* 大陆性气候

continual /kənˈtɪnjuəl/ *adjective* 形容词
happening often 经常发生的；频繁的： *We have had continual problems with this machine.* 我们这台机器常常出故障。
▸ **continually** /kənˈtɪnjuəli/ *adverb* 副词： *He is continually late for work.* 他上班经常迟到。

continue 0┳ /kənˈtɪnjuː/ *verb* 动词 (**continues, continuing, continued** /kənˈtɪnjuːd/)
1 to not stop happening or doing something 继续；持续： *We continued working until five o'clock.* 我们一直工作到五点钟。 ◇ *The rain continued all afternoon.* 雨下了整整一下午。
2 to go further in the same direction（朝相同方向）走： *We continued along the path until we came to the river.* 我们沿着小路一直走到河边。
3 to start again after stopping（中止后）继续，重新开始： *Let's have lunch now and continue the meeting this afternoon.* 我们现在吃午饭吧，下午再继续开会。

continuous 0┳ /kənˈtɪnjuəs/ *adjective* 形容词
not stopping 连续不断的；持续的： *a continuous line* 一条延续不断的线 ◇ *a continuous noise* 不停的嘈杂声
▸ **continuously** /kənˈtɪnjuəsli/ *adverb* 副词： *It rained continuously for five hours.* 雨连续下了五个小时。

A B **C** D E F G H I J K L M N O P Q R S T U V W X Y Z

contraceptive /ˌkɒntrəˈseptɪv/ *noun* 名词
a drug or an object that stops a woman from becoming pregnant 避孕药；避孕用具
▶ **contraception** /ˌkɒntrəˈsepʃn/ *noun* 名词 (*no plural* 不用复数形式) the ways of stopping a woman from becoming pregnant 避孕；节育

contract ⚬͞ /ˈkɒntrækt/ *noun* 名词
an official piece of paper that says that somebody agrees to do something 合同；合约： *The company has signed a contract to build the new road.* 这家公司已经签约修建新路。

contradict /ˌkɒntrəˈdɪkt/ *verb* 动词 (contradicts, contradicting, contradicted)
to say that something is wrong or not true 反驳；驳斥： *I didn't dare contradict him, but I think he was wrong.* 我不敢反驳他，但我认为他是错的。

contrary¹ /ˈkɒntrəri/ *adjective* 形容词
contrary to something very different from something; opposite to something 相反的；相对立的： *He didn't stay in bed, contrary to the doctor's orders.* 他不遵医嘱，没有卧床。

contrary² /ˈkɒntrəri/ *noun* 名词
(*no plural* 不用复数形式)
on the contrary the opposite is true; certainly not 与此相反；恰恰相反： *'You look ill.' 'On the contrary, I feel fine!'* "你气色不好。""恰恰相反，我很好！"

contrast¹ ⚬͞ /ˈkɒntrɑːst/ *noun* 名词
a difference between things that you can see clearly 明显差异： *There is an obvious contrast between the cultures of East and West.* 东西方之间的文化差异明显。

contrast² ⚬͞ /kənˈtrɑːst/ *verb* 动词 (contrasts, contrasting, contrasted)
to look at or think about two or more things together and see the differences between them 对比；对照： *The book contrasts life today with life 100 years ago.* 这本书把现今的生活同 100 年前的生活作了对比。

contribute ⚬͞ /kənˈtrɪbjuːt; ˈkɒntrɪbjuːt/ *verb* 动词 (contributes, contributing, contributed)
to give something when other people are giving too 贡献；捐献： *We contributed £10 each to the disaster fund.* 我们每人捐了 10 英镑给救灾基金。

contribution /ˌkɒntrɪˈbjuːʃn/ *noun* 名词
something that you give when other people are giving too 贡献；捐赠： *Would you like to make a contribution to the charity?* 你想捐钱给慈善机构吗？

control¹ ⚬͞ /kənˈtrəʊl/ *noun* 名词
1 (*no plural* 不用复数形式) the power to make people or things do what you want 控制；支配： *Who has control of the government?* 谁掌握着政府的大权？ ◇ *The driver lost control and the bus went into the river.* 司机控制不了车子，公共汽车掉进河里。
2 controls (*plural* 用复数形式) the parts of a machine that you press or move to make it work 操纵装置： *the controls of an aeroplane* 飞机的操纵装置
be or 或 **get out of control** to be or become impossible to deal with 失去控制： *The situation got out of control and people started fighting.* 场面失控了，人们开始打斗起来。
be in control to have the power or ability to deal with something 控制；掌管： *The police are now in control of the area after last night's violence.* 昨晚的暴力事件之后，警方现在已经控制了该地区。
be under control If things **are under control**, you are able to deal with them successfully. 处于控制之下： *Don't worry, everything's under control.* 别担心，一切都在掌握中。

control² ⚬͞ /kənˈtrəʊl/ *verb* 动词 (controls, controlling, controlled /kənˈtrəʊld/)
to make people or things do what you want 控制；操纵： *He can't control his dog.* 他管不住自己的狗。 ◇ *This switch controls the heating.* 这个开关是控制暖气的。
▶ **controller** /kənˈtrəʊlə(r)/ *noun* 名词
a person who controls something 控制者；操纵者： *an air traffic controller* 空中交通管制人员

control freak /kənˈtrəʊl friːk/ *noun* 名词 (*informal* 非正式)
a person who always wants to be in control of their own and other people's lives, and to organize how things are done 好管事的人；控制狂

controversial /ˌkɒntrəˈvɜːʃl/ *adjective* 形容词
Something that is **controversial** makes people argue and disagree with each other. 引起争论的；有争议的：
a controversial new law 一条受争议的新法规

controversy /ˈkɒntrəvɜːsi; kənˈtrɒvəsi/ *noun* 名词 (*plural* 复数形式 controversies)
public discussion and disagreement

about something（公开的）争论，争议:
*The government's plans caused a lot of
controversy.* 政府的计划引起了很大的
争议。

convenience /kən'viːniəns/ *noun* 名词
(*no plural* 不用复数形式)
being easy to use or making things easy
for somebody 方便；便利: *For
convenience, I usually do all my shopping
in the same place.* 为方便起见，我通常
所有的东西都在一个地方买。

convenient /kən'viːniənt/ *adjective*
形容词
1 useful, easy or quick to do; not causing
problems 方便的；便利的: *Let's meet on
Friday. What's the most convenient time
for you?* 我们星期五见面吧。什么时候你
最方便?
2 near to a place or easy to get to 附近
的；近便的: *The house is very convenient
for the station.* 这所房子离车站很近。
○ OPPOSITE **inconvenient** 反义词为
inconvenient
▶ **conveniently** /kən'viːniəntli/ *adverb*
副词: *We live conveniently close to the
shops.* 我们住的地方到商店很方便。

convent /'kɒnvənt/ *noun* 名词
a place where religious women (called
nuns) live and work 女修道院

conversation ○╍ /ˌkɒnvə'seɪʃn/
noun 名词
a talk between two or more people 交谈；
谈话: *She had a long conversation with
her friend on the phone.* 她在电话里和朋友
聊了很长时间。

conversion /kən'vɜːʃn/ *noun* 名词
changing something into another thing
转变；转换: *the conversion of pounds
into dollars* 英镑兑换成美元

convert /kən'vɜːt/ *verb* 动词 (converts,
converting, converted)
to change something into another thing
转换；改换: *They converted the house
into two flats.* 他们把房子改建成两个
套房了。

convict /kən'vɪkt/ *verb* 动词 (convicts,
convicting, convicted)
to decide in a court of law that somebody
has done something wrong 宣判…有罪:
*She was convicted of murder and sent to
prison.* 她因谋杀罪被判入狱。

convince ○╍ /kən'vɪns/ *verb* 动词
(convinces, convincing, convinced
/kən'vɪnst/)
to make somebody believe something
使相信；使信服: *I couldn't convince*

him *that I was right.* 我无法让他相信我是
对的。

convinced /kən'vɪnst/ *adjective* 形容词
completely sure about something 确信；
坚信: *I'm convinced that I have seen
her somewhere before.* 我肯定以前在哪儿
见过她。

cook¹ ○╍ /kʊk/ *verb* 动词 (cooks,
cooking, cooked /kʊkt/)
to make food ready to eat by heating it
做饭；烹饪: *My father cooked the dinner.*
我父亲做了晚餐。 ◇ *I am learning to cook.*
我在学烹饪。
▶ **cooked** /kʊkt/ *adjective* 形容词:
cooked chicken 煮熟的鸡

> ♫ WORD BUILDING 词汇扩充
> There are many ways to cook food.
> 烹调食物有多种方法。
> You can **bake** bread and cakes and
> you can **roast** meat in an **oven**. 用烤箱
> （oven）烘烤面包和蛋糕说 bake，烤肉
> 说 roast。
> You can **boil** vegetables in a **saucepan**.
> 用平底锅（saucepan）煮蔬菜说 boil。
> You can **fry** fish, eggs, etc. in a **frying
> pan**. 用长柄煎锅（frying pan）煎鱼、
> 鸡蛋等说 fry。

cook² /kʊk/ *noun* 名词
a person who cooks 做饭的人；厨师:
She works as a cook in a big hotel. 她在一
家大旅馆里当厨师。 ◇ *He is a good cook.*
他很会做饭。

cooker ○╍ /'kʊkə(r)/ (*British* 英式英语)
(*American* 美式英语 stove) *noun* 名词
a piece of kitchen equipment for cooking
using electricity or gas. It has places for
heating pans on the top and an oven for
cooking food inside it. 炉具: *an electric
cooker* 电炉 ○ Look at Picture Dictionary
page **P10**. 见彩页 P10。

cookery /'kʊkəri/ *noun* 名词 (*no plural*
不用复数形式)
the skill or activity of preparing and
cooking food 烹饪术；烹饪；烹调:
cookery lessons 烹饪课

cookie ○╍ /'kʊki/ *American English for*
BISCUIT 美式英语，即 biscuit ○ Look at
Picture Dictionary page **P6**. 见彩页 P6。

cooking ○╍ /'kʊkɪŋ/ *noun* 名词 (no
plural 不用复数形式)
1 making food ready to eat 烹饪；烹调:
Who does the cooking in your family?
你们家谁做饭?
2 the food that you cook 饭菜: *He missed*

his mother's cooking when he left home. 他离家时非常想念母亲烧的饭。

cool¹ 0‑ᴡ /kuːl/ *adjective* 形容词 (cooler, coolest)

1 a little cold; not hot or warm 凉的; 凉爽的: *cool weather* 凉爽的天气 ◊ *I'd like a cool drink.* 我想要冷饮。 ➲ Look at the note at **cold¹**. 见 cold¹ 条的注释。

2 not excited or angry 冷静的; 镇静的 ⊃ SAME MEANING **calm** 同义词为 calm

3 (*informal* 非正式) very good or fashionable 酷的; 棒的: *Those are cool shoes you're wearing!* 你穿的那双鞋子真酷!

4 (*informal* 非正式) People say **Cool!** to show that they think something is a good idea. (表示赞同) 妙极的, 棒极的: *'We're planning to go out for lunch tomorrow.' 'Cool!'* "我们打算明天出去吃午饭。" "太棒了!"

cool² /kuːl/ *verb* 动词 (cools, cooling, cooled /kuːld/)

to make something less hot; to become less hot (使) 变凉: *Take the cake out of the oven and leave it to cool.* 把蛋糕从烤箱里拿出来放凉。

cool down

1 to become less hot 变凉: *We swam in the river to cool down after our long walk.* 我们走了很长的路之后, 到河里游泳凉快一下。

2 to become less excited or angry 冷静下来; 平静下来

cooperate /kəʊˈɒpəreɪt/ *verb* 动词 (cooperates, cooperating, cooperated)

to work together with someone else in a helpful way 合作; 协作: *The two companies agreed to cooperate with each other.* 这两家公司同意互相合作。 ◊ *If everyone cooperates, we'll be finished by lunchtime.* 如果每个人都配合的话, 我们到午饭时间就可以完成。

cooperation /kəʊˌɒpəˈreɪʃn/ *noun* 名词 (*no plural* 不用复数形式)

help that you give by doing what somebody asks you to do 配合; 协助: *Thank you for your cooperation.* 感谢你的协助。

cooperative /kəʊˈɒpərətɪv/ *adjective* 形容词

helpful by doing what you are asked to do 配合的; 协助的

cope /kəʊp/ *verb* 动词 (copes, coping, coped /kəʊpt/)

to deal with something, although it is difficult 应付; 处理: *He finds it difficult*

to **cope with** all the pressure at work. 他觉得很难应付所有的工作压力。

copied *form of* COPY² * copy² 的不同形式

copies *form of* COPY * copy 的不同形式

copper /ˈkɒpə(r)/ *noun* 名词 (*no plural* 不用复数形式)

a common metal with a colour between brown and red 铜: *copper wire* 铜线

copy¹ 0‑ᴡ /ˈkɒpi/ *noun* 名词 (*plural* 复数形式 copies)

1 a thing that is made to look exactly like another thing 复制品; 复印件: *This isn't a real painting by Van Gogh. It's only a copy.* 这幅画不是凡·高的真迹, 只是一件复制品。 ◊ *The secretary made two copies of the letter.* 秘书把信复印了两份。

2 one example of a book or newspaper (书或报纸) 一本, 一份: *Two million copies of this newspaper are sold every day.* 这报纸每天卖两百万份。

copy² 0‑ᴡ /ˈkɒpi/ *verb* 动词 (copies, copying, copied /ˈkɒpid/, has copied)

1 to write, draw or make something exactly the same as something else 抄写; 复制; 复印: *The teacher asked us to copy the list of words into our books.* 老师叫我们把那些词语抄在本子上。

2 to do or try to do the same as somebody else 模仿; 仿效 ⊃ SAME MEANING **imitate** 同义词为 imitate: *He copies everything his brother does.* 他模仿他哥哥的一举一动。

cord /kɔːd/ *noun* 名词

1 strong thick string 粗线; 绳索

2 *American English for* FLEX 美式英语, 即 flex

core 果核

core 果心

apples 苹果

core /kɔː(r)/ *noun* 名词
the middle part of some kinds of fruit, where the seeds are 果核；果心：
an apple core 苹果核

cork /kɔːk/ *noun* 名词
1 (*no plural* 不用复数形式) a light soft material that comes from the outside of a particular tree 软木
2 (*plural* 复数形式 corks) a round piece of **cork** that you put in a bottle to close it 软木塞

corkscrew 开瓶起子

corkscrew 开瓶起子
cork 软木塞

corkscrew /ˈkɔːkskruː/ *noun* 名词
a thing that you use for pulling CORKS out of bottles 开瓶起子；瓶塞钻

corn /kɔːn/ *noun* 名词 (*no plural* 不用复数形式)
1 (*British* 英式英语) the seeds of plants that are grown for their grain, for example WHEAT 谷粒
2 *American English for* MAIZE 美式英语，即 maize

corner 角落；拐角

The lamp is in the **corner**. 灯在角落里。

The bank is on the **corner**. 银行在拐角处。

corner 0→ /ˈkɔːnə(r)/ *noun* 名词
a place where two lines, walls or roads meet 角；角落；拐角： *Put the lamp in the corner of the room.* 把灯放在房间的角落里。 ◇ *The shop is on the corner of East Avenue and Union Street.* 那家商店位于东大街和联合街的拐角处。 ◇ *He drove round the corner at top speed.* 他以高速开车转弯。

cornflakes /ˈkɔːnfleɪks/ *noun* 名词 (*plural* 用复数形式)
small pieces of dried food that you eat with milk and sugar for breakfast 玉米片（加牛奶和糖作早餐食用）

corporation /ˌkɔːpəˈreɪʃn/ *noun* 名词
a big company 大公司

corpse /kɔːps/ *noun* 名词
the body of a dead person （人的）尸体

correct¹ 0→ /kəˈrekt/ *adjective* 形容词
right or true; with no mistakes 对的；正确的；无误的： *What is the correct time, please?* 请问现在的确切时间是几点？ ◇ *All your answers were correct.* 你的答案全部正确。 ○ OPPOSITE **incorrect** 反义词为 incorrect
▶ **correctly** /kəˈrektli/ *adverb* 副词： *Have I spelt your name correctly?* 你的名字我拼对了没有？ ○ OPPOSITE **incorrectly** 反义词为 incorrectly

correct² 0→ /kəˈrekt/ *verb* 动词 (corrects, correcting, corrected)
to show where the mistakes are in something and make it right 改正；纠正；修改： *The class did the exercises and the teacher corrected them.* 全班同学做了练习后，老师给他们批改。 ◇ *Please correct me if I make a mistake.* 假如我出错，请纠正我。

correction /kəˈrekʃn/ *noun* 名词
a change that makes something right or better 改正；纠正；修改： *The teacher made a few corrections to my essay.* 老师在我的文章上作了一些修改。

correspond /ˌkɒrəˈspɒnd/ *verb* 动词 (corresponds, corresponding, corresponded)
to be the same, or almost the same, as something 和…相一致；符合： *Does the name on the envelope correspond with the name inside the letter?* 信封上的名字与信里的名字一致吗？

correspondence /ˌkɒrəˈspɒndəns/ *noun* 名词 (*no plural* 不用复数形式)
the letters a person sends and receives 通信；来往书信： *Her secretary reads all*

her correspondence. 她的秘书阅读她的所有信件。

corridor /ˈkɒrɪdɔː(r)/ *noun* 名词
a long narrow part inside a building with rooms on each side of it 走廊；过道

cosmetics /kɒzˈmetɪks/ *noun* 名词 (*plural* 用复数形式)
special powders or creams that you use on your face or hair to make yourself more beautiful 化妆品；美容品

cost¹ 0→ /kɒst/ *noun* 名词
1 (*plural* 复数形式 costs) the money that you have to pay for something 成本；费用；花费: *The cost of the repairs was very high.* 修理费非常高。⊃ Look at the note at **price**. 见 price 条的注释。
2 (*no plural* 不用复数形式) what you lose or give to have another thing 代价: *He saved the child at the cost of his own life.* 他救了孩子，却牺牲了自己的生命。
at all costs no matter what you must do to make it happen 不惜任何代价: *We must win at all costs.* 我们无论如何都要赢。

cost² 0→ /kɒst/ *verb* 动词 (costs, costing, cost, has cost)
1 to have the price of 价钱为: *This plant cost $4.* 这棵植物售价 4 元。◇ *How much did the book cost?* 那本书多少钱？
2 to make you lose something 使损失: *One mistake cost him his job.* 一次过失让他丢了工作。

costly /ˈkɒstli/ *adjective* 形容词 (costlier, costliest)
costing a lot of money 昂贵的；花费大的 ⊃ SAME MEANING **expensive** 同义词为 expensive: *The repairs will be very costly.* 修理会花很多钱。

costume /ˈkɒstjuːm/ *noun* 名词
the special clothes that people wear in a country or at a certain time（某国或某时期的）服装: *The actors wore beautiful costumes.* 演员穿着漂亮的服装。◇ *the national costume of Japan* 日本的民族服装 ⊃ Look also at **swimming costume**. 亦见 swimming costume。

cosy (*British* 英式英语) (*American* 美式英语 cozy) /ˈkəʊzi/ *adjective* 形容词 (cosier, cosiest)
warm and comfortable 温暖舒适的: *a cosy room* 温暖舒适的房间

cot /kɒt/ (*British* 英式英语) (*American* 美式英语 crib) *noun* 名词
a bed with high sides for a baby 婴儿床 ⊃ Look at **cradle**. 见 cradle。

cottage /ˈkɒtɪdʒ/ *noun* 名词
a small house in the country 小屋；村舍 ⊃ Look at the picture at **path**. 见 path 的插图。

cotton 0→ /ˈkɒtn/ *noun* 名词 (*no plural* 不用复数形式)
1 a natural cloth or thread that is made from the soft white hairs around the seeds of a plant that grows in hot countries 棉布；棉线: *a cotton shirt* 棉衬衫 ◇ *a reel of cotton* 一轴棉线
2 *American English for* COTTON WOOL 美式英语，即 cotton wool

cotton wool /ˌkɒtn ˈwʊl/ *noun* 名词 (*no plural* 不用复数形式) (*British* 英式英语) (*American* 美式英语 cotton)
soft light material made from cotton that you often use for cleaning your skin 药棉；脱脂棉: *The nurse cleaned the cut with cotton wool.* 护士用脱脂棉清洗了伤口。

couch /kaʊtʃ/ *noun* 名词 (*plural* 复数形式 couches)
a long comfortable seat for two or more people to sit on 长沙发 ⊃ SAME MEANING **sofa** 同义词为 sofa

couch potato /ˈkaʊtʃ pəteɪtəʊ/ *noun* 名词 (*informal* 非正式)
a person who spends a lot of time sitting and watching television 老泡在电视机前的人；电视迷

cough¹ 0→ /kɒf/ *verb* 动词 (coughs, coughing, coughed /kɒft/)

🔍 PRONUNCIATION 读音说明
The word **cough** sounds like **off**.
* cough 读音像 off。

to send air out of your throat with a sudden loud noise 咳嗽: *The smoke made me cough.* 烟呛得我直咳嗽。

cough² 0→ /kɒf/ *noun* 名词
when you send air out of your throat with a sudden loud noise 咳嗽: *I've got a bad cough.* 我咳嗽得很厉害。◇ *He gave a little cough before he started to speak.* 他轻轻地咳了一下，然后开始演讲。

could 0→ /kʊd/ *modal verb* 情态动词

🔍 PRONUNCIATION 读音说明
The word **could** sounds like **good**, because we don't say the letter l in this word. * could 读音像 good，因为 l 在这里不发音。

1 the word for 'can' in the past * can 的过去式: *He could run very fast when he* *was young.* 他年轻时跑得很快。◇ *I could hear the birds singing.* 我能听到鸟儿在歌唱。

2 a word that you use to ask something in a polite way（礼貌地请求）能，可以：*Could you open the door?* 您开一下门好吗？◇ *Could I have another drink, please?* 请再给我一杯好吗？

3 a word that shows what is or may be possible 可能：*I don't know where Mum is. She could be in the kitchen.* 我不知道妈妈在哪里。她可能在厨房。◇ *It could rain tomorrow.* 明天可能会下雨。➲ Look at the note at **modal verb**. 见 modal verb 条的注释。

couldn't /'kʊdnt/ *short for* COULD NOT
* could not 的缩略式：*It was dark and I couldn't see anything.* 天很黑，我什么都看不见。

could've /'kʊdəv/ (*informal* 非正式) *short for* COULD HAVE * could have 的缩略式：*He could've gone to university but he didn't want to.* 他原本可以上大学，但他不想。

council /'kaʊnsl/ *noun* 名词
a group of people who are chosen to work together and to make rules and decide things 议会；政务委员会：*The city council is planning to widen the road.* 市政务会正计划拓宽这条道路。

councillor (*British* 英式英语) (*American* 美式英语 **councilor**) /'kaʊnsələ(r)/ *noun* 名词
a member of a COUNCIL 市议员；政务委员会委员

count¹ 0➔ /kaʊnt/ *verb* 动词 (counts, counting, counted)

1 to say numbers one after the other in the correct order（按顺序）数数：*The children are learning to count from one to ten.* 孩子们正在学习从一数到十。

2 to look at people or things to see how many there are 清点总数：*I have counted the chairs – there are 32.* 我数了数椅子——有 32 把。

3 to include somebody or something when you are finding a total 把…算入；包括：*There were twenty people on the bus, not counting the driver.* 不算司机，公共汽车上总共有二十人。

4 to be important or accepted 重要；获得认可：*Every point in this game counts.* 这场比赛的每一分都很重要。◇ *Your throw won't count if you go over the line.* 要是越过那条线，你的投掷会判作无效。

count on somebody or 或 **something** to feel sure that somebody or something

will do what you want 依赖；指望：*Can I count on you to help me?* 我指望你帮忙了，可以吗？

count² /kaʊnt/ *noun* 名词
a time when you count things 计数：*After an election there is a count of all the votes.* 选举后要统计选票。

keep count of something to know how many there are of something 记得数目：*Try to keep count of the number of tickets you sell.* 要记住你卖了多少票。

lose count of something to not know how many there are of something 没记得数目

count³ /kaʊnt/ *noun* 名词
a man in some countries who has a special title 伯爵：*Count Dracula* 德拉库拉伯爵

countable /'kaʊntəbl/ *adjective* 形容词
(*grammar* 语法) **Countable** nouns are ones that you can use in the plural or with *a* or *an*, for example *chair* and *idea*.（名词）可数的 ➲ OPPOSITE **uncountable** 反义词为 uncountable

counter /'kaʊntə(r)/ *noun* 名词
1 a long high table in a shop, bank or bar, that is between the people who work there and the customers 柜台：*The man behind the counter in the bank was very helpful.* 银行柜台后面的那个职员很乐意帮忙。

2 a small round thing that you use when you play some games 筹码

counterclockwise /ˌkaʊntə'klɒkwaɪz/ *American English for* ANTICLOCKWISE 美式英语，即 anticlockwise

countess /'kaʊntəs/ *noun* 名词 (*plural* 复数形式 **countesses**)
a woman who has a special title. She may be married to a COUNT or an EARL. 女伯爵；伯爵夫人

countless /'kaʊntləs/ *adjective* 形容词
very many 无数的；数不尽的：*I have tried to phone him countless times.* 我尝试给他打过无数次电话。

country 0➔ /'kʌntri/ *noun* 名词
1 (*plural* 复数形式 **countries**) an area of land with its own people and government 国家：*France, Spain and other European countries* 法国、西班牙和其他欧洲国家

🔎 WHICH WORD? 词语辨析
Country or **nation**? 用 country 还是 nation?

A B C D E F G H I J K L M N O P Q R S T U V W X Y Z

These words are very similar, but we use **nation** when we want to refer to the people as well as the land. 两者非常相似，但 nation 可以指人民和国家: *The whole nation seemed to be watching the match on TV.* 全国人民似乎都在看电视上的那场比赛。

2 the country (*no plural* 不用复数形式) land that is away from towns and cities 乡下；乡村: *Do you live in the town or in the country?* 你住在城里还是乡下？

countryside 0→ /ˈkʌntrisaɪd/ *noun* 名词 (*no plural* 不用复数形式) land with fields, woods, farms, etc., that is away from towns and cities 乡村；农村: *There are magnificent views over open countryside.* 开阔的乡村景色十分壮丽。

county /ˈkaʊnti/ *noun* 名词 (*plural* 复数形式 **counties**) one of the parts of Britain, Ireland or the US which has its own local government （英国、爱尔兰的）郡；（美国的）县: *the county of Oxfordshire* 牛津郡 ◇ *Orange County, California* 加州奥兰治县

couple 0→ /ˈkʌpl/ *noun* 名词 **1 a couple** two or a small number of people or things 两个；几个: *I invited a couple of friends to lunch.* 我请了几个朋友吃午饭。 ◇ *I'll be back in a couple of minutes.* 我几分钟后回来。 **2** two people who are married or in a romantic relationship （一对）夫妻，情侣: *A young couple live next door.* 一对年轻夫妇住在隔壁。

coupon /ˈkuːpɒn/ *noun* 名词 a small piece of paper that you can use to buy things at a lower price, or that you can collect and use instead of money to buy things 优惠券；代币券

courage /ˈkʌrɪdʒ/ *noun* 名词 (*no plural* 不用复数形式) not being afraid, or not showing that you are afraid when you do something dangerous or difficult 勇气 ⊃ SAME MEANING **bravery** 同义词为 bravery: *She showed great courage in the face of danger.* 她面对危险时显得十分勇敢。 ▶ **courageous** /kəˈreɪdʒəs/ *adjective* 形容词 ⊃ SAME MEANING **brave** 同义词为 brave: *a courageous young man* 勇敢的小伙子

courgette /kɔːˈʒet/ (*British* 英式英语) (*American* 美式英语 **zucchini**) *noun* 名词 a long vegetable that is green on the outside and white on the inside 密especial西

葫芦；小胡瓜 ⊃ Look at Picture Dictionary page **P9**. 见彩页 P9。

course 0→ /kɔːs/ *noun* 名词 **1** (*plural* 复数形式 **courses**) a set of lessons on a certain subject 课程: *He's taking a course in computer programming.* 他正在学电脑程序设计课程。 **2** (*no plural* 不用复数形式) the direction that something moves in 行进方向: *We followed the course of the river.* 我们沿着河道走去。 ◇ *The plane had to change course because of the storm.* 飞机因遇到暴风雨而要改变航向。 **3** (*no plural* 不用复数形式) the time when something is happening 期间: *The telephone rang six times during the course of the evening.* 整个晚上电话响了六次。 **4** (*plural* 复数形式 **courses**) one separate part of a meal 一道菜: *a three-course meal* 有三道菜的一顿饭 ◇ *I had chicken for my main course.* 我主菜吃的是鸡。 **5** (*plural* 复数形式 **courses**) a piece of ground for some kinds of sport 运动场地: *a golf course* 高尔夫球场 ◇ *a racecourse* 赛马场 **of course** certainly 当然: *Of course I'll help you.* 我当然会帮助你。 ◇ *'Can I use your telephone?' 'Of course you can.'* "我能借用你的电话吗？" "当然可以。" ◇ *'Are you angry with me?' 'Of course not!'* "你生我的气了吗？" "当然没有！"

coursebook /ˈkɔːsbʊk/ *noun* 名词 (*British* 英式英语) a book that teachers and students use in class 教科书；课本

court 0→ /kɔːt/ *noun* 名词 **1** the place where a judge or a group of people (called a **jury**) decide if a person has done something wrong, and what the punishment will be 法院；法庭: *The man will appear in court tomorrow.* 那个男人明天出庭。 **2** a piece of ground where you can play certain sports 球场: *a tennis court* 网球场 ◇ *a basketball court* 篮球场 ⊃ Look at the note at **pitch¹**. 见 pitch¹ 条的注释。

courteous /ˈkɜːtiəs/ *adjective* 形容词 polite and showing respect for other people 有礼貌的；恭敬的

courtesy /ˈkɜːtəsi/ *noun* 名词 (*no plural* 不用复数形式) polite behaviour that shows respect for other people 礼貌；谦恭；彬彬有礼

court of law /ˌkɔːt əv ˈlɔː/ *noun* 名词 (*plural* 复数形式 **courts of law**) (*British also* 英式英语亦作 **law court**) a place where a judge or a group of people (called a jury) decide if somebody has done something wrong, and what the punishment will be 法院；法庭

courtyard /'kɔːtjɑːd/ *noun* 名词
an open space without a roof, inside a building or between buildings 庭院；院子；天井

cousin 0= /'kʌzn/ *noun* 名词
the child of your aunt or uncle 堂兄（或弟、姐、妹）；表兄（或弟、姐、妹）
つ You use the same word for both male and female cousins. * cousin 可指男性和女性。

cover¹ 0= /'kʌvə(r)/ *verb* 动词 (covers, covering, covered /'kʌvəd/)
1 to put one thing over another thing to hide it or to keep it safe or warm 掩蔽；遮盖：*Cover the floor with a newspaper before you start painting.* 把报纸铺在地上再刷油漆。◇ *She covered her head with a scarf.* 她用头巾包着头。
2 to be all over something or somebody 覆盖：*Snow covered the ground.* 雪覆盖了地面。◇ *The children were covered in mud.* 孩子们全身都是泥。

cover² 0= /'kʌvə(r)/ *noun* 名词
1 a thing that you put over another thing, for example to keep it safe 覆盖物；套子；罩子：*The computer has a plastic cover.* 这台电脑有个塑料罩。
2 the outside part of a book or magazine （书刊的）封面，封皮：*The book had a picture of a film star on the cover (= the front cover).* 那本书封面上印着一个影星的照片。

coveralls /'kʌvərɔːlz/ *American English for* OVERALLS 美式英语，即 overalls

covering 0= /'kʌvərɪŋ/ *noun* 名词
something that covers another thing 覆盖物：*There was a thick covering of snow on the ground.* 地上积着厚厚的雪。

cow 0= /kaʊ/ *noun* 名词
a big female farm animal that is kept for its milk or meat 母牛；奶牛 つ Look at Picture Dictionary page **P2**. 见彩页 **P2**。

> 🔍 WORD BUILDING 词汇扩充
> The male is called a **bull** and a young cow is called a **calf**. 公牛叫做 bull，小牛叫做 calf。
> Meat from a cow is called **beef** and meat from a calf is called **veal**. 牛肉叫做 beef，小牛肉叫做 veal。

cow （母）牛
horn 角
cow 奶牛
bull 公牛
calf 小牛

coward /'kaʊəd/ *noun* 名词
a person who is afraid when there is danger or a problem 胆小鬼；懦夫

cowboy /'kaʊbɔɪ/ *noun* 名词
a man who rides a horse and looks after cows in some parts of the US （美国某些地区的）牛仔，骑马牧人

cozy *American English for* COSY 美式英语，即 cosy

crab 螃蟹
shell 壳
claw 螯

crab /kræb/ *noun* 名词
an animal that lives in and near the sea. It has a hard shell and ten legs. 蟹；螃蟹

crack¹ /kræk/ *verb* 动词 (cracks, cracking, cracked /krækt/)
1 to break, but not into separate pieces 破裂；裂开：*The glass will crack if you pour boiling water into it.* 这只玻璃杯倒进开水就会裂。◇ *This cup is cracked.* 这个杯子裂了。
2 to make a sudden loud noise 发出爆裂声；噼啪作响
crack down on somebody or 或 **something** to become stricter when dealing with bad or illegal behaviour 严厉打击：*The police are cracking down on drug dealers.* 警方正在严厉打击毒贩。

crack² /kræk/ *noun* 名词
1 a thin line on something where it has broken, but not into separate pieces 裂缝；裂纹：*There's a crack in this glass.* 这只玻璃杯上有裂纹。
2 a narrow space between two things or two parts of something 缝隙；狭缝：*a crack in the curtains* 窗帘间的缝隙
3 a sudden loud noise（突然的）爆裂声，噼啪声：*a crack of thunder* 一声霹雳

cracker /'krækə(r)/ *noun* 名词
1 a thin dry biscuit that you can eat with cheese 薄脆饼干 ᴐ Look at Picture Dictionary page **P6**. 见彩页 **P6**。
2 a long round thing made of coloured paper with a small present inside. It makes a loud noise when two people pull the ends away from each other. 彩包爆竹（外覆彩纸，内装小礼物）：*We often **pull crackers** at Christmas parties.* 我们在圣诞聚会经常拉彩包爆竹玩。

crackle /'krækl/ *verb* 动词 (crackles, crackling, crackled /'krækld/)
to make a lot of short sharp sounds 发出噼啪声：*Dry wood crackles when you burn it.* 干柴一燃烧就噼啪作响。

cradle /'kreɪdl/ *noun* 名词
a small bed for a baby which can be moved from side to side 摇篮 ᴐ Look at **cot**. 见 cot.

craft /krɑːft/ *noun* 名词
a job or activity for which you need skill with your hands 手艺；工艺：*Pottery is a traditional craft.* 制陶是一项传统工艺。

craftsman /'krɑːftsmən/ *noun* 名词 (plural 复数形式 craftsmen /'krɑːftsmən/)
a person who is good at making things with their hands 工匠；手艺人

crafty /'krɑːfti/ *adjective* 形容词 (craftier, craftiest)
clever at getting what you want in a way that is not completely honest 狡诈的；诡计多端的

cram /kræm/ *verb* 动词 (crams, cramming, crammed /kræmd/)
to push too many people or things into a small space 把…塞进；挤满：*She crammed her clothes into a bag.* 她把衣服都塞进了包里。

cramp /kræmp/ *noun* 名词 (no plural 不用复数形式)
a sudden pain that you get in a muscle, for example in your leg, which makes it difficult to move 抽筋；痛性痉挛

crane 起重机

crane /kreɪn/ *noun* 名词
a big machine with a long metal arm for lifting heavy things 起重机；吊车

crash¹ 0ᴏ̄ /kræʃ/ *noun* 名词 (plural 复数形式 crashes)
1 an accident when something that is moving hits another thing 碰撞；相撞：*He was killed in a car crash.* 他死于撞车事故。◊ *a plane crash* 飞机失事
2 a loud noise when something falls or hits another thing（落下或碰撞的）巨响：*I heard a crash as the tree fell.* 树倒下的时候我听到轰的一声。

crash² 0ᴏ̄ /kræʃ/ *verb* 动词 (crashes, crashing, crashed /kræʃt/)
1 to have an accident in a car or other vehicle and hit something 碰撞；撞击：*The bus crashed into a tree.* 公共汽车撞上了树。◊ *I crashed my father's car.* 我把父亲的车子撞了。
2 to fall or hit something with a loud noise（落下或撞击时）发出巨响：*The tree crashed to the ground.* 这棵树轰然一声倒在地上。
3 If a computer **crashes**, it suddenly stops working.（电脑）死机

crash helmet /'kræʃ helmɪt/ *noun* 名词
a hard hat that you wear when riding a motorbike to protect your head 防撞头盔

crate /kreɪt/ *noun* 名词
a big box for carrying bottles or other things 大箱子

crawl¹ /krɔːl/ *verb* 动词 (crawls, crawling, crawled /krɔːld/)
to move slowly on your hands and knees or with your body close to the ground 爬；爬行：*Babies crawl before they can walk.* 婴儿先会爬，然后才学会走路。
◊ *A spider crawled across the floor.* 一只蜘蛛爬过了地板。

A B C D E F G H I J K L M N O P Q R S T U V W X Y Z

crawl 爬行

crawl² /krɔːl/ *noun* 名词 (*no plural* 不用复数形式)
a way of swimming on your front 爬泳；自由泳 ➔ Look also at **breaststroke**. 亦见 breaststroke。

crayon /ˈkreɪən/ *noun* 名词
a soft, thick, coloured pencil 蜡笔：
The children were drawing pictures with crayons. 孩子们在用蜡笔画画。

crazy o⃞ /ˈkreɪzi/ *adjective* 形容词
(**crazier, craziest**) (*informal* 非正式)
1 stupid; not sensible 愚蠢的；疯狂的：
You must be crazy to ride a bike at night with no lights. 你晚上骑车不用灯，准是疯了。
2 very angry 非常气愤的；狂怒的：*My mum will go crazy if I get home late.* 要是我回家晚了，我妈妈就会十分生气。
3 If you are **crazy about** something or somebody, you like them very much. 热衷的；狂热的：*She's crazy about football.* 她热衷于足球。◇ *He's crazy about her.* 他对她很痴迷。➔ SAME MEANING **mad** 同义词为 mad

creak /kriːk/ *verb* 动词 (**creaks, creaking, creaked** /kriːkt/)
to make a noise like a door that needs oil, or like an old wooden floor when you walk on it 发出嘎吱声
▸ **creak** *noun* 名词：*The door opened with a creak.* 门吱的一声开了。

cream¹ o⃞ /kriːm/ *noun* 名词
1 (*no plural* 不用复数形式) the thick liquid on the top of milk 奶油；乳脂
2 (*plural* 复数形式 **creams**) a thick liquid that you put on your skin, for example to keep it soft 护肤霜；润肤膏：*hand cream* 护手霜

cream² o⃞ /kriːm/ *adjective* 形容词
with a colour between white and yellow 奶油色的；淡黄色的：*She was wearing a cream dress.* 她穿着淡黄色的连衣裙。

creamy /ˈkriːmi/ *adjective* 形容词
(**creamier, creamiest**)
1 with cream in it, or thick and smooth like cream 含有奶油的；像奶油的：
a creamy sauce 奶油沙司
2 having a colour like cream 奶油色的；淡黄色的：*creamy skin* 奶油色的皮肤

crease /kriːs/ *verb* 动词 (**creases, creasing, creased** /kriːst/)
If you **crease** something, or it **creases**, untidy lines or folds appear in it. 弄皱；起皱：*Don't sit on my jacket – you'll crease it.* 别坐在我的外衣上，会把它弄皱的。◇ *This shirt creases easily.* 这件衬衫很容易起皱。
▸ **crease** *noun* 名词：*You need to iron this shirt – it's full of creases.* 你得熨熨这件衬衫了 —— 它满是褶痕。

create o⃞ /kriˈeɪt/ *verb* 动词 (**creates, creating, created**)
to make something happen or exist 创造：*Do you believe that God created the world?* 你相信上帝创造世界吗？◇ *The government plans to create more jobs for young people.* 政府计划为年轻人创造更多的就业机会。

creation /kriˈeɪʃn/ *noun* 名词
1 (*no plural* 不用复数形式) making something new 创造：*the creation of the world* 世界的创造
2 (*plural* 复数形式 **creations**) a new thing that somebody has made 创造物；作品：*Mickey Mouse was the creation of Walt Disney.* 米老鼠是沃尔特·迪斯尼创作出来的。

creative /kriˈeɪtɪv/ *adjective* 形容词
A person who is **creative** has a lot of new ideas or is good at making new things. 有创造力的：*She's a very good painter – she's so creative.* 她是非常出色的画家，很有创作力。

creator /kriˈeɪtə(r)/ *noun* 名词
a person who makes something new 创造者：*Walt Disney was the creator of Mickey Mouse.* 沃尔特·迪斯尼是米老鼠的创作者。

creature /ˈkriːtʃə(r)/ *noun* 名词
any living thing that is not a plant 生物；动物：*birds, fish and other creatures* 鸟、鱼和其他动物 ◇ *This story is about creatures from another planet.* 这个故事讲的是来自另一个星球的生物。

credit¹ /ˈkredɪt/ *noun* 名词 (*no plural* 不用复数形式)
1 a way of buying something where you pay for it later 赊购；赊欠：*I bought the television on credit.* 这台电视机我是赊购的。
2 having money in an account（账户）

结余: *No bank charges are made if your account is in credit.* 如果账户内还有存款，银行就不会收取费用。
3 saying that somebody has done something well 称赞: *I did all the work but John got all the credit for it!* 工作都是我做的，但功劳却全归了约翰！

credit² /'kredɪt/ *verb* 动词 (credits, crediting, credited)
to add money to somebody's bank account 把…存入账户: *$500 has been credited to your account.* 已把 500 元存入你的账户。

credit card /'kredɪt kɑ:d/ *noun* 名词
a plastic card from a bank that you can use to buy something and pay for it later 信用卡: *Can I pay by credit card?* 我能用信用卡付账吗? ⊃ Look at the picture at **money**. 见 money 的插图。

creep /kri:p/ *verb* 动词 (creeps, creeping, crept /krept/, has crept)
to move quietly and carefully so that nobody hears or sees you 悄悄地挪动; 蹑手蹑脚地走: *I crept into the room where the children were sleeping.* 我蹑手蹑脚走进孩子睡觉的房间。◇ *The cat crept towards the bird.* 猫悄悄地靠近小鸟。

creepy /'kri:pi/ *adjective* 形容词 (creepier, creepiest) (informal 非正式)
making you feel nervous or afraid 令人毛骨悚然的 ⊃ SAME MEANING **scary** 同义词为 scary: *a creepy ghost story* 令人毛骨悚然的鬼故事

crept *form of* CREEP * creep 的不同形式

crescent /'kresnt; 'kreznt/ *noun* 名词
1 the shape of the moon when it is less than half a circle 月牙形; 新月形 ⊃ Look at the picture at **shape¹**. 见 shape¹ 的插图。
2 a street or line of houses with a curved shape 新月形街道: *I live at 34 Elgin Crescent.* 我住在埃尔金新月街 34 号。

crest /krest/ *noun* 名词
the top part of a hill or a wave 山顶; 顶峰; 浪尖: *surfers riding the crest of the wave* 正在浪峰上冲浪的人

crew /kru:/ *noun* 名词
all the people who work on a ship or a plane （轮船或飞机上的）全体工作人员

crib /krɪb/ *American English for* COT 美式英语, 即 cot

cricket /'krɪkɪt/ *noun* 名词
1 (no plural 不用复数形式) a game for two teams of eleven players who try to hit

a small hard ball with a piece of wood (called a **bat**) on a large field (called a **pitch**) 板球（运动）: *We watched a cricket match.* 我们看了一场板球比赛。⊃ Look at Picture Dictionary page **P14**. 见彩页 P14。⊃ Look at the note at **bat¹**. 见 bat¹ 条的注释。
2 (plural 复数形式 crickets) a small brown insect that jumps and makes a loud high noise by rubbing its wings together 蟋蟀; 蛐蛐
▸ **cricketer** /'krɪkɪtə(r)/ *noun* 名词
a person who plays CRICKET 板球运动员

cried *form of* CRY¹ * cry¹ 的不同形式
cries *form of* CRY * cry 的不同形式

crime /kraɪm/ *noun* 名词
something that somebody does that is against the law 罪; 罪行: *Murder and robbery are serious crimes.* 谋杀和抢劫都是重罪。◇ *They had committed a crime.* 他们犯了罪。

criminal¹ /'krɪmɪnl/ *adjective* 形容词
connected with crime 犯罪的; 犯法的: *Deliberate damage to public property is a criminal offence.* 故意损坏公物是刑事罪行。◇ *She is studying criminal law.* 她正在学习刑法。

criminal² /'krɪmɪnl/ *noun* 名词
a person who does something that is against the law 罪犯

crimson /'krɪmzn/ *adjective* 形容词
with a dark red colour, like blood 深红色的

cripple /'krɪpl/ *verb* 动词 (cripples, crippling, crippled /'krɪpld/)
to damage somebody's body so that they cannot walk or move normally 使残废; 使跛: *She was crippled in an accident.* 她在一起事故中残废了。

crisis /'kraɪsɪs/ *noun* 名词 (plural 复数形式 crises /'kraɪsi:z/)
a time when something very dangerous or serious happens 危机; 危急关头: *a political crisis* 政治危机

crisp¹ /krɪsp/ *adjective* 形容词 (crisper, crispest)
1 hard and dry 脆的: *If you keep the biscuits in a tin, they will stay crisp.* 饼干放在罐子里就可保持酥脆。
2 fresh and not soft 鲜脆的: *crisp apples* 鲜脆的苹果

crisp² /krɪsp/ (British 英式英语) (American 美式英语 **chip, potato chip**) *noun* 名词
a very thin piece of potato cooked in

hot oil and eaten cold. **Crisps** are sold in bags and have many different flavours. 炸薯片: *a packet of crisps* 一包炸薯片

crisps 炸薯片

critic /'krɪtɪk/ *noun* 名词
1 a person who says that somebody or something is wrong or bad 批评者: *critics of the government* 批评政府的人
2 a person who writes about a book, film or play and says if they like it or not 评论家; 评论员: *The critics loved his new film.* 评论家喜爱他的新片。

critical /'krɪtɪkl/ *adjective* 形容词
1 If you are **critical** of somebody or something, you say that they are wrong or bad. 批评的; 挑剔的: *They were very critical of my work.* 他们对我的工作提出了许多批评。
2 very important 极重要的; 关键的 ⊃ SAME MEANING **crucial** 同义词为 crucial: *We have reached a critical stage in our negotiations.* 我们的谈判已经到了关键的阶段。
3 very serious or dangerous 非常严重的; 危急的: *The patient is in a critical condition.* 病人情况危急。
▶ **critically** /'krɪtɪkli/ *adverb* 副词: *She's critically ill.* 她病得很重。

criticism 0ᵇ /'krɪtɪsɪzəm/ *noun* 名词
what you think is bad about somebody or something 批评: *I listened to all their criticisms of my plan.* 我听了他们对我的计划提出的所有批评。

criticize /'krɪtɪsaɪz/ *verb* 动词 (criticizes, criticizing, criticized /'krɪtɪsaɪzd/)
to say that somebody or something is wrong or bad 批评: *She was criticized for not following orders.* 她因不遵守命令而受到批评。

croak /krəʊk/ *verb* 动词 (croaks, croaking, croaked /krəʊkt/)
1 If a FROG (= a small green animal that lives in or near water) **croaks**, it makes a low rough sound. (青蛙)呱呱地叫
2 to speak in a low rough voice 用低哑的声音说话: *'My throat's really sore,'*

he croaked. "我的喉咙痛死了。"他哑着嗓子说道。
▶ **croak** *noun* 名词

crockery /'krɒkəri/ *noun* 名词 (*no plural* 不用复数形式)
plates, cups and dishes 陶器; 瓦器

crocodile /'krɒkədaɪl/ *noun* 名词
a big animal with a long tail and a big mouth with sharp teeth. **Crocodiles** live in rivers in hot countries. 鳄鱼: *A crocodile is a reptile.* 鳄鱼是爬行动物。 ⊃ Look at Picture Dictionary page P3. 见彩页 P3.

crooked /'krʊkɪd/ *adjective* 形容词
not straight 不直的; 弯曲的; 歪的: *She has crooked teeth.* 她的牙齿不齐。 ⊃ Look at the picture at **straight**². 见 straight² 的插图。

crop /krɒp/ *noun* 名词
all the plants of one kind that a farmer grows at one time 庄稼; 作物: *There was a good crop of potatoes last year.* 去年马铃薯收成很好。 ◇ *Rain is good for the crops.* 下雨对庄稼有好处。

cross¹ 0ᵇ /krɒs/ *noun* 名词 (*plural* 复数形式 crosses)
1 a mark like X or † 叉号; 十字形记号: *The cross on the map shows where I live.* 地图上打叉的就是我住的地方。
2 something with the shape X or † 叉形物; 十字形物: *She wears a cross (= a symbol of the Christian religion) around her neck.* 她脖子上戴着一条十字架项链。

cross² /krɒs/ *verb* 动词 (crosses, crossing, crossed /krɒst/)
1 to go from one side of something to the other 穿越; 横过: *Be careful when you cross the road.* 过马路要小心。
2 to put one thing over another thing 交叉: *She sat down and crossed her legs.* 她坐下后双腿交叉着。
cross something out to draw a line through a word or words, for example because you have made a mistake 画掉; 删掉: *I crossed the word out and wrote it again.* 我把那个字画掉,重写了一个。

cross³ /krɒs/ *adjective* 形容词
angry 生气的; 恼怒的 ⊃ SAME MEANING **annoyed** 同义词为 annoyed: *I was cross with her because she was late.* 她来迟了,我很生气。

crossing /'krɒsɪŋ/ *noun* 名词
a place where you can cross over something, for example a road or a river 人行横道; 渡口

A
B
C
D
E
F
G
H
I
J
K
L
M
N
O
P
Q
R
S
T
U
V
W
X
Y
Z

crossroads /'krɒsrəʊdz/ *noun* 名词
(*plural* 复数形式 **crossroads**)
a place where two roads meet and cross
each other 十字路口

crosswalk /'krɒswɔːk/ *American English
for* PEDESTRIAN CROSSING 美式英语，
即 pedestrian crossing

crossword puzzle 纵横填字游戏

clues 提示—

crossword /'krɒswɜːd/ (*also* 亦作
crossword puzzle /'krɒswɜːd pʌzl/) *noun*
名词
a game where you have to write words in
square spaces across and down the page
纵横填字游戏

crouch /kraʊtʃ/ *verb* 动词 (**crouches**,
crouching, **crouched** /kraʊtʃt/)
to bend your legs and back so that your
body is close to the ground 蹲；蹲伏：
I crouched under the table to hide. 我蹲在
桌子底下藏了起来。

crow¹ /krəʊ/ *noun* 名词
a large black bird that makes a loud noise
乌鸦

crow² /krəʊ/ *verb* 动词 (**crows**, **crowing**,
crowed /krəʊd/)
to make a loud noise like a male chicken
(called a **cock**) 啼叫；打鸣

crowd¹ 0━ /kraʊd/ *noun* 名词
a lot of people together 人群：*There was
a large crowd at the football match.* 有一
大群人在看足球赛。

crowd² /kraʊd/ *verb* 动词 (**crowds**,
crowding, **crowded**)
to come together in a big group 聚集：
The journalists **crowded round** *the film
star.* 记者把那影星团团围住。

crowded 0━ /'kraʊdɪd/ *adjective*
形容词
full of people 拥挤的：*The streets were
very crowded.* 街上人头攒动。◇ *a crowded
bus* 挤满人的公共汽车

crown¹ /kraʊn/ *noun* 名词
a circle made of valuable metal and
stones (called **jewels**) that a king or queen
wears on his or her head 王冠；皇冠

crown² /kraʊn/ *verb* 动词 (**crowns**,
crowning, **crowned** /kraʊnd/)
to put a **crown** on the head of a new king
or queen, as a sign that he or she is the
new ruler 为⋯加冕：*Elizabeth II was
crowned in 1952.* 伊丽莎白二世于 1952 年
加冕。

crucial /'kruːʃl/ *adjective* 形容词
very important 至关重要的；关键的
⊃ SAME MEANING **critical** 同义词为
critical：*a crucial moment* 紧要关头

crude /kruːd/ *adjective* 形容词 (**cruder**,
crudest)
1 simple and not showing much skill or
care 粗略的；大概的：*The method was
crude but effective.* 这方法虽然简略但挺
有效。
2 rude in a way that many people do not
like 粗俗的；粗鲁的：*crude jokes* 粗俗的
笑话

crude oil /ˌkruːd 'ɔɪl/ *noun* 名词
(*no plural* 不用复数形式)
oil that is in its natural state, before it is
treated with chemicals 原油（开采出来未
经提炼的石油）

cruel 0━ /'kruːəl/ *adjective* 形容词
(**crueller**, **cruellest**)
A person who is **cruel** is unkind and likes
to hurt other people or animals. 残忍的；
残酷的：*I think it's cruel to keep animals
in cages.* 我觉得把动物关在笼子里很残忍。
▶ **cruelly** /'kruːəli/ *adverb* 副词：*He was
cruelly treated when he was a child.*
他小时候受过虐待。

cruelty /'kruːəlti/ *noun* 名词 (*no plural*
不用复数形式)
behaviour that is unkind and hurts other
people or animals 残忍；残酷

cruise¹ /kruːz/ *noun* 名词
a holiday when you travel on a ship and
visit a lot of different places 乘船度假：
They **went on a world cruise**. 他们乘船
环球旅游去了。

cruise² /kruːz/ *verb* 动词 (**cruises**,
cruising, **cruised** /kruːzd/)
to travel on a ship as a holiday, visiting
different places 乘船度假：*They cruised
around the Caribbean.* 他们乘船游览加勒
比海地区。

crumb /krʌm/ *noun* 名词
a very small piece of bread, cake or
biscuit（面包、蛋糕或饼干的）碎屑

crumble /'krʌmbl/ *verb* 动词 (**crumbles**,
crumbling, **crumbled** /'krʌmbld/)
to break into very small pieces 破碎；

变成碎屑: *The old castle walls are crumbling.* 那座古堡的城墙在逐渐坍塌。

crumple /ˈkrʌmpl/ *verb* 动词 (crumples, crumpling, crumpled /ˈkrʌmpld/)
to be pressed or to press something into an untidy shape 压皱; (使) 起皱: *She crumpled the paper into a ball and threw it away.* 她把那张纸揉成团后扔掉了。

crunch /krʌntʃ/ *verb* 动词 (crunches, crunching, crunched /krʌntʃt/)
1 to make a loud noise when you eat something that is hard 嘎吱嘎吱地嚼 (硬食物): *She crunched her apple noisily.* 她嘎吱嘎吱地啃着苹果。
2 to make a noise like the sound of something being crushed 发出碎裂声: *The snow crunched under our feet as we walked.* 我们行走着，脚下的雪嘎吱作响。

crush 0► /krʌʃ/ *verb* 动词 (crushes, crushing, crushed /krʌʃt/)
to press something very hard so that you break or damage it 压碎; 压坏: *She sat on my hat and crushed it.* 她把我的帽子坐扁了。

crust /krʌst/ *noun* 名词
the hard part on the outside of bread 面包皮 ► Look at the picture at **bread**. 见 bread 的插图。
▶ **crusty** /ˈkrʌsti/ *adjective* 形容词 with a hard **crust** 有硬面包皮的: *fresh crusty bread* 刚出炉的脆皮面包

crutch /krʌtʃ/ *noun* 名词 (plural 复数形式 crutches)
a long stick that you put under your arm to help you walk when you have hurt your leg 拐杖: *He broke his leg and now he's on crutches.* 他的腿断了，现在得靠腋杖走路。 ► Look at the picture at **plaster¹**. 见 plaster¹ 的插图。

cry¹ 0► /kraɪ/ *verb* 动词 (cries, crying, cried /kraɪd/, has cried)
1 to have drops of water falling from your eyes because you are unhappy or hurt 哭: *The baby cries a lot.* 那婴儿经常哭。
2 to shout or make a loud noise 喊叫; 嚷: *'Help!' he cried.* "救命!"他喊道。
◇ *She cried out in pain.* 她疼得叫了起来。

cry² 0► /kraɪ/ *noun* 名词 (plural 复数形式 cries)
a loud noise that you make to show strong feelings such as pain, fear or excitement 叫喊; 叫声: *He gave a cry of pain.* 他发出痛苦的叫声。 ◇ *We heard her cries and ran to help.* 我们听到她喊就跑过去帮忙。

crystal /ˈkrɪstl/ *noun* 名词
1 a shape that some substances make when they become solid 结晶; 晶体: *salt crystals* 盐的结晶体
2 a kind of rock that looks like glass 水晶

cub /kʌb/ *noun* 名词
a young animal such as a LION, a BEAR, a FOX, etc. 幼兽

cube /kjuːb/ *noun* 名词
1 a shape like a box with six square sides all the same size 立方体; 正方体
2 the number that you get if you multiply a number by itself twice 立方: *The cube of 5 (= 5³) is 125 (= 5 x 5 x 5).* * 5 的立方是 125。
▶ **cubic** /ˈkjuːbɪk/ *adjective* 形容词: *a cubic metre (= a space like a cube that is one metre long on each side)* 一立方米

cubicle /ˈkjuːbɪkl/ *noun* 名词
a small room that is made by separating off part of a larger room 隔间: *a shower cubicle* 淋浴间

cuckoo /ˈkʊkuː/ *noun* 名词 (plural 复数形式 cuckoos)
a bird that makes a sound like its name 布谷鸟; 杜鹃鸟

cucumber /ˈkjuːkʌmbə(r)/ *noun* 名词
a long vegetable with a green skin, that we often eat in salads 黄瓜 ► Look at Picture Dictionary page **P9**. 见彩页 P9。

cuddle /ˈkʌdl/ *verb* 动词 (cuddles, cuddling, cuddled /ˈkʌdld/)
to hold somebody or something in your arms to show love 拥抱; 搂抱 ► SAME MEANING **hug** 同义词为 hug: *He cuddled his baby.* 他搂着自己的小婴孩。
▶ **cuddle** *noun* 名词: *I gave her a cuddle.* 我拥抱了她一下。

cuff /kʌf/ *noun* 名词
the end part of a sleeve, near your hand 袖口 ► Look at the picture at **shirt**. 见 shirt 的插图。

cultivate /ˈkʌltɪveɪt/ *verb* 动词 (cultivates, cultivating, cultivated)
1 to use land for growing plants 耕种 耕作: *Only a small area of the island was cultivated.* 岛上只有一小片地耕种过。
2 to keep and care for plants 种植; 栽培
▶ **cultivation** /ˌkʌltɪˈveɪʃn/ *noun* 名词 (no plural 不用复数形式): *cultivation of the land* 土地耕种

cultural /ˈkʌltʃərəl/ *adjective* 形容词
1 connected with the ideas, customs and way of life of a group of people or a country 文化的: *There are many cultural*

differences between our two countries. 我们两国之间存在着很多文化差异。 ⊃ Look at **multicultural**. 见 multicultural。
2 connected with art, music or literature 文化艺术的

culture ⊶ /'kʌltʃə(r)/ *noun* 名词
1 (*plural* 复数形式 cultures) the customs, ideas and way of life of a group of people or a country 文化，文明（指风俗、生活方式等）： *the language and culture of the Aztecs* 阿兹特克人的语言和文化
2 (*no plural* 不用复数形式) art, music, literature and the theatre 文化（指艺术、文学等）： *The city is a centre of culture.* 该市是一个文化中心。

cunning /'kʌnɪŋ/ *adjective* 形容词
clever; good at making people believe something that is not true 狡猾的；诡诈的： *Their plan was quite cunning.* 他们的计划挺阴险。

cups 杯

cup 杯子
handle 柄
saucer 茶碟
cup and saucer 茶杯和茶碟
egg cup 蛋杯
mug 大杯
cup 奖杯

cup ⊶ /kʌp/ *noun* 名词
1 a small round container with a handle, that you can drink from 杯子： *a cup and saucer* 一套杯碟
2 a large metal thing like a cup, that you get for winning a sport 奖杯

cupboard ⊶ /'kʌbəd/ *noun* 名词
a piece of furniture with shelves and doors, where you keep things like clothes or food 橱柜 ⊃ Look at Picture Dictionary page P10. 见彩页 P10。

curb¹ *American English for* KERB 美式英语，即 kerb

curb² /kɜ:b/ *verb* 动词 (curbs, curbing, curbed /kɜ:bd/)
to control or limit something, especially something bad 控制，抑制（尤指不好的

事物）： *He needs to learn to curb his temper.* 他得学会控制自己的脾气。

cure¹ /kjʊə(r)/ *verb* 动词 (cures, curing, cured /kjʊəd/)
1 to make a sick person well again 治愈，治好（病人）： *The doctors can't cure her.* 医生治不好她了。
2 to make an illness go away 治愈（疾病）： *Can this disease be cured?* 这种病能治好吗？

cure² /kjʊə(r)/ *noun* 名词
something that makes an illness go away 疗法；药物： *a cure for cancer* 癌症的疗法

curiosity /ˌkjʊəri'ɒsəti/ *noun* 名词
(*no plural* 不用复数形式)
wanting to know about things 好奇心： *I was full of curiosity about the letter.* 我对那封信十分好奇。

curious /'kjʊəriəs/ *adjective* 形容词
1 If you are **curious**, you want to know about something. 好奇的： *They were very **curious about** the people who lived upstairs.* 他们对住在楼上的人很好奇。
2 strange or unusual 奇怪的；不寻常的 *There was a curious mixture of people in the audience.* 观众中各类人混杂在一起显得很怪。
▸ **curiously** /'kjʊəriəsli/ *adverb* 副词： *'Where are you going?' she asked curiously.* "你去哪儿？"她好奇地问。

curl¹ /kɜ:l/ *verb* 动词 (curls, curling, curled /kɜ:ld/)
to form or make something form into a round or curved shape （使）拳曲；鬈曲： *Does your hair curl naturally?* 你的头发是自然鬈的吗？
curl up to put your arms, legs and head close to your body 蜷着身体： *The cat curled up by the fire.* 猫蜷缩在火炉旁。

curl² /kɜ:l/ *noun* 名词
a piece of hair in a round shape 鬈发

curly ⊶ /'kɜ:li/ *adjective* 形容词 (curlier, curliest)
with a lot of CURLS 多卷的；拳曲的 ⊃ OPPOSITE **straight** 反义词为 straight： *He's got curly hair.* 他有一头鬈发。
⊃ Look at the picture at **hair**. 见 hair 的插图。

currant /'kʌrənt/ *noun* 名词
a very small black dried fruit that is used in cooking 小葡萄干

currency /'kʌrənsi/ *noun* 名词 (*plural* 复数形式 currencies)
the money that a country uses 货币：

The currency of the United States is the dollar. 美国的货币是美元。

current[1] /ˈkʌrənt/ *adjective* 形容词
happening or used now 现时的；当前的；通行的：*current fashions* 流行时尚
▶ **currently** /ˈkʌrəntli/ *adverb* 副词
now; at the moment 现时；当前：*He is currently working in Saudi Arabia.* 他目前在沙特阿拉伯工作。

current[2] /ˈkʌrənt/ *noun* 名词
1 air or water that is moving 气流；水流：*It is dangerous to swim here because of the strong current.* 在这儿游泳很危险，因为水流很急。
2 electricity that is going through a wire 电流

curriculum /kəˈrɪkjələm/ *noun* 名词
(*plural* 复数形式 **curricula** /kəˈrɪkjələ/ or 或 **curriculums**)
all the subjects that you study in a school or college 全部课程：*Latin is not on the curriculum at our school.* 拉丁语不在我们学校的课程范围内。 ➋ Look at **syllabus**. 见 syllabus。

curriculum vitae /kəˌrɪkjələm ˈviːtaɪ/
= **CV**

curry /ˈkʌri/ *noun* 名词 (*plural* 复数形式 **curries**)
an Indian dish of meat or vegetables cooked with spices and often eaten with rice 咖喱：*a chicken curry* 咖喱鸡 ➋ Look at Picture Dictionary page **P7**. 见彩页 P7。

curse /kɜːs/ *noun* 名词
1 a rude word that some people use when they are very angry 咒骂语；骂人的话 ➋ SAME MEANING **swear word** 同义词为 swear word
2 a word or phrase that has a magic power to make something bad happen 诅咒；咒语：*The family seemed to be under a curse* (= lots of bad things happened to them). 这家人仿佛受了诅咒似的。
▶ **curse** *verb* 动词 (curse, cursing, cursed /kɜːst/) to use rude language because you are angry 咒骂：*When he stood up, he hit his head and cursed loudly.* 他站起来时撞了头，便破口大骂。

cursor /ˈkɜːsə(r)/ *noun* 名词
(*computing* 电脑) a small sign on a computer screen that shows where on the screen you are working（荧光屏上的）光标，游标

curtain 0-ᴡ /ˈkɜːtn/ *noun* 名词
a piece of cloth that you can move to cover a window 窗帘：*Could you draw*

the curtains (= open or close the curtains), *please?* 请你拉一下窗帘好吗？

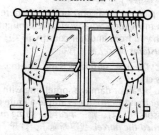

curtains 窗帘

curve[1] 0-ᴡ /kɜːv/ *noun* 名词
a line that is not straight; a bend 曲线；弯曲

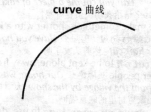

curve 曲线

curve[2] /kɜːv/ *verb* 动词 (curves, curving, curved /kɜːvd/)
to make a round shape; to bend 呈曲线状；弯曲：*The road curves to the right.* 这条路弯向右边。
▶ **curved** /kɜːvd/ *adjective* 形容词：*a table with curved legs* 弯腿的桌子 ◇ *a curved line* 曲线

cushion /ˈkʊʃn/ *noun* 名词
a cloth bag filled with something soft, which you put on a chair 坐垫；垫子

custard /ˈkʌstəd/ *noun* 名词 (*no plural* 不用复数形式)
a sweet yellow sauce made with milk. You eat it with fruit or other sweet dishes. 蛋奶沙司

custom 0-ᴡ /ˈkʌstəm/ *noun* 名词
something that a group of people usually do 风俗；习俗：*the custom of giving presents at Christmas* 圣诞节送礼的习俗 ◇ *It is the custom in that country for women to marry very young.* 女子早婚是那个国家的风俗。

customer 0⭐ /'kʌstəmə(r)/ *noun* 名词
a person who buys things from a shop
顾客；客户

customs /'kʌstəmz/ *noun* 名词 (*plural* 用复数形式)
the place at an airport or a port where you must show what you have brought with you from another country 海关:
a customs officer 海关官员

cut¹ 0⭐ /kʌt/ *verb* 动词 (cuts, cutting, cut, has cut)

1 to break or damage something with something sharp, for example a knife or scissors 切；剪；割: *I cut the string and opened the parcel.* 我剪开绳子，打开了包裹。◇ *I cut the apple in half* (= into two parts). 我把苹果切成两半。◇ *She cut her finger on some broken glass.* 她的手指让碎玻璃割伤了。

2 to take one piece from something bigger using a knife or scissors 切下；剪下: *Can you cut me a piece of cake, please?* 请给我切块蛋糕好吗？

3 to make something shorter with a knife or scissors 切短；剪短: *Have you had your hair cut?* 你头发发了吗？

be cut off to be kept alone, away from other people 被隔绝: *Our house was cut off from the village by the snow.* 大雪把我们家与村里的联系隔断了。

cut down on something to use, do or buy less of something 削减；减少: *You should cut down on sweets and chocolate.* 你应该减少吃糖果和巧克力。

cut something down to **cut** something so that it falls down 砍倒: *We cut down the old tree.* 我们把那棵老树砍倒了。

cut something off to stop the supply of something 中断（供应）: *The workmen cut off the electricity.* 工人把电的供应切断了。

cut something out to take something from the place where it was by using scissors, etc. 剪下: *I cut the picture out of the newspaper.* 我从报纸上剪下了照片。

cut something up to **cut** something into pieces with a knife, etc. 切碎；剁碎

cut² 0⭐ /kʌt/ *noun* 名词

1 an injury on the skin, made by something sharp like a knife 伤口；划口: *He had a deep cut on his leg.* 他腿上有一道很深的口子。

2 a hole or opening in something, made with something sharp 开口；破口: *Make a small cut in the material.* 在布料上剪一个小口。

3 making something smaller or less 削减；减少: *a cut in government spending* 政府开支的削减 ◇ *job cuts* 裁员

cute /kjuːt/ *adjective* 形容词 (cuter, cutest)
pretty and attractive 可爱的: *What a cute little puppy!* 多可爱的小狗啊!

cutlery /'kʌtləri/ *noun* 名词 (*no plural* 不用复数形式) (*British* 英式英语) (*American* 美式英语 flatware)
knives, forks and spoons that you use for eating 餐具（刀、叉和匙）

CV /ˌsiː 'viː/ (*British* 英式英语) (*American* 美式英语 résumé) *noun* 名词
a written list of your education and work experience that you send when you are trying to get a new job 履历；简历: *Send a full CV with your job application.* 随求职信附上详尽的个人履历。 ⊃ **CV** is the short way of writing the Latin words **curriculum vitae**. * CV 是拉丁语 curriculum vitae 的缩写形式。

cyberspace /'saɪbəspeɪs/ *noun* 名词 (*no plural* 不用复数形式)
a place that is not real where emails go when you send them from one computer to another 网络空间

cycle¹ /'saɪkl/ *noun* 名词
a bicycle 自行车 ⊃ SAME MEANING **bike** 同义词为 bike: *We went for a cycle ride at the weekend.* 周末我们骑自行车去了。◇ *a cycle shop* 自行车店

cycle² /'saɪkl/ *verb* 动词 (cycles, cycling, cycled /'saɪkld/)
to ride a bicycle 骑自行车: *I cycle to school every day.* 我每天骑自行车上学。

cycling /'saɪklɪŋ/ *noun* 名词 (*no plural* 不用复数形式)
the sport or activity of riding a bicycle 骑自行车（运动）: *We go cycling most weekends.* 我们周末大多去骑自行车。 ⊃ Look at Picture Dictionary page **P15**. 见彩页 P15。

cyclist /'saɪklɪst/ *noun* 名词
a person who rides a bicycle 骑自行车的人: *He's a keen cyclist* (= he likes cycling). 他热衷于骑自行车。

cyclone /'saɪkləʊn/ *noun* 名词
a very strong wind that moves in a circle and causes a storm 气旋；旋风

cylinder /'sɪlɪndə(r)/ *noun* 名词
a long round shape, like a tube or a tin of food 圆柱；圆筒；圆柱体
▶ **cylindrical** /sɪ'lɪndrɪkl/ *adjective* 形容词: *a cylindrical shape* 圆柱形

Dd

D, d /diː/ *noun* 名词 (*plural* 复数形式 D's, d's /diːz/)
the fourth letter of the English alphabet 英语字母表的第 4 个字母：*'Dog' begins with a 'D'.* * dog 一词以字母 d 开头。

dab /dæb/ *verb* 动词 (dabs, dabbing, dabbed /dæbd/)
to touch something lightly and quickly 轻触；轻拍；轻拭：*She dabbed the cut with cotton wool.* 她用药棉轻轻地擦了擦伤口。

dad /dæd/ *noun* 名词 (*informal* 非正式)
father 爹；爸：*Hello, Dad.* 爸，您好。 ◇ *This is my dad.* 这是我爸。

daddy /'dædi/ *noun* 名词 (*plural* 复数形式 daddies)
a word for 'father' that children use（儿语）爸爸，爹爹

daffodil /'dæfədɪl/ *noun* 名词
a yellow flower that grows in spring 黄水仙

daft /dɑːft/ *adjective* 形容词 (dafter, daftest) (*British* 英式英语) (*informal* 非正式)
silly 傻的；愚蠢的：*I think you're daft to work for nothing!* 我觉得你这样白干活真傻！ ◇ *Don't be daft!* 别犯傻了！

dagger /'dægə(r)/ *noun* 名词
a short pointed knife that people use as a weapon 匕首 ⊃ Look also at **sword**. 亦见 sword。

daily /'deɪli/ *adjective, adverb* 形容词，副词
happening or coming every day or once a day 每日（的）；每日一次（的）：*There are daily flights between London and Tokyo.* 伦敦与东京之间每天都有航班往返。
◇ *a daily newspaper* 日报 ◇ *The museum is open daily from 9 a.m. to 5 p.m.* 博物馆每天上午 9 时至下午 5 时开放。

dainty /'demti/ *adjective* 形容词 (daintier, daintiest)
small and pretty 小巧的：*a dainty little girl* 娇美的小女孩

dairy /'deəri/ *noun* 名词 (*plural* 复数形式 dairies)

a place where milk is kept or where milk products like butter and cheese are made 牛奶场；乳品场

daisy 雏菊

petal 花瓣

stem 茎

daisy /'deɪzi/ *noun* 名词 (*plural* 复数形式 daisies)
a small flower with a yellow centre, which usually grows wild in grass 雏菊

dam /dæm/ *noun* 名词
a wall that is built across a river to hold the water back 水坝

damage¹ 0🔊 /'dæmɪdʒ/ *noun* 名词 (*no plural* 不用复数形式)
harm or injury that is caused when something is broken or spoiled 破坏；损害：*He had an accident, but he didn't do any damage to his car.* 他出了车祸，但他的车子丝毫没有损坏。

damage² 0🔊 /'dæmɪdʒ/ *verb* 动词 (damages, damaging, damaged /'dæmɪdʒd/)
to break or harm something 破坏；损害：*The house was badly damaged by fire.* 房子被大火严重烧坏了。
▸ **damaging** /'dæmɪdʒɪŋ/ *adjective* 形容词：*Cars have a damaging effect on the environment.* 汽车对环境有破坏性的影响。

A
B
C
D
E
F
G
H
I
J
K
L
M
N
O
P
Q
R
S
T
U
V
W
X
Y
Z

damn /dæm/ *exclamation* 感叹词
a rude word that people sometimes use
when they are angry （表示愤怒）该死
的，讨厌的: *Damn! I've lost my key!*
真讨厌！我把钥匙丢了!

damp /dæmp/ *adjective* 形容词 (**damper**,
dampest)
a little wet 潮湿的: *a cold damp house*
又冷又潮的房子

dance¹ 0── /dɑːns/ *verb* 动词 (**dances**,
dancing, **danced** /dɑːnst/)
to move your body to music 跳舞: *Ian
dances well.* 伊恩跳得很好。◇ *I danced
with her all night.* 我和她跳了一整夜舞。
▶ **dancing** /'dɑːnsɪŋ/ *noun* 名词 (*no plural*
不用复数形式): *Will there be dancing at
the party?* 聚会上会安排跳舞吗?

dance² 0── /dɑːns/ *noun* 名词
1 movements that you do to music 舞蹈
2 a party where people dance 舞会: *My
parents met at a dance.* 我父母是在舞会上
认识的。

dancer 0── /'dɑːnsə(r)/ *noun* 名词
a person who dances 跳舞者；舞蹈演员:
Nureyev was a famous ballet dancer.
努里耶夫是著名的芭蕾舞演员。◇ *I'm not
a very good dancer.* 我不怎么会跳舞。

dandelions 蒲公英

dandelion /'dændɪlaɪən/ *noun* 名词
a small yellow wild flower 蒲公英

dandruff /'dændrʌf/ *noun* 名词
(*no plural* 不用复数形式)
small pieces of dead skin in a person's
hair 头皮屑

danger 0── /'deɪndʒə(r)/ *noun* 名词
1 (*no plural* 不用复数形式) the possibility
that something bad may happen 危险:
*You may be in danger if you travel alone
late at night.* 深夜一个人出门可能有危险。
2 (*plural* 复数形式 **dangers**) a person or

thing that may bring harm or trouble
危险的人；危险因素: *Smoking is a
danger to health.* 吸烟有害健康。

dangerous 0── /'deɪndʒərəs/ *adjective*
形容词
A person or thing that is **dangerous** may
hurt you. 危险的；造成危险的: *It's
dangerous to drive a car at night without
any lights.* 晚上驾车不开灯很危险。◇
a dangerous illness 危疾
▶ **dangerously** *adverb* 副词: *She drives
dangerously.* 她开车不安全。

dare /deə(r)/ *verb* 动词 (**dares**, **daring**,
dared /deəd/)

> 🔎 **GRAMMAR** 语法说明
>
> The negative is **daren't** /deənt/ or
> **don't dare** or **doesn't dare**. 否定式为
> daren't /deənt/、don't dare 或 doesn't
> dare: *They daren't ask her for any
> more money.* 他们不敢再向她要钱。
> ◇ *He doesn't dare tell anyone that he's
> broken a window.* 他不敢告诉别人他
> 打破了窗户。
> In the past tense it is **didn't dare**.
> 过去时用 didn't dare。

dare do something to be brave
enough to do something 敢于做某事:
I daren't tell Mum that I've lost her key.
我不敢告诉妈妈我把她的钥匙弄丢了。◇
I didn't dare ask for more money. 我不敢
再多要钱了。
dare somebody to do something
to ask somebody to do something
dangerous or silly to see if they are brave
enough 激某人做（危险或愚蠢）事:
I dare you to jump off that wall! 我谅你
不敢从那堵墙上跳下来!
don't you dare words that you use for
telling somebody very strongly not to do
something （表示不准）你敢，谅你不敢:
Don't you dare read my letters! 够胆你就
看我的信!
how dare you words that show you
are very angry about something that
somebody has done （表示愤怒）你竟
敢: *How dare you speak to me like that!*
你竟敢这样跟我说话!

daring /'deərɪŋ/ *adjective* 形容词
not afraid to do dangerous things 敢于冒
险的；大胆的: *a daring attack* 大胆的袭击
⊃ SAME MEANING **brave** 同义词为 brave

dark¹ 0── /dɑːk/ *adjective* 形容词 (**darker**,
darkest)
1 with no light, or not much light 黑暗
的；阴暗的: *It was so dark that I couldn't*

see anything. 暗得我什么都看不见。◇
It gets dark very early in the winter. 冬天天黑得很早。 ➲ OPPOSITE **light** 反义词为 light

2 A **dark** colour is nearer to black than to white. 深色的： *a dark green skirt* 深绿色的裙子 ◇ *He's got dark brown eyes.* 他有一双深褐色的眼睛。 ➲ OPPOSITE **light, pale** 反义词为 light 和 pale

3 A person who is **dark** has brown or black hair or skin. （头发或皮肤）棕色的，黝黑的： *a thin, dark woman* 黑黑瘦瘦的女人 ➲ OPPOSITE **fair** 反义词为 fair

dark² 0ᵧ /dɑːk/ *noun* 名词 (*no plural* 不用复数形式)
the **dark** where there is no light 黑暗： *Cats can see in the dark.* 猫在黑暗中也看得见东西。 ◇ *Are you afraid of the dark?* 你怕黑吗？
after dark after the sun goes down in the evening 天黑以后
before dark before the sun goes down in the evening 天黑以前： *Make sure you get home before dark.* 你得天黑以前回家。

darkness /'dɑːknəs/ *noun* 名词 (*no plural* 不用复数形式)
when there is no light 黑暗： *The whole house was in darkness.* 整个房屋一片漆黑。

darling /'dɑːlɪŋ/ *noun* 名词
a name that you call somebody that you love 亲爱的；宝贝： *Are you all right, darling?* 亲爱的，你没事吧？

dart /dɑːt/ *verb* 动词 (darts, darting, darted)
to move quickly and suddenly 猛冲；飞奔： *He darted across the road.* 他猛然冲过马路。

darts 掷镖游戏

dart 飞镖   **dartboard** 镖靶

darts /dɑːts/ *noun* 名词 (*plural* 用复数形式)
a game in which you throw a small metal arrow (called a **dart**) at a round board

with numbers on it (called a **dartboard**) 掷镖游戏

dash¹ /dæʃ/ *noun* 名词 (*plural* 复数形式 dashes)
1 a sudden short run somewhere 飞奔；急奔： *The robber made a dash for the door.* 劫匪直奔门口。
2 a mark (–) that you use in writing 破折号

dash² /dæʃ/ *verb* 动词 (dashes, dashing, dashed /dæʃt/)
to run quickly somewhere 飞奔；急奔： *I dashed into a shop when it started to rain.* 开始下雨的时候，我急忙跑进了一家商店。◇ *I must dash – I'm late for work.* 我得赶紧走了，上班要迟到了。

dashboard /'dæʃbɔːd/ *noun* 名词
the part of a car in front of the driver where most of the switches and controls are （汽车的）仪表板

data /'deɪtə/ *noun* 名词 (*plural* 用复数形式)
facts or information 数据；资料： *We are studying the data that we have collected.* 我们正在研究搜集到的数据。

database /'deɪtəbeɪs/ *noun* 名词
information that is stored in a computer in an organized system that lets you look at it and use it in different ways （贮存在电脑中的）数据库： *Information about every car is stored in the police database.* 每辆汽车的信息都贮存在警方的数据库中。

date 0ᵧ /deɪt/ *noun* 名词
1 the number of the day, the month and sometimes the year 日期；日子： *'What's the date today?' 'The first of February.'* "今天几号？" "二月一日。"◇ *Today's date is 11 December 2009.* 今天是 2009 年 12 月 11 日。◇ *What is your date of birth?* 你的出生日期是哪天？ ➲ Look at Study Pages **S9-S10**. 见研习专页 S9-S10。
2 a romantic meeting when two people go out somewhere 约会（谈恋爱）： *He's asked her out on a date.* 他已找她约会。
3 a small sweet brown fruit that comes from a tree which grows in hot countries 海枣（热带果实） ➲ Look at Picture Dictionary page **P8**. 见彩页 P8。
out of date
1 not modern 过时的： *The machinery they use is completely out of date.* 他们用的机器完全过时。
2 too old, so that you cannot use it 过期；失效的： *This ticket is out of date.* 这张票过期了。
up to date
1 modern 时髦的；最新式的： *The new*

A B C **D** E F G H I J K L M N O P Q R S T U V W X Y Z

kitchen will be right up to date, with all the latest gadgets. 新厨房会很时髦，将配备所有最新的器具。
2 with the newest information 有最新信息的：*Is this list of names up to date?* 这份表格是最新的吗？

daughter 0️⃣ /'dɔːtə(r)/ *noun* 名词

🔍 **PRONUNCIATION 读音说明**
The word **daughter** sounds like **water**, because we don't say the letters gh in this word. * daughter 读音像 water，因为 gh 在这里不发音。

a girl or woman who is somebody's child 女儿：*They have two daughters and a son.* 他们有两个女儿一个儿子。◇ *My oldest daughter is a doctor.* 我的大女儿是医生。

daughter-in-law /'dɔːtər ɪn lɔː/ *noun* 名词 (*plural* 复数形式 **daughters-in-law**)
the wife of your son 儿媳妇

dawn /dɔːn/ *noun* 名词
the time in the early morning when the sun comes up 黎明；拂晓

day 0️⃣ /deɪ/ *noun* 名词 (*plural* 复数形式 **days**)
1 a time of 24 hours from midnight to the next midnight 一天；一日：*There are seven days in a week.* 一星期有七天。◇ *I went to Italy for a few days.* 我去意大利待了几天。◇ *'What day is it today?' 'Tuesday.'* "今天星期几？""星期二。"

🔍 **WORD BUILDING 词汇扩充**
The days of the week are: **Monday, Tuesday, Wednesday, Thursday, Friday, Saturday, Sunday.** 一星期中的七天分别是星期一（Monday）、星期二（Tuesday）、星期三（Wednesday）、星期四（Thursday）、星期五（Friday）、星期六（Saturday）、星期日（Sunday）。

2 the time when it is light outside 白天；白昼：*Most people work during the day and sleep at night.* 大多数人白天工作晚上睡觉。
3 a time in the past 时期；时代：*In my grandparents' day, not many people had cars.* 在我祖父母那个年代，有汽车的人不多。
one day
1 on a certain day in the past（指过去）有一天：*One day, a letter arrived.* 有一天，来了一封信。

🔍 **SPEAKING 表达方式说明**
We often use **one day** at the beginning

of a story. * one day 常用于故事的开头。
2 (*also* 亦作 **some day**) at some time in the future（指将来）有朝一日：*I hope to become a doctor one day.* 我希望有一天能当上医生。◇ *Some day I'll be rich and famous.* 总有一天我会名利双收。
the day after tomorrow not tomorrow, but the next day 后天
the day before yesterday not yesterday, but the day before 前天
the other day a few days ago 几天前：*I went to London the other day.* 几天前我去了趟伦敦。
these days (*informal* 非正式) used to talk about the present, especially when you are comparing it with the past 如今；现今：*These days kids grow up so quickly.* 现在的孩子长得真快。
➋ SAME MEANING **nowadays** 同义词为 nowadays

daybreak /'deɪbreɪk/ *noun* 名词 (*no plural* 不用复数形式)
the time of day when light first appears 破晓；天亮

daydream /'deɪdriːm/ *noun* 名词
happy thoughts that make you forget about what you should be doing now 白日梦；幻想：*She stared out of the window, lost in a daydream.* 她凝视窗外，沉浸在幻想中。
▶ **daydream** *verb* 动词 (**daydreams, daydreaming, daydreamed** /'deɪdriːmd/)：*He daydreamed about being so rich that he could buy anything he wanted.* 他幻想自己富有得可以想买什么就买什么。

daylight /'deɪlaɪt/ *noun* 名词 (*no plural* 不用复数形式)
the light from the sun during the day 日光：*These colours look different in daylight.* 这些颜色在日光下看起来不一样。

day off /ˌdeɪ 'ɒf/ *noun* 名词 (*plural* 复数形式 **days off**)
a day when you do not go to work or school 休假日；休息日

daytime /'deɪtaɪm/ *noun* 名词 (*no plural* 不用复数形式)
the time when it is day and not night 白天；白昼；日间：*I prefer to study in the daytime and go out in the evening.* 我比较喜欢白天学习，晚上出去。

dazzle /'dæzl/ *verb* 动词 (**dazzles, dazzling, dazzled** /'dæzld/)

If a light **dazzles** you, it shines brightly in your eyes so that you cannot see for a short time. 使目眩；使眼花： *I was dazzled by the car's lights.* 车灯把我的眼睛晃花了。

dead[1] 🔑 /ded/ ***adjective*** 形容词
1 not alive now 死的；枯萎的： *All my grandparents are dead.* 我的祖父母和外祖父母都过世了。◇ *Throw away those dead flowers.* 把那些谢了的花扔掉吧。◇ *Survivors helped to bury **the dead*** (= the dead people). 幸存者帮忙埋葬死者。
2 (*informal* 非正式) very quiet 死气沉沉的： *This town is dead: everywhere is closed after ten o'clock at night.* 这个镇死气沉沉的，晚上十点钟后哪儿都关门了。
a dead end a street that is only open at one end 死胡同

dead[2] /ded/ ***adverb*** 副词 (*informal* 非正式) completely or very 完全；非常： *I'm dead tired.* 我累死了。

deadline /'dedlaɪn/ ***noun*** 名词
a day or time before which you must do something 截止日期；最后期限： *The deadline for finishing this essay is next Tuesday.* 这篇文章的交稿期限是下星期二。

deadly[1] /'dedli/ ***adjective*** 形容词 (**deadlier**, **deadliest**)
Something that is **deadly** may kill people or other living things. 致命的；致死的： *a deadly weapon* 致命的武器

deadly[2] /'dedli/ ***adverb*** 副词 (*informal* 非正式)
extremely 极其；非常： *I'm deadly serious.* 我可是非常认真的。

deaf /def/ ***adjective*** 形容词
not able to hear anything or not able to hear very well 聋的；失聪的；耳背的： *My grandma's starting to **go deaf**.* 我奶奶耳朵开始不灵了。◇ *television subtitles for **the deaf*** (= people who cannot hear) 为失聪者加配的电视字幕
▶ **deafness** /'defnəs/ ***noun*** 名词 (*no plural* 不用复数形式)： *In old age she was troubled by deafness.* 她晚年受耳聋困扰。

deafen /'defn/ ***verb*** 动词 (**deafens**, **deafening**, **deafened** /'defnd/)
to make a very loud noise so that somebody cannot hear well 使震耳欲聋： *We were deafened by the loud music.* 喧闹的音乐都快把我们的耳朵震聋了。

deal[1] 🔑 /di:l/ ***verb*** 动词 (**deals**, **dealing**, **dealt** /delt/, **has dealt**)
1 to give cards to players in a game of cards 发（牌）： *Start by dealing seven cards to each player.* 先给每个玩家发七张牌。
2 to buy and sell something in business 做买卖；经营： *Our firm **deals with** customers all over the world.* 我们公司和世界各地的顾客都有生意往来。◇ *We **deal in** insurance.* 我们从事保险生意。
deal out to give something to a number of people 分发；分配： *The profits will be dealt out among us.* 利润会在我们之间分配。
deal with something
1 to take action in a particular situation in order to solve a problem or do a particular job 处理；应付： *I am too busy to deal with this problem now.* 我现在太忙，顾不上这个问题。
2 to be about a special subject 论及；关于： *The first chapter of the book deals with letter writing.* 这本书的第一章讲的是如何写信。

deal[2] /di:l/ ***noun*** 名词
an agreement, usually about buying, selling or working 协议；交易： *Let's **make a deal** – I'll help you today if you help me tomorrow.* 我们来个协议吧——要是你明天帮我，我今天就帮你。
a good deal or 或 **a great deal** a lot 大量；许多： *I've spent a great deal of time on this report.* 我花了很多时间来做这份报告。

dealer /'di:lə(r)/ ***noun*** 名词
a person who buys and sells things 交易商： *a car dealer* 汽车经销商

dear[1] 🔑 /dɪə(r)/ ***adjective*** 形容词 (**dearer**, **dearest**)

> **PRONUNCIATION** 读音说明
> The word **dear** sounds just like **deer**.
> * dear 读音同 deer。

1 Dear a word that you use before a person's name at the beginning of a letter（用于书信开头收信人名字之前）亲爱的： *Dear Mr Carter, ...* 亲爱的卡特先生：… ◇ *Dear Sir or Madam, ...* 敬启者：…
2 that you love very much 亲爱的；珍视的： *She was a dear friend.* 她曾是我的好朋友。
3 (*British* 英式英语) costing a lot of money 价格高的；昂贵的 ➲ SAME MEANING **expensive** 同义词为 expensive： *Those strawberries are too dear.* 那些草莓太贵了。➲ OPPOSITE **cheap** 反义词为 cheap

dear[2] /dɪə(r)/ ***exclamation*** 感叹词
something you say if you are surprised, upset or disappointed（惊讶、不安、

A
B
C
D
E
F
G
H
I
J
K
L
M
N
O
P
Q
R
S
T
U
V
W
X
Y
Z

失望等时说.) 啊，哎呀，天哪：*Oh dear! It's started raining again.* 天哪，又开始下雨了。◇ *Dear me! What a mess!* 哎呀！真是一团糟！

dear³ /dɪə(r)/ *noun* 名词 (*informal* 非正式)
a word that you use when you are speaking to somebody that you love（称呼所爱的人）亲爱的：*Hello, dear.* 你好，亲爱的。

death 0━ /deθ/ *noun* 名词
when a life finishes 死亡：*He became manager of the company after his father's death.* 他父亲死后他成了公司的经理。◇ *There are thousands of deaths in car accidents every year.* 每年有许许多多的人死于车祸。

deathly /'deθli/ (**deathlier, deathliest**) *adjective* 形容词
like death 死一般的：*There was a deathly silence.* 当时一片死寂。

debate /dɪ'beɪt/ *noun* 名词
a public meeting where people talk about something important 争论；辩论
▸ **debate** *verb* 动词 (**debates, debating, debated**)：*Politicians will be debating the new law later this week.* 政界将于本周稍后时间围绕新法展开辩论。

debit card /'debɪt kɑːd/ *noun* 名词
a plastic card that you can use to pay for things directly from your bank account 借记卡：*Can I pay by debit card?* 我能用借记卡付款吗？

debt 0━ /det/ *noun* 名词
money that you must pay back to somebody 借款；欠款；债务：*The company has borrowed a lot of money and it still has debts.* 这家公司贷过很多款，现在还有债务。
in debt If you are **in debt**, you must pay money to somebody. 欠债

decade /'dekeɪd/ *noun* 名词
a period of ten years 十年：*The country has become richer in the past decade.* 这个国家在过去十年更为富裕了。

decaffeinated /ˌdiː'kæfɪneɪtɪd/ *adjective* 形容词
(used about coffee or tea) with all or most of the CAFFEINE (= the substance that makes you feel awake) taken out（咖啡或茶）脱咖啡因的：*I only drink decaffeinated coffee in the evenings.* 晚上我只喝脱咖啡因的咖啡。

decay /dɪ'keɪ/ *verb* 动词 (**decays, decaying, decayed** /dɪ'keɪd/)
to become bad or be slowly destroyed

腐烂；腐朽：*If you don't clean your teeth, they will decay.* 不刷牙，牙齿会蛀掉的。
▸ **decay** *noun* 名词 (*no plural* 不用复数形式)：*tooth decay* 蛀牙

deceive /dɪ'siːv/ *verb* 动词 (**deceives, deceiving, deceived** /dɪ'siːvd/)

🔍 SPELLING 拼写说明
Remember! When the sound is /iː/ (which rhymes with 'be'), there is a spelling rule: **I before E, except after C** so you spell **deceive** with EI (not IE). 记住：读音是 /iː/（与 be 押韵）时，拼写规则是：i 在 e 前面，除非 c 在前。因此，deceive 拼写中作 ei（而不是 ie）。

to deliberately make somebody believe something that is not true 欺骗；蒙骗：*She deceived me into thinking she was a police officer.* 她把我骗倒，让我以为她是警察。◇ *You're deceiving yourself if you think he'll change his mind.* 如果你以为他会改变主意，那你是在欺骗自己。

December 0━ /dɪ'sembə(r)/ *noun* 名词
the twelfth month of the year 十二月

decent /'diːsnt/ *adjective* 形容词
1 good enough; right 像样的；体面的：*You can't wear jeans for a job interview – you should buy some decent clothes.* 你不可以穿牛仔裤去参加求职面试，应该买些像样的衣服。
2 honest and good 诚实的；正派的：*decent people* 正直的人

decide 0━ /dɪ'saɪd/ *verb* 动词 (**decides, deciding, decided**)
to choose something after thinking about the possibilities 决定：*I can't decide what colour to paint my room.* 我决定不了我的房间刷什么颜色。◇ *We've decided to go to France for our holidays.* 我们已经决定去法国度假。◇ *She decided that she didn't want to come.* 她决定不来了。

decimal /'desɪml/ *noun* 名词
part of a number, written after a small round mark (called a **decimal point**) 小数：*Three quarters written as a decimal is 0.75.* 四分之三用小数表示就是 0.75。

🔍 SPEAKING 表达方式说明
We say '0.75' as 'nought point seven five'. * 0.75 读作 nought point seven five.

decision 0━ /dɪ'sɪʒn/ *noun* 名词
choosing something after thinking; deciding 决定；抉择：*I must make a*

decision about what I'm going to do when I leave school. 我得定下来离校以后该做什么。

deck /dek/ *noun* 名词
1 one of the floors of a ship, plane or bus （船、飞机或公共汽车的）一层: *He stood on the lower deck of the ship and looked out to sea.* 他站在下层甲板上，放眼向大海望去。
2 (*American* 美式英语) (*British* 英式英语 **pack**) a set of 52 cards for playing games 一副纸牌

deckchair 折叠椅

deckchair /'dektʃeə(r)/ *noun* 名词
a chair that you use outside, for example on the beach. You can fold it up and carry it. （户外用的）折叠椅

declare 0➔ /dɪ'kleə(r)/ *verb* 动词 (**declares, declaring, declared** /dɪ'kleəd/)
1 to say very clearly what you think or what you will do, often to a lot of people 表明；宣称；宣布: *He declared that he was not a thief.* 他声称自己不是小偷。◇ *The country declared war on its enemy.* 该国向敌人宣战了。
2 In an airport or port you **declare** things that you have bought in another country so that you can pay tax on them. （在机场或港口）申报（应纳税品）: *Have you anything to declare?* 你有什么物品要申报吗？
▸ **declaration** /ˌdeklə'reɪʃn/ *noun* 名词: *a declaration of independence* 独立宣言

decorate 0➔ /'dekəreɪt/ *verb* 动词 (**decorates, decorating, decorated**)
1 to make something look nicer by adding beautiful things to it 装饰；装潢: *We decorated the room with flowers.* 我们用花把房间装点了一下。
2 to put paint or paper on the walls of a room 粉刷；糊墙纸: *I am decorating the kitchen.* 我在粉刷厨房。

decoration /ˌdekə'reɪʃn/ *noun* 名词
a beautiful thing that you add to something to make it look nicer 装饰品: *Christmas decorations* 圣诞节的装饰品

decrease /dɪ'kriːs/ *verb* 动词 (**decreases, decreasing, decreased** /dɪ'kriːst/)
to become or to make something smaller or less （使）减少，降低: *The number of people in the village has decreased from 200 to 100.* 村里的人数从 200 人减少到 100 人。 ⊃ OPPOSITE **increase** 反义词为 increase
▸ **decrease** /'diːkriːs/ *noun* 名词: *There was a decrease in the number of people living in the village.* 住在村里的人减少了。 ⊃ OPPOSITE **increase** 反义词为 increase

deed /diːd/ *noun* 名词 (*formal* 正式)
a thing that somebody does that is usually very good or very bad 行为；行动: *Doing the shopping for her grandmother was a good deed.* 帮她奶奶买东西是件善事。

deep 0➔ /diːp/ *adjective* 形容词 (**deeper, deepest**)
1 Something that is **deep** goes down a long way. 深的: *Be careful: the water is very deep.* 小心，水很深。◇ *There were deep cuts in his face.* 他脸上有很深的伤口。 ⊃ Look at the picture at **shallow.** 见 shallow 的插图。
2 You use **deep** to say or ask how far something is from the top to the bottom. 有…深: *The hole was about six metres deep and three metres wide.* 这个洞大约六米深、三米宽。 ⊃ The noun is **depth.** 名词为 depth。
3 A **deep** sound is low and strong. （声音）低沉的: *He has a deep voice.* 他声音低沉。 ⊃ OPPOSITE **high** 反义词为 high
4 A **deep** colour is strong and dark. 深色的: *She has deep blue eyes.* 她有一双深蓝色的眼睛。 ⊃ OPPOSITE **pale** or **light** 反义词为 pale 或 light
5 If you are in a **deep** sleep, it is difficult for somebody to wake you up. 酣睡的；沉睡的: *She was in such a deep sleep that she didn't hear me calling her.* 她睡得很熟，没听见我叫她。
6 Deep feelings are very strong. （情感）强烈的: *deep sadness* 深深的悲痛

deeply 0➔ /'diːpli/ *adverb* 副词
strongly or completely 强烈地；非常；极其: *They were deeply disturbed by the accident.* 事故让他们深感不安。 ◇ *He is sleeping very deeply.* 他睡得很香。

deer /dɪə(r)/ *noun* 名词 (*plural* 复数形式 **deer**)

A B C D E F G H I J K L M N O P Q R S T U V W X Y Z

A
B
C
D
E
F
G
H
I
J
K
L
M
N
O
P
Q
R
S
T
U
V
W
X
Y
Z

🔍 PRONUNCIATION 读音说明

The word **deer** sounds just like **dear**.
* deer 读音同 dear。

a wild animal that eats grass and has horns that look like branches (called antlers) 鹿

deer 鹿

defeat 🔑 /dɪˈfiːt/ *verb* 动词 (defeats, defeating, defeated)
to win a fight or game against a person or group of people 打败；战胜：*The army defeated the rebels.* 军队击败了叛军。
▶ **defeat** *noun* 名词：*It was another defeat for the team.* 这个队又一次落败了。

defence (*British* 英式英语) (*American* 美式英语 **defense**) /dɪˈfens/ *noun* 名词
fighting against people who attack, or keeping away dangerous people or things 防御；保卫：*They fought the war in defence of their country.* 他们为保卫祖国而战。

defend /dɪˈfend/ *verb* 动词 (defends, defending, defended)
1 to fight to keep away people or things that attack 防御；保卫：*They defended the city against the enemy.* 他们为保卫城市抗击敌人。
2 to say that somebody has not done something wrong 辩护：*My sister defended me when my father said I was lazy.* 父亲说我懒，姐姐为我辩护。◇ *He had a lawyer to defend him in court.* 他有律师在法庭上为他辩护。
3 to try to stop another person or team scoring goals or points in a game （比赛中）防守

defense *American English for* DEFENCE 美式英语，即 defence

defiant /dɪˈfaɪənt/ *adjective* 形容词
refusing to do what somebody tells you 违抗的；反抗的：*From the age of fifteen she became more defiant.* 从十五岁开始她就变得更叛逆。

defied (*also* 还有 **defies**) *forms of* DEFY
* defy 的不同形式

define /dɪˈfaɪn/ *verb* 动词 (defines, defining, defined /dɪˈfaɪnd/)
to say what a word means 下定义：*How do you define 'rich'?* 你认为怎样才是"富有"？

definite 🔑 /ˈdefɪnət/ *adjective* 形容词
Something that is **definite** is clear, fixed and unlikely to change. 确定的；肯定的 ⊃ SAME MEANING **certain** 同义词为 certain：*I want a definite answer, 'yes' or 'no'.* 我要一个明确的答复，"是"还是"不是"。

definite article /ˌdefɪnət ˈɑːtɪkl/ *noun* 名词
(*grammar* 语法) in English grammar, the word 'the' 定冠词（the） ⊃ Look at **indefinite article**. 见 indefinite article。

definitely 🔑 /ˈdefɪnətli/ *adverb* 副词
certainly 肯定；确实；绝对：*I'll definitely consider your advice.* 我肯定会考虑你的建议。◇ *It's definitely the best restaurant in the town.* 这绝对是镇上最好的餐馆。

definition /ˌdefɪˈnɪʃn/ *noun* 名词
a group of words that tell you what another word means 定义；释义

defy /dɪˈfaɪ/ *verb* 动词 (defies, defying, defied /dɪˈfaɪd/, has defied)
If you **defy** somebody or something, you do something that they say you should not do. 违抗；反抗：*She defied her parents and stayed out all night.* 她不听父母的话，整夜都没回家。

degree 🔑 /dɪˈɡriː/ *noun* 名词
1 a measurement of temperature 度，度数（温度单位）：*Water boils at 100 degrees Celsius (100°C).* 水在 100 摄氏度沸腾。
2 a measurement of angles (= the space between two lines that meet) 度，度数（角的量度单位）：*There are 90 degrees (90°) in a right angle.* 直角是 90 度。
3 Universities and colleges give **degrees** to students who have completed special courses there. 大学学位：*She has a degree in Mathematics.* 她拥有数学学位。

delay[1] /dɪˈleɪ/ *noun* 名词 (*plural* 复数形式 **delays**)
a time when somebody or something is

late 耽搁；延误；延迟: *There was a long delay at the airport.* 在机场耽搁了很长时间。◇ *You must pay the money without delay* (= immediately). 你得马上付钱。

delay² /dɪˈleɪ/ *verb* 动词 (delays, delaying, delayed /dɪˈleɪd/)

1 to make somebody or something late 使迟到；使耽搁: *My train was delayed for two hours because of the bad weather.* 由于天气恶劣，我坐的火车延误了两个小时。

2 to not do something until a later time 延迟；推迟: *Can we delay our meeting until next week?* 我们能把会议推迟到下星期吗？

delete /dɪˈliːt/ *verb* 动词 (deletes, deleting, deleted)
to remove something that is written or that is stored on a computer 删去；删除: *I deleted some important files on my computer by accident.* 我不小心把电脑上的一些重要文件删除了。

deliberate /dɪˈlɪbərət/ *adjective* 形容词
If something is **deliberate** then it is planned and not done by mistake. 故意的；蓄意的: *Was it an accident or was it deliberate?* 这是无意的还是成心的？

deliberately 0ᵣ /dɪˈlɪbərətli/ *adverb* 副词
If you do something **deliberately**, you wanted or planned to do it. 故意；蓄意: *The police think that somebody started the fire deliberately.* 警方认为是有人故意放火。

delicate /ˈdelɪkət/ *adjective* 形容词
1 If something is **delicate**, you can break or damage it very easily. 易碎的；脆弱的: *I've got delicate skin, so I use special soap.* 我皮肤容易过敏，所以我用特定的肥皂。
2 light and pleasant; not strong 柔和的；清淡可口的；清香的: *delicate colours like pale pink and pale blue* 像淡粉红和浅蓝等柔和的颜色 ◇ *The food had a delicate flavour.* 这食物味道清淡可口。

delicatessen /ˌdelɪkəˈtesn/ *noun* 名词
a shop that sells special, unusual or foreign food, especially cold cooked meat and cheeses（出售冷藏熟肉、干酪等特色或外国食品的）熟食店

delicious /dɪˈlɪʃəs/ *adjective* 形容词
very good to eat 美味的；可口的: *This soup is delicious.* 这个汤真鲜。

delight¹ /dɪˈlaɪt/ *noun* 名词 (no plural 不用复数形式)

great happiness 高兴；愉快 ⊃ SAME MEANING **joy** 同义词为 joy: *The children shrieked with delight when they saw the puppy.* 孩子看到小狗时高兴得大声尖叫。

delight² /dɪˈlaɪt/ *verb* 动词 (delights, delighting, delighted)
to make somebody very pleased or happy 使高兴；使愉快

delighted /dɪˈlaɪtɪd/ *adjective* 形容词
very pleased or happy 高兴的；愉快的: *I'm delighted to meet you.* 很高兴跟你见面。

delightful /dɪˈlaɪtfl/ *adjective* 形容词
very pleasant or attractive 使人高兴的；令人愉快的 ⊃ SAME MEANING **lovely** 同义词为 lovely: *We stayed in a delightful little hotel.* 我们住在一个舒适的小旅馆。

deliver 0ᵣ /dɪˈlɪvə(r)/ *verb* 动词 (delivers, delivering, delivered /dɪˈlɪvəd/)
to take something to the place where it must go 递送；传送: *The postman delivered two letters this morning.* 邮递员今天上午送了两封信。
▸ **delivery** /dɪˈlɪvəri/ *noun* 名词 (plural 复数形式 deliveries): *We are waiting for a delivery of bread.* 我们正等着送面包来。

demand¹ 0ᵣ /dɪˈmɑːnd/ *noun* 名词
saying strongly that you must have something（强烈的）要求: *a demand for higher pay* 涨工资的要求
in demand wanted by a lot of people 有很大需求: *Good teachers are always in demand.* 优秀教师总是很抢手。

demand² 0ᵣ /dɪˈmɑːnd/ *verb* 动词 (demands, demanding, demanded)
to say strongly that you must have something 强烈要求: *The workers are demanding more money.* 工人要求增加工资。◇ *She demanded to see the manager.* 她要求见经理。

demo /ˈdeməʊ/ *noun* 名词 (plural 复数形式 demos) (informal 非正式) short for DEMONSTRATION * demonstration 的缩略式: *All the students went on the demo.* 所有的学生都参加了游行示威。

democracy /dɪˈmɒkrəsi/ *noun* 名词 (plural 复数形式 democracies)
1 a system of government where the people choose their leader by voting 民主制度
2 a country with a government that the people choose 民主国家

democrat /ˈdeməkræt/ *noun* 名词
1 a person who wants DEMOCRACY 民主主义者

A
B
C
D
E
F
G
H
I
J
K
L
M
N
O
P
Q
R
S
T
U
V
W
X
Y
Z

2 Democrat (*politics* 政治) a person in the Democratic Party in the US （美国）民主党党员 ⊃ Look at **republican** (2). 见 republican 第 2 义。

democratic /ˌdeməˈkrætɪk/ *adjective* 形容词
If a country, etc. is **democratic**, all the people in it can choose its leaders or decide about the way it is organized. 民主的；民主政体的

the Democratic Party /ðə ˌdeməˈkrætɪk pɑːti/ *noun* 名词 (*no plural* 不用复数形式)
(*politics* 政治) one of the two main political parties in the US （美国）民主党 ⊃ Look at **Republican Party**. 见 Republican Party。

demolish /dɪˈmɒlɪʃ/ *verb* 动词 (**demolishes, demolishing, demolished** /dɪˈmɒlɪʃt/)
to break a building so that it falls down 拆毁；拆除: *The warehouse is due to be demolished next year.* 这个仓库明年将会拆除。
▸ **demolition** /ˌdeməˈlɪʃn/ *noun* 名词 (*no plural* 不用复数形式): *The demolition of the factory will make room for more houses.* 拆除工厂将腾出地方来建造更多的房屋。

demonstrate /ˈdemənstreɪt/ *verb* 动词 (**demonstrates, demonstrating, demonstrated**)
1 to show something clearly 示范；演示: *He demonstrated how to operate the machine.* 他示范了如何操作这台机器。
2 to walk or stand in public with a group of people to show that you have strong feelings about something 示威 ⊃ SAME MEANING **protest** 同义词为 protest: *Thousands of people demonstrated against the war.* 成千上万的人参加了反战示威。

demonstration /ˌdemənˈstreɪʃn/ (*also informal* 非正式亦作 **demo**) *noun* 名词
1 a group of people walking or standing together in public to show that they have strong feelings about something 示威: *anti-government demonstrations* 反政府示威游行
2 showing how to do something, or how something works 示范；演示: *He gave us a cookery demonstration.* 他给我们做了烹饪示范。

den /den/ *noun* 名词
the place where a wild animal lives 兽穴

denied (*also* 还有 **denies**) *forms of* DENY * deny 的不同形式

denim /ˈdenɪm/ *noun* 名词 (*no plural* 不用复数形式)
strong cotton material that is used for making jeans and other clothes. **Denim** is often blue. 蓝粗棉布；牛仔布: *a denim jacket* 牛仔布夹克 ⊃ Look at Picture Dictionary page **P5**. 见彩页 **P5**。

dense /dens/ *adjective* 形容词
1 with a lot of things or people close together 稠密的；密集的: *dense forests* 茂密的森林
2 thick and difficult to see through 浓密的: *The accident happened in dense fog.* 事故在浓雾中发生。

dent /dent/ *noun* 名词
a place where a flat surface, especially metal, has been hit and pushed in but not broken 凹陷；凹痕；凹坑: *There's a big dent in the side of my car.* 我的汽车车身有一大片凹痕。
▸ **dent** *verb* 动词 (**dents, denting, dented**): *I dropped the tin and dented it.* 我把罐头摔瘪了。

dental /ˈdentl/ *adjective* 形容词
connected with teeth 牙齿的: *dental care* 牙齿护理

dentist ⊶ /ˈdentɪst/ *noun* 名词
1 a person whose job is to look after your teeth 牙医 ⊃ Look at Picture Dictionary page **P12**. 见彩页 **P12**。 ⊃ Look at the note at **tooth**. 见 tooth 条的注释。
2 the dentist's (*no plural* 不用复数形式) the place where a dentist works 牙科诊所: *I have to go to the dentist's today.* 今天我得去看牙医。

deny /dɪˈnaɪ/ *verb* 动词 (**denies, denying, denied** /dɪˈnaɪd/, **has denied**)
to say that something is not true 否认；否定: *He denied that he had stolen the car.* 他否认偷了那辆车。 ◊ *They denied breaking the window.* 他们不承认窗户是他们打破的。 ⊃ OPPOSITE **admit** 反义词为 admit

deodorant /diˈəʊdərənt/ *noun* 名词
a liquid that you put on your body to stop bad smells （消除体臭的）除臭剂

depart /dɪˈpɑːt/ *verb* 动词 (**departs, departing, departed**)
to leave a place 离开；起程: *The next train to Birmingham departs from platform 3.* 下一班开往伯明翰的火车从 3 号月台开出。

> 🔊 SPEAKING 表达方式说明
> It is more usual to say **leave**. 较常用 leave。

➔ OPPOSITE **arrive** 反义词为 arrive

department 0━ /dɪ'pɑ:tmənt/ *noun* 名词
one of the parts of a university, school, government, shop, big company, etc. （学校、企业等的）部门，处，系；（政府的）部门，局，科: *The book department is on the second floor.* 图书部在三楼。◇ *the sales department* 销售部门

department store /dɪ'pɑ:tmənt stɔ:(r)/ *noun* 名词
a big shop that sells a lot of different things 百货商店: *Harrods is a famous department store in London.* 哈罗德是伦敦著名的百货公司。

departure /dɪ'pɑ:tʃə(r)/ *noun* 名词
leaving a place 离开；起程: *Passengers should check in at least one hour before departure.* 乘客应在起飞前至少一小时办理登机手续。➔ OPPOSITE **arrival** 反义词为 arrival

depend 0━ /dɪ'pend/ *verb* 动词 (depends, depending, depended)
depend on somebody or 或 **something**
1 to need somebody or something 依靠；依赖: *She still depends on her parents for money because she hasn't got a job.* 她仍然靠父母的钱生活，因为她没有工作。
2 to trust somebody; to feel sure that somebody or something will do what you want 信任；信赖: *I know I can depend on my friends to help me.* 我知道我可以靠朋友帮忙。
it depends, that depends words that you use to show that something is not certain 那得看情况；视乎情况: *I don't know whether I'll see him. It depends what time he gets here.* 我不知道我是否会见他。那得看他什么时候到这里。◇ *'Can you lend me some money?' 'That depends. How much do you want?'* "你能借我一点钱吗？" "那得看情况了。你要多少？"

dependant /dɪ'pendənt/ *noun* 名词
a person, especially a child, who depends on another person for a home, food, money, etc. 受扶养者: *Do you have any dependants?* 你有没有要扶养的人？

dependent /dɪ'pendənt/ *adjective* 形容词
If you are **dependent** on somebody or something, you need them. 依靠的；

依赖的: *A baby is completely **dependent** on its parents.* 婴儿完全依赖父母的照顾。

deposit¹ /dɪ'pɒzɪt/ *noun* 名词
1 money that you pay to show that you want something and that you will pay the rest later 订金: *We paid a deposit on the flat.* 我们支付了买公寓的订金。
2 extra money that you pay when you rent something. You get it back if you do not damage or lose what you have rented. （租赁的）押金: *If you damage the car they will keep your deposit.* 要是你把车撞了，他们会没收你的押金。
3 money that you pay into a bank 存款: *I'd like to make a deposit, please.* 我想存点钱。

deposit² /dɪ'pɒzɪt/ *verb* 动词 (deposits, depositing, deposited)
to put something somewhere to keep it safe 存放: *The money was deposited in the bank.* 这笔钱存入了银行。

depot /'depəʊ/ *noun* 名词
a place where a lot of goods or vehicles are stored 仓库；车库

depress /dɪ'pres/ *verb* 动词 (depresses, depressing, depressed /dɪ'prest/)
to make somebody feel sad 使抑郁；使沮丧: *This wet weather really depresses me.* 这种阴雨天真的让我很郁闷。

depressed /dɪ'prest/ *adjective* 形容词
very unhappy for a long period of time 抑郁的；沮丧的: *He's been very depressed since he lost his job.* 他自从丢了工作后一直垂头丧气。

depressing /dɪ'presɪŋ/ *adjective* 形容词
Something that is **depressing** makes you feel very unhappy. 使人抑郁的；令人沮丧的: *That film about the war was very depressing.* 那部战争片看了让人感到很沮丧。

depression /dɪ'preʃn/ *noun* 名词 (no plural 不用复数形式)
a feeling of unhappiness that lasts for a long time 抑郁；沮丧: *She often suffers from depression.* 她常常感到抑郁。

depth /depθ/ *noun* 名词
how deep something is; how far it is from the top of something to the bottom 深度: *What is the depth of the swimming pool?* 这个游泳池有多深？◇ *The hole was 2m in depth.* 这个洞有 2 米深。➔ The adjective is **deep**. 形容词为 deep。

deputy /'depjuti/ *noun* 名词 (plural 复数形式 **deputies**)
the person in a company, school, etc.,

A
B
C
D
E
F
G
H
I
J
K
L
M
N
O
P
Q
R
S
T
U
V
W
X
Y
Z

who does the work of the leader when they are not there 副手；代理：*a deputy headmaster* 副校长

derivative /dɪˈrɪvətɪv/ *noun* 名词
a word that is made from another word 派生词；衍生字：*'Sadness' is a derivative of 'sad'.* * sadness 是 sad 的派生词。

descend /dɪˈsend/ *verb* 动词 (descends, descending, descended) (*formal* 正式)
to go down 下来；下去；下降：*The plane started to descend.* 飞机开始降落了。

> 🔊 SPEAKING 表达方式说明
> It is more usual to say **go down**. 较常用 go down。

descendant /dɪˈsendənt/ *noun* 名词
Your **descendants** are your children, your children's children (called grandchildren) and everybody in your family who lives after you. 后裔；后代：*Queen Elizabeth II is a descendant of Queen Victoria.* 英女王伊丽莎白二世是维多利亚女王的后裔。

descent /dɪˈsent/ *noun* 名词
going down 下降：*The plane began its descent to Munich airport.* 飞机开始向慕尼黑机场降落。

describe 🔊 /dɪˈskraɪb/ *verb* 动词 (describes, describing, described /dɪˈskraɪbd/)
to say what somebody or something is like or what happened 描述；形容：*Can you describe the man you saw?* 你能不能描述一下你见过的那名男子？ ◇ *She described the accident to the police.* 她向警方讲述了这次事故。

description 🔊 /dɪˈskrɪpʃn/ *noun* 名词
words that tell what somebody or something is like or what happened 描述；形容：*I gave the police a description of the thief.* 我向警方描述了那个小偷的样子。

desert¹ 🔊 /ˈdezət/ *noun* 名词

> 🔊 SPELLING 拼写说明
> Remember! You spell **desert** with one **S**. 记住：desert 拼写中只有一个 s。

a large, dry area of land with very few plants 沙漠；荒漠：*the Sahara Desert* 撒哈拉沙漠

desert² /dɪˈzɜːt/ *verb* 动词 (deserts, deserting, deserted)
to leave a person or place when it is wrong to go 抛弃；离弃：*He deserted his wife and children.* 他抛弃了妻儿。

deserted /dɪˈzɜːtɪd/ *adjective* 形容词
empty, because all the people have left 无人的：*At night the streets are deserted.* 晚上街头空无一人。

desert island /ˌdezət ˈaɪlənd/ *noun* 名词
an island where nobody lives, in a hot part of the world（热带的）荒岛

deserve /dɪˈzɜːv/ *verb* 动词 (deserves, deserving, deserved /dɪˈzɜːvd/)
to be good or bad enough to have something 值得；应得：*You have worked very hard and you deserve a rest.* 你已经干得很辛苦，应该休息一下了。 ◇ *They stole money from old people, so they deserve to go to prison.* 他们偷老人的钱，应该进监狱。

design¹ 🔊 /dɪˈzaɪn/ *noun* 名词

> 🔊 PRONUNCIATION 读音说明
> The word **design** sounds like **fine**, because we don't say the letter g in this word. * design 读音像 fine，因为 g 在这里不发音。

1 a drawing that shows how to make something 设计图：*Have you seen the designs for the new shopping centre?* 你看过新购物中心的设计方案了吗？
2 a pattern of lines, shapes and colours on something 图案：*The wallpaper has a design of blue and green squares on it.* 壁纸上的图案是蓝色和绿色的格子。

design² 🔊 /dɪˈzaɪn/ *verb* 动词 (designs, designing, designed /dɪˈzaɪnd/)
to draw a plan that shows how to make something 设计；制图：*The building was designed by a German architect.* 这栋楼是由一个德国建筑师设计的。

designer /dɪˈzaɪnə(r)/ *noun* 名词
a person whose job is to make drawings that show how something will be made 设计者；设计师：*a fashion designer* 时装设计师

desire 🔊 /dɪˈzaɪə(r)/ *noun* 名词
a feeling of wanting something very much 渴望；欲望；愿望：*a desire for peace* 对和平的渴求

desk 🔊 /desk/ *noun* 名词
1 a type of table, often with drawers, that you sit at to write or work 书桌；办公桌：*The pupils took their books out of their desks.* 学生从书桌里拿出课本。
2 a table or place in a building where somebody gives information, etc. 问讯台；服务台：*Ask at the information desk.* 到问讯处询问。

desk 书桌

despair /dɪ'speə(r)/ **noun** 名词 (no plural 不用复数形式)
a feeling of not having hope 绝望: *He was in despair because he had no money and nowhere to live.* 他一无钱二无住处，感到绝望了。
▶ **despair verb** 动词 (despairs, despairing, despaired /dɪ'speəd/):
We began to despair of ever finding somewhere to live. 我们开始对找到住处不抱希望了。

desperate /'despərət/ **adjective** 形容词
1 If you are **desperate**, you have no hope and you are ready to do anything to get what you want. 不顾一切的；孤注一掷的: *She is so desperate for a job that she will work anywhere.* 她急切想找一份工作，在哪儿干都行。
2 very serious 极严重的；危急的: *There is a desperate need for food in some parts of Africa.* 非洲有些地区迫切需要食物。
▶ **desperately** /'despərətli/ **adverb** 副词: *He is desperately unhappy.* 他非常不开心。

desperation /ˌdespə'reɪʃn/ **noun** 名词 (no plural 不用复数形式)
the feeling of having no hope, that makes you do anything to get what you want （因绝望而）不顾一切: *In desperation, she sold her ring to get money for food.* 走投无路之下，她把戒指卖了，拿钱去买吃的。

despise /dɪ'spaɪz/ **verb** 动词 (despises, despising, despised /dɪ'spaɪzd/)
to hate somebody or something 憎恨；厌恶；鄙视: *I despise people who tell lies.* 我讨厌说谎的人。

despite /dɪ'spaɪt/ **preposition** 介词
although something happened or is true; not noticing or not caring about something 尽管；即使 ⊃ SAME MEANING **in spite of** 同义词为 in spite of: *We*

decided to go out despite the bad weather. 尽管天气不好，我们还是决定出门。

dessert /dɪ'zɜːt/ **noun** 名词

> 🔍 SPELLING 拼写说明
> Remember! You spell **dessert** with **SS**.
> 记住：dessert 拼写中有 ss。

something sweet that you eat at the end of a meal （饭后）甜点，甜食 ⊃ SAME MEANING **pudding** 同义词为 pudding: *We had ice cream for dessert.* 我们的饭后甜食是冰激凌

dessertspoon /dɪ'zɜːtspuːn/ **noun** 名词
a spoon that you use for eating DESSERTS 点心匙 ⊃ Look at the picture at **spoon**. 见 spoon 的插图。

destination /ˌdestɪ'neɪʃn/ **noun** 名词
the place where somebody or something is going 目的地；终点: *They were very tired when they finally reached their destination.* 他们终于到达目的地时都筋疲力尽了。

destroy ○┰ /dɪ'strɔɪ/ **verb** 动词 (destroys, destroying, destroyed /dɪ'strɔɪd/)
to break something completely so that you cannot use it again or so that it is gone 毁灭；摧毁: *The house was destroyed by fire.* 那所房子被大火烧毁了。

destruction /dɪ'strʌkʃn/ **noun** 名词 (no plural 不用复数形式)
breaking something completely so that you cannot use it again or so that it is gone 毁灭；毁坏: *the destruction of the city by bombs* 炸弹对城市的毁坏

detach /dɪ'tætʃ/ **verb** 动词 (detaches, detaching, detached /dɪ'tætʃt/)
to separate something from another thing that it is joined to （使）分开，脱离: *Please complete and detach the form below.* 请填好下面的表格并撕下。⊃ OPPOSITE **attach** 反义词为 attach

detached /dɪ'tætʃt/ **adjective** 形容词
A **detached** house stands alone and is not joined to any other house. （房子）独立的，不连接的

detail ○┰ /'diːteɪl/ **noun** 名词
1 one of the very small parts that make the whole of something 细节: *Tell me quickly what happened – I don't need to know all the details.* 快告诉我发生了什么事，我不需要知道所有的细节。
2 details (plural 用复数形式) information about something 详情: *For more details,*

A
B
C
D
E
F
G
H
I
J
K
L
M
N
O
P
Q
R
S
T
U
V
W
X
Y
Z

please telephone this number. 欲知详情，请拨打此号码。

in detail with all the small parts 详细地: *Tell me about your plan in detail.* 把你的计划详细地告诉我。

detailed /'di:teɪld/ *adjective* 形容词
giving a lot of information 详细的；细致的: *a detailed description* 详细的描述

detect /dɪ'tekt/ *verb* 动词 (detects, detecting, detected)
to discover or notice something that is difficult to see 发现；查出: *The tests detected a small amount of blood on his clothes.* 化验发现他衣服上有些微血迹。

detective /dɪ'tektɪv/ *noun* 名词
a person whose job is to find out who did a crime. **Detectives** are usually police officers. 侦探；（尤指）警探: *Sherlock Holmes is a famous detective in stories.* 福尔摩斯是故事中的著名侦探。

detention /dɪ'tenʃn/ *noun* 名词
the punishment of being kept at school after the other children have gone home 放学后留校，留堂（作为对学生的惩罚）: *They can't give me a detention for this.* 他们不能因为这事就罚我留堂。

detergent /dɪ'tɜːdʒənt/ *noun* 名词
a powder or liquid that you use for washing things 洗涤剂；洗衣粉

deteriorate /dɪ'tɪəriəreɪt/ *verb* 动词 (deteriorates, deteriorating, deteriorated)
to get worse 转坏；恶化: *Her health deteriorated as she got older.* 她的健康状况随着年岁渐长而恶化。

determination 0ᵐ /dɪˌtɜːmɪ'neɪʃn/ *noun* 名词 (*no plural* 不用复数形式)
being certain that you want to do something 决心；果断；坚定: *She has shown great determination to succeed.* 她表现出争取成功的莫大决心。

determined 0ᵐ /dɪ'tɜːmɪnd/ *adjective* 形容词
very certain that you want to do something 坚决；坚定: *She is determined to win the match.* 她决心要赢得比赛。

detest /dɪ'test/ *verb* 动词 (detests, detesting, detested)
to hate somebody or something 厌恶；憎恨；讨厌: *They have always detested each other.* 他们一直彼此讨厌。

detour /'di:tʊə(r)/ *noun* 名词
a longer way to a place when you cannot go by the usual way 绕行的路；迂回路:

The bridge was closed so we had to make a detour. 桥给封了，我们只好绕道而行。

devastate /'devəsteɪt/ *verb* 动词 (devastates, devastating, devastated)
1 to destroy something or damage it very badly 摧毁；严重破坏: *War devastated the country.* 战争重创了这个国家。
2 to make somebody extremely upset and shocked 使悲痛；使震惊不已: *This tragedy has devastated the community.* 这一悲剧让当地社会震惊不已。
▶ **devastating** /'devəsteɪtɪŋ/ *adjective* 形容词: *The storm had a devastating effect on the island.* 暴风雨给该岛造成了毁灭性的影响。

develop 0ᵐ /dɪ'veləp/ *verb* 动词 (develops, developing, developed /dɪ'veləpt/)
1 to grow slowly, increase, or change into something else; to make somebody or something do this（使）发育，成长，发展: *Children develop into adults.* 儿童长大成人。
2 to begin to have something 开始出现: *She developed the disease at the age of 27.* 她 27 岁时得了这个病。
3 When a photograph is **developed**, special chemicals are used on the film so that you can see the picture. 使显影；冲洗，冲印（胶卷）

developing country /dɪˌveləpɪŋ 'kʌntri/ *noun* 名词
a country that is poor and is just starting to have modern industries 发展中国家

development 0ᵐ /dɪ'veləpmənt/ *noun* 名词
1 (*no plural* 不用复数形式) becoming bigger or more complete; growing 发展；发育；壮大: *We studied the development of babies in their first year of life.* 我们研究了婴儿头一年的成长过程。
2 (*plural* 复数形式 developments) something new that happens 事态发展；进展情况: *There are new developments in science almost every day.* 在科学的领域里，几乎每天都有新的发展。

device /dɪ'vaɪs/ *noun* 名词
a tool or piece of equipment that you use for doing a special job 器具；仪器；设备: *a device for opening tins* 开罐器

devil /'devl/ *noun* 名词 the Devil (*no plural* 不用复数形式)
the most powerful evil spirit, according to some religions 魔鬼

devote /dɪ'vəʊt/ *verb* 动词 (devotes, devoting, devoted)

to give a lot of time or energy to something 奉献（时间或精力）；致力于：*She devoted her life to helping the poor.* 她一生致力于帮助穷人。

devoted /dɪˈvəʊtɪd/ *adjective* 形容词
If you are **devoted** to somebody or something, you love them very much. 挚爱的；对…全心全意的：*John is devoted to his wife and children.* 约翰深爱他的妻儿。

dew /djuː/ *noun* 名词 (*no plural* 不用复数形式)
small drops of water that form on plants and grass in the night 露水；露珠：*In the morning, the grass was wet with dew.* 清晨，草上有露水，湿漉漉的。

diabetes /ˌdaɪəˈbiːtiːz/ *noun* 名词 (*no plural* 不用复数形式)
a disease that makes it difficult for your body to control the level of sugar in your blood 糖尿病

diagonal /daɪˈægənl/ *adjective* 形容词
If you draw a **diagonal** line from one corner of a square to another, you make two triangles. （直线）对角的；对角线的 ⊃ Look at the picture at **line¹**. 见 line¹ 的插图。
▶ **diagonally** /daɪˈægənəli/ *adverb* 副词
Walk diagonally across the field to the far corner and then turn left. 斜着穿过这块地到远端的拐角处，然后左转。

diagram ⊶ /ˈdaɪəgræm/ *noun* 名词
a picture that explains something 图解；示意图：*This diagram shows all the parts of an engine.* 这幅图把发动机的所有部件都显示出来了。

dial¹ /ˈdaɪəl/ *noun* 名词
a round part of a clock or other piece of equipment with numbers or letters on it which shows the time, speed, temperature, etc. 表盘；刻度盘；仪表盘：*Check the tyre pressure on the dial.* 检查一下仪表盘上显示的轮胎压。

dial² /ˈdaɪəl/ *verb* 动词 (*British* 英式英语 **dials, dialling, dialled** /ˈdaɪəld/) (*American* 美式英语 **dialing, dialed**)
to use a telephone by pushing buttons or turning the **dial** to call a number 拨，按（电话号码）：*You have dialled the wrong number.* 你拨错号码了。

dialect /ˈdaɪəlekt/ *noun* 名词
the form of a language that people speak in one part of a country 方言：*a local dialect* 当地方言

dialogue (*British* 英式英语) (*American* 美式英语 **dialog**) /ˈdaɪəlɒg/ *noun* 名词
words that people say to each other in a book, play or film（书、戏剧或电影中的）对话，对白

diameter /daɪˈæmɪtə(r)/ *noun* 名词
a straight line across a circle, through the centre 直径 ⊃ Look at the picture at **circle**. 见 circle 的插图。

diamond ⊶ /ˈdaɪəmənd/ *noun* 名词
1 a hard stone that looks like clear glass and is very expensive 钻石；金刚石：*The ring has a large diamond in it.* 戒指上镶着颗大钻石。◇ *a diamond necklace* 钻石项链
2 the shape ◆ 菱形 ⊃ Look at the picture at **shape¹**. 见 shape¹ 的插图。
3 **diamonds** (*plural* 用复数形式) the group of playing cards (called a **suit**) that have red ◆ shapes on them（纸牌的）方块：*the eight of diamonds* 方块八 ⊃ Look at the picture at **playing card**. 见 playing card 的插图。

diaper /ˈdaɪəpə(r)/ *American English for* NAPPY 美式英语，即 nappy

diarrhoea (*American* 美式英语 **diarrhea**) /ˌdaɪəˈrɪə/ *noun* 名词 (*no plural* 不用复数形式)
an illness that makes you go to the toilet very often 腹泻；拉肚子：*an attack of diarrhoea* 腹泻的发作

diary /ˈdaɪəri/ *noun* 名词 (*plural* 复数形式 **diaries**)

> 🔍 SPELLING 拼写说明
>
> Be careful! Don't confuse **diary** and **dairy**. You spell **diary** with **IA**. 注意：不要混淆 diary 和 dairy。diary 拼写中有 ia。

1 a book where you write what you are going to do 记事簿：*I'll look in my diary to see if I'm free tomorrow.* 我会查看一下记事簿，看明天是否有空。
2 a book where you write what you have done each day 日记本：*Do you keep a diary* (= write in a diary every day)? 你写日记吗？

dice /daɪs/ *noun* 名词 (*plural* 复数形式 **dice**)
a small piece of wood or plastic with spots on the sides for playing games 骰子；色子：*Throw the dice.* 掷骰子。⊃ Look at the picture on the next page. 见后页的插图。

dictate /dɪkˈteɪt/ *verb* 动词 (**dictates, dictating, dictated**)
to say words so that another person can write them 口述；口授；听写：*She dictated a letter to her secretary.* 她向秘书口授信稿。

A B C D E F G H I J K L M N O P Q R S T U V W X Y Z

A
B
C
D
E
F
G
H
I
J
K
L
M
N
O
P
Q
R
S
T
U
V
W
X
Y
Z

dice 骰子

dictation /dɪk'teɪʃn/ *noun* 名词
words that you say or read so that
another person can write them down
口述（或口授）的文字；听写： *We had a
dictation in English today* (= a test when
we wrote down what the teacher said).
我们今天做了英语听写测验。

dictator /dɪk'teɪtə(r)/ *noun* 名词
a person who has complete control of
a country 独裁者

dictionary ⛏ /'dɪkʃənri/ *noun* 名词
(*plural* 复数形式 **dictionaries**)
a book that gives words from A to Z and
explains what each word means 词典；
字典： *Look up the words in your
dictionary.* 在词典里查一下这些词。

did form of DO * do 的不同形式

didn't /'dɪdnt/ *short for* DID NOT * did not
的缩略式

die ⛏ /daɪ/ *verb* 动词 (**dies, dying, died**
/daɪd/, **has died**)
to stop living 死；死亡；凋谢： *People,
animals and plants die if they don't have
water.* 人和动植物没有水就会死。◇
She died of cancer. 她死于癌症。
be dying for something (*informal*
非正式) to want to have something very
much 非常想要某物： *It's so hot! I'm dying
for a drink.* 太热了！我真想要喝的。
be dying to do something to want to
do something very much 渴望做某事：
My brother is dying to meet you. 我弟弟很
想见到你。
die down to slowly become less strong
逐渐减弱： *The storm died down.* 暴风雨
渐渐平息了。

diesel /'di:zl/ *noun* 名词
1 (*no plural* 不用复数形式) a type of heavy
oil that is used in some engines instead of
petrol 柴油： *a diesel engine* 柴油发动机
◇ *a taxi that runs on diesel* 柴油出租车
2 (*plural* 复数形式 **diesels**) a vehicle that
uses **diesel** 柴油车： *My new car's a
diesel.* 我的新车是柴油车。

diet /'daɪət/ *noun* 名词
1 the food that you usually eat 日常
饮食；日常食物： *It is important to have
a healthy diet.* 健康饮食很重要。
2 special foods that you eat when you
are ill or when you want to get thinner
（因患病或为减肥而设的）规定饮食：
*You'll need to go on a diet if you want to
lose some weight.* 你要是想减肥就得节食。

difference ⛏ /'dɪfrəns/ *noun* 名词
the way that one thing is not the same as
another thing 差别；差异；不同： *What's
the difference between this computer and
that cheaper one?* 这台电脑与那台便宜点
的有什么不同？◇ *What's the difference in
price between these two bikes?* 这两辆自行
车的价格相差多少？◇ *Sarah looks exactly
like her sister – I can't tell the difference
between them.* 萨拉跟她妹妹长得简直一模
一样。我分不出她们俩。
make a difference to change or have
an effect on somebody or something
改变；影响： *Marriage made a big
difference to her life.* 结婚大大改变了她的
生活。
**make no difference, not make any
difference** to not change anything; to
not be important 没有改变；没有影响：
*It makes no difference to us if the baby is
a girl or a boy.* 宝宝是男是女对我们来说都
一样。

different ⛏ /'dɪfrənt/ *adjective* 形容词
1 not the same 不同的；有差异的： *These
two shoes are different sizes!* 这两只鞋大小
不一样！◇ *Cricket is different from
baseball.* 板球与棒球不同。
2 many and not the same 各种的；
各样的： *They sell 30 different sorts of ice
cream.* 他们出售 30 种不同的冰激凌。
▶ **differently** /'dɪfrəntli/ *adverb* 副词:
*He's very quiet at home but he behaves
differently at school.* 他在家话不多，
在学校却不一样。

difficult ⛏ /'dɪfɪkəlt/ *adjective* 形容词
1 not easy to do or understand 困难的；
难做的；难懂的： *a difficult problem* 难题
◇ *The exam was very difficult.* 这次考试很
难。◇ *It's difficult to learn a new
language.* 学会一门新语言并非易事。
⊃ OPPOSITE **easy** 反义词为 easy
2 A person who is **difficult** is not easy to
please or will not do what you want.
（人）难相处的，难应付的： *She's a very
difficult child.* 她是个很难哄的孩子。

difficulty ⛏ /'dɪfɪkəlti/ *noun* 名词
(*plural* 复数形式 **difficulties**)
a problem; something that is not easy to

do or understand 困难；难题；难事: *I have difficulty understanding German.* 我不怎么懂德语。◇ *My grandfather walks with difficulty now.* 我祖父现在走路有些困难。

dig 挖

spade 锹 —

dig ⊶ /dɪg/ *verb* 动词 (digs, digging, dug /dʌg/, has dug)
to move earth and make a hole in the ground 挖；掘；凿: *You need to dig the garden before you plant the seeds.* 要先把花园的土翻了再下种。◇ *They dug a tunnel through the mountain for the new railway.* 他们为修新铁路开凿了一条穿山隧道。
dig something up to take something from the ground by **digging** 挖出；掘起: *They dug up some Roman coins in their field.* 他们在自家地里挖出一些罗马硬币。

digest /daɪ'dʒest/ *verb* 动词 (digests, digesting, digested)
When your stomach **digests** food, it changes it so that your body can use it. 消化
▶ **digestion** /daɪ'dʒestʃən/ *noun* 名词 (*no plural* 不用复数形式): *Vegetables are usually cooked to help digestion.* 蔬菜通常煮熟后吃以便于消化。

digital /'dɪdʒɪtl/ *adjective* 形容词
1 using an electronic system that changes sounds or pictures into numbers before it stores or sends them 数字的；数码的；数位的: *a digital camera* 数码相机
2 A **digital** clock or watch shows the time in numbers. （钟表）以数字显示的

dignified /'dɪgnɪfaɪd/ *adjective* 形容词
behaving in a calm, serious way that makes other people respect you 庄重的；有尊严的；可敬的

dignity /'dɪgnəti/ *noun* 名词 (*no plural* 不用复数形式)
calm and serious behaviour that makes other people respect you 尊严: *to behave with dignity* 表现得很有尊严

dilemma /dɪ'lemə; daɪ'lemə/ *noun* 名词
a situation when you have to make a difficult choice between two things 进退两难；两难困境: *to be in a dilemma* 处于进退两难的困境

dilute /daɪ'luːt; daɪ'ljuːt/ *verb* 动词 (dilutes, diluting, diluted)
to add water to another liquid 冲淡；稀释: *You need to dilute this paint before you use it.* 这种油漆使用前要稀释。

dim /dɪm/ *adjective* 形容词 (dimmer, dimmest)
not bright or clear 昏暗的；模糊的: *The light was so dim that we couldn't see anything.* 光线太暗，我们什么都看不见。
▶ **dimly** /'dɪmli/ *adverb* 副词: *The room was dimly lit and full of smoke.* 房间里光线昏暗，到处是烟。

din /dɪn/ *noun* 名词 (*no plural* 不用复数形式)
a very loud, unpleasant noise 喧闹声；嘈杂声: *Stop making that terrible din!* 别那么吵啦!

dinghy /'dɪŋi/ *noun* 名词 (*plural* 复数形式 dinghies)
a small open boat 小艇；无篷小船
⊃ Look at the picture at **boat**. 见 boat 的插图。

dining room /'daɪnɪŋ ruːm/ *noun* 名词
a room where people eat 餐厅；饭厅
⊃ Look at Picture Dictionary page **P10**. 见彩页 P10。

dinner ⊶ /'dɪnə(r)/ *noun* 名词
the largest meal of the day. You have **dinner** in the evening, or sometimes in the middle of the day. 正餐，主餐（晚餐或午餐）: *What time do you usually have dinner?* 你一般什么时候吃正餐？◇ *What's for dinner?* 晚饭吃什么？⊃ Look at the note at **meal**. 见 meal 条的注释。

dinosaur /'daɪnəsɔː(r)/ *noun* 名词
a big wild animal that lived a very long time ago 恐龙: *dinosaur fossils* 恐龙化石

dip /dɪp/ *verb* 动词 (dips, dipping, dipped /dɪpt/)
to put something into a liquid for a short time and then take it out again 蘸；浸: *Dip your hand in the water to see how hot it is.* 把手伸进水里看水有多热。

A
B
C
D
E
F
G
H
I
J
K
L
M
N
O
P
Q
R
S
T
U
V
W
X
Y
Z

A
B
C
D
E
F
G
H
I
J
K
L
M
N
O
P
Q
R
S
T
U
V
W
X
Y
Z

diploma /dɪˈpləʊmə/ *noun* 名词
a piece of paper that shows you have passed an exam or finished special studies 文凭；毕业证书： *a teaching diploma* 教育文凭

diplomat /ˈdɪpləmæt/ *noun* 名词
a person whose job is to speak and do things for their country in another country 外交人员；外交官

diplomatic /ˌdɪpləˈmætɪk/ *adjective* 形容词
1 connected with managing relations between countries 外交的： *diplomatic talks* 外交会谈
2 careful not to say or do things that may make people unhappy or angry 善于交际的；圆通的 ⊃ SAME MEANING **tactful** 同义词为 tactful： *a diplomatic answer* 圆通的回答

direct¹ 0̄ₘ /dəˈrekt; daɪˈrekt/ *adjective, adverb* 形容词，副词
1 as straight as possible, without turning or stopping 直达（的）；径直（的）： *Which is the most direct route to the town centre from here?* 从这儿到市中心哪条路最近？ ◇ *We got a direct flight* (= a flight that does not stop) *to Bangkok.* 我们搭乘直飞曼谷的航班。 ◇ *The 6.45 train goes direct to Oxford.* * 6 点 45 分的火车直达牛津。
2 from one person or thing to another person or thing with nobody or nothing between them 直接（的）： *You should keep this plant out of direct sunlight.* 这种植物应避免受阳光直射。 ◇ *They are in direct contact with the hijackers.* 他们与劫机者直接联系。 ⊃ Look at **indirect**. 见 indirect。

direct² 0̄ₘ /dəˈrekt; daɪˈrekt/ *verb* 动词
(**directs, directing, directed**)
1 to manage or control somebody or something 指挥；管理： *A policeman was in the middle of the road, directing the traffic.* 一名警察在路中央指挥交通。
2 to be in charge of actors in a play or a film 导演： *The movie was directed by Quentin Tarantino.* 这部影片是由昆汀廷·达兰蒂诺导演的。
3 to tell somebody how to get to a place 指路；引路： *Can you direct me to the station, please?* 请问到车站怎么走？

direction 0̄ₘ /dəˈrekʃn; daɪˈrekʃn/ *noun* 名词
1 where a person or thing is going or looking 方向；方位： *They got lost because they went in the wrong direction.* 他们走错方向，所以迷了路。

2 directions (*plural* 用复数形式) words that tell you how to get to a place or how to do something 指南；说明： *Let's stop and ask for directions.* 我们停下来问问路吧。 ◇ *Simple directions for building the model are printed on the box.* 盒子上印有制作这个模型的简单说明。

directly 0̄ₘ /dəˈrektli; daɪˈrektli/ *adverb* 副词
in a direct line or way 直接；径直： *He refused to answer my question directly.* 他拒绝直接回答我的问题。 ◇ *The supermarket is directly opposite the bank.* 超市在银行正对面。 ◇ *Lung cancer is directly related to smoking.* 肺癌与吸烟有直接关系。

direct object /dəˌrekt ˈɒbdʒekt; daɪˌrekt ˈɒbdʒekt/ *noun* 名词
(*grammar* 语法) the person or thing that is directly affected by the action of a verb 直接宾语；直接受词： *In 'I met him in town', the word 'him' is the direct object.* 在 I met him in town 中，him 是直接宾语。

director /dəˈrektə(r); daɪˈrektə(r)/ *noun* 名词
1 a person who controls a business or a group of people 董事；理事；经理
2 a person in charge of a film or play who tells the actors what to do 导演

directory /dəˈrektəri; daɪˈrektəri/ *noun* 名词 (*plural* 复数形式 **directories**)
1 a book or list of people's addresses and telephone numbers 通讯录；电话号码簿： *a telephone directory* 电话号码簿
2 (*computing* 电脑) a file containing a group of other files or programs in a computer （文件或程序的）目录

dirt 0̄ₘ /dɜːt/ *noun* 名词 (*no plural* 不用复数形式)
a substance that is not clean, for example mud or dust 污物；污垢；尘土： *The children came in from the garden covered in dirt.* 孩子从花园进来，全身脏兮兮的。

dirty 0̄ₘ /ˈdɜːti/ *adjective* 形容词 (**dirtier, dirtiest**)
not clean 肮脏的；污秽的： *Your hands are dirty – go and wash them!* 你的手脏了，快去洗洗！

dis- /dɪs/ *prefix* 前缀
Dis- at the beginning of a word usually means 'not'. （用作前缀）不，相反： *disagree* 不同意 ◇ *dishonest* 不诚实的

disability /ˌdɪsəˈbɪləti/ *noun* 名词 (*plural* 复数形式 **disabilities**) a physical or mental condition that means you cannot use a part of your body completely or easily, or that you cannot learn easily （身心或学习的） 缺陷，障碍：*people with severe learning disabilities* 有严重学习障碍的人

disabled /dɪsˈeɪbld/ *adjective* 形容词
not able to use a part of your body well 丧失能力的；有残疾的：*Peter is disabled – he lost a leg in an accident.* 彼得有残疾——他在一起事故中失去了一条腿。◇ *The hotel has improved facilities for the disabled* (= people who are disabled). 这家旅馆改进了供残疾人使用的设施。

disadvantage 0┰ /ˌdɪsədˈvɑːntɪdʒ/ *noun* 名词
a problem that makes something difficult or less good 不利因素；缺点：*One disadvantage of living in the country is the lack of public transport.* 住在乡下的一个不便之处就是缺乏公共交通。

disagree 0┰ /ˌdɪsəˈɡriː/ *verb* 动词
(**disagrees, disagreeing, disagreed** /ˌdɪsəˈɡriːd/)
to have a different opinion from somebody else 不同意；有分歧：*I said it was a good film, but Jason disagreed with me.* 我说那部电影很好看，可是贾森却不同意。◇ *My sister and I disagree about everything!* 我和我姐姐在任何问题上意见都不一样！ ◒ OPPOSITE **agree** 反义词为 agree

disagreement 0┰ /ˌdɪsəˈɡriːmənt/ *noun* 名词
a situation where people have different opinions about something and often argue 意见不一；分歧；争论：*My parents sometimes have disagreements about money.* 我父母有时为钱争执。

disappear 0┰ /ˌdɪsəˈpɪə(r)/ *verb* 动词
(**disappears, disappearing, disappeared** /ˌdɪsəˈpɪəd/)

> ✎ SPELLING 拼写说明
> Remember! You spell **disappear** with one **S** and **PP**. 记住：disappear 拼写中有 s 和 pp。

If a person or thing **disappears**, they go away so people cannot see them. 消失；失踪：*The sun disappeared behind the clouds.* 太阳消失在云层中。 ◇ *The police are looking for a woman who disappeared on Sunday.* 警方正在寻找一名星期天失踪的女子。 ◒ OPPOSITE **appear** 反义词为 appear

▸ **disappearance** /ˌdɪsəˈpɪərəns/ *noun* 名词：*Everybody was worried about the child's disappearance.* 大家都为孩子失踪的事担心。

disappoint 0┰ /ˌdɪsəˈpɔɪnt/ *verb* 动词
(**disappoints, disappointing, disappointed**)
to make you sad because what you wanted did not happen 使失望：*I'm sorry to disappoint you, but I can't come to your party.* 很抱歉让你失望了，我不能来参加你的聚会。

disappointed 0┰ /ˌdɪsəˈpɔɪntɪd/ *adjective* 形容词

> ✎ SPELLING 拼写说明
> Remember! You spell **disappointed** with one **S** and **PP**. 记住：disappointed 拼写中有 s 和 pp。

If you are **disappointed**, you feel sad because what you wanted did not happen. 失望的；失意的：*Sue was disappointed when she didn't win the prize.* 苏未能获奖而感到失望。

disappointing 0┰ /ˌdɪsəˈpɔɪntɪŋ/ *adjective* 形容词
If something is **disappointing**, it makes you feel sad because it is not as good as you hoped. 令人失望的；令人扫兴的：*disappointing exam results* 让人感到失望的考试结果

disappointment 0┰ /ˌdɪsəˈpɔɪntmənt/ *noun* 名词
1 (*no plural* 不用复数形式) a feeling of sadness because what you wanted did not happen 失望；扫兴：*She couldn't hide her disappointment when she lost the match.* 她比赛输了，不禁流露出失望的神情。
2 (*plural* 复数形式 **disappointments**) something that makes you sad because it is not what you hoped 令人失望的事物：*Sarah's party was a disappointment – only four people came.* 萨拉的派对真没劲，只来了四个人。

disapproval /ˌdɪsəˈpruːvl/ *noun* 名词
(*no plural* 不用复数形式)
a feeling that something is bad or that somebody is behaving badly 不赞成；反对：*She shook her head in disapproval.* 她摇头表示反对。 ◒ OPPOSITE **approval** 反义词为 approval

disapprove /ˌdɪsəˈpruːv/ *verb* 动词
(**disapproves, disapproving, disapproved** /ˌdɪsəˈpruːvd/)
to think that somebody or something is

A
B
C
D
E
F
G
H
I
J
K
L
M
N
O
P
Q
R
S
T
U
V
W
X
Y
Z

bad 不赞成；反对： *Joe's parents **disapproved** of his new girlfriend.* 乔的父母不喜欢他的新女友。 ⊃ OPPOSITE **approve** 反义词为 approve

disaster 0ᵐ /dɪˈzɑːstə(r)/ *noun* 名词
1 something very bad that happens and that may hurt a lot of people 灾难；灾害： *Floods and earthquakes are natural disasters.* 洪水和地震是自然灾害。
2 a very bad situation or event 灾难性的境况；不幸的事件： *Our holiday was a disaster! It rained all week!* 我们的假期可真倒霉！整个星期都在下雨！

disastrous /dɪˈzɑːstrəs/ *adjective* 形容词
very bad; that causes great trouble 灾难性的；极糟糕的： *The heavy rain brought disastrous floods.* 暴雨造成了洪灾。

disc (*American* 美式英语 **disk**) /dɪsk/ *noun* 名词
1 a round flat object 圆盘；圆片： *He wears an identity disc around his neck.* 他脖子上挂着圆形身份牌。
2 = CD： *This recording is available on disc or cassette.* 这录音有激光唱片和盒式磁带两种形式。

discipline /ˈdɪsəplɪn/ *noun* 名词 (*no plural* 不用复数形式)
the practice of teaching you to control yourself and follow rules 纪律： *Children learn discipline at school.* 儿童在学校里学会遵守纪律。
▶ **discipline** *verb* 动词 (disciplines, disciplining, disciplined /ˈdɪsəplɪnd/): *You must discipline yourself to work harder.* 你必须严格要求自己更努力工作。

disc jockey /ˈdɪsk dʒɒki/ *noun* 名词 (*abbr.* 缩略式 **DJ**)
a person whose job is to play records and talk about music on the radio or in a club (电台或俱乐部的) 音乐节目主持人

disco /ˈdɪskəʊ/ *noun* 名词 (*plural* 复数形式 **discos**)
a place where people dance and listen to pop music 迪斯科舞厅

disconnect /ˌdɪskəˈnekt/ *verb* 动词 (disconnects, disconnecting, disconnected)
to stop a supply of water, gas or electricity going to a piece of equipment or a building 切断（水、燃气或电的供应）： *Your phone will be disconnected if you don't pay the bill.* 如果不付电话费，电话线会被切断。 ⊃ OPPOSITE **connect** 反义词为 connect

discount /ˈdɪskaʊnt/ *noun* 名词
money that somebody takes away from the price of something to make it cheaper 折扣： *Students often get a discount on rail travel.* 学生坐火车经常可以打折。

discourage /dɪsˈkʌrɪdʒ/ *verb* 动词 (discourages, discouraging, discouraged /dɪsˈkʌrɪdʒd/)
to make somebody not want to do something 劝阻；劝止： *Jane's parents tried to discourage her from leaving school.* 简的父母试图劝她不要退学。 ⊃ OPPOSITE **encourage** 反义词为 encourage
▶ **discouraging** /dɪsˈkʌrɪdʒɪŋ/ *adjective* 形容词 making you feel less confident about something 令人泄气的： *The results were discouraging.* 这些结果令人泄气。 ⊃ OPPOSITE **encouraging** 反义词为 encouraging

discover 0ᵐ /dɪˈskʌvə(r)/ *verb* 动词 (discovers, discovering, discovered /dɪˈskʌvəd/)
to find or learn something for the first time 发现；发觉： *Who discovered Australia?* 是谁发现澳大利亚的？ ◇ *I was in the shop when I discovered that I did not have any money.* 我到商店时发觉自己没带钱。

discovery /dɪˈskʌvəri/ *noun* 名词 (*plural* 复数形式 **discoveries**)
finding or learning something for the first time 发现： *Scientists have made an important new discovery.* 科学家有个重大的新发现。

discriminate /dɪˈskrɪmɪneɪt/ *verb* 动词 (discriminates, discriminating, discriminated)
to treat one person or a group in a worse way than others 区别对待；歧视： *This company discriminates against women – it pays them less than men for doing the same work.* 这家公司歧视女性，男女同工不同酬。
▶ **discrimination** /dɪˌskrɪmɪˈneɪʃn/ *noun* 名词 (*no plural* 不用复数形式)： *religious discrimination* (= treating somebody in an unfair way because their religion is not the same as yours) 宗教歧视

discuss 0ᵐ /dɪˈskʌs/ *verb* 动词 (discusses, discussing, discussed /dɪˈskʌst/)
to talk about something 讨论；谈论；商量： *I discussed the problem with my parents.* 我跟父母谈了这个问题。

discussion o—/dɪˈskʌʃn/ *noun* 名词
talking about something seriously or
deeply 讨论；商讨：*We had an
interesting **discussion about** politics.*
我们就政治展开了很有意思的讨论。

disease o—/dɪˈziːz/ *noun* 名词
an illness, especially one that you can
catch from another person 病；疾病：
Malaria and measles are diseases. 疟疾和
麻疹是疾病。

disgrace /dɪsˈɡreɪs/ *noun* 名词 (*no plural*
不用复数形式)
when other people stop thinking well of
you, because you have done something
bad 耻辱；不光彩；丢脸：*He's in disgrace
because he stole money from his brother.*
他真丢人，偷了他哥哥的钱。

disgraceful /dɪsˈɡreɪsfl/ *adjective* 形容词
Something that is **disgraceful** is very bad,
making other people feel sorry and
embarrassed. 可耻的；不光彩的；丢人
的：*The way the football fans behaved
was disgraceful.* 这些足球迷的行为很
丢人。

disguise[1] /dɪsˈɡaɪz/ *verb* 动词 (disguises,
disguising, disguised /dɪsˈɡaɪzd/)
to change the appearance of somebody
or something so that people will not
know who or what they are 假扮；伪装：
*They disguised themselves as guards and
escaped from the prison.* 他们伪装成警
卫，从监狱逃走了。

disguise[2] /dɪsˈɡaɪz/ *noun* 名词
things that you wear so that people do
not know who you are 伪装用品：*She is
so famous that she has to go shopping in
disguise.* 她太出名了，连去购物都得乔装
打扮。

disgust[1] o—/dɪsˈɡʌst/ *noun* 名词
(*no plural* 不用复数形式)
a strong feeling of not liking something
厌恶；反感：*They left the restaurant
in disgust because the food was so bad.*
他们气冲冲地离开了餐馆，因为食物太
糟糕了。

disgust[2] o—/dɪsˈɡʌst/ *verb* 动词
(disgusts, disgusting, disgusted)
to make somebody have a strong
feeling of not liking something 使厌恶；
使反感：*The violence in the film really
disgusted me.* 那部电影中的暴力镜头真
让我反感。

disgusted o—/dɪsˈɡʌstɪd/ *adjective*
形容词
If you are **disgusted**, you have a strong
feeling of not liking something. 厌恶的；

反感的：*I was disgusted to find a fly in
my soup.* 我发现汤里有只苍蝇，觉得很
恶心。

disgusting o—/dɪsˈɡʌstɪŋ/ *adjective*
形容词
very unpleasant 令人恶心的；令人不快
的：*What a disgusting smell!* 多难闻的
气味!

dish o—/dɪʃ/ *noun* 名词 (*plural* 复数形式
dishes)
1 a container for food. You can use a **dish**
to cook food in an oven, or to put food
on the table. 碟；盘
2 the dishes (*plural* 用复数形式) all the
plates, bowls, cups, etc. that you must
wash after a meal （待洗的）餐具：
I'll wash the dishes. 我来洗碗吧。
3 a part of a meal 饭菜；菜肴：*We had
a fish dish and a vegetarian dish.* 我们吃
了一道鱼和一道素菜。

dishcloth /ˈdɪʃklɒθ/ *noun* 名词
a cloth used for washing dirty dishes
洗碗布

dishonest o—/dɪsˈɒnɪst/ *adjective*
形容词
A person who is **dishonest** says things
that are not true, or steals or cheats.
不诚实的；不可靠的 ⊃ OPPOSITE **honest**
反义词为 honest

dishwasher /ˈdɪʃwɒʃə(r)/ *noun* 名词
a machine that washes things like plates,
glasses, knives and forks 洗碗碟机 ⊃ Look
at Picture Dictionary page **P10**. 见彩页
P10。

disinfectant /ˌdɪsɪnˈfektənt/ *noun* 名词
a liquid that you use for cleaning
something very well 消毒剂；杀菌剂

disk o—/dɪsk/ *noun* 名词
(*computing* 电脑) a flat piece of plastic
that stores information for use by a
computer 磁盘；磁碟 ⊃ Look also at
floppy disk and **hard disk**. 亦见 floppy
disk 和 hard disk。

disk drive /ˈdɪsk draɪv/ *noun* 名词
(*computing* 电脑) a piece of electrical
equipment that passes information to or
from a computer disk 磁盘驱动器

diskette /dɪsˈket/ *noun* 名词
(*computing* 电脑) a small flat plastic object
that you can put in your computer's DISK
DRIVE to record and keep information
软（磁）盘；软碟 ⊃ SAME MEANING **floppy
disk** 同义词为 floppy disk

dislike /dɪsˈlaɪk/ *verb* 动词 (dislikes
disliking, disliked /dɪsˈlaɪkt/) (*formal* 正式)

A

to not like somebody or something
不喜欢；厌恶：*I dislike getting up early.*
我不喜欢早起。

▶ **dislike** *noun* 名词：*I have a strong dislike of hospitals.* 我很不喜欢医院。

B

C

D

disloyal /ˌdɪsˈlɔɪəl/ *adjective* 形容词
not supporting your friends, family,
country, etc. 不忠诚的；不忠实的：
He was accused of being disloyal to the government. 他被指控对政府不忠。
⊃ OPPOSITE **loyal** 反义词为 loyal

E

dismal /ˈdɪzməl/ *adjective* 形容词
very bad and making you feel sad 凄凉
的；惨淡的；使人忧郁的：*It was a wet, dismal day.* 那天下着雨，阴沉沉的。

F

G

dismay /dɪsˈmeɪ/ *noun* 名词 (no plural
不用复数形式)
a strong feeling of surprise and worry
诧异；惊愕；不安：*John looked at me in dismay when I told him about the accident.* 我把出事的消息告诉约翰时，
他惊愕地看着我。

H

I

J

▶ **dismayed** /dɪsˈmeɪd/ *adjective* 形容词：
I was dismayed to find that somebody had stolen my bike. 我发现自行车被偷了，感到
很难过。

K

dismiss /dɪsˈmɪs/ *verb* 动词 (dismisses,
dismissing, dismissed /dɪsˈmɪst/)
1 (*formal* 正式) to make somebody leave
their job 解雇；开除 ⊃ SAME MEANING
sack or **fire** 同义词为 sack 或 fire：*He was dismissed for stealing money from the company.* 他因偷公司的钱而被开除了。
2 to allow somebody to leave a place
让…离开；解散：*The lesson finished and the teacher dismissed the class.* 那堂课
结束了，老师宣布下课。

L

M

N

O

disobedient /ˌdɪsəˈbiːdiənt/ *adjective*
形容词
not doing what somebody tells you to do
不服从的；不听话的：*a disobedient child*
不听话的孩子 ⊃ OPPOSITE **obedient** 反义词
为 obedient

P

Q

▶ **disobedience** /ˌdɪsəˈbiːdiəns/ *noun*
名词 (*no plural* 不用复数形式) ⊃ OPPOSITE
obedience 反义词为 obedience

R

S

disobey /ˌdɪsəˈbeɪ/ *verb* 动词 (disobeys,
disobeying, disobeyed /ˌdɪsəˈbeɪd/)
to not do what somebody tells you to do
不服从；违抗：*She disobeyed her parents and went to the party.* 她不听父母的话，
参加派对去了。 ⊃ OPPOSITE **obey** 反义词
为 obey

T

U

V

W

X

Y

disorganized /dɪsˈɔːɡənaɪzd/ *adjective*
形容词
badly planned or not tidy 计划不周的；

Z

缺乏条理的：*The meeting was very disorganized.* 这个会议安排得很糟糕。
⊃ OPPOSITE **organized** 反义词为 organized

dispenser /dɪˈspensə(r)/ *noun* 名词
a machine or container that you can get
things like money or drinks from 自动
取物装置；自动售货机：*a cash dispenser at a bank* 银行的自动提款机 ◇ *a soap dispenser* 皂液器

display¹ /dɪˈspleɪ/ *verb* 动词 (displays,
displaying, displayed /dɪˈspleɪd/)
to show something so that people can see
it 展示；陈列：*All kinds of toys were displayed in the shop window.* 商店橱窗里
陈列着各种各样的玩具。

display² /dɪˈspleɪ/ *noun* 名词 (*plural* 复数
形式 displays)
something that people look at 展示
（物）；陈列（品）：*a firework display*
烟火表演
on display in a place where people can
see it and where it will attract attention
展览；展出：*The paintings are on display in the museum.* 那些画正在博物馆展出。

dispose /dɪˈspəʊz/ *verb* 动词 (disposes,
disposing, disposed /dɪˈspəʊzd/)
dispose of something to throw
something away or give something away
because you do not want it 扔掉；丢弃；
处置：*Where can I dispose of this rubbish?* 我可以把这垃圾扔到哪儿去？
▶ **disposal** /dɪˈspəʊzl/ *noun* 名词 (*no plural* 不用复数形式)：*the disposal of nuclear waste* 核废料的处置

dispute /dɪˈspjuːt; ˈdɪspjuːt/ *noun* 名词
an argument or disagreement between
people with different ideas 争议；争端；
纠纷：*There was a dispute about which driver caused the accident.* 对于是哪个
司机造成事故存在分歧。

dissatisfied /ˌdɪsˈsætɪsfaɪd/ *adjective*
形容词
not pleased with something 不满意的：
I am very dissatisfied with your work.
我对你的工作很不满意。 ⊃ OPPOSITE
satisfied 反义词为 satisfied

dissolve /dɪˈzɒlv/ *verb* 动词 (dissolves,
dissolving, dissolved /dɪˈzɒlvd/)
If a solid **dissolves**, it becomes part of
a liquid.（固体）溶解，溶化：*Sugar dissolves in water.* 糖溶于水。

distance 0̶ᵦ /ˈdɪstəns/ *noun* 名词
1 how far it is from one place to another
place 距离；间距：*It's a short distance from my house to the station.* 从我家到车
站很近。 ◇ *We usually measure distance in*

miles or kilometres. 我们通常用英里或公里来测量距离。

2 a place that is far from somebody or something 远处；远方： *From a distance, he looks quite young.* 他远看颇年轻。
◇ *I could see a light in the distance.* 我看得见远处有灯光。

distant /ˈdɪstənt/ *adjective* 形容词
far away in space or time 遥远的；久远的： *distant countries* 遥远的国家

distinct /dɪˈstɪŋkt/ *adjective* 形容词
1 easy to hear, see or smell; clear 清楚的；清晰的；明显的： *There is a distinct smell of burning in this room.* 这个房间里有股明显的焦味。
2 clearly different 截然不同的： *English and Welsh are two distinct languages.* 英语和威尔士语是两种截然不同的语言。
▶ **distinctly** /dɪˈstɪŋktli/ *adverb* 副词 very clearly 清楚地；清晰地： *I distinctly heard him say his name was Robert.* 我清清楚楚地听到他说他叫罗伯特。

distinguish /dɪˈstɪŋgwɪʃ/ *verb* 动词
(distinguishes, distinguishing, distinguished /dɪˈstɪŋgwɪʃt/)
to see, hear, etc. the difference between two things or people 辨别；区分： *Some people can't distinguish between me and my twin sister.* 有些人分不清我和我的孪生妹妹。

distinguished /dɪˈstɪŋgwɪʃt/ *adjective* 形容词
famous or important 杰出的；著名的： *a distinguished actor* 著名演员

distract /dɪˈstrækt/ *verb* 动词 (distracts, distracting, distracted)
If a person or thing **distracts** you, they stop you thinking about what you are doing. 使分心；使分散注意力： *The noise distracted me from my homework.* 那噪音吵得我无法集中精神做作业。

distress /dɪˈstres/ *noun* 名词 (*no plural* 不用复数形式)
1 a strong feeling of pain or sadness 痛苦；悲伤
2 being in danger and needing help 遇险；遇难： *a ship in distress* 遇险的船
▶ **distress** *verb* 动词 (distresses, distressing, distressed /dɪˈstrest/):
It distressed her to see her mother crying. 看到母亲哭泣她很难过。

distressing /dɪˈstresɪŋ/ *adjective* 形容词
making you feel sad or upset 使人痛苦的；令人苦恼的： *The news of her death was extremely distressing.* 她去世的消息令人悲痛不已。

distribute /dɪˈstrɪbjuːt/ *verb* 动词
(distributes, distributing, distributed)
to give or send things to each person 分发；分配： *New books are distributed on the first day of school.* 开学第一天发新书。
▶ **distribution** /ˌdɪstrɪˈbjuːʃn/ *noun* 名词 (*no plural* 不用复数形式): *the distribution of newspapers* 送报纸

district /ˈdɪstrɪkt/ *noun* 名词
a part of a country or town 地区；区域： *the City of London's financial district* 伦敦城的金融区

disturb ☞ /dɪˈstɜːb/ *verb* 动词 (disturbs, disturbing, disturbed /dɪˈstɜːbd/)
1 to stop somebody doing something, for example thinking, working or sleeping 打扰；干扰： *I'm sorry to disturb you, but there's a phone call for you.* 很抱歉，打扰你了，有电话找你。 ◇ *Do not disturb* (= a notice that you put on a door to tell people not to come in). 请勿打扰。
2 to worry somebody 使烦恼；使担忧： *We were disturbed by the news that John was ill.* 听说约翰病了，我们都很忧心。

disturbance /dɪˈstɜːbəns/ *noun* 名词
1 a thing that stops you doing something, for example thinking, working or sleeping 打扰；干扰
2 when a group of people fight or make a lot of noise and trouble 骚乱；动乱： *The football fans were causing a disturbance outside the stadium.* 足球迷在体育场外闹事。

disused /ˌdɪsˈjuːzd/ *adjective* 形容词
not used any more 不再使用的；废弃的： *a disused railway line* 废弃的铁路线

ditch /dɪtʃ/ *noun* 名词 (*plural* 复数形式 ditches)
a long narrow hole at the side of a road or field that carries away water 沟渠；水沟

dive /daɪv/ *verb* 动词 (dives, diving, dived /daɪvd/)
1 to jump into water with your arms and head first 跳水： *Sam dived into the pool.* 萨姆跳进了游泳池。
2 to swim underwater wearing breathing equipment, collecting or looking at things 潜水： *The main purpose of his holiday to Greece was to go diving.* 他去希腊度假主要是为了潜水。
3 to go to a deeper level underwater 下潜： *The birds were diving for fish.* 那些鸟潜入水中捉鱼。
▶ **diving** *noun* 名词 (*no plural* 不用复数

形式）: *The resort has facilities for sailing, waterskiing and diving.* 这个度假胜地有帆船运动、水橇滑水和潜水的设施。

diving 跳水
diving board 跳水板
swimming costume 游泳衣

diver /'daɪvə(r)/ *noun* 名词
a person who works underwater 潜水员: *Police divers found a body in the lake.* 警方的潜水员在湖里找到了一具尸体。

diversion /daɪ'vɜːʃn/ *noun* 名词
a way that you must go when the usual way is closed（道路关闭时的）临时绕行路: *There was a diversion around the town because of a road accident.* 因为发生了道路事故，该镇开设了临时绕行路。

divert /daɪ'vɜːt/ *verb* 动词 (diverts, diverting, diverted)
to make something go a different way 使转向；使改道: *Our flight was **diverted** to another airport because of the bad weather.* 由于天气恶劣，我们的航班转飞另一个机场去了。

divide 0̶ː /dɪ'vaɪd/ *verb* 动词 (divides, dividing, divided)
1 to share or cut something into smaller parts 分配；分开；分割: *The teacher **divided** the class **into** groups of three.* 老师把全班分成三人一组。◇ *The book is divided into ten chapters.* 这本书分为十章。
2 to go into parts 分裂；分岔: *When the road divides, go left.* 在路的分岔口向左转。
3 to find out how many times one number goes into a bigger number 除以: *36 divided by 4 is 9 (36 ÷ 4 = 9).* * 36 除以 4 等于 9。

divided highway /dɪ,vaɪdɪd 'haɪweɪ/ *American English for* DUAL CARRIAGEWAY 美式英语，即 dual carriageway

divine /dɪ'vaɪn/ *adjective* 形容词
of, like or from God or a god 上帝的；神的: *a divine message* 神谕

diving board /'daɪvɪŋ bɔːd/ *noun* 名词
a board at the side of a swimming pool that you use to jump into the water 跳水板 ᵓ Look at the picture at **dive**. 见 dive 的插图。

division 0̶ː /dɪ'vɪʒn/ *noun* 名词
1 (*no plural* 不用复数形式) sharing or cutting something into parts 分配；分开；分裂: *the division of Germany after the Second World War* 二战后德国的分裂
2 (*no plural* 不用复数形式) (*maths* 数学) finding out how many times one number goes into a bigger number 除法 ᵓ Look at **multiplication** at MULTIPLY. 见 multiply 条的 multiplication。
3 (*plural* 复数形式 divisions) one of the parts of a big company 部门: *He works in the sales division.* 他在销售部工作。

divorce /dɪ'vɔːs/ *noun* 名词
the end of a marriage by law 离婚: *They are getting a divorce.* 他们在办离婚。
▶ **divorce** *verb* 动词 (divorces, divorcing, divorced /dɪ'vɔːst/): *He divorced his wife.* 他跟妻子离婚了。 ᵓ We often say **get divorced**. 常说 get divorced: *They got divorced last year.* 他们去年离婚了。
▶ **divorced** *adjective* 形容词: *I'm not married – I'm divorced.* 我现在单身，我离婚了。

DIY /,diː aɪ 'waɪ/ *noun* 名词 (*no plural* 不用复数形式) (*British* 英式英语)
making, painting or repairing things in your house yourself 自己动手: *a DIY store* (= where you can buy materials for DIY) * DIY 商店 ᵓ **DIY** is short for 'do-it-yourself'. * DIY 是 do-it-yourself 的缩略式。

dizzy /'dɪzi/ *adjective* 形容词 (dizzier, dizziest)
If you feel **dizzy**, you feel that everything is turning round and round and that you are going to fall. 头晕的；眩晕的: *The room was very hot and I started to feel dizzy.* 屋里很热，我开始感到头晕。

DJ /,diː 'dʒeɪ/ *short for* DISC JOCKEY * disc jockey 的缩略式

do¹ 0̶ː /duː/ *verb* 动词 (does /dʌz/, doing, did /dɪd/, has done /dʌn/)
1 to carry out an action 做；干: *What are you doing?* 你在干什么？ ◇ *He did the cooking.* 饭是他煮的。 ◇ *What did you do with my key?* (= where did you put it?) 你把我的钥匙放哪儿了？

2 to have a job or study something 从事；学习：*'What do you do?' 'I'm a doctor.'* "你是干什么的？" "我是医生。" ◊ *She's doing physics, biology and chemistry for A level.* 她正在修读物理、生物和化学的高级证书考试课程。

3 to finish something; to find the answer 完成；解答：*I have done my homework.* 我做完作业了。◊ *I can't do this sum – it's too difficult.* 这道题我算不出来，太难了。

4 to be good enough; to be enough 适合；足够：*Will this soup do for dinner?* 晚餐喝这个汤行吗？

🔎 WHICH WORD? 词语辨析

Do or **make**? 用 do 还是 make？
We use the verb **do** for many of the jobs we do at home. 做家务常用 do。
We **do the shopping**, **the cleaning**, **the washing** and **the ironing**. 购物说 do the shopping, 打扫说 do the cleaning, 洗衣服说 do the washing, 熨衣服说 do the ironing。
We always use **make** for beds. 铺床用 make：*Make your bed after breakfast.* 吃完早饭后把床铺好。

---

be or 或 **have to do with somebody** or 或 **something** to be connected with somebody or something 关于；与…有关：*I'm not sure what his job is – I think it's something to do with computers.* 我不太清楚他是做什么工作的——大概是跟电脑有关吧。◊ *Don't read that letter. It has nothing to do with you!* 别看那封信，它不关你的事！

could do with something to want or need something 想要；需要：*I could do with a drink.* 我想喝杯饮料。

do something up (*British* 英式英语)
1 to fasten something 扣上；绑上：*Do up the buttons on your shirt.* 把你衬衫的扣子扣上。○ OPPOSITE **undo** 反义词为 undo
2 to clean and repair something to make it look newer 修缮；整修：*They bought*

an old house and now they are doing it up. 他们买了栋旧房子，现在正在翻新。

do² 0ᴍ /duː; də/ *verb* 动词 (does /dʌz/, doing, did /dɪd/, has done /dʌn/)
1 a word that you use with another verb to make a question（与动词连用构成疑问句）：*Do you want an apple?* 你要苹果吗？
2 a word that you use with another verb when you are saying 'not'（与动词连用构成否定句）：*I like football but I don't* (= do not) *like tennis.* 我喜欢足球，但不喜欢网球。
3 a word that you use in place of saying something again（用以避免重复）：*She doesn't speak English, but I do* (= I speak English). 她不会说英语，但是我会。◊ *'I like football.' 'So do I.'* "我喜欢足球。" "我也喜欢。" ◊ *'I don't speak Chinese.' 'Neither do I.'* "我不会说中文。" "我也不会。"
4 a word that you use before another verb to make it stronger（用以加强语气）：*You do look nice!* 你真的很好看！

dock /dɒk/ *noun* 名词
a place by the sea or a river where ships go so that people can move things on and off them or repair them 船坞；码头
▸ **dock** (docks, docking, docked /dɒkt/) *verb* 动词 (used about a ship) to sail into a port and stop at the **dock** （船）进港，停靠码头：*The ship had docked at Lisbon.* 船已停靠在里斯本。

doctor 0ᴍ /ˈdɒktə(r)/ *noun* 名词
1 a person whose job is to make sick people well again 医生；大夫：*Doctor Waters sees patients every morning.* 沃特斯医生每天上午看病。⊃ Look at Picture Dictionary page **P12**. 见彩页 P12。

🔎 SPEAKING 表达方式说明

When we talk about visiting the doctor, we say **go to the doctor's**. 去看医生说

---

do				
present tense 现在式		*negative short forms* 缩写否定式		*past tense* 过去式
				did /dɪd/
I	**do**	I	**don't**	
you	**do**	you	**don't**	*present participle* 现在分词
he/she/it	**does** /dʌz/	he/she/it	**doesn't**	**doing**
we	**do**	we	**don't**	
you	**do**	you	**don't**	*past participle* 过去分词
they	**do**	they	**don't**	**done** /dʌn/

A B C D E F G H I J K L M N O P Q R S T U V W X Y Z

A
B
C
D
E
F
G
H
I
J
K
L
M
N
O
P
Q
R
S
T
U
V
W
X
Y
Z

go to the doctor's: *If you're feeling ill, you should go to the doctor's.* 你要是感到不舒服就得去看医生。

2 a person who has the highest degree from a university 博士 ⟳ When you write 'Doctor' as part of a person's name the short form is **Dr.** * doctor 用作称呼时可缩写为 Dr。

document 0━ /ˈdɒkjumənt/ *noun* 名词
1 an official paper with important information on it 文件；证件: *a legal document* 法律文件
2 (*computing* 电脑) a computer file that contains writing 文件

documentary /ˌdɒkjuˈmentri/ *noun* 名词 (*plural* 复数形式 **documentaries**)
a film about true things 纪录片: *I watched an interesting documentary about Japan on TV last night.* 我昨天晚上在电视上看了一部有关日本的纪录片，很有意思。

dodge /dɒdʒ/ *verb* 动词 (**dodges, dodging, dodged** /dɒdʒd/)
to move quickly to avoid something or somebody 闪开；躲开: *He ran across the busy road, dodging the cars.* 他跑过繁忙的马路，左闪右躲避开汽车。

does *form of* DO * do 的不同形式

doesn't /ˈdʌznt/ *short for* DOES NOT * does not 的缩略式

dogs 狗

dog 狗 **puppies** 小狗

dog 0━ /dɒg/ *noun* 名词
an animal that many people keep as a pet or to guard buildings 狗；犬

🔍 **WORD BUILDING** 词汇扩充
A young dog is called a **puppy**. 小狗叫做 puppy。

doll /dɒl/ *noun* 名词
a toy like a very small person 玩偶；玩具娃娃

dollar 0━ /ˈdɒlə(r)/ *noun* 名词 (*symbol* 符号 $)

🔍 **SPELLING** 拼写说明
Remember! You spell **dollar** with **AR**. 记住：dollar 拼写中有 ar。

a unit of money that people use in the US, Canada, Australia and some other countries. There are 100 **cents** in a dollar. 元（货币单位）: *You will be paid in American dollars.* 款项将用美元支付给你。

dolphin 海豚

dolphin /ˈdɒlfɪn/ *noun* 名词
an intelligent animal that lives in the sea 海豚

dome /dəʊm/ *noun* 名词
the round roof of a building 穹顶；圆屋顶: *the dome of St Paul's Cathedral in London* 伦敦圣保罗大教堂的穹顶

domestic /dəˈmestɪk/ *adjective* 形容词
1 not international; only inside one country 本国的；国内的: *a domestic flight* (= to a place in the same country) 国内航班
2 connected with the home or family 家的；家庭的: *Cooking and cleaning are domestic jobs.* 做饭和打扫是家务活。 ◊ *Many cats and dogs are domestic animals* (= animals that live in your home with you). 很多猫和狗是家养宠物。

dominate /ˈdɒmɪneɪt/ *verb* 动词 (**dominates, dominating, dominated**)
to control somebody or something because you are stronger or more important 控制；支配: *The Italian team dominated throughout the second half of the game.* 意大利队在下半场比赛占尽上风。

domino /ˈdɒmɪnəʊ/ *noun* 名词 (*plural* 复数形式 **dominoes**)
one of a set of small flat pieces of wood

or plastic, used to play a game (called **dominoes**) 多米诺骨牌

dominoes 多米诺骨牌

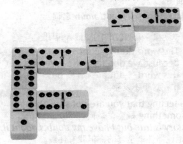

donate /dəʊ'neɪt/ *verb* 动词 (**donates**, **donating**, **donated**)
to give something, especially money, to people who need it 捐赠；捐献: *They donated $10 000 to the hospital.* 他们向医院捐了 10 000 元。
▶ **donation** /dəʊ'neɪʃn/ *noun* 名词: *He made a donation to the charity.* 他给慈善机构捐了款。

done *form of* DO * do 的不同形式

donkey /'dɒŋki/ *noun* 名词 (*plural* 复数形式 **donkeys**)
an animal like a small horse with long ears 驴 ⊃ Look at Picture Dictionary page **P2**. 见彩页 P2。

donor /'dəʊnə(r)/ *noun* 名词
somebody who gives something to help a person or an organization 捐赠者

don't /dəʊnt/ *short for* DO NOT * do not 的缩略式

doodle /'duːdl/ *verb* 动词 (**doodles**, **doodling**, **doodled**)
to make small drawings, especially when you are bored or thinking about something else（尤指无聊或心不在焉时）乱涂，乱画: *I often doodle when I'm on the phone.* 我打电话时常常乱涂乱画。

doom /duːm/ *noun* 名词 (*no plural* 不用复数形式)
death or a terrible event in the future that you cannot avoid 死亡；厄运；劫数

door o‑ /dɔː(r)/ *noun* 名词
the way into a building or room; a piece of wood, glass or metal that you use to open and close the way in to a building, room, cupboard, car, etc. 门口；门: *Can you close the door, please?* 请关上门好吗?

◇ *Sophie knocked on the door. 'Come in,' Peter said.* 索菲敲了敲门。"进来吧。"彼得说。 ◇ *There is somebody at the door.* 门口有人。 ◇ *Will you answer the door* (= go to open the door when somebody knocks or rings the bell)? 你去应门好吗? ⊃ A house often has a **front door** and a **back door**. 房子通常有前门（front door）和后门（back door）。 ⊃ Look at the picture at **house**. 见 house 的插图。
next door in the next house, room or building 隔壁: *Mary lives next door to us.* 玛丽住在我们隔壁。
out of doors outside; not in a building 在户外: *Farmers spend a lot of time out of doors.* 农人大部分时间待在户外。

doorbell /'dɔːbel/ *noun* 名词
a bell outside a house that you ring to tell people inside that you want to go in 门铃

doorknob /'dɔːnɒb/ *noun* 名词
a round object on a door that you use to open and close it 球形门把手

doormat /'dɔːmæt/ *noun* 名词
a piece of material on the floor in front of a door for cleaning your shoes on 门前地垫；门口擦鞋垫

doorstep /'dɔːstep/ *noun* 名词
a step in front of a door outside a building 门阶；门前台阶 ⊃ Look at Picture Dictionary page **P10**. 见彩页 P10。

doorway /'dɔːweɪ/ *noun* 名词
an opening for going into a building or room 门口: *Mike was waiting in the doorway when they arrived.* 他们来到的时候，迈克正在门口等候。

dormitory /'dɔːmətri/ *noun* 名词 (*plural* 复数形式 **dormitories**)
a big bedroom for a lot of people, usually in a school 宿舍（通常在学校）

dosage /'dəʊsɪdʒ/ *noun* 名词
the amount of medicine you should take and how often you should take it（药物）剂量: *the recommended daily dosage* 每日建议剂量

dose /dəʊs/ *noun* 名词
an amount of medicine that you take at one time 一剂（药）: *Take a large dose of medicine before you go to bed.* 临睡前服用一大剂的药。

dot /dɒt/ *noun* 名词
a small round mark 点；小圆点: *The letter 'i' has a dot over it.* 字母 i 上有个小圆点。

A
B
C
D
E
F
G
H
I
J
K
L
M
N
O
P
Q
R
S
T
U
V
W
X
Y
Z

🔍 SPEAKING 表达方式说明

We use **dot** when we say a person's email address. For the address **ann@smith.co.uk** we say 'Ann at smith dot co dot uk'. 口述电邮地址时用 dot, 如 ann@smith.co.uk 读作 Ann at smith dot co dot uk。

on the dot at exactly the right time 准时: *Please be here at nine o'clock on the dot.* 请准时九点钟到这里。

dotted line /ˌdɒtɪd ˈlaɪn/ *noun* 名词
a line of DOTS that sometimes shows where you have to write something 点线; 虚线: *Please sign* (= write your name) *on the dotted line.* 请在虚线上签名。 ⟳ Look at the picture at **wavy**. 见 wavy 的插图。

double¹ ⛏/ˈdʌbl/ *adjective* 形容词

🔍 PRONUNCIATION 读音说明

The word **double** sounds like **bubble**. * double 读音像 bubble。

1 two times as much or as many 两倍的; 双倍的: *a double portion of chips* 双份的炸薯条
2 with two parts that are the same 成双的; 成对的: *double doors* 双扇门 ◇ *Does 'necessary' have double 's'?* * necessary 一词中有两个 s 吗? ◇ *My phone number is double four nine five one* (= 44951). 我的电话号码是 44951。
3 made for two people or things 供两者用的; 双人的: *a double bed* 双人床 ◇ *a double room* 双人房间 ⟳ Look at **single¹** (4). 见 single¹ 第 4 义。

double² /ˈdʌbl/ *verb* 动词 (doubles, doubling, doubled /ˈdʌbld/)
to become, or make something become, twice as much or as many （使）翻倍; 乘以二: *The price of petrol has almost doubled in two years.* 油价两年来几乎翻了一番。

double bass /ˌdʌbl ˈbeɪs/ *noun* 名词
the largest musical instrument with strings, that you usually play standing up 低音提琴

double-click /ˌdʌbl ˈklɪk/ *verb* 动词 (double-clicks, double-clicking, double-clicked /ˌdʌbl ˈklɪkt/)
to quickly press a button twice on a computer control (called a **mouse**) 双击 （鼠标键）: *To start the program, just double-click on the icon.* 要启动程序, 只需双击图标。

double-decker /ˌdʌbl ˈdekə(r)/ *noun* 名词
a bus with two levels 双层公共汽车 ⟳ Look at the picture at **bus**. 见 bus 的插图。

doubt¹ ⛏ /daʊt/ *noun* 名词

🔍 PRONUNCIATION 读音说明

The word **doubt** sounds like **out**, because we don't say the letter b in this word. * doubt 读音像 out, 因为 b 在这里不发音。

a feeling that you are not sure about something 疑惑; 疑问: *She says the story is true but I have my doubts about it.* 她说那件事是真的, 但我有怀疑。
in doubt not sure 不确定; 不肯定: *If you are in doubt, ask your teacher.* 你要是没有把握, 问问老师吧。
no doubt I am sure 无疑; 肯定: *Paul isn't here yet, but no doubt he will come later.* 保罗还没来, 但稍后他一定会来。

doubt² /daʊt/ *verb* 动词 (doubts, doubting, doubted)
to not feel sure about something; to think that something is probably not true or probably will not happen 怀疑; 认为…不大可能: *I doubt if he will come.* 我看他不一定来。

doubtful /ˈdaʊtfl/ *adjective* 形容词
not certain or not likely 不确定; 不大可能: *It is doubtful whether he will walk again.* 很难说他以后还能不能走路。

doubtless /ˈdaʊtləs/ *adverb* 副词
almost certainly 毫无疑问; 几乎肯定地: *Doubtless she'll be late!* 她准要迟到了!

dough /dəʊ/ *noun* 名词 (*no plural* 不用复数形式)
flour, water and other things mixed together, for making bread 生面团

doughnut (*American also* 美式英语亦作 donut) /ˈdəʊnʌt/ *noun* 名词
a small round cake that is cooked in oil 炸面圈; 甜甜圈 ⟳ Look at Picture Dictionary page **P6**. 见彩页 P6。

dove 鸽子

dove /dʌv/ *noun* 名词
a bird that is often used as a sign of peace
鸽子（常用作和平的象征）

down 0-┓ /daʊn/ *adverb, preposition*
副词，介词
1 in or to a lower place; not up 在下面；
向下 *The sun goes down in the evening.*
太阳傍晚下山。◇ *We ran down the hill.*
我们跑下了山。◇ *Put that box down on
the floor.* 把那个箱子放在地上。
2 from standing to sitting or lying 坐或
躺（下）*Sit down.* 坐下 ◇ *Lie down on
the bed.* 躺到床上去。
3 at or to a lower level 下降；减弱
Prices are going down. 价格正在下降。
◇ *Turn that music down!* (= so that it is
not so loud) 把音乐调低点!
4 along 沿着；顺着 *He lives just down
the street.* 他就住在街那头。◇ *Go down
the road till you reach the traffic lights.*
沿着这条路一直走到红绿灯处。
5 on paper; on a list 写（下）*Write
these words down.* 把这些词写下来。
◇ *Have you got me down for the trip?*
你把我列入这次旅行的名单了吗?

downhill /ˌdaʊnˈhɪl/ *adverb* 副词
down, towards the bottom of a hill 往山
下 *My bicycle can go fast downhill.* 我的
自行车下山可以很快。

download /ˌdaʊnˈləʊd/ *verb* 动词
(downloads, downloading, downloaded)
(*computing* 电脑) If you **download** a
computer program or information from
the Internet, you make a copy of it on
your own computer. 下载 *I downloaded
some music files from the Internet.* 我从
网上下载了些音乐文件。

downstairs 0-┓ /ˌdaʊnˈsteəz/ *adverb*
副词
to or on a lower floor of a building 往楼
下；在楼下 *I went downstairs to make
breakfast.* 我下楼去做早饭。
▸ **downstairs** *adjective* 形容词 *She
lives in the downstairs flat.* 她住在楼下的
公寓里。 ● OPPOSITE **upstairs** 反义词为
upstairs

downtown /ˌdaʊnˈtaʊn/ *adverb* 副词
(*American* 美式英语)
in or towards the centre of a city,
especially its main business area 在市
中心；往市中心 *She works downtown.*
她在市中心上班。

downwards 0-┓ /ˈdaʊnwədz/ (*also*
亦作 downward /ˈdaʊnwəd/) *adverb* 副词
towards the ground or towards a lower
level 往下；向下 *She was lying face*

downwards on the grass. 她趴在草地上。
● OPPOSITE **upwards** 反义词为 upwards

doze /dəʊz/ *verb* 动词 (dozes, dozing,
dozed /dəʊzd/)
to sleep lightly for a short time 打瞌睡；
打盹 *My grandfather was dozing in his
armchair.* 我爷爷在扶手椅上打起盹来。
doze off to go to sleep, especially during
the day 打瞌睡，打盹（尤指在日间）：
I dozed off in front of the television. 我在
电视机前打起盹来。
▸ **doze** *noun* 名词 *She had a doze after
lunch.* 她午饭后小睡了一会儿。

dozen /ˈdʌzn/ *noun* 名词 (*plural* 复数形式
dozen)
twelve 一打；十二个 *a dozen red roses*
一打红玫瑰 ◇ *two dozen boxes* 两打箱子
◇ *half a dozen eggs* 半打鸡蛋
dozens of a lot of 许多；很多 *They've
invited dozens of people to the party.* 他们
邀请了许多人参加聚会。

Dr *short way of writing* DOCTOR * Doctor
的缩写形式

draft, drafty *American English for*
DRAUGHT, DRAUGHTY 美式英语，即
draught、draughty

drag 拖；拉

log 原木

drag /dræg/ *verb* 动词 (drags, dragging,
dragged /drægd/)
1 to pull something along the ground
slowly, often because it is heavy 拖；
拉；拽 *He couldn't lift the sack, so
he dragged it out of the shop.* 他提不
起那个大袋，只好把它从商店里拖了
出来。
2 If something **drags**, it seems to go
slowly because it is not interesting.
（因乏味而）显得慢；过得很慢 *Time
drags when you're waiting for a bus.*
等公共汽车的时候，时间过得很慢。

dragon /ˈdrægən/ *noun* 名词
a big, dangerous animal with fire in its
mouth, that you only find in stories 龙

dragonfly /ˈdrægənflaɪ/ *noun* 名词
(*plural* 复数形式 **dragonflies**)

an insect that often flies near water and that has four wings and a long, thin body 蜻蜓

drain¹ /dreɪn/ *verb* 动词 (drains, draining, drained /dreɪnd/)

1 to let liquid flow away from something, so that it becomes dry 使流走；使沥干：*Drain and rinse the pasta.* 把意大利面沥干，再用水冲。

2 to become dry because liquid is flowing away 流干：*Leave the dishes to drain.* 让碟子搁着晾干。

3 to flow away 流走：*The water drained away slowly.* 水慢慢流走了。

drain² /dreɪn/ *noun* 名词
a pipe that carries away dirty water from a building 下水道；排水管：*The drain is blocked.* 下水道堵住了。 ⊃ Look at the picture at **kerb**. 见 kerb 的插图。

drainpipe /'dreɪnpaɪp/ *noun* 名词
a pipe that takes water from the roof of a building to a DRAIN when it rains（从屋顶输送到下水道的）雨水管 ⊃ Look at Picture Dictionary page **P10**. 见彩页 P10。

drama /'drɑːmə/ *noun* 名词
1 (*plural* 复数形式 dramas) a story that you watch in the theatre or on television, or listen to on the radio 戏；剧：*a TV drama* 电视剧

2 (*no plural* 不用复数形式) the study of plays and acting 戏剧（学）：*She went to drama school.* 她曾上戏剧学校。

3 (*plural* 复数形式 dramas) an exciting thing that happens 戏剧性事件：*There was a big drama at school when one of the teachers fell in the swimming pool!* 有个老师掉进了游泳池，事件轰动了全校！

dramatic /drə'mætɪk/ *adjective* 形容词
1 sudden, great or exciting 急剧的；激动人心的：*The finish of the race was very dramatic.* 赛事的结尾十分紧张刺激。

2 of plays or the theatre 戏剧的：*a dramatic society* 戏剧协会
▸ **dramatically** /drə'mætɪkli/ *adverb* 副词：*Prices went up dramatically.* 价格急剧上升。

dramatist /'dræmətɪst/ *noun* 名词
a person who writes plays 剧作家；编剧

drank *form of* DRINK¹ * drink¹ 的不同形式

draught (*British* 英式英语) (*American* 美式英语 draft) /drɑːft/ *noun* 名词
cold air that comes into a room 穿堂风；通风气流：*Can you shut the window? I can feel a draught.* 你能把窗关上吗？我感觉到有股冷风吹进来。
▸ **draughty** (*British* 英式英语) (*American*

美式英语 drafty) /'drɑːfti/ *adjective* 形容词 (draughtier, draughtiest)：*a draughty old house* 透风的老房子

draughts /drɑːfts/ *noun* 名词 (*plural* 用复数形式) (*British* 英式英语) (*American* 美式英语 checkers)
a game that two people play with round flat pieces on a board that has black and white squares on it 国际跳棋；西洋跳棋：*Do you want a game of draughts?* 你想下国际跳棋吗？

draw¹ 0━ /drɔː/ *verb* 动词 (draws, drawing, drew /druː/, has drawn /drɔːn/)

🔎 PRONUNCIATION 读音说明
The word **draw** sounds like **more**.
* draw 读音像 more。

1 to make a picture with a pen or a pencil 画：*She drew a picture of a horse.* 她画了一匹马。 ◇ *He has drawn a car.* 他画了一辆汽车。 ◇ *My sister draws well.* 我姐姐很会画画。

2 to pull or take something from a place 拖；拉；抽；拔：*I drew my chair up closer to the fire.* 我把椅子向炉火旁拉近了点。 ◇ *He drew a knife from his pocket.* 他从口袋里掏出了一把刀。

3 to pull something to make it move 拖动；拉动：*The carriage was drawn by two horses.* 那辆马车是由两匹马拉的。

4 to open or close curtains 拉（窗帘）：*I switched on the light and drew the curtains.* 我开了灯，拉上了窗帘。

5 to move or come 移动；行进：*The train drew into the station.* 火车进站了。

6 to end a game with the same number of points for both players or teams 打成平手：*Liverpool and Tottenham drew in last Saturday's match.* 在上星期六的比赛中利物浦队和托特纳姆队战成平局。

draw back to move away from somebody or something 移开；后退：*He came close but she drew back.* 他走近，她却后退。

draw something out to take money out of a bank 取钱；提款：*I drew out £50 before I went shopping.* 我提取了50英镑才去商店买东西。

draw up to come to a place and stop 到达某处停下：*A taxi drew up outside the house.* 有辆出租车在房子外停了下来。

draw something up to write something 拟订；起草：*They drew up a list of people who they wanted to invite.* 他们将打算邀请的人列了一份名单。

draw² /drɔː/ *noun* 名词
the result of a game when both players or

teams have the same number of points 平局；和局： *The football match ended in a 1–1 draw.* 足球比赛以 1:1 平局结束。

drawer 抽屉

drawer 抽屉

chest of drawers 多屉橱

drawer 0➡ /drɔ:(r)/ *noun* 名词

> 🔍 **PRONUNCIATION 读音说明**
> The word **drawer** sounds like **four**.
> * drawer 读音像 four。

a thing like a box that you can pull out from a cupboard or desk, for example 抽屉： *There's some paper in the top drawer of my desk.* 我书桌的上层抽屉里有些纸。

drawing 0➡ /'drɔ:ɪŋ/ *noun* 名词
1 (*plural* 复数形式 **drawings**) a picture made with a pen or a pencil, but not paint 图画；素描画： *He did a drawing of the old farmhouse.* 他给旧农舍画了一幅素描。
2 (*no plural* 不用复数形式) the art of drawing pictures with a pen or a pencil 绘画；素描艺术： *Katherine is very good at drawing.* 凯瑟琳擅长绘画。

drawing pin /'drɔ:ɪŋ pɪn/ *noun* 名词 (*British* 英式英语) (*American* 美式英语 **thumbtack**)
a short pin with a flat round top, that you use for fastening paper to a wall or board 图钉： *I put the poster up with drawing pins.* 我用图钉把海报钉起来。

drawn *form of* DRAW¹ * draw¹ 的不同形式

dread /dred/ *verb* 动词 (**dreads, dreading, dreaded**)
to be very afraid of something that is going to happen 惧怕；极为担心： *I'm dreading the exams.* 我特别害怕这次考试。

dreadful /'dredfl/ *adjective* 形容词
very bad 糟糕透顶的： *I had a dreadful*

journey – *my train was two hours late!* 我一路上诸事不顺，火车晚点了两个小时！

dreadfully /'dredfəli/ *adverb* 副词
very 非常；极其： *I'm dreadfully sorry, but I must go now.* 实在很抱歉，但我必须走了。

dream¹ 0➡ /dri:m/ *noun* 名词
1 pictures or events which happen in your mind when you are asleep 梦： *I had a dream about school last night.* 我昨天晚上做了一个跟学校有关的梦。

> 🔍 **WORD BUILDING 词汇扩充**
> A bad or frightening dream is called a **nightmare**. 噩梦叫做 nightmare。

2 something nice that you hope for 梦想；理想；愿望： *His dream was to give up his job and live in the country.* 他的梦想是辞掉工作到乡村去生活。

dream² 0➡ /dri:m/ *verb* 动词 (**dreams, dreaming, dreamt** /dremt/ or 或 **dreamed** /dri:md/, **has dreamt** or 或 **has dreamed**)
1 to have a picture or idea in your mind when you are asleep 做梦： *I dreamt about you last night.* 昨晚我梦见你了。 ◇ *I dreamt that I was flying.* 我梦见自己在飞。
2 to hope for something nice in the future 梦想： *She dreams of becoming a famous actress.* 她梦想成为著名演员。

dreary /'drɪəri/ *adjective* 形容词
not at all interesting or attractive 沉闷的；枯燥乏味的： *His voice is so dreary that it sends me to sleep.* 他的声音沉闷得让我要睡觉。

dress¹ 0➡ /dres/ *noun* 名词
1 (*plural* 复数形式 **dresses**) a piece of clothing with a top part and a skirt, that a woman or girl wears 连衣裙 ➔ Look at Picture Dictionary page P5. 见彩页 P5。
2 (*no plural* 不用复数形式) clothes 衣服： *The group of dancers wore Bulgarian national dress.* 那群舞蹈演员穿上了保加利亚的民族服装。

dress² 0➡ /dres/ *verb* 动词 (**dresses, dressing, dressed** /drest/)
1 to put clothes on yourself or another person 穿衣服；给…穿衣服： *I got dressed and went downstairs for breakfast.* 我穿好衣服，下楼去吃早饭。 ◇ *She dressed quickly and went out.* 她匆匆穿上衣服出去了。 ◇ *He washed and dressed the baby.* 他给宝宝洗了澡并穿上衣服。
➔ OPPOSITE **undress** 反义词为 undress
2 to wear a particular style, type or colour

A B C D E F G H I J K L M N O P Q R S T U V W X Y Z

of clothes 穿…的服装： *She dresses like a film star.* 她穿得像个影星。 ◇ *He was **dressed in** black.* 他穿着一身黑衣服。

dress up

1 to put on your best clothes 穿上正装；穿上盛装： *They dressed up to go to the theatre.* 他们穿上了正装去看戏。

2 to put on special clothes for fun, so that you look like another person or a thing 装扮；乔装打扮： *The children dressed up as ghosts.* 孩子装扮成鬼。

dressing /'dresɪŋ/ ***noun*** 名词

1 a thing for covering a part of your body that is hurt （伤口）敷料： *You should put a dressing on that cut.* 你应该在那个划口上盖上敷料。

2 a sauce for food, especially for salads （尤指沙拉的）调料

dressing gown /'dresɪŋ gaʊn/ ***noun*** 名词 (*British* 英式英语) (*American* 美式英语 **robe**)

a piece of clothing like a loose coat with a belt, which you wear before or after a bath, before you get dressed in the morning, etc. 浴衣；晨衣；晨袍： *She got up and put on her dressing gown.* 她起床穿上了晨衣。

dressing table /'dresɪŋ teɪbl/ ***noun*** 名词 (*British* 英式英语)

a piece of bedroom furniture like a table with drawers and a mirror 梳妆台

drew *form of* DRAW[1] * draw[1] 的不同形式

dried *form of* DRY[2] * dry[2] 的不同形式

drier

1 *form of* DRY[1] * dry[1] 的不同形式

2 = DRYER

dries *form of* DRY[2] * dry[2] 的不同形式

driest *form of* DRY[1] * dry[1] 的不同形式

drift /drɪft/ ***verb*** 动词 (**drifts**, **drifting**, **drifted**)

to move slowly in the air or on water 飘移；漂流： *The empty boat drifted out to sea.* 那艘空船漂流到海上了。 ◇ *The balloon drifted away.* 气球飘走了。

drill /drɪl/ ***noun*** 名词

a tool that you use for making holes 钻；钻头；钻床： *an electric drill* 电钻 ◇ *a dentist's drill* 牙钻

▸ **drill** ***verb*** 动词 (**drills**, **drilling**, **drilled** /drɪld/): *Drill two holes in the wall.* 在墙上钻两个洞。

drink[1] 🔑 /drɪŋk/ ***verb*** 动词 (**drinks**, **drinking**, **drank** /dræŋk/, **has drunk** /drʌŋk/)

1 to take in liquid, for example water, milk or coffee, through your mouth 喝；饮： *What do you want to drink?* 你想喝什么？ ◇ *She was drinking a cup of tea.* 她在喝茶。

2 to drink alcohol 喝酒： *'Would you like some wine?' 'No, thank you. I don't drink.'* "你想喝点葡萄酒吗？" "不用了，谢谢。我不喝酒。"

drink[2] 🔑 /drɪŋk/ ***noun*** 名词

1 liquid, for example water, milk or coffee, that you take in through your mouth 饮料： *Would you like a drink?* 你想喝点什么吗？ ◇ *Can I **have a drink** of water?* 可不可以给我一杯水？

2 drink with alcohol in it, for example beer or wine 酒精饮料： *There was lots of food and drink at the party.* 聚会上有很多食物和酒。

drip /drɪp/ ***verb*** 动词 (**drips**, **dripping**, **dripped** /drɪpt/)

1 to fall slowly in small drops 滴下： *Water was dripping through the roof.* 水从屋顶滴落下来。

2 If something **drips**, liquid falls from it in small drops. 滴水： *The tap is dripping.* 水龙头滴着水。

drive[1] 🔑 /draɪv/ ***verb*** 动词 (**drives**, **driving**, **drove** /drəʊv/, **has driven** /'drɪvn/)

1 to control a car, bus, etc. and make it go where you want to go 驾驶；开车： *Can you drive?* 你会开车吗？ ◇ *She usually drives to work.* 她通常开车上班。

2 to take somebody to a place in a car 开车送： *My parents drove me to the airport.* 父母开车送我到机场。

drive[2] 🔑 /draɪv/ ***noun*** 名词

1 a journey in a car 驾车路程；驱车旅程： *It's a long drive from London to Edinburgh.* 从伦敦开车到爱丁堡要走很长时间。 ◇ *We went for a drive in my sister's car.* 我们坐我姐姐的车子去兜风了。

2 a wide hard path or private road that goes from the street to one house （通往住宅的）车道： *You can park your car in the drive.* 你可以把车子停在车道上。

3 (*computing* 电脑) the part of a computer that reads and stores information 驱动器： *I saved my work on the C: drive.* 我把工作存到 C 盘上了。

drive-in /'draɪv ɪn/ ***noun*** 名词 (*American* 美式英语)

a place where you can go to eat or to watch a film while you are sitting in your car 汽车餐馆；汽车影院

driven *form of* DRIVE[1] * drive[1] 的不同形式

driver ο━ /'draɪvə(r)/ *noun* 名词
a person who controls a car, bus, train, etc. 驾驶员；司机；驾驶者：*John is a good driver.* 约翰车开得不错。◇ *a taxi driver* 出租车司机

driver's license /'draɪvəz laɪsns/
American English for DRIVING LICENCE 美式英语，即 driving licence

driving /'draɪvɪŋ/ *noun* 名词 (*no plural* 不用复数形式)
controlling a car, bus, etc. 驾驶；行车：*Driving in the fog can be dangerous.* 在雾中开车可以很危险。

driving licence /'draɪvɪŋ laɪsns/ (*British* 英式英语) (*American* 美式英语 **driver's license**) *noun* 名词
an official document that shows that you are allowed to drive a car, etc. 驾驶执照

driving test /'draɪvɪŋ test/ *noun* 名词
a test that you have to pass before you get your DRIVING LICENCE 驾照考试

droop /druːp/ *verb* 动词 (droops, drooping, drooped /druːpt/)
to bend or hang down 低垂；垂下；耷拉：*Flowers droop if you don't put them in water.* 花不放水里就发蔫。

drop 掉下

drop¹ ο━ /drɒp/ *verb* 动词 (drops, dropping, dropped /drɒpt/)
1 to let something fall 使落下；使掉下：*I dropped my watch and it broke.* 我把手表掉在地上摔坏了。
2 to fall 落下；掉下：*The glass dropped from her hands.* 玻璃杯从她手中掉了下来。
3 to become lower or less 降低；减少：*The temperature has dropped.* 温度下降了。
4 (*also* 亦作 **drop off**) to stop your car and let somebody get out 中途卸客：*Could you drop me at the station?* 你可以让我在车站下车吗？◇ *He dropped me off at the bus stop.* 他让我在公交车站下了车。

5 to stop doing something 停止；终止：*I'm going to drop geography* (= stop studying it) *at school next year.* 我打算明年不修地理课了。
drop in to visit somebody who does not know that you are coming 顺道探访：*We were in the area so we thought we'd drop in and see you.* 我们就在附近，所以想顺便看看你。
drop off to fall asleep 打瞌睡；打盹：*She dropped off in front of the TV.* 她在电视机前打起盹来了。
drop out to stop doing something with a group of people 不再参加；退出：*I dropped out of the football team after I hurt my leg.* 我腿受伤后就退出了足球队。

drop² ο━ /drɒp/ *noun* 名词
1 a very small amount of liquid 滴：*drops of rain* 雨滴 ◇ *a drop of blood* 一滴血
2 a fall in the amount or level of something 下降；减少：*a drop in temperature* 温度的下降 ◇ *a drop in prices* 价格的下跌

drought /draʊt/ *noun* 名词
a long time when there is not enough rain 久旱；旱灾：*Thousands of people died in the drought.* 成千上万的人死于那场旱灾。

drove *form of* DRIVE¹ * drive¹ 的不同形式

drown /draʊn/ *verb* 动词 (drowns, drowning, drowned /draʊnd/)
to die under water because you cannot breathe; to make somebody die in this way 使⋯淹死，溺毙：*The boy fell in the river and drowned.* 男孩掉进河里淹死了。◇ *Twenty people were drowned in the floods.* 洪水淹死了二十人。

drowsy /'draʊzi/ *adjective* 形容词
feeling tired and wanting to sleep 困倦的；昏昏欲睡的：*The heat made him very drowsy.* 炎热的天气使他昏昏欲睡。

drug ο━ /drʌg/ *noun* 名词
1 an illegal chemical substance that people take because it makes them feel happy or excited 毒品：*He doesn't smoke or take drugs.* 他不吸烟，也不吸毒。◇ *Her daughter is on drugs* (= regularly using illegal drugs). 她女儿吸毒成瘾。◇ *Heroin is a dangerous drug.* 海洛因是危险的毒品。
2 a chemical substance used as a medicine, that you take when you are ill to make you better 药品；药物：*drug companies* 药品公司 ◇ *Some drugs can only be obtained with a prescription from a doctor.* 有些药物要有医生处方才能得到。

drug addict /'drʌg ædɪkt/ *noun* 名词
a person who cannot stop using drugs
吸毒成瘾者；瘾君子

drugstore /'drʌgstɔ:(r)/ *noun* 名词
a shop in the US where you can buy
medicines and a lot of other things 药房

drums 鼓

drumstick 鼓槌

drum /drʌm/ *noun* 名词
1 a musical instrument that you hit with
special sticks (called **drumsticks**) or with
your hands 鼓：*He plays the drums in
a band.* 他是一个乐队的鼓手。
2 a big round container for oil 大桶：
an oil drum 油桶

drummer /'drʌmə(r)/ *noun* 名词
a person who plays a DRUM 鼓手

drunk¹ *form of* DRINK¹ * drink¹ 的不同
形式

drunk² 0= /drʌŋk/ *adjective* 形容词
If a person is **drunk**, they have drunk too
much alcohol. （酒）醉：*He gets drunk
every Friday night.* 他每个周五晚上都
喝醉。

dry¹ 0= /draɪ/ *adjective* 形容词 (drier,
driest)
1 with no water or liquid in it or on it
干的；干燥的：*The washing isn't dry yet.*
洗过的衣服还没干。 ⊃ OPPOSITE **wet**
反义词为 wet
2 with no rain 少雨的；干旱的：*dry
weather* 干燥的天气 ⊃ OPPOSITE **wet**
反义词为 wet
3 not sweet 无甜味的；干的：*dry white
wine* 干白葡萄酒

dry² 0= /draɪ/ *verb* 动词 (dries, drying,
dried /draɪd/, has dried)
to become or make something dry （使）
变干；（把…）弄干：*Our clothes were
drying in the sun.* 我们的衣服在太阳底下
晒干。 ◇ *Dry your hands on this towel.*
用这条毛巾把手擦干。
dry out to become completely dry

干透：*Leave your shoes by the fire to dry
out.* 把你的鞋放在火旁烘干。

dry up
1 (used about rivers, lakes, etc.) to
become completely dry（河流、湖泊等）
干涸：*There was no rain for several
months and all the rivers dried up.* 几个月
没有雨，河溪都干涸了。
2 to dry things like plates, knives and
forks with a towel after you have washed
them 擦干（餐具）：*If I wash the dishes,
could you dry up?* 我来洗碗的话，你来擦
干好吗？

dry-clean /,draɪ 'kli:n/ *verb* 动词
(dry-cleans, dry-cleaning, dry-cleaned
/,draɪ 'kli:nd/)
to make clothes clean by using chemicals,
not water 干洗：*I had my suit dry-cleaned.*
我把套装拿去干洗了。

dry-cleaner's /,draɪ 'kli:nəz/ *noun* 名词
a shop where you take clothes and other
things to be DRY-CLEANED 干洗店 ⊃ Look
at Picture Dictionary page **P13**. 见彩页
P13。

dryer (*also* 亦作 **drier**) /'draɪə(r)/ *noun*
名词
a machine for drying something 烘干机；
干燥机：*Take the clothes out of the
washing machine and put them in the
dryer.* 把衣服从洗衣机里拿出来再放进烘干
机里。 ◇ *a hairdryer* 吹风机

dual carriageway /,dju:əl 'kærɪdʒweɪ/
noun 名词 (*British* 英式英语) (*American*
美式英语 **divided highway**)
a wide road with a narrow piece of land
or a fence between the two lines of traffic
（中央有分隔带的）双向车道

duchess /'dʌtʃəs/ *noun* 名词 (*plural* 复数
形式 **duchesses**)
a woman who has a very high position in
society or who is married to a DUKE (= a
man of the highest social position) 女公
爵；公爵夫人：*the Duchess of York* 约克
公爵夫人

duck 鸭子

duck¹ /dʌk/ *noun* 名词
a bird that lives on and near water. You often see **ducks** on farms or in parks. 鸭

🔎 WORD BUILDING 词汇扩充
A young duck is called a **duckling**.
小鸭叫做 duckling。

duck² /dʌk/ *verb* 动词 (ducks, ducking, ducked /dʌkt/)
to move your head down quickly, so that something does not hit you or so that somebody does not see you 迅速低下头；迅速弯下身：*He saw the ball coming towards him and ducked.* 他看见球朝他飞来，赶紧低头闪开。

duckling /'dʌklɪŋ/ *noun* 名词
a young DUCK 小鸭；幼鸭

due /djuː/ *adjective* 形容词
1 because of something; caused by something 由于；因为：*The accident was due to bad driving.* 这起事故是由驾驶不当引起的。
2 If something is **due** at a certain time, you expect it to happen or come then. 预定；预期：*When's the baby due?* 预计宝宝什么时候出生？ ◇ *The new road is due to open in April.* 新路预期四月通车。
3 If an amount of money is **due**, you must pay it. 到期（付款）：*My rent is due at the beginning of the month.* 我月初交房租。
4 ready for something 准备好：*My car is due for a service.* 我的汽车该检修了。

duet /djuˈet/ *noun* 名词
music for two people to sing or play on musical instruments 二重唱（曲）；二重奏（曲）：*James and Olivia sang a duet.* 詹姆斯和奥利维娅表演了二重唱。

dug *form of* DIG * dig 的不同形式

duke /djuːk/ *noun* 名词
a man who has a very high position in society in some parts of Europe 公爵
➲ Look at **duchess**. 见 duchess。

dull /dʌl/ *adjective* 形容词 (duller, dullest)
1 not interesting or exciting 乏味的；无聊的；沉闷的 ➲ SAME MEANING **boring** 同义词为 boring：*Life is never dull in a big city.* 大城市里的生活从不会枯燥。
2 not bright 灰暗的；昏暗的：*It was a dull, cloudy day.* 那天阴沉多云。
3 not strong or loud 隐约的；低沉的：*a dull pain* 隐隐的疼痛

dumb /dʌm/ *adjective* 形容词
1 not able to speak 哑的：*She was born deaf and dumb.* 她天生聋哑。

2 (*informal* 非正式) not intelligent; stupid 笨的；傻的：*That was a dumb thing to do!* 那样做太傻了！

dummy 奶嘴

dummy /'dʌmi/ (*plural* 复数形式 **dummies**) *noun* 名词 (*British* 英式英语) (*American* 美式英语 **pacifier**)
a small rubber object that you put in a baby's mouth to stop it crying 橡皮奶嘴，橡皮奶头（用于安抚婴儿）

dump /dʌmp/ *verb* 动词 (dumps, dumping, dumped /dʌmpt/)
1 to take something to a place and leave it there because you do not want it 丢弃；倾倒：*They dumped their rubbish by the side of the road.* 他们把垃圾扔在路边了。
2 to put something down without being careful 乱扔：*Don't dump your clothes on the floor!* 别把衣服乱扔在地上！
▶ **dump** *noun* 名词 a place where people take things they do not want 垃圾场；废料堆

dune /djuːn/ *noun* 名词
a small hill of sand near the sea or in a desert 沙丘

dungarees /ˌdʌŋgəˈriːz/ *noun* 名词 (*plural* 用复数形式) (*British* 英式英语)
trousers with a part that covers the top of your body 工装裤；背带工作服：*a new pair of dungarees* 一条新的工装裤

dungeon /'dʌndʒən/ *noun* 名词
a prison under the ground, for example in a castle 地牢；城堡地牢

during ☛ /'djʊərɪŋ/ *preposition* 介词
1 all the time that something is happening 在⋯期间：*The sun gives us light during the day.* 太阳在白天给我们光明。
2 at some time while something else is happening 在⋯期间的某个时候：*She died during the night.* 她在夜里死去。◇ *I fell asleep during the film.* 我看电影时睡着了。

dusk /dʌsk/ *noun* 名词 (*no plural* 不用复数形式)
the time in the evening when it is nearly dark 黄昏；傍晚

A B C D E F G H I J K L M N O P Q R S T U V W X Y Z

A B C **D** E F G H I J K L M N O P Q R S T U V W X Y Z

dust¹ 0━ /dʌst/ *noun* 名词 (*no plural* 不用复数形式)

dry dirt that is like powder 灰尘；尘土；尘埃： *The old table was covered in dust.* 旧桌子上铺满灰尘。

dust² /dʌst/ *verb* 动词 (dusts, dusting, dusted)

to take dust off something with a cloth 给…除尘： *I dusted the furniture.* 我擦掉了家具上的灰尘。

dustbin 垃圾桶

dustbin /'dʌstbɪn/ *noun* 名词 (*British* 英式英语) (*American* 美式英语 garbage can, trash can)

a large container for rubbish that you keep outside your house （户外的）垃圾桶，垃圾箱

duster /'dʌstə(r)/ *noun* 名词

a cloth that you use for taking the dust off furniture 抹布；掸子

dustman /'dʌstmən/ *noun* 名词 (*plural* 复数形式 dustmen /'dʌstmən/) (*British* 英式英语)

a person whose job is to take away rubbish from outside people's houses 垃圾清运工

dustpan 畚箕

brush 刷子

dustpan /'dʌstpæn/ *noun* 名词

a flat container with a handle that you use for getting dust or rubbish off the floor 畚箕： *Have you got a dustpan and brush?* 你有畚箕和刷子吗？

dusty /'dʌsti/ *adjective* 形容词 (dustier, dustiest)

covered with dust 布满灰尘的： *The furniture was very dusty.* 家具上满布灰尘。

duty 0━ /'djuːti/ *noun* 名词 (*plural* 复数形式 duties)

1 something that you must do because it is part of your job or because you think it is right 责任；义务： *It's your duty to look after your parents when they get older.* 父母年老时子女有责任照顾他们。◊ *One of the duties of a secretary is to type letters.* 当秘书其中一项职责是打信。

2 money (called tax) that you pay to the government when you bring things into a country from another country 关税；进口税

off duty not working 不值班；不值勤： *The police officer was off duty.* 那个警察当时下了班。

on duty working 值班；值勤： *Some nurses at the hospital are on duty all night.* 医院里有些护士整夜值班。

duty-free /,djuːti 'friː/ *adjective*, *adverb* 形容词，副词

Duty-free goods are things that you can bring into a country without paying money to the government. You can buy goods **duty-free** on planes or ships and at airports. （商品）免税的（地）

duvet /'duːveɪ/ *noun* 名词 (*British* 英式英语)

a thick warm cover for a bed. **Duvets** are often filled with feathers. 羽绒被 ⊃ Look at the picture at **bed**. 见 bed 的插图。

DVD 0━ /,diː viː 'diː/ *noun* 名词

a small plastic disk that you record films and music on. You can play a **DVD** on a computer or a special machine (called a **DVD player**). 数字视盘；数字多功能光盘： *Is the film available on DVD?* 这部电影有 DVD 吗？

dwarf /dwɔːf/ *noun* 名词

1 a person, animal or plant that is much smaller than the usual size 矮子；侏儒；矮生动物；矮生植物

2 (in children's stories) a very small person （童话故事）小矮人： *Snow White and the Seven Dwarfs* 白雪公主和七个小矮人

dye /daɪ/ *verb* 动词 (dyes, dyeing, dyed /daɪd/)

to change the colour of something by using a special liquid or substance 给…染色： *She dyed her hair blonde.* 她把头发染成了金黄色。

▶ **dye** *noun* 名词 a substance that you

use to change the colour of something, for example cloth or hair 染料： *purple hair dye* 紫色染发液

dying *form of* DIE * die 的不同形式

dynamite /'daɪmənaɪt/ *noun* 名词 (*no plural* 不用复数形式) a powerful substance that can explode 炸药： *a stick of dynamite* 一根炸药

Ee

E, e /iː/ *noun* 名词 (*plural* 复数形式 E's, e's /iːz/)

the fifth letter of the English alphabet 英语字母表的第 5 个字母: *'Egg' begins with an 'E'.* * egg 一词以字母 e 开头。

each 0̶ /iːtʃ/ *adjective, pronoun* 形容词，代词

every person or thing in a group 每; 每个；各个: *Each student buys a book and a tape.* 每个学生都买一本书和一盒磁带。 ◇ *He gave a present to each of the children.* 他给每个孩子一份礼物。 ◇ *These T-shirts are £5 each.* 这些 T 恤衫每件 5 英镑。

each other 互相

They are looking at **each other**.
他们相互对视。

each other 0̶ /iːtʃ ˈʌðə(r)/ *pronoun* 代词

used for saying that somebody does the same thing as another person 互相；彼此: *Gary and Susy looked at each other* (= Gary looked at Susy and Susy looked at Gary). 加里和苏茜互相对望。

eager /ˈiːgə(r)/ *adjective* 形容词

If you are **eager** to do something, you want to do it very much. 热切的；渴望的 ◅ SAME MEANING **keen** 同义词为 keen: *She's eager to help with the party.* 她很想为聚会帮忙。

▶ **eagerly** /ˈiːgəli/ *adverb* 副词: *The children were waiting eagerly for the film to begin.* 孩子们都着急地等着电影开始。

▶ **eagerness** /ˈiːgənəs/ *noun* 名词 (*no plural* 不用复数形式): *I couldn't hide my*

eagerness to get home. 我无法掩饰想回家的急切心情。

eagle 雕

—beak 喙

eagle /ˈiːgl/ *noun* 名词

a very large bird that can see very well. It catches and eats small birds and animals. 鹰；雕

ear 0̶ /ɪə(r)/ *noun* 名词

one of the two parts of your body that you use to hear with 耳朵: *Elephants have big ears.* 象有大耳朵。 ◅ Look at Picture Dictionary page **P4**. 见彩页 **P4**。

earache /ˈɪəreɪk/ *noun* 名词 (*no plural* 不用复数形式)

pain inside your ear 耳痛: *I've got earache.* 我耳朵疼。

earl /ɜːl/ *noun* 名词

a British man who has a high social position 伯爵

early 0̶ /ˈɜːli/ *adjective, adverb* 形容词，副词 (**earlier, earliest**)

1 near the beginning of a period of time 早期（的）；初期（的）: *Come in the early afternoon.* 下午早点过来。 ◇ *She was in her early twenties* (= aged between 20 and about 23 or 24). 她那时二十出头。 ◇ *I have to get up early tomorrow.* 我明天得早起。

2 before the usual or right time 提早（的）；提前（的）: *The train arrived ten minutes early.* 火车早到了十分钟。 ◇ *You're early! It's only half past six.* 你来早了！才六点半呢。 ◇ *I was early for the lesson.* 我上课来早了。 ◅ OPPOSITE **late** 反义词为 late

have an early night to go to bed earlier than usual 比平时睡得早: *I'm*

really tired, I think I'll have an early night.
我太累了，我想我会早点睡。

earn 0̄₋ /ɜːn/ *verb* 动词 (earns, earning,
earned /ɜːnd/)

1 to get money by working 挣钱；赚钱：
*How much do teachers earn in your
country?* 在你们国家教师挣多少钱？◇
She earns about £1 500 a month. 她每月
大约挣 1 500 英镑。
2 to get something because you have
worked well or done something good
应得；赢得：*You've earned a holiday!*
假期是你应得的！

earnings /ˈɜːnɪŋz/ *noun* 名词 (*plural*
用复数形式)
money that you earn by working 收入；
工资

earphones /ˈɪəfəʊnz/ *noun* 名词 (*plural*
用复数形式) = HEADPHONES

earrings 耳环

earring /ˈɪərɪŋ/ *noun* 名词
a piece of jewellery that you wear on your
ear 耳环；耳饰：*a pair of silver earrings*
一对银耳环

the earth 地球
northern hemisphere 北半球

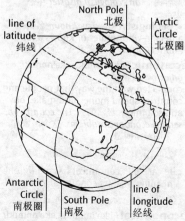

line of
latitude
纬线

North Pole
北极

Arctic
Circle
北极圈

Antarctic
Circle
南极圈

South Pole
南极

line of
longitude
经线

southern hemisphere 南半球

earth 0̄₋ /ɜːθ/ *noun* 名词 (*no plural* 不用
复数形式)

1 usually 通常为 the earth, the Earth this
world; the planet that we live on 世界；
地球：*The moon travels round the earth.*
月亮绕着地球转。◇ *They live in one of the
hottest places on earth.* 他们住在地球上最
热的地方之一。
2 the substance that plants grow in
土壤；泥土 ◯ SAME MEANING **soil** 同义词为
soil：*Cover the seeds with earth.* 用泥土
覆盖种子。

**how, who, what, where, etc. on
earth?** (*informal* 非正式) used in
questions when you are very surprised
or want to say something very strongly
（表示惊讶或加强语气）到底，究竟：
What on earth are you doing? 你究竟在干
什么？◇ *Where on earth is Paul? He's two
hours late!* 保罗到底在哪儿？他已经晚了
两个小时！

earthquake /ˈɜːθkweɪk/ *noun* 名词
a sudden strong shaking of the ground
地震

ease¹ /iːz/ *noun* 名词 (*no plural* 不用复数
形式)

be or 或 **feel at ease** to be or feel
comfortable and relaxed 舒适轻松：
*Everyone was so friendly that I felt
completely at ease.* 所有人都是那么友善，
让我没有半点拘束。

with ease with no difficulty 容易地；
不费劲地 ◯ SAME MEANING **easily** 同义词为
easily：*She answered the questions with
ease.* 她轻而易举地回答了问题。

ease² /iːz/ *verb* 动词
to become or to make something less
painful or serious （使）缓解；减轻：
They waited for the rain to ease. 他们等着
雨势减弱。◇ *This should ease the pain.*
这该会舒缓痛楚。

easel /ˈiːzl/ *noun* 名词
a frame that an artist uses to hold a
picture while it is being painted 画架

easily 0̄₋ /ˈiːzəli/ *adverb* 副词
with no difficulty 容易地；不费劲地：
*I can easily ring and check the time of the
film.* 我打个电话就可以轻松查到电影的
时间。◇ *He passed the test easily.* 他轻松
地通过了测验。◯ The adjective is **easy**.
形容词为 easy。

east 0̄₋ /iːst/ *noun* 名词 (*no plural* 不用
复数形式) (*abbr.* 缩略式 E)

1 the direction you look in to see the sun
come up in the morning 东；东方：
Which way is east? 哪边是东？◇ *There was*

a cold wind from the east. 一股冷风从东面吹来。 ◎ Look at the picture at **compass**. 见 compass 的插图。

2 the East the countries of Asia, for example China and Japan 东方国家（如中国和日本）

▶ **east** *adjective, adverb* 形容词，副词: *They live on the east coast.* 他们住在东岸。 ◊ *an east wind* (= that comes from the east) 东风 ◊ *We travelled east.* 我们向东面走去。

Easter /'i:stə(r)/ *noun* 名词 (*no plural* 不用复数形式)

a Sunday in March or April, and the days around it, when Christians think about Christ coming back to life 复活节: *I'm going on holiday at Easter.* 我打算在复活节去度假。

> ♪ CULTURE 文化资料补充
>
> **Easter** is a popular festival, with many traditions in Britain and the US. 复活节是广泛流行的节日，在英国和美国有很多传统风俗。
> People think about new life and the coming of spring. They celebrate this by eating chocolate eggs. 这个节日象征新生命和春天的到来。人们吃巧克力蛋来庆祝。
> The Monday after **Easter** is called '**Easter Monday**'. In Britain, this is a public holiday. 复活节之后的星期一称Easter Monday，这一天在英国是公共假日。

Easter egg /'i:stər eg/ *noun* 名词
an egg made of chocolate that people give as a present at EASTER 复活节彩蛋（巧克力制成，作为礼物）

eastern 0ㅡ /'i:stən/ *adjective* 形容词
in, of or from the east of a place 东方的；向东的；东部的: *eastern Scotland* 苏格兰东部

easy 0ㅡ /'i:zi/ *adjective* 形容词 (easier, easiest)

1 not difficult to do or understand 容易的；不费劲的: *The homework was very easy.* 作业很容易做。 ◊ *English isn't an easy language to learn.* 英语不是一种容易学的语言。 ◎ OPPOSITE **difficult, hard** 反义词为 difficult 和 hard

2 without problems or pain 舒适的；安逸的: *He has had an easy life.* 他一直过着舒适的生活。 ◎ OPPOSITE **difficult, hard** 反义词为 difficult 和 hard
take it easy, take things easy to relax and not worry or work too much 放松点；

别急；别太担心: *After my exams I'm going to take it easy for a few days.* 我考试之后要放松几天。

eat 0ㅡ /i:t/ *verb* 动词 (eats, eating, ate /et/, has eaten /'i:tn/)

1 to put food in your mouth and swallow it 吃: *Have you eaten all the chocolates?* 你把巧克力都吃了吗？ ◊ *Do you want something to eat?* 你想吃点东西吗？

2 to have a meal 吃饭；用餐: *What time shall we eat?* 我们什么时候吃饭？
eat out to have a meal in a restaurant 在外面吃饭；下馆子: *We don't eat out very often.* 我们不常在外吃饭。

echo /'ekəʊ/ *noun* 名词 (*plural* 复数形式 echoes)

a sound that a surface such as a wall sends back so that you hear it again 回声；回音

▶ **echo** *verb* 动词 (echoes, echoing, echoed /'ekəʊd/): *His footsteps echoed in the empty hall.* 他的脚步声在空荡荡的大厅里回响。

eclipse /ɪ'klɪps/ *noun* 名词
1 a time when the moon comes between the earth and the sun so that we cannot see the sun's light 日食
2 a time when the earth comes between the sun and the moon so that we cannot see the moon's light 月食

ecology /i'kɒlədʒi/ *noun* 名词 (*no plural* 不用复数形式)
the relationship between living things and everything around them; the study of this subject 生态；生态学

▶ **ecological** /ˌi:kə'lɒdʒɪkl/ *adjective* 形容词: *an ecological disaster* 生态灾难

▶ **ecologist** /i'kɒlədʒɪst/ *noun* 名词
a person who studies or knows a lot about ECOLOGY 生态学家

economic /ˌi:kə'nɒmɪk; ˌekə'nɒmɪk/ *adjective* 形容词
connected with the way that people and countries spend money and make, buy and sell things 经济的: *The country has serious economic problems.* 这个国家有严重的经济问题。

> ♪ WHICH WORD? 词语辨析
>
> Be careful! **Economical** has a different meaning. 注意：economical 含义不同。

economical /ˌi:kə'nɒmɪkl; ˌekə'nɒmɪkl/ *adjective* 形容词
costing or using less time, money, etc.

than usual 经济的；节约的：*This car is very economical to run* (= it does not use a lot of petrol). 这辆车很省油。

🔍 **WHICH WORD?** 词语辨析

Be careful! **Economic** has a different meaning. 注意：economic 含义不同。

▶ **economically** /ˌiːkəˈnɒmɪkli; ˌekəˈnɒmɪkli/ *adverb* 副词：*The service could be run more economically.* 这项服务可以用更经济的方法运行。

economics /ˌiːkəˈnɒmɪks; ˌekəˈnɒmɪks/ *noun* 名词 (*no plural* 不用复数形式) the study of the way that people and countries spend money and make, buy and sell things 经济学

economist /ɪˈkɒnəmɪst/ *noun* 名词 a person who studies or knows a lot about ECONOMICS 经济学家；经济专家

economy /ɪˈkɒnəmi/ *noun* 名词 (*plural* 复数形式 **economies**) **1** the way that a country spends its money and makes, buys and sells things 经济：*the economies of Japan and Germany* 日本和德国的经济 **2** using money or things well and carefully 节俭；节约：*We need to make some economies.* 我们得节约一点。

edge 🔑 /edʒ/ *noun* 名词 **1** the part along the end or side of something 边；边缘：*She stood at the water's edge.* 她站在水边。 ◇ *the edge of the table* 桌边 **2** the sharp part of a knife or tool 刀口；刃 **be on edge** to be nervous or worried 紧张不安

edible /ˈedəbl/ *adjective* 形容词 good or safe to eat 可以吃的；适宜食用的：*The food was barely edible* (= almost too bad to eat). 这些食物简直不能入口。

edition /ɪˈdɪʃn/ *noun* 名词 one of a number of books, magazines or newspapers that appear at the same time 版本：*the evening edition of the newspaper* 报纸的晚间版

editor /ˈedɪtə(r)/ *noun* 名词 a person whose job is to prepare or control a book or a newspaper before it is printed 编辑；编者

educate 🔑 /ˈedʒukeɪt/ *verb* 动词 (**educates, educating, educated**) **1** to teach somebody at a school or college 教育：*Where was she educated?* 她在哪儿受教育？

2 to give people information about something 教导；使了解：*We must educate young people about the dangers of smoking.* 我们必须使年轻人了解吸烟的危害。

education 🔑 /ˌedʒuˈkeɪʃn/ *noun* 名词 (*no plural* 不用复数形式) teaching somebody at a school or college （学校的）教育：*He had a good education.* 他受过良好的教育。 ◇ *Education is extremely important.* 教育极其重要。 ▶ **educational** /ˌedʒuˈkeɪʃənl/ *adjective* 形容词：*an educational video* 教学录像

eel /iːl/ *noun* 名词 a long fish that looks like a snake 鳗

effect 🔑 /ɪˈfekt/ *noun* 名词 a change that happens because of something 效应；作用：*We are studying the effects of heat on different metals.* 我们在研究热对不同金属产生的效应。 ◇ *Her shouting had little effect on him.* 她的喊叫对他作用不大。

effective /ɪˈfektɪv/ *adjective* 形容词 Something that is **effective** works well. 有效的：*Cycling is an effective way of keeping fit.* 骑自行车是一种有效的健身方式。 ▶ **effectively** /ɪˈfektɪvli/ *adverb* 副词 in a way that gets the result you wanted 有效地：*She dealt with the situation effectively.* 她有效地应付了那个局面。

efficient /ɪˈfɪʃnt/ *adjective* 形容词 working well without making mistakes or wasting energy 效率高的；能干的：*Our secretary is very efficient.* 我们的秘书很能干。 ◇ *an efficient way of working* 高效率的工作方式 ⊃ OPPOSITE **inefficient** 反义词为 inefficient ▶ **efficiency** /ɪˈfɪʃnsi/ *noun* 名词 (*no plural* 不用复数形式)：*ways of increasing efficiency at the factory* 提高工厂效率的方法 ▶ **efficiently** /ɪˈfɪʃntli/ *adverb* 副词：*Try to use your time more efficiently.* 尝试更有效地利用时间。

effort 🔑 /ˈefət/ *noun* 名词 the physical or mental energy that you need to do something 气力；努力：*Thank you for all your efforts.* 感谢你的所有努力！ ◇ *He made an effort to arrive on time.* 他尽力准时到达。

EFL /ˌiː ef ˈel/ *abbreviation* 缩略式 (*British* 英式英语) **EFL** is short for 'English as a foreign language' (= the teaching of English to

people who speak other languages).
非母语的英语教学（EFL 是 English as a
foreign language 的缩略式）➲ Look at
ESL and **ESOL**. 见 ESL 和 ESOL.

e.g. /ˌi: 'dʒi:/ *abbreviation* 缩略式 short for
FOR EXAMPLE * for example 的缩略式:
*popular sports, e.g. football, tennis and
swimming* 普及的体育运动，如足球、网球
和游泳

egg 蛋

shell 壳

yolk
蛋黄

white
蛋白

egg 蛋

egg /eg/ *noun* 名词
1 a round or OVAL (= almost round)
object that has a baby bird, fish, insect or
snake inside it 蛋，卵: *The hen has laid
an egg.* 母鸡下了个蛋。
2 an egg that we eat, especially from a
chicken 禽蛋；（尤指）鸡蛋: *a boiled
egg* 水煮蛋 ➲ Look at Picture Dictionary
page **P6**. 见彩页 P6。

egg cup /'eg kʌp/ *noun* 名词
a small cup that holds a boiled egg while
you are eating it （放水煮蛋的）蛋杯
➲ Look at the picture at **cup**. 见 cup 的
插图。

eggplant /'egplɑːnt/ *American English for*
AUBERGINE 美式英语，即 aubergine

eight /eɪt/ *number* 数词
8 八

eighteen /ˌeɪ'ti:n/ *number* 数词
18 十八
▸ **eighteenth** /ˌeɪ'ti:nθ/ *pronoun,
adjective, adverb* 代词，形容词，副词 18th
第十八: *He met Emma just before his
eighteenth birthday.* 他就在十八岁生日前
遇见了埃玛。

eighth /eɪtθ/ *pronoun, adjective,
adverb, noun* 代词，形容词，副词，名词
1 8th 第八

2 one of eight equal parts of something;
⅛ 八分之一

eighty /'eɪti/ *number* 数词
1 80 八十
2 the eighties (*plural* 用复数形式) the
numbers, years or temperature between
80 and 89 八十几；八十年代
in your eighties between the ages of 80
and 89 * 80 多岁
▸ **eightieth** /'eɪtiəθ/ *pronoun, adjective,
adverb, noun* 代词，形容词，副词，名词
80th 第八十: *My grandpa just celebrated
his eightieth birthday.* 我爷爷刚庆祝了八十
大寿。

either¹ /'aɪðə(r), 'i:ðə(r)/ *adjective,
pronoun* 形容词，代词
1 one of two things or people （两者的）
任何一个: *There is cake and ice cream.
You can have either.* 有蛋糕和冰激凌，
你可以任选一样。◇ *Either of us will help
you.* 我们俩其中一人会来帮你。
2 each 每个: *There are trees along either
side of the street.* 沿街的两边都是树。

either² /'aɪðə(r), 'i:ðə(r)/ *adverb* 副词
(used in sentences with 'not') also （用于
含有 not 的句子）也: *Lydia can't swim
and I can't either.* 莉迪亚不会游泳，我也
不会。
either … or words that show two
different things or people that you can
choose 要么…要么；不是…就是: *You
can have either tea or coffee.* 你可以喝茶
或咖啡。◇ *I will either write or telephone.*
我要么写信，要么打电话。

elaborate /ɪ'læbərət/ *adjective* 形容词
not simple; with a lot of different parts
复杂的；细致的 ➲ SAME MEANING
complicated 同义词为 complicated:
The carpet has a very elaborate pattern.
这块地毯的图案很复杂。
▸ **elaborately** /ɪ'læbərətli/ *adverb* 副词
The rooms were elaborately decorated.
这些房间都经过精心装饰。

elastic /ɪ'læstɪk/ *noun* 名词 (*no plural*
不用复数形式)
material that becomes longer when you
pull it and then goes back to its usual size
橡皮带；松紧带: *This skirt needs some
new elastic in the waist.* 这条裙子的腰部
需要新的松紧带。
▸ **elastic** *adjective* 形容词: *elastic
material* 弹性材料

elastic band /ɪˌlæstɪk 'bænd/ *noun* 名词
(*British* 英式英语)
a thin circle of rubber that you use for
holding things together 橡皮圈；橡皮筋

⊃ SAME MEANING rubber band 同义词为 rubber band

elbow /'elbəʊ/ *noun* 名词
the part in the middle of your arm where it bends 肘; 肘部: *She fell and broke her elbow.* 她摔倒了，肘部骨折了。 ⊃ Look at Picture Dictionary page **P4**. 见彩页 P4。

elder /'eldə(r)/ *adjective* 形容词
older, especially of two members of the same family （尤指两个家庭成员中）年纪较大的: *My elder brother lives abroad.* 我哥哥住在国外。

elderly /'eldəli/ *adjective* 形容词
(used about people) a polite way of saying 'old' （人）上年纪的: *an elderly lady* 年迈的女士

eldest /'eldɪst/ *adjective* 形容词
oldest of three or more people, especially members of the same family （尤指三个或以上的家庭成员中）年龄最大的: *Their eldest son is at university.* 他们的大儿子在上大学。

elect /ɪ'lekt/ *verb* 动词 (elects, electing, elected)
to choose somebody to be a leader by voting for him or her 选举; 推选: *The new president was elected last year.* 新总统是在去年选出的。

election ☞ /ɪ'lekʃn/ *noun* 名词
a time when people choose somebody to be a leader by voting for him or her 选举: *The election will be held on Wednesday.* 选举将于星期三举行。

⌕ CULTURE 文化资料补充
In Britain, **general elections** are held about every five years. 在英国，大约每五年举行一次大选（general election）。
Voters in each area must choose one person from a list of **candidates** (= a person who wants to be elected) to be the **Member of Parliament** for that area. The head of the UK government is called the **Prime Minister**. 每个地区的选民须从候选人（candidate）名单中选一人作为该地区的议员（Member of Parliament）。英国政府的首脑是首相（Prime Minister）。
In the US, **Presidential elections** are held every four years. The head of the US government is called the **President**. 在美国，每四年举行一次总统选举（Presidential election）。美国政府的首脑是总统（President）。

electric ☞ /ɪ'lektrɪk/ *adjective* 形容词
using or providing electricity 用电的; 电动的; 发电的: *an electric cooker* 电炉具 ◇ *an electric socket* 电源插座

electrical ☞ /ɪ'lektrɪkl/ *adjective* 形容词
of or using electricity 电的; 用电的: *an electrical appliance* (= a machine that uses electricity) 电器

electrician /ɪˌlek'trɪʃn/ *noun* 名词
a person whose job is to make and repair electrical systems and equipment 电工: *John's an electrician. He'll be able to mend the light for you.* 约翰是电工，他能帮你修灯。

electricity ☞ /ɪˌlek'trɪsəti/ *noun* 名词 (*no plural* 不用复数形式)
power that comes through wires. **Electricity** can make heat and light and makes machines work. 电; 电力

electric shock /ɪˌlektrɪk 'ʃɒk/ *noun* 名词
a sudden painful feeling that you get if electricity goes through your body 触电; 电击

electronic ☞ /ɪˌlek'trɒnɪk/ *adjective* 形容词
Electronic equipment includes things like computers and televisions. They use electricity and very small electrical parts (called **microchips** and **transistors**) to make them work. 电子的: *an electronic calculator* 电子计算器

electronics /ɪˌlek'trɒnɪks/ *noun* 名词 (*no plural* 不用复数形式)
the technology that is used to make things like computers and televisions 电子技术: *the electronics industry* 电子工业

elegant /'elɪɡənt/ *adjective* 形容词
with a beautiful style or shape 优雅的; 雅致的: *She looked very elegant in her new black dress.* 她穿上新的黑色连衣裙，看上去很高雅。 ◇ *elegant furniture* 雅致的家具

element /'elɪmənt/ *noun* 名词
1 an important part of something 要素; 基本部分: *Cost was an important element in our decision.* 成本是我们决策时考虑的重要因素。
2 a simple chemical, for example iron or gold 元素: *Water is made of the elements hydrogen and oxygen.* 水是由氢和氧两种元素组成的。

elementary /ˌelɪ'mentri/ *adjective* 形容词
connected with the early stages of learning; not difficult 初级的; 基础的;

A
B
C
D
E
F
G
H
I
J
K
L
M
N
O
P
Q
R
S
T
U
V
W
X
Y
Z

简单的: *an elementary dictionary* 初阶
词典 ◇ *elementary physics* 基础物理

elementary school /ˌelɪˈmentri skuːl/
noun 名词 (*American* 美式英语) (*British*
英式英语 **primary school**)
a school for children aged six to eleven
小学

elephant 象
ear 耳朵
tusk 象牙
trunk 象鼻

elephant /ˈelɪfənt/ *noun* 名词
a very big wild animal from Africa or Asia,
with a long nose (called a **trunk**) that
hangs down 象 ➾ Look at Picture
Dictionary page P3. 见彩页 P3。

elevator /ˈelɪveɪtə(r)/ *American English
for* LIFT[2] (1) 美式英语，即 lift[2] 第 1 义

eleven ⚡ /ɪˈlevn/ *number* 数词
11 十一

▶ **eleventh** /ɪˈlevnθ/ *pronoun, adjective,
adverb* 代词，形容词，副词 11th 第十一

elf /elf/ *noun* 名词 (*plural* 复数形式 **elves**
/elvz/)
a very small person in stories who has
pointed ears and magic powers（故事中
的）小精灵

eliminate /ɪˈlɪmɪneɪt/ *verb* 动词
(**eliminates, eliminating, eliminated**)
to remove something that is not needed
or wanted 清除；排除: *We must try to
eliminate waste.* 我们得尽量清除垃圾。

else ⚡ /els/ *adverb* 副词
1 more; extra 还有; 再有; 另外: *What
else would you like?* 你还想要点什么？
◇ *Is anyone else coming to the party?*
还有其他人来参加聚会吗？
2 different 不同; 别的: *This cafe's
full, let's go somewhere else.* 这个咖啡
馆客满了，我们到别处去吧。◇ *It's not
mine – it must be somebody else's.* 这个
不是我的 —— 一定是别人的。◇ *There
was nothing else to eat so we had eggs*

again. 没有其他吃的，我们就又吃了
鸡蛋。

🔍 GRAMMAR 语法说明
You use **else** after words like **anybody**,
nothing and **somewhere**, and after
question words like **where** and **who**.
* else 用于 anybody、nothing、
somewhere 等词之后，也用于像
where、who 等疑问词之后。

or else if not, then 要不然; 否则 ➾ SAME
MEANING **otherwise** 同义词为 otherwise:
Go now, or else you'll be late. 现在走吧，
要不然你就晚了。

elsewhere /ˌelsˈweə(r)/ *adverb* 副词
in or to another place 在别处; 到别处:
*He can't find a job near home so he's
looking elsewhere.* 他在家附近找不到
工作，于是到别处去找了。

elves *plural of* ELF * elf 的复数形式

email ⚡ (*also* 亦作 **e-mail**) /ˈiːmeɪl/
noun 名词
1 (*no plural* 不用复数形式) a system for
sending messages from one computer to
another 电子邮件（系统）: *to send a
message by email* 用电子邮件发送信息
◇ *What's your email address?* 你的电邮
地址是什么？
2 (*plural* 复数形式 **emails**) a message that
is written on one computer and sent to
another 电子邮件: *I'll send you an email.*
我会给你发电邮的。
▶ **email** (*also* 亦作 **e-mail**) *verb* 动词
(**emails, emailing, emailed** /ˈiːmeɪld/):
Email me when you arrive. 一到就给我发
电邮。◇ *I'll email the documents to her.*
我会用电邮把这些文件传给她。

embarrass ⚡ /ɪmˈbærəs/ *verb* 动词
(**embarrasses, embarrassing,
embarrassed** /ɪmˈbærəst/)
to make somebody feel shy or worried
about what other people think of them
使尴尬; 使窘堪: *Please don't embarrass
me in front of my friends.* 请不要在我的
朋友面前让我难堪。

embarrassed ⚡ /ɪmˈbærəst/
adjective 形容词

🔍 SPELLING 拼写说明
Remember! You spell **embarrassed**
with **RR** and **SS**. 记住: embarrassed
拼写中有 rr 和 ss。

If you are **embarrassed**, you feel shy or
worried about what other people think
of you. 尴尬的; 难堪的: *He felt
embarrassed at being the centre of*

attention. 他因为成了众人注目的中心而感到尴尬。

embarrassing 0━ /ɪmˈbærəsɪŋ/
adjective 形容词
Something that is **embarrassing** makes you feel EMBARRASSED. 让人尴尬的；使人难堪的： *I couldn't remember her name – it was so embarrassing!* 我想不起她的名字了，真是尴尬！

embarrassment 0━
/ɪmˈbærəsmənt/ *noun* 名词 (*no plural* 不用复数形式)
the feeling that you have when you are EMBARRASSED 尴尬；难堪： *His face was red with embarrassment.* 他窘得满脸通红。

embassy /ˈembəsi/ *noun* 名词 (*plural* 复数形式 **embassies**)
a group of people whose job is to speak and act for their government in another country, or the building where they work 使馆官员；大使馆： *To get a visa, you should apply to the American embassy.* 要获取签证，就得到美国大使馆申请。

embrace /ɪmˈbreɪs/ *verb* 动词 (**embraces, embracing, embraced** /ɪmˈbreɪst/) (*formal* 正式)
to put your arms around somebody to show that you love them 拥抱 ➋ SAME MEANING **hug** 同义词为 hug： *She embraced each member of her family in turn.* 她与家人一一拥抱。

embroider /ɪmˈbrɔɪdə(r)/ *verb* 动词 (**embroiders, embroidering, embroidered** /ɪmˈbrɔɪdəd/)
to decorate cloth by sewing patterns on it 在…上刺绣
▶ **embroidered** /ɪmˈbrɔɪdəd/ *adjective* 形容词： *an embroidered blouse* 绣花女衬衫

embroidery 刺绣

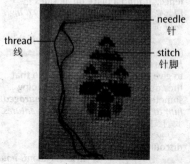

thread 线 — needle 针

— stitch 针脚

embroidery /ɪmˈbrɔɪdəri/ *noun* 名词 (*no plural* 不用复数形式)
patterns that are sewn onto cloth to decorate it 绣花；刺绣图案

embryo /ˈembriəʊ/ *noun* 名词 (*plural* 复数形式 **embryos**)
a human or animal when it is starting to grow before it is born 胚胎

emerald /ˈemərəld/ *noun* 名词
a green JEWEL (= very valuable stone) 祖母绿；绿宝石： *an emerald ring* 绿宝石戒指
▶ **emerald** (*also* 亦作 **emerald green** /ˌemərəld ˈɡriːn/) *adjective* 形容词 bright green 绿宝石色的；翡翠绿的： *an emerald green dress* 翡翠绿的连衣裙

emerge /iˈmɜːdʒ/ *verb* 动词 (**emerges, emerging, emerged** /iˈmɜːdʒd/)
to come out from a place 出现；露出： *The moon emerged from behind the clouds.* 月亮从云层后露出来了。

emergency 0━ /iˈmɜːdʒənsi/ *noun* 名词 (*plural* 复数形式 **emergencies**)
a sudden dangerous situation, when people need help quickly 紧急情况；突发事件： *Come quickly, doctor! It's an emergency!* 医生，快来！有急诊！ ◇ *In an emergency phone 999 for help.* 在紧急情况下拨打 999 求救。 ◇ *an emergency exit* (= a way out of a building that can be used in an emergency) 紧急出口

emergency room /iˈmɜːdʒənsi ruːm/ (*also* 亦作 ER /ˌiː ˈɑː(r)/) *noun* 名词 (*American* 美式英语) (*British* 英式英语 **casualty department**)
the place in a hospital where you go if you have been hurt in an accident or if you have suddenly become ill 急诊室

emigrant /ˈemɪɡrənt/ *noun* 名词
a person who leaves their country to go to live in another country 移居外国的人： *emigrant workers* 移居外国的工人 ➋ Look at **immigrant**. 见 immigrant。

emigrate /ˈemɪɡreɪt/ *verb* 动词 (**emigrates, emigrating, emigrated**)
to leave your country and go to live in another country 移居国外；移民： *They emigrated to Australia in the 1980s.* 他们在 20 世纪 80 年代移民到了澳大利亚。
▶ **emigration** /ˌemɪˈɡreɪʃn/ *noun* 名词 (*no plural* 不用复数形式)： *emigration by poor people in search of work* 穷人为寻求工作而移民 ➋ Look at **immigration**. 见 immigration。

emotion 0━ /iˈməʊʃn/ *noun* 名词
a strong feeling, for example love or

anger 强烈的情感；情绪：*They expressed mixed emotions at the news.* 他们对这个消息表现出复杂的情感。

emotional /ɪˈməʊʃənl/ *adjective* 形容词
1 connected with feelings 感情的；情感的：*emotional problems* 情感问题
2 showing strong feelings, sometimes by crying 情绪激动的：*He got very emotional when we said goodbye.* 我们道别时他很激动。

empathy /ˈempəθi/ *noun* 名词 (*no plural* 不用复数形式)
the ability to understand how other people feel 同感；共鸣

emperor /ˈempərə(r)/ *noun* 名词
a man who rules a group of countries (called an empire) 皇帝：*the Emperor Napoleon* 拿破仑皇帝 ⊃ Look at **empress**. 见 empress。

emphasis /ˈemfəsɪs/ *noun* 名词 (*plural* 复数形式 emphases /ˈemfəsiːz/)
special importance that is given to something 强调；重视 ⊃ SAME MEANING **stress** 同义词为 stress：*Our school places a lot of emphasis on science.* 我们学校特别重视理科。

emphasize /ˈemfəsaɪz/ *verb* 动词 (emphasizes, emphasizing, emphasized /ˈemfəsaɪzd/)
to say something strongly to show that it is important 强调；重视；着重 ⊃ SAME MEANING **stress** 同义词为 stress：*She emphasized the importance of hard work.* 她强调努力的重要性。

empire /ˈempaɪə(r)/ *noun* 名词
a group of countries that is controlled by one country 帝国：*the Roman Empire* 罗马帝国

employ ⊶ /ɪmˈplɔɪ/ *verb* 动词 (employs, employing, employed /ɪmˈplɔɪd/)
to pay somebody to do work for you 雇用；聘用：*The factory employs 800 workers.* 这家工厂雇用了 800 名工人。
⊃ Look at **unemployed**. 见 unemployed。

employee /ɪmˈplɔɪiː/ *noun* 名词
a person who works for somebody 受雇者；雇员：*This company treats its employees very well.* 这家公司对待员工非常好。

employer /ɪmˈplɔɪə(r)/ *noun* 名词
a person or company that pays other people to do work 雇用者；雇主

employment /ɪmˈplɔɪmənt/ *noun* 名词 (*no plural* 不用复数形式)

having a job that you are paid to do 就业；在职；受雇：*It can be hard for young people to find employment.* 年轻人找工作可能很困难。 ⊃ Look at **unemployment**. 见 unemployment。

empress /ˈemprəs/ *noun* 名词 (*plural* 复数形式 empresses)
a woman who rules a group of countries (called an empire), or the wife of an EMPEROR (= a man who rules a group of countries) 女皇；皇后

empty¹ ⊶ /ˈempti/ *adjective* 形容词 (emptier, emptiest)
with nothing or nobody inside or on it 空的：*The hall was almost empty.* 礼堂里几乎什么都没有。 ◇ *an empty box* 空盒子 ⊃ Look at the picture at **full**. 见 full 的插图。

empty² ⊶ /ˈempti/ *verb* 动词 (empties, emptying, emptied /ˈemptid/, has emptied)
1 to take everything out of something 倒空；清空：*The waiter emptied the ashtrays.* 服务员倒掉了烟灰缸里的烟灰。 ◇ *We emptied our bags out onto the floor.* 我们把袋子里的东西都倒在地板上了。
2 to become **empty** 变空：*The film finished and the cinema started to empty.* 电影放完后，电影院开始变得空空荡荡。

enable /ɪˈneɪbl/ *verb* 动词 (enables, enabling, enabled /ɪˈneɪbld/) (*formal* 正式)
to make it possible for somebody to do something 使能够：*Your help enabled me to finish the job.* 你的帮助让我能够完成这项工作。

enclose /ɪnˈkləʊz/ *verb* 动词 (encloses, enclosing, enclosed /ɪnˈkləʊzd/)
1 to put something inside a letter or package 附上；附入：*I enclose a cheque for €100.* 随信附上一张 100 欧元的支票。
2 to put something, for example a wall or fence, around a place on all sides 把…围起来：*The prison is enclosed by a high wall.* 监狱四周有高墙围着。

encourage ⊶ /ɪnˈkʌrɪdʒ/ *verb* 动词 (encourages, encouraging, encouraged /ɪnˈkʌrɪdʒd/)
to give somebody hope or help so that they do something or continue doing something 鼓励；激励：*We encouraged him to write a book about his adventures.* 我们鼓励他把他的冒险经历写成书。
⊃ OPPOSITE **discourage** 反义词为 discourage

▶ **encouragement** /ɪnˈkʌrɪdʒmənt/ *noun* 名词 (*no plural* 不用复数形式)： *Kim's* parents have always **given her a lot of encouragement**. 金的父母一直给她很多鼓励。

▶ **encouraging** /ɪn'kʌrɪdʒɪŋ/ *adjective* 形容词: *Ann's school report is very encouraging.* 安在学校的成绩教人鼓舞。

encyclopedia /ɪn,saɪklə'piːdiə/ *noun* 名词 (*plural* 复数形式 encyclopedias) a book or CD that gives information about a lot of different things 百科全书: *an encyclopedia of world history* 世界历史百科全书

end[1] ⊶ /end/ *noun* 名词 the furthest or last part of something 末端；尽头；结局；结尾: *Turn right at the end of the street.* 在这条街的尽头向右拐。◇ *They were sitting at the other end of the room.* 他们坐在房间的另一端。◇ *I'm going on holiday at the end of June.* 我六月底会去度假。◇ *We were sad because the holiday was coming to an end.* 假期快结束了，我们很不开心。

end to end in a line with the ends touching 首尾相接连成一行: *They put the tables end to end.* 他们把桌子连成一排。

for ... on end for a very long time（长时间）连续地，不断地: *He watches TV for hours on end.* 他一看电视就是几个小时。

in the end finally; at last 最后；最终: *In the end it was midnight when we got home.* 我们最后在午夜时分回到家。

make ends meet to have enough money for your needs 使收支相抵；可维持生计: *After her husband died it was difficult to make ends meet.* 丈夫死后，她生活拮据。

put an end to something to stop something happening 使终止；使结束: *We must put an end to this terrible war.* 我们必须结束这场可怕的战争。

end[2] ⊶ /end/ *verb* 动词 (ends, ending, ended) to stop or to finish something 终止；结束: *What time does the film end?* 电影什么时候结束？◇ *The road ends here.* 这条路到此为止。◇ *Most adverbs in English end in '-ly'.* 英语的副词大多以 -ly 结尾。◇ *We ended our holiday with a few days on the beach.* 我们最后在海滩待了几天，就这样结束了整个假期。

end up to finally be in a place or doing something when you did not plan it 最终成为；结果处于: *If she continues to steal, she'll end up in prison.* 她要是继续偷东西，早晚得进监狱。◇ *I ended up*

doing all the work myself. 最后是我一个人做了所有的工作。

ending /'endɪŋ/ *noun* 名词 the last part of something, for example a word, story or film 结尾；结局: *Nouns with the ending '-ch' form the plural with '-es'.* 以 -ch 结尾的名词，作复数时要加 -es。◇ *The film has a happy ending.* 这部影片的结局是皆大欢喜。

endless /'endləs/ *adjective* 形容词 never stopping or finishing; very long 不停的；无止境的: *The journey seemed endless.* 那次旅程好像没有尽头似的。

▶ **endlessly** /'endləsli/ *adverb* 副词: *He talks endlessly about nothing.* 他没完没了地说着空话。

endure /ɪn'djʊə(r)/ *verb* 动词 (endures, enduring, endured /ɪn'djʊəd/) (*formal* 正式) to suffer something that is painful or uncomfortable, usually without complaining 忍耐；忍受 ⊃ SAME MEANING **bear** 同义词为 bear: *The pain was almost too great to endure.* 痛楚几乎难以忍受。

enemy ⊶ /'enəmi/ *noun* 名词 (*plural* 复数形式 enemies) **1** a person who hates you 敌人；仇人: *He has made a lot of enemies.* 他树敌众多。
2 the enemy (*no plural* 不用复数形式) the army or country that your country is fighting against in a war 敌军；敌国: *The enemy is attacking from the north.* 敌军正从北面进攻。

energetic /,enə'dʒetɪk/ *adjective* 形容词 full of energy so that you can do a lot of things 精力充沛的；充满活力的

energy ⊶ /'enədʒi/ *noun* 名词 (*no plural* 不用复数形式) **1** the ability to be active without getting tired 精力；活力: *Children are usually full of energy.* 儿童一般都精力充沛。
2 the power from electricity, gas, coal, etc. that is used to make machines work and to make heat and light 能量；能源: *It is important to try to save energy.* 节约能源十分重要。◇ *atomic energy* 原子能

engaged /ɪn'geɪdʒd/ *adjective* 形容词 **1** If two people are **engaged**, they have agreed to get married. 已订婚的: *Louise is engaged to Michael.* 路易丝和迈克尔订婚了。◇ *They got engaged last year.* 他们去年订了婚。
2 (*British* 英式英语) (*American* 美式英语 busy) (used about a telephone) being

used（电话）占线的：*I tried to phone him but his number was engaged.* 我尝试给他打电话，可是电话占线了。

engagement /ɪnˈɡeɪdʒmənt/ *noun* 名词

an agreement to marry somebody 订婚

engine ⚙ /ˈendʒɪn/ *noun* 名词

1 a machine that makes things move 发动机；引擎：*a car engine* 汽车引擎
2 the front part of a train which pulls the rest 火车头；机车 ➾ Look at the picture at **train¹**. 见 **train¹** 的插图。

engineer /ˌendʒɪˈnɪə(r)/ *noun* 名词

a person whose job is to plan, make or repair things like machines, roads or bridges 工程师：*My brother is an electrical engineer.* 我弟弟是电机工程师。

engineering /ˌendʒɪˈnɪərɪŋ/ *noun* 名词
(*no plural* 不用复数形式)

planning and making things like machines, roads or bridges 工程：*She's studying chemical engineering at college.* 她在大学修读化学工程。

English /ˈɪŋɡlɪʃ/ *noun* 名词

1 (*no plural* 不用复数形式) the language that is spoken in Britain, the US, Canada, Australia, etc. 英语：*Do you speak English?* 你会说英语吗？
2 the English (*plural* 用复数形式) the people of England 英格兰人

> 🔎 CULTURE 文化资料补充
>
> Be careful! The people of **Scotland** (the **Scots**) and the people of **Wales** (the **Welsh**) are **British**, not **English**. 注意：称苏格兰人（the Scots）和威尔士人（the Welsh）为英国人时要用 British，而不能用 English。

enjoy ⚙ /ɪnˈdʒɔɪ/ *verb* 动词 (**enjoys, enjoying, enjoyed** /ɪnˈdʒɔɪd/)

to like something very much 喜爱；享受：*I enjoy playing football.* 我爱踢足球。◊ *Did you enjoy your dinner?* 这顿饭你喜欢吗？

enjoy yourself to be happy; to have a good time 过得愉快；玩得开心：*I really enjoyed myself at the party.* 我在聚会上真的玩得很开心。

enjoyable ⚙ /ɪnˈdʒɔɪəbl/ *adjective* 形容词

Something that is **enjoyable** makes you happy. 使人快乐的；令人愉快的：*Thank you for a very enjoyable evening.* 今天晚上过得非常愉快，谢谢您！

enjoyment ⚙ /ɪnˈdʒɔɪmənt/ *noun* 名词 (*no plural* 不用复数形式)

a feeling of enjoying something 愉快；快乐；乐趣 ➾ SAME MEANING **pleasure** 同义词为 pleasure：*I get a lot of enjoyment from travelling.* 我从旅行中得到很多乐趣。

enlarge /ɪnˈlɑːdʒ/ *verb* 动词 (**enlarges, enlarging, enlarged** /ɪnˈlɑːdʒd/)

to make something bigger 扩大；增大：*Reading will enlarge your vocabulary.* 阅读可以增加你的词汇量。
▸ **enlargement** /ɪnˈlɑːdʒmənt/ *noun* 名词：*an enlargement of a photograph* 照片的放大

enormous /ɪˈnɔːməs/ *adjective* 形容词

very big 非常大的；巨大的 ➾ SAME MEANING **huge** 同义词为 huge：*an enormous dog* 一条大狗

enormously /ɪˈnɔːməsli/ *adverb* 副词

very or very much 很；非常：*The film was enormously successful.* 这部电影大获成功。

enough ⚙ /ɪˈnʌf/ *adjective, pronoun, adverb* 形容词，代词，副词

> 🔎 PRONUNCIATION 读音说明
>
> The word **enough** sounds like **stuff**, because sometimes the letters **-gh** sound like **f**, in words like **enough**, **rough** and **tough**. * enough 读音像 stuff，因为 -gh 有时会读作 /f/，如 enough、rough、tough 等词。

as much or as many as you need 足够（的）；充足（的）；充分（的）：*There isn't enough food for ten people.* 食物不够十个人吃。◊ *You're too thin – you don't eat enough.* 你太瘦了，你吃得太少了。◊ *Is she old enough to drive?* 她到了可以开车的年龄了吗？

> 🔎 GRAMMAR 语法说明
>
> If you have **enough** of something you have the right amount. * enough 表示数量足够：*There's enough cake for everyone.* 蛋糕够所有人吃。
> In negative sentences **enough** means 'less than'. 在否定句中，not enough 表示"不够"：*The coffee isn't hot enough.* 咖啡不够热。
> For 'more than' we use **too**. 表示"过于"用 too：*The coffee is too hot.* 咖啡太烫了。

➾ Look at the picture at **too**. 见 too 的插图。

enquire (*British* 英式英语) (*American* 美式英语 **inquire**) /ɪnˈkwaɪə(r)/ *verb* 动词 (**enquires, enquiring, enquired** /ɪnˈkwaɪəd/) (*formal* 正式)
to ask for information about something 询问 ➜ SAME MEANING **ask** 同义词为 ask: *Could you **enquire about** train times?* 你能问一下火车时刻吗？

enquire into something to find out information about something 调查；查问: *Journalists have been enquiring into his past.* 记者一直在调查他的过去。

enquiry (*British* 英式英语) (*American* 美式英语 **inquiry**) /ɪnˈkwaɪəri/ *noun* 名词 (*plural* 复数形式 **enquiries**) (*formal* 正式)
a question that you ask to get information about something 查询: *I'll **make** some **enquiries** about dance classes.* 我会查询一下舞蹈班的事。

enrol (*British* 英式英语) (*American* 美式英语 **enroll**) /ɪnˈrəʊl/ *verb* 动词 (**enrols, enrolling, enrolled** /ɪnˈrəʊld/)
to join a group, for example a school, college, course or club. You usually pay money (called a **fee**) when you **enrol**. 注册；登记: *I've **enrolled on** an English course.* 我已经报读了一个英语课程。
➜ In American English, you say 美式英语说: *I've **enrolled in** an English course.* 我已经报读了一个英语课程。

ensure (*British* 英式英语) (*American* 美式英语 **insure**) /ɪnˈʃʊə(r)/ *verb* 动词 (**ensures, ensuring, ensured** /ɪnˈʃʊəd/) (*formal* 正式)
to make certain that something happens 确保；保证 ➜ SAME MEANING **make sure** 同义词为 make sure: *Please ensure that all the lights are switched off before you leave.* 离开前请确保所有的灯都关上。

enter 0— /ˈentə(r)/ *verb* 动词 (**enters, entering, entered** /ˈentəd/)
1 (*formal* 正式) to come or go into a place 进入；进来；进去: *They stopped talking when she entered the room.* 她一进屋他们就不说话了。◇ *Do not enter without knocking.* 进屋前要敲门。

🔎 SPEAKING 表达方式说明
In this sense, it is more usual to say **go in** or **come in**. 就此义而言，较常用 go in 或 come in。

2 to give your name to somebody because you want to do something like take an exam or run in a race 报名参加: *I entered a competition last month and won a prize.* 上个月我报名参加比赛并获了奖。

3 to put information on paper or in a computer 填入；输入: *Please enter your name and address at the top of the form.* 请把你的姓名和地址填写在表格上方。◇ *I've entered the data into the computer.* 我已把数据输入电脑。

enterprise /ˈentəpraɪz/ *noun* 名词
a new plan, project or business 计划；企业: *a business enterprise* 企业规划

entertain 0— /ˌentəˈteɪn/ *verb* 动词 (**entertains, entertaining, entertained** /ˌentəˈteɪnd/)
1 to give food and drink to visitors in your house 招待；款待: *We're entertaining friends this evening.* 今天晚上我们家里请客。
2 to say or do things that other people find interesting or funny 使快乐: *She entertained us all with her funny stories.* 她给我们讲有趣的故事逗大家开心。

entertainer /ˌentəˈteɪnə(r)/ *noun* 名词
a person whose job is to help people have a good time, for example by singing, dancing or telling jokes（歌唱、舞蹈、说笑话等的）演员，表演者，艺人

entertaining /ˌentəˈteɪnɪŋ/ *adjective* 形容词
funny and interesting 有趣的；有意思的: *The talk was informative and entertaining.* 这次演讲内容丰富，又妙趣横生。

entertainment 0— /ˌentəˈteɪnmənt/ *noun* 名词 (*no plural* 不用复数形式)
anything that ENTERTAINS people, for example films, concerts or television 娱乐；娱乐活动: *There isn't much entertainment for young people in this town.* 这个镇上没有什么适合年轻人的娱乐活动。

enthusiasm 0— /ɪnˈθjuːziæzəm/ *noun* 名词 (*no plural* 不用复数形式)
a strong feeling of wanting to do something or liking something 热情；热忱: *The pupils showed great enthusiasm for the new project.* 学生对这个新课题显得兴致勃勃。

enthusiastic 0— /ɪnˌθjuːziˈæstɪk/ *adjective* 形容词
full of enthusiasm 热情的；热衷的: *The kids are very enthusiastic about sport.* 这些孩子热衷于体育运动。

entire /ɪnˈtaɪə(r)/ *adjective* 形容词
whole or complete 全部的；整个的: *We spent the entire day on the beach.* 我们一整天都待在海滩上。

A B C D E F G H I J K L M N O P Q R S T U V W X Y Z

entirely /ɪn'taɪəli/ *adverb* 副词
completely 完全地： *That is an entirely different question.* 那是个截然不同的问题。 ◇ *I entirely agree with you.* 我完全同意你的意见。

entrance /'entrəns/ *noun* 名词
1 (*plural* 复数形式 **entrances**) the door, gate or opening where you go into a place 入口；门口： *I'll meet you at the entrance to the museum.* 我在博物馆门口等你。
2 (*plural* 复数形式 **entrances**) coming or going into a place 进入： *He made his entrance onto the stage.* 他走上了舞台。
3 (*no plural* 不用复数形式) the right to go into a place 进入权： *They were refused entrance to the club because they were wearing jeans.* 他们因为穿着牛仔裤而被拒绝进入会所。

entry /'entri/ *noun* 名词
1 (*no plural* 不用复数形式) the act of going into a place 进入： *The thieves gained entry (= got in) through a window.* 小偷是从窗户进来的。
2 (*no plural* 不用复数形式) the right to go into a place 进入权： *There's a sign that says 'No Entry'.* 有个牌子上写着"禁止入内"。 ◇ *They were refused entry into the country.* 他们被拒绝入境。
3 (*plural* 复数形式 **entries**) a person or thing that is entered in a competition 参赛者；参赛作品： *The standard of the entries was very high.* 参赛作品的水平很高。

envelopes 信封

envelope /'envələʊp/ *noun* 名词
a paper cover for a letter 信封： *Have you written his address on the envelope?* 你把他的地址写在信封上了吗？

envied (*also* 还有 **envies**) *forms of* ENVY
* envy 的不同形式

envious /'enviəs/ *adjective* 形容词
wanting what somebody else has 羡慕的；忌妒的： *She's envious of her sister's success.* 她羡慕她姐姐的成功。 ⟳ The noun and verb are both **envy**. 名词和动词均为 envy。

environment /ɪn'vaɪrənmənt/ *noun* 名词

> 🔍 SPELLING 拼写说明
> Be careful! Remember to put N before M in **environment**. 注意：记住 environment 的拼写中 m 前面有 n。

1 everything around you 环境： *Children need a happy home environment.* 儿童需要有幸福的家庭环境。
2 **the environment** (*no plural* 不用复数形式) the air, water, land, animals and plants around us 自然环境： *We must do more to protect the environment.* 我们必须更加努力保护环境。
▶ **environmental** /ɪn,vaɪrən'mentl/ *adjective* 形容词： *We talked about pollution and other environmental problems.* 我们谈论了污染和其他环境问题。

environmentalist /ɪn,vaɪrən'mentəlɪst/ *noun* 名词
a person who tries to protect the ENVIRONMENT 环境保护主义者；环保人士

environmentally friendly /ɪn,vaɪrənmentəli 'frendli/ (*also* 亦作 **environment-friendly** /ɪn,vaɪrənmənt 'frendli/) *adjective* 形容词
(used about things you buy) not harming the ENVIRONMENT （产品）环保的，对环境无害的： *environmentally friendly packaging* 环保包装

envy /'envi/ *noun* 名词 (*no plural* 不用复数形式)
a sad or angry feeling of wanting what another person has 羡慕；忌妒 ⟳ SAME MEANING **jealousy** 同义词为 jealousy： *I couldn't hide my envy of her success.* 我掩饰不了对她成功的忌妒。 ◇ *They looked with envy at her new clothes.* 他们看到她穿的新衣服，十分羡慕。
▶ **envy** *verb* 动词 (**envies, envying, envied** /'envid/, **has envied**)： *I envy you! You always seem so happy!* 我真羡慕你！你好像总是这么开心！

epic /'epɪk/ *noun* 名词
a long film or book that contains a lot of action 史诗般的电影（或书籍）： *His latest film is a historical epic.* 他最新的影片是一部以历史为题材的巨制。

epidemic /ˌepɪˈdemɪk/ *noun* 名词
a disease that many people in a place have at the same time 流行病: *a flu epidemic* 流行性感冒

episode /ˈepɪsəʊd/ *noun* 名词
a programme on radio or television that is part of a longer story（广播或电视连续剧的）一集: *You can see the final episode of the series on Monday.* 你星期一就能收看这部连续剧的大结局。

equal¹ /ˈiːkwəl/ *adjective* 形容词
the same in size, amount, value or level as something or somebody else 相等的; 同样的: *Women want equal pay for equal work.* 女性要求同工同酬。◇ *Divide the pie into six equal pieces.* 把馅饼分成六等份。

equal² /ˈiːkwəl/ *verb* 动词 (*British* 英式英语 **equals, equalling, equalled** /ˈiːkwəld/) (*American* 美式英语 **equaling, equaled**)
1 to be exactly the same amount as something 等于: *Two plus two equals four (2 + 2 = 4).* 二加二等于四。
2 to be as good as somebody or something 和⋯一样好; 比得上: *This achievement is unlikely ever to be equalled.* 这项成就很可能永远无法匹敌。

equal³ /ˈiːkwəl/ *noun* 名词
a person who has the same ability or rights as somebody else 同等的人: *She treats everyone as her equal.* 她待人如己。

equality /iˈkwɒləti/ *noun* 名词 (*no plural* 不用复数形式)
being the same or having the same rights 平等; 均等: *People are still fighting for racial equality.* 人们仍在努力争取种族平等。

equally /ˈiːkwəli/ *adverb* 副词
1 in the same way 相同地; 同样地: *Diet and exercise are equally important.* 饮食和锻炼同样重要。
2 in equal parts or amounts 平均地; 均等地: *The money was divided equally among her four children.* 那笔钱平分给了她的四个子女。

equator /iˈkweɪtə(r)/ *noun* 名词 (*no plural* 不用复数形式)
the line on maps around the middle of the world. Countries near the **equator** are very hot. 赤道

equip /iˈkwɪp/ *verb* 动词 (**equips, equipping, equipped** /iˈkwɪpt/)
to get or have all the things that are needed for doing something 给⋯配备; 装备: *Before setting out, they equipped*

themselves with a map. 他们在出发前带上了一张地图。◇ *The kitchen is well equipped.* 这个厨房设备齐全。

equipment /iˈkwɪpmənt/ *noun* 名词 (*no plural* 不用复数形式)
special things that you need for doing something 设备; 装备; 仪器: *sports equipment* 运动器材

> **GRAMMAR** 语法说明
> **Equipment** does not have a plural. If you are talking about one item, you say 'a piece of equipment'.
> * equipment 没有复数形式。表示一件设备说 a piece of equipment。

ER /ˌiː ˈɑː(r)/ *abbreviation* 缩略式 (*American* 美式英语) short for EMERGENCY ROOM
* emergency room 的缩略式

er /ɜː(r)/ *exclamation* 感叹词 (*British* 英式英语)
used in writing to show the sound that a person makes when they cannot decide what to say next 嗯（书面用语，表示迟疑）: *Er, do you want to come with us?* 哦，你想跟我们一块去吗?

eraser /iˈreɪzə(r)/ *American English for* RUBBER (2) 美式英语，即 rubber 第 2 义

erect¹ /iˈrekt/ *adjective* 形容词 (*formal* 正式)
standing or pointing straight up 垂直的; 竖直的; 直立的: *He stood with his head erect.* 他昂首站立。

erect² /iˈrekt/ *verb* 动词 (**erects, erecting, erected**) (*formal* 正式)
to build something or to make something stand up straight 建立; 竖立; 搭起: *Police erected barriers to keep the crowds back.* 警方设置路障来阻截人群。

erotic /iˈrɒtɪk/ *adjective* 形容词
causing sexual excitement 引起性欲的; 色情的: *an erotic film* 色情电影

errand /ˈerənd/ *noun* 名词
a short journey to do something for somebody, for example to buy something from a shop 小差事: *I've got to run a few errands for my mum.* 我得为妈妈跑些腿儿。

error /ˈerə(r)/ *noun* 名词 (*formal* 正式)
something that is done wrong 错误; 差错 ⊃ SAME MEANING **mistake** 同义词为 mistake: *The letter was sent to the wrong address because of a computer error.* 由于电脑出了错，这封信送错了地址。◇ *I think you have made an error in calculating the total.* 我想你把总数算错了。

erupt /ɪˈrʌpt/ *verb* 动词 (erupts, erupting, erupted)

When a VOLCANO (= a mountain with a hole in the top) **erupts**, smoke, hot rocks or liquid rock (called **lava**) suddenly come out. （火山）爆发，喷发： *When Mount Vesuvius erupted, it buried Pompeii.* 维苏威火山爆发时把庞贝城埋没了。

▶ **eruption** /ɪˈrʌpʃn/ *noun* 名词: *a volcanic eruption* 火山爆发

escalator /ˈeskəleɪtə(r)/ *noun* 名词
moving stairs that carry people up and down 自动扶梯

escape¹ ⍤ /ɪˈskeɪp/ *verb* 动词 (escapes, escaping, escaped /ɪˈskeɪpt/)
1 to get free from somebody or something 逃走；逃离： *The bird escaped from its cage.* 鸟从笼子里逃走了。 ◇ *Two prisoners escaped, but were later caught.* 两名囚犯越狱，但后来给抓住了。
2 to manage to avoid something dangerous or unpleasant （从危险的或不愉快的事情中）逃脱： *The pilot escaped death by seconds.* 这名飞行员在一瞬间死里逃生。

escape² /ɪˈskeɪp/ *noun* 名词
escaping from a place or a dangerous or unpleasant situation 逃走；逃脱： *As soon as he turned his back, she would make her escape.* 他一转身，她就会跑了。 ◇ *She had a lucky escape* (= something bad almost happened to her) *when a lorry crashed into her car.* 卡车撞到了她的车子，但她幸免于难。

escort¹ /ˈeskɔːt/ *noun* 名词
one or more people or vehicles that go with somebody to protect them 护送者；护卫车队： *The President always travels with an armed escort.* 总统出行时总是由武装卫队护送。

escort² /ɪˈskɔːt/ *verb* 动词 (escorts, escorting, escorted)
to go with somebody, for example to protect them or to make sure that they arrive somewhere 护送；护卫： *The police escorted him out of the building.* 警方护送他离开了大楼。

ESL /ˌiː es ˈel/ *abbreviation* 缩略式
ESL is short for 'English as a second language' (= the teaching of English to speakers of other languages who are living in a country where people speak English). 作为第二语言的英语（教学），英语为第二语言（教学）（ESL 是 English as a second language 的缩略式） ⊃ Look at **EFL**. 见 **EFL**。

ESOL /ˈiːsɒl/ *abbreviation* 缩略式 (*British* 英式英语)
ESOL is short for 'English for speakers of other languages' (= the teaching of English to speakers of other languages). 操其他语言者的英语（教学）（ESOL 是 English for speakers of other languages 的缩略式） ⊃ Look also at **EFL**. 亦见 **EFL**。

especially ⍤ /ɪˈspeʃəli/ *adverb* 副词
1 more than usual or more than others 尤其；特别；格外： *I hate getting up early, especially in winter.* 我讨厌早起，尤其是冬天。 ◇ *She loves animals, especially horses.* 她喜欢动物，尤其是马。
2 for a particular person or thing 专门；特地： *I bought these flowers especially for you.* 这些花我是特地买给你的。

essay /ˈeseɪ/ *noun* 名词
a short piece of writing about a particular subject 文章；短文： *Our teacher asked us to write an essay on our favourite author.* 老师叫我们就我们最喜爱的作家写一篇作文。

essential /ɪˈsenʃl/ *adjective* 形容词
If something is **essential**, it is completely necessary and you must have or do it. 必不可少的；不可或缺的；必要的： *It is essential that you work hard for this exam.* 你必须为这次考试努力。

establish /ɪˈstæblɪʃ/ *verb* 动词 (establishes, establishing, established /ɪˈstæblɪʃt/)
to start something new 建立；创立；设立： *The school was established in 1852.* 这所学校建于 1852 年。

estate /ɪˈsteɪt/ *noun* 名词
1 a large piece of land in the country that one person or family owns 大片私有土地；庄园
2 (*British* 英式英语) land with a lot of houses or factories on it 住宅区；工厂区： *We live on a housing estate.* 我们住在住宅区。 ◇ *an industrial estate* (= where there are a lot of factories) 工业区

estate agent /ɪˈsteɪt eɪdʒənt/ (*British* 英式英语) (*American* 美式英语 **real estate agent**) *noun* 名词
a person whose job is to sell buildings and land for other people 房地产经纪人

estate car /ɪˈsteɪt kɑː(r)/ *noun* 名词 (*British* 英式英语) (*American* 美式英语 **station wagon**)
a long car with a door at the back and space behind the back seat for carrying things 旅行轿车；客货两用小汽车

estimate[1] /'estɪmət/ *noun* 名词
a guess about the size or cost of something before you have all the facts and figures（对大小或成本的）估计：*Can you give me a rough estimate of how many people will be there?* 你能给我粗略估计一下有多少人会在那儿吗？

estimate[2] /'estɪmeɪt/ *verb* 动词
(estimates, estimating, estimated)
to say how much you think something will cost, how big something is, or how long it will take to do something 估计；估算：*The builders estimated that it would take a week to repair the roof.* 建筑工人估计修理屋顶要用一个星期。

estuary /'estʃuəri/ *noun* 名词 (plural 复数形式 estuaries)
the wide part of a river where it goes into the sea 河口：*the Thames Estuary* 泰晤士河河口

etc. 0━ /,et 'setərə/ *abbreviation* 缩略式
You use **etc.** at the end of a list to show that there are other things but you are not going to name them all. 等等：*Remember to take some paper, a pen, etc.* 记住带些纸、笔等东西。

eternal /ɪ'tɜːnl/ *adjective* 形容词
existing or continuing for ever 永久的；永恒的：*They believe in eternal life* (= life after death). 他们相信永生。

ethnic /'eθnɪk/ *adjective* 形容词
connected with or belonging to a particular race of people 民族的；种族的：*London is home to many different ethnic minorities.* 伦敦住着很多不同少数民族的人。

euro 0━ /'jʊərəʊ/ (plural 复数形式 euros) *noun* 名词 (symbol 符号 €)
money that is used in many countries of the European Union 欧元（许多欧盟国家的通用货币）：*All prices are in euros.* 所有价格以欧元标出。

European /,jʊərə'piːən/ *adjective* 形容词
from or connected with Europe 欧洲的：*European languages* 欧洲语言
▸ **European** *noun* 名词：*Many Europeans settled here in the nineteenth century.* 许多欧洲人在十九世纪就于这里定居了。

the European Union /ðə ,jʊərə'piːən 'juːniən/ *noun* 名词 (no plural 不用复数形式) (abbr. 缩略式 EU)
an organization of European countries that encourages TRADE (= the buying and selling of goods) between its members 欧洲联盟；欧盟

evacuate /ɪ'vækjueɪt/ *verb* 动词
(evacuates, evacuating, evacuated)
to take people away from a dangerous place to a safer place 疏散；撤离：*The area near the factory was evacuated after the explosion.* 爆炸发生后，工厂附近地区的人疏散了。
▸ **evacuation** /ɪ,vækju'eɪʃn/ *noun* 名词：*the evacuation of cities during the war* 战时城市人口的撤离

evaporate /ɪ'væpəreɪt/ *verb* 动词
(evaporates, evaporating, evaporated)
If a liquid **evaporates**, it changes into a gas. 蒸发：*Water evaporates if you heat it.* 水加热后会蒸发。

eve /iːv/ *noun* 名词
the day before a special day 前一天；前夕：*24 December is Christmas Eve.* * 12 月 24 日是圣诞节前夕。◇ *I went to a party on New Year's Eve* (= 31 December). 我除夕那天参加了一个聚会。

even[1] 0━ /'iːvn/ *adverb* 副词
1 a word that you use to say that something is surprising 甚至；连；即使：*The game is so easy that even a child can play it.* 这个游戏太容易了，连小孩子都会玩。◇ *He didn't laugh – he didn't even smile.* 他并没有笑出声来 —— 甚至连笑都没笑。
2 a word that you use to make another word stronger 甚至；更加；还：*Their house is even smaller than ours.* 他们的房子比我们的还要小。
even if it does not change anything if 即使；纵然：*Even if you run, you won't catch the bus.* 你即使跑也赶不上那辆公共汽车了。
even so although that is true 尽管如此；即使这样：*I didn't have any lunch, but even so I'm not hungry.* 我没吃午饭，却不觉得饿。
even though although 尽管；即使：*I went to the party, even though I was tired.* 尽管很累，我还是去参加了聚会。

even[2] /'iːvn/ *adjective* 形容词
1 flat and smooth 平滑的：*The game must be played on an even surface.* 这种游戏得在平滑的表面上进行。 ⊃ OPPOSITE **uneven** 反义词为 uneven
2 the same; equal 相等的；均等的；不相上下的：*Sara won the first game and I won the second, so we're even.* 萨拉赢了第一局，我赢了第二局，我们打成了平手。
3 Even numbers can be divided exactly by two. 偶数的：*4, 6 and 8 are even numbers.* * 4、6、8 都是偶数。 ⊃ OPPOSITE **odd** 反义词为 odd

get even with somebody (*informal* 非正式) to hurt somebody who has hurt you 向某人报复

evening /ˈiːvnɪŋ/ *noun* 名词
the part of the day between the afternoon and when you go to bed 傍晚；晚上：*What are you doing **this evening**?* 你今晚做什么？◇ *Most people watch television **in the evening**.* 大多数人晚上看电视。◇ *John came on Monday evening.* 约翰是星期一晚上来的。

event /ɪˈvent/ *noun* 名词
1 something important that happens 重要事情；事件：*My sister's wedding was a big event for our family.* 姐姐的婚礼是我们家的大事。
2 a race or competition 比赛；赛事：*The next event will be the high jump.* 下一项比赛是跳高。

eventually /ɪˈventʃuəli/ *adverb* 副词
after a long time 最后；终于：*The bus eventually arrived two hours late.* 公共汽车最后晚了两小时才到。

ever /ˈevə(r)/ *adverb* 副词
at any time 在任何时候；从来；曾经：*'Have you ever been to Africa?' 'No, I haven't.'* "你去过非洲吗？""没有。" ◇ *I **hardly ever** (= almost never) see Peter any more.* 我几乎再没有见过彼得。
ever since in all the time since 自从：*I have known Lucy ever since we were children.* 我和露西从小就认识了。
ever so, **ever such a** (*informal* 非正式) very 非常；很：*I'm ever so hot.* 我很热。◇ *It's ever such a good film.* 这部电影非常不错。
for ever for all time; always 永远：*I will love you for ever.* 我永远爱你。

evergreen /ˈevəgriːn/ *noun* 名词
a tree or bush that has green leaves all the year 常青树；常青灌木

every /ˈevri/ *adjective* 形容词
1 all of the people or things in a group 每个；每一个：*She knows every student in the school.* 她认识学校里的每一个学生。
2 used for saying how often something happens 每；每隔：*He phones every evening.* 他每天晚上都打电话。◇ *I see Robert **every now and then** (= sometimes, but not often).* 我偶尔见到罗伯特。◇ *She comes **every other day** (= for example on Monday, Wednesday and Friday but not on Tuesday or Thursday).* 她每隔一天来一次。

everybody /ˈevribɒdi/ *pronoun* 代词
each person; all people 每人；人人；所有人：*Everybody knows Tom.* 大家都认识汤姆。◇ *Everybody has a chance to win.* 每个人都有机会赢。

> 🔍 **WHICH WORD?** 词语辨析
>
> **Everybody** or **somebody**? 用 everybody 还是 somebody？
> You use **somebody** for one person. 表示某个人用 somebody：*Somebody is singing outside my window.* 有人在我的窗外唱歌。You use **everybody** for all people. 表示所有人用 everybody：*Everybody was singing 'Happy Birthday'.* 大家都在唱"生日快乐"歌。

everyday /ˈevridei/ *adjective* 形容词
normal; not special 日常的；平常的：*Computers are now part of **everyday** life.* 现在电脑成为日常生活的一部分了。

everyone /ˈevriwʌn/ *pronoun* 代词
= EVERYBODY：*If everyone is here then we can start.* 要是人都到齐，我们就开始吧。

everything /ˈevriθɪŋ/ *pronoun* 代词
each thing; all things 每件事；所有事物；一切：*Sam lost everything in the fire.* 萨姆的所有东西都在火灾中烧毁了。◇ *Everything in that shop is very expensive.* 那家店的每样东西都很贵。

everywhere /ˈevriweə(r)/ *adverb* 副词
in all places or to all places 到处；处处：*I've looked everywhere for my pen, but I can't find it.* 我到处找我的笔，但还是没找到。

evidence /ˈevɪdəns/ *noun* 名词
(*no plural* 不用复数形式)
the facts, signs or objects that make you believe that something is true 证据；证明；根据：*The police searched the room, looking for evidence.* 警方搜查了房间，寻找证据。◇ *There is evidence of a link between smoking and cancer.* 有证据显示吸烟与癌症有关联。

> 📝 **GRAMMAR** 语法说明
>
> **Evidence** does not have a plural so we cannot say 'an evidence'. Instead we say 'a piece of evidence'. * evidence 没有复数形式，所以不说 an evidence，要说 a piece of evidence。

give evidence to say what you know about somebody or something in a court of law（出庭）作证：*The man who saw* the accident will give evidence in court. 事故的目击者将出庭作证。

evident /'evɪdənt/ *adjective* 形容词
easy to see or understand 明显的；显而易见的 ➲ SAME MEANING **obvious** 同义词为 obvious: *It was evident that the damage was very serious.* 破坏显然非常严重。

evidently /'evɪdəntli/ *adverb* 副词
clearly 明显地；显然 ➲ SAME MEANING **obviously** 同义词为 obviously: *She was evidently very upset.* 她显然十分不高兴。

evil 0ⱳ /'iːvl/ *adjective* 形容词
morally bad and cruel 邪恶的；恶毒的：*an evil person* 坏人

exact 0ⱳ /ɪg'zækt/ *adjective* 形容词
completely correct 准确的；精确的：*We need to know the exact time the incident occurred.* 我们需要知道事件发生的确切时间。

exactly 0ⱳ /ɪg'zæktli/ *adverb* 副词
1 You use **exactly** when you are asking for or giving information that is completely correct. 准确地；精确地 ➲ SAME MEANING **precisely** 同义词为 precisely: *Can you tell me exactly what happened?* 你能确切地告诉我发生了什么事吗？◇ *It cost exactly £10.* 买这个花了整整 10 英镑。
2 in every way or detail 正好；恰好 ➲ SAME MEANING **just** 同义词为 just: *This shirt is exactly what I wanted.* 这正是我想要的衬衫。
3 You use **exactly** to agree with somebody. （表示同意）一点不错，正是如此：*'So you mean somebody in this room must be the murderer?' 'Exactly.'* "那么你是说这个房间里有个人一定是杀人凶手？" "正是。"

exaggerate 0ⱳ /ɪg'zædʒəreɪt/ *verb* 动词 (**exaggerates, exaggerating, exaggerated**)

> **🔍 SPELLING** 拼写说明
> Remember! You spell **exaggerate** with **GG**. 记住：exaggerate 拼写中有 gg。

to say that something is bigger, better, worse, etc. than it really is 夸张；夸大：*Don't exaggerate! I was only two minutes late, not twenty.* 别夸大了！我只是晚了两分钟，不是二十分钟。
▸ **exaggeration** /ɪg,zædʒə'reɪʃn/ *noun* 名词：*It's a bit of an exaggeration to say she can't speak English!* 说她不会讲英语，那有点儿夸大其词！

exam 0ⱳ /ɪg'zæm/ *noun* 名词
a test of what you know or can do 考试：

We've got an English exam next week. 我们下星期有英语考试。

> **🔍 WORD BUILDING** 词汇扩充
> You **sit** or **take** an exam. If you do well, you **pass**, and if you do badly, you **fail**. 参加考试用 sit 或 take，考试及格说 pass，不及格说 fail: *I took my exams in June.* 我六月参加了考试。◇ *'Did you pass all your exams?' 'No, I failed History. I've got to take it again in December.'* "你考试都通过了吗？" "没有，历史没及格。我十二月得重考。"

examination 0ⱳ /ɪg,zæmɪ'neɪʃn/ *noun* 名词
1 an act of looking carefully at somebody or something 检查；检验：*a medical examination* 体格检查
2 (*formal* 正式) = EXAM

examine 0ⱳ /ɪg'zæmɪn/ *verb* 动词 (**examines, examining, examined** /ɪg'zæmɪnd/)
1 to look carefully at something or somebody 检查；检验：*The doctor examined her but could find nothing wrong.* 医生给她做了检查，但没发现什么问题。◇ *Have the car examined by an expert before you buy it.* 购车前请专家验一下车。
2 (*formal* 正式) to ask questions to find out what somebody knows or what they can do 考查，测验（某人的知识或能力）：*You will be examined on everything you have learnt this year.* 你们今年学过的东西都要考。

example 0ⱳ /ɪg'zɑːmpl/ *noun* 名词
something that shows what other things of the same kind are like 例子；示例：*This dictionary gives many examples of how words are used in sentences.* 这部词典列举很多例子来说明词语在句中的用法。
for example used for giving an example 例如；譬如：*Do you speak any other languages, for example French or German?* 你会说其他语言吗，例如法语或德语？ ➲ The short way of writing 'for example' is **e.g.** * for example 的缩写形式是 e.g.。

exasperated /ɪg'zæspəreɪtɪd/ *adjective* 形容词
very annoyed or angry 恼怒的；愤怒的：*They were exasperated by all the delays.* 对于所有的延误他们感到非常恼火。

exceed /ɪk'siːd/ *verb* 动词 (**exceeds, exceeding, exceeded**)
to be more than a particular number or

A
B
C
D
E
F
G
H
I
J
K
L
M
N
O
P
Q
R
S
T
U
V
W
X
Y
Z

amount 超过（数目或数量）: *The weight must not exceed 20 kilos.* 重量不得超过 20 公斤。 ⤶ The noun is **excess**. 名词为 excess。

excellent o‑ /'eksələnt/ *adjective* 形容词

🔎 SPELLING 拼写说明
Remember! You spell **excellent** with **LL**. 记住：excellent 拼写中有 ll。

very good 非常好的；出色的；优秀的: *She speaks excellent Spanish.* 她西班牙语 说得非常好。

except o‑ /ɪk'sept/ *preposition* 介词

🔎 WHICH WORD? 词语辨析
Be careful! Don't confuse **except** with **accept**, which sounds very similar. 注意：不要混淆发音相似的 except 和 accept。

not including somebody or something （不包括某人或某事）除…之外: *The restaurant is open every day except Sunday.* 这家餐馆除星期天外每天都营业。◇ *Everyone went to the party except for me.* 除了我之外，大家都参加聚会去了。

except that apart from the fact that 除了；只是: *I don't know what he looks like, except that he's very tall.* 我不知道他 长什么样子，只知道他个子很高。

exception /ɪk'sepʃn/ *noun* 名词
a person or thing that is not the same as the others 例外的人（或事物）: *Most of his films are good but this one is an exception.* 他的大部分影片都很好，可是 这一部例外。

with the exception of somebody or 或 **something** except 除…之外 ⤶ SAME MEANING **apart from** 同义词为 apart from: *I like all vegetables with the exception of cabbage.* 除了卷心菜，我什么 蔬菜都爱吃。

exceptional /ɪk'sepʃənl/ *adjective* 形容词
very good 杰出的；优秀的；卓越的: *She is an exceptional pianist.* 她是个杰出 的钢琴家。

▶ **exceptionally** /ɪk'sepʃənəli/ *adverb* 副词: *He was an exceptionally bright student.* 他以前是个极为聪明的学生。

excess /ɪk'ses/ *noun* 名词 (no plural 不用 复数形式)
more than is necessary or usual 过量；过度: *An excess of stress can make you ill.* 压力过大会让人生病。

▶ **excess** /'ekses/ *adjective* 形容词: *Cut any excess fat off the meat.* 把肉上过多的 肥肉切掉。 ⤶ The verb is **exceed**. 动词为 exceed。

exchange¹ o‑ /ɪks'tʃeɪndʒ/ *noun* 名词
giving or receiving something in return for something else 交换；互换；交流: *a useful exchange of information* 有用的信 息交流 ◇ *We can offer free accommodation in exchange for some help in the house.* 我们可以提供免费住宿，对方就要帮忙做些 家务。 ⤶ Look at **stock exchange**. 见 stock exchange。

exchange² o‑ /ɪks'tʃeɪndʒ/ *verb* 动词 (exchanges, exchanging, exchanged /ɪks'tʃeɪndʒd/)
to give one thing and get another thing for it 交换；交流: *I would like to exchange this skirt for a bigger size.* 我想 把这条裙子换成大一点的。 ◇ *We exchanged phone numbers.* 我们交换了 电话号码。

exchange rate /ɪks'tʃeɪndʒ reɪt/ *noun* 名词
how much money from one country you can buy with money from another country 汇率；兑换率: *The exchange rate is 1.4 euros to the pound.* 汇率是 1.4 欧元 兑 1 英镑。

excite /ɪk'saɪt/ *verb* 动词 (excites, exciting, excited)
to make a person feel very happy or enthusiastic so that they are not calm 使兴奋；使激动: *Please don't excite the children too much or they won't sleep tonight.* 请不要让孩子太兴奋，不然他们 今晚就睡不着了。

excited o‑ /ɪk'saɪtɪd/ *adjective* 形容词
not calm, for example because you are happy about something that is going to happen 兴奋的；激动的: *He's getting very excited about his holiday.* 他对度假 感到十分兴奋。

excitement o‑ /ɪk'saɪtmənt/ *noun* 名词 (no plural 不用复数形式)
a feeling of being excited 兴奋；激动: *There was great excitement in the stadium before the match began.* 比赛开始前体育馆 里群情激奋。

exciting o‑ /ɪk'saɪtɪŋ/ *adjective* 形容词
Something that is **exciting** makes you have strong feelings of happiness and enthusiasm. 令人兴奋的；使人激动的: *an exciting film* 激动人心的影片 ◇ *Her new job sounds very exciting.* 她的新工作听上去 令人兴奋。

exclaim /ɪk'skleɪm/ *verb* 动词 (exclaims, exclaiming, exclaimed /ɪk'skleɪmd/)
to say something suddenly and loudly because you are surprised or angry（因为惊讶或生气）呼喊，惊叫：*'I don't believe it!' she exclaimed.* "我不信！" 她喊道。
▸ **exclamation** /ˌeksklə'meɪʃn/ *noun* 名词： *He gave an exclamation of surprise.* 他发出了一声惊叹。

exclamation mark /ˌeksklə'meɪʃn mɑːk/ (British 英式英语) (American 美式英语 **exclamation point** /ˌeksklə'meɪʃn pɔɪnt/) *noun* 名词
a mark (!) that you use in writing to show loud or strong words, or surprise 感叹号

exclude /ɪk'skluːd/ *verb* 动词 (excludes, excluding, excluded)
1 to deliberately not include something 不包括；将…排除在外：*The price excludes air fares.* 这个价格不含机票。 ⊃ OPPOSITE **include** 反义词为 include
2 to not allow a person to enter a place or do an activity 不让…进入；禁止…参加：*Students were excluded from the meeting.* 学生不能参加这次会议。

excluding ⊶ /ɪk'skluːdɪŋ/ *preposition* 介词
without 不计；不包括：*The meal cost £35, excluding drinks.* 这一餐 35 英镑，不包括饮料。 ⊃ OPPOSITE **including** 反义词为 including

excursion /ɪk'skɜːʃn/ *noun* 名词
a short journey to see something interesting or to enjoy yourself 短途旅行；远足 ⊃ SAME MEANING **trip** 同义词为 trip：*We're going on an excursion to the seaside on Sunday.* 我们星期天去海边游玩。

excuse¹ ⊶ /ɪk'skjuːs/ *noun* 名词

🔍 PRONUNCIATION 读音说明
When the word **excuse** is a noun, it ends with a sound like **juice** or **loose**.
* excuse 作名词时，尾音发音像 juice 或 loose。
When the word **excuse** is a verb, it ends with a sound like **shoes** or **choose**.
* excuse 作动词时，尾音发音像 shoes 或 choose。

words you say or write to explain why you have done something wrong 借口；理由：*You're late! What's your excuse this time?* 你迟到了！这次你的理由是什么？ ◇ *There's no excuse for rudeness.* 怎么说也不该粗鲁无礼。

excuse² ⊶ /ɪk'skjuːz/ *verb* 动词 (excuses, excusing, excused /ɪk'skjuːzd/)
used when you are saying sorry for something that is not very bad 原谅：*Please excuse us for being late – we missed the bus.* 对不起，我们迟到了 —— 我们没赶上公共汽车。
excuse me You use **excuse me** when you want to stop somebody who is speaking, or when you want to speak to somebody you do not know. You can also use **excuse me** to say that you are sorry. 对不起；劳驾；抱歉：*Excuse me, could you tell me the time?* 劳驾，请问现在几点了？ ◇ *Did I stand on your foot? Excuse me.* 我踩到了你的脚吗？对不起。

execute /'eksɪkjuːt/ *verb* 动词 (executes, executing, executed)
to kill a person as a legal punishment 处决；处死：*He was executed for murder.* 他因谋杀罪而被处死。
▸ **execution** /ˌeksɪ'kjuːʃn/ *noun* 名词： *the execution of prisoners* 处决囚犯

executive /ɪɡ'zekjətɪv/ *noun* 名词
an person who has an important position in a business or organization 经理；主管

exercise¹ ⊶ /'eksəsaɪz/ *noun* 名词
1 (no plural 不用复数形式) moving your body to keep it strong and well 锻炼；运动：*Swimming is very good exercise.* 游泳是很好的运动。
2 (plural 复数形式 exercises) a special movement that you do to keep your body strong and well 一套锻炼动作；健身活动：*This exercise is good for your back.* 这套动作对背部有益。
3 (plural 复数形式 exercises) a piece of work that you do to learn something 练习；习题：*Please do exercises 1 and 2 for homework.* 家庭作业请做练习 1 和 2。

exercise² /'eksəsaɪz/ *verb* 动词 (exercises, exercising, exercised /'eksəsaɪzd/)
to move your body to keep it strong and well 锻炼；运动：*They exercise in the park every morning.* 他们每天早晨在公园健身。

exercise book /'eksəsaɪz bʊk/ *noun* 名词
a book that you use at school for writing in 练习本 ⊃ Look at Picture Dictionary page **P11**. 见彩页 P11。

exhaust¹ /ɪɡ'zɔːst/ *noun* 名词
1 (no plural 不用复数形式) the waste gas that comes out of a vehicle, an engine or a machine（车辆、发动机或机器排出的）废气：*car exhaust fumes* 汽车废气
2 (also 亦作 **exhaust pipe** /ɪɡ'zɔːst paɪp/)

(*British* 英式英语) (*American* 美式英语 **tailpipe**) a pipe through which waste gases come out, for example on a car（汽车等的）排气管 ⊃ Look at Picture Dictionary page **P1**. 见彩页 P1.

exhaust[2] /ɪɡˈzɔːst/ *verb* 动词 (exhausts, exhausting, exhausted)
to make you feel very tired 使疲惫不堪；使筋疲力尽: *The long journey exhausted us.* 长途旅行把我们累垮了。
▶ **exhausted** /ɪɡˈzɔːstɪd/ *adjective* 形容词: *I'm exhausted – I think I'll go to bed.* 我累死了 —— 我看我还是睡觉去吧。

exhausting /ɪɡˈzɔːstɪŋ/ *adjective* 形容词
making you feel very tired 使人疲惫不堪的；令人筋疲力尽的: *Teaching young children can be exhausting.* 教小孩子会让人筋疲力尽。

exhibit /ɪɡˈzɪbɪt/ *verb* 动词 (exhibits, exhibiting, exhibited)
to show something in a public place for people to look at 展览；展出: *Her photographs have been exhibited all over the world.* 她的照片在世界各地都展出过。

exhibition ⊶ /ˌeksɪˈbɪʃn/ *noun* 名词
a group of things that are arranged in a place so that people can look at them 展览；展览品: *an exhibition of paintings by Monet* 莫奈画展

exile /ˈeksaɪl/ *noun* 名词
1 (*no plural* 不用复数形式) having to live away from your own country, especially for political reasons or as a punishment 流亡；放逐: *Napoleon spent the last years of his life in exile.* 拿破仑晚年过着流放的生活。
2 (*plural* 复数形式 exiles) a person who has to live away from their own country 流放国外者；被流放者

exist ⊶ /ɪɡˈzɪst/ *verb* 动词 (exists, existing, existed)
to be real; to live 存在；生存: *Does life exist on other planets?* 别的行星上有生命吗？ ◇ *That word does not exist.* 根本没有那个词。

existence /ɪɡˈzɪstəns/ *noun* 名词
(*no plural* 不用复数形式)
being real; existing 存在；存活: *This is the oldest Latin manuscript in existence.* 这是现存最古老的拉丁文手稿。

exit /ˈeksɪt/ *noun* 名词
a way out of a building 出口；太平门: *Where is the exit?* 出口在哪儿？ ◇ *an emergency exit* 紧急出口

exotic /ɪɡˈzɒtɪk/ *adjective* 形容词
strange or interesting because it comes from another country 来自异国的；有异国风味的: *exotic fruits* 异国水果

expand /ɪkˈspænd/ *verb* 动词 (expands, expanding, expanded)
to become bigger or to make something bigger（使）扩大，扩展: *Metals expand when they are heated.* 金属受热会膨胀。 ◇ *We hope to expand the business this year.* 我们希望今年扩大业务。
▶ **expansion** /ɪkˈspænʃn/ *noun* 名词 (*no plural* 不用复数形式): *The city's rapid expansion has caused a lot of problems.* 这个城市的快速发展造成了很多问题。

expect ⊶ /ɪkˈspekt/ *verb* 动词 (expects, expecting, expected)
1 to think that somebody or something will come or that something will happen 期待；预期；预计: *I'm expecting a letter.* 我在等一封信。 ◇ *We expected it to be hot in South Africa, but it was quite cold.* 我们原以为南非会很热，但其实挺冷的。 ◇ *She's expecting a baby* (= she is going to have a baby) *in June.* 她六月份要生孩子。
2 If you are **expected** to do something, you must do it. 指望；要求: *I am expected to work every Saturday.* 我每周六都得上班。
3 (*British* 英式英语) (*informal* 非正式) to think that something will happen or is probably true 猜想；认为: *I expect she'll be late. She usually is.* 我想她会迟到。她经常如此。 ◇ *They haven't had lunch yet, so I expect they're hungry.* 他们还没吃午饭，我想他们准饿了。 ◇ '*Is Ian coming?*' '*Oh yes, I expect so.*' "伊恩会来吗？" "来，我想应该会。"

expectation /ˌekspekˈteɪʃn/ *noun* 名词
a belief that something will happen 期待；盼望: *Against all expectations, we enjoyed ourselves.* 出乎意料的是，我们玩得很开心。

expedition /ˌekspəˈdɪʃn/ *noun* 名词
a journey to find or do something special 远征；探险；考察: *an expedition to the South Pole* 南极考察之行

expel /ɪkˈspel/ *verb* 动词 (expels, expelling, expelled /ɪkˈspeld/)
to send somebody away from a school, a club or a country 开除；驱逐: *The boys were expelled from school for smoking.* 这些男生因吸烟而被学校开除。

expense /ɪkˈspens/ *noun* 名词
1 the cost of something 花费；开销:

Having a car is a big expense. 养一辆车开销很大。

2 expenses (*plural* 用复数形式) money that you spend on a certain thing 费用；开支：*The company pays our **travelling** **expenses**.* 公司支付我们的差旅费。

expensive ᴏ‐ᴡ /ɪkˈspensɪv/ *adjective* 形容词

Something that is **expensive** costs a lot of money. 昂贵的；费用昂贵的：*expensive clothes* 昂贵的衣服 ◇ *The meal was very expensive.* 那顿饭很贵。 ᴏ OPPOSITE **cheap** 反义词为 cheap

experience¹ ᴏ‐ᴡ /ɪkˈspɪəriəns/ *noun* 名词

1 (*no plural* 不用复数形式) knowing about something because you have seen it or done it 经验：*She has four years' teaching experience.* 她有四年教学经验。 ◇ *Do you have much **experience** of working with children?* 与儿童相关的工作经验你多不多？

2 (*plural* 复数形式 experiences) something that has happened to you 经历：*He wrote a book about his experiences in Africa.* 他写了一本书，讲述他在非洲的经历。

experience² ᴏ‐ᴡ /ɪkˈspɪəriəns/ *verb* 动词 (experiences, experiencing, experienced /ɪkˈspɪəriənst/)

If you **experience** something, it happens to you. 经历；体验：*Everyone experiences failure at some time in their lives.* 每个人在人生的某个阶段都会经历失败。

experienced /ɪkˈspɪəriənst/ *adjective* 形容词

If you are **experienced**, you know about something because you have done it many times before. 有经验的；熟练的：*She's an experienced driver.* 她是经验丰富的司机。 ᴏ OPPOSITE **inexperienced** 反义词为 inexperienced

experiment ᴏ‐ᴡ /ɪkˈsperɪmənt/ *noun* 名词

a scientific test that you do to find out what will happen or to see if something is true 实验；试验：*They have to **do experiments** to find out if the drug is safe for humans.* 他们得做实验研究这种药对人体是否安全。

▶ **experiment** *verb* 动词 (experiments, experimenting, experimented)：*I don't think it's right to **experiment on** animals.* 我认为用动物做实验是不对的。

expert ᴏ‐ᴡ /ˈekspɜːt/ *noun* 名词

a person who knows a lot about something 专家；能手：*He's an expert*

on Shakespeare. 他是莎士比亚专家。 ◇ *a computer expert* 电脑高手

explain ᴏ‐ᴡ /ɪkˈspleɪn/ *verb* 动词 (explains, explaining, explained /ɪkˈspleɪnd/)

1 to tell somebody about something so that they understand it 解释；说明；讲解：*The teacher usually **explains** the new words to us.* 老师通常给我们讲解生词。 ◇ *He **explained how** to use the machine.* 他讲解了那台机器的使用方法。

⌕ GRAMMAR 语法说明

We say 'Explain **it** to me'. It is wrong to say 'Explain me it'. 要说 explain it to me，不能说 explain me it。

2 to give a reason for something 说明原因；解释缘由：*I **explained why** we needed the money.* 我说明了我们需要那笔钱的原因。

explanation ᴏ‐ᴡ /ˌekspləˈneɪʃn/ *noun* 名词

something that helps somebody understand something, or a reason for something 解释；说明；理由：*Did they give any **explanation for** their behaviour?* 他们对自己的行为加以解释了吗？

explode ᴏ‐ᴡ /ɪkˈspləʊd/ *verb* 动词 (explodes, exploding, exploded)

to burst suddenly with a very loud noise 爆炸：*A bomb exploded in the city centre, killing two people.* 市中心有枚炸弹爆炸，炸死了两个人。 ᴏ The noun is **explosion**. 名词为 explosion。

exploit /ɪkˈsplɔɪt/ *verb* 动词 (exploits, exploiting, exploited)

to treat somebody badly to get what you want 剥削：*Some employers exploit foreign workers, making them work long hours for low pay.* 有些雇主剥削外籍工人，让他们长时间工作，却付很低的报酬。

explore ᴏ‐ᴡ /ɪkˈsplɔː(r)/ *verb* 动词 (explores, exploring, explored /ɪkˈsplɔːd/)

to travel around a new place to learn about it 探索；考察：*They explored the area on foot.* 他们徒步考察了这个地区。

▶ **exploration** /ˌekspləˈreɪʃn/ *noun* 名词：*the exploration of space* 宇宙探索

explorer /ɪkˈsplɔːrə(r)/ *noun* 名词

a person who travels around a new place to learn about it 探险家；考察者：*The first European explorers arrived in America in the 15th century.* 第一批欧洲探险家在 15 世纪到达美洲。

A
B
C
D
E
F
G
H
I
J
K
L
M
N
O
P
Q
R
S
T
U
V
W
X
Y
Z

A B C D E F G H I J K L M N O P Q R S T U V W X Y Z

explosion 🔑 /ɪk'spləʊʒn/ ***noun*** 名词 the sudden bursting and loud noise of something such as a bomb exploding 爆炸: *There was an explosion and pieces of glass flew everywhere.* 发生了爆炸，玻璃碎片炸得到处都是。 ➲ The verb is **explode**. 动词为 explode。

explosive /ɪk'spləʊsɪv/ ***adjective*** 形容词 Something that is **explosive** can cause an explosion. 引起爆炸的；爆炸性的：*an explosive gas* 易爆气体

▸ **explosive** ***noun*** 名词 a substance that can make things explode 爆炸物；炸药

export[1] /ɪk'spɔːt/ ***verb*** 动词 (**exports**, **exporting**, **exported**)
to sell things to another country 出口；输出：*Japan **exports** cars **to** Britain.* 日本向英国出口汽车。 ➲ OPPOSITE **import** 反义词为 import

▸ **exporter** /ek'spɔːtə(r)/ ***noun*** 名词：*the world's biggest exporter of oil* 世界上最大的石油输出国 ➲ OPPOSITE **importer** 反义词为 importer

export[2] /'ekspɔːt/ ***noun*** 名词
1 (*no plural* 不用复数形式) selling things to another country 出口；输出：*These cars are made **for export**.* 这些汽车是供出口的。
2 (*plural* 复数形式 **exports**) something that you sell to another country 出口产品；输出品：*The country's main exports are tea and cotton.* 这个国家的主要出口产品是茶叶和棉花。 ➲ OPPOSITE **import** 反义词为 import

expose /ɪk'spəʊz/ ***verb*** 动词 (**exposes**, **exposing**, **exposed** /ɪk'spəʊzd/)
to show something that is usually covered or hidden 暴露；揭露：*A baby's skin should not be **exposed to** the sun for too long.* 婴儿的皮肤不应暴露在阳光下太久。 ◇ *The newspaper exposed his terrible secret.* 那家报纸揭露了他那可怕的秘密。

express[1] /ɪk'spres/ ***verb*** 动词 (**expresses**, **expressing**, **expressed** /ɪk'sprest/)
to say or show how you think or feel 表达；表示：*She expressed her ideas well.* 她清楚地表达了她的想法。

express[2] /ɪk'spres/ ***adjective*** 形容词
that goes or is sent very quickly 快速的；特快的：*an express letter* 快递信 ◇ *an express coach* 特快长途汽车

▸ **express** ***adverb*** 副词：*I sent the parcel express.* 我用快递寄出那个包裹。

express[3] /ɪk'spres/ (*plural* 复数形式 **expresses**) (*also* 亦作 **express train**) ***noun*** 名词
a fast train that does not stop at all stations 特快列车

expression 🔑 /ɪk'spreʃn/ ***noun*** 名词
1 the look on your face that shows how you feel 表情；神态：*an expression of surprise* 惊讶的表情
2 a word or group of words; a way of saying something 词语；表达方式；措辞：*The expression 'to drop off' means 'to fall asleep'.* * to drop off 这个词组的意思是 to fall asleep（入睡）。

expressway /ɪk'spresweɪ/ *American English for* MOTORWAY 美式英语，即 motorway

exquisite /ɪk'skwɪzɪt/ ***adjective*** 形容词 extremely beautiful 精美的；精致的：*She has an exquisite face.* 她容貌俊俏。

extend /ɪk'stend/ ***verb*** 动词 (**extends**, **extending**, **extended**)
1 to make something longer or bigger 使伸长；延长；扩大：*I'm extending my holiday for another week.* 我把假期又延长了一个星期。
2 to reach or stretch over an area 延伸；伸展：*The park extends as far as the river.* 公园一直延伸到河边。

extension /ɪk'stenʃn/ ***noun*** 名词
1 (*British* 英式英语) a part that you add to something to make it bigger 延伸部分；扩建部分：*They've built an extension on the back of the house.* 他们在房子后面加以扩建。
2 one of the telephones in a building that is connected to the main telephone 电话分机：*Can I have extension 4110, please?* 请给我转 4110 号分机好吗？

extensive /ɪk'stensɪv/ ***adjective*** 形容词 large in area or amount 宽阔的；宽敞的；大量的：*The house has extensive grounds.* 这栋房子有宽敞的庭院。 ◇ *Many buildings suffered **extensive damage**.* 许多楼房遭到了严重破坏。

extent /ɪk'stent/ ***noun*** 名词 (*no plural* 不用复数形式)
how big something is 大小；程度：*I had no idea of the **full extent of** the problem* (= how big it was). 我不知道这个问题有多严重。

to a certain extent, **to some extent** used to show that you do not think something is completely true 在一定程度上；在某种程度上：*I agree with you to a certain extent.* 我在一定程度上同意你的看法。

exterior /ɪk'stɪəriə(r)/ ***noun*** 名词 the outside part of something, especially

a building （尤指建筑物的）外部，外观：
*We painted the exterior of the house
white.* 我们把房子的外墙刷成了白色。
⊃ OPPOSITE **interior** 反义词为 interior
▸ **exterior** *adjective* 形容词： *an exterior
door* 通向外面的门 ⊃ OPPOSITE **interior**
反义词为 interior

external /ɪkˈstɜːnl/ *adjective* 形容词
on, of or from the outside 外部的；外面
的：*external walls* 外墙 ⊃ OPPOSITE
internal 反义词为 internal

extinct /ɪkˈstɪŋkt/ *adjective* 形容词
If a type of animal or plant is **extinct**,
it does not exist now. （动植物）已灭绝
的，绝种的：*Dinosaurs became extinct
millions of years ago.* 数百万年前恐龙就
灭绝了。

extinguish /ɪkˈstɪŋgwɪʃ/ *verb* 动词
(extinguishes, extinguishing,
extinguished /ɪkˈstɪŋgwɪʃt/) (*formal* 正式)
to make something stop burning 使熄
灭；扑灭 ⊃ SAME MEANING **put out** 同义词
为 put out：*It took several hours to
extinguish the fire.* 几个小时后大火才
扑灭。

extra 0ᴀ /ˈekstrə/ *adjective, adverb*
形容词，副词
more than what is usual 额外（的）；
外加（的）：*I've put an extra blanket on
your bed because it's cold tonight.* 今晚
很冷，我在你的床上多加了一条毯子。◇
*The room costs £30 and you have to pay
extra for breakfast.* 这个房间要 30 英镑，
早餐另计。

extraordinarily /ɪkˈstrɔːdnrəli/ *adverb*
副词
extremely 极其；非常：*She's
extraordinarily clever.* 她聪明绝顶。

extraordinary /ɪkˈstrɔːdnri/ *adjective*
形容词
very unusual or strange 不同寻常的；
奇怪的：*What an extraordinary thing to
say!* 真是咄咄怪事！

extravagant /ɪkˈstrævəgənt/ *adjective*
形容词
If you are **extravagant**, you spend too
much money. 奢侈的；挥霍的：*He's
terribly extravagant – he goes everywhere
by taxi.* 他非常奢侈，到哪儿都坐出租车。
▸ **extravagance** /ɪkˈstrævəgəns/ *noun*
名词 (*no plural* 不用复数形式) the act or
habit of spending too much money
奢侈；挥霍：*There are no limits to his
extravagance.* 他挥霍无度。

extreme 0ᴀ /ɪkˈstriːm/ *adjective*
形容词

1 very great or strong 极度的；极大的：
the extreme cold of the Arctic 北极地区的
严寒
2 If you say that a person is **extreme**, you
mean that their ideas are too strong.
极端的；偏激的
3 as far away as possible 最远的；
尽头的：*They came from the extreme
north of Scotland.* 他们来自苏格兰的最
北部。

extremely 0ᴀ /ɪkˈstriːmli/ *adverb*
副词
very 极其；非常：*He's extremely
good-looking.* 他英俊不凡。

the eye 眼睛

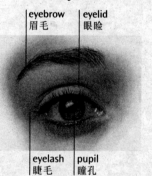

eyebrow 眉毛   eyelid 眼睑
eyelash 睫毛   pupil 瞳孔

eye 0ᴀ /aɪ/ *noun* 名词
one of the two parts in your head that
you see with 眼睛：*She's got blue eyes.*
她有一双蓝眼睛。◇ *Open your eyes!* 睁开
你的眼睛！
catch somebody's eye
1 to make somebody look at you 引起
某人注意：*Try to catch the waiter's eye
the next time he comes this way.* 那名
侍者再往这边来的时候，尽量引起他的
注意。
2 If something **catches your eye**, you
see it suddenly. 吸引某人的目光；让人
突然看到：*Her bright yellow hat caught
my eye.* 她那顶鲜黄色的帽子跃入了我的
眼帘。
in somebody's eyes in the opinion of
somebody 在某人看来：*Richard is 42, but
in his mother's eyes, he's still a little boy!*
理查德 42 岁了，但在母亲的眼里他仍是个
小孩！
keep an eye on somebody or 或
something to look after or watch
somebody or something 照看；留意：

A
B
C
D
E
F
G
H
I
J
K
L
M
N
O
P
Q
R
S
T
U
V
W
X
Y
Z

Will you keep an eye on my bag while I go to the toilet? 我上厕所，你帮我看着包好吗？

see eye to eye with somebody to agree with somebody 与某人看法一致: *Mr Harper doesn't always see eye to eye with his neighbours.* 哈珀先生并非总是与邻居的看法一致。

eyebrow /'aɪbraʊ/ *noun* 名词
one of the two lines of hair above your eyes 眉；眉毛 ⊃ Look at the picture at **eye**. 见 eye 的插图。

eyelash /'aɪlæʃ/ (*also* 亦作 lash) *noun* 名词 (*plural* 复数形式 eyelashes)

one of the hairs that grow in a line on your EYELID 睫毛: *She's got beautiful long eyelashes.* 她的睫毛又长又漂亮。
⊃ Look at the picture at **eye**. 见 eye 的插图。

eyelid /'aɪlɪd/ *noun* 名词
the piece of skin that can move to close your eye 眼睑；眼皮 ⊃ Look at the picture at **eye**. 见 eye 的插图。

eyesight /'aɪsaɪt/ *noun* 名词 (*no plural* 不用复数形式)
the ability to see 视力: *Your eyesight is very good.* 你的视力很好。

F f

F, f /ef/ *noun* 名词
1 (*plural* 复数形式 **F's, f's** /efs/) the sixth letter of the English alphabet 英语字母表的第 6 个字母: *'Father' begins with an 'F'.* * father 一词以字母 f 开头。
2 F short way of writing FAHRENHEIT * Fahrenheit 的缩略形式

fable /'feɪbl/ *noun* 名词
a short story, usually about animals, that teaches people a lesson (called a **moral**) 寓言

fabric /'fæbrɪk/ *noun* 名词
cloth that is used for making things such as clothes and curtains 织物；布料: *cotton fabrics* 棉织物

fabulous /'fæbjələs/ *adjective* 形容词
very good 极好的；绝妙的 ⊃ SAME MEANING **wonderful** 同义词为 wonderful: *The food smells fabulous!* 这食物闻起来香得很！

face¹ 0— /feɪs/ *noun* 名词
1 the front part of your head 脸；面孔: *Have you washed your face?* 你洗脸了吗？ ◇ *She had a smile on her face.* 她面露笑容。 ⊃ Look at Picture Dictionary page **P4**. 见彩页 P4。
2 the front or one side of something（物体的）正面，面: *a clock face* 钟面 ◇ *He put the cards face down on the table.* 他把纸牌正面朝下放在桌子上。

face to face If two people are face to face, they are looking straight at each other. 面对面: *They stood face to face.* 他们面对面站着。

keep a straight face to not smile or laugh when something is funny 绷着脸；忍住不笑: *I couldn't keep a straight face when he dropped his watch in the soup!* 他把手表掉进汤里时，我忍不住笑了起来！

make or 或 **pull a face** to move your mouth and eyes to show that you do not like something 拉长了脸；沉下脸: *She made a face when she saw what was for dinner.* 她一看到正餐的饭菜就拉长了脸。

to somebody's face If you say something **to somebody's face**, you say it when that person is with you. 当着某人的面: *I wanted to say that I was sorry to her face, not on the phone.* 我想当面跟她说对不起，不想在电话里说。

face² 0— /feɪs/ *verb* 动词 (**faces, facing, faced** /feɪst/)
1 to have your face or front towards something 面对；面向: *Can you all face the front of the class, please?* 请你们都面向教室前面好吗？ ◇ *My bedroom faces the garden.* 我的卧室朝向花园。
2 to deal with an unfriendly person or a difficult situation 对付；应付: *I can't face going to work today – I feel too ill.* 我今天上不了班 —— 我病得很厉害。

let's face it (*informal* 非正式) we must agree that it is true 我们得承认；面对现实: *Let's face it – you're not very good at maths.* 老实说，你数学不太好。

facilities /fə'sɪlətiz/ *noun* 名词 (*plural* 用复数形式)
a service, building, piece of equipment, etc. that makes it possible to do something 设施；设备: *Our school has very good sports facilities.* 我们学校的体育设施非常好。

fact 0— /fækt/ *noun* 名词
something that you know has happened or is true 事实；实情: *It's a fact that the earth travels around the sun.* 地球围绕着太阳运行是事实。

in fact, in actual fact used to show that something is true; really 事实上；实际上: *I thought she was Swedish, but in actual fact she's from Norway.* 我以为她是瑞典人，其实她是挪威人。 ◇ *I think I saw him – in fact, I'm sure I did.* 我想我是看见他了，事实上我的确看见了。

factory 0— /'fæktri/ *noun* 名词 (*plural* 复数形式 **factories**)
a place where people make things, usually with machines 工厂；制造厂: *He works at the car factory.* 他在汽车厂工作。

fade /feɪd/ *verb* 动词 (**fades, fading, faded**)
to become lighter in colour or less strong 褪色；变淡；变弱: *Will this shirt fade when I wash it?* 这件衬衫洗的时候会褪色吗？ ◇ *The cheers of the crowd faded away.* 人群的欢呼声逐渐消逝。

Fahrenheit /'færənhaɪt/ *noun* 名词 (*no plural* 不用复数形式) (*abbr.* 缩略式 **F**)
a way of measuring temperature. Water

freezes at 32° **Fahrenheit** and boils at 212° **Fahrenheit**. 华氏温度: *110°F* * 110 华氏度

fail¹ Oₘ /feɪl/ *verb* 动词 (fails, failing, failed /feɪld/)

1 to not pass an exam or test 不及格; 不合格: *She failed her driving test again.* 她再次没通过驾驶考试。◇ *How many students failed last term?* 上一个学期多少学生不及格? ⊃ OPPOSITE **pass** 反义词为 pass

2 to try to do something but not be able to do it 失败; 未能: *He played quite well but failed to win the match.* 他表现相当出色, 可是未能赢得比赛。⊃ OPPOSITE **succeed** 反义词为 succeed

3 to not do something that you should do 未做; 没有做: *The driver failed to stop at a red light.* 那名司机在红灯前没停车。

fail² /feɪl/ *noun* 名词

without fail certainly 务必; 一定: *Be there at twelve o'clock without fail!* 十二点钟务必到达那里!

failure Oₘ /'feɪljə(r)/ *noun* 名词

1 (*no plural* 不用复数形式) lack of success 失败: *The search for the missing children ended in failure.* 寻找那些失踪儿童的行动以失败告终。

2 (*plural* 复数形式 **failures**) a person or thing that does not do well 失败的人(或事物): *I felt that I was a failure because I didn't have a job.* 我觉得自己很失败, 因为我没有工作。

⊃ OPPOSITE **success** 反义词为 success

faint¹ /feɪnt/ *adjective* 形容词 (fainter, faintest)

1 not clear or strong 模糊的; 微弱的: *We could hear the faint sound of music in the distance.* 我们听到远处传来隐约的音乐声。

2 If you feel **faint**, you feel that you are going to fall, for example because you are ill or tired. 昏眩; 晕眩

faint² /feɪnt/ *verb* 动词 (faints, fainting, fainted)

to suddenly become unconscious for a short time, for example because you are weak, ill or shocked 晕倒; 昏倒: *She fainted as soon as she saw the blood.* 她一看到血就晕倒了。

fair¹ Oₘ /feə(r)/ *adjective* 形容词 (fairer, fairest)

1 treating people equally or in the right way 公正的; 公平的: *They didn't get a fair trial.* 他们没有得到公正的审判。◇ *It's not fair! I have to go to bed before*

my sister! 太不公平了! 我得比妹妹先上床睡觉! ⊃ OPPOSITE **unfair** 反义词为 unfair

2 quite good or quite large 相当好的; 相当大的: *They have a fair chance of winning.* 他们的胜算相当大。◇ *They've invited a fair number of people to their party.* 他们邀请了相当多的人参加聚会。

3 (used about a person's skin or hair) light in colour (人的皮肤或头发)浅色的: *He's got fair hair.* 他浅色头发。

⊃ OPPOSITE **dark** 反义词为 dark

4 (used about the weather) bright and not raining (天气)晴朗的

fair² /feə(r)/ *noun* 名词

1 (*also* 亦作 **funfair**) a place outdoors where you can ride on big machines and play games to win prizes. **Fairs** usually travel from town to town. (通常为巡回各地的)露天游乐场

2 a large event where people and businesses show and sell the things they make 商品交易会; 展销会: *a book fair* 书展 ◇ *a world trade fair* 世界交易会

fairly Oₘ /'feəli/ *adverb* 副词

1 quite; not very 相当; 还算: *She speaks French fairly well.* 她法语说得挺不错。◇ *I'm fairly certain it was him.* 我相当肯定那就是他。

2 in a way that is right and honest 公正地; 公平地: *This company treats its workers fairly.* 这家公司对待员工很公平。

⊃ OPPOSITE **unfairly** 反义词为 unfairly

fairy 小仙人

wing 翅膀

fairy /'feəri/ *noun* 名词 (*plural* 复数形式 **fairies**)

a very small person in stories. **Fairies** have wings and can do magic. (故事中的)仙子; 小仙人

fairy tale /ˈfeəri teɪl/ (*also* 亦作 fairy story /ˈfeəri stɔːri/ *plural* 复数形式 fairy stories) *noun* 名词
a story for children that is about magic 童话故事

faith /feɪθ/ *noun* 名词
1 (*no plural* 不用复数形式) feeling sure that somebody or something is good, right or honest 信念；信任：*I've got great faith in your ability to do the job* (= I'm sure that you can do it). 我深信你能胜任这份工作。
2 (*plural* 复数形式 faiths) a religion 宗教；信仰：*the Muslim faith* 伊斯兰教

faithful /ˈfeɪθfl/ *adjective* 形容词
always ready to help your friends and to do what you have promised to do 忠实的；忠诚的：*a faithful friend* 忠实的朋友

faithfully /ˈfeɪθfəli/ *adverb* 副词
Yours faithfully words that you write at the end of a formal letter, before your name（正式信函末署名前的套语）谨启 ⊃ Look at Study Pages S18-S19. 见研习专页 S18-S19。

fake /feɪk/ *noun* 名词
a copy of something that seems real but is not 赝品；假货：*This painting is not really by Van Gogh – it's a fake.* 这幅画不是凡·高的真迹，是赝品。
▸ **fake** *adjective* 形容词：*a fake passport* 假护照

fall¹ /fɔːl/ *verb* 动词 (falls, falling, fell /fel/, has fallen /ˈfɔːlən/)
1 to go down quickly towards the ground 落下；掉下；跌落：*The book fell off the table.* 书从桌上掉了下去。◇ *She fell down the stairs and broke her arm.* 她从楼梯上跌下来，摔断了胳膊。
2 (*also* 亦作 fall over) to suddenly stop standing 跌倒；摔倒；倒下：*He slipped on the ice and fell.* 他在冰上滑倒了。◇ *I fell over and hurt my leg.* 我跌倒把腿摔伤了。
3 to become lower or less 下降；减少：*In the desert the temperature falls quickly at night.* 在沙漠地区，夜晚气温下降很快。◇ *Prices have fallen again.* 价格又下跌了。⊃ OPPOSITE rise 反义词为 rise
fall apart to break into pieces 破碎；解体：*The chair fell apart when I sat on it.* 我一坐上去，椅子就散架了。
fall asleep to start sleeping 入睡：*She fell asleep in the armchair.* 她在扶手椅上睡着了。
fall behind to become slower than others, or not do something when you

should do it 落后；没有及时做：*She's falling behind with her school work.* 她的功课落下了。
fall for somebody to begin to love somebody 爱上某人：*He has fallen for someone he met on holiday.* 他爱上了度假时认识的一个人。
fall in love with somebody to begin to love somebody 爱上某人：*He fell in love with Anna the first time they met.* 他对安娜一见钟情。
fall out with somebody to argue with somebody so that you stop being friends（与某人）吵翻，闹翻：*Jane has fallen out with her best friend.* 简和她最要好的朋友闹翻了。
fall through If a plan **falls through**, it does not happen. 落空；泡汤

fall² /fɔːl/ *noun* 名词
1 a sudden drop from a higher place to a lower place 落下；掉下；跌落：*He had a fall from his horse.* 他从马上摔了下来。
2 becoming lower or less 下降；减少：*a fall in the price of oil* 油价的下跌
3 falls (*plural* 用复数形式) a place where water falls from a high place to a low place 瀑布 ⊃ SAME MEANING waterfall 同义词为 waterfall：*the Victoria Falls* 维多利亚瀑布
4 *American English for* AUTUMN 美式英语，即 autumn

fallen *form of* FALL¹ * fall¹ 的不同形式

false /fɔːls/ *adjective* 形容词
1 not true; wrong 错误的；不正确的：*She gave a false name to the police.* 她向警方报了个假名。◇ *A spider has eight legs – true or false?* 蜘蛛有八条腿，对还是错？⊃ OPPOSITE true 反义词为 true
2 not real or not natural 假的；人造的：*He has false teeth* (= teeth that are made of plastic). 他戴假牙。
false alarm a warning about something bad that does not happen 假警报；虚惊一场：*Everyone thought there was a fire, but it was a false alarm.* 大家都以为失火了，其实只是虚惊一场。

fame /feɪm/ *noun* 名词 (*no plural* 不用复数形式)
being known by many people 名声；名气 ⊃ The adjective is **famous**. 形容词为 famous。

familiar /fəˈmɪliə(r)/ *adjective* 形容词
that you know well 熟悉的：*I heard a familiar voice in the next room.* 我听见隔壁房间传来熟悉的声音。◇ *I'm not familiar with this computer.* 我对这台电脑不怎么

A B C D E F G H I J K L M N O P Q R S T U V W X Y Z

熟悉。 ⟲ OPPOSITE **unfamiliar** 反义词为 unfamiliar

family ⟲ /'fæməli/ *noun* 名词 (*plural* 复数形式 **families**)

1 parents and children 家庭: *How many people are there in your family?* 你家有几口人? ◇ *My family have all got red hair.* 我们家的人都是红头发。 ◇ *His family lives on a farm.* 他家住在农场里。

> ♫ CULTURE 文化资料补充
>
> Sometimes **family** means not just parents and children but other people too, for example grandparents, aunts, uncles and cousins. 有时 family 不仅指父母和子女，还包括其他亲属，如祖父母、外祖父母、姨母、姑母、舅母、姊母、舅父、叔父、伯父、姑父、姨父、同辈表亲或堂亲等。

2 a group of plants or animals （生物分类）科: *Lions belong to the cat family.* 狮子是猫科动物。

family name /'fæməli neɪm/ *noun* 名词 the name that is shared by members of a family 姓 ⟲ SAME MEANING **surname** 同义词为 surname ⟲ Look at the note at **name**[1]. 见 name[1] 条的注释。

family tree /'fæməli 'triː/ *noun* 名词 a plan that shows all the people in a family 家族世系图；族谱

famine /'fæmɪn/ *noun* 名词 A **famine** happens when there is not enough food in a country. 饥荒: *There is a famine in many parts of Africa.* 非洲很多地方出现饥荒。

famous ⟲ /'feɪməs/ *adjective* 形容词 known by many people 出名的；著名的: *Oxford is **famous** for its university.* 牛津因它的大学而闻名。 ◇ *Marilyn Monroe was a famous actress.* 玛丽莲·梦露是著名的演员。 ⟲ The noun is **fame**. 名词为 fame。

fans 扇子；风扇

fan[1] /fæn/ *noun* 名词

1 a person who likes somebody or something, for example a singer or a sport, very much （歌手或体育等的）迷，狂热爱好者: *She was a big fan of the Beatles.* 她是披头士乐队的忠实歌迷。 ◇ *football fans* 足球迷

2 a thing that moves the air to make you cooler 扇子；风扇: *an electric fan* 电风扇

fan[2] /fæn/ *verb* 动词 (**fans**, **fanning**, **fanned** /fænd/) to make somebody or something cooler by moving the air 扇（风）: *I fanned my face with the newspaper.* 我用报纸往脸上扇风。

fanatic /fə'nætɪk/ *noun* 名词 a person who is very enthusiastic about something and may have extreme or dangerous opinions 狂热分子；狂热信徒: *He's a football fanatic.* 他对足球很狂热。 ◇ *a religious fanatic* 宗教狂热分子

fancy[1] /'fænsi/ *verb* 动词 (**fancies**, **fancying**, **fancied** /'fænsid/, **has fancied**) (*British* 英式英语) (*informal* 非正式)

1 to feel that you would like something 想要；想做: *Do you fancy a drink?* 你想喝点什么吗? ◇ *I don't fancy going.* 我不想去。

2 to like somebody in a sexual way 爱慕: *She fancied her friend's brother.* 她喜欢上她朋友的哥哥。

3 a word that shows you are surprised （表示惊奇）真想不到: *Fancy seeing you here!* 真想不到在这儿见到你!

fancy[2] /'fænsi/ *adjective* 形容词 (**fancier**, **fanciest**) not simple or ordinary 复杂的；花巧的；精致的: *She wore a very fancy hat to the wedding.* 她戴了顶别致的帽子参加婚礼。 ◇ *a fancy restaurant* 豪华餐馆

fancy dress /'fænsi 'dres/ *noun* 名词 (*no plural* 不用复数形式) (*British* 英式英语) clothes that you wear at a party so that you look like a different person or a thing 化装舞会服；化装: *He wants to go in fancy dress.* 他想穿化装服去。 ◇ *It was a fancy dress party so I went as Charlie Chaplin.* 那是化装舞会，所以我装扮成查理·卓别林去参加。

fantastic /fæn'tæstɪk/ *adjective* 形容词 (*informal* 非正式) very good; wonderful 极好的；美妙的；出色的 ⟲ SAME MEANING **great** or **brilliant** 同义词为 great 或 brilliant: *We had a* *fantastic holiday*. 我们的假期过得精彩极了。

fantasy /ˈfæntəsi/ *noun* 名词 (*plural* 复数形式 fantasies)
something nice that you think about and that you hope will happen, although it is very unlikely 幻想；想象 ⊃ SAME MEANING **dream** 同义词为 dream: *It was just a fantasy.* 那只是幻想。◇ *She was living in a fantasy world.* 她活在幻想的世界中。

FAQ /ˌef eɪ ˈkjuː/ *abbreviation* 缩略式
FAQ is used in writing to mean 'frequently asked questions'. 常见问题（FAQ 是 frequently asked questions 的缩略式）

far¹ ⊶ /fɑː(r)/ *adverb* 副词 (farther /ˈfɑːðə(r)/ or 或 further /ˈfɜːðə(r)/, farthest /ˈfɑːðɪst/ or 或 furthest /ˈfɜːðɪst/)
1 a long way from somewhere （距离）远: *My house isn't far from the station.* 我家离车站不远。◇ *It's too far to drive in one day.* 那里很远，开一天车也到不了。◇ *I walked much further than you.* 我走得比你远得多。
2 You use **far** to ask about the distance from one place to another place. （用以询问距离）: *How far is it to the coast from here?* 从这儿到海边有多远?

┌─────────────────────────────┐
🔎 WHICH WORD? 词语辨析
We usually use **far** only in questions and negative sentences, and after **too** and **so**. In other sentences we use **a long way**. * far 通常只用于疑问句和否定句，以及 too 和 so 之后，其他句子用 a long way: *It's a long way to walk – let's take the bus.* 走路太远了，咱们坐公共汽车吧。
└─────────────────────────────┘

3 very much 非常；十分: *He's far taller than his brother.* 他比他弟弟高得多。◇ *That's far too expensive.* 那可太贵了。
as far as … to a place 一直到（某处）: *We walked as far as the village and then came back.* 我们一直走到村子，然后返回。◇ *I read as far as the second chapter.* 我读到了第二章。
as far as I know used when you think something is true, but you are not certain 据我所知；依我看: *As far as I know, she's coming, but I may be wrong.* 就我所知，她会来的，但我可能弄错。
by far You use **by far** to show that a person or thing is much better, bigger, etc. than anybody or anything else. 大大地；⋯⋯得多: *She's by far the best player in the team.* 她显然是队中最优秀的选手。
far from it (*informal* 非正式) certainly

not; just the opposite 绝非；完全相反: *'Are you upset?' 'Far from it – I'm delighted.'* "你生气了吗?""恰恰相反 —— 我很高兴。"
far from something almost the opposite of something; not at all 远非；一点也不: *I'm far from certain.* 我一点把握也没有。
so far until now 到目前为止: *So far the work has been easy.* 到目前为止，工作还算容易。

far² ⊶ /fɑː(r)/ *adjective* 形容词 (farther /ˈfɑːðə(r)/ or 或 further /ˈfɜːðə(r)/, farthest /ˈfɑːðɪst/ or 或 furthest /ˈfɜːðɪst/)
1 a long way away 距离远的: *Let's walk – it's not far.* 我们走路去吧，那儿不远。⊃ OPPOSITE **near** 反义词为 near

┌─────────────────────────────┐
🔎 WHICH WORD? 词语辨析
We only use **far** in questions or negative forms. * far 只用于疑问句或否定形式: *Is it far to the beach?* 去海滩远吗?
In positive statements we say **a long way**. 在肯定陈述句中用 a long way: *He lives a long way from the station.* 他住的地方离车站很远。
└─────────────────────────────┘

2 a long way from the centre in the direction mentioned （离中心）远的: *Who's that on the far left of the photo?* 照片上最左边的那个人是谁?

fare /feə(r)/ *noun* 名词
the money that you pay to travel by bus, train, plane, etc. 车费；（飞机等）票价: *My bus fare has gone up.* 我乘坐的公共汽车加了票价。

farewell /ˌfeəˈwel/ *noun* 名词 (*formal* 正式)
goodbye 告别；辞行: *We're having a farewell party for Vanessa.* 我们要给瓦妮莎举行告别聚会。

farm ⊶ /fɑːm/ *noun* 名词
land and buildings where people keep animals and grow crops 农场；养殖场: *They work on a farm.* 他们在农场工作。◇ *farm animals* 农场饲养的动物

farmer ⊶ /ˈfɑːmə(r)/ *noun* 名词
a person who owns or looks after a farm 农场主；农民 ⊃ Look at Picture Dictionary page **P12**. 见彩页 P12。

farmhouse /ˈfɑːmhaʊs/ *noun* 名词
the main house on a farm 农场住宅；农舍

farming ⊶ /ˈfɑːmɪŋ/ *noun* 名词 (*no plural* 不用复数形式)
managing a farm or working on it

农场经营；务农： *farming methods*
耕作方法

farmyard /ˈfɑːmjɑːd/ *noun* 名词
the area beside the main house on a
farm, with buildings or walls around it
农家庭院

farther ⟵ (*also* 还有 **farthest**) *forms of*
FAR * far 的不同形式

fascinate /ˈfæsɪneɪt/ *verb* 动词
(**fascinates, fascinating, fascinated**)
to attract or interest somebody very
much 吸引；迷住： *China has always
fascinated me.* 中国一直令我心驰神往。
◇ *I've always been fascinated by his ideas.*
他的想法总是让我很感兴趣。

fascinating /ˈfæsɪneɪtɪŋ/ *adjective*
形容词
very interesting 有吸引力的；迷人的：
*She told us fascinating stories about her
life.* 她给我们讲了她人生中一些有趣的事。

fascination /ˌfæsɪˈneɪʃn/ *noun* 名词
(*no plural* 不用复数形式)
when you find something or somebody
very interesting 入迷；着迷： *The girls
listened in fascination.* 女孩都听得入迷。

fashion ⟵ /ˈfæʃn/ *noun* 名词
a way of dressing or doing something that
people like and try to copy for a time
时尚；流行样式： *Bright colours are back
in fashion.* 亮丽的色彩又再度流行起来了。
◇ *Some styles never go out of fashion.*
有些款式永远不会过时。 ◇ *a fashion show*
时装表演

fashionable ⟵ /ˈfæʃnəbl/ *adjective*
形容词
popular or in a popular style at the time
流行的；时髦的： *She was wearing a
fashionable black hat.* 她戴着一顶时髦的
黑帽子。 ◯ OPPOSITE **old-fashioned** or
unfashionable 反义词为 old-fashioned
或 unfashionable

▶ **fashionably** /ˈfæʃnəbli/ *adverb* 副词：
He was always fashionably dressed. 他向来
穿戴时髦。

fashion designer /ˈfæʃn dɪzaɪnə(r)/
noun 名词
a person whose job is to design clothes
时装设计师

fast¹ ⟵ /fɑːst/ *adjective* 形容词 (**faster**,
fastest)
1 moving, happening or doing something
very quickly 快的；迅速的： *the fastest
rate of increase for many years* 多年来最
快的增长率 ◇ *a fast learner* 学习很快的人

2 If a clock or watch is **fast**, it shows a
time that is later than the real time.
（钟表）走得快： *My watch is five
minutes fast.* 我的手表快了五分钟。
◯ OPPOSITE **slow** 反义词为 slow

fast² ⟵ /fɑːst/ *adverb* 副词 (**faster**,
fastest)
1 quickly 快；迅速： *Don't drive so fast!*
车子别开得那么快！ ◇ *I can't go any faster.*
我不能走得更快了。 ◯ OPPOSITE **slowly**
反义词为 slowly
2 firmly or deeply 牢固地；深沉地： *The
baby was fast asleep.* 宝宝睡得很香。 ◇
The car was stuck fast in the mud. 汽车
深深陷入淤泥中。

fast³ /fɑːst/ *verb* 动词 (**fasts, fasting,
fasted**)
to not eat food for a certain time 禁食；
斋戒： *Muslims fast during Ramadan.*
穆斯林在斋月期间斋戒。

fasten ⟵ /ˈfɑːsn/ *verb* 动词 (**fastens,
fastening, fastened** /ˈfɑːsnd/)
1 to join or close something so that it will
not come open 系上；扣紧；扎牢：
Please fasten your seat belts. 请系好安全
带。 ◇ *Can you fasten this suitcase for me?*
你帮我把这行李箱关紧行吗？
2 to fix or tie one thing to another thing
把…固定到；使…固定在一起： *Fasten this
badge to your jacket.* 把这枚徽章别在你的
夹克上。

fastener /ˈfɑːsnə(r)/ *noun* 名词
a thing that joins together two parts of
something 纽扣；拉链；扣件： *The
fastener on my skirt has just broken.*
我裙子上的拉链刚坏了。

fast food /ˌfɑːst ˈfuːd/ *noun* 名词
(*no plural* 不用复数形式)
hot food that is served very quickly in
special restaurants, and often taken away
to be eaten in the street 快餐；速食
◯ Look at Picture Dictionary page **P7**.
见彩页 **P7**。

fat¹ ☞ /fæt/ *adjective* 形容词 (fatter, fattest)

with a large round body 肥胖的: *You'll get fat if you eat so much.* 吃这么多会发胖的。 ⇨ OPPOSITE **slim** or **thin** 反义词为 slim 或 thin

> 🔎 WORD BUILDING 词汇扩充
>
> It is not polite to say somebody is **fat**. It is better to say **large** or **plump**. 说一个人 fat 是不礼貌的。用 large 或 plump 较为合适: *She's a rather large lady.* 她是个体态丰腴的女士。 ◇ *He's a bit plump.* 他有点胖。 You can say **chubby** to describe babies and children. 形容婴儿和儿童可用 chubby: *a chubby little girl* 胖乎乎的小女孩

fat² ☞ /fæt/ *noun* 名词

1 (*no plural* 不用复数形式) the soft white substance under the skins of animals and people 脂肪; 肥肉: *Cut the fat off the meat.* 把这块肉上的肥肉切掉。
2 (*plural* 复数形式 **fats**) the substance containing oil that we get from animals, plants, or seeds and use for cooking （食用的）动物油, 植物油: *foods which are low in fat* 低脂食物 ◇ *Heat some fat in a frying pan.* 用煎锅把油加热。

fatal /ˈfeɪtl/ *adjective* 形容词

1 Something that is **fatal** causes death. 致命的: *a fatal car accident* 致命的车祸
2 Something that is **fatal** has very bad results. 导致严重后果的; 毁灭性的: *I made the fatal mistake of signing a document without reading it properly.* 我没仔细看内容就在文件上签名, 铸成了大错。
▸ **fatally** /ˈfeɪtəli/ *adverb* 副词: *She was fatally injured in the crash.* 她在撞车事故中受了极严重的伤。

fate /feɪt/ *noun* 名词

1 (*plural* 复数形式 **fates**) the things, especially bad things, that will happen or have happened to somebody or something 命运; 命中注定的事（尤指环事）: *What will be the fate of the prisoners?* 这些囚犯命运会如何?
2 (*no plural* 不用复数形式) the power that some people believe controls everything that happens 天数; 天意: *It was fate that brought them together again after twenty years.* 天意让他们在二十年后重聚。

father ☞ /ˈfɑːðə(r)/ *noun* 名词

a man who has a child 父亲; 爸爸: *Where do your mother and father live?*

你父母住在哪儿? ⇨ Look at **dad** and **daddy**. 见 dad 和 daddy。

Father Christmas /ˌfɑːðə ˈkrɪsməs/ *noun* 名词

an old man with a red coat and a long white beard. Children believe that he brings presents at Christmas. 圣诞老人

fatherhood /ˈfɑːðəhʊd/ *noun* 名词

(*no plural* 不用复数形式) being a father 父亲的身份; 为人父

father-in-law /ˈfɑːðər ɪn lɔː/ *noun* 名词

(*plural* 复数形式 **fathers-in-law**) the father of your husband or wife 公公; 岳父

faucet /ˈfɔːsɪt/ *American English for* TAP² 美式英语, 即 tap²

fault ☞ /fɔːlt/ *noun* 名词

1 (*no plural* 不用复数形式) If something bad is your **fault**, you made it happen. 失误; 过失: *It's her fault that we are late.* 我们迟到是她的错。 ◇ *It's my fault for being careless.* 粗心大意是我自己的过失。
2 (*plural* 复数形式 **faults**) something that is wrong or bad in a person or thing 缺点; 缺陷; 故障: *There is a serious fault in the machine.* 机器出了严重故障。

faultless /ˈfɔːltləs/ *adjective* 形容词

without any mistakes 完美的; 无可挑剔的 ⇨ SAME MEANING **perfect** 同义词为 perfect: *a faultless performance* 完美的表演

faulty /ˈfɔːlti/ *adjective* 形容词

not working well 有缺陷的; 失灵的: *This light doesn't work – the switch is faulty.* 这盏灯不亮——开关出故障了。

favor *American English for* FAVOUR 美式英语, 即 favour

favorite *American English for* FAVOURITE 美式英语, 即 favourite

favour ☞ (*British* 英式英语) (*American* 美式英语 **favor**) /ˈfeɪvə(r)/ *noun* 名词

something that you do to help somebody 帮忙; 恩惠: *Would you do me a favour and open the door?* 请你帮我把门打开好吗? ◇ *Could I ask you a favour – will you take me to the station this evening?* 请你帮个忙——今天晚上你能送我去车站吗?
be in favour of something to like or agree with something 赞成; 支持: *Are you in favour of higher taxes on cigarettes?* 你赞成对香烟征更高的税吗?

favourable (*British* 英式英语) (*American* 美式英语 **favorable**) /ˈfeɪvərəbl/ *adjective* 形容词

A
B
C
D
E
F
G
H
I
J
K
L
M
N
O
P
Q
R
S
T
U
V
W
X
Y
Z

good, suitable, or acceptable 好的；合适的；可接受的： *She made a favourable impression on his parents.* 她给他父母留下了好印象。

favourite¹ 0━ (*British* 英式英语) (*American* 美式英语 favorite) /ˈfeɪvərɪt/ *adjective* 形容词
Your **favourite** person or thing is the one that you like more than any other. 最喜爱的： *What's your favourite food?* 你最爱吃什么？

favourite² 0━ (*British* 英式英语) (*American* 美式英语 favorite) /ˈfeɪvərɪt/ *noun* 名词
a person or thing that you like more than any other 最喜爱的人（或事物）： *I like all chocolates but these are my favourites.* 凡是巧克力我都喜欢，但我最喜欢这些。

fax /fæks/ *noun* 名词 (*plural* 复数形式 faxes)
a copy of a letter, etc. that you send by telephone lines using a special machine (called a **fax machine**) 传真件；传真电文： *They need an answer today so I'll send a fax.* 他们今天要得到答复，所以我会发一份传真。
▸ **fax** *verb* 动词 (faxes, faxing, faxed /fækst/) to send somebody a **fax** 传真： *Can you fax the drawings to me?* 你能把那些图传真给我吗？

fear¹ 0━ /fɪə(r)/ *noun* 名词
the feeling that you have when you think that something bad might happen 害怕；恐惧；担忧： *I have a terrible fear of dogs.* 我非常怕狗。◇ *He was shaking with fear.* 他吓得发抖。◇ *My fears for his safety were unnecessary.* 我担心他的安全是没有必要的。

fear² /fɪə(r)/ *verb* 动词 (fears, fearing, feared /fɪəd/)
1 to be afraid of somebody or something 害怕；畏惧： *We all fear illness and death.* 我们都害怕生病和死亡。

🗣 SPEAKING 表达方式说明
It is more usual to say **be afraid of** or **be frightened of** somebody or something. 较常用 be afraid of 或 be frightened of。

2 (*formal* 正式) to feel that something bad might happen 担心；担忧： *I fear we will be late.* 恐怕我们要迟到了。

fearful /ˈfɪəfl/ *adjective* 形容词 (*formal* 正式)
afraid or worried about something 担心；

担忧： *They were fearful that they would miss the plane.* 他们担心赶不上飞机。

fearless /ˈfɪələs/ *adjective* 形容词
not afraid of anything 不怕的；无畏的

feast /fiːst/ *noun* 名词
a large special meal for a lot of people 盛宴；宴会： *a wedding feast* 婚筵

feat /fiːt/ *noun* 名词
something you do that is clever, difficult or dangerous 本事；功绩；英勇事迹： *Climbing Mount Everest was an amazing feat.* 攀登珠穆朗玛峰是一项壮举。

feather 羽毛

feather 0━ /ˈfeðə(r)/ *noun* 名词
one of the light, soft things that grow in a bird's skin and cover its body 羽毛

feature 0━ /ˈfiːtʃə(r)/ *noun* 名词
1 an important part of something 特色；特征；特点： *Pictures are a feature of this dictionary.* 插图是本词典的一个特点。
2 one of the parts of your face, for example your eyes, nose or mouth 面容的一部分（如眼、鼻、嘴）： *Her eyes are her best feature.* 她五官中最漂亮的是眼睛。
3 a newspaper or magazine article or TV programme about something（报刊文章、电视节目的）特写，专题节目： *The magazine has a special feature on education.* 这本杂志登载了一篇关于教育的专题文章。

February 0━ /ˈfebruəri/ *noun* 名词
the second month of the year 二月

fed *form of* FEED * feed 的不同形式

federal /ˈfedərəl/ *adjective* 形容词
used for describing a political system in which a group of states or countries are joined together under a central government, but also have their own governments 联邦制的： *a federal system*

of rule 联邦体制 ◇ *the Federal Government of the United States* 美国联邦政府

federation /ˌfedəˈreɪʃn/ *noun* 名词
a group of states or organizations that have joined together 联邦；联合会

fed up /ˌfed ˈʌp/ *adjective* 形容词 (*informal* 非正式)
bored or unhappy, especially with a situation that has continued for too long 厌烦；厌倦：*What's the matter? You look really fed up.* 怎么啦？你看上去很烦恼。◇ *I'm fed up with waiting – let's go.* 我都等烦了，咱们走吧。

fee /fiː/ *noun* 名词
1 the money you pay for professional advice or service from private doctors, lawyers, schools, universities, etc. 专业服务费；咨询费；学费：*We can't afford private school fees.* 我们付不起私立学校的学费。◇ *Most ticket agencies will charge a small fee.* 票务代理大多收取小额服务费。
2 the money that you pay to do something, for example to join a club or visit a museum 会费；入场费：*There is no entrance fee to the gallery.* 这家美术馆不收门票。

feeble /ˈfiːbl/ *adjective* 形容词 (**feebler**, **feeblest**)
not strong 虚弱的；衰弱的 ⊃ SAME MEANING **weak** 同义词为 weak：*a feeble old man* 体弱的老人

feed ⃟ /fiːd/ *verb* 动词 (**feeds**, **feeding**, **fed** /fed/, **has fed**)
to give food to a person or an animal 喂养；饲养：*The baby's crying – I'll go and feed her.* 宝宝哭了，我去给她喂食。

feedback /ˈfiːdbæk/ *noun* 名词 (*no plural* 不用复数形式)
advice or information about how well or badly you have done something 反馈的意见（或信息）：*The teacher will give you feedback on the test.* 老师会讲评你测验的结果。

feel ⃟ /fiːl/ *verb* 动词 (**feels**, **feeling**, **felt** /felt/, **has felt**)
1 to know something because your body tells you 觉得；感到：*How do you feel?* 你感觉如何？◇ *I don't feel well.* 我感到不适。◇ *I'm feeling tired.* 我感到累。◇ *He felt somebody touch his arm.* 他感觉到人碰了碰他的胳膊。
2 used for saying how something seems when you touch it or experience it 摸起来；有⋯感觉：*The water felt cold.* 水有点凉。◇ *This towel feels wet – can I have a dry one?* 这条毛巾摸起来有点湿，可否

给我一条干的？◇ *My coat feels like leather, but it's not.* 我的大衣摸上去像是皮的，但其实不是。
3 to touch something in order to find out what it is like 摸；触摸：*Feel this wool – it's really soft.* 摸摸这毛料，它真的很柔软。
4 to have an opinion about something 以为；认为 ⊃ SAME MEANING **believe** 同义词为 believe：*I feel that we should talk about this.* 我认为我们应该谈谈这件事。
5 to try to find something with your hands instead of your eyes（用手）摸索，寻找：*She felt in her pocket for some matches.* 她在口袋里摸着想找火柴。
feel like something to want something 想要；想做：*Do you feel like going for a walk?* 你想去散步吗？◇ *I don't feel like going out tonight.* 我今晚不想出去。

feeling ⃟ /ˈfiːlɪŋ/ *noun* 名词
1 (*plural* 复数形式 **feelings**) something that you feel inside yourself, like happiness or anger 感情；感觉：*a feeling of sadness* 悲伤的感觉
2 (*no plural* 不用复数形式) the ability to feel in your body 感觉；知觉：*I was so cold that I had no feeling in my feet.* 我冻得脚都失去知觉了。
3 (*plural* 复数形式 **feelings**) an idea that you are not certain about 想法；看法：*I have a feeling that she isn't telling the truth.* 我觉得她没有说实话。
hurt somebody's feelings to do or say something that makes somebody sad 使伤心；伤害⋯的感情：*Don't tell him you don't like his shirt – you'll hurt his feelings.* 别跟他说你不喜欢他的衬衫，你会令他难受的。

feet *plural of* FOOT * foot 的复数形式

fell *form of* FALL¹ * fall¹ 的不同形式

fellow¹ /ˈfeləʊ/ *noun* 名词 (*informal* 非正式)
a man 男人；家伙：*What is that fellow doing?* 那家伙在干什么？

fellow² /ˈfeləʊ/ *adjective* 形容词
used for saying that somebody is the same as you in some way 同类的；同伴的；同事的：*her fellow students* 她的同学

felt¹ *form of* FEEL * feel 的不同形式

felt² /felt/ *noun* 名词 (*no plural* 不用复数形式)
a type of soft thick cloth 毡；毡子

felt-tip pen /ˌfelt tɪp ˈpen/ *noun* 名词
a pen with a soft point 毡头笔 ⊃ Look at Picture Dictionary page **P11**. 见彩页 **P11**。

A B C D E F G H I J K L M N O P Q R S T U V W X Y Z

female ⚓ /'fi:meɪl/ *adjective* 形容词
belonging to the sex that can have babies
女的；女性的；雌性的：*female students*
女学生
▶ **female** *noun* 名词：*My cat is a female.*
我的猫是母的。➲ Look at **male**. 见 male。

feminine /'femənɪn/ *adjective* 形容词
1 typical of a woman or right for a
woman 女性的；适合女性的：*feminine clothes* 女性服装
2 (*grammar* 语法) (in some languages)
belonging to a certain class of nouns,
adjectives or pronouns（某些语言中
名词、形容词或代词）阴性的：*The German word for a flower is feminine.*
德语中表示花的词是阴性的。➲ Look at
masculine. 见 masculine。

fence 栅栏

hedge 树篱

wall 围墙 ｜ gate 栅栏门 ｜ fence 栅栏

fence ⚓ /fens/ *noun* 名词
a thing like a wall that is made of pieces
of wood or metal. **Fences** are put round
gardens and fields. 栅栏；篱笆

fern /fɜːn/ *noun* 名词
a plant with long thin leaves and no
flowers that grows in wet areas 蕨；蕨类
植物

ferocious /fə'rəʊʃəs/ *adjective* 形容词
violent and aggressive 凶猛的；残忍的；
激烈的 ➲ SAME MEANING **fierce** 同义词为
fierce：*a ferocious wild animal* 凶猛的
野兽

ferry /'feri/ *noun* 名词 (*plural* 复数形式
ferries)
a boat that takes people or things on
short journeys across a river or sea
渡船；渡轮：*We went by ferry.* 我们是乘
渡船去的。➲ Look at Picture Dictionary
page **P1**. 见彩页 P1。

fertile /'fɜːtaɪl/ *adjective* 形容词
1 If soil is **fertile**, plants grow well in it.
（土壤）肥沃的
2 Somebody who is **fertile** is able to have
babies. （人）能生育的

fertilizer /'fɜːtəlaɪzə(r)/ *noun* 名词
food for plants 肥料

festival ⚓ /'festɪvl/ *noun* 名词
1 a series of public events, for example
concerts and shows, in one place（音乐、
表演等的）节，会演：*the Cannes Film Festival* 戛纳电影节
2 a time when people celebrate
something, especially a religious event
（尤指宗教的）节日，节庆：*Christmas is an important Christian festival.* 圣诞节是
基督教的重要节日。

fetch /fetʃ/ *verb* 动词 (**fetches**, **fetching**,
fetched /fetʃt/)
to go and bring back somebody or
something 去拿来；去接来；去取：*Can you fetch me my bag?* 你去把我的包拿来
行吗？◇ *I'll fetch your coat for you.* 我去
给你拿大衣。◇ *I went to fetch Andy from the station.* 我到车站去接安迪了。

fête /feɪt/ (*British* 英式英语) *noun* 名词
an event where you can buy things and
play games, often organized to get money
for a particular purpose 露天游乐会；
义卖会：*the school fête* 学校义卖会

fetus *American English for* FOETUS 美式
英语，即 foetus

fever /'fi:və(r)/ *noun* 名词
If you have a **fever**, your body is too hot
because you are ill. 发烧 ➲ SAME MEANING
temperature 同义词为 temperature
▶ **feverish** /'fi:vərɪʃ/ *adjective* 形容词
If you are **feverish**, your body is too hot
because you are ill. 发烧的

few ⚓ /fju:/ *adjective, pronoun* 形容词，
代词 (**fewer**, **fewest**)
not many 很少（的）：*Few people live to the age of 100.* 很少人活到 100 岁。◇
There are fewer buses in the evenings.
晚上公共汽车比较少。◇ *Few of the players played well.* 那些选手没有几个
表现出色。
a few some, but not many 一些；几个：
Only a few people came to the meeting.
只有几个人来开会。◇ *I have read a few of her books.* 我读过她写的几本书。
quite a few quite a lot 相当多；不少：
It's been quite a few years since I saw him last. 我上次见到他已经是好几年前的事了。

fiancé /fi'ɒnseɪ/ *noun* 名词
A woman's **fiancé** is the man she has
promised to marry. 未婚夫

fiancée /fi'ɒnseɪ/ *noun* 名词
A man's **fiancée** is the woman he has
promised to marry. 未婚妻

fib /fɪb/ *noun* 名词 (*informal* 非正式)
something you say that you know is not true; a small lie 谎言；小谎；瞎话：*Don't tell fibs!* 不要撒谎！
▶ **fib** *verb* 动词 (fibs, fibbing, fibbed /fɪbd/) (*informal* 非正式) to tell a small lie 撒谎；说瞎话：*I was fibbing when I said I liked her hat.* 我说喜欢她的帽子，是骗她的呢。

fibber /'fɪbə(r)/ *noun* 名词 (*informal* 非正式)
a person who tells FIBS 撒谎的人

fibre (*British* 英式英语) (*American* 美式英语 **fiber**) /'faɪbə(r)/ *noun* 名词
1 (*no plural* 不用复数形式) the part of your food that helps to move other food through your body and keep you healthy （食物中的）纤维素：*Dried fruits are high in fibre.* 干果含丰富的纤维素。
2 (*plural* 复数形式 **fibres**) one of the many thin threads that form a material 纤维：*cotton fibres* 棉纤维

fiction /'fɪkʃn/ *noun* 名词 (*no plural* 不用复数形式)
stories that somebody writes and that are not true 小说：*I enjoy reading fiction.* 我喜欢看小说。

fiddle /'fɪdl/ *verb* 动词 (fiddles, fiddling, fiddled /'fɪdld/)
to touch something a lot with your fingers, because you are bored or nervous （因厌烦或紧张）摆弄，拨弄：*Stop fiddling with your pen and do some work!* 别摆弄笔了，干点活吧！

fidget /'fɪdʒɪt/ *verb* 动词 (fidgets, fidgeting, fidgeted)
to keep moving your body, hands, or feet because you are nervous, excited, or bored （因紧张、激动或厌烦）坐立不安：*Sit still and stop fidgeting!* 坐好，别晃来晃去！

field ○━ /fiːld/ *noun* 名词
1 a piece of land used for animals or for growing crops, usually surrounded by a fence, trees, etc. （通常圈起来的）田地，耕地，牧场
2 an area of study or knowledge （研究或知识的）领域：*Dr Smith is an expert in her field.* 史密斯博士是其研究领域的专家。
3 a piece of land used for something special 场地；场所：*a sports field* 运动场 ◇ *an airfield* (= a place where planes land and take off) 飞机场

field hockey /'fiːld hɒki/ *American English for* HOCKEY 美式英语，即 hockey

fierce /fɪəs/ *adjective* 形容词 (fiercer, fiercest)
1 angry and wild 凶猛的；凶残的：*a fierce dog* 恶狗
2 very strong 强烈的；猛烈的：*the fierce heat of the sun* 太阳的炽热

fifteen ○━ /ˌfɪf'tiːn/ *number* 数词
15 十五
▶ **fifteenth** /ˌfɪf'tiːnθ/ *pronoun, adjective, adverb* 代词，形容词，副词 15th 第十五

fifth ○━ /fɪfθ/ *pronoun, adjective, adverb* 代词，形容词，副词
1 5th 第五
2 one of five equal parts of something; ⅕ 五分之一

fifty ○━ /'fɪfti/ *number* 数词
1 50 五十
2 the fifties (*plural* 用复数形式) the numbers, years or temperature between 50 and 59 五十几；五十年代：*He was born in the fifties* (= in the 1950s). 他生于 20 世纪 50 年代。
in your fifties between the ages of 50 and 59 * 50 多岁：*Her husband died when she was in her fifties.* 她 50 多岁时丈夫去世。
▶ **fiftieth** /'fɪftiəθ/ *pronoun, adjective, adverb* 代词，形容词，副词 50th 第五十

fig 无花果

fig /fɪg/ *noun* 名词
a soft sweet fruit that is full of small seeds 无花果

fight[1] ○━ /faɪt/ *verb* 动词 (fights, fighting, fought /fɔːt/, has fought)
1 When people **fight**, they try to hurt or kill each other. 打斗；打架；战斗：*Our grandfather fought in the war.* 我们的爷爷打过仗。◇ *My brothers are always fighting.* 我的兄弟总是在打架。
2 to try very hard to stop something 与…斗争：*He fought against the illness for two years.* 他跟疾病抗争了两年。
3 to try very hard to do or get something （为…而）奋斗；争取：*The workers are fighting for better pay.* 工人正在尽力争取加薪。
4 to argue 争吵；吵架：*It's not worth*

A

B

C

D

E

F

G

H

I

J

K

L

M

N

O

P

Q

R

S

T

U

V

W

X

Y

Z

fighting about money. 为钱争吵很不值得。

fight² ⊶ /faɪt/ *noun* 名词
when people try to hurt or kill each other 打斗；打架；战斗: *Don't get into a fight.* 不要打架。◇ *A fight broke out between the two gangs.* 两帮人打了起来。

fighter /'faɪtə(r)/ *noun* 名词
1 (*also* 亦作 **fighter plane** /'faɪtə pleɪn/) a fast plane that shoots at other planes during a war 战斗机；歼击机
2 a person who fights 战士；战斗者

figure ⊶ /'fɪɡə(r)/ *noun* 名词
1 one of the symbols (0–9) that we use to show numbers（从 0 到 9 的）数字: *Shall I write the numbers in words or figures?* 这些数目我用文字写还是用数字写?
2 an amount or price 数额；价格: *What are our sales figures for Spain this year?* 我们今年对西班牙的销售额是多少?
3 the shape of a person's body 身材；体形: *She's got a good figure.* 她身材苗条。
4 a shape of a person that you cannot see clearly（隐约可见的）人影: *I saw a tall figure outside the window.* 我看到窗外有个高大的身影。
5 figures (*plural* 用复数形式) (*informal* 非正式) working with numbers to find an answer 算术 ● SAME MEANING **mathematics** 同义词为 mathematics: *I'm not very good at figures.* 我算术不太好。

figure of speech /ˌfɪɡər əv 'spiːtʃ/ *noun* 名词 (*plural* 复数形式 **figures of speech**)
a word or phrase used in a different way from its usual meaning to create a particular effect 修辞格；修辞手段: *I didn't really mean that she was mad – it was just a figure of speech.* 我并不是说她真的疯了，那不过是打个比方而已。

file¹ ⊶ /faɪl/ *noun* 名词
1 a box or cover for keeping papers in 文件盒；文件夹
2 a collection of information that is stored in a computer and that has a particular name（电脑）文件，文档，档案: *Did you save your file?* 你保存你的文件了吗? ◇ *You can delete that file now.* 你现在可以删除那个文件了。
3 a tool with rough sides that you use for making things smooth 锉；锉刀: *a nail file* 指甲锉
in single file in a line with each person following the one in front 一路纵队: *The children walked into the hall in single file.* 孩子鱼贯走进礼堂。

files 文件夹

file² ⊶ /faɪl/ *verb* 动词 (**files, filing, filed** /faɪld/)
1 to put papers in their correct place, for example in a cover or drawer 把…存档；归档: *Can you file these letters, please?* 请把这些信归档好吗?
2 to walk in a line, one behind the other 排成一行行走: *The students filed into the classroom.* 学生鱼贯走进教室。
3 to make something smooth using a tool with rough sides 锉平；锉光滑: *She filed her nails.* 她把指甲锉光滑了。

filing cabinet 文件柜

file 文件夹

filing cabinet /'faɪlɪŋ kæbɪnət/ *noun* 名词 (*British* 英式英语)
a piece of office furniture with large drawers, in which you keep documents 文件柜

fill ⊶ /fɪl/ *verb* 动词 (**fills, filling, filled** /fɪld/)
1 to make something full 使充满；装满；填满: *Can you fill this glass with water, please?* 请把这个玻璃杯倒满水好吗?
2 to become full 充满: *His eyes filled with tears.* 他眼里含着泪。
fill something in, fill something out to write facts or answers in the spaces that have been left for them 填写: *She*

gave me a form and told me to fill it in.
她给了我一份表格叫我填写。
fill up, **fill something up** to become
full or to make something completely full
（使）充满，填满： *The room soon filled
up.* 房间里很快挤满了人。◇ *He filled up
the tank with petrol.* 他把油箱灌满了
汽油。

filling /ˈfɪlɪŋ/ *noun* 名词
1 the substance that a dentist uses to fill
a hole in your tooth （补牙的）填料：
I've got three fillings in my teeth. 我的牙补
了三处。
2 the food that is put inside a sandwich,
cake, etc. （三明治、蛋糕等的）馅：
a choice of sandwich fillings 可供选择的
三明治馅 ◇ Look at the picture at **pie**.
见 pie 的插图。

film¹ 0ᵣ /fɪlm/ *noun* 名词
1 (*British* 英式英语) (*American* 美式英语
movie) a story shown in moving pictures
that you see on television or at the
cinema 电影；影片： *Let's go and see a
film.* 我们去看电影吧。
2 the thin plastic that you use in a
camera for taking photographs 胶卷；
胶片： *I bought a roll of black and white
film.* 我买了一卷黑白胶卷。

film² 0ᵣ /fɪlm/ *verb* 动词 (films, filming,
filmed /fɪlmd/)
to use a camera to make moving pictures
of a story, news, etc. 拍摄（电影）： *A TV
company are filming outside my house.*
有家电视公司正在我家外面拍摄。

film star /ˈfɪlm stɑː(r)/ (*British* 英式英语)
(*American* 美式英语 movie star) *noun* 名词
an actor or actress who is famous for
being in films 电影明星；影星

filter /ˈfɪltə(r)/ *noun* 名词
a thing used for holding back the solid
parts in a liquid or gas 滤器；过滤器：
a coffee filter 咖啡过滤器
▶ **filter** *verb* 动词 (filters, filtering,
filtered /ˈfɪltəd/): *Filter the water before
you drink it.* 把水过滤后再喝。

filthy /ˈfɪlθi/ *adjective* 形容词 (filthier,
filthiest)
very dirty 肮脏的；污秽的： *Go and wash
your hands. They're filthy!* 去洗洗手。
太脏了!

fin /fɪn/ *noun* 名词
one of the thin flat parts on a fish that
help it to swim 鳍 ◇ Look at the pictures
at **fish** and **shark**. 见 fish 和 shark 的
插图。

final¹ 0ᵣ /ˈfaɪnl/ *adjective* 形容词
not followed by any others 最后的；最终
的 ◇ SAME MEANING **last** 同义词为 last:
This will be our final lesson. 这将是我们
最后的一课。

final² 0ᵣ /ˈfaɪnl/ *noun* 名词
1 the last game or race in a competition,
for the winners of the earlier games or
races 决赛： *We've got through to the
final.* 我们进了决赛。
2 finals (*plural* 用复数形式) (*British* 英式
英语) the exams in your last year at
university 大学毕业考试

finally 0ᵣ /ˈfaɪnəli/ *adverb* 副词
1 after a long time 最终；终于 ◇ SAME
MEANING **in the end** 同义词为 in the end:
After a long wait the bus finally arrived.
等了很长时间，公共汽车终于来了。
2 used before saying the last thing in a
list （用于列举）最后： *And finally,
I would like to thank my parents for all
their help.* 最后，我要感谢父母给我的所有
帮助。

finance¹ /ˈfaɪnæns/ *noun* 名词
1 (*no plural* 不用复数形式) money, or the
activity of managing money 资金；财政；
金融；财务： *an expert in finance* 金融
专家 ◇ *the French Minister of Finance*
法国财政部长
2 finances (*plural* 用复数形式) the money
that you have and that you can spend
财力；财源： *You need to sort out your
finances.* 你要把自己的财政处理好。

finance² /ˈfaɪnæns/ *verb* 动词 (finances,
financing, financed /ˈfaɪnænst/)
to give the money that is needed to pay
for something 提供资金： *The building
was financed by the government.* 这栋大楼
是由政府出资的。

financial 0ᵣ /faɪˈnænʃl/ *adjective*
形容词
connected with money 财政的；金融的；
财务的： *financial problems* 财务问题

find 0ᵣ /faɪnd/ *verb* 动词 (finds, finding,
found /faʊnd/, has found)
1 to see or get something after looking or
trying 找到；找回： *I can't find my
glasses.* 我找不到我的眼镜。◇ *She hasn't
found a job yet.* 她还没找到工作。◇ *Has
anybody found the answer to this
question?* 有人找到这个问题的答案了吗?
2 to see or get something that you did
not expect 发现： *I found some money in
the street.* 我在街上捡到了一些钱。◇
I woke up and found myself in hospital.
我一醒来就发觉自己在医院里了。

A
B
C
D
E
F
G
H
I
J
K
L
M
N
O
P
Q
R
S
T
U
V
W
X
Y
Z

3 used for talking about your opinion or experience 认为；觉得： *I didn't find that book very interesting.* 我不觉得那本书很有趣。◇ *He finds it difficult to sleep at night.* 他感到晚上睡得不好。

find something out to get information about something 获知；弄清： *Can you find out what time the train leaves?* 你能查一下火车什么时候开吗？◇ *Has she found out that you broke the window?* 她有没有发现你打破了窗户？

fine¹ 0🔊 /faɪn/ *adjective* 形容词 (finer, finest)

1 beautiful or of good quality 精美的；漂亮的；高质量的： *There's a fine view from the cathedral.* 从大教堂望去，风景很美。◇ *This is one of Monet's finest paintings.* 这是莫奈最好的画作之一。

2 well or happy 健康的；愉快的： *'How are you?' 'Fine, thanks. And you?'* "你好吗？" "很好，谢谢。你呢？"

3 used for saying that something is good or acceptable 好的；行 ⊃ SAME MEANING OK 同义词为 OK： *'Let's meet on Monday.' 'Fine.'* "我们星期一见吧。" "好的。" ◇ *'Do you want some more milk in your coffee?' 'No, that's fine.'* "你咖啡里还要加点牛奶吗？" "不用了，已经够了。"

4 not raining 晴朗的 ⊃ SAME MEANING sunny 同义词为 sunny： *I hope it stays fine for our picnic.* 我希望我们野餐的时候天气还是这么好。

5 very thin 很细的；纤细的： *I've got very fine hair.* 我头发纤细。 ⊃ OPPOSITE thick 反义词为 thick

6 made of very small pieces 小颗粒的： *Salt is finer than sugar.* 盐比糖细。 ⊃ OPPOSITE coarse 反义词为 coarse

fine² /faɪn/ *noun* 名词
money that you must pay because you have done something wrong 罚款；罚金： *You'll get a fine if you park your car there.* 你要是把车停在那里会被罚款。
▶ **fine** *verb* 动词 (fines, fining, fined /faɪnd/) to make somebody pay a fine 给…罚款： *I was fined £100 for speeding (= driving too fast).* 我因超速驾驶被罚了100英镑。

finger 0🔊 /ˈfɪŋɡə(r)/ *noun* 名词
one of the five parts at the end of your hand 手指 ⊃ Look at Picture Dictionary page **P4**. 见彩页 **P4**。
keep your fingers crossed to hope that somebody or something will be successful 祈求成功： *I'll keep my fingers crossed for you in your exams.* 我会祝你考试顺利。

fingernail /ˈfɪŋɡəneɪl/ *noun* 名词
the thin hard part at the end of your finger 手指甲 ⊃ Look at the picture at **fist**. 见 **fist** 的插图。

fingerprint /ˈfɪŋɡəprɪnt/ *noun* 名词
the mark that a finger makes when it touches something 指纹；指印： *The police found his fingerprints on the gun.* 警方在枪上发现他的指纹。

fingertip /ˈfɪŋɡətɪp/ *noun* 名词
the end of your finger 指尖 ⊃ Look at the picture at **hand¹**. 见 **hand¹** 的插图。

finish¹ 0🔊 /ˈfɪnɪʃ/ *verb* 动词 (finishes, finishing, finished /ˈfɪnɪʃt/)

1 to stop doing something 完成；做好： *I finish work at half past five.* 我五点半下班。◇ *Hurry up and finish your dinner!* 赶快把饭吃完！◇ *Have you finished cleaning your room?* 你把你的房间打扫好了吗？

2 to stop happening 结束；停止： *School finishes at four o'clock.* 学校四点钟放学。 ⊃ OPPOSITE begin or start 反义词为 begin 或 start

finish something off to do or eat the last part of something 做完；吃完： *He finished off the bread.* 他把面包吃光了。

finish with something to stop needing or using something 不再需要；不再使用： *Have you finished with that book?* 那本书你看完了没有？

finish² /ˈfɪnɪʃ/ *noun* 名词 (plural 复数形式 finishes)
the last part or the end of something 最后部分；结尾；结局 ⊃ OPPOSITE start 反义词为 start： *There was a dramatic finish to the race.* 赛跑出现了戏剧性的结局。

fir /fɜː(r)/ (*also* 亦作 **fir tree** /ˈfɜː triː/) *noun* 名词
a tall tree with thin sharp leaves (called needles) that do not fall off in winter 枞；冷杉

fire¹ 0🔊 /ˈfaɪə(r)/ *noun* 名词

1 the heat and bright light that comes from burning things 火： *Many animals are afraid of fire.* 很多动物都怕火。◇ *There was a big fire at the factory last night.* 那家工厂昨晚发生了大火。

2 burning wood or coal that you use for keeping a place warm or for cooking 炉火；灶火： *They lit a fire to keep warm.* 他们生了火取暖。

3 a machine that uses electricity or gas to keep a room warm 取暖器；暖气装置： *Switch on the fire.* 打开取暖器。

catch fire to start to burn 着火；起火：
She dropped her cigarette and the chair caught fire. 她丢下香烟把椅子烧着了。
on fire burning 燃烧着： *My house is on fire!* 我的房子失火了！
put out a fire to stop something from burning 灭火： *We put out the fire with buckets of water.* 我们用一桶桶的水把火扑灭了。
set fire to something, set something on fire to make something start to burn 放火： *Somebody set the house on fire.* 有人放火把房子烧了。

fire² 0➔ /'faɪə(r)/ *verb* 动词 (fires, firing, fired /'faɪəd/)
1 to shoot with a gun 射击；开火；开枪：
*The soldiers **fired** at the enemy.* 士兵向敌人开火了。
2 to tell somebody to leave their job 解雇；开除 ⊃ SAME MEANING **sack** 同义词为 sack： *He was fired because he was always late for work.* 他因为上班老是迟到而遭解雇了。

fire alarm /'faɪər əlɑːm/ *noun* 名词
a bell that rings to tell people that there is a fire 火警钟；火警报警器

fire brigade /'faɪə brɪˌɡeɪd/ (*British* 英式英语) (*American* 美式英语 **fire department** /'faɪə dɪpɑːtmənt/) *noun* 名词
a group of people whose job is to stop fires 消防队： *Call the fire brigade!* 叫消防队来！

fire engine /'faɪər endʒɪn/ (*American also* 美式英语亦作 **fire truck** /'faɪər trʌk/) *noun* 名词
a vehicle that takes people and equipment to stop fires 消防车

fire escape /'faɪər ɪskeɪp/ *noun* 名词
stairs on the outside of a building that people can go down if there is a fire 太平梯（建筑物外供火灾时逃生用）

fire extinguisher /'faɪər ɪkˌstɪŋɡwɪʃə(r)/ *noun* 名词
a metal container with water or chemicals inside for stopping small fires 灭火器

firefighter /'faɪəfaɪtə(r)/ *noun* 名词
a person whose job is to stop fires 消防员

fireman /'faɪəmən/ (*plural* 复数形式 **firemen** /'faɪəmən/) *noun* 名词
a man whose job is to stop fires 消防员

fireplace /'faɪəpleɪs/ *noun* 名词
the place in a room where you light a fire 壁炉

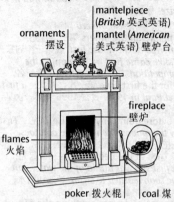

fireplace 壁炉

mantelpiece (*British* 英式英语)
mantel (*American* 美式英语) 壁炉台
ornaments 摆设
fireplace 壁炉
flames 火焰
poker 拨火棍   coal 煤

fire station /'faɪə steɪʃn/ *noun* 名词
a building where fire engines are kept 消防站

fire truck *American English for* FIRE ENGINE 美式英语，即 fire engine

firework /'faɪəwɜːk/ *noun* 名词
a thing that explodes with coloured lights and loud noises, used for entertainment 烟火；烟花： *We watched a firework display in the park.* 我们在公园里观看烟火表演。

firm¹ 0➔ /fɜːm/ *noun* 名词
a group of people working together in a business 公司；企业 ⊃ SAME MEANING **company** 同义词为 company： *My father works for a building firm.* 我父亲在一家建筑公司工作。

firm² 0➔ /fɜːm/ *adjective* 形容词 (firmer, firmest)
1 Something that is **firm** is quite hard or does not move easily. 坚硬的；牢固的；结实的： *Wait until the glue is firm.* 要等到胶水粘固。◇ *The shelf isn't very firm, so don't put too many books on it.* 这个书架不怎么结实，别放太多书上去。
2 showing that you will not change your ideas 坚定的；确定的；严格的： *She's very firm with her children* (= she makes them do what she wants). 她对孩子很严格。◇ *a firm promise* 坚定的承诺
▶ **firmly** /'fɜːmli/ *adverb* 副词： *Nail the pieces of wood together firmly.* 把这些木块钉牢在一起。◇ *'No,' she said firmly.* "不。"她坚定地说。

first¹ 0➔ /fɜːst/ *adjective* 形容词
before all the others 第一的；最初的：

January is the first month of the year. 一月是一年中第一个月份。 ◇ *You've won first prize!* 你赢了一等奖!

first² 0━ /fɜːst/ *adverb* 副词
1 before all the others 第一；首先: *I arrived at the house first.* 我第一个到家。 ◇ *Mike came first* (= he won) *in the competition.* 迈克在比赛中得了第一名。
2 for the first time 一次；首次: *I first met Paul in 1996.* 我在 1996 年第一次见到保罗。
3 before doing anything else 首先: *First fry the onions, then add the potatoes.* 先把洋葱炒一下，然后再放入土豆。
at first at the beginning 起初；起先: *At first she was afraid of the water, but she soon learned to swim.* 她起初怕水，但不久就学会了游泳。
first of all before anything else 第一；首先: *I'm going to cook dinner, but first of all I need to buy some food.* 我来做饭，但我得先去买点菜。

first³ 0━ /fɜːst/ *noun* 名词 (*no plural* 不用复数形式), *pronoun* 代词
the first a person or thing that comes earliest or before all others 第一个人（或事物）: *I was the first to arrive at the party.* 我在聚会上最早到。

first aid /ˌfɜːst 'eɪd/ *noun* 名词 (*no plural* 不用复数形式)
medical help that you give to somebody who is hurt, before a doctor comes 急救

first class /ˌfɜːst 'klɑːs/ *noun* 名词 (*no plural* 不用复数形式)
1 the part of a train, plane, etc. that it is more expensive to travel in 头等座位（或车厢、舱位）: *I got a seat in first class.* 我买了头等舱的票。
2 (*British* 英式英语) the fastest, most expensive way of sending letters 第一类邮件（邮递速度快，邮费高）
▶ **first class** *adverb* 副词: *How much does it cost to send it first class?* 以第一类邮件寄出要多少钱？ ⊃ Look at **second class** and at the note at **stamp¹**. 见 second class 和 stamp¹ 条的注释。

first-class /ˌfɜːst 'klɑːs/ *adjective* 形容词
1 excellent 一流的；优秀的: *a first-class player* 一流的球员 ◇ *I know a place where the food is first-class.* 我知道一个品尝一流美食的地方。
2 connected with the best and most expensive way of travelling on a train, plane or ship 〔座位或舱位〕头等的: *a first-class cabin* 头等舱
3 (*British* 英式英语) connected with the fastest, most expensive way of sending

letters（邮件）第一类的: *a first-class stamp* 第一类邮票

first floor /ˌfɜːst 'flɔː(r)/ *noun* 名词 the first floor
1 (*British* 英式英语) the floor of a building above the floor that is level with the street 二楼: *I live in a flat on the first floor.* 我住在二楼的一套公寓里。
2 (*American* 美式英语) (*British* 英式英语 **ground floor**) the floor of a building that is level with the street 一楼；底层

firstly /'fɜːstli/ *adverb* 副词
used when you are giving the first thing in a list（用于列举）第一，首先: *We were angry firstly because he didn't come, and secondly because he didn't phone.* 我们很生气，一是因为他没来，二是因为他也没打个电话。

first name /'fɜːst neɪm/ (*British* 英式英语) (*American* 美式英语 **given name**) *noun* 名词
the first of your names that come before your family name 名字: *'What is Mr Carter's first name?' 'Paul.'* "卡特先生的名字叫什么？""保罗。" ⊃ Look at the note at **name¹**. 见 name¹ 条的注释。

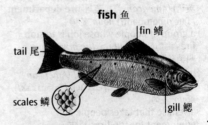

fish 鱼
fin 鳍
tail 尾
scales 鳞
gill 鳃

fish¹ 0━ /fɪʃ/ *noun* 名词 (*plural* 复数形式 **fish** or 或 **fishes**)
an animal that lives and breathes in water, and has thin flat parts (called **fins**) that help it to swim 鱼: *I caught a big fish.* 我捉到一条大鱼。 ◇ *We had fish and chips for dinner.* 我们晚饭吃的是炸鱼薯条。 ⊃ Look at Picture Dictionary page **P7**. 见彩页 P7。

🔍 **WORD BUILDING** 词汇扩充
There are many different types of **fish**. Here are some of them: cod, eel, goldfish, salmon, sardine, shark. Do you know any others? * fish 的种类很多，如: cod（鳕鱼）、eel（鳗）、goldfish（金鱼）、salmon（鲑）、

sardine（沙丁鱼）、shark（鲨鱼）。你还知道别的吗？

fish² 0🔻 /fɪʃ/ *verb* 动词 (fishes, fishing, fished /fɪʃt/)
to try to catch fish 捕鱼；钓鱼

> 🔎 GRAMMAR 语法说明
> When you talk about spending time fishing as a sport, you often say **go fishing**. 钓鱼作为消遣时常说 go fishing： *I go fishing at weekends.* 我周末通常去钓鱼。

▸ **fishing** /ˈfɪʃɪŋ/ *noun* 名词 (*no plural* 不用复数形式)： *Fishing is a major industry in Iceland.* 捕鱼业是冰岛的一个主要产业。

fisherman /ˈfɪʃəmən/ *noun* 名词 (*plural* 复数形式 **fishermen** /ˈfɪʃəmən/)
a person who catches fish as a job or sport 渔民；钓鱼的人

fishing rod /ˈfɪʃɪŋ rɒd/ *noun* 名词
a long thin stick with a thin thread (called a **line**) and a hook, used for catching fish 钓竿

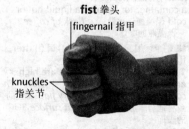

fist 拳头
fingernail 指甲
knuckles 指关节

fist /fɪst/ *noun* 名词
a hand with the fingers closed tightly 拳头： *She banged on the door with her fist.* 她用拳头砰砰地敲门。

fit¹ 0🔻 /fɪt/ *verb* 动词 (fits, fitting, fitted)
1 to be the right size or shape for somebody or something（尺寸或形状）适合，合身： *I tried the dress on, but it didn't fit.* 我试穿了连衣裙，但不合身。
◇ *This key doesn't fit the lock.* 这把钥匙打不开这把锁。
2 to put or fix something somewhere 安装；组装： *They fitted a smoke alarm to the ceiling.* 他们在天花板上装了烟雾警报器。◇ *Can you fit these pieces of the puzzle together?* 你能把这些拼图块件拼起来吗？
fit somebody or 或 **something in**
1 to find time to see somebody or do

something 安排时间（见某人或做某事）： *The doctor can fit you in at 10.30.* 医生可以在 10 点 30 分见你。
2 to find or have enough space for somebody or something 找到足够的空间： *We can't fit in any more chairs.* 我们没有地方可以放更多的椅子了。

fit² 0🔻 /fɪt/ *adjective* 形容词 (fitter, fittest)
1 healthy and strong 健康的；健壮的： *I keep fit by jogging every day.* 我每天慢跑来保持身体健康。
2 good enough 合适的；胜任的 ⊃ SAME MEANING **suitable** 同义词为 suitable： *This food isn't fit to eat.* 这种食物不适宜食用。
◇ *Do you think she's fit for the job?* 你觉得她能胜任这份工作吗？ ⊃ OPPOSITE **unfit** 反义词为 unfit

fit³ /fɪt/ *noun* 名词
1 a sudden illness in which somebody becomes unconscious and may make violent movements 昏厥；痉挛
2 when you cannot stop laughing, coughing, or feeling angry 一阵（忍不住的大笑、咳嗽、怒气）： *We were in fits of laughter.* 我们都笑得前仰后合。◇ *a fit of anger* 一阵愤怒

fitness /ˈfɪtnəs/ *noun* 名词 (*no plural* 不用复数形式)
being healthy and strong 健康；健壮

five 0🔻 /faɪv/ *number* 数词
5 五

fix 0🔻 /fɪks/ *verb* 动词 (fixes, fixing, fixed /fɪkst/)
1 to put something in a place so that it will not move 使固定；安装： *We fixed the shelf to the wall.* 我们把架子固定在墙上。
2 to decide a date or an amount for something 确定；决定 ⊃ SAME MEANING **set** 同义词为 set： *They've fixed a date for the wedding.* 他们已经定下婚礼的日子。
3 to repair something 修理： *The light isn't working – can you fix it?* 这盏灯不亮了，你会修吗？

fixed 0🔻 /fɪkst/ *adjective* 形容词
1 already decided 已定的；固定的： *a fixed price* 固定价格
2 not changing 固定不变的： *He has such fixed ideas that you can't discuss anything with him.* 他很固执己见，你无法和他讨论任何事。

fizzy /ˈfɪzi/ *adjective* 形容词 (fizzier, fizziest)
(used about a drink) containing many small bubbles of gas（饮料）有汽的： *Do you like fizzy drinks?* 你喜欢喝汽水吗？

A
B
C
D
E
F
G
H
I
J
K
L
M
N
O
P
Q
R
S
T
U
V
W
X
Y
Z

flags 旗子

—— flagpole
旗杆

flag �o╾ /flæg/ *noun* 名词
a piece of cloth with a pattern on it which
is joined to a stick (called a **flagpole**).
Every country has its own **flag**. 旗:
The flag is flying for the Queen's birthday.
旗帜正为庆祝女王的生日而飘扬。

flake /fleɪk/ *noun* 名词
a small thin piece of something 小薄片:
huge flakes of snow 大雪花

flame o╾ /fleɪm/ *noun* 名词
a hot bright pointed piece of fire 火焰:
The house was in flames (= burning).
房子一片火海。◇ *The paper burst into
flames* (= began to burn). 纸燃烧了起来。
⊃ Look at the picture at **fireplace**.
见 fireplace 的插图。

flap¹ /flæp/ *noun* 名词
a piece of material, paper, etc. that is
fixed to something at one side only, often
covering an opening（尤指开口处的）
口盖，封舌: *the flap of the envelope*
信封的封舌

flap² /flæp/ *verb* 动词 (flaps, flapping,
flapped /flæpt/)
to move or to make something move up
and down or from side to side 拍打;
扇动: *The sails of the boat flapped in
the wind.* 船帆在风中摆动。◇ *The bird
flapped its wings.* 鸟儿拍打着翅膀。

flare¹ /fleə(r)/ *verb* 动词 (flares, flaring,
flared /fleəd/)
flare up
1 to suddenly burn more strongly
烧旺起来
2 to suddenly start or get worse 突发;
突然加剧: *The pain flared up again.* 疼痛
突然又加剧了。

flare² /fleə(r)/ *noun* 名词
a thing that produces a bright light or
flame, used especially as a signal（尤指
用作信号的）闪光装置，闪光信号灯

flash¹ o╾ /flæʃ/ *verb* 动词 (flashes,
flashing, flashed /flæʃt/)
1 to send out a bright light that comes
and goes quickly; to make something do
this 闪烁; 使闪光: *The light kept flashing
on and off.* 灯光闪烁不停。◇ *She flashed
her headlights at the other driver.* 她向另
一个司机闪车头灯。
2 to appear and disappear very quickly,
or to make something do this 掠过;
使闪现: *I saw something flash past the
window.* 我看见有东西在窗前闪过。
◇ *They flashed the answer up on the TV
screen.* 他们把答案显示在电视屏幕上。

flash² o╾ /flæʃ/ *noun* 名词 (*plural* 复数
形式 flashes)
1 a bright light that comes and goes
quickly 闪光: *a flash of lightning* 一道闪电
2 a bright light that you use with a
camera for taking photographs when it is
dark（照相机的）闪光灯
in a flash very quickly 转瞬间; 刹那间:
The weekend was over in a flash. 周末转眼
就过了。

flashlight /'flæʃlaɪt/ *American English for*
TORCH 美式英语，即 torch

flask /flɑːsk/ *noun* 名词
a container for keeping a liquid hot or
cold 保温瓶; 冰瓶: *a flask of coffee*
一保温瓶的咖啡

flat¹ o╾ /flæt/ *adjective* 形容词 (flatter,
flattest)
1 smooth, with no parts that are higher
or lower than the rest 平的; 平坦的: *The
countryside in Holland is very flat.* 荷兰的
乡村地势十分平坦。◇ *a flat surface* 平坦
的表面
2 a tyre that is **flat** does not have enough
air inside it.（轮胎）瘪了的，撒了气的

flat² o╾ /flæt/ *noun* 名词 (*British* 英式
英语) (*American* 美式英语 apartment)
a group of rooms for living in, usually
on one floor of a house or big building
公寓; 套房; 单元房

🔍 WORD BUILDING 词汇扩充
A tall building with a lot of flats in it is
called a **block of flats**. 公寓楼叫做
block of flats。
---

flat³ /flæt/ *adverb* 副词
with no parts that are higher or lower
than the rest 平坦地: *He lay flat on his
back on the floor.* 他平躺着，仰卧在地板
上。

flatten /'flætn/ *verb* 动词 (flattens,
flattening, flattened /'flætnd/)

to make something flat 使变平；弄平：
I sat on the box and flattened it. 我坐在箱子上，把它坐扁了。

flatter /ˈflætə(r)/ *verb* 动词 (flatters, flattering, flattered /ˈflætəd/)
1 to say nice things about somebody, because you want them to do something 奉承；讨好；恭维
2 If you are **flattered** by something, you like it because it makes you feel important. 感到荣幸：*I'm flattered that she wants my advice.* 她想听我的意见，我倍感荣幸。

flattering /ˈflætərɪŋ/ *adjective* 形容词
making somebody look or sound more attractive or important than they really are 奉承的；讨好的：*flattering remarks* 奉承话

flattery /ˈflætəri/ *noun* 名词 (*no plural* 不用复数形式)
nice things that somebody says when they want you to do something 奉承；恭维

flatware /ˈflætweə(r)/ *American English for* CUTLERY 美式英语，即 cutlery

flavour 0➡ (*British* 英式英语) (*American* 美式英语 flavor) /ˈfleɪvə(r)/ *noun* 名词
the taste of food 味道：*They sell 20 different flavours of ice cream.* 他们出售 20 种不同味道的冰激凌。
▶ **flavour** *verb* 动词 (flavours, flavouring, flavoured /ˈfleɪvəd/): *chocolate-flavoured milk* 巧克力味牛奶

flea /fliː/ *noun* 名词
a very small insect without wings that can jump and that lives on and bites animals and people 跳蚤：*Our cat has got fleas.* 我们的猫身上有跳蚤。

flee /fliː/ *verb* 动词 (flees, fleeing, fled /fled/, has fled)
to run away from something bad or dangerous 逃难；逃生：*During the war, thousands of people fled the country.* 战争期间，成千上万的人逃离了这个国家。

fleece /fliːs/ *noun* 名词
1 the wool coat of a sheep 羊毛
2 a jacket or sweater made from a type of soft warm cloth (also called **fleece**) 绒头织物短上衣（或上衣）

fleet /fliːt/ *noun* 名词
a big group of ships 舰队；船队

flesh /fleʃ/ *noun* 名词 (*no plural* 不用复数形式)
the soft part of your body under your skin 肉

> 🔍 **WORD BUILDING** 词汇扩充
> The flesh of an animal that we eat is called **meat**. 食用的肉叫做 meat。

flew *form of* FLY[1] * fly[1] 的不同形式

flex /fleks/ *noun* 名词 (*British* 英式英语) (*plural* 复数形式 flexes) (*American* 美式英语 **cord**)
a piece of wire covered with plastic, which carries electricity to electrical equipment 花线；皮线

flexible /ˈfleksəbl/ *adjective* 形容词
1 able to change easily 灵活的；容易变动的：*We can start earlier if you like – I can be flexible.* 你想的话，我们可以早点开始。我的时间比较灵活。◇ *flexible working hours* 弹性工作时间
2 able to bend easily without breaking 柔韧的；可弯曲的

flies
1 *form of* FLY[1] * fly[1] 的不同形式
2 *plural of* FLY[2] * fly[2] 的复数形式

flight 0➡ /flaɪt/ *noun* 名词
1 (*plural* 复数形式 flights) a journey in a plane 飞机航程；航班：*Our flight leaves at 10 a.m.* 我们的航班上午 10 点钟起飞。◇ *a direct flight from London to Singapore* 伦敦到新加坡的直飞航班
2 (*no plural* 不用复数形式) flying 飞行：*Have you ever seen an eagle in flight?* 你见过飞翔的鹰吗？
3 a group of steps 一段楼梯：*We carried the sofa up a flight of stairs.* 我们抬着沙发走上了一段楼梯。

flight attendant /ˈflaɪt ətendənt/ *noun* 名词
a person whose job is to serve and take care of passengers on a plane 飞机乘务员；空中服务人员；空服员

fling /flɪŋ/ *verb* 动词 (flings, flinging, flung /flʌŋ/, has flung)
to throw something carelessly or with great force 随手扔；用力扔：*She flung her coat on the chair.* 她把大衣扔在了椅子上。

flip-flop /ˈflɪp flɒp/ (*American* 美式英语 **thong**) *noun* 名词
a simple open shoe with a narrow piece of material that goes between your big toe and the toe next to it 人字拖鞋

flippant /ˈflɪpənt/ *adjective* 形容词
not serious about important things 轻率的：*a flippant answer* 轻率的回答

flipper /ˈflɪpə(r)/ *noun* 名词
1 a flat part of the body of some sea

animals which they use for swimming （某些海洋动物的）鳍肢，鳍足： *Seals have flippers.* 海豹有鳍肢。 ➲ Look at the picture at **seal**[1]. 见 seal[1] 的插图。
2 a flat rubber shoe that you wear to help you swim fast underwater 脚蹼；鸭脚板；蛙鞋 ➲ Look at the picture at **scuba-diving**. 见 scuba-diving 的插图。

flirt /flɜːt/ ***verb*** 动词 (**flirts, flirting, flirted**)
to behave as if you like somebody in a sexual way 调情；打情骂俏： *Jo was **flirting with** him at the party.* 乔在聚会上和他打情骂俏。
▶ **flirt** ***noun*** 名词 a person who **flirts** a lot with different people 爱调情的人

float 0━ /fləʊt/ ***verb*** 动词 (**floats, floating, floated**)
1 to stay on top of a liquid 浮；漂浮： *Wood floats on water.* 木浮于水。
➲ OPPOSITE **sink** 反义词为 sink
2 to move slowly in the air 飘动；飘移： *Clouds were floating across the sky.* 朵朵云彩在天空飘着。

flock /flɒk/ ***noun*** 名词
a group of sheep or birds 羊群；鸟群： *a flock of geese* 一群鹅 ➲ Look at **herd**[1]. 见 herd[1]。

flood[1] 0━ /flʌd/ ***noun*** 名词
1 When there is a **flood**, a lot of water covers the land. 洪水；水灾： *Many homes were destroyed in the flood.* 许多家园在水灾中毁掉了。 ➲ Look at Picture Dictionary page **P16**. 见彩页 P16。
2 a lot of something 大批；大量： *The child was in **floods of tears*** (= crying a lot). 那个孩子哭得泪人儿似的。

flood[2] /flʌd/ ***verb*** 动词 (**floods, flooding, flooded**)
to fill a place with water; to be filled or covered with water 淹没；泛滥： *A pipe burst and flooded the kitchen.* 水管爆裂，厨房到处是水。

floodlight /ˈflʌdlaɪt/ ***noun*** 名词
a powerful light that is used outside, for example near a building or for sports 泛光灯（用于户外照明的强力电灯）

floor 0━ /flɔː(r)/ ***noun*** 名词
1 the part of a room that you walk on 地板；地面： *There weren't any chairs so we sat **on the floor**.* 没有椅子，我们就坐在地板上了。
2 all the rooms at the same height in a building 楼层： *I live on the top floor.* 我住在顶层。 ◇ *Our hotel room was on the sixth floor.* 我们的旅馆房间在七楼。

> **WHICH WORD? 词语辨析**
> The part of a building that is on the same level as the street is called the **ground floor** in British English and the **first floor** in American English. 地面的楼层（一楼）在英式英语中叫做 ground floor，美式英语叫做 first floor。

floorboard /ˈflɔːbɔːd/ ***noun*** 名词
a long flat piece of wood in a wooden floor 木质地板条 ➲ Look at Picture Dictionary page **P10**. 见彩页 P10。

floppy disk /ˌflɒpi ˈdɪsk/ (*also* 亦作 **floppy**) (*plural* 复数形式 **floppies**) ***noun*** 名词
a small flat piece of plastic that stores information for a computer 软（磁）盘；软碟

florist /ˈflɒrɪst/ ***noun*** 名词
1 a person who owns or works in a shop that sells flowers 花店店主；花店店员
2 florist's a shop that sells flowers 花店

flour 0━ /ˈflaʊə(r)/ ***noun*** 名词 (*no plural* 不用复数形式)

> **PRONUNCIATION 读音说明**
> The word **flour** sounds just like **flower**.
> * flour 读音同 flower。

soft white or brown powder that we use to make bread, cakes, etc. 面粉

flourish /ˈflʌrɪʃ/ ***verb*** 动词 (**flourishes, flourishing, flourished** /ˈflʌrɪʃt/)
to develop or grow successfully 繁荣；昌盛；茁壮成长： *Their business is flourishing.* 他们的生意蒸蒸日上。 ◇ *These plants flourish in a sunny position.* 这些植物在阳光充足的位置生长茂盛。

flow[1] 0━ /fləʊ/ ***noun*** 名词 (*no plural* 不用复数形式)
a steady, continuous movement of something in one direction 流；流动： *I used a handkerchief to stop the flow of blood.* 我用手帕止住了血。 ◇ *the steady flow of traffic through the city* 城市中持续平稳的交通流量

flow[2] 0━ /fləʊ/ ***verb*** 动词 (**flows, flowing, flowed** /fləʊd/)
to move in a steady, continuous way in one direction 流；流动： *This river flows into the North Sea.* 这条河流入北海。

flower 0━ /ˈflaʊə(r)/ ***noun*** 名词
the brightly coloured part of a plant that comes before the seeds or fruit 花；花朵： *She gave me a bunch of flowers.*

她给了我一束花。 ⊃ Look at the picture at **plant**¹. 见 plant¹ 的插图。

> 🔎 **WORD BUILDING** 词汇扩充
>
> There are many different types of **flower**. Here are some of them: carnation, daffodil, daisy, rose, tulip, violet. Do you know any others?
> * flower 的种类很多，如：carnation（康乃馨）、daffodil（黄水仙）、daisy（雏菊）、rose（玫瑰）、tulip（郁金香）、violet（紫罗兰）。你还知道别的吗？

flowerpot /'flaʊəpɒt/ *noun* 名词
a container in which you grow plants 花盆

flowery /'flaʊəri/ (*also* 亦作 **flowered** /'flaʊəd/) *adjective* 形容词
covered or decorated with flowers 覆盖着花的；饰以花卉图案的： *She was wearing a flowery dress.* 她穿着花布连衣裙。

flown *form of* FLY¹ * fly¹ 的不同形式

flu /fluː/ *noun* 名词 (*no plural* 不用复数形式)
an illness like a very bad cold that makes your body sore and hot 流行性感冒；流感： *I think I've got flu.* 我想我是得了流感。

fluent /'fluːənt/ *adjective* 形容词
1 able to speak easily and correctly（指人说话）流利的： *Ramon is fluent in English and French.* 拉蒙的英语和法语都很流利。
2 spoken easily and correctly（指语言）通顺的，流畅的： *She speaks fluent Arabic.* 她说一口流利的阿拉伯语。
▸ **fluently** /'fluːəntli/ *adverb* 副词： *She speaks five languages fluently.* 她能流利地说五种语言。

fluff /flʌf/ *noun* 名词 (*no plural* 不用复数形式)
very light, soft pieces of wool, cotton, or fur, or very light and soft new feathers（羊毛、棉花等形成轻软的）绒毛

fluffy /'flʌfi/ *adjective* 形容词 (**fluffier**, **fluffiest**)
feeling or looking very light and soft 毛茸茸的；轻软的： *a fluffy kitten* 毛茸茸的小猫 ◇ *fluffy clouds* 如絮的云朵

fluid /'fluːɪd/ *noun* 名词
a liquid 流质；液体： *The doctor told her to drink plenty of fluids.* 医生叫她多喝流质。

flung *form of* FLING * fling 的不同形式

flush /flʌʃ/ *verb* 动词 (**flushes**, **flushing**, **flushed** /flʌʃt/)
1 to clean a toilet by pressing or pulling a handle that sends water through it 冲厕所： *Remember to flush the toilet.* 记住冲抽水马桶。
2 If you **flush**, your face goes red because you are embarrassed or angry. 脸红： *He flushed with anger.* 他气得满脸通红。

flute 长笛

flute /fluːt/ *noun* 名词
a musical instrument that you hold out to the side and play by blowing 长笛

flutter /'flʌtə(r)/ *verb* 动词 (**flutters**, **fluttering**, **fluttered** /'flʌtəd/)
to make a quick, light movement through the air 飘动；扇动；挥动： *Flags fluttered in the breeze.* 旗帜在微风中飘扬。

fly¹ ∘⇥ /flaɪ/ *verb* 动词 (**flies**, **flying**, **flew** /fluː/, *has* **flown** /fləʊn/)
1 to move through the air 飞；飞行；飞翔： *In autumn some birds fly to warmer countries.* 秋天有些鸟会飞往暖和的地方。
2 to make an aircraft move through the air 驾驶（飞机）： *A pilot is a person who flies an aircraft.* 飞行员是驾驶飞机的。
3 to travel in a plane（乘坐飞机）飞行： *I'm flying to Abu Dhabi tomorrow.* 我明天坐飞机去阿布扎比。
4 to move quickly 迅速移动： *The door suddenly flew open and John came in.* 门猛地一开，约翰便进来了。 ◇ *A stone came flying through the window.* 一块石头从窗外飞了进来。

fly 苍蝇

fly² ∘⇥ /flaɪ/ *noun* 名词 (*plural* 复数形式 **flies**)
1 a small insect with two wings 苍蝇
2 (*British also* 英式英语亦作 **flies**) the part where you fasten a pair of trousers at the front（裤子的）前裆开口： *Your fly is undone!* 你的裤子前裆没拉上！

A B C D E F G H I J K L M N O P Q R S T U V W X Y Z

flying 0-π /ˈflaɪɪŋ/ *adjective* 形容词
able to fly 会飞行的： *flying insects* 飞虫
with flying colours with great success; very well 非常成功： *They all passed the exam with flying colours.* 他们都以优异成绩通过了考试。

flying saucer /ˌflaɪɪŋ ˈsɔːsə(r)/ *noun* 名词
a flying object that some people think they have seen, and that they think has come from another planet 飞碟

flyover /ˈflaɪəʊvə(r)/ (*British* 英式英语) (*American* 美式英语 **overpass**) *noun* 名词
a bridge that carries a road over other roads 跨线桥；立交桥；立体交叉道

foal /fəʊl/ *noun* 名词
a young horse 小马驹

foam /fəʊm/ *noun* 名词 (*no plural* 不用复数形式)
a lot of very small white bubbles that you see when you move liquid quickly 泡沫

focus[1] /ˈfəʊkəs/ *verb* 动词 (**focuses, focusing, focused** /ˈfəʊkəst/)
1 to give all your attention to something 集中注意力；专注于： *to focus on a problem* 集中注意一个问题
2 to move part of a camera, etc. so that you can see things through it clearly （照相机等）调节焦距

focus[2] /ˈfəʊkəs/ *noun* 名词 (*no plural* 不用复数形式)
special attention that is given to somebody or something 焦点： *It was the main **focus of attention** at the meeting.* 那是会议关注的主要焦点。
in focus, out of focus If a photograph is **in focus**, it is clear. If it is **out of focus**, it is not. （相片）聚焦清楚，不清楚

foetus (*British* 英式英语) (*American* 美式英语 **fetus**) /ˈfiːtəs/ (*plural* 复数形式 **foetuses, fetuses**) *noun* 名词
a young human or animal that is still growing inside its mother's body 胎儿

fog /fɒg/ *noun* 名词 (*no plural* 不用复数形式)
thick cloud which forms close to the ground, and which is difficult to see through 雾： *The fog will clear by late morning.* 快到中午的时候雾就会散去。
➲ Look at Picture Dictionary page **P16**. 见彩页 P16。
▸ **foggy** /ˈfɒgi/ *adjective* 形容词 (**foggier, foggiest**): *a foggy day* 雾天 ◇ *It was very foggy this morning.* 今天早上雾很大。

foil /fɔɪl/ *noun* 名词 (*no plural* 不用复数形式)
thin metal paper that is used for covering food 锡纸；箔纸： *Wrap the meat in foil and put it in the oven.* 把肉用箔纸包好再放入烤箱。

fold 折叠

She's **folding** paper. 她在折纸。　a **folding** chair 折叠椅

fold[1] 0-π /fəʊld/ *verb* 动词 (**folds, folding, folded**) (*also* 亦作 **fold up**)
1 to bend something so that one part is on top of another part 折叠： *I folded the letter and put it in the envelope.* 我把信折好放进信封里了。 ◇ *Fold up your clothes.* 把你的衣服叠起来。 ➲ OPPOSITE **unfold** 反义词为 unfold
2 to be able to be made smaller in order to be carried or stored more easily 可折叠： *a folding chair* 折叠椅 ◇ *This table folds up flat.* 这张桌子能折平。
fold your arms If you **fold** your arms, you cross them in front of your chest. 双臂交叉于胸前： *She folded her arms and waited.* 她双臂交叉抱在胸前等着。

fold your arms 交叉双臂

He **folded** his arms.
他双臂交叉在胸前。

fold² 0️⃣ /fəʊld/ *noun* 名词
a line that is made when you bend cloth or paper 褶痕；褶线

folder /'fəʊldə(r)/ *noun* 名词
1 a cover made of cardboard or plastic for keeping papers in 文件夹；纸夹
2 a collection of information or files on one subject that is stored in a computer or on a disk（电脑）文件夹

folk /fəʊk/ *noun* 名词 (*plural* 用复数形式) (*British* 英式英语) (*American* 美式英语 **folks**)
people（泛指）人：*There are a lot of old folk living in this village.* 这个村子里住着很多老人。

folk dance /'fəʊk dɑːns/ *noun* 名词
a traditional dance 土风舞；民间舞蹈：*the folk dances of Turkey* 土耳其的民间舞蹈

folk song /'fəʊk sɒŋ/ *noun* 名词
a traditional song 民歌；民谣

follow 0️⃣ /'fɒləʊ/ *verb* 动词 (**follows, following, followed** /'fɒləʊd/)
1 to come or go after somebody or something 跟着；跟随：*Follow me and I'll show you the way.* 跟我来，我告诉你怎么走。◇ *I think that car is following us!* 我觉得那辆车在跟着我们！◇ *The film will be followed by the news.* 紧接这部影片播出的是新闻报道。
2 to go along a road, path, etc. 沿着：*Follow this road for about a mile and then turn right.* 沿着这条路走大约一英里，然后向右拐。
3 to do what somebody says you should do 遵从；跟从：*I'd like you all to follow my instructions carefully.* 我要你们都小心按照我的指示做。
4 to understand something 理解；明白：*Has everyone followed the lesson so far?* 到目前为止，大家是否都明白这堂课？
as follows as you will now hear or read 如下：*The dates of the meetings will be as follows: 21 March, 3 April, 19 April.* 会议的日期如下：3月21日、4月3日、4月19日。

following 0️⃣ /'fɒləʊɪŋ/ *adjective* 形容词
next 接着的；下一个的：*I saw him the following day.* 接着那天我看见了他。

fond /fɒnd/ *adjective* 形容词 (**fonder, fondest**)
be fond of somebody or 或 **something** to like somebody or something a lot 喜爱：*They are very fond of their uncle.* 他们非常喜欢他们的舅舅。

food 0️⃣ /fuːd/ *noun* 名词 (*no plural* 不用复数形式)
things that people or animals eat 食物；食品：*Let's go and get some food – I'm hungry.* 我们去吃点东西吧，我饿了。◇ *They gave the horses food and water.* 他们给马喂食和饮水。

fool¹ /fuːl/ *noun* 名词
a person who is silly or who does something silly 笨蛋；傻瓜：*You fool! You forgot to lock the door!* 你这个傻瓜！你忘了锁门了！
make a fool of yourself to do something that makes you look silly in front of other people 出丑：*He always makes a fool of himself at parties.* 他总是在聚会上出洋相。

fool² /fuːl/ *verb* 动词 (**fools, fooling, fooled** /fuːld/)
to make somebody believe something that is not true 愚弄；欺骗 ➲ SAME MEANING **trick** 同义词为 trick：*You can't fool me! I know you're lying!* 你骗不了我的！我知道你在撒谎！
fool about, fool around to do silly things 犯傻；干蠢事：*Stop fooling about with that knife.* 别傻乎乎地拿着那把刀舞来舞去了。

foolish /'fuːlɪʃ/ *adjective* 形容词
stupid or silly 傻的；愚蠢的：*a foolish mistake* 愚蠢的错误
▶ **foolishly** /'fuːlɪʃli/ *adverb* 副词：*I foolishly forgot to bring a coat.* 我真笨，忘了带大衣了。

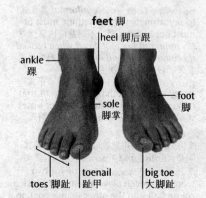

feet 脚
heel 脚后跟
ankle 踝
sole 脚掌
foot 脚
toenail 趾甲
big toe 大脚趾
toes 脚趾

foot 0️⃣ /fʊt/ *noun* 名词
1 (*plural* 复数形式 **feet** /fiːt/) the part of

A
B
C
D
E
F
G
H
I
J
K
L
M
N
O
P
Q
R
S
T
U
V
W
X
Y
Z

your leg that you stand on 脚；足： *I've been walking all day and my feet hurt.* 我走了一整天，脚都走疼了。
2 (*plural* 复数形式 **foot** or 或 **feet**) (*abbr.* 缩略式 **ft**) a measure of length (= 30.48 centimetres). There are twelve INCHES in a **foot**. 英尺（长度单位；1 英尺等于 30.48 厘米或 12 英寸）： *'How tall are you?' 'Five foot six (= five feet and six inches).'* "你有多高？" "五英尺六英寸。"

> ⌕ CULTURE 文化资料补充
>
> In the past, people in Britain used **inches**, **feet**, **yards** and **miles** to measure distances. In the US, people still use these measurements. 英国人过去用英寸（inch）、英尺（foot）、码（yard）、英里（mile）来量度距离。美国人仍然沿用。
>
> In Britain people now use both **centimetres** and **metres** as well as **feet** and **inches** but usually use **miles** instead of **kilometres**. 英国人现在既使用厘米（centimetre）和米（metre），也使用英尺（foot）和英寸（inch），但通常用英里（mile）而不用公里（kilometre）。

3 the lowest part of something 底部 ◑ SAME MEANING **bottom** 同义词为 bottom： *She was standing at the foot of the stairs.* 她站在楼梯底部。
on foot walking 走路；步行： *Shall we go by car or on foot?* 我们开车去还是走路去？
put your feet up to rest 休息： *If you're tired, put your feet up and listen to some music.* 你要是累了，就休息一下，听听音乐。
put your foot down (*informal* 非正式) to say strongly that something must or must not happen 坚决不同意；执意反对： *My mum put her foot down when I asked if I could stay out all night.* 我问妈妈我可否在外面过夜，她坚决表示不行。
put your foot in it (*informal* 非正式) to say or do something by accident that makes somebody embarrassed or upset 说错话让人尴尬；言行不小心冒犯别人

football ⚿ /ˈfʊtbɔːl/ *noun* 名词
1 (*no plural* 不用复数形式) (*British* 英式英语) (*British and American also* 英式和美式英语亦作 **soccer**) a game for two teams of eleven players who try to kick a round ball into the other team's goal on a field (called a **football pitch**) 足球运动： *Peter's playing in a **football match** tomorrow.* 彼得明天要参加足球比赛。

◑ Look at Picture Dictionary page **P14**. 见彩页 P14。
2 *American English for* AMERICAN FOOTBALL 美式英语，即 American football
3 (*plural* 复数形式 **footballs**) a ball for playing this game 足球

footballer /ˈfʊtbɔːlə(r)/ *noun* 名词
a person who plays football 足球运动员： *a professional footballer* 职业足球运动员

footpath /ˈfʊtpɑːθ/ *noun* 名词
a path in the country for people to walk on 人行小道

footprint /ˈfʊtprɪnt/ *noun* 名词
a mark that your foot or shoe makes on the ground 脚印；足迹

footstep /ˈfʊtstep/ *noun* 名词
the sound of a person walking 脚步声： *I heard footsteps and then a knock on the door.* 我听到有脚步声，接着是敲门声。

for¹ ⚿ /fə(r); fɔː(r)/ *preposition* 介词
1 a word that shows who will get or have something （表示受者）给： *These flowers are for you.* 这些花是给你的。
2 a word that shows how something is used or why something is done （表示用途或原因）作…之用，为了： *We had fish and chips for dinner.* 我们晚餐吃的是炸鱼和薯条。◇ *Take this medicine for your cold.* 吃这种药来治感冒吧。◇ *He was sent to prison for murder.* 他因谋杀罪被关进监狱了。
3 a word that shows how long something has been happening （表示一段时间）为时： *She has lived here for 20 years.* 她在这儿住了 20 年了。◑ Look at the note at **since**. 见 since 条的注释。
4 a word that shows how far somebody or something goes （表示距离）： *We walked for miles (= a very long way).* 我们走了很长很长的路。
5 a word that shows where a person or thing is going （表示目的地）往，向： *Is this the train for Glasgow?* 这是开往格拉斯哥的火车吗？
6 a word that shows the person or thing you are talking about 就…而言；对…来说： *It's time for us to go.* 我们该走了。
7 a word that shows how much something is （表示价格）： *I bought this book for £9.* 我花了 9 英镑买这本书。
8 a word that shows that you like an idea 支持；赞成： *Some people were for the strike and others were against it.* 有的人支持罢工，有的人反对。◑ OPPOSITE **against** 反义词为 against
9 on the side of somebody or something

为某一方；代表: *He plays football for Italy.* 他代表意大利队踢球。

10 with the meaning of 意思是: *What is the word for 'table' in German?* "桌子" 这个词用德语怎么说？

for² /fə(r)/ *conjunction* 连词 (*formal* 正式) because 因为；由于: *She was crying, for she knew they could never meet again.* 她哭了起来，因为她知道他们再也见不到面了。

> 🔊 SPEAKING 表达方式说明
> **Because** and **as** are the words that we usually use. * because 和 as 是常用词。

forbid /fə'bɪd/ *verb* 动词 (**forbids**, **forbidding**, **forbade** /fə'bæd/, has **forbidden** /fə'bɪdn/) to say that somebody must not do something 禁止；不准: *My parents have forbidden me to see him again.* 我父母不准我再见他。*Smoking is forbidden* (= not allowed) *inside the building.* 大楼内禁止吸烟。 ⊃ OPPOSITE **allow** 反义词为 allow

force¹ 0┓ /fɔːs/ *noun* 名词
1 (*no plural* 不用复数形式) power or strength 力；力量: *He was killed by the force of the explosion.* 他死于爆炸的威力。◇ *I lost the key so I had to open the door by force.* 我把钥匙丢了，只好破门而入。
2 (*plural* 复数形式 **forces**) a group of people, for example police or soldiers, who do a special job 武装力量；部队: *the police force* 警察部队

force² 0┓ /fɔːs/ *verb* 动词 (**forces**, **forcing**, **forced** /fɔːst/)
1 to make somebody do something that they do not want to do 强迫；迫使: *They forced him to give them the money.* 他们逼他给他们钱。
2 to do something by using a lot of strength 用力；强行: *The thief forced the window open.* 小偷强行把窗打开。

forecast¹ /'fɔːkɑːst/ *noun* 名词
what somebody thinks will happen, based on the information that is available 预报；预测: *The weather forecast said that it would rain today.* 天气预报说今天会下雨。

forecast² /'fɔːkɑːst/ *verb* 动词 (**forecasts**, **forecasting**, **forecast**, has **forecast**) to say what you think will happen, based on the information that is available 预报；预测 ⊃ SAME MEANING **predict** 同义词为 predict: *They've forecast rain tomorrow.* 他们预测明天有雨。
▶ **forecaster** /'fɔːkɑːstə(r)/ *noun* 名词:

*She's a **weather forecaster** on TV.* 她是电视天气预报员。

foreground /'fɔːɡraʊnd/ *noun* 名词
the part of a picture that seems nearest to you（图片中的）前景: *The man in the foreground is my father.* 照片里前面的那个人是我父亲。 ⊃ OPPOSITE **background** 反义词为 background

forehead /'fɔːhed/ *noun* 名词
the part of your face above your eyes 额；前额 ⊃ Look at Picture Dictionary page **P4**. 见彩页 P4。

foreign 0┓ /'fɒrən/ *adjective* 形容词
belonging to or connected with a country that is not your own 外国的；国外的: *We've got some foreign students staying at our house.* 我们家住着一些外国留学生。◇ *a foreign language* 外语

foreigner /'fɒrənə(r)/ *noun* 名词
a person from another country 外国人 ⊃ Look at the note at **stranger**. 见 stranger 条的注释。

forename /'fɔːneɪm/ *noun* (*formal* 正式)
your first name 名 ⊃ Look at the note at **name¹**. 见 name¹ 条的注释。

foresee /fɔː'siː/ *verb* 动词 (**foresees**, **foreseeing**, **foresaw** /fɔː'sɔː/, has **foreseen** /fɔː'siːn/)
to know or guess what will happen in the future 预料；预见 ⊃ SAME MEANING **predict** 同义词为 predict: *Nobody could have foreseen what would happen.* 没有人预料到会发生什么。

forest 0┓ /'fɒrɪst/ *noun* 名词
a large area of land covered with trees 森林: *We went for a walk in the forest.* 我们到林中散步去了。

> 🔊 WORD BUILDING 词汇扩充
> A forest is larger than a **wood**. A **jungle** is a forest in a very hot country. 森林比树林（wood）大。热带丛林叫做 jungle。

forever /fər'evə(r)/ (*also* 亦作 **for ever**) *adverb* 副词
1 for all time 永远 ⊃ SAME MEANING **always** 同义词为 always: *I will love you forever.* 我会永远爱你。
2 (*informal* 非正式) very often 总是；老是: *I can't read because he is forever asking me questions!* 他老问我问题，我都没法看书了！

forgave *form of* FORGIVE * forgive 的不同形式

A
B
C
D
E
F
G
H
I
J
K
L
M
N
O
P
Q
R
S
T
U
V
W
X
Y
Z

forge /fɔːdʒ/ *verb* 动词 (forges, forging, forged /fɔːdʒd/)
to make an illegal copy of something in order to cheat people 伪造；假冒： *The passport had been forged.* 这个护照是伪造的。
forge somebody's signature to sign another person's name, pretending to be that person 伪造签名；冒签

forgery /'fɔːdʒəri/ *noun* 名词
1 (*no plural* 不用复数形式) the crime of making an illegal copy of something in order to cheat people 伪造（罪）
2 (*plural* 复数形式 **forgeries**) something that has been copied in order to cheat people 伪造品；赝品： *This painting is not really by Picasso – it's a forgery.* 这幅画不是毕加索的真迹，是赝品。

forget ⊶ /fə'get/ *verb* 动词 (forgets, forgetting, forgot /fə'gɒt/ , has forgotten /fə'gɒtn/)
1 to not remember something 忘记；遗忘： *I've forgotten her name.* 我忘了她的名字。◇ *Don't forget to do your homework!* 别忘了做家庭作业！
2 to not bring something with you 忘记带： *I had forgotten my glasses.* 我忘了带眼镜。
3 to stop thinking about something 不再想；不放在心上： *Forget about your exams and enjoy yourself!* 别再想着考试的事了，尽情地玩吧！

forgetful /fə'getfl/ *adjective* 形容词
often forgetting things 健忘的 ⊃ SAME MEANING **absent-minded** 同义词为 absent-minded： *My grandmother had become rather forgetful.* 我奶奶已经变得相当健忘。

forgive ⊶ /fə'gɪv/ *verb* 动词 (forgives, forgiving, forgave /fə'geɪv/, has forgiven /fə'gɪvn/)
to stop being angry with somebody for a bad thing that they did 原谅；宽恕： *I can't forgive him for behaving like that.* 我不能原谅他那种行为。

forgiveness /fə'gɪvnəs/ *noun* 名词 (*no plural* 不用复数形式)
the fact that you stop being angry with somebody for a bad thing that they did 原谅；宽恕： *He begged for forgiveness.* 他乞求宽恕。

forgot, forgotten *forms of* FORGET
* forget 的不同形式

fork ⊶ /fɔːk/ *noun* 名词
1 a thing with long points at one end, that you use for putting food in your mouth 餐叉
2 a large tool with points at one end, that you use for digging the ground（钉齿）耙
3 a place where a road or river divides into two parts 分岔处；岔口： *When you get to the fork in the road, go left.* 你到了岔口处就向左拐。

forks 餐叉；叉

form¹ ⊶ /fɔːm/ *noun* 名词
1 a type of something 类型；种类： *Cars, trains and buses are all forms of transport.* 小汽车、火车和公共汽车都是交通工具的种类。
2 a piece of paper with spaces for you to answer questions 表格： *You need to fill in this form to get a new passport.* 你得填好这份表格才能领取新护照。 ⊃ Look at Study Page S20. 见研习专页 S20。
3 the shape of a person or thing 形状；外形： *a cake in the form of a car* 汽车形状的蛋糕
4 one of the ways you write or say a word 词形；形式： *'Forgot' is a form of 'forget'.* * forgot 是 forget 的一种形式。
5 (*British* 英式英语) a class in a school 年级： *Which form are you in?* 你几年级了？

form² ⊶ /fɔːm/ *verb* 动词 (forms, forming, formed /fɔːmd/)
1 to make something or to give a shape to something 形成；使成形： *We formed a line outside the cinema.* 我们在电影院外排成了一行。◇ *In English we usually form the past tense by adding 'ed'.* 英语中一般是通过加 ed 来构成过去时。
2 to grow or take shape 演变；成形： *Ice forms when water freezes.* 水凝结时变冰。
3 to start a group or an organization 组成；组织： *The club was formed last year.* 俱乐部是去年创建的。

formal ⊶ /'fɔːml/ *adjective* 形容词
You use **formal** language or behave in a **formal** way at important or serious times and with people you do not know very well. 正式的；正规的；庄重的： *'Yours*

faithfully' is a formal way of ending a letter. * Yours faithfully 是信函的一种庄重结语。◇ *I wore a suit and tie because it was a formal dinner.* 我穿了西装，戴了领带，因为那是正式的晚宴。 ⊃ OPPOSITE **informal** 反义词为 informal

▸ **formally** /'fɔːməli/ *adverb* 副词: *'How do you do?' she said formally.* "您好！" 她庄重地说。

former /'fɔːmə(r)/ *adjective* 形容词
1 of a time before now 以前的: *the former Prime Minister* 前首相
2 the former the first of two things or people 前者: *He had to choose between losing his job and losing his family. He chose the former.* 他要在失去工作和失去家庭之间作出选择。他选择了前者。 ⊃ OPPOSITE **the latter** 反义词为 the latter

formerly /'fɔːməli/ *adverb* 副词
before this time 以前；从前: *Sri Lanka was formerly called Ceylon.* 斯里兰卡旧称锡兰。

formula /'fɔːmjələ/ *noun* 名词 (*plural* 复数形式 **formulae** /'fɔːmjuliː/ or 或 **formulas**)
1 a group of letters, numbers or symbols that show a rule in mathematics or science 公式；方程式: *The formula for finding the area of a circle is* πr^2. 求圆面积的公式是 πr^2。
2 a list of the substances that you need to make something 配方；处方: *The formula for the new drug has not yet been made public.* 新药的配方尚未公开。

fort /fɔːt/ *noun* 名词
a strong building that was made to protect a place against its enemies 堡垒；碉堡

fortnight /'fɔːtnaɪt/ *noun* 名词 (*British* 英式英语)
a period of two weeks 两星期: *I'm going on holiday for a fortnight.* 我将度假两星期。

▸ **fortnightly** /'fɔːtnaɪtli/ *adjective, adverb* 形容词，副词: *We have fortnightly meetings.* 我们每两周开一次会。

fortress /'fɔːtrəs/ *noun* 名词 (*plural* 复数形式 **fortresses**)
a large strong building that was made to protect a place against its enemies 堡垒；碉堡

fortunate /'fɔːtʃənət/ *adjective* 形容词
lucky 幸运的: *I was very fortunate to get the job.* 我很幸运得到了这份工作。 ⊃ OPPOSITE **unfortunate** 反义词为 unfortunate

▸ **fortunately** /'fɔːtʃənətli/ *adverb* 副词
⊃ SAME MEANING **luckily** 同义词为 luckily: *Fortunately, nobody was hurt in the accident.* 幸好没有人在事故中受伤。

fortune /'fɔːtʃuːn/ *noun* 名词
1 (*no plural* 不用复数形式) things that happen that you cannot control 运气 ⊃ SAME MEANING **luck** 同义词为 luck: *I had the good fortune to get the job.* 我得到了这份工作，真是好运气。
2 (*plural* 复数形式 **fortunes**) a lot of money 一大笔钱；巨款: *He made a fortune selling old cars.* 他靠卖旧车发了财。

tell somebody's fortune to say what will happen to somebody in the future 算命；看相: *The old lady said she could tell my fortune by looking at my hand.* 那个老太太说她能给我看手相。

forty ⊶ /'fɔːti/ *number* 数词

> 🔍 SPELLING 拼写说明
> Remember! There is a **U** in **four**, but no **U** in **forty**. 记住：four 拼写中含有 u，forty 没有。

1 40 四十
2 the forties (*plural* 用复数形式) the numbers, years or temperature between 40 and 49 四十几；四十年代
in your forties between the ages of 40 and 49 * 40 多岁: *I think my teacher must be in his forties.* 我觉得我的老师一定是 40 多岁。

▸ **fortieth** /'fɔːtiəθ/ *pronoun, adjective, adverb* 代词，形容词，副词 40th 第四十

forward¹ ⊶ /'fɔːwəd/ (*also* 亦作 **forwards** /'fɔːwədz/) *adverb* 副词
in the direction that is in front of you 向前: *Move forwards to the front of the train.* 往列车的前边走。 ⊃ OPPOSITE **backwards** 反义词为 backwards

look forward to something to wait for something with pleasure 期待；盼望: *We're looking forward to seeing you again.* 我们期待着再次见到你。

forward² /'fɔːwəd/ *verb* 动词 (**forwards, forwarding, forwarded**)
to send a letter that you receive at one address to another address 转寄，转投（信件）: *Could you forward all my post to me while I'm abroad?* 我出国的时候，你能把我所有的邮件转寄给我吗？

fossil /'fɒsl/ *noun* 名词
a part of a dead plant or an animal that has been in the ground for a very long time and has turned into rock 化石

A B C D E F G H I J K L M N O P Q R S T U V W X Y Z

A
B
C
D
E
F
G
H
I
J
K
L
M
N
O
P
Q
R
S
T
U
V
W
X
Y
Z

foster /'fɒstə(r)/ *verb* 动词 (fosters, fostering, fostered /'fɒstəd/)
1 (*formal* 正式) to let a good feeling or situation develop 促进；培养：*The aim is to foster good relations between the two countries.* 目的是为了促进两国的友好关系。
2 to look after another person's child in your home for a time, without becoming their legal parent 抚育寄养孩童；代养
つ Look at **adopt**. 见 adopt.
▸ **foster** *adjective* 形容词：*her foster parents* 她的寄养父母 ◇ *their foster child* 他们的寄养子女

fought *form of* FIGHT¹ * fight¹ 的不同形式

foul¹ /faʊl/ *adjective* 形容词
1 dirty, or with a bad smell or taste 肮脏的；恶臭的；难闻的：*What a foul smell!* 多难闻的气味啊！
2 very bad 很糟糕的；恶劣的：*We had foul weather all week.* 整个星期天气都很恶劣。

foul² /faʊl/ *verb* 动词 (fouls, fouling, fouled /faʊld/)
(in sport) to do something to another player that is not allowed （体育运动）犯规：*Johnson was fouled twice.* 约翰逊被判了两次犯规。
▸ **foul** *noun* 名词：*He was sent off for a foul on the goalkeeper.* 他对守门员犯规而被罚下场。

found¹ *form of* FIND * find 的不同形式

found² /faʊnd/ *verb* 动词 (founds, founding, founded)
to start a new organization 创建；创办：*This school was founded in 1865.* 这所学校创建于 1865 年。
▸ **founder** /'faʊndə(r)/ *noun* 名词
a person who starts a new organization 创始人；创办人：*the founder and president of the company* 公司的创始人兼总裁

foundation /faʊn'deɪʃn/ *noun* 名词
1 foundations (*plural* 用复数形式) the bricks or stones that form the solid base of a building, under the ground 地基；房基
2 (*no plural* 不用复数形式) the act of starting a new organization 创建；创办

fountain /'faʊntən/ *noun* 名词
water that shoots up into the air and then falls down again. You often see **fountains** in gardens and parks. 喷泉

fountain pen /'faʊntən pen/ *noun* 名词
a pen that you fill with ink 自来水笔

つ Look at Picture Dictionary page **P11**. 见彩页 P11.

four 0➤ /fɔː(r)/ *number* 数词
4 四
on all fours with your hands and knees on the ground 匍匐；趴着：*We went through the tunnel on all fours.* 我们爬着穿过地道。
▸ **fourth** /fɔːθ/ *pronoun, adjective, adverb* 代词，形容词，副词 4th 第四

fourteen 0➤ /ˌfɔː'tiːn/ *number* 数词
14 十四
▸ **fourteenth** /ˌfɔː'tiːnθ/ *pronoun, adjective, adverb* 代词，形容词，副词 14th 第十四

fox 狐狸

fox /fɒks/ *noun* 名词 (*plural* 复数形式 foxes)
a wild animal like a small dog with a long thick tail and red fur 狐；狐狸

fraction /'frækʃn/ *noun* 名词
1 an exact part of a number 分数：¼ (= a quarter) *and* ⅓ (= a third) *are fractions.* * ¼ 和 ⅓ 都是分数。
2 a very small part of something 小部分；一点点：*For a fraction of a second I thought the car would crash.* 有那么一刹那我以为要撞车了。

fountain 喷泉

fracture /ˈfræktʃə(r)/ *noun* 名词
a break in one of your bones 骨折: *She had a fracture of the arm.* 她胳膊骨折了。
▶ **fracture** *verb* 动词 (fractures, fracturing, fractured /ˈfræktʃəd/): *She fell and fractured her ankle.* 她摔了一跤，脚腕骨折了。

fragile /ˈfrædʒaɪl/ *adjective* 形容词
A thing that is **fragile** breaks easily. 易碎的；易损坏的: *Be careful with those glasses. They're very fragile.* 小心那些玻璃杯。它们很容易碎。

fragment /ˈfrægmənt/ *noun* 名词
a very small piece that has broken off something 碎片: *There were fragments of glass everywhere.* 到处都是玻璃碎片。

fragrance /ˈfreɪgrəns/ *noun* 名词
a pleasant smell 芳香；芬芳: *The flowers are chosen for their delicate fragrance.* 选这些花是因为它们气味芳香。

fragrant /ˈfreɪgrənt/ *adjective* 形容词
having a pleasant smell 芳香的；芬芳的: *The air was fragrant.* 空气中弥漫着芳香。

frail /freɪl/ *adjective* 形容词 (frailer, frailest)
not strong or healthy 虚弱的；不健康的 ⊃ SAME MEANING **weak** 同义词为 weak: *a frail old woman* 体弱的老太太

frame¹ 0- /freɪm/ *noun* 名词
1 a thin piece of wood or metal round the edge of a picture, window, mirror, etc. （画、窗、镜等的）框架
2 strong pieces of wood or metal that give something its shape 构架；支架: *the frame of the bicycle* 自行车车架
3 the metal or plastic round the edge of a pair of glasses 眼镜框 ⊃ Look at the picture at **glasses**. 见 glasses 的插图。
frame of mind the way that you feel at a particular time 心境；心情 ⊃ SAME MEANING **mood** 同义词为 mood: *I'm not in the right frame of mind for a party.* 我没心思去参加聚会。

frame² /freɪm/ *verb* 动词 (frames, framing, framed /freɪmd/)
to put a picture in a frame 加上框；给…镶边: *Let's have this photograph framed.* 我们把这张照片镶上框吧。

framework /ˈfreɪmwɜːk/ *noun* 名词
the strong part of something that gives it shape 框架；构架: *The bridge has a steel framework.* 这座桥是钢铁结构的。

frank /fræŋk/ *adjective* 形容词 (franker, frankest)
saying exactly what you think 直率的；坦率的 ⊃ SAME MEANING **honest** or **truthful** 同义词为 honest 或 truthful: *To be frank, I don't like your shirt.* 说老实话，我不喜欢你这件衬衫。
▶ **frankly** /ˈfræŋkli/ *adverb* 副词: *Tell me frankly what you think of my work.* 坦率地告诉我你对我工作的看法。

fraud /frɔːd/ *noun* 名词
1 (*no plural* 不用复数形式) doing things that are not honest to get money 欺诈；诈骗: *His father was sent to prison for fraud.* 他父亲因犯诈骗罪入狱。
2 (*plural* 复数形式 frauds) a person or thing that is not what they seem to be 骗子；冒牌货: *He said he was a police officer but I knew he was a fraud.* 他说他是警察，可是我知道他是冒充的。

fray /freɪ/ *verb* 动词 (frays, fraying, frayed /freɪd/)
If cloth **frays**, the threads become loose at the edges. （布料）磨损，起毛边: *frayed trousers* 磨损的裤子

freak /friːk/ *noun* 名词
1 (*informal* 非正式) a person with a very strong interest in something 狂热爱好者: *a health freak* 极度注重健康的人 ◇ *a computer freak* 电脑迷
2 a person who looks strange or behaves in a very strange way 怪人

freckles /ˈfreklz/ *noun* 名词 (*plural* 用复数形式)
small light brown spots on a person's skin 雀斑: *A lot of people with red hair have freckles.* 很多红头发的人都有雀斑。

free¹ 0- /friː/ *adjective, adverb* 形容词，副词 (freer, freest)
1 able to go where you want and do what you want 自由的；自由自在: *After five years in prison she was finally free.* 她坐了五年牢后终于重获自由了。 ◇ *We set the bird free (= let it go) and it flew away.* 我们把鸟儿放飞了。
2 If something is **free**, you do not have to pay for it. 免费的；不收费: *We've got some free tickets for the concert.* 我们有几张音乐会的赠票。 ◇ *Children under five travel free on trains.* 五岁以下的儿童乘坐火车不收费。
3 not busy 空闲的；有空: *Are you free this afternoon?* 今天下午你有空吗？ ◇ *I don't have much free time.* 我没有什么空闲的时间。
4 not being used 未占用的；空着的: *Excuse me, is this seat free?* 请问这个位子有人坐吗？
free from something, free of something without something bad

免受…的影响；摆脱（不快的事物）：
She was finally free from pain. 她的疼痛终
于消除了。

free² ⊶ /friː/ *verb* 动词 (frees, freeing,
freed /friːd/)
to make somebody or something free
使自由；释放： *He was freed after ten
years in prison.* 他坐了十年牢后获释了。

freedom ⊶ /ˈfriːdəm/ *noun* 名词
(*no plural* 不用复数形式)
being free 自由： *They gave their children
too much freedom.* 他们对孩子太放任了。

freeway /ˈfriːweɪ/ *American English for*
MOTORWAY 美式英语，即 motorway

freeze ⊶ /friːz/ *verb* 动词 (freezes,
freezing, froze /frəʊz/, has frozen
/ˈfrəʊzn/)
1 to become hard because it is so cold.
When water **freezes**, it becomes ice.
冻结；结冰
2 to make food very cold so that it stays
fresh for a long time 冷冻；冷藏： *frozen
vegetables* 冷冻蔬菜
3 to stop suddenly and stay very still
（顿时）停住，不动： *The cat froze when
it saw the bird.* 猫看见鸟就停住不动了。
freeze to death to be so cold that you
die 冻死

freezer /ˈfriːzə(r)/ *noun* 名词
an electric container which keeps food
very cold so that it stays fresh for a long
time 冷冻柜；冰柜 ⊅ Look at **fridge**.
见 fridge。 ⊅ Look at Picture Dictionary
page **P10**. 见彩页 P10。

freezing /ˈfriːzɪŋ/ *adjective* 形容词
very cold 非常冷的： *Can you close the
window? I'm freezing!* 你关一下窗好吗?
我冷死了!

freezing point /ˈfriːzɪŋ pɔɪnt/ *noun* 名词
(*no plural* 不用复数形式)
the temperature at which a liquid freezes
冰点： *Water has a freezing point of 0°
Celsius.* 水的冰点是零摄氏度。

freight /freɪt/ *noun* 名词 (*no plural* 不用
复数形式)
things that lorries, ships, trains and
planes carry from one place to another
（运载的）货物： *a freight train* 货运列车

French fry /ˌfrentʃ ˈfraɪ/ *American
English for* CHIP¹ (1) 美式英语，即 chip¹
第 1 义

frequent /ˈfriːkwənt/ *adjective* 形容词
happening often 常发生的；频繁的： *His
visits became less frequent.* 他来得越来越
少了。

▶ **frequently** /ˈfriːkwəntli/ *adverb* 副词
(*formal* 正式) ⊅ SAME MEANING **often** 同义
词为 often： *Simon is frequently late for
school.* 西蒙上学经常迟到。

fresh ⊶ /freʃ/ *adjective* 形容词 (fresher,
freshest)
1 (used especially about food) made or
picked not long ago; not frozen or in a tin
（食物）新鲜的，未经冷冻的，非罐装的：
I'll make some fresh coffee. 我来煮点新鲜
咖啡。 ◇ *Eat plenty of fresh fruit and
vegetables.* 要多吃新鲜水果和蔬菜。
2 new or different 新颖的；不一样的：
fresh ideas 新颖的想法
3 clean and cool 清新的；凉爽的： *Open
the window and let some fresh air in.*
把窗子打开，让新鲜空气进来。
4 (used about water) not containing salt;
not from the sea （水）淡的，无盐的
▶ **freshly** /ˈfreʃli/ *adverb* 副词： *freshly
baked bread* 刚出炉的面包

freshwater /ˈfreʃwɔːtə(r)/ *noun* 名词
not sea water 淡水

Friday ⊶ /ˈfraɪdeɪ/ *noun* 名词
the day of the week after Thursday and
before Saturday 星期五 ⊅ Look at the
note at **day**. 见 day 条的注释。

fridge /frɪdʒ/ (*American or formal* 美式
英语或正式 **refrigerator**) *noun* 名词
a metal container, usually electric, which
keeps food cold, but not frozen 冰箱；
冷藏柜： *Can you put the milk in the
fridge?* 你把牛奶放进冰箱好吗? ⊅ Look at
freezer. 见 freezer。 ⊅ Look at Picture
Dictionary page **P10**. 见彩页 P10。

fried *form of* FRY * fry 的不同形式

friend ⊶ /frend/ *noun* 名词

> 🔎 **PRONUNCIATION** 读音说明
> The word **friend** sounds like **send**,
> because we don't say the letter **i** in this
> word. * friend 读音像 send，因为 i 在
> 这里不发音。

a person that you like and know very well
朋友： *David is my best friend.* 戴维是我
最要好的朋友。 ◇ *We are very good
friends.* 我们是非常好的朋友。
make friends with somebody
to become a friend of somebody 与…交
朋友： *Have you made friends with any of
the students in your class?* 你和你的同班
同学交朋友了吗?

friendly ⊶ /ˈfrendli/ *adjective* 形容词
(friendlier, friendliest)
kind and helpful 友好的；和蔼可亲的：
My neighbours are very friendly. 我的邻居

都很友善。 ➲ OPPOSITE **unfriendly** 反义词为 unfriendly

be friendly with somebody to be somebody's friend 待⋯如朋友；跟⋯要好： *Jane is friendly with their daughter.* 简和他们的女儿感情很好。

friendship ০ᜢ /ˈfrendʃɪp/ *noun* 名词
the state of being friends with somebody 友谊；友情： *a close friendship* 亲密的友谊 ◇ *Your friendship is very important to me.* 你的友情对我很重要。

fries *form of* FRY * fry 的不同形式

fright /fraɪt/ *noun* 名词
a sudden feeling of fear 惊吓： *I hope I didn't give you a fright when I shouted.* 希望我大声叫喊的时候没吓着你。

frighten ০ᜢ /ˈfraɪtn/ *verb* 动词
(frightens, frightening, frightened /ˈfraɪtnd/)
to make somebody feel afraid 使惊吓；使恐惧 ➲ SAME MEANING **scare** 同义词为 scare： *Sorry, did I frighten you?* 对不起，我吓着你了吗？

frightened ০ᜢ /ˈfraɪtnd/ *adjective* 形容词
afraid 害怕的；恐惧的 ➲ SAME MEANING **scared** 同义词为 scared： *He's frightened of spiders.* 他怕蜘蛛。

frightening ০ᜢ /ˈfraɪtnɪŋ/ *adjective* 形容词
making you feel afraid 使人惊恐的；令人害怕的： *That was the most frightening film I have ever seen.* 那是我看过的最恐怖的电影。

frill /frɪl/ *noun* 名词
a narrow piece of cloth with a lot of folds which decorates the edge of a shirt, dress, etc. （衬衫、连衣裙等）饰边，褶边，褶饰： *a white blouse with frills at the cuffs* 袖口上有褶边的白色女衬衫
▶ **frilly** /ˈfrɪli/ *adjective* 形容词： *a frilly skirt* 带褶边的裙子

fringe /frɪndʒ/ *noun* 名词
1 (*British* 英式英语) (*American* 美式英语 **bangs**) the short hair that hangs down above your eyes 额前短垂发；刘海 ➲ Look at the picture at **hair**. 见 hair 的插图。
2 a line of loose threads that decorate the edge of a piece of cloth or carpet （衣服、地毯等）穗，流苏

frizzy /ˈfrɪzi/ *adjective* 形容词 (frizzier, frizziest)
(used about hair) with a lot of small tight curls （毛发）鬈曲的

fro /frəʊ/ *adverb* 副词
to and fro first one way and then the other way, many times 来回；往返： *She rocked the baby to and fro.* 她来回摇着宝宝。

frog 青蛙

frog /frɒg/ *noun* 名词
a small green animal that lives in and near water. **Frogs** have long back legs and they can jump. 蛙；青蛙

from ০ᜢ /frəm; frɒm/ *preposition* 介词
1 a word that shows where somebody or something starts 从（某起点）： *We travelled from New York to Boston.* 我们从纽约到了波士顿。 ◇ *She began to walk away from him.* 她开始从他身边走开。 ◇ *The tickets cost from $15 to $35.* 票价从 15 元到 35 元不等。
2 a word that shows when something starts 从（某时间）： *The shop is open from 9.30 until 5.30.* 这家店从 9 点 30 分营业至 5 点 30 分。
3 a word that shows who gave or sent something 来自（某人）： *I had a letter from Lyn.* 我收到了琳恩的信。 ◇ *I borrowed a dress from my sister.* 我向姐姐借了一条连衣裙。
4 a word that shows where somebody lives or was born 来自（某地）： *I come from Spain.* 我是西班牙人。
5 a word that shows what is used to make something 由⋯（制成）： *Paper is made from wood.* 纸是用木做的。
6 a word that shows how far away something is 距，离（某地）： *The house is two miles from the village.* 房子距离村子两英里。
7 a word that shows how something changes 由⋯（变成）： *The sky changed from blue to grey.* 天空由蓝色变成了灰色。
8 a word that shows why 由于： *Children are dying from this disease.* 陆续有孩子死于这种病。
9 a word that shows difference 与⋯（不同）： *My book is different from yours.* 我的书和你的不一样。

front /frʌnt/ *noun* 名词

the side or part of something that faces forwards and that you usually see first 正面; 前面: *The book has a picture of a lion on the front.* 书的封面画有一头狮子。◇ *John and I sat in the front of the car and the children sat in the back.* 约翰和我坐在汽车前座，孩子都坐在后座。 ➜ Look at the picture at **back**[1]. 见 **back**[1] 的插图。

in front of somebody or 或 **something**

1 further forward than another person or thing 在⋯前面: *Alice was sitting in front of her mother on the bus.* 艾丽斯在公共汽车上坐在妈妈的前面。

2 when other people are there 当着⋯的面: *Please don't talk about it in front of my parents.* 请不要当着我父母的面说这件事。

▶ **front** *adjective* 形容词: *the front door* 前门 ◇ *the front seat of a car* 汽车前座

frontier /ˈfrʌntɪə(r)/ *noun* 名词

the line where one country joins another country 国界; 边界; 边境

frost /frɒst/ *noun* 名词

ice like white powder that covers the ground when the weather is very cold 霜: *There was a frost last night.* 昨天晚上结霜了。

▶ **frosty** /ˈfrɒsti/ *adjective* 形容词 (**frostier**, **frostiest**): *a frosty morning* 霜冻的早晨

frosting /ˈfrɒstɪŋ/ *American English for* ICING 美式英语，即 icing

frown /fraʊn/ *verb* 动词 (**frowns**, **frowning**, **frowned** /fraʊnd/)

to show feelings of anger or worry by making lines appear above your nose 皱眉; 蹙额: *John frowned at me when I came in. 'You're late,' he said.* 我进来时约翰对我皱着眉，说: "你迟到了。"

▶ **frown** *noun* 名词: *She looked at me with a frown.* 她眉头一皱看着我。

froze *form of* FREEZE * freeze 的不同形式

frozen[1] *form of* FREEZE * freeze 的不同形式

frozen[2] /ˈfrəʊzn/ *adjective* 形容词 (*informal* 非正式)

1 (used about food) kept at a very cold temperature so that it stays fresh for a long time (食物) 冷冻的, 冷藏的: *frozen peas* 冷冻豌豆

2 (used about people) very cold (人) 冻僵，极冷: *I'm frozen stiff.* 我冻僵了。

fruit /fruːt/ *noun* 名词

the part of a plant or tree that holds the seeds. Oranges and apples are types of **fruit**. 果实; 水果 ➜ Look at Picture Dictionary page **P8**. 见彩页 **P8**。

frustrating /frʌˈstreɪtɪŋ/ *adjective* 形容词

making you angry because you cannot do what you want to do 恼人的; 令人沮丧的: *It's very frustrating when you can't say what you mean in a foreign language.* 无法用外语说出想说的话，真是令人沮丧。

fry /fraɪ/ *verb* 动词 (**fries**, **frying**, **fried** /fraɪd/, *has* **fried**)

to cook something in hot oil 炒; 炸; 煎: *Fry the onions in butter.* 用黄油炒洋葱。◇ *fried eggs* 煎蛋

frying pan /ˈfraɪɪŋ pæn/ (*British* 英式英语) (*American* 美式英语 **frypan** /ˈfraɪpæn/) *noun* 名词

a flat metal container with a long handle that you use for frying food 长柄平底煎锅

ft *short way of writing* FOOT (2) * foot 第 2 义的缩写形式

fuel /ˈfjuːəl/ *noun* 名词 (*no plural* 不用复数形式)

anything that you burn to make heat or power. Wood, coal and oil are kinds of **fuel**. 燃料

frying pan 长柄平底煎锅

handle 柄 —

fulfil (*British* 英式英语) (*American* 美式英语 fulfill) /fʊlˈfɪl/ *verb* 动词 (fulfils, fulfilling, fulfilled /fʊlˈfɪld/)
to do what you have planned or promised to do 实现；履行：*Jane fulfilled her dream of travelling around the world.* 简实现了她周游世界的梦想。

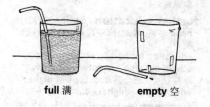

full 满 **empty** 空

full ⚲ /fʊl/ *adjective* 形容词 (fuller, fullest)
1 with a lot of people or things in it, so that there is no more space 满的：*My glass is full.* 我的杯子满了。◇ *The bus was full so we waited for the next one.* 公交车已经满了，我们便等下一班。◇ *These socks are full of holes.* 这些袜子上都是洞。
2 (*British also* 英式英语亦作 full up) having had enough to eat 吃饱了的：*'Would you like anything else to eat?' 'No, thank you, I'm full.'* "你还想吃点什么吗？""不用了，谢谢。我已经饱了。"
3 complete; with nothing missing 完全的；完整的：*Please tell me the full story.* 请把整件事原原本本告诉我。
4 as much, big, etc. as possible 尽量多的；最大量的：*The train was travelling at full speed.* 火车当时正以全速行进。
in full completely; with nothing missing

全部：*Please write your name in full.* 请写下你的全名。

full moon /ˌfʊl ˈmuːn/ *noun* 名词
the time when you can see all of the moon 满月；望月

full stop /ˌfʊl ˈstɒp/ *noun* 名词 (*British* 英式英语) (*American* 美式英语 period)
a mark (.) that you use in writing to show the end of a sentence, or after the short form of a word 句号；句点

full-time /ˌfʊl ˈtaɪm/ *adjective*, *adverb* 形容词，副词
for all the normal working hours of the day or week 全日制（的）；全职（的）：*My mother has a full-time job.* 我母亲有份全职工作。◇ *Do you work full-time?* 你的工作是全职的吗？ ⊃ Look at **part-time**. 见 part-time。

fully ⚲ /ˈfʊli/ *adverb* 副词
completely; totally 完全；全部：*The hotel was fully booked.* 旅馆的房间都订满了。

fun ⚲ /fʌn/ *noun* 名词 (*no plural* 不用复数形式)
pleasure and enjoyment; something that you enjoy 乐趣；玩乐：*Sailing is good fun.* 帆船运动好玩极了。◇ *I'm just learning English for fun.* 我学英语只是为了好玩。◇ *Have fun* (= enjoy yourself)! 玩得开心！
make fun of somebody to laugh about somebody in an unkind way 取笑；拿某人开玩笑：*The other children make fun of him because he wears glasses.* 别的孩子因为他戴眼镜而取笑他。

function¹ /ˈfʌŋkʃn/ *noun* 名词
the special work that a person or thing does 功用；功能：*The function of the heart is to send blood round the body.* 心脏的功能是将血液输送到全身。

function² /ˈfʌŋkʃn/ *verb* 动词 (functions, functioning, functioned /ˈfʌŋkʃnd/)
to work 起作用；运转：*The car engine will not function without oil.* 汽车发动机没有燃油就无法运作。

fund /fʌnd/ *noun* 名词
money that will be used for something special 资金；基金：*a fund to help homeless people* 一个帮助无家可归者的基金 ◇ *The school wants to raise funds for new computers.* 学校想筹集资金购买新电脑。

fundamental /ˌfʌndəˈmentl/ *adjective* 形容词
most important; from which everything else develops 最重要的；基本的；基础的

⊃ SAME MEANING **basic** 同义词为 basic:
*There is **a fundamental difference**
between the two points of view.* 两个观点
有着根本的区别。

fund-raising /ˈfʌnd reɪzɪŋ/ *noun* 名词
(*no plural* 不用复数形式)
the activity of collecting money for a
particular use 资金募集: *fund-raising
activities at school* 在学校的筹款活动

funeral /ˈfjuːnərəl/ *noun* 名词
the time when a dead person is buried or
burned 葬礼；丧礼

funfair /ˈfʌnfeə(r)/ *noun* 名词 = FAIR² (1)

fungus /ˈfʌŋgəs/ *noun* 名词 (*plural* 复数
形式 fungi /ˈfʌngiː; ˈfʌŋgaɪ/)
any plant without leaves, flowers or green
colouring, that grows on other plants or
on other surfaces. MUSHROOMS are **fungi**.
真菌（如蘑菇等）

funnel /ˈfʌnl/ *noun* 名词
1 a tube that is wide at the top to help
you pour things into bottles 漏斗
2 a large pipe on a ship or railway engine
that smoke comes out of（轮船或机车
的）烟囱

funny 0┓ /ˈfʌni/ *adjective* 形容词
(funnier, funniest)
1 making you laugh or smile 好笑的；
滑稽的 ⊃ SAME MEANING **amusing** 同义词
为 amusing: *a funny story* 滑稽的故事
◇ *He's so funny!* 他太有趣了！
2 strange or surprising 奇怪的；使人惊奇
的: *There's a funny smell in this room.*
这个房间有股怪味。

fur 0┓ /fɜː(r)/ *noun* 名词 (*no plural* 不用
复数形式)
the soft thick hair that covers the bodies
of some animals（动物的）毛皮
▶ **furry** /ˈfɜːri/ *adjective* 形容词 (furrier,
furriest): *a furry animal* 毛茸茸的动物

furious /ˈfjʊəriəs/ *adjective* 形容词
very angry 非常生气的；狂怒的: *My
parents were furious with me.* 我父母对我
十分生气。

furnace /ˈfɜːnɪs/ *noun* 名词
a very hot fire in a closed place, used for
heating metals, making glass, etc. 熔炉

furnished /ˈfɜːnɪʃt/ *adjective* 形容词
with furniture already in it 带有家具的:
I rented a furnished flat in the town centre.
我在市中心租了一套带家具的公寓。

furniture 0┓ /ˈfɜːnɪtʃə(r)/ *noun* 名词
(*no plural* 不用复数形式)
tables, chairs, beds, etc. 家具: *They've
bought some furniture for their new*

house. 他们为新房购置了一些家具。
◇ *All the furniture is very old.* 所有的
家具都很旧。

🔍 **GRAMMAR** 语法说明

Furniture does not have a plural, so
we cannot say 'a furniture'. We say
'a piece of furniture' to talk about a
single item. * furniture 没有复数形
式，所以不能说 a furniture。表示一件
家具说 a piece of furniture: *The only
piece of furniture in the room was a
large bed.* 房间里唯一的家具是一张
大床。

---

further 0┓ /ˈfɜːðə(r)/ *adjective, adverb*
形容词，副词
1 at or to a greater distance 较远的；
更远 ⊃ SAME MEANING **farther** 同义词为
farther: *The hospital is further down the
road.* 沿这条路一直走下去就是医院。◇ *We
couldn't go any further because the road
was closed.* 我们无法走得更远，因为路
已经封闭了。
2 more; extra 额外的；更多: *Do you
have any further questions?* 你还有别的
问题吗？

further education /ˌfɜːðər edʒuˈkeɪʃn/
noun 名词 (*abbr.* 缩略式 **FE**) (*British* 英式
英语)
education for people who have left
school but who are not at university
继续教育；进修教育 ⊃ Look at **higher
education**. 见 higher education。

furthest 0┓ *form of* FAR * far 的不同
形式

fury /ˈfjʊəri/ *noun* 名词 (*no plural* 不用
复数形式) (*formal* 正式)
very strong anger 盛怒；大发雷霆: *She
was filled with fury.* 她满腔怒火。

fuse /fjuːz/ *noun* 名词
a small wire inside a piece of electrical
equipment that stops it from working if
too much electricity goes through it
保险丝；熔丝

fuss¹ /fʌs/ *noun* 名词 (*no plural* 不用复数
形式)
a lot of excitement or worry about small
things that are not important 无谓的激动
（或忧虑）；大惊小怪: *He makes a fuss
when I'm five minutes late.* 我迟到五分钟
他就会大发牢骚。

make a fuss of somebody to pay a lot
of attention to somebody 对某人关爱备
至: *Grandad always makes a fuss of me.*
爷爷总是对我无微不至。

fuss² /fʌs/ *verb* 动词 (fusses, fussing, fussed /fʌst/)
to worry and get excited about small things that are not important 大惊小怪:
Stop fussing! 别瞎操心了!

fussy /'fʌsi/ *adjective* 形容词 (fussier, fussiest)
caring a lot about small things that are not important, and difficult to please 吹毛求疵的; 挑剔的: *Rod is fussy about his food* (= there are many things that he will not eat). 罗德很挑食。

future¹ 0━ /'fjuːtʃə(r)/ *noun* 名词
1 the time that will come 将来; 未来: *Nobody knows what will happen in the future.* 谁也不知道将来会发生什么事。

◇ *The company's future is uncertain.* 这家公司前途未卜。
2 the future (*no plural* 不用复数形式) (*grammar* 语法) the form of a verb that shows what will happen after now 将来时; 将来式; 未来式 ⊃ Look at **past²** (2) and **present²** (3). 见 past² 第 2 义和 present² 第 3 义。
in future from now on 今后; 从今以后: *You must work harder in future.* 你今后得更加努力。

future² 0━ /'fjuːtʃə(r)/ *adjective* 形容词
happening or existing in the time that will come 将来的; 未来的: *Have you met John's future wife?* 你见过约翰的未婚妻吗?

A
B
C
D
E
F
G
H
I
J
K
L
M
N
O
P
Q
R
S
T
U
V
W
X
Y
Z

G g

G, g[1] /dʒiː/ *noun* 名词 (*plural* 复数形式 G's, g's /dʒiːz/)
the seventh letter of the English alphabet 英语字母表的第 7 个字母: *'Girl' begins with a 'G'.* * girl 一词以字母 g 开头。

g[2] *short way of writing* GRAM * gram 的缩写形式: *It weighs 100g.* 这东西重 100 克。

gadget /'gædʒɪt/ *noun* 名词
a small machine or useful tool 小器具; 小装置: *Their kitchen is full of electrical gadgets.* 他们的厨房有很多小电器。

gain 0- /geɪn/ *verb* 动词 (gains, gaining, gained /geɪnd/)
1 to get something that you want or need 获得; 取得; 赢得: *I gained useful experience from that job.* 我从那份工作中获得了有益的经验。
2 to get more of something 增加; 增长: *I have gained weight recently.* 我最近体重增加了。

galaxy /'gæləksi/ *noun* 名词 (*plural* 复数形式 galaxies)
a very large group of stars and planets 星系

gale /geɪl/ *noun* 名词
a very strong wind 大风: *The trees were blown down in the gale.* 这些树被大风刮倒了。

gallery /'gæləri/ *noun* 名词 (*plural* 复数形式 galleries)
a place where people can look at or buy art（艺术作品的）陈列室, 展览馆; 画廊: *an art gallery* 美术馆

gallon /'gælən/ *noun* 名词
a unit for measuring liquid. In the UK it is equal to about 4.5 litres; in the US it is equal to about 3.8 litres. 加仑（液量单位; 在英国约等于 4.5 升, 在美国约等于 3.8 升）⊃ Look at the note at **pint**. 见 pint 条的注释。

gallop /'gæləp/ *verb* 动词 (gallops, galloping, galloped /'gæləpt/)
When a horse **gallops**, it runs very fast.（马）奔驰, 疾驰: *The horses galloped round the field.* 马儿在牧场里到处飞奔。

gamble /'gæmbl/ *verb* 动词 (gambles, gambling, gambled /'gæmbld/)
1 to try to win money by playing games that need luck 赌; 赌博: *He gambled a lot of money on the last race.* 他在最后一场赛马压了很多钱。
2 to take a risk, hoping that something will happen 冒风险; 碰运气: *We gambled on the weather staying fine.* 我们碰运气盼望天气会继续好下去。
▶ **gamble** *noun* 名词 something that you do without knowing if you will win or lose 赌; 冒险: *We took a gamble, and it paid off* (= was successful). 我们冒了一次险, 结果成功了。
▶ **gambling** /'gæmblɪŋ/ *noun* 名词 (*no plural* 不用复数形式): *He had heavy gambling debts.* 他因赌博欠债累累。

gambler /'gæmblə(r)/ *noun* 名词
a person who tries to win money by playing games that need luck 赌博的人

game 0- /geɪm/ *noun* 名词
1 (*plural* 复数形式 games) something you play that has rules 游戏; 运动; 比赛: *Shall we have a game of football?* 我们踢场足球好吗? ◇ *Let's play a game!* 咱们玩个游戏吧! ◇ *computer games* 电脑游戏
2 (*no plural* 不用复数形式) wild animals or birds that people kill for sport or food 猎物; 野味

game show /'geɪm ʃəʊ/ *noun* 名词
a television programme in which people play games or answer questions to win prizes（电视）游戏节目, 竞赛节目

gang[1] /gæŋ/ *noun* 名词
1 an organized group of criminals 一帮, 一伙（罪犯）; 犯罪团伙: *a gang of criminals* 一伙罪犯
2 a group of young people who spend a lot of time together and often cause trouble or fight against other groups 青年团伙: *street gangs* 街头团伙
3 (*informal* 非正式) a group of friends 一群朋友: *The whole gang is coming tonight.* 今晚大伙儿都会来。

gang[2] /gæŋ/ *verb* 动词 (gangs, ganging, ganged /gæŋd/)
gang up on or 或 **against somebody**
to join together in a group to hurt or frighten somebody 结伙伤害; 联合起来恐吓: *At school the older boys ganged up*

on him and called him names. 学校里年纪大一些的男孩合伙欺负他，辱骂他。

gangster /'gæŋstə(r)/ *noun* 名词
a member of a group of criminals 匪徒；歹徒

gangway /'gæŋweɪ/ *noun* 名词
1 (*British* 英式英语) the long space between rows of seats in a cinema, theatre, etc. （电影院、剧场等的）座间通道 ⊃ Look at **aisle**. 见 aisle。
2 a bridge that you use for getting on or off a ship （上下船用的）跳板，步桥

gaol /dʒeɪl/ *noun* 名词 (*British* 英式英语)
another word for JAIL * jail 的另一种说法

gap /gæp/ *noun* 名词
a space in something or between two things; a space where something should be 缺口；缝隙；空白处：*The goats got out through a gap in the fence.* 那些山羊从篱笆的豁口钻了出去。◇ *Leave a gap between your car and the next.* 在车与车之间留条道。◇ *Fill in the gaps in the text.* 给文章填空。

gape /geɪp/ *verb* 动词 (gapes, gaping, gaped /geɪpt/)
to look at somebody or something with your mouth open because you are surprised 张口结舌地看：*She gaped at me in astonishment.* 她目瞪口呆地看着我。

gaping /'geɪpɪŋ/ *adjective* 形容词
wide open 大大张开的：*There was a gaping hole in the fence.* 篱笆上有一个很大的豁口。

garage /'gærɑːʒ/ *noun* 名词
1 a building where you keep your car 车库；停车房
2 a place where vehicles are repaired and where you can buy a car or buy petrol and oil （兼营售车、加油的）汽车修理厂

garbage /'gɑːbɪdʒ/ *American English for* RUBBISH (1) 美式英语，即 rubbish 第 1 义

garbage can /'gɑːbɪdʒ kæn/ *American English for* DUSTBIN 美式英语，即 dustbin

garden /'gɑːdn/ *noun* 名词
1 (*British* 英式英语) (*American* 美式英语 yard) a piece of land by your house where you can grow flowers, fruit, and vegetables （住宅旁的）花园，果园，菜园：*Let's have lunch in the garden.* 我们在花园吃午饭吧。⊃ Look at Picture Dictionary page P10. 见彩页 P10。
2 gardens (*plural* 用复数形式) a public park 公园：*Kensington Gardens* 肯辛顿公园

▸ **garden** *verb* 动词 (gardens, gardening, gardened /'gɑːdnd/) to work in a garden 做园艺工作：*My mother was gardening all weekend.* 我母亲整个周末都在干园艺活。

▸ **gardening** /'gɑːdnɪŋ/ *noun* 名词 (*no plural* 不用复数形式) the work that you do in a garden to keep it looking attractive 园艺工作

gardener /'gɑːdnə(r)/ *noun* 名词
a person who works in a garden 园丁；花匠

garlic /'gɑːlɪk/ *noun* 名词 (*no plural* 不用复数形式)
a plant like a small onion with a strong taste and smell, that you use in cooking 蒜；大蒜 ⊃ Look at Picture Dictionary page P9. 见彩页 P9。

garment /'gɑːmənt/ *noun* 名词 (*formal* 正式)
a piece of clothing （一件）衣服

gas /gæs/ *noun* 名词
1 (*plural* 复数形式 gases) a substance like air that is not a solid or a liquid 气体：*Hydrogen and oxygen are gases.* 氢气和氧气都是气体。
2 (*no plural* 不用复数形式) a gas with a strong smell, that you burn to make heat 气体燃料；煤气；天然气：*Do you use electricity or gas for cooking?* 你做饭用电还是用煤气？◇ *a gas fire* 煤气取暖器
3 (*also* 亦作 gasoline /'gæsəliːn/) *American English for* PETROL 美式英语，即 petrol

gasp /gɑːsp/ *verb* 动词 (gasps, gasping, gasped /gɑːspt/)
to breathe in quickly and noisily through your mouth 喘气；喘息：*She gasped in surprise when she heard the news.* 她听到这个消息时吃惊得倒抽了一口气。◇ *He was gasping for air when they pulled him out of the water.* 他们把他从水里拉上来的时候，他急促地喘着气。
▸ **gasp** *noun* 名词：*a gasp of surprise* 惊讶得倒抽一口气

gas station /'gæs steɪʃn/ *American English for* PETROL STATION 美式英语，即 petrol station

gate /geɪt/ *noun* 名词
1 a thing like a door in a fence or wall, that opens so that you can go through 大门；栅栏门：*Please close the gate.* 请关上大门。⊃ Look at the picture at **fence**. 见 fence 的插图。
2 a door in an airport that you go through to reach the plane 登机门；登机口：*Please go to gate 15.* 请到第 15 号登机口。

A B C D E F **G** H I J K L M N O P Q R S T U V W X Y Z

gateway /'geɪtweɪ/ *noun* 名词
a way in or out of a place 出入口；门户

gather /'gæðə(r)/ *verb* 动词 (gathers, gathering, gathered /'gæðəd/)
1 to come together in a group 聚集；集合：*We all gathered round to listen to the teacher.* 我们全部围在一起听老师讲话。
2 to bring together things that are in different places 收集；收拢：*Can you gather up all the books and papers?* 你能把书和纸张都收起来吗？
3 to believe or understand something 认为；理解：*I gather that you know my sister.* 我猜想你认识我的妹妹。

gathering /'gæðərɪŋ/ *noun* 名词
a time when people come together; a meeting 集会；聚会：*a family gathering* 家庭聚会 ◇ *There was a large gathering outside the palace.* 在宫殿外面聚集了很多人。

gauge[1] /geɪdʒ/ *noun* 名词
an instrument that measures how much of something there is 测量仪器；计量器：*Where is the petrol gauge in this car?* 这辆汽车的汽油量表在哪儿？

gauge[2] /geɪdʒ/ *verb* 动词 (gauges, gauging, gauged /geɪdʒd/)
to judge, calculate, or guess something 判断；估计：*It was hard to gauge the mood of the audience.* 很难判断观众的心情。

gave form of GIVE * give 的不同形式

gay /geɪ/ *adjective* 形容词
attracted to people of the same sex 同性恋的 ⊃ SAME MEANING **homosexual** 同义词为 homosexual

gaze /geɪz/ *verb* 动词 (gazes, gazing, gazed /geɪzd/)
to look at somebody or something for a long time 凝视；注视：*She sat and gazed out of the window.* 她坐着凝视窗外。 ◇ *He was gazing at her.* 他盯着她看。 ⊃ Look at the note at **stare**. 见 stare 条的注释。

GCSE /ˌdʒiː siː es 'iː/ *noun* 名词
an examination in one subject that children at schools in the UK take when they are 16 普通中等教育证书：*I've got eight GCSEs.* 我已获得八门学科的普通中等教育证书。 ⊃ 'GCSE' is short for **General Certificate of Secondary Education.** * GCSE 是 General Certificate of Secondary Education 的缩略式。 ⊃ Look at **A level.** 见 A level。

gear /gɪə(r)/ *noun* 名词
1 (*plural* 复数形式 **gears**) the parts in a car engine or a bicycle that control how fast the wheels turn round（汽车或自行车的）排挡，传动装置：*You need to change gear to get up the hill in this car.* 开这辆车上山需要换挡。
2 (*no plural* 不用复数形式) special clothes or equipment that you need for a job or sport（某项活动的）服装，器具，用具：*camping gear* 露营装备

geek /giːk/ *noun* 名词 (*informal* 非正式)
a person who spends a lot of time on a particular interest and who is not popular or fashionable 痴迷…的人；闷蛋；土包子 ⊃ SAME MEANING **nerd** 同义词为 nerd：*a computer geek* 电脑迷

geese plural of GOOSE * goose 的复数形式

gel /dʒel/ *noun* 名词 (*no plural* 不用复数形式)
1 a thick liquid that you put on your hair to keep it in shape（用于头发的）凝胶：*hair gel* 发胶
2 a thick liquid that you can use to wash your body instead of soap（沐浴用的）凝胶：*shower gel* 沐浴露

gem /dʒem/ *noun* 名词
a stone that is very valuable and can be made into jewellery 宝石 ⊃ SAME MEANING **jewel** 同义词为 jewel

gender /'dʒendə(r)/ *noun* 名词
the fact of being male or female 性别

gene /dʒiːn/ *noun* 名词
one of the parts inside a cell that control what a living thing will be like. **Genes** are passed from parents to children. 基因：*The colour of your eyes is decided by your genes.* 眼睛的颜色是由基因决定的。 ⊃ Look at **genetic**. 见 genetic。

general[1] ⊶ /'dʒenrəl/ *adjective* 形容词
1 of, by or for most people or things 全体的；普遍的；一般的：*Is this car park for general use?* 这个停车场是公用的吗？
2 not in detail 概括性的；笼统的：*Can you give me a general idea of what the book is about?* 你能给我介绍一下这本书的梗概吗？
in general usually 通常；大体上：*I don't eat much meat in general.* 我一般很少吃肉。

general[2] /'dʒenrəl/ *noun* 名词
a very important officer in the army（陆军）将军

general election /ˌdʒenrəl ɪ'lekʃn/ *noun* 名词

a time when people choose a new government 大选；普选：*Did you vote in the last general election?* 上一次大选你投票了吗？

general knowledge /ˌdʒenrəl ˈnɒlɪdʒ/ *noun* 名词 (*no plural* 不用复数形式) what you know about a lot of different things 一般知识；常识

generally 0━ /ˈdʒenrəli/ *adverb* 副词 usually; mostly 通常；一般地：*I generally get up at about eight o'clock.* 我通常八点左右起床。

generate /ˈdʒenəreɪt/ *verb* 动词 (generates, generating, generated) to make something such as heat or electricity 产生：*Power stations generate electricity.* 发电厂是发电的。

generation /ˌdʒenəˈreɪʃn/ *noun* 名词 all the people in a family, group or country who were born at about the same time 代；一代：*This photo shows three generations of my family.* 这张照片是我们家三代同堂的合影。◇ *The younger generation don't seem to be interested in politics.* 年轻的一代似乎对政治不感兴趣。

generator /ˈdʒenəreɪtə(r)/ *noun* 名词 a machine that produces electricity 发电机

generosity /ˌdʒenəˈrɒsəti/ *noun* 名词 (*no plural* 不用复数形式) liking to give things to other people 慷慨；大方

generous 0━ /ˈdʒenərəs/ *adjective* 形容词 always ready to give people things or to spend money 慷慨的；大方的：*a generous gift* 丰厚的礼物 ◇ *It was generous of your parents to pay for the meal.* 你父母请了这顿饭，真是大方。 ⊃ OPPOSITE **mean** 反义词为 mean
▶ **generously** /ˈdʒenərəsli/ *adverb* 副词：*Please give generously.* 请慷慨施与。

genetic /dʒəˈnetɪk/ *adjective* 形容词 connected with the parts in the cells of living things (called **genes**) that control what a person, animal or plant will be like 基因的；遗传学的：*The disease has a genetic origin.* 这种疾病有遗传因素。

genetics /dʒəˈnetɪks/ *noun* 名词 (*no plural* 不用复数形式) the scientific study of the way that the development of living things is controlled by qualities that have been passed on from parents to children 遗传学 ⊃ Look at **gene**. 见 gene。

genie /ˈdʒiːni/ *noun* 名词 a spirit with magic powers, especially one that lives in a bottle or a lamp（尤指住在瓶子或灯里的）精灵

genius /ˈdʒiːniəs/ *noun* 名词 (*plural* 复数形式 **geniuses**) a very clever person 天才：*Einstein was a genius.* 爱因斯坦是个天才。

gentle 0━ /ˈdʒentl/ *adjective* 形容词 (gentler, gentlest)
1 quiet and kind 文静的；温柔的：*Be gentle with the baby.* 对宝宝要温柔点。◇ *a gentle voice* 温柔的嗓音
2 not strong or unpleasant 温和的：*It was a hot day, but there was a gentle breeze* (= a soft wind). 天气很热，但有些微风。
▶ **gently** /ˈdʒentli/ *adverb* 副词：*She stroked the kitten very gently.* 她轻轻地抚摩着小猫。

gentleman /ˈdʒentlmən/ *noun* 名词 (*plural* 复数形式 **gentlemen** /ˈdʒentlmən/)
1 a man who is polite and kind to other people 彬彬有礼的人；有教养的人：*He's a real gentleman.* 他是个真正的绅士。
2 (*formal* 正式) a polite way of saying 'man'（对男子的客气称呼）先生：*There is a gentleman here to see you.* 有位先生要见你。◇ *Ladies and gentlemen …* (= at the beginning of a speech) 女士们，先生们… ⊃ Look at **lady**. 见 lady。

gents /dʒents/ *noun* 名词 (*no plural* 不用复数形式) (*British* 英式英语) (*informal* 非正式) **the gents** a public toilet for men（公共）男厕所，男洗手间，男卫生间：*Do you know where the gents is, please?* 请问男厕所在哪儿？ ⊃ Look at **ladies**. 见 ladies。

genuine /ˈdʒenjuɪn/ *adjective* 形容词 real and true 真的；真实的：*The painting was found to be genuine.* 这幅画被认定是真迹。 ⊃ OPPOSITE **fake** 反义词为 fake
▶ **genuinely** /ˈdʒenjuɪnli/ *adverb* 副词 really 真正地：*Do you think he's genuinely sorry?* 你觉得他是真的感到抱歉吗？

geography /dʒiˈɒɡrəfi/ *noun* 名词 (*no plural* 不用复数形式) the study of the Earth and everything on it, such as mountains, rivers, land and people 地理学
▶ **geographical** /ˌdʒiːəˈɡræfɪkl/ *adjective* 形容词：*There is a list of geographical names* (= names of countries, seas, etc.) *at the back of this dictionary.* 本词典的末尾有个地名表。

A
B
C
D
E
F
G
H
I
J
K
L
M
N
O
P
Q
R
S
T
U
V
W
X
Y
Z

A
B
C
D
E
F
G
H
I
J
K
L
M
N
O
P
Q
R
S
T
U
V
W
X
Y
Z

geology /dʒiˈɒlədʒi/ *noun* 名词 (*no plural* 不用复数形式)
the study of rocks and soil and how they were made 地质学
▶ **geologist** /dʒiˈɒlədʒɪst/ *noun* 名词
a person who studies or knows a lot about GEOLOGY 地质学家

geometry /dʒiˈɒmətri/ *noun* 名词 (*no plural* 不用复数形式)
the study in mathematics of things like lines, shapes and angles 几何学

geranium /dʒəˈreɪniəm/ *noun* 名词
a plant with red, white or pink flowers 天竺葵；老鹳草

germ /dʒɜːm/ *noun* 名词
a very small living thing that can make you ill 细菌；病菌： *flu germs* 流感病菌

German measles /ˌdʒɜːmən ˈmiːzlz/ *noun* 名词 (*no plural* 不用复数形式)
a disease that causes red spots all over the body 德国麻疹；风疹： *Jane's got German measles.* 简患了风疹。

gesture[1] /ˈdʒestʃə(r)/ *noun* 名词
a movement of your head or hand to show how you feel or what you want 手势；示意动作： *The boy made a **rude gesture** before running off.* 那男孩在跑掉前做了个粗野的手势。

gesture[2] /ˈdʒestʃə(r)/ *verb* 动词 (gestures, gesturing, gestured)
to point at something or make a sign to somebody 指向；做手势；示意： *She asked me to sit down and **gestured** towards a chair.* 她叫我坐下，并指着一张椅子。

get ⚷ /get/ *verb* 动词 (gets, getting, got /gɒt/, has got) (*British* 英式英语) (*American* 美式英语 has gotten /ˈgɒtn/)
1 to buy or take something 买；带： *Will you get some bread when you go shopping?* 你去买东西时买些面包好吗？
2 to receive something 收到；接到： *I got a lot of presents for my birthday.* 我收到了很多生日礼物。
3 to go and bring back somebody or something 去接；去取 ⊃ SAME MEANING **fetch** 同义词为 fetch： *Jenny will get the children from school.* 珍妮会去学校接孩子。
4 to become 变得： *He is getting fat.* 他越来越胖了。◇ *Mum got angry.* 妈妈生气了。◇ *It's getting cold.* 天气越来越冷。
5 to arrive somewhere 到达： *We got to London at ten o'clock.* 我们十点钟到了伦敦。
6 a word that you use with part of

another verb to show that something happens to somebody or something （与另一动词连用）被： *She got caught by the police.* 她被警察抓住了。
7 to make somebody do something 使，让（某人做某事）： *I got Peter to help me.* 我让彼得来帮我。
8 to start to have an illness 感染；患上： *I think I'm getting a cold.* 我看我感冒了。
9 to travel on something such as a train or a bus 乘坐： *I didn't walk – I got the bus.* 我不是步行去的——我坐公共汽车。
10 to understand or hear something 理解；听懂： *I don't get the joke.* 我听不懂这个笑话。

get away with something to do something bad and not be punished for it 做（坏事）而未受惩罚： *He lied but he got away with it.* 他撒了谎，却没人把他怎么样。
get back to return 返回；回来： *When did you get back from your holiday?* 你是什么时候度完假回来的？
get in to reach a place 到达；抵达 ⊃ SAME MEANING **arrive** 同义词为 arrive： *My train got in at 7.15.* 我的火车 7 点 15 分到。
get in, get into something to climb into a car 钻进，登上（汽车）： *Tom got into the car.* 汤姆上了车。
get off, get off something to leave something such as a train, bus, or bicycle 下（火车、公车或自行车等）： *Where did you get off the bus?* 你是在哪站下车的？
get on
1 words that you use to say or ask how well somebody does something（谈及或问及某人）进展，进步： *Patrick is getting on well at school.* 帕特里克在学校表现很好。◇ *How did you get on in the exam?* 你考试考得怎么样？
2 to become old 变老；上年纪： *My grandfather is getting on – he's nearly 80.* 我爷爷年纪越来越大，快 80 岁了。
get on, get onto something to climb onto a bus, train, or bicycle 爬上，登上（公共汽车、火车或自行车）： *I got on the train.* 我上了火车。
get on with somebody to live or work in a friendly way with somebody 与某人和睦相处： *We get on well with our neighbours.* 我们跟邻居相处得很好。
get out, get out of something to leave or go out of a place （从…）出来；离开（某地）： *I opened the door and got out.* 我打开门走了出来。
get out of something to not do something that you do not like 逃避；

摆脱：*I'll come swimming with you if I can get out of cleaning my room.* 我要是不用打扫我的房间，就跟你一起去游泳。
get something out to take something from the place where it was（从…）取出：*She opened her bag and got out a pen.* 她打开包，取出了一支笔。
get over something to become well or happy again after you have been ill or sad（生病或经历不快后）恢复：*He still hasn't got over his wife's death.* 他还没有从丧妻的悲伤中恢复过来。
get through to be able to speak to somebody on the telephone（用电话）接通，打通：*I tried to ring Kate but I couldn't get through.* 我试过给凯特打电话，可是没打通。
get through something to use or finish a certain amount of something 消耗掉；用完；完成：*I got through a lot of work today.* 我今天做了很多工作。
get together to meet; to come together in a group 相聚；聚集：*The whole family got together for Christmas.* 全家人聚在了一起过圣诞。
get up
1 to stand up 站起；起身：*He got up to let an elderly lady sit down.* 他起身给老太太让座。
2 to get out of bed 起床：*What time do you usually get up?* 你通常几点钟起床？
get up to something
1 to do something, usually something bad 做（尤指坏事）：*I must go and see what the children are getting up to.* 我得去看看孩子们在搞什么鬼。
2 to reach a particular place, for example in a book 到达：*I've got up to page 180.* 我读到第 180 页了。
ghetto /ˈgetəʊ/ *noun* 名词 (*plural* 复数形式 **ghettos** or 或 **ghettoes**)
a part of a city where many poor people live 贫民窟
ghost /gəʊst/ *noun* 名词
the form of a dead person that a living person thinks they see 鬼：*Do you believe in ghosts?* 你相信有鬼吗？
▸ **ghostly** /ˈgəʊstli/ *adjective* 形容词：*ghostly noises* 幽灵般的声音
giant¹ /ˈdʒaɪənt/ *noun* 名词
(in stories) a very big tall person（故事中的）巨人
giant² /ˈdʒaɪənt/ *adjective* 形容词
very big 巨大的：*a giant insect* 巨虫
gift 0— /gɪft/ *noun* 名词
1 something that you give to or get from somebody 礼物；赠品 ⊃ SAME MEANING

present 同义词为 present：*This week's magazine comes with a special free gift.* 本周的杂志附有一份特别赠品。
2 the natural ability to do something well 天赋；天才：*She has a gift for languages.* 她有语言天赋。
gigantic /dʒaɪˈgæntɪk/ *adjective* 形容词
very big 巨大的：*gigantic trees* 参天大树

🔍 WORD BUILDING 词汇扩充
Other words that also mean 'very big' are: **enormous**, **huge** and **massive**. 其他表示"巨大"的词语有 enormous、huge 和 massive。

giggle /ˈgɪgl/ *verb* 动词 (**giggles, giggling, giggled** /ˈgɪgld/)
to laugh in a silly way 傻笑：*The children couldn't stop giggling.* 孩子们咯咯地笑个不停。
▸ **giggle** *noun* 名词：*There was a giggle from the back of the class.* 教室后面传来了咯咯笑声。
gill /gɪl/ *noun* 名词
the part on each side of a fish that it breathes through 鳃 ⊃ Look at the picture at **fish**. 见 fish 的插图。
ginger¹ /ˈdʒɪndʒə(r)/ *noun* 名词 (*no plural* 不用复数形式)
a plant with a hot strong taste, that is used in cooking 姜：*a ginger biscuit* 姜味饼干
ginger² /ˈdʒɪndʒə(r)/ *adjective* 形容词
with a colour between brown and orange 姜黄色的：*My brother has got ginger hair.* 我弟弟有一头姜黄色的头发。
gingerbread /ˈdʒɪndʒəbred/ *noun* 名词 (*no plural* 不用复数形式)
a dark brown cake with GINGER in it 姜饼
Gipsy /ˈdʒɪpsi/ = GYPSY
giraffe /dʒəˈrɑːf/ *noun* 名词
a big animal from Africa with a very long neck and long legs 长颈鹿 ⊃ Look at Picture Dictionary page P3. 见彩图 P3。
girl 0— /gɜːl/ *noun* 名词
a female child; a young woman 女孩；姑娘：*They have three children, two girls and a boy.* 他们有三个孩子，两个女孩，一个男孩。◇ *I lived in this house as a girl.* 我还是小女孩的时候住这所房子。
girlfriend 0— /ˈgɜːlfrend/ *noun* 名词
a girl or woman who somebody has a romantic relationship with 女朋友；女情人：*Have you got a girlfriend?* 你有女朋友吗？

Girl Guide /ˌgɜːl ˈgaɪd/ (*British* 英式英语)
= GUIDE¹ (4)

Girl Scout /ˌgɜːl ˈskaʊt/ *American English*
for GUIDE¹ (4) 美式英语，即 guide¹ 第 4 义

give 0ᵐ /gɪv/ *verb* 动词 (gives, giving,
gave /geɪv/, has given /ˈgɪvn/)
1 to let somebody have something 给；
给予；交给: *She gave me a watch for my
birthday.* 我生日时她送了我一块手表。
◊ *I gave my ticket to the man at the door.*
我把票给了站在门口的那个男子。◊ *Give
the letter to your mother when you've read
it.* 你把信读完后交给你母亲。
2 to make a sound or movement 发出
（声音）；做出（动作）: *Jo gave me an
angry look.* 乔愤怒地瞪了我一眼。◊ *He
gave a shout.* 他大叫了一声。◊ *She gave
him a kiss.* 她吻了他一下。
3 to make somebody have or feel
something 使感到: *That noise is giving
me a headache.* 那噪音让我感到头疼。
◊ *Whatever gave you that idea?* 究竟是
什么让你有那种想法的?
give something away to give
something to somebody without getting
money for it 赠送；捐赠: *I've given all
my old clothes away.* 我把我所有的旧衣服
都捐出去了。
give somebody back something,
give something back to somebody
to return something to somebody 还；
归还: *Can you give me back that book
I lent you?* 你可不可以把我借你的那本书
还给我?
give in to accept or agree to something
that you did not want to accept or agree
to 让步；屈服: *My parents finally gave in
and said I could go to the party.* 父母最后
还是让步了，说我可以参加聚会。
give something in (*British* 英式英语)
to give something to the person who is
collecting it 呈上；交上: *We have to give
our essays in today.* 我们今天得交作文。
give something out to give something
to a lot of people 分发: *Could you give
out these books to the class, please?* 请你
把这些书分发给全班同学好吗?
give up to stop trying to do something
放弃: *I give up – what's the answer?*
我认输了，答案是什么?
give something up to stop doing or
having something 停止做某事；放弃
某物: *He's trying to give up smoking.*
他正尝试戒烟。
given name /ˈgɪvn neɪm/ *another word
for* FIRST NAME * first name 的另一种说法

glacier /ˈglæsiə(r)/ *noun* 名词
a large river of ice that moves slowly
down a mountain 冰川

glad /glæd/ *adjective* 形容词
happy about something 高兴；愉快
⊃ SAME MEANING **pleased** 同义词为
pleased: *He was glad to see us.* 他很
高兴见到我们。

🔎 **WORD BUILDING** 词汇扩充
You are usually **glad** or **pleased** about
a particular event or situation. 对事情
或情况感到欣慰或满意说 glad 或
pleased: *I'm glad that he's feeling
better.* 他感觉好些了，我很高兴。◊
*I'm pleased to say that you've passed
your exam.* 我欣然告诉你，你已经通过
考试。
You use **happy** to describe a state of
mind or before a noun. * happy 用于
描述心情或用在名词之前: *I always feel
happy when the sun is shining.* 阳光
灿烂时我总是心情愉快。◊ *a happy
child* 快乐的孩子

▶ **gladly** /ˈglædli/ *adverb* 副词 If you do
something **gladly**, you are happy to do it.
高兴地；愉快地: *I'll gladly help you.*
我很乐意帮助你。

glamorous /ˈglæmərəs/ *adjective* 形容词
attractive in an exciting way 富有魅力的:
a glamorous model 魅力四射的模特儿
◊ *Making films is less glamorous than
people think.* 拍电影没有想象的那么令人
向往。

glamour (*British* 英式英语) (*American*
美式英语 **glamor**) /ˈglæmə(r)/ *noun* 名词
(*no plural* 不用复数形式)
the quality of seeming to be more
exciting and attractive than ordinary
things and people 魅力；诱惑力: *Young
people are attracted by the glamour of city
life.* 年轻人为缤纷的都市生活所吸引。

glance¹ /glɑːns/ *verb* 动词 (glances,
glancing, glanced /glɑːnst/)
to look quickly at somebody or something
瞥一眼；匆匆一看: *Sue glanced at her
watch.* 苏看了看手表。

glance² /glɑːns/ *noun* 名词
a quick look 一瞥；匆匆一看: *a glance
at the newspaper* 匆匆看一眼报纸
at a glance immediately; with only a
quick look 立刻；一眼；（只）看一眼:
I could see at a glance that he was ill.
我一眼就看出他病了。

glare¹ /gleə(r)/ *verb* 动词 (glares, glaring,
glared /gleəd/)

1 to look at somebody in an angry way 怒目而视: *He glared at the children.* 他生气地瞪着那些孩子。
2 to shine with a bright light that hurts your eyes 发出刺眼的光: *The sun glared down.* 太阳发出刺眼的光芒。

glare² /gleə(r)/ *noun* 名词
1 (*no plural* 不用复数形式) strong light that hurts your eyes 刺眼的光: *the glare of the car's headlights* 汽车头灯刺眼的光
2 (*plural* 复数形式 **glares**) a long, angry look 怒视; 瞪眼: *I tried to say something, but he gave me a glare.* 我试图说句话，可是他瞪了我一眼。

glaring /'gleərɪŋ/ *adjective* 形容词
1 very bad and easy to notice （用于批评）显眼的，显而易见的: *The article was full of glaring mistakes.* 文章处处都是明显的错误。
2 A **glaring** light is very bright and hurts your eyes. 刺眼的: *a glaring white light* 刺眼的白光

glass 玻璃杯

a glass of milk
一杯牛奶

glass /glɑːs/ *noun* 名词
1 (*no plural* 不用复数形式) hard material that you can see through. Bottles and windows are made of **glass**. 玻璃: *I cut myself on some broken glass.* 我被碎玻璃割伤了。◇ *a glass jar* 玻璃罐
2 (*plural* 复数形式 **glasses**) a thing made of glass that you drink from 玻璃杯: *Could I have a glass of milk, please?* 请给我一杯牛奶好吗？◇ *a wine glass* 葡萄酒杯

glasses /'glɑːsɪz/ *noun* (*plural* 用复数形式)
two pieces of glass or plastic (called **lenses**) in a frame that people wear over their eyes to help them see better 眼镜: *Does she wear glasses?* 她戴眼镜吗？
⊃ Look also at **sunglasses**. 亦见 sunglasses。

GRAMMAR 语法说明
Be careful! You cannot say 'a glasses'. You can say **a pair of glasses**. 注意：不说 a glasses，要说 a pair of glasses: *I need a new pair of glasses.* 我需要一副新眼镜。You can also say '*I need some new glasses*'. 也可以说 I need some new glasses。

glasses 眼镜

a pair of glasses 一副眼镜 　　**a pair of sunglasses** 一副太阳镜

frame 眼镜框　　lens 镜片

gleam /gliːm/ *verb* 动词 (**gleams, gleaming, gleamed** /gliːmd/)
to shine with a soft light 发出微光: *The moonlight gleamed on the lake.* 月光映在湖上，泛起粼粼波光。
▸ **gleam** *noun* 名词: *I could see a gleam of light through the trees.* 我看到树缝间透出一丝微光。

glee /gliː/ *noun* 名词 (*no plural* 不用复数形式)
a feeling of happiness, especially when something bad happens to somebody else 高兴; 幸灾乐祸: *She couldn't hide her glee when her rival came last.* 看到自己的对手是最后一名，她不禁喜形于色。

glide /glaɪd/ *verb* 动词 (**glides, gliding, glided**)
1 to move smoothly and quietly 滑行; 滑动: *The dancers glided across the floor.* 舞蹈员在舞池里翩翩起舞。
2 to fly in a GLIDER 滑翔: *I always wanted to go gliding.* 我一直想去滑翔。

glider /'glaɪdə(r)/ *noun* 名词
a plane without an engine 滑翔机

glimmer /'glɪmə(r)/ *noun* 名词
1 a small, weak light 微弱的闪光; 闪烁的微光
2 a small sign of something 微弱的迹象; 一丝; 一线: *There's still a glimmer of hope.* 还有一线希望。
▸ **glimmer** *verb* 动词 (**glimmers, glimmering, glimmered** /'glɪməd/):
A light glimmered in the distance. 灯光在远处忽明忽暗地闪烁。

A B C D E F **G** H I J K L M N O P Q R S T U V W X Y Z

glimpse /glɪmps/ *noun* 名词
a view of somebody or something that is quick and not clear 一瞥；一看：*I caught a glimpse of myself in the mirror.* 我在镜子里瞥见自己。
▸ **glimpse** *verb* 动词 (glimpses, glimpsing, glimpsed /glɪmpst/): *I just glimpsed him in the crowd.* 我刚在人群中瞥见了他。

glisten /'glɪsn/ *verb* 动词 (glistens, glistening, glistened /'glɪsnd/)
(used about wet surfaces) to shine （湿的表面）闪亮，发光：*His eyes glistened with tears.* 他双眼泛着泪光。

glitter /'glɪtə(r)/ *verb* 动词 (glitters, glittering, glittered /'glɪtəd/)
to shine brightly with a lot of small flashes of light 闪亮；闪耀：*The broken glass glittered in the sun.* 碎玻璃在阳光下闪闪发光。
▸ **glitter** *noun* 名词 (*no plural* 不用复数形式)：*the glitter of jewels* 宝石的闪光

glittering /'glɪtərɪŋ/ *adjective* 形容词
1 very impressive or successful 辉煌的；成功的：*a glittering career* 辉煌的事业生涯
2 shining with a lot of small flashes of light 闪闪发光的

global /'gləʊbl/ *adjective* 形容词
of or about the whole world 全球的；全世界的：*Pollution is a global problem.* 污染是全球问题。

global warming /ˌgləʊbl 'wɔːmɪŋ/ *noun* 名词 (*no plural* 不用复数形式)
the fact that the earth's atmosphere is getting hotter because of increases in certain gases 全球气候变暖 ➲ Look at **greenhouse effect**. 见 greenhouse effect。

globe /gləʊb/ *noun* 名词
1 (*plural* 复数形式 globes) a round object with a map of the world on it 地球仪
2 the globe (*no plural* 不用复数形式) the world 地球；世界：*He's travelled all over the globe.* 他到过世界各地。

gloomy /'gluːmi/ *adjective* 形容词 (gloomier, gloomiest)
1 dark and sad 幽暗的；阴暗的：*What a gloomy day!* 多么昏暗闷人的一天！
2 sad and without hope 忧郁的；沮丧的；无望的：*He's feeling very gloomy because he can't get a job.* 他因找不到工作而十分沮丧。
▸ **gloomily** /'gluːmɪli/ *adverb* 副词：*She looked gloomily out of the window at the rain.* 她满脸愁容地看着窗外的雨。

glorious /'glɔːriəs/ *adjective* 形容词
1 (*formal* 正式) famous and full of GLORY 光荣的；荣耀的：*a glorious history* 光荣的历史
2 wonderful or beautiful 壮丽的；壮观的：*The weather was glorious.* 天气好极了。

glory /'glɔːri/ *noun* 名词 (*no plural* 不用复数形式)
1 FAME (= being known by many people) and respect that you get when you do great things 荣耀；光荣：*The winning team came home covered in glory.* 获胜的队伍载誉而归。
2 great beauty 壮丽；瑰丽：*Autumn is the best time to see the forest in all its glory.* 秋天森林绚丽多彩，是游赏的最佳时节。

glossary /'glɒsəri/ *noun* 名词 (*plural* 复数形式 glossaries)
a list of difficult words and their meanings, especially at the end of a book （尤指书后的）词汇表，术语表

glossy /'glɒsi/ *adjective* 形容词 (glossier, glossiest)
smooth and shiny 光亮的；有光泽的：*glossy hair* 富有光泽的头发

gloves 手套

a pair of gloves 一副手套

glove 0┅ /glʌv/ *noun* 名词
a thing that you wear to keep your hand warm or safe 手套：*I need a new pair of gloves.* 我需要一双新手套。◇ *rubber gloves* 橡胶手套

glow /gləʊ/ *verb* 动词 (glows, glowing, glowed /gləʊd/)
to send out soft light or heat without flames or smoke 微微发光；发热：*His*

cigarette glowed in the dark. 他的香烟在黑暗中发出幽幽的光。

▶ **glow** *noun* 名词: *the glow of the sky at sunset* 日落时天空里的霞光

glowing /'gləʊɪŋ/ *adjective* 形容词
saying that somebody or something is very good 热烈赞扬的; 倍加称赞的: *His teacher wrote a glowing report about his work.* 他的老师写了一份报告, 对他的作业倍加称赞。

glue¹ /gluː/ *noun* 名词 (*no plural* 不用复数形式)
a thick liquid that you use for sticking things together 胶水; 糨糊

glue² /gluː/ *verb* 动词 (**glues, gluing, glued** /gluːd/)
to stick one thing to another thing with **glue** (用胶水) 黏合, 粘贴: *Glue the two pieces of wood together.* 把这两块木头粘起来。

glum /glʌm/ *adjective* 形容词 (**glummer, glummest**)
sad and quiet 郁闷的; 闷闷不乐的: *Why are you looking so glum?* 为什么你看起来闷闷不乐的?

▶ **glumly** /'glʌmli/ *adverb* 副词

GM /ˌdʒiː 'em/ *abbreviation* 缩略式
(used about food and plants) grown from cells whose parts that contain information (called **genes**) have been changed (食物和植物) 转基因的, 基因改造的: *GM crops* 转基因农作物 ➋ 'GM' is short for **genetically modified.** * GM 是 genetically modified 的缩略式。

GMT /ˌdʒiː em 'tiː/ *abbreviation* 缩略式
the time system that is used in Britain during the winter and for calculating the time in other parts of the world 格林尼治平时 ➋ 'GMT' is short for **Greenwich Mean Time.** * GMT 是 Greenwich Mean Time 的缩略式。

gnaw /nɔː/ *verb* 动词 (**gnaws, gnawing, gnawed** /nɔːd/)
to bite something for a long time 咬; 啃: *The dog was gnawing a bone.* 狗啃着骨头。

go¹ ⚡ /gəʊ/ *verb* 动词 (**goes, going, went** /went/, **has gone** /gɒn/)
1 to move from one place to another 去; 走: *I went to London by train.* 我是坐火车去伦敦的。◇ *Her new car goes very fast.* 她的新车跑得很快。
2 to travel to a place to do something 去 (做某事): *Paul has gone shopping.* 保罗去买东西了。◇ *Are you going to Dave's party?* 你会去参加戴夫的聚会吗?

◇ *I'll go and make some coffee.* 我去煮点咖啡。
3 to leave a place 离开; 出发: *I must go now – it's four o'clock.* 我得走了, 已经四点了。◇ *What time does the train go?* 火车什么时候开?
4 to become 变为; 变成: *Her hair has gone grey.* 她的头发变灰白了。
5 to have as its place 安置在; 放置于: *'Where do these plates go?' 'In that cupboard.'* "这些盘子放哪儿?" "放那个橱柜里。"
6 to lead to a place 通往: *Does this road go to the station?* 这条路通往车站吗?
7 (used about a machine, etc.) to work (机械等) 运转: *Jane dropped the clock and now it doesn't go.* 简把钟摔了, 现在它不走了。
8 to happen in a certain way 进展; 进行: *How is your new job going?* 你的新工作怎么样? ◇ *The week went very quickly.* 这个星期过得很快。
9 to disappear 消失: *My headache has gone.* 我的头不疼了。
10 to be or look good with something else (与某物) 相配, 协调 ➋ SAME MEANING **match** 同义词为 match: *Does this jumper go with my skirt?* 这件套头毛衣和我的裙子相配吗?
11 to make a certain sound 发出 (某种声音): *Cows go 'moo'.* 牛会"哞哞"地叫。

be going to
1 words that show what you plan to do in the future 打算 (做某事): *Joe's going to cook the dinner tonight.* 乔会做今天晚上的饭。
2 words that you use when you are sure that something will happen in the future 将会: *It's going to rain.* 快下雨了。

go ahead to begin or continue to do something 开始做; 继续进行: *'Can I borrow your pen?' 'Sure, go ahead.'* "我可以借用你的笔吗?" "可以, 拿去用吧。"

go away to leave a person or place; to leave the place where you live for at least one night 走开; 出门: *Go away! I'm doing my homework.* 走开! 我正在做作业呢。◇ *They have gone away for the weekend.* 他们出门度周末了。

go back to return to a place where you were before 回到, 返回 (某处): *We're going back to school tomorrow.* 我们明天返校。

go by to pass 过去; 流逝: *The holidays went by very quickly.* 假期过得很快。

go down well to be something that

people like 受到欢迎: *The film went down very well in the US.* 这部电影在美国很受欢迎。

go off

1 to explode 爆炸: *A bomb went off in the station today.* 今天有一枚炸弹在车站爆炸。

2 When food or drink **goes off**, it becomes too old to eat or drink. （食物或饮料）变质, 变坏: *This milk has gone off – it smells horrible.* 这牛奶变质了, 好难闻。

go off somebody or 或 **something** to stop liking somebody or something 不再喜欢…: *I've really gone off meat lately.* 我近来真的不爱吃肉了。

go on

1 to happen 发生: *What's going on?* 发生什么事?

2 to continue 继续: *I went on working.* 我一直工作下去。

3 words that you use when you want somebody to do something （用于鼓励人做事）来吧: *Oh, go on! Come to the party with me!* 噢, 来呀, 跟我去参加聚会吧!

go out

1 to leave the place where you live or work for a short time, returning on the same day 出去; 外出: *I went out for a walk.* 我出去散步了。 ◊ *We're going out tonight.* 我们今晚外出。

2 to stop shining or burning 熄灭: *The fire has gone out.* 火灭了。

go out with somebody to have somebody as a boyfriend or girlfriend 与…谈恋爱: *She's going out with a boy at school.* 她在跟学校里的一个男生谈恋爱。

go over something to look at or explain something carefully from the beginning to the end 从头到尾检查 ◯ SAME MEANING **go through something** 同义词为 go through something: *Go over your work before you give it to the teacher.* 把作业仔细检查一遍才交给老师。

go round

1 to be enough for everybody 分给所有人: *Is there enough wine to go round?* 酒够大家喝吗?

2 to go to somebody's home 拜访; 探望: *We're going round to Jo's this evening.* 我们今晚到乔的家里去。

go through something

1 to look at or explain something carefully from the beginning to the end 从头到尾检查; 仔细查阅 ◯ SAME MEANING **go over something** 同义词为 go over something: *The teacher went through our homework.* 老师仔细批阅了我们的作业。

2 to have a bad experience 经历（不愉快的事）: *She went through a difficult time when her mother was ill.* 她妈妈生病的时候, 她吃了不少苦。

go up to become higher or more 上涨; 上升 ◯ SAME MEANING **rise** 同义词为 rise: *The price of petrol has gone up again.* 汽油又涨价了。

◯ Look at the note at **been**. 见 been 条的注释。

go² /gəʊ/ *noun* 名词 (*plural* 复数形式 goes) (*British* 英式英语)
the time when a person should move or play in a game or an activity （游戏或活动中）轮到的机会 ◯ SAME MEANING **turn** 同义词为 turn: *Get off the bike – it's my go!* 快从自行车上下来 —— 轮到我骑了!

have a go (*British* 英式英语) (*informal* 非正式) to try to do something 尝试: *I'll have a go at mending your bike.* 我试试修理你的自行车吧。

in one go (*informal* 非正式) all together at one time 一下子; 一举: *They ate the packet of biscuits all in one go.* 他们一下子把整包饼干吃光了。

goal 球门

goalkeeper 守门员

goal 0= /gəʊl/ *noun* 名词

1 the place where the ball must go to win a point in a game like football 球门: *He kicked the ball into the goal.* 他把球踢进了球门。

2 a point that a team wins in a game like football when the ball goes into the goal 进球得分: *Liverpool won by three goals to two.* 利物浦队以三比二获胜。

3 something that you want to do very much 目标; 目的: *She has finally achieved her goal of taking part in the Olympics.* 她终于实现了目标, 参加奥运会。

goalkeeper /ˈgəʊlkiːpə(r)/ *noun* 名词
a player in a game like football who tries

to stop the ball from going into the goal 守门员

goat 山羊

kid 小山羊

goat /gəʊt/ *noun* 名词
an animal with horns. People keep **goats** for their milk. 山羊 ⊃ A young goat is called a **kid**. 小山羊叫做 kid。

god o╾ /gɒd/ *noun* 名词
1 God (*no plural* 不用复数形式) the one great spirit that Christians, Jews and Muslims believe made the world 上帝；天主；真主：*Do you believe in God?* 你信上帝吗？
2 (*plural* 复数形式 **gods**) a spirit or force that people believe has power over them and nature 神：*Mars was the Roman god of war.* 马尔斯是古罗马的战神。

goddess /'gɒdes/ *noun* 名词 (*plural* 复数形式 **goddesses**)
a female god 女神：*Venus was the Roman goddess of love.* 维纳斯是古罗马的爱神。

godparent /'gɒdpeərənt/ (*also* 还有 **godfather** /'gɒdfɑːðə(r)/, **godmother** /'gɒdmʌðə(r)/) *noun* 名词
a person that parents choose to help their child and teach them about the Christian religion 教父；教母；代父；代母

goes *form of* GO * go 的不同形式

goggles /'gɒglz/ *noun* 名词 (*plural* 用复数形式)
big glasses that you wear so that water, dust, or wind cannot get in your eyes 游泳镜；护目镜；风镜：*I always wear goggles when I swim.* 我游泳时都戴泳镜。⊃ Look at the picture at **ski**. 见 ski 的插图。

going *form of* GO¹ * go¹ 的不同形式

gold o╾ /gəʊld/ *noun* 名词 (*no plural* 不用复数形式)
a yellow metal that is very valuable 金；黄金：*Is your ring made of gold?* 你的戒指是金造的吗？◇ *a gold watch* 金表
▶ **gold** *adjective* 形容词 with the colour of gold 金色的；金黄色的：*gold paint* 金漆

golden /'gəʊldən/ *adjective* 形容词
1 made of gold 金制的：*a golden crown* 金王冠
2 with the colour of gold 金色的；金黄色的：*golden hair* 金色的头发

goldfish /'gəʊldfɪʃ/ *noun* 名词 (*plural* 复数形式 **goldfish**)
a small orange fish that people keep as a pet 金鱼

golf /gɒlf/ *noun* 名词 (*no plural* 不用复数形式)
a game that you play by hitting a small ball into holes with a long stick (called a **golf club**) 高尔夫球运动：*My mother plays golf on Sundays.* 我母亲每周日打高尔夫球。
▶ **golfer** /'gɒlfə(r)/ *noun* 名词：*He's a keen golfer.* 他是个高尔夫球爱好者。
⊃ Look at Picture Dictionary page P15. 见彩页 P15。

golf course /'gɒlf kɔːs/ *noun* 名词
a large piece of land, covered in grass, where people play GOLF 高尔夫球场

gone *form of* GO¹ * go¹ 的不同形式

good¹ o╾ /gʊd/ *adjective* 形容词 (**better, best**)
1 done or made very well 做得好的；质量好的：*It's a good knife – it cuts very well.* 这把刀真好，很锋利。◇ *The film was really good.* 这部电影确实不错。
2 pleasant or enjoyable 令人愉快的
⊃ SAME MEANING **nice** 同义词为 nice：*Did you have a good time?* 你玩得开心吗？◇ *The weather was very good.* 天气非常好。
3 able to do something well 能干的；精通的；娴熟的：*She's a good driver.* 她车开得很好。◇ *James is very good at tennis.* 詹姆斯很会打网球。
4 kind, or doing the right thing 善良的；行为端正的：*It's good of you to help.* 你能帮忙真是太好了。◇ *The children were very good while you were out.* 你外出的时候孩子都很听话。
5 right or suitable 合适的；适当的：*This is a good place for a picnic.* 这是个很适合野餐的地方。
6 having a useful or helpful effect 有用的；有好处的：*Fresh fruit and*

vegetables are good for you. 新鲜水果和蔬菜很有益。

7 a word that you use when you are pleased（表示满意）好，不错：*Is everyone here? Good. Now let's begin.* 大家都到了吗？好，我们开始吧。

> **♪ SPEAKING 表达方式说明**
>
> We often say **brilliant, fantastic, great** or **terrific** instead of 'very good'. 常用 brilliant、fantastic、great 或 terrific 来替代 very good。

> **⊃** The adverb is **well**[1]. 副词为 well[1]。

good[2] **0ᴿ** /gʊd/ *noun* 名词 (*no plural* 不用复数形式)
something that is right or helpful 正直的行为；好处；益处：*They know the difference between good and bad.* 他们能区别善恶。

be no good, not be any good to not be useful 没用处；没好处：*This jumper isn't any good. It's too small.* 这件套头毛衣不行，太小了。◇ *It's no good asking Mum for money – she hasn't got any.* 向妈妈要钱也没用，她一分都没有。

do somebody good to make somebody well or happy 对某人有好处：*It will do you good to go to bed early tonight.* 今晚早点睡觉对你有好处。

for good for ever 永远；永久：*She has left home for good.* 她离开了家，再也不回去了。

good afternoon /ˌgʊd ɑːftəˈnuːn/ *exclamation* 感叹词 (*formal* 正式)
words that you say when you see or speak to somebody in the afternoon 下午好

> **♪ SPEAKING 表达方式说明**
>
> We sometimes just say **Afternoon**. 有时只说 Afternoon：*'Good afternoon, Alison.' 'Afternoon, Colin.'*"下午好，艾莉森。""下午好，科林。"
> When we see friends we usually say **Hello** or **Hi** instead of **Good morning** or **Good afternoon**. 朋友见面通常以 Hello 或 Hi 代替 Good morning 或 Good afternoon。
> When we meet somebody we don't know for the first time we say **How do you do?** or **Pleased to meet you**. 初次见面说 How do you do? 或 Pleased to meet you。

goodbye **0ᴿ** /ˌgʊdˈbaɪ/ *exclamation* 感叹词
a word that you say when somebody goes away, or when you go away 再见；再会：

Goodbye! See you tomorrow. 再见！明天见。

> **♪ SPEAKING 表达方式说明**
>
> We sometimes just say **Bye**. 有时只说 Bye：*Bye, Paddy. See you tomorrow.* 再见，帕迪。明天见。

good evening /ˌgʊd ˈiːvnɪŋ/ *exclamation* 感叹词 (*formal* 正式)
words that you say when you see or speak to somebody in the evening 晚上好

> **♪ SPEAKING 表达方式说明**
>
> We sometimes just say **Evening**. 有时只说 Evening：*'Good evening, Mr James.' 'Evening, Miss Evans.'*"晚上好，詹姆斯先生。""晚上好，埃文斯小姐。"

Good Friday /ˌgʊd ˈfraɪdeɪ/ *noun* 名词
the Friday before Easter when Christians remember the death of Christ 耶稣受难日（复活节前的星期五）

good-looking /ˌgʊd ˈlʊkɪŋ/ *adjective* 形容词
(used about people) nice to look at（人）好看的，漂亮的：*He's a good-looking boy.* 他是个漂亮的男孩。 **⊃** SAME MEANING **attractive** 同义词为 attractive **⊃** Look at the note at **beautiful**. 见 beautiful 条的注释。

good morning /ˌgʊd ˈmɔːnɪŋ/ *exclamation* 感叹词 (*formal* 正式)
words that you say when you see or speak to somebody in the morning 早上好 **⊃** Look at the note at **good afternoon**. 见 good afternoon 条的注释。

> **♪ SPEAKING 表达方式说明**
>
> We sometimes just say **Morning**. 有时只说 Morning：*'Good morning, Jack.' 'Morning.'*"早上好，杰克。""早上好。"

good-natured /ˌgʊd ˈneɪtʃəd/ *adjective* 形容词
friendly and kind 和蔼可亲的；和善的

goodness /ˈgʊdnəs/ *noun* 名词 (*no plural* 不用复数形式)
1 being good or kind 善良；美德
2 something in food that is good for your health（有益健康的）精华，养分：*Fresh vegetables have a lot of goodness in them.* 新鲜蔬菜营养丰富。

for goodness' sake words that show anger（表示愤怒）天哪：*For goodness' sake, hurry up!* 天哪，快点吧！

goodness, goodness me words that show surprise（表示吃惊）天哪: *Goodness! What a big cake!* 哇，好大的蛋糕啊!

thank goodness words that show you are happy because a problem or danger has gone away 谢天谢地: *Thank goodness it's stopped raining.* 谢天谢地，雨总算停了。

goodnight /ˌɡʊdˈnaɪt/ *exclamation* 感叹词
words that you say when you leave somebody in the evening or when somebody is going to bed 晚安

> 🔎 SPEAKING 表达方式说明
>
> We sometimes just say **Night** or **Night night**. 有时只说 Night 或 Night night: *'Goodnight, Giles. Sleep well.' 'Night.'* "晚安，贾尔斯。睡个好觉。" "晚安。"

goods 🄾 /ɡʊdz/ *noun* 名词 (*plural* 用复数形式)
1 things that you buy or sell 商品; 货品: *That shop sells electrical goods.* 那家商店售卖电器。
2 things that a train or lorry carries（火车或货车运载的）货物: *a goods train* 货运列车

good-tempered /ˌɡʊd ˈtempəd/ *adjective* 形容词
not often angry 脾气好的: *My dad is very good-tempered.* 我爸爸脾气非常好。

goose /ɡuːs/ *noun* 名词 (*plural* 复数形式 **geese** /ɡiːs/)
a big bird with a long neck. People keep **geese** on farms for their eggs and meat. 鹅 ⊃ Look at Picture Dictionary page P2. 见彩页 P2。

gooseberry /ˈɡʊzbəri/ *noun* 名词 (*plural* 复数形式 **gooseberries**)
a small green fruit with a sharp taste 醋栗 ⊃ Look at Picture Dictionary page P8. 见彩页 P8。

gorgeous /ˈɡɔːdʒəs/ *adjective* 形容词 (*informal* 非正式)
very good or attractive 迷人的; 非常吸引人的 ⊃ SAME MEANING **lovely** 同义词 lovely: *The weather was gorgeous!* 天气好极了! ◇ *What a gorgeous dress!* 多华丽的连衣裙呀!

gorilla /ɡəˈrɪlə/ *noun* 名词
an African animal like a very big black MONKEY 大猩猩（产于非洲）

gorilla 大猩猩

gory /ˈɡɔːri/ *adjective* 形容词 (**gorier, goriest**)
full of violence and blood 血腥的; 暴力的: *It's the goriest film I've ever seen.* 这是我看过的最血腥的影片。

gosh /ɡɒʃ/ *exclamation* 感叹词
a word that shows surprise（表示惊讶）天哪，啊呀: *Gosh! What a big house!* 哇，好大的房子啊!

gossip /ˈɡɒsɪp/ *noun* 名词 (*no plural* 不用复数形式)
talk about other people that is often unkind or not true 流言蜚语; 闲言碎语: *Have you heard the latest gossip about her?* 你听到有关她的最新传言吗?
▶ **gossip** *verb* 动词 (**gossips, gossiping, gossiped** /ˈɡɒsɪpt/): *They were gossiping about Jane's new boyfriend.* 他们闲扯着简的新男友。

got *form of* GET * get 的不同形式

gotten /ˈɡɒtn/ (*American* 美式英语) *form of* GET * get 的不同形式

govern /ˈɡʌvn/ *verb* 动词 (**governs, governing, governed** /ˈɡʌvnd/)
to officially rule or control a country or part of a country 统治; 管治: *Britain is governed by Parliament.* 英国由国会管治。

government 🄾 /ˈɡʌvənmənt/ *noun* 名词 often 常为 the Government
the group of people who officially rule or control a country 政府: *The leaders of the European governments are meeting today in Brussels.* 欧洲各国政府的领导人今天在布鲁塞尔召开会议。

A
B
C
D
E
F
G
H
I
J
K
L
M
N
O
P
Q
R
S
T
U
V
W
X
Y
Z

🔎 **GRAMMAR** 语法说明

Government can be used with a singular or a plural verb. * government 可与单数动词或复数动词连用：*The Government has failed to act.* 政府没有采取行动。◇ *The Government are discussing the problem.* 政府正在商讨这个问题。

governor /'gʌvənə(r)/ *noun* 名词
1 a person who rules or controls part of a country (especially in the US) 省长；（尤指美国）州长：*the Governor of California* 加州州长
2 a person who controls a place like a prison or school 机构主管；狱长；学校董事

gown 长袍

gown /gaʊn/ *noun* 名词
1 a long dress that a woman wears at a special time（特别场合穿的）长裙，女礼服：*a ball gown* 舞会礼服
2 a long loose piece of clothing that people wear to do a special job. Judges, doctors and teachers sometimes wear **gowns**.（法官或教师的）长袍；（医生的）罩衣

GP /ˌdʒiː 'piː/ *noun* 名词
a doctor who treats all types of illnesses and works in a town or village, not in a hospital 全科医生；普通医师 ⊃ GP is short for 'General Practitioner'. * GP 是 general practitioner 的缩略式。

grab /græb/ *verb* 动词 (grabs, grabbing, grabbed /græbd/)
to take something in a rough and sudden way 抓住；抢夺：*The thief grabbed her bag and ran away.* 小偷抢了她的包就跑了。

grace /greɪs/ *noun* 名词 (no plural 不用复数形式)
1 a beautiful way of moving 优美；优雅：*She dances with grace.* 她舞姿优美。
2 thanks to God that people say before or after they eat（饭前或饭后的）谢恩祷告：*Let's say grace.* 我们做谢恩祷告吧。

graceful /'greɪsfl/ *adjective* 形容词
A person or thing that is **graceful** moves in a smooth and beautiful way. 优美的；优雅的：*a graceful dancer* 姿态优美的舞蹈演员
▶ **gracefully** /'greɪsfəli/ *adverb* 副词：*He moves very gracefully.* 他动作非常优雅。

gracious /'greɪʃəs/ *adjective* 形容词
(used about people's behaviour) kind and polite（人的行为）和蔼有礼的：*a gracious smile* 慈祥的微笑
▶ **graciously** /'greɪʃəsli/ *adverb* 副词：*She accepted the invitation graciously.* 她落落大方地接受了邀请。

grade¹ ⊶ /greɪd/ *noun* 名词
1 the level or quality of something 等级；级别：*Which grade of petrol does your car use?* 你的车用哪一等级的汽油？◇ *We use only high-grade materials.* 我们只用高级材料。
2 a number or letter that a teacher gives for your work to show how good it is 成绩等级；评分等级 ⊃ SAME MEANING **mark** 同义词为 mark：*She got very good grades in all her exams.* 她所有的考试成绩都非常好。
3 (*American* 美式英语) (*British* 英式英语 **year**) a class in a school in the US where all the children are the same age 年级：*My sister is in the fifth grade.* 我妹妹读五年级。

grade² /greɪd/ *verb* 动词 (grades, grading, graded)
to sort things or people into sizes or kinds 分级；分类：*The eggs are graded by size.* 这些蛋按大小分等级。

gradual /'grædʒuəl/ *adjective* 形容词
happening slowly 逐渐的；渐进的：*There has been a gradual increase in prices.* 价格已经逐渐上涨。⊃ OPPOSITE **sudden** 反义词为 sudden

gradually /'grædʒuəli/ *adverb* 副词
slowly, over a long period of time 逐渐
地；逐步地：*Life gradually returned to
normal.* 生活逐渐恢复了正常。

graduate¹ /'grædʒuət/ *noun* 名词
1 a person who has finished studying at a
university or college and who has passed
their last exams 大学毕业生：*an Oxford
graduate* 牛津大学毕业生
2 (*American* 美式英语) a person who has
finished their school studies（中学、
小学）毕业生：*a high school graduate*
高中毕业生

graduate² /'grædʒueɪt/ *verb* 动词
(graduates, graduating, graduated)
to finish your studies at a university or
college and pass your last exams 大学
毕业：*I graduated from Exeter University
last year.* 我去年毕业于埃克塞特大学。

graffiti 涂鸦

graffiti /grə'fi:ti/ *noun* 名词 (*plural*
用复数形式)
words or pictures that people write or
draw on walls（墙上的）涂鸦：*The walls
were covered with graffiti.* 墙上布满了
涂鸦。

grain 0– /greɪn/ *noun* 名词
1 (*no plural* 不用复数形式) the seeds of
a plant that we eat, for example rice or
WHEAT 谷物；谷粒：*The animals are fed
on grain.* 这些牲畜以谷物喂饲。
2 (*plural* 复数形式 grains) a very small
hard piece of something 颗粒；细粒：
a grain of sand 一粒沙 ◇ *grains of rice*
米粒

gram 0– (*also* 亦作 gramme) /græm/
(*abbr.* 缩略式 g) *noun* 名词
a measure of weight. There are 1 000
grams in a kilogram. 克：*30 g of butter*
* 30 克黄油

grammar 0– /'græmə(r)/ *noun* 名词
(*no plural* 不用复数形式)

> 🔎 SPELLING 拼写说明
> Remember! You spell **grammar** with
> **AR** at the end, not **ER**. 记住：grammar
> 以 ar 结尾，而非 er。

the rules that tell you how to put words
together when you speak or write 语法；
文法

grammar school /'græmə skʊl/ *noun*
名词
(in Britain, especially in the past) a school
for children between the ages of 11 and
18 who are good at studying（尤指旧时
英国的）文法学校（招收 11 至 18 岁成绩
较好的学生）

grammatical /grə'mætɪkl/ *adjective*
形容词
1 connected with grammar 语法的：
*What is the grammatical rule for making
plurals in English?* 英语中构成复数的语法
规则是怎样的？
2 correct because it follows the rules of
grammar 符合语法的：*The sentence 'They
is happy' is not grammatical.* * They is
happy 这个句子不合语法。
▶ **grammatically** /grə'mætɪkli/ *adverb*
副词：*The sentence is grammatically
correct.* 这个句子语法上是对的。

gran /græn/ *noun* 名词 (*British* 英式英语)
(*informal* 非正式)
grandmother 奶奶；外婆

grand /grænd/ *adjective* 形容词 (grander,
grandest)
very big, important or rich 非常大的；
重大的；宏伟的：*They live in a grand
house in the centre of London.* 他们住在
伦敦市中心的一座豪华大宅里。

grandad /'grændæd/ *noun* 名词 (*British*
英式英语) (*informal* 非正式)
grandfather 爷爷；外公

grandchild /'græntʃaɪld/ *noun* 名词
(*plural* 复数形式 grandchildren
/'græntʃɪldrən/)
the child of your son or daughter（外）
孙子；（外）孙女

granddaughter 0– /'grændɔ:tə(r)/
noun 名词
the daughter of your son or daughter
（外）孙女

grandfather 0– /'grænfɑ:ðə(r)/ (*also
informal* 非正式亦作 grandpa /'grænpɑ:/)
noun 名词

the father of your mother or father
（外）祖父

grandmother ⊶ /'grænmʌðə(r)/
(*also informal* 非正式亦作 **grandma**
/'grænmɑː/) *noun* 名词
the mother of your mother or father
（外）祖母

grandpa *another word for* GRANDFATHER
* grandfather 的另一种说法

grandparent /'grænpeərənt/ *noun* 名词
the mother or father of your mother or
father （外）祖母；（外）祖父

grandson ⊶ /'grænsʌn/ *noun* 名词
the son of your son or daughter
（外）孙子

grandstand /'grænstænd/ *noun* 名词
lines of seats, with a roof over them,
where you sit to watch a sport （有顶的）
大看台

granny (*also* 亦作 **grannie**) /'græni/ *noun*
名词 (*plural* 复数形式 **grannies**) (*informal*
非正式)
grandmother 奶奶；外婆

grant[1] /grɑːnt/ *verb* 动词 (**grants**,
granting, **granted**) (*formal* 正式)
to give somebody what they have asked
for 批准；同意: *They granted him a visa
to leave the country.* 他们给他签发了出国
签证。
take somebody or 或 **something for
granted** to be so used to somebody or
something that you forget you are lucky
to have them （因习以为常而）不把…当
回事；认为…理所当然: *We tend to take
our comfortable lives for granted.* 我们往往
认为舒适生活是理所当然的。

grapes 葡萄

a bunch of grapes 一串葡萄

grant[2] /grɑːnt/ *noun* 名词
money that you are given for a special
reason 拨款: *a student grant* (= to help
pay for study at university) 学生助学金

grape /greɪp/ *noun* 名词
a small green or purple fruit that we eat
or make into wine 葡萄: *a bunch of
grapes* 一串葡萄 ⊃ Look at Picture
Dictionary page **P8**. 见彩页 P8。

grapefruit /'greɪpfruːt/ *noun* 名词 (*plural*
复数形式 **grapefruit** or 或 **grapefruits**)
a fruit that looks like a big orange, but is
yellow 葡萄柚；西柚 ⊃ Look at Picture
Dictionary page **P8**. 见彩页 P8。

grapevine /'greɪpvaɪn/ *noun* 名词
the grapevine the way that news is
passed from one person to another 小道
消息: *I heard it on the grapevine that
you are getting married.* 我听传闻说你要
结婚了。

graphs 图表

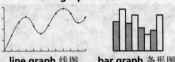

line graph 线图   **bar graph** 条形图

graph /grɑːf/ *noun* 名词
a picture that shows how numbers or
amounts are different from each other
图表

graphics /'græfɪks/ *noun* 名词 (*plural*
用复数形式)
drawings, pictures and diagrams,
especially those which are produced by
a computer （尤指电脑制作的）图像

grasp /grɑːsp/ *verb* 动词 (**grasps**, **grasping**,
grasped /grɑːspt/)
1 to hold something tightly 抓紧；抓牢:
*Claire grasped my arm to stop herself from
falling.* 克莱尔抓住了我的胳膊以防摔倒。
2 to understand something 理解；明白；
领会: *He couldn't grasp what I was
saying.* 他弄不明白我的意思。
▶ **grasp** *noun* 名词 (*no plural* 不用复数
形式): *The ball fell from my grasp.* 那个球
从我手中滑掉了。

grass ⊶ /grɑːs/ *noun* 名词 (*no plural*
不用复数形式)
a plant with thin green leaves that covers
fields and gardens. Cows and sheep eat
grass. 草；青草: *Don't walk on the grass.*
不要践踏草坪。

▶ **grassy** /'grɑːsi/ *adjective* 形容词
covered with grass 长满草的

grasshopper /'grɑːshɒpə(r)/ *noun* 名词
an insect that can jump high in the air
and makes a sound with its back legs 蚱蜢

grate /greɪt/ *verb* 动词 (grates, grating,
grated)
If you **grate** food, you rub it over a metal
tool (called a **grater**) so that it is in very
small pieces. 擦碎，磨碎（食物）: *Can
you grate some cheese?* 你能把干酪擦成丝
吗？ ◇ *grated carrot* 胡萝卜丝

grateful ⊶ /'greɪtfl/ *adjective* 形容词
If you are **grateful**, you feel or show
thanks to somebody. 感激的；感谢的:
*We are grateful to you for the help you
have given us.* 我们感谢您给予的帮助。
⊃ The noun is **gratitude**. 名词为
gratitude。 ⊃ OPPOSITE **ungrateful**
反义词为 ungrateful

grater /'greɪtə(r)/ *noun* 名词
a kitchen tool with holes in it that is used
to cut food into very small pieces by
rubbing it across its surface 礤床儿，磨碎
器（厨房用具）

gratitude /'grætɪtjuːd/ *noun* 名词
(*no plural* 不用复数形式)
the feeling of wanting to thank somebody
for something 感激之情；感谢: *We gave
David a present to show our gratitude for
all his help.* 我们送给戴维一份礼物，感谢
他对我们的一切帮助。

grave[1] /greɪv/ *noun* 名词
a hole in the ground where a dead
person's body is buried 坟墓: *We put
flowers on the grave.* 我们在坟上放了花。
⊃ Look at **tomb**. 见 tomb。

grave[2] /greɪv/ *adjective* 形容词 (graver,
gravest) (*formal* 正式)
very bad or serious 严重的；严峻的: *The
children were in grave danger.* 孩子们的
处境极为凶险。

> 🔊 SPEAKING 表达方式说明
> **Serious** is the word that we usually
> use. * serious 是常用词。

gravel /'grævl/ *noun* 名词 (*no plural* 不用
复数形式)
very small stones that are used for
making paths and roads（用于铺路的）
砾石，碎石

gravestone /'greɪvstəʊn/ *noun* 名词
a piece of stone on a GRAVE that shows
the name of the dead person 墓碑

graveyard /'greɪvjɑːd/ *noun* 名词
a piece of land, usually near a church,
where dead people are buried 墓地

gravity /'grævəti/ *noun* 名词 (*no plural*
不用复数形式)
the force that pulls everything towards
the earth 重力；地球引力

gravy /'greɪvi/ *noun* 名词 (*no plural* 不用
复数形式)
a hot brown sauce that you eat with meat
肉汁（一种伴肉食用的调味汁）

gray ⊶ *American English for* GREY 美式
英语，即 grey

graze /greɪz/ *verb* 动词 (grazes, grazing,
grazed /greɪzd/)
1 to eat grass 吃草: *The sheep were
grazing in the fields.* 羊群在牧场里吃草。
2 to hurt your skin by rubbing it against
something rough 擦伤: *He fell and
grazed his arm.* 他摔倒，把胳膊擦伤了。
▶ **graze** *noun* 名词: *She's got a graze on
her knee.* 她膝盖上有处擦伤。

grease /griːs/ *noun* 名词 (*no plural* 不用
复数形式)
fat from animals, or any thick substance
that is like oil 油脂: *You will need very
hot water to get the grease off these plates.*
你得用很烫的水才能把这些盘子上的油
洗掉。

greasy /'griːsi/ *adjective* 形容词 (greasier,
greasiest)
covered with or containing a lot of GREASE
沾满油的；多油的；油腻的: *Greasy food
is not good for you.* 油腻食物不利于健康。
◇ *greasy hair* 油性头发

great ⊶ /greɪt/ *adjective* 形容词
(greater, greatest)

> 🔊 PRONUNCIATION 读音说明
> The word **great** sounds like **late**.
> * great 读音像 late。

1 very large 大的；巨大的: *It's a great
pleasure to meet you.* 见到你非常高兴。
2 important or special 重要的；伟大的；
卓越的: *Einstein was a great scientist.*
爱因斯坦是伟大的科学家。
3 (*informal* 非正式) very; very good 非常
的；非常好的: *He knows a great many
people.* 他认识很多人。 ◇ *There's a great
big dog in the garden!* 花园里有条很大的
狗！ ◇ *They are great friends.* 他们是很
要好的朋友。
4 (*informal* 非正式) very nice or enjoyable
好极的；美妙的；令人愉快的 ⊃ SAME
MEANING **wonderful** 同义词为
wonderful: *I had a great weekend.*

A
B
C
D
E
F

G

H
I
J
K
L
M
N
O
P
Q
R
S
T
U
V
W
X
Y
Z

我周末过得非常开心。◇ *It's great to see you!* 见到你太好了!

great- /greɪt/ *prefix* 前缀
a word that you put before other words to show some members of a family. For example, your **great-grandmother** is the mother of your grandmother or grandfather, and your **great-grandson** is the son of your grandson or granddaughter. (用于家庭成员的称呼前,表示再隔一代的亲属关系。例如 great-grandmother 指祖父母或外祖父母的母亲,great-grandson 指孙子孙女或外孙子外孙女的儿子。)

greatly /'greɪtli/ *adverb* 副词
very much 很;非常: *I wasn't greatly surprised to see her there.* 在那儿见到她我并不太感到意外。

greed /gri:d/ *noun* 名词 (*no plural* 不用复数形式)
the feeling that you want more of something than you need 贪婪;贪心

greedy /'gri:di/ *adjective* 形容词 (**greedier**, **greediest**)
A **greedy** person wants or takes more of something than they need. 贪婪的;贪心的: *She's so greedy – she's eaten all the chocolates!* 她太贪心了,把所有的巧克力都吃了!

green¹ 0ᵦ /gri:n/ *adjective* 形容词 (**greener**, **greenest**)
1 with the colour of leaves and grass 绿色的: *My brother has green eyes.* 我弟弟的眼睛是绿色的。◇ *a dark green shirt* 深绿色衬衫
2 covered with grass or other plants 长满青草的;绿油油的: *green fields* 绿油油的田野
3 connected with protecting the environment or the natural world 环保的: *green products* (= that do not damage the environment) 环保产品

green² /gri:n/ *noun* 名词
the colour of leaves and grass 绿色: *She was dressed in green.* 她穿着一身绿色的衣服。

greengrocer /'gri:ngrəʊsə(r)/ *noun* 名词
1 a person who sells fruit and vegetables 果菜商
2 **greengrocer's** a shop that sells fruit and vegetables 蔬菜水果店

greenhouse /'gri:nhaʊs/ *noun* 名词 (*plural* 复数形式 **greenhouses** /'gri:nhaʊzɪz/)
a building made of glass, where plants grow 温室;暖房

the greenhouse effect /ðə 'gri:nhaʊs ɪfekt/ *noun* 名词 (*no plural* 不用复数形式)
the problem of the earth's atmosphere getting warmer all the time because of the harmful gases that go into the air 温室效应

greenhouse gas /'gri:nhaʊs 'gæs/ *noun* 名词 (*plural* 复数形式 **greenhouse gases**)
one of the harmful gases that are making the earth's atmosphere get warmer 温室气体

green onion /'gri:n ʌnjən/ *noun* 名词
American English for SPRING ONION 美式英语,即 spring onion

greet /gri:t/ *verb* 动词 (**greets**, **greeting**, **greeted**)
to say hello when you meet somebody 打招呼: *He greeted me with a smile.* 他向我微笑致意。

greeting /'gri:tɪŋ/ *noun* 名词
1 friendly words that you say when you meet somebody 问候语: *'Hello' and 'Good morning' are greetings.* "哈罗"和"早上好"都是问候语。
2 **greetings** (*plural* 用复数形式) friendly words that you write to somebody at a special time 祝词;贺词: *a greetings card* (= a card that you send at Christmas or on a birthday, for example) 贺卡

grew *form of* GROW * grow 的不同形式

grey 0ᵦ (*American also* 美式英语亦作 gray) /greɪ/ *adjective* 形容词 (**greyer**, **greyest**)
with a colour like black and white mixed together 灰色的: *a grey skirt* 灰色的裙子 ◇ *The sky was grey.* 天空灰沉沉的。◇ *He's starting to go grey* (= to have grey hair). 他的头发开始变灰白了。
▶ **grey** *noun* 名词: *He was dressed in grey.* 他穿着一身灰色的衣服。

grid /grɪd/ *noun* 名词
lines that cross each other to make squares, for example on a map 网格;方格

grief /gri:f/ *noun* 名词 (*no plural* 不用复数形式)
great sadness, especially because somebody has died 悲痛,悲伤(尤指因某人逝世)

grieve /gri:v/ *verb* 动词 (**grieves**, **grieving**, **grieved** /gri:vd/)
to feel great sadness, especially because somebody has died (尤指因某人逝世)悲痛,悲伤: *She is grieving for her dead son.* 她因儿子去世感到万分悲痛。

grill¹ /grɪl/ *noun* 名词
the part of a cooker, or a special metal object, that you use to GRILL food 烤架

grill² /grɪl/ *verb* 动词 (grills, grilling, grilled /grɪld/)
to cook food such as meat and fish on metal bars under or over heat 烧烤; 炙烤: *grilled steak* 烤牛排

grim /grɪm/ *adjective* 形容词 (grimmer, grimmest)
1 (used about a person) very serious and not smiling (人)严肃的, 不苟言笑的: *a grim expression* 严肃的表情
2 (used about a situation) very bad and making you feel worried (形势)严峻的, 令人担忧的: *The news is grim.* 这则消息令人担忧。

grin /grɪn/ *verb* 动词 (grins, grinning, grinned /grɪnd/)
to have a big smile on your face 露齿而笑; 咧着嘴笑: *She grinned at me.* 她朝我粲然一笑。
▶ **grin** *noun* 名词: *He had a big grin on his face.* 他脸上挂着灿烂的笑容。

grind /graɪnd/ *verb* 动词 (grinds, grinding, ground /graʊnd/, has ground)
to make something into very small pieces or powder by crushing it 磨碎; 碾碎: *They ground the wheat into flour.* 他们把小麦磨成面粉。◇ *ground coffee* 咖啡粉

grip /grɪp/ *verb* 动词 (grips, gripping, gripped /grɪpt/)
to hold something tightly 抓紧; 握紧: *Marie gripped my hand as we crossed the road.* 过马路的时候, 玛丽紧紧抓着我的手。
▶ **grip** *noun* 名词 (*no plural* 不用复数形式): *He kept a **tight grip** on the rope.* 他紧紧抓住绳子。

gripping /'grɪpɪŋ/ *adjective* 形容词
very exciting, in a way that holds your attention 激动人心的; 吸引人的: *a gripping adventure film* 扣人心弦的冒险片

grit /grɪt/ *noun* 名词 (*no plural* 不用复数形式)
very small pieces of stone 沙粒; 沙砾

groan /grəʊn/ *verb* 动词 (groans, groaning, groaned /grəʊnd/)
to make a deep sad sound, for example because you are unhappy or in pain 呻吟; 叹息: *'I've got a headache,' he groaned.* "我头疼。" 他哼哼着说。
▶ **groan** *noun* 名词: *She gave a groan, then lay still.* 她发出一声呻吟, 就躺着不动了。

grocer /'grəʊsə(r)/ *noun* 名词
1 a person who has a shop that sells food and other things for the home 食品杂货商
2 grocer's a shop that sells food and other things for the home 食品杂货店
⊃ Look at Picture Dictionary page **P13**. 见彩页 P13。

groceries /'grəʊsəriz/ *noun* 名词 (*plural* 用复数形式)
food and other things for the home that you buy regularly 食品杂货: *Can you help me unload the groceries from the car, please?* 请你帮我把食物和日用品从车上搬下来好吗?

groom /gru:m/ *noun* 名词
1 a person whose job is to look after horses 马倌; 马夫
2 a man on the day of his wedding 新郎
⊃ SAME MEANING **bridegroom** 同义词为 bridegroom

groove /gru:v/ *noun* 名词
a long thin cut in the surface of something hard (硬质物体表面的)沟, 槽

grope /grəʊp/ *verb* 动词 (gropes, groping, groped /grəʊpt/)
to try to find something by using your hands, when you cannot see (因看不见)摸索: *He groped around for the light switch.* 他摸索着找电灯开关。

ground¹ *form of* GRIND * grind 的不同形式

ground² 0━ /graʊnd/ *noun* 名词
1 (*no plural* 不用复数形式) the surface of the earth 地面: *We sat on the ground to eat our picnic.* 我们坐在地上吃野餐。◇ *The ground was too dry for the plants to grow.* 土地太干燥, 植物生长不了。
2 (*plural* 复数形式 grounds) a piece of land that is used for something special (某种用途的)场地: *a sports ground* 运动场 ◇ *a playground* (= a place where children play) 操场
3 grounds (*plural* 用复数形式) the land around a large building (建筑物周围的)场地, 庭院: *the grounds of the hospital* 医院的院子

ground floor /,graʊnd 'flɔ:(r)/ *noun* 名词 (*British* 英式英语) (*American* 美式英语 first floor)
the part of a building that is at the same level as the street 地面的楼层; 底层; 一楼: *My office is on the ground floor.* 我的办公室在一楼。

A B C D E F G H I J K L M N O P Q R S T U V W X Y Z

A B C D E F **G** H I J K L M N O P Q R S T U V W X Y Z

group 0━ /gru:p/ *noun* 名词

> 🔍 PRONUNCIATION 读音说明
> The word **group** sounds like **loop**.
> * group 读音像 loop。

1 a number of people or things together 组；群；批：*A group of people were standing outside the shop.* 商店外站着一群人。
2 a number of people who play music together 乐队；乐团 ⊃ SAME MEANING **band** 同义词为 band

grow 0━ /grəʊ/ *verb* 动词 (grows, growing, grew /gru:/, has grown /grəʊn/)
1 to become bigger 长大；长高；发育：*Children grow very quickly.* 孩子长得很快。
2 When a plant **grows** somewhere, it lives there. (植物)生长：*Oranges grow in warm countries.* 柑橘生长在暖和的国家。
3 to plant something in the ground and look after it 种植；栽种：*We grow vegetables in our garden.* 我们在园子里种蔬菜。
4 to allow your hair or nails to grow 留，蓄（头发或指甲）：*Mark has grown a beard.* 马克留胡子了。
5 to become 变成；变得 ⊃ SAME MEANING **get** 同义词为 get：*It was growing dark.* 天渐渐黑了。

grow into something to get bigger and become something 逐渐成长为：*Kittens grow into cats.* 小猫长成大猫。
grow out of something to become too big to do or wear something 长大而不再做某事；长大了而穿不上：*She's grown out of her shoes.* 她的鞋已经穿不下了。
grow up to become an adult; to change from a child to a man or woman 长大成人；成年：*I want to be a doctor when I grow up.* 我长大后想当医生。

growl /graʊl/ *verb* 动词 (growls, growling, growled /graʊld/)
If a dog **growls**, it makes a low angry sound. (狗)低声吼叫：*The dog growled at the stranger.* 那条狗对着陌生人吼叫。
▶ **growl** *noun* 名词：*The dog gave a low growl.* 狗低声吼叫了一下。

grown-up /ˈgrəʊn ʌp/ *noun* 名词
a man or woman, not a child 成人
⊃ SAME MEANING **adult** 同义词为 adult：*Ask a grown-up to help you.* 找个大人帮你吧。
▶ **grown-up** /ˌgrəʊn ˈʌp/ *adjective* 形容词：*She has a grown-up son.* 她有个儿子已经成年。

growth 0━ /grəʊθ/ *noun* 名词
(*no plural* 不用复数形式)
the process of getting bigger 成长；发育；增长：*A good diet is important for children's growth.* 良好的饮食对儿童的发育很重要。◇ *population growth* 人口增长

grub /grʌb/ *noun* 名词
1 (*plural* 复数形式 **grubs**) a young insect when it comes out of the egg (昆虫的)幼虫；蛆
2 (*no plural* 不用复数形式) (*informal* 非正式) food 食物

grubby /ˈgrʌbi/ *adjective* 形容词 (grubbier, grubbiest)
dirty 肮脏的；污秽的：*grubby hands* 脏手

grudge /grʌdʒ/ *noun* 名词
a feeling of anger towards somebody, because of something bad that they have done to you in the past 不满；怨恨：*I don't bear him a grudge about what happened.* 我并没有因为所发生的事而对他心存怨恨。

gruesome /ˈgru:səm/ *adjective* 形容词
very unpleasant and shocking 恐怖的；可怕的：*a gruesome murder* 骇人听闻的谋杀案

grumble /ˈgrʌmbl/ *verb* 动词 (grumbles, grumbling, grumbled /ˈgrʌmbld/)
to say many times that you do not like something 嘟囔；发牢骚：*She's always grumbling about her boss.* 她总是在发牢骚，说老板的不是。

grumpy /ˈgrʌmpi/ *adjective* 形容词 (grumpier, grumpiest)
a little angry 不悦的；脾气坏的 ⊃ SAME MEANING **bad-tempered** 同义词为 bad-tempered：*She gets grumpy when she's tired.* 她累了就容易发怒。

grunt /grʌnt/ *verb* 动词 (grunts, grunting, grunted)
to make a short rough sound, like a pig makes 发出哼声；咕哝
▶ **grunt** *noun* 名词：*He gave a grunt of pain.* 他发出痛苦的哼声。

guarantee¹ /ˌgærənˈti:/ *noun* 名词
1 a promise that something will happen 保证；担保：*I want a guarantee that you will do the work today.* 我要你保证今天会做这工作。
2 a written promise by a company that it will repair a thing you have bought, or give you a new one, if it goes wrong 保证书；保修单：*a two-year guarantee* 两年的保修证明 ◇ *The computer is still under guarantee.* 这台电脑还在保修期内。

guarantee² /ˌɡærənˈtiː/ *verb* 动词
(guarantees, guaranteeing, guaranteed
/ˌɡærənˈtiːd/)
1 to promise that something will be done
or will happen 保证；担保： *I can't
guarantee that I will be able to help you,
but I'll try.* 我不能保证一定能帮你，但我
会尽力而为。
2 to say that you will repair a thing that
somebody buys, or give them a new one,
if it goes wrong 提供保修： *The television
is guaranteed for three years.* 这台电视机
保修三年。

guard¹ ⚬┓ /ɡɑːd/ *noun* 名词

> 🔎 PRONUNCIATION 读音说明
> The word **guard** sounds just like the
> beginning of the word **garden**. * guard
> 读音同 garden 的起首部分。

1 a person who keeps somebody or
something safe from other people, or
who stops somebody from escaping
警卫；看守： *There are security guards
outside the bank.* 银行外面有警卫守着。
◇ *The soldiers were on guard outside the
palace* (= guarding the palace). 士兵在
宫殿外戒备着。
2 (*British* 英式英语) a person whose job is
to look after people and things on a train
列车长
be on your guard to be ready if
something bad happens 警惕；提防

guard² ⚬┓ /ɡɑːd/ *verb* 动词 (guards,
guarding, guarded)
to keep somebody or something safe
from other people, or to stop somebody
from escaping 保卫；守卫： *The house
was guarded by two large dogs.* 这所房子
有两条大狗看守着。

guardian /ˈɡɑːdiən/ *noun* 名词
a person who looks after a child with no
parents （儿童的）监护人

guerrilla /ɡəˈrɪlə/ *noun* 名词
a person who is not in an army but who
fights secretly against the government or
an army 游击队员

guess ⚬┓ /ɡes/ *verb* 动词 (guesses,
guessing, guessed /ɡest/)
to give an answer when you do not know
if it is right 猜；猜测： *Can you guess how
old he is?* 你猜他多大？
▶ **guess** *noun* 名词 (*plural* 复数形式
guesses): *If you don't know the answer,
have a guess!* 你要是不知道答案，就猜一
下吧！

guest ⚬┓ /ɡest/ *noun* 名词
1 a person that you invite to your home
or to a party or special event 客人；
宾客： *There were 200 guests at the
wedding.* * 200 名宾客参加了婚礼。
2 a person who is staying in a hotel
（旅馆的）客人，房客

guest house /ˈɡest haʊs/ *noun* 名词
(*plural* 复数形式 guest houses /ˈɡest
haʊzɪz/)
a small hotel 小旅馆

guidance /ˈɡaɪdns/ *noun* 名词 (*no plural*
不用复数形式)
help and advice 指导；咨询： *I want
some guidance on how to find a job.* 我想
咨询一下如何找工作。

guide¹ ⚬┓ /ɡaɪd/ *noun* 名词
1 a book that tells you about something,
or how to do something 指南；手册：
a guide to birdwatching 观鸟指南
2 (*also* 亦作 guidebook /ˈɡaɪdbʊk/) a book
that tells you about a place you are
visiting 旅游指南；旅游手册： *a guide to
Bangkok* 曼谷旅游指南
3 a person who shows other people
where to go and tells them about a place
导游；向导： *The guide took us round the
castle.* 导游带领我们参观了城堡。
4 Guide (*also* 亦作 Girl Guide) (*British*
英式英语) (*American* 美式英语 Girl Scout)
a member of a special club for girls
(called the Girl Guides) which does a lot
of activities with them, for example
camping 女童子军

guide² ⚬┓ /ɡaɪd/ *verb* 动词 (guides,
guiding, guided)
to show somebody where to go or what
to do 引领；指路；指导： *He guided us
through the busy streets to our hotel.*
他带领我们穿过繁忙的街道到了我们下榻的
旅馆。

guidelines /ˈɡaɪdlaɪnz/ *noun* 名词 (*plural*
用复数形式)
official advice or rules on how to do
something 指导方针；指导原则

guilt /ɡɪlt/ *noun* 名词 (*no plural* 不用复数
形式)
1 the feeling you have when you know
that you have done something wrong
内疚；愧疚： *She felt terrible guilt after
stealing the money.* 她偷了钱以后深感
内疚。
2 the fact of having broken the law
有罪： *The police could not prove his
guilt.* 警方无法证明他有罪。 ⊃ OPPOSITE
innocence 反义词为 innocence

A
B
C
D
E
F
G
H
I
J
K
L
M
N
O
P
Q
R
S
T
U
V
W
X
Y
Z

guilty ⚓ /ˈgɪlti/ *adjective* 形容词
(guiltier, guiltiest)
1 If you feel **guilty**, you feel that you have done something wrong. 内疚的；愧疚的:
*I feel **guilty about** lying to her.* 我对她撒了谎，感到愧疚。
2 If you are **guilty**, you have broken the law. 有罪的；犯了罪的: *He is **guilty of** murder.* 他犯了谋杀罪。 ⊃ OPPOSITE **innocent** 反义词为 innocent

guinea pig /ˈgɪni pɪg/ *noun* 名词
1 a small animal with short ears and no tail, that people often keep as a pet 天竺鼠，豚鼠（耳短无尾，常作宠物饲养）⊃ Look at Picture Dictionary page **P2**. 见彩页 P2。
2 a person who is used in an experiment 实验对象

guitars 吉他

bass guitar 低音吉他

guitar 吉他   electric guitar 电吉他

guitar /gɪˈtɑː(r)/ *noun* 名词
a musical instrument with strings 吉他:
*I **play the guitar** in a band.* 我在乐队里弹吉他。
▶ **guitarist** /gɪˈtɑːrɪst/ *noun* 名词 a person who plays the GUITAR 吉他手

gulf /gʌlf/ *noun* 名词
a large part of the sea that has land almost all the way around it 海湾:
the Gulf of Mexico 墨西哥湾

gull /gʌl/ (*also* 亦作 **seagull**) *noun* 名词
a large grey or white bird that lives by the sea 海鸥

gulp /gʌlp/ *verb* 动词 (gulps, gulping, gulped /gʌlpt/)
to eat or drink something quickly 匆匆吞下；狼吞虎咽: *He **gulped** down a cup of tea and left.* 他一口气喝了一杯茶就走了。
▶ **gulp** *noun* 名词: *She took a **gulp of** coffee.* 她喝了一大口咖啡。

gum /gʌm/ *noun* 名词
1 (*plural* 复数形式 **gums**) Your **gums** are the hard pink parts of your mouth that hold the teeth. 牙龈；齿龈
2 (*no plural* 不用复数形式) thick liquid that you use for sticking pieces of paper together（粘纸用的）粘胶 ⊃ SAME MEANING **glue** 同义词为 glue ⊃ Look also at **chewing gum**. 亦见 chewing gum。

gun ⚓ /gʌn/ *noun* 名词
a weapon that shoots out pieces of metal (called **bullets**) to kill or hurt people or animals 枪；炮: *He aimed the gun at the bird and fired.* 他瞄准了那只鸟然后开枪。

gunman /ˈgʌnmən/ *noun* 名词 (*plural* 复数形式 **gunmen** /ˈgʌnmən/)
a man who uses a gun to rob or kill people 持枪歹徒

gunpowder /ˈgʌnpaʊdə(r)/ *noun* 名词 (*no plural* 不用复数形式)
powder that explodes. It is used in guns and FIREWORKS. 火药

gush /gʌʃ/ *verb* 动词 (gushes, gushing, gushed /gʌʃt/)
to flow out suddenly and strongly 喷出；涌出: *Blood was **gushing from** the cut in her leg.* 她腿上的伤口血流如注。

gust /gʌst/ *noun* 名词
a sudden strong wind 一阵强风: *A **gust** of wind blew his hat off.* 一阵狂风把他的帽子刮走了。

guts /gʌts/ *noun* 名词 (*plural* 用复数形式) (*informal* 非正式)
the courage to do something difficult or unpleasant 勇气；胆量: *It takes **guts** to admit you're wrong.* 承认自己犯错需要很大的勇气。

gutter /ˈgʌtə(r)/ *noun* 名词
1 a pipe under the edge of a roof to carry away water when it rains 檐沟；天沟；檐槽
2 the lower part at the edge of a road where water is carried away when it rains（路旁）排水沟

guy /gaɪ/ *noun* 名词
1 (*informal* 非正式) a man 男人；家伙: *He's a nice **guy**!* 他人不错!
2 **guys** (*plural* 用复数形式) (*informal* 非正式) used when speaking to a group of men and women or boys and girls 伙计们；兄弟姐妹们: *Come on **guys**, let's go.* 快点，伙计们，咱们走吧!

gym /dʒɪm/ *noun* 名词
1 (*plural* 复数形式 gyms) (*also formal*
正式亦作 gymnasium /dʒɪm'neɪziəm/)
a room or building with equipment for
doing physical exercise 健身房；体育馆
2 (*no plural* 不用复数形式)
= GYMNASTICS: *a gym class* 体操课

gymnastics /dʒɪm'næstɪks/ *noun* 名词
(*also* 亦作 gym) (*no plural* 不用复数形式)
exercises for your body 体操：
a gymnastics competition 体操比赛

⊃ Look at Picture Dictionary page **P15**.
见彩页 **P15**。

▸ **gymnast** /'dʒɪmnæst/ *noun* 名词
a person who does GYMNASTICS 体操
运动员

Gypsy (*also* 亦作 Gipsy) /'dʒɪpsi/ *noun*
名词 (*plural* 复数形式 Gypsies)
Gypsies are people who travel around
from one place to another and live in
homes with wheels (called caravans).
吉卜赛人

A
B
C
D
E
F
G
H
I
J
K
L
M
N
O
P
Q
R
S
T
U
V
W
X
Y
Z

H h

H, h /eɪtʃ/ *noun* 名词 (*plural* 复数形式 H's, h's /ˈeɪtʃɪz/)
the eighth letter of the English alphabet 英语字母表的第 8 个字母: *'Hat' begins with an 'H'.* ◆ hat 一词以字母 h 开头。

habit o━ /ˈhæbɪt/ *noun* 名词
something that you do very often 习惯: *Smoking is a bad habit.* 吸烟是一种坏习惯。 ◇ *She's got a habit of phoning me when I'm in bed.* 她习惯了在我睡觉的时候给我打电话。

habitat /ˈhæbɪtæt/ *noun* 名词
the natural place where a plant or an animal lives （动植物的）生存环境, 栖息地

hack /hæk/ *verb* 动词 (hacks, hacking, hacked /hækt/)
1 to cut something or somebody in a rough and violent way 砍；劈: *I hacked the dead branches off the tree.* 我把枯枝从树上砍了下来。
2 to use a computer to get into somebody else's computer in order to damage it or get secret information 非法侵入（他人的电脑系统）: *He hacked into the bank's computer system.* 他侵入了这家银行的电脑系统。

had *form of* HAVE ✻ have 的不同形式

hadn't /ˈhædnt/ *short for* HAD NOT ✻ had not 的缩略式

haggle /ˈhægl/ *verb* 动词 (haggles, haggling, haggled /ˈhægld/)
to argue with somebody until you agree about the price of something 讲价: *Tourists were haggling over the price of a carpet.* 游客正在就一块地毯讨价还价。

ha! ha! /ˌhɑː ˈhɑː/ *exclamation* 感叹词
words that you write to show that somebody is laughing 哈！哈！（笑声）

hail /heɪl/ *noun* 名词 (*no plural* 不用复数形式)
frozen rain that falls in small hard balls (called **hailstones**) 雹；冰雹
▶ **hail** *verb* 动词 (hails, hailing, hailed /heɪld/): *It's hailing.* 下冰雹了。

hair o━ /heə(r)/ *noun* 名词
1 (*no plural* 不用复数形式) all the hairs on a person's head 头发: *She's got long black hair.* 她留着乌黑的长发。

hair 头发

She has a ponytail.
她留着马尾辫。

She has long, straight hair.
她一头长直发。

fringe (*British* 英式英语)
bangs (*American* 美式英语) 刘海
She has pigtails/plaits (*British* 英式英语)
braids (*American* 美式英语).
她留着辫子。

parting 分缝
beard 胡须
He has wavy hair.
他留着波浪形的头发。

He has short, curly hair.
他一头短的鬈发。

moustache (*British* 英式英语) mustache (*American* 美式英语) 髭
He is bald.
他秃顶了。

2 (*plural* 复数形式 **hairs**) one of the long thin things that grow on the skin of people and animals 毛；毛发：*There's a hair in my soup.* 我的汤里有根毛。

> 🔍 **WORD BUILDING** 词汇扩充
>
> You wash your hair with **shampoo** and make it tidy with a **hairbrush** or a **comb**. 洗发水叫做 shampoo，发刷叫做 hairbrush，梳子叫做 comb。
> Some words that you can use to talk about the colour of a person's hair are **black**, **dark**, **brown**, **ginger**, **red**, **fair**, **blonde** and **grey**. 描述头发颜色可以用 black（黑色）、dark（深色）、brown（棕色）、ginger（姜黄色）、red（红褐色）、fair（浅色）、blonde（金黄色）和 grey（灰白色）。

hairbrush /'heəbrʌʃ/ *noun* 名词 (*plural* 复数形式 **hairbrushes**)
a brush that you use to make your hair tidy 发刷 ⊃ Look at the picture at **brush¹**. 见 brush¹ 的插图。

haircut /'heəkʌt/ *noun* 名词
1 when somebody cuts your hair 理发：*I need a haircut.* 我该理发了。
2 the way that your hair is cut 发型；发式：*I like your new haircut.* 我喜欢你的新发型。

hairdresser /'heədresə(r)/ *noun* 名词
1 a person whose job is to wash, cut and arrange people's hair 理发师；美发师 ⊃ Look at **barber**. 见 barber。
2 hairdresser's the place where you go to have your hair cut 理发店；美发店：*I'm going to the hairdresser's tomorrow.* 我打算明天去理发。

hairdryer (*also* 亦作 **hairdrier**) /'heədraɪə(r)/ *noun* 名词
a machine that dries your hair by blowing hot air on it（吹干头发的）吹风机

hairstyle /'heəstaɪl/ *noun* 名词
the way that your hair is cut and arranged 发型；发式

hairy /'heəri/ *adjective* 形容词 (**hairier**, **hairiest**)
covered with a lot of hair 多毛的：*He has got very hairy legs.* 他腿上毛很多。

half¹ ⊶ /hɑːf/ *noun, adjective, pronoun* 名词，形容词，代词 (*plural* 复数形式 **halves** /hɑːvz/)

> 🔍 **PRONUNCIATION** 读音说明
>
> The word **half** sounds like **staff**, because we don't say the letter **l** in this word. * half 读音像 staff，因为 l 在这里不发音。

one of two equal parts of something; ½ 半；一半：*Half of six is three.* 六的一半是三。◊ *I lived in that flat for two and a half years.* 我在那套公寓住了两年半。◊ *The journey takes an hour and a half.* 行程要一个半小时。◊ *I've been waiting more than half an hour.* 我已经等了半个多小时了。◊ *She gave me half of her apple.* 她把苹果分了一半给我。◊ *Half this money is yours.* 这笔钱有一半是你的。
in half so that there are two equal parts 成为相等的两半：*Cut the cake in half.* 把蛋糕切成两半。⊃ The verb is **halve**. 动词为 halve。

half past ⋯点半

It's **half past** nine. 现在是九点半。

half² ⊶ /hɑːf/ *adverb* 副词
50%; not completely 半；不完全：*The bottle is half empty.* 瓶子是半空的。◊ *He's half German* (= one of his parents is German). 他有一半德国血统。
half past 30 minutes after an hour on the clock（时间）⋯点半：*It's half past nine.* 现在是九点半。

half-price /ˌhɑːf 'praɪs/ *adjective, adverb* 形容词，副词
for half the usual price 半价（的）：*You can get half-price tickets one hour before the show.* 演出前一个小时可买到半票。

half-term /ˌhɑːf 'tɜːm/ *noun* 名词 (*British* 英式英语)
a short school holiday in the middle of a three-month period of school (called a **term**)（学校的）期中假

half-time /ˌhɑːf 'taɪm/ *noun* 名词 (*no plural* 不用复数形式)

a short time in the middle of a game like football, when play stops （体育比赛的）中场休息时间

halfway /ˌhɑːˈfweɪ/ *adverb* 副词
in the middle 在…的中间；在中途；到一半：*They live **halfway between** London and Oxford.* 他们住在伦敦和牛津的中间。◇ *She went out **halfway through** the lesson.* 她课上到一半就出去了。

hall 0━ /hɔːl/ *noun* 名词
1 the room in a house that is near the front door and has doors to other rooms 门厅；正门过道：*You can leave your coat in the hall.* 你可以把大衣留在门厅里。
2 a big room or building where a lot of people meet 礼堂；大厅：*a concert hall* 音乐厅 ◇ *We did our exams in the school hall.* 我们在学校礼堂考试。

hallo = HELLO

Halloween (*also* 亦作 **Hallowe'en**) /ˌhæləʊˈiːn/ *noun* 名词 (*no plural* 不用复数形式)
the night of 31 October 万圣节前夕
（10 月 31 日晚）

> ◯ **CULTURE** 文化资料补充
> People used to believe that dead people appeared from their graves at **Halloween**. Children now dress up as witches, ghosts, etc. and go to people's houses saying '**trick or treat**' and the people give them sweets. 人们过去认为鬼魂会在万圣节前夕从坟墓中出来。现在，小孩会装扮成女巫、鬼魂等，挨家挨户说 trick or treat（不请吃就捣蛋），然后就可以分到糖果。

halt /hɔːlt/ *noun* 名词 (*no plural* 不用复数形式)
come to a halt to stop 停止；停下：*The car came to a halt in front of the school.* 汽车在学校门前停了下来。
▸ **halt** *verb* 动词 (halts, halting, halted) (*formal* 正式)：*She halted just outside the gate.* 她就在大门外停了下来。

halve /hɑːv/ *verb* 动词 (halves, halving, halved /hɑːvd/)
to divide something into two parts that are the same 把…分成两等分：*There were two of us, so I halved the orange.* 我们有两个人，所以我把橙分成了两半。◯ The noun is **half**. 名词为 half.

halves *plural of* HALF[1] * half[1] 的复数形式

ham /hæm/ *noun* 名词 (*no plural* 不用复数形式)
meat from a pig's leg that you can keep for a long time because salt or smoke was used to prepare it 火腿 ◯ Look at the note at **pig**. 见 pig 条的注释。

hamburger /ˈhæmbɜːɡə(r)/ *noun* 名词 (*also* 亦作 **burger**)
meat cut into very small pieces and made into a flat round shape. You often eat it in a round piece of bread (called a **roll**). 汉堡肉饼；汉堡包：*A hamburger and chips, please.* 请给我一份汉堡包和炸薯条。

hammer 锤子

hammer[1] 0━ /ˈhæmə(r)/ *noun* 名词
a tool with a handle and a heavy metal part, that you use for hitting nails into things 锤子；榔头

hammer[2] /ˈhæmə(r)/ *verb* 动词 (hammers, hammering, hammered /ˈhæməd/)
1 to hit something with a hammer （用锤子）敲，锤打：*I **hammered** the nail **into** the wood.* 我把钉子钉进木头里去了。
2 to hit something hard 用力敲打：*He **hammered on** the door until somebody opened it.* 他使劲地敲门，直到有人来开门为止。

hammock /ˈhæmək/ *noun* 名词
a bed made of cloth or rope that you hang up at the two ends 吊床

hamster /ˈhæmstə(r)/ *noun* 名词
a small animal that people keep as a pet. A **hamster** can keep food in the sides of its mouth. 仓鼠（宠物，会将食物藏于嘴边颊囊）◯ Look at Picture Dictionary page **P2**. 见彩页 P2。

hand[1] 0━ /hænd/ *noun* 名词
1 (*plural* 复数形式 **hands**) the part at the end of your arm that has four **fingers** and a **thumb** 手：*She held the letter in her hand.* 她把信握在手里。
2 **a hand** (*no plural* 不用复数形式) (*informal* 非正式) some help 帮助：*Could you give me **a hand** with my homework?*

你教我做作业好吗？◇ *Do you need a* *hand?* 你需要帮忙吗？

3 (*plural* 复数形式 **hands**) one of the parts of a clock or watch that move to show the time （钟表）指针 ➾ Look at the picture at **alarm clock**. 见 alarm clock 的插图。

by hand without using a machine 手工制作；手工： *The curtains were made by hand.* 这些窗帘是手工缝制的。

get out of hand to become difficult to control 变得难以控制： *The party got out of hand.* 派对失控了。

hand in hand with your hand in another person's hand 手拉手： *They were walking hand in hand.* 他们手拉手走着。

hands up
1 put one hand in the air if you can answer the question 举手（回答问题）
2 put your hands in the air because somebody has a gun （持枪者命令他人）举起手来

hold hands 牵手

They're **holding hands**.
他们手拉着手。

hold hands to have another person's hand in your hand 牵手

in good hands well looked after 得到很好的照顾： *Don't worry – your son is in good hands.* 不要担心，你儿子得到很好的照顾。

on hand near and ready to help 随时提供帮助： *There is a doctor on hand 24 hours a day.* 一天 24 小时都有医生值班。

on the one hand … on the other hand words that show the good and bad things about something （表示事物好坏两方面）一方面…另一方面…： *On the one hand cars are very useful; on the other*

hand they cause an awful lot of pollution. 一方面，汽车很有用；但另一方面，汽车会造成大量的污染。

hand 手

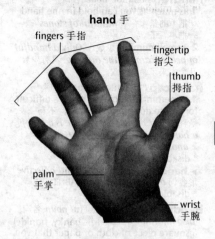

fingers 手指
fingertip 指尖
thumb 拇指
palm 手掌
wrist 手腕

hand[2] /hænd/ *verb* 动词 (**hands, handing, handed**)
to put something into somebody's hand 交；递： *Can you hand me the scissors, please?* 请你把剪刀递给我好吗？◇ *I handed the money to the shop assistant.* 我把钱交给了售货员。

hand something down to pass something from an older person to a younger one 把…传给（年纪较小者）： *He never had any new clothes – they were all handed down from his older brothers.* 他从来没穿过新衣服，所穿的都是几个哥哥留下的。

hand something in to give something to somebody 提交；呈交；上交： *The teacher asked us to hand in our homework.* 老师叫我们交作业。

hand something out to give something to many people 分发： *Please hand out these books.* 请把这些书发出去。

hand something over to give something to somebody 把…交给；移交： *'Hand over your weapons!'* "把武器交出来！"

handbag /'hændbæg/ *noun* 名词 (*British* 英式英语) (*American* 美式英语 **purse**)
a small bag that a woman uses for carrying things like money and keys （女用）小手提包

handcuffs /'hændkʌfs/ *noun* 名词 (*plural* 用复数形式)

A B C D E F G H I J K L M N O P Q R S T U V W X Y Z

two metal rings with a chain that the police put on a prisoner's arms so that they cannot use their hands 手铐

handful /'hændfʊl/ *noun* 名词
1 as much as you can hold in one hand 一把（的量）：*a handful of* stones 一把小石子
2 a small number 少数：*Only a handful of people came to the meeting.* 只有少数几个人来了参加会议。

handicap /'hændikæp/ *noun* 名词
1 something that makes it more difficult for you to do something 障碍；不利条件：*Not being able to drive is a bit of a handicap.* 不会开车可不太方便。
2 another word for DISABILITY
* disability 的另一种说法
▶ **handicapped** /'hændikæpt/ *adjective* 形容词 another word for DISABLED
* disabled 的另一种说法

handkerchief /'hæŋkətʃɪf/ *noun* 名词
(*also informal* 非正式亦作 **hanky, hankie**)
a square piece of cloth or paper that you use for clearing (**blowing**) your nose 手帕；纸巾

handles 把手；柄
handles 把手   **knobs** 旋钮

door handle 门把手

handle 柄
knob 旋钮
knob 旋钮
knob 球形把手

handle¹ /'hændl/ *noun* 名词
the part of a thing that you hold in your hand 把手；柄：*I turned the handle and opened the door.* 我转动把手，打开了门。◇ *Hold that knife by the handle.* 握着那把刀的刀柄。

handle² /'hændl/ *verb* 动词
(**handles, handling, handled** /'hændld/)
1 to touch something with your hands （用手）触，拿：*Always wash your hands before you handle food.* 拿食物前要洗手。
2 to control or deal with somebody or something 控制；处理：*He's not very good at handling pressure.* 他不善于应付压力。

handlebars /'hændlbɑːz/ *noun* 名词
(*plural* 用复数形式)
the part at the front of a bicycle or motorbike that you hold when you are riding it（自行车或摩托车的）把手，车把 ⊃ Look at the picture at **bicycle**. 见 bicycle 的插图。

hand luggage /'hænd lʌgɪdʒ/ *noun* 名词
(*British* 英式英语) (*American* 美式英语 **carry-on bag**) (*no plural* 不用复数形式)
a small bag that you carry with you on a plane 手提行李

handmade /ˌhænd'meɪd/ *adjective* 形容词
made by a person, not by a machine 手工制作的：*handmade chocolates* 手制巧克力

handsome /'hænsəm/ *adjective* 形容词
attractive 英俊的；帅气的 ⊃ SAME MEANING **good-looking** 同义词为 good-looking：*a handsome man* 英俊的男子 ⊃ Look at the note at **beautiful**. 见 beautiful 条的注释。

hands-on /ˌhændz 'ɒn/ *adjective* 形容词
doing something yourself, rather than watching somebody else do it 实际操作的：*She needs some hands-on experience.* 她需要一些实际经验。

handwriting /'hændraɪtɪŋ/ *noun* 名词
(*no plural* 不用复数形式)
the way you write 笔迹；字迹：*Her handwriting is difficult to read.* 她写的字很难辨读。

handy /'hændi/ *adjective* 形容词 (**handier, handiest**)
1 useful 有用的；好用的：*This bag will be handy for carrying my books.* 用这个袋子装我的书会很凑手。
2 near and easy to find or reach 近便；便利：*Have you got a pen handy?* 你手头有钢笔吗？
come in handy to be useful 有用处；用得着：*Don't throw that box away – it might come in handy.* 别把那个箱子扔掉，可能以后会派得上用场。

hang 0═ /hæŋ/ *verb* 动词
1 (hangs, hanging, hung /hʌŋ/, has hung) to fix something, or to be fixed at the top so that the lower part is free 悬挂；吊：*Hang your coat up in the hall.* 把你的大衣挂在门厅里。◇ *I hung the washing on the line to dry.* 我把洗好的衣服挂在晒衣绳上晾干。
2 (hangs, hanging, hanged /hæŋd/, has hanged) to kill yourself or another person by putting a rope around the neck and allowing the body to drop downwards 绞死；上吊：*She was hanged for murder.* 她因谋杀罪被处以绞刑。
hang about, hang around (*informal* 非正式) to stay somewhere with nothing special to do 闲荡：*My plane was late so I had to hang about in the airport all morning.* 飞机误点了，所以我一上午都在机场闲待着。
hang on (*informal* 非正式) to wait for a short time 等一下：*Hang on – I'm not ready.* 等一等，我还没有准备好。
hang on to somebody or 或 **something** to hold somebody or something firmly 抓紧：*Hang on to your purse.* 把钱包攥紧。
hang up to end a telephone call by putting the telephone down 挂断电话

hanger /ˈhæŋə(r)/ *noun* 名词 (*also* 亦作 **coat hanger**)
a piece of metal, wood or plastic with a hook. You use it for hanging clothes on. 衣架 ⊃ Look at the picture at **coat hanger**. 见 coat hanger 的插图。

hang-glider /ˈhæŋ ɡlaɪdə(r)/ *noun* 名词
1 a very large piece of material on a frame, which you hang from and fly through the air 悬挂式滑翔机
2 a person who does HANG-GLIDING 悬挂式滑翔运动员
▶ **hang-gliding** /ˈhæŋ ɡlaɪdɪŋ/ *noun* 名词 (*no plural* 不用复数形式)：*I'd love to try hang-gliding.* 我很想试一试悬挂式滑翔。⊃ Look at Picture Dictionary page P15. 见彩页 P15。

hanky (*also* 亦作 hankie /ˈhæŋki/) *noun* 名词 (*plural* 复数形式 hankies) (*informal* 非正式)
another word for HANDKERCHIEF
* handkerchief 的另一种说法

happen 0═ /ˈhæpən/ *verb* 动词
(happens, happening, happened /ˈhæpənd/)
to take place, usually without being planned first 发生：*How did the accident happen?* 事故是怎么发生的？◇ *Did you*

hear what **happened** to me yesterday? 你听说我昨天发生了什么事吗？
happen to do something to do something by chance 碰巧；恰好：*I happened to meet Tim yesterday.* 我昨天刚巧碰见蒂姆了。

happily /ˈhæpɪli/ *adverb* 副词
1 in a happy way 快乐地；高兴地：*Everyone was smiling happily.* 大家都开心地笑着。
2 it is lucky that 幸运地 ⊃ SAME MEANING **fortunately** 同义词为 fortunately：*Happily, the accident was not serious.* 幸好事故不算严重。⊃ OPPOSITE **unhappily** 反义词为 unhappily

happiness 0═ /ˈhæpinəs/ *noun* 名词 (*no plural* 不用复数形式)
the feeling of being happy 幸福；快乐；高兴

happy 0═ /ˈhæpi/ *adjective* 形容词 (happier, happiest)
1 feeling pleased or showing that you are pleased 快乐的；高兴的：*She looks very happy.* 她看起来很开心。◇ *That was one of the happiest days of my life.* 那是我一生中最快乐的日子之一。⊃ OPPOSITE **unhappy** or **sad** 反义词为 unhappy 或 sad ⊃ Look at the note at **glad**. 见 glad 条的注释。
2 a word that you use to say that you hope somebody will enjoy a special time（表示祝愿）：*Happy New Year!* 新年快乐！◇ *Happy Christmas!* 圣诞快乐！◇ *Happy Birthday!* 生日快乐！

harbour (*British* 英式英语) (*American* 美式英语 **harbor**) /ˈhɑːbə(r)/ *noun* 名词
a place where ships can stay safely in the water 海港；港口；港湾

hard[1] 0═ /hɑːd/ *adjective* 形容词 (harder, hardest)
1 not soft 硬的；坚固的：*These apples are very hard.* 这些苹果非常硬。◇ *I couldn't sleep because the bed was too hard.* 我没法睡着，因为床太硬了。⊃ OPPOSITE **soft** 反义词为 soft
2 difficult to do or understand 难做的；难懂的：*The exam was very hard.* 这次考试很难。◇ *hard work* 困难的工作 ⊃ OPPOSITE **easy** 反义词为 easy
3 full of problems 困难重重的；艰苦的；艰难的：*He's had a hard life.* 他命途多舛。⊃ OPPOSITE **easy** 反义词为 easy
4 not kind or gentle 严厉的；苛刻的：*She is very hard on her children.* 她对孩子都很严厉。⊃ OPPOSITE **soft** 反义词为 soft

A
B
C
D
E
F
G
H
I
J
K
L
M
N
O
P
Q
R
S
T
U
V
W
X
Y
Z

hard² ⊶ /hɑːd/ *adverb* 副词
1 a lot 努力地；艰苦地： *She works very hard.* 她工作非常努力。◇ *You must try harder!* 你得再加把劲!
2 strongly 猛力地；猛烈地： *It's raining hard.* 雨下得很大。◇ *She hit him hard.* 她重重地打他。

hardback /'hɑːdbæk/ *noun* 名词
a book with a hard cover 精装书 ⊃ Look at **paperback**. 见 paperback。

hard disk /ˌhɑːd 'dɪsk/ *noun* 名词
(*computing* 电脑) a disk inside a computer that stores information (called **data**) and programs 硬盘；硬磁盘

harden /'hɑːdn/ *verb* 动词 (hardens, hardening, hardened /'hɑːdnd/)
to become hard 变硬： *Wait for the cement to harden.* 等混凝土变硬。

hard-hearted /ˌhɑːd 'hɑːtɪd/ *adjective* 形容词
not kind to other people and not thinking about their feelings 铁石心肠的；无情的

hardly ⊶ /'hɑːdli/ *adverb* 副词
almost not; only just 几乎不；几乎没有；刚刚： *She spoke so quietly that I could hardly hear her.* 她说话声小得我几乎听不到。◇ *There's hardly any* (= almost no) *coffee left.* 咖啡几乎喝光了。◇ *We hardly ever go out nowadays.* 我们现在几乎不怎么出去了。

hardware /'hɑːdweə(r)/ *noun* 名词
(*no plural* 不用复数形式)
the electronic parts of a computer system, rather than the programs that work on it（电脑）硬件 ⊃ Look at **software**. 见 software。

hare /heə(r)/ *noun* 名词
an animal like a RABBIT (= a small animal with long ears). **Hares** are bigger and have longer ears and can run very fast. 野兔 ⊃ Look at the picture at **rabbit**. 见 rabbit 的插图。

harm¹ ⊶ /hɑːm/ *noun* 名词 (*no plural* 不用复数形式)
hurt or damage 伤害；损害： *Make sure the children don't come to any harm.* 要确保孩子不受到任何伤害。
there is no harm in doing something nothing bad will happen if you do something 做某事没有坏处： *I don't know if she'll help you, but there's no harm in asking.* 我不知道她会不会帮助你，但问一问也无妨。

harm² ⊶ /hɑːm/ *verb* 动词 (harms, harming, harmed /hɑːmd/)
to hurt or damage somebody or something 伤害；损害： *These chemicals harm the environment.* 这些化学品会损害环境。

harmful ⊶ /'hɑːmfl/ *adjective* 形容词
Something that is **harmful** can hurt or damage people or things. 有害的；导致损害的： *Strong sunlight can be harmful to young babies.* 强烈的阳光可能对婴儿有害。

harmless /'hɑːmləs/ *adjective* 形容词
not dangerous 无害的；无危险的： *Don't be frightened – these insects are harmless.* 不用惊慌，这些昆虫不伤人。

harmony /'hɑːməni/ *noun* 名词
1 (*no plural* 不用复数形式) a state of agreement or of living together in peace 融洽；和睦；和谐： *The different races live together in harmony.* 不同种族的人和睦相处。
2 (*plural* 复数形式 harmonies) musical notes that sound nice together 和声： *They sang in harmony.* 他们用和声唱。

harp 竖琴

harp /hɑːp/ *noun* 名词
a large musical instrument that has many strings stretching from the top to the bottom of a frame. You play the **harp** with your fingers. 竖琴

harsh /hɑːʃ/ *adjective* 形容词 (harsher, harshest)
1 not kind; cruel 严厉的；残酷的： *a harsh punishment* 严厉的惩罚
2 rough and unpleasant to see or hear 刺眼的；刺耳的： *a harsh voice* 刺耳的噪音
▶ **harshly** /'hɑːʃli/ *adverb* 副词： *Alec*

laughed harshly. 亚历克大笑，声音很刺耳。

harvest /'hɑːvɪst/ *noun* 名词
1 the time when grain, fruit, or vegetables are ready to cut or pick 收获季节；收割；收获：*The apple harvest is in September.* 苹果的收获期是九月份。
2 all the grain, fruit, or vegetables that are cut or picked 收成；收获量：*We had a good harvest this year.* 我们今年收成很好。
▶ **harvest** *verb* 动词 (harvests, harvesting, harvested)：*When do they harvest the wheat?* 他们什么时候收割小麦？

has *form of* HAVE * have 的不同形式

hasn't /'hæznt/ *short for* HAS NOT * has not 的缩略式

hassle¹ /'hæsl/ *noun* 名词 (*informal* 非正式)
something that annoys you because it takes time or effort 麻烦；困难：*It's a real hassle having to change trains.* 要转火车真麻烦。

hassle² /'hæsl/ *verb* 动词 (hassles, hassling, hassled /'hæsld/) (*informal* 非正式)
to annoy somebody by asking them many times to do something（不断）烦扰，麻烦：*I wish he'd stop hassling me about that essay!* 我希望他不要为了那篇文章再来烦我了！

haste /heɪst/ *noun* 名词 (*no plural* 不用复数形式) (*formal* 正式)
doing things too quickly, especially because you do not have enough time 仓促；匆忙：*The letter was written in haste* (= quickly). 这封信是匆匆忙忙写的。

hasty /'heɪsti/ *adjective* 形容词 (hastier, hastiest)
1 said or done quickly 匆忙的；仓促的：*We ate a hasty lunch, then left.* 我们匆匆吃过午饭就离开了。
2 If you are **hasty**, you do something too quickly. 草率的；草草了事的：*Don't be too hasty. This is a very important decision.* 别太草率，这是个非常重要的决定。
▶ **hastily** /'heɪstɪli/ *adverb* 副词：*He hastily changed the subject.* 他匆匆转换了话题。

hat ⊶ /hæt/ *noun* 名词
a thing that you wear on your head 帽子：*She's wearing a hat.* 她戴着一顶帽子。

hats 帽子

sun hats 遮阳帽　　　　**hood** 风帽

helmet 头盔　　**crash helmet** 防撞头盔

beret 贝雷帽　　**baseball cap** 棒球帽　　**cap** 制服帽

hatch /hætʃ/ *verb* 动词 (hatches, hatching, hatched /hætʃt/)
When baby birds, insects, or fish **hatch**, they come out of an egg. （雏鸟、幼虫或小鱼）孵出，出壳

hate¹ ⊶ /heɪt/ *verb* 动词 (hates, hating, hated)
to have a very strong feeling of not liking somebody or something 厌恶；憎恨；讨厌：*Most cats hate water.* 猫大多不喜欢水。◇ *I hate waiting for buses.* 我讨厌等公共汽车。 ⊃ OPPOSITE **love** 反义词为 love

hate² ⊶ /heɪt/ *noun* 名词 (*no plural* 不用复数形式)
a very strong feeling of not liking somebody or something 厌恶；憎恨；仇恨 ⊃ SAME MEANING **hatred** 同义词为 hatred：*Her love for him had turned to hate.* 她对他已经由爱转成了恨。 ⊃ OPPOSITE **love** 反义词为 love

hatred /'heɪtrɪd/ *noun* 名词 (*no plural* 不用复数形式)
a very strong feeling of not liking somebody or something 厌恶；憎恨；仇恨 ⊃ SAME MEANING **hate** 同义词为 hate：*He had a deep hatred of injustice.* 他对不公正的现象深恶痛绝。

haul /hɔːl/ *verb* 动词 (hauls, hauling, hauled /hɔːld/)
to pull something heavy 拖，拉，拽（重物）：*They hauled the boat out of the river.* 他们把船从河里拖了上来。

A
B
C
D
E
F
G
H
I
J
K
L
M
N
O
P
Q
R
S
T
U
V
W
X
Y
Z

have

present tense 现在式	short forms 缩写	negative short forms 缩写否定式
I **have**	I**'ve**	I **haven't**
you **have**	you**'ve**	you **haven't**
he/she/it **has** /hæz/	he**'s**/she**'s**/it**'s**	he/she/it **hasn't**
we **have**	we**'ve**	we **haven't**
you **have**	you**'ve**	you **haven't**
they **have**	they**'ve**	they **haven't**

past tense short forms 过去式缩写	past tense 过去式	present participle 现在分词
I**'d**	**had** /hæd/	**having**
you**'d**		
he**'d**/she**'d**/it**'d**		past participle 过去分词
we**'d**		
you**'d**		**had**
they**'d**		

haunt /hɔːnt/ *verb* 动词 (**haunts, haunting, haunted**)

1 If a place is **haunted**, people think that there are GHOSTS (= spirits of dead people) there. （鬼魂）出没: *A ghost haunts the castle.* 那座城堡闹鬼。
2 If something sad or unpleasant **haunts** you, you often think of it. （不快的事情）挥之不去，萦绕心头: *Her unhappy face still haunts me.* 她那张伤心的脸依然缠扰着我。

▶ **haunted** /'hɔːntɪd/ *adjective* 形容词: *a haunted house* 闹鬼的房子

have[1] ⚡ /həv; hæv/ *verb* 动词
a word that you use with parts of other verbs to show that something happened or started in the past （与过去分词连用构成完成时）: *I haven't seen that film.* 我没看过那部电影。◇ *Have you ever been to Italy?* 你去过意大利吗？◇ *We've been in England for six months.* 我们已经在英国待了半年。◇ *When we arrived, Paul had already left.* 我们到达时，保罗已经走了。

have[2] ⚡ /hæv/ *verb* 动词 (**has** /hæz/, **having, had** /hæd/, **has had**)

1 (*also* 亦作 **have got**) to own or keep something 有；拥有: *She has blue eyes.* 她有一双蓝眼睛。◇ *They've got (= have got) a big car.* 他们有辆大型轿车。◇ *Do you have any brothers and sisters?* 你有兄弟姐妹吗？
2 a word that you use with many nouns to talk about doing something （与许多名词连用，表示做某事）: *What time do you have breakfast?* 你什么时候吃早餐？◇ *Let's have a drink.* 我们喝一杯吧。◇ *I had*

a shower. 我冲了个澡。◇ *Jill and I have had a fight.* 我和吉尔吵了一架。
3 a word that you use with many nouns to talk about experiencing something （与许多名词连用）经历: *Have fun!* 玩得开心点! ◇ *He has had an accident.* 他出事故了。◇ *Did you have a good holiday?* 你假期过得好吗？◇ *I have an idea.* 我有个主意。◇ *Have you got time to help me?* 你有时间帮我吗？
4 (*also* 亦作 **have got**) to be ill with something 患，得（病）: *She's got (= has got) a headache.* 她头痛。◇ *I have flu.* 我患了流感。

have something done to let somebody do something for you 让人做某事: *I had my hair cut yesterday.* 我昨天理发了。◇ *Have you had your car mended?* 你让人把车修好了吗？

haven't /'hævnt/ *short for* HAVE NOT
* have not 的缩略式

have to ⚡ /'hæv tə/ *strong form and before vowels* 强读式和在元音前念 /'hæv tuː/ *modal verb* 情态动词 (*British also* 英式英语亦作 **have got to**)
used for saying that somebody must do something or that something must happen 必须；不得不: *I have to go to school on Saturday mornings.* 我每周六上午都得上学。◇ *We don't have to get up early tomorrow.* 我们明天不必早起。◇ *Have we got to pay for this now?* 我们必须现在付钱吗？◇ *We had to do lots of boring exercises.* 我们不得不做很多枯燥的练习。➲ Look at the note at **must**. 见 must 条的注释。

hawk /hɔːk/ *noun* 名词
a big bird that catches and eats other birds and small animals 鹰; 隼

hay /heɪ/ *noun* 名词 (*no plural* 不用复数形式)
dry grass that is used as food for farm animals（作饲料的）干草, 草料

hay fever /ˈheɪ fiːvə(r)/ *noun* 名词 (*no plural* 不用复数形式)
an illness like a cold. Grass and other plants can cause **hay fever**. 枯草热; 花粉病

hazard /ˈhæzəd/ *noun* 名词
a danger 危险; 危害: *Ice is a hazard for drivers*. 路上结冰会对司机构成危险。
◇ *a fire hazard* 火灾隐患

hazardous /ˈhæzədəs/ *adjective* 形容词
dangerous 危险的; 有害的: *Motor racing is a hazardous sport*. 赛车是危险的运动。

haze /heɪz/ *noun* 名词 (*no plural* 不用复数形式)
air that is difficult to see through because of heat, dust or smoke 薄雾; 霾; 烟雾

hazelnut /ˈheɪzlnʌt/ *noun* 名词
a small nut that you can eat 榛子 ➋ Look at the picture at **nut**. 见 nut 的插图。

he /hiː/ *pronoun* 代词 (*plural* 复数形式 they)
the man or boy that the sentence is about 他: *I saw Mike when he arrived*. 迈克来的时候我看见了他。 ◇ *'Where's John?' 'He's (= he is) at home.'* "约翰在哪里？" "他在家。"

head¹ /hed/ *noun* 名词
1 the part of your body above your neck 头; 头部: *She turned her head to look at me*. 她转过头来看我。 ➋ Look at Picture Dictionary page **P4**. 见彩页 P4。

> **♪ CULTURE 文化资料补充**
> In Britain and America you **nod your head** (= move it up and down) to say 'yes' or to show that you agree, and you **shake your head** (= move it from side to side) to say 'no' or to show that you disagree. 在英美国家, nod your head（点头）表示同意或赞成, shake your head（摇头）表示不同意或不赞成。

2 your mind or brain 头脑; 脑筋: *A strange thought came into his head*. 他脑海里出现了一个奇怪的念头。 ◇ ***Use your head** (= think)!* 动脑筋想想！
3 the top, front or most important part 顶端; 前端; 最重要部分: *She sat at the head of the table*. 她坐在上座。
4 the most important person 首脑; 领袖: *The Pope is the head of the Catholic church*. 教皇是天主教的首脑。
5 *usually* 通常为 Head (*British* 英式英语) the person in charge of a school or college 校长; 院长 ➋ SAME MEANING **headmaster, headmistress, head teacher** 同义词为 headmaster、headmistress 和 head teacher: *I've been called in to see the Head*. 我接到通知去见校长。
6 heads (*plural* 用复数形式) the side of a coin that has the head of a person on it 硬币正面（有人头像）

> **♪ SPEAKING 表达方式说明**
> You say '**heads or tails?**' when you are throwing a coin in the air to decide something, for example who will start a game. 掷硬币作决定时, 例如由谁开始一场比赛会说 heads or tails?（正面还是反面？）。

a head, per head for one person 每人: *The meal cost €30 a head*. 这顿饭每人 30 欧元。

go to your head to make you too pleased with yourself 使飘飘然; 冲昏头脑: *Stop telling him how clever he is, it will go to his head!* 不要再跟他说他有多么聪明, 不然他会沾沾自喜的!

head first with your head before the rest of your body 头在前; 头朝下

head² /hed/ *verb* 动词 (heads, heading, headed)
1 to move in the direction mentioned 向（…方向）行进: *Let's head for home*. 我们回家吧。 ◇ *Where are you heading?* 你去哪里?
2 to be at the front or top of a group 排在前面（或首位）: *Michael's name heads the list*. 迈克尔的名字居于名单之首。
3 to hit a ball with your head 用头顶（球）

headache /ˈhedeɪk/ *noun* 名词
a pain in your head 头痛: *I've got a headache*. 我头痛。

heading /ˈhedɪŋ/ *noun* 名词
the words at the top of a piece of writing to show what it is about（文章的）标题

headlight /ˈhedlaɪt/ (*also* 亦作 headlamp /ˈhedlæmp/) *noun* 名词
one of the two big bright lights on the front of a car（汽车的）头灯, 前灯

A B C D E F G H I J K L M N O P Q R S T U V W X Y Z

⊃ Look at Picture Dictionary page **P1**. 见彩页 P1。

headline /'hedlam/ *noun* 名词
1 the words in big letters at the top of a newspaper story （报纸的）大字标题
2 the headlines (*plural* 用复数形式)
the most important news on radio or television （广播或电视的）新闻摘要:
Here are the news headlines. 以下是新闻摘要。

headmaster /ˌhed'mɑːstə(r)/ *noun* 名词
(*British* 英式英语) (*American* 美式英语 **principal**)
a man who is in charge of a school （男）校长

headmistress /ˌhed'mɪstrəs/ *noun* 名词
(*plural* 复数形式 **headmistresses**) (*British* 英式英语) (*American* 美式英语 **principal**)
a woman who is in charge of a school （女）校长

headphones
(*also* 亦作 **earphones**) 耳机

headphones /'hedfəʊnz/ (*also* 亦作 **earphones**) *noun* 名词 (*plural* 用复数形式)
things that you put over your head and ears so that you can listen to music without other people hearing it 耳机

headquarters /ˌhed'kwɔːtəz/ *noun* 名词 (*plural* 用复数形式) (*abbr.* 缩略式 **HQ**)
the main offices where the leaders of an organization work 总部；总公司: *The company's headquarters are in London.* 这家公司的总部设在伦敦。

head teacher /ˌhed 'tiːtʃə(r)/ *noun* 名词
(*British* 英式英语) (*British also* 英式英语亦作 **Head**) (*American* 美式英语 **principal**)
a person who is in charge of a school 校长

headway /'hedweɪ/ *noun* 名词 (*no plural* 不用复数形式)
make headway to go forward or make progress 取得进展；有所进步: *We haven't*

made much headway in our discussions. 我们的讨论没什么进展。

heal /hiːl/ *verb* 动词 (**heals**, **healing**, **healed** /hiːld/)
to become well again; to make something well again （使）康复，复原: *The cut on his leg healed slowly.* 他腿上的伤口慢慢愈合。

health ○━ /helθ/ *noun* 名词 (*no plural* 不用复数形式)
the condition of your body 身体状况; 健康: *Smoking is bad for your health.* 吸烟危害健康。 **⊃** Look at Study Pages **S16-S17**. 见研习专页 S16-S17。

healthy ○━ /'helθi/ *adjective* 形容词 (**healthier**, **healthiest**)
1 well; not often ill 健康的; 健壮的:
healthy children 健康的孩子
2 helping to make or keep you well 有益健康的: *healthy food* 健康食品
⊃ OPPOSITE **unhealthy** 反义词为 unhealthy

heap¹ /hiːp/ *noun* 名词
1 a lot of things on top of one another in an untidy way （凌乱的）一堆: *She left her clothes in a heap on the floor.* 她把衣服丢在地上乱成一堆。 **⊃** Look at the note at **pile¹**. 见 pile¹ 条的注释。
2 heaps (*plural* 用复数形式) (*informal* 非正式) a lot 许多; 大量 **◆** SAME MEANING **loads** 同义词为 loads: *We've got heaps of time.* 我们有很多时间。

heap² /hiːp/ *verb* 动词 (**heaps**, **heaping**, **heaped** /hiːpt/)
to put a lot of things on top of one another 堆积; 堆放: *She heaped food onto my plate.* 她在我的盘子里盛满了食物。

hear ○━ /hɪə(r)/ *verb* 动词 (**hears**, **hearing**, **heard** /hɜːd/, **has heard**)

🔊 PRONUNCIATION 读音说明
The word **hear** sounds just like **here**.
* hear 读音同 here。

1 to notice sounds with your ears 听见; 听到: *Can you hear that noise?* 你听见那个声音吗? ◇ *I heard somebody laughing in the next room.* 我听见隔壁有笑声。

🔊 WHICH WORD? 词语辨析
Hear or **listen**? 用 hear 还是 listen?
Hear and **listen** are used in different ways. When you **hear** something, sounds come to your ears. * hear 和 listen 用法不同。hear 表示被动地听: *I heard the door close.* 我听到门关上了。

When you **listen to** something, you are trying to hear it. * listen to 表示主动去听: *I **listen to** the radio every morning.* 我每天早上听收音机。

2 to be told about something 听说; 得知: *Have you heard the news?* 你听到那个消息了吗?

hear from somebody to get a letter or a phone call from somebody 接到某人的来信(或电话): *Have you heard from your sister?* 你听到你妹妹的音信了吗?

hear of somebody or 或 **something** to know about somebody or something 听说过: *Who is he? I've never heard of him.* 他是谁? 我没听说过他。

will not hear of something will not agree to something 不同意: *My father wouldn't hear of me paying for the meal.* 我父亲不会同意吃饭由我付账。

hearing /'hɪərɪŋ/ *noun* 名词 (*no plural* 不用复数形式)
the ability to hear 听力; 听觉: *Speak louder – her hearing isn't very good.* 说大声点 —— 她听力不太好。

hearing aid /'hɪərɪŋ eɪd/ *noun* 名词
a small machine that fits inside the ear and helps people to hear better 助听器

heart 0➔ /hɑːt/ *noun* 名词

🔎 PRONUNCIATION 读音说明
The word **heart** sounds like **start**.
* heart 读音像 start。

1 the part of the body that makes the blood go round inside 心; 心脏: *Your heart beats faster when you run.* 跑步时心跳会加快。
2 your feelings 内心; 心肠: *She has a kind heart* (= she is kind). 她心地善良。
3 the centre; the middle part 中心; 中央: *They live in the heart of the countryside.* 他们住在乡村青树翠蔓之中。
4 the shape ♥ 心形
5 hearts (*plural* 用复数形式) the group of playing cards (called a **suit**) that have red shapes like hearts on them 红桃牌; 红心牌: *the six of hearts* 红桃六 ⊃ Look at the picture at **playing card**. 见 playing card 的插图。

break somebody's heart to make somebody very sad 使某人伤心; 使某人心碎: *It broke his heart when his wife died.* 他妻子去世时他悲痛万分。

by heart so that you know every word 凭记忆; 靠背诵: *I have learned the poem by heart.* 我把这首诗背下来了。

lose heart to stop hoping 丧失信心;

灰心; 气馁: *Don't lose heart – you can still win if you try.* 别泄气, 你再努力还是能赢的。

your heart sinks you suddenly feel unhappy (表示难过) 心里一沉: *My heart sank when I saw the first question on the exam paper.* 我一看到试卷的第一题心就往下沉了。

heartache /'hɑːteɪk/ *noun* 名词 (*no plural* 不用复数形式)
a strong feeling of sadness 痛心; 伤心

heart attack /'hɑːt ətæk/ *noun* 名词
a sudden dangerous illness, when your heart stops working properly 心脏病发作: *She had a heart attack and died.* 她心脏病发作死了。

heartbeat /'hɑːtbiːt/ *noun* 名词
the movement or sound of your heart as it pushes blood around your body 心搏; 心跳声

heartbroken /'hɑːtbrəʊkən/ *adjective* 形容词
extremely sad because of something that has happened 心碎的; 极为悲伤的: *Maggie was heartbroken when her grandfather died.* 爷爷去世的时候, 玛吉悲痛欲绝。

heartless /'hɑːtləs/ *adjective* 形容词
not kind; cruel 无情的; 冷酷的

heat¹ 0➔ /hiːt/ *noun* 名词
1 (*no plural* 不用复数形式) the feeling of something hot 热: *the heat of the sun* 太阳的热力
2 (*no plural* 不用复数形式) hot weather 炎热的天气: *I love the heat.* 我喜欢炎热的天气。 ⊃ OPPOSITE **cold** 反义词为 cold
3 (*plural* 复数形式 **heats**) one of the first parts of a race or competition (赛跑或竞赛的)预赛, 分组赛

heat² 0➔ /hiːt/ (*also* 亦作 **heat up**) *verb* 动词 (**heats**, **heating**, **heated**)
to make something hot; to become hot 加热; 变热: *I heated some milk in a saucepan.* 我用煮锅热了一些牛奶。 ◇ *Wait for the oven to heat up before you put the food in.* 等烤箱热了后再把食物放进去。

heater /'hiːtə(r)/ *noun* 名词
a thing that makes a place warm or that heats water 加热器; 热水器; 暖气装置: *Switch on the heater if you feel cold.* 你要是觉得冷就把暖气打开。 ◇ *a water heater* 热水器

heath /hiːθ/ *noun* 名词
a big piece of wild land where there are no farms 荒地; 荒野

heating /'hiːtɪŋ/ *noun* 名词 (*no plural* 不用复数形式)
a system for making a building warm 供暖系统: *What kind of heating do you have?* 你们有哪种供暖系统？ ⊃ Look at **central heating**. 见 central heating。

heave /hiːv/ *verb* 动词 (**heaves, heaving, heaved** /hiːvd/)
to lift or pull something heavy 举起，拖，拉（重物）: *We heaved the suitcase up the stairs.* 我们把行李箱拖上楼梯。

heaven 0━ /'hevn/ *noun* 名词 (*no plural* 不用复数形式)
the place where many people believe God lives and where good people go to when they die 天堂；天国 ⊃ Look at **hell**. 见 hell。
Good Heavens! words that you use to show surprise（表示惊奇）天哪，我的天: *Good Heavens! I've won £100!* 天哪！我赢了 100 英镑！

heavy 重

light 轻　　　heavy 重

scales (*British* 英式英语)
scale (*American* 美式英语)
磅秤

heavy 0━ /'hevi/ *adjective* 形容词 (**heavier, heaviest**)
1 weighing a lot; difficult to lift or move 重的；沉的: *I can't carry this bag – it's too heavy.* 我拿不动这个袋子，它太重了。 ⊃ OPPOSITE **light** 反义词为 light
2 larger, stronger or more than usual（比一般）大的，强的，多的: *heavy rain* 大雨 ◇ *The traffic was very heavy this morning.* 今天上午交通非常繁忙。 ⊃ OPPOSITE **light** 反义词为 light
▸ **heavily** /'hevəli/ *adverb* 副词: *It was raining heavily.* 雨下得很大。

heavy metal /,hevi 'metl/ *noun* 名词 (*no plural* 不用复数形式)
a kind of very loud rock music 重金属摇滚乐

hectare /'hekteə(r)/ *noun* 名词
a measure of land. There are 10 000 square metres in a **hectare**. 公顷（等于 10 000 平方米）

hectic /'hektɪk/ *adjective* 形容词
very busy 忙碌的；繁忙的: *I had a hectic day at work.* 我今天工作忙得不可开交。

he'd /hiːd/ *short for* HE HAD; HE WOULD
* he had 和 he would 的缩略式

hedge /hedʒ/ *noun* 名词
a line of small trees planted around the edge of a garden or field 树篱 ⊃ Look at the picture at **fence**. 见 fence 的插图。

hedgehog /'hedʒhɒg/ *noun* 名词
a small animal covered with sharp hairs (called **prickles**) 刺猬

heel /hiːl/ *noun* 名词
1 the back part of your foot 足跟；脚后跟 ⊃ Look at the picture at **foot**. 见 foot 的插图。
2 the back part of a shoe under the **heel** of your foot （鞋的）后跟 ⊃ Look at the picture at **shoe**. 见 shoe 的插图。
3 the part of a sock that covers the **heel** of your foot （袜子的）后跟

height 0━ /haɪt/ *noun* 名词

🔎 PRONUNCIATION 读音说明
The word **height** sounds like **white**.
* height 读音像 white。

1 (*plural* 复数形式 **heights**) how far it is from the bottom to the top of somebody or something 身高；高度: *What is the height of this mountain?* 这座山有多高？ ◇ *The wall is two metres in height.* 这堵墙有两米高。 ◇ *She asked me my height, weight and age.* 她问了我的身高、体重和年龄。 ⊃ The adjective is **high**. 形容词为 high。
2 (*plural* 复数形式 **heights**) a high place 高处: *I'm afraid of heights.* 我惧高。
3 (*no plural* 不用复数形式) the strongest or most important part of something 顶点；极点: *the height of summer* 盛夏时节

heir /eə(r)/ *noun* 名词
a person who gets money or property when another person dies （财产的）继承人: *He's the heir to a large fortune.* 他是一大笔财产的继承人。
▸ **heiress** /'eəres/ *noun* 名词 (*plural* 复数形式 **heiresses**) an HEIR who is a woman 女继承人

held *form of* HOLD[1] * hold[1] 的不同形式

helicopter /ˈhelɪkɒptə(r)/ *noun* 名词
a kind of small aircraft that can go straight up in the air. It has long metal parts on top that turn to help it fly. 直升机 ➲ Look at Picture Dictionary page **P1**. 见彩页 **P1**。

hell /hel/ *noun* 名词 (no plural 不用复数形式)
the place where some people believe that bad people go when they die 地狱 ➲ Look at **heaven**. 见 heaven。

he'll /hiːl/ *short for* HE WILL * he will 的缩略式

hello ⚬━ /həˈləʊ/ *exclamation* 感叹词
a word that you say when you meet somebody or when you answer the telephone（见面问候或打电话时说）喂，你好 ➲ Look at the note at **good afternoon**. 见 good afternoon 条的注释。

helmet /ˈhelmɪt/ *noun* 名词
a hard hat that keeps your head safe 头盔；防护帽

help¹ ⚬━ /help/ *verb* 动词 (**helps, helping, helped** /helpt/)
1 to do something useful for somebody; to make somebody's work easier 帮助；帮忙：*Will you help me with the washing-up?* 你能帮我洗碗吗？ ◇ *She helped me to carry the box.* 她帮我提箱子。
2 a word that you shout when you are in danger（遇险时求援）救命，来人：*Help! I can't swim!* 救命！我不会游泳！
can't help If you **can't help** doing something, you cannot stop yourself doing it. 忍不住（做某事）：*It was so funny that I couldn't help laughing.* 太有趣了，我忍不住笑了起来。
help yourself to take something that you want 自便；随便取用：*Help yourself to a drink.* 随便取喝的吧。 ◇ *'Can I have a sandwich?' 'Of course. Help yourself!'* "我可以吃一份三明治吗？" "当然可以，请自便！"

help² ⚬━ /help/ *noun* 名词 (no plural 不用复数形式)
1 the act of helping somebody 帮助；帮忙：*Thank you for all your help.* 感谢你的一切帮助。 ◇ *Do you need any help?* 要帮忙吗？
2 a person or thing that helps 有帮助的人（或事物）：*He was a great help to me when I was ill.* 我生病的时候他没少帮我。

helpful ⚬━ /ˈhelpfl/ *adjective* 形容词
A person or thing that is **helpful** wants to help you or be useful to you. 有帮助的；

有用的：*The woman in the shop was very helpful.* 店里的那个女人非常热心。 ◇ *helpful advice* 有用的建议 ➲ OPPOSITE **unhelpful** 反义词为 unhelpful
▶ **helpfully** /ˈhelpfəli/ *adverb* 副词：*She helpfully suggested that I try the local library.* 她很热心地建议我试试本地的图书馆。

helping /ˈhelpɪŋ/ *noun* 名词
the amount of food on your plate（食物的）一份，一客：*I had a big helping of pie.* 我吃了一大份馅饼。

helpless /ˈhelpləs/ *adjective* 形容词
not able to do things without help 无助的；无自理能力的：*Babies are totally helpless.* 婴儿完全不能照顾自己。

hem /hem/ *noun* 名词
the bottom edge of something like a skirt or trousers, that is folded and sewn（衣物等底边的）褶边，卷边

hemisphere /ˈhemɪsfɪə(r)/ *noun* 名词
one half of the earth（地球的）半球：*the northern hemisphere* 北半球 ➲ Look at the picture at **earth**. 见 earth 的插图。

hen /hen/ *noun* 名词
a female bird, especially a chicken, that people keep on farms for its eggs 母鸡；雌禽 ➲ Look at the note at **chicken**. 见 chicken 条的注释。

her¹ ⚬━ /hɜː(r)/ *pronoun* 代词 (plural 复数形式 **them**)
a word that shows the woman or girl that you have just talked about（用作宾语）她：*Tell Jane that I'll see her tonight.* 告诉简我今天晚上会去看她。 ◇ *I wrote to her yesterday.* 我昨天给她写了封信。

her² /hɜː(r)/ *adjective* 形容词
of or belonging to the woman or girl that you have just talked about 她的：*That's her book.* 那是她的书。 ◇ *Jill has hurt her leg.* 吉尔把腿弄伤了。

herb /hɜːb/ *noun* 名词
a plant whose leaves, seeds, etc. are used in medicine or in cooking 药草；香草 ➲ Look at **spice**. 见 spice。 ➲ Look at Picture Dictionary page **P6**. 见彩页 **P6**。

herd¹ /hɜːd/ *noun* 名词
a big group of animals of the same kind 兽群；牧群：*a herd of cows* 一群奶牛 ➲ Look at **flock**. 见 flock。

herd² /hɜːd/ *verb* 动词 (**herds, herding, herded**)
to move people or animals somewhere in a group 使成群地移动：*The prisoners*

were herded onto the train. 囚犯被成批赶上了火车。

here 0━ /hɪə(r)/ *adverb* 副词

in, at or to this place 在这里；向这里：*Your glasses are here.* 你的眼镜在这里。◇ *Come here, please.* 请到这里来。◇ *Here's my car.* 这是我的车子。◇ *Here comes the bus.* 公共汽车来了。⊃ Look at **there** (2). 见 there 第 2 义。

here and there in different places 在各处；到处：*There were groups of people here and there along the beach.* 沿着海滩到处都是一群群的人。

here goes (*informal* 非正式) words that you say before you do something exciting or dangerous（宣称开始令人兴奋或危险的活动）看我的：*'Here goes,' said Sue, and jumped into the river.* "看我的。" 苏说完就跳进河里了。

here you are words that you say when you give something to somebody 给你：*'Can I borrow a pen, please?' 'Yes, here you are.'* "请问我能借用一支笔吗？" "行，给你。"

hero /'hɪərəʊ/ *noun* 名词 (*plural* 复数形式 **heroes**)
1 a person, especially a man, who has done something brave or good 英雄：*Everybody said that Mark was a hero after he rescued his sister from the fire.* 马克从大火中把妹妹救出来后，大家都说他是个英雄。
2 the most important man or boy in a book, play or film（小说、戏剧或电影的）男主人公，男主角 ⊃ Look at **heroine**. 见 heroine。

heroic /həˈrəʊɪk/ *adjective* 形容词
very brave 英勇的

heroin /'herəʊɪn/ *noun* 名词 (*no plural* 不用复数形式)
a very strong illegal drug 海洛因

heroine /'herəʊɪn/ *noun* 名词
1 a woman who has done something brave or good 女英雄
2 the most important woman or girl in a book, play or film（小说、戏剧或电影的）女主人公，女主角：*The heroine is played by Sandra Bullock.* 女主角由桑德拉•布洛克扮演。

hers 0━ /hɜːz/ *pronoun* 代词
something that belongs to her 她的：*Gina says this book is hers.* 吉纳说这本书是她的。◇ *Are these keys hers?* 这些钥匙是她的吗？

herself 0━ /hɜːˈself/ *pronoun* 代词 (*plural* 复数形式 **themselves** /ðəmˈselvz/)
1 a word that shows the same woman or girl that you have just talked about 她自己：*She fell and hurt herself.* 她摔伤了。
2 a word that makes 'she' stronger（用以强调）她自己：*'Who told you that Jane was married?' 'She told me herself.'* "谁告诉你简结婚了？" "她本人告诉我的。"

by herself
1 without other people（她）独自，单独 ⊃ SAME MEANING **alone** 同义词为 alone：*She lives by herself.* 她一个人住。
2 without help（她）独立地：*She can carry the box by herself.* 她能自己拿这个箱子。

he's /hiːz/ *short for* HE IS; HE HAS * he is 和 he has 的缩略式

hesitate /'hezɪteɪt/ *verb* 动词 (**hesitates, hesitating, hesitated**)
to stop for a moment before you do or say something because you are not sure about it 犹豫；迟疑不决：*He hesitated before answering the question.* 他回答问题前犹豫了一下。
▶ **hesitation** /ˌhezɪˈteɪʃn/ *noun* 名词 (*no plural* 不用复数形式)：*They agreed without hesitation.* 他们毫不犹豫地同意了。

hexagon /'heksəgən/ *noun* 名词
a shape with six sides 六边形；六角形
▶ **hexagonal** /heksˈægənl/ *adjective* 形容词 with six sides 六边形的；六角形的：*a hexagonal box* 六边形的盒子

hey /heɪ/ *exclamation* 感叹词 (*informal* 非正式)
a word that you say to make somebody listen to you, or when you are surprised（用于引起注意或表示惊讶）嘿：*Hey! Where are you going?* 嘿！你去哪里？

hi /haɪ/ *exclamation* 感叹词 (*informal* 非正式)
a word that you say when you meet somebody（用于打招呼）喂，嗨，你好 ⊃ SAME MEANING **hello** 同义词为 hello：*Hi Tony! How are you?* 嗨，托尼！你好吗？

hibernate /'haɪbəneɪt/ *verb* 动词 (**hibernates, hibernating, hibernated**)
When an animal **hibernates**, it goes to sleep for the winter.（动物）冬眠

hiccup (*also* 亦作 **hiccough**) /'hɪkʌp/ *noun* 名词

a sudden noise that you make in your throat. You sometimes get **hiccups** when you have eaten or drunk too quickly. 嗝；呃逆

hide 🔑 /haɪd/ *verb* 动词 (hides, hiding, hid /hɪd/, has hidden /'hɪdn/)

1 to put something where people cannot find it 藏；隐藏：*I hid the money under the bed.* 我把钱藏了在床底下。

2 to be or get in a place where people cannot see or find you 躲藏；藏匿：*Somebody was hiding behind the door.* 有人躲在门后。

3 to not tell or show something to somebody 掩饰；隐瞒：*She tried to hide her feelings.* 她竭力掩藏自己的感情。

hide-and-seek /ˌhaɪd n 'siːk/ *noun* 名词 (*no plural* 不用复数形式)

a children's game in which one player covers his or her eyes while the other players hide, and then tries to find them 捉迷藏

hideous /'hɪdiəs/ *adjective* 形容词
very ugly 十分丑陋的：*That shirt is hideous!* 那件衬衫真难看！

hiding /'haɪdɪŋ/ *noun* 名词 (*no plural* 不用复数形式)
be in hiding, go into hiding to be in, or to go into a place where people will not find you 躲藏起来：*The escaped prisoners are believed to be in hiding.* 据信囚犯越狱后躲起来了。

hi-fi /'haɪ faɪ/ *noun* 名词
a machine for playing records, tapes and CDs 高保真音响设备

high¹ 🔑 /haɪ/ *adjective* 形容词 (higher, highest)

1 Something that is **high** has a long distance between the top and the bottom. 高的：*a high wall* 高墙 ◇ *Mount Everest is the highest mountain in the world.* 珠穆朗玛峰是世界上最高的山峰。 ➋ The noun is **height**. 名词为 height。 ➋ OPPOSITE **low** 反义词为 low

2 You use **high** to say or ask how far something is from the bottom to the top. 有…高：*The table is 80 cm high.* 桌子高 80 厘米。 ➋ The noun is **height**. 名词为 height。

🔎 **WHICH WORD?** 词语辨析

Tall or **high**? 用 tall 还是 high？ We use **tall**, not **high**, to talk about people. 指人用 tall，不用 high：*How tall are you?* 你有多高？ ◇ *He's 1.72 metres tall.* 他身高 1.72 米。

3 far from the ground （离地面）高的：*a high shelf* 高的架子 ➋ OPPOSITE **low** 反义词为 low

4 more than the usual level or amount （水平或数量）高于一般的：*The car was travelling at high speed.* 汽车当时以高速行驶。 ◇ *high temperatures* 高温 ➋ OPPOSITE **low** 反义词为 low

5 A **high** sound is not deep. 高音的：*I heard the high voice of a child.* 我听到小孩的尖嗓音。 ➋ OPPOSITE **low** 反义词为 low

high² /haɪ/ *adverb* 副词
a long way above the ground （离地面）高：*The plane flew high above the clouds.* 飞机在云层之上高飞。 ➋ OPPOSITE **low** 反义词为 low

high and low everywhere 到处；各处：*I've looked high and low for my keys, but I can't find them anywhere.* 我到处找钥匙，可就是找不到。

higher education /ˌhaɪər edʒu'keɪʃn/ *noun* 名词 (*no plural* 不用复数形式)
education at a college or university after the age of 18 （尤指达到学位水平的）高等教育 ➋ Look at **further education**. 见 further education.

high jump /'haɪ dʒʌmp/ *noun* 名词 (*no plural* 不用复数形式)
a sport where people jump over a high bar 跳高

highlands /'haɪləndz/ *noun* 名词 (*plural* 用复数形式)
the part of a country with hills and mountains 高地；高原：*the Scottish Highlands* 苏格兰高地

highlight /'haɪlaɪt/ *noun* 名词
the best or most exciting part of something 最好（或最激动人心）的部分：*The highlight of our holiday was a visit to the palace.* 我们假期最精彩的活动是参观那座宫殿。

highly 🔑 /'haɪli/ *adverb* 副词
1 very or very much 很；非常：*Their children are highly intelligent.* 他们的孩子都很聪明。 ◇ *She has a highly paid job.* 她有一份高薪的工作。

2 very well 非常好：*I think very highly*

of your work (= I think it is very good).
我很欣赏你的工作。

Highness /ˈhaɪnəs/ *noun* 名词 (*plural*
复数形式 **Highnesses**)
a word that you use when speaking to or
about a royal person（对王室成员的
尊称）殿下：*Yes, Your Highness.* 是的,
殿下。

high school /ˈhaɪ skuːl/ *noun* 名词
1 a school in the US and some other
countries for young people between the
ages of 14 and 18（美国等的）中学，高中
2 often used in Britain in the names of
schools for young people between the
ages of 11 and 18（英国的）中学 ⊃ SAME
MEANING **secondary school** 同义词为
secondary school

high street /ˈhaɪ striːt/ *noun* 名词
(*British* 英式英语) (*American* 美式英语
main street)
the main street of a town, where most
shops, banks, etc. are（城镇商业区的）
大街：*There is a butcher's on the high
street.* 大街上有家肉店。

high-tech (*also* 亦作 **hi-tech**) /ˌhaɪ ˈtek/
adjective 形容词 (*informal* 非正式)
using the most modern methods and
machines, especially electronic ones
（尤指电子方面）高技术的，高科技的：
*The country's future is in high-tech
industries.* 这个国家的未来在于高科技
行业。

highway /ˈhaɪweɪ/ *noun* 名词 (*American*
美式英语)
a big road between towns（城镇之间
的）公路

hijack /ˈhaɪdʒæk/ *verb* 动词 (**hijacks**,
hijacking, **hijacked** /ˈhaɪdʒækt/)
to take control of a plane or a car and
make the pilot or driver take you
somewhere 劫持（飞机或汽车）
▸ **hijacker** /ˈhaɪdʒækə(r)/ *noun* 名词:
*The hijackers threatened to blow up the
plane.* 劫机者扬言要炸掉飞机。

hike /haɪk/ *noun* 名词
a long walk in the country 远足；徒步
旅行：*We went on a ten-mile hike at the
weekend.* 我们周末远足去了，走了十英里
路。
▸ **hike** *verb* 动词 (**hikes**, **hiking**, **hiked**
/haɪkt/): *They went hiking in Wales for
their holiday.* 他们假期去了威尔士徒步
旅行。 ⊃ Look at Picture Dictionary page
P15. 见彩页 P15。

hill ⊶ /hɪl/ *noun* 名词
a high piece of land that is not as high

as a mountain 小山；山丘：*I pushed
my bike up the hill.* 我推着自行车上了
小山坡。◇ *Their house is at the top of the
hill.* 他们的房子在小山顶上。 ⊃ Look also
at **uphill** and **downhill**. 亦见 uphill 和
downhill。
▸ **hilly** /ˈhɪli/ *adjective* 形容词 (**hillier**,
hilliest)：*The countryside is very hilly
around here.* 这一带乡村有很多丘陵。

him ⊶ /hɪm/ *pronoun* 代词 (*plural* 复数
形式 **them**)
a word that shows a man or boy（用作
宾语）他：*Where's Andy? I can't see him.*
安迪在哪儿呢？我见不到他。◇ *I spoke to
him yesterday.* 我昨天和他谈过话。

himself ⊶ /hɪmˈself/ *pronoun* 代词
(*plural* 复数形式 **themselves** /ðəmˈselvz/)
1 a word that shows the same man or
boy that you have just talked about
他自己：*Paul looked at himself in the
mirror.* 保罗照了照镜子。
2 a word that makes 'he' stronger（用以
强调）他自己：*Did he make this cake
himself?* 这个蛋糕是他自己做的吗？
by himself
1 without other people（他）独自，单独
⊃ SAME MEANING **alone** 同义词为 alone：
Dad went shopping by himself. 爸爸一个人
去买东西了。
2 without help（他）独立地：*He did it
by himself.* 这是他自己做的。

hinder /ˈhɪndə(r)/ *verb* 动词 (**hinders**,
hindering, **hindered** /ˈhɪndəd/)
to make it more difficult to do something
阻碍；妨碍：*Teachers are hindered by a
lack of resources.* 教师因资料不足而令教学
受阻。

Hindu /ˈhɪnduː/ *noun* 名词
a person who follows the religion of
HINDUISM 印度教教徒

Hinduism /ˈhɪnduːɪzəm/ *noun* 名词
(*no plural* 不用复数形式)
the main religion of India 印度教

hinge /hɪndʒ/ *noun* 名词
a piece of metal that joins a lid to a box
or a door to a frame so that you can open
and close it 铰链；合叶

hint¹ /hɪnt/ *noun* 名词
1 something that you say, but not in
a direct way 暗示；示意：*Sam keeps
dropping hints* (= making hints) *about
wanting a bike for his birthday.* 萨姆不断
暗示自己生日想要一辆自行车。
2 a small amount of something 少量：
There's a hint of garlic in the soup. 汤里
有点蒜味。

hint² /hɪnt/ *verb* 动词 (hints, hinting, hinted)
to say something, but not in a direct way 暗示; 示意: *Sarah hinted that she might be leaving.* 萨拉暗示她可能会离开。

hip /hɪp/ *noun* 名词
the place where your leg joins the side of your body 臀部; 髋 ⊃ Look at Picture Dictionary page P4. 见彩页 P4。

hippie (*also* 亦作 **hippy**) /ˈhɪpi/ *noun* 名词 (*plural* 复数形式 **hippies**)
a person who refuses to accept the western way of life. **Hippies** often have long hair, wear brightly coloured clothes and take illegal drugs. 嬉皮士（拒绝西方社会生活方式的人。他们一般留长发、穿着鲜艳服装、吸毒）

hippopotamus /ˌhɪpəˈpɒtəməs/ *noun* 名词 (*plural* 复数形式 **hippopotamuses** or 或 **hippopotami** /ˌhɪpəˈpɒtəmaɪ/) (*informal* 非正式 **hippo** /ˈhɪpəʊ/)
a large African animal with thick skin that lives near water 河马 ⊃ Look at Picture Dictionary page P3. 见彩页 P3。

hire /ˈhaɪə(r)/ *verb* 动词 (hires, hiring, hired /ˈhaɪəd/)
1 to pay to use something for a short time（短期）租用, 租借: *We hired a car when we were on holiday.* 我们度假时租了一辆车。
2 to pay somebody to do a job for you 雇用; 聘用: *We hired somebody to mend the roof.* 我们雇了个人来修屋顶。
hire something out to let somebody use something for a short time, in return for money 出租: *They hire out bicycles.* 他们出租自行车。
▸ **hire** *noun* 名词 (*no plural* 不用复数形式): *Have you got any boats for hire?* 你们有船出租吗? ⊃ Look at **rent²**. 见 rent²。

his¹ /hɪz/ *adjective* 形容词
of or belonging to the man or boy that you have just talked about 他的: *John came with his sister.* 约翰和他妹妹一起来了。◇ *He has hurt his arm.* 他胳膊受伤了。

his² /hɪz/ *pronoun* 代词
something that belongs to him 他的: *Are these books yours or his?* 这些书是你的还是他的?

hiss /hɪs/ *verb* 动词 (hisses, hissing, hissed /hɪst/)
to make a noise like a very long S 发嘶嘶声: *The cat hissed at me.* 猫对着我发出嘶嘶声。

▸ **hiss** *noun* 名词 (*plural* 复数形式 **hisses**): *the hiss of steam* 蒸汽的嘶嘶声

historian /hɪˈstɔːriən/ *noun* 名词
a person who knows a lot about history 历史学家

historic /hɪˈstɒrɪk/ *adjective* 形容词
important in history 具有历史意义的: *It was a historic moment when man first walked on the moon.* 人类首次在月球上行走是具有历史意义的时刻。

historical /hɪˈstɒrɪkl/ *adjective* 形容词
connected with real people or events in the past 历史的; 有关历史的: *She writes historical novels.* 她写历史小说。

history /ˈhɪstri/ *noun* 名词 (*no plural* 不用复数形式)
1 all the things that happened in the past 历史: *It was an important moment in history.* 那是历史上的重要时刻。
2 the study of things that happened in the past 历史学: *History is my favourite subject.* 历史是我最喜欢的学科。

hit¹ /hɪt/ *verb* 动词 (hits, hitting, hit, has hit)
to touch somebody or something hard 打; 击; 撞: *He hit me on the head with a book.* 他用书打我的头。◇ *The car hit a wall.* 汽车撞墙了。◇ *I hit my knee on the door.* 我的膝盖撞到门上了。

hit² /hɪt/ *noun* 名词
1 touching somebody or something hard 打; 击; 撞: *That was a good hit!* (= in a game of cricket or baseball, for example) 那真是漂亮的一击!
2 a person or a thing that a lot of people like 很受欢迎的人（或事物）: *This song was a hit in the US.* 这首歌曾在美国风靡一时。
3 (*computing* 电脑) a result of a search on a computer, especially on the Internet（尤指互联网的）搜索结果

hitchhike /ˈhɪtʃhaɪk/ *verb* 动词 (hitchhikes, hitchhiking, hitchhiked /ˈhɪtʃhaɪkt/) (*also* 亦作 **hitch** /hɪtʃ/) (hitches, hitching, hitched /hɪtʃt/)
to travel by asking for free rides in cars and lorries 搭便车; 搭顺风车: *We hitchhiked across Europe.* 我们搭便车环游欧洲。

▸ **hitchhiker** /ˈhɪtʃhaɪkə(r)/ *noun* 名词: *We picked up a hitchhiker.* 我们载上了一个搭便车的人。

HIV /ˌeɪtʃ aɪ ˈviː/ *abbreviation* 缩略式
the VIRUS (= a very small thing that can make you ill) that causes AIDS (= a serious illness which destroys the body's

ability to fight infection) 人体免疫缺损病毒；艾滋病病毒

be HIV-positive to have HIV 艾滋病病毒检测呈阳性反应

hive /haɪv/ *noun* 名词 (*also* 亦作 **beehive**)
a box where BEES (= black and yellow insects) live 蜂房；蜂箱

hoard /hɔːd/ *noun* 名词
a secret store of something, for example food or money （秘密）贮藏的东西
▶ **hoard** *verb* 动词 (**hoards**, **hoarding**, **hoarded**) to save and keep things secretly （秘密地）贮藏：*The old man hoarded the money in a box under his bed.* 老人把钱暗藏于床下的盒子里。

hoarse /hɔːs/ *adjective* 形容词
If your voice is **hoarse**, it is rough and quiet, for example because you have a cold. 沙哑的；嘶哑的：*He spoke in a hoarse whisper.* 他用沙哑的嗓音低声说着。

hoax /həʊks/ *noun* 名词 (*plural* 复数形式 **hoaxes**)
a trick that makes somebody believe something that is not true 骗局；恶作剧：*There wasn't really a bomb in the station – it was a hoax.* 车站里并没有炸弹——只是一场恶作剧。

hobby ⚡ /ˈhɒbi/ *noun* 名词 (*plural* 复数形式 **hobbies**)
something that you like doing in your free time 业余爱好：*My hobbies are reading and swimming.* 我平时爱好阅读和游泳。

hockey /ˈhɒki/ *noun* 名词 (*no plural* 不用复数形式)
1 (*British* 英式英语) (*American* 美式英语 **field hockey**) a game for two teams of eleven players who hit a small hard ball with long curved sticks on a field (called a **pitch**) 曲棍球运动
2 *American English for* ICE HOCKEY 美式英语，即 ice hockey

hold¹ ⚡ /həʊld/ *verb* 动词 (**holds**, **holding**, **held** /held/, **has held**)
1 to have something in your hand or arms 拿着；抓住；握；抱：*She was holding a gun.* 她拿着枪。◇ *He held the baby in his arms.* 他怀里抱着婴儿。
2 to keep something in a certain way 使保持：*Hold your hand up.* 把手举起来。◇ *Try to hold the camera still.* 尽量拿稳相机。
3 to support the weight of somebody or something 支撑…的重量：*Are you sure that branch will hold you?* 你确定那根树枝撑得住你的重量吗？

4 to have space for a certain number or amount 容纳；包含：*The car holds five people.* 这辆车能坐五人。
5 to make something happen 召开；举办；进行：*The meeting was held in the town hall.* 会议在市政厅举行。
◇ *It's impossible to hold a conversation with him.* 根本无法与他交谈。

hold somebody or 或 **something back** to stop somebody or something from moving forwards 阻挡；拦阻：*The police held back the crowd.* 警察把人群拦住了。

Hold it! (*informal* 非正式) Wait! Don't move! 等一等！不要动！

hold on
1 (*informal* 非正式) to wait 等一下 ⊃ SAME MEANING **hang on** 同义词为 hang on：*Hold on, I'm coming.* 等一下，我这就来。
2 to keep holding something tightly 抓紧：*The child held on to her mother's hand.* 孩子紧紧抓住妈妈的手。

hold somebody or 或 **something up**
1 to make somebody or something late 使耽搁；使延误：*The plane was held up for 40 minutes.* 飞机延误了40分钟。
2 to try to steal from a place, using a gun 持枪抢劫：*Two men held up a bank in Bristol today.* 两名持枪男子今天抢劫了布里斯托尔的一家银行。

hold² ⚡ /həʊld/ *noun* 名词 (*no plural* 不用复数形式)
the part of a ship or plane where goods are kept （船或飞机的）货舱

get hold of somebody to find somebody so that you can speak to them 跟某人联系：*I'm trying to get hold of Peter but he's not at home.* 我尝试联系彼得，可他不在家。

get hold of something
1 (*also* 亦作 **take hold of something**) to take something in your hands 抓住；握住：*Get hold of the rope!* 抓住绳子！
2 to find something 找到：*I can't get hold of the book I need.* 我找不到我要的那本书。

hold-up /ˈhəʊld ʌp/ *noun* 名词
1 something that makes you wait 阻滞；延误 ⊃ SAME MEANING **delay** 同义词为 delay：*There was a long hold-up on the motorway.* 高速公路上堵车很久了。
2 when somebody tries to rob somebody using a gun 持枪抢劫：*There's been a hold-up at the local supermarket.* 本地的那家超市发生了持枪抢劫。

hole ⚡ /həʊl/ *noun* 名词
an empty space or opening in something

洞；孔；坑： *I'm going to **dig a hole** in the garden.* 我准备在花园里挖一个坑。 ◇ *My socks are full of holes.* 我的袜子满是窟窿。

holiday 0➔ /'hɒlədeɪ/ ***noun*** 名词
1 (*British* 英式英语) (*American* 美式英语 **vacation**) a time when you do not go to work or school, and often go and stay away from home 假期： *The school holidays start next week.* 学校下星期开始放假。 ◇ *We're going to the coast for our **summer holiday**.* 我们打算去海边过暑假。 ◇ *Mrs Smith isn't here this week. She's **on holiday**.* 史密斯太太本周不在，她去度假了。
2 a day when most people do not go to work or school, especially because of a religious or national celebration 假日（尤指宗教或国家的庆典日）： *Next Monday is a holiday.* 下星期一是假日。

> **CULTURE** 文化资料补充
> A day when everybody has a holiday is called a **public holiday** in Britain and the US. In Britain it is also called a **bank holiday**. 在英美国家公共假日叫做 public holiday，在英国也叫做 bank holiday。

hollow /'hɒləʊ/ ***adjective*** 形容词
with an empty space inside 中空的；空心的： *A drum is hollow.* 鼓的中间是空的。

holly /'hɒli/ ***noun*** 名词 (*no plural* 不用复数形式)
a plant that has leaves with a lot of sharp points, and red BERRIES (= small round fruit) 冬青

> **CULTURE** 文化资料补充
> People often put **holly** in their houses at Christmas. 圣诞节时人们常在家里摆放冬青。

holy /'həʊli/ ***adjective*** 形容词 (**holier**, **holiest**)
1 very special because it is about God or a god 与上帝（或神）有关的；神圣的： *The Bible is the holy book of Christians.* 《圣经》是基督徒的圣书。
2 A **holy** person lives a good and religious life.（人）圣洁的

home[1] 0➔ /həʊm/ ***noun*** 名词
1 the place where you live 家： *Simon **left home** (= stopped living in his parents' house) **at the age of 18**.* 西蒙 18 岁就离开家了。
2 a place where they look after people, for example children who have no parents, or old people 养育院；养老院： *My grandmother lives in an old people's home.* 我外婆住在养老院里。
at home in your house or flat 在家： *I stayed at home yesterday.* 我昨天在家。 ◇ *Is Sara at home?* 萨拉在家吗？

home[2] 0➔ /həʊm/ ***adverb*** 副词
to the place where you live 回家；到家

> **GRAMMAR** 语法说明
> Be careful! We do not use **to** before **home**. 注意：home 前不加 to： *Let's **go home**.* 咱们回家吧。 ◇ *What time did you **get home** last night?* 你昨晚什么时候回家的？

home[3] /həʊm/ ***adjective*** 形容词
connected with your home or your country 家的；本国的： *What is your home address?* 你家的地址是什么？ ◇ *home cooking* 家常饭菜

homeless /'həʊmləs/ ***adjective*** 形容词
If you are **homeless**, you have nowhere to live. 无家的： *The floods made many people homeless.* 洪水使很多人无家可归。

home-made /ˌhəʊm 'meɪd/ ***adjective*** 形容词
made in your house, not bought in a shop 自制的；家里做的： *home-made bread* 自制面包

home page /'həʊm peɪdʒ/ ***noun*** 名词
the first of a number of pages of information on the Internet that belongs to a person or an organization. A **home page** contains connections to other pages of information.（网站）主页，首页

homesick /'həʊmsɪk/ ***adjective*** 形容词
sad because you are away from home 想家的；思乡的

homework /'həʊmwɜːk/ ***noun*** 名词 (*no plural* 不用复数形式)
work that a teacher gives to you to do at home 家庭作业： *Have you **done** your French **homework**?* 你做了法语作业没有？
➲ Look at the note at **housework**.
见 housework 条的注释。

homosexual /ˌhəʊmə'sekʃuəl/ ***adjective*** 形容词
attracted to people of the same sex 同性恋的

honest 0➔ /'ɒnɪst/ ***adjective*** 形容词
A person who is **honest** says what is true and does not steal, lie or cheat. 诚实的；老实的；正直的： *She's a very honest person.* 她非常诚实。 ◇ ***Be honest*** *– do you really like this dress?* 说实话，你是不

是真的喜欢这件连衣裙? ⊃ OPPOSITE
dishonest 反义词为 dishonest

▶ **honestly** /'ɒnɪstli/ *adverb* 副词: *Try to answer the questions honestly.* 要尽量老老实实回答问题。◇ *Honestly, I don't know where your money is.* 说实话,我并不知道你的钱在哪儿。

▶ **honesty** /'ɒnəsti/ *noun* 名词 (*no plural* 不用复数形式): *I have serious doubts about his honesty.* 我对他的诚实深存怀疑。

honey /'hʌni/ *noun* 名词 (*no plural* 不用复数形式)
the sweet food that is made by insects (called **bees**) 蜂蜜

honeymoon /'hʌnimuːn/ *noun* 名词
a holiday for two people who have just got married 蜜月

honour (*British* 英式英语) (*American* 美式英语 **honor**) /'ɒnə(r)/ *noun* 名词 (*no plural* 不用复数形式)
1 respect from other people for something good that you have done 尊敬;荣誉: *They fought for the honour of their country.* 他们曾为祖国的荣誉而战。
2 something that makes you proud and pleased 荣幸;光荣: *It was a great honour to be invited to Buckingham Palace.* 获邀到白金汉宫真是莫大的荣幸。
in honour of somebody or 或 **something** to show that you respect somebody or something 出于对…的敬意: *There is a party tonight in honour of our visitors.* 今晚有个欢迎来宾的宴会。

hood /hʊd/ *noun* 名词
1 the part of a coat or jacket that covers your head and neck 风帽、兜帽(大衣或夹克的一部分,可拉起蒙住头颈)⊃ Look at the picture at **hat**. 见 hat 的插图。
2 *American English for* BONNET (1) 美式英语、即 bonnet 第 1 义

hoof /huːf/ *noun* 名词 (*plural* 复数形式 **hoofs** or 或 **hooves** /huːvz/)
the hard part of the foot of horses and some other animals (马等动物的)蹄 ⊃ Look at the picture at **horse**. 见 horse 的插图。

hook ⊶ /hʊk/ *noun* 名词
a curved piece of metal or plastic for hanging things on, or for catching fish with 钩;钩子;钓钩: *Hang your coat on that hook.* 把大衣挂在那个钩子上。
◇ *a fish hook* 鱼钩
off the hook If a telephone is **off the hook**, the part that you speak into (called

the **receiver**) is not in place so that the telephone will not ring. (电话听筒)没挂上

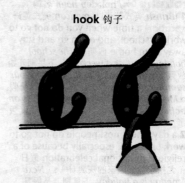

hook 钩子

hooligan /'huːlɪɡən/ *noun* 名词
a young person who behaves in a noisy way and fights other people 小流氓;阿飞: *football hooligans* 足球流氓

hooray (*also* 亦作 **hurray**) /həˈreɪ/ *exclamation* 感叹词 (*also* 亦作 **hurrah** /həˈrɑː/)
a word that you shout when you are very pleased about something 好极了;好哇: *Hooray! She's won!* 好极了!她赢了!

hoot /huːt/ *noun* 名词
the sound that a car's horn or an OWL (= a type of bird) makes 喇叭声;猫头鹰的叫声

▶ **hoot** *verb* 动词 (hoots, hooting, hooted): *The driver hooted at the dog.* 司机对着狗按喇叭。

hoover /'huːvə(r)/ *verb* 动词 (*British* 英式英语) (hoovers, hoovering, hoovered /'huːvəd/)
to clean a carpet or the floor with a machine that sucks up the dirt 用真空吸尘器打扫

▶ **Hoover**™ *noun* 名词 ⊃ SAME MEANING **vacuum cleaner** 同义词为 vacuum cleaner: *The Hoover needs a new bag.* 这个吸尘器需要换个新袋子了。

hooves *plural of* HOOF * hoof 的复数形式

hop /hɒp/ *verb* 动词 (hops, hopping, hopped /hɒpt/)
1 (used about a person) to jump on one foot (人)单脚跳
2 (used about an animal or bird) to jump with two or all feet together (动物或鸟)

齐足跳行：*The frog hopped onto the stone.* 青蛙跳上了石头。
▸ **hop** *noun* 名词 a short jump 短跳

hop 单脚跳行

hope¹ ০⌐ /həʊp/ *verb* 动词 (**hopes**, **hoping**, **hoped** /həʊpt/)
to want something to happen or be true 希望；期望：*I hope that you have a nice holiday.* 我希望你假期愉快。◇ *I hope to see you tomorrow.* 我希望明天能见你。
◇ *She's hoping for a bike for her birthday.* 她希望生日能得到一辆自行车。◇ *'Do you think it will rain?' 'I hope not.'* "你看会下雨吗？" "希望不会。" ◇ *'Will you be at the party?' 'I'm not sure – I hope so.'* "你会参加那个聚会吗？" "还说不准，我希望能去。"

hope² ০⌐ /həʊp/ *noun* 名词
1 (*plural* 复数形式 **hopes**) a feeling of wanting something to happen and thinking that it will 希望；期望：*There's little hope of finding survivors.* 找到幸存者的希望很渺茫了。◇ *Don't give up hope; you may still pass.* 不要觉得没有希望，也许你还是可以通过的。
2 (*no plural* 不用复数形式) a person or thing that gives you hope 被寄予希望的人（或事物）：*Can you help me? You're my only hope.* 你能帮我吗？你是我唯一的希望了。

hopeful /'həʊpfl/ *adjective* 形容词
If you are **hopeful**, you think that something that you want will happen. 抱有希望；满怀希望：*I'm hopeful about getting a job.* 我对找到工作抱有希望。

hopefully /'həʊpfəli/ *adverb* 副词
1 (*informal* 非正式) I hope; we hope 我希望；但愿：*Hopefully he won't be late.* 但愿他不会迟到。
2 hoping that what you want will happen 怀着希望地：*The cat looked hopefully at our plates.* 猫眼巴巴地看着我们的盘子。

hopeless /'həʊpləs/ *adjective* 形容词
1 with no hope of success 没有成功希望的；无望的：*a hopeless situation* 无可

挽救的局面 ◇ *It's hopeless trying to work with all this noise!* 要在这样的噪声下工作简直不可能！
2 (*informal* 非正式) very bad 极差的；糟糕透顶：*I'm hopeless at tennis.* 我网球打得糟透了。
▸ **hopelessly** /'həʊpləsli/ *adverb* 副词：*We got hopelessly lost in the forest.* 我们在森林里完全迷路了。

horizon /hə'raɪzn/ *noun* 名词
the line between the earth or sea and the sky 地平线：*We could see a ship on the horizon.* 我们看得见地平线上出现一艘船。

horizontal /ˌhɒrɪ'zɒntl/ *adjective* 形容词
going from side to side, not up and down 水平的；横的：*a horizontal line* 水平线 ⊃ Look at **vertical**. 见 vertical。 ⊃ Look at the picture at **line**¹. 见 line¹ 的插图。

hormone /'hɔːməʊn/ *noun* 名词
a substance in your body that influences the way you grow and develop 激素；荷尔蒙

horn ০⌐ /hɔːn/ *noun* 名词
1 one of the hard pointed things that some animals have on their heads （某些动物头上的）角 ⊃ Look at the picture at **cow**. 见 cow 的插图。
2 a thing in a car or other vehicle that makes a loud sound to warn people （汽车等的）喇叭：*Don't sound your horn late at night.* 深夜开车不要按喇叭。
3 a musical instrument with a curved metal tube that you blow into （乐器）号

horoscope /'hɒrəskəʊp/ *noun* 名词
something that tells you what will happen, using the planets and your date of birth 占星预言：*Have you read your horoscope today?* (= in a newspaper, for example) 你今天看了你的星座运势吗？

horrible /'hɒrəbl/ *adjective* 形容词 (*informal* 非正式)
very bad or unpleasant 极坏的；糟糕的；十分讨厌的：*What horrible weather!* 多么糟糕的天气！◇ *I had a horrible dream.* 我做了个可怕的梦！

horrid /'hɒrɪd/ *adjective* 形容词 (*informal* 非正式)
very bad or unpleasant 极坏的；糟糕的；十分讨厌的 ⊃ SAME MEANING **horrible** 同义词为 horrible：*Don't be so horrid!* 别那么令人讨厌！

horrific /hə'rɪfɪk/ *adjective* 形容词
very shocking or frightening 令人震惊的；令人惊骇的：*a horrific accident* 骇人听闻的事故

A B C D E F G H I J K L M N O P Q R S T U V W X Y Z

A
B
C
D
E
F
G
H
I
J
K
L
M
N
O
P
Q
R
S
T
U
V
W
X
Y
Z

horrify /'hɒrɪfaɪ/ *verb* 动词 (horrifies, horrifying, horrified /'hɒrɪfaɪd/, has horrified)
to shock and frighten somebody 使震惊; 惊吓: *Everyone was horrified by the murders.* 大家对这些谋杀案都感到十分震惊。

horror /'hɒrə(r)/ *noun* 名词 (*no plural* 不用复数形式)
a feeling of fear or shock 恐惧; 震惊: *They watched in horror as the child ran in front of the bus.* 他们惊恐地看着那个孩子在公共汽车前面跑。
horror film, **horror story** a film or a story which tries to frighten or shock you for entertainment 恐怖电影; 恐怖故事

horse 马

| reins 缰绳 | mane 鬃 | saddle 马鞍 | tail 尾巴 |

hoof 蹄

horse ⚫☞ /hɔːs/ *noun* 名词
a big animal that can carry people and pull heavy things 马: *Can you ride a horse?* 你会骑马吗?

🔎 WORD BUILDING 词汇扩充
A young horse is called a **foal**. The sound a horse makes is **neigh**. 小马驹叫做 foal, 马的叫声叫做 neigh。

horseback /'hɔːsbæk/ *noun* 名词
on horseback sitting on a horse 骑着马: *We saw a lot of policemen on horseback.* 我们看到很多骑着马的警察。

horse riding /'hɔːs raɪdɪŋ/ (*British* 英式英语) (*American* 美式英语 **horseback riding** /'hɔːsbæk raɪdɪŋ/) (*British and American also* 英式和美式英语亦作 **riding**) *noun* 名词 (*no plural* 不用复数形式)
the sport or activity of riding a horse for pleasure 骑马: *She goes horse riding at the weekends.* 她周末都去骑马。 ⊃ Look

at Picture Dictionary page **P15**. 见彩页 P15。

horseshoe /'hɔːʃuː/ *noun* 名词
a piece of metal like a U that a horse wears on its foot 马蹄铁; 马掌

hose /həʊz/ (*also* 亦作 **hosepipe** /'həʊzpaɪp/) *noun* 名词
a long soft tube that you use to bring water, for example in the garden or when there is a fire (软)水管; 水龙带

hospitable /hɒ'spɪtəbl/ *adjective* 形容词
friendly and kind to visitors 好客的; 殷勤的

hospital ⚫☞ /'hɒspɪtl/ *noun* 名词
a place where doctors and nurses look after people who are ill or hurt 医院: *My brother is in hospital – he's broken his leg.* 我弟弟在医院里, 他腿骨折了。 ◇ *The ambulance took her to hospital.* 救护车把她送到医院去了。

🔎 WORD BUILDING 词汇扩充
If you are very ill or you **have an accident** you go **to hospital** (Be careful! In British English, you do not say **to the hospital**). 患重病或出了事故 (have an accident) 会去医院 (go to hospital) (注意: 英式英语不说 go to the hospital)。
A doctor gives you **treatment** and you are called a **patient**. You might need to **have an operation**. The room in a hospital where people sleep is called a **ward**. 治疗叫做 treatment, 病人叫做 patient, 做手术叫做 have an operation, 病房叫做 ward。

hospitality /,hɒspɪ'tæləti/ *noun* 名词 (*no plural* 不用复数形式)
being friendly to people who are visiting you, and looking after them well 好客; 殷勤: *We thanked them for their hospitality.* 我们感谢他们的盛情款待。

host /həʊst/ *noun* 名词
a person who invites people to their house, for example to a party 主人: *Ian, our host, introduced us to the other guests.* 主人伊恩把我们介绍给其他客人了。 ⊃ Look at **hostess**. 见 hostess。

hostage /'hɒstɪdʒ/ *noun* 名词
a prisoner that you keep until people give you what you want 人质: *Several passengers were taken hostage.* 几名乘客被扣为人质了。 ◇ *They held his daughter hostage until he paid them the money.* 他们扣住他女儿当人质, 直到他付赎金为止。

hostel /ˈhɒstl/ *noun* 名词
a place like a cheap hotel where people can stay 廉价旅馆；招待所：*a youth hostel* 青年旅舍

hostess /ˈhəʊstəs/ *noun* 名词 (*plural* 复数形式 **hostesses**)
a woman who invites people to her house, for example to a party 女主人 ⊃ Look at **host**. 见 host。⊃ Look also at **air hostess**. 亦见 air hostess。

hostile /ˈhɒstaɪl/ *adjective* 形容词
very unfriendly 敌意的；敌对的：*a hostile crowd* 怀有敌意的人群

hot ০┐ /hɒt/ *adjective* 形容词 (**hotter, hottest**)
1 having a high temperature 温度高的；热的：*I'm hot. Can you open the window?* 我很热，你把窗户打开行吗？◇ *It's hot today, isn't it?* 今天很热，是吧？◇ *hot water* 热水 ⊃ OPPOSITE **cold** 反义词为 cold

> ⚲ **WHICH WORD?** 词语辨析
> **Warm, hot** or **boiling**? 用 warm、hot 还是 boiling？
> **Warm** means quite hot, especially in a pleasant way. * warm 表示温暖的，尤指暖和舒适的：*Sit by the fire. You'll soon be warm.* 坐到炉火边来吧，你很快就会暖和起来。
> **Boiling** means extremely hot, often in an unpleasant way. * boiling 表示极热的，常指热得令人难受的：*Turn the heating down – it's boiling in here!* 把暖气调低吧，这里热死了！

2 Hot food has a strong, burning taste. 辣的 ⊃ SAME MEANING **spicy** 同义词为 spicy：*a hot curry* 辛辣的咖喱菜

hot-air balloon /ˌhɒt ˈeə bəluːn/
= BALLOON (2) ⊃ Look at Picture Dictionary page **P1**. 见彩页 P1。

hot dog /ˈhɒt dɒg/ *noun* 名词
a hot SAUSAGE (= meat made into a long, thin shape) that you eat in a long bread roll 热狗（香肠面包）⊃ Look at Picture Dictionary page **P7**. 见彩页 P7。

hotel ০┐ /həʊˈtel/ *noun* 名词
a place where you pay to sleep and eat 旅馆；酒店：*I stayed at a hotel near the airport.* 我住在机场附近的一家旅馆。

hotline /ˈhɒtlaɪn/ *noun* 名词
a special telephone line that people can call to get advice or information 热线

hour ০┐ /ˈaʊə(r)/ *noun* 名词
1 a measure of time. There are 60 minutes in an **hour**. 小时：*The journey took two hours.* 路程花了两个小时。◇ *I've been waiting for an hour.* 我等了一小时了。◇ *half an hour* 半小时

2 hours (*plural* 用复数形式) the time when somebody is working, or when a shop or office is open（办公或营业）时间：*Our office hours are 9 a.m. to 5 p.m.* 我们的上班时间是上午 9 时至下午 5 时。

3 the hour (*no plural* 不用复数形式) the time when a new **hour** starts (= 1 o'clock, 2 o'clock, etc.) 整点：*Buses are on the hour and at twenty past the hour.* 每小时整点和二十分时都有公共汽车开出。

for hours (*informal* 非正式) for a long time 很长时间：*I've been waiting for hours.* 我等了很长时间了。

hourly /ˈaʊəli/ *adjective, adverb* 形容词，副词
happening or coming once an hour 每小时一次（的）：*There is an hourly bus to the airport.* 开往机场的公共汽车每小时一班。◇ *Trains run hourly.* 火车每小时一趟。

house 房屋
chimney 烟囱　　drainpipe 雨水管　　roof 屋顶
front door 前门　　window 窗户

house ০┐ /haʊs/ *noun* 名词 (*plural* 复数形式 **houses** /ˈhaʊzɪz/)
1 a building where a person or a family lives 房屋；房子；住宅：*How many rooms are there in your house?* 你家的房子有几个房间？◇ *We're having dinner at Jane's house tonight.* 我们今晚在简的家吃饭。

> ⚲ **WORD BUILDING** 词汇扩充
> A small house is called a **cottage**.
> A house with only one floor is called

a **bungalow**. 小房屋叫做 cottage，平房叫做 bungalow: *My grandparents live in a bungalow near the sea.* 我的爷爷和奶奶住在海边的一所平房。
A tall building where lots of people live is called a **block of flats** or an **apartment block**. 公寓楼叫做 block of flats 或 apartment block: *They live on the third floor of an apartment block.* 他们住在一栋公寓楼的四楼。

2 a building that has a special use 特定用途的建筑物: *an opera house* 歌剧院

housekeeper /'haʊskiːpə(r)/ *noun* 名词
a person whose job is to look after somebody else's house 管家

housewife /'haʊswaɪf/ *noun* 名词 (*plural* 复数形式 **housewives** /'haʊswaɪvz/)
a woman who stays at home and looks after her family 家庭主妇

housework /'haʊswɜːk/ *noun* 名词 (*no plural* 不用复数形式)
work that you do in your house, for example cleaning and washing 家务活

🔍 **WHICH WORD?** 词语辨析
Be careful! Work that a teacher gives you to do at home is called **homework**. 注意: 家庭作业叫做 homework。

housing /'haʊzɪŋ/ *noun* 名词 (*no plural* 不用复数形式)
flats and houses for people to live in 住房; 住宅: *We need more housing for young people.* 我们需要为年轻人提供更多的住宅。

housing estate /'haʊzɪŋ ɪsteɪt/ *noun* 名词 (*British* 英式英语)
a big group of houses that were built at the same time （统建的）住宅区: *We live on a housing estate.* 我们住在一个住宅区里。

hover /'hɒvə(r)/ *verb* 动词 (**hovers**, **hovering**, **hovered** /'hɒvəd/)
to stay in the air in one place 盘旋; 翱翔: *A helicopter hovered above the building.* 直升机在大楼上空盘旋。

hovercraft /'hɒvəkrɑːft/ *noun* 名词 (*plural* 复数形式 **hovercraft**)
a kind of boat that moves over the top of water on air that it pushes out 气垫船

how 0➡ /haʊ/ *adverb* 副词
1 in what way 怎样; 如何: *How does this machine work?* 这台机器是怎样运行的? ◇ *She told me how to get to the station.* 她把去车站的路告诉了我。 ◇ *Do*

you know how to spell 'essential'? 你知道 essential 这个词怎么拼吗?
2 a word that you use to ask if somebody is well （用以问好）: *'How is your sister?' 'She's very well, thank you.'* "你妹妹怎么样?" "她很好，谢谢。"

🔍 **WHICH WORD?** 词语辨析
You use **how** only when you are asking about somebody's health. * how 只用于问及健康状况。
When you are asking somebody to describe another person or a thing you use **what … like?**. 请对方描述某人或某物用 what … like?: *'What is your sister like?' 'She's tall with brown hair.'* "你妹妹长得怎么样?" "她个子高，头发是棕色的。"

3 a word that you use to ask if something is good （询问事物的好坏）: *How was the film?* 那部电影怎么样?
4 a word that you use to ask questions about things like age, amount or time （询问年龄、数量、时间等）: *How old are you?* 你多大了? ◇ *How many brothers and sisters have you got?* 你有几个兄弟姐妹? ◇ *How much does this cost?* 这个要多少钱? ◇ *How long have you lived here?* 你在这里住了多长时间了?
5 a word that shows surprise or strong feeling （表示惊讶或加强语气）: *How kind of you to help!* 你来帮忙，真是太好了!

how about … ? words that you use when you suggest something （用于提出建议）: *How about a drink?* 喝点东西怎么样? ◇ *How about going for a walk?* 出去散步好不好?

how are you? do you feel well? 你好吗?: *'How are you?' 'Fine, thanks.'* "你好吗?" "很好，谢谢。"

how do you do? polite words that you say when you meet somebody for the first time （初次见面时的问候语）你好

🔍 **SPEAKING** 表达方式说明
When somebody says **How do you do?**, you also answer **How do you do?** and you shake hands. Some people say **Pleased to meet you** when they meet. 对方说 How do you do? 时，应以 How do you do? 回答，然后互相握手。也有人见面时说 Pleased to meet you。

however 0➡ /haʊ'evə(r)/ *adverb* 副词
1 it does not matter how 不管怎样; 无论如何: *I never win, however hard I try.* 不管我怎么努力，却始终赢不了。

2 but 但是；然而；不过：*She's very intelligent. However, she's quite lazy.* 她很聪明，不过比较懒。
3 a way of saying 'how' more strongly（强调 how 的说法）究竟，到底

> 🔍 **GRAMMAR** 语法说明
>
> When **ever** is used like this to say **how** more strongly, we write it as a separate word. * ever 用于强调 how 时应分开书写：*How ever did you manage to find me?* 你究竟是怎么找到我的?

howl /haʊl/ *verb* 动词 (howls, howling, howled /haʊld/)
to make a long, loud sound, like a dog makes 嚎叫；呼啸：*The dogs howled all night.* 这些狗嚎叫了一夜。◇ *The wind howled around the house.* 狂风在房子周围呼啸。
▶ **howl** *noun* 名词：*He let out a howl of anger.* 他发出一声愤怒的吼叫。

HQ /ˌeɪtʃ ˈkjuː/ *short for* HEADQUARTERS * headquarters 的缩略式

huddle /ˈhʌdl/ *verb* 动词 (huddles, huddling, huddled /ˈhʌdld/)
to get close to other people because you are cold or frightened（因寒冷或恐惧）挤在一起：*We huddled together for warmth.* 我们挤在一起取暖。

hug /hʌɡ/ *verb* 动词 (hugs, hugging, hugged /hʌɡd/)
to put your arms around somebody to show that you love them 拥抱；搂抱：*She hugged her parents and said goodbye.* 她拥抱了父母，然后说再见。
▶ **hug** *noun* 名词：*Come and give me a hug.* 过来给我一个拥抱。

huge ⬦ /hjuːdʒ/ *adjective* 形容词
very big 非常大的；巨大的 ⊃ SAME MEANING **enormous** 同义词为 enormous：*They live in a huge house.* 他们住在一所很大的房子里。
▶ **hugely** /ˈhjuːdʒli/ *adverb* 副词 very 很；非常：*She is hugely popular.* 她非常受欢迎。

hullo = HELLO

hum /hʌm/ *verb* 动词 (hums, humming, hummed /hʌmd/)
1 to sing with your lips closed 哼（曲子）：*You can hum the tune if you don't know the words.* 你要是不知道歌词，就哼哼曲子吧。
2 to make a low continuous sound 发嗡嗡声：*The overhead wires hummed with power.* 头顶上方的电线通电时嗡嗡作响。

▶ **hum** *noun* 名词 (*no plural* 不用复数形式)：*The computer was making a low hum.* 这台电脑发出轻微的嗡嗡声。

human¹ ⬦ /ˈhjuːmən/ *adjective* 形容词
connected with people, not animals or machines 人的：*the human body* 人体

human² ⬦ /ˈhjuːmən/ (*also* 亦作 **human being** /ˌhjuːmən ˈbiːɪŋ/) *noun* 名词
a person 人：*Dogs can hear much better than humans.* 狗的听觉比人的灵敏得多。

the human race /ðə ˌhjuːmən ˈreɪs/ *noun* 名词 (*no plural* 不用复数形式)
all the people in the world 人类

humble /ˈhʌmbl/ *adjective* 形容词 (humbler, humblest)
1 A humble person does not think they are better or more important than other people. 谦逊的；虚心的：*Despite her success she is still very humble.* 尽管她很成功，她还是非常谦虚。
2 simple or poor 简朴的；低微的：*a humble cottage* 简朴的村舍

humid /ˈhjuːmɪd/ *adjective* 形容词
(used about the weather or climate) warm and wet（天气或气候）温暖潮湿的，湿热的 ⊃ SAME MEANING **damp** 同义词为 damp：*The island is hot and humid.* 这个岛又热又潮湿。
▶ **humidity** /hjuːˈmɪdəti/ *noun* 名词 (*no plural* 不用复数形式)：*high levels of humidity* 高湿度

humor *American English for* HUMOUR 美式英语，即 humour

humorous /ˈhjuːmərəs/ *adjective* 形容词
making you smile or laugh 幽默的；诙谐的 ⊃ SAME MEANING **funny** 同义词为 funny：*a humorous story* 滑稽的故事

humour ⬦ (*British* 英式英语) (*American* 美式英语 **humor**) /ˈhjuːmə(r)/ *noun* 名词 (*no plural* 不用复数形式)
1 the quality of being funny or amusing 幽默；诙谐：*a story full of humour* 非常幽默的故事
2 the ability to laugh and know that something is funny 幽默感：*Dave has a good sense of humour.* 戴夫很有幽默感。

hump /hʌmp/ *noun* 名词
a round lump on an animal's or a person's back（人背上）圆形隆起物；（动物）峰：*A camel has a hump on its back.* 骆驼的背上有驼峰。⊃ Look at the picture at **camel**. 见 camel 的插图。

hundred ⬦ /ˈhʌndrəd/ *number* 数词
1 100 一百：*We invited a hundred people*

A
B
C
D
E
F
G
H
I
J
K
L
M
N
O
P
Q
R
S
T
U
V
W
X
Y
Z

to the party. 我们邀请了一百人参加聚会。
◇ *two hundred pounds* 两百英镑 ◇ *four hundred and twenty* 四百二十
2 hundreds (*informal* 非正式) a lot 许多: *I've got **hundreds of** things to do today.* 我今天有许多事要做。 **⊃** Look at **Numbers** on Study Pages **S6-S8**. 见研习专页 S6-S8 "数字" 部分。
▸ **hundredth** /'hʌndrədθ/ *pronoun, adjective, adverb* 代词，形容词，副词 100th 第一百

hung *form of* HANG (1) * hang 第 1 义的不同形式

hunger /'hʌŋgə(r)/ *noun* 名词 (*no plural* 不用复数形式)
the feeling that you want or need to eat 饥饿 (感觉)

🔊 SPEAKING 表达方式说明
Be careful! We say **I am hungry** not **I have hunger**. 注意：要说 I am hungry，不说 I have hunger。
⊃ Look at **thirst**. 见 thirst。

hungry 🔊 /'hʌŋgri/ *adjective* 形容词 (**hungrier, hungriest**)
wanting to eat 饿的；饥饿的: *Let's eat soon – I'm hungry!* 我们快吃饭吧，我饿了! ⊃ Look at **thirsty**. 见 thirsty。

hunt 🔊 /hʌnt/ *verb* 动词 (**hunts, hunting, hunted**)
to chase animals to kill them as a sport or for food 打猎；狩猎: *Young lions have to learn to hunt.* 幼狮得学会猎食。

🔊 SPEAKING 表达方式说明
When you talk about people spending time hunting as a sport, you say **go hunting**. 狩猎作为消遣叫做 go hunting: *They went hunting in the forest.* 他们去森林打猎了。

hunt for something to try to find something 搜寻；寻找: *I've hunted everywhere for my watch but I can't find it.* 我到处找我的手表，可是找不到。
▸ **hunt** *noun* 名词: *a fox hunt* 猎狐 ◇ *a hunt for the missing child* 对该名失踪儿童的搜寻
▸ **hunting** /'hʌntɪŋ/ *noun* 名词 (*no plural* 不用复数形式) the activity of chasing and killing animals 打猎；狩猎

hunter /'hʌntə(r)/ *noun* 名词
a person who HUNTS wild animals 猎人；狩猎者

hurl /hɜːl/ *verb* 动词 (**hurls, hurling, hurled** /hɜːld/)

to throw something very strongly (用力) 扔，抛: *She hurled the book across the room.* 她把那本书从房间的一头扔到另一头。

hurrah, hurray = HOORAY

hurricane /'hʌrɪkən/ *noun* 名词
a storm with very strong winds 飓风: *Hurricane Katrina caused chaos in the city of New Orleans.* 飓风卡特里娜在新奥尔良市造成了混乱局面。 **⊃** Look at the note at **storm**[1]. 见 storm[1] 条的注释。

hurry[1] 🔊 /'hʌri/ *verb* 动词 (**hurries, hurrying, hurried** /'hʌrid/)
to move or do something quickly 赶快；匆忙: *We hurried home after school.* 我们一放学就赶紧回家了。
hurry up to move or do something more quickly because there is not much time 赶快，加速 (做某事): *Hurry up or we'll be late!* 快点儿，要不然我们就迟到了!

hurry[2] 🔊 /'hʌri/ *noun* 名词
in a hurry needing or wanting to do something quickly 迅速；匆忙: *I can't talk to you now – I'm in a hurry.* 我现在不能跟你聊，我正忙着呢。

hurt[1] 🔊 /hɜːt/ *verb* 动词 (**hurts, hurting, hurt, has hurt**)
1 to make somebody or something feel pain 使疼痛；使受伤: *I fell and hurt my leg.* 我把腿摔疼了。 ◇ *Did you **hurt yourself**?* 你弄伤了自己吗? ◇ *These shoes hurt – they are too small.* 这双鞋夹脚，太小了。
2 to feel pain 感到疼痛: *My leg hurts.* 我腿疼。
3 to make somebody unhappy 使不快: *I never meant to **hurt** your **feelings**.* 我从未想过要让你不高兴。

🔊 WHICH WORD? 词语辨析
Hurt or **injured**? 用 hurt 还是 injured? These words are similar in meaning. We usually use **injured** when someone has been hurt in an accident. 这两个词词义相似。在事故中受伤通常用 injured。

hurt[2] /hɜːt/ *adjective* 形容词
1 physically harmed (身体上) 受伤的 ⊃ SAME MEANING **injured** 同义词为 injured: *Was anyone hurt in the accident?* 事故中有人受伤吗?
2 upset (感情上) 受伤的: *I was very hurt by what you said.* 你的话让我感到很难过。

hurtful /'hɜːtfl/ *adjective* 形容词
making somebody feel upset 使人难过

的；伤感情的 ⊃ SAME MEANING **unkind**
同义词为 unkind: *hurtful remarks* 令人
伤心的话

husband ⊶ /ˈhʌzbənd/ *noun* 名词
the man that a woman is married to 丈夫
⊃ Look at **wife**. 见 wife。

hush /hʌʃ/ *verb* 动词 (hushes, hushing,
hushed /hʌʃt/)
a word that you use to tell somebody to
be quiet 安静；别说话；别作声: *Hush
now, and go to sleep.* 别说话了，睡吧。
▶ **hush** *noun* 名词 (*no plural* 不用复数形
式) a situation in which it is completely
quiet 寂静 ⊃ SAME MEANING **silence** 同义词
为 silence: *A hush fell over the room.*
房间内变得鸦雀无声。

hut /hʌt/ *noun* 名词
a small, simple building with one room
小房子

hydraulic /haɪˈdrɔːlɪk/ *adjective* 形容词
Hydraulic equipment is worked by liquid
moving under pressure. 液压的:
hydraulic brakes 液压制动器

hydroelectric /ˌhaɪdrəʊˈlektrɪk/
adjective 形容词
using the power of water to produce
electricity 水力发电的: *hydroelectric
power* 水力发出的电

hydrogen /ˈhaɪdrədʒən/ *noun* 名词
(*no plural* 不用复数形式)
a light gas that you cannot see or smell
氢；氢气: *Water is made of hydrogen
and oxygen.* 水是由氢和氧构成的。

hygiene /ˈhaɪdʒiːn/ *noun* 名词 (*no plural*
不用复数形式)
keeping yourself and things around you
clean 卫生: *Good hygiene is very
important when you are preparing food.*
准备食物的时候要特别注意卫生。

hygienic /haɪˈdʒiːnɪk/ *adjective*
形容词: *hygienic conditions* 卫生状况

hymn /hɪm/ *noun* 名词
a song that Christians sing in church
（基督教的）赞美诗，圣歌

hype /haɪp/ *noun* 名词 (*no plural* 不用
复数形式) (*informal* 非正式)
advertisements that make you think
something is better than it really is 夸张
的广告: *Don't believe the hype – the
film's rubbish!* 别相信那些天花乱坠的
宣传，那部电影很差劲!

hyphen /ˈhaɪfn/ *noun* 名词
a mark (-) that you use in writing. It joins
words together (for example 'left-handed')
or shows that a word continues on the
next line. 连字符

hypnosis /hɪpˈnəʊsɪs/ *noun* 名词
(*no plural* 不用复数形式)
when somebody's mind and actions can
be controlled by another person because
they are in a kind of deep sleep 催眠
（状态）: *She spoke about the attack
under hypnosis.* 她在催眠状态下谈起了
那次袭击的事。

hypocrite /ˈhɪpəkrɪt/ *noun* 名词
a person who pretends to have moral
beliefs that they do not really have 虚伪
的人；伪君子
▶ **hypocrisy** /hɪˈpɒkrəsi/ *noun* 名词
(*no plural* 不用复数形式): *He condemned
the hypocrisy of those politicians who do
one thing and say another.* 他谴责那些
说一套做一套的政客的虚伪。

hysterical /hɪˈsterɪkl/ *adjective* 形容词
so excited or upset that you cannot
control yourself 歇斯底里的；过于激动
的: *hysterical laughter* 歇斯底里的笑声

I i

I, i¹ /aɪ/ *noun* 名词 (*plural* 复数形式 **I's, i's** /aɪz/)
the ninth letter of the English alphabet 英语字母表的第 9 个字母: *'Island' begins with an 'I'.* * island 一词以字母 i 开头。

I² 0━ /aɪ/ *pronoun* 代词 (*plural* 复数形式 **we**)
the person who is speaking 我: *I phoned and said I was busy.* 我打电话说我很忙。◇ *I'll* (= I will) *see you tomorrow.* 我明天见你。◇ *I'm not going to fall, am I?* 我不会摔倒，是吧?

ice 0━ /aɪs/ *noun* 名词 (*no plural* 不用复数形式)
water that has become hard because it is frozen 冰: *Do you want ice in your drink?* 你的饮料要加冰吗?

iceberg /'aɪsbɜːg/ *noun* 名词
a very big piece of ice in the sea 冰山 (海上的巨大冰块)

ice cream 0━ /ˌaɪs 'kriːm/ *noun* 名词
very cold sweet food made from milk 冰激凌；冰淇淋: *Do you like ice cream?* 你喜欢吃冰激凌吗? ◇ *Two chocolate ice creams, please.* 请来两份巧克力冰激凌。➲ Look at Picture Dictionary page **P7**. 见彩页 P7。

ice cube /'aɪs kjuːb/ *noun* 名词
a small piece of ice that you put in a drink to make it cold 小冰块 (用于冷饮)

ice hockey /'aɪs hɒki/ *noun* 名词 (*British* 英式英语) (*American* 美式英语 **hockey**) (*no plural* 不用复数形式)
a game that is played on ice by two teams who try to hit a small flat rubber thing (called a **puck**) into a goal with long wooden sticks 冰球运动；冰上曲棍球

ice lolly /ˌaɪs 'lɒli/ *noun* 名词 (*plural* 复数形式 **ice lollies**) (*British* 英式英语) (*American* 美式英语 **Popsicle**™)
a piece of sweet ice on a stick 冰棍；冰棒

ice rink /'aɪs rɪŋk/ *noun* 名词 (*also* 亦作 **skating rink, rink**) *noun* 名词
a special place where you can ICE-SKATE 溜冰场

ice-skate /'aɪs skeɪt/ *verb* 动词 (**ice-skates, ice-skating, ice-skated**) (*also* 亦作 **skate**)
to move on ice in special boots (called

ice-skates) that have long sharp pieces of metal on the bottom 滑冰；溜冰 ➲ Look at the picture at **skate²**. 见 skate² 的插图。
▸ **ice-skating** /'aɪs skeɪtɪŋ/ (*also* 亦作 **skating**) *noun* 名词 (*no plural* 不用复数形式): *We go ice-skating every weekend in the winter.* 冬天每逢周末我们就去溜冰。➲ Look at Picture Dictionary page **P14**. 见彩页 P14。

icicle /'aɪsɪkl/ *noun* 名词
a long piece of ice that hangs down from something (向下流水结冰而成的) 冰锥，冰柱 ➲ Look at Picture Dictionary page **P16**. 见彩页 P16。

icing /'aɪsɪŋ/ *noun* 名词 (*no plural* 不用复数形式) (*British* 英式英语) (*American* 美式英语 **frosting**)
a sweet substance that you use for covering cakes 糖霜 (装饰糕饼): *a cake with pink icing* 有一层粉红色糖霜的蛋糕

icon /'aɪkɒn/ *noun* 名词
(*computing* 电脑) a small picture on a computer screen that you can use to start a program or open a file 图标；图符；图示: *Double-click on the icon.* 双击图标。

ICT /ˌaɪ siː 'tiː/ *noun* 名词 (*no plural* 不用复数形式) (*British* 英式英语)
the subject at school in which children learn how to use computers, the Internet, video and other technology 信息和通信技术 ➲ **ICT** is short for 'Information and Communications Technology'. * ICT 是 Information and Communications Technology 的缩略式。

icy /'aɪsi/ *adjective* 形容词 (**icier, iciest**)
1 covered with ice 结满冰的: *icy roads* 结满冰的路
2 very cold 冰冷的；冰冻的: *an icy wind* 凛冽的风

ID /ˌaɪ 'diː/ *abbreviation* 缩略式 (*informal* 非正式)
a document that shows who you are 身份证明: *Do you have any ID?* 你有身份证明吗? ◇ *an ID card* 身份证 ➲ **ID** is short for 'identity' or 'identification'. * ID 是 identity 或 identification 的缩略式。

I'd /aɪd/ *short for* I HAD; I WOULD * I had 和 I would 的缩略式

idea 0ₘ /aɪˈdɪə/ *noun* 名词
1 a plan or new thought 主意；想法；构思： *It was a good idea to give Martin a pen for his birthday.* 送马丁一支笔作生日礼物是个好主意。◇ *I've got an idea. Let's have a party!* 我有个主意，我们开个派对吧！
2 a picture in your mind 印象；概念： *The film gives you a good idea of what Iceland is like.* 这部影片详细介绍了冰岛。◇ *I've got no idea* (= I do not know) *where she is.* 我不知道她在哪里。

ideal /aɪˈdiːəl/ *adjective* 形容词
the best or exactly right 理想的；最合适的 ⊃ SAME MEANING **perfect** 同义词为 perfect： *This is an ideal place for a picnic.* 这是野餐的好地方。

identical /aɪˈdentɪkl/ *adjective* 形容词
exactly the same 完全相同的： *These two cameras are identical.* 这两部相机完全一样。◇ *identical twins* 一模一样的双胞胎

identification /aɪˌdentɪfɪˈkeɪʃn/ *noun*
名词 (*no plural* 不用复数形式)
1 the process of showing or finding out who somebody or something is 辨认；识别： *The identification of bodies after the accident was difficult.* 事故后辨认尸体的工作非常困难。
2 (*abbr.* 缩略式 **ID**) a document that shows who you are 身份证明： *Do you have any identification?* 你有身份证明吗？

identify 0ₘ /aɪˈdentɪfaɪ/ *verb* 动词
(identifies identifying identified /aɪˈdentɪfaɪd/, has identified)
to say or know who somebody is or what something is 辨认；识别： *The police have not identified the dead man yet.* 警方尚未辨认出死者的身份。

identity 0ₘ /aɪˈdentəti/ *noun* 名词 (*plural* 复数形式 identities)
who or what a person or thing is 身份；本体： *The identity of the killer is not known.* 现在还不知道杀人凶手是谁。

identity card /aɪˈdentəti kɑːd/ *noun*
名词 (*also* 亦作 **ID card**)
a card that shows who you are 身份证

idiom /ˈɪdiəm/ *noun* 名词
a group of words with a special meaning 习语；成语；惯用语： *The idiom 'break somebody's heart' means 'to make somebody very unhappy'.* 习语 break somebody's heart 的意思是 "使某人非常伤心"。

idiomatic /ˌɪdiəˈmætɪk/ *adjective* 形容词
using language that contains natural expressions 地道的；符合语言习惯的：
She speaks fluent and idiomatic English. 她说一口流利地道的英语。

idiot /ˈɪdiət/ *noun* 名词
a person who is stupid or does something silly 傻瓜；笨蛋： *I was an idiot to forget my key.* 我真是笨蛋，忘了带钥匙。
▸ **idiotic** /ˌɪdiˈɒtɪk/ *adjective* 形容词:
an idiotic mistake 愚蠢的错误

idol /ˈaɪdl/ *noun* 名词
1 a famous person that people love 偶像；崇拜的对象： *He was the pop idol of millions of teenagers.* 他是千千万万青少年的流行音乐偶像。
2 an object that people treat as a god 神像

i.e. /ˌaɪ ˈiː/ *abbreviation* 缩略式
used in writing to mean 'that is' or 'in other words' 也就是；亦即： *You can buy hot drinks, i.e. tea and coffee, on the train.* 火车上可以买到热饮，也就是茶和咖啡。

if 0ₘ /ɪf/ *conjunction* 连词
1 a word that you use to say what is possible or true when another thing happens or is true 如果；假如；要是： *If you press this button, the machine starts.* 如果按这个键，机器就开动了。◇ *If you see him, give him this letter.* 你要是见到他，就把这封信交给他。◇ *If your feet were smaller, you could wear my shoes.* 你的脚要是小一点，就能穿我的鞋子了。◇ *If I had a million pounds, I would buy a big house.* 假如我有一百万英镑，我会买栋大房子。◇ *I may see you tomorrow. If not, I'll see you next week.* 我可能明天见你，不行的话，我下星期才见你。
2 a word that shows a question 是否 ⊃ SAME MEANING **whether** 同义词为 whether： *Do you know if Paul is at home?* 你知道保罗在家吗？◇ *She asked me if I wanted to go to a party.* 她问我想不想去参加聚会。
3 every time 每次 ⊃ SAME MEANING **whenever** 同义词为 whenever： *If I try to phone her she just hangs up.* 每次我给她打电话，她就挂掉。

as if in a way that makes you think something 似乎；好像；仿佛： *She looks as if she has been on holiday.* 她看上去好像刚度完假似的。

if only words that show that you want something very much 如果…就好了；但愿： *If only I could drive!* 我要是会开车多好啊！

igloo /ˈɪɡluː/ *noun* 名词 (*plural* 复数形式 igloos)
a small house that is made out of blocks of snow 冰屋

A
B
C
D
E
F
G
H
I
J
K
L
M
N
O
P
Q
R
S
T
U
V
W
X
Y
Z

ignite /ɪɡˈnaɪt/ *verb* 动词 (ignites, igniting, ignited) (*formal* 正式)
to start burning or to make something start burning 燃烧；点燃： *The gas ignited and caused an explosion.* 煤气烧着了，引起了爆炸。

ignorance /ˈɪɡnərəns/ *noun* 名词 (*no plural* 不用复数形式)
not knowing about something 无知；不知情： *Her ignorance surprised me.* 她的无知令我惊讶。

ignorant /ˈɪɡnərənt/ *adjective* 形容词
not knowing about something 无知的；不了解的： *I'm very ignorant about computers.* 我对电脑一窍不通。

ignore ⊶ /ɪɡˈnɔː(r)/ *verb* 动词 (ignores, ignoring, ignored /ɪɡˈnɔːd/)
to know about somebody or something, but to not do anything about it 忽视；不理会： *He completely ignored his doctor's advice.* 他根本没理会医生的嘱咐。◇ *I said hello to her, but she ignored me!* 我跟她打招呼，她却不理我！

> 🔎 WHICH WORD? 词语辨析
> Be careful! **Ignore** and **be ignorant** are not the same. 注意：ignore 和 be ignorant 并非同义。

il- *prefix* 前缀
You can add **il-** to the beginning of some words to give them the opposite meaning, for example *'illegal'* (= not legal). （用在某些词前构成反义）

ill ⊶ /ɪl/ *adjective* 形容词 (*British* 英式英语) (*American* 美式英语 **sick**)
not well; not in good health 有病；不舒服： *Mark is in bed because he is ill.* 马克卧病在床。◇ *I feel too ill to go to work.* 我病得不舒服，不能上班了。◇ *Josie was taken ill* (= became ill) *on holiday.* 乔西在假期里病了。⊃ The noun is **illness**. 名词为 illness。⊃ Look at Study Pages **S16-S17**. 见研学专页 S16-S17。

I'll /aɪl/ *short for* I SHALL; I WILL * I shall 和 I will 的缩略式

illegal ⊶ /ɪˈliːɡl/ *adjective* 形容词
not allowed by law 不合法的；非法的；违法的： *It's illegal to drive through a red light.* 开车闯红灯是违法的。 ⊃ OPPOSITE **legal** 反义词为 legal
▶ **illegally** /ɪˈliːɡəli/ *adverb* 副词： *She entered the country illegally.* 她是非法入境的。

illegible /ɪˈledʒəbl/ *adjective* 形容词
difficult or impossible to read 字体难以

辨认的；字迹模糊的： *Your handwriting is completely illegible.* 你写的字完全无法辨认。 ⊃ OPPOSITE **legible** 反义词为 legible

illiterate /ɪˈlɪtərət/ *adjective* 形容词
not able to read or write 不会读写的；文盲的

illness ⊶ /ˈɪlnəs/ *noun* 名词
1 (*no plural* 不用复数形式) being ill 病；疾病： *I missed a lot of school because of illness last year.* 我去年因病耽误了很多课业。
2 (*plural* 复数形式 **illnesses**) a type or period of illness 疾病；患病期： *She died after a long illness.* 她久病不愈去世了。

ill-treat /ˌɪl ˈtriːt/ *verb* 动词 (ill-treats, ill-treating, ill-treated)
to do cruel things to a person or an animal 虐待： *This dog has been ill-treated.* 这条狗受过虐待。

illusion /ɪˈluːʒn/ *noun* 名词
a false idea or belief 错误的观念；幻想： *I have no illusions about the situation – I know it's serious.* 我对形势不抱幻想，我知道是很严峻的。

illustrate /ˈɪləstreɪt/ *verb* 动词 (illustrates, illustrating, illustrated)
to add pictures to show something more clearly 给…配插图；用插图说明： *The book is illustrated with colour photographs.* 这本书配有彩色照片。

illustration /ˌɪləˈstreɪʃn/ *noun* 名词
a picture in a book 插图： *This dictionary has a lot of illustrations.* 这本词典有很多插图。

im- *prefix* 前缀
You can add **im-** to the beginning of some words to give them the opposite meaning, for example *'impatient'* (= not patient). （用在某些词前构成反义）

I'm /aɪm/ *short for* I AM * I am 的缩略式

image ⊶ /ˈɪmɪdʒ/ *noun* 名词
1 the impression that a person or an organization gives to the public （人或组织给予公众的）形象，印象： *He's very different from his public image.* 他和他的公众形象截然不同。
2 a picture in people's minds of somebody or something （心目中的）形象，印象： *A lot of people have an image of London as cold and rainy.* 很多人对伦敦的印象是寒冷多雨。
3 a picture on paper or in a mirror 画面；图像；影象；映象： *images of war* 战争的画面

imaginary /ɪˈmædʒɪnəri/ *adjective*
形容词
not real; only in your mind 想象的；
幻想的；虚构的：*The film is about an imaginary country.* 这部电影讲述的是一个虚构的国家。

imagination ⚟ /ɪˌmædʒɪˈneɪʃn/ *noun* 名词
the ability to think of new ideas or make pictures in your mind 想象力；想象：*He has a lively imagination.* 他的想象力很丰富。◇ *You didn't really see a ghost – it was just your imagination.* 你并非真的见到鬼，那只不过是你的想象而已。

imaginative /ɪˈmædʒɪnətɪv/ *adjective*
形容词
having or showing imagination 富于想象力的：*imaginative ideas* 有创意的想法

imagine ⚟ /ɪˈmædʒɪn/ *verb* 动词
(imagines, imagining, imagined /ɪˈmædʒɪnd/)
1 to make a picture of something in your mind 想象；设想：*Can you imagine life without electricity?* 你能想象生活中没有电吗？◇ *I closed my eyes and imagined I was lying on a beach.* 我闭上眼睛，想象自己躺在海滩上。
2 to see, hear, or think something that is not true 胡乱猜想；猜测：*I never said that, you're imagining things.* 我从没说过那样的话，你在胡思乱想。

imitate /ˈɪmɪteɪt/ *verb* 动词 (imitates, imitating, imitated)
to copy somebody or something 模仿；仿效：*Children learn by imitating adults.* 孩子通过模仿大人来学习。

imitation /ˌɪmɪˈteɪʃn/ *noun* 名词
something that you make to look like another thing 仿制品；赝品 ⊃ SAME MEANING **copy** 同义词为 copy：*It's not a real diamond, it's only an imitation.* 这不是真钻石，只是仿制品。◇ *imitation leather* 人造革

immature /ˌɪməˈtjʊə(r)/ *adjective* 形容词
behaving in a way that is not sensible and is typical of younger people 不成熟的；幼稚的：*He's very immature for his age.* 就他的年龄而言，他十分不成熟。
⊃ OPPOSITE **mature** 反义词为 mature

immediate ⚟ /ɪˈmiːdiət/ *adjective*
形容词
happening now or very soon 立刻的；立即的：*I can't wait – I need an immediate answer.* 我不能等，我需要即时的答复。

immediately ⚟ /ɪˈmiːdiətli/ *adverb*
副词

Remember! You spell **immediately** with **MM**. 记住：immediately 拼写中有 mm。

now 立刻；马上 ⊃ SAME MEANING **at once** 同义词为 at once：*Come to my office immediately!* 马上到我办公室来！

immense /ɪˈmens/ *adjective* 形容词
very big 极大的；巨大的：*immense problems* 巨大的困难

immensely /ɪˈmensli/ *adverb* 副词
very or very much 很；非常：*We enjoyed the party immensely.* 我们在聚会上玩得很开心。

immigrant /ˈɪmɪɡrənt/ *noun* 名词
a person who comes to another country to live there（外来）移民；外侨：*Many immigrants to Britain have come from Asia.* 移居英国的人有很多来自亚洲。

immigration /ˌɪmɪˈɡreɪʃn/ *noun* 名词
(no plural 不用复数形式)
coming to another country to live there 移居（入境）：*The government is trying to control immigration.* 政府正尝试控制移民人数。

immoral /ɪˈmɒrəl/ *adjective* 形容词
(used about people and their behaviour) not honest or good（人或行为）不道德的：*It's immoral to steal.* 偷盗是不道德的。⊃ OPPOSITE **moral** 反义词为 moral

immortal /ɪˈmɔːtl/ *adjective* 形容词
living or lasting for ever 永生的；永恒的；不朽的

immune /ɪˈmjuːn/ *adjective* 形容词
If you are **immune** to a disease, you cannot get it.（对某种疾病）免疫：*You're immune to measles if you've had it before.* 得过麻疹的人会有免疫力。

immunize /ˈɪmjunaɪz/ *verb* 动词
(immunizes, immunizing, immunized /ˈɪmjunaɪzd/)
to protect somebody from a disease by putting a substance that protects the body (called a vaccine) into their blood（通过注射疫苗）使免疫

impact /ˈɪmpækt/ *noun* 名词
the effect that something has 影响；作用：*I hope this campaign will have an impact on young people.* 我希望这场运动能对年轻人起作用。

impatient ⚟ /ɪmˈpeɪʃnt/ *adjective*
形容词
not wanting to wait for something 不耐烦的；没有耐心的：*Don't be so impatient!*

The bus will be here soon. 别那么不耐烦! 公共汽车很快就会来。 ⊃ OPPOSITE **patient** 反义词为 patient

▶ **impatience** /ɪmˈpeɪ∫ns/ *noun* 名词 (*no plural* 不用复数形式): *He couldn't hide his impatience.* 他掩饰不了自己的不耐烦。

▶ **impatiently** /ɪmˈpeɪ∫ntli/ *adverb* 副词: 'Hurry up!' she said impatiently. "快点!" 她不耐烦地说。

imperative¹ /ɪmˈperətɪv/ *adjective* 形容词
very important 非常重要的 ⊃ SAME MEANING **vital** 同义词为 vital: *It is imperative that you see a doctor immediately.* 你得马上去看医生。

imperative² /ɪmˈperətɪv/ *noun* 名词 (*grammar* 语法) the form of a verb that you use for telling somebody to do something 祈使语气: *'Listen!' and 'Go away!' are in the imperative.* * Listen! 和 Go away! 都是祈使语气。

the imperfect /ðɪ ɪmˈpɜːfɪkt/ *noun* 名词 (*no plural* 不用复数形式) (*grammar* 语法) the form of the verb that is used to talk about an action in the past that is not finished or that lasted for a long time 过去未完成时; 未完成式: *In the sentence 'I was having a bath', the verb is in the imperfect.* 在 I was having a bath 一句中, 动词用的是过去未完成时。

impertinent /ɪmˈpɜːtɪnənt/ *adjective* 形容词 (*formal* 正式)
rude and not showing respect 粗鲁无礼的; 不敬的 ⊃ SAME MEANING **cheeky** 同义词为 cheeky: *Don't be impertinent!* 别那么没礼貌!

imply /ɪmˈplaɪ/ *verb* 动词 (implies implying implied /ɪmˈplaɪd/, has implied)
to suggest something without actually saying it 暗示; 暗指: *He asked if I had any work to do. He was implying that I was lazy.* 他问我有没有事情做, 言下之意就是说我懒惰。

impolite /ˌɪmpəˈlaɪt/ *adjective* 形容词
rude 不礼貌的; 粗鲁的: *It was impolite of him to ask you to leave.* 他叫你离开是不礼貌的。 ⊃ OPPOSITE **polite** 反义词为 polite

import /ɪmˈpɔːt/ *verb* 动词 (imports importing imported)
to buy things from another country and bring them into your country 进口; 输入: *Britain imports oranges from Spain.* 英国从西班牙进口橙子。 ⊃ OPPOSITE **export** 反义词为 export

▶ **import** /ˈɪmpɔːt/ *noun* 名词: *What are your country's main imports?* 你们国家主要的进口产品有哪些? ⊃ OPPOSITE **export** 反义词为 export

▶ **importer** /ɪmˈpɔːtə(r)/ *noun* 名词: *an importer of electrical goods* 电器进口商

importance /ɪmˈpɔːtns/ *noun* 名词 (*no plural* 不用复数形式)
the quality of being important 重要; 重要性: *Oil is of great importance to industry.* 石油对工业非常重要。

important /ɪmˈpɔːtnt/ *adjective* 形容词
1 If something is **important**, you must do, have or think about it. 重要的: *It is important to sleep well the night before an exam.* 考试前夕睡好觉是很重要的。 ◇ *I think that happiness is more important than money.* 我认为幸福比金钱重要。
2 powerful or special 有权力的; 有影响力的: *The prime minister is a very important person.* 首相是很有影响力的人物。

impossible /ɪmˈpɒsəbl/ *adjective* 形容词
If something is **impossible**, you cannot do it, or it cannot happen. 不可能的; 无法做到的; 不可能发生的: *It's impossible for me to finish this work by five o'clock.* 我不可能在五点钟以前完成这项工作。 ◇ *The house was impossible to find.* 那所房子找也找不到。 ⊃ OPPOSITE **possible** 反义词为 possible

impractical /ɪmˈpræktɪkl/ *adjective* 形容词
not sensible or realistic 不明智的; 不现实的: *It would be impractical to take our bikes on the train.* 把我们的自行车带上火车是不切实际的。

impress /ɪmˈpres/ *verb* 动词 (impresses impressing impressed /ɪmˈprest/)
to make somebody admire and respect you 使钦佩; 使敬佩: *We were very impressed by your work.* 你的工作给我们留下了深刻的印象。

impression /ɪmˈpre∫n/ *noun* 名词
feelings or thoughts you have about somebody or something 印象; 感想: *What was your first impression of the city?* 你对这座城市的第一印象怎么样? ◇ *I get the impression that she's not very happy.* 我觉得她不太开心。 ◇ *He made a good impression on his first day at work.* 他第一天上班就给人留下了好印象。

impressive /ɪmˈpresɪv/ *adjective* 形容词

If somebody or something is **impressive**, you admire them. 令人敬佩的；令人赞叹的：an *impressive building* 壮观的大楼 ◇ *Your work is very impressive.* 你的工作十分出色。

imprison /ɪmˈprɪzn/ *verb* 动词 (imprisons, imprisoning, imprisoned /ɪmˈprɪznd/)
to put somebody in prison 监禁；关押：*He was imprisoned for killing his wife.* 他因杀害妻子而入狱。
▶ **imprisonment** /ɪmˈprɪznmənt/ *noun* 名词 (*no plural* 不用复数形式)：*two years' imprisonment* 两年监禁

improbable /ɪmˈprɒbəbl/ *adjective* 形容词
not likely to be true or to happen 不太真实的；不太可能（发生）的：*an improbable explanation* 牵强的解释

improve ⟋ /ɪmˈpruːv/ *verb* 动词 (improves, improving, improved /ɪmˈpruːvd/)
to become better or to make something better 改进；改善：*Your English has improved a lot this year.* 你的英语今年有很大的进步。◇ *You must improve your spelling.* 你得减少拼写错误。

improvement ⟋ /ɪmˈpruːvmənt/ *noun* 名词
a change that makes something better than it was before 改进；改善：*There has been a big improvement in Sam's work.* 萨姆的工作有了很大的进步。

impulse /ˈɪmpʌls/ *noun* 名词
a sudden strong wish to do something 冲动；一时的念头：*She felt an impulse to run away.* 她有一股冲动想逃跑。

impulsive /ɪmˈpʌlsɪv/ *adjective* 形容词
doing things suddenly and without thinking carefully 冲动的；未经深入考虑的：*It was an impulsive decision.* 那是一时冲动作出的决定。

in¹ ⟋ /ɪn/ *preposition* 介词
1 a word that shows where somebody or something is 在…里：*a country in Africa* 非洲的一个国家 ◇ *He put his hand in the water.* 他把手放入水中。◇ *She was lying in bed.* 她躺在床上。
2 making all or part of something 构成…的整体（或部分）：*There are 100 centimetres in a metre.* * 1 米等于 100 厘米。
3 a word that shows when something happens（表示时间）在…期间：*My birthday is in May.* 我的生日在五月。◇ *He started school in 1987.* 他 1987 年开始上学。

4 a word that shows how long something takes 在（一段时间）之后：*I'll be ready in ten minutes.* 我十分钟后就准备好。
5 a word that shows what clothes somebody is wearing 穿着：*He was dressed in a suit.* 他穿着一套西装。
6 a word that shows how somebody or something is（表示状态）：*This room is in a mess.* 这个房间乱七八糟。◇ *Jenny was in tears* (= she was crying). 珍妮哭了。◇ *Sit in a circle.* 坐成一圈。
7 a word that shows somebody's job（表示职业）：*He's in the army.* 他在陆军服役。
8 a word that shows in what way or in what language 以（某种方式或语言）：*Write your name in capital letters.* 用大写字母写出你的名字。◇ *They were speaking in French.* 他们在用法语交谈。

in² ⟋ /ɪn/ *adverb* 副词
1 to a place, from outside 到里面；进入：*I opened the door and went in.* 我开门走了进去。
2 at home or at work 在家；在上班：*Nobody was in when we called.* 我们打电话的时候家里没人。

in- /ɪn/ *prefix* 前缀
You can add **in-** to the beginning of some words to give them the opposite meaning, for example '*incomplete*' (= not complete). （用在某些词前构成反义）

inability /ˌɪnəˈbɪləti/ *noun* 名词 (*no plural* 不用复数形式)
not being able to do something 无能；不能：*He has an inability to talk about his problems.* 他无法谈论自己的问题。 ⊃ The adjective is **unable**. 形容词为 unable。

inaccurate /ɪnˈækjərət/ *adjective* 形容词
not correct; with mistakes in it 不正确的；不准确的；有错误的：*The report in the newspaper was inaccurate.* 报纸上的这篇报道并不准确。 ⊃ OPPOSITE **accurate** 反义词为 accurate

inadequate /ɪnˈædɪkwət/ *adjective* 形容词
not enough, or not good enough 不足的；不够好的：*These shoes are inadequate for cold weather.* 这双鞋冷天穿不够暖。 ⊃ OPPOSITE **adequate** 反义词为 adequate

inappropriate /ˌɪnəˈprəʊpriət/ *adjective* 形容词
not suitable 不适当的；不合适的：*Isn't that dress rather inappropriate for a formal occasion?* 那条连衣裙在正式场合穿实在不得体吧？ ⊃ OPPOSITE **appropriate** 反义词为 appropriate

incapable /ɪnˈkeɪpəbl/ *adjective* 形容词
not able to do something 没有能力:
He's incapable of lying. 他不会说谎。
⊃ OPPOSITE **capable** 反义词为 capable

incentive /ɪnˈsentɪv/ *noun* 名词
something that makes you want to do something 激励；推动因素: *People need incentives to save money.* 人需要有鼓励因素来推动他们储蓄。

inch /ɪntʃ/ *noun* 名词 (*plural* 复数形式 inches)
a measure of length (= 2.54 centimetres). There are twelve **inches** in a **foot**. 英寸（长度单位；1 英寸等于 2.54 厘米，12 英寸为 1 英尺）: *I am five foot six inches tall.* 我身高五英尺六英寸。◇ *a twelve-inch ruler* 十二英寸的尺子 ⊃ Look at the note at **foot**. 见 foot 条的注释。

incident /ˈɪnsɪdənt/ *noun* 名词
something that happens, especially something bad or unusual（尤指不好或不寻常的）事件: *There were a number of incidents after the football match.* 足球赛后发生了多起骚乱事件。

incidentally /ˌɪnsɪˈdentli/ *adverb* 副词
a word that you say when you are going to talk about something different（引出新话题）顺便提一句 ⊃ SAME MEANING **by the way** 同义词为 by the way: *Incidentally, have you been to that new cinema yet?* 顺便问一下，你去过那家新影院吗？

inclined /ɪnˈklaɪnd/ *adjective* 形容词
1 wanting to do something 倾向于；有意于: *I'm inclined to agree with you.* 我倾向于同意你的意见。
2 likely to do something 很可能（做某事）: *She's inclined to change her mind a lot.* 她动不动就改变主意。

include 0ᴍ /ɪnˈkluːd/ *verb* 动词
(**includes**, **including**, **included**)
1 to have somebody or something as one part of the whole 包括；包含: *The price of the room includes breakfast.* 房价包括早餐。
2 to make somebody or something part of a group 使成为…的一部分: *Did you include the new girl in the list?* 你把新来的女孩列入名单了吗？ ⊃ OPPOSITE **exclude** 反义词为 exclude

including 0ᴍ /ɪnˈkluːdɪŋ/ *preposition* 介词
with; if you count 包括: *There were five people in the car, including the driver.* 车上有五个人，包括司机。 ⊃ OPPOSITE **excluding** 反义词为 excluding

inclusive /ɪnˈkluːsɪv/ *adjective* 形容词
including everything or the thing mentioned 全部包括在内的；包括…的: *The price is inclusive of meals.* 价格包括了餐费。

income /ˈɪnkʌm/ *noun* 名词
all the money that you receive for your work, for example 收入；所得: *It's difficult for a family to live on one income.* 一家人靠一人的工资生活很困难。

income tax /ˈɪnkʌm tæks/ *noun* 名词
(*no plural* 不用复数形式)
the money that you pay to the government from the money that you earn（个人）所得税

incomplete /ˌɪnkəmˈpliːt/ *adjective* 形容词
not finished; with parts missing 未完成的；不完整的: *This list is incomplete.* 这份名单不完整。 ⊃ OPPOSITE **complete** 反义词为 complete

inconsiderate /ˌɪnkənˈsɪdərət/ *adjective* 形容词
(used about a person) not thinking or caring about other people and their feelings（人）不为别人着想的，不体贴的: *It's inconsiderate of you to make so much noise.* 你发出这么大的声音，太不顾及别人了。 ⊃ OPPOSITE **considerate** 反义词为 considerate

inconsistent /ˌɪnkənˈsɪstənt/ *adjective* 形容词
not always the same 不一致的；反复无常的: *She's so inconsistent – sometimes she's really friendly and sometimes she's not.* 她太反复无常了，态度时好时坏。 ⊃ OPPOSITE **consistent** 反义词为 consistent

inconvenient /ˌɪnkənˈviːniənt/ *adjective* 形容词
causing you problems or difficulty 不方便的；引起麻烦的: *Is this an inconvenient time? I can call back later.* 现在不方便吗？我可以稍后再打电话来。 ⊃ OPPOSITE **convenient** 反义词为 convenient
▸ **inconvenience** /ˌɪnkənˈviːniəns/ *noun* 名词 (*no plural* 不用复数形式): *We apologize for any inconvenience caused by the delay.* 我们为此次延误造成的不便道歉。

incorrect /ˌɪnkəˈrekt/ *adjective* 形容词
not right or true 不对的；不正确的: *There were several incorrect answers.* 有好几题都答错了。 ⊃ OPPOSITE **correct** 反义词为 correct
▸ **incorrectly** /ˌɪnkəˈrektli/ *adverb* 副词: *Her name was spelled incorrectly.* 她的名字

拼错了。 ⊃ OPPOSITE **correctly** 反义词为 correctly

increase 0̶ /ɪnˈkriːs/ *verb* 动词 (increases, increasing, increased /ɪnˈkriːst/)

> 🔍 PRONUNCIATION 读音说明
>
> Be careful how you say this word. When **increase** is a verb, you say the second part of the word louder: in**CREASE**. When **increase** is a noun, you say the first part of the word louder: **IN**crease. 注意：increase 作动词时，重音放在第二个音节，即 in**CREASE**；作名词时，重音放在第一个音节，即 **IN**crease。

to become bigger or more; to make something bigger or more （使）增长，增多，增加：*The number of women who go out to work has increased.* 女性就业人数增多了。◇ *I'm going to* ***increase*** *your pocket money to £5.* 我打算把你的零花钱增加到 5 英镑。

▶ **increase** /ˈɪnkriːs/ *noun* 名词：*There has been an* ***increase*** *in road accidents.* 道路交通事故增多了。◇ *a price increase* 涨价 ⊃ OPPOSITE **decrease** 反义词为 decrease

increasingly /ɪnˈkriːsɪŋli/ *adverb* 副词 more and more 越来越…；愈加…：*This city is becoming increasingly dangerous.* 这个城市变得越来越危险了。

incredible /ɪnˈkredəbl/ *adjective* 形容词
1 impossible or very difficult to believe 不能相信的；难以置信的 ⊃ SAME MEANING **unbelievable** 同义词为 unbelievable：*I found his story completely incredible.* 我觉得他讲的事简直不可思议。
2 (*informal* 非正式) very large or very good 极大的；极好的：*She earns an incredible amount of money.* 她赚的钱多极了。◇ *The hotel was incredible.* 那家旅馆太棒了。

▶ **incredibly** /ɪnˈkredəbli/ *adverb* 副词 (*informal* 非正式) extremely 极端地；极其：*He's incredibly clever.* 他极其聪明。

incubator /ˈɪŋkjubeɪtə(r)/ *noun* 名词 a special machine that hospitals use to keep small or weak babies alive （医院里给弱小或体弱的婴儿用的）恒温箱

indecisive /ˌɪndɪˈsaɪsɪv/ *adjective* 形容词 not able to make decisions easily 无决断力的；犹疑不决的

indeed 0̶ /ɪnˈdiːd/ *adverb* 副词
1 a word that makes a positive thing that you say stronger 的确；确实 ⊃ SAME MEANING **certainly** 同义词为 certainly：*'Did you have a good holiday?' 'I did indeed.'* "你假期过得好吗？" "好极了。"
2 a word that makes 'very' stronger （强调 very 的语气）真的，非常：*Thank you very much indeed.* 非常感谢你。◇ *She's very happy indeed.* 她真的很开心。

indefinite /ɪnˈdefɪnət/ *adjective* 形容词 not clear or certain 不确切的；不明确的：*Our plans are still rather indefinite.* 我们的计划仍相当不确定。

indefinite article /ɪnˌdefɪnət ˈɑːtɪkl/ *noun* 名词 (*grammar* 语法) the name for the words 'a' and 'an' 不定冠词（即 a 和 an）⊃ Look at **definite article**. 见 definite article。

indefinitely /ɪnˈdefɪnətli/ *adverb* 副词 for a long time, perhaps for ever 无限期地：*I can't wait indefinitely.* 我不可能无止境地等下去。

independence /ˌɪndɪˈpendəns/ *noun* 名词 (*no plural* 不用复数形式) being free from another person, thing or country 独立；自主：*America declared its* ***independence*** *from Britain in 1776.* 美国于 1776 年脱离英国，宣告独立。

independent 0̶ /ˌɪndɪˈpendənt/ *adjective* 形容词

> 🔍 SPELLING 拼写说明
>
> Remember! You spell **independent** with three **E's**. 记住：independent 拼写中有三个 e。

1 not controlled by another person, thing or country 独立的；自主的：*Mozambique became independent in 1975.* 莫桑比克于 1975 年取得独立。
2 not needing or wanting help 自立的：*She lives alone now and she is very independent.* 她现在独自生活，自立能力很强。

index /ˈɪndeks/ *noun* 名词 (*plural* 复数形式 **indexes**) a list of words from A to Z at the end of a book. It tells you what things are in the book and where you can find them. （书末尾的）索引

index finger /ˈɪndeks fɪŋɡə(r)/ *noun* 名词 (*plural* 复数形式 **index fingers**) the finger next to your thumb 食指

indicate /ˈɪndɪkeɪt/ *verb* 动词 (indicates, indicating, indicated)
1 to show that something is true, exists or will happen 表明；显示；预示：*Black*

clouds **indicate that** it's going to rain. 乌云密布显示将要下雨。
2 to make somebody notice something, especially by pointing to it 指示，指出（尤指用手指）: *The receptionist indicated the place where I should sign.* 接待员指示我该在哪里签名。
3 (*British* 英式英语) to show that your car is going to turn by using a light 打行车转向信号: *You should indicate left now.* 你现在该打左转弯的灯。

indication /ˌɪndɪˈkeɪʃn/ *noun* 名词 something that shows something 指示；迹象 ⊃ SAME MEANING **sign** 同义词为 sign: *He gave no **indication** that he was angry.* 他当时并没有流露出生气的样子。

indicator /ˈɪndɪkeɪtə(r)/ *noun* 名词 a light on a car that shows that it is going to turn left or right 转向灯；方向灯

indifferent /ɪnˈdɪfrənt/ *adjective* 形容词 not interested in or caring about somebody or something 不感兴趣的；漠不关心的: *He seemed completely **indifferent to** my feelings.* 他似乎毫不在乎我的感受。

indigestion /ˌɪndɪˈdʒestʃən/ *noun* 名词 (*no plural* 不用复数形式) pain in your stomach caused by something you have eaten 消化不良: *Onions **give** me **indigestion**.* 吃洋葱使我消化不良。

indignant /ɪnˈdɪɡnənt/ *adjective* 形容词 angry because somebody has done or said something that you do not like or agree with 愤怒的；愤慨的: *She was indignant when I said she was lazy.* 我说她懒，她就生气了。
▶ **indignantly** /ɪnˈdɪɡnəntli/ *adverb* 副词: *'I'm not late,' he said indignantly.* "我并没有迟到。"他愤愤地说。
▶ **indignation** /ˌɪndɪɡˈneɪʃn/ *noun* 名词 (*no plural* 不用复数形式) a feeling of anger and surprise 气愤；愤慨

indirect /ˌɪndəˈrekt; ˌɪndaɪˈrekt/ *adjective* 形容词 not straight or direct 不直接的；间接的: *We came by an **indirect** route.* 我们是绕道过来的。◇ *These problems are an **indirect** result of the war.* 这些问题是战争间接造成的结果。⊃ OPPOSITE **direct** 反义词为 direct
▶ **indirectly** /ˌɪndəˈrektli; ˌɪndaɪˈrektli/ *adverb* 副词: *These events affect us all, directly or indirectly.* 这些事件直接或间接地影响到我们。

indirect object /ˌɪndərekt ˈɒbdʒɪkt/ *noun* 名词

(*grammar* 语法) a person or thing that an action is done to or for 间接宾语；间接受词: *In the sentence 'I sent him a letter', 'him' is the indirect object.* 在 I sent him a letter 一句中，him 是间接宾语。⊃ Look at **direct object**. 见 direct object。

indirect speech /ˌɪndərekt ˈspiːtʃ/ *another word for* REPORTED SPEECH
* reported speech 的另一种说法

individual¹ 0= /ˌɪndɪˈvɪdʒuəl/ *adjective* 形容词
1 considered separately and not as part of a group 单独的；个别的: *Each individual student gets their own study plan.* 每个学生都有自己的学习计划。
2 for only one person or thing 供一人用的: *an individual portion of cheese* 一人分量的奶酪
▶ **individually** /ˌɪndɪˈvɪdʒuəli/ *adverb* 副词: *The teacher spoke to each student individually.* 老师跟每个学生单独谈了一下。

individual² /ˌɪndɪˈvɪdʒuəl/ *noun* 名词 one person 个人: *Teachers must treat each child as an individual.* 老师必须把每个小孩看作独立的个体。

indoor /ˈɪndɔː(r)/ *adjective* 形容词 done or used inside a building 室内的；户内的: *an indoor swimming pool* 室内游泳池 ◇ *indoor games* 室内游戏 ⊃ OPPOSITE **outdoor** 反义词为 outdoor

indoors /ˌɪnˈdɔːz/ *adverb* 副词 in or into a building 在室内；进入室内: *Let's go indoors. I'm cold.* 我们进屋吧，我冷了。⊃ OPPOSITE **outdoors** 反义词为 outdoors

industrial /ɪnˈdʌstriəl/ *adjective* 形容词
1 connected with making things in factories 工业的: *industrial machines* 工业机器
2 with a lot of factories 工业发达的: *Leeds is an industrial city.* 利兹是个工业城市。

industry 0= /ˈɪndəstri/ *noun* 名词
1 (*no plural* 不用复数形式) the work of making things in factories 工业: *Is there much industry in your country?* 你们国家工业发达吗？
2 (*plural* 复数形式 industries) all the companies that make the same thing 行业: *Japan has a big car industry.* 日本汽车业规模很大。

inefficient /ˌɪnɪˈfɪʃnt/ *adjective* 形容词 A person or thing that is **inefficient** does not work well or in the best way. 效率低的: *This washing machine is very old and*

inefficient. 这台洗衣机很旧，效率又低。
⊃ OPPOSITE **efficient** 反义词为 efficient

inevitable /ɪn'evɪtəbl/ *adjective* 形容词
If something is **inevitable**, it will certainly happen. 不可避免的；必然发生的：*The accident was inevitable – he was driving too fast.* 那起事故无法避免，他当时开得太快了。
▶ **inevitably** /ɪn'evɪtəbli/ *adverb* 副词：*Building the new hospital inevitably cost a lot of money.* 建造这座新医院不免花了很多钱。

inexperienced /ˌɪnɪk'spɪəriənst/ *adjective* 形容词
If you are **inexperienced**, you do not know about something because you have not done it many times before. 缺乏经验的：*a young inexperienced driver* 无经验的年轻司机 ⊃ OPPOSITE **experienced** 反义词为 experienced

inexplicable /ˌɪnɪk'splɪkəbl/ *adjective* 形容词
Something that is **inexplicable** cannot be explained or understood. 无法解释的；费解的：*I found his behaviour inexplicable.* 我觉得他的行为令人费解。

infant /'ɪnfənt/ *noun* 名词 (formal 正式)
a baby or very young child 婴儿；幼儿

infant school /'ɪnfənt skuːl/ *noun* 名词
(British 英式英语)
a school for children between the ages of five and seven 幼儿学校（学生年龄介于五岁到七岁）

infect /ɪn'fekt/ *verb* 动词 (infects, infecting, infected)
to give a disease to somebody 传染；使感染：*Thousands of people have been infected with the virus.* 成千上万的人感染了这种病毒。

infected /ɪn'fektɪd/ *adjective* 形容词
full of small living things (called **germs**) that can make you ill 受感染的；带菌的：*Clean that cut or it could become infected.* 把那伤口清洗一下，否则可能受感染。

infection ⊶ /ɪn'fekʃn/ *noun* 名词
an illness that affects one part of the body 感染；传染（病）：*Mike has an ear infection.* 迈克的耳朵受感染了。

infectious /ɪn'fekʃəs/ *adjective* 形容词
An **infectious** disease goes easily from one person to another. 传染的；感染的

inferior /ɪn'fɪəriə(r)/ *adjective* 形容词
not as good or important as another person or thing 较差的；次等的：*Lisa's so clever she always makes me feel inferior.*

莉萨太聪明了，她总让我感到自卑。
⊃ OPPOSITE **superior** 反义词为 superior

infinite /'ɪnfɪnət/ *adjective* 形容词
with no end; too much or too many to count or measure 无尽的；无穷的；无数的：*There is an infinite number of stars in the sky.* 天上有无数的星星。

infinitely /'ɪnfɪnətli/ *adverb* 副词
very much 非常：*DVDs are infinitely better than videos.* 数字光盘要比录像带好很多。

infinitive /ɪn'fɪnətɪv/ *noun* 名词
(grammar 语法) the simple form of a verb 不定式；不定词：*'Eat', 'go' and 'play' are all infinitives.* ＊eat、go 和 play 都是不定式。

> 🔍 GRAMMAR 语法说明
> We sometimes use the **infinitive** with *to*, and sometimes without, depending on what comes before it. 不定式有时跟 *to*，有时则不跟，这取决于它前面的词：*He can sing.* 他会唱歌。◇ *He wants to sing.* 他想唱歌。

infinity /ɪn'fɪnəti/ *noun* 名词 (no plural 不用复数形式)
space or time without end（空间或时间）无限，无垠

inflammable /ɪn'flæməbl/ *adjective* 形容词
An **inflammable** substance burns easily. 易燃的；可燃的：*Petrol is highly inflammable.* 汽油非常易燃。

inflate /ɪn'fleɪt/ *verb* 动词 (inflates, inflating, inflated) (formal 正式)
to fill something with air or gas 使充气：*He inflated the tyre.* 他给轮胎充了气。

> 🔍 SPEAKING 表达方式说明
> It is more usual to say **blow up** or **pump up**. 较常用 blow up 或 pump up：*I pumped up my bicycle tyres.* 我给自行车轮胎打了气。

inflation /ɪn'fleɪʃn/ *noun* 名词 (no plural 不用复数形式)
a general rise in prices in a country 通货膨胀：*The government is trying to control inflation.* 政府正设法控制通货膨胀。

influence¹ ⊶ /'ɪnfluəns/ *noun* 名词
1 (no plural 不用复数形式) the power to change what somebody believes or does 影响；影响力；作用：*Television has a strong influence on people.* 电视对人有很大的影响。
2 (plural 复数形式 influences) a person or thing that can change somebody or

something 有影响的人（或事物）：*Paul's new girlfriend is a good **influence on** him.* 保罗的新女友对他有好的影响。

influence² /'ɪnfluəns/ *verb* 动词 (influences, influencing, influenced /'ɪnfluənst/)
to change the way that somebody thinks or the way that something happens 影响；对…起作用：*She is easily influenced by her friends.* 她很容易受朋友影响。

influential /ˌɪnfluˈenʃl/ *adjective* 形容词
having power or influence 有影响力的：*Her father's very influential.* 她父亲非常具影响力。

inform 0━ /ɪnˈfɔːm/ *verb* 动词 (informs, informing, informed /ɪnˈfɔːmd/)
to tell somebody something 告诉；通知：*You should **inform** the police **of** the accident.* 你应该向警方报告这起事故。

informal 0━ /ɪnˈfɔːml/ *adjective* 形容词
relaxed and friendly; suitable for a relaxed occasion 友好随便的；非正式的：*I wear informal clothes, like jeans and T-shirts, at weekends.* 我周末穿牛仔裤和T恤衫之类的休闲服装。◇ *an informal letter* 非正式信函

🔊 SPEAKING 表达方式说明
Some words and expressions in this dictionary are labelled **informal**. You use them when speaking and writing to people you know well, but not in serious writing or official letters. 本词典中的一些词语和表达方式标示为informal（非正式），它们一般用于跟熟人的交谈和通信，而不用于严肃的书面文章或公函。

▸ **informally** /ɪnˈfɔːməli/ *adverb* 副词
We have discussed the matter informally. 我们非正式地谈过这件事。

information 0━ /ˌɪnfəˈmeɪʃn/ *noun* 名词 (no plural 不用复数形式)
facts about people or things 信息；资讯；资料：*Can you give me some **information about** trains to London?* 你能不能给我一些往伦敦列车的信息？

🔊 GRAMMAR 语法说明
Be careful! You cannot say 'an information'. You say **some information** or **a piece of information**. 注意：不说an information，要说some information 或 a piece of information：*She gave me an interesting piece of information.* 她向我提供了一则有趣的信息。

informative /ɪnˈfɔːmətɪv/ *adjective* 形容词
giving useful information 提供有用信息的：*The talk was very informative.* 这次演讲很长见识。

ingredient /ɪnˈɡriːdiənt/ *noun* 名词
one of the things that you put in when you make something to eat（烹饪的）用料，配料：*The ingredients for this cake are flour, butter, sugar and eggs.* 做这种蛋糕的材料包括面粉、黄油、糖、鸡蛋。

inhabit /ɪnˈhæbɪt/ *verb* 动词 (inhabits, inhabiting, inhabited)
to live in a place 居住在；栖居于：*Is the island inhabited (= does anybody live there)?* 这个岛有人住吗？ ◇ *The South Pole is inhabited by penguins.* 南极有企鹅栖息。

inhabitant /ɪnˈhæbɪtənt/ *noun* 名词
a person or an animal that lives in a place 居民；栖居的动物：*The town has 30 000 inhabitants.* 这个镇上有三万居民。

inhale /ɪnˈheɪl/ *verb* 动词 (inhales, inhaling, inhaled /ɪnˈheɪld/) (formal 正式)
to take air, smoke, etc. into your body by breathing 吸入；吸气：*Be careful not to inhale the fumes from the paint.* 小心别吸入油漆的气味。

inherit /ɪnˈherɪt/ *verb* 动词 (inherits, inheriting, inherited)
to get money or things from somebody who has died 继承：*Sabine **inherited** some money **from** her grandmother.* 萨拜因继承了她祖母的一些钱。

▸ **inheritance** /ɪnˈherɪtəns/ *noun* 名词 (no plural 不用复数形式) money or things that you get from somebody who has died 遗产；继承物：*She spent her inheritance in just one year.* 她在一年内就把继承的钱花光了。

initial¹ /ɪˈnɪʃl/ *adjective* 形容词
first 最初的；开始的：*My initial reaction was to say 'no'.* 我最初的反应就是说"不"。

▸ **initially** /ɪˈnɪʃəli/ *adverb* 副词 ⊃ SAME MEANING **at first** 同义词为at first：*Initially, the system worked well.* 一开始，系统运行得不错。

initial² /ɪˈnɪʃl/ *noun* 名词
the first letter of a person's name（姓名的）首字母：*John Waters' initials are J.W.* John Waters 的首字母是J.W.。

inject /ɪnˈdʒekt/ *verb* 动词 (injects, injecting, injected)
to put a drug into a person's body using a

special needle (called a syringe) （给…）
注射（药物）

▸ **injection** /ɪnˈdʒekʃn/ *noun* 名词: *The
doctor gave the baby an injection*. 医生给
婴儿打了一针。

injure /ˈɪndʒə(r)/ *verb* 动词 (**injures**,
injuring, **injured** /ˈɪndʒəd/)
to hurt yourself or somebody else,
especially in an accident （尤指事故中）
使受伤，伤害: *She injured her arm when
she was playing tennis*. 她打网球的时候
伤了胳膊。◇ *Joe was injured in a car
accident*. 乔在车祸中受了伤。

▸ **injured** /ˈɪndʒəd/ *adjective* 形容词:
The injured woman was taken to hospital.
受伤的女子被送往医院了。

injury ⊶ /ˈɪndʒəri/ *noun* 名词 (*plural*
复数形式 **injuries**)
damage to the body of a person or an
animal （身体的）伤害: *He had serious
head injuries*. 他头部受了重伤。

injustice /ɪnˈdʒʌstɪs/ *noun* 名词 (*no plural*
不用复数形式)
the fact of a situation not being fair or
right 不公正；不公平: *the struggle
against injustice* 反对不公平的斗争

ink /ɪŋk/ *noun* 名词 (*no plural* 不用复数
形式)
coloured liquid for writing and printing
墨水；油墨: *Please write in black or blue
ink*. 请用黑笔或蓝笔书写。 ⊃ Look at the
picture at **pen**. 见 pen 的插图。

inland /ˌɪnˈlænd/ *adverb* 副词
in or towards the middle of a country
在内陆；向内地: *The village lies a few
miles inland*. 村子位于内陆几英里处。

▸ **inland** /ˈɪnlənd/ *adjective* 形容词 in the
middle of a country, not near the sea
内陆的；内地的: *an inland lake* 内陆湖

inn /ɪn/ *noun* 名词 (*British* 英式英语)
a pub, usually in the country and often
one where you can stay the night （通常
指乡下的）小旅馆，小酒馆

> 🔑 CULTURE 文化资料补充
>
> **Inn** is an old word that we do not use
> much now, except in the names of
> pubs, hotels and restaurants. * inn 是
> 旧词，现在不常用，只用于酒吧、旅馆
> 和餐馆的名称。

inner /ˈɪnə(r)/ *adjective* 形容词
inside; towards or close to the centre
内部的；朝里的；接近中心的: *the inner
ear* 内耳 ⊃ OPPOSITE **outer** 反义词为 outer

inner city /ˌɪnə ˈsɪti/ *noun* 名词 (*plural*
复数形式 **inner cities**)
the poor areas near the centre of a big
city 内城区（大城市中心的贫穷区域）:
the problems of the inner cities 内城区
存在的问题

▸ **inner-city** *adjective* 形容词: *an
inner-city school* 内城区的学校

innocent /ˈɪnəsnt/ *adjective* 形容词
If you are **innocent**, you have not done
anything wrong. 清白的；无辜的；无罪
的: *He claims he's innocent of the crime*.
他声称自己没有犯罪。 ⊃ OPPOSITE **guilty**
反义词为 guilty

▸ **innocence** /ˈɪnəsns/ *noun* 名词
(*no plural* 不用复数形式): *The prisoner's
family are convinced of her innocence*.
女囚犯的家属认定她是清白的。 ⊃ OPPOSITE
guilt 反义词为 guilt

input /ˈɪnpʊt/ *noun* 名词
time, ideas or work that you put into
something to make it successful 投入；
输入: *Her specialist input to the
discussions was very useful*. 她在讨论中
提出的专业意见十分有用。

inquest /ˈɪnkwest/ *noun* 名词
an official process to find out how
somebody died 死因调查；验尸: *An
inquest was held to discover the cause of
death*. 对死亡原因进行了调查。

inquire, inquiry /ɪnˈkwaɪə(r)/,
/ɪnˈkwaɪəri/ *another word for* ENQUIRE,
ENQUIRY * enquire 和 enquiry 的另一种
说法

inquisitive /ɪnˈkwɪzətɪv/ *adjective* 形容词
wanting to find out as much as possible
about things 好打听的；刨根问底的:
*Don't be so inquisitive – it's none of your
business!* 别这么追根问底的，这与你
无关！

insane /ɪnˈseɪn/ *adjective* 形容词
seriously mentally ill 精神失常的；疯癫的
⊃ SAME MEANING **mad** 同义词为 mad:
The prisoners were slowly going insane.
囚犯慢慢地变得精神错乱。

insect ⊶ /ˈɪnsekt/ *noun* 名词
a very small animal that has six legs
昆虫: *Ants, flies, butterflies and beetles
are all insects*. 蚂蚁、苍蝇、蝴蝶和甲虫
都是昆虫。

> 🔑 WORD BUILDING 词汇扩充
>
> There are many different types of
> **insect**. Here are some of them: ant,
> bee, butterfly, cockroach, flea, fly. Do
> you know any others? * insect 的种类

A
B
C
D
E
F
G
H
I
J
K
L
M
N
O
P
Q
R
S
T
U
V
W
X
Y
Z

很多，如：ant（蚂蚁）、bee（蜜蜂）、butterfly（蝴蝶）、cockroach（蟑螂）、flea（跳蚤）、fly（苍蝇）。你还知道别的吗？

insecure /ˌɪnsɪˈkjʊə(r)/ *adjective* 形容词
1 worried and not sure about yourself 缺乏信心的；没把握的：*Many teenagers feel **insecure about** their appearance.* 许多青少年对自己的外表缺乏信心。
2 not safe or firm 不安全的；不牢固的：*This ladder looks a bit insecure.* 这把梯子看上去有点不安全。 ◗ OPPOSITE **secure** 反义词为 secure
▸ **insecurity** /ˌɪnsɪˈkjʊərəti/ *noun* 名词 (*no plural* 不用复数形式)：*She had feelings of insecurity.* 她觉得没有安全感。

insensitive /ɪnˈsensətɪv/ *adjective* 形容词
not knowing or caring how another person feels 不顾他人感受的；冷漠的：*That was a very insensitive remark.* 讲那种话太不通人情了。 ◇ *She's completely insensitive to my feelings.* 她全然不顾我的感受。 ◗ OPPOSITE **sensitive** 反义词为 sensitive

insert /ɪnˈsɜːt/ *verb* 动词 (**inserts, inserting, inserted**) (*formal* 正式)
to put something into something or between two things 插入；嵌入：*Insert the CD into the computer.* 把光碟放入电脑。

inside[1] 0— /ɪnˈsaɪd/ *preposition, adverb, adjective* 介词，副词，形容词
in, on or to the inside of something 在里面；向里面；里面的：*What's inside the box?* 盒子里是什么？ ◇ *It's raining – let's **go inside** (= into the building).* 下雨了，我们进去吧。 ◇ *the inside pocket of a jacket* 夹克的内袋 ◗ Look at **outside[2]** and **outside[3]**. 见 outside[2] 和 outside[3]。

inside out 里面朝外

inside[2] 0— /ɪnˈsaɪd/ *noun* 名词
the part near the middle of something 里面；内部：*The door was locked from the inside.* 门从里面反锁了。 ◇ *There's a label somewhere **on the inside**.* 里面某个地方有个标签。 ◗ Look at **outside[1]**. 见 outside[1]。
inside out with the wrong side on the outside 里面朝外：*You've got your jumper on inside out.* 你把套头毛衣穿反了。

insignificant /ˌɪnsɪɡˈnɪfɪkənt/ *adjective* 形容词
of little value or importance 微不足道的；无足轻重的：*an insignificant detail* 无关紧要的细节 ◗ OPPOSITE **significant** 反义词为 significant

insist /ɪnˈsɪst/ *verb* 动词 (**insists, insisting, insisted**)
1 to say very strongly that something must happen or be done 坚持；坚决要求：*Paul **insisted on** driving me to the station.* 保罗坚持要开车送我去车站。
2 to say very strongly that something is true, when somebody does not believe you 坚称（某事属实）：*He **insists that** he didn't take the money.* 他坚称自己没拿那笔钱。

insolent /ˈɪnsələnt/ *adjective* 形容词 (*formal* 正式)
not showing respect 轻慢的；无礼的；粗野的 ◗ SAME MEANING **rude** 同义词为 rude：*He gave her an insolent stare.* 他侮慢地瞪了她一眼。

inspect /ɪnˈspekt/ *verb* 动词 (**inspects, inspecting, inspected**)
to look at something carefully 审视；查看：*I inspected the car before I bought it.* 我买这辆车之前仔细检查过了。
▸ **inspection** /ɪnˈspekʃn/ *noun* 名词：*The police made an inspection of the house.* 警察把房子检查了一遍。

inspector /ɪnˈspektə(r)/ *noun* 名词
1 a person whose job is to see that things are done correctly 检查员；视察员：*a factory inspector* 工厂检验员
2 a police officer （警察）督察

inspiration /ˌɪnspəˈreɪʃn/ *noun* 名词
a person or thing that makes you want to do something or gives you good ideas 灵感；启发灵感的人（或事物）：*The beauty of the mountains is a great **inspiration to** many artists.* 群山的美景是许多艺术家重要的灵感来源。

inspire /ɪnˈspaɪə(r)/ *verb* 动词 (**inspires, inspiring, inspired** /ɪnˈspaɪəd/)
1 to make somebody want to do something 激发；鼓励：*His wife **inspired** him to write this poem.* 他妻子激发他创作了这首诗。

2 to make somebody feel or think something 使产生感觉（或情感）；启发；启迪： *Her words inspired us all with hope.* 她的话赋予了我们所有人希望。
▸ **inspiring** /ɪnˈspaɪərɪŋ/ *adjective* 形容词： *an inspiring teacher* 启发能力强的老师

install /ɪnˈstɔːl/ *verb* 动词 (installs, installing, installed /ɪnˈstɔːld/)
to put a new thing in its place so it is ready to use 安装： *They have installed a new computer system.* 他们安装了新的电脑系统。

instalment (*British* 英式英语) (*American* 美式英语 **installment**) /ɪnˈstɔːlmənt/ *noun* 名词
1 a regular payment that you make for something （分期付款的）一期付款： *She's paying for her new car in monthly instalments.* 她正以每月分期支付购买新车的款项。
2 one part of a story on radio or television, or in a magazine （连载故事的）一回，一集，一期： *Don't miss next week's exciting instalment.* 下周那一集很精彩，不要错过。

instance /ˈɪnstəns/ *noun* 名词
for instance as an example 例如： *There are several interesting places to visit around here – Warwick, for instance.* 这附近有好几处有趣的地方可以游览，例如沃里克。

instant¹ /ˈɪnstənt/ *adjective* 形容词
1 happening very quickly 立即的；立刻的： *The film was an instant success.* 这部电影一上映就大获成功。
2 (*used about food*) quick and easy to prepare （食品）速食的，方便的： *an instant meal* 快餐 ◇ *instant coffee* 速溶咖啡
▸ **instantly** /ˈɪnstəntli/ *adverb* 副词 immediately; at once 立刻；马上： *The driver was killed instantly.* 司机当场死了。

instant² /ˈɪnstənt/ *noun* 名词
a very short time 瞬间；片刻 ⊃ SAME MEANING 同义词 **moment** 同义词 moment： *She thought for an instant before she answered.* 她想了一下才回答。

instead ⊶ /ɪnˈsted/ *adverb, preposition* 副词，介词
in the place of somebody or something 代替；顶替；反而： *We haven't got any coffee. Would you like tea instead?* 我们没有咖啡了。喝茶好吗？ ◇ *He's been playing football all afternoon instead of studying.* 他踢了一下午足球而没有温习。◇ *Can you

go to the meeting instead of me?* 你能替我去开会吗？

instinct /ˈɪnstɪŋkt/ *noun* 名词
something that makes people and animals do certain things without thinking or learning about them 本能；天性： *Birds build their nests by instinct.* 鸟天生会筑巢。
▸ **instinctive** /ɪnˈstɪŋktɪv/ *adjective* 形容词： *Animals have an instinctive fear of fire.* 动物生来就怕火。

institute /ˈɪnstɪtjuːt/ *noun* 名词
a group of people who meet to study or talk about a special thing; the building where they meet （专门于某范畴的）机构，研究所： *the Institute of Science* 科学研究所

institution /ˌɪnstɪˈtjuːʃn/ *noun* 名词
a big organization like a bank, hospital, prison or school （银行、医院等）大机构： *Many financial institutions are based in London.* 许多金融机构的总部设在伦敦。

instruct /ɪnˈstrʌkt/ *verb* 动词 (instructs, instructing, instructed)
1 to tell somebody what they must do 命令；指示： *He instructed the driver to wait.* 他吩咐司机等着。
2 (*formal* 正式) to teach somebody something 传授；教导： *Children must be instructed in road safety.* 孩子必须接受道路安全的教育。

instruction ⊶ /ɪnˈstrʌkʃn/ *noun* 名词
1 instructions (*plural* 用复数形式) words that tell you what you must do or how to do something 指示；命令；用法说明： *Read the instructions on the back of the packet carefully.* 仔细阅读包装袋背面的说明。◇ *You should always follow the instructions.* 你应该时刻按指示行事。
2 (*no plural* 不用复数形式) teaching or being taught something 指导；传授： *driving instruction* 驾驶指导

instructor /ɪnˈstrʌktə(r)/ *noun* 名词
a person who teaches you how to do something 教练；导师： *a driving instructor* 驾驶教练

instrument ⊶ /ˈɪnstrəmənt/ *noun* 名词
1 a thing that you use for doing a special job 器械；仪器；器具： *surgical instruments* (= used by doctors) 外科器械
2 a thing that you use for playing music 乐器： *Violins and trumpets are musical instruments.* 小提琴和小号是乐器。◇

A B C D E F G H I J K L M N O P Q R S T U V W X Y Z

What instrument do you play? 你会哪种乐器?

insult 0┳ /ɪn'sʌlt/ ***verb*** 动词 (insults, insulting, insulted)
to be deliberately rude to somebody 侮辱；辱骂：*She insulted my brother by saying he was fat.* 她侮辱我弟弟，说他是胖子。
▸ **insult** /'ɪnsʌlt/ ***noun*** 名词：*The boys shouted insults at each other.* 那些男孩相互对骂。

insurance /ɪn'ʃʊərəns/ ***noun*** 名词 (*no plural* 不用复数形式)
an agreement where you pay money to a company so that it will give you a lot of money if something bad happens 保险：*When I crashed my car, the insurance paid for the repairs.* 我撞了车，保险公司支付了修理费。

insure /ɪn'ʃʊə(r)/ ***verb*** 动词 (insures, insuring, insured /ɪn'ʃʊəd/)
1 to pay money to a company, so that it will give you money if something bad happens 给…投保：*Have you **insured** your house **against** fire?* 你给房子投火险了吗?
2 *American English for* ENSURE 美式英语，即 ensure

intellectual /ˌɪntə'lektʃuəl/ ***adjective*** 形容词
connected with a person's ability to think and understand things 智力的；脑力的：*a child's intellectual development* 儿童的智力发展

intelligence /ɪn'telɪdʒəns/ ***noun*** 名词 (*no plural* 不用复数形式)
being able to think, learn and understand quickly and well 智力；智慧：*He is a man of great intelligence.* 他是个睿智的人。◇ *an intelligence test* 智力测试

intelligent 0┳ /ɪn'telɪdʒənt/ ***adjective*** 形容词
able to think, learn and understand quickly and well 聪明的；聪颖的：*Their daughter is very intelligent.* 他们的女儿很聪明。◇ *an intelligent question* 机智的问题
▸ **intelligently** /ɪn'telɪdʒəntli/ ***adverb*** 副词：*They solved the problem very intelligently.* 他们很机智地解决了问题。

intend 0┳ /ɪn'tend/ ***verb*** 动词 (intends, intending, intended)
to plan to do something 打算；有意：*When do you **intend to** go to London?* 你打算什么时候去伦敦? ➲ The noun is **intention**. 名词为 intention。
be intended for somebody or **something** to be planned or made for a particular person or reason 为…设计（或制作）的：*This dictionary is intended for elementary learners of English.* 本词典是为英语初学者编写的。

intense /ɪn'tens/ ***adjective*** 形容词
very great or strong 极大的；强烈的：*intense pain* 剧痛 ◇ *The heat from the fire was intense.* 炉火的热力很强。
▸ **intensely** /ɪn'tensli/ ***adverb*** 副词：*I found the film intensely boring.* 我觉得这部电影无聊透顶。

intensive /ɪn'tensɪv/ ***adjective*** 形容词
involving a lot of work in a short time 密集的；集中的：*an intensive English course* 英语强化课程

intention 0┳ /ɪn'tenʃn/ ***noun*** 名词
what you plan to do 意图；计划：*They **have no intention of** getting married.* 他们不打算结婚。 ➲ The verb is **intend**. 动词为 intend。

intentional /ɪn'tenʃənl/ ***adjective*** 形容词
done on purpose, not by mistake 故意的；存心的 ➲ SAME MEANING **deliberate** 同义词为 deliberate：*I'm sorry I upset you – it wasn't intentional!* 对不起，让你生气了——我不是有意的!
▸ **intentionally** /ɪn'tenʃənəli/ ***adverb*** 副词 ➲ SAME MEANING **deliberately** 同义词为 deliberately：*They broke the window intentionally.* 他们故意把窗户打破了。

interactive /ˌɪntər'æktɪv/ ***adjective*** 形容词
(*computing* 电脑) involving direct communication both ways, between the computer and the person using it（电脑与人之间）交互式的，互动的：*interactive computer games* 互动电脑游戏

interest[1] 0┳ /'ɪntrəst/ ***noun*** 名词
1 (*no plural* 不用复数形式) wanting to know or learn about somebody or something 兴趣；关注：*He read the story **with interest**.* 他津津有味地读那个故事。◇ *He **takes** no **interest in** politics.* 他对政治毫无兴趣。
2 (*plural* 复数形式 interests) something that you like doing or learning about 爱好；兴趣：*His interests are computers and rock music.* 他的爱好是电脑和摇滚乐。
3 (*no plural* 不用复数形式) the extra money that you pay back if you borrow money or that you receive if you put money in a bank 利息

interest² 0= /'ɪntrəst/ *verb* 动词
(interests, interesting, interested)
to make somebody want to know more
使感兴趣；使关注： *Religion doesn't
interest her.* 宗教吸引不到她的兴趣。

interested 0= /'ɪntrəstɪd/ *adjective*
形容词
wanting to know more about somebody
or something 感兴趣的： *Are you
interested in cars?* 你对汽车感兴趣吗？

interesting 0= /'ɪntrəstɪŋ/ *adjective*
形容词
A person or thing that is **interesting**
makes you want to know more about
them. 有趣的；有意思的： *This book is
very interesting.* 这本书很有趣。◇ *That's
an interesting idea!* 那是个有趣的想法！
➔ OPPOSITE **boring** 反义词为 boring

interfere /,ɪntə'fɪə(r)/ *verb* 动词
(interferes, interfering, interfered
/,ɪntə'fɪəd/)
1 to try to do something with or for
somebody, when they do not want your
help 干涉；干预： *Don't interfere! Let
John decide what he wants to do.* 别插手！
让约翰自己决定他想做什么。
2 to stop something from being done
well 妨碍；干扰： *His interest in football
often interferes with his studies.* 他喜欢
足球，常常因此而影响了学业。
▸ **interference** /,ɪntə'fɪərəns/ *noun* 名词
(*no plural* 不用复数形式)： *I don't want
any interference in my affairs!* 我不想有
任何人干涉我的事情！

interior /ɪn'tɪəriə(r)/ *noun* 名词
the inside part 内部；里面： *We painted
the interior of the house white.* 我们把房子
内部刷成了白色。
▸ **interior** *adjective* 形容词： *interior
walls* 内墙 ➔ OPPOSITE **exterior** 反义词为
exterior

intermediate /,ɪntə'miːdiət/ *adjective*
形容词
coming between two things or levels
中间的；中级的： *She's in an intermediate
class.* 她在中级班。

internal /ɪn'tɜːnl/ *adjective* 形容词
of or on the inside 内部的；里面的： *He
has internal injuries (= inside his body).*
他有内伤。 ➔ OPPOSITE **external** 反义词为
external
▸ **internally** /ɪn'tɜːnəli/ *adverb* 副词：
The matter was dealt with internally.
这件事内部解决了。

international 0= /,ɪntə'næʃnəl/
adjective 形容词

between different countries 国际的： *an
international football match* 国际足球比赛
◇ *an international flight* 国际航班
▸ **internationally** /,ɪntə'næʃnəli/ *adverb*
副词： *an internationally famous
musician* 蜚声国际的音乐家

Internet 0= /'ɪntənet/ *noun* 名词 the
Internet (*also informal* 非正式亦作 the
Net) (*no plural* 不用复数形式)
(*computing* 电脑) the international system
of computers that makes it possible for
you to see information from all around
the world on your computer and to send
information to other computers 互联网；
因特网；网路： *You can find out almost
anything on the Internet.* 在互联网上几乎
可以找到任何东西。◇ *Do you have
Internet access?* 你能上网吗？

interpret /ɪn'tɜːprɪt/ *verb* 动词
(interprets, interpreting, interpreted)
1 to say in one language what somebody
has said in another language 口译；
传译： *I can't speak Italian – can you
interpret for me?* 我不会说意大利语——
你可不可以帮我翻译一下？
2 to explain the meaning of something
阐释；解释： *You have to interpret the
facts, not just repeat them.* 你得诠释这些
事实，而不仅仅是重复一遍。

interpretation /ɪn,tɜːprɪ'teɪʃn/ *noun*
名词
an explanation of something 阐释；
解释： *What's your interpretation of
these statistics?* 你怎么解释这些统计
数据？

interpreter /ɪn'tɜːprɪtə(r)/ *noun* 名词
a person whose job is to translate what
somebody is saying into another
language 口译员；传译员

interrupt 0= /,ɪntə'rʌpt/ *verb* 动词
(interrupts, interrupting, interrupted)
1 to stop somebody speaking or doing
something by saying or doing something
yourself 打断；插嘴；打扰： *Please don't
interrupt me when I'm speaking.* 我说话的
时候请不要打断我。
2 to stop something for a time 使暂停；
使中断： *The game was interrupted by
rain.* 比赛因下雨而中断。
▸ **interruption** /,ɪntə'rʌpʃn/ *noun* 名词：
*I can't do my homework here. There are
too many interruptions.* 我在这里无法做
功课，干扰太多了。

interval /'ɪntəvl/ *noun* 名词
1 a period of time between two events
间隔时间；间隙： *There was an interval*

of several weeks between the attacks.
两次袭击相隔了几个星期。
2 (*British* 英式英语) a short time between
two parts of a play or concert （戏剧或
音乐会的）中场休息，幕间休息

interview¹ 0━ /'mtəvju:/ *noun* 名词
1 a meeting when somebody asks you
questions to decide if you will get a job
面试；面谈：*I've got a job interview
tomorrow.* 我明天有个求职面试。
2 a meeting when somebody answers
questions for a newspaper or for a
television or radio programme 采访；
访谈：*There was an interview with the
Prime Minister on TV last night.* 昨天晚上
电视播放了对首相的采访。

interview² /'mtəvju:/ *verb* 动词
(interviews, interviewing, interviewed
/'mtəvju:d/)
to ask somebody questions in an
interview 对…进行面试；主持；采访：
They interviewed six people for the job.
他们给六个申请这份工作的人做了面试。
▸ **interviewer** /'mtəvju:ə(r)/ *noun* 名词：
*The interviewer asked me why I wanted
the job.* 主持面试的人问我为什么要申请
这份工作。

intestine /m'testm/ *noun* 名词
the tube in your body that carries food
away from your stomach to the place
where it leaves your body 肠

intimate /'mtɪmət/ *adjective* 形容词
(used about people) having a close
relationship（人）亲密的，密切的 ⊃ SAME
MEANING **close** 同义词为 close：*They're
intimate friends.* 他们是很亲密的朋友。

into 0━ /'mtə; 'mtu; 'mtu:/ *preposition*
介词
1 to the middle or the inside of
something 进入；到…里面：*Come into
the house.* 进屋吧。◇ *I went into town.*
我进了城。◇ *He fell into the river.* 他掉进
了河里。
2 in the direction of something 朝；向；
对着：*Please speak into the microphone.*
请对着麦克风讲话。
3 against something 撞上；碰上：*The car
crashed into a tree.* 车子撞上了一棵树。
4 a word that shows how somebody or
something changes （表示状态的变化）：
*When it is very cold, water changes into
ice.* 天气寒冷时水就结成冰。◇ *They made
the room into a bedroom.* 他们把房间改成
了卧室。
5 a word that you use when you divide a
number （用于除法）除：*4 into 12 is 3.*
* 12 除以 4 等于 3。

be into something (*informal* 非正式)
to like something; to be interested in
something 喜欢；感兴趣：*What sort
of music are you into?* 你喜欢哪一类
音乐？

intolerable /m'tɒlərəbl/ *adjective* 形容词
so bad or difficult that you cannot accept
it 无法忍受的；不能容忍的 ⊃ SAME
MEANING **unbearable** 同义词为
unbearable：*The situation was
intolerable.* 这种情况令人无法容忍。

intranet /'mtrənet/ *noun* 名词
(*computing* 电脑) a system of computers
inside an organization that makes it
possible for people to share information
内联网（机构内部共享信息的电脑系统）
⊃ Look at **Internet**. 见 Internet。

intransitive /m'trænsətɪv/ *adjective*
形容词
(*grammar* 语法) An **intransitive** verb does
not have an object. （动词）不及物的
⊃ Look at **transitive**. 见 transitive。

intrigue /m'tri:g/ *verb* 动词 (intrigues,
intriguing, intrigued /m'tri:gd/)
to make somebody very interested 激起
兴趣：*His story intrigued me.* 他讲的故事
让我听得入了迷。

introduce 0━ /,mtrə'dju:s/ *verb* 动词
(introduces, introducing, introduced
/,mtrə'dju:st/)
1 to bring people together for the first
time and tell each of them the name of
the other 介绍；引见：*She introduced
me to her brother.* 她把我介绍给她哥哥。
◇ *He introduced himself to me* (= told me
his name). 他向我作了自我介绍。

🔎 **SPEAKING** 表达方式说明
When we introduce people we say **this
is** not 'he is' or 'she is' and not 'here is'.
介绍别人时说 this is，而不是 he is、she
is、here is：*Jane, this is Bob.* 简，
这是鲍勃。◇ *Bob, this is Jane.* 鲍勃，
这是简。
When you meet someone for the first
time, you can say **Hello**, **How do you
do?** or **Pleased to meet you.** 初次见面
打招呼可说 Hello、How do you do? 或
Pleased to meet you。

2 to bring in something new 引入；实施；
推行：*This law was introduced in 2002.*
这项法规是 2002 年开始实施的。

introduction 0━ /,mtrə'dʌkʃn/ *noun*
名词
1 (*no plural* 不用复数形式) bringing in
something new 引进；采用；推行：*the*

introduction of computers into schools
学校开始使用电脑

2 (*plural* 复数形式 introductions) bringing
people together to meet each other
介绍；引见

3 (*plural* 复数形式 introductions) a piece
of writing at the beginning of a book that
tells you about the book（书的）序言，
导论

intruder /ɪnˈtruːdə(r)/ *noun* 名词
a person who enters a place without
permission 闯入者；侵入者: *Police say
the intruder was not armed.* 警方说那名
闯入者没有携带武器。

invade /ɪnˈveɪd/ *verb* 动词 (invades,
invading, invaded)
to go into another country to attack it
入侵；侵略: *They invaded the country
with tanks and guns.* 他们以坦克和大炮
入侵那个国家。 ⊃ The noun is **invasion**.
名词为 invasion。
  ▸ **invader** /ɪnˈveɪdə(r)/ *noun* 名词: *They
prepared to repel the invaders.* 他们准备好
驱赶侵略者。

invalid¹ /ɪnˈvælɪd/ *adjective* 形容词
not legally or officially acceptable（法律
上）无效的；不被官方承认的: *I'm afraid
your passport is invalid.* 恐怕你的护照失效
了。 ⊃ OPPOSITE **valid** 反义词为 valid

invalid² /ˈɪnvəlɪd/ *noun* 名词
a person who has been very ill for a long
time and needs another person to look
after them 不能自理的病人；久病衰弱的人

invaluable /ɪnˈvæljuəbl/ *adjective* 形容词
very useful 极有用的；宝贵的: *Your help
was invaluable.* 你的帮助难能可贵。

  🔍 WHICH WORD? 词语辨析
  Be careful! **Invaluable** is not the
  opposite of **valuable**. The opposite of
  valuable is **worthless**. 注意: valuable
  的反义词并非 invaluable，而是
  worthless。

invariably /ɪnˈveəriəbli/ *adverb* 副词
always or almost always 一直；几乎总是:
He invariably arrives late. 他差不多每次都
迟到。

invasion /ɪnˈveɪʒn/ *noun* 名词
a time when an army from one country
goes into another country to attack it
（武装）入侵；侵略: *Germany's
invasion of Poland in 1939* * 1939 年德国
对波兰的入侵 ⊃ The verb is **invade**. 动词
为 invade。

invent 0━ /ɪnˈvent/ *verb* 动词 (invents,
inventing, invented)
1 to make or think of something for the
first time 发明；创造: *Who invented the
bicycle?* 谁发明了自行车?
2 to say something that is not true
编造；捏造: *I realized that he had
invented the whole story.* 我意识到他说的
事全是瞎编的。
  ▸ **inventor** /ɪnˈventə(r)/ *noun* 名词:
Marconi was the inventor of the radio.
马可尼是无线电通讯的发明者。

invention /ɪnˈvenʃn/ *noun* 名词
1 (*plural* 复数形式 inventions) a thing
that somebody has made for the first
time 发明（物）
2 (*no plural* 不用复数形式) inventing
something 发明；创造: *The invention of
the telephone changed the world.* 电话的
发明改变了整个世界。

inverted commas /ɪnˌvɜːtɪd ˈkɒməz/
noun 名词 (*plural* 用复数形式) (*British*
英式英语)
the signs " " or ' ' that you use in writing
before and after words that somebody
said 引号 ⊃ SAME MEANING **quotation
marks** 同义词为 quotation marks

invest /ɪnˈvest/ *verb* 动词 (invests,
investing, invested)
to give money to a business or bank so
that you will get more money back 投资:
He invested all his money in the company.
他把自己所有的钱都投资在这家公司。
  ▸ **investment** /ɪnˈvestmənt/ *noun* 名词:
an investment of €10 000 * 10 000 欧元
的投资

investigate 0━ /ɪnˈvestɪɡeɪt/ *verb*
动词 (investigates, investigating,
investigated)
to try to find out about something 调查；
侦查: *The police are investigating the
murder.* 警方正在调查这起谋杀案。
  ▸ **investigation** /ɪnˌvestɪˈɡeɪʃn/ *noun*
名词: *They are carrying out an
investigation into the fire.* 他们正在对
这起火灾展开调查。

invisible /ɪnˈvɪzəbl/ *adjective* 形容词
If something is **invisible**, you cannot see
it. 看不见的；隐形的: *Wind is invisible.*
风是看不见的。 ⊃ OPPOSITE **visible** 反义词
为 visible

invitation 0━ /ˌɪnvɪˈteɪʃn/ *noun* 名词
If you have an **invitation** to go
somewhere, somebody has spoken or
written to you and asked you to go. 书面
（或口头）邀请；请柬: *Joe sent me an*

A B C D E F G H I J K L M N O P Q R S T U V W X Y Z

invitation to his party. 乔给我发了请帖，让我去参加他的聚会。

invite ⚪ /ɪnˈvaɪt/ *verb* 动词 (invites, inviting, invited)
to ask somebody to come to a party, to your house, etc. 邀请: *Anna invited me to her party*. 安娜邀请我参加她的聚会。◇ *Let's invite them for dinner*. 我们邀请他们吃饭吧。

invoice /ˈɪnvɔɪs/ *noun* 名词
a list that shows how much you must pay for things that somebody has sold you, or for work that somebody has done for you 发票；（发货或服务）费用清单

involve ⚪ /ɪnˈvɒlv/ *verb* 动词 (involves, involving, involved /ɪnˈvɒlvd/)
1 to have something as a part 包含；使成为一部分: *The job involves using a computer*. 这份工作需要使用电脑。
2 If you **involve** somebody in something, you make them take part in it. 使参与；涉及: *I want to involve more people in the concert*. 我希望更多人参与音乐会。

involved /ɪnˈvɒlvd/ *adjective* 形容词
taking part in something; being part of something or connected with something 参与；有关联: *I'm very involved in local politics*. 我积极参与本地的政治事务。◇ *We need to interview the people involved*. 我们需要采访相关人员。

inwards /ˈɪnwədz/ (*also* 亦作 **inward** /ˈɪnwəd/) *adverb* 副词
towards the inside or centre 向内；向中心: *The doors open inwards*. 这些门向里面开。 ⊃ OPPOSITE **outwards** or **outward** 反义词为 outwards 或 outward

IOU /ˌaɪ əʊ ˈjuː/ *noun* 名词 (*informal* 非正式式)
a piece of paper that shows you promise to pay somebody the money you owe them 借据；欠条 ⊃ IOU is a way of writing 'I owe you'. * IOU 是 I owe you 的缩写形式。

IPA /ˌaɪ piː ˈeɪ/ *abbreviation* 缩略式
a system of symbols to show how words sound 国际音标 ⊃ IPA is short for 'International Phonetic Alphabet'. * IPA 是 International Phonetic Alphabet 的缩略式。

IQ /ˌaɪ ˈkjuː/ *noun* 名词
a way of measuring how intelligent somebody is 智商: *She has an IQ of 128*. 她的智商是 128。

ir- *prefix* 前缀
You can add **ir-** to the beginning of some words to give them the opposite meaning,

for example *irregular* (= not regular). （用在某些词前构成反义）

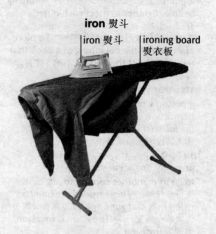

iron 熨斗
iron 熨斗 | ironing board 熨衣板

iron¹ ⚪ /ˈaɪən/ *noun* 名词

> 🔍 **PRONUNCIATION** 读音说明
> The word **iron** sounds like **lion**, because we don't say the letter **r** in this word. * iron 读音像 lion，因为 r 在这里不发音。

1 (*no plural* 不用复数形式) a strong hard metal 铁: *The gates are made of iron*. 这些门是用铁做的。◇ *an iron bar* 铁棒
2 (*plural* 复数形式 **irons**) a piece of electrical equipment that gets hot and that you use for making clothes smooth 熨斗: *a steam iron* 蒸汽熨斗

iron² ⚪ /ˈaɪən/ *verb* 动词 (irons, ironing, ironed /ˈaɪənd/)
to make clothes smooth using an IRON 熨；烫平: *Can you iron this shirt for me?* 你能帮我熨熨这件衬衫吗？
▸ **ironing** /ˈaɪənɪŋ/ *noun* 名词 (*no plural* 不用复数形式) clothes that need to be IRONED 待熨的衣服: *I usually do the ironing on Sunday evening*. 我通常星期天晚上熨衣服。

ironic /aɪˈrɒnɪk/ *adjective* 形容词
If you are **ironic**, you say the opposite of what you mean because you want to make people laugh or show them you are annoyed. 反语的；讽刺的: *When I said it was a beautiful day, I was being ironic*. 我说天色不错其实是在说反话。

ironing board /ˈaɪənɪŋ bɔːd/ *noun* 名词
a special long table where you IRON

clothes 熨衣板 ➲ Look at the picture at **iron¹**. 见 iron¹ 的插图。

irony /ˈaɪrəni/ *noun* 名词 (*plural* 复数形式 **ironies**)
a strange or unusual part of a situation that is different from what you expect 有讽刺意味的情况；奇异可笑之处： *The irony is that when she finally agreed to go out with him, he discovered he didn't like her that much.* 讽刺的是，她终于答应和他交往时，他却发现自己并不那么喜欢她。

irregular /ɪˈregjələ(r)/ *adjective* 形容词
1 happening at different times 不定期的；无规律的： *Their visits were irregular.* 他们来访的时间不定。 ➲ OPPOSITE **regular** 反义词为 regular
2 A word that is **irregular** does not have the usual verb forms or plural. （语法）不规则的： *'Catch' is an irregular verb.* * catch 是不规则动词。➲ OPPOSITE **regular** 反义词为 regular

irrelevant /ɪˈreləvənt/ *adjective* 形容词
not connected with something and not important 无关的；无关紧要的： *Your point is completely **irrelevant** to the discussion.* 你的观点与这次讨论毫不相干。 ➲ OPPOSITE **relevant** 反义词为 relevant

irritable /ˈɪrɪtəbl/ *adjective* 形容词
becoming angry easily 暴躁的；易怒的： *He's very irritable in the mornings.* 他早上很容易发火。

irritate /ˈɪrɪteɪt/ *verb* 动词 (irritates, irritating, irritated)
1 to make somebody quite angry 使恼怒；惹怒： *He irritates me when he asks so many questions.* 他问那么多问题，烦死我了。
2 to make a part of your body hurt a little 刺激（身体部位）；使过敏： *Cigarette smoke irritates my eyes.* 香烟的烟熏得我眼睛刺痛。
▶ **irritation** /ˌɪrɪˈteɪʃn/ *noun* 名词: *This plant can cause irritation to your skin.* 这种植物能引起皮肤过敏。

is *form of* BE * be 的不同形式

Islam /ˈɪzlɑːm/ *noun* 名词 (*no plural* 不用复数形式)
the religion of Muslim people. **Islam** teaches that there is only one God and that Muhammad is his PROPHET (= the person that God has chosen to give his message to people). 伊斯兰教
▶ **Islamic** /ɪzˈlæmɪk/ *adjective* 形容词: *Islamic law* 伊斯兰教戒律

island ⚷ /ˈaɪlənd/ *noun* 名词

> 🔍 PRONUNCIATION 读音说明
> The word **island** sounds like **highland**, because we don't say the letter s in this word. * island 读音像 highland，因为 s 在这里不发音。

a piece of land with water all around it 岛： *the Greek islands* 希腊的岛屿

Isle /aɪl/ *noun* 名词
an island 岛： *the British Isles* 不列颠群岛

> 🔍 CULTURE 文化资料补充
> **Isle** is usually used in names of islands. * Isle 通常用于岛屿的名称。

isn't /ˈɪznt/ *short for* IS NOT * is not 的缩略式

isolated /ˈaɪsəleɪtɪd/ *adjective* 形容词
far from other people or things 隔绝的；孤立的；偏远的： *an isolated house in the mountains* 群山中与世隔绝的一所房子

isolation /ˌaɪsəˈleɪʃn/ *noun* 名词 (*no plural* 不用复数形式)
being away from other people or things 隔绝；隔离： *A lot of old people live in isolation.* 很多老年人过着离群索居的生活。

issue¹ ⚷ /ˈɪʃuː/ *noun* 名词
1 an important problem that people talk about 问题；议题： *Pollution is a serious issue.* 环境污染是个重要议题。
2 a magazine or newspaper of a particular day, week, or month （报刊的）一期： *Have you read this week's issue?* 你看过这期的周刊了吗？

issue² /ˈɪʃuː/ *verb* 动词 (issues, issuing, issued /ˈɪʃuːd/)
to give or say something officially （正式）发放，发布： *The soldiers were **issued** with uniforms.* 士兵都发了军服。 ◇ *The police have **issued** a statement.* 警方已发布一项声明。

IT /ˌaɪ ˈtiː/ *noun* 名词 (*no plural* 不用复数形式)
the study or use of computers and other electronic equipment to store and send information 信息技术；资讯科技 ➲ IT is short for 'Information Technology'. * IT 是 Information Technology 的缩略式。

it ⚷ /ɪt/ *pronoun* 代词 (*plural* 复数形式 they, them)
1 a word that shows a thing or animal 它（指事物或动物）： *I've got a new shirt. It's (= it is) blue.* 我有件新衬衫，是蓝色

A

的。◊ *Where's the coffee? I can't find it.* 咖啡放哪里了？我找不到。

2 a word that points to an idea that follows（用以代指下文）: *It's difficult to learn Japanese.* 日语很难学。

3 a word that shows who somebody is（用以明确身份）: *'Who's on the telephone?' 'It's Jo.'* "电话那头是谁？""是乔。"

4 a word at the beginning of a sentence about time, the weather or distance（用于句首表示时间、天气或距离）: *It's six o'clock.* 六点钟了。◊ *It's hot today.* 今天很热。◊ *It's 100 kilometres to London.* 距离伦敦 100 公里。

italics /ɪˈtælɪks/ *noun* 名词 (*plural* 用复数形式)

a type of writing or printing in which the letters do not stand straight up 斜体: *This sentence is in italics.* 本句用了斜体。

▶ **italic** /ɪˈtælɪk/ *adjective* 形容词: *italic writing* 斜体书写

itch /ɪtʃ/ *verb* 动词 (itches, itching, itched /ɪtʃt/)

to have a feeling on your skin that makes you want to rub or scratch it 发痒: *My nose itches.* 我的鼻子发痒。◊ *This jumper makes me itch.* 我穿这件套衫会觉得痒。

▶ **itch** *noun* 名词 (*plural* 复数形式 itches): *I've got an itch.* 我觉得痒。

▶ **itchy** /ˈɪtʃi/ *adjective* 形容词: *itchy skin* 发痒的皮肤

it'd /ˈɪtəd/ *short for* IT HAD; IT WOULD * it had 和 it would 的缩略式

item /ˈaɪtəm/ *noun* 名词

1 one thing in a list or group of things（清单或一组事物中的）一件，一项: *She had the most expensive item on the menu.* 她点了菜单上最贵的一道菜。◊ *an item of clothing* 一件衣服

2 a piece of news 一则（新闻）；一条（信息）: *There was an interesting news item about Spain.* 有则关于西班牙的新闻很有意思。

it'll /ˈɪtl/ *short for* IT WILL * it will 的缩略式

its /ɪts/ *adjective* 形容词

of the thing or animal that you have just talked about 它的: *The dog has hurt its leg.* 狗的腿受伤了。◊ *The company has its factory in Hull.* 这家公司在赫尔设有工厂。

WHICH WORD? 词语辨析

Its or **it's**? 用 its 还是 it's?

Be careful! **It's** is a short way of saying *it is* or *it has*. 注意：it's 是 it is 或 it has 的缩略式: *It's (= it is) cold today.* 今天很冷。◊ *It's (= it has) been raining.* 一直在下雨。

Its means 'belonging to it'. * its 指"它的": *The bird has broken its wing.* 鸟的翅膀折断了。

it's /ɪts/ *short for* IT IS; IT HAS * it is 和 it has 的缩略式

itself /ɪtˈself/ *pronoun* 代词 (*plural* 复数形式 themselves /ðəmˈselvz/)

1 a word that shows the same thing or animal that you have just talked about 它自己: *The cat was washing itself.* 猫正在清理自己。

2 a word that makes 'it' stronger（表示强调）它本身: *The hotel itself was nice but I didn't like the town.* 旅馆本身很不错，但我不喜欢这个市镇。

by itself

1 alone 独自；单独: *The house stands by itself in the forest.* 房子孤零零地坐落在森林中。

2 without being controlled by a person 自动: *The machine will start by itself.* 机器会自动启动。

I've /aɪv/ *short for* I HAVE * I have 的缩略式

ivory /ˈaɪvəri/ *noun* 名词 (*no plural* 不用复数形式)

the hard white substance that the long teeth (called tusks) of an ELEPHANT (= a very large grey animal with big ears) are made of 象牙

ivy 常春藤

ivy /ˈaɪvi/ *noun* 名词 (*no plural* 不用复数形式)

a plant with dark green leaves, that climbs up walls or trees 常春藤

J j

J, j /dʒeɪ/ *noun* 名词 (*plural* 复数形式 J's, j's /dʒeɪz/)
the tenth letter of the English alphabet 英语字母表的第 10 个字母: *'Jam' begins with a 'J'.* * jam 一词以字母 j 开头。

jab /dʒæb/ *verb* 动词 (jabs, jabbing, jabbed /dʒæbd/)
to push at somebody with a sudden rough movement 戳；刺；捅: *She jabbed me in the stomach with her elbow.* 她用胳膊肘捅了一下我的腹部。
▶ **jab** *noun* 名词: *I felt a jab in my ribs.* 我感到肋骨被人戳了一下。

jack /dʒæk/ *noun* 名词
the playing card that has a picture of a young man on it（纸牌中的）J 牌，杰克: *the jack of hearts* 红桃杰克

jacket 0← /ˈdʒækɪt/ *noun* 名词
a short coat with sleeves 夹克；短上衣 ➔ Look at Picture Dictionary page **P5**. 见彩页 P5。

jacket potato /ˌdʒækɪt pəˈteɪtəʊ/ *noun* 名词 (*plural* 复数形式 jacket potatoes)
another word for BAKED POTATO * baked potato 的另一种说法

jagged /ˈdʒægɪd/ *adjective* 形容词
rough, with a lot of sharp points 凹凸不平的；锯齿状的；嶙峋的: *jagged rocks* 嶙峋的岩石

jaguar /ˈdʒægjuə(r)/ *noun* 名词
a large wild cat with black spots that lives in Central and South America 美洲豹；美洲虎 ➔ Look at Picture Dictionary page **P3**. 见彩页 P3。

jail /dʒeɪl/ *noun* 名词
a prison 监狱: *He was sent to jail for two years.* 他被判入狱两年。
▶ **jail** *verb* 动词 (jails, jailing, jailed /dʒeɪld/): *She was jailed for killing her husband.* 她因杀死丈夫而入狱。

jam¹ 0← /dʒæm/ *noun* 名词
1 (*no plural* 不用复数形式) sweet food made from fruit and sugar. You eat jam on bread. 果酱: *a jar of strawberry jam* 一罐草莓酱 ➔ Look at Picture Dictionary page **P6**. 见彩页 P6。
2 (*plural* 复数形式 jams) a situation in which you cannot move because there

are too many people or vehicles 拥挤；交通堵塞；堵车

jam² /dʒæm/ *verb* 动词 (jams, jamming, jammed /dʒæmd/)
1 to push something into a place where there is not much space 将…塞进去: *She jammed all her clothes into a suitcase.* 她把所有的衣服都塞进了行李箱。
2 to fix something or to become fixed so that you cannot move it（使）卡住，不能动弹: *I can't open the window. It's jammed.* 这扇窗我打不开，它卡住了。

janitor /ˈdʒænɪtə(r)/ *American English for* CARETAKER 美式英语，即 caretaker

January 0← /ˈdʒænjuəri/ *noun* 名词
the first month of the year 一月

jar /dʒɑː(r)/ *noun* 名词
a glass container for food 玻璃罐；广口瓶: *a jar of coffee* 一罐咖啡 ◇ *a jam jar* 果酱瓶 ➔ Look at the picture at **container**. 见 container 的插图。

javelin /ˈdʒævlɪn/ *noun* 名词
a long pointed stick that people throw as a sport 标枪

jaw /dʒɔː/ *noun* 名词
one of the two bones in the head of a person or animal that hold the teeth 颌 ➔ Look at Picture Dictionary page **P4**. 见彩页 P4。

jazz /dʒæz/ *noun* 名词 (*no plural* 不用复数形式)
a kind of music with a strong beat 爵士乐: *a jazz band* 爵士乐队

jealous /ˈdʒeləs/ *adjective* 形容词
1 angry or sad because you are afraid of losing somebody's love 吃醋的；妒忌的: *Sarah's boyfriend gets jealous if she speaks to other boys.* 萨拉要是跟别的男孩说话，她男朋友就会吃醋。
2 angry or sad because you want what another person has 忌妒的；妒羡的 ➔ SAME MEANING **envious** 同义词为 envious: *Ben was jealous of his brother's new car.* 本忌妒哥哥有辆新车。
▶ **jealousy** /ˈdʒeləsi/ *noun* 名词 (*no plural* 不用复数形式): *He felt sick with jealousy.* 他妒火中烧。

A
B
C
D
E
F
G
H
I
J
K
L
M
N
O
P
Q
R
S
T
U
V
W
X
Y
Z

jeans 0̶ᴄ /dʒiːnz/ *noun* 名词 (*plural* 用复数形式)
trousers made of strong cotton material (called **denim**). **Jeans** are usually blue. 牛仔裤: *a pair of jeans* 一条牛仔裤 ◇ *He wore jeans and a T-shirt.* 他穿了牛仔裤和 T 恤衫。 ⊃ Look at Picture Dictionary page **P5**. 见彩页 P5。

Jeep™ /dʒiːp/ *noun* 名词
a strong car that can go well over rough land 吉普车;越野车

jeer /dʒɪə(r)/ *verb* 动词 (jeers, jeering, jeered /dʒɪəd/)
to laugh or shout at someone in an unkind way that shows you do not respect them 嘲笑;讥讽: *The crowd jeered at him.* 群众嘲笑他。

jelly /'dʒeli/ *noun* 名词 (*British* 英式英语) (*American* 美式英语 jello, Jell-O™ /'dʒeləʊ/) (*no plural* 不用复数形式)
a soft food made from fruit juice and sugar, that shakes when you move it 果冻

jellyfish 水母

jellyfish /'dʒelifɪʃ/ *noun* 名词 (*plural* 复数形式 jellyfish or 或 jellyfishes)
a sea animal with a body like JELLY and long thin parts that can STING (= hurt) you 水母;海蜇

jerk /dʒɜːk/ *verb* 动词 (jerks, jerking, jerked /dʒɜːkt/)
to move quickly or suddenly; to pull or make something move like this 猛然一动;急拉;猛推: *The car jerked forward.* 汽车猛地向前一颠。 ◇ *She jerked the door open.* 她猛然拉开了门。
▶ **jerk** *noun* 名词: *The bus started with a jerk.* 公共汽车开动时猛地抖动了一下。

jersey /'dʒɜːzi/ *noun* 名词 (*plural* 复数形式 jerseys)
a warm piece of clothing with sleeves, that you wear on the top part of your body. **Jerseys** are often made of wool. (羊毛) 套头衫 ⊃ Look at the note at **sweater**. 见 sweater 条的注释。

Jesus /'dʒiːzəs/ (*also* 亦作 Jesus Christ /,dʒiːzəs 'kraɪst/, Christ) *noun* 名词
the man who Christians believe is the Son of God 耶稣

jet /dʒet/ *noun* 名词
1 a type of fast modern plane 喷射式飞机
2 liquid or gas that comes very fast out of a small hole 喷射的水(或气体): *a jet of gas* 一股喷射气体 ◇ *jets of water* 一股股喷射的水

jet lag /'dʒet læg/ *noun* 名词 (*no plural* 不用复数形式)
the feeling of being very tired after a long plane journey (长途飞行后的) 时差反应

jetty /'dʒeti/ *noun* 名词 (*plural* 复数形式 jetties)
a platform at the edge of a river, the sea, etc. where people get on and off boats 突码头;突堤;栈桥

Jew /dʒuː/ *noun* 名词
a person who follows the religion of Judaism 犹太人;犹太教徒
▶ **Jewish** /'dʒuːɪʃ/ *adjective* 形容词: *She is Jewish.* 她是犹太人。

jewel /'dʒuːəl/ *noun* 名词
a beautiful stone that is very valuable 宝石 ⊃ SAME MEANING **gem** 同义词为 gem

🔎 WORD BUILDING 词汇扩充
There are many different types of **jewel**. Here are some of them: diamond, emerald, pearl, ruby.
* jewel 的种类很多,如: diamond (钻石)、emerald (绿宝石)、pearl (珍珠)、ruby (红宝石)。

jeweler, jewelry *American English for* JEWELLER, JEWELLERY 美式英语,即 jeweller、jewellery

jeweller (*British* 英式英语) (*American* 美式英语 jeweler) /'dʒuːələ(r)/ *noun* 名词
1 a person who sells, makes or repairs jewellery and watches 珠宝钟表商;珠宝钟表匠
2 jeweller's a shop that sells jewellery and watches 珠宝钟表店

jewellery 0̶ᴄ (*British* 英式英语) (*American* 美式英语 jewelry) /'dʒuːəlri/ *noun* 名词 (*no plural* 不用复数形式)

objects that people wear to decorate their fingers, ears, arms, etc. 珠宝；首饰：
a piece of gold jewellery 一件黄金首饰

jigsaw puzzle 拼图

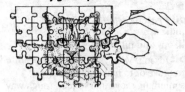

jigsaw /ˈdʒɪɡsɔː/ (*also* 亦作 jigsaw puzzle /ˈdʒɪɡsɔː pʌzl/) *noun* 名词
a picture in many pieces that you put together 拼图

jingle /ˈdʒɪŋɡl/ *verb* 动词 (jingles, jingling, jingled /ˈdʒɪŋɡld/)
to make a pleasant sound like small bells; to cause something to make this sound （使）发出叮当声：*She jingled the coins in her pocket.* 她把口袋里的硬币弄得叮当响。

job ⊶ /dʒɒb/ *noun* 名词
1 the work that you do for money 工作；职业：*She got a job as a waitress.* 她找到了一份服务员的工作。◇ *Peter's just lost his job.* 彼得刚丢了工作。

> 🔎 **WORD BUILDING 词汇扩充**
> When you **apply for a job** you fill in an **application form** or you send a letter and your **CV** (a list of your experience and education). 申请工作（apply for a job）时，要填写申请表（application form）或寄求职信和简历（CV）。
> You **have an interview** and the **employer** asks for **references** (letters from other people saying what you can do). Some jobs are **full-time** and some are **part-time**. 进行面试（have an interview）时，雇主（employer）会索要推荐信（reference）。有些工作是全职的（full-time），有些则是兼职的（part-time）。
> If you **get the sack**, you lose your job because you are bad at it. When you reach a certain age, you **retire** (stop working). 工作表现差会遭解雇（get the sack）。到达一定年龄会退休（retire）。

> To find out what someone's job is, we say: **What do you do?** 询问别人从事什么工作说 What do you do?

2 something that you must do （待做的）事情，活儿：*I have a lot of jobs to do in the house.* 家里有很多活儿要我做。
⊃ Look at the note at **work²**. 见 work² 条的注释。
it's a good job (*informal* 非正式) it is a good or lucky thing 幸亏；幸好：*It's a good job you reminded me – I had completely forgotten!* 幸亏你提醒了我，我已经忘得一干二净!
make a good job of something to do something well 做得好：*You made a good job of the painting.* 你油漆刷得很好。
out of a job without paid work 失业
⊃ SAME MEANING **unemployed** 同义词为 unemployed

> 🔎 **WORD BUILDING 词汇扩充**
> There are many different types of **job**. Here are some of them: builder, chef, doctor, librarian, pilot, teacher. Do you know any others? * job 的种类很多，如：builder（建筑工人）、chef（厨师）、doctor（医生）、librarian（图书馆管理员）、pilot（飞行员）、teacher（教师）。你还知道别的吗?

⊃ Look at Picture Dictionary page **P12**. 见彩页 P12。

jockey /ˈdʒɒki/ *noun* 名词 (*plural* 复数形式 jockeys)
a person who rides horses in races 赛马骑师

jogging 慢跑

jog /dʒɒɡ/ *verb* 动词 (jogs, jogging, jogged /dʒɒɡd/)

A

1 to run slowly for exercise 慢跑（以锻炼身体）： *I jogged round the park.* 我绕着公园慢跑。◇ *I go jogging every morning.* 我每天早晨都去慢跑。

B

2 to push or touch something a little, so that it moves 轻撞；轻碰： *She jogged my arm and I spilled my drink.* 她碰了一下我的胳膊，我把饮料弄洒了。

C

▸ **jog** *noun* 名词 a slow run for exercise 慢跑（以锻炼身体）： *She goes for a jog before breakfast.* 她吃早饭前会去慢跑。

D

E

F

join 0➔ /dʒɔɪn/ *verb* 动词 (joins, joining, joined /dʒɔɪnd/)

1 to bring or fix one thing to another thing 连接；接合： *The tunnel joins Britain to France.* 这条隧道把英国连接到法国。◇ *Join the two pieces of wood together.* 把两块木头连接起来。

G

H

I

2 to come together with somebody or something 与⋯一起；结合；会合： *Will you join us for dinner?* 你会和我们一起吃晚饭吗？◇ *This road joins the motorway soon.* 这条路很快会和高速公路连通。

J

3 to become a member of a group 参加；加入： *He joined the army.* 他参军了。◇ *I've joined an aerobics class.* 我参加了健美操班。

K

join in to do something with other people 参与；加入： *Everyone started singing but Frank refused to join in.* 大家都开始唱歌了，但弗兰克却拒绝加入。

L

M

N

joint[1] /dʒɔɪnt/ *adjective* 形容词 involving two or more people together 联合的；共同的： *The report was a joint effort* (= we worked on it together). 这份报告是大家共同努力的成果。◇ *My wife and I have a joint account* (= a shared bank account). 我和妻子有个联名账户。

O

P

Q

R

joint[2] /dʒɔɪnt/ *noun* 名词

1 a part of your body where bones come together, for example your elbow or your knee 关节

S

2 a place where two parts of something join together 接合处；接头： *the joints of the pipe* 管子的接头

T

U

3 (*British* 英式英语) a big piece of meat that you cook 大块烤肉： *a joint of beef* 一大块烤牛肉

V

W

joke[1] 0➔ /dʒəʊk/ *noun* 名词 something that you say or do to make people laugh, for example a funny story that you tell 笑话： *She told us a joke.* 她给我们讲了个笑话。◇ *I didn't get the joke* (= understand it). 我不明白这个笑话有什么好笑的。

X

Y

Z

joke[2] 0➔ /dʒəʊk/ *verb* 动词 (jokes, joking, joked /dʒəʊkt/)

to tell funny stories; to say things that are funny but not true 说笑话；开玩笑： *They were laughing and joking together.* 他们嘻嘻哈哈地开着玩笑。◇ *I didn't mean what I said – I was only joking.* 我说那些话并不是认真的，我是开玩笑而已。

jolly /'dʒɒli/ *adjective* 形容词 (jollier, jolliest)

happy and full of fun 愉快的；高兴的

jolt /dʒəʊlt/ *verb* 动词 (jolts, jolting, jolted) to move or to make somebody or something move in a sudden rough way （使）震动，摇动，颠簸 ⊃ SAME MEANING **jerk** 同义词为 jerk： *The bus jolted to a stop.* 公共汽车猛地一颠停了下来。◇ *The crash jolted us forwards.* 撞击使我们猛然向前晃。

▸ **jolt** *noun* 名词： *The train stopped with a jolt.* 火车车身一晃停住了。

jot /dʒɒt/ *verb* 动词 (jots, jotting, jotted) **jot something down** to write something quickly 匆匆写下： *I jotted down his phone number.* 我迅速写下了他的电话号码。

journal /'dʒɜːnl/ *noun* 名词 a magazine about one particular thing （某专业的）期刊： *a medical journal* 医学期刊

journalism /'dʒɜːnəlɪzəm/ *noun* 名词 (*no plural* 不用复数形式) the work of collecting and reporting news for newspapers, television, etc. 新闻业；新闻工作

journalist 0➔ /'dʒɜːnəlɪst/ *noun* 名词 a person whose job is to collect and report news for newspapers, television, etc. 新闻记者；新闻工作者

journey 0➔ /'dʒɜːni/ *noun* 名词 (*plural* 复数形式 journeys) the act of travelling from one place to another 旅程；行程 *Did you have a good journey?* 你的旅程愉快吗？ ⊃ Look at the note at **travel**. 见 travel 条的注释。

joy /dʒɔɪ/ *noun* 名词 (*no plural* 不用复数形式) a very happy feeling 快乐；愉快；喜悦： *Their children give them so much joy.* 子女给他们带来无穷喜悦。

▸ **joyful** /'dʒɔɪfl/ *adjective* 形容词 very happy 快乐的；令人愉快的： *a joyful occasion* 令人开心的场合

joyriding /'dʒɔɪraɪdɪŋ/ *noun* 名词 (*no plural* 不用复数形式) the crime of stealing a car and driving

around in a fast, dangerous way 窃车兜风
（偷车以开快车或危险驾驶）
▶ **joyrider** /ˈdʒɔɪraɪdə(r)/ *noun* 名词
a person who steals a car and drives it
in a fast, dangerous way 偷车兜风的人

joystick /ˈdʒɔɪstɪk/ *noun* 名词
a handle that you move to control
something, for example a computer game
（电脑游戏等的）操纵杆；游戏手柄

Judaism /ˈdʒuːdeɪɪzəm/ *noun* 名词
(*no plural* 不用复数形式)
the religion of the Jewish people 犹太教

judge¹ 0ₒ /dʒʌdʒ/ *noun* 名词
1 the person in a court of law who
decides how to punish somebody 法官：
The judge sent him to prison for 20 years.
法官判了他入狱 20 年。 ⊃ Look at Picture
Dictionary page **P12**. 见彩页 P12。
2 a person who chooses the winner of
a competition 裁判员；评判员

judge² 0ₒ /dʒʌdʒ/ *verb* 动词 (judges,
judging, judged /dʒʌdʒd/)
1 to have or to form an opinion about
somebody or something 判断；评定：
*It's difficult to judge how long the project
will take.* 很难判断项目要花多长时间。
2 to decide who or what wins a
competition 裁判；评判： *The
headmaster judged the painting
competition.* 校长担任绘画比赛的评判。

judgement 0ₒ (*also* 亦作 judgment)
/ˈdʒʌdʒmənt/ *noun* 名词
1 (*no plural* 不用复数形式) your ability to
form opinions or make sensible decisions
判断力；眼光： *Use your judgement*
(= you decide). 运用你的判断力。 ◇ *In my
judgement, she will do the job very well.*
我认为她会把这份工作做得很好。
2 (*plural* 复数形式 judgements) the
decision of a judge in a court of law
判决；裁决

judo /ˈdʒuːdəʊ/ *noun* 名词 (*no plural* 不用
复数形式)
a sport where two people fight and try
to throw each other onto the floor 柔道
⊃ Look at Picture Dictionary page **P15**.
见彩页 P15。

jug /dʒʌg/ *noun* 名词 (*British* 英式英语)
(*American* 美式英语 pitcher)
a container with a handle that you use
for holding or pouring liquids （有柄的）
壶： *a milk jug* 奶壶 ◇ *a jug of water*
一壶水

juggle /ˈdʒʌgl/ *verb* 动词 (juggles,
juggling, juggled /ˈdʒʌgld/)
to keep two or more things in the air by

throwing and catching them quickly
玩抛接杂耍
▶ **juggler** /ˈdʒʌglə(r)/ *noun* 名词 a person
who JUGGLES 玩抛接杂耍的人

juggler 玩抛接杂耍的人

juice 0ₒ /dʒuːs/ *noun* 名词 (*no plural*
不用复数形式)

> 🔎 **PRONUNCIATION** 读音说明
> The word **juice** sounds like **loose**.
> * juice 读音像 loose。

the liquid from fruit and vegetables
果汁；蔬菜汁： *a glass of orange juice*
一杯橙汁 ⊃ Look at Picture Dictionary
page **P6**. 见彩页 P6。

juicy /ˈdʒuːsi/ *adjective* 形容词 (juicier,
juiciest)
full of juice 多汁的： *big juicy tomatoes*
多汁的大西红柿

jukebox /ˈdʒuːkbɒks/ *noun* 名词 (*plural*
复数形式 jukeboxes)
a machine in a pub, bar, etc. that plays
music when you put money in it （酒吧
等的）投币式自动点唱机

July 0ₒ /dʒuˈlaɪ/ *noun* 名词
the seventh month of the year 七月

jug 壶

A
B
C
D
E
F
G
H
I
J
K
L
M
N
O
P
Q
R
S
T
U
V
W
X
Y
Z

A
B
C
D
E
F
G
H
I
J
K
L
M
N
O
P
Q
R
S
T
U
V
W
X
Y
Z

jumble¹ /'dʒʌmbl/ *verb* 动词 (jumbles, jumbling, jumbled /'dʒʌmbld/)

jumble something up to mix things so that they are untidy or in the wrong place 使混乱；使杂乱无章: *His clothes were all jumbled up in the cupboard.* 他的衣服都杂乱地堆放在衣橱里。

jumble² /'dʒʌmbl/ *noun* 名词 (*no plural* 不用复数形式)

a lot of things that are mixed together in an untidy way 乱成一团的东西: *a jumble of old clothes and books* 一堆杂乱的旧衣服和书

jumble sale /'dʒʌmbl seɪl/ *noun* 名词 (*British* 英式英语) (*American* 美式英语 **rummage sale**)

a sale of things that people do not want any more. Clubs, churches and schools often have **jumble sales** to make money. 旧物义卖（社团、教会和学校为筹款而举办）

jumbo jet /ˌdʒʌmbəʊ 'dʒet/ *noun* 名词
a very big plane that can carry a lot of people 大型客机

jump 跳

jump ०━ /dʒʌmp/ *verb* 动词 (jumps, jumping, jumped /dʒʌmpt/)

1 to move quickly off the ground, using your legs to push you up 跳；跃: *The cat jumped onto the table.* 猫跳到了桌子上。 ◇ *The horse jumped over the wall.* 马跃过了墙。

2 to move quickly 快速移动: *He jumped into the car and drove away.* 他跳上车，然后开走了。

3 to move suddenly because you are surprised or frightened（因吃惊或害怕）猛地一动；吓一跳: *A loud noise made me jump.* 一声巨响把我吓了一跳。

jump at something to accept an opportunity or an offer with enthusiasm 迫不及待地接受（机会或提议）: *Of course I jumped at the chance to work in*

New York for a year. 能去纽约工作一年，我当然马上接受了这个机会。

▸ **jump** *noun* 名词: *With a huge jump the horse cleared the fence.* 马一跃而起，越过了障碍物。

jumper /'dʒʌmpə(r)/ *noun* 名词
a warm piece of clothing with sleeves, that you wear on the top part of your body. **Jumpers** are often made of wool. （长袖）套头毛衣 ⊃ Look at the note at **sweater**. 见 sweater 条的注释。 ⊃ Look at Picture Dictionary page P5. 见彩页 P5。

jump rope /'dʒʌmp rəʊp/ *American English for* SKIPPING ROPE 美式英语，即 skipping rope

junction /'dʒʌŋkʃn/ *noun* 名词
a place where roads or railway lines meet （道路或铁路的）交叉路口，汇合处: *Turn right at the next junction.* 在下一个交叉路口向右拐。

June ०━ /dʒuːn/ *noun* 名词
the sixth month of the year 六月

jungle /'dʒʌŋgl/ *noun* 名词
a thick forest in a hot part of the world （热带）丛林，密林: *the jungles of South America and Africa* 南美洲和非洲的丛林

junior /'dʒuːniə(r)/ *adjective* 形容词
1 having a lower position in an organization （职位）较低的: *a junior doctor* 初级医生
2 of or for children below a particular age 青少年的: *the junior athletics championships* 青少年田径锦标赛 ⊃ OPPOSITE **senior** 反义词为 senior

junior school /'dʒuːniə skuːl/ *noun* 名词 (*British* 英式英语)
a school for children between the ages of seven and eleven 小学

junk /dʒʌŋk/ *noun* 名词 (*no plural* 不用复数形式)
things that are old or useless 旧物；无用的东西: *The cupboard is full of junk.* 柜子里全是没用的东西。

junk food /'dʒʌŋk fuːd/ *noun* 名词 (*no plural* 不用复数形式) (*informal* 非正式)
food that is quick and easy to prepare and eat but that is bad for your health 垃圾食品（制作、食用方便却有损健康）

jury /'dʒʊəri/ *noun* 名词 (*plural* 复数形式 **juries**)
a group of people in a court of law who decide if somebody has done something wrong or not 陪审团: *The jury decided that the woman was guilty of killing her*

husband. 陪审团裁决该名女子杀害丈夫罪名成立。

just¹ ○┅ /dʒʌst/ *adverb* 副词
1 exactly 正好；恰好：*This jacket is just my size.* 这件夹克正合我的尺码。◇ *You're just in time.* 你来得正是时候。◇ *She looks just like her mother.* 她长得就像她母亲。
2 a very short time before 刚刚；刚才：*I've just heard the news.* 我刚听到这个消息。◇ *Jim isn't here – he's just gone out.* 吉姆不在这里，他刚出去。
3 at this or that moment; now or very soon 此时；那时；现在；即将：*I'm just going to make some coffee.* 我这就去煮些咖啡。◇ *She phoned just as I was going to bed.* 我正要睡觉的时候她来电话了。
4 by a small amount 刚好：*I got here just after nine.* 我到这里时刚好过了九点。◇ *I only just caught the train.* 我刚好赶上火车。
5 a word that makes what you say stronger（表示加强语气）：*Just look at that funny little dog!* 快看看那条好玩的小狗吧！
6 only 只是；仅仅：*It's just a small present.* 这只不过是一份小礼物。
just about (*informal* 非正式) almost; very nearly 几乎；差不多：*I've met just about everyone.* 我几乎每个人都见过。
just a minute, just a moment used for asking somebody to wait for a short time 等一等；请稍候：*Just a minute – there's someone at the door.* 等一下，门口有人。

just now
1 at this moment; now 此时；现在：*I can't talk to you just now. I'm busy.* 我现在没法跟你说话，我很忙。
2 a short time before 刚刚；刚才：*Where's Liz? She was here just now.* 莉兹去哪里了？她刚才还在这里。

just² /dʒʌst/ *adjective* 形容词
fair and right 公正的；正当的：*a just punishment* 应有的惩罚 ⊃ OPPOSITE **unjust** 反义词为 unjust

justice /'dʒʌstɪs/ *noun* 名词 (*no plural* 不用复数形式)
1 treatment of people in a fair way 公正；公道；正义：*the struggle for justice* 争取正义的斗争 ⊃ OPPOSITE **injustice** 反义词为 injustice
2 the law 法律；司法：*the criminal justice system* 刑事审判制度

justify /'dʒʌstɪfaɪ/ *verb* 动词 (justifies, justifying, justified /'dʒʌstɪfaɪd/, has justified)
to be or give a good reason for something 证明⋯有理（或正当）：*Can you justify what you did?* 你能证明你所做的事是正当的吗？

K k

K, k /keɪ/ *noun* 名词 (*plural* 复数形式 K's, k's /keɪz/)
the eleventh letter of the English alphabet 英语字母表的第 11 个字母: *'King' begins with a 'K'.* * king 一词以字母 k 开头。

kangaroo 袋鼠

kangaroo /ˌkæŋɡəˈruː/ *noun* 名词 (*plural* 复数形式 **kangaroos**)
an Australian animal that jumps on its strong back legs and carries its babies in a pocket on its front 袋鼠

karate /kəˈrɑːti/ *noun* 名词 (*no plural* 不用复数形式)
a Japanese sport where people fight with their hands and feet 空手道（源自日本的徒手格斗术）

kebab /kɪˈbæb/ *noun* 名词
small pieces of meat, vegetables, etc. that are cooked on a thin stick 烤肉串 ➲ Look at Picture Dictionary page P7. 见彩页 P7。

keen /kiːn/ *adjective* 形容词 (**keener, keenest**)
1 wanting to do something; interested in something 渴望；热衷于: *Ian was keen to go out but I wanted to stay at home.* 伊恩很想出去，可我却想待在家里。◇ *Louise is a keen swimmer.* 路易丝很喜欢游泳。
2 very good or strong 灵敏的；敏锐的；强烈的: *keen eyesight* 敏锐的视觉
be keen on somebody or 或 **something** (*informal* 非正式) to like somebody or something very much 喜爱；对…着迷: *Tom's very keen on Anna.* 汤姆很喜欢安娜。

keep /kiːp/ *verb* 动词 (**keeps, keeping, kept** /kept/, **has kept**)
1 to stay in a particular state or condition 保持；处于: *Keep still* (= don't move) *while I take your photo.* 不要动，我来给你拍照。◇ *We tried to keep warm.* 我们尽量保暖。
2 to make somebody or something stay in a particular state or condition 使保持: *Keep this door closed.* 这扇门要一直关着。◇ *I'm sorry to keep you waiting.* 对不起，让你久等了。
3 to continue to have something 保留；保存: *You can keep that book – I don't need it.* 那本书你可以留着，我不用了。
4 to put or store something in a particular place 放置；存放: *Where do you keep the coffee?* 你把咖啡放哪儿了?
5 to continue doing something; to do something many times 继续，重复（做某事）: *Keep driving until you see the cinema, then turn left.* 开车一直向前，看到电影院就向左转。◇ *She keeps forgetting my name.* 她老是记不住我的名字。
6 to look after and buy food and other things for a person or an animal 供养；饲养: *It costs a lot to keep a family of four.* 要养活一家四口花费很大。◇ *They keep sheep and pigs on their farm.* 他们的农场饲养羊和猪。
7 to stay fresh 保持新鲜: *Will this fish keep until tomorrow?* 这条鱼留到明天还行吗?
keep away from somebody or 或 **something** to not go near somebody or something 避免接近；远离: *Keep away from the river, children.* 孩子们，不要靠近河边。
keep somebody from doing something to stop somebody from doing something 阻止某人做某事: *You can't keep me from going out!* 你不能不让我出去!
keep going to continue 继续: *I was very tired but I kept going to the end of the race.* 我已经很累了，但是仍坚持跑到了终点。

keep off something to not go on something 不接近（或接触）： *Keep off the grass!* 不要践踏草坪!

keep on doing something to continue doing something; to do something many times 继续（或重复）做某事： *We kept on driving all night!* 我们通宵开车没有停下! ◇ *That man keeps on looking at me.* 那个男的目不转睛地看着我。

keep out to stay outside 留在外面; 不进入： *The sign on the door said 'Danger. Keep out!'* 门上的牌写着"危险! 禁止入内!"。

keep somebody or 或 **something out** to stop somebody or something from going in 使…不进入： *We put a fence round the garden to keep the sheep out.* 我们在花园周围竖起了篱笆，不让羊进来。

keep up with somebody or 或 **something** to go as fast as another person or thing so that you are together 跟上; 赶上： *Don't walk so quickly – I can't keep up with you.* 别走得那么快，我跟不上你了。

keeper /ˈkiːpə(r)/ *noun* 名词
a person who looks after something 看守人; 保管人： *He's a keeper at the zoo – he looks after the lions.* 他是动物园的饲养员 —— 他喂养狮子。 ◒ Look also at **goalkeeper**. 亦见 goalkeeper。

kerb 路缘

pavement (*British* 英式英语)
sidewalk (*American* 美式英语) 人行道

drain 下水道　kerb (*British* 英式英语)
curb (*American* 美式英语)
路缘

kennel /ˈkenl/ *noun* 名词
a small house where a dog sleeps 狗窝; 犬舍

kept *form of* KEEP * keep 的不同形式

kerb (*British* 英式英语) (*American* 美式英语 **curb**) /kɜːb/ *noun* 名词
the edge of a path next to a road 路缘： *They stood on the kerb waiting to cross the road.* 他们站在路缘，等着过马路。

kerosene /ˈkerəsiːn/ *American English for* PARAFFIN 美式英语，即 paraffin

ketchup /ˈketʃəp/ *noun* 名词 (*no plural* 不用复数形式)
a cold sauce made from tomatoes 番茄酱 ◒ Look at Picture Dictionary page P7. 见彩页 P7。

kettle 水壶

kettle /ˈketl/ *noun* 名词
a container with a handle, for boiling water（烧水用的）水壶： *I'll go and put the kettle on* (= fill it with water and make it start to get hot). 我去烧壶水。

keys 钥匙

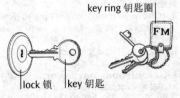

key ring 钥匙圈

lock 锁　key 钥匙

key[1] 0-ᵣ /kiː/ *noun* 名词
1 a piece of metal that opens or closes a lock 钥匙： *He turned the key and opened the door.* 他转动钥匙把门打开了。

2 one of the parts of a computer, a piano or other musical instrument that you press with your fingers（电脑、钢琴等的）键：*Pianos have black and white keys.* 钢琴有黑键和白键。 ᗄ Look at the picture at **saxophone**. 见 saxophone 的插图。

3 answers to questions 答案：*Check your answers with the key at the back of the book.* 把你所做的与书后的答案核对一下。

key² /kiː/ *verb* 动词 (keys, keying, keyed /kiːd/)

key something in to put words or numbers into a computer by pressing the keys 输入；键入：*Key in your password.* 输入密码。

keyboard /'kiːbɔːd/ *noun* 名词
1 all the keys on a computer or piano 键盘；琴键 ᗄ Look at Picture Dictionary page P11. 见彩页 P11。
2 a musical instrument like a small electrical piano 键盘式电子乐器；电子琴：*a keyboard player* 电子琴手

keyhole /'kiːhəʊl/ *noun* 名词
a hole in a lock where you put a key 锁眼；钥匙孔

key ring /'kiː rɪŋ/ *noun* 名词
a metal ring that you keep keys on 钥匙圈；钥匙环

kg *short way of writing* KILOGRAM
* kilogram 的缩写形式

khaki /'kɑːki/ *adjective* 形容词
having the pale brown-green or brown-yellow colour of a soldier's uniform 暗绿色的；黄褐色的：*khaki uniforms* 黄褐色卡其军装
▶ **khaki** *noun* 名词 (*no plural* 不用复数形式)

kick¹ 0̄ /kɪk/ *verb* 动词 (kicks, kicking, kicked /kɪkt/)
1 to hit somebody or something with your foot 踢：*I kicked the ball to Chris.* 我把球踢给了克里斯。
2 to move your foot or feet up and down quickly 踢蹬；踢腿：*The child was kicking and screaming.* 那个孩子又踢又叫。

kick off to start a game of football（足球比赛）开球，开始

kick somebody out (*informal* 非正式) to make somebody leave a place 使离开；逐出；开除：*The boys were kicked out of the cinema because they were noisy.* 那些男孩子太吵了，被撵出了电影院。

kick² 0̄ /kɪk/ *noun* 名词
1 a movement with your foot or your leg, usually to hit something with your foot

踢；踢脚；踢腿：*If the door won't open, give it a kick.* 门要是打不开，就踢它一下。
2 (*informal* 非正式) a feeling of excitement 兴奋；快感：*He gets a kick out of driving fast cars.* 开快车给他带来很大快感。

kick-off /'kɪk ɒf/ *noun* 名词
the start of a game of football（足球比赛的）开球，开赛：*Kick-off is at 2.30 this afternoon.* 足球比赛今天下午 2 时 30 分开始。

kid¹ /kɪd/ *noun* 名词
1 (*informal* 非正式) a child 小孩：*How old are your kids?* 你的小孩几岁了？
2 a young GOAT (= a small animal with horns that lives in mountain areas) 小山羊 ᗄ Look at the picture at **goat**. 见 goat 的插图。

kid² /kɪd/ *verb* 动词 (kids, kidding, kidded) (*informal* 非正式)
to say something that is not true as a joke 开玩笑；戏弄：*I didn't mean it. I was only kidding.* 我并没有这个意思，只是闹着玩而已。

kidnap /'kɪdnæp/ *verb* 动词 (kidnaps, kidnapping, kidnapped /'kɪdnæpt/)
to take somebody away and hide them, so that their family or friends will pay money to free them 绑架；劫持
▶ **kidnapper** /'kɪdnæpə(r)/ *noun* 名词：*The kidnappers are demanding a ransom of $1 million.* 绑匪索要 100 万元的赎金。

kidney /'kɪdni/ *noun* 名词 (*plural* 复数形式 kidneys)
one of the parts inside your body that takes waste liquid from your blood 肾脏

kill 0̄ /kɪl/ *verb* 动词 (kills, killing, killed /kɪld/)
to make somebody or something die 杀死；杀害：*The police do not know who killed the old man.* 警方不知道杀害那名老人的凶手是谁。◇ *Three people were killed in the accident.* 事故中有三人死亡。
▶ **killer** /'kɪlə(r)/ *noun* 名词 a person, animal or thing that kills 杀手；导致死亡的人（或动物、事物）

kilo /'kiːləʊ/ *noun* 名词 (*plural* 复数形式 kilos) *short way of writing* KILOGRAM
* kilogram 的缩写形式

kilobyte /'kɪləbaɪt/ *noun* 名词 (*abbr.* 缩略式 KB, Kb)
a measure of computer memory or information. There are 1 024 **bytes** in a **kilobyte**. 千字节（电脑贮存量单位，等于 1 024 个字节）

kilogram 0╌ (*British also* 英式英语
亦作 **kilogramme**) /'kɪləgræm/ (*also* 亦作
kilo /'kiːləʊ/) (*plural* 复数形式 **kilos**) *noun*
名词 (*abbr.* 缩略式 **kg**)
a measure of weight. There are 1 000
grams in a **kilogram**. 千克；公斤：
I bought two kilos of potatoes. 我买了两
公斤土豆。◊ *1 kg of bananas* * 1 公斤香蕉

kilometre 0╌ (*British* 英式英语)
(*American* 美式英语 **kilometer**)
/'kɪləmiːtə(r); kɪˈlɒmɪtə(r)/ *noun* 名词
(*abbr.* 缩略式 **km**)
a measure of length. There are 1 000
metres in a **kilometre**. 千米；公里：
They live 100 km from Paris. 他们住在
离巴黎 100 公里的地方。

kilt /kɪlt/ *noun* 名词
a skirt that men in Scotland sometimes
wear 苏格兰男式格呢褶裙

kin /kɪn/ *noun* 名词 (*no plural* 不用复数
形式) (*formal* 正式)
the people in your family 家属；亲属：
*Who is your **next of kin** (= your closest
relative)?* 谁是你的直系亲属？

kind¹ 0╌ /kaɪnd/ *noun* 名词
a group of things or people that are the
same in some way 种类 ⟹ SAME MEANING
sort or **type** 同义词为 sort 或 type：*What
kind of music do you like?* 你喜欢什么类型
的音乐？◊ *The shop sells ten different
kinds of bread.* 这家商店出售十种不同的
面包。
kind of (*informal* 非正式) words that you
use when you are not sure about
something 有点；稍微：*He looks kind of
tired.* 他看上去有点累了。

kind² 0╌ /kaɪnd/ *adjective* 形容词
(**kinder, kindest**)
friendly and good to other people 友好
的；亲切的；和蔼的：*'Can I carry your
bag?' 'Thanks. That's very kind of you.'*
"我帮你拿包行吗？""谢谢，你真
好。"◊ *Be **kind** to animals.* 要善待动物。
⟹ OPPOSITE **unkind** 反义词为 unkind

kind-hearted /ˌkaɪnd ˈhɑːtɪd/ *adjective*
形容词
kind and generous to other people 善良
的；仁慈的；宽容的

kindly /'kaɪndli/ *adverb, adjective* 副词，
形容词
1 in a kind way 友好地；亲切地；
和蔼地：*She kindly drove me to the
station.* 她体贴地开车把我送到车站。
2 (**kindlier, kindliest**) kind and friendly
亲切友善的；和蔼的：*a kindly old man*
慈祥的老先生

kindness 0╌ /'kaɪndnəs/ *noun* 名词
the quality of being kind 善良；仁慈；
宽容：*Thank you for your kindness.* 谢谢
您的好意。

king 0╌ /kɪŋ/ *noun* 名词
a man from a royal family who rules a
country 国王：*King Henry VIII* 国王亨利
八世 ⟹ Look at **queen**. 见 queen。

kingdom /'kɪŋdəm/ *noun* 名词
a country where a king or queen rules
王国：*the United Kingdom* 联合王国

kiosk /'kiːɒsk/ *noun* 名词
a small shop in a street where you can
buy things like sweets and newspapers
through a window（出售糖果、报纸等
的）小卖亭；报亭

kiss 0╌ /kɪs/ *verb* 动词 (**kisses, kissing,
kissed** /kɪst/)
to touch somebody with your lips to
show love or to say hello or goodbye 吻；
亲吻：*She kissed me on the cheek.* 她吻了
我的面颊。◊ *They kissed, and then he left.*
他们接吻，然后他走了。
▸ **kiss** *noun* 名词 (*plural* 复数形式
kisses)：*Give me a kiss!* 亲亲我吧！

kit /kɪt/ *noun* 名词
1 the clothes or things that you need to
do something 全套衣服；成套工具：
Where's my football kit? 我的足球服在
哪里呢？◊ *There's a hammer in the tool
kit.* 那套工具中有一把锤子。
2 a set of small pieces that you put
together to make something 成套零件：
a kit for making a model aeroplane 一套
飞机模型的零件

kite 风筝

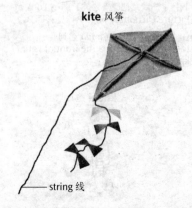

string 线

A
B
C
D
E
F
G
H
I
J
K
L
M
N
O
P
Q
R
S
T
U
V
W
X
Y
Z

kitchen ⊶ /'kɪtʃɪn/ *noun* 名词
a room where you cook food 厨房
⊃ Look at Picture Dictionary page **P10**.
见彩页 P10。

kite /kaɪt/ *noun* 名词
a toy that you fly in the wind on a long
piece of string 风筝 ⊃ Look at the picture
on the previous page. 见前页的插图。

kitten /'kɪtn/ *noun* 名词
a young cat 小猫 ⊃ Look at the picture at
cat. 见 cat 的插图。

kiwi fruit /'kiːwi fruːt/ (*also* 亦作 kiwi)
noun 名词 (*plural* 复数形式 kiwi fruit)
a small green fruit with black seeds and
rough brown skin 猕猴桃；奇异果
⊃ Look at Picture Dictionary page **P8**.
见彩页 P8。

km *short way of writing* KILOMETRE
* kilometre 的缩写形式

knead /niːd/ *verb* 动词 (kneads, kneading,
kneaded)
to press and stretch a mixture of flour
and water (called dough) to make bread
揉，捏（面团）

> 🔊 **PRONUNCIATION** 读音说明
> If a word starts with the letters **KN**, the
> **K** is always silent. So the word **knead**
> sounds just like **need**, **know** sounds
> just like **no** and **knight** sounds just like
> **night**. 以 kn 开头的词，k 都不发音，
> 因此 knead 读音同 need，know 读音同
> no，knight 读音同 night。

knee ⊶ /niː/ *noun* 名词
the part in the middle of your leg where
it bends 膝；膝盖: *I fell and cut my knee.*
我摔了一跤，把膝盖划破了。 ⊃ Look at
Picture Dictionary page **P4**. 见彩页 P4。

kneecap /'niːkæp/ *noun* 名词
the bone that covers the front of your
knee 膝盖骨；髌骨

kneel 跪

kneel /niːl/ *verb* 动词 (kneels, kneeling,
knelt /nelt/ *or* 或 kneeled /niːld/, has
knelt *or* 或 has kneeled)
to bend your legs and rest on one or both
of your knees 跪；跪下: *He knelt down to
pray.* 他跪下来祈祷。 ◇ *Jane was kneeling
on the floor.* 简跪在地上。

knew *form of* KNOW * know 的不同形式

knickers /'nɪkəz/ *noun* 名词 (*plural
用复数形式*) (*British* 英式英语) (*American
美式英语* panties)
a piece of underwear for women that
covers the lower part of the body but not
the legs 女式短衬裤 ⊃ SAME MEANING
pants 同义词为 pants: *a pair of knickers*
一条女式短衬裤

knife 刀

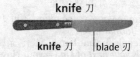

knife 刀 | blade 刃

knife ⊶ /naɪf/ *noun* 名词 (*plural* 复数
形式 knives /naɪvz/)
a sharp metal thing with a handle that
you use to cut things or to fight 刀:
a knife and fork 一副刀叉

knight /naɪt/ *noun* 名词
a soldier of a high level who rode a horse
and fought for his king a long time ago
（古代的）骑士

knit 编织

knitting needle
编织针

stitches
针脚 | wool 毛线

knit /nɪt/ *verb* 动词 (knits, knitting,
knitted)
to make clothes from wool using two long
sticks (called knitting needles) 编织；
针织: *My grandmother knitted this hat
for me.* 我奶奶给我织了这顶帽子。
▸ **knitting** /'nɪtɪŋ/ *noun* 名词 (*no plural*

不用复数形式）: *I usually do some knitting while I'm watching television.* 我通常一边看电视一边织点东西。

knitting needle /ˈnɪtɪŋ niːdl/ *noun* 名词
one of two metal or plastic sticks that you use for making clothes from wool 编织针 ⊃ Look at the picture at **knit**. 见 knit 的插图。

knives *plural of* KNIFE * knife 的复数形式

knob /nɒb/ *noun* 名词
1 a round thing that you turn to control part of a machine（机器的）旋钮: *the volume control knob* 音量控制旋钮
2 a round handle on a door or drawer（门或抽屉的）球形把手 ⊃ Look at the picture at **handle**¹. 见 handle¹ 的插图。

knock¹ 0━ /nɒk/ *verb* 动词 (knocks, knocking, knocked /nɒkt/)
1 to hit something and make a noise 敲；击: *I knocked on the door, but nobody answered.* 我敲了敲门，可是没人应。
2 to hit something hard, usually by accident（常指意外地）碰，撞: *I knocked my head on the door.* 我的头撞到了门上。◇ *She knocked a glass off the table.* 她把玻璃杯从桌上碰掉了。

knock somebody down, knock somebody over to hit somebody so that they fall onto the ground 把某人撞倒（或击倒）: *The boy was knocked down by a car.* 那个男孩给汽车撞倒了。

knock something down to break a building so that it falls down 推倒，拆毁（建筑物）⊃ SAME MEANING **demolish** 同义词为 demolish: *They're knocking down the old houses.* 他们正在拆除那些老房子。

knock somebody out to make somebody fall asleep or become unconscious 使入睡；使不省人事: *The blow knocked him out.* 那一拳把他打晕了。

knock something over to hit something so that it falls over 把…撞倒（或碰掉）: *I knocked over a vase of flowers.* 我把一瓶花碰倒了。

knock² 0━ /nɒk/ *noun* 名词
the action of hitting something; the sound that this makes 敲；敲打声；撞击声: *I heard a knock at the door.* 我听见了敲门声。

knot¹ 0━ /nɒt/ *noun* 名词
a place where you have tied two pieces of rope, string, etc. tightly together（绳子、线等的）结: *I tied a knot in the rope.* 我在绳子上打了个结。◇ *Can you undo*

this knot (= make it loose)? 你能解开这个结吗?

knot 结

rope 绳子   knot 结

knot² /nɒt/ *verb* 动词 (knots, knotting, knotted)
to tie a knot in something 把…打成结: *He knotted the ends of the rope together.* 他把绳子两头系了在一起。

know 0━ /nəʊ/ *verb* 动词 (knows, knowing, knew /njuː/, has known /nəʊn/)
1 to have information in your head 知道；了解: *I don't know her name.* 我不知道她的名字。◇ *He knows a lot about cars.* 他对汽车很在行。◇ *Do you know how to use this machine?* 你会操作这台机器吗? ◇ *Did you know that he's going to live abroad?* 你知道他要去国外生活吗?
2 to be familiar with a person or place 熟悉；认识: *I have known Mario for six years.* 我认识马里奥已经六年了。◇ *I know Paris quite well.* 我对巴黎相当熟悉。◇ *I liked him when I got to know him* (= started to know him). 我开始了解他后就喜欢上他了。

I know (*informal* 非正式) used to agree with something somebody has just said（表示同意）我知道，我理解: *'What a ridiculous situation!' 'I know.'* "事情真荒唐！""的确是。"

let somebody know to tell somebody about something 让某人知道: *Let me know if you need any help.* 你需要帮忙的话就告诉我一声。

you know words that you use when you are thinking about what to say next（说话人考虑接着说什么时用）: *Well, you know, it's hard to explain.* 唉，你知道，这很难解释。

know-all /ˈnəʊ ɔːl/ (*British* 英式英语) (*American* 美式英语 **know-it-all** /ˈnəʊ ɪt ɔːl/) *noun* 名词
an annoying person who behaves as if they know everything 自以为无所不知的人；万事通

knowledge 0━ /ˈnɒlɪdʒ/ *noun* 名词
(*no plural* 不用复数形式)
what you know and understand about

A
B
C
D
E
F
G
H
I
J

K

L
M
N
O
P
Q
R
S
T
U
V
W
X
Y
Z

something 知识；学问：*He has a good knowledge of European history.* 他精通欧洲历史。◇ *He did it without my knowledge* (= I did not know). 他是瞒着我干的。

knowledgeable /'nɒlɪdʒəbl/ *adjective* 形容词
knowing a lot 博学的；有见识的：*She's very knowledgeable about* history. 她的历史知识很丰富。

known *form of* KNOW * know 的不同形式

knuckle /'nʌkl/ *noun* 名词
one of the parts where your fingers bend or where they join your hand 指节；指关节 ⊃ Look at the picture at **fist**. 见 fist 的插图。

koala /kəʊ'ɑːlə/ *noun* 名词
an Australian animal with large ears and thick grey fur that lives in trees 树袋熊；考拉；无尾熊 ⊃ Look at Picture Dictionary page **P3**. 见彩页 P3。

Koran (*also* 亦作 Qur'an) /kə'rɑːn/ *noun* 名词 (*no plural* 不用复数形式)
the Koran the most important book in the Islamic religion 《古兰经》

kph *abbreviation* 缩略式
a way of measuring how fast something is moving. **Kph** is short for 'kilometres per hour' 每小时千米（或公里）数（kph 是 kilometres per hour 的缩略式）

kung fu /ˌkʌŋ 'fuː/ *noun* 名词 (*no plural* 不用复数形式)
a Chinese style of fighting in which people use their hands and feet as weapons 功夫（中国拳术）

L, l¹ /el/ *noun* 名词 (*plural* 复数形式 L's, l's /elz/)
the twelfth letter of the English alphabet 英语字母表的第 12 个字母: *'Lake' begins with an 'L'.* * lake 一词以字母 l 开头。

l² *short way of writing* LITRE * litre 的缩写形式

lab /læb/ (*informal* 非正式) *short for* LABORATORY * laboratory 的缩略式

label 标签

label 标签

label¹ /'leɪbl/ *noun* 名词
a piece of paper or material on something that tells you about it 标签; 标记: *The label on the bottle says 'Made in Mexico'.* 瓶上的标签写着"墨西哥制造"。◇ *The washing instructions are on the label.* 洗涤说明在标签上。

label² /'leɪbl/ *verb* 动词 (*British* 英式英语 labels, labelling, labelled /'leɪbld/) (*American* 美式英语 labeling, labeled)
to put a LABEL on something 在…上贴标签: *I labelled all the boxes with my name and address.* 我在所有的箱子上贴上了我的姓名和地址。

labor *American English for* LABOUR 美式英语, 即 labour

laboratory /lə'bɒrətri/ *noun* 名词 (*plural* 复数形式 laboratories) (*also informal* 非正式亦作 lab)
a special room where scientists work 实验室: *a research laboratory* 研究实验室

laborer *American English for* LABOURER 美式英语, 即 labourer

labour (*British* 英式英语) (*American* 美式英语 labor) /'leɪbə(r)/ *noun* 名词 (*no plural* 不用复数形式)
hard work that you do with your hands and body 劳动; 体力劳动: *manual labour* (= work using your hands) 体力劳动

labourer (*British* 英式英语) (*American* 美式英语 laborer) /'leɪbərə(r)/ *noun* 名词
a person who does hard work with their hands and body 体力劳动者: *a farm labourer* 农场工人

the Labour Party /ðə 'leɪbə pɑːti/ *noun* 名词
(*politics* 政治) one of the important political parties in Britain 工党 (英国主要政党之一) ➷ Look at **Conservative Party** and **Liberal Democrats**. 见 Conservative Party 和 Liberal Democrats。

lace 鞋带; 花边

shoelaces 鞋带　　　**lace collar** 花边领

lace /leɪs/ *noun* 名词
1 (*no plural* 不用复数形式) very thin cloth with holes that form a pretty pattern 网眼织物; 花边; 蕾丝: *lace curtains* 网眼纱帘 ◇ *a handkerchief with lace round the edge* 花边手帕
2 (*plural* 复数形式 laces) a string that you use for tying your shoe 鞋带: *Do up your laces or you'll trip over them.* 把鞋带系好, 不然会绊倒的。

lack¹ 0━ /læk/ *noun* 名词 (*no plural* 不用复数形式)
the state of not having something or of not having enough of something 缺乏;

A
B
C
D
E
F
G
H
I
J
K
L
M
N
O
P
Q
R
S
T
U
V
W
X
Y
Z

短缺: *There is a **lack** of good teachers.*
优秀教师短缺。

lack² /læk/ *verb* 动词 (**lacks, lacking,
lacked** /lækt/)
to have none or not enough of something
没有; 缺乏: *He **lacked** confidence.* 他信心
不足。

lacking /'lækɪŋ/ *adjective* 形容词
1 having none or not enough of
something 短缺; 不足: *He is certainly
not **lacking** in intelligence.* 他当然不是
没有头脑的人。
2 not present or available 缺少; 得不到:
*I feel there is something **lacking** in my life.*
我觉得自己的生活中缺了点什么。

lad /læd/ *noun* 名词
a boy or young man 男孩; 小伙子

ladders 梯子

rung
横档

step
梯级

ladder 梯子   **stepladder** 折梯

ladder /'lædə(r)/ *noun* 名词
a thing that you climb up when you want
to reach a high place. A **ladder** is made of
two tall pieces of metal or wood with
shorter pieces between them (called
rungs). 梯子

ladies /'leɪdiz/ *noun* 名词 (*British* 英式
英语)
the ladies a public toilet for women
(公共)女厕所, 女洗手间, 女卫生间:
Where is the ladies, please? 请问女厕所在
哪里? ⊃ Look at **gents**. 见 **gents**。

ladle /'leɪdl/ *noun* 名词
a spoon in the shape of a cup with a long
handle, used for serving soup 长柄勺;
汤勺

lady ⊶ /'leɪdi/ *noun* 名词 (*plural* 复数
形式 **ladies**)

1 a polite way of saying 'woman'(对女子
的客气称呼)女士, 小姐, 夫人: *an old
lady* 一位老夫人 ⊃ Look at **gentleman**.
见 **gentleman**。
2 Lady a title given to a woman with a
high social position(对社会地位高的女性
的称呼)夫人, 女士, 小姐: *The former
prime minister became Lady Thatcher.*
前首相成了撒切尔夫人。 ⊃ Look at **Lord**.
见 **Lord**。

ladybird /'leɪdibɜːd/ (*British* 英式英语)
(*American* 美式英语 **ladybug** /'leɪdibʌg/)
noun 名词
a small red or yellow insect with black
spots 瓢虫

lager /'lɑːgə(r)/ *noun* 名词
1 (*no plural* 不用复数形式) a light beer
拉格啤酒; 贮陈啤酒: *I'll have a pint of
lager, please.* 请给我来一品脱拉格啤酒。
2 (*plural* 复数形式 **lagers**) a glass, bottle
or can of **lager** 一杯(或一瓶、一罐)
拉格啤酒

laid *form of* LAY¹ * lay¹ 的不同形式

laid-back /ˌleɪd 'bæk/ *adjective* 形容词
(*informal* 非正式)
calm and relaxed; not worried 放松的;
无忧的; 悠闲的

lain *form of* LIE¹ * lie¹ 的不同形式

lake ⊶ /leɪk/ *noun* 名词
a big area of water with land all around it
湖; 湖泊: *Lake Victoria* 维多利亚湖 ◊ *We
went swimming in the lake.* 我们到湖里游
泳去了。

ladle 长柄勺

lamb /læm/ *noun* 名词

⌕ PRONUNCIATION 读音说明
The word **lamb** sounds like **ham**,
because we don't say the letter **b** in

this word. * lamb 读音像 ham，因为 b 在这里不发音。

1 (*plural* 复数形式 **lambs**) a young sheep 羔羊；小羊 ➲ Look at the picture at **sheep**. 见 sheep 的插图。
2 (*no plural* 不用复数形式) meat from a **lamb** 羊羔肉： *We had roast lamb for lunch.* 我们午餐吃了烤羔羊肉。

lame /leɪm/ ***adjective*** 形容词
not able to walk properly 瘸的；跛的： *My horse is lame.* 我的马跛了。

lamp 0-▬ /læmp/ ***noun*** 名词
a thing that gives light 灯： *It was dark, so I switched on the lamp.* 天黑了，所以我开了灯。 ➲ Look at Picture Dictionary page **P10**. 见彩页 P10。

lamp post /ˈlæmp pəʊst/ ***noun*** 名词
a tall thing in the street with a light on the top 路灯柱： *The car skidded and hit a lamp post.* 那辆汽车打滑撞上了路灯柱。

lampshade /ˈlæmpʃeɪd/ ***noun*** 名词
a cover for a lamp 灯罩 ➲ Look at the picture at **light**[1]. 见 light[1] 的插图。

land[1] 0-▬ /lænd/ ***noun*** 名词
1 (*no plural* 不用复数形式) the part of the earth that is not the sea 陆地： *After two weeks in a boat, we were happy to be back* ***on land***. 我们坐了两个星期的船后，回到陆地上非常高兴。
2 (*no plural* 不用复数形式) a piece of ground 土地： *They bought a piece of land and built a house on it.* 他们买了一块地，在上面盖了一所房子。 ◇ *farming land* 耕地
3 (*plural* 复数形式 **lands**) (*formal* 正式) a country 国家： *She returned to the land where she was born.* 她回到了祖国。

land[2] 0-▬ /lænd/ ***verb*** 动词 (**lands, landing, landed**)
1 to come down from the air or to bring something down to the ground（使）着陆，降落： *The plane* ***landed at*** *Heathrow airport.* 飞机降落在希思罗机场。 ◇ *The pilot landed the plane safely.* 飞行员驾驶飞机安全着陆。 ◇ *He fell off the ladder and landed on his back.* 他从梯子上摔了下来，背部着地。
2 to go onto land or to put something onto land from a ship 登陆；上岸： *The soldiers landed on the beaches in Normandy.* 一众士兵在诺曼底海滩登陆了。

landing /ˈlændɪŋ/ ***noun*** 名词
1 the area at the top of stairs in a building 楼梯平台： *There's a telephone on the landing.* 楼梯平台处有部电话。 ➲ Look at the picture at **staircase**. 见 staircase 的插图。
2 coming down onto the ground in a plane 着陆；降落： *The plane made an* ***emergency landing*** *in a field.* 飞机在田地里紧急迫降。 ➲ OPPOSITE **take-off** 反义词为 take-off

landlady /ˈlændleɪdi/ ***noun*** 名词 (*plural* 复数形式 **landladies**)
a woman who rents a house or room to people for money 女房东

landlord /ˈlændlɔːd/ ***noun*** 名词
a man who rents a house or room to people for money 房东

landmark /ˈlændmɑːk/ ***noun*** 名词
a big building or another thing that you can see easily from far away 地标；标志性建筑；标志性物体： *Big Ben is one of London's most famous landmarks.* 大本钟是伦敦最著名的地标之一。

landscape /ˈlændskeɪp/ ***noun*** 名词
everything you can see in an area of land 风景；景色： *The Scottish landscape is very beautiful.* 苏格兰景色非常秀丽。

lane /leɪn/ ***noun*** 名词
1 a narrow road in the country 乡间小路
2 one part of a wide road 车道： *We were driving in the middle lane of the motorway.* 我们在高速公路的中车道上行驶。

language 0-▬ /ˈlæŋɡwɪdʒ/ ***noun*** 名词
1 (*plural* 复数形式 **languages**) words that people from a particular country say and write（某国家的）语言： *'Do you speak any foreign languages?' 'Yes, I speak French and Italian.'* "你会说外语吗？" "我会说法语和意大利语。"
2 (*no plural* 不用复数形式) words that people use to speak and write 语言文字： *This word is not often used in spoken language.* 这个词在口语中不怎么用。

lantern /ˈlæntən/ ***noun*** 名词
a light in a container made of glass or paper, that usually has a handle so you can carry it 灯笼；提灯 ➲ Look at the picture at **light**[1]. 见 light[1] 的插图。

lap /læp/ ***noun*** 名词
1 the flat part at the top of your legs when you are sitting 大腿（朝上的一面）： *The child was sitting* ***on*** *his mother's* ***lap***. 孩子坐在妈妈的大腿上。
2 one journey around a track in a race（跑道的）一圈： *There are three more laps to go in the race.* 比赛还剩三圈。

laptop /ˈlæptɒp/ *noun* 名词
a small computer that is easy to carry
便携式电脑；笔记本电脑

large ⚡ /lɑːdʒ/ *adjective* 形容词 (larger, largest)
big 大的；大规模的： *They live in a large house.* 他们住在一所大房子里。◇ *She has a large family.* 她有一个大家庭。◇ *Have you got this shirt in a large size?* 这款衬衫你们有大号的吗？ ⊃ OPPOSITE **small** 反义词为 small

largely /ˈlɑːdʒli/ *adverb* 副词
mostly 主要地；很大程度上；多半 ⊃ SAME MEANING **mainly** 同义词为 mainly： *The room is largely used for meetings.* 这个房间大多用于开会。

laser /ˈleɪzə(r)/ *noun* 名词
an instrument that makes a very strong line of light (called a **laser beam**). Some **lasers** are used to cut metal and others are used by doctors in operations.
激光器

lash *short for* EYELASH * eyelash 的缩略式

last¹ /lɑːst/ *adjective* 形容词
1 after all the others 最后的；最末的： *December is the last month of the year.* 十二月是一年中最后的一个月。 ⊃ OPPOSITE **first** 反义词为 first
2 just before now; most recent 刚过去的；最近的： *It's June now, so last month was May.* 现在是六月，所以上个月是五月。◇ *I was at school last week, but this week I'm on holiday.* 我上星期上课，这个星期放假。◇ *Did you go out last (= yesterday) night?* 你昨晚出去了吗？
3 The **last** person or thing is the only one left. 唯一剩下的： *Who wants the last cookie?* 还剩一块饼干，谁要吃？
▶ **lastly** /ˈlɑːstli/ *adverb* 副词 finally, as the last thing 最后；最后一点： *Lastly, I want to thank my parents for all their help.* 最后，我要感谢父母给我的所有帮助。

last² ⚡ /lɑːst/ *adverb* 副词
1 after all the others 最后； *He finished last in the race.* 他是最后一个完成比赛的。
2 at a time that is nearest to now 最近一次；上一次： *I last saw Penny in 2003.* 我上次见到彭妮是在 2003 年。

last³ ⚡ /lɑːst/ *noun* 名词 the last (*plural* 复数形式 the last)
a person or thing that comes after all the others; what comes at the end 最后来的人（或发生的事）： *I was the last to arrive at the party.* 我是聚会上最后一个到的。

at last in the end; after some time 最终；终于 ⊃ SAME MEANING **finally** 同义词为 finally： *She waited all week, and at last the letter arrived.* 她等了整整一星期，信终于来了。

last⁴ ⚡ /lɑːst/ *verb* 动词 (lasts, lasting, lasted)
1 to continue for a time 持续；延续： *The film lasted for three hours.* 电影放了三个小时。◇ *How long did the game last?* 比赛进行了多长时间？
2 to be enough for a certain time 够用；足够维持： *We have enough food to last us till next week.* 我们的食物足够我们吃到下星期。

lasting /ˈlɑːstɪŋ/ *adjective* 形容词
continuing for a long time 持久的；耐久的： *Their trip to India made a lasting impression on them.* 他们的印度之行给他们留下了难忘的印象。

last name /ˈlɑːst neɪm/ *noun* 名词
the part of your name that other members of your family also have 姓 ⊃ SAME MEANING **surname** 同义词为 surname： *My first name's Alison, my last name's Waters.* 我姓沃特斯，名字叫艾利森。◇ ⊃ Look at the note at **name¹**. 见 name¹ 条的注释。

late ⚡ /leɪt/ *adjective, adverb* 形容词，副词 (later, latest)
1 near the end of a time 接近末期（的）；晚期（的）： *They arrived in the late afternoon.* 他们是傍晚到的。◇ *She's in her late twenties* (= between the age of 25 and 29). 她快 30 岁了。 ⊃ OPPOSITE **early** 反义词为 early
2 after the usual or right time 迟；晚： *I went to bed late last night.* 我昨晚很晚才睡。◇ *I was late for school today* (= I arrived late). 我今天上学迟到了。◇ *My train was late.* 我那趟火车晚点了。 ⊃ OPPOSITE **early** 反义词为 early
3 no longer alive; dead 已故的；去世的： *Her late husband was a doctor.* 她已故的丈夫是位医生。
a late night an evening when you go to bed later than usual 睡得比平时晚的夜晚
at the latest no later than a time or a date 最晚；最迟： *Please be here by twelve o'clock at the latest.* 请最迟在十二点钟到这里。

lately /ˈleɪtli/ *adverb* 副词
recently 近来： *Have you seen Mark lately?* 你最近见过马克吗？◇ *The weather has been very bad lately.* 近来天气一直很糟糕。

later¹ 0── /'leɪtə(r)/ *adverb* 副词
at a time in the future; after the time you are talking about 以后；后来；随后：
See you later. 回头见。◇ *His father died later that year.* 那年晚些时候他父亲去世了。 ➜ OPPOSITE **earlier** 反义词为 earlier
later on (*informal* 非正式) at a time in the future; after the time you are talking about 以后；后来；随后： *I'm going out later on.* 我过一会儿会出去。

later² 0── /'leɪtə(r)/ *adjective* 形容词
1 coming after something else or at a time in the future 以后的；后来的： *The match has been postponed to a later date.* 比赛延期举行了。
2 near the end of a period of time 接近末期的；晚年的： *the later part of the twentieth century* 二十世纪末叶
➜ OPPOSITE **earlier** 反义词为 earlier

latest /'leɪtɪst/ *adjective* 形容词
the newest or most recent 最近的；最新的： *the latest fashions* 最新时尚

Latin /'lætɪn/ *noun* 名词 (*no plural* 不用复数形式)
the language that people used a long time ago in ancient Rome 拉丁语： *Do you study Latin at school?* 你在学校学拉丁语吗？
▸ **Latin** *adjective* 形容词： *Spanish, Italian and other Latin languages* (= that developed from Latin) 西班牙语、意大利语和其他拉丁语系的语言

Latin American /ˌlætɪn ə'merɪkən/ *adjective* 形容词
from the parts of Central and South America where people speak Spanish or Portuguese 拉丁美洲的

latitude /'lætɪtjuːd/ *noun* 名词 (*no plural* 不用复数形式)
the distance of a place north or south of the line around the middle of the earth (called the **equator**). **Latitude** is measured in degrees. 纬度 ➜ Look at **longitude**. 见 longitude。➜ Look at the picture at **earth**. 见 earth 的插图。

latter¹ /'lætə(r)/ *adjective* 形容词
nearer to the end of a period of time 后期的；后来的 ➜ SAME MEANING **later** 同义词为 later： *She lived in Sweden in the latter part of her life.* 她晚年住在瑞典。

latter² /'lætə(r)/ *noun* 名词 (*no plural* 不用复数形式)
the latter the second of two things or people 后者： *I studied both French and German, but I preferred the latter.* 我学过法语和德语，但我比较喜欢后者。➜ Look at **former**. 见 former。

laugh¹ 0── /lɑːf/ *verb* 动词 (laughs, laughing, laughed /lɑːft/)
to make sounds to show that you are happy or that you think something is funny 笑；发笑： *His jokes always make me laugh.* 他的笑话总是让我哈哈大笑。
laugh at somebody or 或 **something** to laugh to show that you think somebody or something is funny or silly 因⋯发笑；嘲笑；讥笑： *The children laughed at the clown.* 孩子们给小丑逗得笑了起来。◇ *They all laughed at me when I said I was afraid of dogs.* 我说我怕狗，他们都取笑我。

laugh² 0── /lɑːf/ *noun* 名词
the sound you make when you are happy or when you think something is funny 笑声： *My brother has a loud laugh.* 我弟弟笑声很响。◇ *She told us a joke and we all had a good laugh* (= laughed a lot). 她给我们讲了个笑话，我们都大笑了一番。
for a laugh as a joke; for fun 开玩笑；逗趣： *The boys put a spider in her bed for a laugh.* 那些男孩闹着玩，把一只蜘蛛放在她床上。

laughter /'lɑːftə(r)/ *noun* 名词 (*no plural* 不用复数形式)
the sound of laughing 笑声： *I could hear laughter in the next room.* 我听得到隔壁有笑声。

launch /lɔːntʃ/ *verb* 动词 (launches, launching, launched /lɔːntʃt/)
1 to start something new 发起；发动；推出： *The magazine was launched last year.* 这份杂志是去年创刊的。
2 to put a ship into the water or a SPACECRAFT (= a vehicle that travels in space) into the sky 使(船)下水；发射(航天器)： *This ship was launched in 2005.* 这艘船于 2005 年下水。

launderette /lɔːn'dret/ (*British* 英式英语) (*American* 美式英语 **Laundromat**™ /'lɔːndrəmæt/) *noun* 名词
a shop where you pay to wash and dry your clothes in machines 自助洗衣店；投币式洗衣房

laundry /'lɔːndri/ *noun* 名词 (*no plural* 不用复数形式)
clothes and sheets that you must wash or that you have washed 要洗的衣物；洗好的衣物 ➜ SAME MEANING **washing** 同义词为 washing： *a pile of dirty laundry* 一堆脏衣物

A B C D E F G H I J K **L** M N O P Q R S T U V W X Y Z

lava /ˈlɑːvə/ *noun* 名词 (*no plural* 不用复数形式)

hot liquid rock that comes out of a mountain with an opening at the top (called a volcano)（火山喷出的）熔岩，岩浆

lavatory /ˈlævətri/ *noun* 名词 (*plural* 复数形式 lavatories) (*British* 英式英语) (*formal* 正式)

a large bowl with a seat that you use when you need to empty waste from your body, or the room that it is in 抽水马桶；厕所：*Where's the lavatory, please?* 请问厕所在哪里？ ⇨ Look at the note at **toilet**. 见 toilet 条的注释。

law 0ⁿ /lɔː/ *noun* 名词

1 the law (*no plural* 不用复数形式) all the rules of a country 法律：*Stealing is against the law* (= illegal). 盗窃是违法的。◇ *You're breaking the law* (= doing something illegal). 你这样做是犯法的。

2 a rule of a country that says what people may or may not do 法律；法规；法令：*There is a law against carrying guns.* 有禁止携带枪支的法规。

law court /ˈlɔː kɔːt/ *noun* 名词 (*British* 英式英语) = COURT OF LAW

lawn /lɔːn/ *noun* 名词

an area of short grass in a garden or park（花园或公园的）草地，草坪：*They were sitting on the lawn.* 他们坐在草地上。

lawnmower 割草机

lawnmower
(*also* 亦作 **mower**) 割草机

lawnmower /ˈlɔːnməʊə(r)/ (*also* 亦作 **mower**) *noun* 名词

a machine that you use to cut grass in a garden or park 割草机；剪草机

lawyer 0ⁿ /ˈlɔːjə(r)/ *noun* 名词 (*American also* 美式英语亦作 **attorney**)

a person who has studied the law and who helps people or talks for them in a court of law 律师 ⇨ Look at Picture Dictionary page P12. 见彩页 P12。

lay¹ 0ⁿ /leɪ/ *verb* 动词 (lays, laying, laid /leɪd/, has laid)

1 to put somebody or something carefully on another thing 放置，安放（在…上）：*I laid the papers on the desk.* 我把文件放在了桌上。

> **WHICH WORD?** 词语辨析
> **Lay** or **lie**? 用 lay 还是 lie?
> **Lay** has an object. * lay 后接宾语：
> *He is **laying a carpet** in our new house.* 他在给我们的新房子铺地毯。The past simple is **laid**. * lay 过去式为 laid：*She laid the baby down gently on the bed.* 她把婴儿轻轻地放到床上了。
> **Lie** does not have an object. * lie 后不接宾语：*He is lying on the beach.* 他躺在海滩上。The past simple is **lay**. * lie 过去式为 lay：*She was tired so she lay on the bed.* 她累了，就躺到床上去了。

2 to make an egg 下（蛋）；产（卵）：*Birds and insects lay eggs.* 鸟下蛋，昆虫产卵。

lay the table (*British* 英式英语) to put knives, forks, plates and other things on the table before you eat（用餐前）摆好餐具 ⇨ SAME MEANING **set the table** 同义词为 set the table

lay² *form of* LIE¹ * lie¹ 的不同形式

layer 0ⁿ /ˈleɪə(r)/ *noun* 名词

something flat that lies on another thing or that is between other things 层；表层；夹层：*The table was covered with a thin layer of dust.* 桌子上有一层薄薄的灰尘。◇ *The cake has a layer of jam in the middle.* 这个蛋糕中间有一层果酱。 ⇨ Look also at **ozone layer**. 亦见 ozone layer。

lazy 0ⁿ /ˈleɪzi/ *adjective* 形容词 (lazier, laziest)

A person who is **lazy** does not want to work. 不愿工作的；懒惰的：*Don't be so lazy – come and help me!* 别那么懒，过来帮我！◇ *My teacher said I was lazy.* 老师说我懒散。

▸ **laziness** /ˈleɪzinəs/ *noun* 名词 (*no plural* 不用复数形式)

lb *short way of writing* POUND (2) * pound 第 2 义的缩写形式

lead¹ 0ⁿ /liːd/ *verb* 动词 (leads, leading, led /led/, has led)

> **PRONUNCIATION** 读音说明
> The word **lead** usually sounds like

feed or need. 在通常情况下，lead 读音像 feed 或 need。
However, when it means a soft grey metal or the part inside a pencil, it sounds like **red** or **said**. 但当 lead 解作"铅"或"铅笔芯"时，读音像 red 或 said。

1 to take a person or an animal somewhere by going with them or in front of them 带领；引领；领路：*He led me to the classroom.* 他领了我进教室。
2 to go to a place 通向；通往：*This path leads to the river.* 这条小路通往河边。
3 to make something happen 导致；造成：*Smoking can lead to heart disease.* 吸烟能引致心脏病。
4 to have a particular type of life 过（某种生活）：*They lead a very busy life.* 他们过着非常忙碌的生活。
5 to be the first or the best, for example in a race or game 领先；居首位：*Who's leading in the race?* 赛跑谁领先？
6 to control a group of people 控制；领导；率领；掌管：*The team was led by Gwen Hollis.* 这队由格温·霍利斯带领。

lead² /liːd/ *noun* 名词
1 (*no plural* 不用复数形式) the first place or position in front of other people 领先地位；首位：*The French runner has gone into the lead.* 那名法国赛跑选手已经领先了。◇ *Who is in the lead* (= winning)? 现在谁领先？
2 (*plural* 复数形式 **leads**) (*British* 英式英语) (*American* 美式英语 **leash**) (*plural* 复数形式 **leashes**) a long piece of leather or a chain that you tie to a dog's neck so that it walks with you 牵狗带；牵狗链：*All dogs must be kept on a lead.* 所有狗都得套上牵狗带。
3 (*plural* 复数形式 **leads**) a long piece of wire that brings electricity to things like lamps and machines 电线；导线

lead³ /led/ *noun* 名词
1 (*no plural* 不用复数形式) (*symbol* 符号 **Pb**) a soft grey metal that is very heavy. **Lead** is used to make things like water pipes and roofs. 铅
2 (*plural* 复数形式 **leads**) the grey part inside a pencil 铅笔芯

leader 0ᜓ /ˈliːdə(r)/ *noun* 名词
1 a person who controls a group of people 领导者；领袖：*They chose a new leader.* 他们选出了新领袖。
2 a person or thing that is the first or the best 领先者；最佳的人（或事物）：*The leader is ten metres in front of the other*

runners. 跑在最前面的比其他选手领先十米。

leadership /ˈliːdəʃɪp/ *noun* 名词 (*no plural* 不用复数形式)
the state or position of being the person who controls a group of people 领导；领导地位：*The country is under new leadership* (= has new leaders). 这个国家有了新的领导人。

leading /ˈliːdɪŋ/ *adjective* 形容词
best or most important 最好的；最重要的：*He's one of the leading experts in this field.* 他是这个领域的其中一位权威专家。

leaf 0ᜓ /liːf/ *noun* 名词 (*plural* 复数形式 **leaves** /liːvz/)
one of the flat green parts that grow on a plant or tree 叶；叶子：*Leaves fall from the trees in autumn.* 秋天树叶会掉落。

leaflet /ˈliːflət/ *noun* 名词
a piece of paper with writing on it that gives information about something 传单：*I picked up a leaflet on local museums and art galleries.* 我取了一张介绍当地博物馆和美术馆的宣传单。

league /liːg/ *noun* 名词
1 a group of teams that play against each other in a sport（体育队伍的）联合会；（体育运动的）联赛：*the football league* 足球联赛
2 a group of people or countries that work together to do something 联盟；同盟：*the League of Nations* 国际联盟

leak¹ /liːk/ *verb* 动词 (**leaks, leaking, leaked** /liːkt/)
1 to have a hole that liquid or gas can go through 漏；渗漏；泄漏：*The roof of our house leaks when it rains.* 我们的房顶一下雨就漏水。◇ *The boat is leaking.* 船正在入水。
2 (used about liquid or gas) to go out through a hole 漏；（液体）渗漏；（气体）泄漏：*Water is leaking from the pipe.* 水从管子里漏出来。

leak² /liːk/ *noun* 名词
a small hole that liquid or gas can get through 漏洞：*There's a leak in the pipe.* 管子上有个漏洞。
▸ **leaky** /ˈliːki/ *adjective* 形容词：*a leaky roof* 漏水的屋顶

lean¹ 0ᜓ /liːn/ *verb* 动词 (**leans, leaning, leant** /lent/ or 或 **leaned** /liːnd/, **has leant** or 或 **has leaned**)
1 to not be straight; to bend forwards, backwards or to the side 倾斜；前仰（或后仰）：*She leaned out of the window and waved.* 她探身窗外，挥手致意。

A
B
C
D
E
F
G
H
I
J
K
L
M
N
O
P
Q
R
S
T
U
V
W
X
Y
Z

2 to put your body or a thing against another thing 靠着；倚着： *Lean your bike against the wall.* 把你的自行车靠在墙上。

lean 倚靠；倾身

She is **leaning** against a tree. 她倚着树站。

He is **leaning** out of the window. 他探身窗外。

lean² /liːn/ *adjective* 形容词 (**leaner, leanest**)
1 thin and healthy 瘦而健康的： *He is tall and lean.* 他长得又高又瘦。
2 Lean meat does not have very much fat. （肉）脂肪少的，瘦的

leant *form of* LEAN¹ * lean¹ 的不同形式

leap /liːp/ *verb* 动词 (**leaps, leaping, leapt** /lept/ or 或 **leaped** /liːpt/, **has leapt** or 或 **has leaped**)
to jump high or a long way 跳；跳跃： *The cat leapt onto the table.* 那只猫跳上了桌子。
▶ **leap** *noun* 名词： *With one leap, he was over the top of the wall.* 他一跳就跃过了墙头。

leapt *form of* LEAP * leap 的不同形式

leap year /ˈliːp jɪə(r)/ *noun* 名词
a year when February has 29 days. **Leap years** happen every four years. 闰年

learn ⃝ /lɜːn/ *verb* 动词 (**learns, learning, learnt** /lɜːnt/ or 或 **learned** /lɜːnd/, **has learnt** or 或 **has learned**)

> 🔊 PRONUNCIATION 读音说明
> The word **learn** sounds like **turn**.
> * learn 读音像 turn。

1 to find out something, or how to do something, by studying or by doing it often 学；学习；学会： *When did you learn to swim?* 你什么时候学会游泳的？ ◇ *I learnt English at school.* 我在学校学过英语。 ◇ *Learn this list of words for homework* (= so you can remember them). 家庭作业是要学会这些词语。

2 to hear about something 得知；获悉： *I was sorry to learn of your father's death.* 听说你父亲去世了，我非常难过。

learner /ˈlɜːnə(r)/ *noun* 名词
a person who is learning 学习者： *This dictionary is for learners of English.* 本词典是为学习英语的人编写的。

leash /liːʃ/ *American English for* LEAD² (2)
美式英语，即 lead²第 2 义

least ⃝ /liːst/ *adjective, pronoun, adverb* 形容词，代词，副词
1 the smallest amount of something 最小（的）；最少（的）： *Sue has a lot of money, Jane has less, and Kate has the least.* 苏有很多钱，简的少一些，凯特最少。 ⊃ OPPOSITE **most** 反义词为 most
2 less than all others 最小；最少： *I bought the least expensive tickets.* 我买了最便宜的票。 ⊃ OPPOSITE **most** 反义词为 most

at least
1 not less than 至少；最少： *It will cost at least €150.* 这东西至少要花 150 欧元。
2 although other things are bad 起码；无论如何；反正： *We're not rich, but at least we're happy.* 我们不富裕，但起码很快乐。

not in the least not at all 一点也不；丝毫也不： *'Are you angry?' 'Not in the least!'* "你生气了吗？" "一点也没有！"

leather ⃝ /ˈleðə(r)/ *noun* 名词
(*no plural* 不用复数形式)
the skin of an animal that is used to make things like shoes, jackets or bags 皮革： *a leather jacket* 皮夹克

leave¹ ⃝ /liːv/ *verb* 动词 (**leaves, leaving, left** /left/, **has left**)
1 to go away from a place or a person 离开： *The train leaves at 8.40.* 火车于 8 点 40 分开出。 ◇ *At what age do most people leave school in your country?* 你们国家大多数人是几岁毕业离校的？ ◇ *We are leaving for France tomorrow.* 我们明天起程去法国。
2 to let somebody or something stay in the same place or in the same way 使保留，使处于（某处或某种状态）： *Leave the door open, please.* 请让门开着。
3 to forget to bring something with you 忘了带；落下： *I left my books at home.* 我把书忘在家里了。 ◇ *I can't find my glasses. Maybe I left them behind at work.* 我找不到眼镜，可能是忘在办公室了。
4 to make something stay; to not use something 留下备用；不使用： *Leave some cake for me!* 留点蛋糕给我！
5 to give something to somebody when

you die 遗赠；遗留: *She **left** all her money to her two sons.* 她把所有的钱留给了两个儿子。
6 to give the responsibility for something to another person 把（责任）交给；交托；委托: *I'll **leave** it to you to organize the food.* 安排伙食的事我就交给你了。
be left to still be there after everything else has gone 剩下: *There is only one piece of cake **left**.* 只剩一块蛋糕了。
leave somebody or 或 **something alone** to not touch, annoy or speak to somebody or something 不碰；不打扰；不与…说话: *Leave me **alone** – I'm busy!* 别打扰我，我正忙着呢！◇ *Leave that bag **alone** – it's mine!* 别碰那个袋子——它是我的!
leave somebody or 或 **something out** to not put in or do something; to not include somebody or something 不包括；漏掉: *The other children **left** him out of the game.* 别的孩子不跟他玩游戏。◇ *I **left** out question 3 in the exam because it was too difficult.* 我没做第 3 道试题，因为太难了。

leave² /liːv/ *noun* 名词 (no plural 不用复数形式)
a period of time when you are allowed to be away from work for a holiday or for a special reason 假期；休假: *I have 25 days' **leave** each year.* 我每年有 25 天假。◇ *She's not working – she's on sick **leave**.* 她没上班，请了病假。

leaves plural of LEAF * leaf 的复数形式

lecture /ˈlektʃə(r)/ *noun* 名词
a talk to a group of people to teach them about something 讲座；讲课；演讲: *She gave a fascinating **lecture** on Spanish history.* 她做了一次有关西班牙历史的精彩讲座。
▶ **lecture** verb 动词 (lectures, lecturing, lectured /ˈlektʃəd/): *Professor Sims **lectures** in Modern Art.* 西姆斯教授讲授现代艺术。

lecturer /ˈlektʃərə(r)/ *noun* 名词
a person who gives talks to teach people about a subject, especially as a job in a university 讲课者；演讲人；（尤指大学的）讲师: *He is a university **lecturer**.* 他是大学讲师。

led form of LEAD¹ * lead¹ 的不同形式

ledge /ledʒ/ *noun* 名词
a long narrow flat place, for example under a window or on the side of a mountain （窗）台；（山边）突出的岩石，岩架: *a window **ledge*** 窗台

leek /liːk/ *noun* 名词
a vegetable like a long onion that is white at one end and green at the other 韭葱: *leek and potato soup* 韭葱土豆汤

left¹ form of LEAVE¹ * leave¹ 的不同形式

left² 0━ /left/ *adjective, adverb* 形容词, 副词
on the side where your heart is in the body 左边的；向左边: *I've broken my **left** arm.* 我的左臂骨折了。◇ *Turn **left** at the church.* 在教堂那里向左转。 ⊃ OPPOSITE **right** 反义词为 right

left³ 0━ /left/ *noun* 名词 (no plural 不用复数形式)
the left side or direction 左边；左方: *In Britain we drive **on the left**.* 在英国汽车靠左侧行驶。◇ *The house is **on your left**.* 那所房子在你左边。 ⊃ OPPOSITE **right** 反义词为 right

left-hand /ˈleft hænd/ *adjective* 形容词
of or on the left 左手的；左边的: *Your heart is on the **left-hand** side of your body.* 心脏在身体的左侧。 ⊃ OPPOSITE **right-hand** 反义词为 right-hand

left-handed /ˌleft ˈhændɪd/ *adjective, adverb* 形容词, 副词
using your left hand more easily than your right hand, for example when you write 惯用左手（的）；左撇子的: *Are you **left-handed**?* 你是左撇子吗? ◇ *I can't write **left-handed**.* 我左手不会写字。
⊃ OPPOSITE **right-handed** 反义词为 right-handed

leg 0━ /leg/ *noun* 名词
1 one of the long parts of the body of a person or an animal that is used for walking and standing 腿: *A spider has eight **legs**.* 蜘蛛有八条腿。◇ *She sat down and crossed her **legs**.* 她坐了下来，盘着腿。 ⊃ Look at Picture Dictionary page P4. 见彩页 P4。
2 one of the parts of a pair of trousers that covers your leg 裤腿；裤管: *a trouser **leg*** 一条裤腿
3 one of the long parts that a table or chair stands on （桌椅的）腿: *a table **leg*** 桌子腿

legal 0━ /ˈliːgl/ *adjective* 形容词
1 using or connected with the law 法律的；与法律有关的: *legal advice* 法律意见
2 allowed by the law 合法的: *In many parts of the US it is **legal** to carry a gun.* 在美国很多地方，携带枪支是合法的。
⊃ OPPOSITE **illegal** or **against the law** 反义词为 illegal 或 against the law

▶ **legally** /ˈliːɡəli/ *adverb* 副词: *They are not legally married.* 他们没有合法结婚。

legend /ˈledʒənd/ *noun* 名词
1 an old story that is perhaps not true 传说；传奇故事: *the legend of Robin Hood* 罗宾汉传奇
2 a very famous person 传奇人物: *He was a legend in the world of music.* 他是乐坛传奇人物。

legible /ˈledʒəbl/ *adjective* 形容词
clear enough to read 清晰可读的；清楚的: *legible writing* 清晰的笔迹 ⊃ OPPOSITE **illegible** 反义词为 illegible

leisure /ˈleʒə(r)/ *noun* 名词 (*no plural* 不用复数形式)
the time when you are not working and can do what you want 空闲；闲暇: *leisure activities* 休闲活动

leisure centre /ˈleʒə sentə(r)/ (*British* 英式英语) *noun* 名词
a public building where people can go to do sports and other activities in their free time 休闲活动中心

lemon ⊶ /ˈlemən/ *noun* 名词
a yellow fruit with SOUR (= sharp tasting) juice that is used for giving flavour to food and drink 柠檬: *lemon juice* 柠檬汁 ⊃ Look at Picture Dictionary page **P8**. 见彩页 P8。

lemonade /ˌleməˈneɪd/ *noun* 名词 (*no plural* 不用复数形式)
1 (*British* 英式英语) a sweet clear drink with bubbles in it（柠檬味）汽水: *a glass of lemonade* 一杯柠檬味汽水
2 a drink that is made from fresh lemon juice, sugar and water 柠檬饮料

lend ⊶ /lend/ *verb* 动词 (**lends, lending, lent** /lent/, **has lent**)
to give something to somebody for a short time 借给；借出: *I lent the book to Jo.* 我把书借给了乔。 ◇ *Rick lent me his car for an hour.* 里克把他的汽车借给了我一个小时。 ⊃ Look at the note and the picture at **borrow**. 见 borrow 的注释和插图。

length ⊶ /leŋθ/ *noun* 名词 (*no plural* 不用复数形式)
how long something is 长度: *The table is two metres in length.* 这张桌子两米长。 ◇ *We measured the length of the garden.* 我们测量了花园的长度。 ⊃ The adjective is **long**. 形容词为 long。

lengthen /ˈleŋθən/ *verb* 动词 (**lengthens, lengthening, lengthened** /ˈleŋθnd/)
to become or to make something longer

（使）变长；加长: *I need to lengthen this skirt.* 我需要把这条裙子加长。

lengthy /ˈleŋθi/ *adjective* 形容词 (**lengthier, lengthiest**)
very long 冗长的；漫长的: *a lengthy meeting* 冗长的会议

lens /lenz/ *noun* 名词 (*plural* 复数形式 **lenses**)
a special piece of glass in things like cameras or glasses. It makes things look bigger, smaller or clearer when you look through it. 透镜；镜片 ⊃ Look at the picture at **glasses**. 见 glasses 的插图。

Lent /lent/ *noun* 名词 (*no plural* 不用复数形式)
a period of 40 days starting in February or March, when some CHRISTIANS stop doing or eating certain things for religious reasons （基督教的）人斋期，四旬斋

lent *form of* LEND * lend 的不同形式

lentil /ˈlentl/ *noun* 名词
a small round dried seed. You cook **lentils** in water before you eat them. 小扁豆；兵豆: *lentil soup* 兵豆汤

leopard /ˈlepəd/ *noun* 名词
a wild animal like a big cat with yellow fur and dark spots. **Leopards** live in Africa and southern Asia. 豹 ⊃ Look at Picture Dictionary page **P3**. 见彩页 P3。

leotard /ˈliːətɑːd/ *noun* 名词
a piece of clothing that fits the body tightly from the neck to the tops of the legs. **Leotards** are worn by dancers or by women doing some sports. （舞蹈演员或某些体育运动的女运动员穿的）紧身连衣裤 ⊃ Look at Picture Dictionary page **P5**. 见彩页 P5。

less¹ ⊶ /les/ *adjective, pronoun* 形容词，代词
a smaller amount of something 较少的；更少的；较少的数量: *A poor person has less money than a rich person.* 穷人比富人钱少。 ◇ *The doctor advised him to drink less beer.* 医生建议他少喝啤酒。 ⊃ OPPOSITE **more** 反义词为 more ⊃ Look at **least**. 见 least。

less² ⊶ /les/ *adverb* 副词
not so much 较少；更少；不及: *It rains less in summer.* 夏天下雨较少。 ◇ *I'm too fat – I must try to eat less.* 我太胖了，得尽量少吃点。 ◇ *He's less intelligent than his sister.* 他不如他姐姐聪明。 ⊃ OPPOSITE **more** 反义词为 more ⊃ Look at **least**. 见 least。

lessen /ˈlesn/ **verb** 动词 (lessens, lessening, lessened /ˈlesnd/)
to become or to make something less（使）减少，降低，减轻：*This medicine will lessen the pain.* 这种药会减轻疼痛。

lesson ⚷ /ˈlesn/ **noun** 名词
a time when you learn something with a teacher 课：*We have a French lesson after lunch.* 我们午饭后有节法语课。◇ *She gives piano lessons.* 她教钢琴课。◇ *I'm taking driving lessons.* 我在上驾驶课程。

let ⚷ /let/ **verb** 动词 (lets, letting, let, has let)
1 to allow somebody or something to do something 让；允许：*Her parents won't let her stay out after 11 o'clock.* 她父母不准她晚上 11 点后还待在外面。◇ *Let me carry your bag.* 我来帮你拿包吧。◇ *Let the dog in* (= let it come in). 把狗放进来吧。

> 🔑 GRAMMAR 语法说明
> You cannot use **let** in the passive. You must use **allow** and **to**. 被动语态不用 let，要用 allow 加 to：*They let him take the exam again.* 他们让他再次参加考试。◇ *He was allowed to take the exam again.* 他获准再次参加考试。

➡ Look at the note at **allow**. 见 allow 条的注释。
2 *let's* used for making suggestions about what you and other people can do（用于提出建议）：*Let's go to the cinema tonight.* 咱们今晚去看电影吧。

> 🔑 GRAMMAR 语法说明
> The negative is **let's not**. 否定式为 let's not：*Let's not go out this evening.* 咱们今晚别出去了吧。

3 to allow somebody to use your house or land if they pay you 出租：*Have you got any rooms to let?* 你有房间出租吗？
let somebody down to not do something that you promised to do for somebody 失信于人；使某人失望：*Claire has let me down. We agreed to meet at eight o'clock but she didn't come.* 克莱尔让我很失望。我们说好了八点钟见面，她却没来。
let go of somebody or 或 **something**, **let somebody** or 或 **something go** to stop holding somebody or something 放开：*Let go of my hand!* 放开我的手！◇ *Let me go. You're hurting me!* 放开我，你弄疼我了！
let somebody off to not punish somebody 放过；饶恕：*He wasn't sent to*

prison – the judge let him off. 他没被关进监狱——法官放了他一马。

lethal /ˈliːθl/ **adjective** 形容词
Something that is **lethal** can cause a lot of damage or death. 破坏性极大的；致命的 ➡ SAME MEANING **deadly** 同义词为 deadly：*a lethal weapon* 致命的武器

letter ⚷ /ˈletə(r)/ **noun** 名词
1 a piece of writing that one person sends to another person 信；信件：*He got a letter from his cousin this morning.* 他今天上午收到表哥的信。◇ *I'm writing a thank-you letter for the flowers she sent me.* 我正在写感谢信，谢谢她送花给我。
2 a sign in writing that represents a sound in a language 字母：*Z is the last letter in the English alphabet.* z 是英语字母表的最后一个字母。

> 🔍 WORD BUILDING 词汇扩充
> A, B and C are **capital** letters, and a, b, and c are **small** letters. * A、B、C 是大写（capital）字母，a、b、c 是小写（small）字母。

letter box /ˈletə bɒks/ **noun** 名词 (plural 复数形式 **letter boxes**) (British 英式英语) (American 美式英语 **mailbox**)
1 a private box outside a house or a building, or a hole in a door for putting letters through（屋外的）信箱，（门上的）投信口 ➡ Look at Picture Dictionary page **P10**. 见彩页 P10。
2 a small box near the main door of a building or by the road where letters are left for the owner to collect（建筑物大门口或路旁供收信人取信的）信箱
3 (British 英式英语) = POSTBOX

lettuce /ˈletɪs/ **noun** 名词
a plant with big green leaves that you eat cold in salads 莴苣；生菜 ➡ Look at Picture Dictionary page **P9**. 见彩页 P9。

level¹ ⚷ /ˈlevl/ **noun** 名词
1 the amount, size or number of something 数量；大小；数目：*a low level of unemployment* 低失业数字
2 how high something is 高度；水平；级别；层次：*The town is 500 metres above sea level.* 这个镇海拔 500 米。◇ *an elementary-level English class* 初级英语班

level² ⚷ /ˈlevl/ **adjective** 形容词
1 with no part higher than another part 平的；平坦的 ➡ SAME MEANING **flat** 同义词为 flat：*We need level ground to play football on.* 我们需要找块平地踢足球。◇ *This shelf isn't level.* 这块搁板不平。

A B C D E F G H I J K L M N O P Q R S T U V W X Y Z

A
B
C
D
E
F
G
H
I
J
K
L
M
N
O
P
Q
R
S
T
U
V
W
X
Y
Z

2 at the same height, standard or position 等高的；水平相等的；地位相同的：*The two teams are level with 40 points each.* 两队各得 40 分打成了平局。
◇ *His head is **level with** his mother's shoulder.* 他的个头到他母亲的肩膀。

level crossing /ˌlevl ˈkrɒsɪŋ/ (*British* 英式英语) (*American* 美式英语 **railroad crossing**) *noun* 名词
a place where a railway line goes over a road （铁路的）道口，平面交叉

lever /ˈliːvə(r)/ *noun* 名词
1 a handle that you pull or push to make a machine work 操纵杆；控制杆：*Pull this lever.* 拉一下这个控制杆。
2 a bar for lifting something heavy or opening something. You put one end under the thing you want to lift or open, and push the other end. 杠杆

liable /ˈlaɪəbl/ *adjective* 形容词
be liable to do something to be likely to do something 可能做某事：*We're all liable to have accidents when we are very tired.* 我们在非常疲劳的时候都很容易出事故。

liar /ˈlaɪə(r)/ *noun* 名词
a person who says or writes things that are not true (called **lies**) 说谎者；撒谎者：*I don't believe her – she's a liar.* 我不信她的话 —— 她老撒谎。 ⊃ The verb is **lie**. 动词为 lie。

liberal /ˈlɪbərəl/ *adjective* 形容词
A person who is **liberal** lets other people do and think what they want. 开明的；开通的：*Kim's parents are very liberal, but mine are quite strict.* 金的父母很开明，我的父母却相当严厉。

the Liberal Democrats /ðə ˌlɪbərəl ˈdeməkræts/ *noun* 名词 (*plural* 用复数形式) (*politics* 政治) one of the important political parties in Britain （英国）自由民主党 ⊃ Look at **Conservative Party** and **Labour Party**. 见 Conservative Party 和 Labour Party。

liberate /ˈlɪbəreɪt/ *verb* 动词 (**liberates, liberating, liberated**)
to make somebody or something free 解放；使自由：*The city was liberated by the advancing army.* 军队向前挺进，解放了那座城市。

liberty /ˈlɪbəti/ *noun* 名词 (*no plural* 不用复数形式)
being free to go where you want and do what you want 自由 ⊃ Look at **freedom**. 见 freedom。

librarian /laɪˈbreəriən/ *noun* 名词
a person who works in a library 图书馆管理员

library ⊶ /ˈlaɪbrəri/ *noun* 名词 (*plural* 复数形式 **libraries**)
a room or building where you go to borrow or read books 图书馆

🔍 WHICH WORD? 词语辨析
Be careful! You cannot buy books from a **library**. The place where you buy books is called a **bookshop** or a **bookstore**. 注意：买书不去图书馆（library），而是去书店（bookshop 或 bookstore）。

lice *plural of* LOUSE * louse 的复数形式

licence /ˈlaɪsns/ (*British* 英式英语) (*American* 美式英语 **license**) *noun* 名词
an official piece of paper that shows you are allowed to do or have something 执照；许可证：*Do you have a licence for this gun?* 你这支枪有许可证吗？

license /ˈlaɪsns/ *verb* 动词 (**licenses, licensing, licensed** /ˈlaɪsnst/)
to give somebody official permission to do or have something 授权；批准；许可：*This shop is licensed to sell guns.* 这间店有售枪执照。

license plate /ˈlaɪsns pleɪt/ *American English for* NUMBER PLATE 美式英语，即 number plate

lick /lɪk/ *verb* 动词 (**licks, licking, licked** /lɪkt/)
to move your tongue over something 舔：*The cat was licking its paws.* 猫在舔自己的爪子。
▶ **lick** *noun* 名词：*Can I have a lick of your ice cream?* 我能舔一口你的冰激凌吗？

lids 盖

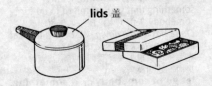

lid ⊶ /lɪd/ *noun* 名词
the top part of a box, pot or other container that covers it and that you can take off （盒、罐等的）盖；盖子 ⊃ Look also at **eyelid**. 亦见 eyelid。

lie¹ 0→ /laɪ/ *verb* 动词 (lies, lying, lay /leɪ/, has lain /leɪn/)

1 to put your body flat on something so that you are not sitting or standing 躺下: *He lay on the bed.* 他躺在床上。 ⊃ Look at the note at **lay¹**. 见 lay¹ 条的注释。

2 to have your body flat on something 躺着; 平卧着: *The baby was lying on its back.* 婴儿仰卧着。

3 to be or stay in a position or state 处于; 位于: *The hills lie to the north of the town.* 群山位于镇子的北面。

lie down to put or have your body flat so that you can rest 躺下: *She lay down on the bed.* 她躺到床上。

lie² 0→ /laɪ/ *verb* 动词 (lies, lying, lied /laɪd/, has lied)

to say something that you know is not true 说谎; 撒谎: *He lied about his age. He said he was 16 but really he's 14.* 他谎报了年龄。他说自己 16 岁，其实只有 14 岁。 ◇ *Don't ever lie to me again!* 别再向我撒谎了！ ⊃ A person who lies is a **liar**. 说谎者叫做 liar。

lie³ 0→ /laɪ/ *noun* 名词

something you say that you know is not true 谎言; 谎话: *She told me a lie.* 她向我撒了一谎。

lieutenant /lefˈtenənt/ (*abbr.* 缩略式 Lieut., Lt) *noun* 名词

an officer at a middle level in the army or navy 陆军中尉; 海军上尉

life 0→ /laɪf/ *noun* 名词 (*plural* 复数形式 lives /laɪvz/)

1 (*no plural* 不用复数形式) People, animals and plants have **life** while they are alive, but things like stone, metal and water do not. 生命: *Do you believe there is life after death?* 你相信死后还有生命吗？ ◇ *Is there life on other planets?* 其他行星上有生命吗？

2 (*plural* 复数形式 lives) being alive 性命: *Many people lost their lives* (= died) *in the fire.* 很多人在这场火灾中丧命。 ◇ *The doctor saved her life* (= stopped her dying). 医生挽救了她的生命。

3 (*plural* 复数形式 lives) the time that somebody is alive 一生; 有生之年: *He has lived here all his life.* 他在这里住了一辈子。

4 (*plural* 复数形式 lives) the way that you live or the experiences that you have when you are alive 生活（方式）: *They were very happy throughout their married life.* 他们的婚姻生活一直都非常幸福。 ◇ *They lead a busy life.* 他们过着忙碌的生活。

5 (*no plural* 不用复数形式) energy; being busy and interested 活力; 生命力: *Young children are full of life.* 幼童充满活力。

lifebelt /ˈlaɪfbelt/ *noun* 名词

a big ring that you hold or wear if you fall into water to stop you from dying in the water (**drowning**) 救生圈

lifeboat /ˈlaɪfbəʊt/ *noun* 名词

a boat that goes to help people who are in danger at sea 救生艇; 救生船

lifeguard /ˈlaɪfɡɑːd/ *noun* 名词

a person at a beach or a swimming pool whose job is to help people who are in danger in the water （海滩或泳池的）救生员

life jacket /ˈlaɪf dʒækɪt/ (*American also* 美式英语亦作 **life vest** /ˈlaɪf vest/) *noun* 名词

a special jacket with no sleeves that can be filled with air. You wear it to help you float if you fall in the water. 救生衣

lifestyle /ˈlaɪfstaɪl/ *noun* 名词

the way that you live 生活方式: *They have a healthy lifestyle.* 他们有健康的生活方式。

lifetime /ˈlaɪftaɪm/ *noun* 名词

all the time that you are alive 一生; 终生: *There have been a lot of changes in my grandma's lifetime.* 我奶奶一生中经历了许多改变。

lift¹ 0→ /lɪft/ *verb* 动词 (lifts, lifting, lifted)

to move somebody or something to a higher position 举起; 提起; 抬起: *I can't lift this box. It's too heavy.* 这个箱子我搬不动，太重了。 ◇ *Lift your arm up.* 把你的胳膊抬高。

lift² 0→ /lɪft/ (*British* 英式英语) *noun* 名词

1 (*American* 美式英语 **elevator**) a machine that takes people and things up and down in a high building 电梯; 升降机: *Shall we use the stairs or take the lift?* 我们爬楼梯还是乘电梯？

2 (*American* 美式英语 **ride**) a free journey in another person's car 免费搭车; 搭便车: *Can you give me a lift to the station?* 你能捎我去车站吗？

lift-off /ˈlɪft ɒf/ *noun* 名词

the moment when a SPACECRAFT (= a vehicle that can travel into space) leaves the ground （航天器的）发射，起飞，升空

light¹ 0→ /laɪt/ *noun* 名词

1 (*no plural* 不用复数形式)

🔊 PRONUNCIATION 读音说明

The word **light** sounds like **white**.
* light 读音像 white。

the energy from the sun, a lamp, etc. that

allows us to see things 光；光线：*Strong sunlight is bad for the eyes.* 强烈的阳光对眼睛有害。◇ *The light was not very good so it was difficult to read.* 光线不太好，所以很难阅读。

2 (*plural* 复数形式 **lights**) a thing that gives light, for example an electric lamp 发光体；灯

> 🔎 **WHICH WORD?** 词语辨析
>
> A light can be **on** or **off**. 灯可以开着（on）或关掉（off）。
> You can **put**, **turn** or **switch** a light **on**, **off** or **out**. 开灯可用动词 put/turn/switch on，关灯可用动词 put out、switch off 或 turn off/out：*Turn the lights off before you go to bed.* 睡觉前把灯关掉。◇ *It's getting dark. Shall I switch the light on?* 天黑了，我开灯好吗?

⊃ Look also at **traffic lights**. 亦见 traffic lights。

3 (*plural* 复数形式 **lights**) something, for example a match, that you use to start a cigarette burning 点火物；打火机；火柴：*Do you have a light?* 你有火吗?

set light to something to make something start to burn 点燃

lights 灯
lampshade 灯罩

light bulb
灯泡

ceiling light
吊灯

lamp
灯

lantern
提灯

torch (*British* 英式英语)
flashlight (*American* 美式英语)
手电筒

light² 0﹣ /laɪt/ *adjective* 形容词 (**lighter**, **lightest**)

1 full of natural light 明亮的；光线充足的：*In summer it's light until about ten o'clock.* 夏天的时候，约十点钟天还是亮的。◇ *The room has a lot of windows so it's very light.* 这个房间有很多窗，所以很

亮堂。⊃ OPPOSITE **dark** 反义词为 dark

2 with a pale colour 浅色的：*a light blue shirt* 浅蓝色的衬衫 ⊃ OPPOSITE **dark** 反义词为 dark。

3 easy to lift or move 轻的；不重的：*Will you carry this bag for me? It's very light.* 你帮我拿这个包好吗? 它很轻的。⊃ OPPOSITE **heavy** 反义词为 heavy。⊃ Look at the picture at **heavy**. 见 heavy 的插图。

4 not very much or not very strong 少量的；轻微的：*light rain* 小雨 ◇ *I had a light breakfast.* 我吃了个轻便的早餐。

▶ **lightly** /ˈlaɪtli/ *adverb* 副词：*She touched me lightly on the arm.* 她轻轻碰了碰我的胳膊。

light³ 0﹣ /laɪt/ *verb* 动词 (**lights**, **lighting**, **lit** /lɪt/ or 或 **lighted**, has **lit** or 或 has **lighted**)

1 to make something start to burn 点火；点燃：*Will you light the fire?* 你来生火好吗? ◇ *She lit a candle.* 她点亮了蜡烛。

2 to give light to something 照亮：*The room is lit by two big lamps.* 房间有两盏大灯照着。

light bulb /ˈlaɪt bʌlb/ *noun* 名词
the glass part of an electric lamp that gives light 电灯泡 ⊃ Look at the picture at **light¹**. 见 light¹ 的插图。

lighten /ˈlaɪtn/ *verb* 动词 (**lightens**, **lightening**, **lightened** /ˈlaɪtnd/)
to become lighter or to make something lighter in colour or weight（使）变明亮，变成淡色，变轻

lighten up (*informal* 非正式) to become happier or less worried about something（使）高兴起来，不那么忧虑

lighter /ˈlaɪtə(r)/ *noun* 名词
a thing for lighting cigarettes 打火机

lighthouse /ˈlaɪthaʊs/ *noun* 名词 (*plural* 复数形式 **lighthouses** /ˈlaɪthaʊzɪz/)
a tall building by or in the sea, with a strong light to show ships that there are rocks 灯塔

lighting /ˈlaɪtɪŋ/ *noun* 名词 (*no plural* 不用复数形式)
the kind of lights that a place has 照明；灯光：*electric lighting* 电力照明

lightning /ˈlaɪtnɪŋ/ *noun* 名词 (*no plural* 不用复数形式)
a sudden bright light in the sky when there is a storm 闪电：*He was struck* (= hit) *by lightning.* 他给闪电击中了。⊃ Look at Picture Dictionary page **P16**. 见彩页 P16。⊃ Look also at **thunder¹**. 亦见 thunder¹。

like¹ ⊶ /laɪk/ *verb* 动词 (likes, liking, liked /laɪkt/)
to feel that somebody or something is good or nice; to enjoy something 喜欢; 喜爱: *Do you like your new teacher?* 你喜欢你的新老师吗? ◇ *I don't like carrots.* 我不爱吃胡萝卜。◇ *I like playing tennis.* 我喜欢打网球。 ⊃ OPPOSITE **dislike** 反义词为 dislike

if you like used to agree with somebody or to suggest something (表示同意或提出建议) 你要是愿意的话: *'Shall we go out tonight?' 'Yes, if you like.'* "我们今晚出去好吗?" "好啊,听你的。"

🔎 GRAMMAR 语法说明
Would like is a more polite way of saying **want**. * would like 是表示 want 的礼貌说法: *Would you like some coffee?* 你想来点儿咖啡吗? ◇ *I'd like to speak to the manager.* 我想跟经理说话。

like² ⊶ /laɪk/ *preposition, conjunction* 介词, 连词
1 the same as somebody or something 像; 和…相似: *She is wearing a dress like mine.* 她穿的连衣裙和我的相似。◇ *John looks like his father.* 约翰长得像他父亲。 ⊃ Look at **unlike**. 见 unlike。
2 in the same way as somebody or something 像…一样: *She acted like a child.* 她表现得像个孩子。
3 for example 例如; 比如: *I bought a lot of things, like books and clothes.* 我买了很多东西, 比如书和衣服。

what is … like? words that you say when you want to know more about somebody or something (想得知更多信息) …怎么样?: *'What's that book like?' 'It's very interesting.'* "那本书怎么样?" "很有趣。"

likeable /'laɪkəbl/ *adjective* 形容词
If a person is **likeable**, they are friendly and easy to like. (人)可爱的, 讨人喜欢的

likelihood /'laɪklihʊd/ *noun* 名词 (no plural 不用复数形式)
the chance of something happening 可能; 可能性: *There is very little likelihood of you passing this exam* (= it is very unlikely that you will pass). 你不大可能通过这次考试。

likely ⊶ /'laɪkli/ *adjective* 形容词 (likelier, likeliest)
If something is **likely**, it will probably happen. 很可能的: *It's likely that she*

will agree. 她很可能会同意。◇ *They are likely to be late.* 他们很可能会迟到。 ⊃ OPPOSITE **unlikely** 反义词为 unlikely

likeness /'laɪknəs/ *noun* 名词 (no plural 不用复数形式)
being or looking the same 相像; 相似: *There's a strong likeness between John and his brother.* 约翰和他弟弟长得非常像。

likewise /'laɪkwaɪz/ *adverb* 副词 (formal 正式)
the same 同样地; 一样: *I sat down and John did likewise.* 我坐下, 约翰也坐下了。

liking /'laɪkɪŋ/ *noun* 名词 (no plural 不用复数形式)
the feeling that you like somebody or something 喜欢; 爱好: *She has a liking for spicy food.* 她喜欢吃辣。

lily /'lɪli/ *noun* 名词 (plural 复数形式 lilies)
a plant with big white or coloured flowers 百合花

limb /lɪm/ *noun* 名词
an arm or a leg 肢; 臂; 腿

lime /laɪm/ *noun* 名词
a small green fruit like a lemon 酸橙 ⊃ Look at Picture Dictionary page **P8**. 见彩页 P8。

limit¹ ⊶ /'lɪmɪt/ *noun* 名词
the most that is possible or allowed 限额; 限度: *There is a limit to the amount of pain we can bear.* 我们能忍受的疼痛是有限度的。◇ *What is the speed limit* (= how fast are you allowed to go)? 最高限速是多少?

limit² ⊶ /'lɪmɪt/ *verb* 动词 (limits, limiting, limited)
to do or have no more than a certain amount or number 限制; 限定: *There are only 100 seats, so we must limit the number of tickets we sell.* 总共只有 100 个座位, 所以我们得限制票的售量。

limp¹ /lɪmp/ *adjective* 形容词
not firm or strong 不直挺的; 绵软的: *Her whole body went limp and she fell to the ground.* 她全身无力, 倒在了地上。

limp² /lɪmp/ *verb* 动词 (limps, limping, limped /lɪmpt/)
to walk with difficulty because you have hurt your foot or leg 瘸着走; 跛行; 蹒跚
▶ **limp** *noun* 名词: *He walks with a limp.* 他走路一瘸一拐的。

line¹ ⊶ /laɪn/ *noun* 名词
1 a long thin mark like this — 线; 线条: *Draw a straight line.* 画一条直线。◇ *The ball went over the line.* 球出界了。

2 people or things beside each other or one after the other 排；行；列 ○ SAME MEANING **queue** 同义词为 queue: *There was a long **line** of people waiting at the Post Office.* 邮局里等候的人排成了长队。

3 all the words that are beside each other on a page（页面上的）一行文字: *How many lines are there on this page?* 这一页有多少行字? ○ *I don't know the next line of the poem.* 我不知道这首诗的下一句。

4 a long piece of string or rope 一截线；一段绳: *Hang the washing on the line to dry.* 把洗好的衣服晾在绳子上。

5 a very long wire for telephones or electricity 电话线路；电线: *I tried to phone him but the line was busy.* 我给他打过电话，但是一直占线。

6 a section of railway track that a train moves along 轨道；铁道: *The accident was caused by a cow on the line.* 事故是因铁轨上有一头牛引起的。

lines 线

→→→
parallel 平行线

horizontal 水平线　　**vertical** 垂直线　　**diagonal** 对角线

line² /laɪn/ *verb* 动词 (lines, lining, lined /laɪnd/)

1 to cover the inside of something with a different material 给…做衬里；在里面铺垫: *The boots are **lined** with fur.* 这双靴子有毛衬里。

2 to stand or be in lines along something 站成一排；成一列: *People lined the streets to watch the race.* 人们沿街站着观看赛跑。

line up to stand in a line or make a line 站成一排；排队: *We lined up to buy tickets.* 我们排队买票。

linen /'lɪnɪn/ *noun* 名词 (*no plural* 不用复数形式)

1 a kind of strong cloth 亚麻布: *a white linen jacket* 白色亚麻夹克

2 sheets and other things made of cloth that you use in the home 家居织品: *bedlinen* 床单及枕套

liner /'laɪnə(r)/ *noun* 名词

1 a big ship that carries people a long way 客轮；邮轮 ○ Look at Picture Dictionary page **P1**. 见彩页 **P1**。

2 a bag that you put inside something to keep it clean 衬袋: *a dustbin liner* 垃圾桶衬袋

linger /'lɪŋgə(r)/ *verb* 动词 (lingers, lingering, lingered /'lɪŋgəd/)

to stay somewhere for a long time 存留；逗留；流连: *The smell of her perfume lingered in the room.* 房间里仍飘溢着她的香水味。

lining /'laɪnɪŋ/ *noun* 名词

material that covers the inside of something 衬里；内衬: *My coat has a thick lining so it's very warm.* 我的大衣有一层厚厚的衬里，所以很暖和。 ○ Look at Picture Dictionary page **P5**. 见彩页 **P5**。

link¹ /lɪŋk/ *noun* 名词

1 something that joins things or people together 联系；关联: *There's a link between smoking and heart disease.* 吸烟和心脏病有关联。

2 (*computing* 电脑) a place where one electronic document on the Internet is connected to another one（网页的）链接: *To visit our other website, click on this link.* 要访问我们另一个网站，点击此链接。

3 one of the round parts in a chain（链条的）一环，一节 ○ Look at the picture at **chain¹**. 见 chain¹ 的插图。

link² /lɪŋk/ *verb* 动词 (links, linking, linked /lɪŋkt/)

to join one person or thing to another 将…连接起来: *The computers are linked together in a network.* 这些电脑联网了。

lion 狮子

mane 鬃毛　coat 毛皮　tail 尾巴　paw 爪　claw 爪子

lion /'laɪən/ *noun* 名词

a large animal of the cat family that lives in parts of Africa and Asia. **Lions** have yellow fur, and the males have a lot of

Study pages 研习专页

Contents 目录

Prepositions of place 方位介词

1 Who's who? 谁是谁?

Use the sentences on the right to work out the names of the people in the picture. One of them has been done for you. 根据右边句子提供的信息，辨别图中的人是谁。其中一人的名字已经列出来。

- Sarah is next to a boy.
- Tom has no one beside him on his right.
- James is in front of Diana.
- Jack is behind Jill.
- Diana is between Tom and another boy.

1 _____ *Tom* _____
2 _____
3 _____
4 _____
5 _____
6 _____

2 Describing pictures 描述图画

A Practise your shapes and prepositions. Complete the sentences with a preposition from the box. 图形和介词练习。将框中介词填入句中的空格。

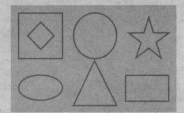

between	~~in~~	below
on top of	above	

1 The diamond is _____ *in* _____ the square.

2 The circle is _____ the triangle.

3 The square is _____ the oval.

4 The rectangle is _____ the star.

5 The triangle is _____ the oval and the rectangle.

B Describe the pictures using a preposition from the box to complete the sentences. 用框中介词完成下列各图的描述。

against	opposite	under
among	below	

1 The temperature is _____ zero.

2 The girl is leaning _____ the wall.

3 The cat is _____ the table.

4 The house is _____ the trees.

5 Kim is _____ Tom.

Prepositions of movement 移动方向介词

1 Where are they going? 他们去哪里?

All the prepositions in the box describe movement. Use each one to describe what the children are doing in the picture.
框中所有的介词都表达移动方向。用这些介词描述图中孩子的活动。

towards	through	out of
round	down	into
over	along	~~up~~
across		

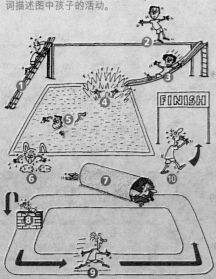

He's/she's ...

1 going ____*up*____ the ladder.

2 going _____ the pole.

3 going _____ the slide.

4 going _____ the pool.

5 swimming _____ the pool.

6 getting _____ the pool.

7 going _____ the tunnel.

8 climbing _____ the wall.

9 running _____ the track.

10 going _____ the finish.

---

2 Giving and following directions 指示和辨别方向

Look at the map below. Use the words in the box to complete the paragraph, explaining how to get from the station to the café. 参看下图，用框中的词语完成指示，说明从车站到咖啡馆的路线。

left again	down this road
~~right~~	on the right
turn left	take the second turning

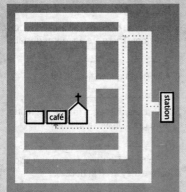

Go out of the station and turn ¹ ___*right*___.

Go to the end of this road and

² _____. At the

crossroads, turn ³ _____.

Walk ⁴ _____ and then

⁵ _____ on the right. Go

straight on, past the first turning on the

right. The café is ⁶ _____,

next to the church.

Exam practice 考试练习

These exercises can help you prepare for Cambridge Young Learners English Tests (Movers, Starters and Flyers), KET and ESOL Skills for Life Exams. 以下练习可帮助准备剑桥少儿英语考试（一级、二级、三级）、英语入门考试和 ESOL 考试。

Part 1 第一部分

Which notice (A–I) says this (1–6)?
哪则提示与下列句子配对？

▶ This trip is not possible because of bad weather.

   _G_

1 Be careful as you walk here. _____

2 You cannot leave your car here all day.

   _____

3 It is not safe to swim here. _____

4 You can get something without paying for it.

   _____

5 You must arrive early if you want to eat dinner here.

   _____

6 You can watch and listen to music here.

   _____

A *Just add hot milk and stir*

B ★ Jazz band playing live tonight ★

C TAKE CARE SLIPPERY PATH

D *Car Parking – 1 hour maximum*

E ⚠ Warning! – Very spicy

F **Danger!** Jellyfish in the water

G *Nature walk cancelled because of rain*

H NO FOOD SERVED AFTER 8PM

I Buy two cups of coffee and get one **free**!

Part 2 第二部分

Read the descriptions of some types of home. What is the word for each one? The first letter is already there. There is one space for each other letter in the word. 阅读下列对不同住所的描述。每种住所的名称是什么？首字母已经提供，在每一空格上填写一个字母。

▶ You can attach this to the back of your car and take it to different places on holiday. You can sleep in it.

   c _a_ _r_ _a_ _v_ _a_ _n_

1 In Antarctica, people often live in this. It is made of blocks of snow.

   i __ __ __ __

2 When people go camping they sleep in this. It is made of cloth.

   t __ __ __

3 In this type of house, all the rooms are on one floor. There are no rooms upstairs.

   b __ __ __ __ __ __ __

4 A king or a queen lives in this.

   p __ __ __ __ __ __

5 A bird keeps its eggs in this. It is made from grass, leaves and straw.

   n __ __ __

6 People lived in these many years ago, before they lived in houses.

   c __ __ __ __

Photocopiable © Oxford University Press

Part 3 第三部分

Read the text, then answer the questions.
阅读下文并回答问题。

Jessica Whitmore: Travel Writer

Jessica Whitmore spends most of her time travelling around the world. Newspapers and magazines pay her to go to different countries and write about them. Why? Because she is a travel writer.

Jessica explains how she became a travel writer. She says: 'It was an accident! After I finished university, I worked in a bank. But I hated it. One day I saw an advertisement for volunteers to teach in Africa. So I went! I was a teacher in a school in Tanzania for 2 years. While I was there, I also visited Uganda, Kenya and Zambia. It was fantastic. When I came back to England, I wrote articles about all the things that I saw. I sent the articles to a newspaper and they printed them. That was 20 years ago.'

Jessica has been to more than 70 countries and written thousands of articles about them. She says, 'I love my job. The best thing is that I meet lots of people from many countries. Every day is different. I'm so lucky.'

▶ Jessica Whitmore is 47 years old.
A Right   B Wrong   C Doesn't say
___C___

1 Jessica worked in a bookshop after she finished university.
A Right   B Wrong   C Doesn't say
_____

2 Jessica saw the advertisement for teachers in Africa in a newspaper.
A Right   B Wrong   C Doesn't say
_____

3 Jessica was a teacher in Tanzania for 2 years.
A Right   B Wrong   C Doesn't say
_____

4 When Jessica was in Africa, she visited Uganda, Ethiopia and Zambia.
A Right   B Wrong   C Doesn't say
_____

5 Jessica learnt how to speak the language in Tanzania.
A Right   B Wrong   C Doesn't say
_____

6 Jessica loves her job because she meets people from different countries.
A Right   B Wrong   C Doesn't say
_____

Part 4 第四部分

Complete the letter. Write **one** word for each space.
完成此信。在每个空格填上一词。

Dear Dan,

I arrived ▶ ___in___ Australia two weeks ago and I am having a fantastic time! The people here ¹_____ very friendly. It is very hot and ²_____ are many things to do. I was in Sydney for one week. I saw Sydney Opera House and the Botanical Gardens. Sydney ³_____ a beautiful and exciting city. Everyone here does lots of sport. People run in the parks and swim or surf ⁴_____ the sea.

Tomorrow I ⁵_____ going to visit a little island. I will go by boat with some other people. We will ⁶_____ in a tent on the beach. I hope we catch some fish for our ⁷_____!

I ⁸_____ write again soon.

Love Elizabeth

Numbers 数字

1 One or first? 用 one 还是 first?

He has **three** children.
他有三个孩子。

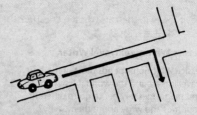

Take the **third** turning on the right.
在右边第三个转弯处拐进去。

A Write the missing numbers and words in this table. 在下表填上数目和文字。

1	one	_1st_	**first**
2	two	_____	**second**
3	three	_____	**third**
4	four	_____	**fourth**
5	five	**5th**	_____
6	six	6th	sixth
7	_____	7th	seventh
8	eight	**8th**	_____
9	nine	9th	ninth
10	ten	10th	tenth
11	eleven	11th	eleventh
12	twelve	**12th**	_twelfth_
13	thirteen	13th	thirteenth
14	_____	14th	fourteenth
15	fifteen	15th	fifteenth
16	sixteen	**16th**	_____
17	_____	17th	seventeenth
18	eighteen	18th	eighteenth
19	nineteen	19th	nineteenth
20	twenty	20th	twentieth
21	twenty-one	**21st**	_____
30	_____	30th	thirtieth
40	_____	40th	fortieth
50	fifty	50th	fiftieth
60	sixty	60th	sixtieth
70	seventy	70th	seventieth
80	eighty	**80th**	_____
90	ninety	90th	ninetieth
100	a/one hundred	_____	**hundredth**
101	_____	_____	**hundred and first**
200	two hundred	200th	two hundredth
_____	**a/one thousand**	**1 000th**	
_____	**a/one million**	1 000 000th	millionth

B One or first? Use the number at the end of each sentence to fill the gap, and write the number out in full. 用 one 还是 first？用句末提供的数字在空位填上数字的英文全写。

1 Their first two children were boys, but their ___third___ was a girl. (3)

2 'What number house do you live at?' 'At number ___twelve___.' (12)

3 I live on the _____ floor of that apartment building over there. (5)

4 We're planning a big party for our grandmother's _____ birthday. (60)

5 It's my father's birthday tomorrow. He's going to be _____. (49)

6 For the _____ time, please turn your music down! (100)

7 I've seen that film about _____ times, I think. (7)

8 They hold a market here on the _____ Sunday of every month. (2)

2 Large numbers 大数目

This is how we say large numbers. 大数目的读法：

267 *two hundred and sixty-seven*
4 302 *four thousand three hundred and two*

Write out the answers to the questions below in full. Practise saying them.
写出下列问题答案的全写，然后练习朗读。

1 There are seven days in a week. How many days are there in one year?

_____

2 There are ninety degrees (90°) in a right angle. How many degrees are there in a semicircle?

_____

3 What do you get if you subtract one hundred and fifty from ten thousand?

_____

3 Saying '0' 0 的读法

■ We usually say **nought** or **zero**.
通常读作 nought 或 zero：
nought point five (0.5)
three, two, one, zero!

■ In telephone numbers we usually say **o** (you say it like 'oh').
在电话号码中通常读作 o（读音像 oh）：
two nine oh three five

■ When we talk about temperature we usually use **zero**.
表示温度时通常读作 zero：
three degrees below zero

■ In scores of games like football, we say **nil**.
表示足球等运动的比分时读作 nil：
The score was two-nil.

4 Fractions and mathematical expressions
分数和数学表达法

A Where should these diagrams go in the box below? Write the numbers 1–7 next to the correct written fractions. 以下框中的图表达什么？把 1–7 写在正确的分数前面。

____ $1/2$ a half

____ $1/8$ a/one eighth

____ $1/3$ a/one third

____ $1/16$ a/one sixteenth

____ $1/4$ a/one quarter

____ $3/4$ three quarters

____ $1 2/5$ one and two fifths

B Here are the most common mathematical expressions.
以下是最常见的数学表达法：

Symbols 符号		We write: 写作	We say: 读作
.	point	3.2	*three point two*
+	plus	5 + 6	*five plus six*
–	minus	10 – 4	*ten minus four*
×	multiplied by **or** times	4 × 6	*four multiplied by six* **or** *four times six*
÷	divided by	4 ÷ 2	*four divided by two*
%	per cent	78%	*seventy-eight per cent*
=	equals	1 + 3 = 4	*one plus three equals four*

What are the answers to these sums?
这些算术题的答案是什么？

1 What is twenty divided by five?   _____

2 What is seventy-two plus thirteen?   _____

3 What is fifty per cent of three hundred?   _____

4 What is twelve minus four point two?   _____

5 What is six multiplied by nine?   _____

6 What is seventy-five per cent expressed as a fraction?   _____

Time and dates 时间和日期

1 What time is it? 几点了？

There are usually two ways of telling the time. Can you fill in the missing words below? 表达时间有两种常用的方式。你能填上所缺的文字吗？

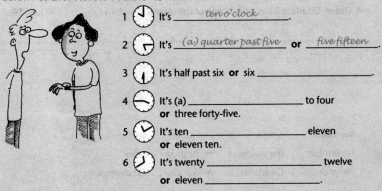

1 It's ___ten o'clock___.

2 It's ___(a) quarter past five___ or ___five fifteen___.

3 It's half past six or six _____.

4 It's (a) _____ to four
   or three forty-five.

5 It's ten _____ eleven
   or eleven ten.

6 It's twenty _____ twelve
   or eleven _____.

---

2 What's the date? 今天几号？

- There are different ways to **say** dates.
  日期有不同的读法：

April 2009

M	1	8	15	22	29
T	2	9	16	23	30
W	3	10	17	(24)	
T	4	11	18	25	
F	5	12	19	26	
S	6	13	20	27	
S	7	14	21	28	

the twenty-fourth of April, two thousand and nine

April the twenty-fourth, two thousand and nine

- We can **write** the date in any of these ways. 写日期可用以下方式：

British English 英式英语	**American English** 美式英语
24 April	April 24
24th April	April 24th
24/4/09	4/24/09

- We say years like this.
  年份用以下的方式读出：

  1706 *seventeen oh six*
  1800 *eighteen hundred*
  1998 *nineteen ninety-eight*
  2015 *twenty fifteen*

A Complete these sentences with the dates written out in full.
填上日期的全写，完成以下句子。

1 Today's date is _____.

2 My date of birth is _____.

B Match the events on the left with the correct date on the right, then practise reading the dates correctly. 将左边的事件与右边的日期配对，然后练习朗读日期。

1 Man landed on the moon on	2 June, 1953.
2 William Shakespeare was born on	August 6, 1991.
3 The first website appeared on	23rd April, 1564.
4 Queen Elizabeth II became Queen of the United Kingdom on	20 July, 1969.

3 Prepositions of time 时间介词

Can you add more to each column?
你能在每栏中填上更多的用语吗？

in	at	on	—
the morning	6 o'clock	2nd June	next week
September	the weekend	my birthday	today
summer	Christmas	Wednesday	this afternoon

Telephoning 打电话

1 Asking for and saying telephone numbers
询问和读出电话号码

Which **three** of the following are correct ways of asking for somebody's phone number?
下列询问电话号码的句子，哪三句正确？

- What's your phone?
- What's your number?
- What number are you?
- What's your phone number?
- What's your mobile?
- What's your mobile number?

Notice how we usually answer the question.
常见的回答有：

- My (phone) number is ...
  36920 three six nine two **oh**
- My mobile number is ...
  25844 two five eight **double four**

Now write your own phone number(s) out in full here. 填上你电话号码的（英文）全写：

_____

_____

2 Using the telephone 打电话

Choose the right word or phrase to complete the text below.
选择适当的用语来完成下文。

When you want to ¹ **make a phone call /** ~~do a phone call~~, you ² **pick up / pick out** the receiver and ³ **ring / dial** the number. The telephone ⁴ **sounds / rings** and the person you are phoning answers it. When you have finished speaking, you ⁵ **hang on / hang up**.

If the person you want to speak to is already ⁶ **at the phone / on the phone**, it is ⁷ **engaged / occupied**. If they are not at home, you can often ⁸ **take a message / leave a message**, asking them to ⁹ **talk you back / call you back** later.

3 Talking on the telephone 通电话

Put the sentences in the correct order. Write the numbers in the spaces.
给以下句子排序，将数字写在空格上。

A ___ Oh hello, Sally. It's John.
  _1_ Hello. 56767.
  ___ Sally speaking.
  ___ Hello. Is Sally there, please?

B ___ I'm sorry — he's out. Can I take a message?
  _1_ Good morning, Dr Lee's surgery.
  ___ Who's calling?
  ___ No, thank you. I'll call back later.
  ___ Hello. Can I speak to Dr Lee, please?
  ___ It's Mr White.

Words that go together 词语搭配

1 Prepositions 介词

Many words are followed by a preposition. This dictionary helps you learn which preposition follows a word, so that you can learn them together. 许多词语后接介词。本词典帮助你学习词语后面该用什么介词，让你整个搭配一并掌握。

about	for	on
at	in	with
by	of	

Choose prepositions from the box to complete the sentences. You can use each one more than once. 用框中的介词完成句子。介词可重复使用。

A Adjectives with prepositions 形容词接介词

1 She's very good ___at___ maths.

2 The room was full _____ people.

3 I don't think he's very interested _____ politics.

4 Are you excited _____ your birthday next week?

5 I'm tired _____ this game. Let's play something else.

6 Be careful _____ those plates — don't drop them!

7 She sleeps with the light on. She's afraid _____ the dark.

8 I'm worried _____ Tom. Do you think he'll be ok?

B Verbs with prepositions 动词接介词

1 I agree ___with___ you — I think this one is too expensive.

2 She sat down and asked _____ a cup of coffee.

3 He smiled _____ her and walked away.

4 Thank you _____ all your help, I really appreciate it.

5 I'm not sure when I'll arrive. It depends _____ the traffic.

6 I'll be ten minutes. Will you wait _____ me?

7 They are always arguing _____ money.

8 Does your little brother believe _____ Santa Claus?

2 Verb + noun 动词 + 名词

A Match the verbs in column A with a noun in column B. 将 A 栏中的动词与 B 栏中的名词配对。

A	B
take	your exams
give	a cold
make	a lie
do	a mess
say	your homework
tell	goodbye
pass	somebody a call
catch	a photo

B Now use the same verbs and nouns to complete these sentences. Don't forget to put the verb into the correct tense! 用配对好的动词和名词完成以下句子。别忘了动词使用正确时态!

1 I have to go now, but I'll _give you a call_ later.

2 What will you do if you don't _____?

3 Smile at the camera, I want to _____.

4 I was surprised when he left without _____.

5 Stop splashing the water, you're _____.

6 I think she _____. She's never been to New York.

7 Mum doesn't let me watch TV until I've _____.

8 You keep sneezing — have you _____?

3 Finding information in the dictionary 在本词典查找信息

You will find useful information on words that go together in this dictionary. Look at the entries for 'appetite' and 'bedside' below. 在本词典中可以找到有关词语搭配的有用信息。看下面 appetite 和 bedside 的条目:

appetite /'æpɪtaɪt/ *noun* 名词
the feeling that you want to eat 食欲;
胃口: *Swimming always **gives me an appetite*** (= makes me hungry). 我一游泳就容易饿。

→ appetite
The words '**give** (somebody) **an appetite**' are printed in darker letters, which means that these words often go together.
* give (somebody) an appetite 用黑体列出，表示这些词经常连用。

bedside /'bedsaɪd/ *noun* 名词 (*no plural* 不用复数形式)
the area that is next to a bed 床边: *She sat at his bedside all night long.* 她整夜守候在他的床边。 ◇ *A book lay open on the **bedside table**.* 床头柜上摊放着一本书。

→ bedside
When the word 'bedside' is used, it is often in the phrase '**bedside table**'.
The example sentence shows you this.
* bedside 常用以构成短语 bedside table，例句说明了这一点。

A Look up these words in the dictionary. What phrases are marked in the example sentences to show that these words often go together? The first one has been done for you. 在本词典中查找这些词语。示例中标示了哪些短语，表示这些词经常连用？第一题已经完成。

answer (*noun*)	*answer to (something)*
	no answer
bed	
bread	
computer	
diet	
hardly	
holiday	
morning	

B Now use some of the phrases that you found in the last exercise to complete the sentences. 从上一练习选出合适的短语完成句子。

1 I tried calling her mobile phone but there was
   no answer.

2 It's eleven o'clock and I'm really tired. I think I'll
   _____.

3 Mavis went to the shop to buy _____.

4 Are you going to write the letter by hand or are you going to do it _____?

5 Rosa's only twelve, I think she's too young to
   _____.

6 I _____ watch TV. I prefer to listen to the radio or read a book.

7 Where shall we go _____ this year?

8 He starts work at 10.30 _____ and finishes at 9.30 at night.

Education 教育

1 School Subjects 学校科目

A There are eleven school subjects hidden in the grid below. You can read them across [→] or down [↓]. Two have been found for you. Can you find the other **nine**?
下列格子中隐藏了十一门学校科目，格子可以横看或竖看。其中有两门已经标出，你能找出其余九门学科吗？

```
I B W A M U B E J Y N E
M A T H E M A T I C S N
U R E L V P R A C H T G
S H S P O R T G I E T L
I B L V D K E B O M O I
C I S H E P H Y S I C S
W O D I M U N Q U S A H
O L R S F A D O S T E A
H O C T L E R T C R A F
R G E O G R A P H Y P Y
B Y H R O A M X N U K E
G P S Y H I A F T D U Z
```

B Complete the following sentences so that they are true for you.
根据自己的情况完成下列句子。

■ My favourite subject at school is/was _____.

■ I am/was not very good at _____.

■ I will always remember my _____ teacher because _____.

2 The Education System 教育制度

A Here are the types of school in Britain and the US which children go to at different ages. Put the two sets into the correct order, starting with the one for the youngest children. 下表列出英国和美国不同年龄的学生所上学校的类型。将两组学校按就读年龄从小到大排序。

In Britain ... 在英国	In the US ... 在美国
___ secondary school	___ elementary school
_1_ nursery school	___ high school
___ college/university	_4_ college/university
___ primary school	___ nursery school

B Use the words or phrases from the box above each paragraph to complete the information about the education system in Britain and the US.
以下是有关英美教育制度的信息。用每段上面框中的词语填空。

terms   private school   attend

In Britain, children must ¹_____ school between the ages of five and sixteen. Most schools are free, but some parents choose to send their children to a ²_____, which they pay for. The school year is divided into three ³_____.

GCSE   A level   pupils

When they are eleven, ⁴_____ move from primary to secondary school. At the age of sixteen everyone must take ⁵_____ (General Certificate of Secondary Education) exams. After this, they can take ⁶_____ (Advanced level) exams when they are eighteen.

graduate   degree   university

Students who get good results in their A levels go to ⁷_____, usually for three or four years. If they pass their exams, students ⁸_____ with a ⁹_____ in the subject they have studied.

public schools   semesters   grades

In the US, school is compulsory between the ages of six and sixteen. Schools that are free are called ¹⁰_____. All through the year, teachers give the students ¹¹_____ showing how well they have done in tests, homework and classroom work. The school year is divided into two ¹²_____.

Health 健康

1 How are you? 你好吗?

A Which of the following are ways of asking about somebody's health?
以下哪些是询问他人健康状况的说法?

- [ ] How are you?
- [ ] How are your feelings?
- [ ] How are you feeling?
- [ ] How do you feel?
- [ ] What do you feel?

B Here are some answers to the questions. Choose a column for each answer. The first one has been done for you.
以下是一些回答。将这些回答填入对应的栏中。第一题已经完成。

I'm sick.   I'm ill.
I'm ok.   I'm fine.
I feel great.   I'm not very well.
I feel awful.   I'm not too bad, thanks.
Very well, thank you.

☺	😐	☹
	I'm not too bad, thanks.	

2 What's the matter? 你怎么了?

A If you think somebody is not well, you can ask 'What's the matter?'. You can answer this question with one of the sentences below. Fill in the gap with a part of the body. 若感到某人身体不舒服,可以问 What's the matter?。以下是其中一些回答。在空位填上表示身体部位的词语。

- My _____ hurts.
- My _____ aches.
- I've got a pain in my _____.

B There are special words for pain in some parts of the body. Can you work out what they are from the example given? 某些身体部位的疼痛会用特定的词。你能从下列例子中想出是什么词吗?

▶ She's got a pain in her tooth.
  She's got toothache

1 My head hurts.
  I've got a _____.

2 My back ached.
  I had _____.

3 His ear hurts.
  He's got _____.

4 She had a pain in her stomach.
  She had _____.

Photocopiable © Oxford University Press

3 Going to the doctor's 看医生

Use these words and phrases to complete the paragraph. 用以下词语填空。

temperature
~~make an appointment~~
examine
symptoms
get better
medicine
write a prescription

When you are ill, the best thing to do is **1** _make an appointment_ to see a doctor. He or she will ask you to explain your **2**_____, for example if you have any aches or pains. Your doctor might **3**_____ you, or take your **4**_____. If you need treatment, the doctor will **5**_____ so that you can get some **6**_____. If you do what the doctor says, you should **7**_____ soon.

Writing letters and emails 写信和写电邮

1 A formal letter 正式信函

54 North Street
Northampton
NN9 5DB

23 March 2009

**your address
(but not your name)**
发信人地址
（不写姓名）

**the name or title
of the person
you are writing
to, and their
address** 收信人
姓名或头衔和
地址

Sarah Jackson
Rainbow Fashions
42 High Street
Northampton
NN3 4HY

the date 日期

Dear Ms Jackson

I am writing in response to your advertisement for a
full-time sales assistant, and I enclose my CV in the
hope that you will consider me for the position.

As you can see from my CV, I worked for two years at
Stanwick's department store in London, where I was
an assistant manager. I would be happy to attend an
interview at any time.

I look forward to hearing from you.

Yours sincerely

your signature
发信人签名

Victoria Dawson

Victoria Dawson

your full name
发信人全名

2 An informal letter 非正式信函

*54 North Street
Northampton
NN9 5DB*

23/3/09

**your address
(but not your name)**
发信人地址
（不写姓名）

Dear Jason,

*Just a quick note to thank you for
dinner in Oxford last Saturday. It was
great to see you, and I'm glad you're
enjoying your course.*

the date 日期

*On Sunday morning, Alan and I went
to the Science Museum, and then we
went for a long walk along the river.
We had a lovely time and we didn't
want to come home!*

Hope to see you soon.

Love Vicky

*PS Good luck with your exams next
month.*

You can also end with
亦可用下列结束语：

- Love from
- Lots of love
- Best wishes
- Yours

3 Formal beginnings and endings 正式的开头和结尾

Formal or informal? 正式还是非正式?

A Which of the following can be used to begin and end **formal** letters? Mark each with ✓ or ✗. 以下哪些用语可用于正式信函的开头和结尾? 请用 ✓ 或 ✗ 表示。

___ Dear Sir		___ Yours faithfully	
___ Dear Madam		✓ Yours sincerely	
___ Dear Sir or Madam		___ Your faithful	
✗ Dear Miss		___ Yours hopefully	
___ Dear Ms Jackson		___ Yours truly	

Formal or informal? 正式还是非正式?

B Which of each pair of phrases is suitable for a **formal** letter and which for an **informal** letter? Write F for 'formal' or I for 'informal'. The first one has been done for you. 右面各对表达之中，哪个适用于正式信函，哪个适用于非正式信函? 正式的写上 F，非正式的则写上 I。第一题已经完成。

_I_ Lots of love, Vicky	_F_ Yours faithfully, Victoria Dawson
___ Dear Mr Khan	___ Dear Ali
___ I enclose a cheque for …	___ Here's some money for …
___ I'm writing to you …	___ I am writing to you …
___ Could you …?	___ I would be grateful if you could …
___ Write back soon!	___ I look forward to hearing from you.

---

4 Emails 电邮

Emails are often informal. Fill in the gaps in the email below with the informal phrases from the box. 电邮一般为非正式的。用框中的非正式用语在电邮中填空。

Must go
Hi Carlos
keep in touch
what's more
Bye for now
to hear from you

Saying an email address 电邮地址的读法
You say this email address as 'Vicky **dot** Dawson **at** freemail **dot** com'. 这个电邮地址读作 Vicky dot Dawson at freemail dot com。

From: Vicky.Dawson@freemail.com
Sent: 23 March 2009 19:05
To: Carlos.Sanchez43@youserve.com
Subject: Re: Greetings from Thailand!

¹ *Hi Carlos*

It was great ² _____. Thailand sounds fantastic, especially the beaches. I wish I was there too, because the weather's awful here and I'm worn out! I've got college most days and, ³ _____, I'm working in the café four evenings a week. It's hard work!

⁴ _____, I've got an essay to write, but ⁵ _____.

⁶ _____

Vicky x   :-)

Filling in forms 填写表格

1 Different types of form 不同的表格

A We often need to fill in forms. Match each verb on the left with the correct information on the right to find out some reasons why. 我们经常需要填写表格。将左边的动词与右边的信息配对，找出一些填写表格的原因？

1 to **order** ___ A a job

2 to **apply** for ___ B a member of a club

3 to **become** ___ C something from website or a catalogue

B These forms are called different names. Can you complete the words? The missing letters are in the boxes. 以下表格名称各异。你能使用框中的字母补全表格的名称吗？

lpptcaoii

1 an **a**__ __ __ __ __ __ __ __ __ **n** form

e d r

2 an **o** __ __ __ **r** form

m h b r e e i s

3 a **m** __ __ __ __ __ __ __ __ **p** form

2 Understanding forms 理解表格的内容

Here are some words and phrases that you will see on forms. Fill in the gaps to find out what they mean. 以下词语常见于表格之中。填空以了解各词语的含义。

nationality	last name	password
sign	in capitals	initials
signature	~~first name~~	tick

1 My name is Sara Esposito. Sara is my
   first name, and Esposito is my
   _____. My _____ are SE.

2 If you are born in Britain your
   _____ is British.

3 If you write something _____,
   you use BIG LETTERS LIKE THIS.

4 A _____ is a secret word that
   only you should know.

5 A sign like this ✓ is called a _____.

6 At the end of a form you usually have
   to _____ your name. This is
   called your _____.

3 Filling in a form 填写表格

You see this notice at your college. Read it and fill in the form. 你在校园看到这则布告。阅读布告并填写表格。

Make new friends and improve your English!

Fill in this form and we will find you an English speaker who is learning your language.

You can then meet up for a language exchange.

Language exchange application

First name _____   Last name _____

Nationality _____   Age _____

Daytime telephone number _____

Email address _____

What is your first language? _____

How long have you been learning English? _____

What are your reasons for learning English?
(Write 10–20 words.)

_____

What area of English would you most like to practise?
Please tick the one(s) that are important for you.

☐ speaking   ☐ listening   ☐ reading

☐ grammar   ☐ writing   ☐ pronunciation

Signature _____   Date _____

hair around their head and neck (called a **mane**). 狮; 狮子

lip ⊶ /lɪp/ *noun* 名词
one of the two soft red parts above and below your mouth 嘴唇: *to kiss somebody on the lips* 吻某人的嘴唇
⊃ Look at Picture Dictionary page **P4**. 见彩页 P4。

lipstick 口红

lipstick /'lɪpstɪk/ *noun* 名词 (*no plural* 不用复数形式)
colour that women sometimes put on their lips 口红; 唇膏: *She put on some lipstick.* 她涂了点口红。

liquid ⊶ /'lɪkwɪd/ *noun* 名词
anything that is not a solid or a gas. Water, oil and milk are **liquids**. 液体
▶ **liquid** *adjective* 形容词: *liquid soap* 洗手液

liquorice (*British* 英式英语) (*American* 美式英语 **licorice**) /'lɪkərɪʃ/ *noun* 名词
a black substance that comes from a plant and is used in some sweets 甘草 (用于制作糖果)

liquor store /'lɪkə stɔ:(r)/ *noun* 名词
American English for OFF-LICENCE 美式英语，即 off-licence

list¹ ⊶ /lɪst/ *noun* 名词
a lot of names or other things that you write or say, one after another 名单; 清单: *a shopping list* (= of things that you must buy) 购物单

list² ⊶ /lɪst/ *verb* 动词 (lists, listing, listed)
to write or say things in a list 列举; 列出清单: *Please list the items in alphabetical order.* 请把各项目按字母顺序列出来。

listen ⊶ /'lɪsn/ *verb* 动词 (listens, listening, listened /'lɪsnd/)

to hear something when you are trying to hear it 听; 倾听: *I was **listening to** the radio.* 我当时在听收音机。◇ *Listen! I want to tell you something.* 听着! 我有事情要告诉你。⊃ Look at the note at **hear**. 见 hear 条的注释。

lit *form of* LIGHT³ * light³ 的不同形式

liter *American English for* LITRE 美式英语，即 litre

literature ⊶ /'lɪtrətʃə(r)/ *noun* 名词 (*no plural* 不用复数形式)
books, plays and poetry 文学: *He is studying English literature.* 他在修读英国文学。

litre ⊶ (*British* 英式英语) (*American* 美式英语 **liter**) /'li:tə(r)/ *noun* 名词 (*abbr.* 缩略式 l)
a measure of liquid 升 (液量单位): *three litres of water* 三升水 ◇ *20 l* * 20 升

litter¹ /'lɪtə(r)/ *noun* 名词
1 (*no plural* 不用复数形式) pieces of paper and other rubbish that people leave in a public place (公共场所乱扔的) 垃圾，废弃物: *The park was full of litter after the concert.* 演唱会过后，公园里到处都是垃圾。
2 (*plural* 复数形式 litters) all the baby animals that are born to the same mother at the same time (动物一胎所生的) 一窝幼崽: *Our dog had a litter of six puppies.* 我们家的狗一窝生了六只小狗。

litter² /'lɪtə(r)/ *verb* 动词 (litters, littering, littered /'lɪtəd/)
to be or to make something untidy with **litter** 使凌乱; 乱扔 (垃圾): *My desk was littered with papers.* 我的书桌上乱堆着文件。

litter bin /'lɪtə bɪn/ (*British* 英式英语) (*American* 美式英语 **trash can**) *noun* 名词
a container to put rubbish in, in the street or a public building (街道上或公共建筑物内的) 垃圾箱，废物箱

little¹ ⊶ /'lɪtl/ *adjective* 形容词
1 not big 小的 ⊃ SAME MEANING **small** 同义词为 small: *a little table* 小桌子
2 young 年幼的; 幼小的: *a little girl* 小女孩 ◇ *my little* (= younger) *brother* 我弟弟
3 (used about distance or time) short (距离) 近的; (时间) 短暂的: *Do you mind waiting a little while?* 你稍微等一会儿好吗?

little² ⊶ /'lɪtl/ *pronoun, adjective* 代词，形容词
not much 不多的; 很少的: *I did very*

little today. 我今天没干多少事。◇ *We have very little money.* 我们钱很少。

a little a small amount of something 少量；少许；一点： *I've got some ice cream. Would you like a little?* 我有些冰激凌。你想来一点吗？ ◇ *I speak a little French.* 我会说一点法语。

little by little slowly 慢慢地；逐渐地： *Little by little she started to feel better.* 她一点一点地好起来了。

little³ 0ᵥ /ˈlɪtl/ ***adverb*** 副词
not much 不多；稍许： *I'm tired – I slept very little last night.* 我累了，昨晚睡得很少。

a little rather; to a small degree 有点；稍微 ⊃ SAME MEANING **a bit** 同义词为 a bit： *This skirt is a little too short for me.* 这条裙子我穿有点太短了。

live¹ 0ᵥ /lɪv/ ***verb*** 动词 (lives, living, lived /lɪvd/)
1 to have your home somewhere 住；居住： *Where do you live?* 你住在哪里？ ◇ *He still lives with his parents.* 他仍与父母一起住。
2 to be or stay alive 生存；活着： *You can't live without water.* 没有水就不能生存。 ◇ *He lived to the age of 93.* 他活到了 93 岁。
3 to spend your life in a certain way （以某种方式）生活，过活： *They live a quiet life in the country.* 他们在乡下过着宁静的生活。

live on something
1 to eat something as your only food 以食…为生： *Cows live on grass.* 牛靠吃草维生。
2 to have enough money to buy what you need to live 靠（…钱）生活： *They live on £70 a week.* 他们每周靠 70 英镑维持生计。

live² /laɪv/ ***adjective*** 形容词
1 not dead 活的： *Have you ever touched a real live snake?* 你摸过活蛇吗？
2 If a radio or television programme is **live**, you see or hear it at the same time as it happens. 现场直播的；实况转播的： *The match is going out live on TV.* 这场比赛将在电视上直播。
3 with electricity passing through it 通电的；带电的： *Don't touch that wire – it's live!* 不要碰那根电线——有电！

lively /ˈlaɪvli/ ***adjective*** 形容词 (livelier, liveliest)
full of life; always moving or doing things 生气勃勃的；活跃的： *The children are very lively.* 孩子们精力非常充沛。

liver /ˈlɪvə(r)/ ***noun*** 名词
1 (*plural* 复数形式 livers) the part inside your body that cleans the blood 肝脏
2 (*no plural* 不用复数形式) the **liver** of an animal that you can cook and eat as food （动物供食用的）肝

lives *plural of* LIFE * life 的复数形式

living¹ 0ᵥ /ˈlɪvɪŋ/ ***adjective*** 形容词
alive; not dead 活的；活着的： *Some people say he is the greatest living writer.* 有人说他是在世的最伟大作家。

living² /ˈlɪvɪŋ/ ***noun*** 名词
1 money to buy the things you need in life 生计；谋生： ***How did he earn a living?*** 他如何谋生？
2 the way that you live 生活方式： ***The cost of living*** *has risen in recent years.* 生活费用在最近几年上涨了。

living room /ˈlɪvɪŋ ruːm/ (*British also* 英式英语亦作 sitting room) ***noun*** 名词
a room in a house where people sit together and watch television or talk, for example 起居室；客厅 ⊃ SAME MEANING **lounge** 同义词为 lounge ⊃ Look at Picture Dictionary page **P10**. 见彩页 P10。

lizard 蜥蜴

lizard /ˈlɪzəd/ ***noun*** 名词
a small animal that has four legs, a long tail and rough skin 蜥蜴

load¹ 0ᵥ /ləʊd/ ***noun*** 名词
1 something that is carried 负载；负荷： *The truck brought another load of wood.* 卡车运来另一车木头。
2 loads (*plural* 用复数形式) (*informal* 非正式) a lot 大量；许多： *We've got **loads** of time.* 我们有很多时间。

load² 0ᵥ /ləʊd/ ***verb*** 动词 (loads, loading, loaded)
1 to put things in or on something, for example a car or a ship 装上；给…装货： *Two men loaded the furniture into the van.* 两个男人把家具装上了运货车。 ◇ *They're loading the plane now.* 他们正在往飞机上

装货。 ⇒ OPPOSITE **unload** 反义词为 unload

2 to put bullets in a gun or film in a camera 装子弹（或胶卷）

loaf /ləʊf/ *noun* 名词 (*plural* 复数形式 **loaves** /ləʊvz/)
bread that has been baked in one piece 一条（面包）: *a loaf of bread* 一条面包 ⇒ Look at the picture at **bread**. 见 bread 的插图。

loan¹ ☮ /ləʊn/ *noun* 名词
money that somebody lends you 借款; 贷款: *to take out a bank loan* 取得银行贷款

loan² /ləʊn/ *verb* 动词 (**loans**, **loaning**, **loaned** /ləʊnd/)
to give something to somebody for a period of time 借出; 借给 ⇒ SAME MEANING **lend** 同义词为 lend: *A friend loaned me $1 000.* 有个朋友借给我 1 000 元。

loathe /ləʊð/ *verb* 动词 (**loathes**, **loathing**, **loathed** /ləʊðd/)
to hate somebody or something 厌恶; 讨厌: *I loathe modern art.* 我讨厌现代艺术。 ⇒ OPPOSITE **love** 反义词为 love

loaves *plural of* LOAF * loaf 的复数形式

lobby /ˈlɒbi/ *noun* 名词 (*plural* 复数形式 **lobbies**)
an area just inside a big building, where people can meet and wait （大型建筑物的）门厅，大厅: *a hotel lobby* 酒店大堂

lobster 龙虾

lobster /ˈlɒbstə(r)/ *noun* 名词
a large sea animal with a hard shell and eight legs. Its shell is black but it turns red when it is cooked. 龙虾

local ☮ /ˈləʊkl/ *adjective* 形容词
of a place near you 当地的; 本地的; 地方的: *Her children go to the local school.* 她的孩子在当地学校上学。 ◇ *a local newspaper* 地方报纸 ◇ *local government* 当地政府

▸ **locally** /ˈləʊkəli/ *adverb* 副词: *Do you work locally?* 你在本地上班吗?

located /ləʊˈkeɪtɪd/ *adjective* 形容词
in a place 位于: *The factory is located near Glasgow.* 这家工厂位于格拉斯哥附近。

location /ləʊˈkeɪʃn/ *noun* 名词
a place 地点; 位置: *The house is in a quiet location on top of a hill.* 房子坐落在幽静的山顶上。

lock¹ ☮ /lɒk/ *verb* 动词 (**locks**, **locking**, **locked** /lɒkt/)
to close something with a key 锁上: *Don't forget to lock the door when you leave.* 走的时候别忘了锁门。 ⇒ OPPOSITE **unlock** 反义词为 unlock

lock something away to put something in a place that you close with a key 把…锁起来: *The paintings are locked away at night.* 这些油画晚上都要锁起来。

lock somebody in to lock a door so that somebody cannot get out 把某人锁在里面: *The prisoners are locked in.* 囚犯都锁进牢房了。

lock somebody out to lock a door so that somebody cannot get in 把某人锁在门外

lock up to lock all the doors and windows of a building 锁好门窗: *Make sure you lock up before you leave.* 离开前一定要锁好门窗。

lock² ☮ /lɒk/ *noun* 名词
a metal thing that keeps a door, gate or box closed so that you need a key to open it again 锁: *I heard the key turn in the lock.* 我听见钥匙在锁里转动。 ⇒ Look at the picture at **key¹**. 见 key¹ 的插图。

locker /ˈlɒkə(r)/ *noun* 名词
a small cupboard with a lock for keeping things in, for example in a school or at a sports centre （学校、体育馆等的）存物柜，寄物柜

locust /ˈləʊkəst/ *noun* 名词
a large insect that lives in hot countries and flies in very large groups, eating all the plants 蝗虫（热带地区成大群飞去吃掉农作物的大型昆虫）

lodge /lɒdʒ/ *verb* 动词 (**lodges**, **lodging**, **lodged** /lɒdʒd/)
to pay to live in a room in another person's house （付钱）寄宿，寄居: *I lodged with a family when I was studying abroad.* 我在国外读书的时候，寄宿在一户人家里。

A B C D E F G H I J K L M N O P Q R S T U V W X Y Z

A B C D E F G H I J K L M N O P Q R S T U V W X Y Z

▸ **lodger** /ˈlɒdʒə(r)/ ***noun*** 名词 a person who pays to live in a room in another person's house 房客；租房人

loft /lɒft/ ***noun*** 名词
the room or space under the roof of a house 阁楼；顶楼 ➲ SAME MEANING **attic** 同义词为 attic: *My old books are in a box in the loft.* 我的旧书放在阁楼的一个箱子里。 ➲ Look at Picture Dictionary page **P10**. 见彩页 P10。

log 原木

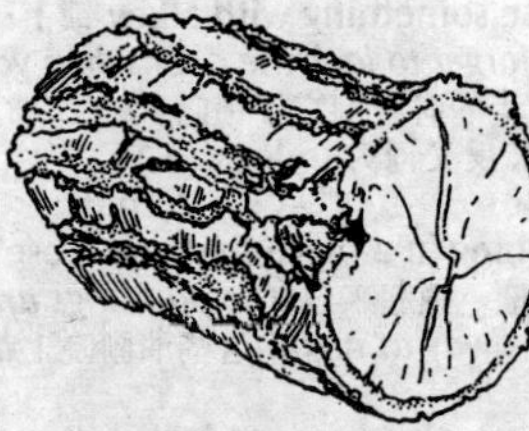

log¹ /lɒg/ ***noun*** 名词
a thick round piece of wood from a tree 原木： *Put another log on the fire.* 往火里再添块木头。

log² /lɒg/ ***verb*** 动词 (**logs**, **logging**, **logged** /lɒgd/)
to keep an official record of things that happen （做正式）记录 ➲ SAME MEANING **record** 同义词为 record: *to log somebody's phone calls* 记录某人的通话
log in, **log on** to type your name, etc. so that you can start using a computer 登录，注册（电脑）： *You need a password to log on.* 登录需要密码。
log off, **log out** to stop using a computer 退出，注销（电脑）： *Make sure you log out before you switch off the computer.* 确保注销后再关电脑。

logical /ˈlɒdʒɪkl/ ***adjective*** 形容词
seeming natural or sensible 合乎逻辑的；合乎情理的： *There is only one logical conclusion.* 只有一个合乎情理的结论。

logo /ˈləʊgəʊ/ ***noun*** 名词 (*plural* 复数形式 **logos**)
a picture or a design that a company or an organization uses as its special sign （公司或组织的）标识，标志： *You will find the company logo on all our products.* 我们所有的产品都有公司的标识。

lollipop /ˈlɒlipɒp/ (*British informal* 英式英语非正式亦作 **lolly** /ˈlɒli/) (*plural* 复数形式 **lollies**) ***noun*** 名词
a big sweet on a stick 棒棒糖 ➲ Look also at **ice lolly**. 亦见 ice lolly。

lonely 0‑ /ˈləʊnli/ ***adjective*** 形容词 (**lonelier**, **loneliest**)
1 unhappy because you are not with other people 孤独的；寂寞的： *She felt very lonely when she first went to live in the city.* 她刚到城里生活的时候感到非常寂寞。
2 far from other places 偏僻的： *a lonely house in the hills* 山中孤零零的房子
➲ Look at **alone**. 见 alone。
▸ **loneliness** /ˈləʊnlinəs/ ***noun*** 名词 (*no plural* 不用复数形式)

long¹ 0‑ /lɒŋ/ ***adjective*** 形容词 (**longer** /ˈlɒŋgə(r)/, **longest** /ˈlɒŋgɪst/)
1 far from one end to the other 长的： *Which is the longest river in the world?* 世界上最长的河是哪一条？ ◇ *She has long black hair.* 她留着乌黑的长发。 ◇ *Tokyo is a long way from London.* 东京与伦敦相距甚远。 ➲ OPPOSITE **short** 反义词为 short ➲ Look at the note at **far**. 见 far 条的注释。
2 You use **long** to ask or talk about how far something is from one end to the other. （询问或谈及长度或距离）： *How long is the table?* 这张桌子有多长？ ◇ *The wall is 5 m long.* 这堵墙 5 米长。 ➲ The noun is **length**. 名词为 length。
3 continuing for a lot of time 长时间的；长期的： *a long film* 放映时间长的电影 ◇ *He's lived here **for a long time**.* 他在这里住了很长时间。 ➲ OPPOSITE **short** 反义词为 short
4 You use **long** to ask or talk about the time from the beginning to the end of something. （询问或谈及时间）： *How long is the lesson?* 这节课时间有多长？

long² 0‑ /lɒŋ/ ***adverb*** 副词 (**longer** /ˈlɒŋgə(r)/, **longest** /ˈlɒŋgɪst/)
for a lot of time 长时间地；长期地： *I can't stay long.* 我不能久留。 ◇ *How long have you been waiting?* 你等了多久了？ ◇ *She moved to the city **long after** her children were born.* 在孩子出生很久以后她才搬进城。 ◇ *My grandfather died **long before** I was born.* 我祖父在我出生很久之前就去世了。
as long as, **so long as** only if 只要： *You can borrow the book as long as you promise not to lose it.* 只要你保证不弄丢这本书，我就把它借给你。
for long for a lot of time 长时间地；长期地： *She went shopping but she was not out for long.* 她买东西去了，但刚出去不久。

long ago many years in the past 很久以前: *Long ago there were no cars.* 很久以前没有汽车。

no longer, not any longer not now; not as before 不再: *She doesn't live here any longer.* 她不再住这儿了。

long³ /lɒŋ/ *verb* 动词 (longs, longing, longed /lɒŋd/)

to want something very much, especially if this does not seem likely 渴望（尤指不太可能得到的事物）: *I long to see my family again.* 我很想再见到我的家人。◇ *She's longing for a letter from her boyfriend.* 她一直盼望着男友的来信。

long-distance /ˌlɒŋ ˈdɪstəns/ *adjective* 形容词

travelling or communicating between places that are far from each other（行程或通讯）长途的，长距离的: *a long-distance phone call* 长途电话

long-haul /ˈlɒŋ hɔːl/ *adjective* 形容词

travelling between places that are a long way from each other 长途的；远距离的: *a long-haul flight* (= a journey on an airplane) 远程航班

longing /ˈlɒŋɪŋ/ *noun* 名词

a strong feeling of wanting something（对…的）渴望，热望 ⊃ SAME MEANING **desire** 同义词为 desire: *a longing for peace* 对和平的渴望

longitude /ˈlɒŋɡɪtjuːd/ *noun* 名词 (no plural 不用复数形式) (abbr. 缩略式 long.)

the distance of a place east or west of a line from the North Pole to the South Pole that passes through Greenwich in London **Longitude** is measured in degrees. 经度 ⊃ Look at **latitude**. 见 latitude。⊃ Look at the picture at **earth**. 见 earth 的插图。

long jump /ˈlɒŋ dʒʌmp/ *noun* 名词 (no plural 不用复数形式)

a sport where you try to jump as far as you can 跳远

loo /luː/ *noun* 名词 (plural 复数形式 loos) (British 英式英语) (informal 非正式)

toilet 厕所；洗手间: *I need to go to the loo.* 我得上厕所。⊃ Look at the note at **toilet**. 见 toilet 条的注释。

look¹ 0— /lʊk/ *verb* 动词 (looks, looking, looked /lʊkt/)

1 to turn your eyes towards somebody or something and try to see them 看；瞧: *Look at this picture.* 看看这幅画。◇ *You should look both ways before you cross the road.* 过马路前要左右张望。⊃ Look at the note at **see**. 见 see 条的注释。

2 to seem to be; to appear 看上去；似乎；显得: *You look tired.* 你看起来累了。◇ *It looks as if it's going to rain.* 看来好像要下雨。

3 You say **look** to make somebody listen to you. （引起注意）喂: *Look, I know you're busy, but I need your help.* 喂，我知道你很忙，但我需要你的帮助。

look after somebody or 或 **something** to take care of somebody or something 照料；照看: *Can you look after my cat when I'm on holiday?* 我度假的时候，你能帮我照看一下我的猫吗？

look for somebody or 或 **something** to try to find somebody or something 寻找: *I'm looking for my keys.* 我在找我的钥匙。

look forward to something to wait for something with pleasure 盼望；期待: *I'm looking forward to seeing you again.* 我期待着再见到你。

look into something to study or try to find out something 仔细研究；调查: *We will look into the problem.* 我们会认真研究这个问题。

look like somebody or 或 **something**

1 to seem to be something 好像；似乎: *That looks like a good film.* 那部电影似乎不错。

2 words that you use to ask about somebody's appearance（询问外表）: *'What does he look like?' 'He's tall with dark hair.'* "他长什么样子？""他个子高，头发乌黑。"

3 to have the same appearance as somebody or something 长得像；与…外表相似: *She looks like her mother.* 她长得像她母亲。

look out! be careful 小心；当心: *Look out! There's a car coming!* 小心！有车来了！

look out for somebody or 或 **something** to pay attention and try to see or find somebody or something 当心；留神注意: *Look out for thieves!* 提防小偷！

look round something to visit a place 参观；游览: *We looked round the museum.* 我们参观了博物馆。

look something up to try to find information in a book （在书中）查找，查阅: *I looked the word up in my dictionary.* 我在词典里查了这个词。

look² 0— /lʊk/ *noun* 名词

1 turning your eyes towards somebody or something; looking 看；瞧: *Have a look at this article.* 看一下这篇文章。◇ *Do you* *want to take a look around?* 你想四处看看吗?

2 trying to find somebody or something 寻找: *I've had a look for your pen, but I can't find it.* 我找过你的笔，可是没找到。

3 the way somebody or something seems 样子; 外观; 外表: *I don't like the look of this weather. I think it's going to rain.* 我不喜欢这样的天气。我看要下雨了。

4 looks(*plural* 用复数形式) a person's appearance 相貌; 容貌: *He has his father's good looks.* 他相貌英俊随他父亲。

loom/luːm/ *noun* 名词
a machine that is used for making cloth by passing pieces of thread across and under other pieces 织布机

loop 圈

loop/luːp/ *noun* 名词
a round shape made by something like string or rope 圈; 环

loose ⊶/luːs/ *adjective* 形容词 (looser, loosest)

> 🔍 SPELLING 拼写说明
> Remember! Don't confuse **loose** with **lose**, which is a verb. 记住: 不要混淆 loose 和动词 lose: *We mustn't lose this game.* 我们绝不能输掉这场比赛。

1 not tied or fixed 松开的; 未固定的: *The dog broke its chain and got loose.* 狗挣脱了链子跑了。 ◇ *One of his teeth is loose.* 他有颗牙松了。

2 not fitting closely 宽松的: *a loose white shirt* 宽松的白衬衫 ⊃ OPPOSITE **tight** 反义词为 tight

▸ **loosely**/luːsli/ *adverb* 副词: *The rope was tied loosely round a tree.* 绳子松松地系在树上。

loosen/luːsn/ *verb* 动词 (loosens, loosening, loosened/luːsnd/)
to become looser or to make something looser (使)变松, 松开: *Can you loosen this knot? It's too tight.* 你能解开这个结吗? 太紧了。 ⊃ OPPOSITE **tighten** 反义词为 tighten

lord/lɔːd/ *noun* 名词
1 Lord(in Britain) a man who has a high position in society (英国)大人, 阁下:

Lord Fraser 弗雷泽阁下 ⊃ Look at **Lady**. 见 **Lady**。

2 the Lord(no plural 不用复数形式) God or Jesus Christ 主; 上帝; 基督

lorry ⊶/lɒri/ *noun* 名词 (plural 复数形式 lorries) (British 英式英语) (American 美式英语 truck)
a big vehicle for carrying heavy things 卡车 ⊃ Look at Picture Dictionary page P1. 见彩页 P1。

lose ⊶/luːz/ *verb* 动词 (loses, losing, lost/lɒst/, has lost)
1 to not be able to find something 遗失; 丢失: *I can't open the door because I've lost my key.* 我丢了钥匙，所以开不了门。

2 to not have somebody or something that you had before 损失; 丧失; 失去: *I lost my job when the factory closed.* 工厂一倒闭我就失业了。

3 to not win 输掉: *Our team lost the match.* 我们队输掉了比赛。

loser/luːzə(r)/ *noun* 名词
a person who does not win a game, race or competition (比赛的)输者, 败方 ⊃ OPPOSITE **winner** 反义词为 winner

loss ⊶/lɒs/ *noun* 名词 (plural 复数形式 losses)
1 losing something 丧失; 遗失; 丢失: *Has she told the police about the loss of her car?* 她丢车的事报警了吗? ◇ *job losses* 失业

2 how much money a business loses 亏损: *The company made a loss of £5 million.* 这家公司亏损了 500 万英镑。 ⊃ OPPOSITE **profit** 反义词为 profit
at a loss If you are at a loss, you do not know what to do or say. 不知所措

lost¹ *form of* LOSE * lose 的不同形式

lost² ⊶/lɒst/ *adjective* 形容词
1 If you are **lost**, you do not know where you are. 迷路的; 迷失方向的: *I took the wrong road and now I'm lost.* 我走错了路, 现在迷路了。 ◇ *Take this map so you don't get lost!* 带上这张地图, 你就不会迷路了!

2 If something is **lost**, you cannot find it. 丢失的; 找不到的

lost property/lɒst 'prɒpəti/ *noun* 名词 (no plural 不用复数形式) (British 英式英语)
things that people have lost or left in a public place 失物: *I left my bag on the train, so I went to the lost property office at the station.* 我把包落在火车上, 于是去了车站的失物招领处。

lot¹ ⊶/lɒt/ *pronoun* 代词 a lot(also informal 非正式亦作 lots) very much; a large amount or number of things or people 大量；许多：*We ate a lot.* 我们吃了很多。

a lot of, **lots of** a large number or amount of things or people 大量；许多：*She's got a lot of friends.* 她有很多朋友。 ◇ *Lots of love from Jane* (= words at the end of a letter). 非常爱你的简（信的结尾）

lot² 0┅ /lɒt/ *adverb* 副词
a lot very much or often 很；非常；经常：*Your flat is a lot bigger than mine.* 你的公寓比我的大多了。◇ *I go to the cinema a lot.* 我经常去看电影。

lotion /ˈləʊʃn/ *noun* 名词
liquid that you put on your skin 护肤液；润肤乳：*suntan lotion* 防晒露

lottery /ˈlɒtəri/ *noun* 名词 (*plural* 复数形式 **lotteries**)
a game where you buy a ticket with numbers on it. You win money if your numbers are chosen. 抽彩给奖法

loud 0┅ /laʊd/ *adjective, adverb* 形容词，副词 (**louder**, **loudest**)
making a lot of noise 大声（的）；响亮（的）；喧闹（的）：*I couldn't hear what he said because the music was too loud.* 音乐太响了，我听不见他说的话。◇ *loud voices* 洪亮的嗓音 ◇ *Please speak a bit louder – I can't hear you.* 请说得大声一点，我听不到你说的话。 ⊃ OPPOSITE **quiet** 反义词为 quiet
out loud so that other people can hear it 大声地：*I read the story out loud.* 我朗读了那则故事。
▶ **loudly** /ˈlaʊdli/ *adverb* 副词：*She laughed loudly.* 她大声笑了起来。

loudspeaker /ˌlaʊdˈspiːkə(r)/ *noun* 名词
a piece of equipment that makes sounds or voices louder 扬声器；扩音器；喇叭：*Music was coming from the loudspeakers.* 音乐是从扩音器里传出来的。

lounge /laʊndʒ/ *noun* 名词
a room in a house where people sit together and watch television or talk, for example 起居室；客厅 ⊃ SAME MEANING **living room, sitting room** 同义词为 living room 和 sitting room

louse /laʊs/ *noun* 名词 (*plural* 复数形式 **lice** /laɪs/)
a small insect that lives on the bodies of people and animals 虱；虱子

lousy /ˈlaʊzi/ *adjective* 形容词 (**lousier**, **lousiest**) (*informal* 非正式)
very bad 极坏的；非常糟糕的 ⊃ SAME

MEANING **awful** 同义词为 awful：*The weather was lousy.* 天气糟透了。

lovable /ˈlʌvəbl/ *adjective* 形容词
easy to love 可爱的；讨人喜欢的：*a lovable little boy* 可爱的小男孩

love¹ 0┅ /lʌv/ *noun* 名词
1 (*no plural* 不用复数形式) the strong warm feeling you have when you like somebody or something very much 爱；喜爱；热爱：*Their love for each other was very strong.* 他们对彼此的爱非常强烈。
2 (*plural* 复数形式 **loves**) a person, a thing or an activity that you love 所爱的人（或事物、活动）：*Who was your first love?* 你的初恋是谁？
3 (*no plural* 不用复数形式) a word in the game of TENNIS that means zero（网球）零分：*The score is 15-love.* 比分是 15 比 0。

be in love with somebody to love somebody 与某人相恋：*He says he is in love with her and they are going to get married.* 他说他爱她，他们打算结婚。

fall in love with somebody to begin to love somebody 爱上某人：*He fell in love with Anna the first time they met.* 他对安娜一见钟情。

love, **love from** (*informal* 非正式) a way of ending a letter to somebody that you know well（信末结语）爱你的：*See you soon. Love, Peter.* 再见。爱你的彼得。

love² 0┅ /lʌv/ *verb* 动词 (**loves**, **loving**, **loved** /lʌvd/)
1 to have a very strong warm feeling for somebody 爱；热爱：*I love him very much.* 我非常爱他。◇ *She loves her parents.* 她爱她的父母。 ⊃ OPPOSITE **hate** 反义词为 hate
2 to like something very much 喜欢；喜爱：*I love skiing.* 我喜欢滑雪。◇ *I would love to go to America.* 我很想去美国。 ⊃ OPPOSITE **hate** 反义词为 hate

love affair /ˈlʌv əfeə(r)/ *noun* 名词
a romantic or sexual relationship between two people who love each other but who are not married 风流韵事；（非夫妻间的）性关系

lovely /ˈlʌvli/ *adjective* 形容词 (**lovelier**, **loveliest**)
beautiful or very nice 可爱的；迷人的；漂亮的；极好的：*That's a lovely dress.* 那是条漂亮的连衣裙。◇ *We had a lovely holiday.* 我们过了一个很棒的假期。◇ *It's lovely to see you again.* 再次见到你太好了。

A B C D E F G H I J K L M N O P Q R S T U V W X Y Z

lover /'lʌvə(r)/ *noun* 名词

1 If two people are **lovers**, they have a sexual relationship but they are not married. 情人；情侣

2 a person who likes something very much 爱好者： *a music lover* 音乐爱好者

loving /'lʌvɪŋ/ *adjective* 形容词
feeling or showing love 爱的；充满爱的： *loving parents* 慈爱的父母

low 0➡ /ləʊ/ *adjective* 形容词 (lower, lowest)

> 🔊 PRONUNCIATION 读音说明
> The word **low** sounds like **go**. * low 读音像 go。

1 near the ground 低的；矮的；接近地面的： *There was a low wall round the garden.* 花园四周有一堵矮墙。◇ *a low bridge* 矮桥 ➊ OPPOSITE **high** 反义词为 high

2 less than usual 低于一般的；比通常少的： *low temperatures* 低温 ◇ *low pay* 低工资 ➊ OPPOSITE **high** 反义词为 high

3 deep or quiet 低沉的；轻声的： *a low sound* 低沉的声音 ◇ *I heard low voices in the next room.* 我听到隔壁有人低沉的说话声。

▶ **low** *adverb* 副词： *The plane flew low over the fields.* 飞机在田野上空低飞。

lower¹ /'ləʊə(r)/ *adjective* 形容词
that is under something or at the bottom of something 下面的；在底部的： *She bit her lower lip.* 她咬了咬下唇。 ➊ OPPOSITE **upper** 反义词为 upper

lower² /'ləʊə(r)/ *verb* 动词 (lowers, lowering, lowered /'ləʊəd/)

1 to move somebody or something down 放下；使下降： *They lowered the boat into the water.* 他们把船放进了水里。

2 to make something less 减少；降低： *Please lower your voice* (= speak more quietly). 请把声音压低一点。 ➊ OPPOSITE **raise** 反义词为 raise

lower case /ˌləʊə 'keɪs/ *noun* 名词 (*no plural* 不用复数形式)
small letters 小写字体： *My email address is all in lower case.* 我的电邮地址全是小写的。 ➊ OPPOSITE **upper case** 反义词为 upper case

loyal /'lɔɪəl/ *adjective* 形容词
A person who is **loyal** does not change their friends or beliefs. （人）忠诚的，忠实的： *a loyal friend* 忠实的朋友 ◇ *He is loyal to the company he works for.* 他忠于所服务的公司。 ➊ OPPOSITE **disloyal** 反义词为 disloyal

▶ **loyalty** /'lɔɪəlti/ *noun* 名词 (*no plural* 不用复数形式)： *Loyalty to your friends is very important.* 对朋友忠诚十分重要。

LP /ˌel 'piː/ *noun* 名词
a record with about 25 minutes of music on each side 密纹唱片（每面约 25 分钟） ➊ Look at **single²**. 见 single²。

L-plate /'el pleɪt/ *noun* 名词
a sign with a big red letter L (for 'learner') on it, that you put on your car when you are learning to drive 红 L 字牌；学车牌

Ltd *abbreviation* 缩略式 (*British* 英式英语)
(used after the name of a British company or business) Limited 有限（责任）公司（用于英国公司或商行名称之后）： *Pierce and Co. Ltd* 皮尔斯有限公司

luck 0➡ /lʌk/ *noun* 名词 (*no plural* 不用复数形式)

1 good things that happen to you that you cannot control 好运；幸运： *We wish you luck in your new career.* 我们祝愿你在新的事业上一帆风顺。

2 things that happen to you that you cannot control; chance 运气；机遇： *to have good luck* 有好运

bad luck, hard luck words that you say to somebody when you are sorry that they did not have good luck（用于对他人表示同情）真倒霉，运气不佳

be in luck to have good things happen to you 运气好；走运： *I was in luck – the shop had the book I wanted.* 我真走运，店里有我要的那本书。

good luck words that you say to somebody when you hope that they will do well 祝某人好运： *Good luck! I'm sure you'll get the job.* 祝你成功！我肯定你会得到这份工作。

lucky 0➡ /'lʌki/ *adjective* 形容词 (luckier, luckiest)

1 having good luck 运气好的；幸运的： *She is lucky to be alive after the accident.* 她能在事故中死里逃生，真是幸运。 ➊ OPPOSITE **unlucky** 反义词为 unlucky

2 bringing success or good luck 带来好运的： *My lucky number is 3.* 我的幸运数字是 3。 ➊ OPPOSITE **unlucky** 反义词为 unlucky

▶ **luckily** /'lʌkɪli/ *adverb* 副词 it is lucky that 幸好；幸而： *I was late, but luckily they waited for me.* 我迟到了，幸好他们等我。

luggage 0➡ /'lʌgɪdʒ/ *noun* 名词 (*no plural* 不用复数形式)
bags and suitcases that you take with you when you travel 行李 ➊ SAME MEANING

A B C D E F G H I J K L M N O P Q R S T U V W X Y Z

baggage 同义词为 baggage: *'How much luggage have you got?' 'Only one suitcase.'* "你有多少行李？""只有一个行李箱。"

> 🔎 GRAMMAR 语法说明
>
> **Luggage** does not have a plural so you cannot say 'a luggage'. If you are talking about one suitcase or bag, you say **a piece of luggage**. * luggage 没有复数形式，因此不能说 a luggage。表示一件行李说 a piece of luggage: *She brought five pieces of luggage with her and she was only staying for one week!* 她随身带了五件行李，可她只待一个礼拜！

lukewarm /ˌluːkˈwɔːm/ *adjective* 形容词
If a liquid is **lukewarm**, it is only slightly warm. （液体）微温的，不冷不热的: *I had to have a lukewarm shower.* 我只能用温水冲了个淋浴。

lump ⚡ /lʌmp/ *noun* 名词
1 a hard piece of something 块: *two **lumps of** sugar* 两块方糖 ◇ *a lump of coal* 一块煤
2 a part in or on your body which has become hard and bigger 肿块: *I've got a lump on my head where I hit it.* 我头上撞过的地方起了个包。

lumpy /ˈlʌmpi/ *adjective* 形容词 (lumpier, lumpiest)
full of or covered with LUMPS 多块状物的；为块状物覆盖的: *The sauce is rather lumpy.* 这调味汁里颗粒相当多。 ⊃ OPPOSITE **smooth** 反义词为 smooth

lunatic /ˈluːnətɪk/ *noun* 名词 (*informal* 非正式)
a person who does stupid and often dangerous things 精神错乱的人；狂人

lunch ⚡ /lʌntʃ/ *noun* 名词 (*plural* 复数形式 lunches)
a meal that you eat in the middle of the day 午饭；午餐: *What would you like for lunch?* 你午饭想吃什么？ ◇ *What time do you usually have lunch?* 你通常什么时候吃午饭？

lunchtime /ˈlʌntʃtaɪm/ *noun* 名词
the time when you eat LUNCH 午餐时间: *I'll meet you at lunchtime.* 我们午饭时间见。

lung /lʌŋ/ *noun* 名词
one of the two parts inside your body that you use for breathing 肺

lurk /lɜːk/ *verb* 动词 (lurks, lurking, lurked /lɜːkt/)
to wait somewhere secretly, especially because you are going to do something bad 埋伏，潜伏（尤指为了干坏事）: *I thought I saw somebody lurking among the trees.* 我想我看见有人藏在树丛中。

luxurious /lʌɡˈʒʊəriəs/ *adjective* 形容词
very comfortable and expensive 十分舒适的；豪华的: *a luxurious hotel* 豪华旅馆

luxury /ˈlʌkʃəri/ *noun* 名词
1 (*no plural* 不用复数形式) a way of living when you have all the expensive and beautiful things you want 奢侈的享受；奢华: *They live in luxury in a beautiful house in Barbados.* 他们住在巴巴多斯一所漂亮的房子里，过着奢华的生活。 ◇ *a luxury hotel* 豪华旅馆
2 (*plural* 复数形式 luxuries) something that is very nice and expensive that you do not really need 奢侈品: *Eating in a restaurant is a luxury for most people.* 在餐馆吃饭对大多数人来说是件奢侈的事。

lying *form of* LIE¹ *and* LIE² * lie¹ 和 lie² 的不同形式

lyrics /ˈlɪrɪks/ *noun* 名词 (*plural* 用复数形式)
the words of a song 歌词: *music and lyrics by Rodgers and Hart* 由罗杰斯和哈特作曲作词

M m

M, m /em/ *noun* 名词 (*plural* 复数形式
M's, m's /emz/)
the thirteenth letter of the English
alphabet 英语字母表中的第 13 个字母:
'*Milk*' *begins with an* '*M*'. * milk 一词以
字母 m 开头。

m *short way of writing* METRE * metre 的
缩写形式

mac /mæk/ *noun* 名词 (*British* 英式英语)
a light coat that you wear when it rains
雨衣 ➾ SAME MEANING **raincoat** 同义词为
raincoat

machine 0﹀ /məˈʃiːn/ *noun* 名词
a thing with moving parts that is made to
do a job. **Machines** often use electricity.
机器（常为电力推动的）: *a washing
machine* 洗衣机 ◇ *This machine does not
work.* 这台机器坏了。

machine gun /məˈʃiːn gʌn/ *noun* 名词
a gun that can send out a lot of bullets
very quickly 机枪；机关枪

machinery /məˈʃiːnəri/ *noun* 名词
(*no plural* 不用复数形式)
machines in general, especially large
ones; the moving parts of a machine
（统称）机器；（尤指）大型机器；
（机器的）活动零件: *industrial
machinery* 工业机械

mad 0﹀ /mæd/ *adjective* 形容词 (**madder**,
maddest)
1 ill in your mind 疯的；神经错乱的；
有精神病的 ➾ SAME MEANING **crazy** 同义词
为 crazy
2 (*British* 英式英语) (*informal* 非正式) very
stupid 极愚蠢的 ➾ SAME MEANING **crazy**
同义词为 crazy: *I think you're mad to go
out in this snow!* 下这么大的雪还出去，
我看你是疯了!
3 (*American* 美式英语) (*informal* 非正式)
very angry 很生气；气愤: *He was mad at
me for losing his watch.* 我把他的手表弄丢
了，他很生气。
be mad about somebody or 或
something (*informal* 非正式) to like
somebody or something very much
（为…）着迷，痴迷；迷恋: *Mina is mad
about computer games.* 明纳对电脑游戏很
痴迷。 ◇ *He's mad about her.* 他爱她爱得
如痴如醉。

drive somebody mad to make
somebody very angry 把某人气疯；使非常
气愤: *This noise is driving me mad!*
这噪音真让我受不了!
go mad (*British* 英式英语) (*informal*
非正式)
1 to become ill in your mind 发疯: *He
went mad and killed himself.* 他发疯，
自杀死了。
2 to become very angry 非常气愤；愤怒:
*Mum will go mad when she finds out what
you did at school.* 妈妈要是知道了你在
学校做过的事，一定会气疯。
like mad (*informal* 非正式) very hard,
fast, much, etc. 非常拼命（或快、厉害
等）: *I had to run like mad to catch the
bus.* 我得拼了命跑才赶上公车。

madam /ˈmædəm/ *noun* 名词 (*no plural*
不用复数形式)
1 (*formal* 正式) a polite way of speaking
to a woman （表示尊称）夫人，女士:
'*Can I help you, madam?*' *asked the shop
assistant.* "夫人，要帮忙吗?"店员
问道。
2 **Madam** a word that you use at the
beginning of a formal letter to a woman
（用于正式信函开头）女士: *Dear
Madam …* 尊敬的女士… ➾ Look at **sir**.
见 sir. ➾ Look at Study Pages S18-S19.
见研习专页 S18-S19.

made *form of* MAKE¹ * make¹ 的不同形式

madly /ˈmædli/ *adverb* 副词
1 in a wild way 疯狂地: *They were
rushing around madly.* 他们疯了似的到处
乱跑。
2 (*informal* 非正式) very much 很；非常:
Richard and Vanessa are madly in love.
理查德和瓦妮莎爱得如痴如狂。

madness /ˈmædnəs/ *noun* 名词 (*no plural*
不用复数形式)
stupid behaviour that could be dangerous
精神失常；疯狂: *It would be madness to
take a boat out in this terrible weather.*
在这么恶劣的天气下驾船出海，简直是
疯了。

magazine 0﹀ /ˌmægəˈziːn/ *noun* 名词
a kind of thin book with a paper cover
that you can buy every week or every

month. It has a lot of different stories and pictures inside. 杂志；期刊

magic ⊶ /'mædʒɪk/ *noun* 名词
(*no plural* 不用复数形式)
1 a special power that can make strange or impossible things happen 魔法；巫术；法术： *He suddenly appeared as if by magic*. 他突然神奇地出现了。
2 clever tricks that somebody can do to entertain people 魔术；戏法
▶ **magic** *adjective* 形容词： *magic tricks* 魔术

magical /'mædʒɪkl/ *adjective* 形容词
1 seeming to have special powers 魔术般的；有神奇力量的： *a herb with magical powers to cure disease* 具有神奇疗效的草药
2 (*informal* 非正式) wonderful and exciting 奇妙的；令人兴奋的： *We spent a magical week in Paris.* 我们在巴黎度过了十分愉快的一周。

magician /mə'dʒɪʃn/ *noun* 名词
1 a person who does clever tricks to entertain people 魔术师；变戏法的人
⊃ SAME MEANING **conjuror** 同义词为 conjuror
2 a man in stories who has strange, unusual powers （故事中的）巫师，术士，施魔法的人

magistrate /'mædʒɪstreɪt/ *noun* 名词
a judge in a court of law who decides how to punish people for small crimes 地方法官

magnet 磁铁

magnet /'mægnət/ *noun* 名词
a piece of metal that can make other metal things move towards it 磁铁；磁石

magnetic /mæg'netɪk/ *adjective* 形容词
having the ability to attract metal objects 有磁性的： *Is this metal magnetic?* 这种金属有磁性吗？

magnificent /mæg'nɪfɪsnt/ *adjective* 形容词
very good or beautiful 壮丽的；宏伟的： *The Taj Mahal is a magnificent building.* 泰姬陵是一座宏伟的建筑。

magnify /'mægnɪfaɪ/ *verb* 动词
(magnifies, magnifying, magnified /'mægnɪfaɪd/, has magnified)
to make something look bigger than it really is 放大： *We magnified the insect under a microscope.* 我们用显微镜放大了昆虫。

magnifying glass 放大镜

magnifying glass /'mægnɪfaɪɪŋ glɑːs/ *noun* 名词 (*plural* 复数形式 magnifying glasses)
a round piece of glass, usually with a handle, that makes things look bigger than they are when you look through it 放大镜

maid /meɪd/ *noun* 名词
a woman whose job is to clean in a hotel or a large house （旅馆或大宅院的）女清洁工

maiden name /'meɪdn neɪm/ *noun* 名词
a woman's family name before she is married （女子的）娘家姓

mail ⊶ /meɪl/ (*British also* 英式英语亦作 post) *noun* 名词 (*no plural* 不用复数形式)
1 the way of sending and receiving letters and packages 邮政；邮递系统： *to send a letter by airmail* 空邮寄信
2 letters and packages that you send or receive 邮件；信件；邮包： *Is there any mail for me?* 有我的信吗？ ⊃ Look also at **email**. 亦见 email。
▶ **mail** *verb* 动词 (mails, mailing, mailed /meɪld/) (*American* 美式英语) to send something in the **mail** 邮寄： *I'll mail the money to you.* 我会把钱寄给你。

mailbox /'meɪlbɒks/ *noun* 名词 (*plural* 复数形式 mailboxes)
1 (*American* 美式英语) (*British* 英式英语 letter box) a private box outside a house or a building or a hole in a door for putting letters through （收信人门前或门

A B C D E F G H I J K L M N O P Q R S T U V W X Y Z

上的）信箱 ➲ Look at Picture Dictionary page **P10**. 见彩页 P10。
2 (*American* 美式英语) (*British* 英式英语 **postbox**) a box in the street where you put letters that you want to send 邮筒；邮箱 ➲ Look at the picture at **postbox**. 见 postbox 的插图。
3 (*computing* 电脑) a computer program that receives and stores email 电子邮箱；电子信箱

mailman /ˈmeɪlmæn/ *American English for* POSTMAN 美式英语，即 postman

main 🔑 /meɪn/ ***adjective*** 形容词
most important 主要的；最重要的： *My main reason for learning English is to get a better job.* 我学英语的主要原因是想找份更好的工作。 ◇ *I had fish for the* ***main course*** (= the most important part of a meal). 我主菜吃的是鱼。

mainly 🔑 /ˈmeɪnli/ ***adverb*** 副词
mostly 主要地；总体上： *The students here are mainly from Japan.* 这里的学生主要来自日本。 ◇ *She eats mainly vegetables.* 她吃蔬菜为主。

main road /ˌmeɪn ˈrəʊd/ ***noun*** 名词
a big important road between towns 大路；主路

main street /ˌmeɪn ˈstriːt/ ***noun*** 名词
American English for HIGH STREET 美式英语，即 high street

maintain /meɪnˈteɪn/ ***verb*** 动词
(**maintains, maintaining, maintained** /meɪnˈteɪnd/)
1 to make something continue at the same level 维持，保持： *If he can maintain this speed, he'll win the race.* 他要是能保持这个速度，就会赢得比赛。
2 to keep something working well 维修；保养： *The roads are well maintained.* 这些路保养得很好。

maintenance /ˈmeɪntənəns/ ***noun*** 名词
(*no plural* 不用复数形式)
keeping something in good condition 维修；保养；维护： *car maintenance* 汽车保养

maize /meɪz/ (*British* 英式英语) (*American* 美式英语 **corn**) ***noun*** 名词 (*no plural* 不用复数形式)
a tall plant with big yellow seeds that you can eat (called **sweetcorn**) 玉蜀黍；玉米

majestic /məˈdʒestɪk/ ***adjective*** 形容词
impressive because of its size or beauty 雄伟的；壮丽的： *a majestic mountain view* 壮丽的山景

Majesty /ˈmædʒəsti/ ***noun*** 名词 (*plural* 复数形式 **Majesties**)
a word that you use to talk to or about a king or queen（对国王或女王的尊称）陛下： *Her Majesty the Queen* 女王陛下

major[1] /ˈmeɪdʒə(r)/ ***adjective*** 形容词
very large, important or serious 重大的；重要的；严重的： *There are airports in all the major cities.* 各主要城市都有飞机场。 ◇ *major problems* 严重的问题 ➲ OPPOSITE **minor** 反义词为 minor

major[2] /ˈmeɪdʒə(r)/ ***noun*** 名词
an officer in the army 陆军少校

majority /məˈdʒɒrəti/ ***noun*** 名词
(*no plural* 不用复数形式)
most things or people in a group 大多数；大部分： *The* ***majority of*** *people agreed with the new law.* 大多数人支持这项新法规。 ➲ OPPOSITE **minority** 反义词为 minority

make[1] 🔑 /meɪk/ ***verb*** 动词 (**makes, making, made** /meɪd/, **has made**)
1 to produce or create something 做；制造；创作： *They make cars in that factory.* 那家工厂制造汽车。 ◇ *He* ***made*** *a box* ***out of*** *some pieces of wood.* 他用几块木头做了个箱子。 ◇ *This shirt is* ***made of*** *cotton.* 这件衬衣是棉制的。
2 to cause something to be or to happen; to produce something 使变得；使成为；产生；引起： *The plane made a loud noise when it landed.* 飞机着陆时发出了巨大的响声。 ◇ *Chocolate makes you fat.* 巧克力会使人发胖。 ◇ *That film made me cry.* 那部电影让我哭了。 ◇ *I made a mistake.* 我犯了一个错误。
3 to force somebody to do something 迫使；强迫： *My father made me stay at home.* 父亲强迫我待在家里。
4 to choose somebody to do a job 选举；任命： *They made him President.* 他们选了他当主席。
5 a word that you use with money, numbers and time（与钱、数字和时间连用）： *She makes* (= earns) *a lot of money.* 她赚很多钱。 ◇ *Five and seven make twelve.* 五加七等于十二。 ◇ *'What's the time?' '****I make it*** *six o'clock.'* "几点钟了？" "我估计是六点钟。"
6 to be able to go somewhere 赶到；抵达；到达： *I'm afraid I can't make the meeting on Friday.* 恐怕我去不了星期五的会议。
make do with something to use something that is not very good, because there is nothing better 凑合；将就： *We didn't have a table, but we made do with*

some boxes. 我们没有桌子，只好用些箱子凑合着。

make something into something to change something so that it becomes a different thing 把…变成；把…改成：*They made the bedroom into an office.* 他们把卧室改成了办公室。

make something or 或 **somebody out** to be able to see, hear or understand something or somebody 看清；听清；弄懂：*It was dark and I couldn't make out the words on the sign.* 太黑了，我看不清牌子上的字。

make something up to tell somebody something that is not true 编造；捏造 ➲ SAME MEANING **invent** 同义词为 invent: *Nobody believes that story – he made it up!* 没人相信那件事 —— 他瞎编！

make up to become friends again after an argument 言归于好：*Jane and Tom had an argument last week, but they've made up now.* 简和汤姆上星期吵了一架，可是现在和好了。◇ *Has she made up with him yet?* 她和他言归于好了吗？ ➲ OPPOSITE **fall out with somebody** 反义词为 fall out with somebody

make² 🔑 /meɪk/ *noun* 名词
the name of the company that made something 品牌：*'What make is your car?' 'It's a Ford.'* "你的汽车是什么牌子的？" "福特。"

maker /'meɪkə(r)/ *noun* 名词
a person, company or machine that makes something 生产者；制造商；制造机：*a film maker* 电影制片人

make-up /'meɪk ʌp/ *noun* 名词 (*no plural* 不用复数形式)
special powders and creams that you put on your face to make yourself more beautiful. Actors also wear **make-up** when they are acting. 化妆品：*She put on her* ***make-up***. 她化了妆。

malaria /mə'leəriə/ *noun* 名词 (*no plural* 不用复数形式)
a serious disease that you get in hot countries from the bite of a small flying insect (called a **mosquito**) 疟疾

male 🔑 /meɪl/ *adjective* 形容词
A **male** animal or person belongs to the sex that does not have babies. 男性的；雄性的；公的：*A cock is a male chicken.* 公鸡是雄性的鸡。
▸ **male** *noun* 名词：*The males of this species are bigger than the females.* 这种动物雄性比雌性大。➲ Look at **female**. 见 female。

mall /mɔːl; mæl/ (*also* 亦作 **shopping mall**) (*American* 美式英语) *noun* 名词
a large building that has a lot of shops, restaurants, etc. inside it 购物中心

mammal /'mæml/ *noun* 名词
any animal that drinks milk from its mother's body when it is young 哺乳动物：*Dogs, horses, whales and people are all mammals.* 狗、马、鲸和人都是哺乳动物。

man 🔑 /mæn/ *noun* 名词
1 (*plural* 复数形式 **men** /men/) an adult male person 男人；成年男子：*I saw a tall man with dark hair.* 我看见一个黑发的高个子男人。
2 (*no plural* 不用复数形式) all humans; people 人；人类：*the damage man has caused to the environment* 人类对环境造成的破坏
3 (*plural* 复数形式 **men**) any person （任何）人：*All men are equal.* 人人平等。

manage 🔑 /'mænɪdʒ/ *verb* 动词 (**manages, managing, managed** /'mænɪdʒd/)
1 to be able to do something that is difficult 能做成，圆满处理（困难的事）：*The box was heavy but she* ***managed to*** *carry it to the car.* 箱子很重，但她还是成功地把它搬上了汽车。
2 to control somebody or something 管理：*She manages a department of 30 people.* 她管理一个 30 人的部门。

management /'mænɪdʒmənt/ *noun* 名词 (*no plural* 不用复数形式)
1 the control of something, for example a business, and the people who work in it 管理；经营：*Teachers must show good classroom management.* 教师必须表现出课堂组织能力。
2 all the people who control a business 管理层；管理人员：*The hotel is now* ***under new management***. 这家酒店现由新的经营者管理。

manager 🔑 /'mænɪdʒə(r)/ *noun* 名词
a person who controls an organization, a business or a shop 经理；管理人；老板：*He is the manager of a shoe shop.* 他是一家鞋店的经理。◇ *a bank manager* 银行经理

managing director /ˌmænɪdʒɪŋ də'rektə(r)/ *noun* 名词
the person who controls a big business or company 总裁；总经理；常务董事

mane /meɪn/ *noun* 名词
the long hair on the neck of some

A B C D E F G H I J K L **M** N O P Q R S T U V W X Y Z

animals, for example horses and LIONS （马）鬃；（狮）鬣 ➲ Look at the pictures at **horse** and **lion**. 见 horse 和 lion 的插图。

mango /ˈmæŋɡəʊ/ ***noun*** 名词 (*plural* 复数形式 **mangoes**)
a fruit that is yellow or red on the outside and yellow on the inside. **Mangoes** grow in hot countries. 芒果 ➲ Look at Picture Dictionary page **P8**. 见彩页 P8。

manic /ˈmænɪk/ ***adjective*** 形容词 (*informal* 非正式)
full of activity and excitement 忙乱的；兴奋的： *Things are manic in the office at the moment.* 这个时候办公室里一片忙乱。

manipulate /məˈnɪpjuleɪt/ ***verb*** 动词 (**manipulates, manipulating, manipulated**)
to influence somebody so that they do or think what you want 操纵；影响： *Politicians know how to manipulate people's opinions.* 政客知道如何操纵民意。

mankind /mænˈkaɪnd/ ***noun*** 名词 (*no plural* 不用复数形式)
all the people in the world 人类

man-made /ˌmæn ˈmeɪd/ ***adjective*** 形容词
made by people; not formed in a natural way 人造的；非天然的；人工的 ➲ SAME MEANING **artificial** 同义词为 artificial: *man-made materials* 人造材料

manner /ˈmænə(r)/ ***noun*** 名词
1 the way that you do something or the way that something happens 方式；方法： *Don't get angry. Let's try to talk about this **in a calm manner**.* 不要生气，咱们心平气和地谈谈这件事吧。
2 manners (*plural* 用复数形式) the way you behave when you are with other people 礼节；礼貌： *It's **bad manners** to talk with your mouth full.* 满口食物跟人说话是不礼貌的。

mansion /ˈmænʃn/ ***noun*** 名词
a very big house 府邸；宅第

mantelpiece /ˈmæntlpiːs/ (*British* 英式英语) (*American* 美式英语 **mantel** /ˈmæntl/) ***noun*** 名词
a narrow shelf above the place where a fire is in a room (called the **fireplace**) 壁炉台： *She has photographs of her children **on the mantelpiece**.* 她在壁炉台上摆着孩子的照片。 ➲ Look at the picture at **fireplace**. 见 fireplace 的插图。

manual[1] /ˈmænjuəl/ ***adjective*** 形容词
using your hands 用手的；手动的： *Do you prefer **manual work** or office work?* 你喜欢体力劳动还是在办公室工作？
▸ **manually** /ˈmænjuəli/ ***adverb*** 副词： *This machine is operated manually.* 这台机器是人工操作的。

manual[2] /ˈmænjuəl/ ***noun*** 名词
a book that tells you how to do something 操作手册；说明书： *Where is the instruction manual for the DVD player?* 这台影碟机的使用说明书在哪里？

manufacture /ˌmænjuˈfæktʃə(r)/ ***verb*** 动词 (**manufactures, manufacturing, manufactured** /ˌmænjuˈfæktʃəd/)
to make things in a factory using machines （用机器）制造，生产： *The company manufactures radios.* 这家公司生产收音机。
▸ **manufacture** ***noun*** 名词 (*no plural* 不用复数形式)： *the manufacture of cars* 汽车制造

manufacturer /ˌmænjuˈfæktʃərə(r)/ ***noun*** 名词
a person or company that makes something 制造者；生产商： *If it doesn't work, send it back to the manufacturers.* 如果坏了，把它送回厂家。

many 🗝 /ˈmeni/ ***adjective, pronoun*** 形容词，代词 (**more, most**)
1 a large number of people or things 许多；大量： *Many people in this country are very poor.* 这个国家很多人很穷。 ◇ *There aren't many students in my class.* 我们班学生不多。 ◇ ***Many of** these books are very old.* 这些书很多都很旧。 ◇ *There are **too many** mistakes in your homework.* 你的家庭作业中错误太多了。
2 a word that you use to ask or talk about the number of people or things （询问或表示人或事物的数量）： ***How many** brothers and sisters have you got?* 你有几个兄弟姐妹？ ◇ *Take **as many** cakes **as** you want.* 你想拿多少个蛋糕就拿多少个。 ➲ Look at **much**[1]. 见 much[1]。

map 🗝 /mæp/ ***noun*** 名词
a drawing of a town, a country or the world that shows things like mountains, rivers and roads 地图： *Can you find Glasgow **on the map**?* 你能在地图上找到格拉斯哥吗？ ◇ *a street **map of** Exeter* 埃克塞特的街道地图

> **WORD BUILDING 词汇扩充**
> A book of maps is called an **atlas**. 地图册叫做 atlas。

➲ Look at Picture Dictionary page **P11**. 见彩页 P11。

marathon /'mærəθən/ *noun* 名词
a very long race when people run about 42 kilometres 马拉松赛跑

marble /'mɑːbl/ *noun* 名词
1 (*no plural* 不用复数形式) a hard attractive stone that is used to make STATUES (= models of people) and parts of buildings 大理石: *Marble is always cold when you touch it.* 大理石摸起来总是冰冷的。
2 (*plural* 复数形式 **marbles**) a small glass ball that you use in a children's game (儿童玩的)玻璃弹子: *The children are playing marbles.* 孩子们在玩弹子游戏。

March ⚬┭ /mɑːtʃ/ *noun* 名词
the third month of the year 三月

march¹ ⚬┭ /mɑːtʃ/ *verb* 动词 (**marches**, **marching**, **marched** /mɑːtʃt/)
1 to walk like a soldier 齐步走；行进: *The soldiers marched along the road.* 士兵沿路行进。
2 to walk somewhere quickly in a determined way 坚决地走: *She marched up to the manager and asked for her money back.* 她毅然走到经理面前要求退款。
3 to walk through the streets in a large group to show that you do not agree with something 游行示威；游行抗议: *They marched through the town shouting 'Stop the war!'* 他们在镇上游行示威，高呼"停止战争！"

march² ⚬┭ /mɑːtʃ/ *noun* 名词 (*plural* 复数形式 **marches**)
1 an organized walk by a large group of people who want to show that they do not agree with something 示威游行；抗议游行: *a peace march* 和平示威游行 ⊃ Look at **demonstration**. 见 demonstration.
2 a journey made by soldiers walking together 行军；行进: *The soldiers were tired after the long march.* 士兵在长途行军后都疲惫不堪。

margarine /ˌmɑːdʒəˈriːn/ *noun* 名词
(*no plural* 不用复数形式)
soft yellow food that looks like butter, but is not made of milk. You put it on bread or use it in cooking. 人造黄油；人造奶油

margin /'mɑːdʒɪn/ *noun* 名词
the space at the side of a page that has no writing or pictures in it (书等的)页边空白，白边

mark¹ ⚬┭ /mɑːk/ *verb* 动词 (**marks**, **marking**, **marked** /mɑːkt/)
1 to put a sign on something by writing or drawing on it (作标记；作记号) *The price is **marked** on the bottom of the box.* 价格标在盒子底部。
2 to show where something is 标明；标示(位置): *This cross marks the place where he died.* 这个十字符号标示出他的死亡地点。
3 to look at school work to see how good it is 给…打分；批改；批阅(学生作业): *The teacher marked all my answers wrong.* 老师在我所有的答案上打了错号。

mark² ⚬┭ /mɑːk/ *noun* 名词
1 a spot or line that spoils the appearance of something 污点；划痕；痕迹: *There's a dirty mark on the front of your shirt.* 你的衬衫正面有一道脏印子。
2 a shape or special sign on something 记号；符号；标记: *This mark shows that the ring is made of silver.* 这个标记表明戒指是银制的。 ◇ *punctuation marks* 标点符号
3 a number or letter that a teacher gives for your work to show how good it is 分数；成绩；等级: *She got very good marks in the exam.* 她在考试中取得很高的分数。

market¹ ⚬┭ /'mɑːkɪt/ *noun* 名词
1 a place where people go to buy and sell things, usually outside 集市；市场: *There is a fruit and vegetable market in the town.* 镇上有个蔬果市场。 ⊃ Look at Picture Dictionary page **P13**. 见彩页 P13。
2 the people who want to buy something 消费群体；市场: *There is a big market for personal computers in the USA.* 在美国，个人电脑的市场很大。

market² /'mɑːkɪt/ *verb* 动词 (**markets**, **marketing**, **marketed**)
to sell something using advertisements 推销；促销: *Companies spend millions marketing their products.* 公司都花大笔的钱来推销产品。

marketing /'mɑːkɪtɪŋ/ *noun* 名词
(*no plural* 不用复数形式)
using advertisements to help a company sell its products 市场营销；促销活动: *She works in the marketing department.* 她在营销部工作。

marmalade /'mɑːməleɪd/ *noun* 名词
(*no plural* 不用复数形式)
a type of soft sweet food (called jam) made from oranges or lemons 橘子酱；酸果酱: *We had toast and marmalade for breakfast.* 我们早餐吃橘子酱吐司。

maroon /məˈruːn/ *adjective, noun*
形容词，名词

A
B
C
D
E
F
G
H
I
J
K
L
M
N
O
P
Q
R
S
T
U
V
W
X
Y
Z

(having) a colour between brown and purple 紫褐色（的）

marriage ⚬ /'mærɪdʒ/ *noun* 名词
1 the time when two people are together as husband and wife 婚姻；结婚： *They had a long and happy marriage.* 他们有过长久而幸福的婚姻。
2 the time when a man and woman become husband and wife 婚礼 ⊃ SAME MEANING **wedding** 同义词为 wedding： *The marriage will take place in church.* 婚礼将在教堂举行。

married ⚬ /'mærid/ *adjective* 形容词
having a husband or a wife 已婚的 ⊃ OPPOSITE **single** or **unmarried** 反义词为 single 或 unmarried
get married to take somebody as your husband or wife 结婚： *Fran and Paul got married last year.* 弗兰和保罗去年结婚了。

marry ⚬ /'mæri/ *verb* 动词 (marries, marrying, married /'mærid/, has married)
to take somebody as your husband or wife （和…）结婚；娶；嫁： *Will you marry me?* 你愿意嫁给我吗？ ◇ *They married when they were very young.* 他们很年轻就结了婚。

> 🔊 SPEAKING 表达方式说明
> It is more usual to say **get married**. 较常用 get married。

marsh /mɑ:ʃ/ *noun* 名词 (plural 复数形式 marshes)
soft wet ground 沼泽；湿地

marvellous (*British* 英式英语) (*American* 美式英语 **marvelous**) /'mɑ:vələs/ *adjective* 形容词
very good 非凡的；绝佳的；了不起的 ⊃ SAME MEANING **wonderful** 同义词为 wonderful： *I had a marvellous holiday.* 我的假期过得很精彩。

mascot /'mæskət/ *noun* 名词
a person, animal or thing that people think brings them good luck 吉祥物；福星

masculine /'mæskjəlɪn/ *adjective* 形容词
1 typical of a man or right for a man 男子汉的；男人的： *a masculine voice* 男性的嗓音
2 (*grammar* 语法) (in some languages) belonging to a certain class of nouns, adjectives or pronouns（某些语言中）阳性的： *The French word for 'sun' is masculine.* 法语中表示"太阳"的词是阳性的。 ⊃ Look at **feminine**. 见 feminine。

mash /mæʃ/ *verb* 动词 (mashes, mashing, mashed /mæʃt/)
to press and mix food to make it soft （把食物）捣烂，捣碎： *mashed potatoes* 土豆泥

masks 面具；口罩

mask /mɑ:sk/ *noun* 名词
a thing that you wear over your face to hide or protect it 面具；面罩；口罩： *a gas mask* 防毒面具 ◇ *The doctors and nurses all wore masks.* 医生和护士都戴口罩。

Mass /mæs/ *noun* 名词 (plural 复数形式 Masses)
an important religious ceremony, especially in the Roman Catholic Church 弥撒： *She goes to Mass every Sunday.* 她每个星期天都去做弥撒。

mass /mæs/ *noun* 名词 (plural 复数形式 masses)
1 a large amount or quantity of something without a clear shape 团；块；堆： *a mass of rock* 一大堆石头
2 masses (plural 用复数形式) (*informal* 非正式) a large amount or number of something 大量；大批 ⊃ SAME MEANING **lots** 同义词为 lots： *I've got masses of work to do.* 我有很多工作要做。

massacre /'mæsəkə(r)/ *noun* 名词
the cruel killing of a lot of people 大屠杀
▶ **massacre** *verb* 动词 (massacres, massacring, massacred /'mæsəkəd/): *The army massacred hundreds of women and children.* 军队屠杀了成百上千的妇女和儿童。

massage /'mæsɑ:ʒ/ *noun* 名词
the act of rubbing somebody's body to get rid of pain or help them relax 按摩： *Do you want me to give you a massage?* 你要我帮你按摩一下吗？
▶ **massage** *verb* 动词 (massages, massaging, massaged /'mæsɑ:ʒd/): *She massaged my back.* 她给我按摩背部。

massive /'mæsɪv/ *adjective* 形容词
very big 极大的；巨大的 ⊃ SAME MEANING **huge** 同义词为 huge： *The house is*

massive – it has 16 bedrooms! 这所房子
非常大，有 16 个卧室！

the mass media /ðə ˌmæs ˈmiːdiə/
noun 名词 (*plural* 用复数形式)
newspapers, television and radio 大众
传媒

mast /mɑːst/ *noun* 名词
1 a tall piece of wood or metal that holds
the sails on a boat 桅杆；船桅 ➲ Look at
the picture at **boat**. 见 boat 的插图。
2 a very tall metal thing that sends out
sounds or pictures for radio or television
（发送无线电或电视信号的）天线杆

master¹ /ˈmɑːstə(r)/ *noun* 名词
1 a man who has people or animals in his
control 主人：*The dog ran to its master.*
狗向主人跑去了。
2 a man who is very good at something
大师；能手：*paintings by the Italian
masters* 意大利绘画大师的作品

master² /ˈmɑːstə(r)/ *verb* 动词 (**masters,**
mastering, mastered /ˈmɑːstəd/)
to learn how to do something well 掌握；
精通：*It takes a long time to master a
foreign language.* 掌握一门外语需要很长
时间。

masterpiece /ˈmɑːstəpiːs/ *noun* 名词
a very good painting, book, film or play
杰作；名著：*'War and Peace' was
Tolstoy's masterpiece.*《战争与和平》是
托尔斯泰的名著。

mat /mæt/ *noun* 名词
1 a small thing that covers a part of the
floor （地板上的）垫子，小地毯：*Wipe
your feet on the doormat before you go in.*
进去前在门口地垫上蹭蹭脚。 ➲ Look at
rug. 见 rug。
2 a small thing that you put under
something on a table （置于桌上的）
小垫子：*a table mat* (= that you put
plates and dishes on) 桌垫 ◇ *a mouse mat*
(= that you rest a computer mouse on)
鼠标垫 ➲ Look at Picture Dictionary page
P11. 见彩页 P11。

match¹ 0━ /mætʃ/ *noun* 名词
1 (*plural* 复数形式 **matches**) a short thin
piece of wood that you use to light a fire
or a cigarette 火柴：*He struck a match
and lit his cigarette.* 他划了根火柴点着
香烟。 ◇ *a box of matches* 一盒火柴
2 (*plural* 复数形式 **matches**) a game
between two people or teams 比赛；
竞赛：*a football match* 足球比赛 ◇
a boxing match 拳击赛
3 (*no plural* 不用复数形式) something that
looks good with something else, for

example because it has the same colour,
shape or pattern 相配的东西：*Your shoes
and dress are a good match.* 你的鞋和
连衣裙很相配。

matches 火柴

match² 0━ /mætʃ/ *verb* 动词 (**matches,**
matching, matched /mætʃt/)
1 to have the same colour, shape or
pattern as something else, or to look
good with something else （颜色、形状
或图案）与…相同，般配，相配：*That
scarf doesn't match your blouse.* 那条围巾
与你的衬衫不相配。
2 to find something that is like another
thing or that you can put with it 给…
配对；找相称的事物：*Match the word
with the right picture.* 把词语与相应的图
配对。
▶ **matching** /ˈmætʃɪŋ/ *adjective* 形容词：
*She was wearing a blue skirt and matching
jacket.* 她穿着蓝裙子和相配的夹克。

matchbox /ˈmætʃbɒks/ *noun* 名词
(*plural* 复数形式 **matchboxes**)
a small box for matches 火柴盒

mate¹ /meɪt/ *noun* 名词
1 (*British* 英式英语) (*informal* 非正式)
a friend 朋友；伙伴：*He went out with
his mates last night.* 他昨晚跟朋友出去了。
2 a person who lives, works or studies
with you 同住者；同事；同学：*André is
one of my classmates.* 安德烈是我的同班
同学。 ◇ *a flatmate* 公寓室友
3 one of two animals that come together
to make young animals （动物的）偶，
伴侣：*In spring the birds look for mates.*
鸟在春天求偶。

mate² /meɪt/ *verb* 动词 (**mates, mating,**
mated)
When animals **mate**, they come together
to make young animals. （动物）交配

material 0━ /məˈtɪəriəl/ *noun* 名词
1 cloth that you use for making clothes
and other things such as curtains 布料；
衣料 ➲ SAME MEANING **fabric** 同义词为
fabric：*I don't have enough material to*

A
B
C
D
E
F
G
H
I
J
K
L
M
N
O
P
Q
R
S
T
U
V
W
X
Y
Z

make a dress. 我没有足够的料子做一条连衣裙。

2 what you use for making or doing something 材料；原料：*Wood and stone are building materials*. 木材和石头是建筑材料。◇ *writing materials* (= pens, pencils and paper, for example) 书写文具

maternal /mə'tɜ:nl/ *adjective* 形容词
1 behaving like a mother 母亲的；像母亲的：*She's not very maternal*. 她不太像个母亲。◇ *maternal love* 母爱
2 A **maternal** relation is from your mother's side of the family. 母亲一方的；母系的：*my maternal grandfather* 我的外祖父 ◌ Look at **paternal**. 见 paternal。

mathematics ◌ /ˌmæθə'mætɪks/ (*formal* 正式) (*British informal* 英式英语非正式亦作 **maths** /mæθs/) (*American informal* 美式英语非正式亦作 **math** /mæθ/) *noun* 名词 (*no plural* 不用复数形式)
the study of numbers, measurements and shapes 数学：*Maths is my favourite subject*. 数学是我最喜欢的学科。
▸ **mathematical** /ˌmæθə'mætɪkl/ *adjective* 形容词：*a mathematical problem* 数学题

matinée /'mætɪmeɪ/ *noun* 名词 (*plural* 复数形式 **matinées**)
an afternoon performance of a play or film（戏剧或电影的）午后场，日场

matter[1] ◌ /'mætə(r)/ *noun* 名词
something that you must talk about or do 问题；事情；情况：*There is a matter I would like to discuss with you*. 有件事我想跟你谈谈。
as a matter of fact words that you use when you say something true, important or interesting 事实上；其实：*I like Dave a lot. As a matter of fact, he's my best friend*. 我很喜欢戴夫。说实话，他是我最好的朋友。
the matter with somebody or 或 **something** the reason for problems or unhappiness, for example（出问题或闹得不愉快的）原因，理由：*Julie's crying. What's the matter with her?* 朱莉在哭，她怎么了？◇ *There is something the matter with my eye*. 我的眼睛有点毛病。
no matter how, what, when, who, etc. words that you use to say that something is always true 不论…；无论…；不管…：*No matter how* (= however) *hard I try, I can't open the door*. 不管我怎么用力，门就是打不开。

matter[2] ◌ /'mætə(r)/ *verb* 动词 (**matters, mattering, mattered** /'mætəd/)
to be important 事关紧要；要紧；重要：*It doesn't matter if you're late – we'll wait for you*. 你来晚了也不要紧，我们会等你的。

mattress /'mætrəs/ *noun* 名词 (*plural* 复数形式 **mattresses**)
the thick soft part of a bed 床垫 ◌ Look at the picture at **bed**. 见 bed 的插图。

mature /mə'tjʊə(r)/ *adjective* 形容词
1 behaving in a sensible way like an adult（思想或行为）成熟的
2 fully grown or fully developed 完全长成的；发育成熟的 ◌ OPPOSITE **immature** 反义词为 immature
▸ **mature** *verb* 动词 (**matures, maturing, matured** /mə'tjʊəd/)：*He has matured a lot since he went to college*. 他上大学后人成熟了不少。

mauve /məʊv/ *adjective* 形容词
pale purple 淡紫色的

maximum /'mæksɪməm/ *noun* 名词 (*no plural* 不用复数形式)
the biggest possible size, amount or number 最大值；最高限度：*This plane can carry a maximum of 150 people*. 这架飞机最多能载 150 人。
▸ **maximum** *adjective* 形容词：*We drove at a maximum speed of 110 kilometres per hour*. 我们以每小时 110 公里的最高速度行驶。◌ OPPOSITE **minimum** 反义词为 minimum

May ◌ /meɪ/ *noun* 名词
the fifth month of the year 五月

may ◌ /meɪ/ *modal verb* 情态动词
1 a word that shows what will perhaps happen or what is possible（表示可能性）也许，可能：*I may go to Spain next year*. 我明年可能去西班牙。◇ *He may not be here*. 他也许不在这里。
2 (*formal* 正式) to be allowed to do something（表示允许）可以：*May I open the window?* 我可以打开窗吗？◇ *You may go now*. 你现在可以走了。◌ Look at the note at **modal verb**. 见 modal verb 条的注释。

maybe ⚓ /'meɪbi/ *adverb* 副词
a word that shows that something may happen or may be true 可能；大概；或许 ⊃ SAME MEANING **perhaps** 同义词为 perhaps: *'Are you going out tonight?' 'Maybe.'* "你今晚会出去吗？""也许吧。" ◇ *Maybe you should phone him.* 你或许应该给他打电话。

🔎 SPEAKING 表达方式说明

You can say **perhaps** or **maybe** to sound more polite. 用 perhaps 或 maybe 显得更有礼貌: *Perhaps/Maybe you could help me with the cooking.* (= Please help me with the cooking.) 或许你可以帮我做饭。

mayonnaise /ˌmeɪə'neɪz/ *noun* 名词
(*no plural* 不用复数形式)
a cold thick sauce made with eggs and oil 蛋黄酱（用蛋和油制成的浓稠冷酱汁）

mayor /meə(r)/ *noun* 名词
the leader of a group of people who control a town or city (called a **council**) 市长；镇长

me ⚓ /miː/ *pronoun* 代词 (*plural* 复数形式 **us**)
the person who is speaking（用作宾语）我: *He telephoned me yesterday.* 他昨天给我打了电话。◇ *Give it to me.* 把它给我。◇ *Hello, it's me.* 喂，是我。

meadow /'medəʊ/ *noun* 名词
a field of grass 草地

meal ⚓ /miːl/ *noun* 名词
food that you eat at a certain time of the day 餐；一顿饭: *What's your favourite meal of the day?* 一天中你最爱吃哪一顿饭？◇ *We had a nice meal in that restaurant.* 我们在那家餐馆享用了一顿美餐。

🔎 CULTURE 文化资料补充

Breakfast, **lunch** and **dinner** (and sometimes **tea** and **supper**) are the usual meals of the day.
Dinner is the main meal. Most people have this in the evening but some people eat their dinner in the middle of the day and call their evening meal **tea** or **supper**. * breakfast 指早餐，lunch 指午餐。dinner 是主餐，大多数人在晚上吃，但也有人在中午吃，后者把晚上吃的那一餐称作 tea 或 supper。

We do not usually say 'a breakfast/lunch/dinner'. 通常不说 a breakfast/lunch/dinner: *Let's have lunch together tomorrow.* 咱们明天一起吃午饭吧。

mean[1] ⚓ /miːn/ *verb* 动词 (**means, meaning, meant** /ment/, **has meant**)
1 to have as a meaning 意思是；意味；表示…的意思: *What does 'medicine' mean?* * medicine 是什么意思？◇ *The red light means that you have to stop here.* 红灯表示必须在这里停下来。
2 to plan or want to say something 本意是；想要说: *She said 'yes' but she really meant 'no'.* 她说"行"，但确实的意思是"不行"。◇ *I don't understand what you mean.* 我不明白你的意思。◇ *We're going on Tuesday, I mean Thursday.* 我们星期二走，不，我是说星期四。
3 to plan or want to do something 想要；打算 ⊃ SAME MEANING **intend** 同义词为 intend: *I didn't mean to hurt you.* 我无意要伤害你。◇ *I meant to phone you, but I forgot.* 我原本想给你打电话，可是忘了。
4 to make something happen 导致；产生…结果: *This snow means there will be no sport today.* 这场雪意味着今天不会有体育活动了。
5 to be important to somebody（对某人）重要: *My family means a lot to me.* 我的家人对我来说很重要。
be meant to
1 If you **are meant to** do something, you should do it. 应该: *You're not meant to smoke on the train.* 在列车上不准吸烟。
2 If something **is meant to** be true, people say it is true. 普遍认为是；看成为: *This is meant to be a good film.* 据说这是一部不错的电影。

mean[2] /miːn/ *adjective* 形容词 (**meaner, meanest**)
1 not liking to give things or to spend money 吝啬的；小气的: *Jim is very mean – he never buys anybody a drink.* 吉姆很吝啬，从来不请人喝一杯。⊃ OPPOSITE **generous** 反义词为 generous
2 unkind 刻薄的: *It was mean of you to say that Peter was fat.* 你说彼得很胖，这话太刻薄了。

meaning ⚓ /'miːnɪŋ/ *noun* 名词
what something means or shows 意思；意义: *This word has two different meanings.* 这个词有两个不同的意思。

means /miːnz/ *noun* 名词 (*plural* 复数形式 **means**)

A B C D E F G H I J K L **M** N O P Q R S T U V W X Y Z

a way of doing something; a way of going somewhere 方法；途径： *Do you have any **means** of transport (= a car, a bicycle etc.)?* 你有自己的交通工具吗？
by means of something by using something 凭借；通过…方法： *We crossed the river by means of a small bridge.* 我们经一座小桥过河。
by no means not at all 一点也不；决不： *I am by no means certain that I can come.* 我能不能来，还完全说不准。

meant *form of* MEAN¹ * mean¹ 的不同形式

meantime /'mi:ntaɪm/ *noun* 名词 (*no plural* 不用复数形式)
in the meantime in the time between two things happening 在此期间；其间；与此同时： *Our house isn't ready, so we're living with my parents in the meantime.* 我们的房子还没竣工，所以在这段时间里我们与我父母一起住。

meanwhile /'mi:nwaɪl/ *adverb* 副词
at the same time as another thing is happening or in the time between two things happening 与此同时；其间： *Peter was at home studying. Omar, meanwhile, was out with his friends.* 彼得在家学习，奥马尔则和朋友出去了。◇ *I'm going to buy a bed next week, but meanwhile I'm sleeping on the floor.* 我下星期会去买床，现在则睡在地板上。

measles /'mi:zlz/ *noun* 名词 (*no plural* 不用复数形式)
an illness that makes small red spots come on your skin 麻疹： *My little brother has got measles.* 我弟弟出麻疹了。

measure¹ ⊶ /'meʒə(r)/ *verb* 动词 (measures, measuring, measured /'meʒəd/)
1 to find the size, weight or amount of somebody or something 测量；量度： *Could you measure the window for me?* 你帮我量一下窗户好吗？
2 to be a certain size or amount 量度为；尺寸是： *This room measures six metres across.* 这个房间宽六米。

measure² ⊶ /'meʒə(r)/ *noun* 名词
1 an action that somebody does in order to achieve something 措施；方法： *The government has **taken measures to** resolve the crisis.* 政府已采取措施来解除危机。
2 a way of showing the size or amount of something 度量单位；计量标准： *A metre is a **measure of** length.* 米是长度单位。

measurement ⊶ /'meʒəmənt/ *noun* 名词

the size of something that is found by measuring it（量得的）尺寸，大小： *What are the **measurements of** the kitchen (= how long and wide is it)?* 厨房的尺寸是多少？

meat ⊶ /mi:t/ *noun* 名词 (*no plural* 不用复数形式)

> 🔊 PRONUNCIATION 读音说明
> The word **meat** sounds just like **meet**.
> * meat 读音同 meet。

the parts of an animal or bird that you can eat（食用的）肉： *You can buy meat at a butcher's.* 在肉店可以买到肉。◇ *I don't eat meat.* 我不吃肉。

mechanic /mə'kænɪk/ *noun* 名词
a person whose job is to repair or work with machines 机械修理工；机械师： *a car mechanic* 汽车修理工

mechanical /mə'kænɪkl/ *adjective* 形容词
moved, done or made by a machine 机械的；机器制造的： *a mechanical toy* 机械玩具
► **mechanically** /mə'kænɪkli/ *adverb* 副词： *The pump is operated mechanically.* 这种水泵靠机械带动。

mechanics /mə'kænɪks/ *noun* 名词 (*no plural* 不用复数形式)
the study of how machines work 机械学

medal /'medl/ *noun* 名词
a piece of metal with words and pictures on it that you get for doing something very good 奖牌；奖章；勋章： *She won a gold medal in the Olympic Games.* 她在奥运会上赢得了一枚金牌。

media /'mi:diə/ *noun* 名词 (*no plural* 不用复数形式)
the media television, radio and newspapers 媒体；新闻媒介： *The media always takes a great interest in the royal family.* 媒体总是对王室很感兴趣。

mediaeval (*British* 英式英语) *form of* MEDIEVAL * medieval 的不同形式

medical ⊶ /'medɪkl/ *adjective* 形容词
connected with medicine, hospitals or doctors 医药的；医学的；医疗的： *a medical student* 医科学生 ◇ *medical treatment* 医疗

medicine ⊶ /'medsn; 'medɪsn/ *noun* 名词
1 (*no plural* 不用复数形式) the science of understanding illnesses and making sick people well again 医学： *He's studying medicine.* 他在学医。

2 (*plural* 复数形式 medicines) special liquids or pills that help you to get better when you are ill 药: *Take this medicine every morning.* 每天早上服用此药。

medieval (*British also* 英式英语亦作 mediaeval) /ˌmedi'i:vl/ *adjective* 形容词
connected with the years between about 1100 and 1500 in Europe 中世纪的（欧洲历史上约 1100 至 1500 年）: *a medieval castle* 中世纪的城堡 ⊃ Look at **Middle Ages**. 见 Middle Ages。

medium ⊶ /'mi:diəm/ *adjective* 形容词
not big and not small （尺寸）中等的: *Would you like a small, medium or large Coke?* 你要小杯、中杯还是大杯的可乐？ ◇ *He is of medium height.* 他中等身材。

meet ⊶ /mi:t/ *verb* 动词 (meets, meeting, met /met/, has met)

> 🔎 PRONUNCIATION 读音说明
> The word **meet** sounds just like **meat**.
> * meet 读音同 meat。

1 to come together by chance or because you have planned it 相遇；会面；相见: *I met Kate in the library today.* 我今天在图书馆碰到了凯特。◇ *Let's meet outside the cinema at eight o'clock.* 咱们八点钟在电影院外面见吧。
2 to see and speak to somebody for the first time 初次见面；结识；相识: *Have you met Anne?* 你跟安妮见过面吗？
3 to go to a place and wait for somebody to arrive 接；迎接: *Can you meet me at the airport?* 你能到机场接我吗？
4 to join together with something 连接；相交: *The two rivers meet in Oxford.* 这两条河在牛津汇合。

meeting ⊶ /'mi:tɪŋ/ *noun* 名词
1 a time when people come together for a special reason, usually to talk about something 会议；集会: *We had a meeting to talk about the plans for the new swimming pool.* 我们开会讨论了修建新游泳池的计划。
2 a time when two or more people come together 会面；相见: *Do you remember your first meeting with your husband?* 你记得和丈夫初次见面的情形吗？

melody /'melədi/ *noun* 名词 (*plural* 复数形式 melodies)
a group of musical notes that make a nice sound when you play or sing them together 旋律；曲调 ⊃ SAME MEANING 同义词为 **tune** 同义词为 tune: *This song has a lovely melody.* 这首歌的旋律很动听。

melon /'melən/ *noun* 名词
a big round yellow or green fruit with a lot of seeds inside 甜瓜 ⊃ Look at Picture Dictionary page P8. 见彩页 P8。

melt ⊶ /melt/ *verb* 动词 (melts, melting, melted)
to warm something so that it becomes liquid; to get warmer so that it becomes liquid （使）融化，熔化: *Melt the butter in a saucepan.* 把黄油放在平底锅里化开。◇ *The snow melted in the sunshine.* 雪在阳光下融化了。

member ⊶ /'membə(r)/ *noun* 名词
a person who is in a group 成员；会员: *I'm a member of the school football team.* 我是校足球队成员。

Member of Parliament /ˌmembər əv 'pɑ:ləmənt/ (*plural* 复数形式 Members of Parliament) *noun* 名词 (*abbr.* 缩略式 MP)
a person that the people of a town or city choose to speak for them in politics 议会议员；议员

membership /'membəʃɪp/ *noun* 名词 (*no plural* 不用复数形式)
being in a group or an organization 成员资格；会员资格: *Membership of the club costs £80 a year.* 俱乐部会费每年80英镑。

memo /'meməʊ/ *noun* 名词 (*plural* 复数形式 memos)
a note that you write to a person who works with you 备忘录: *I sent you a memo about the meeting on Friday.* 我给你发了份星期五会议的备忘录。

memorable /'memərəbl/ *adjective* 形容词
easy to remember because it is special in some way 值得纪念的；难忘的: *Their wedding was a very memorable day.* 他们的婚礼是个十分难忘的日子。

memorial /mə'mɔ:riəl/ *noun* 名词
something that people build or do to help us remember somebody, or something that happened 纪念碑；纪念活动: *The statue is a memorial to all the soldiers who died in the war.* 这尊雕像用来纪念全体阵亡将士。

memorize /'meməraɪz/ *verb* 动词 (memorizes, memorizing, memorized /'meməraɪzd/)
to learn something so that you can remember it exactly 记住；背熟: *We have to memorize a poem for homework.* 我们的家庭作业是背诵一首诗。

A B C D E F G H I J K L M N O P Q R S T U V W X Y Z

A
B
C
D
E
F
G
H
I
J
K
L
M
N
O
P
Q
R
S
T
U
V
W
X
Y
Z

memory 0─┐ /'meməri/ *noun* 名词
(*plural* 复数形式 memories)
1 the ability to remember things
记忆力；记性： *Ruth's got a very good
memory – she never forgets people's
names.* 露丝记性很好，从来不会忘记
别人的名字。
2 something that you remember 回忆；
记得的事： *I have very happy memories
of that holiday.* 我对那次假期留有非常
愉快的回忆。
3 the part of a computer that holds
information （电脑的）存贮器，内存

men *plural of* MAN * man 的复数形式

mend /mend/ *verb* 动词 (mends,
mending, mended)
to make something that is broken
or damaged good again 修理；修补
‽ SAME MEANING **repair** 同义词为 repair:
Can you mend this chair? 你能修这把
椅子吗？

mental 0─┐ /'mentl/ *adjective* 形容词
of or in your mind 精神的；心智的：
mental illness 精神病 ◇ *mental arithmetic*
(= done in your head) 心算
▸ **mentally** /'mentəli/ *adverb* 副词:
He is mentally ill. 他有精神病。

mention 0─┐ /'menʃn/ *verb* 动词
(mentions, mentioning, mentioned
/'menʃnd/)
to speak or write about something
without giving much information 提起；
提及： *Liz mentioned that she was going
to buy a new car.* 利兹提过会买辆新车。◇
He didn't mention Anna in his letter. 他在
信上没提到安娜。
don't mention it polite words that you
say when somebody says 'thank you'
（客气地回答别人的道谢）不客气：
'Thanks very much.' 'Don't mention it.'
"谢谢。""不客气。"
▸ **mention** *noun* 名词: *There was no
mention of the accident in the newspaper.*
报纸没有报道这起事故。

menu /'menjuː/ *noun* 名词 (*plural* 复数
形式 menus)
1 a list of the food that you can choose in
a restaurant 菜单；菜谱： *What's on the
menu tonight?* 今晚菜单上有什么菜？◇
Can I have the menu, please? 请给我一份
菜单好吗？
2 (*computing* 电脑) a list on the screen of
a computer that shows what you can do
菜单；选单： *Go to the menu and click
New.* 到选单处点击"新建"。

merchant /'mɜːtʃənt/ *noun* 名词
a person who buys and sells things,
especially from and to other countries
商人；（尤指）外贸商人： *She's a wine
merchant.* 她是葡萄酒商。

mercy /'mɜːsi/ *noun* 名词 (*no plural* 不用
复数形式)
being kind and not hurting somebody
who has done wrong 仁慈；宽恕；慈悲：
The prisoners begged for mercy. 囚犯请求
宽恕。
be at the mercy of somebody or 或
something to have no power against
somebody or something that is strong
任由…处置；受…摆布；对…无能为力：
Farmers are at the mercy of the weather.
农民靠天吃饭。

mere /mɪə(r)/ *adjective* 形容词
only; not more than 仅仅的；只不过：
*She was a mere child when her parents
died.* 父母去世时，她只不过是个小孩。

merely /'mɪəli/ *adverb* 副词
only 仅仅；只不过 ‽ SAME MEANING **just**
同义词为 just： *I don't want to buy the
book – I am merely asking how much it
costs.* 我并不想买这本书，只不过想问问
价钱。

merge /mɜːdʒ/ *verb* 动词 (merges,
merging, merged /mɜːdʒd/)
to join together with something else
合并；结合： *Three small companies
merged into one large one.* 三家小公司
合并成一家大公司。

merit¹ /'merɪt/ *noun* 名词
the thing or things that are good about
somebody or something 优点；长处：
What are the merits of this plan? 这个计划
有什么好处？

merit² /'merɪt/ *verb* 动词 (merits,
meriting, merited) (*formal* 正式)
to be good enough for something 应得；
值得 ‽ SAME MEANING **deserve** 同义词为
deserve： *This suggestion merits further
discussion.* 这个建议值得进一步讨论。

mermaid /'mɜːmeɪd/ *noun* 名词
a woman in stories who has a fish's tail
and lives in the sea （故事中的）美人鱼

merry /'meri/ *adjective* 形容词 (merrier,
merriest)
happy 高兴的；快乐的： *Merry Christmas!*
圣诞快乐！

merry-go-round /'meri gəʊ raʊnd/
noun 名词
1 (*British* 英式英语) (*also* 亦作
roundabout) (*American* 美式英语

carousel) a big round machine with models of animals or cars on it. Children can ride on it as it turns. 旋转木马
2 *American English for* ROUNDABOUT (2) 美式英语，即 roundabout 第 2 义

merry-go-round 旋转木马

merry-go-round (*British also* 英式英语亦作 **roundabout**)
carousel (*American* 美式英语)
旋转木马

roundabout (*British* 英式英语)
merry-go-round (*American* 美式英语)
旋转平台

mess¹ /mes/ *noun* 名词 (*no plural* 不用复数形式)
1 a lot of untidy or dirty things all in the wrong place 脏乱；杂乱：*Your bedroom is **in a mess**.* 你的卧室又脏又乱。◊ *Don't **make a mess** in the kitchen.* 别把厨房弄得乱七八糟。
2 a person or thing that is untidy or dirty 邋遢的人；脏乱的东西：*My hair is a mess!* 我的头发乱糟糟的！
3 a difficult situation 麻烦；困境：*She's **in a mess** – she's got no money and nowhere to live.* 她陷入了困境——既没钱又没住处。

mess² /mes/ *verb* 动词 (messes, messing, messed /mest/)
mess about, mess around to behave in a silly way 胡闹；瞎闹：*Stop messing around and finish your work!* 别瞎闹了，把你的活儿干完！
mess something up
1 to do something badly or make something go wrong 把…弄糟；搞砸：*The bad weather messed up our plans for the weekend.* 恶劣的天气打乱了我们周末的安排。
2 to make something untidy or dirty

弄乱；弄脏：*Don't mess my hair up!* 别弄乱我的头发！

message ⊶ /'mesɪdʒ/ *noun* 名词
words that one person sends to another 信息；口信；音信：*Could you **give a message** to Jane, please?* 请你给简捎个口信好吗？◊ *Mr Willis is not here at the moment. Can I **take a message**?* 威利斯先生这会儿不在，要我传话吗？

messenger /'mesɪndʒə(r)/ *noun* 名词
a person who brings a message 送信人；通信员；信使

messy /'mesi/ *adjective* 形容词 (messier, messiest)
1 untidy or dirty 凌乱的；脏乱的：*a messy kitchen* 脏乱的厨房
2 making you untidy or dirty 使不整洁的；使脏乱的：*Painting is a messy job.* 绘画是个脏活儿。

met *form of* MEET * meet 的不同形式

metal ⊶ /'metl/ *noun* 名词
a solid substance that is usually hard and shiny, such as iron, tin or gold 金属：*This chair is made of metal.* 这把椅子是金属做的。◊ *a metal box* 金属盒

metallic /mə'tælɪk/ *adjective* 形容词
looking like metal or making a noise like one piece of metal hitting another 金属般的；发出金属撞击声的：*metallic paint* 有金属光泽的颜料

meter /'miːtə(r)/ *noun* 名词
1 a machine that measures or counts something 计量器；计量表：*an electricity meter* 电表
2 *American English for* METRE 美式英语，即 metre

method ⊶ /'meθəd/ *noun* 名词
a way of doing something 方法；办法：*What is the best **method of** cooking beef?* 烹调牛肉的最佳方法是什么？

metre ⊶ (*British* 英式英语) (*American* 美式英语 meter) /'miːtə(r)/ (*abbr.* 缩略式 m) *noun* 名词
a measure of length. There are 100 **centimetres** in a **metre**. 米：*The wall is eight metres long.* 这墙长八米。

metric /'metrɪk/ *adjective* 形容词
using the system of metres, grams and litres to measure things（计量单位）公制的，米制的

miaow /mi'aʊ/ *noun* 名词
a sound that a cat makes（猫叫声）喵
▸ **miaow** *verb* 动词 (miaows, miaowing, miaowed /mi'aʊd/)：*Why is the cat*

x

A B C D E F G H I J K L **M** N O P Q R S T U V W X Y Z

miaowing? 那只猫为什么在喵喵叫？
⊃ Look at **purr**. 见 purr。

mice *plural of* MOUSE * mouse 的复数
形式

microchip /'maɪkrəʊtʃɪp/ *noun* 名词
a very small thing inside a computer or
a machine that makes it work 微芯片

microcomputer /'maɪkrəʊkəmpjuːtə(r)/
noun 名词
a small computer 微型电脑

microphone 麦克风

microphone /'maɪkrəfəʊn/ *noun* 名词
a piece of electrical equipment that
makes sounds louder or records them
so you can listen to them later 麦克风；
话筒；传声器

microscope /'maɪkrəskəʊp/ *noun* 名词
a piece of equipment with special glass in
it, that makes very small things look
much bigger 显微镜： *We looked at the
hair under a microscope.* 我们在显微镜下
观看头发。

microwave /'maɪkrəweɪv/ *(also* 亦作
microwave oven /,maɪkrəweɪv 'ʌvn/)
noun 名词
a type of oven that cooks or heats food
very quickly using electric waves 微波炉

mid- /mɪd/ *adjective* 形容词
(in) the middle of（在）中间的；居中的：
My mother's in her mid-thirties. 我母亲
三十五六岁了。◇ *mid-morning coffee*
上午十点左右喝的咖啡

midday ⊙┅ /,mɪd'deɪ/ *noun* 名词
(*no plural* 不用复数形式)
twelve o'clock in the day 中午；正午：
We met at midday. 我们中午见了面。
⊃ Look at **midnight**. 见 midnight。

middle ⊙┅ /'mɪdl/ *noun* 名词
1 the part that is the same distance from
the sides, edges or ends of something

中间；中部： *A peach has a stone in the
middle*. 桃子的中心有核。
2 the time after the beginning and before
the end（时间段的）中间： *The phone
rang in the middle of the night*. 午夜时分
电话响了。

**be in the middle of doing
something** to be busy doing something
忙于做某事： *I can't speak to you now –
I'm in the middle of cooking dinner.* 我现在
不能跟你谈话，我正忙着做饭呢。
▸ **middle** *adjective* 形容词： *There are
three houses and ours is the middle one.*
那里有三所房子，我们的是中间那所。

middle-aged /,mɪdl 'eɪdʒd/ *adjective*
形容词
not old and not young; between the ages
of about 40 and 60 中年的（40 岁至 60 岁
左右）： *a middle-aged man* 中年男子

the Middle Ages /ðə ,mɪdl 'eɪdʒɪz/
noun 名词 (*plural* 用复数形式)
the years between about 1100 and 1500
in Europe 中世纪（欧洲历史上约 1100 至
1500 年的时期）⊃ Look at **medieval**.
见 medieval。

middle name /'mɪdl neɪm/ *noun* 名词
a name that comes between your first
name and your family name 中名（名和
姓之间的名字）

middle school /'mɪdl skuːl/ *noun* 名词
(*British* 英式英语)
a school for children between the ages
of 9 and 13 中间学校（9 岁到 13 岁儿童
入读）

midnight ⊙┅ /'mɪdnaɪt/ *noun* 名词
(*no plural* 不用复数形式)
twelve o'clock at night 午夜；子夜： *We
left the party at midnight*. 我们午夜时离开
了聚会。⊃ Look at **midday**. 见 midday。

midway /,mɪd'weɪ/ *adverb* 副词
in the middle of 在中间；在中途 ⊃ SAME
MEANING **halfway** 同义词 halfway：
*The village is midway between Girona and
Barcelona.* 这个村子位于赫罗纳和巴塞罗
那之间。

midwife /'mɪdwaɪf/ *noun* 名词 (*plural*
复数形式 **midwives** /'mɪdwaɪvz/)
a person whose job is to help women give
birth to babies 助产士；接生员；产婆

might ⊙┅ /maɪt/ *modal verb* 情态动词
1 used as the form of 'may' when you
repeat later what somebody has said
（间接引语中用作 may 的过去式）：
He said he might be late (= his words
were 'I may be late'), *but he was early.*
他说他可能会迟到，结果早来了。

2 a word that shows what will perhaps happen or what is possible 可能：*Don't run because you might fall.* 别跑，你可能会摔倒。◇ *'Where's Anne?' 'I don't know – she might be in the kitchen.'* "安妮在哪里？""我不知道，可能在厨房里吧。"
3 (*British* 英式英语) (*formal* 正式) a word that you use to ask something in a very polite way（用于客气的提问）可以：*Might I say something?* 我可以说句话吗？ ⊃ Look at the note at **modal verb**. 见 modal verb 条的注释。

mighty /ˈmaɪti/ *adjective* 形容词 (mightier, mightiest) (*formal* 正式)
very great, strong or powerful 巨大的；强大的；有力的：*He hit him with a mighty blow across his shoulder.* 他一拳重重地打在他的肩膀上。

migrate /maɪˈɡreɪt/ *verb* 动词 (migrates, migrating, migrated)
1 (used about animals and birds) to move from one part of the world to another every year（动物和鸟类）迁徙
2 (used about large numbers of people) to go to live and work in another place（大批人）移民，移居，迁移
▶ **migration** /maɪˈɡreɪʃn/ *noun* 名词：*the annual migration of the reindeer* 驯鹿每年一次的迁徙

mild /maɪld/ *adjective* 形容词 (milder, mildest)
1 not strong 不浓的；清淡的：*This cheese has a mild taste.* 这种奶酪味道清淡。
2 not too hot and not too cold 温和的；和煦的：*a mild winter* 和暖的冬天

mile 0━ /maɪl/ *noun* 名词
a measure of length that is used in Britain and the USA (= 1.6 kilometres) 英里（长度单位；1 英里等于 1.6 公里）：*We live three miles from the sea.* 我们住的地方离海边三英里。 ⊃ Look at the note at **foot**. 见 foot 条的注释。

military /ˈmɪlətri/ *adjective* 形容词
connected with soldiers or the army, navy, etc. 军事的；军队的：*a military camp* 军营 ◇ *military action* 军事行动

milk¹ 0━ /mɪlk/ *noun* 名词 (*no plural* 不用复数形式)
the white liquid that a mother makes in her body to give to her baby. People drink the **milk** of cows and some other animals. 奶；牛奶：*Do you want milk in your coffee?* 你的咖啡要加奶吗？ ⊃ Look at Picture Dictionary page **P6**. 见彩页 P6。

milk² /mɪlk/ *verb* 动词 (milks, milking, milked /mɪlkt/)

to take milk from a cow or another animal（给牛或其他动物）挤奶

milkman /ˈmɪlkmən/ *noun* 名词 (*plural* 复数形式 milkmen /ˈmɪlkmən/)
(in Britain) a person who takes milk to people's houses every day 送奶人

milkshake /ˈmɪlkʃeɪk/ *noun* 名词
a drink made of milk with the flavour of chocolate or fruit added to it 奶昔：*a strawberry milkshake* 草莓奶昔 ⊃ Look at Picture Dictionary page **P6**. 见彩页 P6。

milky /ˈmɪlki/ *adjective* 形容词 (milkier, milkiest)
with a lot of milk in it 含奶多的：*milky coffee* 牛奶咖啡

mill /mɪl/ *noun* 名词
1 a building where a machine makes flour from grain 磨坊；面粉厂 ⊃ Look also at **windmill**. 亦见 windmill。
2 a factory where one material is made, for example cloth or paper 工厂；制造厂：*a paper mill* 造纸厂

millennium /mɪˈleniəm/ *noun* 名词 (*plural* 复数形式 millennia /mɪˈleniə/ or 或 millenniums)

🔍 SPELLING 拼写说明
Remember! You spell **millennium** with **LL** and **NN**. 记住：millennium 拼写中有 ll 和 nn。

a period of a thousand years 一千年；千年期

millimetre (*British* 英式英语) (*American* 美式英语 millimeter) /ˈmɪlimiːtə(r)/ (*abbr.* 缩略式 mm) *noun* 名词
a measure of length. There are ten millimetres in a **centimetre**. 毫米：*60 mm * 60 毫米

million 0━ /ˈmɪljən/ *number* 数词
1 1 000 000; one thousand thousand 一百万：*About 56 million people live in this country.* 大约有 5 600 万人住在这个国家。◇ *millions of dollars* 数百万元 ◇ *six million pounds* 六百万英镑

🔍 GRAMMAR 语法说明
We say **six million pounds** (without 's'), but **millions of** pounds. 要说 six million pounds（million 不加 s），但形容数量大时用 millions of pounds。

2 millions (*informal* 非正式) a lot 极多；大量：*I have millions of things to do.* 我有很多很多事情要做。

millionaire /ˌmɪljəˈneə(r)/ *noun* 名词
a person who has more than a million

pounds, dollars, etc.; a very rich person
百万富翁；大富豪

millionth 0― /'mɪljənθ/ *adjective,
pronoun, noun* 形容词，代词，名词
1 000 000th 第一百万的；第一百万；百万
分之一：*Our millionth customer will
receive a prize.* 我们的第一百万位顾客将
得到一份奖品。

mime /maɪm/ *noun* 名词 (no plural 不用
复数形式)
a way of telling a story or telling
somebody something by moving your
face, hands and body, without speaking
哑剧；默剧：*The show is a combination
of dance and mime.* 演出结合了舞蹈和
哑剧。
▶ **mime** *verb* 动词 (mimes, miming,
mimed /maɪmd/): *He mimed that he
was hungry.* 他用哑剧形式表示肚子饿了。

mimic /'mɪmɪk/ *verb* 动词 (mimics,
mimicking, mimicked /'mɪmɪkt/)
to copy the way somebody moves and
speaks in an amusing way 滑稽地模仿
▶ **mimic** *noun* 名词：*Sally's a brilliant
mimic.* 萨莉很擅长滑稽模仿。

mince /mɪns/ *noun* 名词 (no plural 不用
复数形式) (British 英式英语)
meat that has been cut into very small
pieces 绞碎的肉；肉末
▶ **mince** *verb* 动词 (minces, mincing,
minced /mɪnst/): *Mince the beef finely.*
把牛肉绞成细末。

mind[1] 0― /maɪnd/ *noun* 名词
the part of you that thinks and
remembers 头脑；思想：*He has a very
quick mind.* 他思维敏捷。
be or 或 **go out of your mind**
(informal 非正式) to be or become mad
or very worried 心智失常；发疯：*Where
were you? I was going out of my mind with
worry.* 你去哪里了？我担心得快要疯了。
change your mind to have an idea,
then decide to do something different
改变主意：*I planned a holiday in France
and then changed my mind and went to
Italy.* 我原本打算去法国度假，后来改变
主意去意大利了。
have something on your mind to be
worried about something 担忧；操心：
I've got a lot on my mind at the moment.
我现在有很多事要操心。
make up your mind to decide
something 下定决心；拿定主意：*Shall I
buy the blue shirt or the red one? I can't
make up my mind.* 我该买蓝色的那件衬衫
还是红色的那件？我拿不定主意。

mind[2] 0― /maɪnd/ *verb* 动词 (minds,
minding, minded)
1 to feel unhappy or angry about
something 介意：*Do you mind if I smoke?*
我吸烟，你介意吗？◇ *I don't mind the
heat at all.* 我根本不在乎高温。
2 to be careful of somebody or
something 当心；注意 ⊃ SAME MEANING
watch 同义词为 watch：*Mind the step!*
注意台阶！
**do you mind ... ?, would you
mind ... ?** please could you...? 请你…
好吗；可否请你…：*It's cold – would you
mind closing the window?* 这里很冷，请你
关上窗户好吗？
I don't mind it is not important to me
which thing 我无所谓；都可以：*'Do you
want tea or coffee?' 'I don't mind.'* "你要
茶还是咖啡？" "都可以。"
mind out (British 英式英语) (informal
非正式) used to tell somebody to get out
of the way or to be careful 让开；当心：
Mind out! There's a dog in the road. 小心！
路上有条狗。
never mind don't worry; it doesn't
matter 没关系；不要紧：*'I forgot your
book.' 'Never mind, I don't need it today.'*
"我忘了带你的书。" "没关系，我今天
不用。"

mine[1] 0― /maɪn/ *pronoun* 代词
something that belongs to me 我的：
That bike is mine. 那辆自行车是我的。◇
Are those books mine or yours? 那些书是
我的还是你的？

mine[2] 0― /maɪn/ *noun* 名词
1 a very big hole in the ground where
people work to get things like coal, gold
or diamonds 矿；矿井：*a coal mine* 煤矿
2 a bomb that is hidden under the
ground or under water 地雷；水雷
▶ **mine** *verb* 动词 (mines, mining, mined
/maɪnd/): *Diamonds are mined in South
Africa.* 钻石是在南非开采的。

miner /'maɪnə(r)/ *noun* 名词
a person who works in a mine 矿工；
采矿者

mineral /'mɪnərəl/ *noun* 名词
Minerals are things like coal, gold, salt or
oil that come from the ground and that
people use. 矿物；矿物质

mineral water /'mɪnərəl wɔːtə(r)/ *noun*
名词 (no plural 不用复数形式)
water with MINERALS in it, that comes
from the ground 矿泉水：*a bottle of
mineral water* 一瓶矿泉水 ⊃ Look at
Picture Dictionary page **P6**. 见彩页 P6。

mingle /'mɪŋgl/ *verb* 动词 (mingles, mingling, mingled /'mɪŋgld/)
to mix with other things or people 混合；掺杂：*The colours **mingled together** to make brown.* 这些颜色混在一起就成了棕色。◇ *Policemen **mingled with** the crowd.* 警察混在人群之中。

mini- /'mɪni/ *prefix* 前缀
very small 迷你的；极小的：*The school has a minibus that can carry twelve people.* 学校有辆可载十二人的中巴。

miniature /'mɪnətʃə(r)/ *adjective* 形容词
very small; much smaller than usual 微型的；小型的：*a miniature railway* 微型铁路

minimize /'mɪnɪmaɪz/ *verb* 动词 (minimizes, minimizing, minimized /'mɪnɪmaɪzd/)
to make something as small as possible 使减少到最低限度：*We want to **minimize** the risk to the public.* 我们想尽量减少对公众造成的危害。

minimum /'mɪnɪməm/ *noun* 名词
(no plural 不用复数形式)
the smallest size, amount or number that is possible 最小值；最低限度：*We need a **minimum** of six people to play this game.* 我们至少要有六个人才能玩这个游戏。
▸ **minimum** *adjective* 形容词：*What is the **minimum** age for leaving school in your country?* 在你们国家，离开学校的最低年龄是多少？ ⊃ OPPOSITE **maximum** 反义词为 maximum

miniskirt /'mɪniskɜːt/ *noun* 名词
a very short skirt 超短裙；迷你裙

minister /'mɪnɪstə(r)/ *noun* 名词
1 one of the most important people in a government 部长；大臣：*the Minister of Education* 教育部长 ⊃ Look at **prime minister**. 见 prime minister。
2 a priest in some Christian churches（某些基督教教会的）牧师

ministry /'mɪnɪstri/ *noun* 名词 (plural 复数形式 ministries)
a part of the government that controls one special thing（政府的）部：*the Ministry of Defence* 国防部

minor /'maɪnə(r)/ *adjective* 形容词
not very big or important 较小的；次要的：*Don't worry – it's only a **minor** problem.* 别担心，这只是个小问题。◇ *a **minor** road* 小路 ⊃ OPPOSITE **major** 反义词为 major

minority /maɪ'nɒrəti/ *noun* 名词 (plural 复数形式 minorities)
the smaller part of a group 少数；少数人：*Only a **minority** of the students speak English.* 只有少数学生说英语。 ⊃ OPPOSITE **majority** 反义词为 majority

mint /mɪnt/ *noun* 名词
1 (no plural 不用复数形式) a small plant with a strong fresh taste and smell, that you put in food and drinks 薄荷：*mint sauce* 薄荷酱
2 (plural 复数形式 mints) a sweet made from this 薄荷糖

minus¹ /'maɪnəs/ *preposition* 介词
1 (maths 数学) less; when you take away 减；减去：*Six **minus** two is four* (6 - 2 = 4). 六减二等于四。 ⊃ Look at **plus**. 见 plus。
2 below zero 零下：*The temperature will fall to **minus** ten degrees.* 温度将降至零下十度。

minus² /'maɪnəs/ *adjective* 形容词
(maths 数学) lower than zero 负的；小于零的：*a **minus** number* 负数

minute¹ **0-** /'mɪnɪt/ *noun* 名词
1 a measure of time. There are 60 seconds in a **minute** and 60 **minutes** in an hour. 分钟；分：*It's nine **minutes** past six.* 现在是六点零九分。◇ *The train leaves **in ten minutes**.* 火车十分钟后开出。
2 a short time 一会儿 ⊃ SAME MEANING **moment** 同义词为 moment：*Just a **minute** – I'll get my coat.* 等一下，我去拿大衣。◇ *Have you got a **minute**? I'd like to talk to you.* 你有空吗？我想跟你谈谈。
in a minute very soon 很快；马上：*I'll be ready **in a minute**.* 我马上就好。
the minute as soon as 一⋯就：*Phone me **the minute** you arrive.* 你一到就给我打电话。

minute² /maɪ'njuːt/ *adjective* 形容词
very small 极小的；微小的 ⊃ SAME MEANING **tiny** 同义词为 tiny：*I can't read his writing – it's **minute**.* 我看不清他的字——写得太小了。

miracle /'mɪrəkl/ *noun* 名词
a wonderful and surprising thing that happens and that you cannot explain 奇迹：*It's a **miracle that** he wasn't killed.* 他没死，真是个奇迹。

miraculous /mɪ'rækjələs/ *adjective* 形容词
wonderful and surprising 奇迹般的；不可思议的：*a **miraculous** escape* 奇迹般的逃脱
▸ **miraculously** *adverb* 副词：***Miraculously**, no one was hurt.* 不可思议的是，没有人受伤。

mirror ⊶ /ˈmɪrə(r)/ *noun* 名词
a piece of special glass where you can see yourself 镜子: *Look in the mirror.* 照照镜子。 ⇨ Look at Picture Dictionary page **P10**. 见彩页 P10。

mis- /mɪs/ *prefix* 前缀
You can add **mis-** to the beginning of some words to show that something is done wrong or badly, for example *misunderstand* (= not understand correctly). （用在某些词前表示错误地、糟糕地）

misbehave /ˌmɪsbɪˈheɪv/ *verb* 动词
(misbehaves, misbehaving, misbehaved /ˌmɪsbɪˈheɪvd/)
to behave badly 行为不端: *Children who misbehaved were punished.* 调皮捣蛋的孩子受到了惩罚。 ⇨ OPPOSITE **behave** 反义词为 behave

mischief /ˈmɪstʃɪf/ *noun* 名词 (*no plural* 不用复数形式)
bad behaviour that is not very serious 淘气; 恶作剧: *Don't get into mischief while I'm out!* 我外出时不许捣蛋!

mischievous /ˈmɪstʃɪvəs/ *adjective* 形容词
A **mischievous** child likes to annoy people, but not in a serious way. （孩子）顽皮的、捣蛋的 ⇨ SAME MEANING **naughty** 同义词为 naughty: *He gave a mischievous grin.* 他淘气地咧着嘴笑。

miserable /ˈmɪzrəbl/ *adjective* 形容词
1 feeling very sad 痛苦的; 悲惨的: *I waited in the rain for an hour, feeling cold, wet and miserable.* 我在雨中等了一个小时, 又冷又湿, 难受极了。
2 making you feel sad 使人难受的: *miserable weather* 叫人难受的天气

misery /ˈmɪzəri/ *noun* 名词 (*no plural* 不用复数形式)
great unhappiness 痛苦; 悲惨: *the misery of war* 战争带来的苦难

misfortune /ˌmɪsˈfɔːtʃuːn/ *noun* 名词 (*formal* 正式)
something bad that happens; bad luck 厄运; 不幸: *He has known great misfortune.* 他遭遇过极大的不幸。

mislead /ˌmɪsˈliːd/ *verb* 动词 (misleads, misleading /ˌmɪsˈliːdɪŋ/, has misled)
to make somebody believe something that is not true 误导; 使误信: *You misled me when you said you could give me a job.* 你说你能给我一份工作, 让我误以为真。

Miss ⊶ /mɪs/ *noun* 名词
a word that you use before the name of a girl or woman who is not married （用于未婚女子姓氏前的称呼）小姐: *Dear Miss Smith, …* 亲爱的史密斯小姐: … ⇨ Look at the note at **Ms**. 见 Ms 条的注释。

miss ⊶ /mɪs/ *verb* 动词 (misses, missing, missed /mɪst/)
1 to not hit or catch something 未击中; 未抓住: *I tried to hit the ball but I missed.* 我想要打那个球, 但没击中。
2 to not see or hear something 未看到; 未听到: *You missed a good programme on TV last night.* 你昨晚错过了一档精彩的电视节目。 ◇ *Our house is the one on the corner – you can't miss it.* 我们的房子是在拐角的那所, 你不会找不到的。
3 to be too late for a train, bus, plane or boat 错过, 未赶上（交通工具）: *I just missed my bus.* 我只差了一步, 没能赶上公共汽车。 ⇨ OPPOSITE **catch** 反义词为 catch
4 to feel sad about somebody or something that has gone 想念; 怀念: *I'll miss you when you leave.* 你走后我会想你的。
miss something out to not put in or do something; to not include something 不包括…在内; 遗漏: *I didn't finish the exam – I missed out two questions.* 我没答完试卷, 漏了两道题。

missile /ˈmɪsaɪl/ *noun* 名词
1 a powerful weapon that can be sent long distances through the air and then explodes 导弹: *nuclear missiles* 核导弹
2 a thing that you throw at somebody to hurt them （攻击用的）投掷物

missing ⊶ /ˈmɪsɪŋ/ *adjective* 形容词
lost, or not in the usual place 找不到的; 丢失的; 失踪的: *The police are looking for the missing child.* 警方正在寻找那名失踪的孩子。 ◇ *My purse is missing. Have you seen it?* 我的钱包不见了。你有没有见过?

mission /ˈmɪʃn/ *noun* 名词
a journey to do a special job 使命; 任务: *They were sent on a mission to the moon.* 他们被送往月球执行任务。

missionary /ˈmɪʃənri/ *noun* 名词 (*plural* 复数形式 missionaries)
a person who goes to another country to teach people about a religion 传教士

mist /mɪst/ *noun* 名词
thin cloud near the ground, that is difficult to see through 薄雾; 雾气: *Early in the morning, the fields were covered in mist.* 清晨, 田野笼罩在薄雾之中。
▶ **misty** *adjective* 形容词 (mistier, mistiest): *a misty morning* 薄雾弥漫的

早晨 ⊃ Look at Picture Dictionary page **P16**. 见彩页 P16。

mistake¹ 0━ /mɪˈsteɪk/ *noun* 名词
something that you think or do that is wrong 错误；失误: *You have **made a lot** **of spelling mistakes** in this letter.* 你在这封信中拼错了很多字。◊ *It was **a mistake** to go by bus – the journey took two hours!* 坐公共汽车去实在失策——路上竟花了两个小时!

> 🔎 **WHICH WORD?** 词语辨析
> **Mistake** or **fault**? 用 mistake 还是 fault?
> When you **make a mistake** you do something wrong. 犯错说 make a mistake: *Try not to make any mistakes in your exam.* 在考试中尽量别出错。
> If you do something bad it is **your fault**. 某人的过失说 somebody's fault: *It's my fault we're late. I lost the tickets.* 我们迟到都是我的错,我把票弄丢了。

by mistake when you did not plan to do it 错误地;无意中: *Sorry, I took your book by mistake.* 对不起,我错拿了你的书。

mistake² 0━ /mɪˈsteɪk/ *verb* 动词
(mistakes, mistaking, mistook /mɪˈstʊk/, has mistaken /mɪˈsteɪkən/)
to think that somebody or something is a different person or thing 将…错误地当成: *I'm sorry – I **mistook** you **for** my cousin.* 对不起,我误认你是我表妹了。

mistaken /mɪˈsteɪkən/ *adjective* 形容词
wrong 错误的;不正确的: *I said she was Spanish but I was mistaken – she's Portuguese.* 我说她是西班牙人,但原来我弄错了,她是葡萄牙人。◊ *a case of **mistaken identity** (= when people think that a person is somebody else)* 认错人的情况

misunderstand /ˌmɪsʌndəˈstænd/ *verb* 动词 (misunderstands, misunderstanding, misunderstood /ˌmɪsʌndəˈstʊd/, has misunderstood)
to not understand something correctly 误解;误会: *I'm sorry, I misunderstood what you said.* 对不起,我误解了你的话。

misunderstanding /ˌmɪsʌndəˈstændɪŋ/ *noun* 名词
a situation in which somebody does not understand something correctly 误解;误会: *I think **there's been a** **misunderstanding**. I ordered two tickets,*

not four. 我看是搞错了,我订的是两张票,不是四张。

mitten /ˈmɪtn/ *noun* 名词
a thing that you wear to keep your hand warm. It has one part for your thumb and another part for your other fingers. 连指手套 ⊃ Look at **glove**. 见 glove。

mix 0━ /mɪks/ *verb* 动词 (mixes, mixing, mixed /mɪkst/)
1 to put different things together to make something new 使混合;使掺和: *Mix yellow and blue paint **together** to make green.* 把黄的和蓝的颜料调在一起配成绿色。
2 to join together to make something new 混合;融合: *Oil and water don't mix.* 油和水不相融。
3 to be with and talk to other people 交往;相处: *In my job, I **mix with** a lot of different people.* 我在工作中要与许多不同的人打交道。

mix somebody or 或 **something up**
to think that one person or thing is a different person or thing 误以为…是;将…混淆: *People often mix Mark **up with** his brother.* 人们常把马克和他的弟弟弄混了。

mix something up to make things untidy 弄乱: *Don't mix up my papers!* 别把我的文件弄乱了!

mixed 0━ /mɪkst/ *adjective* 形容词
containing different kinds of people or things 混合的;混杂的: *a mixed salad* 什锦沙拉 ◊ *Is their school mixed (= with boys and girls together)?* 他们学校是男女同校吗?

mixer /ˈmɪksə(r)/ *noun* 名词
a machine that mixes things together 搅拌器;混合机: *a food mixer* 食物搅拌器

mixture 0━ /ˈmɪkstʃə(r)/ *noun* 名词
something that you make by mixing different things together 混合物: *Air is a **mixture of** gases.* 空气是多种气体的混合。◊ *a cake mixture* 蛋糕配料

mm *short way of writing* MILLIMETRE * millimetre 的缩写形式

moan /məʊn/ *verb* 动词 (moans, moaning, moaned /məʊnd/)
1 to make a long sad sound when you are hurt or very unhappy (因疼痛或悲伤而) 呻吟: *He was **moaning with** pain.* 他痛苦地呻吟着。
2 (*informal* 非正式) to talk a lot about something in a way that annoys other people 抱怨;发牢骚 ⊃ SAME MEANING

complain 同义词为 complain: *He's always **moaning about** the weather.* 他老是抱怨天气不好。
▶ **moan** *noun* 名词: *I heard a loud moan.* 我听到很大的呻吟声。

mob /mɒb/ *noun* 名词
a big noisy group of people who are shouting or fighting 暴民

mobile /'məʊbaɪl/ *adjective* 形容词
able to move easily from place to place 可移动的；流动的: *A mobile library visits the village every week.* 流动图书馆每星期都到村子里来。

mobile phone 移动电话

mobile phone ⚫╾ /ˌməʊbaɪl 'fəʊn/ (*British* 英式英语) (*British also* 英式英语亦作 **mobile** /'məʊbaɪl/) (*American* 美式英语 **cellphone**) *noun* 名词
a telephone that you can carry around with you 移动电话；手机: *I'll ring you on your mobile tonight.* 我今晚会打你手机。

mock /mɒk/ *verb* 动词 (mocks, mocking, mocked /mɒkt/) (*formal* 正式)
to laugh at somebody or something in an unkind way 嘲笑；嘲弄: *The other children mocked her old-fashioned clothes.* 别的孩子嘲笑她穿着土气。

modal verb /ˌməʊdl 'vɜːb/ *noun* 名词
a verb, for example 'might', 'can' or 'must', that you use with another verb 情态动词

> 🔍 **GRAMMAR** 语法说明
>
> **Can**, **could**, **may**, **might**, **should**, **must**, **will**, **shall**, **would** and **ought to** are modal verbs. 情态动词有 can、could、may、might、should、must、will、shall、would 和 ought to。
> Modal verbs do not have an 's' in the 'he/she' form: *She can drive* (NOT She cans drive). 情态动词与 he/she 连用时不加 s: *She can drive.* （不说 She cans drive.）。
> After modal verbs (except **ought to**), you use the infinitive without 'to': *I must go now* (NOT I must to go). 情态动词后面的不定式不跟 to（ought to 除外）: *I must go now.* （不说 I must to go.）。
> You make questions and negative sentences without 'do' or 'did': *Will you come with me?* (NOT Do you will come?) ◇ *They might not know* (NOT They don't might know). 疑问句和否定句不用 do 或 did: *Will you come with me?* （不说 Do you will come?）; *They might not know.* （不说 They don't might know.）。

model¹ ⚫╾ /'mɒdl/ *noun* 名词
1 a small copy of something （比实物小的）模型: *a **model** of the Taj Mahal* 泰姬陵的模型 ◇ *a **model** aeroplane* 飞机模型
2 one of the cars, machines, etc. that a certain company makes （汽车、机器等的）型号: *Have you seen their **latest model**?* 你见过他们最新的型号吗?
3 a person who wears clothes at a special show or for photographs, so that people will see them and buy them （时装表演或拍照的）模特儿
4 a person who sits or stands so that an artist can draw, paint or photograph them （绘画或摄影的）模特儿

model² /'mɒdl/ *verb* 动词 (models, modelling, modelled /'mɒdld/)
to wear and show clothes as a model 做时装模特儿: *Kate **modelled** swimsuits at the fashion show.* 凯特在时装表演中展示泳装。

modem /'məʊdem/ *noun* 名词
a piece of equipment that uses a telephone line to connect two computers 调制解调器

moderate /'mɒdərət/ *adjective* 形容词
not too much and not too little 中等的；适度的: *Cook the vegetables over a **moderate** heat.* 用中火煮这些蔬菜。

modern ⚫╾ /'mɒdn/ *adjective* 形容词
of the present time; of the kind that is usual now 现代的；时新的: *modern art* 现代艺术 ◇ *The airport is very modern.* 这个机场非常先进。

modest /'mɒdɪst/ *adjective* 形容词
not talking much about good things that

you have done or about things that you can do well 谦虚的; 谦逊的: *You didn't tell me you could sing so well – you're very modest!* 你没告诉我你唱歌唱得这么好，你太谦虚了！

▸ **modestly** *adverb* 副词: *He spoke quietly and modestly about his success.* 他低声谦虚地谈到了自己的成功经历。

▸ **modesty** /ˈmɒdəsti/ *noun* 名词 (*no plural* 不用复数形式): *She accepted the prize with her usual modesty.* 她以一贯的谦逊态度接受了奖项。

moist /mɔɪst/ *adjective* 形容词
a little wet 微湿的; 湿润的: *Keep the earth moist or the plant will die.* 保持土壤湿润，否则植物会枯死。

moisture /ˈmɔɪstʃə(r)/ *noun* 名词 (*no plural* 不用复数形式)
small drops of water on something or in the air（物体表面或空气中的）水分，潮气，湿气

mold, moldy *American English for* MOULD, MOULDY 美式英语，即 mould、mouldy

mole /məʊl/ *noun* 名词
1 a small grey or brown animal that lives under the ground and makes tunnels 鼹鼠（穴居地下，会挖地道）
2 a small dark spot on a person's skin 痣

molecule /ˈmɒlɪkjuːl/ *noun* 名词
the smallest part into which a substance can be divided without changing its chemical nature 分子 ⊃ Look at **atom**. 见 atom。

mom /mɒm/ *American English for* MUM 美式英语，即 mum

moment 0← /ˈməʊmənt/ *noun* 名词
a very short time 片刻; 瞬间 ⊃ SAME MEANING **minute** 同义词为 minute: *He thought for a moment before he answered.* 他想了片刻才回答。◇ *Can you wait a moment?* 你等一会儿行吗？

at the moment now 现在; 此刻: *She's on holiday at the moment, but she'll be back next week.* 她现在度假，下星期回来。

in a moment very soon 很快; 马上: *He'll be here in a moment.* 他很快就会来。

the moment as soon as 一…就: *Tell Jim to phone me the moment he arrives.* 告诉吉姆，叫他一到就给我打电话。

mommy /ˈmɒmi/ (*also* 亦作 **momma** /ˈmɒmə/) *American English for* MUMMY 美式英语，即 mummy

monarch /ˈmɒnək/ *noun* 名词
a king or queen 君主; 国王; 女王

monarchy /ˈmɒnəki/ *noun* 名词 (*plural* 复数形式 **monarchies**)
a country that has a king or queen 君主制国家; 君主国

monastery /ˈmɒnəstri/ *noun* 名词 (*plural* 复数形式 **monasteries**)
a place where religious men (called monks) live together 隐修院; 修道院; 寺院

Monday 0← /ˈmʌndeɪ/ *noun* 名词
the day of the week after Sunday and before Tuesday, the first day of the working week 星期一 ⊃ Look at the note at **day**. 见 day 条的注释。

money 金钱

credit card 信用卡

chequebook (*British* 英式英语)
checkbook (*American* 美式英语) 支票簿

coins 硬币

note (*British* 英式英语)
bill (*American* 美式英语) 纸币

money 0← /ˈmʌni/ *noun* 名词 (*no plural* 不用复数形式)

🔎 **PRONUNCIATION** 读音说明
The word **money** sounds like **funny**.
* money 读音像 funny。

what you use when you buy or sell something 钱; 金钱; 货币: *How much money did you spend?* 你花了多少钱？◇ *This jacket cost a lot of money.* 这件夹克花了不少钱。◇ *The film made a lot of money.* 这部电影赚了很多钱。

🔎 **WORD BUILDING** 词汇扩充
Money consists of **coins** (small round metal things) and **notes** (pieces of paper). This is called **cash**. 钱包括硬币（coin）和纸币（note）。这些称为现金（cash）: *I haven't got much cash. Can I pay by cheque?* 我现金不多，可以用支票支付吗？

The coins that you have in your purse are called **change**. 币值小的硬币称为零钱（change）： *Have you got any change for the phone?* 你有零钱打电话吗?
The money somebody gives you in a shop if you pay too much is also called **change**. 付钱时找回的钱也叫做 change： *Here's your change.* 这是找给你的钱。

monitor /ˈmɒnɪtə(r)/ *noun* 名词
a machine that shows pictures or information on a screen like a television 显示屏；显示器： *a PC with a 17-inch colour monitor* 带 17 英寸彩色显示器的个人电脑 ⇨ Look at Picture Dictionary page **P11**. 见彩页 P11。

monk /mʌŋk/ *noun* 名词
a religious man who lives with other religious men in a special building (called a **monastery**) 修士；僧侣

monkey 猴子

monkey /ˈmʌŋki/ *noun* 名词 (*plural* 复数形式 monkeys)
an animal with a long tail, that can climb trees 猴子

monotonous /məˈnɒtənəs/ *adjective* 形容词
always the same and therefore very boring 单调乏味的： *It's a very monotonous job.* 这是份很枯燥的工作。

monsoon /ˌmɒnˈsuːn/ *noun* 名词
the season when very heavy rain falls in Southern Asia （南亚的）雨季

monster /ˈmɒnstə(r)/ *noun* 名词
an animal in stories that is big, ugly and frightening （传说中的）怪物，怪兽

month 0⃟ /mʌnθ/ *noun* 名词
1 one of the twelve parts of a year 月；月份： *December is the last month of the year.* 十二月是一年中的最后一个月。◇ *We went on holiday last month.* 我们上个月度假去了。

The **months** of the year are: January, February, March, April, May, June, July, August, September, October, November, December.
一年中的月份（month）分别是一月（January）、二月（February）、三月（March）、四月（April）、五月（May）、六月（June）、七月（July）、八月（August）、九月（September）、十月（October）、十一月（November）、十二月（December）。

2 about four weeks 一个月的时间： *She was in hospital for a month.* 她在医院住了一个月。

monthly /ˈmʌnθli/ *adjective, adverb* 形容词，副词
happening or coming every month or once a month 每月的；每月一次（的）： *a monthly magazine* 月刊 ◇ *I am paid monthly.* 我领的是月薪。

monument /ˈmɒnjumənt/ *noun* 名词
a thing that is built to help people remember a person or something that happened 纪念性建筑；纪念碑；纪念像： *This is a monument to Queen Victoria.* 这是维多利亚女王纪念碑。

moo /muː/ *noun* 名词
the sound that a cow makes （牛叫声）哞
▶ **moo** *verb* 动词 (moos, mooing, mooed /muːd/): *Cows were mooing in the barn.* 牛在棚子里哞哞叫。

mood 0⃟ /muːd/ *noun* 名词
the way that you feel at a particular time 情绪；心情： *Dad is in a bad mood because he's lost his glasses.* 爸爸心情不好，因为他的眼镜丢了。◇ *Our teacher was in a very good mood today.* 我们老师今天心情非常好。◇ *I'm not in the mood for a party.* 我没有心情参加派对。

moody /ˈmuːdi/ *adjective* 形容词 (moodier, moodiest)
If you are **moody**, you often change and become angry or unhappy without warning. 情绪多变的；喜怒无常的： *Teenagers can be very moody.* 青少年情绪易变。

moon 0⃟ /muːn/ *noun* 名词 the moon (*no plural* 不用复数形式)
the big object that shines in the sky at night 月亮；月球： *When was the first landing on the moon?* 人类首次登月是在什么时候?

moonlight /'muːnlaɪt/ *noun* 名词
(*no plural* 不用复数形式)
the light from the moon 月光

moor[1] /mʊə(r)/ *noun* 名词
wild land on hills that has grass and low
plants, but not many trees 旷野；高沼；
漠泽： *We went walking on the Yorkshire
moors.* 我们在约克郡的旷野散步。

moor[2] /mʊə(r)/ *verb* 动词 (moors,
mooring, moored /mʊəd/)
to tie a boat or ship to something so that
it will stay in one place 使（船）停泊；
系泊

mop 拖把

mop /mɒp/ *noun* 名词
a thing with a long handle that you use
for washing floors 拖把；墩布
▶ **mop** *verb* 动词 (mops, mopping,
mopped /mɒpt/)： *I mopped the floor.*
我拖了地板。

moped /'məʊped/ *noun* 名词
a vehicle like a bicycle with a small
engine 机动自行车；摩托自行车 ⊃ Look
at the picture at **motorbike**. 见 motorbike
的插图。

moral[1] ☛ /'mɒrəl/ *adjective* 形容词
connected with what people think is right
or wrong 道德的： *Some people do not eat
meat for moral reasons.* 有些人出于道德
原因不吃肉。◇ *a moral problem* 道德
问题
▶ **morally** /'mɒrəli/ *adverb* 副词： *It's
morally wrong to tell lies.* 说谎在道德上是
不对的。

moral[2] /'mɒrəl/ *noun* 名词
1 morals (*plural* 用复数形式) ideas about
what is right and wrong 道德（思想）：
These people have no morals. 这些人没有
道德。
2 a lesson about what is right and wrong,
that you can learn from a story or from
something that happens 寓意；教益：
The moral of the story is that we should be

kind to animals. 这则故事的寓意是我们
应当善待动物。

more[1] ☛ /mɔː(r)/ *adjective, pronoun*
形容词，代词
a bigger amount or number of something
更多（的）；更大（的）；较多（的）；
较大（的）： *You've got more money
than I have.* 你的钱比我的多。◇ *Can I
have some more sugar in my tea?* 我的
茶里能再加点糖吗？◇ *We need two
more chairs.* 我们还需要两把椅子。◇
There aren't any more chocolates. 没有
巧克力了。⊃ Look at **most**[1]. 见 most[1].
⊃ OPPOSITE **less or fewer** 反义词为 less 或
fewer

more[2] ☛ /mɔː(r)/ *adverb* 副词
1 a word that makes an adjective or
adverb stronger（构成形容词或副词的
比较级）更，更加： *Your book was more
expensive than mine.* 你的书比我的贵。◇
Please speak more slowly. 请讲慢一点。
2 a bigger amount or number（数量上）
更多，更大；更甚： *I like Anna more
than her brother.* 我喜欢安娜多于她哥哥。
⊃ Look at **most**[2]. 见 most[2]. ⊃ OPPOSITE
less 反义词为 less

more or less almost, but not exactly
大概；差不多 ⊃ SAME MEANING **roughly**
同义词为 roughly： *We are more or less
the same age.* 我们年龄相仿。

not any more not any longer 不再：
They don't live here any more. 他们不再住
在这里了。

once more (*formal* 正式) again 又；
再一次： *Spring will soon be here once
more.* 春天又快到了。

morning ☛ /'mɔːnɪŋ/ *noun* 名词
the first part of the day, between the time
when the sun comes up and the middle
of the day (midday) 早晨；上午： *I went
swimming this morning.* 我今天上午去游
泳了。◇ *I'm going to London tomorrow
morning.* 我明天早上去伦敦。◇ *The letter
arrived on Tuesday morning.* 信是星期二
上午寄到的。◇ *I felt ill all morning.* 我整
个上午都感到不适。◇ *I start work at nine
o'clock in the morning.* 我上午九点开始
工作。

in the morning tomorrow during the
morning 明天早晨；明天上午： *I'll see you
in the morning.* 明天上午见。

mortgage /'mɔːɡɪdʒ/ *noun* 名词
money that you borrow to buy a house
按揭（房屋抵押贷款）

Moslem /'mɒzləm/ = MUSLIM

mosque /mɒsk/ *noun* 名词
a building where Muslims go to say their prayers 清真寺

mosquito 蚊子

mosquito /məˈskiːtəʊ/ *noun* 名词 (*plural* 复数形式 **mosquitoes**)
a small flying insect that bites people and animals and drinks their blood 蚊子

moss /mɒs/ *noun* 名词 (*no plural* 不用复数形式)
a soft green plant that grows like a carpet on things like trees and stones 苔藓；地衣

most¹ 0= /məʊst/ *adjective*, *pronoun* 形容词，代词
the biggest amount or number of something 最多（的）；最大（的）：*Jo did a lot of work, but I did **the most**.* 乔做了很多工作，可是我做得最多。◇ *He was ill for **most** of last week.* 他上周大部分时间都病了。 ⊃ Look at **more¹**. 见 more¹。
⊃ OPPOSITE **least** 反义词为 least
at most, at the most not more than a certain number, and probably less 至多；不超过：*We can stay two days at the most.* 我们顶多能逗留两天。
make the most of something to use something in the best way 充分利用：*We only have one free day, so let's make the most of it.* 我们只有一天的自由时间，所以咱们好好利用吧。

most² 0= /məʊst/ *adverb* 副词
more than all others 最：*It's the most beautiful garden I have ever seen.* 这是我见过的最漂亮的花园。◇ *Which part of your holiday did you enjoy most?* 你假期过得最愉快的是哪段时间？ ⊃ OPPOSITE **least** 反义词为 least

mostly 0= /ˈməʊstli/ *adverb* 副词
almost all 差不多所有；大多：*The students in my class are mostly Japanese.* 我班上的学生大多是日本人。

motel /məʊˈtel/ *noun* 名词
a hotel for people who are travelling by car 汽车旅馆

moth /mɒθ/ *noun* 名词
an insect with big wings that flies at night 蛾；飞蛾

mother 0= /ˈmʌðə(r)/ *noun* 名词
a woman who has a child 母亲；妈妈：*My mother is a doctor.* 我妈妈是医生。 ⊃ Look at **mum** and **mummy**. 见 mum 和 mummy。

motherhood /ˈmʌðəhʊd/ *noun* 名词 (*no plural* 不用复数形式)
the state of being a mother 母亲身份

mother-in-law /ˈmʌðər ɪn lɔː/ *noun* 名词 (*plural* 复数形式 **mothers-in-law**)
the mother of your husband or wife 婆婆；岳母

motion /ˈməʊʃn/ *noun* 名词 (*no plural* 不用复数形式)
movement 运动；移动：*The motion of the boat made her feel sick.* 船的颠簸让她想吐。◇ *Please remain seated while the bus is **in motion** (= moving).* 公共汽车行驶时请坐在座位上。

motivate /ˈməʊtɪveɪt/ *verb* 动词 (**motivates, motivating, motivated**)
to make somebody want to do something 驱使；推动；激发：*The best teachers know how to **motivate** children **to learn**.* 最优秀的教师懂得如何激励学生学习。

motive /ˈməʊtɪv/ *noun* 名词
a reason for doing something 动机：*Was there a **motive** for the murder?* 这起谋杀有动机吗？

motor /ˈməʊtə(r)/ *noun* 名词
the part inside a machine that makes it move or work 发动机；马达：*an electric motor* 电动机 ◇ *The washing machine doesn't work. It needs a new motor.* 洗衣机坏了，得换新的发动机。

> 🔎 SPEAKING 表达方式说明
> We usually use **engine**, not **motor**, when we are talking about cars and motorbikes. 指汽车和摩托车的发动机通常用 engine 而非 motor。

motorbike 0= /ˈməʊtəbaɪk/ (*also formal* 正式亦作 **motorcycle** /ˈməʊtəsaɪkl/) *noun* 名词
a vehicle with two wheels and an engine 摩托车

motorboat /ˈməʊtəbəʊt/ *noun* 名词
a small fast boat that has a MOTOR 摩托艇；汽艇 ⊃ Look at the picture at **boat**. 见 boat 的插图。

motorcyclist /ˈməʊtəsaɪklɪst/ *noun* 名词
a person who rides a motorbike 骑摩托车的人；摩托车手

motorbike 摩托车

motorbike 摩托车   **moped** 摩托自行车

scooter 小型摩托车

motorist /'məʊtərɪst/ *noun* 名词
a person who drives a car 开车的人；
驾车者

motor racing /'məʊtə reɪsɪŋ/ *noun* 名词
(*no plural* 不用复数形式)
a sport where people drive cars very fast
on a special road (called a track) to try to
win races 赛道汽车赛：*He watched motor
racing on TV.* 他在电视上看了赛车。

motorway /'məʊtəweɪ/ (*British* 英式英语)
(*American* 美式英语 expressway, freeway)
noun 名词
a wide road where vehicles can travel fast
高速公路：*The motorway around London
is called the M25.* 环绕伦敦的高速公路叫做
M25。

mould 霉

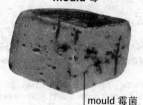

mould 霉菌

mould¹ /məʊld/ (*British* 英式英语)
(*American* 美式英语 mold) *noun* 名词
1 (*plural* 复数形式 moulds) a container
that you pour liquid into. The liquid then
becomes hard (sets) and takes the shape
of the container. 模具；模子：*They
poured the chocolate into a heart-shaped
mould.* 他们把巧克力倒入了心形模子。
2 (*no plural* 不用复数形式) a soft green,

grey or blue substance that grows on food
that is too old 霉；霉菌
  ▶ **mouldy** /'məʊldi/ *adjective* 形容词:
mouldy cheese 发霉的干酪

mould² /məʊld/ (*British* 英式英语)
(*American* 美式英语 mold) *verb* 动词
(**moulds, moulding, moulded**)
to make something soft into a certain
shape 使成形；塑造：*The children
moulded animals out of clay.* 孩子们把
黏土捏成了动物形状。

mound /maʊnd/ *noun* 名词
1 a small hill; a large pile of earth 小丘；
小山冈；土墩
2 a pile of things 一堆；一摞：*a mound
of newspapers* 一摞报纸

Mount /maʊnt/ (*abbr.* 缩略式 Mt) *noun*
名词
You use **Mount** before the name of a
mountain.（用于名称）山，峰：*Mount
Everest* 珠穆朗玛峰 ◇ *Mt Etna* 埃特纳火山

mount /maʊnt/ *verb* 动词 (**mounts,
mounting, mounted**)
1 (*also* 亦作 mount up) to increase 增加；
上升：*Tension in the area is mounting.*
该地区的紧张局势不断升级。◇ *My debts
were beginning to mount up.* 我的债务开始
增加了。
2 to get on a horse or a bicycle 骑上，
跨上（马或自行车）

mountain 山

mountain 0̶ /'maʊntən/ *noun* 名词
a very high hill 高山；山岳：*Everest is the
highest mountain in the world.* 珠穆朗玛峰
是世界上最高的山峰。◇ *We climbed the
mountain.* 我们登上了那座山。

mountain bike /'maʊntən baɪk/ *noun*
名词
a bicycle with a strong frame and wide
tyres that you can use to ride over rough
ground 山地自行车；越野单车

A B C D E F G H I J K L **M** N O P Q R S T U V W X Y Z

A
B
C
D
E
F
G
H
I
J
K
L
M
N
O
P
Q
R
S
T
U
V
W
X
Y
Z

mountaineer /ˌmaʊntəˈnɪə(r)/ *noun* 名词
a person who climbs mountains 登山者；登山运动员
▶ **mountaineering** /ˌmaʊntəˈnɪərɪŋ/ *noun* 名词 (*no plural* 不用复数形式)： *He took up mountaineering as a boy.* 他小时候就开始登山运动了。

mourn /mɔːn/ *verb* 动词 (mourns, mourning, mourned /mɔːnd/)
to feel very sad, usually because somebody has died 哀悼；伤逝： *She is still mourning for her husband.* 她仍在哀悼她丈夫。
▶ **mourning** /ˈmɔːnɪŋ/ *noun* 名词 (*no plural* 不用复数形式)： *They are in mourning for their son.* 他们在哀悼儿子。

mice 鼠标；老鼠

mouse ⚓ /maʊs/ *noun* 名词 (*plural* 复数形式 mice /maɪs/)
1 a small animal with a long tail 老鼠；耗子： *Our cat caught a mouse.* 我们的猫捉到了一只老鼠。
2 a thing that you move with your hand to tell a computer what to do 鼠标

moustache /məˈstɑːʃ/ *noun* 名词 (*British* 英式英语) (*American* 美式英语 mustache)
the hair above a man's mouth, below his nose 上唇的胡子；髭： *He has got a moustache.* 他嘴上边留着小胡子。 ➾ Look at the picture at **hair**. 见 hair 的插图。

mouth ⚓ /maʊθ/ *noun* 名词 (*plural* 复数形式 mouths /maʊðz/)
1 the part of your face below your nose that you use for eating and speaking 嘴；口： *Open your mouth, please!* 请张开嘴！ ➾ Look at Picture Dictionary page **P4**. 见彩页 P4。
2 the place where a river goes into the sea 河口；入海口： *the mouth of the Thames* 泰晤士河河口

mouthful /ˈmaʊθfʊl/ *noun* 名词
the amount of food or drink that you can put in your mouth at one time 一口（食物或饮料）： *She only had a mouthful of cake.* 她只吃了一口蛋糕。

move¹ ⚓ /muːv/ *verb* 动词 (moves, moving, moved /muːvd/)
1 to go from one place to another; to change the way you are standing or sitting 移动；改变位置： *Don't get off the bus while it's moving.* 公共汽车未停稳时不要下车。 ◇ *We moved to the front of the cinema.* 我们换到了电影院的前面去坐。
2 to put something in another place or another way 使移动；挪动： *Can you move your car, please?* 请你把你的汽车挪一挪好吗？
3 to go to live in another place 搬家；搬迁： *They sold their house in London and moved to Liverpool.* 他们卖掉伦敦的房子，搬到利物浦去了。 ◇ *We are moving house soon.* 我们快搬家了。
move in to go to live in a house or flat 迁入；搬进住宅： *I've got a new flat – I'm moving in next week.* 我买了套新公寓，下周就搬进去。
move out to leave a house or flat where you were living 迁出；搬出去

move² ⚓ /muːv/ *noun* 名词
1 a change of place or position 移动；挪动： *The police are watching every move she makes.* 警方监视着她的一举一动。
2 a change in the place where you live 搬家；搬迁： *We need a big van for the move.* 我们搬家需要一辆大客货车。
get a move on (*informal* 非正式) hurry 赶紧；赶快： *Get a move on or you'll be late for work!* 赶快，不然你上班就迟到了！

movement ⚓ /ˈmuːvmənt/ *noun* 名词
1 moving or being moved 活动；动作： *The old man's movements were slow and painful.* 那个老人行动缓慢而痛苦。
2 a group of people who have the same ideas or beliefs（具有共同思想或信念的）运动： *a political movement* 政治运动

movie ⚓ /ˈmuːvi/ *noun* 名词 (*American* 美式英语)
1 (*British* 英式英语 film) a film that you see at the cinema 电影；影片： *Would you like to see a movie?* 你想看电影吗？
2 the movies (*plural* 用复数形式) (*British* 英式英语 the cinema) (*no plural* 不用复数形式) the place where you go to watch a

film 电影院: *We went to the movies last night.* 我们昨晚去看电影了。

movie theater /'muːvi θɪətə(r)/ *American English for* CINEMA * 美式英语，即 cinema

moving /'muːvɪŋ/ *adjective* 形容词 making you feel something strongly, especially sadness 动人的；令人感动的: *It's a very moving story.* 这个故事非常感人。

mow /məʊ/ *verb* 动词 (mows, mowing, mowed /məʊd/, has mown /məʊn/) to cut grass with a machine 用割草机割（草）: *Sally is mowing the grass.* 萨莉正在割草。

mower /'məʊə(r)/ *noun* 名词 a machine that cuts grass 割草机；剪草机 ⊃ SAME MEANING **lawnmower** 同义词为 lawnmower ⊃ Look at the picture at **lawnmower**. 见 lawnmower 的插图。

MP /,em 'piː/ *short for* MEMBER OF PARLIAMENT * Member of Parliament 的缩略式

mph /,em piː 'eɪtʃ/ *abbreviation* 缩略式 a way of measuring how fast something is moving. **Mph** is short for **miles per hour**. 每小时英里数（mph 是 miles per hour 的缩略式）: *The train was travelling at 125 mph.* 火车正以每小时 125 英里的速度行驶。

MP3 /,em piː 'θriː/ *noun* 名词 (*also* 亦作 **MP3 file** /,em piː 'θriː faɪl/) a type of computer file which holds music * MP3（音乐）文件；MP3 档案

MP3 player /,em piː 'θriː pleɪə(r)/ *noun* 名词 a piece of computer equipment that can play MP3 FILES * MP3 播放器

Mr 0➞ /'mɪstə(r)/ *noun* 名词 a word that you use before the name of a man（用于男子姓名前的称呼）先生: *Mr Richard Waters* 理查德·沃特斯先生 ◇ *Mr Holland* 霍兰先生

Mrs 0➞ /'mɪsɪz/ *noun* 名词 a word that you use before the name of a woman who is married（用于已婚女性姓名前的称呼）太太，夫人: *Mrs Sandra Garcia* 桑德拉·加西亚夫人 ◇ *Mrs Nolan* 诺兰太太

Ms /məz; mɪz/ *noun* 名词 a word that you can use before the name of any woman, instead of **Mrs** or **Miss**（用于已婚或未婚女性姓名前的称呼）女士: *Ms Fiona Green* 菲奥纳·格林女士

🔎 **GRAMMAR** 语法说明

Miss, Mrs, Ms and **Mr** are all titles that we use in front of somebody's family name, NOT their first name, unless it is included with the family name.
* Miss、Mrs、Ms 和 Mr 后接姓氏而不是名字，但也可后接名字加姓: *Is there a Miss (Tamsin) Hudson here?* 这里有位叫（塔姆辛·）赫德森的小姐吗？ ◇ *Hello, Miss Hudson, come this way.* 你好，赫德森小姐，请往这边走。(NOT 不说 *Miss Tamsin*)

MSc /,em es 'siː/ *abbreviation* 缩略式 a second university degree that you get by doing a course or a piece of research in a science subject. **MSc** is short for **Master of Science**. 理科硕士（MSc 是 Master of Science 的缩略式）

Mt *short way of writing* MOUNT * Mount 的缩写形式

much¹ 0➞ /mʌtʃ/ *adjective, pronoun* 形容词，代词 (more, most) a big amount of something; a lot of something 大量；许多: *I haven't got much money.* 我没有多少钱。 ◇ *There was so much food that we couldn't eat it all.* 食物多得我们吃不完。 ◇ *Eat as much as you can.* 你能吃多少就吃多少。 ◇ *How much paper do you want?* 你要多少纸？ ◇ *How much is this shirt?* 这件衬衫多少钱？

🔎 **GRAMMAR** 语法说明

We usually use **much** only in negative sentences, in questions, and after 'too', 'so', 'as' and 'how'. * much 通常只用于否定句、疑问句或在 too、so、as、how 之后。
In other sentences we use **a lot** (of). 其他情况用 a lot (of): *She's got a lot of money.* 她有很多钱。

⊃ Look at **many**. 见 many。

much² 0➞ /mʌtʃ/ *adverb* 副词 a lot 很；非常: *I don't like him very much.* 我不太喜欢他。 ◇ *Your flat is much bigger than mine.* 你的公寓比我的大多了。 ◇ *'Do you like it?' 'No, not much.'* "你喜欢这个吗？" "不，不太喜欢。"

muck /mʌk/ *verb* 动词 (mucks, mucking, mucked /mʌkt/) (*British* 英式英语) (*informal* 非正式式)

muck about, muck around to behave in a silly way 游手好闲；胡混: *Stop mucking about and come and help me!* 别胡闹了，过来帮我一把！

A B C D E F G H I J K L M N O P Q R S T U V W X Y Z

mud ⚬┄ /mʌd/ *noun* 名词 (*no plural* 不用复数形式)
soft wet earth 泥; 污泥: *Phil came home from the football match covered in mud.* 菲尔在足球比赛后回到家里，浑身是泥。

muddle /'mʌdl/ *verb* 动词 (**muddles, muddling, muddled** /'mʌdld/)
1 (*also* 亦作 **muddle something up**) to put things in the wrong order or mix them up 弄乱; 搅混: *Their letters were all muddled up together in a drawer.* 他们的信都混放在一个抽屉里。
2 (*also* 亦作 **muddle somebody up**) (*informal* 非正式) to mix somebody's ideas so that they cannot understand or think clearly 使困惑; 使糊涂 ⊃ SAME MEANING **confuse** 同义词为 confuse: *Don't ask so many questions – you're muddling me.* 别问那么多问题——你把我弄糊涂了。
muddle somebody or 或 **something up** to think that one person or thing is a different person or thing 混淆; 分不清: *I always muddle Jane up with her sister.* 我总是把简和她妹妹搞混。
▶ **muddle** *noun* 名词: *I was in such a muddle that I couldn't find anything.* 我真是糊涂了，什么都找不到。

muddy /'mʌdi/ *adjective* 形容词 (**muddier, muddiest**)
covered with mud 满是泥的; 泥泞的: *When it rains, the roads get very muddy.* 这些路一下雨就会满是泥泞。

muesli /'mjuːzli/ *noun* 名词 (*no plural* 不用复数形式)
food made from grain, fruit and nuts that you eat with milk for breakfast 牛奶什锦早餐（谷物、水果、坚果加牛奶）

mug¹ /mʌg/ *noun* 名词
a big cup with straight sides 大杯; 马克杯: *a mug of tea* 一大杯茶 ⊃ Look at the picture at **cup**. 见 cup 的插图。

mug² /mʌg/ *verb* 动词 (**mugs, mugging, mugged** /mʌgd/)
to attack somebody in the street and take their money 拦路抢劫
▶ **mugger** *noun* 名词: *Watch out for muggers, especially at night.* 要当心劫匪，尤其是在晚上。

mule /mjuːl/ *noun* 名词
an animal that is used for carrying heavy loads and whose parents are a horse and a DONKEY (= an animal like a small horse with long ears) 骡子

multicultural /ˌmʌlti'kʌltʃərəl/ *adjective* 形容词
for or including people from many different countries and cultures 多元文化的; 多种文化融合的: *We live in a multicultural society.* 我们生活在多元文化的社会中。

multimedia /ˌmʌlti'miːdiə/ *adjective* 形容词
using sound, pictures and film as well as words on a screen 多媒体的: *The firm produces multimedia software for schools.* 这家公司生产供学校用的多媒体软件。

multiple-choice /ˌmʌltɪpl 'tʃɔɪs/ *adjective* 形容词
A **multiple-choice** exam or question gives you three or four different answers and you have to choose the right one. （试题）多项选择的

multiply ⚬┄ /'mʌltɪplaɪ/ *verb* 动词 (**multiplies, multiplying, multiplied** /'mʌltɪplaɪd/, **has multiplied**)
to make a number bigger by a certain number of times 乘; 使相乘: *Two multiplied by three is six (2 x 3 = 6).* 二乘以三等于六。◇ *Multiply three and seven together.* 把三与七相乘。⊃ Look at **divide**. 见 divide。
▶ **multiplication** /ˌmʌltɪplɪ'keɪʃn/ *noun* 名词 (*no plural* 不用复数形式): *Today we did multiplication and division.* 我们今天做了乘法和除法。

multi-storey /ˌmʌlti 'stɔːri/ *adjective* 形容词 (*British* 英式英语)
with many floors 多层的: *a multi-storey car park* 多层停车场

mum /mʌm/ (*British* 英式英语) (*American* 美式英语 **mom**) *noun* 名词 (*informal* 非正式)
mother 妈妈: *This is my mum.* 这是我妈妈。◇ *Can I have an apple, Mum?* 妈，我能吃个苹果吗？

mumble /'mʌmbl/ *verb* 动词 (**mumbles, mumbling, mumbled** /'mʌmbld/)
to speak quietly in a way that is not clear, so that people cannot hear you well 嘟哝; 口齿不清地说: *She mumbled something, but I didn't hear what she said.* 她叽里咕噜说了些话，但我听不清她说的是什么。

mummy /'mʌmi/ (*British* 英式英语) (*American* 美式英语 **mommy**) *noun* 名词 (*plural* 复数形式 **mummies**) (*informal* 非正式)
a word for 'mother' that children use （儿语）妈咪

mumps /mʌmps/ *noun* 名词 (*no plural* 不用复数形式)

an illness that children get which makes your neck swell (= get bigger) 腮腺炎

murder¹ 0̄ /'mɜːdə(r)/ *noun* 名词
the crime of killing somebody deliberately 谋杀（罪）；凶杀：*He was sent to prison for the **murder** of a police officer.* 他因谋杀一名警察而关进了监狱。

murder² 0̄ /'mɜːdə(r)/ *verb* 动词
(murders, murdering, murdered /'mɜːdəd/)
to kill somebody deliberately 谋杀；杀害：*She was murdered with a knife.* 她被人用刀杀死了。
▶ **murderer** /'mɜːdərə(r)/ *noun* 名词：*The police have caught the murderer.* 警方已经抓到凶手了。

murmur /'mɜːmə(r)/ *verb* 动词 (murmurs, murmuring, murmured /'mɜːməd/)
to speak in a low quiet voice 低语；嗬嗬地说：*'I love you,' she murmured.* "我爱你。"她低声地说。
▶ **murmur** *noun* 名词：*I heard the **murmur** of voices from the next room.* 我听见隔壁房间传来了嗬嗬细语声。

muscle 0̄ /'mʌsl/ *noun* 名词
one of the parts inside your body that are connected to the bones and which help you to move 肌肉：*Riding a bicycle is good for developing the leg muscles.* 骑自行车有助于锻炼腿部肌肉。

museum 0̄ /mju'ziːəm/ *noun* 名词
a building where people can look at old or interesting things 博物馆：*Have you ever been to the British Museum?* 你去过大英博物馆吗？

mushroom /'mʌʃrʊm/ *noun* 名词
a plant with a flat top and no leaves that you can eat as a vegetable 蘑菇 ➾ Look at Picture Dictionary page P9. 见彩页 P9。

music 0̄ /'mjuːzɪk/ *noun* 名词
(no plural 不用复数形式)
1 the sounds that you make by singing, or by playing instruments 音乐；乐曲：*What sort of music do you like?* 你喜欢什么类型的音乐？
2 signs on paper to show people what to sing or play 乐谱：*Can you read music?* 你懂乐谱吗？

> 🔎 WORD BUILDING 词汇扩充
> There are many different types of **music**. Here are some of them: classical, heavy metal, jazz, opera, reggae, rock. Do you know any others? * music 的种类很多，如：classical（古典音乐）、heavy metal（重金属音乐）、jazz（爵士乐）、opera

（歌剧）、reggae（雷盖音乐）、rock（摇滚乐）。你还知道别的吗？

musical¹ 0̄ /'mjuːzɪkl/ *adjective* 形容词
1 connected with music 音乐的：*musical instruments* (= the piano, the guitar or the trumpet, for example) 乐器
2 good at making music 有音乐天赋的：*Sophie's very musical.* 索菲很有音乐才能。

musical² /'mjuːzɪkl/ *noun* 名词
a play or film that has singing and dancing in it 音乐剧；音乐片；歌舞剧：*We went to see the musical 'Chicago'.* 我们去看了音乐剧《芝加哥》。

musician 0̄ /mju'zɪʃn/ *noun* 名词
a person who writes music or plays a musical instrument 音乐家；作曲家；乐师

Muslim /'mʊzlɪm/ *noun* 名词
a person who follows the religion of Islam 穆斯林；伊斯兰教信徒
▶ **Muslim** *adjective* 形容词：*the Muslim way of life* 穆斯林的生活方式

must 0̄ /məst; mʌst/ *modal verb* 情态动词
1 a word that you use to tell somebody what to do or what is necessary（表示命令或需要）必须：*You must look before you cross the road.* 过马路前一定要先看清楚交通情况。

> 🔎 GRAMMAR 语法说明
> You use **must not** or the short form **mustn't** /'mʌsnt/ to tell people **not** to do something. 告诉别人不要做某事用 must not 或缩略式 mustn't /'mʌsnt/：*You mustn't be late.* 你不许迟到。
> When you want to say that somebody can do something if they want, but that it is not necessary, you use **don't have to**. 表示某人可以做某事，但并非必要，用 don't have to：*You **don't have to do your homework today*** (= you can do it today if you want, but it is not necessary). 你不一定要今天做家庭作业。

2 a word that shows that you are sure something is true（表示确信某事属实）肯定，一定：*You must be tired after your long journey.* 你走了这么长的路一定累了。
◇ *I can't find my keys. I must have left them at home.* 我找不到钥匙，准是忘在家里了。 ➾ Look at the note at **modal verb**. 见 modal verb 条的注释。

mustache *American English for*
MOUSTACHE 美式英语，即 moustache

mustard /ˈmʌstəd/ *noun* 名词 (*no plural*
不用复数形式)
a thick yellow sauce with a very strong
taste, that you eat with meat 芥末酱
つ Look at Picture Dictionary page **P7**.
见彩页 P7。

mustn't /ˈmʌsnt/ *short for* MUST NOT
* must not 的缩略式

mutter /ˈmʌtə(r)/ *verb* 动词 (mutters,
muttering, muttered /ˈmʌtəd/)
to speak in a low quiet voice that is
difficult to hear 低声含糊地说；嘀咕：
*He muttered something about going home,
and left the room.* 他嘀咕着说要回家，
然后就离开了房间。

my ☞ /maɪ/ *adjective* 形容词
of or belonging to me 我的： *Where is
my watch?* 我的手表在哪儿？ ◇ *These
are my books, not yours.* 这些是我的书，
不是你的。 ◇ *I've hurt my arm.* 我弄伤了
胳膊。

myself ☞ /maɪˈself/ *pronoun* 代词
(*plural* 复数形式 ourselves)
1 a word that shows the same person as
the one who is speaking （指说话者本
人）我自己： *I hurt myself.* 我把自己弄伤
了。 ◇ *I bought myself a new shirt.* 我给
自己买了件新衬衫。
2 a word that makes 'I' stronger （用以
强调）我自己，亲自： *'Did you buy this

cake?' 'No, I made it myself.'* "这个蛋糕你
是买的吗？" "不是，我亲自做的。"
by myself
1 without other people （我）独自，单独
つ SAME MEANING **alone** 同义词为 alone：
I live by myself. 我一个人住。
2 without help （我）独立地： *I made
dinner by myself.* 我自己做了晚饭。

mysterious ☞ /mɪˈstɪəriəs/ *adjective*
形容词
Something that is **mysterious** is strange
and you do not know about it or
understand it. 神秘的；难以理解的：
*Several people said they had seen
mysterious lights in the sky.* 有几个人说看
见天空中有神秘的光。
▶ **mysteriously** *adverb* 副词： *The
plane disappeared mysteriously.* 那架飞机
离奇失踪了。

mystery /ˈmɪstri/ *noun* 名词 (*plural* 复数
形式 mysteries)
something strange that you cannot
understand or explain 谜；神秘的事物；
不可理解之事： *The police say that the
man's death is still a mystery.* 警方说那名
男子的死仍是个谜。

myth /mɪθ/ *noun* 名词
1 a very old story 神话： *Greek myths*
希腊神话
2 a story or belief that is not true 不真实
的事；错误的观念： *It's a myth that
money makes you happy.* 金钱能带来幸福
的想法是错误的。

N n

N, n /en/ *noun* 名词 (*plural* 复数形式 N's, n's /enz/)
the fourteenth letter of the English alphabet 英语字母表的第 14 个字母: *'Nice' begins with an 'N'.* * nice 一词以字母 n 开头。

nag /næg/ *verb* 动词 (nags, nagging, nagged /nægd/)
to keep asking somebody to do something 唠叨；絮叨: *My parents are always **nagging** me to work harder.* 我父母一直唠叨我，要我更努力些。

nail 钉子

nail 0➔ /neɪl/ *noun* 名词
1 the hard part at the end of a finger or toe 指甲；趾甲: *toenails* 趾甲 ◇ *fingernails* 指甲
2 a small thin piece of metal with one sharp end which you hit into wood (with a tool called a **hammer**) to fix things together 钉；钉子
▸ **nail** *verb* 动词 (nails, nailing, nailed /neɪld/): *I nailed the pieces of wood together.* 我把木板钉在了一起。

nail polish /'neɪl pɒlɪʃ/ (*British also* 英式英语亦作 **nail varnish** /'neɪl vɑːnɪʃ/) *noun* 名词
a coloured liquid that people put on their nails 指甲油；趾甲油

naked /'neɪkɪd/ *adjective* 形容词
not wearing any clothes 赤裸的；裸露的
⊃ SAME MEANING **nude** 同义词为 nude

name¹ 0➔ /neɪm/ *noun* 名词
a word or words that you use to call or talk about a person or thing 名字；名称: *My name is Chris Eaves.* 我叫克里斯·伊夫斯。 ◇ *What's your name?* 你叫什么名字? ◇ *Do you know the name of this flower?* 你知道这种花的名称吗?

call somebody names to say bad, unkind words about somebody 辱骂；谩骂: *Joe cried because the other children were calling him names.* 乔哭了，因为别的孩子骂他。

name² 0➔ /neɪm/ *verb* 动词 (names, naming, named /neɪmd/)
1 to give a name to somebody or something 命名；给…取名: *They named their baby Sophie.* 他们给婴儿起名叫索菲。 ◇ *They named him Michael after his grandfather* (= gave him the same name as his grandfather). 他们以孩子祖父的名字给孩子取名为迈克尔。
2 to know and say the name of somebody or something 说出…的名字; 说出…的名称: *The headmaster could name every one of his 600 pupils.* 校长叫得出全校 600 名学生的名字。

namely /'neɪmli/ *adverb* 副词
You use **namely** when you are going to name a person or thing that you have just said something about. 即；也就是: *Only two students were late, namely Sergio and Antonio.* 只有两名学生迟到，就是塞吉奥和安东尼奥。

nanny /'næni/ *noun* 名词 (*plural* 复数形式 nannies)
a woman whose job is to look after the children of a family 保姆

A
B
C
D
E
F
G
H
I
J
K
L
M
N
O
P
Q
R
S
T
U
V
W
X
Y
Z

nap /næp/ *noun* 名词
a short sleep that you have during the day （日间的）小睡，打盹：*I had a nap after lunch.* 我午饭后小睡了一会儿。

napkin /'næpkɪn/ *noun* 名词 (*British* 英式英语)
a piece of cloth or paper that you use when you are eating to clean your mouth and hands and to keep your clothes clean 餐巾；餐巾纸 ⊃ SAME MEANING **serviette** 同义词为 serviette

nappy /'næpi/ *noun* 名词 (*British* 英式英语) (*plural* 复数形式 **nappies**) (*American* 美式英语 **diaper**)
a piece of cloth or strong paper that a baby wears around its bottom and between its legs 尿布：*Does his nappy need changing?* 他的尿布要换了吗？

narrow ⊶ /'nærəʊ/ *adjective* 形容词 (**narrower**, **narrowest**)
1 not far from one side to the other 窄的；狭窄的：*The bridge was very narrow.* 那座桥很窄。◇ *a narrow ribbon* 狭长的丝带 ⊃ OPPOSITE **broad** or **wide** 反义词为 broad 或 wide
2 by a small amount 勉强的；刚好的：*We had a narrow escape – the car nearly hit a tree.* 我们侥幸逃过一劫——车子险些撞到树上。◇ *a narrow defeat* 以极小的差距落败

narrowly /'nærəʊli/ *adverb* 副词
only by a small amount 勉强地；刚刚：*They narrowly escaped injury.* 他们差点儿受伤了。

narrow-minded /,nærəʊ 'maɪndɪd/ *adjective* 形容词
not wanting to accept ideas or opinions that are different from your own 心胸狭窄的；气量小的：*The people in this town are very narrow-minded.* 这个镇上的人心胸狭隘。⊃ OPPOSITE **broad-minded** 反义词为 broad-minded

nasty /'nɑːsti/ *adjective* 形容词 (**nastier**, **nastiest**)
bad; not nice 极差的；糟糕的 ⊃ SAME MEANING **horrible** 同义词为 horrible：*There's a nasty smell in this room.* 这个房间有一股难闻的气味。◇ *Don't be so nasty!* 别那么讨厌！

nation /'neɪʃn/ *noun* 名词
a country and all the people who live in it 国家；国民 ⊃ Look at the note at **country**. 见 country 条的注释。

national ⊶ /'næʃnəl/ *adjective* 形容词
connected with all of a country; typical of a country 全国的；国家的；民族的：*She wore Greek national costume.* 她穿上了希腊民族服装。◇ *national newspapers* 全国性的报纸

national anthem /,næʃnəl 'ænθəm/ *noun* 名词
the official song of a country 国歌

nationality /,næʃə'næləti/ *noun* 名词 (*plural* 复数形式 **nationalities**)
the state of belonging to a certain country 国籍：*'What nationality are you?' 'I'm Australian.'* "你是哪国人？" "我是澳大利亚人。"

national park /,næʃnəl 'pɑːk/ *noun* 名词
a large area of beautiful land that is protected by the government so that people can enjoy it 国家公园

native[1] /'neɪtɪv/ *adjective* 形容词
connected with the place where you were born 出生地的：*I returned to my native country.* 我回到了祖国。◇ *My native language is German.* 我的母语是德语。

native[2] /'neɪtɪv/ *noun* 名词
a person who was born in a place 当地人；本地人：*He's a native of Liverpool.* 他是土生土长的利物浦人。

Native American /,neɪtɪv ə'merɪkən/ *noun* 名词
a member of the group of people who were living in America before people from Europe arrived there 美洲土著居民

native speaker /,neɪtɪv 'spiːkə(r)/ *noun* 名词
a person who speaks a language as their first language 说本族语的人；母语使用者：*All our teachers are Spanish native speakers.* 我们所有的老师都是以西班牙语为母语的。

natural ⊶ /'nætʃrəl/ *adjective* 形容词
1 made by nature, not by people 自然生成的；天然的：*This part of Scotland is an area of great natural beauty.* 苏格兰的这一地区有壮丽的自然风光。◇ *Earthquakes and floods are natural disasters.* 地震和洪水是自然灾害。
2 normal or usual 正常的；自然的：*It's natural for parents to feel sad when their children leave home.* 孩子离开家，父母觉得难过是很正常的。⊃ OPPOSITE **unnatural** 反义词为 unnatural

naturally /'nætʃrəli/ *adverb* 副词
1 in a way that you would expect 顺理成章地；自然地；当然地 ⊃ SAME MEANING **of course** 同义词为 of course：*Naturally, I get upset when things go wrong.* 事情出差错时，我当然会感到不安。

2 in a way that is not made or caused by people 天然地；非人为地： *Is your hair naturally curly?* 你的鬈发是天生的吗？
3 in a normal way 正常地；自然地： *Try to stand naturally while I take a photo.* 我拍照的时候，尽量站得自然点。

nature 0— /'neɪtʃə(r)/ *noun* 名词
1 (*no plural* 不用复数形式) all the plants, animals, etc. in the world and all the things that happen in it that are not made or caused by people 世间的万物；自然界；大自然： *the beauty of nature* 大自然之美
2 (*plural* 复数形式 natures) the way a person or thing is 天性；本性；本质： *Our cat has a very friendly nature.* 我们的猫天性温驯。

naughty /'nɔːti/ *adjective* 形容词 (naughtier, naughtiest)
A **naughty** child does bad things or does not do what you ask them to do. （儿童）顽皮的，淘气的： *She's the naughtiest child in the class.* 她是班上最顽皮的孩子。

naval /'neɪvl/ *adjective* 形容词
connected with a navy 海军的： *a naval officer* 海军军官

navigate /'nævɪgeɪt/ *verb* 动词 (navigates, navigating, navigated)
to use a map or some other method to find which way a ship, a plane or a car should go 导航；确定方位： *Long ago, explorers used the stars to navigate.* 很久以前，探险家依靠星星来导航。
▶ **navigation** /ˌnævɪ'geɪʃn/ *noun* 名词 (*no plural* 不用复数形式) deciding which way a ship or other vehicle should go by using a map, etc. 导航；领航： *navigation skills* 导航技能
▶ **navigator** /'nævɪgeɪtə(r)/ *noun* 名词
a person who decides which way a ship, etc. should go （船舶等的）导航者，领航员： *Dad's usually the navigator when we go somewhere in the car.* 我们开车出去的时候，爸爸通常负责指路。

navy 0— /'neɪvi/ *noun* 名词 (*plural* 复数形式 navies)
the ships that a country uses when there is a war, and the people who work on them 海军： *Mark is in the navy.* 马克在海军服役。

navy blue /ˌneɪvi 'bluː/ (*also* 亦作 navy /'neɪvi/) *adjective* 形容词
dark blue 海军蓝的；深蓝色的

near 0— /nɪə(r)/ *adjective, adverb, preposition* 形容词、副词、介词 (nearer, nearest)

not far away; close to somebody or something 在附近（的）；接近（的）： *Let's walk to my house. It's quite near.* 我们走路去我家吧，挺近的。◇ *Where's the nearest hospital?* 最近的医院在哪儿？◇ *My parents live quite near.* 我父母住在附近。◇ *I don't need a car because I live near the city centre.* 我不需要汽车，因为我住在市中心附近。

nearby 0— /'nɪəbaɪ/ *adjective* 形容词
not far away; close 附近的；邻近的： *We took her to a nearby hospital.* 我们把她送到附近的一家医院。
▶ **nearby** /ˌnɪə'baɪ/ *adverb* 副词： *Let's go and see Tim – he lives nearby.* 我们去看看蒂姆吧——他住在附近。

nearly 0— /'nɪəli/ *adverb* 副词
almost; not quite 几乎；差不多： *I'm nearly 16 – it's my birthday next week.* 我快 16 岁了，下星期过生日。◇ *She was so ill that she nearly died.* 她病得很厉害，差点儿丧命。
not nearly not at all 远非；一点也不： *The book wasn't nearly as good as the film.* 这本书远不如电影好。

neat /niːt/ *adjective* 形容词 (neater, neatest)
1 with everything in the right place and done carefully 整洁的；整齐的 ⟹ SAME MEANING **tidy** 同义词为 tidy： *Keep your room neat and tidy.* 保持你的房间干净整齐。◇ *She has very neat handwriting.* 她写字很工整。
2 (*American* 美式英语) (*informal* 非正式) good; nice 好的；棒的： *That's a really neat car!* 那车真不错！
▶ **neatly** *adverb* 副词： *Write your name neatly.* 工整地写上你的名字。

necessarily /ˌnesə'serəli/ *adverb* 副词
not necessarily not always 不一定；未必： *Big men aren't necessarily strong.* 大个子的男人不一定强壮。

necessary 0— /'nesəsəri/ *adjective* 形容词
If something is **necessary**, you must have it or do it. 必要的；必须的： *Warm clothes are necessary in winter.* 保暖的衣服是冬天里必备的。

necessity /nə'sesəti/ *noun* 名词 (*plural* 复数形式 necessities)
something that you must have 必不可少的东西；必需品： *Food and clothes are necessities of life.* 食物和衣服是生活必需品。

neck 0— /nek/ *noun* 名词
1 the part of your body between your

A
B
C
D
E
F
G
H
I
J
K
L
M
N
O
P
Q
R
S
T
U
V
W
X
Y
Z

shoulders and your head 颈; 脖子:
Helen wore a thick scarf round her neck.
海伦脖子上围着一条厚围巾。 ⊃ Look at
Picture Dictionary page **P4**. 见彩页 P4。
2 the part of a piece of clothing that goes
round your neck 衣领; 领子: *The neck's
too tight.* 这领子太紧了。
3 the thin part at the top of a bottle 瓶颈

necklaces 项链

necklace /'nekləs/ *noun* 名词
a piece of jewellery that you wear round
your neck 项链: *a diamond necklace*
钻石项链

need¹ ☞ /niːd/ *verb* 动词 (needs,
needing, needed)
1 If you **need** something, you must have
it. 需要（某物）: *All plants and animals
need water.* 所有动植物都需要水。 ◇ *You
don't need your coat – it's not cold.* 你不用
穿大衣 —— 天不冷。
2 If you **need** to do something, you must
do it. 必须（做某事）: *James is very ill.
He needs to go to hospital.* 詹姆斯病得很
重，他需要上医院。 ◇ *'Do we need to pay
now, or can we pay next week?' 'You don't
need to pay now.'* "我们得现在付钱，还是
可以下周再付？" "你不必现在付钱。"

need² ☞ /niːd/ *noun* 名词
a situation in which you must have
something or do something 需要; 必要:
*the growing need for new books and
equipment* 对新书和新设备日益增加的需求
◇ *There's no need for you to come.* 你不必
来。 ◇ *She's in need of a rest.* 她需要休息。

needle ☞ /'niːdl/ *noun* 名词
1 a small thin piece of metal that you use
for sewing cloth 针; 缝纫针: *Put the
thread through the eye* (= hole) *of the
needle.* 把线穿过针眼。 ⊃ Look at the

picture at **sew**. 见 sew 的插图。 ⊃ Look
also at **knitting needle**. 亦见 knitting
needle。
2 a small thin piece of metal that forms
part of an instrument （仪器的）指针,
针状物: *The compass needle points north.*
罗盘的指针指向北方。 ◇ *a hypodermic
needle* (= for taking blood or giving drugs)
皮下注射器针头
3 a very thin pointed leaf on a tree that
stays green all year （常青树的）针叶:
pine needles 松针

needless /'niːdləs/ *adjective* 形容词
not necessary; able to be avoided 不必要
的; 可以避免的: *needless suffering* 不必
要的痛苦 ◇ *The problem is the cost,
needless to say* (= it is not necessary to
say this, because it is obvious). 不用说,
问题在于所涉及的费用。
▸ **needlessly** *adverb* 副词: *Many people
died needlessly.* 许多人白白地丧命了。

needn't /'niːdnt/ *short for* NEED NOT
* need not 的缩略式: *You needn't go if
you don't want to.* 你不想去就不必去了。

negative¹ ☞ /'negətɪv/ *adjective*
形容词
1 bad or harmful 坏的; 有害的: *The
whole experience was definitely more
positive than negative.* 整个经历当然是
利多于弊。 ⊃ OPPOSITE **positive** 反义词为
positive
2 only thinking about the bad qualities of
somebody or something 消极的; 负面
的: *If you go into the match with a
negative attitude, you'll never win.* 要是
抱着消极的态度参加比赛，就永远赢不了。
⊃ OPPOSITE **positive** 反义词为 positive
3 using words like 'no', 'not' and 'never'
否定的: *'I don't like British food' is a
negative sentence.* * I don't like British
food 是个否定句。

negative² /'negətɪv/ *noun* 名词
a piece of film that we use to make a
photograph. On a **negative**, dark things
are light and light things are dark. （摄影
胶片的）负片, 底片

neglect /nɪ'glekt/ *verb* 动词 (neglects,
neglecting, neglected)
to not take care of somebody or
something 疏于照顾; 未予看管: *The dog
was dirty and thin because its owner had
neglected it.* 那条狗由于主人疏于照顾而又
脏又瘦。
▸ **neglect** *noun* 名词 (no plural 不用复数
形式): *The house was in a state of
neglect.* 房子处于无人照管的状态。

▶ **neglected** *adjective* 形容词: *neglected children* 无人照看的孩子

negotiate /nɪˈgəʊʃieɪt/ (negotiates, negotiating, negotiated) *verb* 动词
to reach an agreement by talking with other people 谈判；协商；磋商: *We have negotiated a deal.* 我们已经达成交易。◇ *The unions were **negotiating with** the management **over** pay.* 工会正与资方就工资问题进行谈判。

neigh /neɪ/ *verb* 动词 (neighs, neighing, neighed /neɪd/)
When a horse **neighs**, it makes a long high sound. （马）嘶鸣
▶ **neigh** *noun* 名词

neighbor, neighboring *American English for* NEIGHBOUR, NEIGHBOURING 美式英语，即 neighbour、neighbouring

neighborhood *American English for* NEIGHBOURHOOD 美式英语，即 neighbourhood

neighbour 0ᵐ (*British* 英式英语) (*American* 美式英语 **neighbor**) /ˈneɪbə(r)/ *noun* 名词
a person who lives near you 邻居: *Don't make so much noise or you'll wake the neighbours.* 别那么大声，会吵醒邻居的。

> 🔎 **WHICH WORD?** 词语辨析
> Your **next-door neighbour** is the person who lives in the house next door to your house. 隔壁的邻居叫做 next-door neighbour。

neighbourhood (*British* 英式英语) (*American* 美式英语 **neighborhood**) /ˈneɪbəhʊd/ *noun* 名词
a part of a town; the people who live there 街区；城区；街坊四邻: *They live in a friendly neighbourhood.* 他们住在一个邻里关系和睦的小区。

neighbouring (*British* 英式英语) (*American* 美式英语 **neighboring**) /ˈneɪbərɪŋ/ *adjective* 形容词
near or next to 邻近的；毗邻的: *people from neighbouring villages* 邻村的村民

neither¹ 0ᵐ /ˈnaɪðə(r); ˈniːðə(r)/ *adjective, pronoun* 形容词，代词
not one and not the other of two things or people 两者都不: *Neither book is very interesting.* 两本书都很无趣。◇ *Neither of the boys was there.* 两个男孩都不在那里。

neither² 0ᵐ /ˈnaɪðə(r); ˈniːðə(r)/ *adverb* 副词
also not 也不: *Lydia can't swim and neither can I.* 莉迪亚不会游泳，我也不会。

◇ *'I don't like rice.' 'Neither do I.'* "我不喜欢米饭。""我也不喜欢。"
neither … nor not … and not …和…都不；既不…也不…: *Neither Paul nor I went to the party.* 保罗和我都没有参加聚会。

neon /ˈniːɒn/ *noun* 名词 (*no plural* 不用复数形式) (*symbol* 符号 Ne)
a type of gas that is used in bright lights and signs 氖；氖气

nephew /ˈnefjuː/ *noun* 名词
the son of your brother or sister 侄子；外甥

nerd /nɜːd/ *noun* 名词 (*informal* 非正式)
a person who spends a lot of time on a particular interest and who is not popular or fashionable （对某事痴迷的）怪人；落伍的人 ⊃ SAME MEANING **geek** 同义词为 geek

nerve 0ᵐ /nɜːv/ *noun* 名词
1 (*plural* 复数形式 **nerves**) one of the long thin things inside your body that carry feelings and messages to and from your brain 神经
2 nerves (*plural* 用复数形式) a feeling of worry or fear 神经紧张: *John breathed deeply to **calm** his **nerves**.* 约翰深呼吸来稳定情绪。
3 (*no plural* 不用复数形式) the state of being brave or calm when there is danger 胆量；勇气: *You need a lot of nerve to be a racing driver.* 当赛车手要有过人的胆量。
get on somebody's nerves to annoy somebody 烦扰；使心神不定: *Stop making that noise – you're getting on my nerves!* 别弄出那种声音，你弄得我心烦意乱!

nerve-racking /ˈnɜːv rækɪŋ/ *adjective* 形容词
making you very nervous or worried 令人焦虑不安的；令人提心吊胆的: *It was a nerve-racking drive up the mountain.* 开车上那座山真让人胆战心惊。

nervous 0ᵐ /ˈnɜːvəs/ *adjective* 形容词
1 worried or afraid 紧张的；焦虑的；担忧的: *I'm quite **nervous about** starting my new job.* 我将要开始新的工作，心情十分紧张。
2 connected with the NERVES in your body 神经的: *the nervous system* 神经系统
▶ **nervously** /ˈnɜːvəsli/ *adverb* 副词: *He laughed nervously, not knowing what to say.* 他不知道该说什么，紧张地干笑了起来。
▶ **nervousness** /ˈnɜːvəsnəs/ *noun* 名词 (*no plural* 不用复数形式): *He tried to hide*

A

B

C

D

E

F

G

H

I

J

K

L

M

N

O

P

Q

R

S

T

U

V

W

X

Y

Z

his nervousness. 他试图掩藏自己的紧张情绪。

nest¹ /nest/ *noun* 名词
a place where a bird, snake, insect, etc. keeps its eggs or its babies（鸟、蛇、昆虫等的）巢，窝，穴：*a bird's nest* 鸟巢

nest² /nest/ *verb* 动词 (nests, nesting, nested)
to make and live in a **nest** 筑巢：*The ducks are nesting by the river.* 鸭子正在河边筑巢。

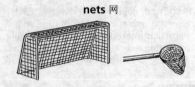

nets 网

net 0━ /net/ *noun* 名词
1 material that has very large spaces between the threads; a piece of this material that we use for a particular purpose 网；网状物：*a fishing net* 渔网 ◇ *a tennis net* 网球网 ◇ *He kicked the ball into the back of the net.* 他一脚把球踢入网中。
2 the Net (*informal* 非正式) = INTERNET

netball /'netbɔːl/ *noun* 名词 (*no plural* 不用复数形式)
a game where two teams of seven players, usually women, try to throw a ball through a high round net（女子）无挡板篮球

nettle /'netl/ *noun* 名词
a wild plant covered with hairs that can hurt you if you touch them 荨麻

network /'netwɜːk/ *noun* 名词
a number of things or people that form a single system or that are closely connected 网络；关系网：*the rail network* 铁路网 ◇ *computer networks* 电脑网络 ◇ *a network of friends* 朋友圈子

neutral¹ /'njuːtrəl/ *adjective* 形容词
1 not supporting either side in an argument or war 中立的；不偏袒的：*I don't take sides when my brothers argue – I remain neutral.* 我的兄弟吵架时我谁也不帮 —— 我保持中立。
2 having or showing no strong qualities, emotions or colour 不带情感的；中性的；不鲜艳的：*a neutral tone of voice* 平静的语气 ◇ *neutral colours* 素净的颜色

neutral² /'njuːtrəl/ *noun* 名词 (*no plural* 不用复数形式)
the position in which no power is being sent from a vehicle's engine to its wheels（车辆）空挡：*Put the car in neutral.* 把排挡置于空挡位。

never 0━ /'nevə(r)/ *adverb* 副词
not at any time; not ever 从不；从未；决不：*She never works on Saturdays.* 她星期六向来不工作。◇ *I've never been to America.* 我从未去过美国。◇ *I will never forget you.* 我永远不会忘记你。

nevertheless /ˌnevəðə'les/ *adverb* 副词 (*formal* 正式)
but 尽管如此；然而 ⊃ SAME MEANING **however** 同义词为 however：*They played very well. Nevertheless, they didn't win.* 他们表现得很出色，可是他们并没有胜出。

new 0━ /njuː/ *adjective* 形容词 (newer, newest)
1 not existing before 新的；刚出现的：*Have you seen his new film?* 你看过他的新影片吗？◇ *I bought a new pair of shoes yesterday.* 我昨天买了双新鞋。
2 different from before 新颖的；有别于以前的：*Our new flat is much bigger than our old one.* 我们的新公寓比旧的大很多。◇ *The teacher usually explains the new words to us.* 老师通常给我们解释生词。
3 doing something for the first time 新任的；初来乍到的：*New parents are often tired.* 新手父母经常累。◇ *He's new to the job and still needs help.* 他刚开始做这份工作，还需要帮助。

newcomer /'njuːkʌmə(r)/ *noun* 名词
a person who has just come to a place 新来的人

newly /'njuːli/ *adverb* 副词
not long ago 新近；最近 ⊃ SAME MEANING **recently** 同义词为 recently：*Our school is newly built.* 我们学校是新建的。

new moon /ˌnjuː 'muːn/ *noun* 名词
the time when you can see only the first thin part of the moon 新月（期）

news 0━ /njuːz/ *noun* 名词 (*no plural* 不用复数形式)
1 information about things that have just happened 消息；音信：*Have you heard the news? Stewart is getting married.* 你听说了吗？斯图尔特要结婚了。◇ *I've got some good news for you.* 我有好消息要告诉你。

> 🔎 GRAMMAR 语法说明
> Be careful! You cannot say 'a news'. To talk about a single item, you can say

some news or **a piece of news**. 注意：
不说 a news，可以说 some news 或
a piece of news： *Julie told us an*
interesting piece of news. 朱莉告诉我们
一条很有意思的消息。

2 the news (*no plural* 不用复数形式)
a programme on television or radio that
tells people about important things that
have just happened（电视或电台的）
新闻节目： *We heard about the plane*
crash on the news. 我们在新闻上听到飞机
失事的消息。

break the news to be the first person
to tell somebody about something
important 最先透露消息： *Have you*
broken the news to your wife? 你最先把
那件事告诉你妻子了吗？

newsagent /ˈnjuːzeɪdʒənt/ *noun* 名词
1 a person who sells things like
newspapers, magazines, sweets and
cigarettes 报刊经销商；书报店店员
2 newsagent's a shop that sells things
like newspapers, magazines, sweets and
cigarettes 报刊经销店；书报店

newspaper 0━ /ˈnjuːspeɪpə(r)/ *noun*
名词
1 (*plural* 复数形式 newspapers) large
pieces of paper with news, advertisements
and other things printed on them 报纸：
a daily newspaper 日报
2 (*no plural* 不用复数形式) paper taken
from old **newspapers** 旧报纸： *We*
wrapped the plates in newspaper before
packing them. 我们用旧报纸把盘子包了
起来再装箱。

new year (*also* 亦作 New Year) /ˌnjuː
ˈjɪə(r)/ *noun* 名词 (*no plural* 不用复数形式)
the beginning of the year 新年： *Happy*
New Year! 新年快乐！ ◇ *We will get in*
touch in the new year. 我们在新年的时候
会互相联系。

━━━━━━━━━━━━━━━━━━━━━━
🖉 WHICH WORD? 词语辨析
1 January is called **New Year's Day** and
31 December is called **New Year's Eve**.
元旦（1月1日）叫做 New Year's
Day，除夕（12月31日）叫做 New
Year's Eve。
━━━━━━━━━━━━━━━━━━━━━━

next¹ 0━ /nekst/ *adjective* 形容词
1 coming after this one 下一个的；接下
来的： *I'm going on holiday next week.*
我下周去度假。 ◇ *Take the next road on*
the right. 在下个路口右转。
2 nearest to this one 最近的： *I live in the*
next village. 我住在离这里最近的村子里。

next to somebody or 或 **something** at
the side of somebody or something 在…
旁；毗邻 ➲ SAME MEANING **beside** 同义词
为 beside： *The bank is next to the post*
office. 银行在邮局旁边。

next² 0━ /nekst/ *adverb* 副词
straight after this 紧接着；随后： *I've*
finished this work. What shall I do next?
我把这件工作做完了。下一步做什么呢？

next³ 0━ /nekst/ *noun* 名词 (*no plural*
不用复数形式)
the person or thing that comes after this
one 下一个（人或事物）： *Susy came first*
and Paul was the next to arrive. 苏茜第一
个到，然后就是保罗。

next door /ˌnekst ˈdɔː(r)/ *adverb* 副词
in or to the nearest house 在隔壁： *Who*
lives next door? 隔壁住的是谁？
▶ **next-door** *adjective* 形容词： *They're*
my **next-door** *neighbours.* 他们是我的隔壁
邻居。

nib /nɪb/ *noun* 名词
the metal point of a pen, where the
coloured liquid (called ink) comes out
钢笔尖 ➲ Look at Picture Dictionary page
P11. 见彩页 P11。

nibble /ˈnɪbl/ *verb* 动词 (nibbles, nibbling,
nibbled /ˈnɪbld/)
to eat something in very small bites
小口咬；一点点地吃： *The mouse nibbled*
the cheese. 老鼠把奶酪啃了。

nice 0━ /naɪs/ *adjective* 形容词 (nicer,
nicest)
pleasant, good or kind 令人愉快的；
好的；和蔼的： *Did you have a nice*
holiday? 你假期过得愉快吗？ ◇ *I met a*
nice boy at the party. 我在聚会上邂逅了
一个很不错的男孩。 ◇ *It's nice to see you.*
很高兴见到你。

━━━━━━━━━━━━━━━━━━━━━━
🖉 SPEAKING 表达方式说明
We often say **great**, **lovely** or
wonderful instead of 'very nice'.
* great、lovely 和 wonderful 比 very
nice 更常用： *The party was great.*
那次聚会棒极了。 ◇ *We had a lovely*
weekend. 我们周末过得很愉快。 ◇ *It was*
a wonderful show. 那是一场精彩的
表演。
━━━━━━━━━━━━━━━━━━━━━━

nice and ... words that show that you
like something（表示喜欢）： *It's nice*
and warm by the fire. 在炉火边真是暖和
又舒适。
▶ **nicely** *adverb* 副词： *You can have a*
cake if you ask nicely (= in a polite way).

A B C D E F G H I J K L M **N** O P Q R S T U V W X Y Z

A
B
C
D
E
F
G
H
I
J
K
L
M
N
O
P
Q
R
S
T
U
V
W
X
Y
Z

你要是有礼貌地说想要蛋糕，就给你一块。

nickname /ˈnɪkneɪm/ *noun* 名词
a name that your friends or family sometimes call you instead of your real name 绰号；外号
▶ **nickname** *verb* 动词 (nicknames, nicknaming, nicknamed /ˈnɪkneɪmd/):
She was nicknamed 'The Ice Queen'. 她外号叫"冰王后"。

nicotine /ˈnɪkətiːn/ *noun* 名词 (*no plural* 不用复数形式)
a poisonous chemical in cigarettes that makes it difficult to stop smoking 尼古丁

niece /niːs/ *noun* 名词
the daughter of your brother or sister 侄女；外甥女 ⊃ Look at **nephew**. 见 nephew。

night ☛ /naɪt/ *noun* 名词
1 the part of the day when it is dark and most people sleep 夜；夜晚：*These animals come out at night.* 这些动物晚上出来活动。◇ *The baby cried all night.* 婴儿哭了一整夜。◇ *She stayed at my house last night.* 她昨晚在我家过夜。
2 the part of the day between late afternoon and when you go to bed 晚上，晚间（傍晚至睡觉前的时段）：*We went to a party on Saturday night.* 我们星期六晚上参加了聚会。◇ *He doesn't get home until 8 o'clock at night.* 他到晚上 8 点才到家。⊃ **Tonight** means the night or evening of today. * tonight 指今天晚上。

nightclub /ˈnaɪtklʌb/ *noun* 名词
a place where you can go late in the evening to drink and dance 夜总会
⊃ SAME MEANING **club** 同义词为 club

nightdress /ˈnaɪtdres/ (*plural* 复数形式 nightdresses) (*also* 亦作 nightie /ˈnaɪti/) *noun* 名词
a loose dress that a woman or girl wears in bed 女式睡衣；睡袍

nightlife /ˈnaɪtlaɪf/ *noun* 名词 (*no plural* 不用复数形式)
things to do in the evenings in a particular area, such as dancing or going to bars 夜生活：*What's the nightlife like round here?* 这一带有什么夜生活？

nightly /ˈnaɪtli/ *adjective, adverb* 形容词，副词
happening or coming every night 每夜（的）；每晚（的）：*a nightly TV show* 每晚播放的电视节目

nightmare /ˈnaɪtmeə(r)/ *noun* 名词
1 a dream that frightens you 噩梦；

梦魇：*I had a nightmare last night.* 我昨晚做了个噩梦。
2 something that is very bad or frightening 可怕的经历；可怕的事：*Travelling through the snow was a nightmare.* 那次雪中之行如噩梦般可怕。

night-time /ˈnaɪt taɪm/ *noun* 名词 (*no plural* 不用复数形式)
the time when it is dark 夜间；夜晚：*She is afraid to go out at night-time.* 她不敢在夜间外出。 ⊃ OPPOSITE **daytime** 反义词为 daytime

nil /nɪl/ *noun* 名词 (*no plural* 不用复数形式)
the number 0, especially when it is the score in games such as football 零，零分（尤指足球等比赛的比分）：*Our team won the match by two goals to nil.* 我们队以二比零赢了比赛。

nine ☛ /naɪn/ *number* 数词
9 九
▶ **ninth** /naɪnθ/ *pronoun, adjective, adverb* 代词，形容词，副词 9th 第九

nineteen ☛ /ˌnaɪnˈtiːn/ *number* 数词
19 十九
▶ **nineteenth** /ˌnaɪnˈtiːnθ/ *pronoun, adjective, adverb* 代词，形容词，副词 19th 第十九

ninety ☛ /ˈnaɪnti/ *number* 数词
1 90 九十
2 the nineties (*plural* 用复数形式) the numbers, years or temperature between 90 and 99 九十几；九十年代
in your nineties between the ages of 90 and 99 * 90 多岁：*My grandmother is in her nineties.* 我外婆 90 多岁了。
▶ **ninetieth** /ˈnaɪntiəθ/ *pronoun, adjective, adverb* 代词，形容词，副词 90th 第九十

nip /nɪp/ *verb* 动词 (nips, nipping, nipped /nɪpt/)
1 to give somebody a quick painful bite 咬：*The dog nipped his leg.* 狗咬了他的腿。
2 (*British* 英式英语) to go somewhere quickly 快速前往：*I'm just nipping to the shops.* 我正要赶去商店。

nipple /ˈnɪpl/ *noun* 名词
one of the two small dark circles on either side of your chest. A baby can get milk from its mother through the **nipples**. 乳头

nitrogen /ˈnaɪtrədʒən/ *noun* 名词 (*no plural* 不用复数形式) (*symbol* 符号 N)
the gas that forms about 80% of the air 氮；氮气

No. (also 亦作 **no.**) short way of writing NUMBER[1] (1) * number[1] 第 1 义的缩写形式

no[1] 0🔊 /nəʊ/ exclamation 感叹词
1 used for giving a negative reply or statement （用于否定的回答或陈述）不，不是，没有 ⊃ OPPOSITE **yes** 反义词为 yes: 'Do you want a drink?' 'No, thank you.' "你想喝点东西吗？" "不了，谢谢。" ◇ 'He's Italian.' 'No, he isn't. He's French.' "他是意大利人。" "不，他是法国人。"
2 something that you say when something bad happens or to show you are surprised or shocked （坏事发生时表示惊讶或震惊）：Oh no! I've broken my watch! 糟糕！我把手表弄坏了！

no[2] 0🔊 /nəʊ/ adjective 形容词
1 not one; not any 没有；无: I have no money – my purse is empty. 我没钱，钱包是空的。◇ No visitors may enter without a ticket. 无票者不得进入。
2 used for saying that something is not allowed 不准；禁止: The sign said 'No Smoking'. 牌子上写着"禁止吸烟"。

no[3] /nəʊ/ adverb 副词
not any 不: My flat is no bigger than yours. 我的公寓并不比你的大。

noble /ˈnəʊbl/ adjective 形容词 (**nobler, noblest**)
1 good, honest and caring about other people 崇高的；高尚的: noble thoughts 崇高的思想
2 belonging to the highest social class 贵族的；高贵的: a man of noble birth 出身高贵的人

nobody 0🔊 /ˈnəʊbədi/ pronoun 代词
no person; not anybody 没有人；没有任何人 ⊃ SAME MEANING **no one** 同义词为 no one: Nobody in our class speaks Greek. 我们班上没人会说希腊语。◇ There was nobody at home. 家里没人。

nod /nɒd/ verb 动词 (**nods, nodding, nodded**)
to move your head down and up again quickly as a way of saying 'yes' or 'hello' to somebody 点头: 'Do you understand?' asked the teacher, and everybody nodded. "你们懂了吗？"老师问道。大家都点了点头。

nod off to go to sleep 打盹；打瞌睡: Grandma nodded off in her chair. 奶奶在椅子上打瞌睡。

▶ **nod** noun 名词: Jim gave me a nod when I arrived. 我到的时候，吉姆向我点了点头。

noise 0🔊 /nɔɪz/ noun 名词
a sound, especially one that is loud or unpleasant 声响；噪音: I heard a noise upstairs. 我听到楼上有声音。◇ Don't make so much noise! 别那么吵！

noisy 0🔊 /ˈnɔɪzi/ adjective 形容词 (**noisier, noisiest**)
making a lot of noise; full of noise 吵闹的；嘈杂的 ⊃ OPPOSITE **quiet** 反义词为 quiet: The children are very noisy. 这些孩子非常吵闹。◇ The restaurant was too noisy. 那家饭店太吵了。

▶ **noisily** /ˈnɔɪzɪli/ adverb 副词: He ate his dinner noisily. 他吃饭的时候发出了很大的声音。

nomad /ˈnəʊmæd/ noun 名词
a member of a group of people that moves with its animals from place to place 游牧部落的人

▶ **nomadic** /nəʊˈmædɪk/ adjective 形容词: nomadic tribes 游牧部落

non- /nɒn/ prefix 前缀
You can add **non-** to the beginning of some words to give them the opposite meaning, for example （加在某些词前构成反义）：non-alcoholic drinks (= drinks containing no alcohol) 不含酒精的饮料 ◇ a non-smoker (= a person who does not smoke) 不吸烟的人 ◇ This train is non-stop (= does not stop before the end of the journey). 这班列车是直通车。

none 0🔊 /nʌn/ pronoun 代词
not any; not one 丝毫没有；一个都没有: She has eaten all the chocolates – there are none in the box. 她把巧克力吃光了——盒子里一块也没有了。◇ I went to four shops, but none of them had the book I wanted. 我去了四家书店，但都没有我要的书。

nonsense 0🔊 /ˈnɒnsns/ noun 名词 (no plural 不用复数形式)
words or ideas that have no meaning or that are not true 胡说八道；瞎说；谬论: It's nonsense to say that Jackie is lazy. 说杰基懒惰，那真是胡说八道。

noodles /ˈnuːdlz/ noun 名词 (plural 用复数形式)
long thin lines of food made from flour, eggs and water (called pasta), which are used especially in Chinese and Italian cooking 面条: Would you prefer rice or noodles? 你喜欢吃米饭还是面条？ ⊃ Look at Picture Dictionary page **P6**. 见彩页 P6。

A B C D E F G H I J K L M N O P Q R S T U V W X Y Z

noon /nuːn/ *noun* 名词 (*no plural* 不用复数形式)

twelve o'clock in the middle of the day 正午；中午 ⊃ SAME MEANING **midday** 同义词为 midday: *I met him at noon.* 我中午跟他见面了。

no one ⚬━ /ˈnəʊ wʌn/ *pronoun* 代词

no person; not anybody 没有人；没有任何人 ⊃ SAME MEANING **nobody** 同义词为 nobody: *There was no one in the classroom.* 教室里没有人。◇ *No one saw me go into the house.* 谁也没看见我走进那所房子。

nor ⚬━ /nɔː(r)/ *conjunction* 连词

used after 'neither' and 'not' to mean 'also not'（用于 neither 或 not 之后）也不: *If Alan doesn't go, nor will Lucy.* 要是艾伦不去，露西也不会去。◇ *'I don't like eggs.' 'Nor do I.'* "我不爱吃鸡蛋。" "我也不爱。" ◇ *Neither Tom nor I eat meat.* 汤姆和我都不吃肉。

normal ⚬━ /ˈnɔːml/ *adjective* 形容词

usual and ordinary; not different or special 正常的；典型的；一般的: *I will be home at the normal time.* 我会在平常的时间回来。

normally ⚬━ /ˈnɔːməli/ *adverb* 副词

1 usually 通常；一般情况下: *I normally go to bed at about eleven o'clock.* 我一般在十一点左右睡觉。

2 in the usual or ordinary way 正常地: *He isn't behaving normally.* 他举止失常。

north ⚬━ /nɔːθ/ *noun* 名词 (*no plural* 不用复数形式) (*abbr.* 缩略式 N)

the direction to your left when you watch the sun rise; a place in this direction 北方: *the north of England* 英格兰的北部 ⊃ Look at the picture at **compass**. 见 compass 的插图。

▸ **north** *adjective*, *adverb* 形容词，副词: *They live in North London.* 他们住在伦敦北部。◇ *a north wind* (= that comes from the north) 北风 ◇ *We travelled north from London to Scotland.* 我们从伦敦北行至苏格兰。

north-east /ˌnɔːθ ˈiːst/ *noun* 名词 (*no plural* 不用复数形式) (*abbr.* 缩略式 NE)

the direction between north and east; a place in this direction 东北；东北方；东北部: *He lives in the north-east.* 他住在东北地区。⊃ Look at the picture at **compass**. 见 compass 的插图。

▸ **north-east** *adjective*, *adverb* 形容词，副词: *north-east Scotland* 苏格兰东北部

▸ **north-eastern** /ˌnɔːθ ˈiːstən/ *adjective* 形容词: *north-eastern regions* 东北地区

northern ⚬━ /ˈnɔːðən/ *adjective* 形容词

connected with, in or from the north 北方的；向北的；北部的: *Newcastle is in northern England.* 纽卡斯尔位于英格兰北部。

the North Pole /ðə ˌnɔːθ ˈpəʊl/ *noun* 名词 (*no plural* 不用复数形式)

the point on the Earth's surface which is furthest north 北极 ⊃ Look at **South Pole**. 见 South Pole。⊃ Look at the picture at **earth**. 见 earth 的插图。

north-west /ˌnɔːθ ˈwest/ *noun* 名词 (*no plural* 不用复数形式)

the direction between north and west; a place in this direction 西北；西北方；西北部: *She's from the north-west.* 她来自西北地区。⊃ Look at the picture at **compass**. 见 compass 的插图。

▸ **north-west** *adjective*, *adverb* 形容词，副词: *north-west London* 伦敦的西北部

▸ **north-western** /ˌnɔːθ ˈwestən/ *adjective* 形容词: *north-western France* 法国的西北部

nose ⚬━ /nəʊz/ *noun* 名词

1 the part of your face, above your mouth, that you use for breathing and smelling 鼻；鼻子: *Blow your nose!* (= Clear your nose by blowing through it.) 擤擤你的鼻子！⊃ Look at Picture Dictionary page **P4**. 见彩页 P4。

2 the front part of a plane 飞机头部

nostril /ˈnɒstrəl/ *noun* 名词

one of the two holes in your nose 鼻孔 ⊃ Look at Picture Dictionary page **P4**. 见彩页 P4。

nosy /ˈnəʊzi/ *adjective* 形容词 (nosier, nosiest)

too interested in other people's lives, in a way which is annoying 好管闲事的；爱打听的: *'Where are you going?' 'Don't be so nosy!'* "你去哪里？" "少管闲事！"

not ⚬━ /nɒt/ *adverb* 副词

used for forming negative sentences or phrases（构成否定句或否定的短语）不，没有: *I'm not hungry.* 我不饿。◇ *They did not arrive.* 他们没有到。◇ *I can come tomorrow, but not on Tuesday.* 我明天能来，但星期二不行。◇ *'Are you angry with me?' 'No, I'm not.'* "你生我的气吗？" "没有。"

not at all

1 used as a reply when somebody has
thanked you for something（别人道谢时
的回答）不客气，没关系： *'Thanks for
your help.' 'Oh, not at all.'* "谢谢你的
帮助。" "噢，不客气。"
2 no; not a little bit 一点也不；根本不：
'Are you tired?' 'Not at all.' "你累了吗？"
"一点也不累。"

note¹ 0─┐/nəʊt/ *noun* 名词
1 words that you write quickly to help
you remember something 笔记；记录：
*I **made a note** of her address.* 我记下了她
的地址。◇ *The teacher told us to **take
notes**.* 老师叫我们做笔记。
2 a short letter 便条；短笺： *Dave sent
me a note to thank me for the present.*
戴夫给我寄了封短信，感谢我送他礼物。
3 (*British* 英式英语) (*American* 美式英语
bill) a piece of paper money 纸币： *He
gave me a $20 note.* 他给了我一张 20 元
的钞票。◇ Look at the picture at **money**.
见 money 的插图。
4 a short piece of extra information
about something in a book 注释；注解：
Look at the note on page 39. 见第 39 页的
注释。
5 one sound in music; the written symbol
for one sound 单音；音符： *I can play a
few notes.* 我会弹奏几个音。◇ *What's this
note?* 这个音符是什么？

note² 0─┐/nəʊt/ *verb* 动词 (notes, noting,
noted)
to notice and remember something
注意；留意： *Please **note that** all the
shops are closed on Mondays.* 请留意所有
商店星期一都不开门。
note something down to write
something so that you can remember it
写下；记下： *The police officer noted
down my name and address.* 警察把我的
名字和地址记了下来。

notebook /ˈnəʊtbʊk/ *noun* 名词
1 a small book that you can write in
笔记本
2 a very small computer that you can
carry with you and use anywhere 笔记本
电脑

notepad /ˈnəʊtpæd/ *noun* 名词
pieces of paper that you can write on,
joined together in a block 记事本；便条本

notepaper /ˈnəʊtpeɪpə(r)/ *noun* 名词
(*no plural* 不用复数形式)
paper that you write letters on 信纸；
信笺

nothing 0─┐/ˈnʌθɪŋ/ *pronoun* 代词
not anything; no thing 没有什么；没有
东西： *There's nothing in this bottle – it's
empty.* 这个瓶子里什么都没有，是空的。
◇ *I've finished all my work and I've got
nothing to do.* 我把工作都做完了，没事可
做了。◇ *Don't leave the baby there **with
nothing on** (= not wearing any clothes) –
he'll get cold.* 别让宝宝在那儿光着身子——
他会着凉的。
be 或 **have nothing to do with
somebody** or 或 **something** to have no
connection with somebody or something
与⋯无关： *That question has nothing to
do with what we're discussing.* 那个问题与
我们正在讨论的内容毫不相干。◇ *Keep
out of this – it's nothing to do with you.*
别掺和，这与你毫无关系。
for nothing
1 for no money 不花钱；免费 ➋ SAME
MEANING **free** 同义词为 free： *You can
have these books for nothing. I don't want
them.* 这些书免费赠送，我不要了。
2 without a good result 徒劳：
*I went to the station for nothing – she
wasn't on the train.* 我白跑了一趟车站——
她不在那列火车上。
nothing but only 只是；仅仅： *He eats
nothing but salad.* 他只吃沙拉。
nothing like not the same as somebody
or something in any way 完全不像： *He's
nothing like his brother.* 他一点也不像
哥哥。

notice¹ 0─┐/ˈnəʊtɪs/ *noun* 名词
1 (*plural* 复数形式 notices) a piece of
writing that tells people something
通告；通知；启事： *The notice on the
wall says 'NO SMOKING'.* 墙上的告示写着
"禁止吸烟"。
2 (*no plural* 不用复数形式) a warning that
something will happen; the amount of
time before it happens 预告；警告；
通知期： *We only had two weeks' notice
of the exam.* 我们在考试之前两星期才得到
通知。◇ *We left for Scotland **at very short
notice** and I forgot my coat.* 我们临时得到
通知，要赶往苏格兰，仓促间我忘了带大
衣。◇ *He's **handed in** his notice* (= he
has said officially that he will leave his
job). 他已提交了辞呈。

A
B
C
D
E
F
G
H
I
J
K
L
M
N
O
P
Q
R
S
T
U
V
W
X
Y
Z

A B C D E F G H I J K L M **N** O P Q R S T U V W X Y Z

take no notice to not pay attention to something 不理会 ⊃ SAME MEANING **ignore** 同义词为 ignore: *Take no notice of what she said.* 别理会她说的话。

notice² ○╌ /ˈnəʊtɪs/ *verb* 动词 (notices, noticing, noticed /ˈnəʊtɪst/)
to see or pay attention to somebody or something 看到；注意到: *Did you notice what she was wearing?* 你注意到她穿什么衣服了吗? ◇ *I noticed that he was driving a new car.* 我注意到他开着一辆新车。

noticeable /ˈnəʊtɪsəbl/ *adjective* 形容词
easy to see 显而易见的；显眼的: *I've got a mark on my shirt. Is it noticeable?* 我衬衫上有块污渍，显眼吗?

noticeboard /ˈnəʊtɪsbɔːd/ (*British* 英式英语) (*American* 美式英语 **bulletin board**) *noun* 名词
a board on a wall for information 布告板；告示牌: *The teacher put the exam results on the noticeboard.* 老师把考试成绩贴在布告板上。

notorious /nəʊˈtɔːriəs/ *adjective* 形容词
well known for being bad 臭名昭著的；声名狼藉的: *a notorious criminal* 恶名昭彰的罪犯
▸ **notoriously** *adverb* 副词: *This road is notoriously dangerous.* 众所周知，这条路很危险。

nought /nɔːt/ *noun* 名词
the number 0 零: *We say 0.5 as 'nought point five'.* * 0.5 读作"零点五"。

noun /naʊn/ *noun* 名词
(*grammar* 语法) a word that is the name of a person, place, thing or idea 名词: *'Anne', 'London', 'cat' and 'happiness' are all nouns.* * Anne、London、cat 和 happiness 都是名词。

novel¹ ○╌ /ˈnɒvl/ *noun* 名词
a book that tells a story about people and things that are not real （长篇）小说: *'David Copperfield' is a novel by Charles Dickens.* 《大卫·科波菲尔》是查尔斯·狄更斯写的小说。

novel² /ˈnɒvl/ *adjective* 形容词
new, different and interesting 新颖的；与众不同的: *a novel idea* 新颖的点子

novelist /ˈnɒvəlɪst/ *noun* 名词
a person who writes novels 小说家

November ○╌ /nəʊˈvembə(r)/ *noun* 名词
the eleventh month of the year 十一月

now¹ ○╌ /naʊ/ *adverb* 副词
1 at this time 现在；目前；此刻: *I can't see you now – can you come back later?*

我现在无法见你，你过一会儿再来行吗? ◇ *She was in Paris but she's living in Rome now.* 她之前在巴黎，目前则住在罗马。 ◇ *Don't wait – do it now!* 别等了，马上做! ◇ *From now on* (= after this time) *your teacher will be Mr Hancock.* 从现在起你们的老师就是汉考克先生。
2 used when you start to talk about something new, or to make people listen to you （用以转换话题或引起注意）喂，哎: *I've finished writing this letter. Now, what shall we have for dinner?* 我这封信写好了。那么，我们晚饭吃什么? ◇ *Be quiet, now!* 喂，安静点!
now and again, now and then sometimes, but not often 有时；偶尔: *We go to the cinema now and again.* 我们偶尔去看电影。

now² /naʊ/ (*also* 亦作 **now that**) *conjunction* 连词
because something has happened 既然: *Now that Mark has arrived we can start dinner.* 既然马克已经来了，我们就开饭吧。

nowadays /ˈnaʊədeɪz/ *adverb* 副词
at this time 现今；如今: *A lot of people work with computers nowadays.* 如今很多人用电脑工作。

nowhere ○╌ /ˈnəʊweə(r)/ *adverb* 副词
not anywhere; at, in or to no place 无处；哪里都不: *There's nowhere to stay in this village.* 这个村子里没有地方可以落脚。
nowhere near not at all 远非；绝不: *Ruichi's English is nowhere near as good as yours.* 鲁伊吉的英语远远没有你的好。

nuclear ○╌ /ˈnjuːkliə(r)/ *adjective* 形容词
1 using the energy that is made when the central part of an ATOM (= one of the very small things that everything is made of) is broken 原子能的；核能的: *nuclear energy* 核能 ◇ *nuclear weapons* 核武器
2 connected with the centre of ATOMS (= one of the very small things that everything is made of) 核子的: *nuclear physics* 核物理学

nucleus /ˈnjuːkliəs/ (*plural* 复数形式 **nuclei** /ˈnjuːkliaɪ/) *noun* 名词
the centre of a cell or an ATOM (= one of the very small things that everything is made of) 细胞核；原子核

nude /njuːd/ *adjective* 形容词
not wearing any clothes 裸体的；一丝不挂的 ⊃ SAME MEANING **naked** 同义词为 naked

nudge /nʌdʒ/ *verb* 动词 (nudges, nudging, nudged /nʌdʒd/)
to touch or push somebody or something with your elbow (= the pointed part where your arm bends) （用肘）轻触，轻推: *Nudge me if I fall asleep in the film.* 我看电影时要是睡着了你就推推我。
▶ **nudge** *noun* 名词: *Liz gave me a nudge.* 利兹用肘碰了我一下。

nuisance /'njuːsns/ *noun* 名词
a person or thing that causes you trouble 讨厌的人（或事物）: *I've lost my keys. What a nuisance!* 我钥匙丢了，真烦人!

numb /nʌm/ *adjective* 形容词
not able to feel anything 失去知觉的; 麻木的: *My fingers were numb with cold.* 我的手指冻僵了。

number¹ ⃛ /'nʌmbə(r)/ *noun* 名词
1 (*abbr.* 缩略式 No. or 或 no.) a word or symbol that represents a quantity or shows the position of something in a series; a number to identify something 数; 数字; 号码; 编号: *Choose a number between ten and one hundred.* 在十到一百之间选一个数。◇ *My phone number is Oxford 56767.* 我的电话号码是牛津 56767。◇ *I live at no. 47.* 我住在 47 号。
2 a group of more than one person or thing 若干; 数量: *A large number of our students come from Japan.* 我们的学生中很多人来自日本。◇ *There are a number of ways you can cook an egg.* 鸡蛋有几种烹调方法。

number² /'nʌmbə(r)/ *verb* 动词 (numbers, numbering, numbered /'nʌmbəd/)
to give a number to something 标号; 给…编号: *Number the pages from one to ten.* 把各页从一到十编上号码。

number plate /'nʌmbə pleɪt/ (*British* 英式英语) (*American* 美式英语 **license plate**) *noun* 名词
the flat piece of metal on the front and back of a car that has numbers and letters on it (its **registration number**) （车辆的）牌照，号码牌 ⊃ Look at Picture Dictionary page P1. 见彩页 P1。

numerous /'njuːmərəs/ *adjective* 形容词 (*formal* 正式)
many 许多的; 大量的

nun /nʌn/ *noun* 名词
a woman who has given her life to God instead of getting married. Most **nuns** live together in a special building (called a **convent**). 修女 ⊃ Look at **monk**. 见 monk。

nurse¹ ⃛ /nɜːs/ *noun* 名词
a person whose job is to look after people who are sick or hurt 护士; 护理员: *My sister works as a nurse in a hospital.* 我妹妹在医院里当护士。 ⊃ Look at Picture Dictionary page P12. 见彩页 P12。

nurse² /nɜːs/ *verb* 动词 (nurses, nursing, nursed /nɜːst/)
to look after somebody who is sick or hurt 护理; 看护: *I nursed my father when he was ill.* 父亲生病时我照料他。

nursery /'nɜːsəri/ *noun* 名词 (*plural* 复数形式 nurseries)
1 a place where small children and babies can stay when their parents are at work 托儿所
2 a place where people grow and sell plants 苗圃

nursery rhyme /'nɜːsəri raɪm/ *noun* 名词
a song or poem for young children 童谣; 儿歌

nursery school /'nɜːsəri skuːl/ *noun* 名词
a school for children between the ages of about two and five 幼儿园

nursing /'nɜːsɪŋ/ *noun* 名词 (*no plural* 不用复数形式)
the job of being a nurse 护理工作; 看护: *He has decided to go into nursing when he leaves school.* 他决定毕业后从事护理工作。

nuts 坚果

almond 杏仁

walnut 核桃

shell 壳

peanut 花生

hazelnut 榛子

nut ⃛ /nʌt/ *noun* 名词
1 a dry fruit that has a hard outside part with a seed inside. Many types of **nut** can

A
B
C
D
E
F
G
H
I
J
K
L
M
N
O
P
Q
R
S
T
U
V
W
X
Y
Z

be eaten. 坚果： *walnuts, hazelnuts and peanuts* 核桃、榛子和花生

2 a metal ring that you put on the end of a long piece of metal (called a **bolt**) to fix things together 螺母；螺帽 ⊃ Look at the picture at **bolt**. 见 bolt 的插图。

nutritious /njuˈtrɪʃəs/ *adjective* 形容词 (used about food) good for you （食物）

有营养的，营养丰富的： *tasty and nutritious meals* 美味而有营养的饭菜

nylon /ˈnaɪlɒn/ *noun* 名词 (*no plural* 不用复数形式)

very strong material that is made by machines and is used for making clothes, rope, brushes and other things 尼龙： *a nylon fishing line* 尼龙钓线

Oo

O, o¹ /əʊ/ *noun* 名词 (*plural* 复数形式 O's, o's /əʊz/)
the fifteenth letter of the English alphabet 英语字母表的第 15 个字母: *'Orange' begins with an 'O'.* * orange 一词以字母 o 开头。

O² /əʊ/ *exclamation, noun* 感叹词，名词
1 = OH
2 a way of saying the number '0' 零 ('0' 的一种说法)

oak /əʊk/ *noun* 名词
1 (*plural* 复数形式 oaks) a kind of large tree 橡树；栎树
2 (*no plural* 不用复数形式) the wood of an **oak** tree 橡木；栎木: *an oak table* 橡木桌子

OAP /ˌəʊ eɪ 'piː/ (*British* 英式英语) *short for* OLD-AGE PENSIONER * old-age pensioner 的缩略式

oar /ɔː(r)/ *noun* 名词
a long stick with a flat end that you use for moving a boat through water (called **rowing**) 船桨；桨 ⊃ Look at the picture at **rowing boat**. 见 rowing boat 的插图。

oasis /əʊ'eɪsɪs/ *noun* 名词 (*plural* 复数形式 oases /əʊ'eɪsiːz/)
a place in a desert where there is water and plants grow（沙漠中的）绿洲

oath /əʊθ/ *noun* 名词
a formal promise 誓言: *He swore an oath of loyalty.* 他宣誓效忠。

oats /əʊts/ *noun* 名词 (*plural* 用复数形式)
a plant with seeds that we use as food for people and animals 燕麦: *We make porridge from oats.* 我们用燕麦来做麦片粥。

obedient /ə'biːdiənt/ *adjective* 形容词
doing what somebody tells you to do 顺从的；服从的: *He was an obedient child.* 他是个听话的孩子。 ⊃ OPPOSITE **disobedient** 反义词为 disobedient
▸ **obedience** /ə'biːdiəns/ *noun* 名词 (*no plural* 不用复数形式): *Teachers expect complete obedience from their pupils.* 老师要求学生绝对服从。
▸ **obediently** /ə'biːdiəntli/ *adverb* 副词: *I called the dog and it followed me obediently.* 我唤那条狗，它就很听话地跟着我。

obese /əʊ'biːs/ *adjective* 形容词
(used about people) very fat, in a way that is not healthy（人）病态肥胖的

obey /ə'beɪ/ *verb* 动词 (obeys, obeying, obeyed /ə'beɪd/)
to do what somebody tells you to do; to follow an order or rule 服从；顺从；遵守: *He always obeyed his parents.* 他一直听他父母的话。 ◇ *You must obey the law.* 必须遵守法律。

object¹ 0── /'ɒbdʒɪkt/ *noun* 名词

> 🔊 **PRONUNCIATION** 读音说明
> When the word **object** is a noun, you say the first part of the word louder: **OBject**. When the word **object** is a verb, you say the second part of the word louder: **objECT**. * object 作名词时，重音放在第一个音节：OBject；作动词时，重音放在第二个音节：objECT。

1 a thing that you can see and touch 物体；物品: *There was a small round object on the table.* 桌上有个小的圆形物品。
2 what you plan to do 目标；目的 ⊃ SAME MEANING **aim** 同义词为 aim: *His object in life is to become as rich as possible.* 他的人生目标就是要挣取最多的钱。
3 (*grammar* 语法) the person or thing that is affected by an action. In the sentence 'Jane painted the door', the **object** of the sentence is 'the door'. 宾语，受词（在 Jane painted the door 一句中，宾语是 the door）⊃ Look at **subject** (3). 见 subject 第 3 义。

object² /əb'dʒekt/ *verb* 动词 (objects, objecting, objected)
to not like something; to not agree with something 不喜欢；不赞成；反对: *I objected to their plan.* 我反对他们的计划。

objection /əb'dʒekʃn/ *noun* 名词
a reason why you do not like something or do not agree with something 不喜欢的理由；反对意见: *I have no objections to the plan.* 我对这个计划没有异议。

objective /əb'dʒektɪv/ *noun* 名词
something that you are trying to achieve

A
B
C
D
E
F
G
H
I
J
K
L
M
N
o
P
Q
R
S
T
U
V
W
X
Y
Z

目标；目的 ➲ SAME MEANING **aim** 同义词为 aim

obligation /ˌɒblɪˈɡeɪʃn/ *noun* 名词
something that you must do 义务；责任： *We have an **obligation** to help.* 我们有责任提供援助。

obligatory /əˈblɪɡətri/ *adjective* 形容词 (*formal* 正式)
If something is **obligatory**, you must do it because it is the law or a rule. 必须做的；强制的 ➲ SAME MEANING **compulsory** 同义词为 compulsory

oblige /əˈblaɪdʒ/ *verb* 动词 (obliges, obliging, obliged /əˈblaɪdʒd/)
to force somebody to do something 强制；迫使： *The law **obliges** parents **to** send their children to school.* 法律规定父母必须送子女入学。

obliged /əˈblaɪdʒd/ *adjective* 形容词
forced to do something; feeling that you must do something 有需要；感到有义务： *We **felt obliged** to offer our help.* 我们觉得有义务伸手相助。

oblivious /əˈblɪviəs/ *adjective* 形容词
not noticing or realizing something 未注意；未意识到： *She was completely **oblivious of** all the trouble she had caused.* 她完全没有察觉自己所造成的一切麻烦。

oblong /ˈɒblɒŋ/ *noun* 名词
a shape with two long sides, two short sides and four angles of 90° 长方形；矩形 ➲ SAME MEANING **rectangle** 同义词为 rectangle
▸ **oblong** *adjective* 形容词： *This page is oblong.* 这一页是长方形的。

obnoxious /əbˈnɒkʃəs/ *adjective* 形容词
extremely unpleasant 极讨厌的；可憎的： *He really is an **obnoxious** person.* 他真的很令人讨厌。

observant /əbˈzɜːvənt/ *adjective* 形容词
good at noticing things 善于观察的；观察力敏锐的： *That's very **observant** of you!* 你真有眼力！

observation /ˌɒbzəˈveɪʃn/ *noun* 名词 (*no plural* 不用复数形式)
when you watch somebody or something carefully 观察；监视： *The police kept the house **under observation**.* 警方监视着这所房子。 ◇ *His powers of **observation** are excellent.* 他观察力很强。

observe /əbˈzɜːv/ *verb* 动词 (observes, observing, observed /əbˈzɜːvd/) (*formal* 正式)
to watch or see somebody or something

看到；观察；注意到： *The police **observed** a man leaving the house.* 警察注意到一名男子离开了那所房子。

obsess /əbˈses/ *verb* 动词 (obsesses, obsessing, obsessed /əbˈsest/)
to completely fill your mind 使痴迷；使迷恋： *Debbie is **obsessed** with football.* 戴比对足球很痴迷。

obsession /əbˈseʃn/ *noun* 名词
a person or thing that you think about all the time 使人痴迷的人（或事物）： *Cars are his **obsession**.* 他迷恋汽车。

obstacle /ˈɒbstəkl/ *noun* 名词
something that makes it difficult for you to do something or go somewhere 障碍；阻碍： *Not speaking a foreign language was a major **obstacle to** her career.* 不会说外语曾是她事业上的主要障碍。

obstinate /ˈɒbstɪnət/ *adjective* 形容词
not changing your ideas; not doing what other people want you to do 固执的；顽固的 ➲ SAME MEANING **stubborn** 同义词为 stubborn： *He's too **obstinate** to say he's sorry.* 他太固执了，拒不道歉。

obstruct /əbˈstrʌkt/ *verb* 动词 (obstructs, obstructing, obstructed)
to be in the way so that somebody or something cannot go past 阻挡；阻塞： *Please move your car – you're **obstructing** the traffic.* 请开走你的车子 —— 你阻碍交通了。
▸ **obstruction** /əbˈstrʌkʃn/ *noun* 名词 a thing that stops somebody or something from going past 障碍；障碍物： *The train had to stop because there was an **obstruction** on the line.* 因为铁轨上有障碍物，火车非得停下来不可。

obtain 0→ /əbˈteɪn/ *verb* 动词 (obtains, obtaining, obtained /əbˈteɪnd/) (*formal* 正式)
to get something 获得；得到： *Where can I **obtain** tickets for the play?* 这出戏剧的票哪里有卖？

obtuse angle /əbˌtjuːs ˈæŋɡl/ *noun* 名词
an angle between 90° and 180° 钝角（介于 90° 至 180°） ➲ Look at **acute angle** and **right angle**. 见 acute angle 和 right angle.

obvious 0→ /ˈɒbviəs/ *adjective* 形容词
easy to see or understand 明显的；显然的；易懂的 ➲ SAME MEANING **clear** 同义词为 clear： *It's **obvious** that she's not happy.* 她显然很不开心。
▸ **obviously** /ˈɒbviəsli/ *adverb* 副词： *There has **obviously** been a mistake.* 显然是出错了。

occasion 0̶ /əˈkeɪʒn/ *noun* 名词
1 a time when something happens 某次；…的时候：*I've been to Paris on three or four occasions.* 我去过巴黎三四次。
2 a special time 特别的时刻：*A wedding is a big family occasion.* 婚礼是家庭中的大事。

occasional /əˈkeɪʒənl/ *adjective* 形容词
happening sometimes, but not very often 偶尔；偶然的：*We get the occasional visitor.* 我们偶尔有客人来。

occasionally /əˈkeɪʒnəli/ *adverb* 副词
sometimes, but not often 偶尔；有时候：*I go to London occasionally.* 我偶尔到伦敦去。

occupation /ˌɒkjuˈpeɪʃn/ *noun* 名词
1 (*plural* 复数形式 occupations) (*formal* 正式) a job 职业；工作：*What is your mother's occupation?* 你母亲做什么工作?
2 (*plural* 复数形式 occupations) something that you do in your free time 消遣；业余活动：*Fishing is his favourite occupation.* 钓鱼是他最喜爱的消遣。
3 (*no plural* 不用复数形式) when a country or army takes or has control of an area or building 侵占；占领：*the Roman occupation of Britain* 罗马人对不列颠的占领
4 (*no plural* 不用复数形式) (*formal* 正式) the fact of living in a house, room, etc. （房子、房间等的）使用，占用：*The new house is now ready for occupation.* 新房子现在可以入住了。

occupy /ˈɒkjupaɪ/ *verb* 动词 (occupies, occupying, occupied /ˈɒkjupaɪd/, has occupied)
1 to fill a space or period of time 占用（空间或时间）⊃ SAME MEANING **take up** 同义词为 take up：*The bed seemed to occupy most of the room.* 这张床似乎占去了大半个房间。
2 to keep somebody busy 使忙碌：*She occupied herself reading.* 她以看书来打发时间。
3 (*formal* 正式) to live or work in a room or building 占有，使用（房间或建筑物）：*Who occupies these offices?* 这些办公室是谁用的?
4 to take or have control of an area or building 侵占；占领：*Protestors occupied the TV station.* 抗议者占领了电视台。
▸ **occupied** /ˈɒkjupaɪd/ *adjective* 形容词
1 busy 忙于：*This work will keep me occupied all week.* 这项工作会让我忙上整个星期。

2 being used 使用中：*Excuse me – is this seat occupied?* 请问，这个座位有人吗?

occur 0̶ /əˈkɜː(r)/ *verb* 动词 (occurs, occurring, occurred /əˈkɜːd/) (*formal* 正式)
to happen 发生：*The accident occurred this morning.* 事故是今天早上发生的。
occur to somebody to come into somebody's mind 出现在脑海中；想起：*It occurred to me that* you might like to come. 我突然想到你可能想过来。

ocean 0̶ /ˈəʊʃn/ *noun* 名词
a very big sea 大海；海洋：*the Atlantic Ocean* 大西洋

o'clock 0̶ /əˈklɒk/ *adverb* 副词
used after the numbers one to twelve for saying the time（用于时间）…点钟，…点整：*I left home at four o'clock and arrived in London at half past five.* 我四点钟离开家，五点半到了伦敦。

> 🔾 GRAMMAR 语法说明
> Be careful! **O'clock** is only used with full hours. You cannot say 'at half past five o'clock'. 注意：o'clock 只用于整点，不说 at half past five o'clock。

octagon /ˈɒktəɡən/ *noun* 名词
a shape with eight straight sides 八边形；八角形
▸ **octagonal** /ɒkˈtæɡənl/ *adjective* 形容词：*an octagonal coin* 八角形硬币

October 0̶ /ɒkˈtəʊbə(r)/ *noun* 名词
the tenth month of the year 十月

octopus 章鱼

tentacle 触手

octopus /ˈɒktəpəs/ *noun* 名词 (*plural* 复数形式 octopuses)
a sea animal with eight arms 章鱼

odd 0̶ /ɒd/ *adjective* 形容词 (odder, oddest)
1 strange or unusual 奇怪的；异乎寻常的 ⊃ SAME MEANING **peculiar** 同义词为 peculiar：*It's odd that he left without*

A B C D E F G H I J K L M N

O

P Q R S T U V W X Y Z

telling anybody. 他谁也没告诉就走了，真奇怪。

2 not able to be divided by two 奇数的: *1, 3, 5 and 7 are all **odd numbers**.* * 1、3、5 和 7 都是奇数。 ⊃ OPPOSITE **even** 反义词为 even

3 not with the pair or set it belongs to; not matching 不成对的; 不相配的: *You're wearing **odd socks**!* 你穿的袜子不成对!

the odd one out one that is different from all the others 与众不同者; 异类: *'Apple', 'orange', 'cabbage' – which is the odd one out?* 苹果、橙子、卷心菜，哪一个不是同类?

oddly /'ɒdli/ *adverb* 副词
in a strange or unusual way 古怪地; 怪异地: *She behaved very oddly.* 她的行为十分古怪。

odds /ɒdz/ *noun* 名词
the odds used for saying how likely something is 可能性; 机会: *The odds are that he'll win* (= he'll probably win). 他很可能会赢。 ◇ *The odds are against us* (= we will probably not succeed). 我们成功的机会不大。

odds and ends /ˌɒdz ənd 'endz/ *noun* 名词 (*plural* 用复数形式) (*British* 英式英语) (*informal* 非正式)
different small things that are not important 零碎的东西: *a box of odds and ends* 一箱零星杂物

of 0— /əv; ɒv/ *preposition* 介词
1 belonging to or connected with somebody or something（表示相关或所属关系）…的: *the back of the chair* 椅背 ◇ *What's the name of this mountain?* 这座山的名称是什么? ◇ *the plays of Shakespeare* 莎士比亚的戏剧 ◇ *the arrival of the president* 总统的到来

2 used after an amount, etc.（用于数量等之后）: *a litre of water* 一升水 ◇ *the fourth of July* 七月四日

3 used for saying what something is or what something is made of（用于表示性质或构成）: *a piece of wood* 一块木头 ◇ *a cup of tea* 一杯茶 ◇ *Is this shirt made of cotton?* 这件衬衫是棉的吗?

4 used for giving your opinion about somebody's behaviour（表示对某人行为的看法）: *That's very kind of you.* 你真好。

5 used for showing that somebody or something is part of a group（表示作为一部分）: *one of the girls* 其中的一个女孩 ◇ *some of his friends* 他的一些朋友

6 used with some adjectives and verbs

（与某些形容词和动词连用）: *I'm proud of you.* 我为你感到自豪。 ◇ *This perfume smells of roses.* 这种香水是玫瑰味的。

off¹ 0— /ɒf/ *preposition, adverb* 介词, 副词
1 away from a place; at a distance in space or time 离开;（空间或时间上）离: *My birthday is not far off.* 我的生日快到了。 ◇ *I must be off soon* (= leave). 我得马上走了。

2 down or away from something 从…落下（或离开）: *He fell off the roof.* 他从屋顶摔了下来。 ◇ *We got off the bus.* 我们下了公共汽车。 ◇ *The thief ran off.* 小偷跑了。

3 used for talking about removing something（表示除去某物）: *If you're hot, take your coat off.* 你觉得热，就把大衣脱了吧。 ◇ *Can you clean that paint off the carpet?* 你清除地毯上的那块油漆吗? ⊃ OPPOSITE **on** 反义词为 on

4 not connected; not working 未连接; 不运行: *Make sure the lights are off before you go.* 走之前一定要把灯关掉。 ⊃ OPPOSITE **on** 反义词为 on

5 not at work or school 没有上班（或上学）: *I had the day off yesterday.* 我昨天休假。

6 joined to something and leading from it 与…相连: *The bathroom is off the bedroom.* 浴室连着卧室。

off² 0— /ɒf/ *adjective* 形容词
not fresh enough to eat or drink（食物或饮料）不新鲜, 变质: *The milk's off.* 牛奶变质了。

offence 0— (*British* 英式英语) (*American* 美式英语 **offense**) /ə'fens/ *noun* 名词
1 (*plural* 复数形式 **offences**) an illegal action 违法行为; 罪行 ⊃ SAME MEANING **crime** 同义词为 crime: *He has committed an offence.* 他犯了罪。

2 (*no plural* 不用复数形式) when a person is angry or unhappy because of what somebody has said or done 得罪; 冒犯: *He took offence when I refused his help.* 我不肯让他帮忙，他就生气了。

offend /ə'fend/ *verb* 动词 (**offends, offending, offended**)
to make somebody feel angry or unhappy; to hurt somebody's feelings 得罪; 冒犯: *I hope they won't be offended if I don't come.* 如果我不去，我希望他们不会生气。

offense *American English for* OFFENCE 美式英语, 即 offence

offensive /əˈfensɪv/ *adjective* 形容词
rude in a way that makes somebody feel upset, angry or insulted 冒犯的；侮辱的：
offensive language 冒犯的语言

offer¹ ⍥ /ˈɒfə(r)/ *verb* 动词 (offers, offering, offered /ˈɒfəd/)
to say or show that you will do or give something if another person wants it 主动提出；自愿给予：*She offered me a cake.* 她给了我一块蛋糕。◇ *I offered to help her.* 我主动提出要帮助她。

offer² ⍥ /ˈɒfə(r)/ *noun* 名词
1 when you offer to do or give something if another person wants it 主动提议；建议：*Thanks for the offer, but I don't need any help.* 谢谢你的好意，但我并不需要帮助。
2 an amount of money that you say you will give for something 出价；报价：*They've made an offer for the house.* 他们已经给房子报了价。
on offer
1 for sale or available 可买到；可使用：*The college has a wide range of courses on offer.* 这所学院开设了各式各样的课程。
2 (*British* 英式英语) for sale at a lower price than usual for a certain time 打折出售；减价销售

office ⍥ /ˈɒfɪs/ *noun* 名词
1 a place where people work, usually at desks 办公室；办公楼：*I work in an office.* 我在办公室上班。
2 a place where you can buy something or get information 办事处；服务处；问询处 ⊃ Look at **post office** and **ticket office**. 见 post office 和 ticket office。
3 Office one part of the government （政府的）部：*the Foreign Office* 外交部

officer ⍥ /ˈɒfɪsə(r)/ *noun* 名词
1 a person in the army, navy or air force who gives orders to other people 军官：*a naval officer* 海军军官
2 a person who does important work, especially for the government （尤指政府的）官员：*a prison officer* 典狱官员 ◇ *police officers* 警察

official¹ ⍥ /əˈfɪʃl/ *adjective* 形容词
connected with government or with a particular organization or a person in authority 官方的；正式的；公事的：*an official government report* 政府报告 ◇ *an official announcement* 官方公告
▸ **officially** /əˈfɪʃəli/ *adverb* 副词：*He has now heard officially that he's got the job.* 他刚接到正式通知，他获得了这份工作。

official² /əˈfɪʃl/ *noun* 名词
a person who does important work, especially for the government （尤指政府的）官员：*government officials* 政府官员

off-licence /ˈɒf laɪsns/ (*British* 英式英语) (*American* 美式英语 **liquor store**) *noun* 名词
a shop where you can buy drinks like beer and wine 外卖酒店

often ⍥ /ˈɒfn/ *adverb* 副词
many times 常常；经常：*We often play football on Sundays.* 我们星期天常常踢足球。◇ *I've often seen her on the train.* 我常在火车上见到她。◇ *I don't write to him very often.* 我不常给他写信。◇ *How often do you visit her?* 你多长时间去看她一次？

every so often sometimes, but not often 有时；偶尔：*Every so often she phones me.* 她偶尔给我来个电话。

oh ⍥ /əʊ/ *exclamation* 感叹词
1 used for showing a strong feeling, like surprise or fear （表示惊讶、恐惧等）啊，哎哟：*Oh no! I've lost my keys!* 哎哟，我丢了钥匙！
2 used before other words, for example when you are thinking what to say （表示思索）哦，嗯：*'What time is it?' 'Oh, about two o'clock.'* "几点了？" "嗯，两点左右吧。"
Oh dear used for showing that you are surprised or unhappy （表示惊讶或不愉快）哎呀，天哪：*Oh dear – have you hurt yourself?* 哎呀，你伤到自己了吗？
Oh well used when you are not happy about something, but you cannot change it （表示无奈）唉，好啦：*'I'm too busy to go out tonight.' 'Oh well, I'll see you tomorrow then.'* "我太忙了，今晚不能出去。" "唉，好吧，那么我们明天见。"

oil ⍥ /ɔɪl/ *noun* 名词 (no plural 不用复数形式)
1 a thick liquid that comes from under the ground or the sea. We use oil for energy and to make machines work smoothly. 石油；原油；润滑油
2 a thick liquid that comes from plants or animals and that we use in cooking （食用的）动物油，植物油：*Fry the onions in oil.* 把洋葱在油里炸一下。

oil painting /ˈɔɪl peɪntɪŋ/ *noun* 名词
a picture that has been done with paint made from oil 油画

oil rig /ˈɔɪl rɪɡ/ *noun* 名词
a special building or a platform with

A
B
C
D
E
F
G
H
I
J
K
L
M
N
O
P
Q
R
S
T
U
V
W
X
Y
Z

machines that dig for oil under the sea or on land 石油钻塔；钻井平台

oil slick /'ɔɪl slɪk/ *noun* 名词
a large amount of oil on the sea after an accident（海上）浮油

oil well /'ɔɪl wel/ *noun* 名词
a hole that is made deep in the ground or under the sea in order to get oil 油井

oily /'ɔɪli/ *adjective* 形容词 (oilier, oiliest)
like oil or covered with oil 像油的；油乎乎的： *an oily liquid* 油状液体 ◇ *oily hands* 沾满油的手

ointment /'ɔɪntmənt/ *noun* 名词
a smooth substance that you put on sore skin or on an injury to help it get better 药膏；软膏

OK¹ 0━ (*also* 亦作 **okay**) /əʊˈkeɪ/ *exclamation* 感叹词 (*informal* 非正式)
yes 对；好；行 C SAME MEANING **all right** 同义词为 all right： *'Shall we go to the party?' 'OK.'* "我们去参加聚会好吗？" "好啊。"

OK² 0━ (*also* 亦作 **okay**) /əʊˈkeɪ/ *adjective, adverb* 形容词，副词 (*informal* 非正式)
1 safe and well; calm or happy 安然无恙；平安；快乐 C SAME MEANING **all right** 同义词为 all right： *'How's your mum?' 'OK, thanks.'* "你妈妈怎么样？" "还好，谢谢。"
2 all right; acceptable 行；好的；可以： *Is it okay to sit here?* 坐这儿行吗？

old 0━ /əʊld/ *adjective* 形容词 (older, oldest)
1 having lived for a long time 老的；年纪大的： *My grandfather is very old.* 我爷爷很老了。 ◇ *My sister is older than me.* 我姐姐比我大。 C OPPOSITE **young** 反义词为 young
2 made or bought a long time ago 旧的；古老的： *an old house* 老房子 C OPPOSITE **new** 反义词为 new
3 You use **old** to show the age of somebody or something. （表示年龄）： *He's nine years old.* 他九岁了。 ◇ *How old are you?* 你多大了？ ◇ *a six-year-old boy* 六岁的男孩
4 done or had before now 以前的；原先的： *My old job was more interesting than this one.* 我以前的那份工作比这份有意思。 C OPPOSITE **new** 反义词为 new
5 known for a long time 相识时间长的： *Jane is an old friend – we were at school together.* 简是老朋友，我们以前是同学。
▸ **the old** *noun* 名词 (*plural* 用复数形式)
old people 老年人

old age /ˌəʊld 'eɪdʒ/ *noun* 名词 (*no plural* 不用复数形式)
the part of your life when you are old 老年；晚年： *He's enjoying life in his old age.* 他在安享晚年。 C OPPOSITE **youth** 反义词为 youth

old-age pension /ˌəʊld eɪdʒ 'penʃn/ *noun* 名词 (*no plural* 不用复数形式)
money that you get from a government or a company when you are old and do not work any more (when you are retired) 养老金
▸ **old-age pensioner** /ˌəʊld eɪdʒ 'penʃənə(r)/ *noun* 名词 (*abbr.* 缩略式 **OAP**)
a person who has an OLD-AGE PENSION 领养老金者

old-fashioned 0━ /ˌəʊld 'fæʃnd/ *adjective* 形容词
not modern 过时的；老式的 C OPPOSITE **fashionable** 反义词为 fashionable： *old-fashioned clothes* 过时的衣服 ◇ *My parents are rather old-fashioned.* 我父母比较守旧。

olive /'ɒlɪv/ *noun* 名词
a small green or black fruit, that people eat or make into oil 橄榄 C Look at Picture Dictionary page **P6**. 见彩页 P6。

olive oil /ˌɒlɪv 'ɔɪl/ *noun* 名词 (*no plural* 不用复数形式)
oil that is produced from OLIVES 橄榄油： *Fry the onions in a little olive oil.* 用少量橄榄油炒一下洋葱。 C Look at Picture Dictionary page **P6**. 见彩页 P6。

the Olympic Games /ði əˌlɪmpɪk 'ɡeɪmz/ (*also* 亦作 **the Olympics** /ði əˈlɪmpɪks/) *noun* 名词 (*plural* 用复数形式)
an international sports competition that is organized every four years in a different country 奥林匹克运动会；奥运会

omelette /'ɒmlət/ *noun* 名词
a dish made of eggs mixed together and then fried 煎蛋卷： *a cheese omelette* 奶酪蛋卷

omit /ə'mɪt/ *verb* 动词 (omits, omitting, omitted) (*formal* 正式)
to not include something 省略；漏掉 C SAME MEANING **leave out** 同义词为 leave out： *Omit question 2 and do question 3.* 第 2 题略去，做第 3 题。

on 0━ /ɒn/ *preposition, adverb* 介词，副词
1 used for showing where something is 在⋯上： *Your book is on the table.* 你的书在桌上。 ◇ *The number is on the door.* 号码在门上。 ◇ *There is a good film on TV tonight.* 今天晚上电视上有部精彩的影片。

◇ *I've got a cut on my hand.* 我手上有个伤口。

2 used for showing when 在（某时）: *My birthday is on 6 May.* 我的生日是 5 月 6 日。 ◇ *I'll see you on Monday.* 星期一见。 ⊃ Look at Study Pages **S9-S10**. 见研习专页 S9-S10。

3 used with ways of travelling and types of travel （与交通工具和出行方式连用）: *He got on the train.* 他上了火车。 ◇ *I came here on foot* (= walking). 我是走路来的。

4 used for showing that somebody or something continues （表示持续）: *You can't stop here – drive on.* 你不能停在这里，继续开吧。

5 working; being used 在运行；使用中: *All the lights were on.* 所有的灯都开着。 ⊃ OPPOSITE **off** 反义词为 off

6 using something 通过；使用: *I bought it on the Internet.* 这是我在网上买的。 *I was on the phone to Jania.* 我在跟贾妮亚通电话。 ◇ *He saw it on TV.* 他在电视上看到了这件事。

7 about 关于: *a book on cars* 关于汽车的书

8 covering your body 穿着；戴着: *Put your coat on.* 把大衣穿上。

9 happening 发生: *What's on at the cinema?* 电影院在放映什么?

10 when something happens 在…时候; 一…就: *She telephoned me on her return from New York.* 她从纽约一回来就给我打电话。

on and on without stopping 不停地; 持续地: *He went* (= talked) *on and on about his girlfriend.* 他滔滔不绝地谈论着他的女朋友。

once¹ 0━ /wʌns/ *adverb* 副词

1 one time 一次: *I've only been to Spain once.* 我只去过一次西班牙。 ◇ *He phones us once a week* (= once every week). 他每周给我们打一次电话。

2 at some time in the past 曾经; 一度: *This house was once a school.* 这所房子曾经是学校。

at once

1 immediately 立即; 马上 ⊃ SAME MEANING **now** 同义词为 now: *Come here at once!* 马上到这里来!

2 at the same time 同时: *I can't do two things at once!* 我不能同时干两件事!

for once this time only 仅此一次: *For once I agree with you.* 只有这一次我同意你的意见。

once again, once more again; one more time 再次; 再一次: *Can you explain it to me once more?* 你能再给我解释一次吗?

once or twice a few times; not often 一两次; 几次: *I've only met them once or twice.* 我只见过他们几次。

once upon a time (used at the beginning of a children's story) a long time ago （用于儿童故事的开头）从前, 很久以前: *Once upon a time there was a beautiful princess …* 很久以前, 有一位漂亮的公主…

once² /wʌns/ *conjunction* 连词
as soon as; when 一…就; 当…的时候: *Once you've finished your homework you can go out.* 你一做完家庭作业就可以出去。

one¹ 0━ /wʌn/ *number, adjective* 数词, 形容词

1 the number 1 一: *One and one make two* (1 + 1 = 2). 一加一等于二。 ◇ *Only one person spoke.* 只有一个人说话。

2 a person or thing, especially when they are part of a group （尤指一组中的）一个人, 一件事物: *One of my friends is ill.* 我的一个朋友病了。 ◇ *I've lost one of my books.* 我丢了一本书。

3 only 唯一: *You are the one person I can trust.* 你是我唯一可以信任的人。

4 used for talking about a particular time, without saying exactly when （表示不确切的某个时间）: *I'll come over one evening.* 那天晚上我会过来的。

one by one first one, then the next, etc.; separately 一个一个地; 逐一: *Please come in one by one.* 请一个一个进来。

one² 0━ /wʌn/ *pronoun* 代词

1 used instead of the name of a person or thing （用以代替所说的人或事物）: *I've got some bananas. Do you want one?* 我有些香蕉。你要一根吗? ◇ *'Can I borrow a book?' 'Yes. Which one?'* "我可以借本书吗?" "可以。哪一本?" ◇ *The questions are hard – leave the ones you can't do.* 这些问题很难回答, 把你不会做的留着吧。

2 (*formal* 正式) people in general; I （泛指）人; 本人: *One feels quite helpless.* 人们觉得很无助。

🔊 SPEAKING 表达方式说明

It is very formal to use **one** in this way and it sounds rather old-fashioned. * one 的这种用法非常正式, 而且听起来有些过时。
We usually say 'you' for 'people in general' and 'I' when you are talking about yourself. 通常用 you 泛指人, 用 I 表示自己。

one another 0━ /ˌwʌn əˈnʌðə(r)/
pronoun 代词
each other 互相；彼此： *We looked at one another.* 我们彼此看着对方。

oneself /wʌnˈself/ *pronoun* 代词 (*formal* 正式)
used with 'one' for saying that an action involves the person doing it （与 one 连用）自己，自身： *One has to ask oneself if such action is necessary.* 大家必须问一下自己，这样的行动是否必要。

by oneself
1 alone; without other people 单独；独自
2 without help 独立地

one-way /ˌwʌn ˈweɪ/ *adjective* 形容词
allowing travel in one direction only 单行的；单程的： *a one-way street* 单行道 ◇ *a one-way ticket* 单程票

onion 0━ /ˈʌnjən/ *noun* 名词
a round vegetable with many layers and a strong smell. Cutting **onions** can make you cry. 洋葱 ⊃ Look at Picture Dictionary page **P9**. 见彩图 P9。

online /ˌɒnˈlaɪn/ *adjective, adverb* 形容词，副词
using a computer or the Internet 网上（的）；在线（的）；联网（的）： *Online shopping is both cheap and convenient.* 网上购物既便宜又方便。◇ *Bookings can be made online.* 预订可在网上进行。

only¹ 0━ /ˈəʊnli/ *adjective* 形容词
with no others 唯一的；仅有的： *She's the only girl in her class.* 她是班上唯一的女生。

only² 0━ /ˈəʊnli/ *adverb* 副词
and nobody or nothing else; no more than 只；仅： *I invited twenty people to the party, but only five came.* 我邀请了二十个人参加聚会，可是只来了五个人。◇ *We can't have dinner now. It's only four o'clock!* 我们不能现在吃晚饭。才四点钟！◇ *We only waited five minutes.* 我们只等了五分钟。

only just
1 not long ago 刚刚；刚才： *We've only just arrived.* 我们刚刚到。
2 almost not 几乎不；差点儿没有： *We only just had enough money to pay for the meal.* 我们的钱几乎不够付那顿饭的饭费。

only³ /ˈəʊnli/ *conjunction* 连词 (*informal* 非正式)
but 只是： *I like this bag, only it's too expensive.* 我喜欢这个包，只是太贵了。

only child /ˌəʊnli ˈtʃaɪld/ *noun* 名词
(*plural* 复数形式 **only children**)
a child who has no brothers or sisters 独生子（或女）： *I'm an only child.* 我是独生子。

onto 0━ (*also* 亦作 **on to**) /ˈɒntə; ˈɒntu/
preposition 介词
to a place on somebody or something 到…上： *The bottle fell onto the floor.* 瓶子掉到地上了。◇ *The cat jumped onto the table.* 猫跳到桌子上去了。

onwards /ˈɒnwədz/ (*also* 亦作 **onward** /ˈɒnwəd/) *adverb* 副词
1 and after 从…开始： *I shall be at home from eight o'clock onwards.* 我从八点钟起会在家。
2 forward; further 往前；朝前： *The soldiers marched onwards until they came to a bridge.* 士兵一直向前行进，来到一座桥前。

oops /ʊps/ *exclamation* 感叹词
a word you say when something has gone wrong, for example when somebody has fallen over or has dropped something （出差错时说）哎哟： *Oops! Are you ok?* 哎哟！你没事吧？

ooze /uːz/ *verb* 动词 (**oozes, oozing, oozed**)
1 If a thick liquid **oozes** from something, it comes out slowly. 渗出；慢慢流出： *Blood was oozing from the wound.* 血从伤口慢慢流了出来。
2 to show a lot of a particular quality 充满（某特质）： *She walked into the party oozing confidence.* 她走进聚会场所，显得一脸自信。

open¹ 0━ /ˈəʊpən/ *adjective* 形容词
1 not closed, so that people or things can go in or out 开着的： *Leave the windows open.* 让窗户开着。◇ *The book lay open on the table.* 那本书在桌上摊开放着。◇ *an open box* 打开的盒子
2 able to be used or done; available 开放；营业；公开： *The bank is open from 9 a.m. to 4 p.m.* 这家银行的营业时间为上午 9 时至下午 4 时。◇ *The competition is open to all children under the age of 14.* 这项比赛欢迎所有 14 岁以下的儿童参加。
3 not hiding your thoughts and feelings 坦诚的；直率的： *She's a very open person.* 她为人直率。
4 away from towns and people; with not many buildings or trees 开阔的；空旷的： *We were in open country.* 我们在空旷的地方。
5 not yet decided 未决定；尚在考虑：

'Where shall we go on Friday?' 'Let's leave it open.' "我们星期五去哪里？""到时再说吧。"

in the open air outside 在户外；在露天： *We had our lunch in the open air.* 我们在户外吃午饭。

open² 0̶ /ˈəʊpən/ *verb* 动词 (**opens, opening, opened** /ˈəʊpənd/)

1 to move, or to move something, so that something is not closed or covered 开；打开；开启： *The door opened and a man came in.* 门开了，一个男子走了进来。◇ *It was hot, so I opened a window.* 天气很热，所以我打开了窗户。◇ *Open your eyes!* 睁开你的眼睛！◇ *Open your books at page 10.* 把书翻到第 10 页。

2 to make it possible for people to enter a place 开门；开放；为……揭幕： *Banks don't open on Sundays.* 银行星期天不开门。◇ *The President opened the new hospital.* 总统为新医院揭幕。

3 to start something; to start 开始；启动；以…开头： *I'd like to open a bank account.* 我想开一个银行账户。◇ *How do you open a file in this program?* 怎么打开这个程序中的文件？◇ *The story opens with a murder.* 这个故事以一起谋杀案揭开序幕。 ⊃ OPPOSITE **close** or **shut** 反义词为 close 或 shut

open³ /ˈəʊpən/ *noun* 名词 (*no plural* 不用复数形式)

out in the open outside; in the countryside 在户外；露天；在野外： *Children need to play out in the open.* 孩子需要在户外玩耍。

into the open not hidden or secret 公开；为人所知： *They intend to bring their complaints out into the open.* 他们想把心中的种种不快说出来。

open-air /ˌəʊpən ˈeə(r)/ *adjective* 形容词 outside 户外的；露天的： *an open-air concert* 露天音乐会

opener /ˈəʊpnə(r)/ *noun* 名词 a small tool that you use for opening tins or bottles 开罐器；开瓶器： *a tin-opener* 罐头起子

opening /ˈəʊpnɪŋ/ *noun* 名词

1 a space in something where people or things can go in and out 孔；洞；豁口 ⊃ SAME MEANING **hole** 同义词为 hole： *The cattle got out through an opening in the fence.* 牛从篱笆上的豁口跑了出去。

2 a ceremony to celebrate the start of a public event or the first time a new building, road, etc. is used 开幕式；落成典礼： *the opening of the Olympic Games* 奥运会开幕式

openly /ˈəʊpənli/ *adverb* 副词 not secretly; without trying to hide anything 公开地；坦诚地；毫不隐瞒地： *She told me openly that she didn't agree.* 她直率地告诉我她不同意。

opera /ˈɒprə/ *noun* 名词 a play where the actors sing most of the words to music 歌剧： *Do you like opera?* 你喜欢歌剧吗？◇ *We went to see an opera by Verdi.* 我们去看了一出威尔地的歌剧。

opera house /ˈɒprə haʊs/ *noun* 名词 a building where you can see OPERAS 歌剧院

operate 0̶ /ˈɒpəreɪt/ *verb* 动词 (**operates, operating, operated**)

1 to work; to make something work （使）运作，运转；操作： *I don't know how this machine operates.* 我不知道这台机器是如何运行的。◇ *These switches operate the heating.* 这些开关控制暖气设备。

2 to cut into somebody's body to take out or repair a part inside 动手术： *Doctors will operate on her leg tomorrow.* 医生明天给她做腿部手术。

> 🔎 WORD BUILDING 词汇扩充
>
> A doctor who **operates** on people in hospital is called a **surgeon**. A surgeon's work is called **surgery**. 在医院给病人做手术（operate）的外科医生叫做 surgeon，外科手术叫做 surgery。

operation 0̶ /ˌɒpəˈreɪʃn/ *noun* 名词

1 cutting into somebody's body to take out or repair a part inside 手术： *He had an operation on his eye.* 他的眼睛做过手术。

2 an event that needs a lot of people or planning （有组织的）行动，活动： *a military operation* 军事行动

operator /ˈɒpəreɪtə(r)/ *noun* 名词

1 a person who makes a machine work 操作人员： *a machine operator* 机器操作员

2 a person who works for a telephone company and helps to connect people making calls （电话的）接线员： *What number do you dial for the operator?* 找接线员拨什么号码？

3 a person or company that runs a particular business （某种生意的）经营者，公司： *a tour operator* 经营旅游业者 ◇ *a bus operator* 公共汽车公司

opinion 0̶ /əˈpɪniən/ *noun* 名词 what you think about something 意见；

想法；看法 ⊃ SAME MEANING **view** 同义词
为 view：*In my opinion, she's wrong.*
我认为她错了。◇ *What's your opinion of
his work?* 你对他的工作有什么意见？◇
He had strong opinions on everything.
他对什么事都很有自己的一套想法。

opponent /ə'pəʊnənt/ *noun* 名词
the person against you in a fight or
competition 对手；竞争者：*The first
team beat their opponents easily.* 第一队
轻易战胜了对手。

opportunity 0- /,ɒpə'tju:nəti/ *noun*
名词 (*plural* 复数形式 opportunities)
a chance to do something; a time when
you can do something that you want to
do 机会；时机：*I didn't get the
opportunity to visit them.* 我没有机会拜访
他们。◇ *It was a golden* (= perfect)
opportunity and I decided to take it.
这是难得的好机会，我决定要好好把握。

oppose /ə'pəʊz/ *verb* 动词 (opposes,
opposing, opposed /ə'pəʊzd/)
to try to stop or change something
because you do not like it 反对；抵制；
阻挠：*A lot of people opposed the new
law.* 很多人反对新法。

opposed /ə'pəʊzd/ *adjective* 形容词
disagreeing strongly with something and
trying to stop it 反对：*I am opposed to
the plan.* 我反对这个计划。
as opposed to (*formal* 正式) words that
you use to show that you are talking
about one thing, not something different
不同于；而不是：*She teaches at the
college, as opposed to the university.*
她在学院任教，而不是在大学。

opposite 对面

They're sitting **opposite** each other.
他们相对而坐。

opposite[1] 0- /'ɒpəzɪt/ *adjective*,
adverb, *preposition* 形容词，副词，介词

1 across from where somebody or
something is; on the other side 对面
（的）；另一边（的）：*The church is on
the opposite side of the road from my flat.*
教堂在我公寓那侧马路的对面。◇ *You sit
here, and I'll sit opposite.* 你坐这里，我坐
你对面。◇ *The bank is opposite the
supermarket.* 银行在超市的对面。
2 as different as possible 相反的；截然
不同的：*North is the opposite direction
to south.* 北是南的相反方向。

opposite[2] 0- /'ɒpəzɪt/ *noun* 名词
a word or thing that is as different as
possible from another word or thing
反义词；相反的事物：*'Hot' is the opposite
of 'cold'.* * hot 是 cold 的反义词。

opposition /,ɒpə'zɪʃn/ *noun* 名词
(*no plural* 不用复数形式)
disagreeing with something and trying to
stop it 反对；反抗：*There was a lot of
opposition to the plan.* 有很多人反对这个
计划。

opt /ɒpt/ *verb* 动词 (opts, opting, opted)
to choose to do something 选择：*She
opted for a career in medicine.* 她选择了
医学事业。

optician /ɒp'tɪʃn/ *noun* 名词
1 a person who examines your eyes to
find out how well you can see and who
sells glasses 验光师；配镜师
2 optician's the shop where an **optician**
works and where you can buy glasses
眼镜店 ⊃ Look at Picture Dictionary page
P13. 见彩页 P13。

optimism /'ɒptɪmɪzəm/ *noun* 名词
(*no plural* 不用复数形式)
the feeling that good things will happen
乐观；乐观主义 ⊃ OPPOSITE **pessimism**
反义词为 pessimism

optimist /'ɒptɪmɪst/ *noun* 名词
a person who thinks that good things
will happen 乐观的人；乐观主义者
⊃ OPPOSITE **pessimist** 反义词为 pessimist

optimistic /,ɒptɪ'mɪstɪk/ *adjective* 形容词
If you are **optimistic**, you think that good
things will happen. 乐观的 ⊃ OPPOSITE
pessimistic 反义词为 pessimistic：*I'm
optimistic about winning.* 我对获胜是
乐观的。

option /'ɒpʃn/ *noun* 名词
a thing that you can choose 可选择的事物

⊃ SAME MEANING **choice** 同义词为 choice: *You **have the option of** studying full-time or part-time.* 你可以选择全日制或兼读课程。

optional /ˈɒpʃənl/ *adjective* 形容词
If something is **optional**, you can choose it or not choose it. 可选择的：*All students must learn English, but German is optional.* 所有学生都得学英语，但德语是选修的。 ⊃ OPPOSITE **compulsory** 反义词为 compulsory

or ⊶ /ɔː(r)/ *conjunction* 连词
1 a word that joins possibilities 或；或者；还是：*Is it blue or green?* 是蓝的还是绿的？ ◊ *Are you coming or not?* 你来不来？ ◊ *You can have soup, salad or sandwiches.* 你可以要汤、沙拉或者三明治。 ◊ *She hasn't phoned or written for weeks.* 她已经好几个星期没有打电话或写信了。
2 if not 否则；不然 ⊃ SAME MEANING **otherwise** 同义词为 otherwise：*Go now, or you'll be late.* 现在就走，要不然你会迟到。

oral /ˈɔːrəl/ *adjective* 形容词
spoken; not written 口头的；口语的：*the oral exam* 口试

orange¹ ⊶ /ˈɒrɪndʒ/ *noun* 名词
1 a round fruit with a colour between red and yellow, and a thick skin 橙子；柑橘：*orange juice* 橙汁 ⊃ Look at Picture Dictionary page **P8**. 见彩页 P8。
2 a colour between red and yellow 橙色；橘黄色

orange² ⊶ /ˈɒrɪndʒ/ *adjective* 形容词
with a colour that is between red and yellow 橙色的；橘黄色的：*orange paint* 橘黄色的颜料

orbit /ˈɔːbɪt/ *noun* 名词
the path of a planet or an object that is moving around another thing in space（天体等运行的）轨道
▸ **orbit** *verb* 动词 (orbits, orbiting, orbited) to move around something in space 沿轨道运动；环绕（天体等）运行：*The spacecraft is orbiting the moon.* 航天器环绕着月球运行。

orchard /ˈɔːtʃəd/ *noun* 名词
a piece of land where fruit trees grow 果园

orchestra /ˈɔːkɪstrə/ *noun* 名词
a big group of people who play different musical instruments together 管弦乐队

ordeal /ɔːˈdiːl/ *noun* 名词
a very bad or unpleasant thing that

happens to somebody 折磨；煎熬；苦难：*He was lost in the mountains for a week without food or water – it was a terrible ordeal.* 他在深山中迷了路，一个星期没有食物和水，饱受折磨。

order¹ ⊶ /ˈɔːdə(r)/ *noun* 名词
1 (*no plural* 不用复数形式) the way that you place people or things together 顺序；次序：*The names are in alphabetical order.* 姓名是按字母顺序排列的。 ◊ *List the jobs in order of importance.* 把工作按重要性排列。
2 (*no plural* 不用复数形式) when everything is in the right place or everybody is doing the right thing 条理；秩序：*Our teacher likes order in the classroom.* 我们的老师喜欢教室里秩序井然。 ◊ *Are these papers in order* (= correct and tidy)? 这些文件整理好了吗？
3 (*plural* 复数形式 **orders**) words that tell somebody to do something 命令；指令：*He gave the order for work to begin.* 他下令开始工作。 ◊ *Soldiers have to obey orders.* 军人必须服从命令。
4 (*plural* 复数形式 **orders**) when you ask a company to send or supply goods to you 订单；订货；订购：*I'd like to place an order for some books.* 我想订些书。
5 (*plural* 复数形式 **orders**) when you ask for food or drink in a restaurant, bar, etc. 点菜：*The waiter took our order.* 服务员记下了我们点的菜。
in order to so that you can do something 以便；为了：*We arrived early in order to buy our tickets.* 为了买票我们到得很早。
out of order (used about a machine, etc.) not working（机器等）出问题，出故障：*I couldn't ring you – the phone was out of order.* 我没法给你打电话，因为电话坏了。

order² ⊶ /ˈɔːdə(r)/ *verb* 动词 (orders, ordering, ordered /ˈɔːdəd/)
1 to tell somebody that they must do something 命令；指示：*The student was ordered to leave the classroom.* 那名学生被勒令离开教室。
2 to ask a company to send or supply goods to you 订购；订货：*The shop didn't have your book – I ordered it.* 书店没有你要的书，所以我订了一本。
3 to ask for food or drink in a restaurant, bar, etc. 叫，点（食品或饮料）：*I ordered some coffee.* 我点了咖啡。

ordinary ⊶ /ˈɔːdnri/ *adjective* 形容词
not special or unusual 普通的；平常的；

一般的 ⊃ SAME MEANING **normal** 同义词为 normal: *Simon was wearing a suit, but I was in my ordinary clothes.* 西蒙穿着西装，我却穿着平常的衣服。

out of the ordinary unusual 异乎寻常 ⊃ SAME MEANING **strange** 同义词为 strange: *Did you see anything out of the ordinary?* 你看到有什么是不同寻常的吗？

ore /ɔː(r)/ *noun* 名词
rock or earth from which you get metal 矿石；矿砂；矿：*iron ore* 铁矿石

organ /ˈɔːgən/ *noun* 名词
1 a part of your body that has a special purpose, for example your heart 器官：*the body's internal organs* 身体内脏
2 a musical instrument, usually in a church, that is played like a piano 管风琴（常见于教堂）

organic /ɔːˈgænɪk/ *adjective* 形容词
1 grown in a natural way, without using chemicals 有机的；绿色的；不使用化学品的：*organic vegetables* 有机蔬菜
2 containing living things 有机物的；生物的：*Improve the soil by adding organic matter.* 加入有机物成分以改良土壤。

organism /ˈɔːgənɪzəm/ *noun* 名词
a living thing, especially a very small one that you can only see with a special instrument (called a **microscope**) 有机体；生物；（尤指）微生物

organization /ˌɔːgənaɪˈzeɪʃn/ *noun* 名词
1 (*plural* 复数形式 **organizations**) a group of people who work together for a special purpose 组织；机构：*He works for an organization that helps old people.* 他在一家帮助长者的机构工作。
2 (*no plural* 不用复数形式) the activity of planning or arranging something; the way that something is planned or arranged 安排；组织；筹备：*She's busy with the organization of her daughter's wedding.* 她正忙着筹备女儿的婚礼。

organize /ˈɔːgənaɪz/ *verb* 动词 (**organizes, organizing, organized** /ˈɔːgənaɪzd/)
to plan or arrange something 组织；筹备；安排：*Our teacher has organized a visit to the museum.* 我们老师安排了一次参观博物馆的活动。

organized /ˈɔːgənaɪzd/ *adjective* 形容词
with everything planned or arranged 有组织的；有条理的：*She's very organized.* 她是个很有条理的人。

⊃ OPPOSITE **disorganized** 反义词为 disorganized

oriental /ˌɔːriˈentl/ *adjective* 形容词
connected with the eastern part of the world, especially China and Japan 东方的（尤指中国和日本）：*oriental art* 东方艺术

origin /ˈɒrɪdʒɪn/ *noun* 名词
1 the time, way or place that something first existed 起源；源头；起因：*the origins of life on earth* 地球上生命的起源
2 the country, race, culture, etc. that a person comes from 原籍；血统；出身：*His family is of French origin.* 他家是法国后裔。

original /əˈrɪdʒənl/ *adjective* 形容词
1 first; earliest 最初的；原来的：*I have the car now, but my sister was the original owner.* 这辆车现在是我的，但原先的车主是我姐姐。
2 new and different 创新的；独创的：*His poems are very original.* 他的诗别具一格。
3 real, not copied 真正的；非复制的：*original paintings* 绘画真迹
▶ **original** *noun* 名词：*This is a copy of the painting – the original is in the National Gallery.* 这幅画是复制品——原作藏于国家美术馆。

originally /əˈrɪdʒənəli/ *adverb* 副词
in the beginning 最初；原来：*The school was originally very small.* 这所学校当初非常小。◇ *I'm from London originally.* 我原本来自伦敦。

ornament /ˈɔːnəmənt/ *noun* 名词
a thing that we have because it is beautiful, not because it is useful 装饰物；装饰品；摆设：*china ornaments* 瓷器装饰品 ⊃ Look at the picture at **fireplace**. 见 fireplace 的插图。
▶ **ornamental** /ˌɔːnəˈmentl/ *adjective* 形容词：*There is an ornamental pond in the garden.* 花园中有个观赏池塘。

orphan /ˈɔːfn/ *noun* 名词
a child whose parents are dead 孤儿

orphanage /ˈɔːfənɪdʒ/ *noun* 名词
a home for children whose parents are dead 孤儿院

ostrich /ˈɒstrɪtʃ/ *noun* 名词 (*plural* 复数形式 **ostriches**)
a very big bird from Africa that cannot fly but can run fast because it has long legs 鸵鸟

other /ˈʌðə(r)/ *adjective, pronoun* 形容词，代词
as well as or different from the one or

ones I have said 其他；另外；别的：
Carmen is Spanish, but the other students in my class are Japanese. 卡门是西班牙人，但我班上其余的学生都是日本人。◇ *I can only find one shoe. Have you seen the other one?* 我只找到一只鞋。你有看到另一只吗？◇ *I saw her on the other side of the road.* 我看见她在马路对面。*John and Claire arrived at nine o'clock, but the others* (= the other people) *were late.* 约翰和克莱尔九点钟就到了，但其他人都迟到了。

other than except; apart from 除了；除…以外：*I haven't told anybody other than you.* 除了你，我对谁也没说过。

some ... or other (*informal* 非正式) words that show you are not sure（表示不肯定）：*I can't find my glasses. I know I put them somewhere or other.* 我找不到我的眼镜。我好像把它放在什么地方了。

the other day not many days ago 前几天 ➾ SAME MEANING **recently** 同义词为 recently：*I saw your brother the other day.* 我前几天见到了你的弟弟。

otherwise¹ 0╼ /'ʌðəwaɪz/ *adverb* 副词
1 in all other ways 此外；除此之外：*The house is a bit small, but otherwise it's very nice.* 房子有点小，但除此之外都很不错。
2 in a different way 在其他方面；另；亦：*Most people agreed, but Rachel thought otherwise.* 大多数人都同意了，但雷切尔却有不一样的看法。

otherwise² /'ʌðəwaɪz/ *conjunction* 连词
if not 否则；不然 ➾ SAME MEANING **or** 同义词为 or：*Hurry up, otherwise you'll be late.* 快点，不然你会迟到的。

ouch /aʊtʃ/ *exclamation* 感叹词
You say '**ouch**' when you suddenly feel pain.（表示突然感到疼痛）哎哟：*Ouch! That hurts!* 哎哟！疼死了！

ought to 0╼ /'ɔːt tə; 'ɔːt tu/ *modal verb* 情态动词

⟡ PRONUNCIATION 读音说明
The word **ought** sounds like **sport**.
* ought 读音像 sport。

1 words that you use to tell or ask somebody what is the right thing to do（表示给予或寻求建议）应该，应当 ➾ SAME MEANING **should** 同义词为 should：*It's late – you ought to go home.* 时候不早了，你该回家了。◇ *You oughtn't to argue.* 你不应该争辩。
2 words that you use to say what you think will happen or what you think is

true（表示可能性）应该会，应当是 ➾ SAME MEANING **should** 同义词为 should：*Tim has worked very hard, so he ought to pass the exam.* 蒂姆很用功，所以他应该会通过考试。◇ *That film ought to be good.* 那部电影应该很好看。 ➾ Look at the note at **modal verb**. 见 modal verb 条的注释。

ounce /aʊns/ *noun* 名词 (*abbr.* 缩略式 **oz**)
a measure of weight (= 28.35 grams). There are 16 **ounces** in a **pound**. 盎司（重量单位；1 盎司等于 28.35 克，16 盎司为 1 磅）：*four ounces of flour* 四盎司面粉 ➾ Look at the note at **pound**. 见 pound 条的注释。

our 0╼ /ɑː(r); 'aʊə(r)/ *adjective* 形容词
belonging to us 我们的：*This is our house.* 这是我们的房子。

ours 0╼ /ɑːz; 'aʊəz/ *pronoun* 代词
something that belongs to us 我们的（东西）：*Your car is the same as ours.* 你们的车跟我们的一样。

ourselves 0╼ /ɑː'selvz; ˌaʊə'selvz/ *pronoun* 代词 (*plural* 用复数形式)
1 used when you and another person or other people do an action and are also affected by it 我们自己：*We made ourselves some coffee.* 我们给自己煮了些咖啡。
2 a word that makes 'we' stronger（用于强调）我们自己，亲自：*We built the house ourselves.* 房子是我们自己建的。

by ourselves
1 alone; without other people（我们）独自，单独：*We went on holiday by ourselves.* 我们独自度假去了。
2 without help（我们）独立地

out 0╼ /aʊt/ *adjective, adverb* 形容词，副词
1 away from the inside of a place（从…里）出来：*When you go out, please close the door.* 你出去的时候请把门关上。◇ *She opened the box and took out a picture.* 她打开盒子，取出了一张照片。➾ OPPOSITE **in** 反义词为 in
2 not at home or not in the place where you work 不在家；没上班；不在：*I phoned Steve but he was out.* 我给史蒂夫打过电话，但他不在。◇ *I went out to the cinema last night.* 我昨晚出去看电影了。➾ OPPOSITE **in** 反义词为 in
3 not burning or shining 熄灭：*The fire went out.* 火熄灭了。
4 not hidden; that you can see 出来；显露：*Look! The sun is out!* 瞧！太阳出来了！◇ *All the flowers are out* (= open). 花都开了。

A
B
C
D
E
F
G
H
I
J
K
L
M
N
O
P
Q
R
S
T
U
V
W
X
Y
Z

5 in a loud voice 大声地: *She cried out in pain.* 她痛得大叫起来。
⊃ Look also at **out of**. 亦见 out of。

outbreak /'aʊtbreɪk/ *noun* 名词
the sudden start of something bad (不好的事) 爆发，突然发生: *the outbreak of war* 战争的爆发

outdoor /'aʊtdɔ:(r)/ *adjective* 形容词
happening, existing or used outside a building 户外的；室外的；露天的: *an outdoor swimming pool* 室外游泳池 ◇ *Bring outdoor clothing.* 带上户外穿的衣服。⊃ OPPOSITE **indoor** 反义词为 indoor

outdoors 0━ /,aʊt'dɔ:z/ *adverb* 副词
not in a building 在户外；在室外；露天
⊃ SAME MEANING **outside** 同义词为 outside: *In summer we sometimes eat outdoors.* 我们夏天有时候在屋外吃饭。
⊃ OPPOSITE **indoors** 反义词为 indoors

outer /'aʊtə(r)/ *adjective* 形容词
on the outside; far from the centre 外表的；外部的；远离中心的: *Remove the outer leaves from the cabbage.* 择去卷心菜外层的菜叶。 ◇ *outer London* 伦敦的外围地区 ⊃ OPPOSITE **inner** 反义词为 inner

outfit /'aʊtfɪt/ *noun* 名词
a set of clothes that you wear together 全套服装；整套装束: *I've bought a new outfit for the party.* 我为参加聚会买了套新衣服。

outgrow /,aʊt'grəʊ/ *verb* 动词 (outgrows, outgrowing, outgrew /,aʊt'gru:/, has outgrown /,aʊt'grəʊn/)
to become too big or too old for something 长大得容不下；因年长而不再喜欢 ⊃ SAME MEANING **grow out of** 同义词为 grow out of: *She's outgrown her school uniform again.* 她的校服又因为她长大而穿不下了。

outing /'aʊtɪŋ/ *noun* 名词
an organized visit that lasts for less than a day (为时不超过一天的) 外出活动 ⊃ SAME MEANING **trip** 同义词为 trip: *We are going on an outing to the zoo.* 我们将到动物园游玩。

outline /'aʊtlaɪn/ *noun* 名词
a line that shows the shape or edge of something 轮廓: *It was dark, but we could see the dim outline of the castle.* 天黑了，但我们依稀看得到城堡的轮廓。

outlook /'aʊtlʊk/ *noun* 名词
what will probably happen 前景: *The outlook for the economy is not good.* 经济前景并不乐观。

out of 0━ /'aʊt əv/ *preposition* 介词
1 words that show where from 从…出来: *She took a cake out of the box.* 她从盒子里取出了一个蛋糕。 ◇ *She got out of bed.* 她起床了。 ⊃ OPPOSITE **into** 反义词为 into
2 not in 不在；离开；脱离: *Fish can't live out of water.* 鱼离开水就不能活。
3 using something; from 用，以，由 (…制成): *He made a table out of some old pieces of wood.* 他用一些旧木料做了张桌子。
4 from a number or set 从 (数量或组合) 中: *Nine out of ten people think that the government is right.* 十个人里有九个认为政府做得对。
5 because of a particular feeling 出于，因为 (某种情感): *I was just asking out of curiosity.* 我只是出于好奇才问的。
6 without 没有: *We're out of coffee.* 我们没咖啡了。 ◇ *She's been out of work for six months.* 她已经失业六个月了。

output /'aʊtpʊt/ *noun* 名词 (*no plural* 不用复数形式)
the amount of things that somebody or something has made or done 产量；产出: *What was the factory's output last year?* 工厂去年的产量是多少?

outside¹ 0━ /,aʊt'saɪd/ *noun* 名词
the part of something that is away from the middle 外部；外表: *the outside of the packet* 包装袋的外面 ◇ *We've only seen the building from the outside.* 我们只从外面看过这座建筑物。 ⊃ OPPOSITE **inside** 反义词为 inside

outside² 0━ /,aʊt'saɪd/ *adjective* 形容词
away from the middle of something 外部的；外表的: *the outside walls of the house* 房子的外墙 ◇ *an outside toilet* 户外厕所 ⊃ OPPOSITE **inside** 反义词为 inside

outside³ 0━ /,aʊt'saɪd/ *preposition, adverb* 介词，副词
in or to a place that is not inside a building 在 (…) 外面；向 (…) 外面: *I left my bicycle outside the shop.* 我把自行车放在商店外面了。 ◇ *Come outside and see the garden!* 出来看看花园吧! ⊃ OPPOSITE **inside** 反义词为 inside

outskirts /'aʊtskɜ:ts/ *noun* 名词 (*plural* 用复数形式)
the edges of a town or city (市镇的) 边缘地区；市郊: *They live on the outskirts of town.* 他们住在市郊。

outstanding /aʊt'stændɪŋ/ *adjective* 形容词
very good; much better than others 杰出

的；优秀的；出色的 ⊃ SAME MEANING
excellent 同义词为 excellent: *Her work
is outstanding.* 她的工作很出色。

outward /ˈaʊtwəd/ *adjective* 形容词
1 connected with the way things seem to
be 表面的；外表的: *Despite her cheerful
outward appearance, she was in fact very
unhappy.* 尽管她表面上很快乐，但事实上
她很不开心。
2 travelling away from a place that you
will return to later 外出的；向外的:
*There were no delays on the outward
journey.* 这次外出旅程没有任何耽搁。

outwards /ˈaʊtwədz/ *(also 亦作 outward
/ˈaʊtwəd/) adverb* 副词
towards the outside 朝外；向外:
The windows open outwards. 这些窗户
向外开。⊃ OPPOSITE **inwards** or **inward**
反义词为 inwards 或 inward

oval /ˈəʊvl/ *adjective* 形容词
with a shape like an egg 椭圆形的；卵形
的: *an oval mirror* 椭圆形镜子 ⊃ Look at
the picture at **shape**[1]. 见 shape[1] 的插图。
▶ **oval** *noun* 名词: *Draw an oval.* 画一个
椭圆形。

oven ⚊ /ˈʌvn/ *noun* 名词
the part of a cooker shaped like a box
with a door on the front. You put food in
the **oven** to cook or heat it. 烤箱: *Take
the bread out of the oven.* 把面包从烤箱里
取出来。

over[1] ⚊ /ˈəʊvə(r)/ *adverb, preposition*
副词，介词
1 on somebody or something so that it
covers them 覆盖；盖住: *She put a
blanket over the sleeping child.* 她给睡着
的孩子盖上毯子。
2 above something; higher than
something 在⋯上方: *A plane flew over
our heads.* 一架飞机从我们头顶上飞过。◇
There is a picture over the fireplace. 壁炉
上方有一幅画。
3 across; to the other side of something
穿越；跨过: *The dog jumped over the
wall.* 狗跳过了墙。
4 to or in a place 去，在（某处）: *Come
over and see us on Saturday.* 星期六到我们
这儿来坐坐。◇ *Come over here!* 到这儿
来! ◇ *Go over there and see if you can
help.* 到那儿去，看看你是否能帮上忙。
5 down or sideways 倒下；落下；侧向:
I fell over in the street. 我在街上摔倒了。◇
He leaned over to speak to her. 他靠过去
跟她说话。
6 so that the other side is on top 翻转:
You may turn your papers over and begin.
你们可以把试卷翻过来，开始答题。

7 more than a number, price, etc.
（数字、价格等）多于，超过: *She lived
in Spain for over 20 years.* 她在西班牙住了
超过 20 年。◇ *This game is for children of
ten and over.* 这个游戏是给十岁或以上的
儿童玩的。
8 not used; remaining 未用；剩余:
*There are a lot of cakes left over from the
party.* 派对过后剩下了很多蛋糕。
9 used for saying that somebody repeats
something（表示重复）: *He said the
same thing over and over again* (= many
times). 他反复说着同一件事。◇ *You'll
have to start all over again* (= from the
beginning). 你得从头再做。
all over everywhere; in every part 到处；
遍及: *Have you seen my glasses? I've
looked all over.* 你见过我的眼镜吗？所有
的地方我都找过了。◇ *She travels all over
the world.* 她周游世界各地。

over[2] /ˈəʊvə(r)/ *adjective* 形容词
finished 结束: *The exams are over now.*
现在考试都结束了。

over- /ˈəʊvə(r)/ *prefix* 前缀
more than is good; too much 太；过多:
He's been overeating. 他吃得太多了。◇
*You're being over-optimistic – she won't
pass all her exams.* 你太乐观了，她不会
通过所有考试的。

overall[1] /ˌəʊvərˈɔːl/ *adjective* 形容词
including everything 全部的；总体的
⊃ SAME MEANING **total** 同义词为 total:
*The overall cost of the repairs will be about
$350.* 总修理费大约会是 350 元。
▶ **overall** *adverb* 副词: *How much will it
cost overall?* 一共要多少钱？

overalls 连身工作服

overall[2] /ˈəʊvərɔːl/ *noun* 名词 (*British*
英式英语)

A B C D E F G H I J K L M N **O** P Q R S T U V W X Y Z

a kind of coat that you wear over your clothes to keep them clean when you are working （工作时穿的）罩衣: *The laboratory assistant was wearing a white overall.* 实验室助手穿着一件白罩衣。

overalls /'əʊvərɔːlz/ (*British* 英式英语) (*American* 美式英语 **coveralls**) *noun* 名词 (*plural* 用复数形式)
a piece of clothing that covers your legs, body and arms. You wear it over your other clothes to keep them clean when you are working. 连身工作服；工装裤 ➔ Look at the picture on the previous page. 见前页的插图。

overboard /'əʊvəbɔːd/ *adverb* 副词
over the side of a boat and into the water 从船上落入水中: *She fell overboard.* 她从船上掉进了水里。

overcoat /'əʊvəkəʊt/ *noun* 名词
a long warm coat 大衣: *Although it was a hot day, he was wearing an overcoat.* 尽管那天很热，他却穿上了大衣。

overcome /ˌəʊvə'kʌm/ *verb* 动词
(**overcomes**, **overcoming**, **overcame** /ˌəʊvə'keɪm/, has **overcome**)
to find an answer to a difficult thing in your life; to control something 克服: *He overcame his fear of flying.* 他克服了对飞行的恐惧。

overcrowded /ˌəʊvə'kraʊdɪd/ *adjective* 形容词
too full of people 过于拥挤的: *The trains are overcrowded on Friday evenings.* 星期五晚上火车都挤得水泄不通。

overdue /ˌəʊvə'djuː/ *adjective* 形容词
not done by the expected time 过期的；逾期的 ➔ SAME MEANING **late** 同义词为 late: *We had no money and the rent was overdue.* 我们没有钱，拖欠了房租。

overflow /ˌəʊvə'fləʊ/ *verb* 动词
(**overflows**, **overflowing**, **overflowed** /ˌəʊvə'fləʊd/)
to be so full that there is no space 溢出；挤满: *Someone left the tap on and the bath overflowed.* 有人让水龙头一直开着，使得浴缸漫水了。

overgrown /ˌəʊvə'grəʊn/ *adjective* 形容词
covered with plants that have grown too big 植物蔓生的；杂草丛生的: *The house was empty and the garden was overgrown.* 那所房子空着，花园里杂草丛生。

overhead /'əʊvəhed/ *adjective* 形容词
above your head 头顶上的: *an overhead light* 头顶上方的灯

▸ **overhead** /ˌəʊvə'hed/ *adverb* 副词:
A plane flew overhead. 一架飞机从头顶上飞过。

overhear /ˌəʊvə'hɪə(r)/ *verb* 动词
(**overhears**, **overhearing**, **overheard** /ˌəʊvə'hɜːd/, has **overheard**)
to hear what somebody is saying when they are speaking to another person 偶然听到；无意中听到: *I overheard Louise saying that she was unhappy.* 我无意中听到路易丝说自己很不开心。

overlap /ˌəʊvə'læp/ *verb* 动词 (**overlaps**, **overlapping**, **overlapped** /ˌəʊvə'læpt/)
When two things **overlap**, part of one thing covers part of the other thing. 部分重叠；交叠: *The tiles on the roof overlap.* 屋顶上的瓦片交叠着。

overlook /ˌəʊvə'lʊk/ *verb* 动词
(**overlooks**, **overlooking**, **overlooked** /ˌəʊvə'lʊkt/)
1 to not see or notice something 未看见；忽略；未注意到: *He overlooked one important fact.* 他忽略了一个重要的事实。
2 to have a view over something 俯视；俯瞰: *My room overlooks the garden.* 我的房间可以俯瞰花园。

overnight /ˌəʊvə'naɪt/ *adjective*, *adverb* 形容词，副词
for or during the night 在夜间（的）；在晚上（的）: *an overnight journey* 夜间旅程 ◇ *They stayed at our house overnight.* 他们在我们家过夜了。

overpass /'əʊvəpɑːs/ *American English* for FLYOVER 美式英语，即 flyover

overseas /ˌəʊvə'siːz/ *adjective*, *adverb* 形容词，副词
in, to or from another country across the sea 海外的；在（或去、来自）海外: *There are many overseas students in Britain.* 英国有很多外国留学生。◇ *She travels overseas a lot.* 她经常出国。

oversleep /ˌəʊvə'sliːp/ *verb* 动词
(**oversleeps**, **oversleeping**, **overslept** /ˌəʊvə'slept/, has **overslept**)
to sleep too long and not wake up at the right time 睡过头；睡得太久: *I overslept and was late for work.* 我睡过了头，上班迟到了。

overtake /ˌəʊvə'teɪk/ *verb* 动词
(**overtakes**, **overtaking**, **overtook** /ˌəʊvə'tʊk/, has **overtaken** /ˌəʊvə'teɪkən/)
to go past somebody or something that is going more slowly 超过；超越: *The car overtook a bus.* 那辆汽车超过了公共汽车。

overtime /ˈəʊvətaɪm/ *noun* 名词
(*no plural* 不用复数形式)
extra time that you spend at work 加班
（时间）: *I have **done** a lot of **overtime**
this week.* 我这星期经常加班。

overweight /ˌəʊvəˈweɪt/ *adjective*
形容词
too heavy or fat 超重的；太胖的: *The
doctor said I was overweight and that
I should eat less.* 医生说我太胖，应该
少吃点。

overwhelming /ˌəʊvəˈwelmɪŋ/ *adjective*
形容词
very great or strong 巨大的；强烈的:
an overwhelming feeling of loneliness
强烈的孤独感

ow /aʊ/ *exclamation* 感叹词
You say '**ow**' when you suddenly feel
pain.（表示突然感到疼痛）哎哟: *Ow!
You're standing on my foot.* 哎哟! 你踩着
我的脚了。

owe 0̄ /əʊ/ *verb* 动词 (owes, owing,
owed /əʊd/)

> 🔍 PRONUNCIATION 读音说明
> The word **owe** sounds like **go**.
> * owe 读音像 go。

1 to have to pay money to somebody
欠（钱）: *I lent you $10 last week and
$10 the week before, so you **owe** me $20.*
我上星期借了 10 元给你，之前一个星期也
借了 10 元，所以你欠我 20 元。
2 to have something because of a
particular person or thing（将…）归因
于，归功于: *He **owes** his life to the man
who pulled him out of the river.* 他能活下
来，全靠那个男子把他从河里拉了上来。
◇ *She **owes** her success to hard work.* 她的
成功靠的是勤奋。

owl 猫头鹰

owing to /ˈəʊɪŋ tu/ *preposition* 介词
because of 因为；由于: *The train was
late owing to the bad weather.* 火车因天气
恶劣晚点了。

owl /aʊl/ *noun* 名词
a bird that flies at night and eats small
animals 猫头鹰

own¹ 0̄ /əʊn/ *adjective, pronoun*
形容词，代词

> 🔍 PRONUNCIATION 读音说明
> The word **own** sounds like **bone**.
> * own 读音像 bone。

used for emphasizing that something
belongs to a particular person（表示
强调）自己的，本人的: *Is that **your** own
camera or did you borrow it?* 那个照相机
是你自己的还是借的? ◇ *I have **my** own
room now that my sister has left home.*
如今姐姐离开了家，我就有了自己的房间。
◇ *I want a home **of my** own.* 我想有个
属于自己的家。

> 📝 GRAMMAR 语法说明
> Be careful! You cannot use **own** after
> 'a' or 'the'. 注意: own 不能用在 a 或
> the 之后。You cannot say 不说:
> *I would like an own room.* You say
> 而说: *I would like my own room.* or
> 或: *I would like a room of my own.*

get your own back on somebody to
do something bad to somebody who has
done something bad to you（对某人）
还以颜色，报复，报仇: *He said he would
get his own back on me for breaking his
watch.* 他说他把他的手表弄坏了，他会给
我点颜色看。
on your own
1 alone 独自；单独: *She lives on her
own.* 她独自生活。
2 without help 独立地: *I can't move this
box on my own – can you help me?*
我一个人搬不动这个箱子，你能帮我吗?

own² 0̄ /əʊn/ *verb* 动词 (owns, owning,
owned /əʊnd/)
to have something that is yours 有；
拥有: *We don't own our flat – we rent it.*
我们没有自己的房子，我们是租的。◇
I don't own a car. 我没有汽车。
own up to say that you have done
something wrong 承认，招认（干了
坏事）；认错: *Nobody owned up to
breaking the window.* 没有人承认打破了
窗户。

owner 0̄ /ˈəʊnə(r)/ *noun* 名词
a person who has something that belongs

A
B
C
D
E
F
G
H
I
J
K
L
M
N
O
P
Q
R
S
T
U
V
W
X
Y
Z

to them 拥有者；物主：*Who is the owner of that red car?* 那辆红色汽车是谁的？

ox /ɒks/ *noun* 名词 (*plural* 复数形式 oxen /'ɒksn/)
a large male cow that is used for pulling or carrying heavy things 公牛 ⊃ Look at the picture at **plough**. 见 plough 的插图。

oxygen /'ɒksɪdʒən/ *noun* 名词 (*no plural* 不用复数形式) (*symbol* 符号 **O**)
a gas in the air. Animals and plants need **oxygen** to live. 氧；氧气

oyster /'ɔɪstə(r)/ *noun* 名词
a small sea animal with a shell. You can eat some types of **oyster** and others produce shiny white things used to make jewellery (called **pearls**). 牡蛎；蚝

oz *short way of writing* OUNCE * ounce 的缩写形式

ozone /'əʊzəʊn/ *noun* 名词 (*no plural* 不用复数形式)
a poisonous gas which is a form of OXYGEN 臭氧

ozone-friendly /ˌəʊzəʊn 'frendli/ *adjective* 形容词
(used about cleaning products, etc.) not containing chemicals that could harm the OZONE LAYER（洗涤产品等）对臭氧层无害的：*Most aerosol sprays are now ozone-friendly.* 气雾喷剂现在大多对臭氧层无害。

the ozone layer /ðɪ 'əʊzəʊn leɪə(r)/ *noun* 名词 (*no plural* 不用复数形式)
the layer of OZONE high above the surface of the earth, which helps to protect the earth from the bad effects of the sun 臭氧层（存在地球大气层中，可保护地球不受太阳有害物质的侵害）

Pp

P, p[1] /piː/ *noun* 名词 (*plural* 复数形式 P's, p's /piːz/)
the sixteenth letter of the English alphabet 英语字母表的第 16 个字母: *'Pencil' begins with a 'P'.* * pencil 一词以字母 p 开头。

p[2]
1 /piː/ *short for* PENNY, PENCE * penny 和 pence 的缩略式
2 *short way of writing* PAGE * page 的缩写形式

pace[1] /peɪs/ *noun* 名词
1 (*no plural* 不用复数形式) how fast you do something or how fast something happens 速度；步伐；节奏: *We started at a steady pace.* 我们稳步地开始了。
2 (*plural* 复数形式 paces) a step 一步: *Take two paces forward.* 向前走两步。
keep pace with somebody or 或 **something** to go as fast as somebody or something 与…步伐一致: *She couldn't keep pace with the other runners.* 她跟不上其他赛跑选手的步伐。

pace[2] /peɪs/ *verb* 动词
to walk around nervously or angrily （因紧张或生气）踱来踱去，走来走去: *She paced up and down outside.* 她在外面踱来踱去。

pacifier /'pæsɪfaɪə(r)/ *American English for* DUMMY 美式英语，即 dummy

pack[1] 0— /pæk/ *noun* 名词
1 a set of things 一套: *I bought a pack of five exercise books.* 我买了一套五本的练习本。◇ *an information pack* 资讯包
2 (*British* 英式英语) (*American* 美式英语 **deck**) a set of 52 cards for playing games 一副（纸牌）◇ Look at **playing card**. 见 playing card。
3 a group of wild dogs or similar animals 一群（野生动物）: *a pack of wolves* 一群狼
4 *American English for* PACKET 美式英语，即 packet: *a pack of cigarettes* 一包香烟

pack[2] 0— /pæk/ *verb* 动词 (**packs**, **packing**, **packed** /pækt/)
1 to put things into a bag or suitcase before you go somewhere 收拾行李: *Have you packed your suitcase?* 你行李

收拾好了吗？◇ *Don't forget to pack your toothbrush.* 别忘了把牙刷装进行李。
2 to put things into a box, bag, etc. 装箱；打包: *Pack all these books into boxes.* 把这些书都装进箱子里。 ◇ OPPOSITE **unpack** 反义词为 unpack

pack up
1 to stop doing something 收工；停止（做某事）: *At two o'clock we packed up and went home.* 我们两点钟就收工回家了。
2 (*British* 英式英语) (*informal* 非正式) If a machine **packs up**, it stops working. （机器）停止工作，出毛病

package 0— /'pækɪdʒ/ *noun* 名词
something that is wrapped in paper, cardboard or plastic 包裹 ◇ SAME MEANING **parcel** 同义词为 parcel

package holiday /,pækɪdʒ 'hɒlədeɪ/ (*British* 英式英语) (*American* 美式英语 **package tour** /'pækɪdʒ tʊə(r)/) *noun* 名词
a complete holiday that you buy from a single company, instead of paying different companies for your travel, hotel, etc. 包价旅游（旅行社代办交通、住宿等）

packaging /'pækɪdʒɪŋ/ *noun* 名词 (*no plural* 不用复数形式)
material like paper, cardboard or plastic that is used to wrap things that you buy or that you send 包装材料；外包装

packed /pækt/ *adjective* 形容词
full 挤满的: *The train was packed.* 火车里挤满了乘客。

packed lunch /,pækt 'lʌntʃ/ *noun* 名词 (*British* 英式英语)
food that you take to school or work to eat in the middle of the day （带去上学或上班的）自备午餐

packet 0— /'pækɪt/ (*British* 英式英语) (*American* 美式英语 **pack**) *noun* 名词
a small box or bag that you buy things in 小包；小盒；小袋: *a packet of biscuits* 一包饼干 ◇ *an empty crisp packet* 空的薯片袋

packing /'pækɪŋ/ *noun* 名词 (*no plural* 不用复数形式)
1 the act of putting things into a bag or suitcase before you go somewhere

A

B

C

D

E

F

G

H

I

J

K

L

M

N

O

P

Q

R

S

T

U

V

W

X

Y

Z

收拾行李: *Have you **done** your **packing**?*
你行李收拾好了吗？
2 material like paper, cardboard or
plastic that is used to wrap things that
you buy or that you send 包装材料:
The price includes postage and packing.
价格包括邮资和包装费。

pact /pækt/ *noun* 名词
an important agreement to do something
条约；协议；公约: *They **made a pact** not
to tell anyone.* 他们约定不告诉任何人。

pad /pæd/ *noun* 名词
1 a thick flat piece of soft material 软垫；
护垫: *Footballers wear pads on their legs
to protect them.* 足球运动员戴护垫保护
双腿。◇ *I used a pad of cotton wool to
clean the cut.* 我用一块药棉清洗了伤口。
2 pieces of paper that are joined together
at one end 便笺本；拍纸簿: *a writing
pad* 拍纸簿

padded /'pædɪd/ *adjective* 形容词
covered with or containing a layer of
thick soft material 有衬垫的: *a padded
jacket* 有夹层的外套

paddle¹ /'pædl/ *noun* 名词
a piece of wood with a flat end, that you
use for moving a small boat through
water 船桨

paddle² /'pædl/ *verb* 动词 (**paddles,
paddling, paddled** /'pædld/)
1 to move a small boat through water
with a PADDLE 用桨划船: *We paddled up
the river.* 我们沿河划船逆流而上。
2 to walk in water that is not deep 蹚水；
涉水: *The children were paddling in the
sea.* 孩子们在海边蹚着水玩。

padlock 挂锁

padlock /'pædlɒk/ *noun* 名词
a lock that you use on things like gates
and bicycles 挂锁

page ☞ /peɪdʒ/ (*abbr.* 缩略式 **p**) *noun*
名词

one or both sides of a piece of paper in
a book, magazine or newspaper（书刊
的）页，版: *Please turn to page 120.*
请翻到第 120 页。◇ *What page is the story
on?* 那则报道在哪一版？◇ *I'm reading
a 600-page novel.* 我在读一本 600 页的
小说。

paid *form of* PAY¹ * pay¹ 的不同形式

pain ☞ /peɪn/ *noun* 名词
1 (*plural* 复数形式 **pains**) the feeling that
you have in your body when you are hurt
or ill 疼；痛: *I've got a pain in my leg.*
我腿疼。◇ *He's in terrible pain.* 他疼痛
难忍。
2 (*no plural* 不用复数形式) unhappiness
痛苦；悲痛: *Her eyes were full of pain.*
她的眼神充满了痛苦。
be a pain *or* 或 **a pain in the neck**
(*informal* 非正式) a person, thing or
situation that makes you angry or
annoyed 让人恼火的人（或事物、
情况）: *She can be a real pain when
she's in a bad mood.* 她要是心情不好，
会令人非常讨厌。

painful ☞ /'peɪnfl/ *adjective* 形容词
giving pain 令人疼痛的；令人痛苦的:
I've cut my leg – it's very painful. 我把腿
划破了，疼死了。Ↄ OPPOSITE **painless**
反义词为 painless

painkiller /'peɪnkɪlə(r)/ *noun* 名词
a drug that makes pain less strong
止痛药: *She's on painkillers.* 她服用
止痛药。

painless /'peɪnləs/ *adjective* 形容词
not causing pain 无痛的: *a painless
injection* 无痛注射 Ↄ OPPOSITE **painful**
反义词为 painful

paint¹ ☞ /peɪnt/ *noun* 名词
a coloured liquid that you put on things
with a brush, to change the colour or to
make a picture 油漆；颜料: *red paint*
红色颜料 ◇ *Is the paint dry yet?* 油漆
干了吗？

paint 油漆；颜料

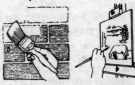

paint² 0🔊 /peɪnt/ *verb* 动词 (paints, painting, painted)

1 to put **paint** on something to change the colour 刷油漆: *We painted the walls grey.* 我们把墙刷成了灰色。
2 to make a picture of somebody or something using **paints** 用颜料作画: *I'm painting a picture of some flowers.* 我在画花。◇ *My sister paints very well.* 我姐姐很会画画。

paintbrush /'peɪntbrʌʃ/ *noun* 名词 (*plural* 复数形式 **paintbrushes**)
a brush that you use for painting 画笔; 漆刷 ⊃ Look at the picture at **brush¹**. 见 brush¹ 的插图。

painter 0🔊 /'peɪntə(r)/ *noun* 名词
1 a person whose job is to paint things like walls or houses 油漆工 ⊃ Look at Picture Dictionary page **P12**. 见彩页 P12。
2 a person who paints pictures 画家 ⊃ SAME MEANING **artist** 同义词为 artist: *Picasso was a famous painter.* 毕加索是著名的画家。

painting 0🔊 /'peɪntɪŋ/ *noun* 名词
a picture that somebody makes with paint 画: *a painting by Rembrandt* 伦勃朗的画 ◇ *He did a painting of the bridge.* 他给那座桥画了一幅画。

pair 0🔊 /peə(r)/ *noun* 名词

> 🔊 **PRONUNCIATION** 读音说明
> The word **pair** sounds just like **pear**.
> * pair 读音同 pear。

1 two things of the same kind that you use together 一双; 一对: *a pair of shoes* 一双鞋 ◇ *a new pair of earrings* 一对新耳环
2 a thing with two parts that are joined together 由两个相同部分组成的物品: *a pair of glasses* 一副眼镜 ◇ *a pair of scissors* 一把剪刀 ◇ *I bought two pairs of trousers.* 我买了两条裤子。
3 two people or animals together（人或动物）双，对: *a pair of ducks* 两只鸭子 ⊃ Look at **couple**. 见 couple。
in pairs with two things or people together 成双; 成对: *Shoes are only sold in pairs.* 鞋子只能成对出售。◇ *The students are working in pairs.* 学生两人一组在学习。

pajamas /pə'dʒɑːməz/ *American English for* PYJAMAS 美式英语，即 pyjamas

pal /pæl/ *noun* 名词 (*informal* 非正式)
a friend 朋友; 哥们儿

palace /'pæləs/ *noun* 名词
a very large house where a king or queen lives 王宫; 宫殿: *The Queen lives at Buckingham Palace.* 女王住在白金汉宫。

palace 宫殿

pale 0🔊 /peɪl/ *adjective* 形容词 (**paler**, **palest**)
1 with not much colour in your face（脸色）苍白的，煞白的 ⊃ SAME MEANING **white** 同义词为 white: *Are you ill? You look pale.* 你病了吗？你气色不好。◇ *She has very pale skin.* 她的皮肤很白。
2 with a light colour; not strong or dark（颜色）浅的，淡的 ⊃ SAME MEANING **light** 同义词为 light: *a pale blue dress* 淡蓝色的连衣裙 ⊃ OPPOSITE **dark** 反义词为 dark

palm /pɑːm/ *noun* 名词
1 the flat part of the front of your hand 手掌; 手心 ⊃ Look at the picture at **hand¹**. 见 hand¹ 的插图。
2 (*also* 亦作 **palm tree** /'pɑːm triː/) a tree that grows in hot countries, with no branches and a lot of big leaves at the top 棕榈树: *a coconut palm* 椰子树

pamphlet /'pæmflət/ *noun* 名词
a very thin book with a paper cover that gives information about something 小册子; 手册

pan 0🔊 /pæn/ *noun* 名词
a metal pot that you use for cooking 平底锅: *a frying pan* 煎锅

pancake /'pænkeɪk/ *noun* 名词
a very thin round thing that you eat. You make **pancakes** with flour, eggs and milk and cook them in a frying pan. 烙饼; 薄饼 ⊃ Look at Picture Dictionary page **P7**. 见彩页 P7。

panda /'pændə/ *noun* 名词 (*plural* 复数形式 **pandas**)

A
B
C
D
E
F
G
H
I
J
K
L
M
N
O
P
Q
R
S
T
U
V
W
X
Y
Z

A
B
C
D
E
F
G
H
I
J
K
L
M
N
O
P
Q
R
S
T
U
V
W
X
Y
Z

a large black and white animal that lives in China 大熊猫

panda 大熊猫

pane /peɪn/ *noun* 名词
a piece of glass in a window（一块）窗玻璃： *a windowpane* 一块窗玻璃

panel /ˈpænl/ *noun* 名词
1 a flat piece of wood, metal or glass that is part of a door, wall or ceiling（门、墙或天花板的）嵌板，镶板
2 a group of people who give their opinions about something or discuss something 咨询小组；评审小组： *Do you have any questions for our panel?* 你有什么问题想问我们的咨询小组吗？◇ *a panel of experts* 专家小组
3 a flat part on a machine, where there are things to help you control it 控制板；仪表盘： *the TV's* ***control panel*** 电视机的控制面板

pang /pæŋ/ *noun* 名词
a sudden strong and painful feeling（突如其来的）剧痛，痛苦： *hunger pangs* 饥肠辘辘 ◇ *a pang of jealousy* 一阵妒火

panic /ˈpænɪk/ *noun* 名词
a sudden feeling of fear that you cannot control and that makes you do things without thinking carefully（突然的）恐慌，惊恐： *There was panic in the shop when the fire started.* 起火时商店内一片恐慌。
▶ **panic** *verb* 动词 (panics, panicking, panicked /ˈpænɪkt/): *Don't panic!* 不要惊慌！

panic-stricken /ˈpænɪk strɪkən/ *adjective* 形容词
very frightened in a way that stops you thinking clearly 惊慌失措的：

Panic-stricken shoppers fled from the scene. 惊慌失措的商店顾客纷纷逃离现场。

pant /pænt/ *verb* 动词 (pants, panting, panted)
to take in and let out air quickly through your mouth, for example after running or because you are very hot 喘气；喘息： *The dog was panting.* 狗在喘着气。

panther /ˈpænθə(r)/ *noun* 名词
a wild animal like a big cat with black fur 黑豹

panties /ˈpæntiz/ *American English for* KNICKERS 美式英语，即 knickers

pantomime /ˈpæntəmaɪm/ *noun* 名词 (*British* 英式英语)
a funny play for children, with singing and dancing. You can usually see **pantomimes** at Christmas. 童话剧（通常在圣诞节期间上演）

pants /pænts/ *noun* 名词 (*plural* 用复数形式)
1 (*British* 英式英语) (*American* 美式英语 **panties, underpants**) a small piece of clothing that you wear under your other clothes, around the middle of your body to cover your bottom 内裤；衬裤 ⊃ SAME MEANING **knickers, underpants** 同义词为 knickers 和 underpants： *a pair of pants* 一条内裤
2 *American English for* TROUSERS 美式英语，即 trousers

paper 0= /ˈpeɪpə(r)/ *noun* 名词
1 (*no plural* 不用复数形式) thin material for writing or drawing on or for wrapping things in 纸： *a sheet of paper* 一张纸 ◇ *a paper bag* 纸袋
2 (*plural* 复数形式 **papers**) a newspaper 报纸： *Have you seen today's paper?* 你看了今天的报纸没有？
3 **papers** (*plural* 用复数形式) important pieces of paper with writing on them 文件；文献： *Her desk was piled high with papers.* 她的书桌上文件堆得高高的。
4 (*plural* 复数形式 **papers**) a group of questions in an exam 试卷： *The English paper was easy.* 英语试题很容易。

paperback /ˈpeɪpəbæk/ *noun* 名词
a book with a paper cover 平装书；简装本 ⊃ Look at **hardback**. 见 hardback。

paper clip /ˈpeɪpə klɪp/ *noun* 名词
a small metal object that you use for holding pieces of paper together 回形针；曲别针 ⊃ Look at Picture Dictionary page **P11**. 见彩页 P11。

paperwork /ˈpeɪpəwɜːk/ *noun* 名词
(*no plural* 不用复数形式)
the written work that you have to do as
part of your job 文书工作: *Teachers have
far too much paperwork.* 老师要做的案头
工作实在太多。

parachute 降落伞

parachute /ˈpærəʃuːt/ *noun* 名词
a thing that you have on your back when
you jump out of a plane and that opens,
so that you fall to the ground slowly
降落伞

parade /pəˈreɪd/ *noun* 名词
a line of people who are walking together
for a special reason, while other people
watch them 游行（群众为特别原因结队
而行）: *a military parade* 阅兵

paradise /ˈpærədaɪs/ *noun* 名词
(*no plural* 不用复数形式)
the place where some people think good
people go after they die 天堂；天国
⊃ SAME MEANING **heaven** 同义词为 heaven

paraffin /ˈpærəfɪn/ (*British* 英式英语)
(*American* 美式英语 **kerosene**) *noun* 名词
(*no plural* 不用复数形式)
a type of oil that people burn to produce
heat or light 煤油

paragraph /ˈpærəɡrɑːf/ *noun* 名词
a group of lines of writing. A **paragraph**
always begins on a new line. （文章）
段，段落

parallel /ˈpærəlel/ *adjective* 形容词
Parallel lines are straight lines that are
always the same distance from each
other. 平行的 ⊃ Look at the picture at
line¹. 见 line¹ 的插图。

paralyse /ˈpærəlaɪz/ (*British* 英式英语)
(*American* 美式英语 **paralyze**) *verb* 动词
(paralyses, paralysing, paralysed
/ˈpærəlaɪzd/)
to make a person unable to move all or
part of their body 使瘫痪；使麻痹: *After
the accident she was **paralysed from the
waist down**.* 那起事故后她腰部以下都
瘫痪了。

▸ **paralysis** /pəˈræləsɪs/ *noun* 名词
(*no plural* 不用复数形式): *The disease can
cause paralysis.* 这种病可导致瘫痪。

paramedic /ˌpærəˈmedɪk/ *noun* 名词
a person who is not a doctor or a nurse,
but who looks after people who are hurt
or ill until they get to a hospital 护理
人员；医务辅助人员

parcel 包裹

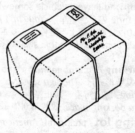

parcel /ˈpɑːsl/ (*American also* 美式英语
亦作 **package**) *noun* 名词
something with paper around it, that you
send or carry 包裹；小包: *She sent a
parcel of books to her aunt.* 她给姨妈寄去
了一包书。

pardon¹ /ˈpɑːdn/ *exclamation* 感叹词
1 (*British* 英式英语) (*American* 美式英语
pardon me) What did you say? 请再说
一遍: *'You're very quiet.' 'Pardon?' 'I said,
you're very quiet.'* “你话很少。”
“什么？” “我说你话很少。”
2 (*British and American also* 英式和美式
英语亦作 **pardon me**) I'm sorry 抱歉；
对不起: *Pardon me, I didn't see you
standing there.* 对不起，我没看见你站在
那里。

pardon² /ˈpɑːdn/ *verb* 动词 (pardons,
pardoning, pardoned /ˈpɑːdnd/) (*formal*
正式)
to officially decide not to punish
somebody for something bad that they
have done 赦免: *Two hundred prisoners
were pardoned by the king.* 两百名囚犯
获得了国王特赦。 ⊃ SAME MEANING
forgive 同义词为 forgive

parent ⚭ /ˈpeərənt/ *noun* 名词
a mother or father 父亲；母亲：*Her parents live in Italy.* 她父母亲住在意大利。

parenthood /ˈpeərənthʊd/ *noun* 名词
(*no plural* 不用复数形式)
being a parent 父母身份

parish /ˈpærɪʃ/ *noun* 名词 (*plural* 复数形式 **parishes**)
an area that has its own church and priest 堂区；教区

park¹ ⚭ /pɑːk/ *noun* 名词
a place with grass and trees, where anybody can go to walk, play games or relax 公园：*We had a picnic in the park.* 我们在公园野餐了。◇ *Hyde Park* 海德公园

park² ⚭ /pɑːk/ *verb* 动词 (parks, parking, parked /pɑːkt/)
to stop and leave a vehicle somewhere for a time 停车；泊车：*You can't park in this street.* 这条街上不准停车。◇ *My car is parked opposite the bank.* 我的车停在银行对面。

▶ **parking** /ˈpɑːkɪŋ/ *noun* 名词 (*no plural* 不用复数形式)：*The sign says 'No Parking'.* 牌上写着"禁止停车"。◇ *I can't find a parking space.* 我找不到停车位。

parking lot /ˈpɑːkɪŋ lɒt/ *American English for* CAR PARK 美式英语，即 car park

parking meter /ˈpɑːkɪŋ miːtə(r)/ *noun* 名词
a machine beside the road that you put money into when you park your car next to it 停车收费器

parking ticket /ˈpɑːkɪŋ tɪkɪt/ *noun* 名词
a piece of paper that orders you to pay money (called a **fine**) for parking your car where it is not allowed 违章停车罚款单

parliament /ˈpɑːləmənt/ *noun* 名词
the people who make the laws in a country 议会；国会：*the French parliament* 法国议会

🔎 CULTURE 文化资料补充
In the United Kingdom, the group of people who make the laws meet in the **Houses of Parliament** in London. 在英国，议会负责立法，在伦敦的议会大厦（Houses of Parliament）开会。The two parts of the Houses of Parliament are called the **House of Commons** (where the **Members of Parliament** meet) and the **House of Lords**. 议会分下议院（House of Commons）和上议院（House of

Lords）两院。下院议员（Members of Parliament）在下议院开会。

parrot /ˈpærət/ *noun* 名词
a bird with very bright feathers that can copy what people say 鹦鹉 ⊃ Look at Picture Dictionary page **P2**. 见彩页 P2。

parsley /ˈpɑːsli/ *noun* 名词 (*no plural* 不用复数形式)
a type of plant (called a **herb**) with small green leaves that you use in cooking or for decorating food 欧芹

part¹ ⚭ /pɑːt/ *noun* 名词
1 some, but not all of something; one of the pieces of something 部分：*We spent part of the day on the beach.* 那天我们部分时间在海滩度过。◇ *Which part of Spain do you come from?* 你是西班牙哪个地区的人？
2 a piece of a machine 零件；部件：*Is there a shop near here that sells bicycle parts?* 附近有没有卖自行车零件的商店？
3 the person you are in a play or film （戏剧或电影的）角色：*She played the part of Ophelia.* 她扮演奥菲莉亚一角。
4 *American English for* PARTING (2) 美式英语，即 parting 第 2 义

take part in something to do something together with other people 参加；参与：*All the students took part in the concert.* 所有学生都参加了这次音乐会。

part² /pɑːt/ *verb* 动词 (parts, parting, parted) (*formal* 正式)
to go away from each other 分离；离别：*We parted at the airport.* 我们在机场分了手。

part with something to give something to somebody else, especially something that you would prefer to keep 放弃，交出（尤指舍不得的东西）：*Read the contract very carefully before you part with any money.* 仔细看清合同后再交钱。

partial /ˈpɑːʃl/ *adjective* 形容词
not complete 部分的；不完全的：*The evening was only a partial success.* 晚会只取得了部分成功。

▶ **partially** *adverb* 副词 ⊃ SAME MEANING **partly** 同义词为 partly：*The road was partially blocked by a fallen tree.* 部分道路被倒下的一棵树挡住了。

participant /pɑːˈtɪsɪpənt/ *noun* 名词
a person who does something together with other people 参加者；参与者：*All participants in the event will receive a*

certificate. 这次活动的所有参加者将获得一份证书。

participate /pɑːˈtɪsɪpeɪt/ *verb* 动词
(participates, participating, participated)
(*formal* 正式)
to do something together with other people 参加；参与 ➲ SAME MEANING **take part** 同义词为 take part：*Ten countries participated in the discussions.* 十个国家参加了会谈。

▶ **participation** /pɑːˌtɪsɪˈpeɪʃn/ *noun* 名词 (*no plural* 不用复数形式)：*Your participation is greatly appreciated.* 热烈欢迎您的参与。

participle /pɑːˈtɪsɪpl/ *noun* 名词
(*grammar* 语法) a form of a verb 分词（现在分词或过去分词）：*The present participle of 'eat' is 'eating' and the past participle is 'eaten'.* * eat 的现在分词是 eating，过去分词是 eaten。

particular ⚬╼ /pəˈtɪkjələ(r)/ *adjective* 形容词
1 one only, and not any other 特定的；特指的：*You need a particular kind of flour to make bread.* 做面包需要用特定的面粉。
2 more than usual 特别的；格外的 ➲ SAME MEANING **special** 同义词为 special：*The road is very icy, so take particular care when you are driving.* 路上结满了冰，所以开车要格外小心。
3 If you are **particular**, you want something to be exactly right. 挑剔；讲究：*He's very particular about the food he eats.* 他对吃的东西非常讲究。
in particular more than others 尤其；特别 ➲ SAME MEANING **especially** 同义词为 especially：*Is there anything in particular you want to do this weekend?* 这个周末你有什么特别想做的事吗？

particularly ⚬╼ /pəˈtɪkjələli/ *adverb* 副词
more than usual or more than others 尤其；特别；格外 ➲ SAME MEANING **especially** 同义词为 especially：*I'm particularly tired today.* 我今天特别累。◇ *I don't particularly like fish.* 我不那么喜欢吃鱼。

parties plural of PARTY * party 的复数形式

parting /pɑːtɪŋ/ *noun* 名词
1 a time when people leave each other 离别；分手：*We had a sad parting at the airport.* 我们在机场伤心地道别了。
2 (*British* 英式英语) (*American* 美式英语 **part**) a line in your hair that you make by brushing it in different directions using

a plastic or metal thing (called a **comb**)（头发的）分缝，分线；发缝：*He has a side parting.* 他头发梳偏分。

partly ⚬╼ /pɑːtli/ *adverb* 副词
not completely but in some way 部分地；不完全地：*The window was partly open.* 窗户半开着。◇ *The accident was partly my fault.* 事故部分责任在我。

partner ⚬╼ /pɑːtnə(r)/ *noun* 名词
1 your husband, wife, boyfriend or girlfriend 配偶；伴侣
2 one of the people who owns a business（生意的）合伙人
3 a person you are dancing with, or playing a game with 搭档；同伴；舞伴

partnership /pɑːtnəʃɪp/ *noun* 名词
being partners 伙伴关系；合伙人身份：*The two sisters went into partnership and opened a shop.* 她们姐妹俩合伙开了家店。

part of speech /ˌpɑːt əv ˈspiːtʃ/ *noun* 名词 (*plural* 复数形式 **parts of speech**)
(*grammar* 语法) one of the groups that words are divided into, for example 'noun', 'verb', 'adjective', etc. 词类，词性（如名词、动词、形容词等）

part-time /ˌpɑːt ˈtaɪm/ *adjective, adverb* 形容词，副词
for only a part of the day or week 部分时间（的）；兼职（的）：*I've got a part-time job as a secretary.* 我有一份做秘书的兼职工作。◇ *Jane works part-time.* 简做兼职工作。➲ Look at **full-time**. 见 full-time。

party ⚬╼ /pɑːti/ *noun* 名词 (*plural* 复数形式 **parties**)
1 a time when friends meet, usually in somebody's home, to eat, drink and enjoy themselves 聚会；派对：*We're having a party this Saturday. Can you come?* 我们这个星期六有个聚会。你能来吗？◇ *a birthday party* 生日派对
2 (*politics* 政治) a group of people who have the same ideas about politics 政党；党派：*He's a member of the Labour Party.* 他是工党党员。

🔎 **CULTURE** 文化资料补充
The main **political parties** in Britain are the **Labour Party**, the **Conservative Party** (also called the **Tory Party**) and the **Liberal Democrats**. 英国的主要政党（political party）有工党（Labour Party）、保守党（Conservative Party，也称 Tory Party）和自由民主党（Liberal Democrats）。

A
B
C
D
E
F
G
H
I
J
K
L
M
N
O
P
Q
R
S
T
U
V
W
X
Y
Z

In the US the main **parties** are the **Republicans** and the **Democrats**. 美国的主要政党是共和党（Republicans）和民主党（Democrats）。

3 a group of people who are travelling or working together（一同工作、旅行的）团体，团队：*a party of tourists* 旅行团

pass¹ 0➔ /pɑːs/ *verb* 动词 (passes, passing, passed /pɑːst/)

1 to go by somebody or something 走过；经过；路过：*She passed me in the street.* 她在街上与我擦肩而过。◇ *Do you pass any shops on your way to the station?* 你去车站会路经任何商店吗？

2 to go or move in a particular direction（沿某方向）移动：*A plane passed overhead.* 一架飞机从头顶上空飞过。◇ *The train passes through Oxford on its way to London.* 列车开往伦敦的路上会经过牛津。

3 to give something to somebody 将⋯传给；把⋯递给：*Could you pass me the salt, please?* 请把盐递给我好吗？

4 (in some sports) to kick, hit or throw the ball to somebody on your team（某些体育运动）传球

5 If time **passes**, it goes by.（时间）消逝，过去：*A week passed before his letter arrived.* 过了一个星期他的信才到。

6 to spend time 度过，消磨，打发（时间）：*How did you pass the time in hospital?* 你住院时是怎么打发时间的？

7 to do well enough in an examination or test 通过（考试）；及格；合格：*Did you pass your driving test?* 你通过驾照考试了吗？ ⊃ OPPOSITE **fail** 反义词为 fail

pass away to die 去世；逝世：*The old man passed away in his sleep.* 老头儿在睡梦中去世了。

pass something on to give or tell something to another person 转交；转告：*Will you pass on a message to Mike for me?* 你替我向迈克转告一句话好吗？

pass out to suddenly become unconscious 失去知觉；昏迷 ⊃ SAME MEANING **faint** 同义词为 faint

pass² /pɑːs/ *noun* 名词 (plural 复数形式 passes)

1 doing well enough in an exam（考试）及格，合格：*How many passes did you get in your exams?* 你考试有几门及格？ ⊃ OPPOSITE **fail** 反义词为 fail

2 a special piece of paper or card that says you can go somewhere or do something 通行证：*You need a pass to*

get into the factory. 需要通行证才能进入这家工厂。

3 kicking, throwing or hitting a ball to somebody in a game 传球

4 a road or way through mountains 关口；山路：*the Brenner Pass* 布伦纳山口

passage 0➔ /'pæsɪdʒ/ *noun* 名词

1 a narrow way, for example between two buildings 通道；走廊

2 a short part of a book, a speech or a piece of music 段落；章节；乐段：*We studied a passage from the story for homework.* 我们研究了故事中的一个段落作为家庭作业。

passenger 0➔ /'pæsɪndʒə(r)/ *noun* 名词

a person who is travelling in a car, bus, train or plane but not driving or flying it 乘客；旅客：*The plane was carrying 200 passengers.* 飞机上载有 200 名乘客。

passer-by /,pɑːsə 'baɪ/ *noun* 名词 (plural 复数形式 passers-by)

a person who is walking past you in the street 过路人；路人：*I asked a passer-by where the Science Museum was.* 我向一个路人打听了科学馆在哪里。

passion /'pæʃn/ *noun* 名词

a very strong feeling, usually of love, but sometimes of anger or hate 强烈情感；激情

passionate /'pæʃənət/ *adjective* 形容词

having or showing very strong feelings 充满激情的：*a passionate kiss* 热吻

passive /'pæsɪv/ *noun* 名词 (no plural 不用复数形式)

(*grammar* 语法) the form of a verb that shows that the action is done by a person or thing to another person or thing 被动语态：*In the sentence 'The car was stolen', the verb is in the passive.* 在 The car was stolen 一句中，动词用了被动语态。 ⊃ OPPOSITE **active** 反义词为 active

passport 0➔ /'pɑːspɔːt/ *noun* 名词

a small book with your name and photograph in it. You must take it with you when you travel to other countries. 护照

password /'pɑːswɜːd/ *noun* 名词

a secret word that allows you to go into a place or start using a computer 密码；口令：*Never tell anybody your password.* 不要把密码告诉任何人。

past¹ 0➔ /pɑːst/ *adjective* 形容词

1 connected with the time that has gone

过去的；以前的：*We will forget your past mistakes.* 我们不会计较你以前的过失。
2 just before now 刚过去的 ⊃ SAME MEANING **last** 同义词为 last：*He has been ill for the past week.* 过去一星期他一直病着。

past² 0➤ /pɑːst/ *noun* 名词 (*no plural* 不用复数形式)
1 the time before now, and the things that happened then 过去；昔日；往事：*We learn about the past in history lessons.* 我们在历史课上了解过去的事。◇ *In the past, many people had large families.* 以前，很多人拥有大家庭。
2 (*also* 亦作 **the past tense**) the form of a verb that you use to talk about the time before now 过去时；过去式：*The past tense of the verb 'go' is 'went'.* 动词 go 的过去时是 went。⊃ Look at **future¹** (2) and **present²** (3). 见 future¹ 第 2 义和 present² 第 3 义。

past³ 0➤ /pɑːst/ *preposition, adverb* 介词，副词
1 a word that shows how many minutes after the hour（用于时间，表示整点后）过…分钟：*It's two minutes past four.* 现在是四点过两分。◇ *It's half past seven.* 现在是七点半。
2 from one side to the other of somebody or something; on the other side of somebody or something 从一边到另一边；经过：*Go past the cinema, then turn left.* 走过电影院之后向左拐。◇ *The bus went past without stopping.* 公共汽车一直开过去，没有停下来。

pasta /'pæstə/ *noun* 名词 (*no plural* 不用复数形式)
an Italian food that is made from flour, water and sometimes eggs, which comes in many different shapes 意大利面食：*pasta with tomato sauce* 番茄酱意大利面 ⊃ Look at Picture Dictionary page **P7**. 见彩页 P7。

paste¹ /peɪst/ *noun* 名词
a soft wet substance, usually made from powder and liquid, and sometimes used for sticking paper to things 面糊；糨糊：*Mix the flour with milk to make a paste.* 把面粉和牛奶和成面糊。

paste² /peɪst/ *verb* 动词 (**pastes, pasting, pasted**)
1 to stick something to something else using paste 粘贴：*Paste the picture into your books.* 把图片粘到你的书上。
2 (*computing* 电脑) to copy or move writing or pictures into a computer document from somewhere else 粘贴；

贴上：*You can cut and paste the tables into your essay.* 你可以把这些图表剪贴到你的文章中。

pastime /'pɑːstaɪm/ *noun* 名词
something that you like doing when you are not working 消遣 ⊃ SAME MEANING **hobby** 同义词为 hobby：*Painting is her favourite pastime.* 她闲暇时最爱绘画。

past participle /ˌpɑːst 'pɑːtɪsɪpl/ *noun* 名词
(*grammar* 语法) the form of a verb that in English is used with 'have' to make a tense (called the **perfect tense**) 过去分词：*'Gone' is the past participle of 'go'.* * gone 是 go 的过去分词。

the past perfect /ðə ˌpɑːst 'pɜːfɪkt/ *noun* 名词 (*no plural* 不用复数形式)
(*grammar* 语法) the form of a verb that describes an action that was finished before another thing happened 过去完成时；过去完成式：*'The film had already started when we got there' is in the past perfect.* * The fillm had already started when we got there 用了过去完成时。

pastry /'peɪstri/ *noun* 名词
1 (*no plural* 不用复数形式) a mixture of flour, fat and water that is rolled flat and used for making a special type of food (called a **pie**) 油酥面团 ⊃ Look at the picture at **pie**. 见 pie 的插图。
2 (*plural* 复数形式 **pastries**) a small cake made with **pastry** 油酥糕点

the past tense /ðə ˌpɑːst 'tens/ *noun* 名词 (*no plural* 不用复数形式)
(*grammar* 语法) the form of a verb that you use to talk about the time before now 过去时；过去式：*The past tense of 'sing' is 'sang'.* * sing 的过去时是 sang。

pat /pæt/ *verb* 动词 (**pats, patting, patted**)
to touch somebody or something lightly with your hand flat 轻拍：*She patted the dog on the head.* 她轻轻拍了拍狗的头。⊃ Look at the picture at **stroke²**. 见 stroke² 的插图。
▶ **pat** *noun* 名词：*He gave me a pat on the shoulder.* 他轻轻拍了拍我的肩膀。

patch /pætʃ/ *noun* 名词 (*plural* 复数形式 **patches**)
1 a small piece of something that is not the same as the other parts（与周围不同的）小块，小片：*a black cat with a white patch on its back* 背上有块白斑的黑猫
2 a piece of cloth that you use to cover a hole in things like clothes 补丁；补块：*I sewed a patch on my jeans.* 我在牛仔裤上打了个补丁。

A B C D E F G H I J K L M N O P Q R S T U V W X Y Z

A
B
C
D
E
F
G
H
I
J
K
L
M
N
O
P
Q
R
S
T
U
V
W
X
Y
Z

pâté /'pæteɪ/ *noun* 名词 (*no plural* 不用复数形式)
thick food made from meat, fish or vegetables, that you eat on bread 酱（肉糜、鱼酱或蔬菜泥，涂于面包上食用）: *duck pâté* 鸭肉酱

paternal /pə'tɜːnl/ *adjective* 形容词
1 like a father or connected with being a father 父亲般的；父亲的: *paternal love* 父爱
2 A **paternal** relation is part of your father's family. 父系的: *my paternal grandmother* (= my father's mother) 我的祖母

path 小径

path 小径—— cottage 村舍

path 0━ /pɑːθ/ *noun* 名词 (*plural* 复数形式 paths /pɑːðz/)
a way across a piece of land, where people can walk 小路；小径: *a path through the woods* 树林中的小径

pathetic /pə'θetɪk/ *adjective* 形容词 (*informal* 非正式)
very bad or weak 差劲的；软弱无力的: *That was a pathetic performance – they deserved to lose!* 他们表现差劲，输了活该！

patience /'peɪʃns/ *noun* 名词 (*no plural* 不用复数形式)
staying calm and not getting angry when you are waiting for something, or when you have problems 耐心；耐性: *Learning to play the piano takes hard work and patience.* 学弹钢琴需要勤奋和耐心。 ◇ *She was walking so slowly that her sister finally lost patience with her* (= became angry with her). 她走得太慢，以致她姐姐终于不耐烦了。 ⊃ OPPOSITE **impatience** 反义词为 impatience

patient¹ 0━ /'peɪʃnt/ *adjective* 形容词
able to stay calm and not get angry when you are waiting for something or when you have problems 有耐心的；有耐性的: *Just sit there and be patient. Your mum will be here soon.* 耐心地在那边坐一会儿，你妈妈马上就来。 ⊃ OPPOSITE **impatient** 反义词为 impatient
▸ **patiently** /'peɪʃntli/ *adverb* 副词: *She waited patiently for the bus.* 她耐心地等着公共汽车。

patient² 0━ /'peɪʃnt/ *noun* 名词
a sick person that a doctor is looking after 病人

patio /'pætiəʊ/ *noun* 名词 (*plural* 复数形式 patios)
a flat hard area outside a house where people can sit and eat（屋外的）露台，平台

patriotic /ˌpeɪtri'ɒtɪk/ *adjective* 形容词
having or showing a great love for your country 爱国的

patrol /pə'trəʊl/ *noun* 名词
a group of people or vehicles that go round a place to see that everything is all right 巡逻队；巡逻车队: *an army patrol* 陆军巡逻队
on patrol the act of going round a place to see that everything is all right 巡逻: *During the carnival there will be 30 police officers on patrol.* 狂欢节期间将有 30 名警察执行巡逻任务。
▸ **patrol** *verb* 动词 (patrols, patrolling, patrolled /pə'trəʊld/): *A guard patrols the gate at night.* 警卫夜间在大门口巡逻。

patter /'pætə(r)/ *noun* 名词 (*no plural* 不用复数形式)
quick light sounds 啪嗒啪嗒的响声: *I heard the patter of children's feet on the stairs.* 我听到了孩子们在楼梯上啪嗒啪嗒的脚步声。
▸ **patter** *verb* 动词 (patters, pattering, pattered /'pætəd/): *Rain pattered against the window.* 雨点啪嗒啪嗒轻敲着窗户。

pattern 0━ /'pætn/ *noun* 名词
1 the way in which something happens or develops 模式: *Her days all seemed to follow the same pattern.* 她每天的生活似乎都是同一个模式。
2 shapes and colours on something 图案；花样: *The curtains had a pattern of flowers and leaves.* 窗帘上有花和叶子的图案。
3 a thing that you copy when you make something 图样；底样: *I bought some*

material and a pattern to make a new skirt. 我买了布料和纸样来做新裙子。

patterned /ˈpætənd/ *adjective* 形容词
with shapes and colours on it 有图案的；带花样的： *a patterned shirt* 有图案的衬衫

pause /pɔːz/ *verb* 动词 (pauses, pausing, paused /pɔːzd/)
to stop talking or doing something for a short time 暂停；中止： *He paused for a moment before answering my question.* 他顿了一会儿才回答我的问题。
▸ **pause** *noun* 名词 a period of time when you stop talking or stop what you are doing 停顿；暂停： *There was a long pause before she spoke.* 她停了好一会儿才说话。

pave /peɪv/ *verb* 动词 (paves, paving, paved /peɪvd/)
to cover an area of ground with flat stones (called **paving stones**) or bricks（用砖石）铺（地）： *There is a paved area near the house.* 房子附近有块石板地。

pavement /ˈpeɪvmənt/ (*British* 英式英语) (*American* 美式英语 **sidewalk**) *noun* 名词
the part at the side of a road where people can walk（马路边的）人行道 ⟳ Look at the picture at **kerb**. 见 kerb 插图。

paw /pɔː/ *noun* 名词
the foot of an animal, for example a dog or a cat（动物的）爪 ⟳ Look at the pictures at **cat** and **lion**. 见 cat 和 lion 插图。

pay¹ 0╺ /peɪ/ *verb* 动词 (pays, paying, paid /peɪd/, has paid)
to give somebody money for something, for example something they are selling you or work that they do 付钱；支付： *How much did you pay for your car?* 你的汽车花了多少钱？ ◇ *I paid the builder for mending the roof.* 我把修理屋顶的钱付给建筑工人了。 ◇ *She has a very well-paid job.* 她有一份薪水很高的工作。
pay somebody back to hurt somebody who has hurt you 报复： *One day I'll pay her back for lying to me!* 她对我撒了谎，总有一天我会治治她的！
pay somebody or 或 **something back** to give back the money that somebody has lent to you 还钱： *Can you lend me £10? I'll pay you back* (= pay it back to you) *next week.* 你能借我 10 英镑吗？我下星期还给你。

pay² 0╺ /peɪ/ *noun* 名词 (no plural 不用复数形式)
the money that you get for working 工资；薪水： *There are millions of workers on low pay.* 很多工人的工资都很低。

> 🔎 **WORD BUILDING** 词汇扩充
>
> **Pay** is the general word for money that you **earn** (= get regularly for work that you have done). * pay 泛指所挣（earn）的钱。
> If you are paid each week you get **wages**. If you are paid each month you get a **salary**. 按周领取的工资叫做 wages，按月领取的叫 salary。

payment 0╺ /ˈpeɪmənt/ *noun* 名词
1 (no plural 不用复数形式) paying or being paid 付款；收款： *This cheque is in payment for the work you have done.* 这张支票是给你做这项工作的酬金。
2 (plural 复数形式 **payments**) an amount of money that you pay 支付的款项；付款额： *I make monthly payments of £50.* 我每月支付 50 英镑。

payphone /ˈpeɪfəʊn/ *noun* 名词
a telephone that you put money in to make a call（公用）付费电话

PC /ˌpiː ˈsiː/ *noun* 名词
1 a small computer. **PC** is short for 'personal computer'. 个人电脑（PC 是 personal computer 的缩略式）
2 (*British* 英式英语) a police officer. **PC** is short for 'police constable'. 警员（PC 是 police constable 的缩略式）： *PC Smith* 警员史密斯

PE /ˌpiː ˈiː/ *noun* 名词 (no plural 不用复数形式)
sport and exercise that are done as a subject at school. **PE** is short for 'physical education'. 体育（科）（PE 是 physical education 的缩略式）： *We have PE on Tuesdays.* 我们每周二上体育课。

pea /piː/ *noun* 名词
a very small round green vegetable. **Peas** grow in long, thin cases (called **pods**). 豌豆 ⟳ Look at Picture Dictionary page **P9**. 见彩页 P9。

peace 0╺ /piːs/ *noun* 名词 (no plural 不用复数形式)
1 a time when there is no war or fighting between people or countries 和平；太平： *The two countries eventually made peace* (= agreed to stop fighting). 两国最终停战和解了。
2 the state of being quiet and calm 安静；宁静；平静： *the peace and quiet of the countryside* 乡村的宁静 ◇ *Go away and leave me in peace!* 走开，让我静一静！

peaceful 🔊 /'piːsfl/ *adjective* 形容词
1 with no fighting 和平的：*a peaceful demonstration* 和平示威
2 quiet and calm 安静的；宁静的：*It's so peaceful here.* 这里好宁静。
▶ **peacefully** /'piːsfəli/ *adverb* 副词：*She's sleeping peacefully.* 她睡得正香。

peach /piːtʃ/ *noun* 名词 (*plural* 复数形式 **peaches**)
a soft round fruit with a yellow and red skin and a large stone in the centre 桃；桃子 ⊃ Look at Picture Dictionary page **P8**. 见彩页 P8。

peacock /'piːkɒk/ *noun* 名词
a large bird with beautiful long blue and green feathers in its tail 孔雀 ⊃ Look at Picture Dictionary page **P2**. 见彩页 P2。

peak /piːk/ *noun* 名词
1 the time when something is highest, biggest, etc. 高峰；顶峰；巅峰：*The traffic is at its peak between five and six in the evening.* 傍晚五六点钟是交通高峰时段。
2 the pointed top of a mountain 山峰：*snowy mountain peaks* 白雪皑皑的山峰
3 the front part of a hat that sticks out above your eyes 帽舌；帽檐

peanut /'piːnʌt/ *noun* 名词
a nut that you can eat 花生：*salted peanuts* 咸花生 ⊃ Look at the picture at **nut**. 见 nut 的插图。

peanut butter /ˌpiːnʌt 'bʌtə(r)/ *noun* 名词 (*no plural* 不用复数形式)
a thick soft substance made from PEANUTS that you eat on bread 花生酱

pear /peə(r)/ *noun* 名词

> 🔊 PRONUNCIATION 读音说明
> The word **pear** sounds just like **pair**.
> * pear 读音同 pair。

a fruit that is green or yellow on the outside and white on the inside 梨 ⊃ Look at Picture Dictionary page **P8**. 见彩页 P8。

pearl /pɜːl/ *noun* 名词
a small round white thing that grows inside the shell of a fish (called an **oyster**). **Pearls** are valuable and are used to make jewellery. 珍珠：*a pearl necklace* 珍珠项链

peasant /'peznt/ *noun* 名词
a poor person who lives in the country and works on a small piece of land 农民；小农

pebble /'pebl/ *noun* 名词
a small round stone 鹅卵石；砾石

peck /pek/ *verb* 动词 (**pecks, pecking, pecked** /pekt/)
When a bird **pecks** something, it eats or bites it quickly. （鸟）啄，啄食：*The hens were pecking at the corn.* 母鸡啄着玉米。

peculiar /pɪ'kjuːliə(r)/ *adjective* 形容词
strange; not usual 奇怪的；不寻常的 ⊃ SAME MEANING **odd** 同义词为 odd：*What's that peculiar smell?* 那是什么怪味？

pedal /'pedl/ *noun* 名词
a part of a bicycle or other machine that you move with your feet （自行车、机器等的）踏板，脚蹬子 ⊃ Look at the picture at **bicycle**. 见 bicycle 的插图。

pedestrian /pə'destriən/ *noun* 名词
a person who is walking in the street 行人；步行者

pedestrian crossing /pəˌdestriən 'krɒsɪŋ/ (*British* 英式英语) (*American* 美式英语 **crosswalk**) *noun* 名词
a place where cars must stop so that people can cross the road 人行横道

pedestrian precinct /pəˌdestriən 'priːsɪŋkt/ *noun* 名词 (*British* 英式英语)
a part of a town where there are a lot of shops and where cars cannot go 步行区；行人专用区

peel[1] /piːl/ *verb* 动词 (**peels, peeling, peeled** /piːld/)
1 to take the outside part off a fruit or vegetable （给水果或蔬菜）剥皮，去皮：*Can you peel the potatoes?* 你能给土豆削皮吗？
2 to come off in thin pieces 脱落；剥落：*The paint is peeling off the walls.* 墙上的油漆逐渐剥落了。

peel[2] /piːl/ *noun* 名词 (*no plural* 不用复数形式)
the outside part of some fruit and vegetables （某些水果、蔬菜的）皮：*orange peel* 橙子皮 ◇ *potato peel* 土豆皮 ⊃ Look at Picture Dictionary page **P8**. 见彩页 P8。

peep /piːp/ *verb* 动词 (**peeps, peeping, peeped** /piːpt/)
to look at something quickly or secretly 偷看；窥视：*I peeped through the window and saw her.* 我从窗户窥探，看到了她。
▶ **peep** *noun* 名词 (*no plural* 不用复数形式)：*Have a peep in the bedroom and*

see if the baby is awake. 往卧室里瞥一眼，看宝宝醒来没有。

peer /pɪə(r)/ ***verb*** 动词 (**peers**, **peering**, **peered** /pɪəd/)
to look closely at something because you cannot see well 仔细看；端详： *I peered outside but I couldn't see anything because it was dark.* 我往外仔细瞧，可是因为天黑什么也看不见。

peg /peg/ ***noun*** 名词
1 a small thing on a wall or door where you can hang things 挂钩： *Your coat is on the peg.* 你的大衣挂在钩子上。
2 a small wooden or plastic thing that holds wet clothes on a line when they are drying 晾衣夹子： *a clothes peg* 晾衣夹

pen 钢笔

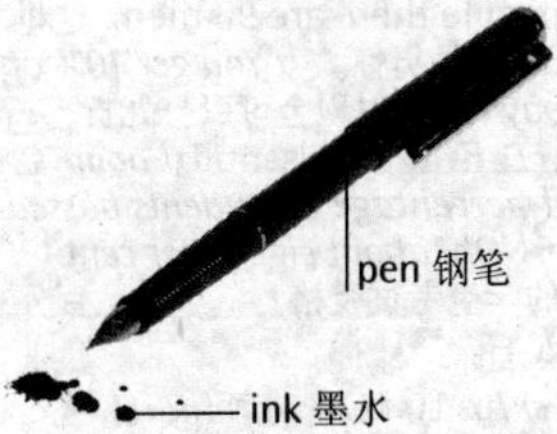

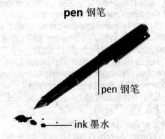

pen 🔑 /pen/ ***noun*** 名词
1 a thing that you use for writing with a coloured liquid (called **ink**) 笔；钢笔；墨水笔
2 a small piece of ground with a fence around it for keeping farm animals in 畜栏；圈

penalty /ˈpenlti/ ***noun*** 名词 (*plural* 复数形式 **penalties**)
1 a punishment 惩罚；处罚： *The **penalty for** travelling without a ticket is £300* (= you must pay £300). 无票乘车罚款 300 英镑。
2 (in sport) a punishment for one team and an advantage for the other team because a player has broken a rule （体育运动）判罚；点球： *Beckham stepped forward to **take the penalty*** (= try to score the goal). 贝克汉姆上前踢点球了。

pence *plural of* PENNY * penny 的复数形式

pencil 🔑 /ˈpensl/ ***noun*** 名词
a thin object that you use for writing or drawing. **Pencils** are usually made of wood and have a black or coloured point. 铅笔 ➲ Look at **pen**. 见 pen。

pencil 铅笔

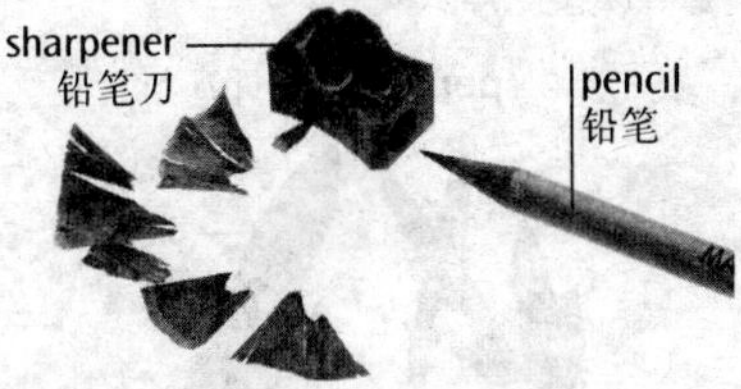

penetrate /ˈpenɪtreɪt/ ***verb*** 动词 (**penetrates**, **penetrating**, **penetrated**)
to go through or into something 穿入；穿透： *The knife penetrated deep into his chest.* 刀深深地刺进了他的胸膛。

penfriend /ˈpenfrend/ (*British* 英式英语) (*American* 美式英语 **pen pal** /ˈpen pæl/) ***noun*** 名词
a person that you make friends with by writing letters but you have probably never met them 笔友（靠书信联系，彼此可能从未见面）

penguin 企鹅

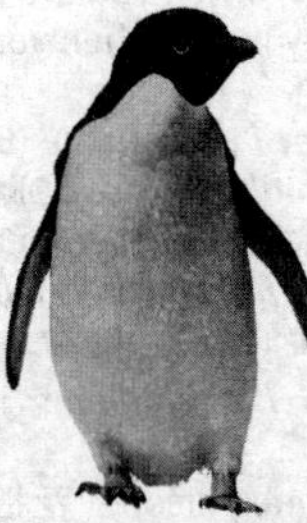

penguin /ˈpeŋgwɪn/ ***noun*** 名词
a black and white bird that lives in very cold places. **Penguins** can swim but they cannot fly. 企鹅

penicillin /ˌpenɪˈsɪlɪn/ ***noun*** 名词 (*no plural* 不用复数形式)
a drug that is used to stop infections and to treat illnesses 青霉素；盘尼西林

penis /ˈpiːnɪs/ ***noun*** 名词 (*plural* 复数形式 **penises**)
the part of a man's or a male animal's body that is used for getting rid of waste liquid and for having sex 阴茎

penknife /ˈpennaɪf/ ***noun*** 名词 (*plural* 复数形式 **penknives** /ˈpennaɪvz/)

A B C D E F G H I J K L M N O P Q R S T U V W X Y Z

A
B
C
D
E
F
G
H
I
J
K
L
M
N
O
P
Q
R
S
T
U
V
W
X
Y
Z

a small knife that you can carry in your pocket 小折刀

penknife 小折刀

—— blade 刀

penny ○┬ /'peni/ (*abbr.* 缩略式 **p**) *noun* 名词 (*plural* 复数形式 **pence** /pens/ or 或 **pennies**)
a small coin that people use in Britain. There are 100 **pence** in a **pound**. 便士（英国硬币；100 便士等于 1 英镑）: *These pencils cost 40 pence each.* 这些铅笔每支 40 便士。◇ *Can you lend me 50p?* 你能借给我 50 便士吗?

pension /'penʃn/ *noun* 名词
money that you get from a government or a company when you are old and do not work any more (when you are **retired**) 养老金；退休金
▶ **pensioner** /'penʃənə(r)/ (*British* 英式英语) (*British also* 英式英语亦作 **old-age pensioner** /,əʊld eɪdʒ 'penʃənə(r)/) *noun* 名词: *Many pensioners live in poverty.* 许多领养老金的人生活贫困。

people ○┬ /'piːpl/ *noun* 名词 (*plural* 用复数形式)
more than one person（泛指）人: *How many people came to the meeting?* 有多少人来开会了? ◇ *People often arrive late at parties.* 参加聚会的人经常迟到。

pepper /'pepə(r)/ *noun* 名词
1 (*no plural* 不用复数形式) powder with a hot taste that you put on food 胡椒粉: *salt and pepper* 盐和胡椒粉 ⊃ Look at Picture Dictionary page **P6**. 见彩页 P6。
2 (*plural* 复数形式 **peppers**) a red, green or yellow vegetable that is almost empty inside 甜椒；柿子椒；灯笼椒 ⊃ Look at Picture Dictionary page **P9**. 见彩页 P9。

peppermint /'pepəmɪnt/ *noun* 名词
1 (*no plural* 不用复数形式) a plant with a strong fresh taste and smell. It is used to make things like sweets and medicines. 胡椒薄荷；薄荷

2 (*plural* 复数形式 **peppermints**) a sweet with the flavour of **peppermint** 薄荷糖

per /pə(r)/ *preposition* 介词
for each; in each 每；每一: *These apples cost 40p per pound.* 这些苹果每磅 40 便士。◇ *I was driving at 60 miles per hour.* 当时我的车速是每小时 60 英里。

perceive /pə'siːv/ *verb* 动词 (**perceives**, **perceiving**, **perceived** /pə'siːvd/) (*formal* 正式)
to understand or think of something or somebody in a particular way 理解为；认为；视为: *My comments were perceived as criticism.* 我的评论被视作指责。

per cent /pə 'sent/ *noun* 名词 (*no plural* 不用复数形式) (*symbol* 符号 **%**)
in each hundred 百分之…: *90 per cent of the people who work here are men* (= in 100 men there are 90 men). 在这里工作的人 90% 是男性。◇ *You get 10% off if you pay cash.* 付现金可以打九折。
▶ **percentage** /pə'sentɪdʒ/ *noun* 名词: *'What percentage of students passed the exam?' 'Oh, about eighty per cent.'* "百分之几的学生考试及格?""噢，百分之八十左右。"

perch¹ /pɜːtʃ/ *verb* 动词 (**perches**, **perching**, **perched** /pɜːtʃt/)
to sit on something narrow or uncomfortable（在窄小处上）坐；（不稳地）坐；（鸟）栖息，停留: *The bird perched on a branch.* 那只鸟停在树枝上。◇ *We perched on high stools.* 我们坐在高脚凳上。

perch² /pɜːtʃ/ *noun* 名词 (*plural* 复数形式 **perches**)
a place where a bird sits（鸟的）栖息处，栖木

perfect ○┬ /'pɜːfɪkt/ *adjective* 形容词
1 so good that it cannot be better; with nothing wrong 完美的；无瑕的: *Her English is perfect.* 她的英语非常地道。◇ *It's perfect weather for a picnic.* 这种天气最适合野餐。
2 made from 'has', 'have' or 'had' and the PAST PARTICIPLE of a verb（动词）完成时的，完成式的: *perfect tenses* 完成时

the perfect /ðə 'pɜːfɪkt/ (*also* 亦作 **the perfect tense** /ðə ,pɜːfɪkt 'tens/) *noun* 名词 (*no plural* 不用复数形式)
(*grammar* 语法) the form of the verb that is made with 'has', 'have' or 'had' and the PAST PARTICIPLE 完成时；完成式: *'I've finished' is in the perfect tense.* * I've finished 用的是完成时。◇ Look at **past**

perfect and **present perfect**. 见 past perfect 和 present perfect。

perfection /pəˈfekʃn/ *noun* 名词
(*no plural* 不用复数形式)
the state of being perfect 完美；完善：
The meat was cooked to perfection. 这肉烹煮得恰到好处。

perfectly /ˈpɜːfɪktli/ *adverb* 副词
1 completely 完全地；非常 ⊃ SAME MEANING **quite** 同义词为 quite： *I'm perfectly all right.* 我完全没事。
2 in a perfect way 完美地；圆满地： *She played the piece of music perfectly.* 她把那首乐曲演奏得很完美。

perform 0━ /pəˈfɔːm/ *verb* 动词
(**performs, performing, performed** /pəˈfɔːmd/)
1 to do something such as a piece of work or a task 做；履行；执行： *Doctors performed a complicated operation to save her life.* 医生做了复杂的手术来挽救她的生命。
2 to be in something such as a play or a concert 表演；演出： *The band is performing at the Odeon tonight.* 乐队今晚在奥迪昂电影院演出。◇ *The play will be performed every night next week.* 这出戏下周每晚上演。

performance 0━ /pəˈfɔːməns/ *noun* 名词
1 (*plural* 复数形式 **performances**) a time when a play, etc. is shown, or music is played in front of a lot of people 表演；演出： *We went to the evening performance of the play.* 我们去看了那出戏的晚场演出。
2 (*no plural* 不用复数形式) how well you do something 表现： *My parents were pleased with my performance in the exam.* 父母对我的考试成绩很满意。

performer /pəˈfɔːmə(r)/ *noun* 名词
a person who is in something such as a play or a concert 表演者；演员

perfume /ˈpɜːfjuːm/ *noun* 名词
1 a liquid with a nice smell that you put on your body 香水： *a bottle of perfume* 一瓶香水
2 a nice smell 香味

perhaps 0━ /pəˈhæps/ *adverb* 副词
a word that you use when you are not sure about something 可能；大概；也许 ⊃ SAME MEANING **maybe** 同义词为 maybe： *I don't know where she is – perhaps she's still at work.* 我不知道她在哪里，或许还在上班。◇ *There were three*

men, or perhaps four. 那时有三个男人，也许是四个。

period 0━ /ˈpɪəriəd/ *noun* 名词
1 an amount of time 一段时间；时期： *This is a difficult period for him.* 对他来说这是个困难时期。◇ *What period of history are you studying?* 你在学习哪段时期的历史？
2 a lesson in school 一节课： *We have five periods of German a week.* 我们每周有五节德语课。
3 the time when a woman loses blood from her body each month 月经
4 *American English for* FULL STOP 美式英语，即 full stop

perm /pɜːm/ *noun* 名词
the treatment of hair with special chemicals to make it curly 烫发；鬈发： *I think I'm going to have a perm.* 我想我会去烫个头发。
▸ **perm** *verb* 动词 (**perms, perming, permed** /pɜːmd/): *Have you had your hair permed?* 你烫过头发吗？

permanent 0━ /ˈpɜːmənənt/ *adjective* 形容词
continuing for ever or for a very long time without changing 永久的；经久不变的： *I'm looking for a permanent job.* 我在找一份固定的工作。⊃ Look at **temporary**. 见 temporary。
▸ **permanently** /ˈpɜːmənəntli/ *adverb* 副词： *Has he left permanently?* 他走了再不回来吗？

permission 0━ /pəˈmɪʃn/ *noun* 名词
(*no plural* 不用复数形式)
allowing somebody to do something 准许；许可： *She gave me permission to leave early.* 她允许我早点儿走。◇ *You may not leave the school without permission.* 未经批准你不得擅离学校。

permit¹ /pəˈmɪt/ *verb* 动词 (**permits, permitting, permitted**) (*formal* 正式)
to let somebody do something 允许；准许 ⊃ SAME MEANING **allow** 同义词为 allow： *You are not permitted to smoke in the hospital.* 医院里不准吸烟。

permit² /ˈpɜːmɪt/ *noun* 名词
a piece of paper that says you can do something or go somewhere 许可证： *Have you got a work permit?* 你有工作许可证吗？

persevere /ˌpɜːsɪˈvɪə(r)/ *verb* 动词
(**perseveres, persevering, persevered** /ˌpɜːsɪˈvɪəd/)
to continue trying to do something that is difficult 坚持： *If you persevere with your*

studies, you could go to university. 只要你对学业孜孜以求，就能上大学。

persistent /pə'sɪstənt/ *adjective* 形容词
1 determined to continue doing something even though people tell you to stop 坚持不懈的；执著的：*She's a very persistent child – she just never gives up.* 她是个执著的孩子，永不言弃。
2 lasting for a long time 持续的：*a persistent cough* 久咳

person 0ᴙ /'pɜːsn/ *noun* 名词 (*plural* 复数形式 **people** /'piːpl/)
a man or woman 人：*I think she's the best person for the job.* 我觉得她是这份工作的最佳人选。◇ *We've invited a few people to dinner.* 我们邀请了几个人来吃饭。

in person seeing somebody, not just speaking on the telephone or writing a letter 亲自；亲身；当面：*I want to speak to her in person.* 我想当面跟她说。

personal 0ᴙ /'pɜːsənl/ *adjective* 形容词
of or for one person 个人的；私人的：*That letter is personal and you have no right to read it.* 那是私人信件，你无权翻阅。◇ *Please keep all your personal belongings with you.* 请保管阁下所有的随身物品。

personal computer /ˌpɜːsənl kəm'pjuːtə(r)/ = PC (1)

personality /ˌpɜːsə'næləti/ *noun* 名词 (*plural* 复数形式 **personalities**)
1 the qualities that a person has that make them different from other people 性格；个性：*Mark has a great personality.* 马克的品格很高尚。
2 a famous person 名人：*a television personality* 电视明星

personally /'pɜːsənəli/ *adverb* 副词
1 You say **personally** when you are saying what you think about something. 就本人而言；就个人来说：*Personally, I like her, but a lot of people don't.* 就我个人来说，我喜欢她，可是很多人不喜欢。
2 done by you yourself, and not by somebody else acting for you 亲自：*I will deal with this matter personally.* 我会亲自处理这件事。

personal stereo /ˌpɜːsənl 'steriəʊ/ *noun* 名词 (*plural* 复数形式 **personal stereos**)
a small machine for listening to music. You can carry it with you and listen through wires (called **headphones**) that go in your ears. 随身听

personnel /ˌpɜːsə'nel/ *noun* 名词 (*plural* 用复数形式)
the people who work for a large business or organization（大公司或机构的）全体人员，职员：*military personnel* 军事人员

persuade 0ᴙ /pə'sweɪd/ *verb* 动词 (persuades, persuading, persuaded)
to make somebody think or do something by talking to them 劝说；说服：*The shop assistant persuaded me to buy the most expensive pair of jeans.* 店员游说我买最贵的牛仔裤。

persuasion /pə'sweɪʒn/ *noun* 名词 (*no plural* 不用复数形式)
the process of making somebody think or do something 劝说；说服：*After a lot of persuasion she agreed to come.* 好说歹说，她才同意来。

pessimism /'pesɪmɪzəm/ *noun* 名词 (*no plural* 不用复数形式)
thinking that bad things will happen 悲观；悲观主义 ⊃ OPPOSITE **optimism** 反义词为 optimism

▶ **pessimist** /'pesɪmɪst/ *noun* 名词：*Lisa's such a pessimist.* 莉萨太悲观了。
⊃ OPPOSITE **optimist** 反义词为 optimist

▶ **pessimistic** /ˌpesɪ'mɪstɪk/ *adjective* 形容词：*Don't be so pessimistic – of course it's not going to rain!* 别那么悲观，当然不会下雨的！⊃ OPPOSITE **optimistic** 反义词为 optimistic

pest /pest/ *noun* 名词
1 an insect or animal that damages plants or food 害虫；害兽；害鸟
2 (*informal* 非正式) a person or thing that makes you a little angry 讨厌鬼；麻烦的事物：*My little sister's a real pest!* 我妹妹真讨厌！

pester /'pestə(r)/ *verb* 动词 (pesters, pestering, pestered /'pestəd/)
to annoy somebody by asking them for something many times 缠扰；烦扰：*Journalists pestered the neighbours for information.* 记者缠着邻居打听消息。

pet 0ᴙ /pet/ *noun* 名词
1 an animal that you keep in your home 宠物：*I've got two pets – a cat and a goldfish.* 我养了两个宠物：一只猫和一条金鱼。⊃ Look at Picture Dictionary page P2. 见彩页 P2。
2 a child that a teacher or a parent likes best 宠儿：*She's the teacher's pet.* 她是最受老师宠爱的学生。

petal /'petl/ *noun* 名词
one of the coloured parts of a flower 花瓣 ⊃ Look at the picture at **plant¹**. 见 plant¹ 的插图。

petition /pəˈtɪʃn/ *noun* 名词
a special letter from a group of people that asks for something 请愿书:
*Hundreds of people signed the **petition for a new pedestrian crossing**.* 数百人签名请愿要求设置新的人行横道。

petrol 0━ /ˈpetrəl/ (*British* 英式英语) (*American* 美式英语 **gas, gasoline**) *noun* 名词 (*no plural* 不用复数形式)
a liquid that you put in a car to make it go 汽油

petrol station /ˈpetrəl steɪʃn/ (*American* 美式英语 **gas station**) *noun* 名词
a place where you can buy PETROL 加油站

phantom /ˈfæntəm/ *noun* 名词
a spirit of a dead person that people think they see 鬼魂；幽灵 ⊃ SAME MEANING **ghost** 同义词为 ghost

pharmacist /ˈfɑːməsɪst/ = CHEMIST (1)

pharmacy /ˈfɑːməsi/ *noun* 名词 (*plural* 复数形式 **pharmacies**)
a shop, or part of a shop, which sells medicines and drugs 药房；药店；（商店）医药柜台

phase /feɪz/ *noun* 名词
a time when something is changing or growing 阶段；时期: *She's going through a difficult phase just now.* 她正在经历一段困难时期。

PhD /ˌpiː eɪtʃ ˈdiː/ *abbreviation* 缩略式
a high level university degree that you get by doing an important piece of work in a particular subject 博士学位 ⊃ 'PhD' is short for **Doctor of Philosophy**. * PhD 是 Doctor of Philosophy 的缩略式。

philosopher /fəˈlɒsəfə(r)/ *noun* 名词
a person who studies PHILOSOPHY 哲学家

philosophy /fəˈlɒsəfi/ *noun* 名词
1 (*no plural* 不用复数形式) the study of ideas about the meaning of life 哲学
2 (*plural* 复数形式 **philosophies**) a set of beliefs that a person has about life 人生哲学；生活的信条: *Enjoy yourself and don't worry about tomorrow – that's my philosophy!* 尽情享受，不为明天忧虑，这就是我的人生哲学!

phone¹ 0━ /fəʊn/ (*also* 亦作 **telephone**) *noun* 名词
an instrument that you use for talking to somebody who is in another place 电话:
The phone's ringing – can you answer it? 电话铃在响，你可不可以去接一下?
be on the phone 在打电话: *Anna was **on the phone** for an hour.* 安娜打了一个小时的电话。

phone² 0━ /fəʊn/ *verb* 动词 (**phones, phoning, phoned** /fəʊnd/) (*British also* 英式英语亦作 **phone up**)
to speak to somebody by phone 打电话 ⊃ SAME MEANING **call** 同义词为 call: *I phoned Di last night.* 我昨晚给迪打了电话。◇ *I was just phoning up for a chat.* 我打电话过来只是想聊聊。◇ *Could you phone back later?* 你过一会儿再打电话来好吗?

phone book /ˈfəʊn bʊk/ (*also* 亦作 **telephone book, telephone directory**) *noun* 名词
a book of people's names, addresses and telephone numbers 电话簿

phone box /ˈfəʊn bɒks/ (*plural* 复数形式 **phone boxes**) (*also* 亦作 **telephone box**) *noun* 名词
a public telephone in the street 公用电话间；公用电话亭

phone call /ˈfəʊn kɔːl/ (*also* 亦作 **telephone call**) *noun* 名词
when you use the phone to talk to somebody （一通）电话；（一次）通话: *I need to **make a phone call**.* 我得打个电话。

phonecard /ˈfəʊnkɑːd/ *noun* 名词
a small plastic card that you can use to pay for a call to somebody from a phone box （打公共电话的）电话卡

phone number /ˈfəʊn nʌmbə(r)/ (*also* 亦作 **telephone number**) *noun* 名词
the number of a particular phone that you use when you want to make a call to it 电话号码: *What's your phone number?* 你的电话号码是什么?

phonetic /fəˈnetɪk/ *adjective* 形容词
using special signs to show how to say words 音标的；标示语音的: *The phonetic alphabet is on a chart on the classroom wall.* 音标列在教室墙上的图表中。

phonetics /fəˈnetɪks/ *noun* 名词 (*no plural* 不用复数形式)
the study of the sounds that people make when they speak 语音学

photo 0━ /ˈfəʊtəʊ/ *noun* 名词 (*plural* 复数形式 **photos**) (*informal* 非正式)
= PHOTOGRAPH

photocopier /ˈfəʊtəʊkɒpiə(r)/ *noun* 名词
a machine that makes copies of documents by photographing them 复印机；影印机

photocopy /ˈfəʊtəʊkɒpi/ *noun* 名词 (*plural* 复数形式 **photocopies**)
a copy of something on paper that you

A
B
C
D
E
F
G
H
I
J
K
L
M
N
O
P
Q
R
S
T
U
V
W
X
Y
Z

make with a PHOTOCOPIER 复印本；影印件

▸ **photocopy** *verb* 动词 (photocopies, photocopying, photocopied /ˈfəʊtəʊkɒpid/, has photocopied): *Can you photocopy this letter for me?* 你可不可以给我复印这封信？

photograph 0-ᴡ /ˈfəʊtəɡrɑːf/ (*also* 亦作 **photo**) *noun* 名词
a picture that you take with a camera 照片；相片： *I took a photo of the Eiffel Tower.* 我拍了一张埃菲尔铁塔的照片。

▸ **photograph** *verb* 动词 (photographs, photographing, photographed /ˈfəʊtəɡrɑːft/): *The winner was photographed holding his prize.* 获胜者捧着奖品照了一张相。

photographer 0-ᴡ /fəˈtɒɡrəfə(r)/ *noun* 名词
a person who takes photographs, especially as a job 摄影师；拍照者

photographic /ˌfəʊtəˈɡræfɪk/ *adjective* 形容词
connected with photographs or photography 照片的；摄影的： *photographic equipment* 摄影器材

photography /fəˈtɒɡrəfi/ *noun* 名词 (*no plural* 不用复数形式)
taking photographs 摄影；摄影术

phrasal verb /ˌfreɪzl ˈvɜːb/ *noun* 名词
(*grammar* 语法) a verb that joins with another word or words to make a verb with a new meaning 短语动词： *'Look after' and 'take off' are phrasal verbs.* * look after 和 take off 是短语动词。

phrase 0-ᴡ /freɪz/ *noun* 名词

> 🔊 **PRONUNCIATION** 读音说明
> The word **phrase** sounds like **days**.
> * phrase 读音像 days。

(*grammar* 语法) a group of words that you use together as part of a sentence 短语；词组： *'First of all' and 'a bar of chocolate' are phrases.* * first of all 和 a bar of chocolate 是词组。

physical 0-ᴡ /ˈfɪzɪkl/ *adjective* 形容词
connected with things that you feel or do with your body 身体的；肉体的： *physical exercise* 体育锻炼

▸ **physically** /ˈfɪzɪkli/ *adverb* 副词： *I'm not physically fit.* 我现在身体不好。

physical education /ˌfɪzɪkl edʒuˈkeɪʃn/ (*abbr.* 缩略式 **PE**) *noun* 名词 (*no plural* 不用复数形式)

sport and exercise that are done as a subject at school 体育（科）

physicist /ˈfɪzɪsɪst/ *noun* 名词
a person who studies or knows a lot about PHYSICS 物理学家

physics /ˈfɪzɪks/ *noun* 名词 (*no plural* 不用复数形式)
the scientific study of things like heat, light and sound 物理学

pianist /ˈpɪənɪst/ *noun* 名词
a person who plays the piano 钢琴演奏者；钢琴家

piano 钢琴

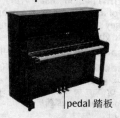

pedal 踏板

piano 0-ᴡ /piˈænəʊ/ *noun* 名词 (*plural* 复数形式 **pianos**)
a big musical instrument that you play by pressing black and white bars (called **keys**) 钢琴： *Can you play the piano?* 你会弹钢琴吗？

pick¹ 0-ᴡ /pɪk/ *verb* 动词 (picks, picking, picked /pɪkt/)

1 to take the person or thing you like best 挑选；选择 ⊃ SAME MEANING **choose** 同义词为 choose： *They picked Simon as their captain.* 他们选西蒙当队长。

2 to take a flower, fruit or vegetable from the place where it grows 采，摘（花、水果或蔬菜）： *I've picked some flowers for you.* 我给你采了些花。

pick on somebody (*informal* 非正式) to treat somebody in an unfair or cruel way 欺负某人；故意刁难某人： *Sally gets picked on by the other kids.* 萨莉被别的孩子欺负。

pick somebody or 或 **something out** to be able to see somebody or something among a lot of others 认出某人；辨别出某物： *Can you pick out my father in this photo?* 你能在这张照片上认出我父亲吗？

pick somebody up to come to get somebody, especially in a car （尤指开车）接（某人）： *My father picks me up from school.* 父亲到学校来接我。

pick somebody or 或 **something up**
to take and lift somebody or something
抱起某人；拿起某物: *She picked up the
kitten and stroked it.* 她抱起小猫轻轻抚摩
它。◇ *The phone stopped ringing just as I
picked it up.* 我刚拿起电话，它就不响了。
pick something up to learn something
without really studying it（未经正式学习
而）学到某事物: *Did you pick up any
Japanese while you were in Tokyo?* 你在
东京的时候学点儿日语了吗?

pick² /pɪk/ *noun* 名词 (*no plural* 不用复数
形式)
the one that you choose; your choice
选中的人（或事物）；选择
take your pick to choose what you like
随意挑选: *We've got orange juice,
lemonade or milk. Take your pick.* 我们有
橙汁、柠檬味汽水和牛奶，你随便挑吧。

pickaxe (*British* 英式英语) (*American*
美式英语 **pickax**) /ˈpɪkæks/ *noun* 名词
a large sharp metal tool with a wooden
handle which is used for breaking rocks
or hard ground 镐，尖嘴镐，鹤嘴锄
（碎石或刨土用）

picket /ˈpɪkɪt/ *noun* 名词
a person or group of people who stand
outside the place where they work when
there is a STRIKE (= an organized protest),
and try to stop other people going in
（罢工行动的）纠察队员，纠察队
▶ **picket** *verb* 动词 (**pickets, picketing,
picketed**): *Workers were picketing the
factory.* 工人在工厂外任纠察执行罢工。

pickpocket /ˈpɪkpɒkɪt/ *noun* 名词
a person who steals things from people's
pockets 扒手

picnic /ˈpɪknɪk/ *noun* 名词
a meal that you eat outside, away from
home 野餐: *We had a picnic by the river.*
我们在河边野餐。
▶ **picnic** *verb* 动词 (**picnics, picnicking,
picnicked** /ˈpɪknɪkt/): *We picnicked on the
beach yesterday.* 我们昨天在海滩野餐。

picture¹ ⚬̄ /ˈpɪktʃə(r)/ *noun* 名词
a drawing, painting or photograph 图画；
图片；照片: *Julie drew a picture of her
dog.* 朱莉给她的狗画了一幅画。◇ *They
showed us some pictures (= photographs)
of their wedding.* 他们给我们看了一些他们
婚礼的照片。◇ *I took a picture (= a
photograph) of the house.* 我给房子拍了
一张照片。➔ Look at Picture Dictionary
page **P10**. 见彩页 P10。

picture² /ˈpɪktʃə(r)/ *verb* 动词 (**pictures,
picturing, pictured** /ˈpɪktʃəd/)

to imagine something in your mind
想象；设想: *I can just picture them lying
on the beach.* 我完全可以想象到他们躺在
海滩上的情景。

pie 馅饼

pastry
油酥面团

filling
馅

pie /paɪ/ *noun* 名词
a type of food made of meat, fruit or
vegetables covered with PASTRY (= a
mixture of flour, butter and water)
（肉或蔬果）馅饼，派: *an apple pie*
苹果派

piece ⚬̄ /piːs/ *noun* 名词

> 🔎 **SPELLING 拼写说明**
>
> Remember! **I** comes before **E** in **piece**.
> 记住: **piece** 中的 i 在 e 前面。
> Use the phrase **a piece of pie** to help
> you remember. 可用词组 a piece of pie
> 来帮助记忆。

1 a part of something（表示一部分）
块，片，件: *Would you like another
piece of cake?* 你要再来一块蛋糕吗? ◇
a piece of broken glass 一块碎玻璃
2 one single thing（表示单一的量）张，
条，件: *Have you got a piece of paper?*
你有纸吗? ◇ *That's an interesting piece of
news.* 那是一则有趣的新闻。
3 a coin 硬币: *a 50p piece* 一枚 50 便士
的硬币
fall to pieces to become very old and in
bad condition; to break 变得破旧不堪；
破碎: *The chair fell to pieces when I sat
on it.* 这把椅子我一坐就散了。
in pieces broken 破成碎片: *The teapot
lay in pieces on the floor.* 茶壶破成碎片，
散落地上。
take something to pieces to divide
something into its parts 拆开…成各部分:
*I took the bed to pieces because it was too
big to go through the door.* 因为床太大
不能通过这道门，我把它拆了。

pier /pɪə(r)/ *noun* 名词
a long structure that is built from the

land into the sea, where people can walk or get on and off boats 码头；突堤

pier 码头

pile 摞

pierce /pɪəs/ *verb* 动词 (pierces, piercing, pierced /pɪəst/)
to make a hole in something with a sharp point 扎穿；刺破；穿透：*The nail pierced her skin.* 钉子戳破了她的皮肤。◇ *I'm going to have my ears pierced.* 我准备去打耳洞。

piercing /'pɪəsɪŋ/ *adjective* 形容词
A **piercing** sound is very loud and unpleasant. （声音）刺耳的，尖利的：*a piercing cry* 刺耳的喊叫

pig 0→ /pɪg/ *noun* 名词
1 a fat animal that people keep on farms for its meat 猪 ⊃ Look at Picture Dictionary page **P2**. 见彩页 P2。

> 🔍 **WORD BUILDING** 词汇扩充
> A young pig is called a **piglet**. 小猪叫做 piglet。
> Meat from a pig is called **pork**, **bacon** or **ham**. 猪肉叫做 pork，咸猪肉叫做 bacon，火腿叫做 ham。

2 an unkind person or a person who eats too much 讨厌的人；贪吃的人：*You've eaten all the biscuits, you pig!* 你把饼干都吃光了，你这头馋猪！

pigeon /'pɪdʒɪn/ *noun* 名词
a grey bird that you often see in towns 鸽子

piglet /'pɪglət/ *noun* 名词
a young pig 小猪；猪崽儿

pigsty /'pɪgstaɪ/ (*also* 亦作 **sty**) *noun* 名词
(*plural* 复数形式 **pigsties**)
a small building where pigs live 猪圈；猪栏

pigtail /'pɪgteɪl/ *noun* 名词
hair that you twist together (called **plait**) and tie at the sides or at the back of your head 辫子 ⊃ Look at the picture at **hair**. 见 hair 的插图。

pile¹ 0→ /paɪl/ *noun* 名词
a lot of things on top of one another; a large amount of something 堆；摞；大量：*Clothes lay in piles on the floor.* 衣服一堆堆放在地上。◇ *a pile of earth* 一堆泥土

> 🔍 **WHICH WORD?** 词语辨析
> **Pile** or **heap**? 用 pile 还是 heap？
> A **pile** may be tidy or untidy. A **heap** is untidy. * pile 可指整齐或不整齐的一堆，而 heap 指不整齐的一堆。

pile² 0→ /paɪl/ *verb* 动词 (piles, piling, piled /paɪld/)
to put a lot of things on top of one another 堆放；摞起：*She piled the boxes on the table.* 她把盒子叠在桌子上。

pilgrim /'pɪlgrɪm/ *noun* 名词
a person who travels a long way to a place because it has a special religious meaning 朝圣者；朝觐者

pilgrimage /'pɪlgrɪmɪdʒ/ *noun* 名词
a journey that a PILGRIM makes 朝圣

pill /pɪl/ *noun* 名词
a small round hard piece of medicine that you swallow 药丸；药片 ⊃ SAME MEANING **tablet** 同义词为 tablet：*Take one of these pills before every meal.* 这些药片每顿饭前服一片。

pillar 柱

pillar 柱

pillar /'pɪlə(r)/ *noun* 名词
a tall strong piece of stone, wood or metal that holds up a building 柱子；支柱

pillar box /'pɪlə bɒks/ *noun* 名词 (*plural* 复数形式 **pillar boxes**) (*British* 英式英语)
a tall red box in the street for sending letters 邮筒；信筒 ➜ SAME MEANING **postbox** 同义词为 postbox

pillow /'pɪləʊ/ *noun* 名词
a soft thing that you put your head on when you are in bed 枕头

pillowcase /'pɪləʊkeɪs/ *noun* 名词
a cover for a PILLOW 枕套

pilot ০━ /'paɪlət/ *noun* 名词
a person who flies a plane 飞行员 ➜ Look at Picture Dictionary page **P12**. 见彩页 P12。

pimple /'pɪmpl/ *noun* 名词
a small spot on your skin 丘疹；粉刺

pins 针

drawing pin (*British* 英式英语)
thumbtack (*American* 美式英语) 图钉

pin 大头针   **safety pin** 安全别针

pin¹ ০━ /pɪn/ *noun* 名词
a small thin piece of metal with a flat part at one end and a sharp point at the other. You use a **pin** for holding things together or fixing one thing to another. 大头针 ➜ Look also at **drawing pin** and **safety pin**. 亦见 drawing pin 和 safety pin。

pin² /pɪn/ *verb* 动词 (**pins, pinning, pinned** /pɪnd/)
1 to fix things together with a pin or pins （用大头针）钉住，别住：*Could you pin this notice to the board?* 你把这份通知钉在布告板上好吗？
2 to hold somebody or something so that they cannot move 按住，压住（使不能动弹）：*He tried to get away, but they pinned him against the wall.* 他想逃走，可是他们把他紧按在墙上。

pinch 捏

pinch¹ /pɪntʃ/ *verb* 动词 (**pinches, pinching, pinched** /pɪntʃt/)
1 to press somebody's skin tightly between your thumb and finger 拧；捏；掐：*Don't pinch me – it hurts!* 别拧我，很疼的！
2 (*British* 英式英语) (*informal* 非正式) to steal something 偷：*Who's pinched my pen?* 谁偷了我的笔？

pinch² /pɪntʃ/ *noun* 名词 (*plural* 复数形式 **pinches**)
1 the act of pressing somebody's skin tightly between your thumb and finger 拧；捏；掐：*He gave me a pinch on the arm to wake me up.* 他拧了一下我的胳膊来弄醒我。
2 an amount of something you can hold between your thumb and finger 一撮：*Add a pinch of salt to the soup.* 往汤里加一撮盐。

pine /paɪn/ (*also* 亦作 **pine tree** /'paɪn triː/) *noun* 名词
a tall tree with thin sharp leaves (called **needles**) that do not fall off in winter 松树

pineapple /'paɪnæpl/ *noun* 名词
a big fruit that is yellow inside and has a rough brown skin 菠萝；凤梨 ➜ Look at Picture Dictionary page **P8**. 见彩页 P8。

ping-pong /'pɪŋ pɒŋ/ *noun* 名词 (*no plural* 不用复数形式)
a game where players hit a small light ball over a net on a big table 乒乓球运动 ➜ SAME MEANING **table tennis** 同义词为 table tennis

pink ০━ /pɪŋk/ *adjective* 形容词
with a light red colour 粉红色的：*a pink jumper* 粉红色的套头毛衣
▶ **pink** *noun* 名词 (*no plural* 不用复数形式)：*She was dressed in pink.* 她穿着一身粉红色的衣服。

pins and needles /,pɪnz ən 'niːdlz/ *noun* 名词 (*plural* 用复数形式)
a feeling that you sometimes get in a part of your body when you have not moved it

for a long time （身体某部位长时间保持一种姿势后产生的）发麻，麻木

pint /paɪnt/ (*abbr.* 缩略式 **pt**) *noun* 名词
a measure of liquid (= 0.57 litres). There are eight **pints** in a **gallon**. 品脱（容量单位）；1 品脱等于 0.57 升，8 品脱等于 1 加仑：*a pint of beer* 一品脱啤酒 ◇ *two pints of milk* 两品脱牛奶

> 🔎 **CULTURE** 文化资料补充
>
> In the past, people in Britain used **pints** and **gallons** to measure liquids, not **litres**. Nowadays, most people use and understand both ways. 在过去，英国人用品脱（pint）和加仑（gallon）来量液体，不用升（litre）。现在大多数人两种单位都使用。
> People in the US still use **pints** and **gallons**. (But note that an American **pint** = 0.47 litres.) 美国人仍使用品脱（pint）和加仑（gallon）。（但要注意美国的 1 品脱等于 0.47 升。）

pioneer /ˌpaɪəˈnɪə(r)/ *noun* 名词
a person who goes somewhere or does something before other people 拓荒者；先锋；先驱：*the pioneers of the American West* 美国西部的开拓者

pip /pɪp/ *noun* 名词 (*British* 英式英语)
the seed of some fruits. Lemons, oranges and apples have **pips**. （某些水果的）核，籽，种子 ➷ Look at Picture Dictionary page **P8**. 见彩页 P8.

pipe ⚪/paɪp/ *noun* 名词
1 a long tube that takes something such as water, oil or gas from one place to another 管道；管子：*A water pipe is leaking under the ground.* 一根水管在地下漏着水。
2 a tube with a small bowl at one end that is used for smoking TOBACCO (= the dried leaves used for making cigarettes) 烟斗；烟袋：*My grandfather smoked a pipe.* 我祖父以前抽烟斗。

pipeline /ˈpaɪplaɪn/ *noun* 名词
a line of pipes that carry oil or gas a long way 输送管道
in the pipeline Something that is **in the pipeline** is being planned or prepared and will happen soon. 在规划（或筹备）中

pirate /ˈpaɪrət/ *noun* 名词
a person on a ship who robs other ships 海盗

pistol /ˈpɪstl/ *noun* 名词
a small gun 手枪

pit /pɪt/ *noun* 名词
1 a deep hole in the ground （地面上的）洞，坑，井
2 a deep hole that people make in the ground to take out coal 煤矿 ➷ SAME MEANING **mine** 同义词为 mine

pitch¹ /pɪtʃ/ *noun* 名词
1 (*plural* 复数形式 **pitches**) a piece of ground where you play games like football 场地；球场：*a cricket pitch* 板球场

> 🔎 **WORD BUILDING** 词汇扩充
>
> You also play **hockey** and **rugby** on a **pitch**. * pitch 亦指曲棍球场和橄榄球场。
> You play **badminton** and **tennis** on a **court**. 羽毛球场和网球场用 court。

2 (*no plural* 不用复数形式) how high or low a sound is 音高

pitch² /pɪtʃ/ *verb* 动词 (**pitches**, **pitching**, **pitched** /pɪtʃt/)
to put up a tent 搭（帐篷）；扎（营）：*We pitched our tent under a big tree.* 我们在一棵大树下搭起了帐篷。

pitcher /ˈpɪtʃə(r)/ *American English for* JUG 美式英语，即 jug

pity¹ ⚪/ˈpɪti/ *noun* 名词 (*no plural* 不用复数形式)
1 a feeling of sadness for a person or an animal who is in pain or who has problems 可怜；同情；怜悯：*I feel no pity for him – it's his own fault.* 我不可怜他——他这是自作自受。
2 something that makes you feel a little sad or disappointed 可惜；遗憾 ➷ SAME MEANING **shame** 同义词为 shame：*It's a pity you can't come to the party.* 你不能来参加聚会，真可惜。
take pity on somebody to help somebody because you feel sad for them 可怜；同情；怜悯：*I took pity on her and gave her some money.* 我可怜她，就给了她一些钱。

pity² /ˈpɪti/ *verb* 动词 (**pities**, **pitying**, **pitied** /ˈpɪtid/, **has pitied**)
to feel sad for somebody who is in pain or who has problems 可怜；同情；怜悯：*I really pity people who haven't got anywhere to live.* 我非常同情那些无家可归的人。

pizza /ˈpiːtsə/ *noun* 名词 (*plural* 复数形式 **pizzas**)
a flat round piece of bread with tomatoes, cheese and other things on top, that is cooked in an oven 比萨饼

⟳ Look at Picture Dictionary page **P7**. 见彩页 P7。

place¹ /pleɪs/ *noun* 名词
1 a particular area or position 地方；位置；地点： *Put the book back in the right place.* 把书放回原处。
2 a particular building, town or country 地方（指建筑物、城镇或国家）： *Budapest is a very interesting place.* 布达佩斯是一个很有意思的地方。◇ *Do you know a good place to have lunch?* 你能介绍个好地方吃午饭吗？
3 a seat or space for one person 座位；位置： *An old man was sitting in my place.* 有个老人坐在我的位子上。
4 the position that you have in a race, competition or test（赛跑、竞赛或测验的）名次： *Alice finished in second place.* 艾丽斯得了第二名。
in place where it should be; in the right place 归位；在正确位置： *Use tape to hold the picture in place.* 用胶带固定这幅画的位置。
in place of somebody or 或 **something** instead of somebody or something 代替；取代： *You can use milk in place of cream.* 你可以用牛奶代替奶油。
take place to happen 发生；进行： *The wedding of John and Sara will take place on 22 May.* 约翰和萨拉的婚礼将于 5 月 22 日举行。

place² /pleɪs/ *verb* 动词 (places, placing, placed /pleɪst/) (*formal* 正式)
to put something somewhere 放置；安放： *The waiter placed the meal in front of me.* 服务员把饭菜放在我的面前。

plague /pleɪɡ/ *noun* 名词
a disease that spreads quickly and kills many people 瘟疫；死亡率高的传染病

plain¹ /pleɪn/ *adjective* 形容词 (plainer, plainest)
1 easy to see, hear or understand 清楚的；明显的；浅白的 ⟳ SAME MEANING **clear** 同义词为 clear： *It's plain that he's unhappy.* 他显然很不高兴。
2 simple and ordinary 简单的；朴素的： *plain food* 清淡的食物
3 with no pattern; all one colour 无花纹的；单色的： *She wore a plain blue dress.* 她穿了一条净蓝色连衣裙。
4 not pretty 相貌平庸的： *She was a plain child.* 她是个相貌平平的孩子。

plain² /pleɪn/ *noun* 名词
a large piece of flat land 平原

plainly /'pleɪnli/ *adverb* 副词
in a way that is easy to see, hear or understand 清楚地；明显地 ⟳ SAME MEANING **clearly** 同义词为 clearly： *They were plainly very angry.* 他们显然很生气。

plait /plæt/ (*British* 英式英语) (*American* 美式英语 **braid**) *noun* 名词
a long piece of hair that somebody has divided into three parts and put over and under each other 发辫；辫子： *She wears her hair in plaits.* 她梳着辫子。 ⟳ Look at the picture at **hair**. 见 hair 的插图。
▶ **plait** *verb* 动词 (plaits, plaiting, plaited)： *She plaited her hair.* 她把头发编成辫子。

plan¹ /plæn/ *noun* 名词
1 something that you have decided to do and how you are going to do it 计划；打算： *What are your holiday plans?* 你假期准备怎么过？◇ *They have plans to build a new school.* 他们计划修建一所新学校。
2 a map showing a building or a town（建筑物或城镇的）详图： *a street plan of London* 伦敦街道图
3 a drawing that shows how a new building, room or machine will be made 设计图；平面图： *Have you seen the plans for the new shopping centre?* 你看过新购物中心的设计图吗？

plan² /plæn/ *verb* 动词 (plans, planning, planned /plænd/)
to decide what you are going to do and how you are going to do it 计划；筹划： *They're planning a holiday in Australia next summer.* 他们正在计划明年夏天去澳大利亚度假。◇ *I'm planning to go to university.* 我打算上大学。

plane /pleɪn/ *noun* 名词 (*British also* 英式英语亦作 **aeroplane**) (*American* 美式英语 **airplane**)
a vehicle with wings that can fly through the air 飞机： *I like travelling by plane.* 我喜欢坐飞机出行。◇ *What time does your plane land?* 你的飞机什么时候降落？◇ *Our plane took off three hours late.* 我们的航班延误了三小时才起飞。◇ *I caught the next plane to Dublin.* 我赶上了下一班飞机去都柏林。

> 🔎 **WORD BUILDING** 词汇扩充
> A plane **lands** and **takes off** at an **airport**. 飞机在机场（airport）降落（land）和起飞（take off）。

⟳ Look at Picture Dictionary page **P1**. 见彩页 P1。

planet /'plænɪt/ *noun* 名词
a large round object in space that moves

A
B
C
D
E
F
G
H
I
J
K
L
M
N
O
P
Q
R
S
T
U
V
W
X
Y
Z

around the sun or another star 行星: *Earth, Mars and Venus are planets.* 地球、火星和金星是行星。

plank /plæŋk/ *noun* 名词
a long flat piece of wood 木板；板条

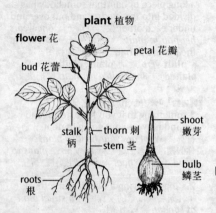

plant 植物
flower 花
petal 花瓣
bud 花蕾
stalk 柄
thorn 刺
stem 茎
shoot 嫩芽
roots 根
bulb 鳞茎

plant¹ 0🔑 /plɑːnt/ *noun* 名词
anything that grows from the ground 植物: *Don't forget to water the plants.* 别忘了给植物浇水。

> 🔎 **WORD BUILDING** 词汇扩充
> There are many different types of **plant**. Here are some of them: bamboo, cactus, grass, moss, seaweed, tree. Do you know any others? * plant 的种类很多，如: bamboo（竹）、cactus（仙人掌）、grass（草）、moss（苔藓）、seaweed（海藻）、tree（树）。你还知道别的吗?

plant² 0🔑 /plɑːnt/ *verb* 动词 (plants, planting, planted)
to put plants or seeds in the ground 种植；栽种: *We planted some roses in the garden.* 我们在花园里种了些玫瑰。

plantation /plɑːnˈteɪʃn/ *noun* 名词
a piece of land where things like tea, bananas or rubber grow 种植园: *a sugar plantation* 甘蔗种植园

plaster¹ /ˈplɑːstə(r)/ *noun* 名词
1 (*no plural* 不用复数形式) a substance that is used for covering walls inside buildings 灰泥；灰浆
2 (*no plural* 不用复数形式) a hard covering around a broken bone; the substance that the covering is made of 熟石膏: *My leg was in plaster.* 我的腿打了石膏。

3 (*plural* 复数形式 **plasters**) (*British* 英式英语) (*American* 美式英语 **Band-Aid™**) a small piece of sticky material that you put over a cut on your body to keep it clean 膏药；创可贴

bandage 绷带
plaster 创可贴
sling 悬带
crutch 腋杖
plaster 石膏

plaster² /ˈplɑːstə(r)/ *verb* 动词 (plasters, plastering, plastered)
1 to cover a wall with PLASTER¹ (1) to make it smooth 在…上抹灰泥
2 to cover a surface with a large amount of something 用…涂抹: *She plastered herself in suntan lotion.* 她往身上抹了防晒露。

plastic 0🔑 /ˈplæstɪk/ *noun* 名词
(*no plural* 不用复数形式)
an artificial material that is used for making many different things 塑料；塑胶: *These chairs are made of plastic.* 这些椅子是塑料制的。 ◊ *plastic cups* 塑料杯

plastic surgery /ˌplæstɪk ˈsɜːdʒəri/ *noun* 名词 (*no plural* 不用复数形式)
medical operations that doctors can do to improve a person's appearance 整容手术；整形外科

plate 盘子

plate 0🔑 /pleɪt/ *noun* 名词
a round dish that you put food on 盘子；碟子 ⊃ Look also at **number plate**. 亦见 number plate。

platform 0🔑 /ˈplætfɔːm/ *noun* 名词
1 the part of a railway station where

people get on and off trains 站台；月台： *The train to London leaves from platform 5.* 往伦敦的列车从 5 号站台开出。

2 a surface that is higher than the floor, where people stand so that other people can see and hear them 讲台；舞台： *The headmaster went up to the platform to make his speech.* 校长走上了讲台讲话。

play[1] 🔑 /pleɪ/ ***verb*** 动词 (**plays, playing, played** /pleɪd/)

1 to have fun; to do something to enjoy yourself 玩；玩耍： *The children were **playing with** their toys.* 孩子在玩玩具。

2 to take part in a game 参加游戏（或运动）；和…比赛： *I like playing tennis.* 我喜欢打网球。◇ *Do you know how to play chess?* 你会下棋吗？

3 to make music with a musical instrument 演奏；弹奏；吹奏： *My sister plays the piano very well.* 我姐姐钢琴弹得很好。

> **GRAMMAR** 语法说明
> Note that we usually say 'play **the** violin, **the** piano, etc.'. 注意：通常说 play the violin、the piano 等（乐器前要加 the）： *I'm learning to play the clarinet.* 我在学吹单簧管。

4 to put a record, CD, DVD, etc. in a machine and listen to it 播放： *Shall I play the CD again?* 我把 CD 再放一遍好吗？

5 to act the part of somebody in a play 扮演（角色）： *Who wants to play the policeman?* 谁想演警察？

play[2] 🔑 /pleɪ/ ***noun*** 名词

1 (*plural* 复数形式 **plays**) a story that you watch in the theatre or on television, or listen to on the radio 戏剧： *We went to see a play at the National Theatre.* 我们去国家大剧院看了出戏剧。

2 (*no plural* 不用复数形式) games; what children do for fun 游戏；玩耍： *work and play* 工作和耍乐

> **GRAMMAR** 语法说明
> Be careful! We **play** football, cards, etc. or we **have a game of** football, cards, etc. (NOT **a play**). 注意：可以说 play football、cards 等或 have a game of football、cards 等（不说 have a play）。

player 🔑 /ˈpleɪə(r)/ ***noun*** 名词

1 a person who plays a game 游戏者；运动员： *football players* 足球运动员

2 a person who plays a musical instrument（乐器的）演奏者： *a trumpet player* 小号手

playful /ˈpleɪfl/ ***adjective*** 形容词
full of fun; not serious 有趣的；爱玩的；闹着玩的： *a playful puppy* 顽皮的小狗 ◇ *a playful remark* 戏言

playground /ˈpleɪɡraʊnd/ ***noun*** 名词
an area where children can play, for example at school（儿童）游乐场，游戏场，操场

playing cards 纸牌

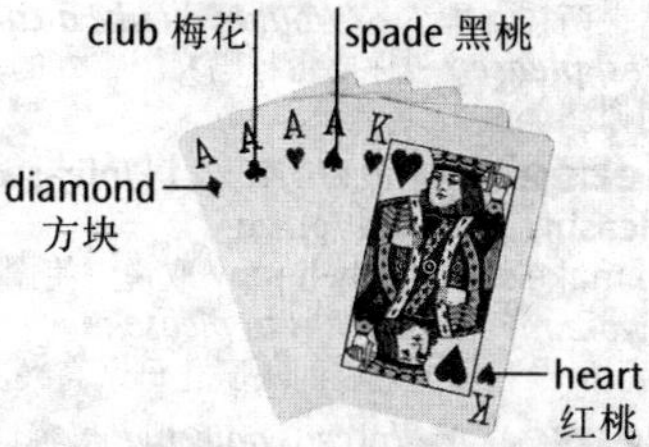
club 梅花
spade 黑桃
diamond 方块
heart 红桃

playing card /ˈpleɪɪŋ kɑːd/ (*also* 亦作 **card**) ***noun*** 名词
one of a set of 52 cards with numbers and pictures on them that you use for playing games 纸牌；扑克牌： *a pack of playing cards* 一副纸牌

playing field /ˈpleɪɪŋ fiːld/ ***noun*** 名词
a large area of grass where people play sports like football 球场；运动场

playtime /ˈpleɪtaɪm/ ***noun*** 名词 (*British* 英式英语) (*American* 美式英语 **recess**)
the time at school between lessons when you can go out and play（学校的）游戏时间，课间休息时间： *She fell over at **playtime**.* 她在课间休息的时候摔了一跤。

plea /pliː/ ***noun*** 名词
asking for something with strong feeling 请求；恳求： *He made a **plea for** help.* 他恳求帮助。

plead /pliːd/ ***verb*** 动词 (**pleads, pleading, pleaded**, *American also* 美式英语亦作 **pled** /pled/)

1 to ask for something in a very strong way 恳求；乞求： *He **pleaded with** his parents **to** buy him a guitar.* 他央求父母给他买把吉他。

2 to say in a court of law that you did or did not do a crime（在法庭上）申辩，辩护： *She pleaded not guilty to murder.* 她不承认犯了谋杀罪。

A B C D E F G H I J K L M N O **P** Q R S T U V W X Y Z

pleasant ☞ /'pleznt/ *adjective* 形容词
nice, enjoyable or friendly 宜人的；
令人愉快的；友好的: *The weather here is very pleasant.* 这里的天气十分宜人。◇ *He's a very pleasant person.* 他为人很友善。
➲ OPPOSITE **unpleasant** 反义词为 unpleasant
▶ **pleasantly** /'plezntli/ *adverb* 副词:
a pleasantly cool room 凉爽宜人的房间

please¹ ☞ /pli:z/ *exclamation* 感叹词
a word that you use when you ask for something politely（表示礼貌地请求）请，请问: *What's the time, please?* 请问现在几点了？◇ *Two cups of coffee, please.* 请来两杯咖啡。◇ *'Would you like a cake?' 'Yes, please.'* "你要蛋糕吗？""好的，谢谢。"

please² ☞ /pli:z/ *verb* 动词 (pleases, pleasing, pleased /pli:zd/)
to make somebody happy 取悦；使愉快: *I wore my best clothes to please my mother.* 我穿上最好的衣服让母亲高兴。

pleased ☞ /pli:zd/ *adjective* 形容词
happy 高兴；满意: *He wasn't very pleased to see me.* 他并不那么乐意见我。◇ *Are you pleased with your new watch?* 你对新手表满意吗？➲ Look at the note at **glad**. 见 glad 条的注释。

pleasure ☞ /'pleʒə(r)/ *noun* 名词
1 (*no plural* 不用复数形式) the feeling of being happy or enjoying something 快乐；愉快；乐趣: *She gets a lot of pleasure from her music.* 她从自己的音乐中得到很多乐趣。
2 (*plural* 复数形式 pleasures) something that makes you happy 开心的事物；乐事: *It was a pleasure to meet you.* 很高兴和你见面。
it's a pleasure You say 'it's a pleasure' as a polite way of answering somebody who thanks you.（表示礼貌的答谢）不用客气: *'Thank you for your help.' 'It's a pleasure.'* "谢谢你的帮助。""不用客气。"
with pleasure You say 'with pleasure' to show in a polite way that you are happy to do something.（表示乐意做某事）没问题，很乐意: *'Can you help me move these boxes?' 'Yes, with pleasure.'* "你能帮我搬这些箱子吗？""好哇，问题。"

pleat /pli:t/ *noun* 名词
a fold that is part of a skirt, a pair of trousers, etc.（裙、裤等的）褶

pled /pled/ *American English for* PLEADED (*form of* PLEAD) 美式英语，即 pleaded（plead 的不同形式）

plenty ☞ /'plenti/ *pronoun* 代词
as much or as many as you need; a lot 大量；充足；很多: *'Do we need more chairs?' 'No, there are plenty.'* "我们还需要椅子吗？""不用了，已经够多了。"◇ *We've got plenty of time to get there.* 我们有充足的时间前往那里。

pliers /'plaɪəz/ *noun* 名词 (*plural* 用复数形式)
a tool for holding things tightly or for cutting wire 钳子；手钳: *Have you got a pair of pliers?* 你有钳子吗？

plod /plɒd/ *verb* 动词 (plods, plodding, plodded)
to walk slowly in a heavy tired way 艰难地行走: *We plodded up the hill in the rain.* 我们冒雨吃力地往山上走。

plot¹ /plɒt/ *noun* 名词
1 what happens in a story, play or film（故事、戏剧或电影的）情节，布局: *This book has a very exciting plot.* 这本书的情节非常紧张刺激。
2 a secret plan to do something bad 阴谋，密谋: *a plot to kill the President* 刺杀总统的阴谋
3 a small piece of land that you use or you plan to use for a special purpose（有特定用途的）小块土地: *She bought a small plot of land to build a house on.* 她买了一小块地来盖房子。◇ *a vegetable plot* 菜圃

plot² /plɒt/ *verb* 动词 (plots, plotting, plotted)
to make a secret plan to do something bad 密谋；暗中策划: *They plotted to rob the bank.* 他们秘密策划抢劫银行。

plough 犁

ox 公牛
plough 犁

plough (*British* 英式英语) (*American* 美式英语 plow) /plaʊ/ *noun* 名词
a large farm tool that is pulled across a field to dig the soil 犁
▶ **plough** *verb* 动词: *The farmer ploughed his fields.* 农夫把田地犁了。

pluck /plʌk/ *verb* 动词 (plucks, plucking, plucked /plʌkt/)
to remove something by pulling it quickly

拔掉；抢夺：*He **plucked** the letter from her hands.* 他从她手里把信抢了过来。◇ *We needed to **pluck** the chicken* (= remove its feathers). 我们得拔鸡毛了。

plugs 插头；塞子

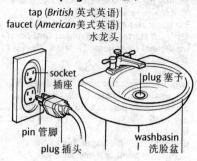

tap (*British* 英式英语)
faucet (*American* 美式英语)
水龙头

socket
插座

plug 塞子

pin 管脚

washbasin
洗脸盆

plug 插头

plug¹ /plʌg/ *noun* 名词
1 a thing with metal pins that joins a lamp, machine, etc. to a place in the wall (called a socket) where there is electricity 插头
2 a round thing that you put in the hole in a bath, to keep the water in （浴缸的）塞子

plug² /plʌg/ *verb* 动词 (plugs, plugging, plugged /plʌgd/)
to fill a hole, so that nothing can get out 堵塞，封堵（孔洞）：*He plugged the hole in the pipe with an old rag.* 他用旧破布堵住了管子上的洞。
plug something in to join a lamp, machine, etc. to the electricity, using a PLUG 把…插上电源；接通…的电源：*Can you plug in the television, please?* 请你把电视机插上电源好吗？ ◒ OPPOSITE **unplug** 反义词为 unplug

plughole /ˈplʌghəʊl/ (*British* 英式英语) *noun* 名词
a hole in a bath where water flows away （浴缸的）排水孔，漏眼

plum /plʌm/ *noun* 名词
a soft round fruit with a stone in the middle 李子；梅子 ◒ Look at Picture Dictionary page **P8**. 见彩页 P8。

plumber /ˈplʌmə(r)/ *noun* 名词
a person whose job is to put in and repair things like water pipes and baths 水暖工；管子工 ◒ Look at Picture Dictionary page **P12**. 见彩页 P12。

plumbing /ˈplʌmɪŋ/ *noun* 名词 (*no plural* 不用复数形式)

1 the pipes that carry water into and around a building （建筑物的）管道系统，自来水管道：*The builders are putting in the plumbing and central heating.* 建筑工人在安装自来水管道和中央供暖系统。
2 the work of a PLUMBER 水暖工程

plump /plʌmp/ *adjective* 形容词 (plumper, plumpest)
quite fat, in a nice way 胖乎乎的；丰满的：*a plump baby* 胖乎乎的婴儿

plunge /plʌndʒ/ *verb* 动词 (plunges, plunging, plunged /plʌndʒd/)
1 to jump or fall suddenly into something 突然跳进（或坠落）：*She plunged into the pool.* 她一头跳进了游泳池。
2 to push something suddenly and strongly into something else 把…猛力插入：*I plunged my hand into the water.* 我一下子把手伸进了水里。

plural ⟐ /ˈplʊərəl/ *noun* 名词
(*grammar* 语法) the form of a word that shows there is more than one 复数；复数形式：*The plural of 'child' is 'children'.* * child 的复数形式是 children。
▶ **plural** *adjective* 形容词：*Most plural nouns in English end in 's'.* 英语中的复数名词大多以 s 结尾。 ◒ OPPOSITE **singular** 反义词为 singular

plus /plʌs/ *preposition* 介词
added to; and 加；和：*Two plus three is five (2 + 3 = 5).* 二加三等于五。 ◇ *All of our class plus half of Class Four are going.* 我们班的所有同学和四班的一半同学都会去。 ◒ Look at **minus¹**. 见 minus¹。

p.m. /ˌpiː ˈem/ *abbreviation* 缩略式
You use **p.m.** after a time to show that it is between midday and midnight. 下午；午后：*The plane leaves at 3 p.m.* 飞机下午 3 点起飞。 ◇ We use **a.m.** for times between midnight and midday. 用 a.m. 表示上午。

pneumonia /njuːˈməʊniə/ *noun* 名词
(*no plural* 不用复数形式)
a serious illness of the LUNGS (= the parts of your body that you breathe with) 肺炎

poach /pəʊtʃ/ *verb* 动词 (poaches, poaching, poached /pəʊtʃt/)
1 to cook food gently in liquid 水煮；炖；煨：*I had a poached egg for breakfast.* 我早餐吃了个水煮蛋。
2 to kill and steal animals, birds or fish from another person's land 偷猎；偷捕
▶ **poacher** *noun* 名词 a person who kills or steals animals, etc. from another person's land 偷猎者：*The elephant had*

A

B

C

D

E

F

G

H

I

J

K

L

M

N

O

P

Q

R

S

T

U

V

W

X

Y

Z

been shot by poachers. 那头象被偷猎者射杀了。

PO Box /piː ˈəʊ bɒks/ *noun* 名词 (*plural* 复数形式 **PO Boxes**)
a box in a post office for keeping the letters of a person or office 邮政信箱：*The address is PO Box 63, Bristol BS7 1JN.* 地址是布里斯托尔 BS7 1JN，邮政信箱 63 号。

pocket 0̅ᴍ /ˈpɒkɪt/ *noun* 名词
the part of a piece of clothing that you can put things in 衣袋；口袋；兜：*I put the key in my pocket.* 我把钥匙放进口袋里了。○ Look at the picture at **shirt**. 见 shirt 的插图。

pick somebody's pocket to steal money from somebody's pocket or bag 扒窃

pocketbook /ˈpɒkɪtbʊk/ *American English for* WALLET 美式英语，即 wallet

pocket money /ˈpɒkɪt mʌni/ *noun* 名词
(*no plural* 不用复数形式)
money that parents give to a child each week to buy things 零花钱：*How much pocket money do you get?* 你有多少零花钱？

pod /pɒd/ *noun* 名词
a long thin case that some plants have, which is filled with seeds 荚；豆荚：*Peas grow in pods.* 豌豆长在荚里面。○ Look at Picture Dictionary page **P9**. 见彩页 P9。

poem 0̅ᴍ /ˈpəʊɪm/ *noun* 名词
words arranged in lines in an artistic way, often with sounds repeated at the ends of lines 诗；韵文：*He wrote poems about the beauty of the countryside.* 他曾写关于乡村美景的诗。

poet /ˈpəʊɪt/ *noun* 名词
a person who writes poems 诗人

poetic /pəʊˈetɪk/ *adjective* 形容词
like a poem 诗歌的；有诗意的：*poetic language* 诗歌语言

poetry 0̅ᴍ /ˈpəʊətri/ *noun* 名词
(*no plural* 不用复数形式)
poems（总称）诗歌，诗作：*Wordsworth wrote beautiful poetry.* 华兹华斯写下了优美的诗篇。

point¹ 0̅ᴍ /pɔɪnt/ *noun* 名词
1 a fact, an idea or an opinion 观点；见解：*You made some interesting points (= said some interesting things) in your essay.* 你在文章中提出了几个有趣的观点。○ Look at **point of view**. 见 point of view。

2 the purpose of, or the reason for, doing something 目的；意图；理由：*The point of going to school is to learn.* 上学的目的是为了学习。○ *What's the point of going to her house? She's not at home.* 去她家干什么？她又不在家。○ *There's no point in waiting for Julie – she isn't coming.* 没必要等朱莉了——她不来。

3 a particular moment in time 时刻；瞬间：*It started to rain and at that point we decided to go home.* 下起雨来了，我们就决定回家去。

4 a particular place 地方；地点：*No parking beyond this point.* 请勿越界停车。

5 a small round mark (.) that we use when writing part of a number (called a decimal) 小数点；点：*2.5 (= two point five)* * 2.5 点 5

6 the sharp end of something 尖端；尖头：*the point of a needle* 针尖

7 a mark that you win in a game or sport（游戏或体育运动的）得分，点：*Our team scored six points.* 我们队得了六分。

be on the point of doing something
If you **are on the point of doing something**, you are going to do it very soon. 正要做某事：*I was on the point of leaving when he turned up.* 他来到的时候我正要离开。

point² 0̅ᴍ /pɔɪnt/ *verb* 动词 (**points, pointing, pointed**)
1 to show where something is using your finger, a stick, etc.（用手指、木棍等）指，指向：*I asked him where the bank was and he pointed across the road.* 我问他银行在哪里，他朝马路的对面指了指。○ *There was a sign pointing towards the city centre.* 有个指向市中心的路标。

2 to hold something towards somebody or something 瞄准：*She was pointing a gun at his head.* 她用枪瞄准他的头。

point something out to tell or show somebody something 指出：*Eva pointed out that my bag was open.* 伊娃指出我的包打开了。

pointed 0̅ᴍ /ˈpɔɪntɪd/ *adjective* 形容词
with a sharp end 尖的；有尖头的：*a long pointed nose* 又长又尖的鼻子

pointless /ˈpɔɪntləs/ *adjective* 形容词
with no use or purpose 无用的；无意义的；徒劳的：*It's pointless telling Paul anything – he never listens.* 跟保罗说什么都没用，他根本不听。

point of view /ˌpɔɪnt əv ˈvjuː/ (*plural* 复数形式 **points of view**) *noun* 名词
an opinion or way of thinking about something 观点；看法；视角：*The book*

*was written **from** the father's **point of view**.*
这本书是从父亲的角度来写的。

poison¹ 0ᵤ /'pɔɪzn/ *noun* 名词
(*no plural* 不用复数形式)
something that will kill you or make you
very ill if you eat or drink it 毒药；有毒
物质：*rat poison* 老鼠药

poison² 0ᵤ /'pɔɪzn/ *verb* 动词 (poisons,
poisoning, poisoned /'pɔɪznd/)
to use **poison** to kill or hurt somebody or
something 毒死；毒害

poisonous 0ᵤ /'pɔɪzənəs/ *adjective*
形容词
Something that is **poisonous** will kill you
or make you very ill if you eat or drink it.
有毒的；导致中毒的：*Some mushrooms
are poisonous.* 有些蘑菇有毒。

poke 探

poke /pəʊk/ *verb* 动词 (pokes, poking,
poked /pəʊkt/)
1 to push somebody or something hard
with your finger or another long thin
thing (用手指或细长物体)捅，戳 *She
poked me in the eye with a pencil.* 她用
铅笔戳了我的眼睛。
2 to push something quickly somewhere
推；捅；探 *Jeff poked his head out of
the window.* 杰夫把头探出了窗外。
▸ **poke** *noun* 名词：*I gave her a poke to
wake her up.* 我捅了她一下把她叫醒。

poker /'pəʊkə(r)/ *noun* 名词
1 (*no plural* 不用复数形式) a game that
people play with cards, usually for money
扑克牌游戏
2 (*plural* 复数形式 pokers) a metal stick
that you use for moving the wood in a
fire 通条；拨火棍 ⊃ Look at the picture at
fireplace. 见 fireplace 的插图。

polar /'pəʊlə(r)/ *adjective* 形容词
connected with the areas around the top
and bottom of the earth (called the **North
Pole** and the **South Pole**) 极地的；北极
（或南极）的：*the polar regions* 极地地区

polar bear /ˌpəʊlə 'beə(r)/ *noun* 名词
a large white animal that lives near the

North Pole 北极熊；白熊 ⊃ Look at
Picture Dictionary page **P3**. 见彩页 P3。

pole /pəʊl/ *noun* 名词
1 a long thin piece of wood or metal.
Poles are often used to hold something
up. 杆子；柱子；棍：*a flag pole* 旗杆 ◇
tent poles 帐篷支柱 ⊃ Look at the picture
at **ski**. 见 ski 的插图。
2 one of two places at the top and
bottom of the earth 地极：*the North Pole*
北极 ◇ *the South Pole* 南极

police 0ᵤ /pə'liːs/ *noun* 名词 (*plural*
用复数形式)
the official organization whose job is to
make sure that people do not break the
laws of a country 警察部门；警方：*Have
the police found the murderer?* 警方找到
杀人凶手了吗？◇ *a police car* 警车

police constable /pəˌliːs 'kʌnstəbl/
(*abbr.* 缩略式 **PC**) *noun* 名词
an ordinary police officer 警员；警察：
PC Nolan 警员诺兰

police force /pə'liːs fɔːs/ *noun* 名词
all the police officers in a country or part
of a country 警力；警察部队

policeman /pə'liːsmən/ *noun* 名词
(*plural* 复数形式 policemen /pə'liːsmən/)
a man who is a police officer （男）警察
⊃ Look at Picture Dictionary page **P12**.
见彩页 P12。

police officer /pə'liːs ɒfɪsə(r)/ *noun*
名词
a man or woman who works in the police
警察

police station /pə'liːs steɪʃn/ *noun* 名词
an office where police officers work
警察局；派出所：*They took the men to
the police station for questioning.* 他们把
那些人带往警察局盘问。

policewoman /pə'liːswʊmən/ *noun*
名词 (*plural* 复数形式 policewomen)
a woman who is a police officer 女警察

policy /'pɒləsi/ *noun* 名词 (*plural* 复数形式
policies)
the plans of a government or
organization 政策；方针：*What is the
government's **policy** on education?* 政府的
教育政策是怎样的？

polish¹ /'pɒlɪʃ/ *noun* 名词 (*no plural* 不用
复数形式)
a cream or liquid that you put on
something to make it shine 擦光剂；
上光剂；亮光剂：*furniture polish* 家具
上光剂

polish² /'pɒlɪʃ/ *verb* 动词 (polishes, polishing, polished /'pɒlɪʃt/)
to rub something so that it shines 擦亮；磨光: *Have you polished your shoes?* 你把鞋子擦了吗?

polite ○━ /pə'laɪt/ *adjective* 形容词
speaking or behaving in a way that shows respect 有礼貌的；客气的: *It is polite to say 'please' when you ask for something.* 有求于别人的时候，说声"请"才算有礼貌。 ⊃ OPPOSITE **impolite** or **rude** 反义词为 impolite 或 rude
▸ **politely** /pə'laɪtli/ *adverb* 副词: *He asked politely for a glass of water.* 他礼貌地要了一杯水。
▸ **politeness** /pə'laɪtnəs/ *noun* 名词 (*no plural* 不用复数形式): *He stood up out of politeness and offered her his seat.* 他出于礼貌站了起来，把座位让给她。

political ○━ /pə'lɪtɪkl/ *adjective* 形容词
connected with politics or the government 政治的；政府的: *political parties* 政党 ◇ *his political beliefs* 他的政治信仰
▸ **politically** /pə'lɪtɪkli/ *adverb* 副词: *a politically powerful country* 政治强国

politician ○━ /ˌpɒlə'tɪʃn/ *noun* 名词
a person who works in politics 从政者；政治人物: *Politicians of all parties supported us.* 所有党派的政治人物都支持我们。

politics ○━ /'pɒlətɪks/ *noun* 名词
(*no plural* 不用复数形式)
1 the work and ideas that are connected with government 政治；政务: *Are you interested in politics?* 你对政治感兴趣吗?
2 the study of government 政治学: *She studied Politics at university.* 她在大学读政治学。 ⊃ Look at the notes at **congress**, **election** and **party**. 见 congress、election 和 party 条的注释。

poll /pəʊl/ *noun* 名词
1 a way of discovering opinions by asking a group of people questions 民意测验；民意调查: *A recent poll showed that 73% were unhappy with the government.* 最近的一次民意调查显示，有 73% 的人对政府不满意。
2 an election; the number of votes in an election 选举投票；投票数: *The country will go to the polls* (= vote) *in June.* 该国将在六月举行选举。

pollen /'pɒlən/ *noun* 名词 (*no plural* 不用复数形式)
the yellow powder in flowers that is taken to other flowers by insects or by the wind 花粉

pollute /pə'luːt/ *verb* 动词 (pollutes, polluting, polluted)
to make the air, rivers, etc. dirty and dangerous 污染: *Many of Britain's rivers are polluted with chemicals from factories.* 英国很多河流都遭工厂排出的化学物污染。

pollution /pə'luːʃn/ *noun* 名词 (*no plural* 不用复数形式)
1 the action of making the air, rivers, etc. dirty and dangerous 污染: *We must stop the pollution of our beaches.* 我们必须制止海滩的污染。
2 dirty and dangerous chemicals, gases, etc. that harm the environment 污染物

polystyrene /ˌpɒli'staɪriːn/ *noun* 名词 (*no plural* 不用复数形式)
soft white plastic that is used for packing things so that they do not get broken 聚苯乙烯（作包装物品用）

pond /pɒnd/ *noun* 名词
a small area of water 池塘: *We have a fish pond in our garden.* 我们花园里有个鱼塘。

pony /'pəʊni/ *noun* 名词 (*plural* 复数形式 ponies)
a small horse 小型马；矮种马

ponytail /'pəʊniteɪl/ *noun* 名词
long hair that you tie at the back of your head so that it hangs down 马尾辫 ⊃ Look at the picture at **hair**. 见 hair 的插图。

pool¹ ○━ /puːl/ *noun* 名词
1 (*also* 亦作 **swimming pool**) a place that has been built for people to swim in 游泳池: *Karen dived into the pool.* 卡伦一头跳进了泳池。
2 a small area of liquid or light on the ground 一摊（液体）；一小片（光）: *She was lying in a pool of blood.* 她倒在血泊之中。

pool² /puːl/ *verb* 动词 (pools, pooling, pooled /puːld/)
to collect money or ideas together from different people 收集，集中（钱或想法）: *First we'll work in pairs, then we'll pool our ideas.* 我们先两人一组分头工作，然后大家一起集思广益。

poor ○━ /pɔː(r)/ *adjective* 形容词 (poorer, poorest)
1 with very little money 贫穷的；贫困的: *She was too poor to buy clothes for her children.* 她穷得没钱给孩子买衣服。 ◇

*She gave her life to helping **the poor*** (= poor people). 她一生致力于帮助穷人。 ⊃ The noun is **poverty**. 名词为 poverty。 ⊃ OPPOSITE **rich** 反义词为 rich

2 a word that you use when you feel sad because somebody has problems （表示怜悯）可怜的，不幸的: *Poor Tina! She's feeling ill.* 可怜的蒂娜！她感到不舒服。

3 bad 不好的；差的；次的: *My grandfather is in very poor health.* 我祖父身体很差。

poorly¹ /'pɔːli/ *adverb* 副词 badly 差劲地；糟糕地: *The street is poorly lit.* 这条街道的光线很暗。

poorly² /'pɔːli/ *adjective* 形容词 (*British* 英式英语) (*informal* 非正式) ill 不适；不舒服: *She felt poorly.* 她感到不舒服。

pop¹ /pɒp/ *noun* 名词
1 (*no plural* 不用复数形式) (*also* 亦作 **pop music**) modern music that is most popular among young people 流行音乐: *What's your favourite **pop group**?* 你最喜欢的流行乐队是哪个？ ◇ *a pop singer* 流行歌手

2 (*plural* 复数形式 **pops**) a short sharp sound 砰；啪；噗: *The cork came out of the bottle with a loud pop.* 瓶塞砰的一声进了出来。

pop² /pɒp/ *verb* 动词 (**pops, popping, popped** /pɒpt/)
1 to burst, or to make something burst, with a short sharp sound （使）爆破，发爆破声: *The balloon will pop if you put a pin in it.* 气球用针一戳就会爆。

2 to come or go somewhere quickly 匆匆来（或去）: *She's just popped out to the shops.* 她刚匆匆去了商店。

3 to put something somewhere quickly （迅速地）放，搁: *Katie **popped** a sweet **into** her mouth.* 凯蒂一下子把糖果放进嘴里了。

pop in to make a short visit 短暂到访: *We were near Tim's house so we **popped in** for a cup of coffee.* 我们在蒂姆家附近，于是进了他家喝杯咖啡。

pop up (*informal* 非正式) to appear suddenly 突然出现: *The menu pops up when you double-click on the link.* 双击这个链接，选单就会弹出来。 ◇ *New restaurants were popping up everywhere.* 一下子到处都开了新餐馆。

popcorn /'pɒpkɔːn/ *noun* 名词 (*no plural* 不用复数形式) light white balls of cooked grain (from a plant called maize), which are covered in salt or sugar 爆（玉）米花

pope /pəʊp/ *noun* 名词 the head of the Roman Catholic Church （罗马天主教）教宗，教皇: *Pope Benedict* 教宗本笃

Popsicle™ /'pɒpsɪkl/ *American English for* ICE LOLLY 美式英语，即 ice lolly

popular ⊶ /'pɒpjələ(r)/ *adjective* 形容词 liked by a lot of people 受欢迎的；流行的；当红的: *Football is a popular sport in Britain.* 足球运动在英国很受欢迎。 ⊃ OPPOSITE **unpopular** 反义词为 unpopular

popularity /ˌpɒpju'lærəti/ *noun* 名词 (*no plural* 不用复数形式) being liked by many people 受欢迎；普及；流行

population /ˌpɒpju'leɪʃn/ *noun* 名词 the number of people who live in a place 人口: *What is the population of your country?* 你们国家人口有多少？

porch /pɔːtʃ/ *noun* 名词
1 (*British* 英式英语) a small area at the door of a house or a church, that is covered by a roof and often has walls （房屋或教堂的）门廊，门厅

2 *American English for* VERANDA 美式英语，即 veranda

pork /pɔːk/ *noun* 名词 (*no plural* 不用复数形式) meat from a pig 猪肉: *pork sausages* 猪肉香肠 ⊃ Look at the note at **pig**. 见 pig 条的注释。

porridge /'pɒrɪdʒ/ *noun* 名词 (*no plural* 不用复数形式) a soft food made by boiling grain with liquid 麦片粥: *porridge oats* 燕麦粥

port ⊶ /pɔːt/ *noun* 名词 a town or city by the sea, where ships arrive and leave 港口城市；港市: *Liverpool is a large port in the North of England.* 利物浦是英格兰北部一个大的港口城市。

portable /'pɔːtəbl/ *adjective* 形容词 able to be moved or carried easily 便携的；手提的: *a portable television* 便携式电视机

porter /'pɔːtə(r)/ *noun* 名词
1 a person whose job is to carry people's bags in places like railway stations and hotels （火车站、旅馆等的）行李员，搬运工

2 (*British* 英式英语) a person whose job is to look after the entrance of a hotel or

A
B
C
D
E
F
G
H
I
J
K
L
M
N
O
P
Q
R
S
T
U
V
W
X
Y
Z

other large building（旅馆或大型建筑物的）门卫，门房

portion /'pɔːʃn/ *noun* 名词
a part of something that one person gets 部分；一份：*He gave a **portion** of the money to each of his children.* 他给他的孩子每人一部分钱。◊ *a large **portion** of chips* 一大份薯条

portrait /'pɔːtreɪt/ *noun* 名词
a painting or picture of a person 肖像；画像

posh /pɒʃ/ *adjective* 形容词 (posher, poshest)
1 expensive and of good quality 豪华的：*a **posh** restaurant* 豪华的餐馆
2 (*British* 英式英语) connected with a high social class, in a way that ordinary people do not like 上流社会的；上等人的：*They thought she was too **posh**.* 他们认为她上等阶层的作风太明显了。

position 0┐ /pə'zɪʃn/ *noun* 名词
1 the place where somebody or something is 位置：*Can you show me the **position** of your village on the map?* 你能指给我看你们村在地图上的位置吗？◊ *Is everyone **in position** (= in the right place)?* 大家都各就各位了吗？
2 the way that somebody or something is sitting, standing, facing, etc. 姿势；摆放方位：*She was still sitting in the same **position** when I came back.* 我回来的时候，她还是同一个姿势坐着。◊ *Keep the box in an upright **position**.* 把箱子竖着放。
3 how things are at a certain time 处境；局面；状况：*He's in a difficult **position** – he hasn't got enough money to finish his studies.* 他身处困境，没有足够的钱来完成学业。
4 a job 职位；职务：*There have been over a hundred applications for the **position** of Sales Manager.* 已有一百多人申请销售经理一职。

positive 0┐ /'pɒzətɪv/ *adjective* 形容词
1 thinking or talking about the good parts of a situation 正面的；乐观的；积极的：*It's important to stay positive.* 保持乐观是很重要的。◊ *The teacher was very **positive** about my work.* 老师对我的作业抱非常肯定的态度。◯ OPPOSITE **negative** 反义词为 negative
2 completely certain 确定；肯定：*Are you **positive** that you closed the door?* 你确定把门关上了吗？◯ SAME MEANING **sure** 同义词为 sure

positively *adverb* 副词 /'pɒzətɪvli/ (*informal* 非正式)
really; extremely 非常；极度：*The idea is positively stupid.* 这个主意愚蠢到家。

possess /pə'zes/ *verb* 动词 (possesses, possessing, possessed /pə'zest/) (*formal* 正式)
to have or own something 有；拥有：*He lost everything that he possessed in the fire.* 他在火灾中失去了拥有的一切。

possession /pə'zeʃn/ *noun* 名词

> 🔎 SPELLING 拼写说明
> Remember! You spell **possession** with **SS** and **SS**. 记住：possession 拼写中有两个 ss。

1 (*no plural* 不用复数形式) (*formal* 正式) the fact of having or owning something 具有；拥有；占有：*The **possession** of drugs is a crime.* 藏有毒品是犯罪行为。
2 possessions (*plural* 用复数形式) the things that you have or own 财物；财产 ◯ SAME MEANING **belongings** 同义词为 belongings

possibility 0┐ /ˌpɒsə'bɪləti/ *noun* 名词 (*plural* 复数形式 possibilities)
something that might happen 可能；可能性：*There's a **possibility that** it will rain, so take your umbrella.* 可能会下雨，把雨伞带上吧。

possible 0┐ /'pɒsəbl/ *adjective* 形容词
able to happen or to be done 可能的；可能发生的；可能做到的：*Is it **possible** to get to Birmingham by train?* 坐火车能到伯明翰去吗？◊ *I'll phone you **as soon as possible**.* 我会尽快给你打电话。◯ OPPOSITE **impossible** 反义词为 impossible

possibly 0┐ /'pɒsəbli/ *adverb* 副词
1 perhaps 可能；或许：*'Will you be free tomorrow?' 'Possibly.'* "你明天有空吗？""可能有。"
2 in a way that can be done 尽量；尽可能：*I'll come as soon as I possibly can.* 我会尽快过来。

post¹ 0┐ /pəʊst/ *noun* 名词
1 (*British* 英式英语) (*American* 美式英语 mail) (*no plural* 不用复数形式) the official system for sending and receiving letters, packages, etc. 邮政体系；邮递；邮寄：*I sent your present by post.* 我把你的礼物寄出去了。
2 (*British* 英式英语) (*American* 美式英语 mail) (*no plural* 不用复数形式) all the letters and packages that you send or receive 邮件；信件：*Did you get any post*

this morning? 你今天早上收到邮件了吗？
3 (*plural* 复数形式 **posts**) a job, especially an important one in a large organization 职位；（尤指）要职： *a government post* 政府职位
4 (*plural* 复数形式 **posts**) a piece of wood or metal that stands in the ground to hold something or to show where something is 柱子；杆： *The sign had fallen off the post.* 指示牌从杆上掉了下来。 ◇ *a lamp post* 路灯柱 ➲ Look also at **signpost**. 亦见 signpost。

post² 0━ /pəʊst/ ***verb*** 动词 (**posts, posting, posted**)
1 (*British* 英式英语) (*American* 美式英语 **mail**) to send a letter or package by post 邮寄；递送： *Could you **post** this **letter** for me?* 你帮我寄这封信好吗？
2 to send somebody to a place to do a job 派送；派驻： *Sara's company have **posted** her **to** Japan for two years.* 萨拉的公司已经派她到日本工作两年。

postage /ˈpəʊstɪdʒ/ ***noun*** 名词 (*no plural* 不用复数形式)
money that you pay to send a letter or package 邮资；邮费

postal /ˈpəʊstl/ ***adjective*** 形容词
connected with sending and receiving letters, packages, etc. 邮政的；邮递的： *postal collections* 邮递员收件

postbox 邮筒；邮箱

postbox (*British* 英式英语) 邮筒

mailbox (*American* 美式英语) 邮箱

postbox /ˈpəʊstbɒks/ ***noun*** 名词 (*plural* 复数形式 **postboxes**) (*British* 英式英语) (*British also* 英式英语亦作 **letter box**) (*American* 美式英语 **mailbox**)
a box in the street where you put letters that you want to send 邮筒；邮箱

postcard /ˈpəʊstkɑːd/ ***noun*** 名词
a card with a picture on one side, that you write on and send by post 明信片： *She sent me a postcard from California.* 她从加利福尼亚州给我寄来了一张明信片。

postcard 明信片

postcode /ˈpəʊstkəʊd/ (*British* 英式英语) (*American* 美式英语 **zip code**) ***noun*** 名词
a group of numbers and letters that you write at the end of an address 邮政编码；邮递区号

poster /ˈpəʊstə(r)/ ***noun*** 名词
a big piece of paper on a wall, with a picture or words on it 海报；招贴画

postgraduate /ˌpəʊstˈgrædʒuət/ ***noun*** 名词
a student at a university who has already done a degree 研究生

postman /ˈpəʊstmən/ (*plural* 复数形式 **postmen** /ˈpəʊstmən/) (*American* 美式英语 **mailman**) ***noun*** 名词
a person whose job is to take (**deliver**) letters and packages to people's homes 邮递员；邮差

post office 0━ /ˈpəʊst ɒfɪs/ ***noun*** 名词
a building where you go to send letters and packages and to buy stamps 邮政局

postpone /pəˈspəʊn/ ***verb*** 动词 (**postpones, postponing, postponed** /pəˈspəʊnd/)
to say that something will happen later than you planned 推迟；延期： *The match was postponed because of the weather.* 比赛因天气而延期举行了。

pot 0━ /pɒt/ ***noun*** 名词
1 a deep round container for cooking 锅： *a big **pot of** soup* 一大锅汤
2 a container that you use for a special thing（有特定用途的）罐，壶，盆：

a teapot 茶壶 ◇ *a pot of* paint 一罐油漆 ◇ *a plant pot* 花盆

pots 盆；罐；壶

plant pot 花盆

yogurt pot
酸奶罐

coffee pot 咖啡壶

potato 0🔊 /pəˈteɪtəʊ/ *noun* 名词 (*plural* 复数形式 **potatoes**)
a white vegetable with a brown or red skin that grows underground 马铃薯；土豆：*a baked potato* 烤土豆 ◇ *mashed potato* 土豆泥 ⊃ Look at Picture Dictionary page **P9**. 见彩页 **P9**。

potato chip /pəˈteɪtəʊ tʃɪp/ (*American* 美式英语) *noun* 名词 = CRISP²

potential¹ /pəˈtenʃl/ *adjective* 形容词
possible; likely to happen or exist 潜在的；可能的：*potential students* 潜在的学生

potential² /pəˈtenʃl/ *noun* 名词 (*no plural* 不用复数形式)
qualities or possibilities that exist and can be developed 潜力；潜质；可能性：*She has great potential* as a musician. 她大有潜质成为一名乐师。

pottery /ˈpɒtəri/ *noun* 名词 (*no plural* 不用复数形式)
1 cups, plates and other things that are made from CLAY (= heavy earth that becomes hard when it is baked in an oven) 陶器：*This shop sells beautiful pottery.* 这家商店出售精美的陶器。
2 the activity of making cups, plates and other things from CLAY 陶器制造；陶艺：*Her hobby is pottery.* 她爱好陶艺。

poultry /ˈpəʊltri/ *noun* 名词 (*plural* 用复数形式)
birds such as chickens that people keep on farms for their eggs or their meat 家禽

pounce /paʊns/ *verb* 动词 (**pounces, pouncing, pounced** /paʊnst/)
to jump on somebody or something suddenly 猛扑：*The cat pounced on the bird.* 猫猛然向鸟扑去。

pound 0🔊 /paʊnd/ *noun* 名词
1 (*symbol* 符号 £) money that people use in Britain. There are 100 **pence** in a **pound**. 英镑（英国货币单位：1 英镑等于 100 便士）：*The computer cost six hundred pounds.* 这台电脑价值六百英镑。◇ *a ten-pound note* 一张十英镑的纸币 ◇ *a pound coin* 一英镑的硬币 ◇ *I spent £40 today.* 我今天花了 40 英镑。
2 (*symbol* 符号 **lb**) a measure of weight (= 0.454 kilograms). There are 16 **ounces** in a **pound**. 磅（重量单位：1 磅等于 0.454 公斤或 16 盎司）：*You need half a pound of flour.* 你需要半磅面粉。◇ *2lbs sugar* 两磅糖

🔍 **CULTURE** 文化资料补充
Many older people in Britain still use **ounces**, **pounds** and **stone** to measure weight. 在英国，许多年纪较大的人仍用盎司（ounce）、磅（pound）和英石（stone）来量度重量，而不用克（gram）或公斤（kilogram）。
In the US, people use **ounces** and **pounds**, but not **stone**. 美国人也用盎司（ounce）和磅（pound），但不用英石（stone）。

pour 倒

pour 0🔊 /pɔː(r)/ *verb* 动词 (**pours, pouring, poured** /pɔːd/)
1 to make liquid flow out of or into something 倒，注，灌（液体）：*She poured water into the teapot.* 她把水倒进了茶壶。◇ *She poured me a cup of tea.* 她给我倒了一杯茶。◇ *Pour the sauce over the meat.* 把调味汁浇在肉上。

2 to flow quickly 涌流： *Oil poured out of the damaged ship.* 油从毁坏的船里涌了出来。◇ *Tears were **pouring down** her cheeks.* 眼泪顺着她的面颊簌簌地落下。
3 to rain very hard （雨）倾盆而下： *It's pouring.* 正下着倾盆大雨。◇ *It poured with rain all day.* 整天大雨滂沱。

poverty /'pɒvəti/ *noun* 名词 (*no plural* 不用复数形式)
the state of being poor 贫穷；贫困： *There are many people living in poverty in this city.* 这座城市有许多人生活在贫困之中。

powder 0★ /'paʊdə(r)/ *noun* 名词
a dry substance like flour that is made of a lot of very small pieces 粉末： *Crush the spices to a powder.* 将香料碾成粉末。◇ *Can you get some more washing powder* (= for washing clothes)? 你能再拿些洗衣粉吗？

power 0★ /'paʊə(r)/ *noun* 名词
1 (*no plural* 不用复数形式) the ability to control people or things; the ability to do things 控制力；影响力；能力： *The president has a lot of power.* 总统有很大的影响力。◇ *I did **everything in my power*** (= everything I could do) *to help her.* 我已竭尽全力帮助她。
2 (*plural* 复数形式 **powers**) the right to do something 权力： *Police officers have the **power to** arrest people.* 警察有逮捕人的权力。
3 (*plural* 复数形式 **powers**) a strong person or country 有权力的人；强国： *There is a meeting of **world powers** in Rome next week.* 下周世界强国将在罗马召开会议。
4 (*no plural* 不用复数形式) the energy or strength that somebody or something has 能量；力量： *The ship was helpless against the **power of the storm**.* 那艘船只能听凭威力强大的暴风雨摆布。
5 (*no plural* 不用复数形式) energy that can be collected and used for making machines work, making electricity, etc. 能；能量： *nuclear power* 核能

powerful 0★ /'paʊəfl/ *adjective* 形容词
1 having a lot of strength or power 强有力的；权力大的： *The car has a very powerful engine.* 这辆车的发动机功率很大。◇ *The president is very powerful.* 总统很有权力。
2 having a strong effect 有强烈作用的；强效的： *a powerful drug* 特效药

powerless /'paʊələs/ *adjective* 形容词
not able to do anything 无能为力： *I was powerless to help.* 我无力相助。

power point /'paʊə pɔɪnt/ (*British* 英式英语) *noun* 名词
a place in a wall where you connect a lamp, machine, etc. to the electricity 电源插座 ⊃ SAME MEANING **socket** 同义词为 socket

power station /'paʊə steɪʃn/ *noun* 名词
a place where electricity is made 发电站；发电厂

PR /,piː 'ɑː(r)/ *abbreviation* 缩略式 = PUBLIC RELATIONS

practical 0★ /'præktɪkl/ *adjective* 形容词
1 connected with doing or making things, not just with ideas 实际的；实践的： *Have you got any **practical experience** of teaching?* 你有实际的教学经验吗？
2 sensible or suitable; likely to be successful 可行的；实用的： *Your plan isn't practical.* 你的计划不切实际。⊃ OPPOSITE **impractical** 反义词为 impractical
3 good at making and repairing things 手巧的： *She's a very practical person and has made a lot of improvements to the house.* 她手很巧，使房子生色不少。

practically /'præktɪkli/ *adverb* 副词
almost; nearly 几乎；差不多： *Don't go out – lunch is practically ready!* 不要出去，午饭差不多好了！◇ *It rained practically every day of our holiday.* 我们度假时几乎每天都下雨。

practice 0★ /'præktɪs/ *noun* 名词
(*no plural* 不用复数形式)

> 🖊 SPELLING 拼写说明
>
> Remember! Don't confuse **practice**, which is a noun in British English, with **practise**, which is a verb. 记住：不要混淆英式英语中的名词 practice 和动词 practise： *Our football practice is on Monday, but we should practise every day.* 虽然我们的足球训练在星期一，但我们应该每天都练习。
>
> In American English you spell both the verb and the noun **practice**. 在美式英语中，动词和名词拼法相同，均为 practice。

doing something many times so that you will do it well 练习；训练： *You need lots of practice when you're learning to play a musical instrument.* 学习演奏一种乐器需要大量练习。

out of practice not good at something, because you have not done it for a long time 生疏；疏于练习

A
B
C
D
E
F
G
H
I
J
K
L
M
N
O
P
Q
R
S
T
U
V
W
X
Y
Z

practise 0━ /'præktɪs/ (British 英式 英语) (American 美式英语 practice) *verb* 动词 (practises, practising, practised /'præktɪst/)
to do something many times so that you will do it well 练习；训练：*If you want to play the piano well, you must practise every day.* 如果你想把钢琴弹好，就得每天 练习。 ⊃ Look at the note at **practice**. 见 practice 条的注释。

praise /preɪz/ *verb* 动词 (praises, praising, praised /preɪzd/)
to say that somebody or something is good 赞扬；称赞：*She was praised for her hard work.* 她的努力受到了赞扬。
▸ **praise** *noun* 名词 (no plural 不用复数 形式)：*The book has received a lot of praise.* 这本书大获好评。

pram /præm/ (British 英式英语) (American 美式英语 baby carriage) *noun* 名词
a thing that a baby lies in to go out. It has wheels so that you can push it. 婴儿车 ⊃ Look at the picture at **pushchair**. 见 pushchair 的插图。

prawn /prɔːn/ *noun* 名词 (British 英式英语) (American 美式英语 shrimp)
a small sea animal that is pink after it has been cooked 对虾；明虾

pray /preɪ/ *verb* 动词 (prays, praying, prayed /preɪd/)
to speak to God or a god 祈祷；祷告：*They prayed to God for help.* 他们祈求 上帝保佑。

prayer 0━ /preə(r)/ *noun* 名词
1 (plural 复数形式 prayers) words that you say when you speak to God or a god 祷告，祷文（指内容）：*They said a prayer for world peace.* 他们为世界和平 祷告。
2 (no plural 不用复数形式) the act of PRAYING 祈祷，祷告（指行为）：*the power of prayer* 祈祷的力量 ◇ *They knelt in prayer.* 他们跪着祈祷。

preach /priːtʃ/ *verb* 动词 (preaches, preaching, preached /priːtʃt/)
to talk about God or a god to a group of people 布道；讲道

preacher /'priːtʃə(r)/ *noun* 名词
a person who gives religious talks in public 布道者；传道者：*Our preacher tonight is Reverend Jones.* 今晚给我们讲道 的是琼斯牧师。

precaution /prɪ'kɔːʃn/ *noun* 名词
something that you do so that bad things will not happen 预防措施：*I took the precaution of locking all the windows*

when I went out. 我出门时把所有窗户都 锁好了，以防万一。

precious /'preʃəs/ *adjective* 形容词
1 very valuable or expensive 宝贵的； 贵重的：*Diamonds are precious stones.* 钻石是一种宝石。
2 that you consider to be very special 珍爱的：*My family is very precious to me.* 我的家庭在我心中占据着十分重要的 位置。

precise /prɪ'saɪs/ *adjective* 形容词
exactly right 准确的；精确的：*I gave him precise instructions on how to get to my house.* 我给了他明确的指示如何去我家。

precisely /prɪ'saɪsli/ *adverb* 副词
exactly 准确地；确切地：*They arrived at two o'clock precisely.* 他们是两点整到的。

predict /prɪ'dɪkt/ *verb* 动词 (predicts, predicting, predicted)
to say what you think will happen 预测； 预计；预言：*She predicted that it would rain, and she was right.* 她早说过要下雨， 果不其然。
▸ **prediction** /prɪ'dɪkʃn/ *noun* 名词：
The results confirmed our predictions. 结果证实了我们的预测。

prefect /'priːfekt/ *noun* 名词 (British 英式 英语)
an older student in a school who has duties such as making sure that younger students behave （在学校中负责维持纪律 等的）学长

prefer 0━ /prɪ'fɜː(r)/ *verb* 动词 (prefers, preferring, preferred /prɪ'fɜːd/)
to like one thing or person better than another 喜欢…多于…；较喜欢：*Would you prefer tea or coffee?* 你要茶还是咖啡？ ◇ *I would prefer to stay at home.* 我宁愿 待在家里。 ◇ *He prefers going out to studying.* 他喜欢出去玩多于学习。

preferable /'prefrəbl/ *adjective* 形容词
better or more suitable 更好；更合适：
I think living in the country is preferable to living in the city. 我认为在乡下生活比 在城市生活好。
▸ **preferably** /'prefrəbli/ *adverb* 副词：
Phone me on Sunday morning, but preferably not too early! 星期日早上打电话 给我，但最好别太早！

preference /'prefrəns/ *noun* 名词
a feeling that you like one thing or person better than another 偏爱；偏好：*We have lemonade and orange juice – do you have a preference?* 我们有柠檬味汽水和 橙汁，你喜欢哪样？

prefix /'priːfɪks/ *noun* 名词 (*plural 复数形式* **prefixes**)
(*grammar 语法*) a group of letters that you add to the beginning of a word to make another word 前缀；词首： *The prefix 'im-' means 'not', so 'impossible' means 'not possible'.* 前缀 im- 的意思是 not，所以 impossible 的意思就是 not possible.
➔ Look at **suffix**. 见 suffix.

pregnancy /'pregnənsi/ (*plural 复数形式* **pregnancies**) *noun* 名词
the state of being pregnant 怀孕；妊娠： *Many women feel sick during pregnancy.* 许多妇女怀孕时感到恶心。

pregnant 0➤ /'pregnənt/ *adjective* 形容词
If a woman is **pregnant**, she has a baby growing in her body. 怀孕的；妊娠的： *She's five months pregnant.* 她怀孕五个月了。

prejudice /'predʒudɪs/ *noun* 名词
a strong idea that you do not like somebody or something, for a reason that is wrong or unfair 偏见；成见： *She was a victim of racial prejudice.* 她是种族偏见的受害者。

prejudiced /'predʒədɪst/ *adjective* 形容词
having a strong idea that you do not like somebody or something, for a reason that is wrong or unfair 有偏见的；有成见的： *He is prejudiced against me because I'm a woman.* 他因为我是女的而对我有偏见。

preparation 0➤ /ˌprepə'reɪʃn/ *noun* 名词
1 (*no plural 不用复数形式*) making something ready 准备；预备： *I packed my bags in preparation for the journey.* 我收拾好行李，为旅行作准备。
2 preparations (*plural 用复数形式*) what you do to get ready for something 准备工作： *They began to make preparations for the wedding last year.* 他们去年开始筹备婚礼。

prepare 0➤ /prɪ'peə(r)/ *verb* 动词
(**prepares**, **preparing**, **prepared** /prɪ'peəd/)
to make somebody or something ready; to make yourself ready 准备；筹备；预备： *Martin is in the kitchen preparing the dinner.* 马丁正在厨房准备晚餐。◇ *I prepared well for the exam.* 我为考试做好了准备。

prepared 0➤ /prɪ'peəd/ *adjective* 形容词
ready; able to deal with something 做好准备的： *I wasn't prepared for all these problems.* 对于这些困难我感到措手不及。

prepared to do something happy to do something 乐意做某事： *I'm not prepared to give you any money.* 我无意给你钱。➔ SAME MEANING **willing** 同义词为 willing

preposition /ˌprepə'zɪʃn/ *noun* 名词
(*grammar 语法*) a word that you use before a noun or pronoun to show where, when, how, etc. 介词： *In the sentence 'He travelled from London to Munich', 'from' and 'to' are prepositions.* 在 He travelled from London to Munich 一句中，from 和 to 是介词。

prescribe /prɪ'skraɪb/ *verb* 动词
(**prescribes**, **prescribing**, **prescribed** /prɪ'skraɪbd/)
to say that somebody must take a medicine 给…开药；开药方： *The doctor prescribed some tablets.* 医生开了些药片。

prescription /prɪ'skrɪpʃn/ *noun* 名词
a piece of paper that a doctor gives to you with the name of your medicine on it 处方；药方

presence /'prezns/ *noun* 名词 (*no plural 不用复数形式*)
the fact of being in a place 在场；出席： *an experiment to test for the presence of oxygen* 测试是否有氧气存在的实验 ◇ *Mother did not allow arguing in her presence* (= when she was there). 母亲不允许她在场时有人争吵。

present¹ 0➤ /'preznt/ *adjective* 形容词

> 🔎 **PRONUNCIATION** 读音说明
>
> When the word **present** is a noun or an adjective, you say the first part of the word louder: **PRESent**. * present 作名词或形容词时，重音放在第一个音节：PRESent。
> When the word **present** is a verb, you say the second part of the word louder: **preSENT**. * present 作动词时，重音放在第二个音节：preSENT。

1 in a place 出现；在场；出席： *The whole class was present.* 全班同学都到了。➔ OPPOSITE **absent** 反义词为 absent
2 being or happening now 当前的；现在的 ➔ SAME MEANING **current** 同义词为 current： *What is your present job?* 你现在的工作是什么？

present² 0➤ /'preznt/ *noun* 名词
1 (*plural 复数形式* **presents**) something that you give to somebody or get from somebody 礼物；礼品 ➔ SAME MEANING **gift** 同义词为 gift： *What can I get him for*

a birthday present? 我给他准备什么生日礼物好呢?

presents 礼物

bow 蝴蝶结　　ribbon 丝带

wrapping paper 包装纸

2 (*no plural* 不用复数形式) the time now 现在;目前: *I can't help you at present – I'm too busy.* 我现在无法帮你,我太忙了。
3 the present (*also* 亦作 **the present tense**) (*no plural* 不用复数形式) (*grammar* 语法) the form of a verb that you use to talk about what is happening or what exists now 现在时;现在式 ⊃ Look at **future**[1] (2) and **past**[2] (2). 见 future[1] 第 2 义和 past[2] 第 2 义。

present[3] 0－ /prɪ'zent/ *verb* 动词 (**presents, presenting, presented**)
to give something to somebody, especially in a formal ceremony 授予;颁发;献给: *The prizes were **presented** to the winners.* 奖项颁发给了优胜者。◇ *They **presented** their teacher **with** some flowers.* 他们向老师献了花。

presentation /ˌprezn'teɪʃn/ *noun* 名词
1 the act of giving something to somebody, especially in a formal ceremony 颁发: *The presentation of the prizes will take place at 7.30.* 颁奖仪式将于 7 点 30 分举行。
2 a meeting where somebody shows or explains something to the people listening 展示会;发布会;报告: *Each student has to give a short **presentation** on a subject of their choice.* 每名学生要就自己所选的题目做一个简短的报告。

presenter /prɪ'zentə(r)/ *noun* 名词
a person whose job is to introduce programmes on TV or radio (电视或广播)节目主持人

presently /'prezntli/ *adverb* 副词
1 soon 很快;马上: *He will be here presently.* 他马上就到。
2 now 现在: *She's presently working in a cafe.* 她现在在一家小餐馆工作。

present participle /ˌpreznt 'pɑ:tɪsɪpl/ *noun* 名词
(*grammar* 语法) the form of a verb that ends in *-ing* 现在分词

the present perfect /ðə ˌpreznt 'pɜ:fɪkt/ *noun* 名词 (*no plural* 不用复数形式)
(*grammar* 语法) the form of a verb for things that began in the past and continue now. We make it with the present tense of *have* and a past participle of the verb. 现在完成时;现在完成式: *'They have finished' is in the present perfect.* * They have finished 用了现在完成时。

the present tense /ðə ˌpreznt 'tens/ (*also* 亦作 **the present**) *noun* 名词 (*no plural* 不用复数形式)
(*grammar* 语法) the form of a verb that you use to talk about what is happening or what exists now 现在时;现在式

preservation /ˌprezə'veɪʃn/ *noun* 名词 (*no plural* 不用复数形式)
the act of keeping something safe or in good condition 保存;保养: *the preservation of rare birds* 对稀有鸟类的保护

preserve /prɪ'zɜ:v/ *verb* 动词 (**preserves, preserving, preserved** /prɪ'zɜ:vd/)
to keep something safe or in good condition 保存;保养: *They managed to preserve most of the paintings.* 他们设法让大部分油画保存下来。

president 0－ /'prezɪdənt/ *noun* 名词
1 the leader of a country that does not have a king or queen (called a **republic**) 总统;国家主席: *the President of the United States of America* 美国总统
2 the person with the highest position in an organization or a company 最高负责人;会长;主席;总裁
▶ **presidential** /ˌprezɪ'denʃl/ *adjective* 形容词: *the presidential elections* 总统选举

press[1] 0－ /pres/ *noun* 名词
1 the press (*no plural* 不用复数形式) newspapers and magazines and the people who write them 报界;新闻界: *She told her story to the press.* 她向新闻界讲述了她的经历。
2 (*plural* 复数形式 **presses**) a machine for printing things like books and newspapers 印刷机
3 (*plural* 复数形式 **presses**) the act of pushing something 按压;摁: *Give the doorbell a press.* 按一下门铃吧。

press² 0🔊 /pres/ *verb* 动词 (presses, pressing, pressed /prest/)
1 to push something 按；摁： *If you press this button, the door will open.* 按下这个按钮，门就会开。◇ *She pressed her face against the window.* 她把脸贴在了窗户上。 ⊃ Look at the picture at **squeeze**. 见 squeeze 的插图。
2 to make clothes flat and smooth using an iron 熨平： *This suit needs pressing.* 这套西服需要熨一下。

press conference /'pres kɒnfərəns/ *noun* 名词
a meeting when a famous or important person answers questions from newspaper and TV journalists 记者招待会；新闻发布会

press-up /'pres ʌp/ (*British* 英式英语) (*American* 美式英语 **push-up**) *noun* 名词
a type of exercise in which you lie on your front and push your body up with your arms 俯卧撑： *I do twenty press-ups every morning.* 我每天早上做二十下俯卧撑。

pressure 0🔊 /'preʃə(r)/ *noun* 名词
1 the force that presses on something 压力；挤压： *The pressure of the water caused the dam to crack.* 水压导致大坝决了口。
2 the force that a gas or liquid has when it is contained inside something 压力；压强： *He has high blood pressure* (= the force with which blood travels round your body). 他有高血压。◇ *You should check the tyre pressures* (= the amount of air in the car tyres) *regularly.* 你应该定期检查轮胎的气压。
3 a feeling of worry because of the things you have to do 心理压力： *She's under a lot of pressure at work.* 她工作上承受着很大的压力。◇ *financial pressures* 经济压力

presume /prɪ'zjuːm/ *verb* 动词 (presumes, presuming, presumed /prɪ'zjuːmd/)
to think that something is true, although you are not certain 假设；假定： *She's not home yet so I presume she's still at work.* 她还没回家，所以我猜她还在工作呢。

pretend 0🔊 /prɪ'tend/ *verb* 动词 (pretends, pretending, pretended)
to try to make somebody believe something that is not true 假装；佯装： *He didn't want to talk, so he pretended to be asleep.* 他不想说话，就假装睡着了。◇ *I pretended that I was enjoying myself.* 我装出乐在其中的样子。

pretty¹ 0🔊 /'prɪti/ *adverb* 副词 (*informal* 非正式)
quite; fairly 相当；颇： *It's pretty cold today.* 今天天气颇冷。

pretty² 0🔊 /'prɪti/ *adjective* 形容词 (prettier, prettiest)
nice to look at 好看的；漂亮的： *a pretty little girl* 漂亮的小女孩 ◇ *These flowers are very pretty.* 这些花儿非常好看。 ⊃ Look at the note at **beautiful**. 见 beautiful 条的注释。

prevent 0🔊 /prɪ'vent/ *verb* 动词 (prevents, preventing, prevented)
to stop somebody from doing something; to stop something happening 阻止；防止；预防： *Her parents want to prevent her from getting married.* 她父母想阻止她结婚。◇ *It is easier to prevent disease than to cure it.* 预防疾病比治疗疾病容易。

prevention /prɪ'venʃn/ *noun* 名词 (*no plural* 不用复数形式)
stopping somebody from doing something or stopping something from happening 预防；防止： *crime prevention* 防止罪行 ◇ *the prevention of cruelty to animals* 防止虐待动物

preview /'priːvjuː/ *noun* 名词
1 a chance to see a play, film, etc. before it is shown to the general public （戏剧、电影等的）预演，预映
2 a chance to see what something will be like before it happens or is shown 预览： *Click on the print preview button.* 点击"打印预览"按钮。

previous 0🔊 /'priːviəs/ *adjective* 形容词
coming or happening before or earlier 先前的；以往的： *Who was the previous owner of the car?* 这辆车之前的车主是谁？
▶ **previously** *adverb* 副词： *I work in a factory now, but previously I was a secretary.* 我现在于工厂上班，但之前是秘书。

prey /preɪ/ *noun* 名词 (*no plural* 不用复数形式)
an animal or bird that another animal or bird kills for food 被捕食的动物；猎物： *Zebra are prey for lions.* 斑马是狮子捕食的动物。

price 0🔊 /praɪs/ *noun* 名词
how much money you pay to buy something 价格；价钱；物价： *The price is £15.* 价钱是 15 英镑。◇ *Prices in this country are very high.* 这个国家的物价非常高。

A
B
C
D
E
F
G
H
I
J
K
L
M
N
O
P
Q
R
S
T
U
V
W
X
Y
Z

🔎 **WHICH WORD?** 词语辨析

Price, **cost** or **charge**? 用 price、cost 还是 charge？

The **price** of something is the amount of money that you must pay to buy something. We usually say *How much?* or *How much is it?* if we want to know the **price** of something. * price 指购买某物需要支付的价钱。询问某物的价格通常说 How much? 或 How much is it?。

You use **cost** when you are talking about paying for services or about prices without saying an exact sum of money. 表示服务费或没有说明具体金额的价钱时用 cost: *The cost of electricity is going up.* 电费在上升。

A **charge** is the amount of money that you must pay to use something. * charge 是使用某物需要付出的钱: *Is there a charge for parking here?* 在这里停车要收费吗?

priceless /ˈpraɪsləs/ *adjective* 形容词
extremely valuable 无价的；极珍贵的：*priceless jewels* 价值连城的珠宝

prick /prɪk/ *verb* 动词 (**pricks, pricking, pricked** /prɪkt/)
to make a very small hole in something, or to hurt somebody, with a sharp point 扎（破）；刺（破）：*I pricked my finger on a needle.* 我的手指让针扎破了。
▶ **prick** *noun* 名词：*She felt the prick of a needle.* 她感到针刺的疼痛。

prickle /ˈprɪkl/ *noun* 名词
a sharp point on a plant or an animal （动植物上的）刺，针：*A hedgehog has prickles.* 刺猬身上有刺。

prickly /ˈprɪkli/ *adjective* 形容词
covered with PRICKLES 多刺的：*a prickly cactus* 多刺的仙人掌

pride /praɪd/ *noun* 名词 (*no plural* 不用复数形式)
1 the feeling that you are proud of something that you or others have got or have done 自豪；骄傲；得意：*She showed us her painting with great pride.* 她非常自豪地给我们看她的画。
2 the feeling that you are better than other people 傲慢；自负

priest 0🔒 /priːst/ *noun* 名词
a person who leads people in their religion 神父；司祭；司铎：*a Buddhist priest* 佛教僧侣

primary /ˈpraɪməri/ *adjective* 形容词
first; most important 首要的；最重要的；

主要的：*The primary aim of this course is to improve your spoken English.* 这个课程的主要目标是提高英语口语水平。

primary school /ˈpraɪməri skuːl/ (*British* 英式英语) *noun* 名词
a school for children between the ages of five and eleven 小学 ➲ Look at **secondary school**. 见 secondary school。

prime minister 0🔒 /ˌpraɪm ˈmɪnɪstə(r)/ *noun* 名词
the leader of the government in some countries, for example in Britain 首相；总理

primitive /ˈprɪmətɪv/ *adjective* 形容词
very simple; not developed 简陋的；原始的：*The cooking facilities were very primitive.* 烹饪设备非常简陋。 ◇ *primitive beliefs* 原始的信仰

prince /prɪns/ *noun* 名词
1 a man in a royal family, especially the son of a king or queen 王子；亲王；王孙：*the Prince of Wales* 威尔士亲王
2 a man from a royal family who is the ruler of a small country （小国的）君主，国君

princess /ˌprɪnˈses/ *noun* 名词 (*plural* 复数形式 **princesses**)
a woman in a royal family, especially the daughter of a king or queen or the wife of a PRINCE 公主；郡主；王妃

principal¹ /ˈprɪnsəpl/ *adjective* 形容词
most important 最重要的；主要的：*My principal reason for going to Rome was to learn Italian.* 我去罗马的主要原因是学意大利语。

principal² /ˈprɪnsəpl/ *noun* 名词
a person who is in charge of a school or college （学校、学院的）校长，院长

principally /ˈprɪnsəpli/ *adverb* 副词
mainly; mostly 主要地：*She sometimes travels to Europe, but she works principally in Africa.* 她有时候到欧洲去，可是主要在非洲工作。

principle /ˈprɪnsəpl/ *noun* 名词
1 a rule about how you should live 原则；准则：*He has very strong principles.* 他很有原则。 ◇ *I refuse to lie about it; it's against my principles.* 我绝不为此事撒谎，那违背我的原则。
2 a rule or fact about how something happens or works 原理；法则：*scientific principles* 科学原理

print¹ 0🔒 /prɪnt/ *verb* 动词 (**prints, printing, printed**)
1 to put words or pictures onto paper

using a machine. Books, newspapers and magazines are **printed**. 打印；印制；印刷 **2** to write with letters that are not joined together 用印刷体写（字母之间笔画不相连接）: *Please print your name and address clearly.* 请用印刷体把你的名字和地址写清楚。

print² /prɪnt/ *noun* 名词
1 (*no plural* 不用复数形式) letters that a machine makes on paper 印刷字体: *The print is too small to read without my glasses.* 字印得太小了，我不戴眼镜看不清。 **2** (*plural* 复数形式 **prints**) a mark where something has pressed on something（压出的）印迹，印记: *footprints in the snow* 雪地上的足迹 ◇ *The police are looking for prints* (= fingerprints). 警方正在寻找指纹。 **3** (*plural* 复数形式 **prints**) a copy on paper of a painting or photograph 版画；（冲印出的）相片

printer /'prɪntə(r)/ *noun* 名词
1 a machine that prints words from a computer 打印机；印表机 **2** a person or company that prints things like books or newspapers 印刷商；印刷公司

priority 0→ /praɪ'ɒrəti/ *noun* 名词
1 (*plural* 复数形式 **priorities**) something that you think is more important than other things and that you must do first 最重要的事；优先考虑的问题: *Education is a top priority.* 教育是当务之急。 **2** (*no plural* 不用复数形式) being more important than somebody or something or coming before somebody or something else 优先；优先权: *We give priority to families with small children.* 我们会优先考虑有幼儿的家庭。 ◇ *Emergency cases take priority over other patients in hospital.* 医院里的急诊病人比其他病人得到优先诊治。

prison 0→ /'prɪzn/ *noun* 名词
a place where criminals must stay as a punishment 监狱；牢房 ⊃ SAME MEANING **jail** 同义词为 jail: *He was sent to prison for robbing a bank.* 他因抢劫银行被判入狱。 ◇ *She was in prison for 15 years.* 她坐了 15 年牢。

prisoner 0→ /'prɪznə(r)/ *noun* 名词
a person who is in prison as a punishment; a person who is not free 囚犯；被囚禁的人: *The number of prisoners serving life sentences has fallen.* 服无期徒刑的犯人数目下降了。 ◇ *He was*

taken prisoner by rebel soldiers. 他被叛军俘虏了。

private 0→ /'praɪvət/ *adjective* 形容词
1 for one person or a small group of people only, and not for anybody else 私人的；私有的；专用的: *You shouldn't read his letters – they're private.* 你不应该看他的信，那都是私人信件。 ◇ *This is private property.* 这是私人领地。 **2** alone; without other people there 单独的；私下的: *I would like a private meeting with the manager.* 我想跟经理单独会面。 **3** not connected with your job 与工作无关的；私人的: *She never talks about her private life at work.* 她上班的时候从不谈自己的私生活。 **4** not controlled or paid for by the government 私有的；私立的；私营的: *a private hospital* 私立医院 ◇ *private schools* 私立学校
in private alone; without other people there 私下；单独: *Can I speak to you in private?* 我能私下跟你谈谈吗？
▶ **privately** /'praɪvətli/ *adverb* 副词: *Let's go into my office – we can talk more privately there.* 咱们到我办公室去吧。那里谈话更私密。

privilege /'prɪvəlɪdʒ/ *noun* 名词
something special that only one person or a few people may do or have 特权；特别待遇: *Prisoners who behave well have special privileges.* 表现好的犯人会有特别优待。
▶ **privileged** /'prɪvəlɪdʒd/ *adjective* 形容词: *I feel very privileged to be playing for the national team.* 能为国家队效力，我很荣幸。

prize 0→ /praɪz/ *noun* 名词
something that you give to the person who wins a game, race, etc. 奖励；奖品；奖金: *I won first prize in the painting competition.* 我获得了绘画比赛一等奖。 ◇ *Did you win a prize?* 你获奖了吗？

probable 0→ /'prɒbəbl/ *adjective* 形容词
likely to happen or to be true 很可能的: *It is probable that he will be late.* 他很可能会迟到。 ⊃ OPPOSITE **improbable** 反义词为 improbable

probably 0→ /'prɒbəbli/ *adverb* 副词
almost certainly 很可能；几乎可以肯定: *I will probably see you on Thursday.* 我很可能星期四见你。

problem 0→ /'prɒbləm/ *noun* 名词
1 something that is difficult; something

A
B
C
D
E
F
G
H
I
J
K
L
M
N
O
P
Q
R
S
T
U
V
W
X
Y
Z

A B C D E F G H I J K L M N O P Q R S T U V W X Y Z

that makes you worry 棘手的问题；麻烦；难题： *She has a lot of problems. Her husband is ill and her son is in prison.* 她有很多难处。她丈夫病了，儿子又进了监狱。◇ *There is a problem with my telephone – it doesn't work.* 我的电话有问题，它坏了。
2 a question that you must answer by thinking about it 问题；习题： *I can't solve this problem.* 我解答不了这个问题。

proceed /prə'si:d/ *verb* 动词 (proceeds, proceeding, proceeded) (*formal* 正式)
1 to continue doing something 继续做： *We're not sure whether we want to* **proceed with** *the sale of the house.* 我们不确定是否还想把房子卖掉。
2 to do something next, after having done something else first 接着做： *Once he had calmed down, he* **proceeded to** *tell us what had happened.* 他一冷静下来，就告诉我们发生了什么事。

process 0→ /'prəʊses/ *noun* 名词 (*plural* 复数形式 processes)
a number of actions, one after the other, for doing or making something 过程；步骤；流程： *He explained the process of building a boat.* 他讲解了造船的工序。◇ *Learning a language is usually a slow process.* 语言学习通常是一个缓慢的过程。

procession /prə'seʃn/ *noun* 名词
a line of people or cars that are moving slowly along（人或车辆的）队伍，行列： *We watched the carnival procession.* 我们观看了狂欢节的游行。

produce¹ 0→ /prə'dju:s/ *verb* 动词 (produces, producing, produced /prə'dju:st/)
1 to make or grow something 生产；制造；出产： *This factory produces cars.* 这家厂生产汽车。◇ *What does the farm produce?* 这个农场出产什么？
2 to make something happen 产生；引起： *His hard work produced good results.* 努力使他取得了好成绩。
3 to bring something out to show it 出示；展示： *She produced a ticket from her pocket.* 她从口袋里掏出一张票来。
4 to organize something like a play or film 制作（戏剧、电影等）： *The play was produced by Peter Gordon.* 这出戏是由彼得•戈登监制的。

produce² /'prɒdju:s/ *noun* 名词 (*no plural* 不用复数形式)
food that you grow on a farm or in a garden to sell 农产品： *fresh farm produce* 新鲜的农产品

producer /prə'dju:sə(r)/ *noun* 名词
1 a person who organizes something like a play or film（戏剧、电影等的）制片人，制作人，监制： *a television producer* 电视节目制作人
2 a company or country that makes or grows something 生产商；制造公司；产地： *Brazil is an important producer of coffee.* 巴西是重要的咖啡出产国。

product 0→ /'prɒdʌkt/ *noun* 名词
something that people make or grow to sell 产品；制品： *The company has just launched a new product.* 这家公司刚推出一款新产品。

production 0→ /prə'dʌkʃn/ *noun* 名词
1 (*no plural* 不用复数形式) the action of making or growing something 生产；制造： *the production of oil* 石油的生产
2 (*plural* 复数形式 productions) a play, film, etc.（戏剧、电影等的）出品，制作

productive /prə'dʌktɪv/ *adjective* 形容词
doing, achieving or producing a lot 有效益的；多产的： *The meeting was very productive.* 会议很有成效。

profession 0→ /prə'feʃn/ *noun* 名词
a job that needs a lot of studying and special training 职业；专业工作： *She's a doctor* **by profession**. 她的职业是医生。

professional 0→ /prə'feʃənl/ *adjective* 形容词
1 connected with a profession 专业的；职业的： *I got professional advice from a lawyer.* 我得到了律师的专业意见。
2 doing something for money as a job 职业的： *a professional footballer* 职业足球运动员 ⊃ OPPOSITE **amateur** 反义词为 amateur
▸ **professionally** /prə'feʃənəli/ *adverb* 副词： *He plays the piano professionally.* 他钢琴弹得很熟练。

professor /prə'fesə(r)/ *noun* 名词
1 (*British* 英式英语) a university teacher of the highest level 教授： *Professor Oliver* 奥利弗教授 ◇ *He's professor of Psychology at Birmingham University.* 他是伯明翰大学的心理学教授。
2 (*American* 美式英语) a teacher at a college or university（学院或大学的）讲师，教员

profile /'prəʊfaɪl/ *noun* 名词
the shape of a person's face when you see it from the side 侧面轮廓；侧影

profit 0→ /'prɒfɪt/ *noun* 名词
money that you get when you sell something for more than it cost to buy

or make 利润；赢利；盈余：*They made a profit of £10.* 他们赚了 10 英镑。

profitable /ˈprɒfɪtəbl/ *adjective* 形容词
If something is **profitable**, it brings you money. 赚钱的；有利可图的：*a profitable business* 赚钱的生意

program[1] ⚙ /ˈprəʊɡræm/ *noun* 名词
1 (*computing* 电脑) a set of instructions that you give to a computer 程序；编码指令：*Load the program into the computer.* 把程序载入电脑。
2 *American English for* PROGRAMME 美式英语，即 programme

program[2] /ˈprəʊɡræm/ *verb* 动词
(**programs, programming, programmed** /ˈprəʊɡræmd/)
to give a set of instructions to a computer 编写程序；设计程序

programer *American English for* PROGRAMMER 美式英语，即 programmer

programme ⚙ (*British* 英式英语)
(*American* 美式英语 **program**) /ˈprəʊɡræm/ *noun* 名词
1 something on television or radio （电视或广播）节目：*Did you watch that programme about Japan on TV last night?* 你昨晚看了那个关于日本的电视节目吗？
2 a piece of paper or a little book that tells people at a play or concert what they are going to see or hear （戏剧或音乐会的）节目单
3 a plan of things to do 计划；方案：*What is your programme for tomorrow?* 你明天有什么安排？

programmer (*British* 英式英语)
(*American* 美式英语 **programer**)
/ˈprəʊɡræmə(r)/ *noun* 名词
a person whose job is to write programs for a computer 程序设计员；编程人员

progress[1] ⚙ /prəˈɡres/ *verb* 动词
(**progresses, progressing, progressed** /prəˈɡrest/)
1 to improve or develop 进步；改进；进展：*Students can progress at their own speed.* 学生可按各自的速度进步。
2 to move forwards; to continue 前进；行进；继续：*She became more tired as the evening progressed.* 夜越深她感到越疲倦。

progress[2] ⚙ /ˈprəʊɡres/ *noun* 名词
(*no plural* 不用复数形式)
1 improvement or development 进步；发展；进程：*Jo has made good progress in maths this year.* 乔今年数学进步很大。
2 movement forward 前行；前进；行进：*She watched her father's slow progress*

down the steps. 她看着父亲慢慢地走下台阶。
in progress happening now 进行中：*Quiet please – examination in progress.* 请肃静！考试正进行中。

prohibit /prəˈhɪbɪt/ *verb* 动词 (**prohibits, prohibiting, prohibited**) (*formal* 正式)
to say that people must not do something 禁止 ⊃ SAME MEANING **forbid** 同义词为 forbid：*Smoking is prohibited in the theatre.* 剧院里禁止吸烟。

project ⚙ /ˈprɒdʒekt/ *noun* 名词
1 a big plan to do something 项目；方案：*a project to build a new airport* 兴建新机场的方案 ◇ *The research project will be funded by the government.* 研究项目将由政府资助。
2 a piece of work that you do at school. You find out a lot about something and write about it. （学生的）专题研究：*We did a project on Africa.* 我们做了一个关于非洲的专题研究。

projector /prəˈdʒektə(r)/ *noun* 名词
a machine that shows films or pictures on a wall or screen 放映机；投影仪

prominent /ˈprɒmɪnənt/ *adjective* 形容词
1 easy to see, for example because it is bigger than usual 显眼的；突出的：*prominent teeth* 龅牙
2 important and famous 重要的；著名的；杰出的：*a prominent writer* 杰出的作家

promise[1] ⚙ /ˈprɒmɪs/ *verb* 动词
(**promises, promising, promised** /ˈprɒmɪst/)
to say that you will certainly do or not do something 许诺；承诺；答应：*She promised to give me the money today.* 她答应今天给我钱。◇ *I promise that I'll come.* 我保证我一定来。◇ *Promise me you won't be late!* 答应我你不会迟到！

promise[2] ⚙ /ˈprɒmɪs/ *noun* 名词
when you say that you will certainly do or not do something 承诺；诺言；许诺：*He kept his promise* (= did what he said). 他信守诺言。◇ *You broke your promise – how can I trust you?* 你食言了，我怎么还能信任你呢？

promote /prəˈməʊt/ *verb* 动词 (**promotes, promoting, promoted**)
1 to help to sell a product or make it more popular by advertising it or offering it at a special price 促销；推销：*The band has gone on tour to promote their new album.* 乐队开始了巡回演出，宣传他们的新专辑。

A B C D E F G H I J K L M N O P Q R S T U V W X Y Z

A
B
C
D
E
F
G
H
I
J
K
L
M
N
O
P
Q
R
S
T
U
V
W
X
Y
Z

2 to give somebody a more important job 提拔；擢升；晋升：*She worked hard, and after a year she was promoted to manager.* 她工作勤奋，一年后就晋升为经理了。

▶ **promotion** /prə'məʊʃn/ *noun* 名词: *The new job is a promotion for me.* 新职位对我来说是晋升。

prompt /prɒmpt/ *adjective* 形容词 quick 迅速的；及时的：*She gave me a prompt answer.* 她很快回答了我。

promptly /'prɒmptli/ *adverb* 副词 quickly; not late 立即；迅速；及时：*We arrived promptly at two o'clock.* 我们在两点钟准时到达。

pronoun /'prəʊnaʊn/ *noun* 名词 (*grammar* 语法) a word that you use in place of a noun 代词；代名词：*'He', 'it', 'me' and 'them' are all pronouns.* * he、it、me 和 them 都是代词。

pronounce 0ᵣ /prə'naʊns/ *verb* 动词 (**pronounces, pronouncing, pronounced** /prə'naʊnst/) to make the sound of a letter or word 发音；读（音）：*How do you pronounce your name?* 你的名字怎么念？ ◇ *You don't pronounce the 'b' at the end of 'comb'.* * comb 末尾的 b 不发音。

pronunciation /prə,nʌnsi'eɪʃn/ *noun* 名词 how you say a word or words 发音；读音：*What's the correct pronunciation of this word?* 这个词的正确发音是什么？ ◇ *His pronunciation is very good.* 他的发音非常好。

proof 0ᵣ /pruːf/ *noun* 名词 (*no plural* 不用复数形式) something that shows that an idea is true 证据；证明：*Do you have any proof that you are the owner of this car?* 你有证据证明你是这辆车的车主吗？ ⊃ The verb is **prove**. 动词为 prove.

propeller /prə'pelə(r)/ *noun* 名词 a part that is connected to the engine on a ship or a plane. It turns round very fast to make the ship or plane move. （轮船或飞机的）螺旋桨，推进器 ⊃ Look at the picture at **toy**. 见 toy 的插图。

proper 0ᵣ /'prɒpə(r)/ *adjective* 形容词 **1** right or correct 合适的；适宜的；恰当的：*I haven't got the proper tools to mend the car.* 我没有合适的工具来修理这辆车。 **2** (*British* 英式英语) (*informal* 非正式) real 真正的：*He hasn't got any proper friends.* 他没有真正的朋友。

properly 0ᵣ /'prɒpəli/ *adverb* 副词 well or correctly 正确地；适当地：*Close the door properly.* 把门关好。 ◇ *I can't see properly without my glasses.* 不戴眼镜我看不清楚。

property 0ᵣ /'prɒpəti/ *noun* 名词 **1** (*no plural* 不用复数形式) something that you have or own 所有物；财产；财物：*This book is the property of James Waters.* 这本书属詹姆斯·沃特斯所有。 **2** (*plural* 复数形式 **properties**) a building and the land around it 房产

prophet /'prɒfɪt/ *noun* 名词 a person that God chooses to give his message to people 先知

proportion /prə'pɔːʃn/ *noun* 名词 **1** a part of something 比例；部分；份额：*A large proportion of* (= many) *people agree.* 大部分人同意。 **2** the amount or size of one thing compared to another thing （数量或大小之间的）比例：*What is the proportion of men to women in the factory?* 这家工厂的男女比例是多少？

proposal /prə'pəʊzl/ *noun* 名词 **1** a plan or idea about how to do something 建议；提议：*a proposal to build a new station* 修建新车站的提议 **2** when you ask somebody to marry you 求婚

propose /prə'pəʊz/ *verb* 动词 (**proposes, proposing, proposed** /prə'pəʊzd/) **1** (*formal* 正式) to say what you think should happen or be done 建议；提议 ⊃ SAME MEANING **suggest** 同义词为 suggest: *I proposed that we should meet again on Monday.* 我建议我们星期一再开会。 **2** to ask somebody to marry you 求婚: *He proposed to me!* 他向我求婚了！

prose /prəʊz/ *noun* 名词 (*no plural* 不用复数形式) (*language* 语言) writing that is not poetry 散文：*He wrote poetry and prose.* 他写过诗歌和散文。

prosecute /'prɒsɪkjuːt/ *verb* 动词 (**prosecutes, prosecuting, prosecuted**) to say officially in a court of law that somebody has done something illegal 起诉；对（某人）提起公诉：*He was prosecuted for theft.* 他因盗窃而被起诉。

prosperous /'prɒspərəs/ *adjective* 形容词 rich and successful 繁荣的；兴旺的；兴盛的

protect 0̄**ṛ** /prə'tekt/ *verb* 动词
(**protects, protecting, protected**)
to keep somebody or something safe
保护；防护： *Parents try to **protect** their
children **from** danger.* 父母努力保护子女
远离危险。◇ *Wear a hat to **protect** your
head **against** the sun.* 戴上帽子以防头部
晒着。

protection 0̄**ṛ** /prə'tekʃn/ *noun* 名词
(*no plural* 不用复数形式)
keeping somebody or something safe
保护；防护： *He was put **under** police
protection.* 他受到了警方的保护。

protein /'prəʊtiːn/ *noun* 名词
a substance in foods such as meat, fish
and beans. **Protein** helps you to grow
and stay healthy. 蛋白质

protest¹ 0̄**ṛ** /'prəʊtest/ *noun* 名词
an action that shows publicly that you do
not like or approve of something 抗议：
*She took part in a **protest against** the war.*
她参加了反战抗议。

protest² 0̄**ṛ** /prə'test/ *verb* 动词
(**protests, protesting, protested**)
to say or show strongly that you do
not like something 抗议；反对： *They
protested against the government's plans.*
他们反对政府的计划。

Protestant /'prɒtɪstənt/ *noun* 名词
a person who believes in the Christian
God and who is not a Roman Catholic
新教教徒

proud 0̄**ṛ** /praʊd/ *adjective* 形容词
(**prouder, proudest**)
1 pleased about something that you or
others have done or about something
that you have 自豪的： *They are very
proud of their new house.* 他们为自己的
新房子感到非常自豪。
2 thinking that you are better than other
people 骄傲自大的；傲慢的： *She was too
proud to say she was sorry.* 她太骄傲了，
赔个不是都不肯。 ᴐ The noun is **pride**.
名词为 pride。
▸ **proudly** *adverb* 副词： *'I made this
myself,' he said proudly.* "这是我自己做
的。"他自豪地说。

prove 0̄**ṛ** /pruːv/ *verb* 动词 (**proves,
proving, proved** /pruːvd/, **has proved** or
或 **has proven** /'pruːvn/)
to show that something is true 证明；
证实： *The blood on his shirt **proves that**
he is the murderer.* 他衬衫上的血迹证明
他就是杀人凶手。 ᴐ The noun is **proof**.
名词为 proof。

proverb /'prɒvɜːb/ *noun* 名词
a short sentence that people often say,
that gives help or advice 谚语；格言：
'Waste not, want not' is an English proverb.
"勤俭节约，吃穿不缺"是句英语谚语。

provide 0̄**ṛ** /prə'vaɪd/ *verb* 动词
(**provides, providing, provided**)
to give something to somebody who
needs it 提供；供给： *I'll **provide** the food
for the party.* 我会提供聚会的食物。◇ *The
company have **provided** me **with** a car.*
公司为我配了一辆车。

provided /prə'vaɪdɪd/ (*also* 亦作
providing /prə'vaɪdɪŋ/) *conjunction* 连词
only if 只要；假如： *I'll go **provided that**
the children can come with me.* 要是孩子可
跟我一起去我就去。◇ *Phone me when you
get home, providing it's not too late.* 要是
不太晚的话，你一到家就给我打个电话。

province /'prɒvɪns/ *noun* 名词
a part of a country 省： *Canada has ten
provinces.* 加拿大有十个省。
▸ **provincial** /prə'vɪnʃl/ *adjective* 形容词
connected with a PROVINCE 省的；省级
的： *the provincial government* 省政府

provision /prə'vɪʒn/ *noun* 名词 (*no plural*
不用复数形式)
when something is given to somebody
who needs it 提供；供给： *The
government is responsible for the provision
of health care.* 政府负责提供医疗保健
服务。

provoke /prə'vəʊk/ *verb* 动词 (**provokes,
provoking, provoked** /prə'vəʊkt/)
to cause particular feelings or behaviour
激起；引发： *Dairy products may provoke
allergic reactions in some people.* 奶制品
可致使某些人出现过敏反应。

prowl /praʊl/ *verb* 动词 (**prowls,
prowling, prowled** /praʊld/)
(used about an animal that is hunting or
a person who is waiting for a chance to
do something bad) to move around an
area quietly so that nobody sees or hears
you（猎食中的动物或图谋不轨的人）
潜行： *I could hear someone prowling
around outside.* 我听到有人在外面悄悄地
蹑来蹑去。

PS /ˌpiː 'es/ *noun* 名词
You write **PS** at the end of a letter, after
your name, when you want to add
something.（用于信末）附言，又及：
... Love from Paul. PS I'll bring the car.
爱你的保罗。又及：我会把车开来。

A
B
C
D
E
F
G
H
I
J
K
L
M
N
O
P
Q
R
S
T
U
V
W
X
Y
Z

psychiatrist /saɪˈkaɪətrɪst/ *noun* 名词
a doctor who helps people who have a
mental illness 精神科医生；精神病学家

psychologist /saɪˈkɒlədʒɪst/ *noun* 名词
a person who studies PSYCHOLOGY 心理
学家

psychology /saɪˈkɒlədʒi/ *noun* 名词
(*no plural* 不用复数形式)
the study of the mind and how it works
心理学

psychopath /ˈsaɪkəpæθ/ *noun* 名词
a person who has a serious mental illness
that makes them behave in a violent way
towards other people 精神变态者；精神
失常者

pt *short way of writing* PINT * pint 的缩写
形式

PTO /ˌpiː tiː ˈəʊ/ *abbreviation* 缩略式
the abbreviation for 'please turn over';
written at the bottom of a page to tell
you to turn to the next page（位于页末）
请翻页，请见下页，见反面（PTO 是
please turn over 的缩略式）

pub 0= /pʌb/ *noun* 名词 (*British* 英式英语)
a place where people go to drink and
meet their friends 酒吧；酒馆：*They've
gone to the pub for a drink.* 他们去酒吧喝
酒了。◇ *On Sundays, we often go out for
a pub lunch.* 在星期天，我们通常下酒馆
吃午饭。

> 🔎 CULTURE 文化资料补充
>
> In Britain, you can buy alcoholic drinks
> like **beer** or **wine** in a **pub** if you are
> over the age of 18. In a lot of pubs you
> can also buy food. 在英国，18 岁以上
> 的人可以在酒吧（pub）买啤酒（beer）
> 或葡萄酒（wine）等含酒精的饮料。在
> 许多酒吧里还能买到食物。

public¹ 0= /ˈpʌblɪk/ *adjective* 形容词
connected with everybody; for everybody
公众的；公共的；公用的：*a public
telephone* 公用电话 ◇ *Smoking is not
allowed in public places.* 公共场所不准
吸烟。

▶ **publicly** /ˈpʌblɪkli/ *adverb* 副词 to
everybody; not secretly 公开地；公然地：
*She spoke publicly about her friendship
with the Prince.* 她公开谈论与王子的友谊。

public² 0= /ˈpʌblɪk/ *noun* 名词
the public (*no plural* 不用复数形式)
people in general; everybody 公众；
民众：*The palace is open to the public
between 10 a.m. and 4 p.m.* 宫殿从上午
10 时至下午 4 时向公众开放。

in public when other people are there
公开地；当众：*I don't want to talk
about it in public.* 我不想公开谈论这
件事。

publication /ˌpʌblɪˈkeɪʃn/ *noun* 名词
1 (*no plural* 不用复数形式) when a book,
magazine, etc. is made and sold 出版；
发行：*He became very rich after the
publication of his first book.* 他在第一本书
出版以后变得非常有钱。
2 (*plural* 复数形式 publications) a book,
magazine, etc. 出版物

public convenience /ˌpʌblɪk
kənˈviːniəns/ *noun* 名词
a toilet for everybody to use, for example
in the street 公共厕所

publicity /pʌbˈlɪsəti/ *noun* 名词 (*no plural*
不用复数形式)
giving information about something so
that people know about it 宣传；报道：
*There was a lot of publicity for the new
film.* 新电影做了大量宣传。

public relations /ˌpʌblɪk rɪˈleɪʃnz/
noun 名词 (*no plural* 不用复数形式) (*abbr.*
缩略式 PR)
the business of providing information
about somebody or something, in order
to give people a good impression of them
公关工作（或活动）：*She works in public
relations.* 她从事公关工作。

public school /ˌpʌblɪk ˈskuːl/ *noun* 名词
1 (in Britain, especially in England)
a private school for young people
between the ages of 13 and 18, whose
parents pay for their education. The
students often live at the school while
they are studying.（英国，尤指英格兰
的）公学（为 13 到 18 岁青少年而设的
私立付费学校，学生常寄宿）
2 (in the US, Australia, Scotland and other
countries) a free local school paid for
by the government（美国、澳大利亚、
苏格兰等的）免费公立学校

public transport /ˌpʌblɪk ˈtrænspɔːt/
noun 名词 (*no plural* 不用复数形式)
buses and trains that everybody can use
公共交通工具：*I usually travel by public
transport.* 我通常乘坐公交出门。

publish 0= /ˈpʌblɪʃ/ *verb* 动词
(publishes, publishing, published
/ˈpʌblɪʃt/)
1 to prepare and print a book, magazine
or newspaper for selling 出版；发行：
*This dictionary was published by Oxford
University Press.* 本词典由牛津大学出版社
出版。

2 to make information available to the public, especially on the Internet（尤指在互联网上）公布，发表

▶ **publisher** /ˈpʌblɪʃə(r)/ *noun* 名词: *The publisher is OUP.* 出版者为牛津大学出版社。

pudding /ˈpʊdɪŋ/ *noun* 名词 (*British* 英式英语)
1 something sweet that you eat at the end of a meal（餐末的）甜点，甜食
◯ SAME MEANING **dessert** 同义词为 dessert: *'What's for pudding?' 'Fruit.'* "甜点是什么？" "水果。"
2 a hot sweet dish, often like a cake, that you eat at the end of a meal 布丁: *Christmas pudding* 圣诞布丁

puddle /ˈpʌdl/ *noun* 名词
a small pool of rain or other liquid on the ground 水洼；小水坑

puff¹ /pʌf/ *verb* 动词 (**puffs, puffing, puffed** /pʌft/)
1 to smoke a cigarette, pipe, etc. 吸，抽（香烟、烟斗等）: *He sat puffing his cigar.* 他坐着抽雪茄。
2 (used about air, smoke, wind, etc.) to blow or come out in clouds（空气、烟、风等）冒出，喷出: *Smoke was puffing out of the chimney.* 烟囱正冒着烟。◇ *Stop puffing cigarette smoke in my face.* 别对着我的脸喷烟雾。
3 (*informal* 非正式) to breathe quickly or loudly, especially after you have been running 喘气；气喘吁吁；急促喘息: *She was puffing as she ran up the hill.* 她气喘吁吁地往山上跑。

puff² /pʌf/ *noun* 名词
a small amount of air, wind, smoke, etc. that is blown from somewhere 一股，一缕（空气、风、烟等）: *a puff of smoke* 一缕青烟

pull 拉

pull¹ 0━ /pʊl/ *verb* 动词 (**pulls, pulling, pulled** /pʊld/)
1 to move somebody or something strongly towards you 拉；拖；拽: *She pulled the drawer open.* 她拉开了抽屉。
2 to go forward, moving something behind you 牵引；拉动: *The cart was pulled by two horses.* 车子由两匹马拉着。
3 to move something somewhere 拉；拖动: *He pulled up his trousers.* 他提了提裤子。

pull down to destroy a building 拆毁，拆除（建筑物）: *The old school has been pulled down.* 那所旧学校已经拆了。

pull in to drive a car to the side of the road and stop 把车停在路边: *I pulled in to look at the map.* 我在路边把车停下，看一下地图。

pull somebody's leg (*informal* 非正式) to try to make somebody believe something that is not true, for fun 捉弄和…开玩笑: *I didn't really see an elephant – I was only pulling your leg!* 我并没有真的看到大象，只是和你开个玩笑！

pull yourself together to control your feelings after being upset 使自己镇定下来: *Pull yourself together and stop crying.* 振作起来，别哭了。

pull up to stop a car 停车: *The driver pulled up at the traffic lights.* 司机在红绿灯处停了车。

pull² 0━ /pʊl/ *noun* 名词
an action of pulling something 拉；拖；拽: *Give the rope a pull.* 拉一下绳子。

pullover /ˈpʊləʊvə(r)/ *noun* 名词
a warm piece of clothing with sleeves, that you wear on the top part of your body. **Pullovers** are often made of wool. 套头毛衣 ◯ Look at the note at **sweater**. 见 sweater 条的注释。

pulse /pʌls/ *noun* 名词
the beating of your heart that you feel in different parts of your body, especially in your wrist 脉搏: *The nurse felt* (= measured) *his pulse.* 护士给他量了脉搏。

pump¹ /pʌmp/ *noun* 名词
a machine that moves a liquid or gas into or out of something 泵；抽水机；打气筒: *a bicycle pump* 自行车打气筒 ◇ *a petrol pump* 汽油泵

pump² /pʌmp/ *verb* 动词 (**pumps, pumping, pumped** /pʌmpt/)
to force a gas or a liquid to go in a particular direction 用泵输送（气体

A
B
C
D
E
F
G
H
I
J
K
L
M
N
O
P
Q
R
S
T
U
V
W
X
Y
Z

或液体）: *Your heart **pumps** blood **around** your body.* 心脏把血液输送到全身。

pump something up to fill something with air, using a pump 为…充气; 给…打气: *I pumped up my bicycle tyres.* 我给自行车轮胎打了气。

pumpkin /'pʌmpkɪn/ *noun* 名词
a very large round vegetable with a thick orange skin 南瓜 ⊃ Look at Picture Dictionary page **P9**. 见彩页 P9。

pun /pʌn/ *noun* 名词
a funny use of a word that has two meanings, or that sounds the same as another word 双关语

punch 拳打

punch /pʌntʃ/ *verb* 动词 (punches, punching, punched /pʌntʃt/)
1 to hit somebody or something hard with your closed hand (your fist) 拳打; 以拳痛击: *He punched me on the nose.* 他一拳打在我的鼻子上。
2 to make a hole in something with a special tool 给…打孔: *The ticket collector punched my ticket.* 收票员在我的票上打了孔。
▶ **punch** *noun* 名词 (*plural* 复数形式 punches): *a punch on the chin* 打在下巴上的一拳

punctual /'pʌŋktʃuəl/ *adjective* 形容词
arriving or doing something at the right time; not late 准时的; 守时的: *Please try to be punctual for your classes.* 请尽量准时上课。
▶ **punctually** /'pʌŋktʃuəli/ *adverb* 副词: *They arrived punctually at seven o'clock.* 他们七点钟准时到达。

punctuate /'pʌŋktʃueɪt/ *verb* 动词 (punctuates, punctuating, punctuated)
to put full stops, question marks, etc. in your writing （给…）加标点符号

punctuation /ˌpʌŋktʃu'eɪʃn/ *noun* 名词 (*no plural* 不用复数形式)
using PUNCTUATION MARKS when you are writing 标点符号的使用

punctuation mark /ˌpʌŋktʃu'eɪʃn mɑːk/ *noun* 名词
one of the marks that you use in your writing, for example a full stop or question mark 标点符号

puncture /'pʌŋktʃə(r)/ *noun* 名词 (*British* 英式英语)
a hole in a tyre, that lets the air go out （轮胎上的）小孔, 小洞: *My bike has got a puncture.* 我的自行车车胎扎了。
▶ **puncture** *verb* 动词 (punctures, puncturing, punctured /'pʌŋktʃəd/) to make a PUNCTURE in something 在…上扎孔（或穿孔）: *A piece of glass punctured the tyre.* 一块玻璃把轮胎扎破了。

punish ⊶ /'pʌnɪʃ/ *verb* 动词 (punishes, punishing, punished /'pʌnɪʃt/)
to make somebody suffer because they have done something wrong 惩罚; 处罚: *The children were punished for telling lies.* 孩子们因撒谎受到了惩罚。

punishment ⊶ /'pʌnɪʃmənt/ *noun* 名词
an act or a way of punishing somebody 惩罚; 处罚: *What is the punishment for murder in your country?* 在你们国家谋杀罪会处以什么刑罚？ ◇ *The child was sent to bed as a punishment for being naughty.* 那个孩子太顽皮, 被罚上床睡觉去了。

pupil ⊶ /'pjuːpl/ *noun* 名词
1 a person who is learning at school, especially a child 学生（尤指小学生）: *There are 30 pupils in the class.* 班上有 30 个学生。 ⊃ Look at the note at **student**. 见 student 条的注释。 ⊃ Look at Picture Dictionary page **P11**. 见彩页 P11。
2 the round black hole in the middle of your eye 瞳孔; 眸子 ⊃ Look at the picture at **eye**. 见 eye 的插图。

puppet 木偶

puppet /'pʌpɪt/ *noun* 名词
a small model of a person or animal that you move by pulling strings or by putting your hand inside 木偶

puppy /'pʌpi/ *noun* 名词 (*plural* 复数形式 **puppies**)
a young dog 小狗；幼犬 ➋ Look at the picture at **dog**. 见 dog 的插图。

purchase¹ /'pɜːtʃəs/ *noun* 名词 (*formal* 正式)
the action of buying something; something that you have bought 购买；购买的东西: *She **made** several **purchases** and then left the store.* 她买了几件东西就离开了商店。

purchase² /'pɜːtʃəs/ *verb* 动词 (**purchases, purchasing, purchased** /'pɜːtʃəst/) (*formal* 正式)
to buy something 买；购买: *The company has purchased three new shops.* 这家公司购入了三间新店。

pure 0━ /pjʊə(r)/ *adjective* 形容词 (**purer, purest**)
1 not mixed with anything else 纯的；纯粹的: *This shirt is pure cotton.* 这件衬衫是纯棉的。
2 clean and healthy 洁净的；纯净的: *pure mountain air* 山区纯净的空气
3 complete or total 完全的；纯粹的: *What she said was pure nonsense.* 她说的全是胡扯。

purely /'pjʊəli/ *adverb* 副词
only or completely 仅仅；完全: *He doesn't like his job – he does it purely for the money.* 他并不喜欢自己的工作，纯粹是为了挣钱。

purple 0━ /'pɜːpl/ *adjective* 形容词
with a colour between red and blue 紫色的
▶ **purple** *noun* 名词: *She often wears purple.* 她经常穿紫色的衣服。

purpose 0━ /'pɜːpəs/ *noun* 名词
the reason for doing something 意图；目的: *What is the purpose of your visit?* 你这次来访的目的是什么?
on purpose because you want to; not by accident 故意；有意地 ➋ SAME MEANING **deliberately** 同义词为 **deliberately**: *'You've broken my pen!' 'I'm sorry, I didn't do it on purpose.'* "你弄坏了我的笔! " "对不起，我不是故意的。"

purposely /'pɜːpəsli/ *adverb* 副词
on purpose; deliberately 故意地；蓄意地

purr /pɜː(r)/ *verb* 动词 (**purrs, purring, purred** /pɜːd/)
When a cat **purrs**, it makes a low sound that shows that it is happy. (猫满足地) 发出呼噜声

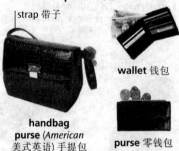
purse 钱包
strap 带子
wallet 钱包
handbag
purse (*American* 美式英语) 手提包
purse 零钱包

purse /pɜːs/ *noun* 名词
1 (*British* 英式英语) a small bag made of leather, plastic, etc. for carrying money, credit cards, etc., used especially by women (尤指女用的) 钱包
2 *American English for* HANDBAG 美式英语，即 handbag

pursue /pə'sjuː/ *verb* 动词 (**pursues, pursuing, pursued** /pə'sjuːd/) (*formal* 正式)
to follow somebody or something because you want to catch them 追赶；追逐 ➋ SAME MEANING **chase** 同义词为 chase: *The police pursued the stolen car for several kilometres.* 警方追赶那辆被盗汽车，追了好几公里。

push 推

push 0━ /pʊʃ/ *verb* 动词 (**pushes, pushing, pushed** /pʊʃt/)
1 to use force to move somebody or something forward or away from you

A
B
C
D
E
F
G
H
I
J
K
L
M
N
O
P
Q
R
S
T
U
V
W
X
Y
Z

推；推动：*The car broke down so we had to push it to a garage.* 车子坏了，我们唯有把它推到修理厂去。◇ *He pushed me over!* 他把我推倒了！
2 to press something with your finger 按；摁：*Push the red button to stop the bus.* 按红色的按钮让公共汽车停下来。
▶ **push** *noun* 名词 (*plural* 复数形式 pushes): *She gave him a push and he fell.* 她推了他一下，他摔倒了。

pushchair 幼儿小推车

pushchair
折叠式幼儿小推车

pram 婴儿车

pushchair /ˈpʊʃtʃeə(r)/ (*British* 英式英语) (*American* 美式英语 **stroller**) *noun* 名词
a chair on wheels in which a young child is pushed along 折叠式婴儿车 ⊃ SAME MEANING **buggy** 同义词为 buggy

push-up /ˈpʊʃ ʌp/ *noun* 名词 *American English for* PRESS-UP 美式英语，即 press-up

pussy /ˈpʊsi/ *noun* 名词 (*plural* 复数形式 pussies)
a word for 'cat' that children use（儿语）猫咪

put ⊶ /pʊt/ *verb* 动词 (puts, putting, put, has put)
1 to move something to a place or position 放；放置：*She put the book on the table.* 她把书放在桌子上。◇ *He put his hand in his pocket.* 他把手插进口袋。
2 to write something 写；记：*Put your name at the top of the page.* 把你的名字写在这页纸的上端。
put something away to put something back in its usual place 把…放回原处：*She put the box away in the cupboard.* 她把盒子放回柜子里。
put something down to stop holding something and put it on another thing,

for example on the floor or a table 放下；搁下：*Let me put my bags down first.* 让我先把包放下。
put somebody off to make somebody not like someone or something 使讨厌；使反感：*The accident put me off driving.* 那次事故之后我就不喜欢开车了。
put something off to not do something until later 推迟；延迟 ⊃ SAME MEANING **delay** 同义词为 delay：*He put off his holiday because the children were ill.* 由于孩子都生病，所以他把假期推迟了。
put something on
1 to take clothes and wear them 穿上；戴上：*Put on your coat.* 穿上你的大衣。◇ *Put your shoes on.* 把你的鞋子穿上。⊃ OPPOSITE **take something off** 反义词为 take something off
2 to make a piece of electrical equipment start to work 打开，开动（电器）：*I put on the TV.* 我开了电视。◇ *Put the lights on.* 开灯。◇ *Shall we put some music on?* 我们放点音乐好吗？
put something out to stop a fire or to stop a light shining 使熄灭；关上（灯）：*She put out the fire with a bucket of water.* 她用一桶水把火浇灭了。◇ *Put the lights out before you go.* 走之前把灯都关掉。
put somebody through to connect somebody on the telephone to the person they want to speak to 给…接通电话：*Can you put me through to the manager, please?* 请帮我接通经理的电话好吗？
put somebody up to let somebody sleep in your home 留某人过夜：*Can you put me up for the night?* 你能让我在你家过夜吗？
put up with somebody or 或 **something** to have pain or problems without complaining 容忍；忍受：*We can't change the bad weather, so we have to put up with it.* 我们对糟糕的天气毫无办法，只好忍着吧。

puzzle¹ /ˈpʌzl/ *noun* 名词
1 something that is difficult to understand or explain 不解之谜；谜团：*Janet's reason for leaving her job is a puzzle to me.* 珍妮特辞职的原因对我来说是个谜。
2 a game that is difficult and makes you think a lot 智力游戏；谜 ⊃ Look also at **crossword** and **jigsaw**. 亦见 crossword 和 jigsaw。

puzzle² /ˈpʌzl/ *verb* 动词 (puzzles, puzzling, puzzled /ˈpʌzld/)
to make you feel that you cannot understand or explain something 使困惑；使迷惑不解: *Tim's illness puzzled his doctors.* 蒂姆的病让他的医生都感到不解。

puzzled /ˈpʌzld/ *adjective* 形容词
not able to understand or explain something 困惑的；迷惑不解的: *She had a **puzzled look** on her face.* 她满脸困惑。

puzzling /ˈpʌzlɪŋ/ *adjective* 形容词
difficult to understand or explain 令人困惑的；费解的

pyjamas (*British* 英式英语) (*American* 美式英语 **pajamas**) /pəˈdʒɑːməz/ *noun* 名词 (*plural* 用复数形式)
a loose jacket and trousers that you wear in bed 睡衣裤 ➲ Look at Picture Dictionary page **P5**. 见彩页 P5。

pyramid /ˈpɪrəmɪd/ *noun* 名词
a shape with a flat bottom and three or four sides that come to a point at the top 锥体；棱锥体: *the pyramids of Egypt* 埃及的金字塔

pyramid 金字塔

Q q

Q, q /kjuː/ *noun* 名词 (*plural* 复数形式 Q's, q's/kjuːz/)
the seventeenth letter of the English alphabet 英语字母表的第 17 个字母：
'*Queen*' begins with a '*Q*'. * queen 一词以字母 q 开头。

quack /kwæk/ *noun* 名词
the sound that a DUCK (= a bird that lives on or near water) makes（鸭子的）嘎嘎声，呱呱声
▶ **quack** *verb* 动词 (quacks, quacking quacked/kwækt/)

quaint /kweɪnt/ *adjective* 形容词
(quainter, quaintest)
old-fashioned, usually in an attractive way 古色古香的：*a quaint little cottage* 老式而别致的小村舍

qualification /ˌkwɒlɪfɪˈkeɪʃn/ *noun* 名词
an examination that you have passed, or training or knowledge that you need to do a special job 资格；资历：*He left school with no qualifications.* 他中学肄业。

qualified /ˈkwɒlɪfaɪd/ *adjective* 形容词
having passed the exams or done the training necessary to do a particular job 具备相关资历的；合格的：*She's a qualified nurse.* 她是一名合格护士。

qualify /ˈkwɒlɪfaɪ/ *verb* 动词 (qualifies, qualifying, qualified /ˈkwɒlɪfaɪd/, has qualified)
to get the right knowledge and training and pass exams so that you can do a certain job 取得资格；具备资格：*Anna has qualified as a doctor.* 安娜已经取得医生的资格。

quality ০➣ /ˈkwɒləti/ *noun* 名词
(*no plural* 不用复数形式)
how good or bad something is 质量；品质：*The quality of her work is excellent.* 她工作很出色。◇ *This furniture isn't very good quality.* 这件家具质量不太好。

quantity ০➣ /ˈkwɒntəti/ *noun* 名词
(*plural* 复数形式 quantities)
how much of something there is 数量
つ SAME MEANING **amount** 同义词为 amount：*I only bought a small quantity of cheese.* 我只买了少量的干酪。

quarrel[1] /ˈkwɒrəl/ *noun* 名词
an argument or a disagreement with

somebody 争吵；吵架；口角：*He had a quarrel with his wife about money.* 为了钱的事，他和妻子吵了一架。

quarrel[2] /ˈkwɒrəl/ *verb* 动词 (*British* 英式英语 quarrels, quarrelling, quarrelled /ˈkwɒrəld/) (*American* 美式英语 quarreling, quarreled)
to argue or disagree with somebody 争吵；吵架：*He quarrelled with his wife about money.* 为了钱的事，他和妻子吵架了。◇ *The children are always quarrelling.* 孩子们总是在拌嘴。

quarry /ˈkwɒri/ *noun* 名词 (*plural* 复数形式 quarries)
a place where people cut stone, sand, etc. out of the ground 采石场

quarter ০➣ /ˈkwɔːtə(r)/ *noun* 名词
1 one of four equal parts of something; ¼ 四分之一：*a mile and a quarter* * 1.25 英里 ◇ *The film starts in three quarters of an hour.* 电影四十五分钟后开演。
2 three months 三个月；季度；季：*You get a telephone bill every quarter.* 你每季度会收到一次电话账单。
3 a part of a town（城镇的）区：*the Chinese quarter* 华人区
(a) **quarter past** (*British* 英式英语) 15 minutes after the hour（正点之后）过 15 分钟，过一刻：*It's quarter past two.* 两点一刻了。◇ *I'll meet you at a quarter past.* 我一刻钟的时候见你。
つ In American English you say **a quarter after**. 美式英语说 a quarter after：*It's a quarter after seven.* 七点一刻了。
(a) **quarter to** (*British* 英式英语) 15 minutes before the hour（正点之前）差 15 分钟，差一刻：*It's quarter to nine.* 八点四十五分了。 つ In American English you say **a quarter of**. 美式英语说 a quarter of：*It's a quarter of four now.* 现在是三点四十五分。

quarter-final /ˌkwɔːtə ˈfaɪnl/ *noun* 名词
one of the four matches between the eight players or teams left in a competition 四分之一决赛；半准决赛
つ Look at **semi-final**. 见 semi-final。

quay /kiː/ *noun* 名词 (*plural* 复数形式 quays)
a place in a port where ships go so that

people can move things on and off them
码头

queen ⊶ /kwi:n/ *noun* 名词
1 a woman from a royal family who
rules a country 女王: *Queen Elizabeth II*
(= the second), *the Queen of England*
英国女王伊丽莎白二世
2 the wife of a king 王后

quench /kwentʃ/ *verb* 动词 (quenches,
quenching, quenched /kwentʃt/)
quench your thirst to drink as much as
you need so that you stop feeling thirsty
解渴; 止渴

query¹ /'kwɪəri/ *noun* 名词 (*plural* 复数
形式 queries)
a question 疑问; 询问: *Phone me if
you have any queries.* 要是有任何疑问就
打电话给我。

query² /'kwɪəri/ *verb* 动词 (queries,
querying, queried /'kwɪərid/)
to ask a question about something that
you think is wrong 提出疑问; 质疑: *We
queried the bill but the waitress said it was
correct.* 我们怀疑账单有问题, 可是女服务
员却说正确无误。

question¹ ⊶ /'kwestʃən/ *noun* 名词
1 something that you ask 问题: *They
asked me a lot of questions.* 他们问了
我很多问题。◇ *She didn't answer my
question.* 她没有回答我的问题。◇ *What is
the answer to question 3?* 第 3 题的答案
是什么?
2 something that you need to deal with;
something that is being discussed (待处
理的)问题; 议题: *The question is, how
can we raise the money?* 问题是, 我们
该如何筹集这笔钱? ◇ *It's a question of
time – we need to finish the work today.*
这是时间问题 —— 我们得在今天完成这项
工作。
in question that we are talking about
讨论中的: *On the day in question I was
in London.* 在说到的那天, 我在伦敦。
out of the question not possible
不可能: *No, I won't give you any more
money. It's out of the question!* 不行,
我不会再给你钱了。决不可能!

question² ⊶ /'kwestʃən/ *verb* 动词
(questions, questioning, questioned
/'kwestʃənd/)
1 to ask somebody questions about
something 问; 提问: *The police
questioned him about the stolen car.*
警方查问了他关于那辆被盗汽车的事。
2 to feel doubt about something 怀疑;
质疑: *She told me she was the child's*

mother so I didn't question her right to be
there. 她告诉我她是那个孩子的母亲, 我就
没有怀疑她是否有权待在那里了。

question mark /'kwestʃən mɑ:k/ *noun*
名词
the sign (?) that you write at the end of
a question 问号

questionnaire /ˌkwestʃə'neə(r)/ *noun*
名词
a list of questions for people to answer so
that information can be collected from
the answers 问卷; 调查表: *Please fill in
(= write the answers on) the
questionnaire.* 请填写问卷。

question tag /'kwestʃən tæg/ *noun* 名词
(*grammar* 语法) words such as 'is it?' or
'didn't you?' that you put on the end of
a sentence to make it into a question
反意疑问成份, 附加疑问成份 (放在句末,
使句子变成问句): *In the sentence 'You're
French, aren't you?', 'aren't you' is a
question tag.* 在 You're French, aren't you?
这句中, aren't you 是反意疑问成份。

queue¹ /kju:/ *noun* 名词 (*British* 英式英语)
(*American* 美式英语 line)
a line of people who are waiting to do
something 等候的长队: *We stood in the
queue for the cinema.* 我们排队买电影票。

queue² /kju:/ (*also* 亦作 queue up) *verb*
动词 (queues, queuing, queued /kju:d/)
(*British* 英式英语)
to stand in a QUEUE 排队等候: *We queued
for a bus.* 我们排队等公共汽车。

quiche /ki:ʃ/ *noun* 名词 (*plural* 复数形式
quiches /'ki:ʃɪz/)
a type of food made of PASTRY (= a
mixture of flour, fat and water) filled with
egg and milk with cheese, onion, etc. and
cooked in the oven. You can eat **quiche**
hot or cold. 开口馅饼 (馅料有蛋、牛奶、
奶酪、洋葱等) ◇ Look at Picture
Dictionary page P7. 见彩页 P7。

quick ⊶ /kwɪk/ *adjective, adverb*
形容词, 副词 (quicker, quickest)
taking little time 快的; 迅速的 ⊃ SAME
MEANING **fast** 同义词为 fast: *It's quicker
to travel by plane than by train.* 搭飞机比
坐火车快。◇ *Can I make a quick
telephone call?* 我能打个很短的电话吗?
⊃ OPPOSITE **slow** 反义词为 slow
▸ **quickly** *adverb* 副词: *Come as quickly
as you can!* 赶紧过来!

quid /kwɪd/ *noun* 名词 (*plural* 复数形式
quid) (*British* 英式英语) (*informal* 非正式)
(money) a pound 一英镑: *It costs five
quid.* 这个要五英镑。

A
B
C
D
E
F
G
H
I
J
K
L
M
N
O
P
Q
R
S
T
U
V
W
X
Y
Z

A
B
C
D
E
F
G
H
I
J
K
L
M
N
O
P
Q
R
S
T
U
V
W
X
Y
Z

quiet[1] 0– /'kwaɪət/ *adjective* 形容词
(quieter, quietest)
1 making very little noise 安静的；轻声
的：*Be quiet – the baby's asleep.* 安静点，
宝宝睡着了。◇ *a quiet voice* 轻柔的嗓音
つ OPPOSITE **loud** or **noisy** 反义词为 loud
或 noisy
2 without many people or without many
things happening 寂静的；宁静的；清静
的：*London is very quiet on Sundays.*
星期天的伦敦非常宁静。
▶ **quietly** /'kwaɪətli/ *adverb* 副词：
Please close the door quietly. 请轻轻关门。

quiet[2] /'kwaɪət/ *noun* 名词 (*no plural* 不用
复数形式)
when there is no noise 安静；宁静；
寂静：*I need quiet when I'm working.*
我工作的时候需要安静。◇ *I go to the
library for a little* **peace and quiet**.
我到图书馆去清静一下。

quilt /kwɪlt/ *noun* 名词
a bed cover with soft material inside
加衬芯床罩；被子

quit /kwɪt/ *verb* 动词 (quits, quitting, quit,
has quit) (*informal* 非正式)
to leave a job or place; to stop doing
something 离职；离开；停止；戒掉：
*She **quit** as coach.* 她辞去了教练的工作。
◇ *We've nearly finished – we're not going
to* **quit** *now!* 我们快完成了，我们现在不会
放弃！

quite 0– /kwaɪt/ *adverb* 副词
1 not very; rather 颇；相当 つ SAME
MEANING **fairly** 同义词为 fairly：*It's quite
warm today, but it's not hot.* 今天相当暖
和，但并不热。◇ *He plays the guitar quite
well.* 他吉他弹得挺好的。◇ *We waited
quite a long time.* 我们等了很长时间。
2 completely 完全；十分：*Dinner is **not**
quite ready.* 晚饭还没完全准备好。
quite a few or 或 **quite a lot** a fairly
large amount or number 很多；相当多：
There were quite a few people at the party.

参加聚会的人相当多。◇ *They drank **quite**
a lot of wine.* 他们喝了不少葡萄酒。

quiver /'kwɪvə(r)/ *verb* 动词 (quivers,
quivering, quivered /'kwɪvəd/)
to shake slightly 微微颤动；抖动；
哆嗦 つ SAME MEANING **tremble** 同义词为
tremble：*Her lip quivered and then she
started to cry.* 她嘴唇微颤，然后哭了
起来。

quiz /kwɪz/ *noun* 名词 (*plural* 复数形式
quizzes)
a game where you try to answer
questions 知识竞赛；智力游戏：*a quiz
on television* 电视智力游戏节目

quota /'kwəʊtə/ *noun* 名词
the limited number or amount of people
or things that is officially allowed 配额；
限额；定额：*We have already reached
our quota – we cannot take any more
people.* 我们的名额已满，不能再收人了。

quotation /kwəʊ'teɪʃn/ (*also* 亦作 quote
/kwəʊt/) *noun* 名词
words that you say or write, that another
person said or wrote before 引语；引文：
That's a quotation from a poem by Keats.
那句引文摘录自济慈的诗。

quotation marks /kwəʊ'teɪʃn mɑːks/
(*also* 亦作 quotes) *noun* 名词 (*plural*
用复数形式)
the signs (" ") or (' ') that you use in
writing before and after the exact words
that someone has said 引号

quote /kwəʊt/ *verb* 动词 (quotes, quoting,
quoted)
to repeat exactly something that another
person said or wrote 引用；引述：*She
quoted from the Bible.* 她引用了《圣经》
里的语句。◇ *Don't **quote** me, but she's
wrong.* 不要说这是我说的，可是她错了。

the Qur'an /ðə kə'rɑːn/ *noun* 名词
(*no plural* 不用复数形式) = KORAN

R r

A
B
C
D
E
F
G
H
I
J
K
L
M
N
O
P
Q
R
S
T
U
V
W
X
Y
Z

R, r /ɑː(r)/ *noun* 名词 (*plural* 复数形式 **R's, r's** /ɑːz/)
the eighteenth letter of the English alphabet 英语字母表的第 18 个字母: 'Rose' begins with an 'R'. * rose 一词以字母 r 开头。

rabbi /'ræbaɪ/ *noun* 名词 (*plural* 复数形式 **rabbis**)
a teacher or leader of the Jewish religion 拉比（犹太教的经师或领袖）

rabbit 兔子

hare 野兔　　　**rabbit** 兔子

rabbit /'ræbɪt/ *noun* 名词
a small animal with long ears. **Rabbits** live in holes under the ground. 兔子

rabies /'reɪbiːz/ *noun* 名词 (*no plural* 不用复数形式)
a serious disease that people can get if a dog or another animal with the disease bites them 狂犬病；恐水症: *The dog had rabies.* 这条狗有狂犬病。

race¹ 0━ /reɪs/ *noun* 名词
1 a competition to see who can run, drive, ride, etc. fastest 赛跑；速度比赛: *Who won the race?* 赛跑谁赢了？ ◇ *a horse race* 赛马
2 the races (*British* 英式英语) (*plural* 用复数形式) horse races or dog races 赛马；赛狗: *He likes going to the races.* 他喜欢去看赛马。
3 a group of people of the same kind, for example with the same colour skin, language or customs 种族；人种: *People of many different races live together in this country.* 在这个国家里，很多不同种族的人生活在一起。

race² 0━ /reɪs/ *verb* 动词 (**races, racing, raced** /reɪst/)
1 to run, drive, ride, etc. in a competition to see who is the fastest 进行速度比赛: *The cars raced round the track.* 车子环绕跑道进行比赛。 ◇ *I'll race you to the other end of the pool.* 我要跟你比谁先游到泳池的对岸。
2 to move, or to move somebody or something, very fast （使）快速移动: *He raced up the stairs.* 他飞快地跑上楼去。 ◇ *The ambulance raced the injured woman to hospital.* 救护车把那名受伤女子迅速送往医院去了。

racecourse /'reɪskɔːs/ (*also* 亦作 **racetrack** /'reɪstræk/) *noun* 名词
a place where you go to see horse races 赛马场；赛马跑道

racial /'reɪʃl/ *adjective* 形容词
connected with people's race; happening between people of different races 种族的；种族间的: *racial differences* 种族差异

racing /'reɪsɪŋ/ *noun* 名词 (*no plural* 不用复数形式)
the sport of taking part in races 赛跑；赛车；赛马: *a racing car* 赛车

racism /'reɪsɪzəm/ *noun* 名词 (*no plural* 不用复数形式)
the belief that some groups (**races**) of people are better than others 种族主义
▶ **racist** *noun* 名词: *He's a terrible racist.* 他是个偏激的种族主义者。
▶ **racist** *adjective* 形容词: *a racist comment* 种族主义的评论

rack /ræk/ *noun* 名词
a kind of shelf, made of bars, that you put things on 支架；架子: *I got on the train and put my bag on the luggage rack.* 我上了火车，把包放上行李架了。

racket (*also* 亦作 **racquet**) /'rækɪt/ *noun* 名词
a thing that you use for hitting the ball in sports such as TENNIS, BADMINTON and SQUASH （网球、羽毛球、壁球等的）球拍 ➔ Look at the picture on the next page. 见下页的插图。

racket 球拍

radar /'reɪdɑː(r)/ *noun* 名词 (*no plural* 不用复数形式)
a way of finding where a ship or an aircraft is and how fast it is travelling by using radio waves 雷达

radiation /ˌreɪdi'eɪʃn/ *noun* 名词 (*no plural* 不用复数形式)
dangerous energy that some substances send out 辐射: *High levels of radiation have been recorded near the nuclear power station.* 这座核电站附近检测到了高强度的辐射。

radiator /'reɪdieɪtə(r)/ *noun* 名词
1 a metal thing with hot water inside that makes a room warm 散热器；暖气片 ➲ Look at Picture Dictionary page **P10**. 见彩页 P10。
2 a part of a car that has water in it to keep the engine cold（汽车发动机的）冷却器，水箱

radio 0ᴡ /'reɪdiəʊ/ *noun* 名词
1 (*no plural* 不用复数形式) sending or receiving sounds that travel a long way through the air by special waves 无线电传送: *The captain of the ship sent a message by radio.* 船长用无线电发送了一条信息。
2 (*plural* 复数形式 radios) a piece of equipment that brings voices or music from far away so that you can hear them 收音机: *We listened to an interesting programme on the radio.* 我们收听了一档很有意思的广播节目。◇ *Can you turn on the radio?* 你可不可以打开收音机?

radioactive /ˌreɪdiəʊ'æktɪv/ *adjective* 形容词
sending out dangerous energy 放射性的；有辐射的: *the disposal of radioactive waste* 放射性废料的处理

radius /'reɪdiəs/ *noun* 名词 (*plural* 复数形式 radii /'reɪdiaɪ/)
the length of a straight line from the centre of a circle to the outside 半径

➲ Look at **diameter**. 见 diameter。
➲ Look at the picture at **circle**. 见 circle 的插图。

raffle /'ræfl/ *noun* 名词
a way of making money for a charity by selling tickets with numbers on them. Later some numbers are chosen and the tickets with these numbers on them win prizes. （为慈善机构筹款的）抽彩

raft /rɑːft/ *noun* 名词
a flat boat with no sides and no engine 木排；筏

rag /ræg/ *noun* 名词
1 a small piece of old cloth that you use for cleaning 抹布
2 rags (*plural* 用复数形式) clothes that are very old and torn 破旧衣服: *She was dressed in rags.* 她穿着破衣烂衫。

rage /reɪdʒ/ *noun* 名词
very strong anger 暴怒；狂怒: *Sue stormed out of the room in a rage.* 苏怒气冲冲地冲出了房间。

raid /reɪd/ *noun* 名词
a sudden attack on a place 突袭；劫掠: *a bank raid* 抢劫银行
▸ **raid** *verb* 动词 (raids, raiding, raided): *Police raided the house looking for drugs.* 警方突击搜查那所房子以缉查毒品。

rail /reɪl/ *noun* 名词
1 (*plural* 复数形式 rails) a long piece of wood or metal that is fixed to the wall or to something else 横杆: *Hang your towel on the rail in the bathroom.* 把你的毛巾挂在浴室的横杆上。
2 rails (*plural* 用复数形式) the long pieces of metal that trains go on 铁轨；轨道
3 (*no plural* 不用复数形式) trains as a way of travelling 铁路运输；火车: *We decided to travel by rail.* 我们决定了坐火车出行。

railings /'reɪlɪŋz/ *noun* 名词 (*plural* 用复数形式)
a fence made of long pieces of metal（金属）栏杆，围栏

railroad /'reɪlrəʊd/ *American English for* RAILWAY 美式英语，即 railway

railroad crossing /'reɪlrəʊd krɒsɪŋ/ *American English for* LEVEL CROSSING 美式英语，即 level crossing

railway 0ᴡ /'reɪlweɪ/ *noun* 名词
1 (*also* 亦作 railway line) the metal lines that trains go on from one place to another 铁路；铁道
2 a train service that carries people and things 铁路运输: *a railway timetable* 列车时刻表

railway station /ˈreɪlweɪ steɪʃn/ *noun* 名词
a place where trains stop so that people can get on and off 火车站

rain¹ 0── /reɪn/ *noun* 名词 (*no plural* 不用复数形式)
the water that falls from the sky 雨；雨水

rain² 0── /reɪn/ *verb* 动词 (rains, raining, rained /reɪnd/)
When it **rains**, water falls from the sky. 下雨：*It's raining.* 下雨了。◇ *It rained all day.* 下了一整天雨。⊃ Look at Picture Dictionary page **P16**. 见彩页 P16。

rainbow /ˈreɪnbəʊ/ *noun* 名词
a half circle of colours in the sky when rain and sun come together 虹；彩虹 ⊃ Look at Picture Dictionary page **P16**. 见彩页 P16。

raincoat /ˈreɪnkəʊt/ *noun* 名词
a light coat that you wear when it rains 雨衣 ⊃ SAME MEANING **mac** 同义词为 mac

raindrop /ˈreɪndrɒp/ *noun* 名词
one drop of rain 雨点；雨滴

rainforest /ˈreɪnfɒrɪst/ *noun* 名词
a forest in a hot part of the world where there is a lot of rain（热带）雨林：*the Amazon rainforest* 亚马孙雨林

rainy /ˈreɪni/ *adjective* 形容词 (rainier, rainiest)
with a lot of rain 下雨的；多雨的：*a rainy day* 雨天

raise 0── /reɪz/ *verb* 动词 (raises, raising, raised /reɪzd/)
1 to move something or somebody up 举起；抬起：*Raise your hand if you want to ask a question.* 想发问就举手。⊃ OPPOSITE **lower** 反义词为 lower
2 to make something bigger, higher, stronger, etc. 增加；提高：*They've raised the price of petrol.* 他们已经把油价提高。◇ *She raised her voice* (= spoke more loudly). 她提高了嗓门。⊃ OPPOSITE **lower** 反义词为 lower
3 to get money from other people for a particular purpose 募集（资金）；筹款：*We raised £1 000 for the hospital.* 我们为医院筹集了 1 000 英镑。
4 to start to talk about something 提起；提出：*He raised an interesting question.* 他提了个有趣的问题。
5 to look after a child or an animal until they are an adult 抚养；养育：*It's difficult to raise a family with so little money.* 靠这么少的钱来养家糊口很困难。

raisin /ˈreɪzn/ *noun* 名词
a small dried fruit (called a **grape**) 葡萄干

rake /reɪk/ *noun* 名词
a tool with a long handle that you use in a garden for collecting leaves or for making the soil flat 耙子
▶ **rake** *verb* 动词 (rakes, raking, raked /reɪkt/): *Rake up the dead leaves.* 把枯叶耙在一起。

rally /ˈræli/ *noun* 名词 (*plural* 复数形式 rallies)
1 a group of people walking or standing together to show that they feel strongly about something 公众集会；群众大会：*a peace rally* 和平集会
2 a race for cars or motorcycles（汽车或摩托车）拉力赛

RAM /ræm/ *noun* 名词 (*no plural* 不用复数形式)
(*computing* 电脑) the type of memory that allows a computer to work 内存；随机存贮器：*32 megabytes of RAM* * 32 兆的内存

ram /ræm/ *noun* 名词
a male sheep 公绵羊

ramp /ræmp/ *noun* 名词
a path that you use instead of steps to go up or down 坡道；斜坡：*I pushed the wheelchair up the ramp.* 我把轮椅推上了坡道。

ran *form of* RUN¹ * run¹ 的不同形式

ranch /rɑːntʃ/ *noun* 名词
a very large farm, especially in the US or Australia, where cows, horses or sheep are kept（尤指美国或澳大利亚的）大牧场，大农场

random /ˈrændəm/ *adjective* 形容词
without any special plan 随机的；随意的；任意的：*She chose a few books at random.* 她随便挑了几本书。

rang *form of* RING² * ring² 的不同形式

range¹ /reɪndʒ/ *noun* 名词
1 different things of the same kind（同一类的）一系列：*This shop sells a range of bicycles.* 这家店出售各种各样的自行车。
2 how far you can see, hear, shoot, travel, etc.（感官的）范围；射程；达到的距离：*The gun has a range of five miles.* 这尊炮的射程是五英里。
3 the amount between the highest and the lowest 范围；幅度：*The age range of the children is between eight and twelve.* 这些孩子的年龄范围在八至十二岁之间。
4 a line of mountains or hills 山脉

A B C D E F G H I J K L M N O P Q R S T U V W X Y Z

range² /reɪndʒ/ *verb* 动词 (ranges,
ranging, ranged /reɪndʒd/)
to be at different points between two
things 在…之间变动: *The ages of the
students in the class range from 18 to 50.*
班上学生的年龄在 18 至 50 岁之间。

rank /ræŋk/ *noun* 名词
how important somebody is in a group of
people, for example in an army（军队等
的）级别，地位: *General is one of the
highest ranks in the army.* 将军是最高军衔
之一。

ransom /ˈrænsəm/ *noun* 名词
the money that you must pay so that
a criminal will free a person that they
have taken 赎金: *The kidnappers have
demanded a ransom of a million pounds.*
绑匪已经索要一百万英镑的赎金。

rap¹ /ræp/ *noun* 名词
1 a quick knock 快速的敲击；拍打:
I heard a rap on the door. 我听见急促的
敲门声。
2 (*music* 音乐) a type of modern music in
which singers speak the words of a song
very quickly 说唱乐；饶舌音乐: *a rap
song* 说唱歌曲

rap² /ræp/ *verb* 动词 (raps, rapping,
rapped /ræpt/)
1 to hit something quickly and lightly,
making a noise 轻敲: *She rapped on the
door.* 她轻轻地拍门。
2 (*music* 音乐) to speak the words of a rap
song（说唱乐中）念白；唱饶舌歌

rape /reɪp/ *verb* 动词 (rapes, raping,
raped /reɪpt/)
to force somebody to have sex when they
do not want to 强奸；强暴
▶ **rape** *noun* 名词: *He was sent to prison
for rape.* 他因强奸罪被判入狱。

rapid /ˈræpɪd/ *adjective* 形容词
happening or moving very quickly 迅速
的；快速的: *She made rapid progress
and was soon the best in the class.* 她进步
很快，不久就成为班上最优秀的学生。
⊃ OPPOSITE **slow** 反义词为 slow
▶ **rapidly** *adverb* 副词: *The snow
rapidly disappeared.* 雪很快就不见了。

rare ☞ /reə(r)/ *adjective* 形容词 (rarer,
rarest)
1 If something is **rare**, you do not find or
see it often. 稀少的；罕见的: *Pandas are
rare animals.* 大熊猫是稀有动物。◇
It's rare to see snow in April. 四月份下雪
很少见。⊃ OPPOSITE **common** 反义词为
common
2 Meat that is **rare** is not cooked for very

long, so that the inside is still red.（肉）
半熟的，煮得很嫩的

rarely ☞ /ˈreəli/ *adverb* 副词
not very often 不常；很少: *We rarely
agree with each other.* 我们很少看法一致。

rash¹ /ræʃ/ *noun* 名词 (*plural* 复数形式
rashes)
a lot of small red spots on your skin 疹;
皮疹

rash² /ræʃ/ *adjective* 形容词 (rasher,
rashest)
If you are **rash**, you do things too quickly
and without thinking about the possible
result. 轻率的；鲁莽的: *You were very
rash to leave your job before you had
found a new one.* 你没找到新工作就辞职，
真是太轻率了。

raspberry /ˈrɑːzbəri/ *noun* 名词 (*plural*
复数形式 raspberries)
a small soft red fruit that grows on
bushes 覆盆子；山莓；悬钩子: *raspberry
jam* 山莓酱

rat 老鼠

rat /ræt/ *noun* 名词
an animal like a big mouse 老鼠；大鼠；
耗子

rate /reɪt/ *noun* 名词
1 the speed of something or how often
something happens 速度；频率；比率:
*The crime rate was lower in 2004 than in
2005.* * 2004 年的犯罪率比 2005 年低。
2 the amount that something costs or
that somebody is paid 价格；费用: *The
basic rate of pay is £10 an hour.* 基本工资
是每小时 10 英镑。
at any rate (*informal* 非正式) anyway;
whatever happens 无论如何；不管怎样:
*I hope to be back before ten o'clock –
I won't be late at any rate.* 我希望十点钟
之前回来——无论如何我不会迟到。

rather ☞ /ˈrɑːðə(r)/ *adverb* 副词
more than a little but not very 颇；相当
⊃ SAME MEANING **quite** 同义词为 quite:
We were rather tired after our long journey.
我们走了很长的路，挺累的。◇ *It's rather
a small room.* 那是个相当小的房间。

🔎 SPEAKING 表达方式说明

If you use **rather** with a positive word, it sounds as if you are surprised and pleased. * rather 与褒义词连用有感到惊喜或欣然的意思： *The new teacher is rather nice.* 新老师人挺好的。

rather than in the place of; instead of 而不是： *Could I have tea rather than coffee?* 我不要咖啡要茶行吗？

would rather would prefer to do something 宁愿；较喜欢： *I'd rather go by train than by bus.* 我宁愿坐火车也不愿搭公共汽车。

ration¹ /'ræʃn/ *noun* 名词
a small amount of something that you are allowed to have when there is not enough for everybody to have what they want（因供应有限而实行的）配给量： *food rations* 食物配给量

ration² /'ræʃn/ *verb* 动词 (rations, rationing, rationed /'ræʃnd/)
to control the amount of something that somebody is allowed to have, for example because there is not enough for everyone to have as much as they want 定量配给；限量供应： *Eggs were rationed during the war.* 战争期间，鸡蛋是限量配给的。

rational /'ræʃnəl/ *adjective* 形容词
based on facts; sensible 理性的；合理的；明智的： *There must be a rational explanation for why he's behaving like this.* 他这样做一定有合理的解释。

rattle¹ /'rætl/ *verb* 动词 (rattles, rattling, rattled /'rætld/)
to make a sound like hard things hitting each other or to shake something so that it makes this sound（使）哗啦啦响，咔嗒响： *The windows were rattling all night in the wind.* 窗户整夜被风刮得咔嗒作响。◇ *She rattled the money in the tin.* 她摇动铁罐里的钱币，发出哗啦啦的声响。

rattle² /'rætl/ *noun* 名词
1 the noise of hard things hitting each other（硬物撞击的）哗啦声，咔嗒声： *the rattle of empty bottles* 空瓶子相碰的咔嗒声
2 a toy that a baby can shake to make a noise 拨浪鼓

rattlesnake /'rætlsneɪk/ *noun* 名词
a poisonous American snake that makes a noise like a RATTLE with its tail when it is angry or afraid 响尾蛇

raw /rɔː/ *adjective* 形容词

🔎 PRONUNCIATION 读音说明

The word **raw** sounds like **more**. * raw 读音像 more。

1 not cooked 生的；未煮熟的： *raw meat* 生肉
2 in its natural state; not yet made into anything 自然状态的；未经加工的： *raw sugar* 原糖

ray /reɪ/ *noun* 名词 (plural 复数形式 rays)
a line of light or heat 光线；（热的）射线： *the sun's rays* 太阳光线

razor /'reɪzə(r)/ *noun* 名词
a sharp thing that people use to cut hair off their bodies (to shave) 剃须刀；除毛刀： *an electric razor* 电动剃须刀

razor blade /'reɪzə bleɪd/ *noun* 名词
the thin metal part of a RAZOR that cuts 剃须刀刀片

Rd short way of writing ROAD * road 的缩写形式

re- /riː/ *prefix* 前缀
You can add **re-** to the beginning of some words to give them the meaning 'again'. 再；又；重新： *We had to **rebuild** (= build again) the fence after the storm.* 暴风雨过后我们得重修篱笆。◇ *Your homework is all wrong. Please **redo** it (= do it again).* 你的家庭作业全错了，请你重做。

reach¹ 0— /riːtʃ/ *verb* 动词 (reaches, reaching, reached /riːtʃt/)
1 to arrive somewhere 到达；抵达： *It was dark when we reached Paris.* 我们到达巴黎时已经天黑了。◇ *Have you reached the end of the book yet?* 这本书你读完了吗？
2 to put out your hand to do or get something 伸出手（做某事或够某物）： *I **reached for** the telephone.* 我伸手去拿电话。
3 to be able to touch something 够得着： *Can you get that book from the top shelf for me? I **can't reach**.* 你能帮我把架子顶层的那本书拿下来吗？我够不着。

reach² /riːtʃ/ *noun* 名词 (no plural 不用复数形式)
beyond reach, out of reach too far away to touch 够不到： *Keep this medicine out of children's reach.* 把这药放在小孩够不着的地方。
within reach near enough to touch or go to 够得着；靠近： *Is the beach within reach of the hotel?* 海滩在旅馆附近吗？

A
B
C
D
E
F
G
H
I
J
K
L
M
N
O
P
Q
R
S
T
U
V
W
X
Y
Z

A
B
C
D
E
F
G
H
I
J
K
L
M
N
O
P
Q
R
S
T
U
V
W
X
Y
Z

react /ri'ækt/ *verb* 动词 (reacts, reacting, reacted)
to say or do something because something has happened 作出反应；回应： *How did Paul react to the news?* 保罗对这消息怎么回应？

reaction 0ᴿ /ri'ækʃn/ *noun* 名词
what you say or do because of something that has happened 反应；回应： *What was her reaction when you told her about the accident?* 你告诉她这起事故的时候，她有什么反应？ ◇ *What was his reaction to the news?* 他对这条新闻有什么反应？

read 0ᴿ /riːd/ *verb* 动词 (reads, reading, read /red/, has read)
1 to look at words and understand them 阅读： *Have you read this book? It's very interesting.* 你读过这本书吗？可有意思呢。
2 to say words that you can see 朗读；诵读： *I read a story to the children.* 我给孩子子读了一则故事。

read something out to read something to other people （向别人）朗读，宣读： *The teacher read out the list of names.* 老师宣读了名单。

▶ **reading** *noun* 名词 (*no plural* 不用复数形式)： *My interests are reading and football.* 我的爱好是阅读和足球。

reader /'riːdə(r)/ *noun* 名词
1 a person who reads something 读者
2 a book for reading at school 读本；读物

readily /'redɪli/ *adverb* 副词
quickly and easily 轻而易举地；便利地： *Most vegetables are readily available at this time of year.* 大多数蔬菜在这个时节都可以很方便地买到。

ready 0ᴿ /'redi/ *adjective* 形容词
1 prepared and able to do something 准备好；准备妥当： *I'll be ready to leave in five minutes.* 我五分钟后就可以准备好出发。 ◇ *I must go and get ready to go out.* 我得去准备出门了。
2 finished so that you can use it 已完成；可以使用： *Dinner will be ready soon.* 晚饭很快就好了。
3 happy to do something 乐意；愿意 ⊃ SAME MEANING **willing** 同义词为 willing： *He's always ready to help.* 他总是乐意帮忙。

ready-made /,redi 'meɪd/ *adjective* 形容词
already prepared and ready to use 已做好的；现成的： *ready-made meals* 现成的饭菜

real 0ᴿ /rɪəl/ *adjective* 形容词
1 existing, not just imagined 真实存在的；现实的： *The film is about events that happened in real life.* 电影讲述的是真人真事。
2 actually true, not only what people think is true 真实的；确实的： *The name he gave to the police wasn't his real name.* 他提供给警方的名字不是他的真名。
3 natural; not false or a copy 真的；天然的；非假冒的： *This ring is real gold.* 这枚戒指是真金的。
4 big or complete 大的；十足的： *I've got a real problem.* 我遇到大问题了。

real estate agent /'rɪəl ɪsteɪt eɪdʒənt/ *American English for* ESTATE AGENT 美式英语，即 estate agent

realistic /,riːə'lɪstɪk/ *adjective* 形容词
sensible and accepting what is possible in a particular situation 务实的；现实的： *We have to be realistic about our chances of winning.* 我们必须实事求是地估计我们获胜的机会。

reality 0ᴿ /ri'æləti/ *noun* 名词
(*no plural* 不用复数形式)
the way that something really is, not how you would like it to be 现实： *I enjoyed my holiday, but now it's back to reality.* 我假期玩得很开心，可是现在回到现实了。 ◇ *She looked very confident but in reality she was extremely nervous.* 她看上去信心十足，但事实上她紧张极了。

realize 0ᴿ /'riːəlaɪz/ *verb* 动词 (realizes, realizing, realized /'rɪəlaɪzd/)
to understand or know something 理解；认识到；意识到： *When I got home, I realized that I had lost my key.* 我回到家，才发现钥匙丢了。 ◇ *I didn't realize you were American.* 我不知道你是美国人。

▶ **realization** /,riːəlaɪ'zeɪʃn/ *noun* 名词 (*no plural* 不用复数形式)： *the sudden realization of what he had done* 突然意识到他自己做了些什么

really 0ᴿ /'rɪəli/ *adverb* 副词
1 in fact; actually 事实上；真正地： *Do you really love him?* 你真的爱他吗？
2 very or very much 非常；十分： *I'm really hungry.* 我很饿。 ◇ *'Do you like this music?' 'Not really.'* "你喜欢这乐曲吗？" "不太喜欢。"
3 a word that shows you are interested or surprised （表示感兴趣或惊讶）： *'I'm going to China next year.' 'Really?'* "我明年会去中国。" "真的吗？"

rear¹ /rɪə(r)/ *noun* 名词 (*no plural* 不用复数形式)
the back part of something 后部： *The kitchen is at the rear of the house.* 厨房在

房子的后面。 ➲ OPPOSITE **front** 反义词为 front

rear² /rɪə(r)/ ***adjective*** 形容词
at the back of something 后部的: *the rear window of a car* 后车窗

rear³ /rɪə(r)/ ***verb*** 动词 (**rears**, **rearing**, **reared** /rɪəd/)
to care for and educate young children 抚养; 养育 ➲ SAME MEANING **bring somebody up**, **raise** 同义词为 bring somebody up 和 raise: *She reared three children without any help.* 她独力抚养了三个孩子。

reason 🔑 /ˈriːzn/ ***noun*** 名词
a cause or an explanation for why you do something or why something happens 原因; 理由: *The reason I didn't come to the party was that I was ill.* 我没有参加聚会是因为我病了。 ◇ *Is there any* ***reason why*** *you were late?* 你迟到了, 有什么原因吗? ◇ *She gave no* ***reasons for*** *her decision.* 她没有对她的决定作出任何解释。

reasonable 🔑 /ˈriːznəbl/ ***adjective*** 形容词
1 fair and ready to listen to what other people say 讲理的; 明事理的: *I tried to be reasonable even though I was very angry.* 尽管我很生气, 我还是尽力保持理智。
2 fair or right in a particular situation 公道的; 合理的: *I think $100 is a reasonable price.* 我觉得 100 元是个合理的价格。
➲ OPPOSITE **unreasonable** 反义词为 unreasonable

reasonably /ˈriːznəbli/ ***adverb*** 副词
1 quite, but not very 还算; 尚可 ➲ SAME MEANING **fairly** 同义词为 fairly: *The food was reasonably good.* 食物还算不错。
2 in a reasonable way 通情达理地; 合理地: *Don't get angry – let's talk about this reasonably.* 不要生气, 咱们讲道理, 好好谈这件事吧。

reassure /ˌriːəˈʃʊə(r)/ ***verb*** 动词 (**reassures**, **reassuring**, **reassured** /ˌriːəˈʃʊəd/)
to say or do something to make somebody feel safer or happier 使安心; 使消除顾虑: *The doctor reassured her that she was not seriously ill.* 医生让她放心, 说她的病不严重。
▶ **reassurance** /ˌriːəˈʃʊərəns/ ***noun*** 名词 (*no plural* 不用复数形式): *He needs reassurance that he is right.* 他需要别人肯定他做得对。

rebel¹ /ˈrebl/ ***noun*** 名词
a person who fights against the people in control, for example the government 叛乱分子; 造反者; 反政府的人

rebel² /rɪˈbel/ ***verb*** 动词 (**rebels**, **rebelling**, **rebelled** /rɪˈbeld/)
to fight against the people in control, for example the government or your parents 造反; 反抗; 反叛: *She* ***rebelled against*** *her parents by refusing to go to university.* 她跟父母作对, 拒绝上大学。

rebellion /rɪˈbeljən/ ***noun*** 名词
a time when some of the people in a country fight against their government 叛乱; 反叛: *Hundreds of people died in the rebellion.* 数以百计的人死于这场叛乱。

recall /rɪˈkɔːl/ ***verb*** 动词 (**recalls**, **recalling**, **recalled** /rɪˈkɔːld/) (*formal* 正式)
to remember something 记起; 回忆起: *I don't recall the name of the hotel.* 我不记得旅馆的名字了。

receipt /rɪˈsiːt/ ***noun*** 名词
a piece of paper that shows you have paid for something 收据; 收条: *Can I have a receipt?* 可不可以给我一张收据?

receive 🔑 /rɪˈsiːv/ ***verb*** 动词 (**receives**, **receiving**, **received** /rɪˈsiːvd/) (*formal* 正式)

> **SPELLING** 拼写说明
> Remember! When the sound is /iː/, there is a spelling rule: **I before E, except after C**, so you spell **receive** with **EI** (not **IE**). 记住: 读音是 /iː/ 时, 拼写规则是: "i 在 e 前面, 除非 c 在前"。因此, receive 拼写中作 ei (而不是 ie)。

to get or accept something that somebody has given or sent to you 接到; 收到 ➲ SAME MEANING **get** 同义词为 get: *Did you receive my letter?* 你收到我的信了吗?

receiver /rɪˈsiːvə(r)/ ***noun*** 名词
the part of a telephone that you use for listening and speaking (电话的)听筒, 受话器

recent 🔑 /ˈriːsnt/ ***adjective*** 形容词
that happened or began only a short time ago 近来的; 最近的: *Is this a recent photo of your son?* 这是你儿子的近照吗?

recently 🔑 /ˈriːsntli/ ***adverb*** 副词
not long ago 最近; 不久前: *She worked here until quite recently.* 她不久以前还在这里工作。

reception /rɪˈsepʃn/ ***noun*** 名词
1 (*no plural* 不用复数形式) the place

A B C D E F G H I J K L M N O P Q R S T U V W X Y Z

where you go first when you arrive at a hotel or an office building（旅馆或办公楼的）服务台，接待处：*Leave your key in reception if you go out.* 出去时把钥匙交到服务台。
2 (*plural* 复数形式 **receptions**) a big important party 招待会；宴会：*The wedding reception will be held at the castle.* 婚宴将在城堡中举行。

receptionist /rɪˈsepʃənɪst/ *noun* 名词
a person in a hotel, an office, etc. whose job is to answer the telephone and to help people when they arrive 接待员

recess /rɪˈses/ *American English for* PLAYTIME 美式英语，即 playtime

recipe /ˈresəpi/ *noun* 名词
a piece of writing that tells you how to cook something 食谱；烹饪法

reckless /ˈrekləs/ *adjective* 形容词
A person who is **reckless** does dangerous things without thinking about what could happen. 鲁莽的；不顾后果的：*reckless driving* 鲁莽驾驶

reckon /ˈrekən/ *verb* 动词 (**reckons, reckoning, reckoned** /ˈrekənd/)
1 (*informal* 非正式) to believe something because you have thought about it 想；认为：*It's very late. I reckon she isn't coming.* 很晚了，我想她不会来了。
2 to use numbers to find an answer 估计；估算 ⊃ SAME MEANING **calculate** 同义词为 calculate：*We reckoned the journey would take about half an hour.* 我们估计行程大约花半个小时。

recognition /ˌrekəɡˈnɪʃn/ *noun* 名词 (*no plural* 不用复数形式)
1 knowing what something is or who somebody is when you see it or them 认出；识别：*I said hello to her, but there was no sign of recognition on her face.* 我跟她打了个招呼，她却似乎没认出我来。
2 knowing that something is true 承认；认可：*There is a general recognition of the need to change the law.* 普遍认为该项法律需要修改。

recognize 0﹣ /ˈrekəɡnaɪz/ *verb* 动词 (**recognizes, recognizing, recognized** /ˈrekəɡnaɪzd/)
1 to know again somebody or something that you have seen or heard before 认出；识别；辨认出：*I didn't recognize you without your glasses.* 你没戴眼镜，我都没认出你来。
2 to know that something is true 承认；

意识到：*They recognize that there is a problem.* 他们意识到出了问题。

recommend 0﹣ /ˌrekəˈmend/ *verb* 动词 (**recommends, recommending, recommended**)

> 🔎 SPELLING 拼写说明
> Remember! You spell **recommend** with one **C** and **MM**. 记住：recommend 拼写中有一个 c 和 mm。

1 to tell somebody that a person or thing is good or useful 推荐；举荐：*Can you recommend a hotel near the airport?* 你能推荐一家机场附近的旅馆吗？
2 to tell somebody in a helpful way what you think they should do 建议；劝告 ⊃ SAME MEANING **advise** 同义词为 advise：*I recommend that you see a doctor.* 我建议你去看医生。

recommendation /ˌrekəmenˈdeɪʃn/ *noun* 名词
saying that something is good or useful 推荐；举荐：*We stayed at this hotel on their recommendation* (= because they said it was good). 我们听取他们的推荐住进了这家旅馆。

record¹ 0﹣ /ˈrekɔːd/ *noun* 名词

> 🔊 PRONUNCIATION 读音说明
> When the word **record** is a noun, you say the first part of the word louder: **RE**cord. * record 作名词时，重音放在第一个音节：RECord。
> When the word **record** is a verb, you say the second part of the word louder: re**CORD**. * record 作动词时，重音放在第二个音节：reCORD。

1 notes about things that have happened 记录；记载：*Keep a record of all the money you spend.* 把你所有的花费都记录下来。
2 a thin, round piece of plastic that makes music when you play it on a special machine 唱片：*Put another record on.* 放另一张唱片。◇ *a record company* 唱片公司
3 the best, fastest, highest, lowest, etc. that has been done in a sport（体育比赛中的）纪录：*She holds the world record for long jump.* 她保持着跳远的世界纪录。◇ *He did it in record time* (= very fast). 他以历来最快的速度完成了。◇ *She's hoping to break the record for the 100 metres* (= to do it faster than anyone has done before). 她希望打破 100 米的纪录。

record² 0ᵐ /rɪˈkɔːd/ *verb* 动词 (records, recording, recorded)
1 to write notes about or make pictures of things that happen so you can remember them later 记录；记载: *In his diary he recorded everything that he did.* 他在日记中把做过的事都记下来了。
2 to put music or a film on a tape, a CD or a DVD so that you can listen to or watch it later 录制；录（音）；录（像）: *I recorded a programme from the TV.* 我录了一档电视节目。

record-breaking /ˈrekɔːd breɪkɪŋ/ *adjective* 形容词
the best, fastest, highest, etc. ever 破纪录的: *We did the journey in record-breaking time.* 我们以破纪录的时间完成了旅程。

recorder 竖笛

recorder /rɪˈkɔːdə(r)/ *noun* 名词
a musical instrument that children often play. You blow through it and cover the holes in with your fingers. 竖笛 ➔ Look also at **tape recorder** and **video** (2). 亦见 tape recorder 和 video 第 2 义。

recording /rɪˈkɔːdɪŋ/ *noun* 名词
sounds or pictures on a tape, CD or film 录音；录像: *a new recording of Mozart's 'Don Giovanni'* 莫扎特的《唐·乔凡尼》新录音

record player /ˈrekɔːd pleɪə(r)/ *noun* 名词
a machine that you use for playing records 唱机

recover 0ᵐ /rɪˈkʌvə(r)/ *verb* 动词 (recovers, recovering, recovered /rɪˈkʌvəd/)
1 to become well or happy again after you have been ill or sad 康复；痊愈；复原: *She is slowly recovering from her illness.* 她病后正慢慢康复。
2 to get back something that was lost 找回；寻回: *Police never recovered the stolen car.* 警方一直找不到那辆失车。

recovery /rɪˈkʌvəri/ *noun* 名词 (no plural 不用复数形式)

when you feel well or happy again after you have been ill or sad 恢复；康复；痊愈: *He made a quick recovery after his operation.* 他手术后恢复得很快。

recreation /ˌrekriˈeɪʃn/ *noun* 名词 (no plural 不用复数形式)
relaxing and enjoying yourself, when you are not working 娱乐；消遣: *recreation activities such as swimming and yoga* 游泳、瑜伽之类的消遣活动

recruit¹ /rɪˈkruːt/ *verb* 动词 (recruits, recruiting, recruited)
to find new people to join a company or an organization 招募；征召；招聘: *The army are recruiting new officers.* 陆军正在征募新军官。

recruit² /rɪˈkruːt/ *noun* 名词
a person who has just joined the army, the navy or the police 新兵；新警员: *the training of new recruits* 新兵训练

rectangle /ˈrektæŋgl/ *noun* 名词
a shape with two long sides, two short sides and four angles of 90 degrees 长方形；矩形
▶ **rectangular** /rekˈtæŋgjələ(r)/ *adjective* 形容词: *This page is rectangular.* 本页是长方形的。

recycle /ˌriːˈsaɪkl/ *verb* 动词 (recycles, recycling, recycled /ˌriːˈsaɪkld/)
to do something to materials like paper and glass so that they can be used again 再利用；回收利用: *Old newspapers can be recycled.* 旧报纸可以回收利用。

recycled /ˌriːˈsaɪkld/ *adjective* 形容词
Something that is **recycled** has been used before. 再利用的；再生的: *recycled paper* 再生纸

red 0ᵐ /red/ *adjective* 形容词 (redder, reddest)
1 having the colour of blood 红的；红色的: *She's wearing a bright red dress.* 她穿着鲜红色的连衣裙。◇ *red wine* 红葡萄酒
2 Red hair has a colour between red, orange and brown. （毛发）红褐色的
▶ **red** *noun* 名词: *Lucy was dressed in red.* 露西穿着一身红色的衣服。

reduce 0ᵐ /rɪˈdjuːs/ *verb* 动词 (reduces, reducing, reduced /rɪˈdjuːst/)
to make something smaller or less 缩小；减少: *I bought this shirt because the price was reduced from £20 to £12.* 我买了这件衬衫，因为它的价格从 20 英镑减到 12 英镑。◇ *Reduce speed now* (= words on a road sign). 现在开始减速（路牌上的

A B C D E F G H I J K L M N O P Q R S T U V W X Y Z

A
B
C
D
E
F
G
H
I
J
K
L
M
N
O
P
Q
R
S
T
U
V
W
X
Y
Z

标示）。 ⇨ OPPOSITE **increase** 反义词为
increase

reduction /rɪ'dʌkʃn/ *noun* 名词
making something smaller or less 缩小；
减少： *price reductions* 减价 ◇ *There has
been some **reduction** in unemployment.*
失业人数有所减少。

redundant /rɪ'dʌndənt/ *adjective* 形容词
without a job because you are not
needed any more 被裁减的；被裁退的：
*When the factory closed, 300 people were
made redundant.* 工厂倒闭时，300 人给
裁退了。

reed /riːd/ *noun* 名词
a tall plant, like grass, that grows in or
near water 芦苇

reel 卷轴

a reel of cotton 一轴棉线

reel /riːl/ *noun* 名词
a thing with round sides that holds cotton
for sewing, film for cameras, etc. 卷轴；
卷盘；卷筒： *a reel of cotton* 一轴棉线

refer ⚬ʀ /rɪ'fɜː(r)/ *verb* 动词 (refers,
referring, referred /rɪ'fɜːd/)
refer to somebody or 或 **something**
1 to talk about somebody or something
提到；说起： *When I said that some
people are stupid, I wasn't referring to you!*
我说有些人很蠢时，并不是指你呀！
2 to describe or be connected with
somebody or something 意指；指涉：
*The word 'child' here refers to anybody
under the age of 16.* 此处 child 一词指
16 岁以下的人。
3 to look in a book or ask somebody for
information 查阅；参考；查询 ⇨ SAME
MEANING **consult** 同义词为 consult：
*If you don't understand a word, you may
refer to your dictionaries.* 要是不知道一个
词的意思，可以查词典。

referee /ˌrefə'riː/ *noun* 名词
a person who watches a game such as
football to make sure the players obey
the rules （足球等比赛的）裁判 ⇨ Look at
umpire. 见 umpire。

reference /'refrəns/ *noun* 名词
1 (*plural* 复数形式 **references**) what
somebody says or writes about something
谈到（或写到）的事： *The book is full of
references to her childhood in India.* 书中
多处谈到她在印度的童年往事。
2 (*no plural* 不用复数形式) looking at
something for information 参考；查阅：
*Keep these instructions for future
reference.* 把这些说明资料保管好以备
后用。
3 (*plural* 复数形式 **references**)
If somebody gives you a **reference**, they
write about you to somebody who may
give you a new job. 推荐信；介绍信：
Did your boss give you a good reference?
你的老板有没有给你写一封赞扬你的
推荐信？

reference book /'refrəns bʊk/ *noun*
名词
a book where you look for information
参考书；工具书： *A dictionary is a
reference book.* 词典是工具书。

reflect /rɪ'flekt/ *verb* 动词 (reflects,
reflecting, reflected)
1 to show a picture of somebody or
something in a mirror, water or glass
反映；映出（影像）： *She could see
herself reflected in the mirror.* 她看到自己
在镜子中的影像。
2 to send back light, heat or sound 反射
（光、热或声）： *The windows reflected
the bright morning sunshine.* 窗户反射着
早晨灿烂的阳光。
3 to show something 反映；显示；表明：
*His music reflects his interest in African
culture.* 他的音乐反映出他对非洲文化的
兴趣。

reflection /rɪ'flekʃn/ *noun* 名词
1 (*plural* 复数形式 **reflections**) a picture
that you see in a mirror or on a shiny
surface 映像；映照出的影像： *He admired
his reflection in the mirror.* 他欣赏着自己
在镜中的样子。
2 (*no plural* 不用复数形式) sending back
light, heat or sound （光、热或声的）反射
3 a thing that shows what somebody or
something is like 反映；显示： *Your
clothes are a **reflection** of your personality.*
穿着能体现人的个性。

reform[1] /rɪ'fɔːm/ *verb* 动词 (reforms,
reforming, reformed /rɪ'fɔːmd/)
to change something to make it better
改革；革新；改良： *The government wants
to reform the education system in this
country.* 政府想要改革国家的教育制度。

reform² /rɪˈfɔːm/ *noun* 名词
a change to something to make it better
改革；变革；改良：*economic reform*
经济改革

refresh /rɪˈfreʃ/ *verb* 动词 (refreshes,
refreshing, refreshed /rɪˈfreʃt/)
to make somebody feel less tired, less
hot or full of energy again 使恢复精力；
使凉爽：*A sleep will refresh you after
your long journey.* 长途旅程后睡一觉能
让你恢复体力。

refreshed /rɪˈfreʃt/ *adjective* 形容词
If you feel **refreshed**, you feel less tired,
less hot or full of energy again. 精神焕发
的；凉爽的：*He looked refreshed after
a good night's sleep.* 睡了一晚好觉之后，
他显得精神焕发。

refreshing /rɪˈfreʃɪŋ/ *adjective* 形容词
making you feel less tired or less hot
使人精神焕发的；使人清爽凉快的：
a cool, refreshing drink 清凉提神的饮料

refreshments /rɪˈfreʃmənts/ *noun* 名词
(*plural* 用复数形式)
food and drinks that are available in
a place like a cinema or theatre, or at
a public event（电影院、剧院等公共场所
销售的）点心，茶点，小吃：*Light
refreshments will be served during the
break.* 休息期间会有茶点供应。

refrigerator /rɪˈfrɪdʒəreɪtə(r)/ *noun* 名词
American English for FRIDGE 美式英语，即
fridge

refuge /ˈrefjuːdʒ/ *noun* 名词
a place where you are safe from
somebody or something 避难所；庇护
处：*We took refuge from the hot sun
under a tree.* 我们躲到树下，避开火辣辣的
太阳。

refugee /ˌrefjuˈdʒiː/ *noun* 名词
a person who must leave their country
because of danger, for example a war
难民

refund /ˈriːfʌnd/ *noun* 名词
money that is paid back to you, because
you have paid too much or because you
are not happy with something you have
bought 退款；返还款：*The watch didn't
work properly so I took it back to the shop
and got a refund.* 手表走得不准，我便拿去
还给商店，并取回退款。
▸ **refund** /rɪˈfʌnd/ *verb* 动词 (refunds,
refunding, refunded): *We will refund
your money in full.* 你的钱我们会全数
退还。

refusal /rɪˈfjuːzl/ *noun* 名词
saying 'no' when somebody asks you
to do or have something 拒绝；回绝：
a refusal to pay 拒绝付钱

refuse¹ ⊶ /rɪˈfjuːz/ *verb* 动词 (refuses,
refusing, refused /rɪˈfjuːzd/)
to say 'no' when somebody asks you to do
or have something 拒绝；回绝：*I asked
Matthew to help, but he refused.* 我请马修
帮忙，可是他拒绝了。◇ *The shop
assistant refused to give me my money
back.* 售货员不肯把钱退给我。

refuse² /ˈrefjuːs/ *noun* 名词 (*no plural*
不用复数形式) (*formal* 正式)
things that you throw away 废弃物；垃圾
➡ SAME MEANING **rubbish** 同义词为
rubbish

regard¹ /rɪˈɡɑːd/ *verb* 动词 (regards,
regarding, regarded)
to think about somebody or something
in a certain way 将⋯视为；将⋯看作：
I regard her as my best friend. 我把她看成
是我最好的朋友。

regard² /rɪˈɡɑːd/ *noun* 名词
1 (*no plural* 不用复数形式) (*formal* 正式)
attention to or care for somebody or
something 关心；关注：*She shows
no regard for other people's feelings.*
她不顾及别人的感受。
2 (*no plural* 不用复数形式) what you feel
when you admire or respect somebody or
something 敬佩；尊敬：*I have great
regard for his work* (= I think it is very
good). 我非常欣赏他的作品。
3 regards (*plural* 用复数形式) used to
send good wishes to somebody at the end
of a letter or an email, or when you ask
somebody to give your good wishes to
another person who is not there（用于
信函或电邮结尾或请人转达的）致意，
问候：*With kind regards, Yours ...* 谨此
致意，⋯敬上 ◇ *Please give my regards to
your parents.* 请代我向你父母问好。

regarding /rɪˈɡɑːdɪŋ/ *preposition* 介词
(*formal* 正式)
about somebody or something 关于；
有关 ➡ SAME MEANING **concerning** 同义词
为 concerning: *Please contact us if you
require further information regarding this
matter.* 欲知有关此事的更多信息，请联系
我们。

regardless /rɪˈɡɑːdləs/ *adverb* 副词
in spite of problems or difficulties 不管；
不顾：*The weather was terrible, but we
carried on regardless.* 天气非常糟糕，
但我们并不在意，照常进行。

A B C D E F G H I J K L M N O P Q R S T U V W X Y Z

A
B
C
D
E
F
G
H
I
J
K
L
M
N
O
P
Q
R
S
T
U
V
W
X
Y
Z

reggae /'regeɪ/ *noun* 名词 (*no plural* 不用复数形式)
(*music* 音乐) a type of West Indian music 雷盖音乐；雷鬼

regiment /'redʒɪmənt/ *noun* 名词
a group of soldiers in an army（军队的）团

region ⚬─ /'riːdʒən/ *noun* 名词
a part of a country or of the world（国家或世界的）地区，区域：*tropical regions of the world* 世界上的热带地区

regional /'riːdʒənl/ *adjective* 形容词
belonging a certain REGION 地区的；区域的

register¹ /'redʒɪstə(r)/ *verb* 动词
(registers, registering, registered /'redʒɪstəd/)
1 to put a name on an official list 登记；注册：*I would like to register for the English course.* 我想登记修读英语课程。
2 to show a number or amount 显示（读数）：*The thermometer registered 30°C.* 温度计显示为 30 摄氏度。

register² /'redʒɪstə(r)/ *noun* 名词
an official list of names 名册；登记表；注册簿：*The teacher keeps a register of all the students in the class.* 老师有全班学生的名册。

registration /ˌredʒɪ'streɪʃn/ *noun* 名词
(*no plural* 不用复数形式)
putting a name on an official list 登记；注册：*the registration of births, marriages and deaths* 出生、婚姻和死亡登记

registration number /ˌredʒɪ'streɪʃn nʌmbə(r)/ (*British* 英式英语) *noun* 名词
the numbers and letters on the front and back of a car or other vehicle（车辆的）牌照号码

regret¹ /rɪ'gret/ *verb* 动词 (regrets, regretting, regretted)
to feel sorry about something that you did or did not do 后悔；感到遗憾：*He regrets selling his car.* 他后悔把车卖了。◇ *I don't regret what I said to her.* 我不后悔跟她说了那些话。

regret² /rɪ'gret/ *noun* 名词
a sad feeling about something that you did or did not do 后悔；遗憾：*Do you have any regrets about leaving your job?* 对于辞职你感到后悔吗？

regular ⚬─ /'regjələ(r)/ *adjective* 形容词
1 happening again and again with the same amount of space or time in between 规则的；有规律的；定期的：*a regular heartbeat* 正常的心跳 ◇ *A light flashed at regular intervals.* 有盏灯有规律地发出闪光。 ➲ OPPOSITE **irregular** 反义词为 irregular
2 going somewhere or doing something often 频繁的；经常的：*I've never seen him before – he's not one of my regular customers.* 我以前从来没见过他。他不是我的老顾客。
3 usual 通常的；平常的：*Who is your regular doctor?* 通常给你看病的是哪位医生？
4 (*grammar* 语法) A word that is **regular** has the usual verb forms or plural.（动词、名词等）规则的，按规则变化的：*'Work' is a regular verb.* * work 是规则动词。 ➲ OPPOSITE **irregular** 反义词为 irregular
▶ **regularly** /'regjələli/ *adverb* 副词：*We meet regularly every Friday.* 我们定期逢星期五见面。

regulation /ˌregju'leɪʃn/ *noun* 名词
an official rule that controls what people do 规章；规则；条例：*You can't smoke here – it's against fire regulations.* 这里不准吸烟，那是违反消防条例的。

rehearsal /rɪ'hɜːsl/ *noun* 名词
a time when you practise something such as a play or a piece of music before you do it in front of other people（戏剧、音乐等的）排练，排演：*There's a rehearsal for the play tonight.* 今晚那出戏要进行彩排。

rehearse /rɪ'hɜːs/ *verb* 动词 (rehearses, rehearsing, rehearsed /rɪ'hɜːst/)
to practise something such as a play or a piece of music before you do it in front of other people 排练；排演：*We are rehearsing for the concert.* 我们正在为音乐会排练。

reign¹ /reɪn/ *noun* 名词
a time when a king or queen rules a country 君主统治时期：*The reign of Queen Elizabeth II began in 1952.* 女王伊丽莎白二世于 1952 年即位。

reign² /reɪn/ *verb* 动词 (reigns, reigning, reigned /reɪnd/)
to be king or queen of a country（国王或女王）统治，当政：*Queen Victoria reigned for over sixty years.* 维多利亚女王在位超过六十年。

rein /reɪn/ *noun* 名词
a long thin piece of leather that a horse wears on its head so that the person riding it can control it（马的）缰绳 ➲ Look at the picture at **horse**. 见 horse 的插图。

reindeer 驯鹿

reindeer /ˈremdɪə(r)/ *noun* 名词 (*plural* 复数形式 reindeer)
a big animal that lives in very cold countries. **Reindeer** are brown and have long horns on their heads. 驯鹿

reject /rɪˈdʒekt/ *verb* 动词 (rejects, rejecting, rejected)
to say that you do not want somebody or something 拒绝接受；不予考虑：*He rejected my offer of help.* 我主动提出帮忙，他拒绝了。
▶ **rejection** /rɪˈdʒekʃn/ *noun* 名词：*David got a rejection from Leeds University.* 戴维没有被利兹大学录取。

relate /rɪˈleɪt/ *verb* 动词 (relates, relating, related)
to show or to make a connection between two or more things 显示…之间的联系；把…联系起来：*I found it difficult to relate the two ideas in my mind.* 我觉得很难把这两个概念联系起来。
relate to somebody or 或 **something**
to be connected to somebody or something 涉及；与…相关：*We don't need to listen to this, as it doesn't relate to our situation.* 我们没必要听这个，因为这跟我们的处境不相关。

related /rɪˈleɪtɪd/ *adjective* 形容词
in the same family; connected 有亲属关系的；相关的：*'Are those two boys related?' 'Yes, they're brothers.'* "那两个男孩有亲属关系吗？""有，他们是两兄弟。"

relation /rɪˈleɪʃn/ *noun* 名词
1 a connection between two things （事物之间的）关系，联系，关联：*There is no relation between the size of the countries and the number of people who live there.* 国家的面积与人口的多少并无关联。
2 a person in your family 亲戚；亲属
⊃ SAME MEANING **relative** 同义词为 relative

relationship /rɪˈleɪʃnʃɪp/ *noun* 名词
the way people, groups or countries behave with each other or how they feel about each other （人、团体或国家之间的）关系，联系：*I have a good relationship with my parents.* 我跟父母关系很好。◇ *The book is about the relationship between an Indian boy and an English girl.* 这本书讲述一个印度男孩和一个英格兰女孩之间的关系。

relative /ˈrelətɪv/ *noun* 名词
a person in your family 亲戚，亲属
⊃ SAME MEANING **relation** 同义词为 relation

relatively /ˈrelətɪvli/ *adverb* 副词
quite, especially when compared to others 相当地；相对地：*This room is relatively small.* 这个房间相对较小。

relax /rɪˈlæks/ *verb* 动词 (relaxes, relaxing, relaxed /rɪˈlækst/)
1 to rest and be calm; to become less worried or angry 放松；休息；冷静：*After a hard day at work I spent the evening relaxing in front of the television.* 辛苦工作了一天之后，晚上我就悠闲地看看电视。
2 to become less tight or to make something become less tight （使）放松，松开：*Let your body relax.* 放松你的身体。

relaxation /ˌriːlækˈseɪʃn/ *noun* 名词 (*no plural* 不用复数形式)
time spent resting and being calm 放松；休息；消遣：*You need more rest and relaxation.* 你需要多休息，多放松。

relaxed /rɪˈlækst/ *adjective* 形容词
calm and not worried 放松的；冷静的：*She felt relaxed after her holiday.* 她度假后感到轻松多了。

relaxing /rɪˈlæksɪŋ/ *adjective* 形容词
helping you to rest and become less worried 令人放松的；轻松的：*a quiet, relaxing holiday* 平静轻松的假期

release¹ /rɪˈliːs/ *verb* 动词 (releases, releasing, released /rɪˈliːst/)
to let a person or an animal go free 释放；使自由：*He was released from prison last month.* 他上个月获释出狱。

release² /rɪˈliːs/ *noun* 名词
when a person or an animal is allowed to go free 释放；获释：*the release of the prisoners* 囚犯的释放

relevant /ˈreləvənt/ *adjective* 形容词
connected with what you are talking or

A
B
C
D
E
F
G
H
I
J
K
L
M
N
O
P
Q
R
S
T
U
V
W
X
Y
Z

writing about; important 相关的；切题的；重要的： *We need somebody who can do the job well – your age is not relevant.* 我们需要一个能胜任的人——你的年龄无关紧要。 ○ OPPOSITE **irrelevant** 反义词为 irrelevant

reliable /rɪˈlaɪəbl/ *adjective* 形容词
that you can trust 可靠的；值得信赖的： *My car is very reliable.* 我的车子很牢靠。 ◇ *He is a reliable person.* 他是个值得信赖的人。 ○ OPPOSITE **unreliable** 反义词为 unreliable ○ The verb is **rely**. 动词为 rely。

relied *form of* RELY * rely 的不同形式

relief 0ᵐ /rɪˈliːf/ *noun* 名词 (*no plural* 不用复数形式)
1 the good feeling you have when pain or worry stops（痛楚或忧虑过后的）宽慰，轻松，解脱： *It was a great relief to know she was safe.* 知道她安全，总算是放下心头大石了。
2 food or money that is given to people who need it 救援物资；救济金： *Many countries sent relief to the victims of the disaster.* 许多国家给灾民送去了救援物资。

relies *form of* RELY * rely 的不同形式

relieve /rɪˈliːv/ *verb* 动词 (relieves, relieving, relieved /rɪˈliːvd/)
to make a bad feeling or a pain stop or get better 解除；减轻；缓和： *These pills should relieve the pain.* 这些药片应该能减轻疼痛。

relieved /rɪˈliːvd/ *adjective* 形容词
feeling happy because a problem or danger has gone away 感到宽慰的；放心的；如释重负的： *I was relieved to hear that you weren't hurt in the accident.* 听说你在事故中没有受伤，我就放心了。

religion 0ᵐ /rɪˈlɪdʒən/ *noun* 名词
1 (*no plural* 不用复数形式) believing in a god or gods and the activities connected with this 宗教信仰
2 (*plural* 复数形式 religions) one of the ways of believing in a god or gods 宗教： *Christianity, Islam and other world religions* 基督教、伊斯兰教和世界上的其他宗教

religious 0ᵐ /rɪˈlɪdʒəs/ *adjective* 形容词
1 connected with religion 宗教的： *a religious leader* 宗教领袖
2 having a strong belief in a religion 笃信宗教的；虔诚的： *My parents are very religious.* 我父母很虔诚。

reluctance /rɪˈlʌktəns/ *noun* 名词 (*no plural* 不用复数形式)
not wanting to do something 不情愿；勉强： *He agreed, but with great reluctance.* 他同意了，却十分勉强。

reluctant /rɪˈlʌktənt/ *adjective* 形容词
If you are **reluctant** to do something, you do not want to do it. 不情愿的；勉强的： *He was reluctant to give me the money.* 他不愿意把钱给我。
▸ **reluctantly** *adverb* 副词： *She reluctantly agreed to help with the cleaning.* 她勉强答应帮忙打扫。

rely 0ᵐ /rɪˈlaɪ/ *verb* 动词 (relies, relying, relied /rɪˈlaɪd/, has relied)
rely on somebody or 或 **something**
1 to need somebody or something 依靠；依赖 ○ SAME MEANING **depend on somebody** or **something** 同义词为 depend on somebody 或 something： *I rely on my parents for money.* 我的钱都是靠父母给的。
2 to feel sure that somebody or something will do what they say they will do 信赖；信任： *You can rely on him to help you.* 你可以信任他来帮你。 ○ The adjective is **reliable**. 形容词为 reliable。

remain 0ᵐ /rɪˈmeɪn/ *verb* 动词 (remains, remaining, remained /rɪˈmeɪnd/) (*formal* 正式)
1 to stay in the same way; to not change 仍然是；保持不变： *I asked her a question but she remained silent.* 我问了她一个问题，可是她保持沉默。
2 to stay after other people or things have gone 留下；剩下： *After the fire, very little remained of the house.* 火灾过后，房子烧得所剩无几。

remaining /rɪˈmeɪnɪŋ/ *adjective* 形容词
continuing to exist or stay after other people or things have gone or been used 剩下的；余下的： *They spent the remaining two days of their holiday on the beach.* 他们假期的最后两天在海滩上度过。

remains /rɪˈmeɪnz/ *noun* 名词 (*plural* 用复数形式)
what is left when most of something has gone 剩余物；残留物；遗迹： *the remains of an old church* 古老教堂的遗迹

remark¹ 0ᵐ /rɪˈmɑːk/ *noun* 名词
something that you say 言论；谈论 ○ SAME MEANING **comment** 同义词为 comment： *He made a remark about the food.* 他对食物作了评论。

remark² /rɪˈmɑːk/ *verb* 动词 (remarks, remarking, remarked /rɪˈmɑːkt/)
to say something 说；谈论；评论 ⊃ SAME MEANING **comment** 同义词为 comment：
'It's cold today,' he remarked. "今天很冷。"他说。

remarkable /rɪˈmɑːkəbl/ *adjective* 形容词
unusual and surprising in a good way 了不起的；非凡的：*a remarkable discovery* 非凡的发现
▶ **remarkably** /rɪˈmɑːkəbli/ *adverb* 副词：*She speaks French remarkably well.* 她法语说得好极了。

remedy /ˈremədi/ *noun* 名词 (*plural* 复数形式 remedies)
something that makes you better when you are sick or in pain 疗法；药物：*He gave me a remedy for toothache.* 他给了我一个治牙疼的方子。

remember ⚬ /rɪˈmembə(r)/ *verb* 动词 (remembers, remembering, remembered /rɪˈmembəd/)
to keep something in your mind or bring something back into your mind 记得；想起：*Can you remember his name?* 你记得他的名字吗？ ◇ *I remember posting the letter.* 我记得把信寄了。 ◇ *Did you remember to go to the bank?* 你记得去银行了吗？ ⊃ OPPOSITE **forget** 反义词为 forget

remind ⚬ /rɪˈmaɪnd/ *verb* 动词 (reminds, reminding, reminded)
1 to help somebody remember something that they must do 提醒；提示：*Please remind me to buy some bread on the way home.* 请提醒我在回家时顺便去买些面包。
2 to make somebody remember somebody or something 使想起；唤起记忆：*She reminds me of her mother.* 她让我想起她的母亲。

reminder /rɪˈmaɪndə(r)/ *noun* 名词
something that makes you remember something 提醒人的事物；引起回忆的事物：*Eddie kept the ring as a reminder of happier days.* 埃迪保存着那枚戒指，好让自己回想起过去的美好时光。

remorse /rɪˈmɔːs/ *noun* 名词 (*no plural* 不用复数形式)
the feeling you have when you are sorry for doing something wrong 懊悔；自责：*She was filled with remorse for what she had done.* 她对自己所做的事深感懊悔。
⊃ Look at **guilt**. 见 guilt。

remote /rɪˈməʊt/ *adjective* 形容词 (remoter, remotest)
far away from where other people live 遥远的；偏远的：*a remote island in the Pacific Ocean* 太平洋上一个偏远的岛

remote control 遥控器

remote control /rɪˌməʊt kənˈtrəʊl/ *noun* 名词 (*no plural* 不用复数形式)
1 a way of controlling something from a distance 遥控：*The doors can be opened by remote control.* 这些门可靠遥控打开。
2 (*also informal* 非正式亦作 **remote**) a piece of equipment that you use for controlling something from a distance 遥控器；遥控设备：*Pass me the remote control – I'll see what's on the other channel.* 把遥控器递给我，我来看看另一个频道播什么。

remotely /rɪˈməʊtli/ *adverb* 副词
at all; in any way 完全；一点也：*I'm not remotely interested in your opinions.* 我对你的意见根本不感兴趣。

removal /rɪˈmuːvl/ *noun* 名词
when you take something off or away 移除；去除；挪走：*the removal of a car that was blocking the exit* 把挡住出口的汽车拖走

remove ⚬ /rɪˈmuːv/ *verb* 动词 (removes, removing, removed /rɪˈmuːvd/)
to take somebody or something off or away from somebody or something 移除；去掉；脱下：*The statue was removed from the museum.* 雕像从博物馆搬走了。 ◇ *Please remove your shoes before entering the temple.* 进庙前请先脱鞋。 ⊃ SAME MEANING Less formal verbs are **take away** or **take off**. 较为非正式的同义动词为 take away 或 take off。

renew /rɪˈnjuː/ *verb* 动词 (renews, renewing, renewed /rɪˈnjuːd/)
to get or give something new in the place of something old 更新；更换：*If you want to stay in the country for another month*

you must renew your visa. 若你想在这个国家再待一个月，就得续签签证。

rent¹ 0̄ᵣ /rent/ *noun* 名词
the money that you pay to live in a place or to use something that belongs to another person 租金；房租：*How much is your rent?* 你的租金是多少？

rent² 0̄ᵣ /rent/ *verb* 动词 (**rents, renting, rented**)
1 to pay to live in a place or to use something that belongs to another person 租用；租借：*I rent a house on the edge of town.* 我在市郊租了一所房子。
2 to let somebody live in a place or use something that belongs to you, if they pay you 出租：*He rents rooms in his house to students.* 他把屋里的房间租给学生。 ⭥ Look at **hire**. 见 hire.

rep /rep/ *noun* 名词 (*informal* 非正式)
a person whose job is to travel around an area selling their company's products 推销员；销售代表

repaid *form of* REPAY * repay 的不同形式

repair¹ 0̄ᵣ /rɪ'peə(r)/ *verb* 动词 (**repairs, repairing, repaired** /rɪ'peəd/)
to make something that is broken or damaged good again 修理；修复；修缮 ⭥ SAME MEANING **mend** 同义词为 mend：*Can you repair my bike?* 你能给我修理自行车吗？

repair² /rɪ'peə(r)/ *noun* 名词
something you do to fix something that is broken or damaged 修理；修复；修缮：*The school is closed for repairs to the roof.* 学校因维修房顶关闭了。

repay /rɪ'peɪ/ *verb* 动词 (**repays, repaying, repaid** /rɪ'peɪd/, **has repaid**)
1 to pay back money to somebody 还（钱）；偿还：*to repay a loan* 偿还贷款
2 to do something for somebody to show your thanks 回报；报答：*How can I repay you for all your help?* 对你的一切帮助我怎么才能报答呢？

repayment /rɪ'peɪmənt/ *noun* 名词
paying somebody back, or the money that you pay them 偿还款项；还款：*monthly repayments* 每月还款

repeat 0̄ᵣ /rɪ'piːt/ *verb* 动词 (**repeats, repeating, repeated**)
1 to say or do something again 重复：*He didn't hear my question, so I repeated it.* 他没听见我的问题，所以我重复了一遍。
2 to say what another person has said 复述；跟读：*Repeat this sentence after me.* 跟我读这个句子。

▸ **repeat** *noun* 名词：*I think I've seen this programme before – it must be a repeat.* 我想我以前看过这个节目 —— 这肯定是重播。

repeated /rɪ'piːtɪd/ *adjective* 形容词
happening or done many times 重复的；反复发生的：*There have been repeated accidents on this stretch of road.* 这一路段发生过多起事故。
▸ **repeatedly** /rɪ'piːtɪdli/ *adverb* 副词：*I've asked him repeatedly not to leave his bicycle here.* 我三番五次叫他不要把自行车放在这里。

repetition /ˌrepə'tɪʃn/ *noun* 名词
saying or doing something again 重复：*to learn by repetition* 通过重复来学习

replace 0̄ᵣ /rɪ'pleɪs/ *verb* 动词 (**replaces, replacing, replaced** /rɪ'pleɪst/)
1 to take the place of somebody or something 代替；取代：*Teachers will never be replaced by computers in the classroom.* 课堂上电脑永远取代不了老师。
2 to put a new or different person or thing in the place of another 更换；替换：*The watch was broken so the shop replaced it with a new one.* 手表坏了，商店于是给换了一块新的。
3 to put something back in the place where it was before 放回原处：*Please replace the books on the shelf when you have finished with them.* 书看完后请放回架子上。

replacement /rɪ'pleɪsmənt/ *noun* 名词
a new or different person or thing that takes the place of another 接替者；替代品：*Sue is leaving the company next month so we need to find a replacement.* 苏下个月离开公司，所以我们得找个人接替她。

replay /'riːpleɪ/ *noun* 名词 (*British* 英式英语)
(*sport* 体育运动) a game that is played again because nobody won the first time （因未决出胜负而进行的）重赛

reply¹ 0̄ᵣ /rɪ'plaɪ/ *verb* 动词 (**replies, replying, replied** /rɪ'plaɪd/, **has replied**)
to say or write something as an answer to somebody or something 回答；答复：*I wrote to Jane but she hasn't replied.* 我给简写了封信，可她还没回信。

reply² 0̄ᵣ /rɪ'plaɪ/ *noun* 名词 (*plural* 复数形式 **replies**)
an answer 回答；答复：*Have you had a reply to your letter?* 你收到回信了吗？ ◊ *What did you say in reply to his question?* 他的问题你是怎么回答的？

A
B
C
D
E
F
G
H
I
J
K
L
M
N
O
P
Q
R
S
T
U
V
W
X
Y
Z

report¹ 0— /rɪ'pɔːt/ *verb* 动词 (reports, reporting, reported)
to give people information about something that has happened 汇报; 报告; 报道: *We **reported** the accident **to** the police.* 我们向警方报告了这起事故。

report² 0— /rɪ'pɔːt/ *noun* 名词
1 something that somebody says or writes about something that has happened 报告; 报道: *Did you read the newspaper reports about the earthquake?* 你看了报纸上有关地震的报道吗?
2 (*British* 英式英语) something that teachers write about a student's work (学生的) 成绩报告单

reported speech /rɪ,pɔːtɪd spiːtʃ/ *noun* 名词 (*no plural* 不用复数形式) (*also* 亦作 **indirect speech**)
(*grammar* 语法) saying what somebody has said, rather than repeating their exact words. In **reported speech**, 'I'll come later' becomes 'He said he'd (= he would) come later'. 间接引语; 间接叙述法

reporter /rɪ'pɔːtə(r)/ *noun* 名词
a person who writes in a newspaper or speaks on the radio or television about things that have happened 记者; 通讯员 ➷ Look at **journalist**. 见 journalist。

represent 0— /,reprɪ'zent/ *verb* 动词 (represents, representing, represented)
1 to speak or do something in place of another person or other people 代表: *It is an honour for athletes to represent their country.* 作为运动员，能代表国家参赛是一份光荣。
2 to be an example or a sign of something 象征; 表示: *The yellow lines on the map represent roads.* 地图上黄线代表道路。

representative /,reprɪ'zentətɪv/ *noun* 名词
a person who speaks or does something for a group of people 代表: *There were representatives from every country in Europe at the meeting.* 会上有来自欧洲每一个国家的代表。

reproduce /,riːprə'djuːs/ *verb* 动词 (reproduces, reproducing, reproduced /,riːprə'djuːst/)
1 to make a copy of something 复制
2 When people, animals or plants **reproduce**, they have young ones. 繁殖; 生育

reproduction /,riːprə'dʌkʃn/ *noun* 名词 (*no plural* 不用复数形式)
producing babies or young animals or plants 繁殖; 生育: *We are studying plant*

reproduction at school. 我们正在学校学植物的繁殖。

reptile /'reptaɪl/ *noun* 名词
any animal with cold blood that lays eggs. Snakes are **reptiles**. 爬行动物

> 🔎 **WORD BUILDING** 词汇扩充
>
> There are many different types of **reptile**. Here are some of them: alligator, crocodile, lizard, snake, tortoise, turtle. Do you know any others? * reptile 的种类很多，如: alligator (钝吻鳄)、crocodile (鳄鱼)、lizard (蜥蜴)、snake (蛇)、tortoise (陆龟)、turtle (海龟)。你还知道别的吗?

republic /rɪ'pʌblɪk/ *noun* 名词
a country where people choose the government and the leader (the president) 共和国: *the Republic of Ireland* 爱尔兰共和国 ➷ Look at **monarchy**. 见 monarchy。

republican /rɪ'pʌblɪkən/ *noun* 名词
1 a person who wants a REPUBLIC 拥护共和政体的人; 共和主义者
2 Republican (*politics* 政治) a person in THE REPUBLICAN PARTY in the US (美国) 共和党党员 ➷ Look at **democrat** (2). 见 democrat 第 2 义。

the Republican Party /ðə rɪ'pʌblɪkən pɑːti/ *noun* 名词 (*no plural* 不用复数形式) (*politics* 政治) one of the two main political parties in the US (美国) 共和党 ➷ Look at **Democratic Party**. 见 Democratic Party。

repulsive /rɪ'pʌlsɪv/ *adjective* 形容词
making you feel disgusted; very unpleasant 令人厌恶的; 令人反感的: *What a repulsive smell!* 多么恶心的气味!

reputation /,repju'teɪʃn/ *noun* 名词
what people think or say about somebody or something 名声; 名誉: *This restaurant has a good reputation.* 这家餐馆口碑不错。

request¹ 0— /rɪ'kwest/ *noun* 名词
asking for something in a polite or formal way 请求; 要求: *They made a request for money.* 他们提出要钱。

request² 0— /rɪ'kwest/ *verb* 动词 (requests, requesting, requested) (*formal* 正式)
to ask for something 请求; 要求: *Passengers are requested not to smoke* (= a notice in a bus). 请勿吸烟 (公共汽车上的告示)

A
B
C
D
E
F
G
H
I
J
K
L
M
N
O
P
Q
R
S
T
U
V
W
X
Y
Z

🔍 SPEAKING 表达方式说明

It is more usual to say **ask for**. 较常用
ask for。

require 0━ /rɪˈkwaɪə(r)/ *verb* 动词
(requires, requiring, required /rɪˈkwaɪəd/)
(*formal* 正式)
to need something 需要；要求： *Do you
require anything else?* 你还需要别的
什么吗?

🔍 SPEAKING 表达方式说明

Need is the word that we usually use.
* need 是常用词。

requirement /rɪˈkwaɪəmənt/ *noun*
名词
something that you need or that you
must have 所需的东西；必备的条件；
要求

rescue[1] 0━ /ˈreskjuː/ *verb* 动词 (rescues,
rescuing, rescued)
to save somebody or something from
danger 营救；援救： *She rescued the child
when he fell in the river.* 她在那孩子掉进
河里时救起了他。

rescue[2] 0━ /ˈreskjuː/ *noun* 名词
saving somebody or something from
danger 营救；援救： *The police came to
his rescue.* 警方救了他。

research[1] 0━ /rɪˈsɜːtʃ; ˈriːsɜːtʃ/ *noun*
名词 (*no plural* 不用复数形式)
studying something carefully to find out
more about it 研究；调查： *scientific
research* 科学研究

research[2] 0━ /rɪˈsɜːtʃ/ *verb* 动词
(researches, researching, researched
/rɪˈsɜːtʃt/)
to study something carefully to find out
more about it 研究；调查： *Scientists are
researching the causes of the disease.*
科学家正在研究这种疾病的成因。
▶ **researcher** /rɪˈsɜːtʃə(r)/ *noun* 名词

resemblance /rɪˈzembləns/ *noun* 名词
looking like somebody or something else
相似；相像： *There's no resemblance
between my two brothers.* 我两个哥哥
长得一点儿也不像。

resemble /rɪˈzembl/ *verb* 动词
(resembles, resembling, resembled
/rɪˈzembld/)
to look like somebody or something else
和…相似；像： *Lisa resembles her mother.*
莉萨长得像她母亲。

🔍 SPEAKING 表达方式说明

It is more usual to say **look like**. 较常用
look like。

resent /rɪˈzent/ *verb* 动词 (resents,
resenting, resented)
to feel angry about something because
you think it is not fair（觉得不公平而）
愤恨，感到气愤；愤愤不平： *I resented
her criticism of my work.* 她对我工作提出
批评令我气愤。

resentment /rɪˈzentmənt/ *noun* 名词
(*no plural* 不用复数形式)
a feeling of anger about something that
you think is not fair 愤恨；怨恨

reservation /ˌrezəˈveɪʃn/ *noun* 名词
a room, seat, table or another thing that
you have asked somebody to keep for
you 预订（房间、座位等）： *I called the
restaurant and made a reservation for
a table for two.* 我给餐馆打电话，预订了
一张两人的餐桌。

reserve[1] 0━ /rɪˈzɜːv/ *verb* 动词
(reserves, reserving, reserved /rɪˈzɜːvd/)
1 to keep something for a special reason
or to use later 预留；保留： *Those seats
are reserved.* 那些是预留座位。
2 to ask for a seat, table, room, etc. to be
kept for you at a future time 预订（座位、
房间等）つ SAME MEANING **book** 同义词为
book： *I would like to reserve a single
room for tomorrow night, please.* 我要预订
一间明晚的单人房。

reserve[2] /rɪˈzɜːv/ *noun* 名词
1 something that you keep to use later
储备；贮存物品： *reserves of food* 食物
储备
2 an area of land where the animals and
plants are protected by law（动植物的）
保护区： *a nature reserve* 自然保护区
3 (*sport* 体育运动) a person who will play
in a game if another person cannot play
替补队员；后备选手
in reserve for using later 储备；备用：
*Don't spend all the money – keep some in
reserve.* 别把钱都花光——留点以备后用。

reserved /rɪˈzɜːvd/ *adjective* 形容词
If you are **reserved**, you keep your
feelings hidden from other people. 内向
的；内敛的；矜持的

reservoir /ˈrezəvwɑː(r)/ *noun* 名词
a big lake where a town or city keeps
water to use later 水库

residence /ˈrezɪdəns/ *noun* 名词
1 (*plural* 复数形式 residences) (*formal*

正式) a large house, usually where an important or famous person lives 宅第；住所；府邸： *The Prime Minister's official residence is 10 Downing Street.* 英国首相的官邸是唐宁街 10 号。

2 (*no plural* 不用复数形式) having your home in a particular place 居住；定居： *The family applied for permanent residence in the United States.* 这家人申请了在美国永久定居。◇ *a university **hall of residence*** (= a place where students live) 大学学生宿舍

resident /ˈrezɪdənt/ *noun* 名词
a person who lives in a place 居民

residential /ˌrezɪˈdenʃl/ *adjective* 形容词
A **residential** area is one where there are houses rather than offices or factories. 住宅的

resign /rɪˈzaɪn/ *verb* 动词 (resigns, resigning, resigned /rɪˈzaɪnd/)
to leave your job 辞职： *The director has resigned.* 董事已经辞职。

resign yourself to something to accept something that you do not like but that you cannot change 无奈地接受： *There were a lot of people at the doctor's so John resigned himself to a long wait.* 诊所里人很多，约翰只好慢慢等。

resignation /ˌrezɪɡˈneɪʃn/ *noun* 名词
saying that you want to leave your job 辞职： *a letter of resignation* 辞职信 ◇ *to hand in your resignation* (= to give your employer a letter saying that you want to leave your job) 递交辞呈

resist /rɪˈzɪst/ *verb* 动词 (resists, resisting, resisted)
1 to try to stop something happening or to fight against somebody or something 阻止；抵制；抵抗： *The government are resisting pressure to change the law.* 政府正在顶住要求修改法律的压力。
2 to stop yourself doing or having something that you want to do or have 忍住（不做）；抑制住： *I can't resist chocolate.* 我完全抗拒不了巧克力。

resistance /rɪˈzɪstəns/ *noun* 名词
(*no plural* 不用复数形式)
when people try to stop something happening; fighting against somebody or something 阻止；抵制；反抗；抵抗： *There was a lot of resistance to the plan to build a new airport.* 兴建新机场的计划广受非议。

resolution /ˌrezəˈluːʃn/ *noun* 名词
something that you decide to do or not to do 决定；决议： *Julie made a resolution*

to study harder. 朱莉下定决心要更加努力学习。

resolve /rɪˈzɒlv/ *verb* 动词 (resolves, resolving, resolved /rɪˈzɒlvd/) (*formal* 正式)
to decide to do or not to do something 决心；决定： *He resolved never to do it again.* 他决定再也不这么做了。

resort /rɪˈzɔːt/ *noun* 名词
a place where a lot of people go on holiday 旅游胜地；度假胜地： *a popular seaside resort* 受欢迎的海滨度假胜地
a last resort the only person or thing left that can help 可求助的最后一个人；最后的方法： *Nobody else will lend me the money, so I am asking you as a last resort.* 谁都不会借钱给我了，我只好抱着最后的希望向你求助。

resource /rɪˈsɔːs, rɪˈzɔːs/ *noun* 名词
something that a person, an organization or a country has and can use 资源： *Oil is one of our most important natural resources.* 石油是我们最重要的自然资源之一。

respect¹ 0ᵐ /rɪˈspekt/ *noun* 名词
(*no plural* 不用复数形式)
1 thinking that somebody or something is very good or clever 尊敬；敬意： *I have a lot of respect for your father.* 我非常尊敬你的父亲。
2 being polite to somebody or something 尊重： *You should treat old people with more respect.* 你应该更加尊重老年人。

respect² 0ᵐ /rɪˈspekt/ *verb* 动词 (respects, respecting, respected)
to have a good opinion of somebody or something 尊敬；敬重 ⊃ SAME MEANING **admire** 同义词为 admire： *I respect him for his honesty.* 我敬重他为人诚实。

respectable /rɪˈspektəbl/ *adjective* 形容词
If a person or thing is **respectable**, people think they are good or correct. 体面的；得体的；德高望重的： *She comes from a respectable family.* 她出身望族。

respectful /rɪˈspektfl/ *adjective* 形容词
If you are **respectful**, you are polite to other people and in different situations. 表示敬意的；尊敬的： *The crowd listened in respectful silence.* 群众肃然静听。

respond /rɪˈspɒnd/ *verb* 动词 (responds, responding, responded) (*formal* 正式)
to do or say something to answer somebody or something 回应；回答 ⊃ SAME MEANING **reply** 同义词为 reply：

A B C D E F G H I J K L M N O P Q R S T U V W X Y Z

A
B
C
D
E
F
G
H
I
J
K
L
M
N
O
P
Q

R

S
T
U
V
W
X
Y
Z

I said 'hello', but he didn't respond. 我跟他打招呼，他却没有回应。

response /rɪ'spɒns/ *noun* 名词
an answer to somebody or something 回应；回答 ⊃ SAME MEANING **reply** 同义词为 reply: *I wrote to them but I've had no response.* 我给他们写了信，但一直没有回音。

responsibility 0━ /rɪ,spɒnsə'bɪləti/ *noun* 名词
a duty to deal with or take care of somebody or something, so that it is your fault if something goes wrong 责任；职责: *Who has responsibility for the new students?* 谁负责新生？◇ *The dog is my brother's responsibility.* 我弟弟负责照看这条狗。

responsible 0━ /rɪ'spɒnsəbl/ *adjective* 形容词
1 having the duty to take care of somebody or something, so that it is your fault if something goes wrong 有责任；负责: *The driver is responsible for the lives of the people on the bus.* 公共汽车司机对乘客的生命负有责任。
2 being the person who made something bad happen（对过失）负有责任: *Who was responsible for the accident?* 谁该为这起事故负责？
3 A **responsible** person is somebody that you can trust and rely on. 负责任的；有责任心的: *We need a responsible person to look after our son.* 我们需要一个尽责的人照看儿子。

rest¹ 0━ /rest/ *noun* 名词
1 the rest the part that is left or the ones that are left 剩余部分；其余的人（或事物）: *If you don't want the rest, I'll eat it.* 剩下的如果你不吃的话，我就吃啦。◇ *I liked the beginning, but the rest of the film wasn't very good.* 我喜欢电影的开头，但其余部分就不怎么样。◇ *Jason watched TV and the rest of us went for a walk.* 贾森看电视，我们其他人去散步了。
2 a time when you relax, sleep or do nothing 休息；歇息: *After walking for an hour, we stopped for a rest.* 走了一小时后，我们停下来休息了。

rest² 0━ /rest/ *verb* 动词 (rests, resting, rested)
1 to relax, sleep or do nothing after an activity or an illness 休息；歇息: *We worked all morning and then rested for an hour before starting work again.* 我们工作了一上午，然后休息一小时便又继续工作。
2 to be on something; to put something

on or against another thing（使）倚着；靠在（…上）: *His arms were resting on the table.* 他双臂靠在桌子上。

restaurant 0━ /'restrɒnt/ *noun* 名词
a place where you buy a meal and eat it 餐馆；饭馆

> ⌕ **WORD BUILDING** 词汇扩充
>
> You usually go to a **restaurant** for a special meal. 上饭馆通常是去吃特别的饭菜。
> You can get a quick or cheap meal at a **cafe**, a **sandwich bar**, a **takeaway** or a **fast-food restaurant**. 吃快餐或廉价餐可以到小餐馆（cafe）、三明治店（sandwich bar）、外卖店（takeaway）或快餐店（fast-food restaurant）。

restful /'restfl/ *adjective* 形容词
making you feel relaxed and calm 使人放松的；闲适宁静的: *a restful holiday* 悠闲的假日

restless /'restləs/ *adjective* 形容词
not able to stay still or relax because you are bored or nervous 坐立不安的；不耐烦的: *The children always get restless on long journeys.* 长途旅行时，孩子们总是躁动不安。

restore /rɪ'stɔː(r)/ *verb* 动词 (restores, restoring, restored /rɪ'stɔːd/)
to make something as good as it was before 恢复；修复: *The old palace has been restored.* 旧宫殿已经修复好。

restrain /rɪ'streɪn/ *verb* 动词 (restrains, restraining, restrained /rɪ'streɪnd/)
to stop somebody or something from doing something; to control somebody or something 抑制；控制: *I couldn't restrain my anger.* 我抑制不住愤怒。

restrict /rɪ'strɪkt/ *verb* 动词 (restricts, restricting, restricted)
to allow only a certain amount, size, sort, etc. 限制；限定 ⊃ SAME MEANING **limit** 同义词为 limit: *Our house is very small, so we had to restrict the number of people we invited to the party.* 我们的房子很小，所以得限制邀请来参加聚会的人数。

restriction /rɪ'strɪkʃn/ *noun* 名词
a rule to control somebody or something 限制；约束: *There are a lot of parking restrictions in the city centre.* 在市中心停车有很多限制。

restroom /'restruːm/ *noun* 名词 (*American* 美式英语)
a room with a toilet in a public place, for

example a restaurant or theatre（餐馆、剧院等公共场所的）洗手间、卫生间

result¹ 0➔ /rɪˈzʌlt/ *noun* 名词
1 something that happens because of something else 结果： *The accident was a result of bad driving.* 那起事故是由驾驶不当引起的。◇ *I woke up late and as a result I was late for school.* 我起床晚了，结果上课迟到。
2 the score at the end of a game, competition or exam（比赛）得分；（考试）成绩： *football results* 足球比赛的结果 ◇ *When will you know your exam results?* 你什么时候会知道考试成绩？

result² 0➔ /rɪˈzʌlt/ *verb* 动词 (results, resulting, resulted)
result in something to make something happen 造成；导致 ⊃ SAME MEANING **cause** 同义词为 cause： *The accident resulted in the death of two drivers.* 事故造成了两名司机死亡。

resume /rɪˈzjuːm/ *verb* 动词 (resumes, resuming, resumed /rɪˈzjuːmd/) (*formal* 正式)
to start something again after stopping for a period of time（中断后）恢复，继续： *to resume negotiations* 恢复谈判

résumé /ˈrezjumeɪ/ *noun* 名词 *American English for* CV 美式英语，即 CV

— **retire** 0➔ /rɪˈtaɪə(r)/ *verb* 动词 (retires, retiring, retired /rɪˈtaɪəd/)
to stop working because you are a certain age 退休： *My grandfather retired when he was 65.* 我祖父 65 岁时退休了。
▸ **retired** *adjective* 形容词： *a retired teacher* 退休教师

retirement /rɪˈtaɪəmənt/ *noun* 名词 (*no plural* 不用复数形式)
the time in a person's life after they have reached a certain age and have stopped working 退休（生活）： *We all wish you a long and happy retirement.* 我们大家祝愿你的退休生活长久而幸福。

retreat /rɪˈtriːt/ *verb* 动词 (retreats, retreating, retreated)
to move back or away from somebody or something, for example because you have lost a fight 撤退；退却： *The enemy is retreating.* 敌人正在撤退。
▸ **retreat** *noun* 名词： *The army is now in retreat.* 军队正在撤退。

return¹ 0➔ /rɪˈtɜːn/ *verb* 动词 (returns, returning, returned /rɪˈtɜːnd/)
1 to come or go back to a place 返回；回来；回去： *They returned from Italy last week.* 他们上周从意大利回来了。

2 to give, put, send or take something back 归还；带回；送回；放回： *Will you return this book to the library?* 你把这本书归还给图书馆好吗？

return² 0➔ /rɪˈtɜːn/ *noun* 名词
1 (*no plural* 不用复数形式) coming or going back to a place 返回；回来；归来： *They met me at the airport on my return to Britain.* 我回到英国的时候，他们在机场接我。
2 (*no plural* 不用复数形式) giving, putting, sending or taking something back 归还；带回；送回；放回： *the return of the stolen money* 被盗钱款的归还
3 (*plural* 复数形式 returns) (*British* 英式英语) (*British also* 英式英语亦作 return ticket) (*American* 美式英语 round trip, round-trip ticket) a ticket to travel to a place and back again 往返票： *A return to London, please.* 请给我一张到伦敦的往返票。 ⊃ OPPOSITE **single** 反义词为 single
in return as a way of thanking somebody for something they have done for you or paying them for something they have given you 作为回报： *Can I buy you lunch in return for all your help?* 为感谢你所有的帮助，我请你吃午饭好吗？
many happy returns words that you say to wish somebody a happy birthday 生日快乐；长寿如意

reunion /riːˈjuːniən/ *noun* 名词
a meeting of people who have not seen each other for a long time 团聚；重逢： *We had a family reunion on my aunt's birthday.* 姑妈生日那天我们全家团聚了。

reunite /ˌriːjuːˈnaɪt/ *verb* 动词 (reunites, reuniting, reunited)
to come together or to bring people together again（使）重逢，团聚： *The missing child was found and reunited with his parents.* 失踪的孩子找到了，并与父母团聚了。

Rev. *short way of writing* REVEREND
* Reverend 的缩写形式

reveal /rɪˈviːl/ *verb* 动词 (reveals, revealing, revealed /rɪˈviːld/)
to tell something that was a secret or show something that was hidden 透露；揭露；揭示： *She refused to reveal any names to the police.* 她不肯向警方透露任何名字。

revenge /rɪˈvendʒ/ *noun* 名词 (*no plural* 不用复数形式)
something bad that you do to somebody who has done something bad to you

A
B
C
D
E
F
G
H
I
J
K
L
M
N
O
P
Q
R
S
T
U
V
W
X
Y
Z

报复；报仇： *He wants to **take his
revenge** on his enemies.* 他想找敌人报仇。

Reverend /'revərənd/ *adjective* 形容词
(*abbr.* 缩略式 Rev.)
the title of a Christian priest （对基督教
神职人员的尊称）尊敬的

reverse¹ /rɪ'vɜːs/ *verb* 动词 (reverses,
reversing, reversed /rɪ'vɜːst/)
1 to turn something the other way round
使颠倒；倒转；掉转： *Writing is reversed
in a mirror.* 从镜子里看字是反的。
2 to go backwards in a car, etc.; to make
a car, etc. go backwards （使汽车等）
倒退；倒车： *I reversed the car into the
garage.* 我把车子倒进了车库。
reverse the charges (*British* 英式英语)
to make a telephone call that the person
you are telephoning will pay for 打对方付
费的电话： *I want to reverse the charges,
please.* 我想打一个由对方付费的电话。

reverse² /rɪ'vɜːs/ *noun* 名词 (*no plural*
不用复数形式)
1 the complete opposite of what
somebody just said, or of what you expect
相反的情况： *Of course I don't dislike you –
quite the reverse* (= I like you very much).
我当然不讨厌你 —— 事实刚好相反呢。
2 the control in a car or other vehicle that
allows it to move backwards （汽车等的）
倒挡，后退装置： *Leave the car in reverse
while it's parked on this hill.* 汽车停在这个
斜坡上的时候要挂上倒挡。

review¹ /rɪ'vjuː/ *noun* 名词
1 looking at something or thinking about
something again to see if it needs
changing 重新审视；检讨： *There will be
a review of your contract after six months.*
六个月后会对你的合同审核一次。
2 a piece of writing in a newspaper or
magazine that says what somebody
thinks about a book, film, play, etc.
（书、电影、戏剧等的）评论： *The film
got very good reviews.* 这部影片大获好评。

review² /rɪ'vjuː/ *verb* 动词 (reviews,
reviewing, reviewed /rɪ'vjuːd/)
1 to look at something or think about
something again to see if it needs
changing 复查；重新审视；检讨： *Your
salary will be reviewed after one year.*
你的薪金一年后会重新评定。
2 to write about a new book, film, etc.,
giving your opinion of it （对书、电影
等）作评论： *The play was reviewed in the
national newspapers.* 全国性报纸都对这出
戏作了评论。

revise /rɪ'vaɪz/ *verb* 动词 (revises,
revising, revised /rɪ'vaɪzd/)
1 to change something to make it better
or more correct 修改；修订： *The book
has been revised for this new edition.*
该书为这个新版作了修订。
2 (*British* 英式英语) to study again
something that you have learnt, before
an exam （考试前）复习，温习： *I'm
revising for the Geography test.* 我在为
地理测验复习功课。

revision /rɪ'vɪʒn/ *noun* 名词 (*no plural*
不用复数形式) (*British* 英式英语)
studying something again that you have
already learnt, in order to prepare for an
exam 复习；温习： *I need to do some
revision for the History exam.* 我需要为
历史考试复习一下。

revive /rɪ'vaɪv/ *verb* 动词 (revives,
reviving, revived /rɪ'vaɪvd/)
to become or make somebody or
something well or strong again （使）
复苏，复活： *They tried to revive him, but
he was already dead.* 他们试图救活他，
可是他已经死了。

revolt /rɪ'vəʊlt/ *verb* 动词 (revolts,
revolting, revolted)
to fight against the people in control
反抗；反叛；起义： *The army is revolting
against the government.* 军队正起来反抗
政府。
▶ **revolt** *noun* 名词： *The army quickly
stopped the revolt.* 军队很快镇压了叛乱。

revolting /rɪ'vəʊltɪŋ/ *adjective* 形容词
extremely unpleasant; so bad that it
makes you feel sick 令人极其反感的；
令人作呕的 ⊃ SAME MEANING **disgusting**
同义词为 disgusting： *This meat tastes
revolting.* 这肉的味道令人作呕。

revolution /ˌrevə'luːʃn/ *noun* 名词
1 a fight by people against their
government in order to put a new
government in its place 革命： *The French
Revolution was in 1789.* 法国大革命发生在
1789 年。
2 a big change in the way of doing things
（方法的）巨变，大变革： *the Industrial
Revolution* 工业革命

revolutionary /ˌrevə'luːʃənəri/ *adjective*
形容词
1 connected with a political REVOLUTION (1)
革命的
2 producing great changes; very new
and different 产生巨变的；革新的：
a revolutionary new scheme to ban cars

from the city centre 禁止汽车进入市中心
的革命性新计划

revolve /rɪˈvɒlv/ *verb* 动词 (revolves,
revolving, revolved /rɪˈvɒlvd/)
to move around in a circle 旋转；环绕：
The earth revolves around the sun. 地球
绕太阳转动。

revolver /rɪˈvɒlvə(r)/ *noun* 名词
a type of small gun 左轮手枪

reward¹ /rɪˈwɔːd/ *noun* 名词
a present or money that somebody gives
you because you have done something
good or worked hard 奖励；报酬：*She is
offering a £50 reward to anyone who finds
her dog.* 她正悬赏 50 英镑寻找她的狗。

reward² /rɪˈwɔːd/ *verb* 动词 (rewards,
rewarding, rewarded)
to give something to somebody because
they have done something well or worked
hard 奖励；奖赏：*His parents bought him
a bike to reward him for passing his exam.*
他父母给他买了一辆自行车，奖励他通过
考试。

rewind /ˌriːˈwaɪnd/ *verb* 动词 (rewinds,
rewinding, rewound /ˌriːˈwaʊnd/, has
rewound)
to make a video or a tape go backwards
倒（录像带或录音带）；倒带：*Please
rewind the tape at the end of the film.*
电影播放完毕后请倒带。

rheumatism /ˈruːmətɪzəm/ *noun* 名词
(*no plural* 不用复数形式)
an illness that causes pain in the muscles
and where your bones join together (your
joints) 风湿（病）

rhino /ˈraɪnəʊ/ *noun* 名词 (*plural* 复数形式
rhinos) (*informal* 非正式) short for
RHINOCEROS * rhinoceros 的缩略式

rhinoceros 犀牛

horn
角

rhinoceros /raɪˈnɒsərəs/ *noun* 名词
(*plural* 复数形式 rhinoceros or 或
rhinoceroses)

a big wild animal from Africa or Asia, with
thick skin and a horn on its nose 犀牛

rhyme¹ /raɪm/ *noun* 名词
1 a word that has the same sound as
another sound, for example 'bell' and
'well' 同韵词；押韵词
2 a short piece of writing where the
lines end with the same sounds 韵文：
a children's rhyme 儿歌

rhyme² /raɪm/ *verb* 动词 (rhymes,
rhyming, rhymed /raɪmd/)
1 to have the same sound as another
word（字词）押韵：*'Chair' rhymes with
'bear'.* * chair 和 bear 押韵。
2 to have lines that end with the same
sounds（诗句）押韵：*This poem doesn't
rhyme.* 这首诗不押韵。

rhythm /ˈrɪðəm/ *noun* 名词
a regular pattern of sounds that come
again and again 节奏；韵律：*This music
has a good rhythm.* 这首乐曲的节奏很棒。

rib /rɪb/ *noun* 名词
one of the bones around your chest 肋骨

ribbon /ˈrɪbən/ *noun* 名词
a long thin piece of material for tying
things or making something look pretty
带子；丝带：*She wore a pink ribbon in
her hair.* 她头发上绑着粉红色的饰带。

rice 0— /raɪs/ *noun* 名词 (*no plural* 不用
复数形式)
short, thin white or brown grain from a
plant that grows on wet land in hot
countries. We cook and eat **rice**. 稻米；
大米：*Would you like rice or potatoes with
your chicken?* 你点的鸡肉要配米饭还是
马铃薯？ つ Look at Picture Dictionary
page **P7**. 见彩页 P7。

rich 0— /rɪtʃ/ *adjective* 形容词 (richer,
richest)
1 having a lot of money 富裕的；富有
的：*a rich family* 富裕的家庭 ◇ *It's a
favourite resort for the rich* (= people who
are rich) *and famous.* 这是富豪名流最喜欢
去度假的地方。 つ OPPOSITE **poor** 反义词
为 poor
2 containing a lot of something 富含…
的：*Oranges are rich in vitamin C.* 橙子
含有丰富的维生素 C。
3 Food that is **rich** has a lot of fat or
sugar in it and makes you feel full quickly.
（食物）油腻的，甜腻的：*a rich chocolate
cake* 甜腻的巧克力蛋糕

rid 0— /rɪd/ *adjective* 形容词
get rid of somebody or 或 **something**
to make yourself free of somebody or
something that you do not want; to

A
B
C
D
E
F
G
H
I
J
K
L
M
N
O
P
Q
R
S
T
U
V
W
X
Y
Z

throw something away 除掉；摆脱；扔掉：*This dog is following me – I can't get rid of it.* 这条狗一直跟着我——我甩不掉它。◊ *I got rid of my old coat and bought a new one.* 我把旧大衣扔了，买了件新的。

ridden *form of* RIDE¹ * ride¹ 的不同形式

riddle /'rɪdl/ *noun* 名词
a difficult question that has a clever or funny answer 谜语：*Here's a riddle: What has four legs but can't walk? The answer is a chair!* 猜你这个谜语：四条腿，不会走，是什么呢？谜底是椅子！

ride¹ 0ₙ /raɪd/ *verb* 动词 (rides, riding, rode /rəʊd/, has ridden /'rɪdn/)
1 to sit on a horse or bicycle and control it as it moves 骑（马或自行车）：*I'm learning to ride* (= a horse). 我在学骑马。◊ *Don't ride your bike on the grass!* 别在草地上骑自行车！

> 🔎 SPEAKING 表达方式说明
> When you talk about spending time riding a horse for pleasure, you say **go riding** or **go horse riding** in British English. 在英式英语中，表示骑马游玩说 go riding 或 go horse riding：*I went riding today.* 我今天去骑马了。
> In American English, you say **go horseback riding**. 美式英语说 go horseback riding。

2 to travel in a car, bus or train 乘坐（汽车、公共汽车或火车）：*We rode in the back of the car.* 我们坐在汽车的后座。⊃ When you control a car, bus or train, you **drive** it. 用 drive 表示驾驶汽车、公共汽车或火车。

ride² 0ₙ /raɪd/ *noun* 名词
1 a journey on a horse or bicycle, or in a car, bus or train（骑马、骑车、乘车等的）旅程：*We went for a ride in the woods.* 我们去树林里骑马了。◊ *I had a ride in his new car.* 我坐他的新车兜风了。
2 *American English for* LIFT² (2) 美式英语，即 lift² 第 2 义：*We managed to get a ride into town when we missed the bus.* 我们没赶上公共汽车，但设法搭便车进了城。

rider /'raɪdə(r)/ *noun* 名词
a person who rides a horse or bicycle 骑手；骑马者；骑车者

ridge /rɪdʒ/ *noun* 名词
a long thin part of something that is higher than the rest, for example along the top of hills or mountains 山脊：*We walked along the ridge looking down at*

the valley below. 我们沿着山脊走，俯视下面的山谷。

ridiculous /rɪ'dɪkjələs/ *adjective* 形容词
so silly that it makes people laugh 荒谬的；可笑的：*I look ridiculous in this hat.* 我戴这顶帽子显得很可笑。

riding /'raɪdɪŋ/ (British also 英式英语亦作 horse riding) (American 美式英语 horseback riding) *noun* 名词 (no plural 不用复数形式)
the sport of riding a horse 骑马

rifle /'raɪfl/ *noun* 名词
a long gun that you hold against your shoulder to shoot with 步枪；来复枪

right¹ 0ₙ /raɪt/ *adjective* 形容词

> 🔎 PRONUNCIATION 读音说明
> The word **right** sounds like **quite**.
> * right 读音像 quite。

1 good; fair or what the law allows 正当；妥当：*It's not right to leave young children alone in the house.* 把幼童独留家中是不妥当的。
2 correct or true 正确的；真实的：*That's not the right answer.* 那不是正确答案。◊ *'Are you Mr Johnson?' 'Yes, that's right.'* "你是约翰逊先生吗？" "是的，我就是。"
3 best 最好的；最合适的：*Is she the right person for the job?* 她是这份工作的合适人选吗？
⊃ OPPOSITE **wrong** 反义词为 wrong
4 on or of the side of the body that faces east when a person faces north 右边的：*Most people write with their right hand.* 大多数人用右手写字。⊃ OPPOSITE **left** 反义词为 left

right² 0ₙ /raɪt/ *adverb* 副词
1 exactly 正好；恰好：*He was sitting right next to me.* 他就坐在我旁边。
2 all the way; completely 一直；完全：*Go right to the end of the road.* 一直走到这条路的尽头。
3 immediately 立即；马上：*Wait here – I'll be right back.* 在这里等，我马上回来。◊ *Phone the doctor right away.* 立即打电话给医生。
4 correctly 正确地：*Have I spelt your name right?* 我把你的名字拼对了吗？
⊃ OPPOSITE **wrong** 反义词为 wrong
5 to the right side 往右边；向右边：*Turn right at the end of the street.* 在街的尽头向右转。⊃ OPPOSITE **left** 反义词为 left

right³ 0ₙ /raɪt/ *noun* 名词
1 (no plural 不用复数形式) what is good or fair 正当；公正；正确：*Young children*

have to learn the difference between *right and wrong*. 小孩子得学会分辨是非。 ⊃ OPPOSITE **wrong** 反义词为 wrong

2 (*plural* 复数形式 **rights**) what you are allowed to do, especially by law 权利: *In Britain, everyone **has the right to** vote at 18.* 在英国，年满 18 岁就有选举权。

3 (*no plural* 不用复数形式) the right side or direction 右方; 右边: *We live in the first house **on the right**.* 我们住在右边的第一所房子。 ⊃ OPPOSITE **left** 反义词为 left

right⁴ 0━ /raɪt/ *exclamation* 感叹词 (*British* 英式英语) (*informal* 非正式)
1 yes, I agree; yes, I will（表示同意或遵从）是的，好的: *'I'll see you tomorrow.' 'Right.'* "我明天见你。" "好的。"
2 You say 'right' to make somebody listen to you.（引起注意）嗨，喂: *Are you ready? Right, let's go.* 你准备好了吗？嗨，咱们走吧。

right angle /'raɪt æŋgl/ *noun* 名词 (*maths* 数学) an angle of 90 degrees. *A square has four **right angles**.* 直角 ⊃ Look at the picture at **angle**. 见 angle 的插图。

right-hand /'raɪt hænd/ *adjective* 形容词 of or on the right 右手的; 右边的: *The supermarket is on the **right-hand side** of the road.* 超市在路的右边。

right-handed /,raɪt 'hændɪd/ *adjective* 形容词
If you are **right-handed**, you use your right hand more easily than your left hand, for example for writing. 惯用右手的

rightly /'raɪtli/ *adverb* 副词 correctly 正确地; 无误地: *If I remember rightly, the party was on 15 June.* 要是我没记错的话，那次聚会是在 6 月 15 日。

rigid /'rɪdʒɪd/ *adjective* 形容词
1 not able or not wanting to be changed 死板的; 一成不变的: *The school has very rigid rules.* 这所学校校规很严。
2 hard and not easy to bend or move 坚硬的; 僵硬的: *She was rigid with fear.* 她吓得浑身发僵。

rim /rɪm/ *noun* 名词
the edge of something round（圆形物体的）边缘，边沿: *the rim of a cup* 杯沿

rind /raɪnd/ *noun* 名词
the thick hard skin of some fruits, or some types of cheese and meat 果皮;（奶酪或肉的）外皮: *lemon rind* 柠檬皮

ring¹ 0━ /rɪŋ/ *noun* 名词
1 a circle of metal that you wear on your finger 戒指; 指环: *a wedding ring* 婚戒

2 a circle 圆; 环: *The coffee cup left a ring on the table top.* 咖啡杯在桌面上留下了一圈印迹。
3 a space with seats around it, used for a competition or a performance 圆形竞技场; 圆形表演场: *a boxing ring* 拳击场
4 the sound that a bell makes 铃声; 钟声: *There was a ring at the door.* 门铃响了。

give somebody a ring (*British* 英式英语) (*informal* 非正式) to telephone somebody 给某人打电话: *I'll give you a ring later.* 我稍后会给你打电话。

rings 戒指

ring² 0━ /rɪŋ/ *verb* 动词 (rings, ringing, rang /ræŋ/, has rung /rʌŋ/)
1 (*British* 英式英语) to telephone somebody 给…打电话 ⊃ SAME MEANING **call**, **phone** 同义词为 call 和 phone: *I'll ring you on Sunday.* 我星期天会给你打电话。 ◇ *She rang up yesterday and cancelled the order.* 她昨天打电话来取消了订单。
2 to make a sound like a bell 发出铃声: *The telephone is ringing.* 电话铃在响。
3 to press or move a bell so that it makes a sound 按铃; 摇铃: *We rang the doorbell again but nobody answered.* 我们又按了一次门铃，可是没有人应门。

ring somebody back (*British* 英式英语) to telephone somebody again or to telephone somebody who has telephoned you 再给某人打电话; 给某人回电话: *He isn't here now – can you ring back later?* 他现在不在，你过一会儿再打来好吗？

ringtone /'rɪŋtəʊn/ *noun* 名词
the sound a mobile phone makes when somebody is calling you 手机铃声: *You can download ringtones from the Internet.* 你可以从网上下载手机铃声。

rink /rɪŋk/ *noun* 名词
1 *short for* ICE RINK * ice rink 的缩略式
2 *short for* SKATING RINK * skating rink 的缩略式

rinse /rɪns/ *verb* 动词 (rinses, rinsing, rinsed /rɪnst/)

A B C D E F G H I J K L M N O P Q R S T U V W X Y Z

to wash something with water to take away dirt or soap 冲洗；洗涮：*Wash your hair and rinse it well.* 洗完头发后要冲洗干净。

riot /'raɪət/ *noun* 名词
when a group of people fight and make a lot of noise and trouble 暴乱；骚乱：*There were riots in the streets after the football match.* 足球赛后街上发生了骚乱。
▶ **riot** *verb* 动词 (riots, rioting, rioted): *The prisoners are rioting.* 囚犯正在闹事。

rip /rɪp/ *verb* 动词 (rips, ripping, ripped /rɪpt/)
to pull or tear something quickly and suddenly 猛地撕开；扯破：*I ripped my shirt on a nail.* 我的衬衫让钉子给刮破了。◇ *Joe ripped the letter open.* 乔把信撕开。
rip somebody off (*informal* 非正式)
to cheat somebody by making them pay too much for something 敲诈；敲竹杠：*Tourists complained that they were being ripped off by local taxi drivers.* 游客抱怨遭当地的出租车司机敲竹杠了。 ➋ The noun is **rip-off**. 名词为 rip-off。
rip something up to tear something into small pieces 把⋯撕碎：*She ripped the photo up.* 她把照片撕碎了。

ripe /raɪp/ *adjective* 形容词 (riper, ripest)
Fruit that is ripe is ready to eat. （水果等）成熟的：*These bananas aren't ripe – they're still green.* 这些香蕉还没成熟——还是青的呢。

rip-off /'rɪp ɒf/ *noun* 名词 (*informal* 非正式)
something that costs a lot more than it should 索价过高的东西：*$70 for a T-shirt! What a rip-off!* * 70 元一件 T 恤衫！真是漫天要价！

ripple 涟漪

ripple¹ /'rɪpl/ *noun* 名词
a small wave or movement on the surface of water 波纹；水波；涟漪

ripple² /'rɪpl/ *verb* 动词 (ripples, rippling, rippled /'rɪpld/)
to move in small waves 如小水波般起伏：*The sea rippled and sparkled in the sun.* 大海在阳光下波光粼粼。

rise¹ 0ᵐ /raɪz/ *noun* 名词
when the amount, number or level of something goes up （数量、数字或水平的）上升，上涨，提高 ➋ SAME MEANING **increase** 同义词为 increase：*There has been a sharp rise in the price of oil.* 油价曾经急剧上涨。◇ *a pay rise* 涨工资

rise² 0ᵐ /raɪz/ *verb* 动词 (rises, rising, rose /rəʊz/, has risen /'rɪzn/)
1 to go up; to become higher or more 上升；上涨；提高：*Smoke was rising from the chimney.* 烟从烟囱里升起。◇ *Prices have risen by 20%.* 价格已经上升 20%。
2 to get up from a sitting or lying position 站起来；起床：*She rose to her feet.* 她站起身来。
3 If the sun or moon rises, it moves up in the sky. （太阳或月亮）升起：*The sun rises in the east and sets (= goes down) in the west.* 太阳从东方升起，西方落下。

risk¹ 0ᵐ /rɪsk/ *noun* 名词
the possibility that something bad may happen; a dangerous situation 风险；危险：*Smoking can increase the risk of heart disease.* 吸烟可增加患心脏病的风险。
at risk in danger 有危险：*Children are most at risk from this disease.* 儿童患这种病的风险最高。
take a risk or 或 **risks** to do something when you know that something bad may happen because of it 冒险（做某事）：*Don't take risks when you're driving.* 开车的时候不要冒险。

risk² 0ᵐ /rɪsk/ *verb* 动词 (risks, risking, risked /rɪskt/)
1 to put something or yourself in danger 使面临危险；使冒险：*He risked his life to save the child from the burning house.* 他冒着生命危险从着火的房子里去救那孩子。
2 to do something when you know that something bad may happen because of it 冒⋯的风险：*If you don't work harder, you risk failing the exam.* 如果你不用功点，考试就可能不及格。

risky /'rɪski/ *adjective* 形容词 (riskier, riskiest)
dangerous 冒险的；有风险的

rival /'raɪvl/ *noun* 名词
a person who wants to do better than you

or who is trying to take what you want 竞争对手: *John and Lucy are rivals for the manager's job.* 约翰和露西是经理一职的竞争对手。

river ⊶ /'rɪvə(r)/ *noun* 名词
a long wide line of water that flows into the sea 河; 江: *the River Amazon* 亚马孙河

road ⊶ /rəʊd/ *noun* 名词
the way from one place to another, where cars can go 路; 道路; 公路: *Is this the road to the city centre?* 这是去市中心的路吗? ◇ *My address is 34a Windsor Road, London NW2.* 我的地址是伦敦西北2区温莎路 34a 号。 ⊃ The short way of writing 'Road' in addresses is **Rd**. * Road 在地址中的缩写形式为 Rd: *30 Welton Rd* 韦尔敦路 30 号

> ✏ WORD BUILDING 词汇扩充
> **Street** is another word for **road**.
> * street (街道) 是 road 的另一种说法。
> A country road is often called a **lane**. 乡间小道常用 lane。
> A **motorway** (*British*) or a **freeway** (*American*) is a fast road which you use to travel between cities. * motorway (英式英语) 或 freeway (美式英语) 是城市之间的高速公路。

by road in a car, bus, etc. 乘汽车; 坐公共汽车: *It's a long journey by road – the train is faster.* 乘汽车要很长时间, 坐火车比较快。

roadworks /'rəʊdwɜːks/ *noun* 名词 (*plural* 用复数形式) (*British* 英式英语)
work that involves repairing or building roads 道路检修; 道路施工

roam /rəʊm/ *verb* 动词 (roams, roaming, roamed /rəʊmd/)
to walk or travel with no special plan 闲逛; 游荡: *Dogs were roaming the streets looking for food.* 狗在街上走来走去寻找食物。

roar¹ /rɔː(r)/ *verb* 动词 (roars, roaring, roared /rɔːd/)
to make a loud deep sound 吼叫; 咆哮; 轰鸣: *The lion roared.* 狮子大声咆哮。 ◇ *Everybody roared with laughter.* 所有人都哈哈大笑了。

roar² /rɔː(r)/ *noun* 名词
a loud deep sound 吼叫; 咆哮; 隆隆声: *The lion gave a huge roar.* 狮子大吼了一声。 ◇ *the roar of an aeroplane's engines* 飞机发动机的隆隆声

roast /rəʊst/ *verb* 动词 (roasts, roasting, roasted)
to cook or be cooked in an oven or over a fire 烤; 烘; 焙: *Roast the chicken in a hot oven.* 用烤箱高温烤鸡。
▸ **roast** *adjective* 形容词: *roast beef and roast potatoes* 烤牛肉和烘土豆

rob ⊶ /rɒb/ *verb* 动词 (robs, robbing, robbed /rɒbd/)
to take something that is not yours from a person or place 抢劫; 掠夺; 盗取: *They robbed a bank.* 他们抢劫了一家银行。 ⊃ Look at the note at **steal**. 见 steal 条的注释。

robber /'rɒbə(r)/ *noun* 名词
a person who steals things from a person or a place 劫匪; 强盗; 盗贼: *a bank robber* 银行劫匪 ⊃ Look at the note at **thief**. 见 thief 条的注释。

robbery /'rɒbəri/ *noun* 名词 (*plural* 复数形式 robberies)
taking something that is not yours from a person or place 抢劫; 盗窃: *What time did the robbery take place?* 这起抢劫是在什么时间发生的?

robe /rəʊb/ *noun* 名词
1 a long loose thing that you wear on your body, for example at a special ceremony 袍服; 礼袍: *a graduation robe* 毕业礼袍
2 *American English for* DRESSING GOWN 美式英语, 即 dressing gown

robin /'rɒbɪn/ *noun* 名词
a small brown bird with a red front 知更鸟

robot /'rəʊbɒt/ *noun* 名词
a machine that can work like a person 机器人: *This car was built by robots.* 这辆汽车是由机器人制造的。

rock¹ ⊶ /rɒk/ *noun* 名词
1 (*no plural* 不用复数形式) the very hard material that is in the ground and in mountains 岩石
2 (*plural* 复数形式 rocks) a big piece of rock 巨石; 岩块: *The ship hit the rocks.* 轮船触礁了。
3 (*no plural* 不用复数形式) (*also* 亦作 **rock music**) a sort of modern music with a strong rhythm 摇滚乐: *a rock concert* 摇滚音乐会

rock² /rɒk/ *verb* 动词 (rocks, rocking, rocked /rɒkt/)
to move slowly backwards and forwards or from side to side; to make somebody or something do this (使) 摇晃, 晃动: *The boat was rocking gently on the lake.*

A B C D E F G H I J K L M N O P Q R S T U V W X Y Z

小船在湖面微微摇晃。◇ *I rocked the baby until she went to sleep.* 我轻轻摇着宝宝直到她入睡。

rock and roll (*also 亦作* **rock 'n' roll**) /ˌrɒk ən ˈrəʊl/ *noun* 名词 (*no plural* 不用复数形式)
a type of music with a strong rhythm that was most popular in the 1950s 摇滚乐

rocket /ˈrɒkɪt/ *noun* 名词
1 a vehicle that is used for travelling into space 火箭: *to launch a rocket* 发射火箭 ◇ *a space rocket* 太空火箭
2 a weapon that travels through the air and carries a bomb 火箭武器；火箭（弹）⊃ SAME MEANING **missile** 同义词为 missile
3 an object that shoots high into the air and then explodes with pretty coloured lights (a type of **firework**) 焰火；烟花

rock music /ˈrɒk mjuːzɪk/ = ROCK¹ (3)

rocky /ˈrɒki/ *adjective* 形容词 (**rockier**, **rockiest**)
with a lot of rocks 多岩石的；嶙峋的：
a rocky path 布满石头的小路

rod /rɒd/ *noun* 名词
a long thin straight piece of wood or metal （细直的）杆，竿，棒：*a fishing rod* 钓鱼竿

rode *form of* RIDE¹ * ride¹ 的不同形式

rodent /ˈrəʊdnt/ *noun* 名词
a type of small animal that has strong sharp front teeth, for example a mouse or a RABBIT 啮齿动物（如老鼠或兔子）

role /rəʊl/ *noun* 名词
1 what a person does, for example in an organization or a relationship 职能；角色：*Your role is to welcome guests as they arrive.* 你的任务是迎宾。
2 a person's part in a play or film （演员的）角色：*He played the role of the King.* 他扮演国王这个角色。

rolls 卷；小圆面包

toilet roll
卫生纸卷

bread rolls
小圆面包

roll of tape
一卷胶带

roll¹ /rəʊl/ *noun* 名词
1 something made into a long round shape by turning it around itself many times 卷；卷状物：*a roll of material* 一卷布料 ◇ *a roll of film* 一卷胶卷
2 a small round piece of bread made for one person 小圆面包：*a roll and butter* 小圆面包和黄油

roll² /rəʊl/ *verb* 动词 (**rolls**, **rolling**, **rolled** /rəʊld/)
1 to move along by turning over and over; to make something move in this way （使）滚动，翻滚：*The pencil rolled off the table on to the floor.* 铅笔从桌上滚落到地上。◇ *We rolled the rock down the path.* 我们将石头沿路滚了下去。
2 to turn your body over when you are lying down 翻身；打滚：*She rolled over onto her back.* 她翻过身来仰面躺着。
3 to move on wheels 靠轮子滚动，移动：*The car rolled down the hill.* 汽车滑下山了。
4 to make something into a long round shape or the shape of a ball 卷起来；绕成球状：*Can you help me to roll up this carpet?* 你能帮我把这地毯卷起来吗？
5 to make something flat by moving something heavy on top of it 使平展；压平：*Roll the pastry into a large circle.* 把油酥面团擀成一个大圆片。

Rollerblade™ (*British* 英式英语) (*American* 美式英语 **Roller Blade™**) /ˈrəʊləbleɪd/ *noun* 名词
a boot with a line of small wheels on the bottom 直排滚轴旱冰鞋 ⊃ Look at **roller skate**. 见 roller skate。⊃ Look at the picture at **skate²**. 见 skate² 的插图。
▸ **Rollerblading** *noun* 名词 (*no plural* 不用复数形式)：*to go Rollerblading* 玩直排轮滑

roller coaster /ˈrəʊlə kəʊstə(r)/ *noun* 名词
a metal track that goes up and down and around bends, and that people ride on in a small train for fun 过山车（游乐设施）

roller skate /ˈrəʊlə skeɪt/ (*also 亦作* **skate**) *noun* 名词
a boot with small wheels on the bottom 旱冰鞋；滚轴溜冰鞋 ⊃ Look at **Rollerblade**. 见 Rollerblade。⊃ Look at the picture at **skate²**. 见 skate² 的插图。
▸ **roller skate** (*also 亦作* **skate**) *verb* 动词
to move over a hard surface wearing **roller skates** 滑旱冰；溜旱冰；滚轴溜冰
▸ **roller skating** (*also 亦作* **skating**) *noun* 名词 (*no plural* 不用复数形式)：*At the weekend, they go roller skating at the*

local skating rink. 周末的时候他们去当地的旱冰场溜旱冰。

Roman Catholic /ˌrəʊmən ˈkæθəlɪk/ *noun* 名词
a member of the Christian church that has the Pope as its head 天主教徒
▶ **Roman Catholic** *adjective* 形容词: *a Roman Catholic priest* 天主教神父

romance /rəʊˈmæns/ *noun* 名词
1 a time when two people are in love 恋爱: *a romance between a doctor and a nurse* 医生与护士的恋爱
2 a story about love 爱情故事: *She writes romances.* 她写爱情故事。

romantic o-ᴡ /rəʊˈmæntɪk/ *adjective* 形容词
about love; full of feelings of love 爱情的；浪漫的: *a romantic film* 爱情影片

roof o-ᴡ /ruːf/ *noun* 名词 (*plural* 复数形式 **roofs**)
the top of a building or car, that covers it 顶部；屋顶；车顶 ⇒ Look at Picture Dictionary page **P10**. 见彩页 **P10**。

room o-ᴡ /ruːm/ *noun* 名词
1 (*plural* 复数形式 **rooms**) one of the spaces in a building that has walls around it 房间；室: *How many rooms are there in the new house?* 新房子有几个房间？◇ *a classroom* 教室

> 𝒫 **WORD BUILDING** 词汇扩充
> A house or flat usually has a **living room** (or **sitting room** or **lounge**), **bedrooms**, a **bathroom**, a **toilet**, a **kitchen**, a **hall** and perhaps a **dining room**. 一所房子或一套公寓通常包含有起居室（living room、sitting room 或 lounge）、卧室（bedroom）、浴室（bathroom）、卫生间（toilet）、厨房（kitchen）、门厅（hall），有些还有饭厅（dining room）。
>
> ⇒ Look at Picture Dictionary page **P10**. 见彩页 **P10**。

2 (*no plural* 不用复数形式) space; enough space 空间；足够的空间: *There's no room for you in the car.* 车里没有你的位置了。

rooster /ˈruːstə(r)/ *American English for* COCK 美式英语，即 cock

root o-ᴡ /ruːt/ *noun* 名词
the part of a plant that is under the ground （植物的）根，根茎 ⇒ Look at the picture at **plant¹**. 见 plant¹ 的插图。

rope o-ᴡ /rəʊp/ *noun* 名词
very thick strong string 绳子；绳索

rope 绳子

coil of rope 一圈绳子

rose¹ *form of* RISE² ＊ rise² 的不同形式

rose² /rəʊz/ *noun* 名词
a flower with a sweet smell. It grows on a bush that has sharp points (called **thorns**) on it. 玫瑰；蔷薇

rosy /ˈrəʊzi/ *adjective* 形容词 (**rosier, rosiest**)
pink and looking healthy 粉红的；红润的: *rosy cheeks* 红润的脸颊

rot /rɒt/ *verb* 动词 (**rots, rotting, rotted**)
to become bad and soft, as things do when they die 腐烂；腐败变质 ⇒ SAME MEANING **decay** 同义词为 decay: *the smell of rotting fruit* 腐烂水果的气味

rotate /rəʊˈteɪt/ *verb* 动词 (**rotates, rotating, rotated**)
to move in circles 旋转；转动: *The earth rotates around the sun.* 地球绕太阳转动。
▶ **rotation** /rəʊˈteɪʃn/ *noun* 名词: *the rotation of the earth* 地球的转动

rotten /ˈrɒtn/ *adjective* 形容词
1 old and not fresh; bad 腐烂的；腐败的: *These eggs are rotten – they smell horrible!* 这些蛋坏了——臭极了！
2 (*informal* 非正式) very bad; not nice or kind 糟糕的；恶劣的: *That was a rotten thing to say!* 那么说太难听了！

rough o-ᴡ /rʌf/ *adjective* 形容词 (**rougher, roughest**)

> 𝒫 **PRONUNCIATION** 读音说明
> The word **rough** sounds like **stuff** because sometimes the letters **-gh** sound like **f**, in words like **enough** and **tough**. ＊ rough 读音像 stuff，因为 -gh 有时会读作 /f/，像 enough 和 tough 等词。

1 not smooth or flat 粗糙的；凹凸不平的: *It was difficult to walk on the rough ground.* 在凹凸不平的地面上很难行走。
2 not exactly correct; made or done quickly 粗略的；大致的: *Can you give me a rough idea how much it will cost?*

你能告诉我大概要花多少钱吗？ ◇ *a rough drawing* 草图

3 not gentle or calm 狂暴的；汹涌的：*rough seas* 波涛汹涌的大海

roughly /ˈrʌfli/ *adverb* 副词
1 about; not exactly 大概；粗略地 ⊃ SAME MEANING **approximately** 同义词为 approximately：*The journey should take roughly two hours.* 路程大概要花两个小时。 ⊃ OPPOSITE **exactly** 反义词为 exactly
2 not gently 粗暴地；粗野地：*He pushed me roughly away.* 他粗暴地把我推开了。

round¹ 0̶ₘ /raʊnd/ *adjective* 形容词
having the shape of a circle or a ball 圆形的；球形的：*a round table* 圆桌

round² 0̶ₘ /raʊnd/ (*also* 亦作 *around*) *adverb, preposition* 副词，介词
1 on or to all sides of something, often in a circle 环绕；围绕：*The earth moves round the sun.* 地球绕着太阳转。 ◇ *We sat round the table.* 我们围着桌子坐。 ◇ *The bird flew round and round the room.* 那只鸟在房间里兜着圈飞。
2 in the opposite direction or in another direction 倒转：*I turned round and went home again.* 我转身又回家去了。 ◇ *Turn your chair round.* 把你的椅子转过来。
3 in or to different parts of a place 在各处；到处：*We travelled round France last summer.* 我们去年夏天周游了法国。
4 to or on the other side of something 到另一边；在另一边：*There's a bank just round the corner.* 拐角处就有一家银行。
5 from one person or place to another 依次；逐个：*Pass these photos round the class.* 把这些照片传给全班同学看。
6 (*informal* 非正式) to or at somebody's house 到某人家；在某人家：*Come round* (= to my house) *at eight o'clock.* 八点钟来我家吧。
go round to be enough for everybody 足够分给所有人：*Are there enough cakes to go round?* 蛋糕够分给所有人吗？
round about nearly; not exactly 大约；大概：*It will cost round about £90.* 这大约要 90 英镑。

round³ /raʊnd/ *noun* 名词
1 one part of a game or competition （游戏或比赛的）轮，回合：*the third round of the boxing match* 拳击赛的第三回合
2 a lot of visits, one after another, for example as part of your job 巡访；例行工作：*The postman starts his round at seven o'clock.* 邮递员七点钟开始巡行派送邮件。
3 drinks for all the people in a group （由一人给大家买的）一巡饮料：*I'll buy this round. What would you all like?* 我来请这一巡饮料。你们都想喝些什么？

roundabout /ˈraʊndəbaʊt/ (*British* 英式英语) *noun* 名词
1 (*American* 美式英语 **traffic circle**) a place where roads meet, where cars must drive round in a circle （道路汇合处的）环形路；交通环岛
2 (*American* 美式英语 **merry-go-round**) a round platform for children to play on. They sit or stand on it and somebody pushes it round. 旋转平台（儿童游乐设施）
3 another word for MERRY-GO-ROUND * merry-go-round 的另一种说法 ⊃ Look at the picture at **merry-go-round**. 见 merry-go-round 的插图。

round trip /ˌraʊnd ˈtrɪp/ *noun* 名词
1 a journey to a place and back again 往返旅程：*It's a four-mile round trip to the centre of town.* 从这里去市中心来回要走四英里的路。
2 (*American also* 美式英语亦作 **round-trip ticket**) *American English for* RETURN² (3) 美式英语，即 return² 第 3 义

route 0̶ₘ /ruːt/ *noun* 名词
a way from one place to another 路线；路径：*What is the quickest route from London to Edinburgh?* 从伦敦去爱丁堡走哪条路线最快？

routine /ruːˈtiːn/ *noun* 名词
your usual way of doing things 常规；例行公事：*Make exercise a part of your daily routine.* 让锻炼成为你日常生活的一部分。

row¹ 0̶ₘ /rəʊ/ *noun* 名词

🔊 PRONUNCIATION 读音说明
This meaning of **row** sounds like **no**. 作此义时 row 读音像 no。

a line of people or things 排；列；行：*We sat in the front row of the theatre* (= the front line of seats). 我们坐在剧院的前排。 ◇ *a row of houses* 一排房子

row² /rəʊ/ *verb* 动词 (**rows, rowing, rowed** /rəʊd/)

🔊 PRONUNCIATION 读音说明
This meaning of **row** sounds like **no**. 作此义时 row 读音像 no。

to move a boat through water using long pieces of wood with flat ends (called **oars**) 划（船）：*We rowed across the lake.* 我们从湖的一边划船到另一边。

🔎 SPEAKING 表达方式说明

When you talk about spending time rowing as a sport, you say **go rowing**. 去做划艇运动说 go rowing: *We went rowing on the river.* 我们在河里划船。

row³ /raʊ/ *noun* 名词 (*British* 英式英语)

🔎 PRONUNCIATION 读音说明

This meaning of **row** sounds like **how**. 作此义时 row 读音像 how。

1 (*plural* 复数形式 **rows**) a noisy talk between people who do not agree about something 吵架；争吵 ⊃ SAME MEANING **argument** 同义词为 argument: *She had a row with her boyfriend.* 她跟男朋友吵了一架。

2 (*no plural* 不用复数形式) a loud noise 喧闹；喧嚷: *The children were making a terrible row.* 孩子们吵得要死。

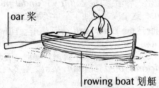

rowing boat 划艇

oar 桨

rowing boat 划艇

rowing boat /ˈrəʊɪŋ bəʊt/ *noun* 名词
a small boat that you move through water using long thin pieces of wood with flat ends (called **oars**) 小划子；划艇

royal ⚬ʀ /ˈrɔɪəl/ *adjective* 形容词
connected with a king or queen 皇家的；王室的；国王的；女王的: *the royal family* 王室

royalty /ˈrɔɪəlti/ *noun* 名词 (*no plural* 不用复数形式)
kings, queens and their families 皇家成员；王室成员

rub ⚬ʀ /rʌb/ *verb* 动词 (**rubs, rubbing, rubbed** /rʌbd/)
to move something backwards and forwards on another thing 擦；搓: *I rubbed my hands together to keep them warm.* 我搓着手取暖。 ◇ *The cat rubbed its head against my leg.* 猫用头蹭我的腿。
rub something out (*British* 英式英语)
to take writing or marks off something by using a rubber or a cloth（用橡皮或布）擦掉: *I rubbed the word out and wrote it again.* 我把字擦掉，重写了一遍。
▶ **rub** *noun* 名词 (*no plural* 不用复数形式): *Give your shoes a rub.* 擦擦你的鞋。

rubber ⚬ʀ /ˈrʌbə(r)/ *noun* 名词
1 (*no plural* 不用复数形式) a strong material that we use to make things like car tyres 橡胶
2 (*plural* 复数形式 **rubbers**) (*British* 英式英语) (*American* 美式英语 **eraser**) a small piece of rubber that you use for taking away marks that you have made with a pencil 橡皮 ⊃ Look at Picture Dictionary page **P11**. 见彩页 P11。

rubber band /ˌrʌbə ˈbænd/ (*British also* 英式英语亦作 **elastic band**) *noun* 名词
a thin circle of rubber that you use for holding things together 橡皮筋；橡皮圈

rubbish ⚬ʀ /ˈrʌbɪʃ/ (*British* 英式英语) *noun* 名词 (*no plural* 不用复数形式)
1 (*American* 美式英语 **garbage, trash**) things that you do not want any more 垃圾；废弃物: *old boxes, bottles and other rubbish* 旧盒子、瓶子和别的一些垃圾 ◇ *Throw this rubbish in the bin.* 把这些垃圾扔到垃圾箱里。
2 something that you think is bad, stupid or wrong 差劲的事物；废话；废物: *You're talking rubbish!* 你胡说八道！

ruby /ˈruːbi/ *noun* 名词 (*plural* 复数形式 **rubies**)
a dark red stone that is used in jewellery 红宝石: *a ruby ring* 红宝石戒指

rucksack /ˈrʌksæk/ *noun* 名词 (*British* 英式英语)
a bag that you carry on your back, for example when you are walking or climbing 背包 ⊃ SAME MEANING **backpack** 同义词为 backpack ⊃ Look at the picture at **backpack¹**. 见 backpack¹ 的插图。

rudder /ˈrʌdə(r)/ *noun* 名词
a flat piece of wood or metal at the back of a boat or a plane. It moves to make the boat or plane go left or right.（船）舵；（飞机）方向舵

rude ⚬ʀ /ruːd/ *adjective* 形容词 (**ruder, rudest**)
1 not polite 无礼的；粗鲁的 ⊃ SAME MEANING **impolite** 同义词为 impolite: *It's rude to walk away when someone is talking to you.* 有人跟你说话时你走开是很没礼貌的。
2 about things like sex or using the toilet 猥亵的；下流的: *rude words* 下流话

A
B
C
D
E
F
G
H
I
J
K
L
M
N
O
P
Q

R

S
T
U
V
W
X
Y
Z

▶ **rudely** *adverb* 副词: *'Shut up!' she said rudely.* "闭嘴!"她粗鲁地说。
▶ **rudeness** *noun* 名词 (*no plural* 不用复数形式): *I would like to apologize for my rudeness.* 我想为我的无礼道歉。

rug 小地毯

rug /rʌg/ *noun* 名词
1 a small piece of thick material that you put on the floor 小地毯 ⊃ Look at **carpet**. 见 carpet。
2 a thick piece of material that you put round your body to keep you warm 厚毯子

rugby /'rʌgbi/ *noun* 名词 (*no plural* 不用复数形式)
a game like football for two teams of 13 or 15 players. In **rugby**, you can kick and carry the ball. 橄榄球运动 ⊃ Look at Picture Dictionary page **P14**. 见彩页 P14。

rugged /'rʌgɪd/ *adjective* 形容词
Rugged land is not smooth, and has a lot of rocks and not many plants on it. (土地)崎岖的,多岩石的

ruin¹ 0̰ /'ruːm/ *verb* 动词 (ruins, ruining, ruined /'ruːmd/)
to damage something badly so that it is no longer good; to destroy something completely 毁坏;破坏;糟蹋: *I spilled coffee on my jacket and ruined it.* 我把咖啡洒在夹克上,衣服给毁了。◇ *The rain ruined our picnic.* 这场雨让我们的野餐泡汤了。

ruin² /'ruːm/ *noun* 名词
a building that has been badly damaged 废墟;残垣断壁: *The old castle is now a ruin.* 旧城堡现在是一片颓垣败瓦。
in ruins badly damaged or destroyed 严重受损;遭毁灭: *The city was in ruins after the war.* 战后那座城市满目疮痍。

ruin 废墟

rule¹ 0̰ /ruːl/ *noun* 名词
1 (*plural* 复数形式 rules) something that tells you what you must or must not do 规则;规矩;规定: *It's against the school rules to smoke.* 吸烟是违反校规的。◇ *to break a rule* (= do something that you should not do) 违反规定
2 (*no plural* 不用复数形式) government 统治;管治: *The country is under military rule.* 这个国家现处于军事统治之下。

rule² 0̰ /ruːl/ *verb* 动词 (rules, ruling, ruled /ruːld/)
to control a country 统治;管治: *Queen Victoria ruled for many years.* 维多利亚女王统治了很多年。

ruler /'ruːlə(r)/ *noun* 名词
1 a long piece of plastic, metal or wood that you use for drawing straight lines or for measuring things 直尺;尺子 ⊃ Look at Picture Dictionary page **P11**. 见彩页 P11。
2 a person who rules a country 统治者

rum /rʌm/ *noun* 名词
a strong alcoholic drink that is made from the sugar plant 朗姆酒(用甘蔗汁酿成的烈性酒)

rumble /'rʌmbl/ *verb* 动词 (rumbles, rumbling, rumbled /'rʌmbld/)
to make a long deep sound 发出隆隆声: *I'm so hungry that my stomach is rumbling.* 我饿得肚子咕噜咕噜直叫。
▶ **rumble** *noun* 名词 (*no plural* 不用复数形式): *the rumble of thunder* 隆隆的雷声

rummage sale /'rʌmɪdʒ seɪl/ *noun* 名词
American English for JUMBLE SALE 美式英语,即 jumble sale

rumour (*British* 英式英语) (*American* 美式英语 rumor) /'ruːmə(r)/ *noun* 名词
something that a lot of people are talking about that is perhaps not true 谣言;

流言: *There's a rumour that our teacher is leaving.* 有传言说我们老师要走了。

run[1] ⟶ /rʌn/ *verb* 动词 (runs, running, ran /ræn/, has run)
1 to move very quickly on your legs 跑; 跑动: *I was late, so I ran to the bus stop.* 我出门晚了，所以跑着去公共汽车站。
2 to control something and make it work 管理; 经营; 操作: *Who runs the business?* 业务由谁经营的?
3 to work 运行; 运转: *The car had stopped but the engine was still running.* 汽车已经停了，但发动机还在转动。
4 to go; to make a journey 行驶: *The buses don't run on Sundays.* 公共汽车星期天停驶。
5 to move something somewhere 移动: *He ran his fingers through his hair.* 他用手指弄头发。
6 to pass or go somewhere 经过; 通向: *The road runs across the fields.* 这条路穿过那些田地。
7 to flow 流动; 流淌: *The river runs into the North Sea.* 这条河流入北海。
run after somebody or 或 **something** to try to catch a person or an animal 追赶; 追逐 ⊃ SAME MEANING **chase** 同义词为 chase: *The dog ran after a rabbit.* 狗追着兔子。
run away to go quickly away from a place 逃走; 逃离 ⊃ SAME MEANING **escape** 同义词为 escape: *She ran away from home when she was 14.* 她 14 岁时离家出走了。
run into somebody to meet somebody by chance 偶然遇见某人: *Guess who I ran into today?* 猜猜我今天碰到谁了?
run into somebody or 或 **something** to crash into somebody or something 撞上: *The bus went out of control and ran into a line of people.* 公共汽车失控，撞到了一排人。
run out of something to have no more of something 用完; 耗尽: *We've run out of coffee. Will you go and buy some?* 我们咖啡喝完了。你去买点行吗?
run over somebody or 或 **something** to hit a person or an animal with your car or other vehicle （汽车等）撞倒, 碾过: *The dog was run over by a bus.* 那条狗被公共汽车轧了。

run[2] ⟶ /rʌn/ *noun* 名词
1 moving very quickly on your legs 跑; 跑步: *I go for a run every morning.* 我每天早上都跑步。
2 a point in the games of BASEBALL and CRICKET （棒球和板球的）一分: *Our*

team won by two runs. 我们队以两分的优势获胜。

rung[1] form of RING[2] * ring[2] 的不同形式

rung[2] /rʌŋ/ *noun* 名词
one of the steps of a LADDER (= a piece of equipment that is used for climbing up something) （梯子的）横档, 梯级 ⊃ Look at the picture at **ladder**. 见 ladder 的插图。

runner /'rʌnə(r)/ *noun* 名词
a person who runs 奔跑的人; 赛跑选手

runner-up /ˌrʌnər 'ʌp/ *noun* 名词 (plural 复数形式 **runners-up** /ˌrʌnəz'ʌp/)
a person or team that comes second in a race or competition 第二名; 亚军

running[1] /'rʌnɪŋ/ *noun* 名词 (no plural 不用复数形式)
the sport of running 跑步（运动）: *Let's go running tomorrow morning.* 我们明天早上去跑步吧。

running[2] /'rʌnɪŋ/ *adjective* 形容词
one after another 连续: *We won the competition for three years running.* 我们连续三年赢得竞赛。

runny /'rʌni/ *adjective* 形容词 (runnier, runniest)
1 If you have a **runny** nose, a lot of liquid comes out of it, for example because you have a cold. 流鼻涕的
2 If a substance is **runny**, it has more liquid than is usual. 太稀的; 呈流质状的; 软的: *Omelettes should be runny in the middle.* 煎蛋卷的中间部分应该是软的。

runway /'rʌnweɪ/ *noun* 名词 (plural 复数形式 **runways**)
a long piece of ground where planes take off and land （飞机）跑道

rural /'rʊərəl/ *adjective* 形容词
connected with the country, not the town 乡村的; 农村的: *The book is about life in rural France.* 这本书写的是法国的乡村生活。 ⊃ Look at **urban**. 见 urban。

rush[1] ⟶ /rʌʃ/ *verb* 动词 (rushes, rushing, rushed /rʌʃt/)
1 to move or do something very quickly or too quickly 迅速移动; 匆忙做: *The children rushed out of school.* 孩子们飞快地跑出了学校。 ◇ *We rushed to finish the work on time.* 我们赶紧把工作按时完成。
2 to take somebody or something quickly to a place 将…迅速送到（某处）: *She was rushed to hospital.* 她被紧急送到医院去了。

rush² 0ᴥ /rʌʃ/ *noun* 名词 (*no plural* 不用复数形式)

1 a sudden quick movement 急速的移动；冲；奔：*At the end of the film there was a rush for the exits.* 电影结束后，观众纷纷涌向出口。

2 a situation when you need to move or do something very quickly 匆忙；仓促 ⊃ SAME MEANING **hurry** 同义词为 hurry：*I can't stop now – I'm in a rush.* 我现在不能停下来，正赶时间呢。

rush hour /rʌʃ auə(r)/ *noun* 名词
the time when the roads are busy because a lot of people are going to or coming from work （上下班时的）交通高峰时段

rust /rʌst/ *noun* 名词 (*no plural* 不用复数形式)
a red-brown substance that you sometimes see on metal that has been wet 锈；铁锈

▸ **rust** *verb* 动词 (rusts, rusting, rusted)：*My bike rusted because I left it out in the rain.* 我的自行车生锈了，因为我把它放在外面给雨淋了。

rustle /rʌsl/ *verb* 动词 (rustles, rustling, rustled /rʌsld/)
to make a sound like dry leaves moving together; to make something make this sound （使）窸窸窣窣地响，沙沙地响：*Stop rustling your newspaper – I can't hear the film!* 别再把报纸弄得沙沙响，我都听不见影片的声音了！

▸ **rustle** *noun* 名词 (*no plural* 不用复数形式)：*the rustle of leaves* 树叶的沙沙声

rusty /rʌsti/ *adjective* 形容词 (rustier, rustiest)
(used about things made of metal) covered with a red-brown substance (called **rust**) because it has got wet （金属物体）生锈的：*a rusty nail* 生锈的钉子

rut /rʌt/ *noun* 名词
a deep track that a wheel makes in the ground 车辙；车印

be in a rut to have a boring life that is difficult to change 生活单调乏味：*I gave up my job because I felt I was stuck in a rut.* 我把工作辞掉了，因为我觉得那样的生活很乏味。

S s

S, s /es/ *noun* 名词 (*plural* 复数形式 S's, s's /'esɪz/)

the nineteenth letter of the English alphabet 英语字母表的第 19 个字母：'*Sun*' begins with an '*S*'. * sun 一词以字母 s 开头。

sack¹ /sæk/ *noun* 名词

a big strong bag for carrying heavy things （装重物的）大袋：*a sack of potatoes* 一大袋土豆

get the sack (*British* 英式英语) (*informal* 非正式) to lose your job 被解雇；被炒鱿鱼：*She got the sack for being late.* 她因迟到被解雇了。

give somebody the sack (*British* 英式英语) (*informal* 非正式) to say that somebody must leave their job 解雇某人；炒某人鱿鱼：*Tony's work wasn't good enough and he was given the sack.* 托尼工作干得不够好，被炒鱿鱼了。

sack² /sæk/ *verb* 动词 (sacks, sacking, sacked /sækt/)

to say that somebody must leave their job 解雇；开除：*The manager sacked her because she was always late.* 因为她老迟到，经理把她解雇了。

sacred /'seɪkrɪd/ *adjective* 形容词

with a special religious meaning 神圣的：*A church is a sacred building.* 教堂是神圣的建筑。

sacrifice /'sækrɪfaɪs/ *verb* 动词 (sacrifices, sacrificing, sacrificed /'sækrɪfaɪst/)

1 to stop doing or having something important so that you can help somebody or to get something else 牺牲；献出：*During the war, many people sacrificed their lives for their country.* 在战争期间，许多人为国捐躯。

2 to kill an animal as a present to a god （向神）献祭，供奉：*They sacrificed a lamb.* 他们祭奉上羊羔。

▶ **sacrifice** *noun* 名词：*They made a lot of sacrifices to pay for their son to go to university.* 他们为供儿子上大学作了很多牺牲。

sad 0ᴡ /sæd/ *adjective* 形容词 (sadder, saddest)

unhappy or making you feel unhappy 悲伤的；难过的；使人悲哀的：*We are*

very *sad* to hear that you are leaving. 听说你要离开，我们十分难过。◇ *a sad story* 让人伤心的故事

▶ **sadly** /'sædli/ *adverb* 副词：*She looked sadly at the empty house.* 她看着空荡荡的房子，心里十分难受。

▶ **sadness** /'sædnəs/ *noun* 名词 (*no plural* 不用复数形式)：*Thoughts of him filled her with sadness.* 一想到他，她就非常伤心。

saddle /'sædl/ *noun* 名词

a seat on a horse or bicycle 马鞍；（自行车）车座 ᴅ Look at the pictures at **bicycle** and **horse**. 见 bicycle 和 horse 的插图。

safari /sə'fɑːri/ *noun* 名词 (*plural* 复数形式 safaris)

a journey to look at or hunt wild animals, usually in Africa （通常指在非洲的）野生动物观光，游猎

safe¹ 0ᴡ /seɪf/ *adjective* 形容词 (safer, safest)

1 not in danger; not hurt 安全；安然无恙：*Don't go out alone at night – you won't be safe.* 晚上不要独自出门，你会有危险。

2 not dangerous 没有危险的；安全的：*Is it safe to swim in this river?* 在这条河里游泳安全吗？◇ *Always keep medicines in a safe place.* 药物一定要放在安全的地方。

safe and sound not hurt or broken 平安无事；安然无恙：*The child was found safe and sound.* 孩子找到了，安然无恙。

▶ **safely** /'seɪfli/ *adverb* 副词：*Phone your parents to tell them you have arrived safely.* 给父母打个电话，告诉他们你已经平安到达了。

safe² /seɪf/ *noun* 名词

a strong metal box with a lock where you keep money or things like jewellery 保险箱；保险柜

safety 0ᴡ /'seɪfti/ *noun* 名词 (*no plural* 不用复数形式)

being safe 安全；平安：*He is worried about the safety of his children.* 他担心子女的安全。

safety belt /'seɪfti belt/ *noun* 名词

a long thin piece of material that you put round your body in a car or a plane to keep you safe in an accident（汽车或飞机

A
B
C
D
E
F
G
H
I
J
K
L
M
N
O
P
Q
R
S
T
U
V
W
X
Y
Z

座位上的）安全带 ⊃ SAME MEANING **seat belt** 同义词为 seat belt

safety pin /'seɪfti pɪn/ *noun* 名词
a pin that you use for joining pieces of cloth together. It has a cover over the point so that it is not dangerous. 安全别针 ⊃ Look at the picture at **pin¹**. 见 pin¹ 的插图。

sag /sæg/ *verb* 动词 (sags, sagging, sagged /sægd/)
to bend or hang down 凹陷；下垂： *The bed is very old and it sags in the middle.* 床很旧，中间陷下去了。

said *form of* SAY¹ * say¹ 的不同形式

sail¹ 0̄ /seɪl/ *verb* 动词 (sails, sailing, sailed /seɪld/)

> ♪ PRONUNCIATION 读音说明
> The word **sail** sounds just like **sale**. * sail 读音同 sale。

1 to travel on water （船）航行；（人）乘船航行： *The ship sailed along the coast.* 船沿着海岸航行。
2 to control a boat with sails 驾驶（帆船）： *We sailed the yacht down the river.* 我们驾驶帆船沿河而下。

> ♪ SPEAKING 表达方式说明
> When you talk about spending time sailing a boat, you say **go sailing**. 驾驶帆船游玩说 go sailing： *We often go sailing on the lake at weekends.* 我们周末常在湖上扬帆出游。

> ▸ **sailing** /'seɪlɪŋ/ *noun* 名词 (*no plural* 不用复数形式) the sport of controlling a boat with sails 帆船运动

sail² 0̄ /seɪl/ *noun* 名词
a big piece of cloth on a boat that catches the wind and moves the boat along 帆 ⊃ Look at the picture at **boat**. 见 boat 的插图。

sailor 0̄ /'seɪlə(r)/ *noun* 名词
a person who sails ships or boats as their job or as a sport 水手；海员；驾船人

saint /seɪnt/ *noun* 名词
(in the Christian religion) a dead person who lived their life in a very good way （基督教的）圣人，圣徒： *Saint Nicholas* 圣尼古拉斯

> ♪ PRONUNCIATION 读音说明
> You usually say /snt/ before names. The short way of writing **Saint** before names is **St**. * saint 用于名称前通常

读作 /snt/，缩写形式为 St： *St George's church* 圣乔治教堂

sake /seɪk/ *noun* 名词
for goodness' sake, for Heaven's sake (*informal* 非正式) something that you say to show you are annoyed （表示气恼）天哪，行行好吧
for the sake of somebody or 或 **something, for somebody's** or 或 **something's sake** to help somebody or something; because of somebody or something 为了…起见；因…的缘故： *The couple stayed together for the sake of their children.* 那对夫妇为了孩子才继续在一起。

salad 0̄ /'sæləd/ *noun* 名词
a dish of cold vegetables that have not been cooked 沙拉： *Do you want chips or salad with your chicken?* 你点的鸡肉要配薯条还是沙拉？ ⊃ Look at Picture Dictionary page **P7**. 见彩页 P7。

salary /'sæləri/ *noun* 名词 (*plural* 复数形式 salaries)
money that you receive every month for the work that you do （按月发放的）薪水，工资

sale 0̄ /seɪl/ *noun* 名词

> ♪ PRONUNCIATION 读音说明
> The word **sale** sounds just like **sail**. * sale 读音同 sail。

1 (*no plural* 不用复数形式) selling something 出售；销售
2 (*plural* 复数形式 sales) a time when a shop sells things for less money than usual 降价销售；大减价： *In the sale, everything is half-price.* 大减价的时候，所有商品半价出售。
for sale If something is **for sale**, its owner wants to sell it. 供出售；待售： *Is this house for sale?* 这所房子在出售吗？
on sale If something is **on sale**, you can buy it in shops. （于商店）出售，上市： *The magazine is on sale at most newsagents.* 这份杂志可在大多数书报亭买到。

sales clerk /'seɪlz klɜːrk/ *American English for* SHOP ASSISTANT 美式英语，即 shop assistant

salesman /'seɪlzmən/ *noun* 名词 (*plural* 复数形式 salesmen /'seɪlzmən/)
a man whose job is to sell things （男）推销员，促销员

salesperson /'seɪlzpɜːsn/ *noun* 名词 (*plural* 复数形式 salespeople) a man or a woman whose job is to sell things 推销员；促销员

saleswoman /'seɪlzwʊmən/ *noun* 名词 (*plural* 复数形式 saleswomen)
a woman whose job is to sell things 女推销员；女促销员

saliva /sə'laɪvə/ *noun* 名词 (*no plural* 不用复数形式)
the liquid in your mouth that helps you to swallow food 唾液；口水

salmon /'sæmən/ *noun* 名词 (*plural* 复数形式 salmon)
a big fish with pink meat that lives in the sea and in rivers 鲑（鱼）；大马哈鱼；三文鱼

salt 0ᵦ /sɔːlt/ *noun* 名词 (*no plural* 不用复数形式)
a white substance that comes from sea water and from the earth. We put it on food to make it taste better. 盐：*Add a little **salt and pepper**.* 加点盐和胡椒粉。
Ə Look at Picture Dictionary page **P6**. 见彩页 P6。

▸ **salty** /'sɔːlti/ *adjective* 形容词 (saltier, saltiest) tasting of salt or containing salt 咸的；含盐的：*Sea water is salty.* 海水是咸的。

salute /sə'luːt/ *verb* 动词 (salutes, saluting, saluted)
to make the special sign that soldiers make, by lifting your hand to your head （士兵式）敬礼：*The soldiers saluted as the Queen walked past.* 女王走过的时候，士兵行礼致敬。

▸ **salute** *noun* 名词：*The soldier gave a salute.* 士兵敬了个礼。

same¹ 0ᵦ /seɪm/ *adjective* 形容词
the same not different; not another 同一的；相同的：*Emma and I like the same kind of music.* 埃玛和我喜欢同一类音乐。◇ *I've lived in the same town all my life.* 我一辈子都住在同一个镇上。◇ *He went to the same school as me.* 他和我上过同一所学校。

same² 0ᵦ /seɪm/ *pronoun* 代词
all or 或 **just the same** in spite of this 虽然这样；尽管如此：*I understand why you're angry. All the same, I think you should say sorry.* 我明白你为什么生气。即便这样，我认为你还是应该赔个不是。

same to you (*informal* 非正式) words that you use for saying to somebody what they have said to you（作为回应）你也一样：*'Have a good weekend.' 'Same to you.'* "周末愉快。""你也一样。"

the same not a different person or thing

同样的人（或事物）：*Do these two words mean the same?* 这两个词意思一样吗？◇ *I'd like one the same as yours.* 你这个东西我也想要一个。

▸ **same** *adverb* 副词 **the same** in the same way 同样：*We treat boys exactly the same as girls.* 男孩女孩我们完全同等对待。

sample /'sɑːmpl/ *noun* 名词
a small amount of something that shows what the rest is like 样品；样本：*a free sample of perfume* 免费的香水样品 ◇ *a blood sample* 血样

sand 0ᵦ /sænd/ *noun* 名词 (*no plural* 不用复数形式)
powder made of very small pieces of rock, that you find on beaches and in deserts 沙；沙子：*Concrete is a mixture of sand and cement.* 混凝土是沙和水泥的混合物。

sandal /'sændl/ *noun* 名词
a light open shoe that you wear in warm weather 凉鞋 Ə Look at the picture at **shoe**. 见 shoe 的插图。

sandwich /'sænwɪtʃ; 'sænwɪdʒ/ *noun* 名词 (*plural* 复数形式 sandwiches)
two pieces of bread with other food between them 三明治：*a cheese sandwich* 奶酪三明治 Ə Look at Picture Dictionary page **P7**. 见彩页 P7。

sandy /'sændi/ *adjective* 形容词 (sandier, sandiest)
with sand 含沙的；多沙的：*a sandy beach* 沙滩

sane /seɪn/ *adjective* 形容词 (saner, sanest)
with a normal healthy mind; not mad 精神正常的；神志清醒的 Ə OPPOSITE **insane** 反义词为 insane

sang *form of* SING * sing 的不同形式

sank *form of* SINK¹ * sink¹ 的不同形式

Santa Claus /'sæntə klɔːz/ *another word for* FATHER CHRISTMAS * Father Christmas 的另一种说法

sarcasm /'sɑːkæzəm/ *noun* 名词 (*no plural* 不用复数形式)
saying the opposite of what you mean because you want to be rude to somebody or to show them you are angry 说反话；讽刺；挖苦

▸ **sarcastic** /sɑː'kæstɪk/ *adjective* 形容词：*There's no need to be sarcastic.* 没必要冷嘲热讽。

sardine /ˌsɑː'diːn/ *noun* 名词
a very small sea fish that you can eat. You often buy **sardines** in tins. 沙丁鱼

A B C D E F G H I J K L M N O P Q R S T U V W X Y Z

A B C D E F G H I J K L M N O P Q R **S** T U V W X Y Z

sari /'sɑːri/ *noun* 名词 (*plural* 复数形式 saris)
a long piece of material that women, particularly Indian women, wear around their bodies as a dress 莎丽（印度女人裹在身上的长巾）

sat *form of* SIT * sit 的不同形式

satchel /'sætʃəl/ *noun* 名词
a bag that children use for carrying books to and from school（儿童用的）书包

satellite /'sætəlaɪt/ *noun* 名词
a piece of electronic equipment that people send into space. **Satellites** travel round the earth and send back pictures or television and radio signals. 人造卫星: *satellite television* 卫星电视

satellite dish /'sætəlaɪt dɪʃ/ *noun* 名词
a piece of equipment that people put on the outside of their houses so that they can receive television signals from a SATELLITE 卫星电视碟形天线 ⊃ Look at Picture Dictionary page **P10**. 见彩页 P10。

satin /'sætɪn/ *noun* 名词 (*no plural* 不用复数形式)
very shiny smooth cloth 缎子

satire /'sætaɪə(r)/ *noun* 名词
1 (*no plural* 不用复数形式) using humour to attack somebody or something that you think is bad or silly 讽刺；讥讽: *political satire* 政治讽刺
2 (*plural* 复数形式 satires) a piece of writing or a play, film, etc. that uses **satire** 讽刺作品: *The play is a satire on political life.* 这出戏是讽刺政治生活的作品。

satisfaction ◐ /ˌsætɪs'fækʃn/ *noun* 名词 (*no plural* 不用复数形式)
being pleased with what you or other people have done 满意；满足: *She finished painting the picture and looked at it with satisfaction.* 她画完了那幅画，看着它很满意。

satisfactory /ˌsætɪs'fæktəri/ *adjective* 形容词
good enough, but not very good 令人满意的；可以接受的: *Her work is not satisfactory.* 她的工作不太令人满意。
⊃ OPPOSITE **unsatisfactory** 反义词为 unsatisfactory

satisfied ◐ /'sætɪsfaɪd/ *adjective* 形容词
pleased because you have had or done what you wanted 满意的；满足的: *The teacher was not satisfied with my work.* 老师对我的作业不满意。

satisfy /'sætɪsfaɪ/ *verb* 动词 (satisfies, satisfying, satisfied /'sætɪsfaɪd/, has satisfied)
to give somebody what they want or need; to be good enough to make somebody pleased 使满足；使满意: *Nothing he does satisfies his father.* 他做什么都不能令他父亲满意。

satisfying /'sætɪsfaɪɪŋ/ *adjective* 形容词
Something that is **satisfying** makes you pleased because it is what you want. 令人满意（或满足）的: *a satisfying result* 令人满意的结果

Saturday ◐ /'sætədeɪ/ *noun* 名词
the day of the week after Friday and before Sunday 星期六 ⊃ Look at the note at **day**. 见 day 条的注释。

sauce ◐ /sɔːs/ *noun* 名词
a thick liquid that you eat on or with other food 调味汁；沙司；酱: *pasta with tomato sauce* 浇番茄酱的意大利面食 ⊃ Look at Picture Dictionary page **P7**. 见彩页 P7。

saucepans 深平底锅

lid 盖子

saucepan /'sɔːspən/ *noun* 名词 (*also* 亦作 pan)
a round metal container for cooking 深平底锅；煮锅

saucer /'sɔːsə(r)/ *noun* 名词
a small round plate that you put under a cup 茶杯碟；茶托 ⊃ Look at the picture at **cup**. 见 cup 的插图。

sauna /'sɔːnə/ *noun* 名词
a room that is hot and filled with steam where people sit to relax and feel healthy 桑拿浴室: *a hotel with a swimming pool and sauna* 有游泳池和桑拿浴室的旅馆

sausage /'sɒsɪdʒ/ *noun* 名词
a mixture of meat, spices, etc. that is pressed into a long, thin skin 香肠；腊肠: *garlic sausage* 蒜味香肠 ◇ *sausages and chips* 香肠和薯条

savage /'sævɪdʒ/ *adjective* 形容词
wild or violent 凶恶的；凶残的: *He was the victim of a savage attack by a large dog.* 他遭到了一条大狗凶残的袭击。

save 0🔑 /seɪv/ *verb* 动词 (saves, saving, saved /seɪvd/)

1 to take somebody or something away from danger 救；拯救；挽救: *He saved me from the fire.* 他把我从大火中救了出来。◇ *The doctor saved her life.* 医生救了她的命。

2 (*also 亦作* **save up**) to keep or not spend money so that you can buy something later 存（钱）；储蓄: *I've saved enough money to buy a car.* 我已存够了买汽车的钱。◇ *I'm saving up for a new bike.* 我在存钱买一辆新自行车。

3 to keep something to use in the future 保留；保存: *Save some of the meat for tomorrow.* 留点肉明天吃。

4 to use less of something 节省；节约: *She saves money by making her own clothes.* 她为了省钱自己做衣服。

5 to stop somebody from scoring a goal, for example in football （足球等）扑救，救球

6 (*computing* 电脑) to store information in a computer by giving it a special instruction 保存（信息）；存盘: *Don't forget to save the file before you close it.* 关闭文件之前别忘了存盘。

savings /ˈseɪvɪŋz/ *noun* 名词 (*plural* 用复数形式)

money that you are keeping to use later 存款；积蓄: *I keep my savings in the bank.* 我把积蓄存在银行。

saw[1] *form of* SEE * see 的不同形式

saw 锯

saw[2] /sɔː/ *noun* 名词

a metal tool for cutting wood 锯

▶ **saw** *verb* 动词 (saws, sawing, sawed /sɔːd/, has sawn /sɔːn/): *She sawed a branch off the tree.* 她锯下了一截树枝。

sawdust /ˈsɔːdʌst/ *noun* 名词 (*no plural* 不用复数形式)

powder that falls when you SAW wood 锯末；锯木屑

saxophone /ˈsæksəfəʊn/ *noun* 名词

a musical instrument made of metal that you play by blowing into it 萨克斯管

saxophone 萨克斯管

key 键

say[1] 0🔑 /seɪ/ *verb* 动词 (says /sez/, saying, said /sed/, has said)

1 to make words with your mouth 说；讲: *You say 'please' when you ask for something.* 向别人提出请求时要说 "请"。◇ *'This is my room,' he said.* "这是我的房间。" 他说。◇ *She said that she was cold.* 她说她冷。

> ♫ **WHICH WORD?** 词语辨析
>
> **Say** or **tell**? 用 say 还是 tell?
> We use **say** with the actual words that are spoken, or before **that** in reported speech. * say 与所说的话连用，或用在间接引语的 that 之前: *'I'm ready,' Tim said.* "我准备好了。" 蒂姆说。◇ *Tim said that he was ready.* 蒂姆说他准备好了。
> Notice that you **say** something **to** somebody. 注意 "跟某人说某事" 作 say something to somebody: *Tim said to Kate that he was ready.* 蒂姆跟凯特说他准备好了。But you **tell** somebody something (without **to**). "告诉某人某事" 则作 tell somebody something（不加 to）: *Tim told Kate that he was ready.* 蒂姆告诉凯特他准备好了。

2 to give information in writing, numbers or pictures 提供（书面信息）；标示: *The notice on the door said 'Private'.* 门上的告示写着 "私人专用"。◇ *The clock says half past three.* 时钟显示的时间是三点半。

that is to say what I mean is … 也就是说；亦即: *I'll see you in a week, that's to say next Monday.* 我们一周后再见，也就是下周一。

say[2] /seɪ/ *noun* 名词

have a say to have the right to help decide something 有决定权；有发言权: *I'd like to have a say in who we invite to*

A
B
C
D
E
F
G
H
I
J
K
L
M
N
O
P
Q
R
S
T
U
V
W
X
Y
Z

the party. 我们请谁来参加聚会，我希望我能发表意见。

saying /ˈseɪɪŋ/ *noun* 名词
a sentence that people often say, that gives advice about something 谚语；格言：*'Love is blind' is an old saying.* "爱情是盲目的" 是句古谚。

scab /skæb/ *noun* 名词
a hard covering that grows over your skin where it is cut or broken 痂

scaffolding /ˈskæfəldɪŋ/ *noun* 名词
(*no plural* 不用复数形式)
metal bars and pieces of wood joined together, where people like painters can stand when they are working on high parts of a building 脚手架（组）；鹰架

scald /skɔːld/ *verb* 动词 (scalds, scalding, scalded)
to burn somebody or something with very hot liquid 烫伤

scales 秤；比例；鳞

bathroom scales
浴室磅秤

scale
比例

kitchen scales
厨房用秤

fish scales
鱼鳞

scale ⚓ /skeɪl/ *noun* 名词
1 the size or level of something 规模；程度：*It was not until morning that the full scale of the damage could be seen.* 直到早晨，破损的程度才完全显露出来。
2 a set of levels or numbers used for measuring something 等级；级别：*Their work is assessed on a scale from 1 to 10.* 他们的工作按 1 到 10 级来评估。
3 scales (*plural* 用复数形式) (*British* 英式英语) (*American* 美式英语 scale) a machine for showing how heavy people or things are 秤；磅秤；天平：*bathroom scales* 浴室磅秤

4 how distances are shown on a map （地图上的）比例，比例尺：*This map has a scale of one centimetre to ten kilometres.* 这张地图的比例是一厘米代表十公里。
5 one of the flat hard things that cover the body of animals like fish and snakes （鱼、蛇等动物的）鳞，鳞片

scalp /skælp/ *noun* 名词
the skin on the top of your head, under your hair 头皮

scan /skæn/ *verb* 动词 (scans, scanning, scanned /skænd/)
1 to look at or read every part of something quickly until you find what you are looking for 浏览；扫视：*Vic scanned the list until he found his own name.* 维克浏览着名单，直至找到自己的名字为止。
2 to pass light over a picture or document using an electronic machine (called a scanner) in order to copy it and put it in the memory of a computer （用扫描仪）扫描（图片或文件）

scandal /ˈskændl/ *noun* 名词
1 (*plural* 复数形式 scandals) something that shocks people and makes them talk about it because they think it is bad 丑闻；丑行：*a sex scandal* 性丑闻
2 (*no plural* 不用复数形式) unkind talk about somebody that gives you a bad idea of them 关于丑行的传言；丑闻

scanner /ˈskænə(r)/ *noun* 名词
1 (*computing* 电脑) a piece of equipment that copies words or pictures from paper into a computer 扫描仪；扫描器
2 a machine that gives a picture of the inside of something. Doctors use one kind of scanner to look inside people's bodies. （医疗等用的）扫描器，扫描设备

scar /skɑː(r)/ *noun* 名词
a mark that is left on your skin by an old cut or wound 伤疤；疤痕：*The operation didn't leave a very big scar.* 手术并没有留下很大的疤痕。
▶ **scar** *verb* 动词 (scars, scarring, scarred /skɑːd/)：*His face was badly scarred by the accident.* 那起事故令他脸上留下了严重的伤疤。

scarce /skeəs/ *adjective* 形容词 (scarcer, scarcest)
difficult to find; not enough 稀少的；缺乏的；不足的：*Food for birds and animals is scarce in the winter.* 冬天鸟兽的食物很少。

scarcely /'skeəsli/ *adverb* 副词
almost not; only just 几乎不；勉强: *He was so frightened that he could scarcely speak.* 他吓得几乎说不出话来。

scare¹ /skeə(r)/ *verb* 动词 (scares, scaring, scared /skeəd/)
to make somebody frightened 使惊吓；使惊恐: *That noise scared me!* 那声响吓了我一跳!

scare² /skeə(r)/ *noun* 名词
1 a feeling of being frightened 惊吓；惊恐: *You gave me a scare!* 你吓了我一跳!
2 a situation where many people are afraid or worried about something 恐慌；恐惧: *a health scare* 健康大恐慌

scarecrow /'skeəkrəʊ/ *noun* 名词
a thing that looks like a person, that farmers put in their fields to frighten birds 稻草人

scared /skeəd/ *adjective* 形容词
frightened 受惊的；害怕的: *Claire is scared of the dark.* 克莱尔怕黑。

scarves 头巾；围巾

scarf 围巾

scarf 头巾

scarf /skɑːf/ *noun* 名词 (plural 复数形式 scarves /skɑːvz/)
a piece of material that you wear around your neck or head 围巾；头巾；披巾

scarlet /'skɑːlət/ *adjective* 形容词
with a bright red colour 猩红色的；鲜红色的

scary /'skeəri/ *adjective* 形容词 (scarier, scariest) (informal 非正式)
frightening 吓人的；恐怖的；可怕的: *a scary ghost story* 让人发毛的鬼故事

scatter /'skætə(r)/ *verb* 动词 (scatters, scattering, scattered /'skætəd/)
1 to throw things so that they fall in a lot of different places 撒；撒播: *Scatter the grass seed over the lawn.* 把草籽撒在草坪上。
2 to move quickly in different directions 散开；四散: *The crowd scattered when it started to rain.* 一开始下雨人群就跑散了。

scene 0← /siːn/ *noun* 名词
1 a place where something happened （某事发生的）地点，现场: *The police arrived at the scene of the crime.* 警方来到了案发现场。
2 part of a play or film （戏剧或电影的）场，镜头，片段: *Act 1, Scene 2 of 'Hamlet'* 《哈姆雷特》第1幕第2场
3 what you see in a place 景观；景象 ⊃ SAME MEANING **view** 同义词为 view: *He painted scenes of life in the countryside.* 他画了乡村生活的情景。

scenery /'siːnəri/ *noun* 名词 (no plural 不用复数形式)
1 the things like mountains, rivers and forests that you see around you in the countryside 自然景色；风景: *What beautiful scenery!* 多么美丽的景色啊!
2 things on the stage of a theatre that make it look like a real place （舞台）布景

scent /sent/ *noun* 名词
1 (plural 复数形式 scents) a smell 气味: *These flowers have no scent.* 这些花没有香味。
2 (no plural 不用复数形式) a liquid with a nice smell, that you put on your body 香水 ⊃ SAME MEANING **perfume** 同义词为 perfume: *a bottle of scent* 一瓶香水
▶ **scented** /'sentɪd/ *adjective* 形容词
having a nice smell 有香味的；芬芳的: *scented candles* 芳香的蜡烛

sceptical /'skeptɪkl/ *adjective* 形容词
having doubts that something is true or that something will happen 怀疑的: *I am sceptical about his chances of winning.* 我对他能否获胜感到怀疑。

schedule /'ʃedjuːl/ *noun* 名词
a plan or list of times when things will happen or be done 日程安排；工作计划: *I've got a busy schedule next week.* 我下周的日程排得很紧。◇ *We're behind schedule* (= late) *with the project.* 我们这个项目的进度落后了。◇ *Filming began on schedule* (= at the planned time). 电影按计划时间开始拍摄。

scheme¹ /skiːm/ *noun* 名词 (British 英式英语)
a plan or a system for doing or organizing something 计划；方案；体系: *a local scheme for recycling newspapers* 当地的报纸回收体系

scheme² /skiːm/ *verb* 动词 (schemes, scheming, schemed /skiːmd/)
to make secret plans to do something

She felt that they were all ... against her. 她觉得他们都在

scholar /'skɒlə(r)/ *noun* 名词
a person who has learned a lot about something 学者: *a famous history scholar* 著名的历史学者

scholarship /'skɒləʃɪp/ *noun* 名词
money that is given to a good student to help them to continue studying 奖学金: *Adrian won a scholarship to university.* 阿德里安获得了上大学的奖学金。

school ⚡ /skuːl/ *noun* 名词
1 (*plural* 复数形式 schools) a place where children go to learn 学校（指中小学）: *Lucy is at school.* 露西在上学。◇ *Which school do you go to?* 你上哪一所学校?
2 (*no plural* 不用复数形式) being at **school** 上学: *I hate school!* 我讨厌上学! ◇ *He left school when he was 16.* 他 16 岁时离开学校。◇ *School starts at nine o'clock.* 学校九点钟开始上课。

🔑 GRAMMAR 语法说明
You usually talk about **school** without 'the' or 'a'. * school 前通常不加 the 或 a: *I enjoyed school.* 我喜欢上学。◇ *Do you walk to school?* 你走路上学吗?
You use 'a' or 'the' when more information about the school is given. 进一步提供关于学校的信息时要加 a 或 the: *Harry goes to the school that his father went to.* 哈里上的是他父亲去的母校。◇ *She teaches at a school for deaf children.* 她在一所聋哑学校教书。

⊃ Look at Study Pages S14-S15. 见研习专页 S14-S15。
3 (*plural* 复数形式 schools) (*American* 美式英语) (*informal* 非正式) a college or university, or the time that you spend there 学院；大学；上大学时期
4 (*plural* 复数形式 schools) a place where you go to learn a special thing 专科学校: *a language school* 语言学校

schoolboy /'skuːlbɔɪ/ *noun* 名词
a boy who goes to school （中小学的）男生

schoolchild /'skuːltʃaɪld/ (*plural* 复数形式 schoolchildren) *noun* 名词
a boy or girl who goes to school （中小学的）学生

schooldays /'skuːldeɪz/ *noun* 名词
(*plural* 用复数形式)
the time in your life when you are at school 学生时代

schoolgirl /'skuːlɡɜːl/ *noun* 名词
a girl who goes to school （中小学的）女生

science ⚡ /'saɪəns/ *noun* 名词
the study of natural things （自然）科学: *I'm interested in science.* 我对自然科学感兴趣。◇ *Biology, chemistry and physics are all sciences.* 生物、化学和物理都属于自然科学。

science fiction /,saɪəns 'fɪkʃn/ *noun* 名词 (*no plural* 不用复数形式)
stories about things like travel in space, life on other planets or life in the future 科幻小说

scientific ⚡ /,saɪən'tɪfɪk/ *adjective* 形容词
of or about science 科学的；关于科学的: *We need more grants for scientific research.* 我们需要更多的科研经费。

scientist ⚡ /'saɪəntɪst/ *noun* 名词
a person who studies science or works with science 科学家；科研人员

scissors 剪刀

a pair of scissors 一把剪刀

scissors ⚡ /'sɪzəz/ *noun* 名词 (*plural* 用复数形式)
a tool for cutting that has two sharp parts that are joined together 剪刀: *These scissors aren't very sharp.* 这把剪刀不是很锋利。

🔑 GRAMMAR 语法说明
Be careful! You cannot say 'a scissors'. You can say **a pair of scissors**. 注意: 不说 a scissors，说 a pair of scissors: *I need a pair of scissors.* 我需要一把剪刀。You can also say '*I need some scissors*'. 也说 I need some scissors。

scold /skəʊld/ *verb* 动词 (scolds, scolding, scolded)
to tell a child in an angry way that they have done something wrong 训斥，责骂

（孩子）: *His mother scolded him for being so naughty.* 他母亲骂他太顽皮。

scoop /skuːp/ *verb* 动词 (scoops, scooping, scooped /skuːpt/)
to use a spoon or your hands to take something up or out （用勺子）舀；（用手）拿，抓: *I scooped some ice cream out of the bowl.* 我从碗里舀了些冰激凌出来。

scooter /'skuːtə(r)/ *noun* 名词
a light motorcycle with a small engine 小型摩托车 ➔ Look at the picture at **motorbike**. 见 motorbike 的插图。

score¹ 0← /skɔː(r)/ *noun* 名词
the number of points, goals, etc. that you win in a game or competition （游戏或竞赛的）得分，比分: *The winner got a score of 320.* 获胜者得了 320 分。◇ *What's the score now?* 现在比分是多少？

score² 0← /skɔː(r)/ *verb* 动词 (scores, scoring, scored /skɔːd/)
to win points, goals, etc. in a game or competition （在游戏或竞赛中）得分: *Brazil scored three goals against France.* 巴西队跟法国队比赛时进了三球。

scoreboard /'skɔːbɔːd/ *noun* 名词
a large board that shows the score during a game or competition （游戏或竞赛的）记分牌

scorn /skɔːn/ *noun* 名词 (no plural 不用复数形式)
a strong feeling that somebody or something is stupid or not good enough 蔑视；鄙视: *He was full of scorn for my idea.* 他对我的主意不屑一顾。
▶ **scornful** /'skɔːnfl/ *adjective* 形容词: *She gave him a scornful look.* 她鄙视地看了他一眼。

scorpion 蝎子

sting 螫针

scorpion /'skɔːpiən/ *noun* 名词
a small animal that looks like an insect and has a sting in its tail 蝎子

Scout /skaʊt/ *noun* 名词
1 the Scouts (*plural* 用复数形式) a special club for boys, and sometimes girls too, which does a lot of activities with them, for example camping 童子军
2 (*British* 英式英语) (*American* 美式英语 **Boy Scout**) a boy or girl who is a member of the **Scouts** 童子军成员

scowl /skaʊl/ *verb* 动词 (scowls, scowling, scowled /skaʊld/)
to look at somebody in an angry way 怒视: *His teacher scowled at him for being late.* 他迟到了，老师生气地瞪着他。
▶ **scowl** *noun* 名词: *He looked up at me with a scowl.* 他抬眼看了看我，面露不悦。

scramble /'skræmbl/ *verb* 动词 (scrambles, scrambling, scrambled /'skræmbld/)
to move quickly up or over something, using your hands to help you （用手快速地）爬，攀爬: *They scrambled over the wall.* 他们爬过了墙。

scrambled eggs /,skræmbld 'egz/ *noun* 名词 (*plural* 用复数形式)
eggs that you mix together with milk and cook in a pan with butter 炒鸡蛋

scrap /skræp/ *noun* 名词
1 (*plural* 复数形式 scraps) a small piece of something 碎片；小块: *a scrap of paper* 一小片纸
2 (*no plural* 不用复数形式) something you do not want any more but that is made of material that can be used again （可循环再用的）废料，废品: *scrap paper* 废纸

scrapbook /'skræpbʊk/ *noun* 名词
a large book with empty pages that you can stick pictures or newspaper articles in 剪贴簿

scrape /skreɪp/ *verb* 动词 (scrapes, scraping, scraped /skreɪpt/)
1 to move a rough or sharp thing across something 刮掉；削去: *I scraped the mud off my shoes with a knife.* 我用小刀把鞋上的泥刮掉。
2 to hurt or damage something by moving it against a rough or sharp thing 擦伤；刮破: *I fell and scraped my knee on the wall.* 我摔了一跤，膝盖撞到墙壁蹭破了。

scratch¹ 0← /skrætʃ/ *verb* 动词 (scratches, scratching, scratched /skrætʃt/)
1 to move your nails across your skin （用指甲）挠，抓，搔: *She scratched her head.* 她挠了挠头。
2 to cut or make a mark on something

A
C
D
E
F
G
H
I
J
K
L
M
N
O
P
Q
R
S
T
U
V
W
X
Y
Z

with a sharp thing 划破；抓伤；留下划痕：*The cat scratched me!* 猫抓伤了我!

scratch² /skrætʃ/ *noun* 名词 (*plural* 复数形式 **scratches**)
a cut or mark that a sharp thing makes 刮伤；划痕：*Her hands were covered in scratches from the cat.* 她双手满是猫的抓痕。
from scratch from the beginning 从头（开始）；从零（开始）：*I threw away the letter I was writing and started again from scratch.* 我把原先在写的信扔了，从头再来。

scream¹ /skriːm/ *verb* 动词 (**screams, screaming, screamed** /skriːmd/)
to make a loud high cry that shows you are afraid or hurt（因害怕或受伤）尖叫：*She saw the snake and screamed.* 她看到蛇，尖叫了起来。◇ *He screamed for help.* 他尖声呼救。

scream² /skriːm/ *noun* 名词
a loud high cry 尖叫（声）：*a scream of pain* 痛苦的尖叫声

screech /skriːtʃ/ *verb* 动词 (**screeches, screeching, screeched** /skriːtʃt/)
to make a loud high sound 发出尖锐的声音：*The car's brakes screeched as it stopped suddenly.* 汽车猛地停下时发出了刺耳的刹车声。

screen 0̄ /skriːn/ *noun* 名词
1 the flat square part of a television or computer where you see pictures or words（电视或电脑的）屏幕，荧光屏，荧幕 ⊃ Look at Picture Dictionary page **P11**. 见彩页 P11。
2 the flat thing on the wall of a cinema, where you see films 银幕
3 a kind of thin wall that you can move around. **Screens** are used to keep away cold, light, etc. or to stop people from seeing something. 屏风；隔板；帘：*The nurse put a screen around the bed.* 护士在床的周围拉上了帘子。

screw 螺丝钉

screw¹ /skruː/ *noun* 名词
a small metal thing with a sharp end, that

you use for fixing things together. You push it into something by turning it with a special tool (called a **screwdriver**). 螺丝钉；螺丝

screw² /skruː/ *verb* 动词 (**screws, screwing, screwed** /skruːd/)
1 to fix something to another thing using a SCREW 用螺丝固定：*The cupboard is screwed to the wall.* 橱柜用螺丝固定在墙上了。
2 to turn something to fix it to another thing 旋紧；拧紧：*Screw the lid on the jar.* 把罐盖拧紧。
screw something up to make paper or material into a ball with your hand 把…揉成团：*He screwed up the letter and threw it in the bin.* 他把信揉成一团扔进了垃圾箱。

screwdriver /'skruːdraɪvə(r)/ *noun* 名词
a tool for turning SCREWS 螺丝刀；改锥

scribble /'skrɪbl/ *verb* 动词 (**scribbles, scribbling, scribbled** /'skrɪbld/)
to write something or make marks on paper quickly and without care 潦草地书写；乱画：*The children scribbled in my book.* 孩子在我的书上乱写乱涂。

script /skrɪpt/ *noun* 名词
the written words that actors speak in a play or film 剧本；脚本

scripture /'skrɪptʃə(r)/ *noun* 名词
the book or books that a particular religion is based on（某宗教的）圣典，经文

scroll /skrəʊl/ *verb* 动词 (**scrolls, scrolling, scrolled** /skrəʊld/)
to move what you can see on a computer screen up or down so that you can look at different parts of it（在电脑屏幕上）滚动；滚屏：*Scroll down to the bottom of the document.* 向下滚动到文件末尾。

scrub /skrʌb/ *verb* 动词 (**scrubs, scrubbing, scrubbed** /skrʌbd/)
to rub something hard to clean it, usually with a brush and soap and water（常指用刷子、肥皂和水用力）擦洗，刷洗：*He scrubbed the floor.* 他刷了地板。

scruffy /'skrʌfi/ *adjective* 形容词 (**scruffier, scruffiest**)
untidy and perhaps dirty 不整洁的；邋遢的：*She was wearing scruffy jeans.* 她穿着脏兮兮的牛仔裤。

scuba-diving /'skuːbə daɪvɪŋ/ *noun* 名词
swimming underwater using special equipment for breathing 戴水肺潜水：

You should never go scuba-diving alone.
千万不要独自去戴水肺潜水。

scuba-diving 戴水肺潜水
tank 氧气罐　flipper 脚蹼

scuba-diving 戴水肺潜水

snorkel 呼吸管
mask 面罩

snorkelling 徒手潜水

sculptor /'skʌlptə(r)/ *noun* 名词
a person who makes shapes from things
like stone or wood 雕刻家；雕塑家

sculpture /'skʌlptʃə(r)/ *noun* 名词
1 (*no plural* 不用复数形式) making shapes
from things like stone or wood 雕刻；
雕塑
2 (*plural* 复数形式 **sculptures**) a shape
made from things like stone or wood
雕刻品；雕塑品

sea 0━ /siː/ *noun* 名词

> 🔍 **PRONUNCIATION** 读音说明
> The word **sea** sounds just like **see**.
> * sea 读音同 see.

1 (*no plural* 不用复数形式) the salt water
that covers large parts of the earth 海；
海洋： *We went for a swim in the sea.*
我们去海里游泳了。◇ *The sea is very
rough today.* 今天海上风浪很大。
2 Sea (*plural* 复数形式 **Seas**) a big area of
salt water（用于名称）海： *the Black Sea*
黑海 ➋ Look at **ocean**. 见 ocean.
at sea travelling on the sea 在海上（航
行）： *We spent three weeks at sea.* 我们
在海上度过了三个星期。

the seabed /ðə ˈsiːbed/ *noun* 名词
(*no plural* 不用复数形式)
the floor of the sea 海底；海床

seafood /'siːfuːd/ *noun* 名词 (*no plural*
不用复数形式)

fish and small animals from the sea that
we eat, especially SHELLFISH (= animals
with shells that live in water) 海鲜，海味
（尤指甲壳类）

seagull 海鸥

seagull /'siːgʌl/ *noun* 名词
a big grey or white bird with a loud cry,
that lives near the sea 海鸥

seal 海豹

flipper 鳍肢

seal¹ /siːl/ *noun* 名词
an animal with short fur that lives in and
near the sea, and that eats fish 海豹

seal² /siːl/ *verb* 动词 (**seals, sealing,
sealed** /siːld/)
to close something tightly by sticking two
parts together 封上；封好： *She sealed
the envelope.* 她封好了信封。

seam /siːm/ *noun* 名词
a line where two pieces of cloth are
joined together（两块布之间的）接缝，
线缝

search¹ 0━ /sɜːtʃ/ *verb* 动词 (**searches,
searching, searched** /sɜːtʃt/)
to look carefully because you are trying
to find somebody or something 搜索；
搜寻；搜查： *I searched everywhere for
my pen.* 我到处寻找我的笔。

search² 0━ /sɜːtʃ/ *noun* 名词 (*plural*
复数形式 **searches**)

B C D E F G H I J K L M N O P Q R **S** T U V W X Y Z

A

C

D

E

F

G

H

I

J

K

L

M

N

O

P

Q

R

S

T

U

V

W

X

Y

Z

when you try to find somebody or
something 搜索；搜寻；搜查： *I found
my keys after a long search.* 我找了好长
时间才找到我的钥匙。◇ *We drove round
the town in search of a cheap hotel.*
我们开车在镇子上到处跑，想找家便宜
的旅馆。◇ *The search for the murder
weapon goes on.* 杀人凶器的搜寻工作
还在继续。

seashell /'si:ʃel/ *noun* 名词
the empty shell of a small animal that
lives in the sea 海贝壳

seashore /'si:ʃɔ:(r)/ *noun* 名词
the seashore (*no plural* 不用复数形式)
the land next to the sea 海岸；海滨： *We
were looking for seashells on the seashore.*
我们在海滨捡贝壳。

seasick /'si:sɪk/ *adjective* 形容词
If you are **seasick**, you feel ill in your
stomach because the boat you are on is
moving a lot. 晕船

seaside /'si:saɪd/ *noun* 名词 (*no plural*
不用复数形式)
an area or a place next to the sea where
people often go on holiday（人们度假常
去的）海边，海滨： *Let's go to the seaside
today.* 我们今天去海边吧。

season ⊶ /'si:zn/ *noun* 名词
1 one of the four parts of the year 季；
季节

> 🔎 WORD BUILDING 词汇扩充
>
> The four seasons are **spring, summer,
> autumn** and **winter**. 一年四季分别是
> 春季（spring）、夏季（summer）、
> 秋季（autumn）、冬季（winter）。

⊃ Look at Picture Dictionary page **P16**.
见彩页 P16。
2 a special time of the year for something
（某些事物的）季节： *The football season
starts in August.* 足球赛季在八月开始。

seat ⊶ /si:t/ *noun* 名词
something that you sit on 座位： *the back
seat of a car* 汽车的后排座位 ◇ *We had
seats at the front of the theatre.* 我们的
座位在剧院的前排。◇ *Please take a seat*
(= sit down). 请就座。

seat belt /'si:t belt/ *noun* 名词
a long thin piece of material that you put
round your body in a car, bus or plane to
keep you safe in an accident（汽车或飞机
座位上的）安全带

seaweed /'si:wi:d/ *noun* 名词 (*no plural*
不用复数形式)
a plant that grows in the sea. There are

many different types of **seaweed**. 海草；
海藻

second¹ ⊶ /'sekənd/ *adjective, adverb*
形容词，副词
next after first 第二： *February is the
second month of the year.* 二月是一年中的
第二个月。◇ *She came second in the race.*
她赛跑得了第二名。

second² ⊶ /'sekənd/ *noun* 名词
(*no plural* 不用复数形式)
a person or thing that comes next after
the first 第二个人（或事物）： *Today is
the second of April* (= April 2nd). 今天是
四月二日。◇ *I was the first to arrive, and
Jim was the second.* 我是第一个到的，吉姆
是第二个。

second³ ⊶ /'sekənd/ *noun* 名词
1 a measure of time. There are 60
seconds in a minute. 秒
2 a very short time 片刻；瞬间： *Wait
a second!* 等一下！◇ *I'll be ready in a
second.* 我马上就好了。

secondary school /'sekəndri sku:l/
noun 名词 (*British* 英式英语)
a school for children between the ages of
11 and 16 or 18 中学

second class /ˌsekənd 'klɑ:s/ *noun* 名词
(*no plural* 不用复数形式)
1 the part of a train, plane, etc. that it is
cheaper to travel in 二等座位（或车厢、
舱位）： *We sat in second class.* 我们坐在
二等车厢。
2 (*British* 英式英语) the cheapest but the
slowest way of sending letters 第二类邮件
（邮费低，邮递速度慢）⊃ Look at the
note at **stamp¹**. 见 stamp¹ 条的注释。
▸ **second-class** *adjective* 形容词：
a second-class ticket 二等座位的票
▸ **second class** *adverb* 副词： *I sent the
letter second class.* 我把信按第二类邮件
寄出。

second-hand /ˌsekənd 'hænd/ *adjective,
adverb* 形容词，副词
not new; used by another person before
二手（的）；用过（的）： *second-hand
books* 旧书 ◇ *I bought this car
second-hand.* 我买的这辆车是二手的。

secondly /'sekəndli/ *adverb* 副词
a word that you use when you are giving
the second thing in a list（用于列举）
第二，其次： *Firstly, it's too expensive and
secondly, we don't really need it.* 首先，
它太贵了；其次，我们不太需要它。

secrecy /'si:krəsi/ *noun* 名词 (*no plural*
不用复数形式)

not telling other people 保密；秘密：
*They worked **in secrecy**.* 他们秘密地工作。

secret¹ 0🔊 /'si:krət/ *noun* 名词
something that you do not or must not
tell other people 秘密；机密： *I can't tell
you where I'm going – it's a secret.* 我不能
告诉你我去哪里，这是秘密。◇ *Can you
keep a secret (= not tell other people)?*
你能保密吗？

in secret without other people knowing
秘密地；暗中；私下地： *They met in
secret.* 他们秘密见了面。

secret² 0🔊 /'si:krət/ *adjective* 形容词
If something is **secret**, other people do
not or must not know about it. 秘密的；
保密的： *They kept their wedding secret
(= they did not tell anybody about it).*
他们对婚礼的事保密。◇ *a secret meeting*
秘密会议

secretarial /ˌsekrə'teəriəl/ *adjective*
形容词
connected with the work of a secretary
秘书的；文秘工作的： *a secretarial college*
文秘学院

secretary 0🔊 /'sekrətri/ *noun* 名词
(*plural* 复数形式 **secretaries**)
1 a person who types letters, answers the
telephone and does other things in an
office 秘书
2 an important person in the government
（政府）大臣： *the **Secretary of State**
(= head of the department) for Education*
教育大臣
3 *American English for* MINISTER (1) 美式
英语，即 minister 第 1 义

secretive /'si:krətɪv/ *adjective* 形容词
If you are **secretive**, you do not like to
tell other people about yourself or your
plans. 不外露的；惯于掩藏自己的： *Mark
is very **secretive about** his job.* 马克对自己
的工作讳莫如深。

secretly 0🔊 /'si:krətli/ *adverb* 副词
without other people knowing 秘密地；
暗中： *We are secretly planning a big
party for her.* 我们正悄悄地为她筹备一个
盛大的聚会。

section 0🔊 /'sekʃn/ *noun* 名词
one of the parts of something 部分：
This section of the road is closed. 这段路
封闭了。

secure /sɪ'kjʊə(r)/ *adjective* 形容词
1 If you are **secure**, you feel safe and you
are not worried. 安心的；无忧虑的： *Do
you feel secure about the future?* 你对未来
有信心吗？◇ OPPOSITE **insecure**
反义词为 insecure

2 safe 安全的；牢靠的： *Don't climb that
ladder – it's not very secure (= it may fall).*
别爬那架梯子，它不太牢靠。◇ *Her job is
secure (= she will not lose it).* 她的工作很
安稳。
3 well locked or protected so that nobody
can go in or out 关紧锁好的；严密把守
的： *This gate isn't very secure.* 这大门
没有关好。

▶ **securely** /sɪ'kjʊəli/ *adverb* 副词： *Are
all the windows securely closed?* 窗户都
关紧了吗？

security /sɪ'kjʊərəti/ *noun* 名词 (*no plural
不用复数形式*)
1 the feeling of being safe 安全感：
Children need love and security. 孩子需要
疼爱，也需要安全感。◇ OPPOSITE
insecurity 反义词为 insecurity
2 things that you do to keep a place safe
保安措施： *We need better security at
airports.* 我们需要加强机场保安工作。

see 0🔊 /si:/ *verb* 动词 (**sees**, **seeing**, **saw**
/sɔ:/, has seen /si:n/)

> 🔊 **PRONUNCIATION** 读音说明
> The word **see** sounds just like **sea**.
> * see 读音同 sea。

1 to know or notice something using your
eyes 看见；见到： *It was so dark that
I couldn't see anything.* 光线太暗，我什么
都看不见。◇ *Can you see that plane?*
你能看见那架飞机吗？

> 🔊 **WHICH WORD?** 词语辨析
> **See**, **look** or **watch**? 用 see、look 还是
> watch？
> When you **see** something, you know
> about it with your eyes, without trying.
> * see 指非刻意地看见： *Suddenly, I saw
> a bird fly past the window.* 突然间，
> 我看见有只鸟从窗里飞过。
> When you **watch** something, you look
> at it for some time. * watch 指长时间
> 地看： *They **watched** the carnival
> procession.* 他们观看了狂欢节的游行。
> When you **look at** something, you turn
> your eyes towards it because you want
> to see it. * look at 指刻意地看： *She
> **looked at** all the pictures in the room.*
> 她看了房间里所有的画。

2 to watch a film, play or television
programme 观看（电影、戏剧或电视
节目）： *I'm going to see a film tonight.*
我今天晚上去看电影。
3 to find out about something 弄清；
了解： *Go and see what time the train
leaves.* 去看看火车什么时候开。

A
C
D
E
F
G
H
I
J
K
L
M
N
O
P
Q
R
S
T
U
V
W
X
Y
Z

meet somebody 拜访；看望；
... going to see my grandma at
... 我们周末去看望我奶奶。◇
... outside the station at ten
o'clock. 我十点钟在车站外面见你。
5 to understand something 理解；明白：
'You have to turn the key this way.'
'I see.' "你得这样转动钥匙才行。"
"我明白了。"

6 to make certain about something
确保：*Please see that you lock the door.*
请务必把门锁上。
I'll see, we'll see I will think about
what you have said and tell you what I
have decided later. 让我（们）考虑一下：
'Will you lend me the money?' 'I'll see.'
"你愿意把钱借给我吗？""我考虑
一下。"
let's see, let me see words that you
use when you are thinking or trying to
remember something 让我（们）想想：
Let's see, where did I put the keys? 让我
想一想，我把钥匙放哪儿了？
seeing that, seeing as (*informal* 非正式)
because 因为；既然：*Seeing that you've
got nothing to do, you can help me!* 既然
你没什么事做，过来帮我吧！
see somebody off to go to an airport
or a station to say goodbye to somebody
who is leaving 给某人送行；送别
see to somebody or 或 **something** to
do what you need to do for somebody or
something 照管；处理：*Sit down – I'll see
to the dinner.* 歇着吧，我来做饭。
see you, see you later (*informal* 非正式)
goodbye 再见：*'Bye Dave!' 'See you!'*
"再见，戴夫！""再见！"

seed ⚬ /siːd/ *noun* 名词
the small hard part of a plant from which
a new plant grows 种子；籽 ➭ Look at
Picture Dictionary page **P8**. 见彩页 P8.

seek /siːk/ *verb* 动词 (**seeks, seeking,
sought** /sɔːt/, **has sought**) (*formal* 正式)
to try to find or get something 寻找；
寻求：*You should seek help.* 你应该寻求
援助。

seem ⚬ /siːm/ *verb* 动词 (**seems,
seeming, seemed** /siːmd/)
to give the impression of being or doing
something 看上去；似乎；好像：*She
seems tired.* 她好像累了。◇ *My mother
seems to like you.* 我母亲似乎喜欢你。◇
Helen seems like (= seems to be) *a nice
girl.* 海伦好像是个不错的女孩。

seen *form of* SEE * see 的不同形式

see-saw /siː sɔː/ *noun* 名词
a piece of equipment for children to play

on which is made of a piece of wood that
moves up and down when a child sits on
each end 跷跷板

segment /'segmənt/ *noun* 名词
one of the sections of an orange, a lemon,
etc. （橙子、柠檬等的）瓣

seize /siːz/ *verb* 动词 (**seizes, seizing,
seized** /siːzd/)
to take something quickly and firmly
快速抓住；紧紧捉住 ➭ SAME MEANING **grab**
同义词为 grab：*The thief seized her bag
and ran away.* 小偷一把夺过她的包就
跑了。

seldom /'seldəm/ *adverb* 副词
not often 不常；很少 ➭ SAME MEANING
rarely 同义词为 rarely：*It seldom snows
in Athens.* 雅典很少下雪。

select /sɪ'lekt/ *verb* 动词 (**selects,
selecting, selected**) (*formal* 正式)
to take the person or thing that you like
best 选择；挑选；选拔 ➭ SAME MEANING
choose 同义词为 choose：*We select only
the finest fruits.* 我们只挑选最好的水果。

selection /sɪ'lekʃn/ *noun* 名词
1 (*no plural* 不用复数形式) taking the
person or thing you like best 选择；
挑选；选拔：*The manager is responsible
for team selection.* 主教练负责队员的
选拔。
2 (*plural* 复数形式 **selections**) a group
of people or things that somebody has
chosen, or a group of things that you
can choose from 选中的人（或事物）；
可供选择的事物：*The shop has a good
selection of CDs.* 这家商店有很多激光唱片
可供选购。

self /self/ *noun* 名词 (*plural* 复数形式
selves /selvz/)
a person's own nature or qualities （自己
的）本来面目，本性，本质：*It's good
to see you back to your old self again*
(= well or happy again). 看到你又恢复了
原样真是太好了。

self- /self/ *prefix* 前缀
by yourself; for yourself 由自己；为自己：
*He is self-taught – he never went to
university.* 他是自学的，从未上过大学。

self-confident /,self 'kɒnfɪdənt/
adjective 形容词
sure about yourself and what you can do
自信的
▸ **self-confidence** /,self 'kɒnfɪdəns/
noun 名词 (*no plural* 不用复数形式)：
*Failing that exam made her lose a lot of
self-confidence.* 那次考试不及格使她的
自信心大受打击。

self-conscious /ˌself ˈkɒnʃəs/ *adjective*
形容词
worried about what other people think
of you 在意别人眼光的；局促不安的；
不自然的： *She walked into her new
school feeling very self-conscious.* 她走进
新学校，感到非常不自在。

self-control /ˌself kənˈtrəʊl/ *noun* 名词
(*no plural* 不用复数形式)
the ability to control yourself and your
emotions 自控能力；自制力

self-defence (*British* 英式英语)
(*American* 美式英语 **self-defense**) /ˌself
dɪˈfens/ *noun* (*no plural* 不用复数形式)
the use of force to protect yourself
自我保护；自卫： *I only hit him in
self-defence.* 我是出于自卫才打了他。

self-employed /ˌself ɪmˈplɔɪd/ *adjective*
形容词
working for yourself, not for somebody
else 个体经营的；自雇的： *He's a
self-employed electrician.* 他是个单干的
电工。

selfish /ˈselfɪʃ/ *adjective* 形容词
thinking too much about what you want
and not about what other people want
自私的： *I'm sick of your selfish behaviour!*
我讨厌你那自私自利的行为！ ➙ OPPOSITE
unselfish 反义词为 unselfish
▸ **selfishly** /ˈselfɪʃli/ *adverb* 副词： *He
behaved very selfishly.* 他表现得很自私。
▸ **selfishness** /ˈselfɪʃnəs/ *noun* 名词
(*no plural* 不用复数形式)： *Her selfishness
made me very angry.* 她的自私使我十分
生气。

self-pity /ˌself ˈpɪti/ *noun* 名词 (*no plural*
不用复数形式)
when you think too much about your
own problems and feel sorry for yourself
自怜

self-service /ˌself ˈsɜːvɪs/ *adjective*
形容词
In a **self-service** shop or restaurant you
take what you want and then pay for it.
（商店）自选的；（餐馆）自助的： *The
cafe is self-service.* 那是个自助小餐馆。

sell 0̸ /sel/ *verb* 动词 (**sells, selling, sold**
/səʊld/, **has sold**)
to give something to somebody who pays
you money for it 卖；出售： *I sold my
guitar for £200.* 我的吉他卖了 200 英镑。
◇ *He sold me a ticket.* 他卖给我一张票。◇
*Newsagents usually sell chocolates and
cigarettes.* 报刊店一般会出售巧克力和
香烟。➙ Look at **buy**. 见 buy。
sell out, be sold out to be sold

completely so that there are no more left
售完；销售一空： *I went to the shop to
buy a newspaper, but they had all sold
out.* 我去商店买报纸，可是都卖光了。◇
The concert was sold out weeks ago.
音乐会的门票几个星期前就卖光了。
sell out of something to sell all that
you have of something 卖光；脱销：
I'm afraid we've sold out of milk. 抱歉，
我们的牛奶已经卖光。

Sellotape™ /ˈseləteɪp/ (*British* 英式英语)
noun 名词 (*no plural* 不用复数形式)
a type of clear tape that you use for
sticking things like paper and cardboard
together 赛勒塔普胶黏带；透明胶带

semester /sɪˈmestə(r)/ *noun* 名词
(*American* 美式英语)
one of the two periods that the school or
college year is divided into 学期 ➙ Look
at **term** (2). 见 term 第 2 义。

semi- /ˈsemi/ *prefix* 前缀
half or part 半；部分： *She's semi-retired
now* (= she only works some of the time).
她现在半退休了。

semicircle /ˈsemisɜːkl/ *noun* 名词
half a circle 半圆；半圆形： *The children
sat in a semicircle.* 孩子们围坐成一个
半圆形。 ➙ Look at the picture at **circle**.
见 circle 的插图。

semicolon /ˌsemiˈkəʊlən/ *noun* 名词
a mark (;) that you use in writing to
separate parts of a sentence 分号

semi-detached /ˌsemi dɪˈtætʃt/
adjective 形容词
A **semi-detached** house is joined to
another house on one side. （房屋）
半独立式的

semi-final /ˌsemi ˈfaɪnl/ *noun* 名词
one of the two games that are played in
a competition to find out who will play in
the last part of the competition (the final)
半决赛；准决赛

senate /ˈsenət/ *noun* 名词
the Senate one of the parts of the
government in some countries, for
example the US 参议院 ➙ Look at
congress (2). 见 congress 第 2 义。

senator /ˈsenətə(r)/ *noun* 名词
Senator a member of the SENATE 参议员

send 0̸ /send/ *verb* 动词 (**sends,
sending, sent** /sent/, **has sent**)
1 to make something go somewhere,
especially a letter or a message 寄；
发送： *I sent a message to John.* 我给
约翰发了条短信。 ◇ *Have you sent your*

parents a postcard? 你给你父母寄明信片了吗?

2 to make somebody go somewhere 派遣; 打发: *My company is **sending me to** New York.* 我的公司要派我去纽约. ◇ *He was **sent to prison** for ten years.* 他被判入狱十年.

send for somebody or 或 **something** to ask for somebody or something to come to you 请某人来; 召唤: *Send for an ambulance!* 叫救护车来!

send something off to post something 寄出: *I'll send the letter off today.* 我今天会把信寄出.

senior 0━ /'si:niə(r)/ *adjective* 形容词
1 more important than others 级别高的; 资深的: *a senior officer in the army* 高级陆军军官
2 older than others 年龄较大的; 年长的: *a senior pupil* 高年级学生
➲ OPPOSITE **junior** 反义词为 junior

senior citizen /ˌsi:niə 'sɪtɪzn/ *noun* 名词
a person who has reached the age when you can stop work 长者; 老年人 ➲ SAME MEANING **pensioner** 同义词为 pensioner

> 🔊 SPEAKING 表达方式说明
>
> Some people think it is polite to say **senior citizens** or **pensioners** instead of **old people**. 有些人认为用 senior citizen 或 pensioner 比 old people 有礼貌.

sensation /sen'seɪʃn/ *noun* 名词
1 a physical feeling (身体的) 感觉; 知觉: *I felt a burning sensation on my skin.* 我皮肤上有种烧灼的感觉.
2 great excitement or interest 轰动; 哗然: *The film caused a sensation.* 这部电影引起了轰动.

sensational /sen'seɪʃnəl/ *adjective* 形容词
very exciting or interesting 轰动的; 引起哗然的: *sensational news* 爆炸性新闻

sense¹ 0━ /sens/ *noun* 名词
1 (plural 复数形式 senses) the power to see, hear, smell, taste or touch 感觉官能 (即视、听、嗅、味、触五觉): *Dogs have a very good sense of smell.* 狗的嗅觉很灵敏.
2 (no plural 不用复数形式) the ability to feel or understand something 意识; 理解力: *The boy had no sense of right and wrong.* 那个男孩不懂得分辨是非. ◇ *I like him – he's got a great sense of humour.* 我喜欢他, 他很有幽默感.
3 (no plural 不用复数形式) the ability

to think carefully about something and to do the right thing 理智; 判断力; 辨别力: *Did anybody **have the sense to** call the police?* 当时有没有人明智地去报警?
4 (plural 复数形式 senses) a meaning 意思; 含义: *This word has four senses.* 这个词有四个意思.

make sense to be possible to understand 有道理; 讲得通: *What does this sentence mean? It doesn't make sense to me.* 这句话是什么意思? 我看不懂.

sense² /sens/ *verb* 动词 (senses, sensing, sensed /senst/)
to understand or feel something 感觉到; 意识到: *I sensed that he was worried.* 我察觉出他很担心.

sensible 0━ /'sensəbl/ *adjective* 形容词
able to think carefully about something and to do the right thing 理智的; 明智的: *It wasn't very sensible of you to run away.* 你溜走并不明智. ◇ *a sensible answer* 合理的回答 ➲ OPPOSITE **silly** 反义词为 silly
▸ **sensibly** /'sensəbli/ *adverb* 副词: *I hope you'll act sensibly.* 我希望你会理智地行动.

sensitive 0━ /'sensətɪv/ *adjective* 形容词
1 understanding other people's feelings and being careful about them 善解人意的; 体贴的: *He's a very sensitive man.* 他是个很体贴的男人. ➲ OPPOSITE **insensitive** 反义词为 insensitive
2 easily becoming worried or unhappy about something, or about things in general 情绪易波动的; 敏感的: *Don't say anything about her hair – she's very sensitive about it.* 千万别提及她的头发, 她对此很敏感. ➲ OPPOSITE **insensitive** 反义词为 insensitive
3 easily hurt or damaged 易受伤害 (或损坏) 的; 过敏的: *She's got very sensitive skin.* 她皮肤很容易过敏.

sent form of SEND * send 的不同形式

sentence¹ 0━ /'sentəns/ *noun* 名词
1 a group of words that tells you something or asks a question. When a **sentence** is written, it always begins with a capital letter and usually ends with a full stop. 句子: *You don't need to write a long letter. A couple of sentences will be enough.* 信不用写得很长, 几句话就行了.
2 the punishment that a judge gives to somebody in a court of law 判决; 判刑: *20 years in prison was a very harsh sentence.* 监禁 20 年是非常重的判刑.

sentence² /'sentəns/ *verb* 动词
(sentences, sentencing, sentenced
/'sentənst/)
to tell somebody in a court of law what
their punishment will be 宣判；判刑：
*The judge sentenced the man to two years
in prison.* 法官判该名男子入狱两年。

sentimental /ˌsentɪ'mentl/ *adjective*
形容词
producing or showing feelings such as
romantic love or pity that are too strong
or not appropriate 多愁善感的；故作伤感
的：*a sentimental love story* 情意缠绵的
爱情故事 ◇ *I'm so sentimental – I always
cry at weddings!* 我这人太容易感动，总爱
在婚礼上哭！

separate¹ ⚷ /'seprət/ *adjective*
形容词
1 away from something; not together or
not joined 分开的：*The cup broke into
three separate pieces.* 杯子碎成了三块。◇
*In my school, the older children are
separate from the younger ones.* 在我的
学校，年龄较大的学生跟年龄较小的是
分开的。
2 different; not the same 不同的；有区别
的：*We stayed in separate rooms in the
same hotel.* 我们住在同一个旅馆里不同的
房间。
▶ **separately** /'seprətli/ *adverb* 副词：
Shall we pay separately or together? 我们
各付各的还是一起付？

separate² ⚷ /'sepəreɪt/ *verb* 动词
(separates, separating, separated)
1 to stop being together 分开；分离
⊃ SAME MEANING **split up** 同义词为 split
up：*My parents separated when I was
a baby.* 我还是婴孩时父母就分开了。
2 to divide people or things; to keep
people or things away from each other
（使）分开；分割；把…隔离 ⊃ SAME
MEANING **split** 同义词为 split：*The teacher
separated the class into two groups.* 老师
把全班分成两组。
3 to be between two things 隔开；阻隔：
*The Mediterranean separates Europe and
Africa.* 欧洲和非洲之间隔着地中海。
▶ **separation** /ˌsepə'reɪʃn/ *noun* 名词：
*The separation from my family and
friends made me very unhappy.* 与家人和
朋友分离使我感到非常难过。

September ⚷ /sep'tembə(r)/ *noun*
名词
the ninth month of the year 九月

sequence /'si:kwəns/ *noun* 名词
a number of things that happen or come
one after another 一系列的事物；一连串

的事物：*an extraordinary sequence of
events* 不寻常的一连串事件 ◇ *Complete the
following sequence: 2, 4, 8 …* 完成以下
序列：2、4、8…

sergeant /'sɑːdʒənt/ *noun* 名词
an officer in the army or the police
（陆军）中士；（警察）巡佐

serial /'sɪəriəl/ *noun* 名词
a story that is told in parts on television
or radio, or in a magazine（电视或广播）
连续剧；（杂志）连载小说 ⊃ Look at
series (2). 见 series 第 2 义。

series ⚷ /'sɪəriːz/ *noun* 名词 (*plural*
复数形式 series)
1 a number of things of the same kind
that come one after another 一系列；
一连串：*I heard a series of shots and
then silence.* 我听到一连串的枪声，然后
是一片寂静。
2 a number of television or radio
programmes, often on the same subject,
that come one after another（电视或
广播）系列节目：*The first episode of
the new series is on Saturday.* 新系列剧的
第一集在星期六播出。◇ *a TV series on
dinosaurs* 关于恐龙的电视系列节目
⊃ Look at **serial**. 见 serial。

serious ⚷ /'sɪəriəs/ *adjective* 形容词
1 very bad 严重的：*That was a serious
mistake.* 那是个严重的错误。◇ *They had a
serious accident.* 他们出了严重事故。
2 important 重要的；重大的：*a serious
decision* 重大的决定
3 not funny 严肃的：*a serious film* 严肃
的影片
4 If you are **serious**, you are not joking or
playing.（人）认真的，严肃的：*Are you
serious about going to live in Spain?* 你是
真的要去西班牙住吗？◇ *You look very
serious. Is something wrong?* 你表情很
严肃，出什么事了？
▶ **seriousness** /'sɪəriəsnəs/ *noun* 名词
(*no plural* 不用复数形式)：*The boy didn't
understand the seriousness of his crime.*
这个男孩不明白自己罪行的严重性。

seriously ⚷ /'sɪəriəsli/ *adverb* 副词
in a serious way 严重地；严肃地；
认真地：*She's seriously ill.* 她病得很重。
◇ *You're not seriously expecting me to
believe that?* 你不是真的以为我会相信
那个吧？◇ *Smoking can seriously damage
your health.* 吸烟会严重损害健康。
take somebody or 或 **something
seriously** to show that you know
somebody or something is important
认真对待：*Don't take what he says too*

A B C D E F G H I J K L M N O P Q R S T U V W X Y Z

seriously – he's always joking. 别对他说的话太认真，他总爱开玩笑。

sermon /'sɜːmən/ *noun* 名词
a talk that a priest gives in church 布道；讲道

servant /'sɜːvənt/ *noun* 名词
a person who works in another person's house, doing work like cooking and cleaning 仆人；佣人

serve 0ᴇ /sɜːv/ *verb* 动词 (serves, serving, served /sɜːvd/)
1 to give food or drink to somebody 提供（饮食）： *Breakfast is served from 7.30 to 9.00 a.m.* 早餐供应时间是早上 7 点 30 分至 9 点。
2 to help somebody in a shop to buy things 接待，服务（顾客）： *Excuse me, Madam. Are you being served?* 请问，女士，有人接待您吗？
3 to do work for other people 为…服务；履行职责： *During the war he served in the army.* 战争期间，他在陆军服役。
it serves you right words that you use to tell somebody that it is right that a bad thing has happened to them 活该；咎由自取： *'I feel ill.' 'It serves you right for eating so much!'* "我不舒服。""活该，谁叫你吃那么多！"

service 0ᴇ /'sɜːvɪs/ *noun* 名词
1 (*plural* 复数形式 **services**) a business that does useful work for all the people in a country or an area 公共服务： *This town has a good bus service.* 这个镇的公共汽车服务很不错。◇ *the postal service* 邮政服务
2 (*no plural* 不用复数形式) the work that somebody does for customers in a shop, restaurant or hotel （对顾客的）服务，招待： *The food was good but the service was very slow.* 食物很好，但是服务太慢。
3 (*no plural* 不用复数形式) help or work that you do for somebody 工作；服务： *She left the company after ten years of service.* 她在公司工作十年后离开了。
4 (*plural* 复数形式 **services**) the time when somebody looks at a car or machine to see that it is working well 保养；检修： *She takes her car to the garage for a service every six months.* 她每隔半年把汽车送到修理厂检修一次。
5 the services (*plural* 用复数形式) the army, navy and air force 武装力量；军队
6 (*plural* 复数形式 **services**) a meeting in a church with prayers and singing 宗教仪式，礼拜（包括祈祷和唱歌）： *We went to the evening service.* 我们去参加了晚祷。
7 services (*plural* 用复数形式) (*British* 英式

英语) a place at the side of a big road where you can stop to buy petrol and food and use the toilets （公路旁的）服务站 ᴐ SAME MEANING **service station** 同义词为 service station

service station /'sɜːvɪs steɪʃn/ *noun* 名词 (*British* 英式英语)
a place at the side of a big road where you can stop to buy food and petrol and use the toilets （公路旁的）服务站

serviette /ˌsɜːviˈet/ *noun* 名词
a piece of cloth or paper that you use when you are eating to clean your mouth and hands and to keep your clothes clean 餐巾；餐巾纸 ᴐ SAME MEANING **napkin** 同义词为 napkin

session /'seʃn/ *noun* 名词
a period of time spent doing a particular activity （某项活动的）一场，一节： *The first swimming session is at nine o'clock.* 第一场游泳九点钟开始。

set¹ 0ᴇ /set/ *verb* 动词 (sets, setting, set, has set)
1 to put something somewhere 放置；使处于： *Dad set the plate in front of me.* 爸爸把盘子摆在我的面前。
2 to put the action of a play, book or film in a particular time and place （戏剧、书或电影）以…为背景： *The film is set in India in the 1920s.* 这部电影以 20 世纪 20 年代的印度为背景。
3 to make something ready to use or to start working 设定；设置： *I set my alarm clock for seven o'clock.* 我把闹钟设定在七点钟闹响。◇ *Can you set the video recorder* (= make it record a programme)? 你能调录录像机吗？
4 to make something happen 使发生；引发： *They set the school on fire* (= made it start to burn). 他们放火烧学校。
5 When the sun **sets**, it goes down from the sky. （太阳）落下，落山 ᴐ OPPOSITE **rise** 反义词为 rise
6 to decide what something will be; to fix something 确定；决定： *Let's set a date for the meeting.* 让我们把开会日期定一下吧。
7 to give somebody work to do 布置，分配（工作）： *Our teacher set us a lot of homework.* 老师给我们布置了很多家庭作业。
8 to become hard or solid 凝固；凝结： *Wait for the cement to set.* 等水泥凝固变硬。

set off, set out to start a journey 启程；出发；动身： *We set off for Oxford at two o'clock.* 我们两点钟启程去牛津。

set the table (*British* 英式英语) to put knives, forks, plates and other things on the table before you eat 摆放餐具 ⊃ SAME MEANING **lay the table** 同义词为 lay the table

set something up to start something 建立；创建： *The company was set up in 1981.* 这家公司创建于 1981 年。

set² 0ᴇ /set/ *noun* 名词
a group of things of the same kind, or a group of things that you use together 成套的组合；一套；一组： *a set of six glasses* 一套六个的玻璃杯 ◇ *a tool set* 一套工具

settee /se'ti:/ *noun* 名词 (*British* 英式英语)
a long soft seat for more than one person 长沙发 ⊃ SAME MEANING **sofa** 同义词为 sofa

setting /'setɪŋ/ *noun* 名词
the place where something is or where something happens 环境；背景： *The house is in a beautiful setting on top of a hill.* 房子坐落在风景秀丽的山顶上。

settle 0ᴇ /'setl/ *verb* 动词 (**settles, settling, settled** /'setld/)
1 to decide something after talking with somebody; to end a discussion or an argument 商定；议定；解决（纷争）： *That's settled then, we'll go on Monday.* 那么就这样定了，我们星期一出发。 ◇ *Have you settled your argument with Rajit?* 你与拉吉特的争论解决了吗？
2 to go to live in a new place and stay there 定居： *Ruth left England and settled in America.* 鲁思离开英格兰，去美国定居了。
3 to come down and rest somewhere 停歇；停留： *The bird settled on a branch.* 鸟停在了树枝上。
4 to pay the money that you owe 结算，付清（账款）： *Have you settled your bill?* 你付清账单了吗？

settle down
1 to sit down or lie down so that you are comfortable 舒适地坐下（或躺下）： *I settled down in front of the television.* 我在电视机前舒舒服服地坐下来。
2 to become calm and quiet 平静下来；安静下来： *The children settled down and went to sleep.* 孩子们安静下来睡觉去了。
3 to begin to have a calm life in one place（在某地）定居下来，开始过安定的生活： *When are you going to get married and settle down?* 你打算什么时候结婚安定下来呢？

settle in to start to feel happy in a new place（在新的地方）安顿下来，开始

适应： *We only moved to this flat last week and we haven't settled in yet.* 我们上星期才搬进这套公寓，还没安顿好呢。

settlement /'setlmənt/ *noun* 名词
1 an agreement about something after talking or arguing（商讨或争论后达成的）协议： *After days of talks, the two sides reached a settlement.* 经过多天的谈判后，双方达成了协议。
2 a group of homes in a place where no people have lived before（拓荒安家的）定居点，聚落： *a settlement in the forest* 森林中的聚落

seven 0ᴇ /'sevn/ *number* 数词
7 七

seventeen 0ᴇ /ˌsevn'ti:n/ *number* 数词
17 十七

seventeenth 0ᴇ /ˌsevn'ti:nθ/ *adjective, adverb, noun* 形容词，副词，名词
17th 第十七

seventh 0ᴇ /'sevnθ/ *adjective, adverb, noun* 形容词，副词，名词
1 7th 第七
2 one of seven equal parts of something; ⅐ 七分之一

seventieth 0ᴇ /'sevntiəθ/ *adjective, adverb, noun* 形容词，副词，名词
70th 第七十

seventy 0ᴇ /'sevnti/ *number* 数词
1 70 七十
2 the seventies (*plural* 用复数形式) the numbers, years or temperature between 70 and 79 七十几；七十年代
in your seventies between the ages of 70 and 79 * 70 多岁

several 0ᴇ /'sevrəl/ *adjective, pronoun* 形容词，代词
more than two but not many 一些；几个： *I've read this book several times.* 这本书我读了好几遍。 ◇ *Several letters arrived this morning.* 今天上午来了几封信。 ◇ *If you need a pen, there are several on the table.* 如果你要用笔，桌上有几支。

severe /sɪ'vɪə(r)/ *adjective* 形容词 (**severer, severest**)
1 not kind or gentle 严厉的；严苛的： *a severe punishment* 严厉的惩罚
2 very bad 严重的；十分恶劣的： *She suffers from severe headaches.* 她患有严重的头痛。 ◇ *We're expecting a severe* (= very cold) *winter.* 我们将面临一个严冬。
▶ **severely** /sɪ'vɪəli/ *adverb* 副词： *They*

punished him severely. 他们严厉地惩罚了他。◇ She was severely injured in the accident. 她在事故中受了重伤。

sewing 缝纫

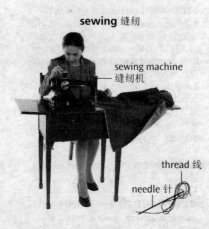

sewing machine 缝纫机

thread 线

needle 针

sew 0— /səʊ/ *verb* 动词 (sews, sewing, sewed /səʊd/, has sewed or 或 has sewn /səʊn/)

> 🔑 **PRONUNCIATION** 读音说明
> The word **sew** sounds just like **so**.
> * sew 读音同 so。

to use a needle and cotton to join pieces of material together or to join something to material 缝；缝制：*He sewed a button on his shirt.* 他把纽扣钉在衬衫上了。◇ *Can you sew?* 你会做针线活吗？

sewing 0— /ˈsəʊɪŋ/ *noun* 名词 (no plural 不用复数形式)
the activity of sewing; something that you sew 缝纫；针线活

sewing machine /ˈsəʊɪŋ məʃiːn/ *noun* 名词
a machine that you use for sewing 缝纫机 ⊃ Look at the picture at **sew**. 见 sew 的插图。

sex 0— /seks/ *noun* 名词
1 (plural 复数形式 sexes) the state of being a male or a female 性别：*What sex is your dog?* 你的狗是公的还是母的？◇ *the male sex* 男性
2 (no plural 不用复数形式) when two people put their bodies together, sometimes to make a baby 性交；性行为：*to have sex* 性交

sexual 0— /ˈsekʃuəl/ *adjective* 形容词
connected with sex 性的；性别的；性行为

的：*a campaign for sexual equality* 争取男女平等的运动 ◇ *the sexual organs* 性器官
▶ **sexually** /ˈsekʃuəli/ *adverb* 副词：*to be sexually active* 性行为活跃

sh! /ʃ/ *exclamation* 感叹词
be quiet!（用以制止别人出声）嘘：*Sh! You'll wake the baby up!* 嘘！你会把宝宝吵醒！

shabby /ˈʃæbi/ *adjective* 形容词 (shabbier, shabbiest)
old and untidy or dirty because it has been used a lot 破旧的；破败的；破烂的：*This coat's getting a bit shabby.* 这件大衣有点破旧了。
▶ **shabbily** /ˈʃæbɪli/ *adverb* 副词：*She was shabbily dressed.* 她穿得破破烂烂的。

shade 背阴

shadow 影子   shade 阴凉处

shade¹ 0— /ʃeɪd/ *noun* 名词
1 (no plural 不用复数形式) a place where it is dark and cool because the sun doesn't shine there 背阴处；阴凉处：*We sat in the shade of a big tree.* 我们坐在大树的树荫下。
2 (plural 复数形式 shades) a thing that keeps strong light from your eyes 遮光物；灯罩：*I bought a new shade for the lamp.* 我买了个新灯罩。
3 (plural 复数形式 shades) how light or dark a colour is 色调；色度：*I'm looking for a shirt in a darker shade of green.* 我正在找一件深绿色的衬衫。
4 shades (plural 用复数形式) (informal 非正式) = SUNGLASSES

shade² /ʃeɪd/ *verb* 动词 (shades, shading, shaded)
to stop light from shining on something 给…遮挡光线：*He shaded his eyes with his hand.* 他用手遮住眼睛。

shadow 0— /ˈʃædəʊ/ *noun* 名词
a dark shape that you see near somebody or something that is in front of the light

阴影；影子：*The dog was chasing its own shadow.* 狗在追着自己的影子。 ⊃ Look at the picture at **shade¹**. 见 shade¹ 的插图。

shady /ˈʃeɪdi/ *adjective* 形容词 (**shadier, shadiest**)
not in the sun 背阴的；遮阳的；阴凉的：*We sat in a shady part of the garden.* 我们坐在花园里的阴凉处。

shake 摇动

They **shook** hands.
他们握手。

He **shook** his head.
他摇头。

shake 0━ /ʃeɪk/ *verb* 动词 (**shakes, shaking shook** /ʃʊk/, **has shaken** /ˈʃeɪkən/)
to move quickly from side to side or up and down; to make something do this （使）摇动，抖动，颤动：*The house shakes when trains go past.* 火车经过时房子会晃动。 ◇ *He was shaking with fear.* 他吓得直哆嗦。 ◇ *Shake the bottle before opening it.* 打开瓶子前先摇一摇。 ◇ *An explosion shook the windows.* 爆炸撼动了窗户。

shake hands to hold somebody's hand and move it up and down when you meet them 握手

shake your head to move your head from side to side to say 'no' 摇头（表示否定）

shaken *form of* SHAKE * shake 的不同形式

shaky /ˈʃeɪki/ *adjective* 形容词 (**shakier, shakiest**)
1 shaking because you are ill or frightened （因生病或恐惧）发抖的，颤抖的：*You've got shaky hands.* 你的手发抖。
2 not firm; not strong 晃动的；不稳固的：*That ladder looks a little shaky.* 那梯子看上去摇摇晃晃的。

shall 0━ /ʃəl；ʃæl/ *modal verb* 情态动词

🔑 GRAMMAR 语法说明
The negative form of **shall** is **shall not** or the short form **shan't** /ʃɑːnt/.
* shall 的否定式为 shall not 或缩写为

shan't /ʃɑːnt/: *I shan't be there.* 我不会在那里的。
The short form of **shall** is **'ll**. We often use this. * shall 的缩略式为 'll，十分常用：*I'll* (= I shall) *see you tomorrow.* 我明天见你。

1 a word that you use when you are asking, offering or suggesting something （表示询问、提议或建议）：*What time shall I come?* 我什么时间过来好呢？ ◇ *Shall I close the window?* 我关上窗好吗？ ◇ *What shall we do tomorrow?* 我们明天做什么好呢？ ◇ *Shall we go now?* 我们现在走好吗？
2 (*formal* 正式) a word that you use instead of 'will' with 'I' and 'we' to show the future （与 I、we 连用，代替 will，表示将来）：*I shall see you tomorrow.* 我明天见你。 ⊃ Look at the note at **modal verb**. 见 modal verb 条的注释。

shallow 浅

shallow 浅   **deep** 深

shallow /ˈʃæləʊ/ *adjective* 形容词 (**shallower, shallowest**)
not deep; with not much water （水）浅的：*This part of the river is shallow – we can walk across.* 这段河很浅，我们可以趟水过去。 ⊃ OPPOSITE **deep** 反义词为 deep

shame 0━ /ʃeɪm/ *noun* 名词 (**no plural** 不用复数形式)
1 the unhappy feeling that you have when you have done something wrong or stupid 羞耻；羞愧；惭愧：*I was filled with* (= felt a lot of) *shame after I lied to my parents.* 我对父母撒了谎之后感到非常羞愧。 ⊃ The adjective is **ashamed**. 形容词为 ashamed。
2 a fact or situation that makes you feel sad or disappointed 憾事；令人失望的情况 ⊃ SAME MEANING **pity** 同义词为 pity：*It's a shame you can't come to the party.* 你不能来参加聚会，真可惜。 ◇ *'Sally's not*

well.' *'What a shame!'* "萨莉不舒服。"
"真糟糕！"

shameless /ˈʃeɪmləs/ *adjective* 形容词
doing bad things without caring what
other people think 不知羞耻的；无耻的；
不要脸的: *It was a shameless attempt to
copy somebody else's work.* 试图抄袭别人
的作品是很无耻的。

shampoo /ʃæmˈpuː/ *noun* 名词 (*plural*
复数形式 **shampoos**)
a special liquid for washing your hair
洗发水；洗发剂: *a bottle of shampoo*
一瓶洗发水

▶ **shampoo** *verb* 动词 (**shampoos**,
shampooing, **shampooed** /ʃæmˈpuːd/):
How often do you shampoo your hair?
你多长时间洗一次头？

shan't /ʃɑːnt/ *short for* SHALL NOT * shall
not 的缩略式

shapes 形状

square 正方形　circle 圆形　oval 椭圆形

rectangle 长方形　star 星形

crescent
新月形　triangle
三角形　diamond
菱形

shape¹ ⚬ᴡ /ʃeɪp/ *noun* 名词
1 (*plural* 复数形式 **shapes**) what you see if
you draw a line round something; the
form of something 形状；外形: *What
shape is the table – round or square?* 那张
桌子是什么形状，是圆的还是方的？ ◇
*I bought a bowl **in the shape of** a fish.*
我买了一个鱼形的碗。◇ *Circles, squares
and triangles are all different shapes.*
圆形、正方形和三角形都是不同的形状。
2 (*no plural* 不用复数形式) the physical
condition of somebody or something
身体状况；状态: *He was **in bad shape**
after the accident.* 他出事故以后身体很

不好。◇ *I like to **keep in shape** (= keep fit)
by exercising every day.* 我要每天锻炼来保
持健康。

out of shape
1 not having the right shape 变形；走样:
*My jumper went out of shape when I
washed it.* 我的套头毛衣洗过之后走样了。
2 (*used about a person*) not in good
physical condition （人）身体不好，
不健康: *I didn't realize how out of shape
I was!* 我没意识到我身体竟然这么差！

shape² ⚬ᴡ /ʃeɪp/ *verb* 动词 (**shapes**,
shaping, **shaped** /ʃeɪpt/)
to give a certain shape to something
使成为…形状: *She **shaped** the clay **into**
a pot.* 她把黏土捏成盆状。

shaped ⚬ᴡ /ʃeɪpt/ *adjective* 形容词
having a certain shape 有…形状的:
*He gave me a birthday card **shaped like**
a cat.* 他送给我一张猫形的生日贺卡。◇
a heart-shaped box of chocolates 心形盒装
巧克力

share¹ ⚬ᴡ /ʃeə(r)/ *verb* 动词 (**shares**,
sharing, **shared** /ʃeəd/)
1 to divide something between two or
more people 分享；分配: ***Share** these
sweets **with** your friends.* 把这些糖与你的
朋友分着吃吧。◇ *We **shared** a large pizza
between three of us.* 我们三个人分吃了
一个大比萨饼。
2 to have or use something with another
person 共有；共用: *I **share** a bedroom
with my sister.* 我和妹妹共用一间卧室。

share² ⚬ᴡ /ʃeə(r)/ *noun* 名词
1 a part of something bigger that each
person has （分得的）一份: *Here is your
share of the money.* 这份钱是你的。◇
*I did my **share** of the work.* 我做完了我那
部分的工作。
2 one of equal parts which the value of
a company is divided into and that are
sold to people who want to own part of
the company 股份；股票: *a fall in share
prices* 股价的下跌

shark 鲨鱼

fin 鳍

shark /ʃɑːk/ *noun* 名词
a big fish that lives in the sea. Some **sharks** have sharp teeth and are dangerous. 鲨鱼

sharp¹ ○━ /ʃɑːp/ *adjective* 形容词
(**sharper, sharpest**)
1 with an edge or point that cuts or makes holes easily 尖利的；锋利的；锐利的： *a sharp knife* 锋利的刀 ◊ *a sharp needle* 尖针 ◔ OPPOSITE **blunt** 反义词为 blunt
2 strong and sudden 剧烈的；骤然的： *a sharp bend in the road* 路上的急转弯 ◊ *I felt a sharp pain in my leg.* 我感到腿上一阵剧痛。
3 clear and easy to see 清晰的；鲜明的： *We could see the sharp outline of the mountains against the sky.* 我们看见天空映衬下群山清晰的轮廓。
4 able to see, hear or learn well 敏锐的；灵敏的；敏捷的： *She's got a very sharp mind.* 她头脑非常机敏。 ◊ *sharp eyes* 敏锐的眼睛
5 sudden and angry 尖锐的；尖刻的；严厉的： *sharp words* 尖锐的言辞
▶ **sharply** /ʃɑːpli/ *adverb* 副词： *The road bends sharply to the left.* 道路陡然向左拐去。 ◊ *'Go away!' he said sharply.* "走开！"他厉声说道。

sharp² /ʃɑːp/ *adverb* 副词
1 exactly 准确地； （时间上）准点地： *Be here at six o'clock sharp.* 六点整到这里。
2 with a big change of direction （方向）急转： *Turn sharp right at the next corner.* 在下一个路口向右急转。

sharpen /ʃɑːpən/ *verb* 动词 (**sharpens, sharpening, sharpened** /ʃɑːpənd/)
to make something sharp or sharper 使（更）锋利（或清晰等）： *They sharpened all the knives.* 他们把所有的刀都磨快了。

sharpener /ʃɑːpnə(r)/ *noun* 名词
a thing that you use for making something sharp 磨具；削具： *a pencil sharpener* 铅笔刀 ◔ Look at Picture Dictionary page **P11**. 见彩页 P11。

shatter /ʃætə(r)/ *verb* 动词 (**shatters, shattering, shattered** /ʃætəd/)
to break into very small pieces; to break something into very small pieces （使）破碎，变成碎片： *The glass hit the floor and shattered.* 玻璃杯掉到地上摔碎了。 ◊ *The explosion shattered the windows.* 爆炸把窗户都震碎了。

shave /ʃeɪv/ *verb* 动词 (**shaves, shaving, shaved** /ʃeɪvd/)
to cut hair off your face or body by cutting it very close with a special knife (called a razor) 剃须；刮脸；除毛： *He shaves every morning.* 他每天早晨都刮胡子。
▶ **shave** *noun* 名词： *I haven't had a shave today.* 我今天还没刮脸。

shaver /ʃeɪvə(r)/ *noun* 名词
an electric tool that you use for SHAVING 电动剃须刀 ◔ Look at **razor**. 见 razor。

shawl /ʃɔːl/ *noun* 名词
a big piece of cloth that a woman wears round her shoulders, or that you put round a baby （女用）披肩，披巾；襁褓

she ○━ /ʃiː/ *pronoun* 代词 (*plural* 复数形式 **they**)
a woman or girl who the sentence is about 她： *'Where's your sister?' 'She's* (= she is) *at work.'* "你妹妹在哪里？" "她在上班。"

shears 园艺剪刀

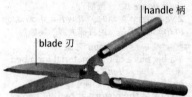

blade 刀　　　handle 柄

shears /ʃɪəz/ *noun* 名词 (*plural* 用复数形式)
a tool like a very large pair of scissors that you use for cutting things in the garden 园艺剪刀

shed¹ /ʃed/ *noun* 名词
a small building where you keep things or animals 贮物的棚屋；畜棚： *We keep our tools in the garden shed.* 我们把工具放在园艺工具棚。

shed² /ʃed/ *verb* 动词 (**sheds, shedding, shed, has shed**)
to lose something because it falls off 脱落；蜕下： *The snake shed its skin.* 蛇蜕皮了。

she'd /ʃiːd/ *short for* SHE HAD; SHE WOULD
* she had 和 she would 的缩略式

sheep ○━ /ʃiːp/ *noun* 名词 (*plural* 复数形式 **sheep**)
an animal that people keep on farms for its meat and its wool 羊；绵羊

A B C D E F G H I J K L M N O P Q R S T U V W X Y Z

A B C D E F G H I J K L M N O P Q R **S** T U V W X Y Z

sheep 绵羊

sheep 绵羊　　**lamb** 羔羊

sheer /ʃɪə(r)/ *adjective* 形容词
1 complete 完全的；纯粹的；十足的:
sheer nonsense 一派胡言
2 very steep 陡峭的: *It was a sheer drop
to the sea.* 那是一道直插大海的陡坡。

sheet 0= /ʃiːt/ *noun* 名词
1 a big piece of thin material for a bed
床单；被单: *I put some clean sheets
on the bed.* 我在床上铺了干净的床单。
⊃ Look at the picture at **bed**. 见 bed 的
插图。
2 a thin flat piece of something like
paper, glass or metal 一张；薄片；薄块:
a sheet of writing paper 一张信纸

shells 壳

shell 壳

seashell 海贝壳　　**snail** 蜗牛

shell 蛋壳　　shell 果壳

chick 小鸡　　**nuts** 坚果

shelf 0= /ʃelf/ *noun* 名词 (*plural* 复数
形式 shelves /ʃelvz/)
a long flat piece of wood on a wall or
in a cupboard, where things can stand
（竖立物品的）架子，搁板: *Put the
plates on the shelf.* 把盘子放在搁板上。◇
bookshelves 书架 ⊃ Look at Picture
Dictionary page **P10**. 见彩页 P10。

shell 0= /ʃel/ *noun* 名词
the hard outside part of birds' eggs and
nuts and of some animals （鸟蛋、坚果
或某些动物的）壳 ⊃ Look also at **seashell**.
亦见 seashell。

she'll /ʃiːl/ *short for* SHE WILL * she will 的
缩略式

shellfish /'ʃelfɪʃ/ *noun* 名词 (*plural* 复数
形式 shellfish)
a kind of animal that lives in water and
that has a shell 水生有壳类动物

shelter[1] /'ʃeltə(r)/ *noun* 名词
1 (*no plural* 不用复数形式) protection
from bad weather or danger 遮蔽；庇护;
避难: *We took shelter from the rain
under a tree.* 我们在树下避雨。◇ *People
ran for shelter when the bombs started to
fall.* 炮弹开始袭来，人们四处奔跑躲避。
2 (*plural* 复数形式 shelters) a place that
protects you from bad weather or danger
遮蔽处；避难处；庇护所: *a bus shelter*
(= for people who are waiting at a bus
stop) 公共汽车候车亭

shelter[2] /'ʃeltə(r)/ *verb* 动词 (shelters,
sheltering, sheltered /'ʃeltəd/)
1 to make somebody or something safe
from bad weather or danger 遮护；庇护:
The trees shelter the house from the wind.
那些树给房子挡风。
2 to go to a place where you will be safe
from bad weather or danger （到某处）
躲避: *Let's shelter from the rain under
that tree.* 咱们到那棵树下去避雨吧。

shelves *plural of* SHELF * shelf 的复数形式

shepherd /'ʃepəd/ *noun* 名词
a person who looks after sheep 牧羊人

she's /ʃiːz/ *short for* SHE IS; SHE HAS * she is
和 she has 的缩略式

shield[1] /ʃiːld/ *noun* 名词
a big piece of metal, wood or leather that
soldiers carried in front of their bodies
when they were fighting in wars long ago.
Some police officers carry **shields** now.
（旧时的）盾；（警用）防暴盾牌

shield[2] /ʃiːld/ *verb* 动词 (shields,
shielding, shielded)
to keep somebody or something safe

from danger or from being hurt 庇护；
掩护：*She shielded her eyes from the sun
with her hand.* 她用手遮住眼睛避开阳光。

shift¹ /ʃɪft/ *verb* 动词 (shifts, shifting,
shifted)
to move something from one place to
another 移动；挪动：*Can you help me to
shift the bed? I want to sweep the floor.*
你能帮我挪一下床吗？我想扫扫地。

shift² /ʃɪft/ *noun* 名词
1 a change in what people think about
something（想法的）改变，转变：*There
has been a shift in public opinion away
from the war.* 公众舆论已经转变，不再
讨论战争。
2 a group of workers who begin work
when another group finishes 轮班职工：
the night shift 夜班职工

shin /ʃɪn/ *noun* 名词
the bone in the front part of your leg
from your knee and your foot 胫骨

shine ⊶ /ʃaɪn/ *verb* 动词 (shines,
shining, shone /ʃɒn/, has shone)
1 to give out light 发光；照耀：*The sun is
shining.* 太阳照耀着。
2 to be bright 发亮：*I polished the silver
until it shone.* 我把银器擦得发亮。
3 to direct a light at somebody or
something 使…照向：*Don't shine your
torch in my eyes!* 别用手电筒照我的眼睛！

shiny ⊶ /ˈʃaɪni/ *adjective* 形容词
(shinier, shiniest)
causing a bright effect when in the sun or
in light 闪闪发亮的；闪耀的：*The new
shampoo leaves your hair soft and shiny.*
这种新洗发液使你的头发柔顺光亮。◇
He's got a shiny new car. 他买了辆锃亮的
新车。

ship ⊶ /ʃɪp/ *noun* 名词
a big boat for long journeys on the sea
大船；轮船；舰：*We went to India by
ship.* 我们坐船去印度了。⊃ Look at
Picture Dictionary page **P1**. 见彩页 P1。
▸ **ship** *verb* 动词 (ships, shipping,
shipped /ʃɪpt/)：*New Zealand ships meat
to Britain.* 新西兰用船把肉类运往英国。

shipping /ˈʃɪpɪŋ/ *noun* 名词 (no plural
不用复数形式)
ships in general or the carrying of goods
by ships 船舶；（货物的）航运，海运：
The port is now open to shipping. 港口现已
通航。◇ *a shipping company* 航运公司

shipwreck /ˈʃɪprek/ *noun* 名词
an accident at sea when a ship breaks
in bad weather or on rocks 船舶失事；
海难

be **shipwrecked** to be on a ship when it
is in a **shipwreck** 遭遇海难：*They were
shipwrecked off the coast of Portugal.* 他们
的船只在葡萄牙海岸附近失事。

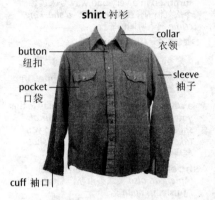

shirt 衬衫

collar
衣领

button
纽扣

sleeve
袖子

pocket
口袋

cuff 袖口

shirt ⊶ /ʃɜːt/ *noun* 名词

🔎 **PRONUNCIATION** 读音说明
The word **shirt** sounds like **hurt**. * shirt
读音像 hurt。

a thin piece of clothing that you wear on
the top part of your body 衬衫

shiver /ˈʃɪvə(r)/ *verb* 动词 (shivers,
shivering, shivered /ˈʃɪvəd/)
to shake because you are cold, frightened
or ill（因寒冷、恐惧或生病）发抖，颤抖：
We were shivering with cold. 我们冷得直
哆嗦。
▸ **shiver** *noun* 名词：*Sue gave a shiver
and pulled her coat around her.* 苏打了个
冷颤，便把大衣裹紧了。

shock¹ ⊶ /ʃɒk/ *noun* 名词
1 a very bad surprise 震惊；惊愕：*The
news of his death came as a shock to all
of us.* 他的死讯传来，我们都感到十分
震惊。
2 a sudden pain when electricity goes
through your body 电休克；触电：
电击：*Don't touch that wire – you'll get
an electric shock.* 别碰那根电线，你会
触电的。

shock² ⊶ /ʃɒk/ *verb* 动词 (shocks,
shocking, shocked /ʃɒkt/)
to give somebody a very bad surprise;
to upset somebody 使震惊；使惊愕；
使难过：*I was shocked by his behaviour.*
我对他的行为感到震惊。

A
B
C
D
E
F
G
H
I
J
K
L
M
N
O
P
Q
R
S
T
U
V
W
X
Y
Z

A
B
C
D
E
F
G
H
I
J
K
L
M
N
O
P
Q
R
S
T
U
V
W
X
Y
Z

▶ **shocked** /ˈʃɒkt/ *adjective* 形容词:
Don't look so shocked – I did warn you!
别那么惊讶, 我提醒过你的!

shocking ⚬ᴛ /ˈʃɒkɪŋ/ *adjective* 形容词
making you feel upset, angry, or
surprised in a very bad way 令人震惊的;
令人气愤的; 使人难过的: *a shocking
crime* 骇人听闻的罪行

shoe ⚬ᴛ /ʃuː/ *noun* 名词

> 🔍 **PRONUNCIATION** 读音说明
> The word **shoe** sounds like **who**. * shoe
> 读音像 who。

a covering made of leather or plastic that
you wear on your foot 鞋: *a pair of
shoes* 一双鞋 ◇ *What size shoes do you
take?* 你穿多大号的鞋? ◇ *a shoe shop*
鞋店

shoelace /ˈʃuːleɪs/ (*also* 亦作 **lace**)
(*American also* 美式英语亦作 **shoestring**
/ˈʃuːstrɪŋ/) *noun* 名词
a long thin piece of material like string
that you tie to close a shoe 鞋带: *Tie
your shoelaces.* 系好你的鞋带。 ⊃ Look at
the picture at **shoe**. 见 shoe 的插图。

shone *form of* SHINE * shine 的不同形式

shook *form of* SHAKE * shake 的不同形式

shoot¹ ⚬ᴛ /ʃuːt/ *verb* 动词 (shoots,
shooting, shot /ʃɒt/, has shot)
1 to fire a gun or another weapon; to
hurt or kill a person or an animal with
a gun 射击; 开枪; 射伤; 枪杀: *She shot*

a bird. 她射中了一只鸟。 ◇ *The police
officer was shot in the arm.* 那名警察的
胳膊中枪了。
2 to move quickly or suddenly 急速
移动; 飞驰: *The car shot past us.*
那辆车从我们旁边飞驰而过。
3 to make a film 拍摄 (电影): *They are
shooting a film about the war.* 他们正在
拍摄一部战争片。

shoot² /ʃuːt/ *noun* 名词
a new part of a plant 嫩芽; 新枝: *The
first shoots appear in spring.* 新芽在春天
长出来。 ⊃ Look at the picture at **plant¹**.
见 plant¹ 的插图。

shop¹ ⚬ᴛ /ʃɒp/ (*British* 英式英语)
(*American* 美式英语 **store**) *noun* 名词
a building where you buy things 商店;
店铺: *a bookshop* 书店 ◇ *Do you need
anything from the shops?* 你要从商店买
什么东西吗?

shop² ⚬ᴛ /ʃɒp/ *verb* 动词 (shops,
shopping, shopped /ʃɒpt/)
to go to buy things from shops (去商店)
买东西, 购物: *I'm **shopping** for some
new clothes.* 我正在商店买新衣服。

> 🔍 **SPEAKING** 表达方式说明
> It is more usual to say **go shopping**.
> 较常用 go shopping。

▶ **shopper** /ˈʃɒpə(r)/ *noun* 名词: *The
streets were full of shoppers.* 街上到处都是
购物的人。

shoes 鞋

slippers 拖鞋

sandal 凉鞋

sole 鞋底 ——

wellingtons (*British* 英式英语)
rubber boots (*American* 美式英语)
长筒橡胶雨靴

buckle
搭扣

boot 靴子

shoelace
(*also* 亦作 **lace**)
鞋带

trainers (*British*
英式英语) **sneakers**
(*American* 美式英语)
运动鞋

shoes 鞋

flip-flops (*British*
英式英语) **thongs**
(*American* 美式英语)
人字拖鞋

shoe 鞋

heel
鞋后跟

shop assistant /ˈʃɒp əsɪstənt/ (*British* 英式英语) (*American* 美式英语 **sales clerk, clerk**) *noun* 名词
a person who works in a shop 店员；售货员 ⊃ Look at Picture Dictionary page **P12**. 见彩页 P12。

shopkeeper /ˈʃɒpkiːpə(r)/ (*British* 英式英语) (*American* 美式英语 **storekeeper**) *noun* 名词
a person who owns a small shop（小商店的）店主

shoplifting /ˈʃɒplɪftɪŋ/ *noun* 名词 (*no plural* 不用复数形式)
the crime of stealing things from shops 店铺行窃（罪）：*He was accused of shoplifting.* 他被控店铺行窃。
▶ **shoplifter** /ˈʃɒplɪftə(r)/ *noun* 名词：*Shoplifters will be prosecuted.* 在本店行窃者会被起诉。

shopping ⌒ /ˈʃɒpɪŋ/ *noun* 名词 (*no plural* 不用复数形式)
1 buying things from shops 买东西；购物：*She does her shopping after work.* 她下班后去商店买东西。◇ *I usually go shopping at the weekend.* 我通常周末去购物。
2 the things that you have bought in a shop（在商店）购买的东西：*Will you carry my shopping for me?* 你帮我提一下买的东西好吗？

shopping centre /ˈʃɒpɪŋ sentə(r)/ (*British* 英式英语) (*American* 美式英语 **shopping mall, mall**) *noun* 名词
a large building that has a lot of shops, restaurants, etc. inside it 购物中心 ⊃ Look at Picture Dictionary page **P13**. 见彩页 P13。

shore /ʃɔː(r)/ *noun* 名词
the land next to the sea or a lake 海岸；湖岸：*The swimmer kept close to the shore.* 那个游泳的人一直没有游离岸边。

short ⌒ /ʃɔːt/ *adjective* 形容词 (**shorter, shortest**)
1 a small distance from one end to the other（长度或距离）短的：*Her hair is very short.* 她的头发很短。◇ *We live a short distance from the beach.* 我们住的地方离海滩很近。⊃ OPPOSITE **long** 反义词为 long
2 less tall than most people 矮的：*I'm too short to reach the top shelf.* 我太矮了，够不着最上层架子。◇ *a short fat man* 矮胖的男子 ⊃ OPPOSITE **tall** 反义词为 tall
3 lasting for only a little time（时间）短的，短暂的；短期的：*The film was very short.* 那部电影很短。◇ *a short holiday*

短假期 ⊃ OPPOSITE **long** 反义词为 long
be short of something to not have enough of something 短缺；不足：*I'm short of money this month.* 我这个月缺钱。
for short as a short way of saying or writing something 简称；简写：*My sister's name is Deborah, but we call her 'Deb' for short.* 我妹妹名叫 Deborah，我们简称她为 Deb。
short for something a short way of saying or writing something 简称；简写：*'Tom' is short for 'Thomas'.* * Tom 是 Thomas 的简称。

shortage /ˈʃɔːtɪdʒ/ *noun* 名词
a situation when there is not enough of something 短缺；不足；缺少：*a water shortage* 用水短缺 ◇ *There is a shortage of good teachers.* 优秀的教师短缺。

short cut /ˌʃɔːt ˈkʌt/ *noun* 名词
a shorter way to get somewhere 近路；捷径：*We took a short cut to school across the field.* 我们穿过田野抄近路去上学。

shorten /ˈʃɔːtn/ *verb* 动词 (**shortens, shortening, shortened** /ˈʃɔːtnd/)
to become shorter or to make something shorter（使）变短，缩短：*The trousers were too long, so I shortened them.* 裤子太长，所以我把它改短了。

shortly /ˈʃɔːtli/ *adverb* 副词
soon 很快；不久：*The doctor will see you shortly, Mr Smith.* 史密斯先生，医生很快就会给你看病。◇ *We left shortly after six o'clock.* 我们六点过后没多久就走了。

shorts /ʃɔːts/ *noun* 名词 (*plural* 用复数形式)
1 short trousers that end above your knees 短裤：*a pair of shorts* 一条短裤 ⊃ Look at Picture Dictionary page **P5**. 见彩页 P5。
2 (*American* 美式英语) a piece of loose clothing that men wear under their trousers 男用平脚内裤

shot¹ *form of* SHOOT¹ * shoot¹ 的不同形式

shot² ⌒ /ʃɒt/ *noun* 名词
1 the action of firing a gun, or the noise that this makes 射击；开枪；开炮；枪炮声：*He fired a shot.* 他开了一枪。
2 the action of kicking or hitting a ball in a sport like football 击球；射门；投篮：*a shot at goal* 射门
3 a photograph 照片：*This is a good shot of you.* 你这张照片拍得不错。

A
B
C
D
E
F
G
H
I
J
K
L
M
N
O
P
Q
R
S
T
U
V
W
X
Y
Z

should /ʃʊd/ *modal verb* 情态动词

> 🔊 PRONUNCIATION 读音说明
> The word **should** sounds like **good**, because we don't say the letter **l** in this word. * should 读音像 good，因为 l 在这里不发音。

> 🔊 GRAMMAR 语法说明
> The negative form of **should** is **should not** or the short form **shouldn't** /ˈʃʊdnt/. * should 的否定形式为 should not 或缩写为 shouldn't /ˈʃʊdnt/。

1 a word that you use to tell or ask somebody what is the right thing to do 应该；应当 ⟳ SAME MEANING **ought to** 同义词为 ought to： *If you feel ill, you should stay in bed.* 你要是觉得不舒服就应该卧床。◇ *You shouldn't eat so much chocolate.* 你不该吃那么多巧克力。◇ *I'm tired. I shouldn't have gone to bed so late.* 我很累，我不应该那么晚睡的。
2 a word that you use to give or ask somebody for advice（表示提出或征询建议）应该： *You should try that new restaurant.* 你应该去试试那家新餐馆。◇ *Should I invite him to the party?* 我该邀请他参加聚会吗？
3 a word that you use to say what you think will happen or what you think is true（表示预期）应该会： *They should be here soon.* 他们应该很快就到。
4 the word that we use for 'shall' in the past, when we say what somebody said（用于间接引语，作 shall 的过去时）： *We asked if we should help her.* 我们问过是否要帮助她。⟳ Look at the note at **modal verb**. 见 modal verb 条的注释。

shoulder /ˈʃəʊldə(r)/ *noun* 名词

> 🔊 PRONUNCIATION 读音说明
> The word **shoulder** sounds like **older**. * shoulder 读音像 older。

the part of your body between your neck and your arm 肩膀；肩部 ⟳ Look at Picture Dictionary page **P4**. 见彩页 P4。

shoulder bag /ˈʃəʊldə bæg/ *noun* 名词
a type of bag that you carry over one shoulder with a long narrow piece of cloth or leather 肩包 ⟳ Look at Picture Dictionary page **P5**. 见彩页 P5。

shouldn't /ˈʃʊdnt/ *short for* SHOULD NOT * should not 的缩略式

should've /ˈʃʊdəv/ *short for* SHOULD HAVE * should have 的缩略式

shout /ʃaʊt/ *verb* 动词 (shouts, shouting, shouted)
to speak very loudly 大声说；叫；喊： *Don't shout at me!* 别冲我大声嚷嚷！◇ *'Go back!' she shouted.* "回去！" 她喊道。
▶ **shout** *noun* 名词： *We heard a shout for help.* 我们听见有人高声呼救。

shove /ʃʌv/ *verb* 动词 (shoves, shoving, shoved /ʃʌvd/)
to push somebody or something in a rough way 推搡；猛推；乱挤： *They shoved him through the door.* 他们连推带搡把他赶了出门。

shovel¹ /ˈʃʌvl/ *noun* 名词
a tool that you use for picking up and moving earth, sand or snow 锹；铲子

shovel² /ˈʃʌvl/ *verb* 动词 (*British* 英式英语 shovels, shovelling, shovelled /ˈʃʌvld/) (*American* 美式英语 shoveling, shoveled)
to move something with a **shovel** 铲；铲起： *We shovelled the snow off the path.* 我们把小路上的雪铲走了。

show¹ /ʃəʊ/ *verb* 动词 (shows, showing, showed /ʃəʊd/, has shown /ʃəʊn/ or 或 has showed)

> 🔊 PRONUNCIATION 读音说明
> The word **show** sounds like **go**. * show 读音像 go。

1 to let somebody see something 出示；展示： *She showed me her holiday photos.* 她给我看了她度假时拍的照片。◇ *You have to show your ticket on the train.* 在火车上要出示车票。
2 to make something clear; to explain something to somebody 显示；表明；演示；解释： *Can you show me how to use the computer?* 你能给我演示一下怎么用这台电脑吗？◇ *Research shows that most people get too little exercise.* 研究表明大多数人缺乏锻炼。
3 to appear or be seen 显现；露出；显出： *The anger showed in his face.* 他脸上露出了生气的样子。
show off to talk loudly or do something silly to make people notice you 招摇；显摆： *Joyce was showing off by driving too fast.* 乔伊斯开车开得飞快来炫耀。
show something off to let people see something that is new or beautiful 炫耀；夸示： *James wanted to show off his new jacket.* 詹姆斯想向人炫耀他的新夹克。
show somebody round to go with somebody and show them everything in a building 领某人参观： *David showed me round the school.* 戴维带我参观了学校。

show up (*informal* 非正式) to arrive
露面；出现：*What time did they show up?*
他们什么时候出现的？

show² ⊶/ʃəʊ/ *noun* 名词
1 something that you watch at the
theatre or on television 演出；表演；
节目：*a comedy show* 喜剧表演 ◇ *Did
you enjoy the show?* 你喜欢这场演出吗？
2 a group of things in one place that
people go to see 展出；展览：*a flower
show* 花展 ◇ *The paintings are on show at
the National Gallery until 15 May.* 画作在
国家美术馆展出至 5 月 15 日。

shower² ⊶/ˈʃaʊə(r)/ *noun* 名词
1 a place where you can wash by
standing under water that falls from
above you 淋浴间；淋浴室：*There's
a shower in the bathroom.* 浴室里有
淋浴间。 ⤷ Look at Picture Dictionary
page **P10**. 见彩页 P10.
2 the act of washing yourself in a shower
淋浴：*I had a shower after the tennis
match.* 我在网球比赛后冲了个澡。
3 rain that falls for a short time 阵雨：
*The day will be cloudy, with occasional
heavy showers.* 日间多云，时有大雨。

shown *form of* SHOW¹ * show¹ 的不同形式

shrank *form of* SHRINK * shrink 的不同
形式

shred /ʃred/ *noun* 名词
a small thin piece of material that has
been cut or torn off （切或撕的）丝，
细条，碎片：*shreds of paper* 碎纸

shrewd /ʃruːd/ *adjective* 形容词
(**shrewder, shrewdest**)
able to make good decisions because you
understand people or situations well
精明的；有眼光的：*She's a very shrewd
businesswoman.* 她是个非常精明的商人。

shriek /ʃriːk/ *verb* 动词 (**shrieks,
shrieking, shrieked** /ʃriːkt/)
to make a loud high cry 尖叫：*She
shrieked with fear* (= because she was
afraid). 她吓得尖叫起来。
▶ **shriek** *noun* 名词：*He gave a shriek of
pain.* 他疼得发出一声尖叫。

shrill /ʃrɪl/ *adjective* 形容词 (**shriller,
shrillest**)
A **shrill** sound is high and loud. 刺耳的；
尖声的：*a shrill whistle* 刺耳的哨子声

shrimp /ʃrɪmp/ *noun* 名词
1 (*British* 英式英语) a small sea animal
with a shell and a lot of legs that turns
pink when you cook it. **Shrimps** are
smaller than PRAWNS. 虾；小虾

2 *American English for* PRAWN 美式英语，
即 prawn

shrine /ʃraɪn/ *noun* 名词
a special place that is important to people
for religious reasons 圣地；圣祠；神庙

shrink 缩小

'Oh no! My T-shirt has **shrunk**!'
不好了！我的 T 恤衫缩水了！

shrink /ʃrɪŋk/ *verb* 动词 (**shrinks,
shrinking, shrank** /ʃræŋk/ or 或 **shrunk**
/ʃrʌŋk/, **has shrunk**)
to become smaller or to make something
smaller （使）收缩，缩小：*My jeans
shrank when I washed them.* 我的牛仔裤
洗后缩水了。

shrivel /ˈʃrɪvl/ *verb* 动词 (*British* 英式英语
shrivels, shrivelling, shrivelled /ˈʃrɪvld/)
(*American* 美式英语 **shriveling, shriveled**)
to become smaller, especially because of
dry conditions 枯萎；干枯：*The plants
shrivelled up and died in the hot weather.*
植物在炎热的天气下枯死了。

shrub /ʃrʌb/ *noun* 名词
a plant like a small low tree 灌木

shrug /ʃrʌɡ/ *verb* 动词 (**shrugs, shrugging,
shrugged** /ʃrʌɡd/)
to move your shoulders to show that
you do not know or do not care about
something 耸肩（表示不知道或不在乎）：
*I asked her where Sam was but she just
shrugged.* 我问她萨姆在哪里，她只是耸了
耸肩。 ⤷ Look at the picture on the next
page. 见下页的插图。
▶ **shrug** *noun* 名词：*He answered my
question with a shrug.* 他耸了耸肩，算是
回答了我的问题。

A B C D E F G H I J K L M N O P Q R **S** T U V W X Y Z

A
B
C
D
E
F
G
H
I
J
K
L
M
N
O
P
Q
R
S
T
U
V
W
X
Y
Z

shrug 耸肩

He **shrugged** his shoulders.
他耸了耸肩。

shrunk *form of* SHRINK * shrink 的不同
形式

shudder /ˈʃʌdə(r)/ *verb* 动词 (**shudders**,
shuddering, **shuddered** /ˈʃʌdəd/)
to shake because you are cold or
frightened, or because of a strong feeling
（因寒冷、恐惧或强烈的感情）发抖，
颤抖： *He shuddered when he saw the
snake.* 他看见了蛇，吓得直发抖。
▶ **shudder** *noun* 名词： *She felt a shudder
of fear.* 她感到一阵恐惧，哆嗦了一下。

shuffle /ˈʃʌfl/ *verb* 动词 (**shuffles**,
shuffling, **shuffled** /ˈʃʌfld/)
1 to walk slowly, without taking your feet
off the ground 拖着脚走： *The old man
shuffled along the road.* 那个老人拖着脚
在路上走。
2 to mix playing cards before a game
洗（牌）： *She shuffled the cards carefully
before dealing them.* 她在发牌前仔细地洗
了牌。

shut¹ ⭘ᆢ /ʃʌt/ *verb* 动词 (**shuts**, **shutting**,
shut, has **shut**)
1 to move, or to move something, so that
it is not open 关闭；关上 ⊃ SAME MEANING
close 同义词为 close： *Could you shut the
door, please?* 请你把门关上好吗？ ◇ *The
door shut behind me.* 那扇门在我走过之后
关上了。
2 to stop being open, so that people
cannot go there 停止营业；关门 ⊃ SAME
MEANING **close** 同义词为 close： *The shops
shut at 5.30.* 这些商店 5 点 30 分关门。
shut down to close and stop working; to
make something close and stop working
（使）停业；倒闭 ⊃ SAME MEANING **close
down** 同义词为 close down： *The factory
shut down last year.* 这家工厂去年倒闭
了。
shut up (*informal* 非正式) to stop talking
住口；闭嘴： *Shut up and listen!* 住口，
听着！

shut² ⭘ᆢ /ʃʌt/ *adjective* 形容词
not open 关闭；关门；停业 ⊃ SAME
MEANING **closed** 同义词为 closed： *The
restaurant is shut today.* 餐馆今天不营业。
◇ *Is the door shut?* 门是关着的吗？

shutter /ˈʃʌtə(r)/ *noun* 名词
a wooden or metal thing that covers the
outside of a window 活动护窗；百叶窗：
Close the shutters at night. 晚上把活动护窗
关上。

shuttle /ˈʃʌtl/ *noun* 名词
1 a plane, bus or train that travels
regularly between two places 定期往返的
航班（或班车、火车）
2 = SPACE SHUTTLE

shy ⭘ᆢ /ʃaɪ/ *adjective* 形容词 (**shyer**,
shyest)
not able to talk easily to people you do
not know 害羞的；羞怯的；腼腆的： *He
was too shy to speak to her.* 他太害羞了，
都不敢跟她说话。 ◇ *a shy smile* 腼腆的
微笑
▶ **shyness** /ˈʃaɪnəs/ *noun* 名词 (*no plural*
不用复数形式)： *As a child she suffered
from terrible shyness.* 她小时候非常害羞。

sick ⭘ᆢ /sɪk/ *adjective* 形容词 (**sicker**,
sickest)
not well 生病的；不舒服的 ⊃ SAME
MEANING **ill** 同义词为 ill： *She's looking
after her sick mother.* 她在照看生病的
母亲。 ◇ *Joe's been off sick* (= away
because of illness) *all week.* 乔因病一整个
星期都没上班。
be sick (*British* 英式英语) When you **are
sick**, food comes up from your stomach
and out of your mouth. 呕吐 ⊃ SAME
MEANING **vomit** 同义词为 vomit
be sick of something to have had or
done too much of something, so that you
do not want it any longer 对…感到厌烦：
I'm sick of watching TV – let's go out.
电视我看腻了，咱们出去吧。
feel sick (*British* 英式英语) to feel that
food is going to come up from your
stomach 想呕吐；恶心

sickness /ˈsɪknəs/ *noun* 名词 (*no plural*
不用复数形式)
being ill 患病；身体不适： *He could not
work for a long time because of sickness.*
他因病长期不能工作。

side 0‑ /saɪd/ *noun* 名词

1 one of the flat outside parts of something（物体的）面：*A box has six sides.* 一个盒子有六个面。

2 the part of something that is not the front, back, top or bottom 侧面：*There is a door at the side of the house.* 房子的侧面有一道门。◇ *There's a scratch on the side of my car.* 我车子的侧面有一道划痕。⊃ Look at the picture at **back¹**. 见 back¹ 的插图。

3 the part of something that is near the edge and away from the middle 边沿；边缘：*I stood at the side of the road.* 我站在路边。

4 the right or left part of something （左或右）边，侧：*He lay on his side.* 他侧身躺着。◇ *We drive on the left side of the road in Britain.* 在英国开车靠左行驶。

5 one of two groups of people who fight, argue or play a game against each other （打斗、争论或比赛的）一方，一派：*I thought you were on my side* (= agreed with me). 我以为你是站在我这边的。◇ *Which side won?* 哪方赢了？

side by side next to each other 并排；并肩：*They walked side by side.* 他们并肩而行。

take sides to show that you agree with one person, and not the other, in a fight or an argument 表态支持一方

sideboard /'saɪdbɔːd/ *noun* 名词
a type of cupboard that you use for storing plates and dishes in the room where you eat (called a **dining room**) 餐具柜 ⊃ Look at Picture Dictionary page **P10**. 见彩页 P10。

sidewalk /'saɪdwɔːk/ *American English for* PAVEMENT 美式英语，即 pavement

sideways /'saɪdweɪz/ *adjective, adverb* 形容词，副词

1 to or from the side 向（或从）一侧（的）；横向（的）：*She looked sideways at the girl next to her.* 她侧眼看了看身旁的女孩。

2 with one of the sides first 侧着（的）；侧面朝前（的）：*We carried the table sideways through the door.* 我们把桌子侧着抬过了那道门。

siege /siːdʒ/ *noun* 名词
a situation when an army stays outside a town or police stay outside a building for a long time so that no one can get in or out （军队或警察对城镇或建筑物）包围，围困，封锁

sieve /sɪv/ *noun* 名词
a type of kitchen tool that you use to remove lumps from food such as flour or soup 滤器；筛子；漏勺

sieve 筛子

sigh /saɪ/ *verb* 动词 (sighs, sighing, sighed /saɪd/)
to let out a deep breath, for example because you are sad, tired or pleased 叹息；叹气

▶ **sigh** *noun* 名词：*'I wish I had more money,' he said with a sigh.* "我要是有更多的钱就好了。"他叹气道。

sight 0‑ /saɪt/ *noun* 名词

1 (*no plural* 不用复数形式) the ability to see 视力；视觉 ⊃ SAME MEANING **eyesight** 同义词为 eyesight：*She has poor sight* (= she cannot see well). 她视力不好。

2 (*no plural* 不用复数形式) seeing somebody or something 看见；看到：*We had our first sight of London from the plane.* 我们在飞机上第一次看到伦敦。

3 (*plural* 复数形式 sights) something that you see 景象；情景：*The mountains were a beautiful sight.* 群山看上去十分壮丽。

4 sights (*plural* 用复数形式) the interesting places in a town or city, that are often visited by tourists 名胜；景点：*When you come to Paris I'll show you the sights.* 你来巴黎的时候，我会带你去观光。

5 (*no plural* 不用复数形式) a position where you can see somebody or something 视力范围；视野：*We watched until they were out of sight* (= we could not see them). 我们看着他们，直到他们消失在我们的视线范围。◇ *Eventually the town came into sight* (= we could see it). 最后终于看到了那个小镇。

at first sight when you see somebody or something for the first time 初次见到：*He fell in love with her at first sight.* 他对她一见钟情。

catch sight of somebody or 或 **something** to see somebody or something suddenly （突然）看见；瞥见：*I caught sight of Fiona in the crowd.* 我在人群中看到了菲奥纳。

lose sight of somebody or 或 **something** to no longer be able to see somebody or something 再也看不见：*After an hour at sea we lost sight of land.*

A
B
C
D
E
F
G
H
I
J
K
L
M
N
O
P
Q
R
S
T
U
V
W
X
Y
Z

A
B
C
D
E
F
G
H
I
J
K
L
M
N
O
P
Q
R
S
T
U
V
W
X
Y
Z

我们在海上航行了一小时后就看不见
陆地了。

sightseeing /'saɪtsiːɪŋ/ *noun* 名词 (*no plural* 不用复数形式)
the activity of visiting interesting buildings and places as a tourist 观光；游览：*to go sightseeing* 去观光 ◇ *Did you have a chance to do any sightseeing?* 你有没有机会出外游览一下？
▶ **sightseer** /'saɪtsiːə(r)/ *noun* 名词
⊃ SAME MEANING **tourist** 同义词为 tourist：*The town was full of sightseers.* 镇上到处都是游客。

sign 标示牌

sign¹ 0━ /saɪn/ *noun* 名词
1 something that tells you that something exists, is happening or may happen in the future 迹象；征兆：*Dark clouds are a sign of rain.* 乌云是下雨的迹象。
2 a thing with writing or a picture on it that tells you something 标示牌；标志：*The sign said 'No Smoking'.* 标示牌上写着"禁止吸烟"。◇ *a road sign* 路标
3 a mark, shape or movement that has a special meaning 符号；记号；手势；示意：*In mathematics, a cross is a plus sign.* 数学中十字形表示加号。◇ *I put up my hand as a sign for him to stop.* 我举手示意要他停下来。

sign² 0━ /saɪn/ *verb* 动词 (signs, signing, signed /saɪnd/)
to write your name in your own way on something 签名；签字；签署：*Sign here, please.* 请在这里签名。◇ *I signed the cheque.* 我在支票上签了名。⊃ The noun is **signature**. 名词为 signature。

signal 0━ /'sɪgnəl/ *noun* 名词
a light, sound or movement that tells you something without words 信号；暗号：*A red light is a signal for cars to stop.* 红灯是停车的信号。

▶ **signal** *verb* 动词 (*British* 英式英语 **signals, signalling, signalled** /'sɪgnəld/) (*American* 美式英语 **signaling, signaled**)：*The policeman signalled to the children to cross the road.* 警察示意孩子们过马路。

signature /'sɪgnətʃə(r)/ *noun* 名词
your name as you usually write it, for example at the end of a letter 签名；署名 ⊃ The verb is **sign**. 动词为 sign。

significance /sɪg'nɪfɪkəns/ *noun* 名词 (*no plural* 不用复数形式)
the importance or meaning of something 重要性；意义：*What is the significance of this discovery?* 这项发现有什么意义？

significant /sɪg'nɪfɪkənt/ *adjective* 形容词
important; with a special meaning 重要的；有特殊意义的：*The police say that the time of the robbery was very significant.* 警方说抢劫发生的时间非常关键。

sign language /'saɪn læŋgwɪdʒ/ *noun* 名词 (*no plural* 不用复数形式)
a language that uses movements of the hands. It is used especially by people who cannot hear. 手语

signpost 路标

signpost /'saɪnpəʊst/ *noun* 名词
a sign beside a road, that shows the way to a place and how far it is 路标；路牌

Sikh /siːk/ *noun* 名词
a person who follows one of the religions of India (called Sikhism) 锡克教教徒

silence 0━ /'saɪləns/ *noun* 名词
1 (*no plural* 不用复数形式) a situation in which there is no sound 寂静；宁静：*I can only work in complete silence.* 我要在完全安静的环境中才能工作。
2 (*plural* 复数形式 silences) a time when nobody speaks or makes a noise 沉默；

缄默: *There was a long silence before she answered the question.* 她沉默了很长时间才回答那个问题。◇ *We ate our dinner in silence.* 我们一声不吭地吃饭。

silent /'saɪlənt/ *adjective* 形容词

1 with no sound; completely quiet 寂静的；无声的: *Everyone was asleep, and the house was silent.* 大家都睡了，房子里静悄悄的。

2 If you are **silent**, you are not speaking. 沉默的；不作声的: *I asked him a question and he was silent for a moment before he answered.* 我问了他一个问题，他沉默了一会才回答。

▶ **silently** /'saɪləntli/ *adverb* 副词: *The cat moved silently towards the bird.* 猫悄悄地向鸟靠近。

silk /sɪlk/ *noun* 名词 (*no plural* 不用复数形式)

a type of thin smooth cloth that is made from the threads that an insect (called a **silkworm**) makes 丝绸；绸缎: *This scarf is made of silk.* 这条围巾是丝绸制的。◇ *a silk shirt* 丝绸衬衫

silky /'sɪlki/ *adjective* 形容词 (**silkier**, **silkiest**)

soft, smooth and shiny, like SILK 柔软光洁的；丝绸般的: *silky hair* 如丝般的秀发

silly /'sɪli/ *adjective* 形容词 (**sillier**, **silliest**)

not sensible or clever; stupid 愚蠢的；傻的；糊涂的: *Don't be so silly!* 别这么傻！◇ *It was silly of you to leave the door open when you went out.* 你出去的时候忘了关门，真糊涂。

silver¹ /'sɪlvə(r)/ *noun* 名词 (*no plural* 不用复数形式)

1 a shiny grey metal that is valuable 银: *a silver necklace* 银项链

2 things that are made of silver, for example knives, forks and dishes 银器；银制品: *The thieves stole some valuable silver.* 那伙盗贼偷走了一些贵重的银器。

silver² /'sɪlvə(r)/ *adjective* 形容词

with the colour of silver 银色的: *silver paper* 锡纸

similar /'sɪmələ(r)/ *adjective* 形容词

the same in some ways but not completely the same 相像的；相似的；类似的: *Rats are similar to mice, but they are bigger.* 大鼠和耗子相似，但个头较大。◇ *Jane and her sister look very similar.* 简和她妹妹长得很相像。

similarity /ˌsɪmə'lærəti/ *noun* 名词 (*plural* 复数形式 **similarities**)

a way that people or things are the same

相像；相似；类似: *There are a lot of* **similarities between** *the two countries.* 这两个国家有很多相似之处。◦ ⊃ OPPOSITE **difference** 反义词为 difference

simmer /'sɪmə(r)/ *verb* 动词 (**simmers**, **simmering**, **simmered** /'sɪməd/)

to cook gently in water that is almost boiling 用文火炖；煨: *Simmer the vegetables for ten minutes.* 把蔬菜用文火炖十分钟。

simple /'sɪmpl/ *adjective* 形容词 (**simpler**, **simplest**)

1 easy to do or understand 简单的；简易: *This dictionary is written in simple English.* 这本词典以简单的英语编写而成。◇ *'How do you open this?' 'I'll show you – it's simple.'* "这个怎么开？" "我演示给你看，很简单。" ⊃ OPPOSITE **difficult** 反义词为 difficult

2 without a lot of different parts or extra things 朴素的；简朴的 ⊃ SAME MEANING **plain** 同义词为 plain: *She wore a simple black dress.* 她穿了一件朴素的黑色连衣裙。◇ *a simple meal* 简单的一餐

simplicity /sɪm'plɪsəti/ *noun* 名词 (*no plural* 不用复数形式)

the quality of being simple 简单；简易；简朴: *I like the simplicity of these paintings.* 我喜欢这些画的朴实风格。

simplify /'sɪmplɪfaɪ/ *verb* 动词 (**simplifies**, **simplifying**, **simplified** /'sɪmplɪfaɪd/, has **simplified**)

to make something easier to do or understand 简化；使简易: *The story has been simplified so that the children can understand it.* 这个故事经过简化，以便儿童也能看懂。

simply /'sɪmpli/ *adverb* 副词

1 a word that you use when you want to show how easy or basic something is（强调简单）仅仅，只 ⊃ SAME MEANING **just** 同义词为 just: *Simply add water and stir.* 只需加水搅动一下就行。

2 in a simple way 简单地；简朴地: *Please explain it more simply.* 请解释得再简单些。

3 really 确实；的确: *The weather was simply terrible – it rained every day!* 天气实在很糟糕，天天都下雨！

simultaneous /ˌsɪml'teɪniəs/ *adjective* 形容词

happening at exactly the same time 同时发生的；共时的；同步的: *The city was hit by three simultaneous explosions.* 该市同时遭到了三起爆炸的袭击。

▶ **simultaneously** /ˌsɪml'teɪniəsli/

A
B
C
D
E
F
G
H
I
J
K
L
M
N
O
P
Q
R
S
T
U
V
W
X
Y
Z

adverb 副词: *'I'm sorry!' they said simultaneously.* "对不起！"他们异口同声地说。

sin /sɪn/ *noun* 名词
something that your religion says you should not do, because it is very bad（宗教不允许的）罪，罪孽，罪恶: *Stealing is a sin.* 偷盗有罪。
▸ **sin** *verb* 动词 (sins, sinning, sinned /sɪnd/): *He knew that he had sinned.* 他知道自己犯了罪。

since 0➔ /sɪns/ *adverb, preposition, conjunction* 副词，介词，连词
1 from a time in the past until a later time in the past or until now 自…开始；从…以来；自那时起: *He has been ill since Sunday.* 他从星期天开始一直病着。◊ *I haven't seen him since 1987.* 我从 1987 年以来就再也没见过他。◊ *She has lived here since she was a child.* 她从小就住在这里。◊ *George went to Canada in 1974 and he has lived there ever since* (= in all the time from then until now). 乔治 1974 年去了加拿大，从那时起就一直住在那儿。◊ *Andy left three years ago and we haven't seen him since.* 安迪三年前走了，从此我们再也没见过他。

> 🔎 **WHICH WORD?** 词语辨析
> **For** or **since**? 用 for 还是 since?
> We use **for** to say how long something has continued, for example in **hours**, **days** or **years**. * for 表示持续的时间，如多少个小时、多少天或多少年: *She has been ill for three days.* 她病了三天了。◊ *I've lived in this house for ten months.* 我在这所房子住了十个月了。◊ *We have been married for ten years.* 我们结婚十年了。
> We use **since** with points of time in the past, for example a **time** on the clock, a **date** or an **event**. * since 表示从过去的某时间点开始，如某钟点、某一天或某一事件: *I have been here since six o'clock.* 我从六点钟开始就一直在这儿了。◊ *She has been alone since her husband died.* 自从丈夫去世后，她一直独自生活。◊ *We have been married since 1996.* 我们 1996 年结婚到现在。

2 because 由于；既然 ⊃ SAME MEANING **as** 同义词为 as: *Since it's your birthday, I'll buy you a drink.* 既然是你的生日，我来请你喝一杯。
3 at a time after another time in the past 此后；之后: *They got married five years ago and have since had three children.* 他们五年前结了婚，至今已有三个孩子。

sincere /sɪnˈsɪə(r)/ *adjective* 形容词
being honest and meaning what you say 真诚的；诚恳的；诚挚的: *Were you being sincere when you said that you loved me?* 你说你爱我的时候是真心的吗?

sincerely /sɪnˈsɪəli/ *adverb* 副词
in a sincere way 真诚地；由衷地；诚恳地: *I am sincerely grateful to you.* 我衷心感激您。
Yours sincerely words that you write at the end of a formal letter, before your name（正式信函末署名前的套语）谨启 ⊃ Look at Study Pages **S18-S19**. 见研习专页 S18-S19。

sing 0➔ /sɪŋ/ *verb* 动词 (sings, singing, sang /sæŋ/, has sung /sʌŋ/)
to make music with your voice 唱（歌）；歌唱: *She sang a song.* 她唱了首歌。◊ *The birds were singing.* 鸟儿在歌唱。

singer 0➔ /ˈsɪŋə(r)/ *noun* 名词
a person who sings, or whose job is singing, especially in public 唱歌的人；歌手；歌唱家: *an opera singer* 歌剧演员

single¹ 0➔ /ˈsɪŋɡl/ *adjective* 形容词
1 only one 单一的；单个的: *He gave her a single red rose.* 他送给她一朵红玫瑰。
2 a word that makes 'every' stronger（用以强调每一个）: *You answered every single question correctly.* 每一个问题你都答对了。
3 not married 单身的；未婚的: *Are you married or single?* 你是已婚还是单身?
4 for one person 单人的: *I would like to book a single room, please.* 劳驾，我想预订个单人间。◊ *a single bed* 单人床 ⊃ Look at **double¹**. 见 double¹。
5 (*British* 英式英语) for a journey to a place, but not back again 单程的: *How much is a single ticket to London, please?* 请问到伦敦的单程票要多少钱? ⊃ Look at **return²**. 见 return²。

single² /ˈsɪŋɡl/ *noun* 名词
1 a ticket for a journey to a place, but not back again 单程票: *A single to Brighton, please.* 请来一张到布赖顿的单程票。⊃ Look at **return²**. 见 return²。
2 a CD, tape, etc. that has only one song on each side; the main song on this CD or tape 单曲唱片（或磁带等）；单曲: *Have you heard Joss Stone's new single?* 你听过乔斯·斯通的新单曲吗? ⊃ Look at **album**. 见 album。

single parent /ˌsɪŋɡl ˈpeərənt/ *noun* 名词
a person who looks after his or her child

or children alone, without help from the other parent 单亲

singular /ˈsɪŋɡjələ(r)/ *noun* 名词
(*no plural* 不用复数形式)
(*grammar* 语法) the form of a word that you use for one person or thing 单数形式: *The singular of 'men' is 'man'.* * men 的单数形式是 man。
▸ **singular** *adjective* 形容词: *'Table' is a singular noun.* * table 是单数名词。
⊃ Look at **plural**. 见 plural。

sink¹ 0̄ /sɪŋk/ *verb* 动词 (sinks, sinking, sank /sæŋk/, has sunk /sʌŋk/)
1 to go down under water 下沉；沉没: *If you throw a stone into water, it sinks.* 石头扔进水里会沉下去。◇ *The fishing boat sank to the bottom of the sea.* 渔船沉到海底了。⊃ OPPOSITE **float** 反义词为 float
2 to make a ship go down under water 使沉没: *The ship was sunk by a torpedo.* 船被鱼雷炸沉了。
3 to go down 下落；下降: *The sun sank slowly behind the hills.* 太阳徐徐地下山了。

sink² /sɪŋk/ *noun* 名词
the place in a kitchen where you wash dishes 洗涤池；洗碗槽 ⊃ Look at Picture Dictionary page **P10**. 见彩页 P10。

sip /sɪp/ *verb* 动词 (sips, sipping, sipped /sɪpt/)
to drink something slowly, taking only a little each time 小口喝；抿: *She sipped her coffee.* 她小口喝着咖啡。
▸ **sip** *noun* 名词: *Can I have a sip of your lemonade?* 我能喝一小口你的柠檬汽水吗？

sir 0̄ /sɜː(r)/ *noun* 名词
1 (*no plural* 不用复数形式) a polite way of speaking to a man, instead of using his name（表示尊称）先生: *'Can I help you, sir?' asked the shop assistant.* "先生，帮忙吗？"店员问道。⊃ Look at **madam**. 见 madam。
2 Sir (*no plural* 不用复数形式) a word that you use at the beginning of a formal letter to a man（用于正式信函开头）先生: *Dear Sir …* 尊敬的先生… ⊃ Look at **madam**. 见 madam。
3 Sir (*no plural* 不用复数形式) the title that is used in front of the name of a man who has received one of the highest British honours（英国贵族头衔）爵士: *Sir Bob Geldof* 鲍勃·格尔多夫爵士 ⊃ Look at **Lady**. 见 Lady。

siren /ˈsaɪrən/ *noun* 名词
a machine that makes a long loud sound

to warn people about something. Police cars and fire engines have **sirens**. 警报器；汽笛

sister 0̄ /ˈsɪstə(r)/ *noun* 名词
1 a girl or woman who has the same parents as you 姐姐；妹妹: *I've got two sisters and one brother.* 我有两个姐妹和一个弟弟。◇ *Jane and Anne are sisters.* 简和安妮是姐妹。
2 Sister (*British* 英式英语) a nurse who has an important job in a hospital 护士长
3 Sister a female member of religious group 修女

sister-in-law /ˈsɪstər ɪn lɔː/ *noun* 名词
(*plural* 复数形式 sisters-in-law)
1 the sister of your wife or husband 大（或小）姨子；大（或小）姑子
2 the wife of your brother 嫂子；弟媳

sit 0̄ /sɪt/ *verb* 动词 (sits, sitting, sat /sæt/, has sat)
1 to rest your weight on your bottom, for example in a chair 坐: *We sat in the garden all afternoon.* 我们整个下午都坐在花园里。◇ *Come and sit next to me.* 坐到我身边来。◇ *She was sitting on the sofa.* 她坐在沙发上。
2 (*British* 英式英语) to do an examination 参加（考试）: *The students will sit their exams in June.* 学生将于六月参加考试。
sit down to move your body downwards so you are sitting 坐下: *She came into the room and sat down.* 她走进房间，坐了下来。
sit up to sit when you have been lying 坐起来: *He sat up in bed and looked at the clock.* 他从床上坐了起来，看了看钟。

site /saɪt/ *noun* 名词
1 a place where a building is, was, or will be（建筑物的）地点，所在地: *a building site* 建筑工地 ◇ *This house was built on the site of an old theatre.* 这所房子建在旧剧院的遗址上。
2 a place where something happened 现场；发生地: *the site of a famous battle* 一场著名战役的遗址
3 = WEBSITE

sitting room /ˈsɪtɪŋ ruːm/ *noun* 名词
(*British* 英式英语) another word for LIVING ROOM * living room 的另一种说法

situated /ˈsɪtʃueɪtɪd/ *adjective* 形容词
in a place 位于；坐落在: *The hotel is situated close to the beach.* 旅馆位于海滩附近。

situation 0̄ /ˌsɪtʃuˈeɪʃn/ *noun* 名词
the things that are happening in a certain place or at a certain time 情况；形势；

局面: *We are in a difficult **situation** at the moment.* 我们此刻处境艰难。

sit-up /'sɪt ʌp/ *noun* 名词
an exercise for the stomach muscles in which you lie on your back with your legs bent, then lift the top half of your body from the floor 仰卧起坐: *To keep fit, she does twenty sit-ups every morning.* 为了健身，她每天早上做二十个仰卧起坐。

six 0━ /sɪks/ *number* 数词 (*plural* 复数形式 sixes)
6 六

sixteen 0━ /ˌsɪks'tiːn/ *number* 数词
16 十六

sixteenth 0━ /ˌsɪks'tiːnθ/ *pronoun, adjective, adverb, noun* 代词, 形容词, 副词, 名词
1 16th 第十六
2 one of sixteen equal parts of something; 1/16 十六分之一

sixth 0━ /sɪksθ/ *pronoun, adjective, adverb, noun* 代词, 形容词, 副词, 名词
1 6th 第六
2 one of six equal parts of something; 1/6 六分之一

sixth form /'sɪksθ fɔːm/ *noun* 名词
(*British* 英式英语)
the classes in the last two years of secondary school, for students between the ages of 16 and 18 第六学级（中学的最后两年，学生在 16 岁到 18 岁之间）

sixtieth 0━ /'sɪkstiəθ/ *pronoun, adjective, adverb* 代词, 形容词, 副词
60th 第六十

sixty 0━ /'sɪksti/ *number* 数词
1 60 六十
2 the sixties (*plural* 用复数形式) the numbers, years or temperature between 60 and 69 六十几；六十年代
in your sixties between the ages of 60 and 69 * 60 多岁: *My mum's in her sixties.* 我妈妈 60 多岁。

size 0━ /saɪz/ *noun* 名词
1 (*no plural* 不用复数形式) how big or small something is 大小: *My bedroom is the same size as yours.* 我的卧室跟你的大小一样。
2 (*plural* 复数形式 sizes) an exact measurement 尺码；号: *Have you got these shoes in a bigger size?* 这双鞋你们有尺码大一点的吗？

skate¹ /skeɪt/ *verb* 动词 (skates, skating, skated)
1 (*also* 亦作 ice-skate) to move on ice wearing skates 滑冰；溜冰: *Can you skate?* 你会溜冰吗? ◇ *They skated across the frozen lake.* 他们滑过冰封的湖面。

2 = ROLLER SKATE

skates 溜冰鞋

ice skates 溜冰鞋 **Rollerblades™** 直排滚轴旱冰鞋 **roller skates** 旱溜冰鞋

skate² /skeɪt/ *noun* 名词
1 a boot with a long sharp piece of metal under it, that you wear for moving on ice 溜冰鞋 ⊃ SAME MEANING **ice skate** 同义词为 ice skate
2 a boot with wheels on the bottom, that you wear for moving quickly on smooth ground 旱冰鞋 ⊃ SAME MEANING **roller skate** 同义词为 roller skate

skateboard 滑板

skateboard /'skeɪtbɔːd/ *noun* 名词
a long piece of wood or plastic on wheels. You stand on it as it moves over the ground. 滑板
▶ **skateboarding** /'skeɪtbɔːdɪŋ/ *noun* 名词 (*no plural* 不用复数形式): *Dave goes skateboarding every weekend.* 戴夫每个周末都去玩滑板。 ⊃ Look at Picture Dictionary page P15. 见彩页 P15。

skating rink /'skeɪtɪŋ rɪŋk/ (*also* 亦作 rink) *noun* 名词
1 a special place where you can SKATE on ice 溜冰场
2 a special place where you can ROLLER SKATE (= move over a hard surface

wearing boots with small wheels on the bottom) 旱冰场；轮式溜冰场

skeleton /'skelɪtn/ *noun* 名词
the bones of a whole animal or person 骨骼；骨架

sketch /sketʃ/ *noun* 名词 (*plural* 复数形式 **sketches**)
a picture that you draw quickly 素描；速写；草图：*The artist is making sketches for his next painting.* 画家正为他的下一幅作品画草图。

▶ **sketch** *verb* 动词 (**sketches, sketching, sketched** /sketʃt/): *He quickly sketched the view from the window.* 他很快勾勒出窗外的景色。

skiing 滑雪
pole 滑雪杆
skier 滑雪者
goggles 护目镜
boot 靴子
ski 滑雪板

ski /skiː/ *noun* 名词 (*plural* 复数形式 **skis**)
one of a pair of long flat pieces of wood, metal or plastic that you fix to boots so that you can move over snow 滑雪板：*a pair of skis* 一副滑雪板

▶ **ski** *verb* 动词 (**skis, skiing** /'skiːɪŋ/, **skied** /skiːd/, has **skied**): *Can you ski?* 你会滑雪吗？ ◇ *We went skiing in Austria.* 我们去奥地利滑雪了。

▶ **skier** /'skiːə(r)/ *noun* 名词：*Marie's a good skier.* 玛丽是个滑雪好手。

skid /skɪd/ *verb* 动词 (**skids, skidding, skidded**)
If a vehicle such as a car or lorry **skids**, it moves suddenly and in a dangerous way to the side, for example because the road is wet. （车辆）打滑，侧滑：*The lorry skidded on the icy road.* 卡车在结冰的路面上打滑了。

skies *plural of* SKY * sky 的复数形式

skilful (*British* 英式英语) (*American* 美式英语 **skillful**) /'skɪlfl/ *adjective* 形容词

very good at doing something 技术好的；熟练的：*a very skilful tennis player* 技术一流的网球高手

▶ **skilfully** (*British* 英式英语) (*American* 美式英语 **skillfully**) /'skɪlfəli/ *adverb* 副词：*He chopped the vegetables quickly and skilfully.* 他快速且熟练地把菜切好。

skill ०ल /skɪl/ *noun* 名词
1 (*no plural* 不用复数形式) the ability to do something well 技巧；技艺：*Flying a plane takes great skill.* 驾驶飞机需要很高的技术。
2 (*plural* 复数形式 **skills**) a thing that you can do well 技能；技术：*What skills do you need for this job?* 这份工作需要什么技能？

skilled /skɪld/ *adjective* 形容词
good at something because you have learned about or done it for a long time 有技能的；熟练的：*skilled workers* 熟练工

skillful, skillfully *American English for* SKILFUL, SKILFULLY 美式英语，即 skilful 和 skilfully

skin ०ल /skɪn/ *noun* 名词
1 the substance that covers the outside of a person or an animal's body 皮；皮肤：*She has dark skin.* 她皮肤黝黑。 ◇ *animal skins* 兽皮
2 the outside part of some fruits and vegetables 果皮；外皮：*a banana skin* 香蕉皮

skinny /'skɪni/ *adjective* 形容词 (**skinnier, skinniest**)
too thin 骨瘦如柴的；皮包骨的：*He's so skinny – he doesn't eat enough.* 他太瘦了——他吃得太少。 ➋ Look at the note at **thin**. 见 thin 条的注释。

skip /skɪp/ *verb* 动词 (**skips, skipping, skipped** /skɪpt/)
1 to move along quickly with little jumps from one foot to the other 蹦蹦跳跳地走：*The children were skipping along the road.* 孩子们在路上蹦蹦跳跳地走。
2 to jump many times over a rope that is turning 跳绳
3 to not do or have something that you should do or have 跳过，略过（应做的事）：*I skipped my class today and went swimming.* 我今天逃课去游泳了。

▶ **skip** *noun* 名词：*She gave a skip and a jump and was off down the street.* 她连蹦带跳顺着大街跑了。

skipping rope /'skɪpɪŋ rəʊp/ (*British* 英式英语) (*American* 美式英语 **jump rope**) *noun* 名词
a rope that you use for SKIPPING 跳绳

A
B
C
D
E
F
G
H
I
J
K
L
M
N
O
P
Q
R
S
T
U
V
W
X
Y
Z

A
B
C
D
E
F
G
H
I
J
K
L
M
N
O
P
Q
R
S
T
U
V
W
X
Y
Z

skirt 0️⃣ /skɜːt/ *noun* 名词

🔍 **PRONUNCIATION** 读音说明

The word **skirt** sounds like **hurt**. * skirt 读音像 **hurt**。

a piece of clothing for a woman or girl that hangs from the waist and covers part of the legs 裙子 ⊃ Look at Picture Dictionary page **P5**. 见彩页 P5。

ski slope /'skiː sləʊp/ *noun* 名词
a part of a mountain where you can SKI (= move over snow on special pieces of wood, metal or plastic) 滑雪坡

skull /skʌl/ *noun* 名词
the bones in the head of a person or an animal 颅骨；头盖骨

sky 0️⃣ /skaɪ/ *noun* 名词 (*plural* 复数形式 **skies**)
the space above the earth where you can see the sun, moon and stars 天；天空: *a beautiful blue sky* 美丽的蓝天 ◊ *There are no clouds in the sky.* 天上没有云。

skyscraper /'skaɪskreɪpə(r)/ *noun* 名词
a very tall building 摩天大楼: *He works on the 49th floor of a skyscraper.* 他在一栋摩天大楼的 50 层上班。

slab /slæb/ *noun* 名词
a thick flat piece of something 厚板；厚片: *stone slabs* 石板 ◊ *a big slab of cheese* 一大块干酪

slack /slæk/ *adjective* 形容词
1 loose 松弛的: *Suddenly the rope went slack.* 绳子突然松了。 ⊃ OPPOSITE **tight** 反义词为 tight
2 not busy 萧条的；冷清的: *Business has been very slack.* 生意一直很冷清。

slam /slæm/ *verb* 动词 (**slams, slamming, slammed** /slæmd/)
to close something or put something down with a loud noise 砰地关上；用力一摔: *She slammed the door angrily.* 她气呼呼地砰的一声关上了门。 ◊ *He slammed the book on the table and went out.* 他啪的一声把书扔到桌上就出去了。

slang /slæŋ/ *noun* 名词 (*no plural* 不用复数形式)
informal words that people use when they are talking. You do not use **slang** when you need to be polite, and you do not usually use it in writing. 俚语: *In British English, 'quid' is slang for 'pound'.* 在英式英语中，quid 是 pound（英镑）的俚语说法。

slant /slɑːnt/ *verb* 动词 (**slants, slanting, slanted**)

Something that **slants** has one side higher than the other or does not stand straight up. 倾斜；歪斜: *My handwriting slants to the left.* 我写的字都向左边。
▶ **slant** *noun* 名词 (*no plural* 不用复数形式): *Cut the flower stems on the slant.* 将花茎斜着剪。

slap 掌掴

slap /slæp/ *verb* 动词 (**slaps, slapping, slapped** /slæpt/)
to hit somebody with the flat inside part of your hand 掌击；掴: *He slapped me on the face.* 他打了我一记耳光。
▶ **slap** *noun* 名词: *She gave me a slap across the face.* 她给了我一个耳光。

slaughter /'slɔːtə(r)/ *verb* 动词 (**slaughters, slaughtering, slaughtered** /'slɔːtəd/)
1 to kill an animal for food 屠宰，宰杀（动物以供食用）
2 to kill a lot of people in a cruel way 屠杀，杀戮（人）
▶ **slaughter** *noun* 名词 (*no plural* 不用复数形式): *We must act to stop this slaughter.* 我们必须采取行动制止这场杀戮。

slave¹ /sleɪv/ *noun* 名词
a person who belongs to another person and must work for that person for no money 奴隶
▶ **slavery** /'sleɪvəri/ *noun* 名词 (*no plural* 不用复数形式): *When did slavery end in America?* 美国的奴隶制是什么时候结束的?

slave² /sleɪv/ *verb* 动词 (**slaves, slaving, slaved** /sleɪvd/)
to work very hard 拼命工作；苦干: *I've been slaving away all day.* 我整天都在拼死拼活地工作。

sledge /sledʒ/ (*American also* 美式英语 亦作 **sled** /sled/) *noun* 名词
a small vehicle with pieces of metal or wood instead of wheels that you sit in to move over snow 雪橇 ⊃ Look at **sleigh**. 见 sleigh。

sleep¹ 0— /sliːp/ *verb* 动词 (sleeps, sleeping, slept /slept/, has slept)
to rest with your eyes closed, as you do at night 睡；睡觉：*I sleep for eight hours every night.* 我每晚睡八个小时。◇ *Did you sleep well?* 你睡得好吗？

> 🔎 **SPEAKING** 表达方式说明
>
> Be careful! We usually say **be asleep** not **be sleeping**. 注意：通常说 be asleep，不说 be sleeping：*I was asleep when you phoned.* 你打电话来的时候我在睡觉。
> We use **go to sleep** or **fall asleep** to talk about starting to sleep. 入睡说 go to sleep 或 fall asleep：*She got into bed and went to sleep.* 她上床睡了。◇ *He fell asleep in front of the fire.* 他在炉火前睡着了。

sleep² 0— /sliːp/ *noun* 名词 (*no plural* 不用复数形式)
the natural condition of rest when your eyes are closed and your mind and body are not active or conscious 睡觉；睡眠：*I didn't get any sleep last night.* 我昨晚一夜没睡。
go to sleep to start to sleep 入睡 ➔ SAME MEANING **fall asleep** 同义词为 fall asleep：*I got into bed and soon went to sleep.* 我上了床，很快就睡着了。

sleeping bag /'sliːpɪŋ bæg/ *noun* 名词
a big warm bag that you sleep in when you go camping 睡袋

sleepless /'sliːpləs/ *adjective* 形容词
without sleep 无眠的；失眠的：*I had a sleepless night.* 我过了一个不眠之夜。

sleepy /'sliːpi/ *adjective* 形容词 (sleepier, sleepiest)
1 tired and ready to sleep 困倦的；瞌睡的：*I felt sleepy after that big meal.* 吃了那顿大餐以后我就觉得困了。
2 quiet, with not many things happening 安静的；不热闹的：*a sleepy little village* 宁静的小村庄

sledge 雪橇

sledge 雪橇   **sleigh**（动物拉）雪橇

sleet /sliːt/ *noun* 名词 (*no plural* 不用复数形式)
snow and rain together 雨夹雪

sleeve 0— /sliːv/ *noun* 名词
the part of a coat, dress or shirt, for example, that covers your arm 袖子；衣袖：*a shirt with short sleeves* 短袖衬衫 ➔ Look at the picture at **shirt**. 见 shirt 插图。

sleigh /sleɪ/ *noun* 名词
a large vehicle with pieces of metal or wood instead of wheels that you sit in to move over snow. A **sleigh** is usually pulled by animals. （通常为动物拉的）雪橇 ➔ Look at the picture at **sledge**. 见 sledge 的插图。

slender /'slendə(r)/ *adjective* 形容词
thin, in an attractive way 苗条的；纤细的：*She has long, slender legs.* 她有一双修长的腿。

slept *form of* SLEEP¹ * sleep¹ 的不同形式

slice 0— /slaɪs/ *noun* 名词
a thin piece that you cut off bread, meat or other food（面包、肉类等）薄片，片：*Would you like a slice of cake?* 给你来片蛋糕好吗？◇ *She cut the bread into slices.* 她把面包切成片。➔ Look at the picture at **bread**. 见 bread 的插图。
▶ **slice** *verb* 动词 (slices, slicing, sliced /slaɪst/)：*Slice the onions.* 把洋葱切成片。

slide¹ 0— /slaɪd/ *verb* 动词 (slides, sliding, slid /slɪd/, has slid)
to move smoothly or to make something move smoothly across something（使）滑行，滑动：*She fell and slid along the ice.* 她在冰上摔倒滑了出去。

slide² /slaɪd/ *noun* 名词
1 a long metal thing that children play on. They climb up steps, sit down, and then SLIDE down the other side. 滑梯 ➔ Look at the picture at **swing²**. 见 swing² 的插图。
2 a small photograph that you show on a screen, using a special machine (called a **projector**) 幻灯片：*a slide show* 幻灯放映

slight /slaɪt/ *adjective* 形容词 (slighter, slightest)
small; not important or serious 轻微的；不重要的：*I've got a slight problem.* 我遇到一点小麻烦。◇ *a slight headache* 轻微的头痛

slightly 0— /'slaɪtli/ *adverb* 副词
a little 略微；稍微：*I'm feeling slightly better today.* 我今天稍微好了一些。

slim¹ /slɪm/ *adjective* 形容词 (slimmer, slimmest)

A B C D E F G H I J K L M N O P Q R **S** T U V W X Y Z

thin, but not too thin 苗条的；修长的：
a tall slim man 高瘦的男人 ➲ Look at the note at **thin**. 见 thin 条的注释。

slim² /slɪm/ *verb* 动词 (**slims, slimming, slimmed** /slɪmd/)
to become thinner 减肥；瘦身：*I've been trying to slim.* 我一直在尝试减肥。

🔍 SPEAKING 表达方式说明
The more usual expression is **lose weight**. 较常用 lose weight。

slime /slaɪm/ *noun* 名词 (*no plural* 不用复数形式)
a thick liquid that looks or smells bad 粘液：*The pond was covered in green slime.* 池塘表面尽是绿色黏糊糊的污水。
▶ **slimy** /'slaɪmi/ *adjective* 形容词 (**slimier, slimiest**)：*a slimy surface* 湿黏的表面

sling¹ /slɪŋ/ *noun* 名词
a piece of cloth that you wear to hold up an arm that is hurt（悬吊受伤手臂的）悬带，吊腕带：*She's got her arm in a sling.* 她的手臂用悬带吊着。➲ Look at the picture at **plaster¹**. 见 plaster¹ 的插图。

sling² /slɪŋ/ *verb* 动词 (**slings, slinging, slung** /slʌŋ/, has slung) (*British* 英式英语) (*informal* 非正式)
to throw something without care 乱扔；随便丢：*He got angry and slung the book at me.* 他生气了，便把书扔向我。

slip¹ /slɪp/ *verb* 动词 (**slips, slipping, slipped** /slɪpt/)
1 to move smoothly over something by accident and fall or almost fall 滑倒；滑跤：*He slipped on the ice and broke his leg.* 他在冰上滑倒，把腿摔断了。
2 to go quickly and quietly so that nobody sees you 悄悄地走；溜走：*Ann slipped out of the room.* 安溜出了房间。◇ *We slipped away when no one was looking.* 我们趁别人没注意溜走了。
3 to put something in a place quickly and quietly 迅速放入；悄悄地塞：*He slipped the money into his pocket.* 他悄悄把钱塞进了口袋。
slip up (*informal* 非正式) to make a mistake 出差错；犯错误

slip² /slɪp/ *noun* 名词
1 a small mistake 差错；疏漏：*It was just a slip.* 那只是个小疏忽。
2 a small piece of paper 纸条：*Write your address on this slip of paper.* 把你的地址写在这张纸条上。

slipper /'slɪpə(r)/ *noun* 名词
a light soft shoe that you wear in the house 拖鞋；室内便鞋：*a pair of slippers*

一双拖鞋 ➲ Look at the picture at **shoe**. 见 shoe 的插图。

slippery /'slɪpəri/ *adjective* 形容词
so smooth or wet that you cannot move on it or hold it easily 滑的：*a slippery floor* 滑的地板 ◇ *The road was wet and slippery.* 马路又湿又滑。

slit /slɪt/ *noun* 名词
a long thin hole or cut 狭长的开口（或切口）
▶ **slit** *verb* 动词 (**slits, slitting, slit, has slit**)：*I slit the envelope open with a knife.* 我用刀裁开了信封。

slither /'slɪðə(r)/ *verb* 动词 (**slithers, slithering, slithered** /'slɪðəd/)
to move by sliding from side to side along the ground like a snake 曲折爬行；蜿蜒滑行；蛇行：*I saw a snake slithering down a rock.* 我看见一条蛇爬到岩石下面去了。

slob /slɒb/ *noun* 名词 (*informal* 非正式)
a lazy, untidy person 懒虫；邋遢鬼：*My brother's such a slob – he never tidies his room.* 我弟弟真是个邋遢鬼，他从来不整理自己的房间。

slogan /'sləʊɡən/ *noun* 名词
a short sentence or group of words that is easy to remember. **Slogans** are used to make people believe something or buy something. 标语；口号：*anti-government slogans* 反政府口号 ◇ *an advertising slogan* 广告标语

slope¹ /sləʊp/ *noun* 名词
a piece of ground that has one end higher than the other, like the side of a hill 斜坡；山坡：*We walked down the mountain slope.* 我们顺着山坡走下去。➲ Look also at **ski slope**. 亦见 ski slope。

slope² /sləʊp/ *verb* 动词 (**slopes, sloping, sloped** /sləʊpt/)
to have one end higher than the other 倾斜：*The field slopes down to the river.* 这片地倾向河边。◇ *a sloping roof* 倾斜的屋顶

sloppy /'slɒpi/ *adjective* 形容词 (**sloppier, sloppiest**)
1 showing a lack of care or effort 马虎的；草率的：*a sloppy piece of work* 粗制滥造的作品
2 Sloppy clothes are loose and comfortable.（衣服）宽大的，松垮的：*a sloppy sweater* 松松垮垮的毛衣

slot /slɒt/ *noun* 名词
a long thin hole that you push something through（投放东西的）扁口：*Put your*

money in the slot and take your ticket.
将钱放入投币口，然后取票。

slot machine /'slɒt məʃi:n/ *noun* 名词
a machine that gives you things like drinks or sweets when you put money in 投币自动售货机

slow¹ 0━ /sləʊ/ *adjective* 形容词 (slower, slowest)

> 🔍 **PRONUNCIATION** 读音说明
> The word **slow** sounds like **go**. * slow 读音像 go。

1 not moving or doing something quickly 慢的；缓慢的：*a slow train* 慢行火车 ◇ *She hasn't finished her work yet – she's very slow.* 她还没做完工作，她很慢。
2 If a clock or watch is **slow**, it shows a time that is earlier than the real time. （钟表）走得慢：*My watch is five minutes slow.* 我的手表慢五分钟。
⊃ Look at **fast¹** and **quick**. 见 fast¹ 和 quick。

▶ **slowly** /'sləʊli/ *adverb* 副词：*The old lady walked slowly up the hill.* 老太太慢慢地走上山。

slow² /sləʊ/ *adverb* 副词
slowly 慢慢地；缓慢地：*Please drive slower.* 请把车开慢些。 ◇ *slow-moving traffic* 缓慢行进的车流

slow³ /sləʊ/ *verb* 动词 (slows, slowing, slowed /sləʊd/)
slow down, **slow somebody** or 或 **something down** to start to go more slowly; to make somebody or something start to go more slowly （使）放慢速度，减慢：*The train slowed down as it came into the station.* 火车进站时慢了下来。 ◇ *Don't talk to me when I'm working – it slows me down.* 我工作的时候别跟我说话，那会把我的进度拖慢。

slug 蛞蝓

slug /slʌg/ *noun* 名词
a small soft animal that moves slowly and eats plants 蛞蝓；缓步虫

slum /slʌm/ *noun* 名词
a poor part of a city where people live in old dirty buildings 贫民窟

slump /slʌmp/ *verb* 动词 (slumps, slumping, slumped /slʌmpt/)

1 (used about prices, sales and the economy) to fall suddenly and by a large amount （价格、销售量等）骤降，暴跌：*Shares slumped to their lowest ever level.* 股价骤降至新低。
2 to fall or sit down suddenly because you are ill, weak or tired （因病弱或疲倦）重重坐下，颓然倒下：*Suddenly the old man slumped to the floor.* 突然间，老人重重地瘫坐在地上。

slung *form of* SLING² * sling² 的不同形式

sly /slaɪ/ *adjective* 形容词
A person who is **sly** tricks people or does things secretly. 狡诈的；狡猾的 ⊃ SAME MEANING **cunning** 同义词为 cunning

smack /smæk/ *verb* 动词 (smacks, smacking, smacked /smækt/)
to hit somebody with the inside part of your hand 用巴掌打；掴：*They never smack their children.* 他们从来不打孩子。

▶ **smack** *noun* 名词：*She gave her son a smack.* 她打了儿子一巴掌。

small 0━ /smɔːl/ *adjective* 形容词 (smaller, smallest)

1 not big; little 小的：*This dress is too small for me.* 这件连衣裙我穿太小了。 ◇ *My house is smaller than yours.* 我的房子比你的小。
2 young 年幼的；幼小的：*They have two small children.* 他们有两个年幼的孩子。

smart /smɑːt/ *adjective* 形容词 (smarter, smartest)

1 (*British* 英式英语) right for a special or an important time; clean and tidy 衣着讲究的；得体的；整洁的：*a smart new suit* 光鲜的新西装 ◇ *He looks very smart in his new jacket.* 他穿着新夹克，显得很帅气。
2 (*American* 美式英语) clever 聪明的；机敏的：*She's not as smart as her sister.* 她不如她妹妹聪明。

▶ **smartly** /'smɑːtli/ *adverb* 副词：*She was very smartly dressed.* 她穿得很体面。

smash /smæʃ/ *verb* 动词 (smashes, smashing, smashed /smæʃt/)

1 to break something into many pieces 打碎；击碎：*The boys smashed the window with their ball.* 那些男孩用球打碎了窗户。
2 to break into many pieces 破碎：*The plate fell on the floor and smashed.* 盘子掉到地上摔碎了。

▶ **smash** *noun* 名词：*The glass hit the floor with a smash.* 玻璃杯掉到地上哗啦一声摔碎了。

smashing /'smæʃɪŋ/ *adjective* 形容词
(*British* 英式英语) (*informal* 非正式)
very good 非常好的 ⊃ SAME MEANING
great 同义词为 great: *The food was
smashing.* 食物非常好吃。

smear /smɪə(r)/ *verb* 动词 (**smears,
smearing, smeared** /smɪəd/)
to spread a soft substance on something,
making it dirty 涂抹（使弄脏）: *The child
had smeared chocolate all over his clothes.*
这个孩子把巧克力抹得满衣服都是。
▶ **smear** *noun* 名词: *She had smears of
paint on her dress.* 她的连衣裙上有油漆
污渍。

smell 0- /smel/ *verb* 动词 (**smells,
smelling, smelt** /smelt/ or 或 **smelled**
/smeld/, **has smelt** or 或 **has smelled**)
1 to have a particular smell 有…气味;
闻起来…: *Dinner smells good!* 饭菜闻起
来很香! ◇ *The perfume smells of roses.*
这香水是玫瑰味的。
2 to notice something with your nose
闻到; 嗅到: *Can you smell smoke?*
你闻到烟味吗?
3 to have a bad smell 有难闻的气味;
发臭: *Your feet smell!* 你的脚很臭!
▶ **smell** *noun* 名词: *There's a smell of
gas in this room.* 这个房间里有煤气味。

smelly /'smeli/ *adjective* 形容词 (**smellier,
smelliest**)
having a bad smell 难闻的; 有臭味的:
smelly socks 臭袜子

smile 0- /smaɪl/ *verb* 动词 (**smiles,
smiling, smiled** /smaɪld/)
to move your mouth to show that you are
happy or that you think something is
funny 微笑: *He smiled at me.* 他向我
微笑。
▶ **smile** *noun* 名词: *She had a big smile
on her face.* 她脸上露出了灿烂的笑容。

smog /smɒg/ *noun* 名词 (*no plural* 不用
复数形式)
dirty poisonous air that can cover a whole
city 烟雾（笼罩城市的有毒空气污染物）

smoke¹ 0- /sməʊk/ *noun* 名词
(*no plural* 不用复数形式)
the grey, white or black gas that you see
in the air when something is burning
烟: *The room was full of smoke.* 房间里
都是烟。◇ *cigarette smoke* 香烟的烟

smoke² 0- /sməʊk/ *verb* 动词 (**smokes,
smoking, smoked** /sməʊkt/)
to breathe in smoke through a cigarette,
etc. and let it out again; to use cigarettes,
etc. in this way, as a habit 吸烟; 抽烟:
He was smoking a cigar. 他抽着雪茄。◇

Do you smoke? 你吸烟吗?
▶ **smoker** /'sməʊkə(r)/ *noun* 名词: *Her
parents are both heavy smokers* (= they
smoke a lot). 她父母烟瘾很大。
⊃ OPPOSITE **non-smoker** 反义词为
non-smoker
▶ **smoking** /'sməʊkɪŋ/ *noun* 名词
(*no plural* 不用复数形式): *No smoking
in the theatre.* 剧院内禁止吸烟。

smoked /sməʊkt/ *adjective* 形容词
Smoked food is put over a wood fire to
give it a special taste. 熏制的: *smoked
salmon* 熏鲑鱼

smoky /'sməʊki/ *adjective* 形容词 (**smokier, smokiest**)
full of smoke 烟雾弥漫的; 浓烟滚滚的:
a smoky room 烟雾弥漫的房间

smolder *verb* 动词 *American English for*
SMOULDER 美式英语, 即 smoulder

smooth 0- /smuːð/ *adjective* 形容词
(**smoother, smoothest**)
1 having a completely flat surface 平滑
的; 光滑的: *Babies have such smooth
skin.* 婴儿的皮肤是多么光滑。◇ *The
surface should be completely smooth.*
表面应该完全平滑。⊃ OPPOSITE **rough**
反义词为 rough
2 (used about a liquid mixture) with no
big pieces in it （液体混合物）均匀的,
无结块的: *Beat the sauce until it is
smooth.* 把调味酱汁搅拌至均匀为止。
⊃ OPPOSITE **lumpy** 反义词为 lumpy
3 A **smooth** movement or journey is even
and comfortable. 顺利流畅的; （旅程）
平稳的: *The weather was good so we had
a very smooth flight.* 天气很好, 我们整个
航程非常平稳。⊃ OPPOSITE **bumpy**
反义词为 bumpy
▶ **smoothly** /'smuːðli/ *adverb* 副词: *The
plane landed smoothly.* 飞机平稳降落了。

smother /'smʌðə(r)/ *verb* 动词 (**smothers,
smothering, smothered** /'smʌðəd/)
1 to kill somebody by covering their face
so that they cannot breathe 使窒息而死;
闷死
2 to cover a thing with too much of
something （用某物）厚厚地覆盖: *He
smothered his cake with cream.* 他在蛋糕
上涂了厚厚一层奶油。

smoulder (*British* 英式英语) (*American*
美式英语 **smolder**) /'sməʊldə(r)/ *verb* 动词
(**smoulders, smouldering, smouldered**
/'sməʊldəd/)
to burn slowly without a flame （无明火
地）闷燃: *A fire smouldered in the grate.*
火在炉条上闷燃着。

smudge /smʌdʒ/ *verb* 动词 (smudges, smudging, smudged /smʌdʒd/)
If something **smudges** or you **smudge** it, it becomes dirty or untidy because you have touched it. 弄脏；擦模糊；变模糊: *Leave the painting to dry or you'll smudge it.* 让画放着干一下，不然你会把它弄脏的。◇ *My lipstick has smudged.* 我的口红糊了。
▶ **smudge** *noun* 名词: *There's a smudge on your cheek.* 你脸颊上有块污迹。

smug /smʌg/ *adjective* 形容词 (smugger, smuggest)
too pleased with yourself, in a way that annoys other people 沾沾自喜；自鸣得意的: *He gave her a smug look.* 他沾沾自喜地看了她一眼。

smuggle /ˈsmʌgl/ *verb* 动词 (smuggles, smuggling, smuggled /ˈsmʌgld/)
to take things secretly into or out of a country when this is against the law 走私；偷运: *They were trying to smuggle drugs into France.* 他们企图把毒品走私到法国。
▶ **smuggler** /ˈsmʌglə(r)/ *noun* 名词: *drug smugglers* 走私毒品的人

snack /snæk/ *noun* 名词
a small quick meal 小吃；点心: *We had a snack on the train.* 我们在火车上吃了些点心。

snack bar /ˈsnæk bɑː(r)/ *noun* 名词
a place where you can buy and eat SNACKS 小吃店；快餐部

snag /snæg/ *noun* 名词
a small problem 小问题；小困难: *It's a beautiful bike – the only snag is, it's very expensive.* 这辆自行车很漂亮，只有一个小问题，就是价格很贵。

snail 蜗牛

—— shell 壳

snail /sneɪl/ *noun* 名词
a small soft animal with a hard shell on its back. **Snails** move very slowly. 蜗牛

snake ⟶ /sneɪk/ *noun* 名词
an animal with a long thin body and no legs 蛇: *Do these snakes bite?* 这些蛇咬人吗?

snake 蛇

snap¹ /snæp/ *verb* 动词 (snaps, snapping, snapped /snæpt/)
1 to break something suddenly with a sharp noise; to be broken in this way （使）吧啦一声断裂，啪地折断: *He snapped the pencil in two.* 他把铅笔啪的一声折成了两截。◇ *Suddenly, the rope snapped.* 突然，绳子啪地绷断了。
2 to say something in a quick angry way 气冲冲地说；没好气地说: *'Go away – I'm busy!' she snapped.* "走开，我正忙着呢！" 她气呼呼地说。
3 to try to bite somebody or something 咬: *The dog snapped at my leg.* 狗冲我的腿咬过来。

snap² /snæp/ *noun* 名词
1 a sudden sound of something breaking （物体断裂时的）吧啦声，喀嚓声
2 (*also* 亦作 **snapshot** /ˈsnæpʃɒt/)
a photograph 快照；抓拍的照片: *She showed us her holiday snaps.* 她给我们看了她度假时拍的照片。

snarl /snɑːl/ *verb* 动词 (snarls, snarling, snarled /snɑːld/)
When an animal **snarls**, it shows its teeth and makes a low angry sound. （动物）龇牙咆叫: *The dogs snarled at the stranger.* 那些狗冲着陌生人厉声吠叫。

snatch /snætʃ/ *verb* 动词 (snatches, snatching, snatched /snætʃt/)
to take something with a quick rough movement 一把夺过；一下抓走 ⊃ SAME MEANING **grab** 同义词为 grab: *A thief snatched her handbag and ran away.* 小偷一下抢过她的手提包就跑了。

sneak /sniːk/ *verb* 动词 (sneaks, sneaking, sneaked /sniːkt/)
to go somewhere very quietly so that nobody sees or hears you 偷偷地走；溜: *She sneaked out of the house without telling her parents.* 她没跟父母说一声就溜出了房子。

sneaker /ˈsniːkə(r)/ *noun* 名词 *American English for* TRAINER (1) 美式英语，即 trainer 第 1 义

A
B
C
D
E
F
G
H
I
J
K
L
M
N
O
P
Q
R
S
T
U
V
W
X
Y
Z

sneer /snɪə(r)/ *verb* 动词 (**sneers**, **sneering**, **sneered** /snɪəd/)

to speak or smile in an unkind way to show that you do not like somebody or something, or that you think they are not good enough 嘲笑；讥笑：*I told her about my idea, but she just sneered at it.* 我把我的想法告诉她，她只报以冷笑。

▶ **sneer** *noun* 名词: *His lips curled in a sneer.* 他嘴角挂着一丝冷笑。

sneeze 打喷嚏

sneeze /sniːz/ *verb* 动词 (**sneezes**, **sneezing**, **sneezed** /sniːzd/)

to make air come out of your nose and mouth with a sudden loud noise, for example because you have a cold 打喷嚏：*Pepper makes you sneeze.* 胡椒粉会使人打喷嚏。

▶ **sneeze** *noun* 名词: *She gave a loud sneeze.* 她打了一个很响的喷嚏。

sniff /snɪf/ *verb* 动词 (**sniffs**, **sniffing**, **sniffed** /snɪft/)

1 to make a noise by suddenly taking in air through your nose. People sometimes **sniff** when they have a cold or when they are crying. （感冒或哭泣时）抽鼻子：*I wish you'd stop sniffing!* 我真希望你别再抽鼻子了！

2 to smell something 嗅；闻：*The dog was sniffing the meat.* 狗闻着那块肉。

▶ **sniff** *noun* 名词: *I heard a loud sniff.* 我听到一声很大声的抽泣声。

snob /snɒb/ *noun* 名词

a person who likes people with a high social position and thinks they are better than other people 势利的人：*Jack's such a snob – he's always going on about his rich relations.* 杰克真是个势利眼，总是没完没了地谈论他有钱的亲戚。

snooker /ˈsnuːkə(r)/ *noun* 名词 (*no plural* 不用复数形式)

a game in which two players try to hit coloured balls into pockets on the edge of a large table, using a long stick (called a **cue**) 斯诺克（供两人打的落袋台球） ⊃ Look at Picture Dictionary page **P15**. 见彩页 P15。

snooze /snuːz/ *verb* 动词 (**snoozes**, **snoozing**, **snoozed** /snuːzd/) (*informal* 非正式)

to sleep for a short time 小睡；打盹

▶ **snooze** *noun* 名词: *I had a snooze after lunch.* 我午饭后打了个盹。

snore /snɔː(r)/ *verb* 动词 (**snores**, **snoring**, **snored** /snɔːd/)

to make a noise in your nose and throat when you are asleep 打鼾；打呼噜：*He was snoring loudly.* 他打着很响的呼噜。

snorkel /ˈsnɔːkl/ *noun* 名词

a short tube that a person swimming just below the surface of the water can use to breathe through （徒手潜水用的）呼吸管

▶ **snorkelling** (*British* 英式英语) (*American* 美式英语 **snorkeling**) /ˈsnɔːklɪŋ/ *noun* 名词 (*no plural* 不用复数形式): *to go snorkelling* 去徒手潜水 ⊃ Look at the picture at **scuba-diving**. 见 scuba-diving 的插图。

snort /snɔːt/ *verb* 动词 (**snorts**, **snorting**, **snorted**)

to make a noise by blowing air through the nose 喷鼻息；发哼声：*The horse snorted.* 马打了个响鼻。

snow 0️⃣ /snəʊ/ *noun* 名词 (*no plural* 不用复数形式)

> 🔊 **PRONUNCIATION** 读音说明
>
> The word **snow** sounds like **go**. * snow 读音像 go。

soft white pieces of frozen water that fall from the sky when it is very cold 雪

▶ **snow** *verb* 动词 (**snows**, **snowing**, **snowed** /snəʊd/): *It often snows in Scotland in winter.* 苏格兰冬天常下雪。◇ *It's snowing!* 下雪了！ ⊃ Look at Picture Dictionary page **P16**. 见彩页 P16。

snowball /ˈsnəʊbɔːl/ *noun* 名词

a ball of snow that children throw at each other 雪球：*The kids were having a snowball fight* (= throwing snowballs at each other). 孩子们在打雪仗。

snowboarding /ˈsnəʊbɔːdɪŋ/ *noun* 名词 (*no plural* 不用复数形式)

the sport of moving down mountains that are covered in snow using a large board that you fasten to both your feet

滑雪板运动 ⇒ Look at Picture Dictionary page **P15**. 见彩页 P15。

snowflake /'snəʊfleɪk/ *noun* 名词
one piece of falling snow 雪花；雪片

snowman /'snəʊmæn/ *noun* 名词 (*plural* 复数形式 snowmen /'snəʊmen/)
the figure of a person that children make out of snow 雪人

snowplough (*British* 英式英语) (*American* 美式英语 **snowplow**) /'snəʊplaʊ/ *noun* 名词
a large vehicle that clears snow away from roads 雪犁，扫雪机（用以清除路上积雪）

snowy /'snəʊi/ *adjective* 形容词 (snowier, snowiest)
with a lot of snow 多雪的：*snowy weather* 下雪的天气

so¹ 0ᴀ /səʊ/ *adverb* 副词
1 a word that makes an adjective or adverb stronger, especially when this produces a particular result（强调形容词或副词）这么，那么，如此：*This bag is so heavy that I can't carry it.* 这个包这么重，我都提不动。◇ *I'm so tired I can't keep my eyes open.* 我累得连眼睛也睁不开了。◇ *Why are you so late?* 你怎么这么晚？

🔎 **WHICH WORD?** 词语辨析
So or **such**? 用 so 还是 such?
You use **so** before an adjective that is used without a noun. 形容词不带名词时用 so：*It was so cold that we stayed at home.* 天气那么冷，我们都待在家里了。◇ *This book is so exciting.* 这本书是多么激动人心。
You use **such** before a noun that has an adjective in front of it. 形容词后接名词时用 such：*It was such a cold night that we stayed at home.* 那是多么寒冷的一夜，我们都待在家里了。◇ *This is such an exciting book.* 这是多么激动人心的一本书。

2 You use 'so' instead of saying words again.（用以代替刚说过的事，避免重复）：*'Is John coming?' 'I think so* (= I think that he is coming).' "约翰来吗？""我想会来。"◇ *'I got it wrong, didn't I?' 'I'm afraid so* (= you did get it wrong).' "我弄错了，是不是？""恐怕是。"
3 also 也：*Julie is a teacher and so is her husband.* 朱莉是教师，她丈夫也是。◇ *'I like this music.' 'So do I.'* "我喜欢这音乐。""我也喜欢。"

🔎 **GRAMMAR** 语法说明
In negative sentences, we use **neither** or **nor**. 否定句中用 neither 或 nor：*Lydia can't swim and neither can I.* 莉迪娅不会游泳，我也不会。◇ *If Alan doesn't go, nor will Lucy.* 要是艾伦不去，露西也不会去。

and so on and other things like that 等等；诸如此类：*The shop sells pens, paper and so on.* 这家商店出售钢笔、纸之类的东西。
not so ... as words that show how two people or things are different 不像…那么…；没有…那么…：*He's not so tall as his brother.* 他没有他哥哥那么高。
or so words that you use to show that a number is not exactly right（数量）…左右，…上下：*Forty or so people came to the party.* 有四十来人参加了聚会。

so² 0ᴀ /səʊ/ *conjunction* 连词
1 because of this or that 因此；所以：*The shop is closed so I can't buy any bread.* 商店关门了，所以我没买到面包。
2 (*also* 亦作 **so that**) in order that 为了；以便：*Speak louder so that everybody can hear you.* 说话大声点，好让大家都听见。◇ *I'll give you a map so you can find my house.* 我给你一张地图，你就能找到我家了。
so what? (*informal* 非正式) why is that important or interesting? 那又怎么样？：*'It's late.' 'So what? There's no school tomorrow.'* "很晚了。""晚了又怎样？反正明天不用上学。"

soak /səʊk/ *verb* 动词 (soaks, soaking, soaked /səʊkt/)
1 to make somebody or something very wet 使湿透：*Soak the plants thoroughly once a week.* 每周给植物浇一次透水。
2 to be in a liquid; to let something stay in a liquid 浸泡：*Leave the dishes to soak in hot water.* 让碟子在热水中泡着。
soak something up to take in a liquid 吸收，吸掉（液体）：*Soak the water up with a cloth.* 用布把水吸掉。

soaked /səʊkt/ *adjective* 形容词
very wet 湿透；湿淋淋：*You're soaked! Come in and get dry.* 你都湿透了！进来弄干吧。

soaking /'səʊkɪŋ/ *adjective* 形容词
very wet 湿透的；湿淋淋的：*This towel is soaking.* 这块毛巾湿淋淋的。

soap 0ᴀ /səʊp/ *noun* 名词 (*no plural* 不用复数形式)

A
B
C
D
E
F
G
H
I
J
K
L
M
N
O
P
Q
R
S
T
U
V
W
X
Y
Z

🔍 **PRONUNCIATION** 读音说明

The word **soap** sounds like **rope**.
* soap 读音像 rope。

a substance that you use with water for washing and cleaning 肥皂： *a bar of soap* 一块肥皂 ➒ Look at the picture at **bar**[1]. 见 bar[1] 的插图。

▶ **soapy** /'səʊpi/ *adjective* 形容词： *soapy water* 肥皂水

soap opera /'səʊp ɒprə/ (*also informal* 非正式亦作 **soap**) *noun* 名词
a story about the lives of a group of people, that is on the TV or radio every day or several times each week 肥皂剧： *Do you watch the soaps?* 你看肥皂剧吗？

soap powder /'səʊp paʊdə(r)/ *noun* 名词 (*no plural* 不用复数形式)
powder that you use for washing clothes 洗衣粉；肥皂粉

soar /sɔ:(r)/ *verb* 动词 (**soars, soaring, soared** /sɔ:d/)
1 to fly high in the sky 高飞；翱翔
2 to go up very fast 急升；猛增： *Prices are soaring.* 价格飞涨。

sob /sɒb/ *verb* 动词 (**sobs, sobbing, sobbed** /sɒbd/)
to cry loudly, making short sounds 啜泣；抽噎
▶ **sob** *noun* 名词： *I could hear her sobs through the wall.* 我隔着墙听到她的抽噎声。

sober /'səʊbə(r)/ *adjective* 形容词
not drunk 没有醉的；清醒的

so-called /ˌsəʊ 'kɔ:ld/ *adjective* 形容词
a word that you use to show that you do not think another word is correct 所谓的： *Her so-called friends did not help her* (= they are not really her friends). 她所谓的朋友并没有帮助她。

soccer /'sɒkə(r)/ *noun* 名词 (*no plural* 不用复数形式) *another word for* FOOTBALL
* football 的另一种说法

sociable /'səʊʃəbl/ *adjective* 形容词
friendly and enjoying being with other people 好交际的；和善的

social 🔊 /'səʊʃl/ *adjective* 形容词
connected with people together in society; connected with being with other people 社会的；社交的： *the social problems of big cities* 大城市的社会问题 ◇ *Anne has a busy social life* (= she goes out with friends a lot). 安妮的社交生活繁忙。

socialize /'səʊʃəlaɪz/ *verb* 动词 (**socializes, socializing, socialized** /'səʊʃəlaɪzd/)
to meet and spend time with people in a friendly way 交际；（与…）交往： *I enjoy socializing with friends.* 我喜欢与朋友来往。

social security /ˌsəʊʃl sɪ'kjʊərəti/ *noun* 名词 (*no plural* 不用复数形式) (*British* 英式英语)
money that a government pays to somebody who is poor, for example because they have no job 社会保障金；社会救济金

social worker /'səʊʃl wɜ:kə(r)/ *noun* 名词
a person whose job is to help people who have problems, for example because they are poor or ill 社会福利工作者

society 🔊 /sə'saɪəti/ *noun* 名词
1 (*no plural* 不用复数形式) a large group of people who live in the same country or area and have the same ideas about how to live 社会： *They carried out research into the roles of men and women in today's society.* 他们就现今社会中男性和女性的角色进行了研究。
2 (*plural* 复数形式 **societies**) a group of people who are interested in the same thing 社团；团体；协会： *a music society* 音乐社团

sock 🔊 /sɒk/ *noun* 名词
a thing that you wear on your foot, inside your shoe 短袜；袜子： *a pair of socks* 一双短袜 ➒ Look at Picture Dictionary page P5. 见彩页 P5。

socket /'sɒkɪt/ *noun* 名词
a place in a wall where you can connect electrical equipment to a power supply （电源）插座 ➒ Look at the picture at **plug**[1]. 见 plug[1] 的插图。

soda /'səʊdə/ (*also* 亦作 **soda water** /'səʊdə wɔ:tə(r)/) *noun* 名词 (*no plural* 不用复数形式)
1 water with bubbles in it that is used for mixing with other drinks 苏打水： *whisky and soda* 威士忌苏打
2 (*American* 美式英语) a sweet drink with bubbles in it that is made from soda water and a fruit flavour 苏打汽水

sofa /'səʊfə/ (*also* 亦作 **couch**) (*British also* 英式英语亦作 **settee**) *noun* 名词
a long soft seat for more than one person 长沙发： *Jane and Bob were sitting on the sofa.* 简和鲍勃坐在长沙发上。

soft 🔊 /sɒft/ *adjective* 形容词 (**softer, softest**)

1 not hard or firm; that moves when you press it 软的; 柔软的: *Warm butter is soft.* 温的黄油是软的。◇ *a soft bed* 软床
2 smooth and nice to touch; not rough 柔滑的; 细滑的: *soft skin* 柔嫩的皮肤 ◇ *My cat's fur is very soft.* 我的猫身上的毛很柔滑。
3 not bright or strong 柔和的: *the soft light of a candle* 柔和的烛光
4 quiet or gentle; not loud 轻柔的: *soft music* 轻柔的音乐 ◇ *He has a very soft voice.* 他的嗓音非常柔润。
5 kind and gentle; not strict 温柔的; 不严厉的: *She's too soft with her class and they don't do any work.* 她对她班上的学生太温和了，他们什么作业也不做。

sofa 长沙发

soft drink /ˌsɒft ˈdrɪŋk/ *noun* 名词
a cold sweet drink that does not have alcohol in it, for example orange juice 软饮料（不含酒精，如橙汁）

soften /ˈsɒfn/ *verb* 动词 (**softens**, **softening**, **softened** /ˈsɒfnd/)
to become softer or to make something softer （使）变软; （使）变柔和: *This cream softens the skin.* 这种护肤霜能令皮肤柔嫩。

softly /ˈsɒftli/ *adverb* 副词
gently or quietly 温和地; 轻柔地: *She spoke very softly.* 她说话声音非常轻柔。

software /ˈsɒftweə(r)/ *noun* 名词
(*no plural* 不用复数形式)
programs for a computer 软件: *There's a lot of new educational software available now.* 现在有很多新的教育软件。

soggy /ˈsɒgi/ *adjective* 形容词 (**soggier**, **soggiest**)
very wet 湿漉漉的; 湿透的

soil 0━ /sɔɪl/ *noun* 名词 (*no plural* 不用复数形式)
what plants and trees grow in; earth 土壤

solar /ˈsəʊlə(r)/ *adjective* 形容词
of or using the sun 太阳的: *solar energy* 太阳能

the solar system /ðə ˈsəʊlə sɪstəm/ *noun* 名词 (*no plural* 不用复数形式)
the sun and the planets that move around it 太阳系

sold *form of* SELL * sell 的不同形式

soldier 0━ /ˈsəʊldʒə(r)/ *noun* 名词
a person in an army 军人; 士兵

sole¹ /səʊl/ *adjective* 形容词
only 唯一的; 仅有的: *His sole interest is football.* 他唯一的爱好就是足球。

sole² /səʊl/ *noun* 名词
1 (*plural* 复数形式 **soles**) the bottom part of your foot or of a shoe 脚掌; 鞋底: *These boots have leather soles.* 这双靴子的底是皮的。 ⊃ Look at the picture at **foot**. 见 foot 的插图。
2 (*plural* 复数形式 **sole**) a flat sea fish that we eat 鳎（可食用比目鱼）

solely /ˈsəʊlli/ *adverb* 副词
only, and not involving anybody or anything else 仅; 只: *I agreed to come solely because of Frank.* 我同意来完全是因为弗兰克。

solemn /ˈsɒləm/ *adjective* 形容词
serious 严肃的; 庄严的: *slow, solemn music* 缓慢而庄严的音乐
▶ **solemnly** /ˈsɒləmli/ *adverb* 副词: *'I've got some bad news for you,' he said solemnly.* "我有坏消息告诉你。"他严肃地说。

solicitor /səˈlɪsɪtə(r)/ *noun* 名词 (*British* 英式英语)
a lawyer whose job is to give legal advice, prepare legal documents and arrange the buying and selling of land, etc. 事务律师、诉状律师（提供法律咨询、准备法律文件、安排土地的购买和出让等）

solid¹ 0━ /ˈsɒlɪd/ *adjective* 形容词
1 hard, not like a liquid or a gas 固体的; 坚固的: *Water becomes solid when it freezes.* 水遇冷会凝结成固体。
2 with no empty space inside; made of the same material inside and outside 实心的; 单一物质构成的: *a solid rubber ball* 实心橡皮球 ◇ *This ring is solid gold.* 这个戒指是纯金的。

solid² 0━ /ˈsɒlɪd/ *noun* 名词
not a liquid or gas 固体: *Milk is a liquid and cheese is a solid.* 牛奶是液体，干酪是固体。

solitary /ˈsɒlətri/ *adjective* 形容词
without others; alone 独自的; 单独的: *She went for a long solitary walk.* 她独自散步，走了很长的路。

solo¹ /ˈsəʊləʊ/ *adjective, adverb* 形容词，副词
alone; without other people 独自（的）；单独（的）： *She flew solo across the Atlantic.* 她独自一人飞越了大西洋。

solo² /ˈsəʊləʊ/ *noun* 名词 (plural 复数形式 solos)
a piece of music for one person to sing or play 独唱（曲）；独奏（曲）： *a guitar solo* 吉他独奏

solution ⚡ /səˈluːʃn/ *noun* 名词
the answer to a question or problem 答案；解决办法： *I can't find a solution to this problem.* 我找不到解决这个问题的办法。

solve ⚡ /sɒlv/ *verb* 动词 (solves, solving, solved /sɒlvd/)
to find the answer to a question or problem 解答；解决： *The police are still trying to solve the crime.* 警方仍在设法破案。

some ⚡ /sʌm/ *adjective, pronoun* 形容词，代词

🔊 PRONUNCIATION 读音说明
The word **some** sounds just like **sum**. * some 读音同 sum。

1 a number or an amount of something 一些；若干： *I bought some tomatoes and some butter.* 我买了些西红柿和黄油。◇ *This cake is nice. Do you want some?* 这个蛋糕味道不错。你想来点吗？

🔊 WHICH WORD? 词语辨析
Some or **any**? 用 some 还是 any？
We use **some** in statements and in questions where we expect the answer to be 'Yes'. * some 用于陈述句和预期得到肯定答案的疑问句： *He gave me some good advice.* 他给了我一些很好的忠告。◇ *Would you like some cake?* 你想来点蛋糕吗？
We use **any** in questions and after 'not' and 'if'. * any 用于疑问句或 not 和 if 后： *Did you buy any apples?* 你有没有买苹果？◇ *I didn't buy any meat.* 我没买肉。◇ *If you have any questions, please ask me at the end of the lesson.* 如有任何疑问，请在课末问我。

2 part of a number or an amount of something 某些；部分；有的： *Some of the children can swim, but the others can't.* 有的孩子会游泳，有的则不会。
3 I do not know which （表示不确定）某个： *There's some man at the door who wants to see you.* 门口有个男的想见你。

some more a little more or a few more 多一些： *Have some more coffee.* 再喝点咖啡吧。◇ *Some more people arrived.* 又来了一些人。

some time quite a long time 相当长的时间： *We waited for some time but she did not come.* 我们等了相当长的时间，但是她没来。

somebody ⚡ /ˈsʌmbədi/ (also 亦作 **someone**) *pronoun* 代词
a person; a person that you do not know 某人；有人： *There's somebody at the door.* 门口有人。◇ *Someone has broken the window.* 有人把窗户打破了。◇ *Ask somebody else* (= another person) *to help you.* 叫别人帮你吧。

somehow ⚡ /ˈsʌmhaʊ/ *adverb* 副词
in some way that you do not know 以某种方式： *We must find her somehow.* 我们怎么也得找到她。

someone ⚡ /ˈsʌmwʌn/ *another word for* SOMEBODY * somebody 的另一种说法

someplace /ˈsʌmpleɪs/ *American English for* SOMEWHERE 美式英语，即 somewhere

somersault /ˈsʌməsɔːlt/ *noun* 名词
a movement when you turn your body with your feet going over your head 滚翻；空翻；筋斗： *The children were doing somersaults on the carpet.* 孩子们在地毯上翻筋斗。

something ⚡ /ˈsʌmθɪŋ/ *pronoun* 代词
a thing; a thing you cannot name 某事；某物： *There's something under the table. What is it?* 桌子底下有个东西，那是什么？◇ *I want to tell you something.* 我有件事想告诉你。◇ *Would you like something else* (= another thing) *to eat?* 你想吃点别的吗？

something like the same as somebody or something in some ways, but not in every way 有点像： *A rat is something like a mouse, but bigger.* 大鼠有点像耗子，但是较大。

sometime /ˈsʌmtaɪm/ *adverb* 副词
at a time that you do not know exactly 某个时间： *I'll phone sometime tomorrow.* 我明天会找个时间打电话。

sometimes ⚡ /ˈsʌmtaɪmz/ *adverb* 副词
not very often 有时；间或： *He sometimes writes to me.* 他有时给我写信。◇ *Sometimes I drive to work and sometimes I go by bus.* 我有时开车上班，有时坐公共汽车去。

somewhere 0ᵣ /'sʌmweə(r)/ *adverb*
副词 (*British* 英式英语) (*American* 美式英语
someplace)

at, in or to a place that you do not know
exactly 某地；某处: *They live somewhere
near London.* 他们住在伦敦附近某处。◇
*'Did she go to Spain last year?' 'No, I think
she went somewhere else* (= to another
place).' "她去年去西班牙了吗？"
"没有，我想她去了别的地方。"

son 0ᵣ /sʌn/ *noun* 名词

> 🔊 **PRONUNCIATION** 读音说明
> The word **son** sounds just like **sun**.
> * son 读音同 sun。

a boy or man who is somebody's child
儿子: *They have a son and two daughters.*
他们有一个儿子和两个女儿。

song 0ᵣ /sɒŋ/ *noun* 名词
1 (*plural* 复数形式 songs) a piece of music
with words that you sing 歌；歌曲: *a pop
song* 流行歌曲
2 (*no plural* 不用复数形式) singing; music
that a person or bird makes 歌唱；声乐:
The story is told through song and dance.
故事通过歌舞来表现。

son-in-law /'sʌn ɪn lɔː/ *noun* 名词 (*plural*
复数形式 sons-in-law)
the husband of your daughter 女婿

soon 0ᵣ /suːn/ *adverb* 副词
not long after now, or not long after
a certain time 不久；马上: *John will be
home soon.* 约翰快到家了。◇ *She arrived
soon after two o'clock.* 两点钟后不久她就
到了。◇ *Goodbye! See you soon!* 再见！
回头见！
as soon as at the same time that; when
一…就…: *Phone me as soon as you get
home.* 你一到家就给我打电话。
sooner or later at some time in the
future 迟早；早晚: *Don't worry – I'm
sure he'll write to you sooner or later.*
不用担心，我肯定他迟早会给你来信的。

soot /sʊt/ *noun* 名词 (*no plural* 不用复数
形式)
black powder that comes from smoke
煤烟子

soothe /suːð/ *verb* 动词 (soothes,
soothing, soothed /suːðd/)
to make somebody feel calmer and less
unhappy 安慰；抚慰: *The baby was
crying, so I tried to soothe her by singing to
her.* 宝宝在哭，所以我唱歌来哄她。
▶ **soothing** /'suːðɪŋ/ *adjective* 形容词:
soothing music 舒缓的音乐

sophisticated /sə'fɪstɪkeɪtɪd/ *adjective*
形容词
1 having a lot of experience of the world
and social situations; knowing about
things like fashion and culture 见多识广
的；老练的；世故的: *She's a very
sophisticated young woman.* 她是个很有
见识的年轻女子。
2 (used about machines, systems, etc.)
clever and complicated (机器、系统等)
精密的: *highly sophisticated computer
systems* 高度精密的电脑系统

sore 0ᵣ /sɔː(r)/ *adjective* 形容词
If a part of your body is **sore**, it gives you
pain. 疼痛的: *My feet were sore after the
long walk.* 我走了那一大段路后脚很疼。◇
I've got a sore throat. 我嗓子疼。

sorrow /'sɒrəʊ/ *noun* 名词 (*no plural*
不用复数形式)
sadness 哀伤；悲痛

sorry 0ᵣ /'sɒri/ *adjective* 形容词
1 feeling sad 遗憾；难过: *I'm sorry you
can't come to the party.* 你不能来参加
聚会，我感到很失望。
2 a word that you use when you feel bad
about something you have done 抱歉；
对不起: *I'm sorry I didn't phone you.*
我没给你打电话，实在很抱歉。◇ *Sorry
I'm late!* 对不起，我迟到了！◇ *I'm sorry
for losing your pen.* 我把你的笔给丢了，
对不起。
3 a word that you use to say 'no' politely
(表示婉言拒绝): *I'm sorry – I can't
help you.* 很抱歉，我帮不了你。
4 a word that you use when you did not
hear what somebody said and you want
them to say it again (请求重复自己没
听清的话): *'My name is Linda Willis.'
'Sorry? Linda who?'* "我叫琳达·
威利斯。" "对不起，琳达什么？"
feel sorry for somebody to feel sad
because somebody has problems 同情
某人；为某人难过: *I felt sorry for her and
gave her some money.* 我同情她，就给了
她一些钱。

sort¹ 0ᵣ /sɔːt/ *noun* 名词
a group of things or people that are the
same in some way; a type or kind 种类；
类型: *What sort of music do you like
best – pop or classical?* 你最爱什么类型的
音乐，流行音乐还是古典音乐？◇ *We
found all sorts of shells on the beach.*
我们在海滩上找到各种各样的贝壳。
sort of (*informal* 非正式) words that you
use when you are not sure about
something 有几分；有点儿: *It's sort of*

long and thin, a bit like a sausage. 那个
东西细细长长的，有点像香肠。

sort² 0➡ /sɔːt/ *verb* 动词 (**sorts**, **sorting**,
sorted)
to put things into groups 把…分类: *The
machine sorts the eggs into large ones and
small ones.* 这台机器按大小把鸡蛋分类。
sort something out
1 (*informal* 非正式) to make something
tidy 整理: *I sorted out my clothes and
put the old ones in a bag.* 我整理好衣服，
把旧的都放进袋子里。
2 to find an answer to a problem 解决
（问题）: *I haven't found a flat yet but
I hope to sort something out soon.* 我还没
找到公寓，但希望能很快解决这件事。

SOS /ˌes əʊ 'es/ *noun* 名词
a call for help from a ship or a plane that
is in danger 紧急求救信号

sought *form of* SEEK * seek 的不同形式

soul /səʊl/ *noun* 名词
1 (*plural* 复数形式 **souls**) the part of a
person that some people believe does not
die when the body dies 灵魂: *Christians
believe that your soul goes to heaven when
you die.* 基督徒相信人死后灵魂会升上
天堂。
2 (*also* 亦作 **soul music** /'səʊl mjuːzɪk/)
(*no plural* 不用复数形式) a kind of music
that was made popular by African
American musicians 灵乐，灵魂音乐
（源于非洲裔美国人）: *a soul singer*
灵乐歌手
not a soul not one person 一个人都
没有: *I looked everywhere, but there
wasn't a soul in the building.* 我到处看了，
大楼里一个人都没有。

sound¹ 0➡ /saʊnd/ *noun* 名词
something that you hear 声音；响声:
I heard the sound of a baby crying.
我听到一名婴儿的哭声。◇ *Light travels
faster than sound.* 光比声传播得快。

sound² 0➡ /saʊnd/ *verb* 动词 (**sounds**,
sounding, **sounded**)
to seem a certain way when you hear it
听起来: *He sounded angry when I spoke
to him on the phone.* 我跟他通电话的
时候，他听上去很生气。◇ *That sounds
like a good idea.* 那个主意听起来不错。◇
*She told me about the book – it sounds
interesting.* 她向我介绍了那本书，听起来
很有意思。

sound³ /saʊnd/ *adjective* 形容词
1 right and good 合理的；可靠的；
良好的: *She gave me some sound advice.*
她给了我一些很合理的建议。

2 healthy or strong 健康的；强健的:
sound teeth 健康的牙齿

sound⁴ /saʊnd/ *adverb* 副词
sound asleep sleeping very well 酣睡；
熟睡: *The children are sound asleep.*
孩子们睡得正香。

soundly /'saʊndli/ *adverb* 副词
completely and deeply 完全；全然；
深深: *I slept very soundly last night.*
我昨晚睡得很沉。

soup 0➡ /suːp/ *noun* 名词 (*no plural*
不用复数形式)

> 🔊 **PRONUNCIATION** 读音说明
>
> The word **soup** sounds like **loop**.
> * soup 读音像 loop。

liquid food that you make by cooking
things like vegetables or meat in water
汤: *tomato soup* 番茄汤 ➲ Look at
Picture Dictionary page **P7**. 见彩页 P7。

sour /'saʊə(r)/ *adjective* 形容词
1 with a sharp taste like a lemon（味道）
酸的: *If it's too sour, put some sugar in it.*
要是太酸就放点糖进去。
2 Sour milk tastes bad because it is not
fresh.（牛奶）变酸的，馊的: *This milk
has gone sour.* 这牛奶馊了。

source /sɔːs/ *noun* 名词
a place where something comes from
来源；源头；出处: *Our information
comes from many sources.* 我们的消息
有很多来源。

south 0➡ /saʊθ/ *noun* 名词 (*no plural*
不用复数形式) (*abbr.* 缩略式 S)
the direction that is on your right when
you watch the sun come up in the
morning 南；南方 ➲ Look at the picture
at **compass**. 见 compass 的插图。
▶ **south** *adjective*, *adverb* 形容词，副词:
Brazil is in South America. 巴西位于
南美洲。◇ *the south coast of England*
英格兰南岸 ◇ *Birds fly south in the winter.*
冬天鸟飞往南方。

south-east /ˌsaʊθ 'iːst/ *noun* 名词
(*no plural* 不用复数形式) (*abbr.* 缩略式 SE)
the direction between south and east;
a place in this direction 东南；东南方；
东南部: *He lives in the south-east.* 他住在
东南部。➲ Look at the picture at
compass. 见 compass 的插图。
▶ **south-east** *adjective*, *adverb* 形容词，
副词: *south-east London* 伦敦东南部
▶ **south-eastern** /ˌsaʊθ 'iːstən/ *adjective*
形容词: *the south-eastern states of the US*
美国的东南部诸州

southern ⊶ /'sʌðən/ *adjective*
形容词
connected with, in or from the south
南方的；向南的；南部的：*Italy is in
southern Europe.* 意大利位于欧洲南部。

the South Pole /ðə ˌsaʊθ 'pəʊl/ *noun*
名词 (*no plural* 不用复数形式)
the point on the Earth's surface which is
furthest south 南极 ⊃ Look at the picture
at **earth**. 见 earth 的插图。

south-west /ˌsaʊθ 'west/ *noun* 名词 (*no
plural* 不用复数形式) (*abbr.* 缩略式 SW)
the direction between south and west;
a place in this direction 西南；西南方；
西南部： *He's from the south-west.* 他来自
西南部。 ⊃ Look at the picture at
compass. 见 compass 的插图。
▸ **south-west** *adjective, adverb* 形容词，
副词： *Our garden faces south-west.* 我们
的花园朝西南。
▸ **south-western** /ˌsaʊθ 'westən/
adjective 形容词

souvenir /ˌsuːvə'nɪə(r)/ *noun* 名词
something that you keep to remember a
place or a special event 纪念物；纪念品：
*I brought back this cowboy hat as a
souvenir of Texas.* 我把这顶牛仔帽带了
回来，算是到得克萨斯州的纪念品。

sow /səʊ/ *verb* 动词 (**sows, sowing, sowed**
/səʊd/, **has sown** /səʊn/ or 或 **has sowed**)
to put seeds in the ground 播种；下种：
The farmer sowed the field with corn. 农民
在田里种上了谷物。

space ⊶ /speɪs/ *noun* 名词
1 (*no plural* 不用复数形式) a place that is
big enough for somebody or something
to go into or onto 空间 ⊃ SAME MEANING
room 同义词为 room： *Is there space for
me in your car?* 你的车还有空儿给我坐吗？
2 (*plural* 复数形式 **spaces**) an empty place
between things 空位： *a parking space*
停车位 ◇ *There is a space here for you to
write your name.* 这里有个空白处让你把
名字写上。
3 (*also* 亦作 **outer space**) (*no plural* 不用
复数形式) the area outside the Earth's
atmosphere where all the other planets
and stars are 太空；外层空间： *space
travel* 太空旅行

spacecraft /'speɪskrɑːft/ *noun* 名词
(*plural* 复数形式 **spacecraft**)
a vehicle that travels in space 航天器；
宇宙飞船；太空船

spaceman /'speɪsmæn/ *noun* 名词 (*plural*
复数形式 **spacemen** /'speɪsmen/) (*also*
还有 **spacewoman** /'speɪswʊmən/, *plural*

复数形式 **spacewomen** /'speɪswɪmɪn/)
(*informal* 非正式)
a person who travels in space 宇航员；
航天员；太空人 ⊃ SAME MEANING
astronaut 同义词为 astronaut

spaceship /'speɪsʃɪp/ *noun* 名词
a vehicle that travels in space 宇宙飞船；
太空船

space shuttle /'speɪs ʃʌtl/ (*also* 亦作
shuttle) *noun* 名词
a vehicle that can travel into space and
land like a plane when it returns to Earth
航天飞机；太空梭

spacious /'speɪʃəs/ *adjective* 形容词
with a lot of space inside 宽敞的：
a spacious kitchen 宽敞的厨房

spade /speɪd/ *noun* 名词
1 a tool that you use for digging 铲子；锹
⊃ Look at the picture at **dig**. 见 dig 的
插图。
2 **spades** (*plural* 用复数形式) the playing
cards that have the shape ♠ on them
（纸牌）黑桃： *the queen of spades* 黑桃 Q
⊃ Look at the picture at **playing card**.
见 playing card 的插图。

spaghetti /spə'geti/ *noun* 名词 (*no plural*
不用复数形式)
a kind of food made from flour and
water, that looks like long pieces of string
意大利细面条： *Shall we have some
spaghetti?* 我们吃点意大利细面条好吗？
⊃ Look at Picture Dictionary page **P7**.
见彩页 P7。

spam /spæm/ *noun* 名词 (*no plural* 不用
复数形式) (*informal* 非正式)
advertisements that companies send by
email to people who have not asked for
them 垃圾电邮

span[1] /spæn/ *noun* 名词
1 the length of time that something
continues 持续时间： *We are looking at
a time span of several months.* 我们在考量
一个为期数个月的期限。
2 the length of something from one end
to another （物件的）宽度，跨度： *The
bird's wingspan is 60cm.* 这只鸟翼展 60
厘米。

span[2] /spæn/ *verb* 动词 (**spans, spanning,
spanned** /spænd/)
1 to continue for a particular length of
time 持续；贯穿： *His career spanned
more than 50 years.* 他的职业生涯长达
50 多年。
2 to form a bridge over something 横跨；
在…上架桥： *The river is spanned by a*

beautiful iron bridge. 河上架起了一座美丽的铁桥。

spanner 扳手

spanner /'spænə(r)/ (*British* 英式英语) (*American* 美式英语 **wrench**) *noun* 名词
a tool that you use for turning small metal rings (called **nuts**) and pins (called **bolts**) that are used for holding things together 扳手，扳子，扳钳（用以拧动螺母和螺栓的工具）

spare[1] /speə(r)/ *adjective* 形容词
1 If something is **spare**, you do not use or need it all the time. 备用的；闲置的：*Have you got a spare tyre in your car?* 你车上有备用轮胎吗？ ◇ *You can stay with us tonight. We've got a spare room.* 你今晚可以住在我们这儿。我们有间空房。
2 Spare time is time when you are not working. 空闲的；闲暇的：*What do you do in your spare time?* 你空闲时做些什么？

spare[2] /speə(r)/ *verb* 动词 (spares, sparing, spared /speəd/)
to be able to give something to somebody 留出；腾出；拨出；抽出：*I can't spare the time to help you today.* 我今天抽不出时间来帮你。 ◇ *Can you spare any change?* 可以给我一些零钱吗？

spark /spɑːk/ *noun* 名词
a very small piece of something that is burning 火花；火星

sparkle /'spɑːkl/ *verb* 动词 (sparkles, sparkling, sparkled /'spɑːkld/)
to shine with a lot of very small points of light 闪烁；闪耀：*The sea sparkled in the sunlight.* 海面在阳光下水光粼粼。 ◇ *Her eyes sparkled with excitement.* 她的眼睛闪耀着激动的光芒。
▶ **sparkle** *noun* 名词 (*no plural* 不用复数形式)：*the sparkle of diamonds* 钻石的熠熠生辉

sparkling /'spɑːklɪŋ/ *adjective* 形容词
1 shining with a lot of very small points of light 闪烁的；闪耀的：*sparkling blue eyes* 亮晶晶的蓝眼睛
2 Sparkling wine or water has a lot of small bubbles in it. （饮料）有汽的，起泡的 ⊃ SAME MEANING **fizzy** 同义词为 fizzy

sparrow /'spærəʊ/ *noun* 名词
a small brown bird 麻雀

spat *form of* SPIT * spit 的不同形式

speak 0ᵣ /spiːk/ *verb* 动词 (speaks, speaking, spoke /spəʊk/, has spoken /'spəʊkən/)
1 to say things; to talk to somebody 说话；谈话；讲话：*Please speak more slowly.* 请说得慢一点。 ◇ *Can I speak to John Smith, please?* (= words that you say on the telephone) 请叫约翰•史密斯来听电话好吗？ ◇ *The head teacher spoke for over an hour.* 校长讲了一个多小时。
2 to know and use a language 说（某种语言）：*I can speak French and Italian.* 我会说法语和意大利语。

speak up to talk louder 大声点说：*Can you speak up? I can't hear you!* 你能说得大声点吗？我听不见！
⊃ The noun is **speech**. 名词为 speech.

speaker 0ᵣ /'spiːkə(r)/ *noun* 名词
1 a person who is talking to a group of people 发言者；演讲者
2 the part of something such as a radio or CD player where the sound comes out 扬声器；喇叭

spear /spɪə(r)/ *noun* 名词
a long stick with a sharp point at one end, used for hunting or fighting 矛；标枪

special 0ᵣ /'speʃl/ *adjective* 形容词
1 not usual or ordinary; important for a reason 特别的；特殊的：*It's my birthday today so we are having a special dinner.* 今天是我生日，所以我们准备吃一顿特别的晚餐。
2 for a particular person or thing 专门的；特设的：*He goes to a special school for deaf children.* 他上的是为失聪儿童开办的特殊学校。

specialist /'speʃəlɪst/ *noun* 名词
a person who knows a lot about something 专家：*She's a specialist in Chinese art.* 她是中国艺术的专家。

specialize /'speʃəlaɪz/ *verb* 动词 (specializes, specializing, specialized /'speʃəlaɪzd/)
specialize in something to study or know a lot about one special thing 专门研究；专攻：*He specialized in criminal law.* 他专攻刑法。

specially /'speʃəli/ (*also* 亦作 especially) *adverb* 副词
1 for a particular person or thing 专门；特意：*I made this cake specially for you.* 这个蛋糕我是特意给你做的。
2 very; more than usual or more than others 非常；格外；尤其 ⊃ SAME MEANING

particularly 同义词为 particularly: *The food was not specially good.* 食物并不是特别好。

species /'spiːʃiːz/ *noun* 名词 (*plural* 复数形式 species)
a group of animals or plants that are the same and can BREED (= make new animals or plants) together（生物分类）种；物种: *a rare **species** of frog* 一种罕见的青蛙

specific /spə'sɪfɪk/ *adjective* 形容词
1 exact and clear 明确的: *He gave us **specific** instructions on how to get there.* 他给我们明确地指示如何去那里。
2 particular 特定的: *Is there anything **specific** that you want to talk about?* 你有什么特别的事情要谈吗？
▶ **specifically** /spə'sɪfɪkli/ *adverb* 副词: *I **specifically** asked you to buy butter, not margarine.* 我特别叮嘱你要买黄油，而不是人造黄油。

specify /'spesɪfaɪ/ *verb* 动词 (specifies, specifying, specified /'spesɪfaɪd/)
to say something clearly or in detail 具体说明；明确指定: *He said he'd be arriving in the morning, but didn't **specify** the time.* 他说他早上到，但没具体说什么时间。

specimen /'spesɪmən/ *noun* 名词
1 one example of a group of things 样本；样品: *specimens of different types of rock* 不同种类的岩石样本
2 a small amount or part of something that shows what the rest is like 抽样；取样 ⊃ SAME MEANING **sample** 同义词为 sample: *The doctor took a **specimen** of blood for testing.* 医生抽了血样进行化验。

speck /spek/ *noun* 名词
a very small bit of something 小点: *specks of dust* 尘粒

spectacles /'spektəklz/ *noun* 名词 (*plural* 用复数形式) (*formal* 正式)
pieces of special glass that you wear over your eyes to help you see better 眼镜 ⊃ SAME MEANING **glasses** 同义词为 glasses: *a pair of **spectacles*** 一副眼镜

spectacular /spek'tækjələ(r)/ *adjective* 形容词
wonderful to see 壮观的；壮丽的: *There was a **spectacular** view from the top of the mountain.* 从山顶上望去，景色十分壮丽。
▶ **spectacularly** /spek'tækjələli/ *adverb* 副词: *This is a **spectacularly** beautiful area.* 这是个景色美得令人赞叹的地区。

spectator /spek'teɪtə(r)/ *noun* 名词
a person who is watching an event, especially a sports event（尤指体育赛事的）观众: *There were 2 000 **spectators** at the football match.* 那场足球比赛有 2 000 名观众入场观看。

sped *form of* SPEED² * speed² 的不同形式

speech /spiːtʃ/ *noun* 名词
1 (*plural* 复数形式 speeches) a talk that you give to a group of people 演说；讲话: *The President made a **speech**.* 总统发表了演说。
2 (*no plural* 不用复数形式) the power to speak, or the way that you speak 说话能力；说话方式: *He has problems with his **speech**.* 他说话有困难。

speed¹ /spiːd/ *noun* 名词
how fast something goes 速度: *The car was travelling at a **speed** of 50 miles an hour.* 当时汽车以每小时 50 英里的速度行驶。 ◇ *a high-**speed** train* (= that goes very fast) 高速列车

speed² /spiːd/ *verb* 动词 (speeds, speeding, sped /sped/ or 或 speeded, has sped or 或 has speeded)
1 to go or move very quickly 快速行进；疾驰: *He **sped** past me on his bike.* 他骑着自行车从我身边飞速驶过。
2 to drive too fast 超速驾驶；超速行车: *The police stopped me because I was **speeding**.* 我开车超速，所以警察把我拦了下来。
speed up, speed something up to go faster; to make something go faster（使）加速: *What can we do to **speed** up the process?* 我们能做些什么来加快流程？

speed limit /'spiːd lɪmɪt/ *noun* 名词
the fastest that you are allowed to travel on a road（道路的）最高速度限制，限速: *The **speed limit** on motorways is 100 kilometres an hour.* 高速公路的限速是每小时 100 公里。

spell¹ /spel/ *verb* 动词 (spells, spelling, spelt /spelt/ or 或 spelled /speld/, has spelt or 或 has spelled)
to use the right letters to make a word 拼写: *'How do you **spell** your name?' 'A-Z-I-Z.'* "你的名字怎么拼？" "A-Z-I-Z。" ◇ *You have **spelt** this word wrong.* 你把这个词拼错了。

spell² /spel/ *noun* 名词
magic words that make somebody change or make them do what you want 咒语；符咒: *The witch cast a **spell** on the prince.* 女巫给王子施了魔咒。

spelling /'spelɪŋ/ *noun* 名词
1 (*plural* 复数形式 spellings) the right way of writing a word 拼法: *Look in your*

A
B
C
D
E
F
G
H
I
J
K
L
M
N
O
P
Q
R
S
T
U
V
W
X
Y
Z

dictionary to find the right spelling. 查词典
找出正确的拼法。
2 (no plural 不用复数形式) the ability to
spell correctly 拼写能力: *You need to
work on your spelling.* 你需要在拼写方面
下点功夫。

spend 0⃞ /spend/ *verb* 动词 (spends,
spending, spent /spent/, has spent)
1 to pay money for something 花，用
（钱）: *Louise **spends** a lot of money **on**
clothes.* 路易丝花很多钱买衣服。
2 to pass time 花，度过（时间）: *I spent
the summer in Italy.* 我在意大利过了
夏天。◇ *He spent a lot of time sleeping.*
他用了很多时间睡觉。

sphere /sfɪə(r)/ *noun* 名词
any round object that is like a ball 球;
球体: *The earth is a sphere.* 地球是一个
球体。

spice 0⃞ /spaɪs/ *noun* 名词
a powder of the seeds from a plant, that
you can put in food to give it a stronger
taste 香料; 调味粉: *They use a lot of
spices, such as chilli and ginger.* 他们使用
很多香料，如辣椒和姜。➲ Look at
Picture Dictionary page **P6**. 见彩页 P6。
▶ **spicy** /'spaɪsi/ *adjective* 形容词 (spicier,
spiciest): *spicy food* 香辣食物

spider 蜘蛛

web 蜘蛛网

spider 蜘蛛

spider 0⃞ /'spaɪdə(r)/ *noun* 名词
a small animal with eight legs, that
catches and eats insects 蜘蛛: *Spiders
spin webs to catch flies.* 蜘蛛结网捕捉
苍蝇。

spied form of SPY² * spy² 的不同形式
spies
1 plural of SPY¹ * spy¹ 的复数形式
2 form of SPY² * spy² 的不同形式

spike /spaɪk/ *noun* 名词
a piece of metal with a sharp point 尖状

物; 尖刺: *The fence has spikes along the
top.* 篱笆顶部有尖刺。

spiky 刺猬式的

spiky hair 刺猬式头发

spiky /'spaɪki/ *adjective* 形容词 (spikier,
spikiest)
1 having sharp points 有尖刺的: *spiky
leaves* 带刺的叶子
2 Spiky hair sticks straight up in the air.
（头发）刺猬式的

spill 洒出

He **spilled** his milk.
他把牛奶洒了。

spill /spɪl/ *verb* 动词 (spills, spilling, spilt
/spɪlt/ or 或 spilled /spɪld/, has spilt or 或
has spilled)
If you **spill** a liquid, it flows out of
something by accident. 洒出; 溅出;
溢出: *I've spilt my coffee!* 我把咖啡洒了!

spin /spɪn/ *verb* 动词 (spins, spinning,
spun /spʌn/, has spun)
1 to turn round quickly; to turn
something round quickly （使）快速
旋转: *She spun round as he entered the
room.* 他进房间时，她猛地转过身来。◇
Spin the wheel. 转动轮子。
2 to make thread from wool or cotton
纺（线）; 纺（纱）: *She spun and dyed
the wool herself.* 毛线是她自纺自染的。
3 If a spider **spins** a WEB (= a thin net
that it makes to catch flies), it produces

thread from its own body to make it.
（蜘蛛）结（网）

spinach /'spɪnɪtʃ/ *noun* 名词 (*no plural* 不用复数形式)
a vegetable with big green leaves 菠菜

spine /spaɪn/ *noun* 名词
the line of bones in your back 脊柱；脊椎

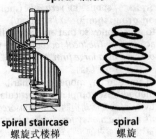

spiral 螺旋形

spiral staircase
螺旋式楼梯

spiral
螺旋

spiral /'spaɪrəl/ *noun* 名词
a long shape that goes round and round as it goes up 螺旋形：*A spring is a spiral.* 弹簧是螺旋形的。
▶ **spiral** *adjective* 形容词：*a spiral staircase* 螺旋式楼梯

spire /'spaɪə(r)/ *noun* 名词
a tall pointed tower on top of a church （教堂顶部的）尖塔，尖顶

spirit ⊶ /'spɪrɪt/ *noun* 名词
1 the part of a person that is not the body. Some people think that your **spirit** does not die when your body dies. 精神；心灵
2 spirits (*plural* 用复数形式) strong alcoholic drinks such as WHISKY 烈酒
3 spirits (*plural* 用复数形式) the way that a person feels 情绪；心境：*She's in high spirits* (= happy) *today.* 她今天情绪高涨。

spiritual /'spɪrɪtʃuəl/ *adjective* 形容词
connected with deep feelings and beliefs rather than the physical body 精神的；心灵的：*Our society often neglects people's spiritual needs.* 我们的社会经常忽视人们的精神需要。

spit /spɪt/ *verb* 动词 (spits, spitting, spat /spæt/, has spat)
to send liquid or food out from your mouth 吐；唾：*He spat on the ground.* 他往地上吐了痰。 ◇ *The baby spat her food out.* 宝宝把食物吐了出来。

spite ⊶ /spaɪt/ *noun* 名词 (*no plural* 不用复数形式)
when somebody deliberately says or does unkind things 恶意；怨恨：*She broke my watch out of spite.* 她为了泄愤把我的手表弄坏了。

in spite of something although something is true; not noticing or caring about something 尽管 ⊃ SAME MEANING **despite** 同义词为 despite：*I slept well in spite of the noise.* 尽管很吵，我还是睡得很好。 ◇ *In spite of the bad weather, we went out.* 尽管天气恶劣，我们还是出门了。

spiteful /'spaɪtfl/ *adjective* 形容词
saying or doing unkind things 恶意的；恶毒的

splash¹ /splæʃ/ *verb* 动词 (splashes, splashing, splashed /splæʃt/)
to throw drops of liquid over somebody or something; to make this happen 溅湿；泼洒：*The car splashed us as it drove past.* 汽车驶过的时候溅了我们一身水。 ◇ *The children were splashing around in the pool.* 孩子们在游泳池里拍打戏水。

splash² /splæʃ/ *noun* 名词 (*plural* 复数形式 splashes)
1 the sound that a person or thing makes when they fall into water 落水声；溅泼声：*Tom jumped into the river with a big splash.* 汤姆扑通一声跳进了河里。
2 a small amount of liquid 溅泼的液体：*There were splashes of paint on the floor.* 地板上有一摊摊颜料。

splendid /'splendɪd/ *adjective* 形容词
very beautiful or very good 壮丽的；极好的：*a splendid palace* 富丽堂皇的宫殿 ◇ *What a splendid idea!* 这主意妙极了！

splinter /'splɪntə(r)/ *noun* 名词
a small thin sharp piece of wood, metal or glass that has broken off a bigger piece （木块、金属或玻璃的）锋利碎片：*I've got a splinter in my finger.* 我的手指扎了根刺。

split¹ /splɪt/ *verb* 动词 (splits, splitting, split, has split)
1 to divide or separate; to make this happen （使）分开；分摊：*I split the wood with an axe.* 我用斧子把木头劈开了。 ◇ *We split the money between us.* 我们把钱分了。 ◇ *The teacher told us to split into groups.* 老师叫我们分组。
2 to tear or break apart; to make this happen （使）裂开：*His jeans split when he sat down.* 他坐下时牛仔裤裂开了。 ◇

How did you split your lip? 你的嘴唇怎么裂开了?
split up to stop being together 分手: *He has split up with his girlfriend.* 他跟女友分手了。

split² /splɪt/ *noun* 名词
a long cut or hole in something 裂缝; 裂口: *There's a big split in the tent.* 帐篷上裂了一个大口子。

spoil ⚡ /spɔɪl/ *verb* 动词 (spoils, spoiling, spoilt /spɔɪlt/ or 或 spoiled /spɔɪld/, has spoilt or 或 has spoiled)
1 to make something less good than before 破坏; 糟蹋: *The mud spoiled my shoes.* 我的鞋子给泥弄污了。◊ *Did the bad weather spoil your holiday?* 恶劣的天气有没有搞砸你的假期?
2 to give a child too much so that they think they can always have what they want 溺爱; 娇惯; 宠坏: *She spoils her grandchildren.* 她总是宠着孙子孙女。

spoilt /spɔɪlt/ *adjective* 形容词
(used about a child) rude and badly behaved because people give them everything they ask for (孩子) 娇惯的, 宠坏的: *a spoilt child* 宠坏了的孩子

spoke¹ *form of* SPEAK * speak 的不同形式

spoke² /spəʊk/ *noun* 名词
one of the thin bars that join the middle part of a wheel to the outside part 辐条; 轮辐 ⊃ Look at the picture at **bicycle**. 见 bicycle 的插图。

spoken ⚡ *form of* SPEAK * speak 的不同形式

spokesman /'spəʊksmən/ *noun* 名词
(*plural* 复数形式 spokesmen /'spəʊksmən/)
(*also* 还有 spokeswoman /'spəʊkswʊmən/, *plural* 复数形式 spokeswomen /'spəʊkswɪmɪn/)
a person who tells somebody what a group of people has decided 发言人

sponge /spʌndʒ/ *noun* 名词
1 a soft thing with a lot of small holes in it, that you use for washing yourself or cleaning things 海绵
2 (*British* 英式英语) (*also* 亦作 sponge cake /'spʌndʒ keɪk/) a soft light cake 海绵蛋糕: *a chocolate sponge* 巧克力海绵蛋糕

spongy /'spʌndʒi/ *adjective* 形容词
soft, like a SPONGE 海绵似的; 柔软吸水的: *The ground was quite spongy.* 地面像海绵似的相当松软。

sponsor¹ /'spɒnsə(r)/ *noun* 名词
1 a person or a company that gives money so that an event will take place

赞助人; 赞助商: *The race organizers are trying to attract sponsors.* 比赛的主办机构正在想方设法拉赞助。
2 a person who agrees to pay money to a charity if somebody else completes a particular activity (慈善活动) 赞助人, 捐助者: *I need sponsors for a bike ride to Brighton in aid of Cancer Research.* 为了替癌症研究院筹款, 我需要有人赞助我赴布赖顿的自行车之旅。

sponsor² /'spɒnsə(r)/ *verb* 动词 (sponsors, sponsoring, sponsored /'spɒnsəd/)
1 to give money so that an event will take place 赞助: *The local football team were sponsored by a large firm.* 当地的足球队是由一家大公司赞助的。
2 to agree to pay money to a charity if somebody else completes a particular activity 为慈善活动捐助: *a sponsored walk to raise money for children in need* 为贫困儿童举办的步行筹款

spoons 勺子

tablespoon 餐勺
soup spoon 汤匙
dessertspoon 点心匙 **teaspoon** 茶匙

spoon ⚡ /spuːn/ *noun* 名词
a thing with a round end that you use for eating, serving or mixing food 勺子; 匙; 调羹: *a wooden spoon* 木勺 ◊ *You need a knife, fork and spoon.* 你需要一副刀、叉、匙。

spoonful /'spuːnfʊl/ *noun* 名词
the amount that you can put in one spoon 一勺的量: *a spoonful of sugar* 一勺糖

sport ⚡ /spɔːt/ *noun* 名词
a physical game or activity that you do to keep your body strong or because you enjoy it 体育运动: *Jane does a lot of sport.* 简做很多运动。◊ *Football, swimming, and tennis are all sports.* 足球、游泳和网球都是体育运动。

A
B
C
D
E
F
G
H
I
J
K
L
M
N
O
P
Q
R
S
T
U
V
W
X
Y
Z

> ⌕ **WORD BUILDING** 词汇扩充
>
> There are many different types of
> **sport**. Here are some of them:
> baseball, football, karate, motor
> racing, rugby, snowboarding. Do you
> know any others? * sport 的种类很多，
> 如：baseball（棒球）、football
> （足球）、karate（空手道）、motor
> racing（赛车）、rugby（橄榄球）、
> snowboarding（滑雪板运动）。你还
> 知道别的吗？

➲ Look at Picture Dictionary pages
P14-P15. 见彩页 P14-P15。

sports car /'spɔːts kɑː(r)/ *noun* 名词
a fast car, usually with a roof that you can
open 跑车（顶篷多可打开）

sports centre /'spɔːts sentə(r)/ *noun*
名词
a big building where you can play a lot of
different sports 体育中心

sportsman /'spɔːtsmən/ *noun* 名词
(*plural* 复数形式 sportsmen /'spɔːtsmən/)
(*also* 还有 sportswoman /'spɔːtswʊmən/,
plural 复数形式 sportswomen
/'spɔːtswɪmɪn/)
a person who plays sport 运动员；体育
运动爱好者

sporty /'spɔːti/ *adjective* 形容词 (sportier,
sportiest)
liking or good at sport 爱好（或擅长）
体育运动的

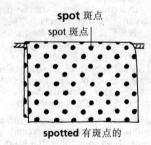

spot 斑点

spot 斑点

spotted 有斑点的

spot¹ 0╌ /spɒt/ *noun* 名词
1 a small round mark 斑点：*a red dress
with white spots* 带白点的红色连衣裙
2 (*British* 英式英语) a small red mark on
your skin（皮肤上的）丘疹，粉刺：*A lot
of teenagers get spots on their faces.* 很多
青少年脸上都长粉刺。
3 a place 地点；场所：*This is a good spot
for a picnic.* 这是野餐的好地方。

spot² /spɒt/ *verb* 动词 (spots, spotting,
spotted)
to see somebody or something suddenly
（突然）看到：*She spotted her friend in
the crowd.* 她在人群中看到她的朋友。

spotless /'spɒtləs/ *adjective* 形容词
completely clean 一尘不染的；洁净的：
She keeps the house spotless. 她把房子收拾
得一尘不染。

spotted /'spɒtɪd/ *adjective* 形容词
with small round marks on it 有斑点的：
a spotted shirt 有花点的衬衫 ➲ Look at
the picture at **spot¹**. 见 spot¹ 的插图。

spotty /'spɒti/ *adjective* 形容词 (spottier,
spottiest) (*British* 英式英语)
with small red marks on your skin 长丘疹
（或粉刺）的：*He's got a very spotty face.*
他脸上长满粉刺。

spout /spaʊt/ *noun* 名词
the narrow part of a container that you
pour liquid out of（盛液体容器的）嘴
➲ Look at the picture at **teapot**. 见 teapot
的插图。

sprain /spreɪn/ *verb* 动词 (sprains,
spraining, sprained /spreɪnd/)
to hurt part of your body by turning it
suddenly 扭伤：*Scott fell and sprained his
ankle.* 斯科特摔了一跤，扭伤了脚踝。

sprang *form of* SPRING² * spring² 的不同
形式

spray 喷雾剂

spray 喷雾液体

can 金属罐

spray¹ /spreɪ/ *noun* 名词 (*no plural* 不用
复数形式)
1 liquid in very small drops that flies
through the air 浪花；水花；飞沫：*spray
from the sea* 海上的浪花
2 liquid in a container that comes out in
very small drops when you press a button
喷雾剂：*a can of hairspray* 一罐喷雾发胶

spray² /spreɪ/ *verb* 动词 (sprays, spraying,
sprayed /spreɪd/)
to make very small drops of liquid fall on

A B C D E F G H I J K L M N O P Q R S T U V W X Y Z

something 喷洒： *Somebody has sprayed paint on my car.* 有人在我的汽车车身喷了油漆。

spread 0-w /spred/ *verb* 动词 (**spreads**, **spreading**, **spread**, **has spread**)

1 to open something so that you can see all of it 展开；摊开： *The bird spread its wings and flew away.* 鸟展翅飞走了。◇ ***Spread out** the map on the table.* 把地图在桌子上摊开。

2 to put a soft substance all over something 涂；抹： *I spread butter on the bread.* 我给面包涂了黄油。

3 to reach more people or places; to make something do this（使）传播，散布，扩散： *Fire quickly spread to other parts of the building.* 大火很快蔓延到大楼的其他地方。◇ *Rats spread disease.* 老鼠能传播疾病。

▸ **spread** *noun* 名词 (*no plural* 不用复数形式)： *Doctors are trying to stop the spread of the disease.* 医生在竭力阻止这种疾病的传播。

spreadsheet /ˈspredʃiːt/ *noun* 名词 (*computing* 电脑) a computer program for working with rows of numbers, used especially for doing accounts 电子表格程序；电子报表软件

spring 弹簧

spring¹ 0-w /sprɪŋ/ *noun* 名词

1 the part of the year after winter, when plants start to grow 春天；春季： *flowers that bloom **in spring*** 春天绽放的花

➲ Look at Picture Dictionary page **P16**. 见彩页 P16。

2 a long thin piece of metal that is bent round and round. A **spring** will go back to the same size and shape after you push or pull it. 弹簧

3 a place where water comes out of the ground 泉： *a mountain spring* 山泉

spring² /sprɪŋ/ *verb* 动词 (**springs**, **springing**, **sprang** /spræŋ/, **has sprung** /sprʌŋ/)

to jump or move suddenly 跳；跃；蹦： ***He sprang to his feet.*** 他霍地站了起来。◇ *Everyone **sprang into action**.* 大家都马上行动起来。

spring onion /ˌsprɪŋ ˈʌnjən/ (*British* 英式英语) (*American* 美式英语 **green onion**) *noun* 名词

a very small onion with long leaves, often eaten raw 大葱

sprinkle /ˈsprɪŋkl/ *verb* 动词 (**sprinkles**, **sprinkling**, **sprinkled** /ˈsprɪŋkld/)

to shake small pieces of something or drops of a liquid on another thing 撒；洒： *Sprinkle some sugar on the fruit.* 在水果上撒点糖。

sprint /sprɪnt/ *verb* 动词 (**sprints**, **sprinting**, **sprinted**)

to run a short distance very fast 短距离快速奔跑

sprout¹ /spraʊt/ *verb* 动词 (**sprouts**, **sprouting**, **sprouted**)

to start to grow（植物）发芽： *New leaves are sprouting on the trees.* 树上正长出新叶。

sprout² /spraʊt/ *noun* 名词 = BRUSSELS SPROUT

sprung *form of* SPRING² * spring² 的不同形式

spun *form of* SPIN * spin 的不同形式

spy¹ /spaɪ/ *noun* 名词 (*plural* 复数形式 **spies**)

a person who tries to learn secrets about another country, person or company 间谍

spy² /spaɪ/ *verb* 动词 (**spies**, **spying**, **spied** /spaɪd/, **has spied**)

to watch a country, person or company and try to learn their secrets 从事间谍活动；搜集情报： *He spied for his government for more than ten years.* 他为他的政府搜集情报十多年。

spy on somebody or 或 **something** to watch somebody or something secretly 暗中监视；窥探： *Have you been spying on me?* 你是不是一直在暗中监视我？

squabble /ˈskwɒbl/ *verb* 动词 (**squabbles**, **squabbling**, **squabbled** /ˈskwɒbld/)

to argue about something that is not important（为琐事）争吵，发生口角： *The children were **squabbling over** the last cake.* 孩子们为最后的一块蛋糕争吵。◇ *Stop **squabbling with** your brother!* 别跟你弟弟吵了！

▸ **squabble** *noun* 名词： *It was a silly squabble about what game to play.* 那是为了玩什么游戏而起的无谓争吵。

squad /skwɒd/ *noun* 名词

a small group of people who work

together 小组；小队：*England's football squad* 英格兰足球队 ◇ *a squad of police officers* 一队警察

square¹ **0ᴍ** /skweə(r)/ *adjective* 形容词

🔍 **PRONUNCIATION** 读音说明
The word **square** ends with the same sound as **stair**. * square 末段的发音和 stair 相同。

1 with four straight sides that are the same length 正方形的： *a square table* 方桌
2 (*abbr.* 缩略式 sq) used for talking about the area of something（面积）平方　*If a room is 5 metres long and 4 metres wide, its area is 20 square metres.* 一个房间长 5 米、宽 4 米，面积就是 20 平方米。
3 (used about something that is square in shape) having sides of a particular length（正方形物体）…见方，边长：*The picture is twenty centimetres square* (= each side is 20cm long). 这幅画二十厘米见方。

square² **0ᴍ** /skweə(r)/ *noun* 名词
1 a shape with four straight sides that are the same length 正方形 ⊃ Look at the picture at **shape¹**. 见 shape¹ 的插图。
2 an open space in a town with buildings around it 广场：*Trafalgar Square is in London.* 特拉法尔加广场位于伦敦。 ◇ *the town square* 镇广场
3 (*maths* 数学) the number that you get when you multiply another number by itself 平方；二次幂：*Four is the square of two* (2 x 2 = 4). 四是二的平方。

squash¹ /skwɒʃ/ *verb* 动词 (squashes, squashing, squashed /skwɒʃt/)
1 to press something hard and make it flat 压扁；挤扁：*She sat on my hat and squashed it.* 她把我的帽子坐扁了。 ⊃ Look at the picture at **squeeze**. 见 squeeze 的插图。
2 to push a lot of people or things into a small space（使）挤进，塞入：*We squashed five people into the back of the car.* 我们让五个人挤进了汽车后座。

squash² /skwɒʃ/ *noun* 名词 (*no plural* 不用复数形式)
1 a game where two players hit a small ball against the wall in a special room 壁球：*the squash courts* 壁球场
2 (*British* 英式英语) a drink made from fruit juice and sugar. You add water before you drink it.（加水冲开的）果汁饮料：*a glass of orange squash* 一杯橙汁饮料

squat 蹲

squat /skwɒt/ *verb* 动词 (squats, squatting, squatted)
1 to sit with your feet on the ground, your legs bent and your bottom just above the ground 蹲：*I squatted down to light the fire.* 我蹲了下来点火。
2 to live in an empty building that is not yours and that you do not pay for 擅自占用（闲置建筑物）

squatter /'skwɒtə(r)/ *noun* 名词
a person who is living in an empty building without the owner's permission 擅自占用他人房子的人

squeak /skwi:k/ *verb* 动词 (squeaks, squeaking, squeaked /skwi:kt/)
to make a short high sound like a mouse 发出短促而尖厉的声音；吱吱叫；嘎吱作响：*The door was squeaking, so I put some oil on it.* 门吱吱作响，我就给它上了点润滑油。
▸ **squeak** *noun* 名词：*the squeak of a mouse* 老鼠吱吱的叫声
▸ **squeaky** /'skwi:ki/ *adjective* 形容词：*He's got a squeaky voice.* 他嗓音又高又尖。

squeal /skwi:l/ *verb* 动词 (squeals, squealing, squealed /skwi:ld/)
to make a loud high sound 高声尖叫：*The children squealed with excitement.* 孩子们兴奋得大声尖叫起来。
▸ **squeal** *noun* 名词：*squeals of delight* 开心的尖叫

squeeze /skwi:z/ *verb* 动词 (squeezes, squeezing, squeezed /skwi:zd/)
1 to press something hard 挤；捏：*Squeeze the lemons and add the juice to the mixture.* 将柠檬榨汁，倒入混合料中。 ◇ *She squeezed his hand.* 她捏了捏他的手。
2 to go into a small space; to push too much into a small space（使）挤进，

A
B
C
D
E
F
G
H
I
J
K
L
M
N
O
P
Q
R
S
T
U
V
W
X
Y
Z

塞进: *Fifty people **squeezed into** the small room*. 五十个人挤进了那个小房间。
◇ *Can you **squeeze** another person **into** your car*? 你的车还能多挤进一个人吗?
▶ **squeeze** *noun* 名词: *She gave my arm a squeeze*. 她捏了一下我胳膊。

squeeze 挤

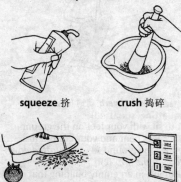

squeeze 挤   **crush** 捣碎

squash 压扁   **press** 按

squid /skwɪd/ *noun* 名词 (*plural* 复数形式 squid or 或 squids)
a sea animal that we eat, with a soft body and ten long parts (called tentacles) 枪乌贼; 鱿鱼

squid 鱿鱼

squirrel /ˈskwɪrəl/ *noun* 名词
a small grey or brown animal with a big thick tail. **Squirrels** live in trees and eat nuts. 松鼠

squirrel 松鼠

squirt /skwɜːt/ *verb* 动词 (squirts, squirting, squirted)
(used about a liquid) to suddenly come out and go onto something or towards

something; to make this happen (使)
(液体) 喷射: *I bit into the orange and juice squirted out*. 我咬了一口橙子, 橙汁喷了出来。 ◇ *He squirted me with water*. 他用水喷我。

St
1 *short way of writing* SAINT * saint 的缩写形式
2 *short way of writing* STREET * street 的缩写形式

stab /stæb/ *verb* 动词 (stabs, stabbing, stabbed /stæbd/)
to push a knife or another sharp thing into somebody or something 刺; 戳; 捅: *He was stabbed in the back*. 他背上被刺了一刀。

stable¹ /ˈsteɪbl/ *adjective* 形容词
not likely to move, fall or change 稳定的; 稳固的; 牢固的: *Don't stand on that table – it's not very stable*. 别站在那张桌子上, 它不太牢。 ➔ OPPOSITE **unstable** 反义词为 unstable

stable² /ˈsteɪbl/ *noun* 名词
a building where you keep horses 马厩; 马房

stack¹ /stæk/ *noun* 名词
a lot of things on top of one another 叠; 摞 ➔ SAME MEANING **pile** 同义词为 pile: *a stack of books* 一叠书

stack² /stæk/ *verb* 动词 (stacks, stacking, stacked /stækt/)
to put things on top of one another 叠放; 摞起: *I stacked the chairs after the concert*. 音乐会之后, 我把椅子摞起来了。

stadium /ˈsteɪdiəm/ *noun* 名词
a place with seats around it where you can watch sport 体育场; 运动场: *a football stadium* 足球比赛场馆

staff /stɑːf/ *noun* 名词 (*plural* 用复数形式)
the people who work in a place 职工; 员工: *The hotel staff were very friendly*. 旅馆的员工非常友善。

staffroom /ˈstɑːfruːm/ *noun* 名词
a room in a school where teachers can work and rest 教员室

stage 0— /steɪdʒ/ *noun* 名词
1 a certain time in a longer set of things that happen 阶段; 时期: *The first stage of the course lasts for two weeks*. 课程的第一阶段为期两周。 ◇ *At this stage I don't know what I'll do when I leave school*. 现阶段我还不知道离校后会做些什么。
2 the part of a theatre where the actors, dancers, etc. perform 舞台: *The audience threw flowers onto the stage*.

观众将鲜花抛向舞台。 ◇ *There were more than 50 people on stage in one scene.* 在一场戏中舞台上的演员有 50 多人。

stagger /ˈstæɡə(r)/ *verb* 动词 (staggers, staggering, staggered /ˈstæɡəd/)
to walk as if you are going to fall 摇摇晃晃地走；蹒跚；踉跄: *He staggered across the room with the heavy box.* 他扛着沉重的箱子跟踉跄跄地走到房间的另一端。

stain /steɪn/ *verb* 动词 (stains, staining, stained /steɪnd/)
to leave a dirty mark that is difficult to remove on something 玷污；留下污渍: *The wine stained the carpet red.* 葡萄酒把地毯染红了一块。
▶ **stain** *noun* 名词: *She had blood stains on her shirt.* 她衬衫上有血迹。

stair 0-ː /steə(r)/ *noun* 名词
1 stairs (*plural* 用复数形式) steps that lead up and down inside a building 楼梯: *I ran up the stairs to the bedroom.* 我跑上楼梯到卧室去了。 ⊃ Look also at **downstairs** and **upstairs**. 亦见 downstairs 和 upstairs。
2 one of the steps in a set of **stairs** 梯级: *How many stairs are there up to the top floor?* 到顶层共有多少级楼梯？

staircase 楼梯

stair 梯级 — banister 楼梯扶手 — landing 楼梯平台

staircase /ˈsteəkeɪs/ (*also* 亦作 stairway /ˈsteəweɪ/) *noun* 名词
a big set of stairs 楼梯

stale /steɪl/ *adjective* 形容词 (staler, stalest)
not fresh 不新鲜的: *stale bread* 不新鲜的面包 ◇ *stale air* 污浊的空气

stalk /stɔːk/ *noun* 名词
one of the long thin parts of a plant that the flowers, leaves or fruit grow on （叶或果实）柄；（花）梗 ⊃ Look at the picture at **plant**[1]. 见 plant[1] 的插图。

stall /stɔːl/ *noun* 名词
a big table with things on it that somebody wants to sell, for example in a street or market 货摊；摊位: *a fruit stall* 水果摊

stammer /ˈstæmə(r)/ *verb* 动词 (stammers, stammering, stammered /ˈstæməd/)
to say the same sound many times when you are trying to say a word 口吃；结结巴巴地说 ⊃ SAME MEANING **stutter** 同义词为 stutter: *'B-b-b-but wait for me,' she stammered.* "可—可—可—可要等等我。" 她结结巴巴地说。

stamp[1] 0-ː /stæmp/ *noun* 名词
1 a small piece of paper that you put on a letter to show that you have paid to send it 邮票: *Could I have three first-class stamps, please?* 请给我三张第一类邮票好吗？ ◇ *He has been collecting stamps since he was eight.* 他从八岁就开始集邮。

> 🔎 **CULTURE** 文化资料补充
> There are two kinds of **stamp** for sending letters to other parts of Britain: **first-class stamps** and **second-class stamps**. First-class stamps are more expensive and the letters arrive more quickly. 英国国内邮寄信件的邮票（stamp）有两种：第一类邮票（first-class stamp）和第二类邮票（second-class stamp）。第一类邮票贵一些，信件会快些送到。
> In Britain and the US you can buy stamps and send letters at a **post office**. 在英国和美国，可以在邮局（post office）购买邮票和邮寄信件。

2 a small piece of wood or metal that you press on paper to make marks or words 图章；印戳: *a date stamp* 日戳

stamp 用力踩

She **stamped** her foot. 她跺脚。

stamp[2] /stæmp/ *verb* 动词 (stamps, stamping, stamped /stæmpt/)
1 to put your foot down very hard 用力踩；跺脚: *She stamped on the*

spider and killed it. 她踩死了蜘蛛。
2 to walk by putting your feet down hard and loudly 踩着脚走: *Mike stamped angrily out of the room.* 迈克气呼呼地踩着脚走出了房间。
3 to press a small piece of wood or metal on paper to make marks or words (在…上) 盖章 (或戳等): *They stamped my passport at the airport.* 他们在机场给我的护照上盖了章。

stand¹ 0-ᴡ /stænd/ *verb* 动词 (stands, standing, stood /stʊd/, has stood)
1 to be on your feet 站; 站立: *She was standing by the door.* 她在门口旁站着。◇ *Stand still while I take your photograph.* 我给你拍照时, 站着别动。
2 (*also* 亦作 stand up) to get up on your feet 站起来; 起立: *The teacher asked us all to stand up.* 老师叫我们全体起立。
3 to be in a place 位于: *The castle stands on a hill.* 城堡坐落在小山上。
4 to put something somewhere 放置: *I stood the ladder against the wall.* 我把梯子靠在墙上。
can't stand somebody or 或 **something** to hate somebody or something 不能容忍; 受不了: *I can't stand this music.* 我受不了这种音乐。
stand by
1 to watch but not do anything 袖手旁观: *How can you stand by while those boys kick the cat?* 那些男孩子踢那猫的时候你怎么能袖手旁观?
2 to be ready to do something 随时待命: *Stand by until I call you!* 随时待命, 等我叫你!
stand by somebody to help somebody when they need it 随时准备帮助: *Julie's parents stood by her when she was in trouble.* 朱莉有麻烦的时候, 她父母在她身边支持她。
stand for something to be a short way of saying or writing something 是…的缩写: *USA stands for 'the United States of America'.* * USA 是 the United States of America 的缩写。
stand out to be easy to see 突出; 显眼: *Joe stands out in a crowd because of his red hair.* 红色的头发令乔在人群中很引人注目。
stand up for somebody or 或 **something** to say that somebody or something is right; to support somebody or something 支持; 维护: *Everyone else said I was wrong, but my sister stood up for me.* 大家都说我错, 只有妹妹支持我。
stand up to somebody to argue or

fight with a more powerful person who is attacking you 奋起反抗

stand² 0-ᴡ /stænd/ *noun* 名词
1 a table or small shop where you can buy things or get information 货摊; 售卖亭: *a news-stand* (= where you can buy newspapers and magazines) 书报亭
2 a piece of furniture that you can put things on 架; 座: *an umbrella stand* 伞架
3 a large structure where people can watch sport from seats arranged in rows that are low near the front and high near the back (体育场的) 看台

standard¹ 0-ᴡ /'stændəd/ *noun* 名词
1 how good somebody or something is 标准; 水平: *Her work is of a very high standard.* 她的工作水准很高。
2 standards (*plural* 用复数形式) a level of behaviour that people think is acceptable 行为标准; 道德水平: *Many people are worried about falling standards in modern society.* 很多人对现代社会中不断下降的道德水平表示担心。

standard² /'stændəd/ *adjective* 形容词
normal; not special 标准的; 普通的; 正常的: *Clothes are sold in standard sizes.* 衣服以标准的尺码出售。

standard of living /ˌstændəd əv 'lɪvɪŋ/ *noun* 名词 (*plural* 复数形式 standards of living)
how rich or poor you are 生活水平: *They have a low standard of living* (= they are poor). 他们生活水平低。

stank *form of* STINK¹ * stink¹ 的不同形式

staple /'steɪpl/ *noun* 名词
a small straight piece of metal that you use for fixing pieces of paper together. You press the **staples** through the paper, using a STAPLER. 订书钉
▶ **staple** *verb* 动词 (staples, stapling, stapled /'steɪpld/): *Staple the pieces of paper together.* 把这些纸订在一起。

stapler /'steɪplə(r)/ *noun* 名词
a tool that you use for fixing pieces of paper together with metal STAPLES 订书机 ⊃ Look at Picture Dictionary page **P11**. 见彩页 P11。

star¹ 0-ᴡ /stɑː(r)/ *noun* 名词
1 one of the small bright lights that you see in the sky at night 恒星; 星
2 a shape with points 星形; 星状物: *a horse with a white star on its forehead* 前额有一块星形白斑的马 ⊃ Look at the picture at **shape¹**. 见 shape¹ 的插图。
3 a famous person, for example an actor or a singer 明星: *a film star* 影星

star² 0➤ /stɑː(r)/ *verb* 动词 (stars, starring, starred/stɑːd/)
1 to be the main actor in a play or film 主演；担任（戏剧或电影的）主角：*He has **starred** in many films.* 他主演过很多电影。
2 to have somebody as a star 由…担任主角：*The film **stars** Julia Roberts.* 这部电影由朱莉娅·罗伯茨主演。

stare 0➤ /steə(r)/ *verb* 动词 (stares, staring, stared/steəd/)
to look at somebody or something for a long time 瞪；盯着看；凝视：*Everybody **stared at** her hat.* 大家都盯着她的帽子看。
◇ *He was **staring** out of the window.* 他凝视着窗外。

> 🔍 **WHICH WORD?** 词语辨析
>
> **Stare** or **gaze**? 用 stare 还是 gaze?
> You usually **stare** at somebody or something if you are surprised or shocked. It is rude to **stare** at people.
> * stare 通常指因惊讶或震惊而凝视某人或某物，这是不礼貌的。
> You often **gaze** at somebody or something that you love or admire.
> * gaze 通常指因喜欢或仰慕而凝视某人或某物。

start¹ 0➤ /stɑːt/ *verb* 动词 (starts, starting, started)
1 to begin to do something 开始，着手（做）：*I **start** work at nine o'clock.* 我九点钟开始上班。◇ *It **started** raining.* 开始下雨了。◇ *She **started** to cry.* 她哭了起来。
2 to begin to happen; to make something begin to happen（使）发生，开始进行：*The film **starts** at 7.30.* 电影 7 点 30 分开演。◇ *The police do not know who **started** the fire.* 警方不知道是谁放的火。
3 to begin to work or move; to make something begin to work or move 开动；发动；启动：*The engine won't **start**.* 引擎发动不起来。◇ *I can't **start** the car.* 这辆车我启动不了。
start off to begin 开始：*The teacher **started off** by asking us our names.* 老师一开始先问了我们的名字。

start² 0➤ /stɑːt/ *noun* 名词
1 the beginning or first part of something 开头；开端：*She arrived after **the start of** the meeting.* 她在会议开始后才来。
2 the act of starting something 开始：*There's lots of work to do, so let's **make a start**.* 有很多工作要做，我们开始吧。
for a start (*informal* 非正式) words that you use when you give your first reason

for something 首先；第一：*'Why can't we go on holiday?' 'Well, **for a start**, we don't have any money.'* "我们为什么不能去度假呢？""嗯，第一，我们没钱。"

starter /'stɑːtə(r)/ (*British* 英式英语) (*American* 美式英语 **appetizer**) *noun* 名词
a small amount of food that you eat as the first part of a meal 开胃小吃；开胃菜：*What would you like as a **starter** – soup or melon?* 你要什么开胃小吃，汤还是甜瓜？

startle /'stɑːtl/ *verb* 动词 (startles, startling, startled/'stɑːtld/)
to make somebody suddenly surprised or frightened 使受惊；使吓一跳：*You **startled** me when you knocked on the window.* 你敲窗时吓了我一跳。

starve /stɑːv/ *verb* 动词 (starves, starving, starved/stɑːvd/)
to die because you do not have enough to eat 饿死：*Millions of people are **starving** in some parts of the world.* 世界上的一些地区有数百万的人正在挨饿。
be starving (*informal* 非正式) to be very hungry 饿得很：*When will dinner be ready? I'm **starving**!* 饭什么时候准备好？我快饿死了！
▸ **starvation** /stɑː'veɪʃn/ *noun* 名词 (*no plural* 不用复数形式)：*The child died of **starvation**.* 那个孩子饿死了。

state¹ 0➤ /steɪt/ *noun* 名词
1 how somebody or something is 状态；状况；情况：*The house was **in a terrible state**.* 那所房子破败不堪。◇ *What **state of mind** is he in?* 他心情如何？
2 a country and its government 国家；政府：*Many schools are owned by the **state**.* 许多学校是公立的。
3 (*also* 亦作 **State**) a part of a country 州：*Texas is a **state** in the USA.* 得克萨斯是美国的一个州。
4 the States (*plural* 用复数形式) (*informal* 非正式) the United States of America 美国

state² 0➤ /steɪt/ *verb* 动词 (states, stating, stated)
to formally say or write something（正式地）陈述，说明，声明：*I **stated** in my letter that I was looking for a job.* 我在信中说明了我正在找工作。

statement 0➤ /'steɪtmənt/ *noun* 名词
something that you say or write, especially formally（尤指正式的）陈述，声明：*The driver **made a statement** to the police about the accident.* 司机向警方写了一份事故的供述。

station 0☞ /'steɪʃn/ *noun* 名词
1 (*also* 亦作 railway station) a place where trains stop so that people can get on and off 火车站
2 a place where buses or coaches start and end their journeys 公共汽车站; 长途汽车站: *the bus station* 公共汽车站
3 a building for some special work 站; 所; 局: *the police station* 警察局 ◇ *the fire station* 消防站 ◇ *a petrol station* 加油站
4 a television or radio company 电视台; 电台

stationary /'steɪʃənri/ *adjective* 形容词
not moving 不动的; 静止的: *a stationary vehicle* 停着的车辆

stationery /'steɪʃənri/ *noun* 名词
(*no plural* 不用复数形式)
paper, pens and other things that you use for writing 文具

station wagon /'steɪʃn wægən/
American English for ESTATE CAR 美式英语, 即 estate car

statistics /stə'tɪstɪks/ *noun* 名词 (*plural* 用复数形式)
numbers that give information about something 统计数字: *Statistics show that women live longer than men.* 统计数字显示, 女性比男性长寿。

statue /'stætʃuː/ *noun* 名词
a model of a person or an animal, made from stone or metal 雕像; 塑像: *the Statue of Liberty in New York* 纽约的自由女神像

stay[1] 0☞ /steɪ/ *verb* 动词 (stays, staying, stayed /steɪd/)
1 to be in the same place and not go away 待; 停留: *Stay here until I come back.* 在这儿待着, 等我回来。◇ *I stayed in bed until ten o'clock.* 我在床上躺到十点钟。
2 to continue in the same way and not change 保持; 继续处于: *I tried to stay awake.* 我尽量保持清醒。
3 to live somewhere for a short time 暂住; 逗留: *I stayed with my friend in Dublin.* 我在都柏林的时候在朋友家暂住。◇ *Which hotel are you staying at?* 你住在哪家旅馆?

stay behind to be somewhere after other people have gone 留下来: *The teacher asked me to stay behind after the lesson.* 老师叫我课后留下。

stay in to be at home and not go out 待在家里; 不外出: *I'm staying in this evening because I'm tired.* 我很累, 今晚不出门了。

stay up to not go to bed 深夜不睡; 熬夜: *We stayed up until after midnight.* 我们半夜后才去睡觉。

stay[2] 0☞ /steɪ/ *noun* 名词 (*plural* 复数形式 stays)
a short time when you live somewhere 逗留; 暂住: *Did you enjoy your stay in London?* 你在伦敦期间过得愉快吗?

steady 0☞ /'stedi/ *adjective* 形容词 (steadier, steadiest)
1 developing or changing at a regular speed (发展或变化) 稳步的, 匀速的: *a steady increase* 稳步的增长
2 not changing or stopping 不变的; 稳定的: *Father now had a steady job.* 父亲现在有了份稳定的工作。◇ *His breathing was steady.* 他呼吸平稳。
3 not moving or shaking 平稳的; 稳固的: *Hold the ladder steady while I stand on it.* 我站在梯子上面时, 把它扶稳。
▶ **steadily** /'stedɪli/ *adverb* 副词: *Prices are falling steadily.* 价格正在稳步下降。

steak /steɪk/ *noun* 名词
a wide flat piece of meat, especially meat from a cow (called **beef**) 肉排; (尤指) 牛排: *I'd like steak and chips, please.* 请给我一份牛排和薯条。

steal 0☞ /stiːl/ *verb* 动词 (steals, stealing, stole /stəʊl/, has stolen /'stəʊlən/)
to secretly take something that is not yours 偷; 窃取: *Her money has been stolen.* 她的钱被偷了。

🔍 **WHICH WORD?** 词语辨析
A person who steals is called a **thief**. 小偷叫做 thief。
A thief **steals** things, but **robs** people and places。* steal 后接所偷的东西, rob 后接被抢劫的人或地方: *They stole my camera.* 他们偷了我的相机。◇ *I've been robbed.* 我被抢了。◇ *They robbed a bank.* 他们抢劫了一家银行。

steam[1] 0☞ /stiːm/ *noun* 名词 (*no plural* 不用复数形式)
the gas that water becomes when it gets very hot 水蒸气; 蒸汽: *There was steam coming from my coffee.* 我的咖啡冒着热气。

steam[2] /stiːm/ *verb* 动词 (steams, steaming, steamed /stiːmd/)
1 to send out STEAM 散发蒸汽; 冒水汽: *a steaming bowl of soup* 一碗热气腾腾的汤
2 to cook something in STEAM 蒸 (食物); 蒸煮: *steamed vegetables* 清蒸蔬菜

steel /stiːl/ *noun* 名词 (*no plural* 不用复数形式)
very strong metal that is used for making things like knives, tools and machines 钢

steep /stiːp/ *adjective* 形容词 (**steeper**, **steepest**)
A **steep** hill, mountain or road goes up quickly from a low place to a high place. （山或道路）陡的，陡峭的: *I can't cycle up the hill – it's too steep.* 这座山我骑自行车上不去，太陡了。
▶ **steeply** /'stiːpli/ *adverb* 副词: *The path climbed steeply up the side of the mountain.* 这条小路沿山边而上，十分陡峭。

steeple /'stiːpl/ *noun* 名词
a tall pointed tower on a church （教堂的）尖塔

steer /stɪə(r)/ *verb* 动词 (**steers**, **steering**, **steered** /stɪəd/)
to make a car, boat, bicycle, etc. go left or right by turning a wheel or handle 驾驶（交通工具）；操纵方向盘

steering wheel /'stɪərɪŋ wiːl/ *noun* 名词
the wheel that you turn to make a car go left or right 方向盘；舵轮

stem /stem/ *noun* 名词
the long thin part of a plant that the flowers and leaves grow on （植物的）茎，梗 ⇨ Look at the picture at **plant**[1]. 见 plant[1] 的插图。

step[1] 0= /step/ *noun* 名词
1 a movement when you move your foot up and put it down in another place to walk, run or dance 迈步；脚步；舞步: *She took a step forward and then stopped.* 她向前迈了一步，然后停了下来。
2 a place to put your foot when you go up or down 台阶；梯级: *These steps go down to the garden.* 这些台阶往下通向花园。⇨ Look at Picture Dictionary page **P10**. 见彩页 P10。
3 one thing in a list of things that you must do 步骤；措施: *What is the first step in planning a holiday?* 安排假期的第一步要做什么?
step by step doing one thing after another; slowly 一步一步地；逐步；循序渐进: *This book shows you how to play the guitar, step by step.* 这本书教人如何循序渐进地学弹吉他。

step[2] 0= /step/ *verb* 动词 (**steps**, **stepping**, **stepped** /stept/)
to move your foot up and put it down in another place when you walk, run or dance 迈步；踩；踏: *You stepped on my foot!* 你踩了我的脚!

stepfather /'stepfɑːðə(r)/ *noun* 名词
a man who has married your mother but who is not your father 继父；后父 ⇨ Look at the note at **stepmother**. 见 stepmother 条的注释。

stepladder /'steplædə(r)/ *noun* 名词
a type of LADDER (= a thing that helps you to climb up something) with two parts, one with steps. The parts are joined together at the top so that it can stand on its own and be folded up when you are not using it. 折梯；活梯 ⇨ Look at the picture at **ladder**. 见 ladder 的插图。

stepmother /'stepmʌðə(r)/ *noun* 名词
a woman who has married your father but who is not your mother 继母；后母

> ✏ **WORD BUILDING** 词汇扩充
> The child from an earlier marriage of your stepmother or stepfather is called your **stepbrother** or **stepsister**. 继母与其前夫或继父与其前妻所生的子女是你的继兄/弟（stepbrother）或继姐/妹（stepsister）。

stereo /'steriəʊ/ *noun* 名词 (*plural* 复数形式 **stereos**)
a machine for playing CDs, tapes or records, with two parts (called **speakers**) where the sound comes from 立体声音响系统: *a car stereo* 车用立体声音响
▶ **stereo** *adjective* 形容词: *a stereo cassette player* 立体声盒式磁带播放机

sterling /'stɜːlɪŋ/ *noun* 名词 (*no plural* 不用复数形式)
the system of money that is used in Britain; the pound 英镑（英国货币）: *You can pay in pounds sterling or in American dollars.* 你可以用英镑或美元支付。

stern /stɜːn/ *adjective* 形容词 (**sterner**, **sternest**)
serious and strict with people; not smiling or friendly 严厉的；不苟言笑的: *a stern expression* 严厉的表情

stew /stjuː/ *noun* 名词
food that you make by cooking meat or vegetables in liquid for a long time 炖肉菜；煨的菜: *beef stew* 炖牛肉 ⇨ Look at Picture Dictionary page **P7**. 见彩页 P7。
▶ **stew** *verb* 动词 (**stews**, **stewing**, **stewed** /stjuːd/): *stewed fruit* 炖水果

steward /'stjuːəd/ *noun* 名词
a man whose job is to look after people

A
B
C
D
E
F
G
H
I
J
K
L
M
N
O
P
Q
R
S
T
U
V
W
X
Y
Z

on a plane or a ship （飞机或轮船上的）乘务员，服务员 ⊃ SAME MEANING **flight attendant** 同义词为 flight attendant

stewardess /'stjuːə'des/ *noun* 名词
(*plural* 复数形式 **stewardesses**)
a woman whose job is to look after people on a plane or a ship （飞机或轮船上的）女乘务员，女服务员 ⊃ SAME MEANING **air hostess**, **flight attendant** 同义词为 air hostess 和 flight attendant

stick¹ 0= /stɪk/ *verb* 动词 (**sticks**, **sticking** **stuck** /stʌk/, has **stuck**)
1 to push a pointed thing into something 插入；刺；扎： *Stick a fork into the meat to see if it's cooked.* 用叉子扎进肉看熟了没有。
2 to join something to something else with a sticky substance; to become joined in this way 粘贴；粘住： *I stuck a stamp on the envelope.* 我在信封上贴了一枚邮票。
3 to be fixed in one place; to not be able to move 卡住；陷住；无法动弹： *This door always sticks.* 这扇门老是卡住。
4 (*informal* 非正式) to put something somewhere 放置： *Stick that box on the floor.* 把那个箱子放在地板上。

stick out to come out of the side or top of something so that you can see it easily 伸出；探出： *The boy's head was sticking out of the window.* 那个男孩把头探出窗外。
stick something out to push something out 使伸出；使突出： *Don't stick your tongue out!* 别把舌头伸出来！
stick to something to continue with something and not change it 坚持；固守： *We're sticking to Peter's plan.* 我们坚持执行彼得的计划。
stick up for somebody or 或 **something** to say that somebody or something is right 支持；捍卫： *Everyone else said I was wrong, but Kim stuck up for me.* 大家都说我错了，只有金支持我。

stick² 0= /stɪk/ *noun* 名词
1 a long thin piece of wood 枝条；木棍；树枝： *We found some sticks and made a fire.* 我们捡了些树枝生起火来。
2 (*British* 英式英语) = WALKING STICK: *The old man walked with a stick.* 那个老人拄着拐棍走路。
3 a long thin object that is used in some sports to hit or control the ball （某些体育运动的）球棍，球棒： *a hockey stick* 曲棍球球棍
4 a long thin piece of something 条状物；棍状物： *a stick of chalk* 一支粉笔

sticker /'stɪkə(r)/ *noun* 名词
a small piece of paper with a picture or words on it, that you can stick onto things 粘贴标签；贴纸

sticky 0= /'stɪki/ *adjective* 形容词
(**stickier**, **stickiest**)
able to stick to things; covered with a substance that can stick to things 黏的；黏糊糊的： *Glue is sticky.* 胶水是黏的。 ◇ *sticky fingers* 黏糊糊的手指

stiff /stɪf/ *adjective* 形容词 (**stiffer**, **stiffest**)
not easy to bend or move 不易弯曲（或活动）的；硬的： *stiff cardboard* 硬纸板

still¹ 0= /stɪl/ *adverb* 副词
1 a word that you use to show that something has not changed 还；仍然；依旧： *Do you still live in London?* 你还住在伦敦吗？ ◇ *Is it still raining?* 还在下雨吗？
2 although that is true （虽然…）还是；但；不过： *She felt ill, but she still went to the party.* 她虽然感到不舒服，但还是参加聚会去了。
3 a word that you use to make another word stronger （加强比较）还要，更： *It was cold yesterday, but today it's colder still.* 昨天很冷，可是今天更冷。

still² 0= /stɪl/ *adjective* 形容词
1 without moving 静止的；不动的： *Please stand still while I take a photo.* 我拍照时，请站着别动。 ◇ *The water was perfectly still.* 水面平静无波。
2 (*British* 英式英语) (used about a drink) not containing any bubbles or gas （饮料）不起泡的，不含气的： *still mineral water* 无汽矿泉水 ⊃ OPPOSITE **fizzy**, **sparkling** 反义词为 fizzy 和 sparkling

▶ **stillness** /'stɪlnəs/ *noun* 名词 (*no plural* 不用复数形式)： *the stillness of the night* 夜间的寂静

sting¹ /stɪŋ/ *verb* 动词 (**stings**, **stinging** **stung** /stʌŋ/, has **stung**)
1 If an insect or a plant **stings** you, it hurts you by pushing a small sharp part into your skin. （昆虫或植物）叮，蜇，刺： *I've been stung by a bee!* 我给蜜蜂蜇了！
2 to feel a sudden sharp pain 感到刺痛： *The smoke made my eyes sting.* 烟熏得我眼睛发疼。

sting² /stɪŋ/ *noun* 名词
1 the sharp part of some insects, that can hurt you （某些昆虫的）螫针，刺： *A wasp's sting is in its tail.* 黄蜂的螫针在它的尾部。 ⊃ Look at the picture at **scorpion**. 见 scorpion 的插图。

2 a hurt place on your skin where an insect or a plant has **stung** you 叮伤；蜇伤；刺伤：*a bee sting* 被蜜蜂蜇伤的地方

stink¹ /stɪŋk/ *verb* 动词 (stinks, stinking, stank /stæŋk/, has stunk /stʌŋk/) (*informal* 非正式)
to have a very bad smell 有臭味；发臭：*That fish stinks!* 那条鱼发腥了！

stink² /stɪŋk/ *noun* 名词 (*informal* 非正式)
a very bad smell 臭味；难闻的气味：*What a terrible stink!* 多难闻的气味！

stir /stɜː(r)/ *verb* 动词 (stirs, stirring, stirred /stɜːd/)
1 to move a spoon or another thing round and round to mix something 搅动；搅拌：*He put sugar in his coffee and stirred it.* 他把糖放进咖啡里搅了搅。
2 to move a little; to make something move a little（使）微动：*The wind stirred the leaves.* 风吹得叶子微微摇动。

stitch¹ /stɪtʃ/ *noun* 名词 (*plural* 复数形式 stitches)
1 a small line or circle of thread that joins or decorates cloth（缝纫的）一针，针脚 ➲ Look at the picture at **embroidery**. 见 embroidery 的插图。
2 a circle of wool that you put round a needle when you are KNITTING (= making clothes from wool)（编织的）一针 ➲ Look at the picture at **knit**. 见 knit 的插图。
3 a short piece of special thread that doctors use to sew the edges of a cut together（缝合伤口的）一针，缝线：*The cut needed eight stitches.* 这道伤口需要缝八针。

stitch² /stɪtʃ/ *verb* 动词 (stitches, stitching, stitched /stɪtʃt/)
to sew something 缝；缝补；缝合：*I stitched a button on my skirt.* 我在我的裙子上缝了一个钮扣。

stock¹ /stɒk/ *noun* 名词
1 things that a shop keeps ready to sell 现货；存货：*We have a large stock of tables and chairs.* 我们有大量的桌子和椅子存货。◇ *I'll see if we have your size in stock.* 我去看一下你要的尺寸有没有货。◇ *I'm afraid that book's out of stock at the moment.* 很抱歉，那本书现在脱销了。
2 (*business* 商业) a share in a company or business that somebody has bought, or the value of those shares 股份；股票；股价：*stocks and shares* 股份与股票 ➲ Look at **stock exchange**. 见 stock exchange。

stock² /stɒk/ *verb* 动词 (stocks, stocking, stocked /stɒkt/)
to keep something ready to sell 存货：*I'm afraid we don't stock umbrellas.* 很抱歉，雨伞我们没货。

stockbroker /'stɒkbrəʊkə(r)/ *noun* 名词 (*business* 商业) a person whose job is to buy and sell shares in companies for other people 证券经纪人；股票经纪人

stock exchange /'stɒk ɪkstʃeɪndʒ/ (*also* 亦作 **stock market** /'stɒk mɑːkɪt/) *noun* 名词 (*no plural* 不用复数形式) (*business* 商业) a place where people buy and sell shares in companies; the business of doing this 证券交易（所）；股票交易（所）：*the London Stock Exchange* 伦敦证券交易所 ◇ *to lose money on the stock market* 在股市中赔钱

stocking /'stɒkɪŋ/ *noun* 名词
a long thin thing that a woman wears over her leg and foot 长筒女袜：*a pair of stockings* 一双长筒袜

stole, stolen *forms of* STEAL * steal 的不同形式

stomach 0== /'stʌmək/ *noun* 名词
1 the part inside your body where food goes after you eat it 胃
2 the front part of your body below your chest and above your legs 腹部；肚子 ➲ Look at Picture Dictionary page **P4**. 见彩页 P4。

stomach ache /'stʌmək eɪk/ *noun* 名词 (*no plural* 不用复数形式)
a pain in your stomach 胃痛；腹痛：*I've got stomach ache.* 我肚子疼。

stone 0== /stəʊn/ *noun* 名词
1 (*no plural* 不用复数形式) the very hard material that is in the ground. **Stone** is sometimes used for building. 石头：*a stone wall* 石墙
2 (*plural* 复数形式 stones) a small piece of **stone** 石块；石子：*The children were throwing stones into the river.* 孩子们正往河里扔石子。
3 (*plural* 复数形式 stones) the hard part in the middle of some types of fruit 果核：*Peaches, plums, cherries and olives all have stones.* 桃子、李子、樱桃和橄榄都有核。 ➲ Look at Picture Dictionary page **P8**. 见彩页 P8。
4 (*plural* 复数形式 stones) a small piece of beautiful rock that is very valuable 宝石：*A diamond is a precious stone.* 钻石是一种宝石。
5 (*plural* 复数形式 stone) (*British* 英式英语) a measure of weight equal to 6.35 kg.

A
B
C
D
E
F
G
H
I
J
K
L
M
N
O
P
Q
R
S
T
U
V
W
X
Y
Z

There are 14 **pounds** in a **stone**. 英石
（重量单位；1 英石等于 6.35 公斤或 14
磅）: *I weigh ten stone.* 我体重十英石。
➲ Look at the note at **pound**. 见 pound 条
的注释。

stony /'stəʊni/ *adjective* 形容词 (**stonier**,
stoniest)
containing a lot of stones; covered with a
lot of stones 多石的；布满石头的: *stony
ground* 多石的地面

stood *form of* STAND¹ * stand¹ 的不同形式

stool /stuːl/ *noun* 名词
a small seat with no back 凳子 ➲ Look at
the picture at **bar¹**. 见 bar¹ 的插图。

stoop /stuːp/ *verb* 动词 (**stoops**, **stooping**,
stooped /stuːpt/)
If you **stoop**, you bend your body forward
and down. 俯身；弯腰: *She stooped to
pick up the baby.* 她弯下腰把宝宝抱了
起来。

stop¹ 0= /stɒp/ *verb* 动词 (**stops**,
stopping, **stopped** /stɒpt/)
1 to finish moving or working; to become
still 停止；停下: *The train stopped at
every station.* 火车每站都停。◇ *The clock
has stopped.* 钟停了。◇ *I stopped to post
a letter.* 我停下来寄了封信。
2 to not do something any more; to finish
不再做；中断: *Stop making that noise!*
别再弄那种声音！
3 to make somebody or something finish
moving or doing something 使停止；
使终止: *Ring the bell to stop the bus.*
按铃让公共汽车停下来。
**stop somebody (from) doing
something** to not let somebody do
something 阻止；阻拦: *My dad stopped
me from going out.* 爸爸不让我出去。

stop² 0= /stɒp/ *noun* 名词
1 the moment when somebody or
something finishes moving 停止；终止:
The train came to a stop. 火车停了下来。
2 a place where buses or trains stop so
that people can get on and off 车站:
I'm getting off at the next stop. 我在
下一站下车。
put a stop to something to make
something finish 使停止；结束:
A teacher put a stop to the fight. 一名
老师制止了那场打斗。

store¹ 0= /stɔː(r)/ *noun* 名词
1 a big shop that sells many different
types of things 百货商店: *Harrods is a
famous London store.* 哈罗德是伦敦著名的
百货商店。
2 (*American* 美式英语) a shop, large or

small 商店；店铺: *a health food store*
保健食品商店
3 things that you are keeping to use later
贮存物；备用物: *a secret store of food*
私存的食物

store² 0= /stɔː(r)/ *verb* 动词 (**stores**,
storing, **stored** /stɔːd/)
to keep something to use later 贮存；
贮藏: *The information is stored on
a computer.* 信息存在一台电脑中。

storekeeper /'stɔːkiːpə(r)/ *American
English for* SHOPKEEPER 美式英语，
即 shopkeeper

storey (*British* 英式英语) (*American* 美式
英语 **story**) /'stɔːri/ *noun* 名词 (*British
plural* 英式英语复数形式 **storeys**)
(*American plural* 美式英语复数形式 **stories**)
one level in a building 楼层: *The building
has four storeys.* 这栋楼有四层。

storm¹ 0= /stɔːm/ *noun* 名词
very bad weather with strong winds and
rain 暴风雨: *a thunderstorm* 雷暴

> 🔑 **WORD BUILDING** 词汇扩充
> When there is a storm, you hear
> **thunder** and see **lightning** in the sky.
> **Cyclones**, **hurricanes**, **tornadoes** and
> **typhoons** are large violent storms.
> 暴风雨时会听到雷声（thunder）并
> 看到天空中的闪电（lightning）。旋风
> （cyclone）、飓风（hurricane）、
> 龙卷风（tornado）和台风（typhoon）
> 都是强烈的风暴。

storm² /stɔːm/ *verb* 动词 (**storms**,
storming, **stormed** /stɔːmd/)
to move in a way that shows you are
angry 气呼呼地走；闯；冲: *He stormed
out of the room.* 他怒气冲冲地冲出了
房间。

stormy /'stɔːmi/ *adjective* 形容词
(**stormier**, **stormiest**)
with strong wind and rain 狂风暴雨的:
a stormy night 风雨交加的夜晚

story 0= /'stɔːri/ *noun* 名词 (*plural* 复数
形式 **stories**)
1 words that tell you about people and
things that are not real（虚构的）故事，
小说: *Hans Christian Andersen wrote
stories for children.* 安徒生是写童话故事
的。◇ *a ghost story* 鬼故事
2 words that tell you about things that
really happened（对真实情况的）描述，
叙述: *My grandmother told me stories
about when she was a child.* 祖母给我讲了
她童年的一些事情。

3 *American English for* STOREY 美式英语，
即 storey

stove /stəʊv/ *noun* 名词
1 a closed metal box in which you burn
wood and coal to heat a room （取暖用
的）炉子，火炉： *a wood-burning stove*
烧柴的炉子
2 *American English for* COOKER 美式英语，
即 cooker

straight¹ ⊶ /streɪt/ *adverb* 副词
1 not in a curve or at an angle; in a
straight line 笔直地；成直线： *Look
straight in front of you.* 向前直看。◇
*Go straight on until you come to the bank,
then turn left.* 一直往前走，到了银行就
向左拐。
2 without stopping or doing anything
else; directly 直接；径直： *Come straight
home.* 直接回家。◇ *She walked straight
past me.* 她径直从我身旁走过。
straight away immediately; now 立即；
马上： *I'll do it straight away.* 我马上
去做。

straight 正

straight 正   **crooked** 歪

straight² ⊶ /streɪt/ *adjective* 形容词
(**straighter, straightest**)
1 with no curve or bend 直的；笔直的：
Use a ruler to draw a straight line. 用尺画
一条直线。◇ *His hair is curly and mine is
straight.* 他的头发是鬈的，我的是直的。
➲ Look at the picture at **hair**. 见 hair 的
插图。
2 with one side as high as the other
水平；垂直： *This picture isn't straight.*
这幅画挂歪了。
3 honest and direct 坦诚的；直率的：
a straight answer to a straight question
问得直率，答得坦诚
get something straight to make sure
that you understand something
completely 搞清楚；弄明白： *Let's get this
straight. Are you sure you left your bike by
the cinema?* 让我们弄清楚，你确定把自行
车忘在电影院旁吗？

straighten /'streɪtn/ *verb* 动词
(**straightens, straightening, straightened**
/'streɪtnd/)
to become or to make something straight
（使）变直，变正

straightforward /ˌstreɪt'fɔːwəd/
adjective 形容词
easy to understand or do 简易的；简单
明了的： *a straightforward question* 简单
的问题

strain¹ /streɪn/ *noun* 名词
1 physical force （物理）压力，作用力：
*The rope broke **under the strain**.* 绳子给
拉断了。
2 worry; problems caused by worry 精神
压力；重负；压力下出现的问题： *His
illness **put** a great **strain on** their marriage.*
他的病给他们的婚姻带来了很大的压力。
3 an injury to part of your body, caused
by making it work too hard 劳损；拉伤；
扭伤： *back strain* 背部拉伤

strain² /streɪn/ *verb* 动词 (**strains,
straining, strained** /streɪnd/)
1 to try very hard 尽力；竭力： *Her voice
was so quiet that I had to strain to hear
her.* 她声音很轻，我要很费力才能听见她
说话。
2 to hurt a part of your body by making it
work too hard 损伤；拉伤；扭伤： *Don't
read in the dark. You'll strain your eyes.*
不要在光线不足的地方看书，这样会损伤
眼睛的。
3 to pour a liquid through something
with small holes in it, to remove any solid
bits 滤；过滤

strand /strænd/ *noun* 名词
one piece of thread or hair 一根，一股，
一缕（线或毛发）

stranded /'strændɪd/ *adjective* 形容词
left in a place that you cannot get away
from 滞留的；无法离开的： *The car broke
down and I was stranded on a lonely road.*
车子抛锚了，我被困在一条无人来往的
路上。

strange ⊶ /streɪndʒ/ *adjective* 形容词
(**stranger, strangest**)
1 unusual or surprising 奇怪的；异常的：
Did you hear that strange noise? 你听见了
那奇怪的声音吗？
2 that you do not know 陌生的；生疏的：
We were lost in a strange town. 我们在陌生
的镇上迷了路。

🔍 **WHICH WORD?** 词语辨析

Be careful! We use **foreign**, not **strange**,
to talk about a person or thing that

A
B
C
D
E
F
G
H
I
J
K
L
M
N
O
P
Q
R
S
T
U
V
W
X
Y
Z

comes from another country. 注意：表示来自另外一个国家的人或事物用 foreign，不用 strange。

strangely /'streɪndʒli/ ***adverb*** 副词
in a surprising or an unusual way 奇怪地；异常地： *He was acting very strangely.* 当时他举止十分反常。◇ *She was strangely quiet.* 她出奇地沉默。

stranger /'streɪndʒə(r)/ ***noun*** 名词
1 a person who you do not know 陌生人
2 a person who is in a place that they do not know 外来人： *I'm a **stranger to** this city.* 我在这个城市人生地疏。

WHICH WORD? 词语辨析
Be careful! We use the word **foreigner**, not **stranger**, for a person who comes from another country. 注意：表示外国人用 foreigner，不用 stranger。

strangle /'stræŋgl/ ***verb*** 动词 (**strangles, strangling, strangled** /'stræŋgld/)
to kill somebody by pressing their neck very tightly 勒死；掐死

strap¹ /stræp/ ***noun*** 名词
a long flat piece of material that you use for carrying something or for keeping something in place 带子： *a leather watch strap* 皮表带 ➲ Look at the pictures at **purse** and **watch²**. 见 purse 和 watch² 的插图。

strap² /stræp/ ***verb*** 动词 (**straps, strapping, strapped** /stræpt/)
to hold something in place with a STRAP 用带子系（或捆、扎）： *I strapped the bag onto the back of my bike.* 我用带子把包捆在自行车的后面。

strategy /'strætədʒi/ ***noun*** 名词 (*plural* 复数形式 **strategies**)
a plan; planning 策略；计策： *What's your **strategy for** passing the exam?* 你用什么策略通过考试？

straw /strɔː/ ***noun*** 名词
1 (*no plural* 不用复数形式) dried plants that animals sleep on or that people use for making things like hats and floor coverings （干燥的）禾秆，麦秆，稻草： *a straw hat* 草帽
2 (*plural* 复数形式 **straws**) a thin paper or plastic tube that you can drink through （喝饮料用的）吸管
the last straw, the final straw the last of several bad things; the thing that finally makes it impossible for you to accept a situation any longer 使人最不堪忍受的一件事；教人终于无法忍受的一件事

strawberry /'strɔːbəri/ ***noun*** 名词 (*plural* 复数形式 **strawberries**)
a soft red fruit with seeds near the surface 草莓 ➲ Look at Picture Dictionary page **P8**. 见彩页 P8。

stray /streɪ/ ***adjective*** 形容词
A **stray** animal is lost or does not have a home. （动物）走失的，无主的： *a stray dog* 流浪狗
▸ **stray** ***noun*** 名词 (*plural* 复数形式 **strays**)
an animal that has no home 流浪动物

streak /striːk/ ***noun*** 名词
a long thin line that is a different colour from the surface it is on 条纹；条痕： *She's got **streaks of** grey in her hair.* 她头发里夹杂着缕缕白发。◇ ***a streak of lightning*** 一道闪电

stream¹ /striːm/ ***noun*** 名词
1 a small river 小河；溪： *a mountain stream* 山涧
2 moving liquid, or moving things or people （液体等事物的）流；人流： ***a stream of** blood* 一股血 ◇ *I've had a **steady stream** of visitors.* 我不断有客人来访。

stream² /striːm/ ***verb*** 动词 (**streams, streaming, streamed** /striːmd/)
to move like water 流；流动： *Tears were **streaming down** his face.* 他脸上淌着泪。

streamline /'striːmlaɪn/ ***verb*** 动词 (**streamlines, streamlining, streamlined** /'striːmlaɪnd/)
1 to give something like a car or boat a long smooth shape so that it can go fast through air or water 使（汽车、船等）成流线型
2 to make an organization or a way of doing things work better by making it simpler 精简，简化（以提高效率）

street 🔑 /striːt/ ***noun*** 名词 (*abbr.* 缩略式 **St**)
a road in a city, town or village with buildings along the sides 大街；街道： *I saw Anna walking down the street.* 我看见安娜沿着大街走去。◇ *I live in Hertford Street.* 我住在赫特福德街。◇ *91 Oxford St, London* 伦敦牛津街 91 号

streetcar /'striːtkɑː(r)/ ***noun*** 名词
American English for TRAM 美式英语，即 tram

street light /'striːt laɪt/ ***noun*** 名词
a light on a tall post in the street 路灯；街灯

strength 0━ /streŋθ/ *noun* 名词
(*no plural* 不用复数形式)
how strong or powerful you are 体力；
力气；力量：*I don't have the **strength** to
lift this box – it's too heavy.* 我的力气不够
大，提不起这个箱子，它太重了。

strengthen /'streŋθn/ *verb* 动词
(strengthens, strengthening,
strengthened /'streŋθnd/)
to become or to make somebody or
something stronger 加强；增强：*The
wind had strengthened overnight.* 夜里
风更大了。

stress¹ /stres/ *noun* 名词 (*no plural* 不用
复数形式)
1 a feeling of worry because of problems
in your life 精神压力；心理负担：*Mum's
been suffering from stress since Dad's been
ill.* 自从爸爸生病以来，妈妈一直承受很大
的压力。
2 saying one word or part of a word more
strongly than another 重音；重读：*In the
word 'dictionary', the stress is on the first
part of the word.* * dictionary 一词的重音
在第一个音节。

stress² /stres/ *verb* 动词 (stresses,
stressing, stressed /strest/)
1 to say something strongly to show that
it is important 强调；着重：*I must stress
how important this meeting is.* 我必须强调
这次会议有多重要。
2 to say one word or part of a word more
strongly than another 重读：*You should
stress the first part of the word 'happy'.*
* happy 一词应该重读第一个音节。

stressful /'stresfl/ *adjective* 形容词
causing a lot of worry 令人担忧的；压力
大的：*a stressful job* 压力大的工作

stretch¹ 0━ /stretʃ/ *verb* 动词
(stretches, stretching, stretched /stretʃt/)
1 to pull something to make it longer or
wider; to become longer or wider 拉长；
拽宽；变长；变宽：*The T-shirt stretched
when I washed it.* 这件T恤衫我洗过后变
长了。
2 to push your arms and legs out as far
as you can 伸展，舒展（胳膊和腿）：
Joe got out of bed and stretched. 乔起床后
伸了伸腰。◇ *The cat stretched out in front
of the fire and went to sleep.* 猫在火炉前
舒展身子睡着了。
3 to cover a large area of land or a long
period of time 延伸；绵延；延续：
The beach stretches for miles. 海滩绵延
数英里。

stretch² /stretʃ/ *noun* 名词 (*plural* 复数
形式 stretches)
a piece of land or water 一片，一段（陆地
或水域）：*This is a beautiful stretch of
countryside.* 这一片乡村景色秀丽。

stretcher /'stretʃə(r)/ *noun* 名词
a kind of bed for carrying somebody who
is ill or hurt 担架：*They carried him to
the ambulance on a stretcher.* 他们用担架
把他抬上了救护车。

strict 0━ /strɪkt/ *adjective* 形容词
(stricter, strictest)
If you are **strict**, you make people do
what you want and do not allow them
to behave badly. 严格的；严厉的：
*Her parents are very strict – she always
has to be home before ten o'clock.* 她父母
很严厉 —— 她总得在十点之前回到家里。
◇ *strict rules* 严格的规则

strictly /'strɪktli/ *adverb* 副词
1 definitely; in a strict way 绝对地；
严格地：*Smoking is strictly forbidden.*
严禁吸烟。
2 exactly 确切地：*That is not strictly true.*
那并非完全属实。

stride /straɪd/ *verb* 动词 (strides, striding,
strode /strəʊd/)
to walk with long steps 大踏步走；阔步
行走：*The police officer strode across the
road.* 警察迈着大步穿过马路。
▶ **stride** *noun* 名词：*He walked with long
strides.* 他阔步走着。

strike¹ /straɪk/ *verb* 动词 (strikes, striking,
struck /strʌk/, has struck)
1 (*formal* 正式) to hit somebody or
something 打；击；碰：*A stone **struck**
me **on** the back of the head.* 一块石头击中
了我的后脑。

🔊 SPEAKING 表达方式说明
Hit is the more usual word, but when
you talk about **lightning** (= the flashes
of light that you see in the sky when
there is a storm), you always use **strike**.
* hit 是较常用的词，但谈及闪电
（lightning）时总是用 strike：*The tree
was struck by lightning.* 那棵树遭闪电
击中了。

2 to stop working because you want more
money or are angry about something
罢工：*The nurses are striking for better
pay.* 护士正在为争取加薪而罢工。
3 to come suddenly into your mind 突然
想到：*It suddenly **struck** me **that** she
looked like my sister.* 我突然发觉她长得像
我的妹妹。

A
B
C
D
E
F
G
H
I
J
K
L
M
N
O
P
Q
R
S
T
U
V
W
X
Y
Z

A
B
C
D
E
F
G
H
I
J
K
L
M
N
O
P
Q
R
S
T
U
V
W
X
Y
Z

4 If a clock **strikes**, it rings a bell a certain number of times so that people know what time it is. （钟）敲响，报时: *The clock struck nine.* 时钟敲了九点。

strike a match to make fire with a match 划火柴

strike² /straɪk/ *noun* 名词
a time when people are not working because they want more money or are angry about something 罢工: *There are no trains today because the drivers are on strike.* 今天火车不开，因为司机在罢工。

striking /'straɪkɪŋ/ *adjective* 形容词
If something is **striking**, you notice it because it is very unusual or interesting. 异乎寻常的；引人注目的；显著的: *That's a very striking hat.* 那帽子很别致。

string 绳子

string 🔒 /strɪŋ/ *noun* 名词
1 very thin rope that you use for tying things 绳子；带子；线: *I tied up the parcel with string.* 我用绳子把包裹捆了起来。◇ *The key was hanging on a string.* 钥匙挂在一根带子上。
2 a line of things on a piece of thread 一串: *a string of blue beads* 一串蓝色的珠子
3 a piece of thin wire on a musical instrument （乐器的）弦: *guitar strings* 吉他的弦

strip¹ /strɪp/ *verb* 动词 (**strips, stripping, stripped** /strɪpt/)
1 (*also* 亦作 **strip off**) to take off your clothes; to take off another person's clothes 脱，扒掉（衣服）: *She stripped off and ran into the sea.* 她脱掉衣服，跑进海里。◇ *They were stripped and searched by the police officers.* 他们被警察脱衣搜身。
2 to take off something that is covering something 除去；剥去: *I stripped the wallpaper off the walls.* 我把墙纸从墙上揭了下来。

strip² /strɪp/ *noun* 名词
a long thin piece of something 条；带；片: *a strip of paper* 纸条

stripe 条纹

stripe 条纹

striped 带条纹的

stripe /straɪp/ *noun* 名词
a long thin line of colour 条纹；线条: *Zebras have black and white stripes.* 斑马身上有黑白条纹。

▶ **striped** /straɪpt/ *adjective* 形容词: *He wore a blue and white striped shirt.* 他穿了蓝白条纹的衬衫。

strode *form of* STRIDE * stride 的不同形式

stroke¹ /strəʊk/ *noun* 名词
1 a movement that you make with your arms, for example when you are swimming or playing sports such as TENNIS （游泳、网球等的）划水，击打
2 a sudden serious illness when the brain stops working properly 中风: *He had a stroke.* 他曾经中风。
3 a sudden successful action or event 突然的成功: *It was a stroke of luck finding your ring again so quickly.* 这么快就找回你的戒指真是幸运。
4 a gentle movement of your hand over a surface 轻抚；抚摸: *He gave the cat a stroke.* 他轻抚了一下猫。

stroke 抚摸

pat 轻拍

stroke² /strəʊk/ *verb* 动词 (**strokes, stroking, stroked** /strəʊkt/)

to move your hand gently over somebody or something to show love 轻抚；抚摸：*She stroked his hair.* 她抚摸着他的头发。

stroll /strəʊl/ *verb* 动词 (**strolls, strolling, strolled** /strəʊld/)
to walk somewhere in a slow relaxed way 散步；漫步；溜达：*We strolled along the beach.* 我们沿着海滩漫步。
▸ **stroll** *noun* 名词：*We went for a stroll by the river.* 我们去了河边散步。

stroller /ˈstrəʊlə(r)/ *noun* 名词 American English for PUSHCHAIR 美式英语，即 pushchair

strong ০ᴥ /strɒŋ/ *adjective* 形容词 (**stronger, strongest**)
1 A **strong** person has a powerful body, and can carry heavy things. （人）强壮的，健壮的，力气大的：*I need somebody strong to help me move this piano.* 我需要找个力气大的人帮我搬这架钢琴。
2 A **strong** object does not break easily. （物体）坚固的，结实的：*Don't stand on that chair – it's not very strong.* 别站在那把椅子上——它不太结实。
3 A **strong** opinion or belief is not easy to change. （观点或信念）坚定的，不易动摇的：*There was strong opposition to the plan.* 这个计划遭到了强烈的反对。
4 powerful 强大的；强劲的：*strong winds* 强风 ◇ *The current was very strong.* 水流很急。
5 having a big effect on the mind or the body 浓烈的；刺激的：*I like strong tea* (= with not much milk in it). 我喜欢喝浓茶。◇ *a strong smell of oranges* 很浓的橙子味
▸ **strongly** /ˈstrɒŋli/ *adverb* 副词：*I strongly believe that he is wrong.* 我坚信他是错的。

struck *form of* STRIKE¹ * strike¹ 的不同形式

structure ০ᴥ /ˈstrʌktʃə(r)/ *noun* 名词
1 (*no plural* 不用复数形式) the way that something is made 结构；构造：*We are studying the structure of a bird's wing.* 我们在研究鸟的翅膀构造。
2 (*plural* 复数形式 **structures**) a building or another thing that people have made with many parts 建筑物；结构体：*The new post office is a tall glass and brick structure.* 新邮局是一栋用玻璃和砖建造的高楼。

struggle /ˈstrʌɡl/ *verb* 动词 (**struggles, struggling, struggled** /ˈstrʌɡld/)
1 to try very hard to do something that is not easy 努力；奋斗：*We struggled to lift the heavy box.* 我们费尽了力气抬起那个重箱子。
2 to move your arms and legs a lot when you are fighting or trying to get free 博斗；扭打；挣脱：*She struggled with her attacker.* 她和袭击者扭打了起来。
▸ **struggle** *noun* 名词：*In 1862 the American slaves won their struggle for freedom.* * 1862 年，美国的奴隶在争取自由的斗争中获得了胜利。

stubborn /ˈstʌbən/ *adjective* 形容词
A **stubborn** person does not change their ideas easily or do what other people want them to do. 固执的；顽固的；倔强的 Ɔ SAME MEANING **obstinate** 同义词为 obstinate：*She's too stubborn to say sorry.* 她脾气犟，不肯说对不起。
▸ **stubbornly** /ˈstʌbənli/ *adverb* 副词：*He stubbornly refused to apologize.* 他怎么都不肯道歉。

stuck¹ *form of* STICK¹ * stick¹ 的不同形式
stuck² /stʌk/ *adjective* 形容词
1 not able to move 卡住；不能移动：*This drawer is stuck – I can't open it.* 这个抽屉卡住了，我打不开。◇ *I was stuck in Italy with no money.* 我身无分文，困在意大利了。
2 not able to do something because it is difficult 难倒；被难住：*If you get stuck, ask your teacher for help.* 要是给难倒了就请教老师。

student ০ᴥ /ˈstjuːdnt/ *noun* 名词
a person who is studying at a school, college or university 学生：*Tim is a history student.* 蒂姆是历史科的学生。

> ♫ WHICH WORD? 词语辨析
>
> **Student** or **pupil**? 用 student 还是 pupil？
> We usually say **student**. We often say **pupil** when talking about children at school. 一般多用 student。pupil 常用来指小学生。

studio /ˈstjuːdiəʊ/ *noun* 名词 (*plural* 复数形式 **studios**)
1 a room where an artist works （艺术家的）工作室
2 a room where people make films, radio and television programmes or records 摄影棚；录音室；演播室；制作室：*a television studio* 电视演播室

study¹ ০ᴥ /ˈstʌdi/ *noun* 名词 (*plural* 复数形式 **studies**)
1 the activity of learning about something 学习；研究：*He's doing a course in Business Studies.* 他正在修读

A B C D E F G H I J K L M N O P Q R S T U V W X Y Z

商学课程。◇ *Biology is **the study of** living things.* 生物学是研究生物的学科。
2 a room in a house where you go to study, read or write 书房

study² 0ᴛ /'stʌdi/ *verb* 动词 (studies, studying, studied /'stʌdid/, has studied)
1 to spend time learning about something 学习；研究：*He studied French at university.* 他在大学学过法语。
2 to look at something carefully 细看；仔细观察：*We must study the map before we leave.* 出发前我们得仔细看看地图。

stuff¹ 0ᴛ /stʌf/ *noun* 名词 (no plural 不用复数形式) (*informal* 非正式)
any material, substance or group of things 东西；物品：*What's this blue stuff on the carpet?* 地毯上这蓝色的东西是什么？◇ *Put your stuff in this bag.* 把你的东西放进这个袋子。

stuff² /stʌf/ *verb* 动词 (stuffs, stuffing, stuffed /stʌft/)
1 to fill something with something 填满；塞满：*The pillow was **stuffed with** feathers.* 枕头塞满了羽毛。
2 (*informal* 非正式) to push something quickly into another thing 把…塞进；把…填进：*He took the money quickly and **stuffed it into** his pocket.* 他匆忙拿了钱，塞进了口袋。

stuffy /'stʌfi/ *adjective* 形容词 (stuffier, stuffiest)
If a room is **stuffy**, it has no fresh air in it. （房间）闷热的，不通风的：*Open the window – it's very stuffy in here.* 把窗户打开，这儿太闷了。

stumble /'stʌmbl/ *verb* 动词 (stumbles, stumbling, stumbled /'stʌmbld/)
to hit your foot against something when you are walking or running, and almost fall 绊脚：*The old lady stumbled as she was going upstairs.* 老太太上楼时绊着了。

stump /stʌmp/ *noun* 名词
the small part that is left when something is cut off or broken 残余部分；残根；残段：*a tree stump* 树墩

stun /stʌn/ *verb* 动词 (stuns, stunning, stunned /stʌnd/)
1 to hit a person or an animal on the head so hard that they cannot see, think or make a sound for a short time 使昏迷；打昏
2 to make somebody very surprised 使震惊；使惊愕：*His sudden death stunned his family and friends.* 他突然去世，使家人亲友十分震惊。

stung *form of* STING¹ * sting¹ 的不同形式

stunk *form of* STINK¹ * stink¹ 的不同形式

stunning /'stʌnɪŋ/ *adjective* 形容词
very beautiful, wonderful 非常迷人的；绝妙的：*a stunning dress* 非常漂亮的连衣裙 ◇ *a stunning victory* 令人惊喜的胜利

stunt /stʌnt/ *noun* 名词
something dangerous or difficult that a person does, especially as part of a film （尤指电影的）特技：*James Bond films are full of exciting stunts.* 《007》系列电影中有很多惊险特技。

stupid 0ᴛ /'stjuːpɪd/ *adjective* 形容词
not intelligent; silly 愚蠢的；笨的；糊涂的：*Don't be so stupid!* 别那么傻！◇ *What a stupid question!* 多么愚蠢的问题！
▶ **stupidity** /stjuː'pɪdəti/ *noun* 名词 (no plural 不用复数形式)：*There are no limits to his stupidity!* 他真是愚蠢至极！
▶ **stupidly** /'stjuːpɪdli/ *adverb* 副词：*I stupidly forgot to close the door.* 我忘了关门，真糊涂。

sturdy /'stɜːdi/ *adjective* 形容词 (sturdier, sturdiest)
strong and healthy; not easy to break 强壮的；结实的；坚固的：*sturdy legs* 强壮的腿 ◇ *sturdy shoes* 结实的鞋子

stutter /'stʌtə(r)/ *verb* 动词 (stutters, stuttering, stuttered /'stʌtəd/)
to say the same sound many times when you are trying to say a word 口吃；结结巴巴地说 ➔ SAME MEANING **stammer** 同义词为 stammer：*'I d-d-don't understand,' he stuttered.* "我不一不一不明白。" 他结结巴巴地说。

sty /staɪ/ *noun* 名词 (plural 复数形式 sties)
= PIGSTY

style 0ᴛ /staɪl/ *noun* 名词
1 a way of doing, making or saying something 方式；作风；风格：*I don't like his style of writing.* 我不喜欢他的写作风格。
2 the shape or kind of something 样式；款式：*This shop has all the latest styles.* 这家商店具备所有最新的款式。◇ *a new hairstyle* 新发型

stylish /'staɪlɪʃ/ *adjective* 形容词
fashionable and attractive 时髦的；新潮的：*Jane's very stylish.* 简非常时髦。

subject 0ᴛ /'sʌbdʒɪkt/ *noun* 名词
1 the person or thing that you are talking or writing about 主题；话题；题目：*What is the subject of the talk?* 这个讲座的主题是什么？
2 something you study at school,

university or college 学科；科目；课程：
I'm studying three subjects: Maths, Physics and Chemistry. 我在修读三个学科：数学、物理和化学。
3 (*grammar* 语法) the word in a sentence that does the action of the verb 主语：
In the sentence 'Sue ate the cake', 'Sue' is the subject. 在 Sue ate the cake 一句中，Sue 是主语。 ⊃ Look at **object¹** (3). 见 object¹ 第 3 义。
4 a person who belongs to a certain country 国民；臣民：*British subjects* 英国国民

submarine /ˌsʌbmə'ri:n/ *noun* 名词
a ship that can travel underwater 潜水艇

subscription /səb'skrɪpʃn/ *noun* 名词
money that you pay, for example to get the same magazine each month or to join a club（杂志等的）订阅费；会员费：*I've got a subscription to 'Vogue' magazine.* 我订阅了《时尚》杂志。

substance 0➔ /'sʌbstəns/ *noun* 名词
any solid, liquid or gas 物质：*Stone is a hard substance.* 石头是坚硬的物质。◇ *chemical substances* 化学物质

substitute /'sʌbstɪtjuːt/ *noun* 名词
a person or thing that you put in the place of another 替代者；替代物：*One player was injured, so a substitute came on.* 一名球员受了伤，所以派上替补球员。
▶ **substitute** *verb* 动词 (substitutes, substituting, substituted)：*You can substitute margarine for butter.* 你可以用人造黄油代替黄油。

subtitles /'sʌbtaɪtlz/ *noun* 名词 (*plural* 用复数形式)
words at the bottom of a film or TV programme that tell you what people are saying（电影或电视的）字幕：*It was a French film with English subtitles.* 那是部带英语字幕的法国影片。

subtle /'sʌtl/ *adjective* 形容词
not large, bright or easy to notice 不易察觉的；暗的；微妙的：*subtle colours* 暗色 ◇ *There has been a subtle change in her behaviour.* 她的行为发生了微妙的变化。

subtract /səb'trækt/ *verb* 动词 (subtracts, subtracting, subtracted)
to take a number away from another number 减；减去 ➔ SAME MEANING **take away** 同义词为 take away：*If you subtract 6 from 9, you get 3.* *9 减 6 得 3。 ⊃ OPPOSITE **add** 反义词为 add
▶ **subtraction** /səb'trækʃn/ *noun* 名词：*The children are learning how to do*

subtraction. 孩子在学习减法。 ⊃ Look at **addition**. 见 addition。

suburb /'sʌbɜːb/ *noun* 名词
one of the parts of a town or city outside the centre 郊区；城外：*We live in the suburbs.* 我们住在郊区。
▶ **suburban** /sə'bɜːbən/ *adjective* 形容词：*suburban areas* 郊区地带

subway /'sʌbweɪ/ *noun* 名词 (*plural* 复数形式 **subways**)
1 American English for UNDERGROUND² 美式英语，即 underground²：*the New York subway* 纽约地铁 ◇ *a subway station* 地铁站
2 (*British* 英式英语) a path that goes under a busy road, so that people can cross safely 地下人行道

succeed 0➔ /sək'siːd/ *verb* 动词 (succeeds, succeeding, succeeded)
to do or get what you wanted to do or get 成功；实现目标：*She finally succeeded in getting a job.* 她终于找到了工作。◇ *I tried to get a ticket for the concert but I didn't succeed.* 我设法去弄张演唱会的入场券，可没弄到手。 ⊃ OPPOSITE **fail** 反义词为 fail

success 0➔ /sək'ses/ *noun* 名词
1 (*no plural* 不用复数形式) doing or getting what you wanted; doing well 成功；胜利：*I wish you success with your studies.* 我祝你学业有成。
2 (*plural* 复数形式 **successes**) somebody or something that does well or that people like a lot 成功的人（或事物）：*The film 'The Matrix' was a great success.* 电影《黑客帝国》大获成功。 ⊃ OPPOSITE **failure** 反义词为 failure

successful 0➔ /sək'sesfl/ *adjective* 形容词

🔎 SPELLING 拼写说明
Remember! You spell **successful** with **CC** and **SS**. 记住：successful 拼写中有 cc 和 ss。

If you are **successful**, you have got or done what you wanted, or you have become popular, rich, etc. 成功的；受欢迎的；发迹的：*a successful actor* 走红的演员 ◇ *The party was very successful.* 派对办得很成功。 ⊃ OPPOSITE **unsuccessful** 反义词为 unsuccessful
▶ **successfully** /sək'sesfəli/ *adverb* 副词：*He completed his studies successfully.* 他顺利完成了学业。

such 0➔ /sʌtʃ/ *adjective* 形容词
1 a word that makes another word

A
B
C
D
E
F
G
H
I
J
K
L
M
N
O
P
Q
R
S
T
U
V
W
X
Y
Z

stronger（加强语气）这么，那么，如此：
He wears such strange clothes. 他穿那么
怪模怪样的衣服。◇ *It was such a nice
day that we decided to go to the beach.*
天气这么好，我们决定去海滩。 ⟳ Look at
the note at **so¹**. 见 **so¹** 条的注释。
2 like this or that 这样的；那样的：
*'Can I speak to Mrs Graham?' 'I'm sorry.
There's no such person here.'* "请给我找
格雷厄姆夫人听电话好吗？" "很抱歉，
这里没有这个人。"
such as words that you use to give an
example 例如；像…之类 ⟳ SAME MEANING
like 同义词为 like：*Sweet foods such as
chocolate can make you fat.* 巧克力之类的
甜食会使人发胖。

suck 0➔ /sʌk/ *verb* 动词 (sucks, sucking,
sucked /sʌkt/)
1 to pull something into your mouth,
using your lips 吸；嘬；吮吸：*The baby
sucked milk from its bottle.* 婴儿吸着奶瓶
中的奶。
2 to hold something in your mouth and
touch it a lot with your tongue 含在嘴里
舔着吃：*She was sucking a sweet.* 她嘴里
呷着一块糖。

sudden 0➔ /'sʌdn/ *adjective* 形容词
happening quickly when you do not
expect it 突然的；忽然的：*His death was
very sudden.* 他死得很突然。◇ *a sudden
change in the weather* 天气的骤变
all of a sudden suddenly 突然；猛地：
*We were watching TV when all of a sudden
the lights went out.* 我们看电视的时候，
灯突然灭了。

suddenly 0➔ /'sʌdənli/ *adverb* 副词
quickly and unexpectedly 突然；忽然；
猛地：*He left very suddenly.* 他走得很
突然。◇ *Suddenly there was a loud noise.*
突然一声巨响。

sue /suː/ *verb* 动词 (sues, suing, sued /suːd/)
to go to a court of law and ask for money
from a person who has done something
bad to you 控告；起诉：*She sued the
company for loss of earnings.* 她因收入的
损失而控告公司。

suede /sweɪd/ *noun* 名词 (no plural 不用
复数形式)
a type of soft leather with a rough surface
绒面革；仿麂皮：*suede boots* 绒面革靴子

suffer 0➔ /'sʌfə(r)/ *verb* 动词 (suffers,
suffering, suffered /'sʌfəd/)
to feel pain, sadness or another
unpleasant feeling 遭受，蒙受（痛苦、
悲伤等）：*She suffers from bad
headaches.* 她头痛得厉害。◇ *It's not*

right for children to suffer. 让孩子受苦是
不对的。

▸ **suffering** /'sʌfərɪŋ/ *noun* 名词
(no plural 不用复数形式)：*They have
experienced so much suffering.* 他们经历过
重重的苦难。

sufficient /sə'fɪʃnt/ *adjective* 形容词
(formal 正式)
as much or as many as you need or want
足够的；充足的 ⟳ SAME MEANING **enough**
同义词为 enough：*There was sufficient
food to last two weeks.* 食物足够维持两个
星期。

suffix /'sʌfɪks/ *noun* 名词 (plural 复数形式
suffixes)
letters that you add to the end of a word
to make another word 后缀；词尾：
*If you add the suffix '-ly' to the adjective
'quick', you make the adverb 'quickly'.*
形容词 quick 加上后缀 -ly 就会构成副词
quickly。 ⟳ Look at **prefix**. 见 prefix。

suffocate /'sʌfəkeɪt/ *verb* 动词
(suffocates, suffocating, suffocated)
to die or to make somebody die because
there is no air to breathe 闷死；（使）
窒息而死

sugar 0➔ /'ʃʊɡə(r)/ *noun* 名词
1 (no plural 不用复数形式) a sweet
substance that comes from certain plants
糖：*Do you take sugar in your coffee?*
你喝咖啡放糖吗？
2 (plural 复数形式 sugars) the amount of
sugar that a small spoon can hold 一匙
糖：*Two sugars, please.* 请加两匙糖。

suggest 0➔ /sə'dʒest/ *verb* 动词
(suggests, suggesting, suggested)
to say what you think somebody should
do or what should happen 建议；提议：
I suggest that you stay here tonight.
我建议你今晚在这里过夜。◇ *Simon
suggested going for a walk.* 西蒙提议去
散散步。◇ *What do you suggest?* 你有什么
建议？

suggestion 0➔ /sə'dʒestʃən/ *noun*
名词
a plan or an idea that somebody thinks of
for somebody else to discuss and consider
建议；提议：*I don't know what to buy
Alison for her birthday. Have you got any
suggestions?* 我不知道给艾莉森买什么生日
礼物好。你有什么建议吗？◇ *May I make
a suggestion?* 我可以提个建议吗？

suicide /'suːɪsaɪd/ *noun* 名词
the act of killing yourself 自杀：
He committed suicide at the age of 23.
他 23 岁时自杀。

suit¹ 0️⃣ /suːt/ *noun* 名词

🔍 PRONUNCIATION 读音说明
The word **suit** sounds like **boot**.
* suit 读音像 boot。

1 a jacket and trousers, or a jacket and skirt, that you wear together and that are made from the same material 西服；套装 ⊃ Look at Picture Dictionary page **P5**. 见彩页 P5。
2 one of the 4 sets that PLAYING CARDS (= cards with numbers and pictures on them that you use for playing games) are divided into（扑克牌中分成四种的）花色：*The four suits are hearts, clubs, diamonds and spades.* 扑克牌的四种花色分别是红桃、梅花、方块和黑桃。⊃ Look at the picture at **playing card**. 见 playing card 的插图。

suit² 0️⃣ /suːt/ *verb* 动词 (suits, suiting, suited)
1 If something **suits** you, it looks good on you. 相配；合身：*Does this hat suit me?* 这顶帽子适合我戴吗？
2 to be right for you; to be what you want or need 适合；对…方便；合…心意：*Would it suit you if I came at five o'clock?* 我要是五点钟来你方便吗？

suitable 0️⃣ /ˈsuːtəbl/ *adjective* 形容词 right for somebody or something 合适的；适宜的：*This film isn't **suitable for** children.* 这部影片儿童不宜。⊃ OPPOSITE **unsuitable** 反义词为 unsuitable
▸ **suitably** /ˈsuːtəbli/ *adverb* 副词：*Tony wasn't suitably dressed for a party.* 托尼的穿着不宜参加聚会。

suitcase 行李箱

suitcase 0️⃣ /ˈsuːtkeɪs/ *noun* 名词 a large bag with flat sides that you carry your clothes in when you travel（旅行用的）行李箱，手提箱

sulfur *noun* 名词 American English for SULPHUR 美式英语，即 sulphur

sulk /sʌlk/ *verb* 动词 (sulks, sulking, sulked /sʌlkt/)
to not speak because you are angry about

something 生闷气；闷闷不乐：*She's been sulking all day because her mum wouldn't let her go to the party.* 因为妈妈不让她参加派对，她一整天都闷闷不乐。
▸ **sulky** /ˈsʌlki/ *adjective* 形容词 (sulkier, sulkiest)：*I can't stand sulky teenagers.* 我忍受不了郁郁寡欢的青少年。

sullen /ˈsʌlən/ *adjective* 形容词 looking bad-tempered and not wanting to speak to people 面有愠色的；闷闷不乐的；郁郁寡欢的：*a sullen expression* 愠怒的表情

sulphur (*British* 英式英语) (*American* 美式英语 **sulfur**) /ˈsʌlfə(r)/ *noun* 名词 (*no plural* 不用复数形式) (*symbol* 符号 S)
a natural yellow substance that smells like bad eggs 硫磺

sum 0️⃣ /sʌm/ *noun* 名词

🔍 PRONUNCIATION 读音说明
The word **sum** sounds just like **some**.
* sum 读音同 some。

1 an amount of money 金额；款项：*£200 000 is a large **sum of money**.* 二十万英镑是一大笔钱。
2 the answer that you have when you add numbers together 和；总数：*The **sum of** two and five is seven.* 二加五的和是七。
3 a simple piece of work with numbers, for example adding or dividing 算术：*Children have to learn how to **do sums**.* 孩子得学会算术。

summary /ˈsʌməri/ *noun* 名词 (*plural* 复数形式 **summaries**)
a short way of telling something by giving only the most important facts 总结；概要：*Here is **a summary of** the news …* 以下是新闻摘要…

summer 0️⃣ /ˈsʌmə(r)/ *noun* 名词 the season that comes between spring and autumn 夏天；夏季：*I am going to Spain **in the summer**.* 我夏天将会去西班牙。◇ *the summer holidays* 暑假 ⊃ Look at Picture Dictionary page **P16**. 见彩页 P16。

summit /ˈsʌmɪt/ *noun* 名词 the top of a mountain 山顶

summon /ˈsʌmən/ *verb* 动词 (summons, summoning, summoned /ˈsʌmənd/) (*formal* 正式)
to order a person to come to a place 召唤；传唤：*The boys were **summoned to** the head teacher's office.* 那些男孩被召唤到校长办公室。

A
B
C
D
E
F
G
H
I
J
K
L
M
N
O
P
Q
R
S
T
U
V
W
X
Y
Z

sun 0ᴙ /sʌn/ *noun* 名词 (*no plural* 不用复数形式)

🔎 PRONUNCIATION 读音说明

The word **sun** sounds just like **son**.
* sun 读音同 son。

1 the sun the big round object in the sky that gives us light in the day, and heat 太阳: *The sun is shining.* 太阳照耀着。
2 light and heat from the sun 阳光: *We sat in the sun all morning.* 我们一上午都坐着晒太阳。

sunbathe /'sʌnbeɪð/ *verb* 动词 (**sunbathes, sunbathing, sunbathed** /'sʌnbeɪðd/)
to lie in the sun so that your skin becomes darker 晒太阳；沐日光浴: *We sunbathed on the beach.* 我们在海滩上晒太阳。
  ▶ **sunbathing** /'sʌnbeɪðɪŋ/ *noun* 名词 (*no plural* 不用复数形式): *Sunbathing is bad for your skin.* 沐日光浴对皮肤有害。

sunburn /'sʌnbɜːn/ *noun* 名词 (*no plural* 不用复数形式)
red painful skin that you get when you have been in the hot sun for too long 晒斑；晒伤 ⊃ Look at **suntan**. 见 suntan。
  ▶ **sunburned** /'sʌnbɜːnd/ (*also* 亦作 **sunburnt** /'sʌnbɜːnt/) *adjective* 形容词: *sunburned shoulders* 晒伤的肩膀

Sunday 0ᴙ /'sʌndeɪ/ *noun* 名词
the day of the week after Saturday and before Monday, thought of as either the first or the last day of the week 星期日；星期天 ⊃ Look at the note at **day**. 见 day 条的注释。

sunflower 向日葵

sunflower /'sʌnflaʊə(r)/ *noun* 名词
a very tall plant with large yellow flowers, which farmers grow for its seeds and their oil, which are used in cooking 向日葵

sung *form of* SING * sing 的不同形式

sunglasses /'sʌnɡlɑːsɪz/ (*also informal* 非正式亦作 **shades**) *noun* 名词 (*plural* 用复数形式)
glasses with dark glass in them that you wear in strong light 太阳镜；墨镜: *a pair of sunglasses* 一副太阳镜 ⊃ Look at the picture at **glasses**. 见 glasses 的插图。

sunk *form of* SINK¹ * sink¹ 的不同形式

sunlight /'sʌnlaɪt/ *noun* 名词 (*no plural* 不用复数形式)
the light from the sun 阳光；日光: *The room was full of sunlight.* 房间里阳光充沛。

sunny /'sʌni/ *adjective* 形容词 (**sunnier, sunniest**)
bright and warm with light from the sun 阳光充足的；晴朗的: *a sunny day* 阳光明媚的一天 ◊ *Tomorrow will be warm and sunny.* 明天天气将会暖和晴朗。

sunrise /'sʌnraɪz/ *noun* 名词 (*no plural* 不用复数形式)
the time in the morning when the sun comes up 日出 ⊃ SAME MEANING **dawn** 同义词为 dawn: *They were up before sunrise.* 他们日出前就起床了。 ⊃ Look at **sunset**. 见 sunset。

sunset /'sʌnset/ *noun* 名词
the time in the evening when the sun goes down 日落: *The park closes at sunset.* 公园在日落时关门。 ⊃ Look at **sunrise**. 见 sunrise。 ⊃ Look at Picture Dictionary page **P16**. 见彩页 P16。

sunshine /'sʌnʃaɪn/ *noun* 名词 (*no plural* 不用复数形式)
the light and heat from the sun 阳光；日光: *We sat outside in the sunshine.* 我们坐在外面晒太阳。

suntan /'sʌntæn/ (*also* 亦作 **tan**) *noun* 名词
When you have a **suntan**, your skin is brown because you have been in the hot sun. (皮肤) 晒黑: *I'm trying to get a suntan.* 我正努力把皮肤晒黑点。 ⊃ Look at **sunburn**. 见 sunburn。
  ▶ **suntanned** /'sʌntænd/ (*also* 亦作 **tanned**) *adjective* 形容词: *suntanned arms* 晒得黝黑的胳膊

super /'suːpə(r)/ *adjective* 形容词 (*informal* 非正式)
very good 极好的；顶呱呱的 ⊃ SAME MEANING **lovely** 同义词为 lovely: *That was a super meal.* 那顿饭好吃极了。

superb /suːˈpɜːb/ ***adjective*** 形容词
very good or beautiful 极好的；秀丽的：*a superb holiday* 美妙的假期 ◇ *The view from the window is superb.* 从窗口望出去，景色十分宜人。

superintendent /ˌsuːpərɪnˈtendənt/ ***noun*** 名词
1 a person who manages and controls a large building（大楼的）主管，负责人：*the superintendent of schools in Dallas* 达拉斯教育局长
2 a police officer with a high position 警司；警长：*Detective Superintendent Nolan* 诺兰探长

superior /suːˈpɪəriə(r)/ ***adjective*** 形容词
better or more important than another person or thing 更好的；优越的；更重要的：*I think ground coffee is* ***superior to*** *instant coffee.* 我觉得即磨咖啡比速溶咖啡好。 ➲ OPPOSITE **inferior** 反义词为 inferior

superlative /suˈpɜːlətɪv/ ***noun*** 名词
(*grammar* 语法) the form of an adjective or adverb that shows the most of something（形容词或副词的）最高级：*'Most intelligent', 'best' and 'fastest' are all superlatives.* * most intelligent、best 和 fastest 都是形容词最高级。
▸ **superlative** ***adjective*** 形容词：*'Youngest' is the superlative form of 'young'.* * youngest 是 young 的最高级形式。 ➲ Look at **comparative**. 见 comparative。

supermarket /ˈsuːpəmɑːkɪt/ ***noun*** 名词
a big shop where you can buy food and other things for your home 超级市场；超市

> **WORD BUILDING** 词汇扩充
> In a supermarket you put the things you want to buy in a **basket** or a **trolley** (*British*) (*American* **cart**) and pay for them all at the **checkout**.
> 在超市里，把要买的东西放进篮子（basket）或手推车（英式英语用 trolley；美式英语用 cart）里，然后到收款台（checkout）付款。

➲ Look at Picture Dictionary page **P13**. 见彩页 P13。

supersonic /ˌsuːpəˈsɒnɪk/ ***adjective*** 形容词
faster than the speed of sound 超音速的：*a supersonic aeroplane* 超音速飞机

superstar /ˈsuːpəstɑː(r)/ ***noun*** 名词
a person such as a singer or film star who is very famous and successful 超级巨星：*Madonna is a global superstar.* 麦当娜是国际巨星。

superstition /ˌsuːpəˈstɪʃn/ ***noun*** 名词
a belief in good and bad luck and other things that cannot be explained 迷信：*People say that walking under a ladder brings bad luck, but it's just a superstition.* 人们说在梯子下面走不吉利，但这不过是迷信的说法。
▸ **superstitious** /ˌsuːpəˈstɪʃəs/ ***adjective*** 形容词：*A lot of people are* ***superstitious about*** *the number 13.* 很多人相信 13 这个数字不吉利。

superstore /ˈsuːpəstɔː(r)/ ***noun*** 名词
a very big shop 大型超市；大型商场：*There's a new computer superstore on the edge of town.* 城边新开了一家电脑商城。

supervise /ˈsuːpəvaɪz/ ***verb*** 动词
(**supervises**, **supervising**, **supervised** /ˈsuːpəvaɪzd/)
to watch somebody or something in order to see that people are working or behaving correctly 监督；监管；指导：*It was his job to supervise the builders.* 监督建筑工人是他的工作。
▸ **supervision** /ˌsuːpəˈvɪʒn/ ***noun*** 名词 (*no plural* 不用复数形式)：*Children must not use the pool without supervision.* 儿童无人看管不得使用此游泳池。
▸ **supervisor** /ˈsuːpəvaɪzə(r)/ ***noun*** 名词：*a factory supervisor* 工厂监督人

supper /ˈsʌpə(r)/ ***noun*** 名词
the last meal of the day 晚饭；晚餐；夜宵：*We had supper and then went to bed.* 我们吃完晚饭就睡觉了。 ➲ Look at the note at **meal**. 见 meal 条的注释。

supply[1] 🔑 /səˈplaɪ/ ***noun*** 名词 (*plural* 复数形式 **supplies**)
a store or an amount of something that you need 供应；供给；供应量：*Food supplies were dropped by helicopter.* 补给食物以直升机空投。 ◇ *The water supply was cut off.* 供水被切断了。

supply[2] /səˈplaɪ/ ***verb*** 动词 (**supplies**, **supplying**, **supplied** /səˈplaɪd/, **has supplied**)
to give or sell something that somebody needs 提供；供应；供给：*The school* ***supplies*** *us* ***with*** *books.* 学校给我们提供书本。 ◇ *The lake* ***supplies*** *water* ***to*** *thousands of homes.* 这个湖为千家万户供水。
▸ **supplier** /səˈplaɪə(r)/ ***noun*** 名词：*We are the region's biggest supplier of computer equipment.* 我们是该地区最大的电脑设备供应商。

A B C D E F G H I J K L M N O P Q R S T U V W X Y Z

A B C D E F G H I J K L M N O P Q R **S** T U V W X Y Z

support¹ 0━ /səˈpɔːt/ *verb* 动词
(**supports, supporting supported**)
1 to say that somebody or something is right or the best 支持；拥护：*Everybody else said I was wrong but Paul supported me.* 大家都说我错，只有保罗支持我。◇ *Which football team do you support?* 你拥护哪支足球队？
2 to help somebody to live by giving things like money, a home or food 供养；抚养：*She has three children to support.* 她得供养三个孩子。
3 to hold somebody or something up, so that they do not fall 支撑；支承：*The bridge isn't strong enough to support heavy lorries.* 这座桥不够结实，不能承受重型卡车。

support² /səˈpɔːt/ *noun* 名词
1 (*no plural* 不用复数形式) help 支持；帮助：*Thank you for all your support.* 谢谢你全力的支持。
2 (*plural* 复数形式 **supports**) something that holds up another thing 支撑物；支柱：*a roof support* 屋顶的支柱

supporter /səˈpɔːtə(r)/ *noun* 名词
a person who supports a political party or a sports team 支持者；拥护者：*football supporters* 足球迷

suppose 0━ /səˈpəʊz/ *verb* 动词
(**supposes, supposing, supposed** /səˈpəʊzd/)
1 to think that something is probably true or will probably happen 认为；推断；猜想：*'Where's Jenny?' 'I don't know – I suppose she's still at work.'* "珍妮在哪里？" "我不知道。我想她还在上班吧。"
2 a word that you use when you agree with something but are not happy about it（表示勉强同意）：*'Can I borrow your pen?' 'Yes, I suppose so – but don't lose it.'* "我能借用你的笔吗？" "行是行，可别弄丢了。"

be supposed to
1 If you **are supposed to** do something, you should do it. 应当；应该：*They were supposed to meet us here.* 他们本应在这里跟我们见面。◇ *You're not supposed to smoke in this room.* 这个房间里不准抽烟。
2 (*informal* 非正式) If something **is supposed to** be true, people say it is true. 被认为；被视为：*This is supposed to be a good restaurant.* 一般认为这家餐馆不错。

supposing /səˈpəʊzɪŋ/ *conjunction* 连词
if something happens or is true 假设；假定：*Supposing we miss the bus, how will we get to the airport?* 假设我们赶不上公共汽车，那怎么去机场呢？

supreme /suːˈpriːm/ *adjective* 形容词
highest or most important 最高的；至高无上的：*the Supreme Court* 最高法院

supremely /suːˈpriːmli/ *adverb* 副词
extremely 极其；极为：*He is supremely confident that he can win.* 他信心十足，认为自己能够胜出。

sure 0━ /ʃʊə(r); ʃɔː(r)/ *adjective* 形容词
(**surer, surest**) *adverb* 副词
1 knowing that something is true or right 肯定；确信 ➹ SAME MEANING **certain** 同义词为 **certain**：*I'm sure I've seen that man before.* 我肯定以前见过那个男子。◇ *If you're not sure how to do it, ask your teacher.* 要是你把握怎样做就问问老师。
2 If you are **sure** to do something, you will certainly do it. 一定；必定：*If you work hard, you're sure to pass the exam.* 你要是努力，就一定能通过考试。

for sure without any doubt 无疑；肯定：*I think he's coming to the party but I don't know for sure.* 我想他会来参加聚会，可是我不能确定。

make sure to check something so that you are certain about it 核实；弄清楚：*I think the party starts at eight, but I'll phone to make sure.* 我想聚会是在八点钟开始，但我会打个电话核实一下。◇ *Make sure you don't leave your bag on the bus.* 千万别把包落在公共汽车上。

sure (*American* 美式英语) (*informal* 非正式) yes 可以；当然：*'Can I borrow this book?' 'Sure.'* "我可以借这本书吗？" "当然可以。"

sure enough as I thought 不出所料；果然：*I said they would be late, and sure enough they were.* 我说过他们会迟到，他们果然迟到了。

surely /ˈʃʊəli; ˈʃɔːli/ *adverb* 副词
a word that you use when you think that something must be true, or when you are surprised（表示确信或惊讶）无疑；必定：*This will surely cause problems.* 这肯定会造成困难的。◇ *Surely you know where your brother works!* 你一定知道你弟弟在哪儿上班！

surf¹ /sɜːf/ *noun* 名词 (*no plural* 不用复数形式)
the white part on the top of waves in the sea 浪尖；浪峰

surf² /sɜːf/ *verb* 动词 (**surfs, surfing, surfed** /sɜːft/) (*also* 亦作 **go surfing**)
to stand or lie on a long piece of wood or plastic (called a **surfboard**) and ride on a

wave 冲浪；进行冲浪运动: *We went surfing in Hawaii.* 我们去了夏威夷冲浪。
surf the Net, surf the Internet to use the Internet （在互联网上）冲浪，浏览: *He spends hours every day surfing the Net.* 他每天花好多时间上网。

▶ **surfer** /'sɜːfə(r)/ *noun* 名词: *The beach is popular with surfers.* 这个海滩很受冲浪者欢迎。

surface 0= /'sɜːfɪs/ *noun* 名词
1 the outside part of something 表面；表层: *the earth's surface* 地球的表面
2 the top of water 水面: *She dived below the surface.* 她潜入了水中。

surfboard /'sɜːfbɔːd/ *noun* 名词
a long piece of wood or plastic that you stand or lie on to ride on a wave 冲浪板 ➲ Look at Picture Dictionary page **P14**. 见彩页 **P14**。

surfing /'sɜːfɪŋ/ *noun* 名词 (*no plural* 不用复数形式)
the sport of riding on waves while standing on a SURFBOARD 冲浪运动: *His hobbies include surfing and photography.* 他的爱好包括冲浪和摄影。 ➲ Look at Picture Dictionary page **P14**. 见彩页 **P14**。

surgeon /'sɜːdʒən/ *noun* 名词
a doctor who cuts your body to take out or repair a part inside. (This is called an **operation**.) 外科医生: *a brain surgeon* 脑外科医生

surgery /'sɜːdʒəri/ *noun* 名词
1 (*no plural* 不用复数形式) cutting a person's body to take out or repair a part inside 外科手术: *He needed surgery after the accident.* 他出事故后需要做手术。
2 (*plural* 复数形式 **surgeries**) a place or time when a doctor or dentist sees patients 诊室；门诊时间: *There is no surgery on Saturdays.* 星期六没有医生应诊。

surname /'sɜːneɪm/ *noun* 名词
the name that a family has 姓 ➲ SAME MEANING **last name, family name** 同义词为 last name 和 family name: *Her name is Kate Smith; Smith is her surname.* 她叫凯特·史密斯。史密斯是她的姓。 ➲ Look at the note at **name¹**. 见 name¹ 条的注释。

surprise¹ 0= /sə'praɪz/ *noun* 名词
1 (*no plural* 不用复数形式) the feeling that you have when something happens suddenly that you did not expect 惊奇；惊讶: *He looked up in surprise when I walked in.* 我走进来的时候，他惊讶地

抬起了头。◇ *To my surprise, everyone agreed with me.* 出乎我的意料，大家都同意我的看法。
2 (*plural* 复数形式 **surprises**) something that happens when you do not expect it 令人惊奇的事；意想不到的事: *Don't tell him about the party – it's a surprise!* 别告诉他聚会的事 —— 这是个惊喜!
take somebody by surprise to happen when somebody does not expect it 使某人吃惊；出乎某人意料: *The news took me completely by surprise.* 这则消息着实让我感到意外。

surprise² 0= /sə'praɪz/ *verb* 动词 (**surprises, surprising, surprised** /sə'praɪzd/)
to do something that somebody does not expect 使惊奇；使惊讶: *I arrived early to surprise her.* 我早到是为了给她惊喜。

surprised 0= /sə'praɪzd/ *adjective* 形容词
If you are **surprised**, you feel or show surprise. 惊奇的；感到意外的: *I was surprised to see Tim yesterday – I thought he was in Canada.* 我昨天见到蒂姆感到很意外，我还以为他在加拿大呢。

surprising 0= /sə'praɪzɪŋ/ *adjective* 形容词
If something is **surprising**, it makes you feel surprise. 使人惊奇的；出人意料的: *The news was surprising.* 这则消息令人惊讶。

▶ **surprisingly** /sə'praɪzɪŋli/ *adverb* 副词: *The exam was surprisingly easy.* 这次考试出奇地容易。

surrender /sə'rendə(r)/ *verb* 动词 (**surrenders, surrendering, surrendered** /sə'rendəd/)
to stop fighting because you cannot win 投降: *After six hours on the roof, the man surrendered to the police.* 那名男子在屋顶与警方对峙六小时后投降了。

▶ **surrender** *noun* 名词 (*no plural* 不用复数形式): *We will not even consider surrender.* 投降我们连想都没想过。

surround 0= /sə'raʊnd/ *verb* 动词 (**surrounds, surrounding, surrounded**)
to be or go all around something 围绕；环绕: *The lake is surrounded by trees.* 这个湖绿树环抱。

surroundings /sə'raʊndɪŋz/ *noun* 名词 (*plural* 用复数形式)
everything around you, or the place where you live 环境: *I don't like seeing animals in a zoo – I prefer to see them in their natural surroundings.* 我不喜欢看

A
B
C
D
E
F
G
H
I
J
K
L
M
N
O
P
Q
R
S
T
U
V
W
X
Y
Z

动物园里的动物，我喜欢看生活在自然环境
中的动物。

survey /'sɜːveɪ/ *noun* 名词 (*plural* 复数
形式 surveys)
asking questions to find out what people
think or do 民意调查: *We did a survey of
people's favourite TV programmes.* 我们对
观众最喜欢的电视节目做了民意调查。

survive 0̄➔ /sə'vaɪv/ *verb* 动词 (survives,
surviving, survived /sə'vaɪvd/)
to continue to live in or after a difficult or
dangerous time 生存；幸存: *Camels can
survive for many days without water.* 骆驼
很多天不喝水也能存活。◇ *Only one
person survived the plane crash.* 飞机失事
后仅一人生还。

▶ **survival** /sə'vaɪvl/ *noun* 名词 (*no plural*
不用复数形式): *Food and water are
necessary for survival.* 要维持生命，食物
和水是必不可少的。

▶ **survivor** /sə'vaɪvə(r)/ *noun* 名词: *The
government sent help to the survivors of
the earthquake.* 政府向地震的生还者提供
援助。

suspect¹ /sə'spekt/ *verb* 动词 (suspects,
suspecting, suspected)
1 to think that something is true, but not
be certain 猜想；觉得: *John wasn't at
college today – I suspect that he's ill.* 约翰
今天没来学校，我看他是病了。
2 to think that somebody has done
something wrong but not be certain 怀疑
（某人干了坏事）: *They suspect Helen
of stealing the money.* 他们怀疑那笔钱是
海伦偷的。➔ The noun is **suspicion** and
the adjective is **suspicious**. 名词为
suspicion，形容词为 suspicious。

suspect² /'sʌspekt/ *noun* 名词
a person who you think has done
something wrong 嫌疑犯；嫌疑分子:
The police have arrested two suspects.
警方已经逮捕两名嫌疑犯。

suspend /sə'spend/ *verb* 动词 (suspends,
suspending, suspended)
1 to hang something from something else
悬挂；吊: *Coloured flags were suspended
from the ceiling.* 彩旗悬挂在天花板上。
2 to stop or delay something for a time
暂停；推迟: *Rail services were suspended
for 24 hours.* 铁路服务暂缓了 24 小时。

suspense /sə'spens/ *noun* 名词 (*no plural*
不用复数形式)
a feeling of excitement or worry that you
have when you are waiting for news or
for something to happen 悬念；焦虑:

Don't keep me in suspense – did you pass?
别卖关子了 —— 你通过了吗?

suspicion /sə'spɪʃn/ *noun* 名词
1 a feeling that somebody has done
something wrong 怀疑；嫌疑: *He was
arrested on suspicion of murder.* 他涉嫌
谋杀被逮捕了。
2 an idea that is not totally certain 感觉；
看法: *We have a suspicion that she is
unhappy.* 我们觉得她并不开心。➔ The
verb is **suspect**. 动词为 suspect。

suspicious /sə'spɪʃəs/ *adjective* 形容词
1 If you are **suspicious**, you do not
believe somebody or something, or you
feel that something is wrong. 怀疑的；
觉得可疑: *The police are suspicious of
her story.* 警方认为她的陈述可疑。
2 A person or thing that is **suspicious**
makes you feel that something is wrong.
可疑的；令人怀疑的: *Anyone who sees
anything suspicious should contact the
police.* 若发现任何可疑的事情，应与警方
联系。

▶ **suspiciously** /sə'spɪʃəsli/ *adverb*
副词: *'What are you doing here?' the
woman asked suspiciously.* "你在这里干
什么?" 那个女子疑惑地问。

swallow¹ 0̄➔ /'swɒləʊ/ *verb* 动词
(swallows, swallowing, swallowed
/'swɒləʊd/)
to make food or drink move down your
throat from your mouth 吞下；咽下:
I can't swallow these tablets without water.
没有水我咽不下这些药片。

swallow² /'swɒləʊ/ *noun* 名词
a small bird with a long tail 燕子

swam *form of* SWIM * swim 的不同形式

swamp /swɒmp/ *noun* 名词
an area of soft wet ground 沼泽；湿地

swan 天鹅

swan /swɒn/ *noun* 名词
a big white bird with a very long neck.
Swans live on rivers and lakes. 天鹅

swap (*also* 亦作 swop) /swɒp/ *verb* 动词
(swaps, swapping, swapped /swɒpt/)
to change one thing for another thing; to
give one thing and get another thing for it
交换；互换： *Do you want to swap chairs
with me* (= you have my chair and I'll
have yours)? 你想跟我换椅子吗？ ◇
I swapped my CD for Tom's (= I had his
and he had mine). 我跟汤姆交换了 CD。
▸ **swap** *noun* 名词： *Why don't we do
a swap?* 我们何不来一个交换？

swarm¹ /swɔːm/ *noun* 名词
a big group of flying insects 一大群
（在飞的昆虫）： *a swarm of bees*
一大群蜜蜂

swarm² /swɔːm/ *verb* 动词 (swarms,
swarming, swarmed /swɔːmd/)
to fly or move quickly in a big group
成群地飞行；大批地移动： *The fans
swarmed into the stadium.* 球迷一窝蜂
涌进了体育馆。

sway /sweɪ/ *verb* 动词 (sways, swaying,
swayed /sweɪd/)
to move slowly from side to side 摇摆；
摇动： *The trees were swaying in the wind.*
树随风摇曳。

swear /sweə(r)/ *verb* 动词 (swears,
swearing, swore /swɔː(r)/, has sworn
/swɔːn/)
1 to say bad words 说脏话；说粗话：
Don't swear at your mother! 不要对你
母亲说脏话！
2 to make a serious promise 发誓：
He swears that he is telling the truth.
他发誓他说的是真话。

swear word /'sweə wɜːd/ *noun* 名词
a bad word 脏话；粗话

sweat /swet/ *verb* 动词 (sweats,
sweating, sweated)
to produce liquid through your skin
because you are hot, ill or afraid 出汗；
流汗： *The room was so hot that everyone
was sweating.* 房间太热，大家都出汗了。
▸ **sweat** *noun* 名词 (*no plural* 不用复数
形式)： *He wiped the sweat from his
forehead.* 他擦掉了额头上的汗。

sweater /'swetə(r)/ *noun* 名词
a warm piece of clothing with long
sleeves, which you wear on the top part
of your body 毛衣；线衣

WORD BUILDING 词汇扩充
Other words for **sweater** are **jersey**,
jumper and **pullover**. **Sweaters** are
often made of wool. A **cardigan** is a
sweater that fastens at the front like a
jacket. 与 sweater 同义的词有 jersey、
jumper 和 pullover。sweater 通常用
羊毛制成。cardigan（开襟毛衣）则像
夹克般在前面系扣。

⊃ Look at Picture Dictionary page **P5**.
见彩页 P5。

sweatshirt /'swetʃɜːt/ *noun* 名词
a warm piece of clothing with long
sleeves made of thick cotton, which
you wear on the top part of your body
（长袖）运动衫 ⊃ Look at Picture
Dictionary page **P5**. 见彩页 P5。

sweaty /'sweti/ *adjective* 形容词
(sweatier, sweatiest)
covered with sweat 满是汗的；汗淋淋的：
sweaty socks 汗湿的袜子 ◇ *I'm all hot and
sweaty – I need a shower.* 我热得浑身是
汗，得冲个澡。

sweep /swiːp/ *verb* 动词 (sweeps,
sweeping, swept /swept/, has swept)
1 to clean something by moving dirt or
rubbish away with a brush 清扫；扫打：
I've swept the floor. 我已经扫地了。
2 to push something along or away
quickly and strongly 横扫；席卷： *The
bridge was swept away by the floods.*
桥被洪水冲走了。
sweep up, sweep something up
to remove dirt or rubbish using a brush
打扫掉；清扫走： *I swept up the broken
glass.* 我扫走了碎玻璃。

sweet¹ /swiːt/ *adjective* 形容词
(sweeter, sweetest)
1 containing or tasting of sugar 含糖的；
甜的： *Honey is sweet.* 蜂蜜是甜的。
2 with a good smell 芳香的；芬芳的：
the sweet smell of roses 玫瑰的芳香
3 attractive; pretty 可爱的；惹人喜爱的
⊃ SAME MEANING **cute** 同义词为 cute：
What a sweet little girl! 多可爱的小女孩
啊！
4 having or showing a kind character
善良的；和善的： *It was sweet of you to
help me.* 你出手相助，真好。

sweet² /swiːt/ *noun* 名词
1 (*British* 英式英语) (*American* 美式英语
candy) a small piece of sweet food 糖果：
*He bought a packet of sweets for the
children.* 他给孩子买了一包糖。
2 sweet food that you eat at the end of

a meal（餐后）甜点，甜食 ⊃ SAME
MEANING **dessert** 同义词为 dessert:
Do you want a sweet? 你想吃甜点吗？

sweetcorn /'swiːtkɔːn/ (*British* 英式英语)
(*American* 美式英语 **corn**) *noun* 名词
(*no plural* 不用复数形式)
the sweet yellow seeds of a tall plant
(called **maize**) that you eat as a vegetable
甜玉米

sweetheart /'swiːthɑːt/ *noun* 名词
(*no plural* 不用复数形式)
a word that you use when speaking to
a person that you love（称呼所爱的人）
亲爱的，宝贝儿: *Do you want a drink,
sweetheart?* 亲爱的，想喝一杯吗？

sweetly /'swiːtli/ *adverb* 副词
in a pretty, kind or nice way 可爱地；
令人愉快地: *She smiled sweetly.* 她笑得
很甜。

swell /swel/ *verb* 动词 (swells, swelling,
swelled /sweld/, has swollen /'swəʊlən/
or 或 has swelled)
swell up to become bigger or thicker
than normal 膨胀；肿胀: *After he hurt
his ankle it began to swell up.* 他的脚踝
弄伤后开始肿起来。

swelling /'swelɪŋ/ *noun* 名词
a place on the body that is bigger or
fatter than it usually is 肿胀部位；浮肿
处: *He's got a swelling on his head where
he fell and hit it.* 他摔倒后头碰了个包。

swept form of SWEEP * sweep 的不同形式

swerve /swɜːv/ *verb* 动词 (swerves,
swerving, swerved /swɜːvd/)
to change direction suddenly so that you
do not hit somebody or something
急转弯；突然转向: *The driver swerved
when he saw the child in the road.* 司机
看到路上有个孩子，立刻转向避开了。

swift /swɪft/ *adjective* 形容词 (swifter,
swiftest)
quick or fast 快的；迅速的: *We made a
swift decision.* 我们迅速作出了决定。
▶ **swiftly** /'swɪftli/ *adverb* 副词: *She ran
swiftly up the stairs.* 她飞快地跑上了楼梯。

swim ⚬ /swɪm/ *verb* 动词 (swims,
swimming, swam /swæm/, has swum
/swʌm/)
to move your body through water 游泳:
Can you swim? 你会游泳吗？ ◇ *I swam
across the lake.* 我游到了湖的对岸。

🔊 SPEAKING 表达方式说明
When you talk about spending time
swimming as a sport, you usually say

go swimming. 表示去游泳通常用 go
swimming: *I go swimming every day.*
我每天都游泳。

▶ **swim** *noun* 名词 (*no plural* 不用复数
形式): *Let's go for a swim.* 咱们去游泳吧。
▶ **swimmer** /'swɪmə(r)/ *noun* 名词:
He's a good swimmer. 他是个游泳高手。
▶ **swimming** /'swɪmɪŋ/ *noun* 名词
(*no plural* 不用复数形式): *Swimming is
my favourite sport.* 游泳是我最喜欢的
运动。 ⊃ Look at Picture Dictionary
page **P14**. 见彩页 P14。

swimming costume /'swɪmɪŋ
kɒstjuːm/ (*also* 亦作 **swimsuit**) *noun* 名词
a piece of clothing that a woman or girl
wears for swimming（女式）游泳衣
⊃ Look at the picture at **dive**. 见 dive 的
插图。

swimming pool ⚬ /'swɪmɪŋ puːl/
(*also* 亦作 **pool**) *noun* 名词
a place that is built for people to swim in
游泳池: *an open-air swimming pool*
露天游泳池

swimming trunks /'swɪmɪŋ trʌŋks/
(*also* 亦作 **trunks**) *noun* 名词 (*plural*
用复数形式)
short trousers that a man or boy wears
for swimming（男式）游泳裤

swimsuit /'swɪmsuːt/ *another word for*
SWIMMING COSTUME * swimming costume
的另一种说法

swing¹ /swɪŋ/ *verb* 动词 (swings,
swinging, swung /swʌŋ/, has swung)
1 to move backwards and forwards or
from side to side through the air; to make
somebody or something do this（使）
摆动，摇摆: *Monkeys were swinging
from the trees.* 猴子在树上荡来荡去。◇
He swung his arms as he walked. 他一边走
一边摆动手臂。
2 to move in a curve 呈弧形运动: *The
door swung open.* 门晃开了。

swing 秋千

slide 滑梯　　**swings** 秋千

swing[2] /swɪŋ/ *noun* 名词
a seat that hangs down and that children can sit on to move backwards and forwards through the air 秋千

swipe /swaɪp/ *verb* 动词 (swipes, swiping, swiped /swaɪpt/) (*informal* 非正式)
1 to hit or try to hit something by swinging your arm 挥拳打；挥臂击:
He swiped at the ball and missed. 他挥棒击球但没击中。
2 to steal something 偷窃

switch 开关

switch[1] 0━ /swɪtʃ/ *noun* 名词 (*plural* 复数形式 switches)
a small thing that you press to turn electricity on or off （电路的）开关:
Where is the light switch? 电灯的开关在哪里?

switch[2] 0━ /swɪtʃ/ *verb* 动词 (switches, switching, switched /swɪtʃt/)
to change to something different 转变；变换: *I switched to another seat because I couldn't see the film.* 我看不到影片，所以换了个座位。
switch something off to make a light or a machine stop working by pressing a SWITCH 关上（电源） ⊃ SAME MEANING **turn something off** 同义词为 turn something off: *I switched the TV off.* 我把电视关了。◇ *Don't forget to switch off the lights!* 别忘了关灯!
switch something on to make a light or a machine work by pressing a SWITCH 打开（电源） ⊃ SAME MEANING **turn something on** 同义词为 turn something on: *Switch the radio on.* 把收音机打开。

switchboard /'swɪtʃbɔːd/ *noun* 名词
the place in a large company where somebody answers telephone calls and sends them to the right people （电话的）交换台，总机

swollen[1] *form of* SWELL * swell 的不同形式

swollen[2] /'swəʊlən/ *adjective* 形容词
(used about a part of the body) thicker or fatter than it usually is （身体部位）肿胀的，胀大的: *a swollen ankle* 肿胀的脚踝

swoop /swuːp/ *verb* 动词 (swoops, swooping, swooped /swuːpt/)
to fly down quickly 向下猛冲；俯冲: *The plane swooped down low over the buildings.* 飞机俯冲到那些大楼的上方。

swop /swɒp/ *verb* 动词 = SWAP

sword /sɔːd/ *noun* 名词

> 🔎 **PRONUNCIATION** 读音说明
> The word **sword** sounds like **cord**, because we don't say the **w**.
> * sword 读音像 cord，因为 w 在这里不发音。

a weapon that looks like a very long sharp knife 剑；长刀

swore, sworn *forms of* SWEAR * swear 的不同形式

swot[1] /swɒt/ *noun* 名词 (*British* 英式英语) (*informal* 非正式)
a person who spends too much time studying 学习狂；书呆子

swot[2] /swɒt/ *verb* 动词 (swots, swotting, swotted) (*British* 英式英语) (*informal* 非正式)
to study hard before an exam （考试前）刻苦学习: *Debbie is swotting for her test next week.* 戴比正在努力学习，准备下星期的测验。

swum *form of* SWIM * swim 的不同形式

swung *form of* SWING[1] * swing[1] 的不同形式

syllable /'sɪləbl/ *noun* 名词
a part of a word that has one VOWEL sound when you say it. 'Swim' has one **syllable** and 'system' has two **syllables**. 音节

syllabus /'sɪləbəs/ *noun* 名词 (*plural* 复数形式 syllabuses)
a list of all the things that you must study on a course 教学大纲

symbol 0━ /'sɪmbl/ *noun* 名词
a mark, sign or picture that has a special meaning 象征；标志；符号: *O is the symbol for oxygen.* * O 是氧的符号。◇ *A dove is the symbol of peace.* 鸽子是和平的象征。

symmetrical /sɪ'metrɪkl/ (*also* 亦作 **symmetric** /sɪ'metrɪk/) *adjective* 形容词
having two halves that are exactly the same 对称的: *symmetrical patterns* 对称的图案

A B C D E F G H I J K L M N O P Q R S T U V W X Y Z

sympathetic /ˌsɪmpə'θetɪk/ *adjective* 形容词
showing that you understand other people's feelings when they have problems 同情的；有同情心的：*Everyone was very sympathetic when I was ill.* 我生病时大家都非常关心我。 ⊃ OPPOSITE **unsympathetic** 反义词为 unsympathetic
▸ **sympathetically** /ˌsɪmpə'θetɪkli/ *adverb* 副词：*He smiled sympathetically.* 他露出同情的微笑。

sympathize /'sɪmpəθaɪz/ *verb* 动词
(sympathizes, sympathizing, sympathized /'sɪmpəθaɪzd/)
to show that you understand somebody's feelings when they have problems 同情；谅解：*I sympathize with you – I've got a lot of work to do too.* 我很同情你，我也有很多工作要做。

sympathy /'sɪmpəθi/ *noun* 名词
(*no plural* 不用复数形式)
understanding of another person's feelings and problems 同情：*Everyone feels a lot of sympathy for the victims.* 大家对受害者深表同情。

symphony /'sɪmfəni/ *noun* 名词 (*plural* 复数形式 symphonies)
a long piece of music for a lot of musicians playing together 交响乐；交响曲：*Beethoven's fifth symphony* 贝多芬的第五交响曲

symptom /'sɪmptəm/ *noun* 名词
something that shows that you have an illness 症状：*A sore throat is often a symptom of a cold.* 嗓子疼通常是感冒的症状。

synagogue /'sɪnəgɒg/ *noun* 名词
a building where Jewish people go to say prayers and learn about their religion 犹太教会堂

synonym /'sɪnənɪm/ *noun* 名词
a word that means the same as another word 同义词；近义词：*'Big' and 'large' are synonyms.* * big 和 large 是同义词。

synthesizer /'sɪnθəsaɪzə(r)/ *noun* 名词
an electronic musical instrument that can produce a lot of different sounds （电子）音响合成器

synthetic /sɪn'θetɪk/ *adjective* 形容词
made by people, not natural 人造的；合成的 ⊃ SAME MEANING **artificial** 同义词为 artificial：*Nylon is a synthetic material, but wool is natural.* 尼龙是人造材料，而羊毛是天然的。

syringe /sɪ'rɪndʒ/ *noun* 名词
a plastic or glass tube with a needle that is used for taking blood out of the body or putting drugs into the body 注射器

syrup /'sɪrəp/ *noun* 名词 (*no plural* 不用复数形式)
a thick sweet liquid made by boiling sugar with water or fruit juice 糖水；糖浆：*peaches in syrup* 糖水桃子

system ⊶ /'sɪstəm/ *noun* 名词
1 a group of things or parts that work together 系统：*the railway system* 铁路系统 ◇ *We have a new computer system at work.* 我们工作的地方有一个新的电脑系统。
2 a group of ideas or ways of doing something 体系；制度；体制：*What system of government do you have in your country?* 你们国家政府是什么体制的？

Tt

T, t /tiː/ *noun* 名词 (*plural* 复数形式 T's, t's /tiːz/)
the twentieth letter of the English alphabet 英语字母表的第 20 个字母: *'Table' begins with a 'T'.* * table 一词以字母 t 开头。

table ○━ /'teɪbl/ *noun* 名词
1 a piece of furniture with a flat top on legs 桌子; 台子; 几: *a coffee table* 咖啡茶几 ○ Look at Picture Dictionary page **P10**. 见彩页 P10。
2 a list of facts or numbers 表格; 列表: *There is a table of irregular verbs at the back of this dictionary.* 本词典末尾有个不规则动词表。

tablecloth /'teɪblklɒθ/ *noun* 名词
a cloth that you put over a table when you have a meal (餐桌的) 桌布, 台布

tablespoon /'teɪblspuːn/ *noun* 名词
a big spoon that you use for putting food on plates 餐勺; 汤匙 ○ Look at the picture at **spoon**. 见 spoon 的插图。

tablet /'tæblət/ *noun* 名词
a small hard piece of medicine that you swallow 药片; 片剂 ○ SAME MEANING **pill** 同义词为 pill: *Take two of these tablets before every meal.* 这些药每顿饭前服两片。

table tennis /'teɪbl tenɪs/ (*also informal* 非正式亦作 ping-pong) *noun* 名词
(*no plural* 不用复数形式)
a game where players use a small round BAT (= a piece of wood) to hit a small light ball over a net on a big table 乒乓球运动

tabloid /'tæblɔɪd/ *noun* 名词
a newspaper with small pages (通俗) 小报

tackle¹ /'tækl/ *verb* 动词 (tackles, tackling, tackled /'tækld/)
1 to try to deal with a difficult problem or situation 应付, 处理 (困难的问题或局面): *How shall we tackle this problem?* 我们该怎么处理这个问题呢?
2 to try to take the ball from somebody in a game like football (足球等) 抢截, 铲断
3 to try to catch and hold somebody 抓获; 擒获: *The police officer tackled*

one of the robbers as he ran out. 警察在其中的一名劫匪跑出来时将其抓住了。

tackle² /'tækl/ *noun* 名词
trying to get the ball from somebody in a game like football (足球等的) 抢截, 抢断, 铲断: *a rugby tackle* 橄榄球中的抢断

tacky /'tæki/ *adjective* 形容词 (tackier, tackiest) (*informal* 非正式)
cheap and of bad quality 质劣的; 蹩脚的: *a shop selling tacky souvenirs* 出售劣质廉价纪念品的商店

tact /tækt/ *noun* 名词 (*no plural* 不用复数形式)
knowing how and when to say things so that you do not hurt people 圆通; 得体; 老练: *She handled the situation with great tact.* 她极其得体地应付了那个局面。

tactful /'tæktfl/ *adjective* 形容词
careful not to say or do things that may make people unhappy or angry 圆通的; 得体的; 不得罪人的: *That wasn't a very tactful thing to say!* 说那种话可不太得体!
○ OPPOSITE **tactless** 反义词为 tactless
▸ **tactfully** /'tæktfəli/ *adverb* 副词:
He tactfully suggested I should lose some weight. 他婉转地建议我该减重了。

tactless /'tæktləs/ *adjective* 形容词
saying or doing things that may make people unhappy or angry 不圆通的; 不得体的; 得罪人的: *It was tactless of you to ask how old she was.* 你问她多大年纪, 真是不得体。 ○ OPPOSITE **tactful** 反义词为 tactful

tag /tæg/ *noun* 名词
a small piece of paper or material fixed to something, that tells you about it 标签; 标牌 ○ SAME MEANING **label** 同义词为 label: *I looked at the price tag to see how much the dress cost.* 我看了一下连衣裙的价格标签, 想知道卖多少钱。

tail ○━ /teɪl/ *noun* 名词
1 the long thin part at the end of an animal's body 尾; 尾巴: *The dog wagged its tail.* 狗摇了摇尾巴。 ○ Look at the pictures at **cat**, **fish¹**, **horse** and **lion**. 见 cat、fish¹、horse 和 lion 的插图。
2 the part at the back of something 尾部; 后部: *the tail of an aeroplane* 机尾

3 tails (*plural* 用复数形式) the side of a coin that does not have the head of a person on it 硬币反面（没有人头像的一面）⊃ OPPOSITE **heads** 反义词为 heads

tailor /'teɪlə(r)/ *noun* 名词
a person whose job is to make clothes for men （男装的）裁缝

tailpipe /'teɪlpaɪp/ *American English for* EXHAUST¹ (2) 美式英语，即 exhaust¹ 第 2 义

take 0━ /teɪk/ *verb* 动词 (takes, taking, took /tʊk/, has taken /'teɪkn/)
1 to move something or go with somebody to another place 拿走；携带；带领；引领：*Take your coat with you – it's cold.* 带上大衣吧，天气很冷。◊ *Mark took me to the station.* 马克带我去了火车站。⊃ Look at the note at **bring**. 见 bring 条的注释。
2 to put your hand round something and hold it 拿；握；抱；接：*Take this money – it's yours.* 把这些钱拿着——是你的。◊ *She took my hand and led me outside.* 她拉着我的手，把我领到外面。
3 to remove something from a place or a person, often without asking them （常指未经允许）拿走；偷走：*Somebody has taken my bike.* 有人把我的自行车拿走了。
4 to eat or drink something 吃；喝；服（药）：*Don't forget to take your medicine.* 别忘了吃药。
5 to agree to have something; to accept something 接受：*If you take my advice you'll forget all about him.* 你要是听我的话，就会把他彻底忘掉。
6 to need an amount of time 需要…时间；费时：*The journey took four hours.* 旅程花了四个小时。◊ *It takes a long time to learn a language.* 学一门语言要花很长时间。
7 to travel in a bus, train, etc. 乘坐，搭乘（公交车、火车等）：*I took a taxi to the hospital.* 我坐了出租车去医院。

take after somebody to be or look like an older member of your family （行为或外貌）像（家中长辈）：*She takes after her mother.* 她长得像她母亲。

take something away to remove something 拿开；移除；挪开：*I took the scissors away from the child.* 我把剪刀从孩子那里拿走了。

take something down to write something that somebody says 写下；记录：*He took down my address.* 他写下了我的地址。

take off When a plane **takes off**, it leaves the ground and starts to fly.

（飞机）起飞 ⊃ OPPOSITE **land** 反义词为 land

take something off
1 to remove clothes from your body 脱下（衣服）：*Take off your coat.* 把你的大衣脱掉。⊃ OPPOSITE **put something on** 反义词为 put something on
2 to have time as a holiday, not working 休假：*I am taking a week off in June.* 我会在六月份休假一周。

take over, take something over to get control of something or look after something when another person stops 接管；接手：*Robert took over the business when his father died.* 罗伯特在他父亲去世后接管了公司。

take up something to use or fill time or space 占用（时间）；占据（空间）：*The bed takes up half the room.* 这张床占半个房间。◊ *The new baby takes up all her time.* 她全部时间都花在刚出生的宝宝身上。

takeaway /'teɪkəweɪ/ *noun* 名词 (*plural* 复数形式 takeaways) (*British* 英式英语) (*American* 美式英语 takeout)
1 a restaurant that sells hot food that you take out with you to eat somewhere else 外卖餐馆：*a Chinese takeaway* 中式外卖店
2 food that you buy at this kind of restaurant 外卖食物：*Let's have a takeaway tonight.* 咱们今晚叫外卖吃吧。
▸ **takeaway** *adjective* 形容词：*a takeaway pizza* 外卖比萨饼

take-off /'teɪk ɒf/ *noun* 名词
the time when a plane leaves the ground and starts to fly （飞机）起飞 ⊃ OPPOSITE **landing** 反义词为 landing

takeout /'teɪkaʊt/ *American English for* TAKEAWAY 美式英语，即 takeaway

tale /teɪl/ *noun* 名词
a story, usually about things that are not true （常指虚构的）故事：*fairy tales* 童话故事

talent /'tælənt/ *noun* 名词
a natural ability to do something very well 天才；天赋：*She has a talent for drawing.* 她有绘画的天分。

talented /'tæləntɪd/ *adjective* 形容词
having a natural ability to do something well 天才的；有才能的：*a talented musician* 天才音乐家

talk¹ 0━ /tɔːk/ *verb* 动词 (talks, talking, talked /tɔːkt/)
to speak to somebody; to say words 说话；讲话；谈话：*She is talking to her friend on the telephone.* 她正在和朋友

通电话。◇ *We **talked about** our holiday.*
我们谈了我们度假的事。

talk² 0➔ /tɔːk/ *noun* 名词
1 when two or more people talk about
something 交谈；谈话；讨论；会谈：
*Dave and I **had a long talk about** the
problem.* 戴夫和我就这个问题作了一次
长谈。◇ *The two countries are **holding
talks** to try and end the war.* 两国正在
谈判，试图结束战争。
2 when a person speaks to a group of
people 讲座；报告： *Professor Wilson
gave an interesting **talk on** Chinese art.*
威尔逊教授做了一个关于中国艺术的讲座，
很有意思。

talkative /'tɔːkətɪv/ *adjective* 形容词
A person who is **talkative** likes to talk
a lot. 话多的；健谈的

tall 0➔ /tɔːl/ *adjective* 形容词 (**taller**,
tallest)
1 higher than other people or things
高的；高大的： *a tall tree* 高大的树 ◇
*Richard is **taller** than his brother.* 理查德
比他弟弟高。◑ OPPOSITE **short** 反义词为
short
2 You use **tall** to say or ask how far it is
from the bottom to the top of somebody
or something. （用以表示或询问高度）
有…高： *How **tall** are you?* 你身高多少？
◇ *She's 1.62 metres **tall**.* 她身高 1.62 米。
◑ Look at the note at **high¹**. 见 high¹ 条的
注释。

tame¹ /teɪm/ *adjective* 形容词 (**tamer**,
tamest)
A **tame** animal is not wild and is not
afraid of people. （动物）驯服的，温驯
的： *The birds are so **tame** they will eat
from your hand.* 这些鸟驯服得会在你的
手上啄食。

tame² /teɪm/ *verb* 动词 (**tames**, **taming**,
tamed /teɪmd/)
to make a wild animal easy to control; to
make something TAME 驯服；驯化

tan¹ /tæn/ *verb* 动词 (**tans**, **tanning**,
tanned /tænd/)
If your skin **tans**, it becomes brown
because you have spent time in the sun.
（人的皮肤）晒黑，晒成褐色： *My skin
tans really easily.* 我的皮肤很容易晒黑。
▸ **tanned** *adjective* 形容词：
*a **tanned** face* 晒黑的脸

tan² /tæn/ (*also* 亦作 **suntan**) *noun* 名词
the brown colour that your skin goes
when you have spent time in the sun
晒成的棕褐色： *to get a tan* 晒黑

tangerine /ˌtændʒə'riːn/ *noun* 名词
a fruit like a small sweet orange, with
a skin that is easy to take off 橘子

tangle /'tæŋgl/ *noun* 名词
many things that have become twisted
together so that you cannot easily
separate the different parts 纠结；乱糟糟
的一团： *My hair is full of **tangles**.* 我的
头发乱糟糟的。
▸ **tangle** *verb* 动词 (**tangles**, **tangling**,
tangled /'tæŋgld/): *Does your hair **tangle**
easily?* 你的头发容易缠结吗？

tangled /'tæŋgld/ *adjective* 形容词
twisted together in an untidy way 缠结
的；紊乱的： *The string is all **tangled**.*
绳子乱成一团了。

tank /tæŋk/ *noun* 名词
1 a large container for holding liquid or
gas （存贮液体或气体的）箱，槽，罐：
a fuel tank (= in a car) 燃料箱 ◑ Look at
the picture at **scuba-diving**. 见
scuba-diving 的插图。
2 a strong heavy vehicle with big guns.
Tanks are used by armies in wars. 坦克

tanker /'tæŋkə(r)/ *noun* 名词
a ship or lorry that carries oil, petrol
or gas in large amounts 运送大量石油（或
汽油、气体）的轮船（或卡车）；油轮；
油罐车： *an oil tanker* 油轮

tantrum /'tæntrəm/ *noun* 名词
If a child has a **tantrum**, they cry and
shout because they are angry. （小孩的）
耍脾气，使性子

tap¹ 0➔ /tæp/ *verb* 动词 (**taps**, **tapping**,
tapped /tæpt/)
to hit or touch somebody or something
quickly and lightly 轻敲；轻拍；轻叩：
*She **tapped** me on the shoulder.* 她轻轻拍
了拍我的肩膀。◇ *I **tapped** on the window.*
我轻轻地敲了敲窗户。

tap² 0➔ /tæp/ (*British* 英式英语)
(*American* 美式英语 **faucet**) *noun* 名词
1 a thing that you turn to make
something like water or gas come out of
a pipe （水、气等的）龙头，旋塞： *Turn
the tap off.* 把水龙头关上。◑ Look at the
picture at **plug¹**. 见 plug¹ 的插图。
2 a light hit with your hand or fingers
轻敲；轻叩： *They heard a **tap** at the door.*
他们听到轻轻的敲门声。

tape¹ 0➔ /teɪp/ *noun* 名词
1 a long thin piece of plastic material,
that is used for recording sound, music or
moving pictures so that you can listen to
or watch it later 磁带；录音带；录像带：
*I have got the concert **on tape**.* 我有那次

演唱会的录像。◇ *Will you play your new music tape?* 你放一下你新买的录音带好吗?

2 a long thin piece of material or paper, used for sticking things together 胶带;胶条: *sticky tape* 粘胶带

tape² /teɪp/ *verb* 动词 (**tapes**, **taping**, **taped** /teɪpt/)

to put sound, music or moving pictures on TAPE so that you can listen to or watch it later 把…录在磁带上 ⊃ SAME MEANING **record** 同义词为 record: *I taped the film that was on TV last night.* 我把昨晚电视上播放的电影录了下来。

tape measure /teɪp meʒə(r)/ *noun* 名词
a long thin piece of plastic, cloth or metal for measuring things 卷尺;皮尺

tape recorder /teɪp rɪˌkɔːdə(r)/ *noun* 名词
a machine that you use for recording and playing sound or music on tape 录音机

tapestry /'tæpəstri/ *noun* 名词 (*plural* 复数形式 **tapestries**)
a piece of cloth with pictures on it made from coloured thread 绒绣;壁毯;织锦

tar /tɑː(r)/ *noun* 名词 (*no plural* 不用复数形式)
a black substance that is thick and sticky when it is hot, and hard when it is cold. **Tar** is used for making roads. 焦油;焦油沥青;柏油

target /'tɑːgɪt/ *noun* 名词
1 a result that you are trying to achieve 目标;指标: *Our target is to finish the job by Friday.* 我们的目标是周五前完成这项工作。
2 a person, place or thing that you try to hit when you are shooting or attacking (射击或攻击的)目标,靶子: *The bomb hit its target.* 炸弹击中了目标。

Tarmac™ /'tɑːmæk/ *noun* 名词 (*no plural* 不用复数形式)
a black material that is used for making the surfaces of roads. It is made with TAR. 塔玛克柏油碎石(用于铺路)

tart /tɑːt/ *noun* 名词
an open PIE (= a type of baked food) filled with sweet food such as fruit 甜果馅饼: *Would you like a piece of apple tart?* 你想要一块苹果馅饼吗?

tartan /'tɑːtn/ *noun* 名词
a special pattern on material that comes from Scotland (源自苏格兰的)花格图案: *a tartan skirt* 花格呢裙

task /tɑːsk/ *noun* 名词
a piece of work that you must do; a job 任务;工作: *I had the task of cleaning the floors.* 我的任务是清洁地板。

taste¹ /teɪst/ *noun* 名词
1 (*plural* 复数形式 **tastes**) the feeling that a certain food or drink gives in your mouth 味道;滋味: *Sugar has a sweet taste and lemons have a sour taste.* 糖有甜味,柠檬有酸味。◇ *I don't like the taste of this cheese.* 我不喜欢这种奶酪的味道。
2 (*no plural* 不用复数形式) the power to know about food and drink with your mouth 味觉: *When you have a cold, you often lose your sense of taste.* 感冒时常会失去味觉。
3 (*plural* 复数形式 **tastes**) a little bit of food or drink 少许尝的东西,一口;一点儿: *Have a taste of the fish to see if you like it.* 尝一口鱼吧,看你喜欢不喜欢。
4 (*no plural* 不用复数形式) being able to choose nice things 鉴赏力;品味: *She has good taste in clothes.* 她对衣着很有品味。

taste² /teɪst/ *verb* 动词 (**tastes**, **tasting**, **tasted**)
1 to have a certain flavour 有…味道: *This tastes of oranges.* 这有橙味。◇ *Honey tastes sweet.* 蜂蜜味道甜。
2 to feel or know a certain food or drink in your mouth 尝出(味道): *Can you taste onions in this soup?* 你能尝出这个汤里有洋葱味吗?
3 to eat or drink a little of something, to test its flavour 品尝;尝: *Taste this cheese to see if you like it.* 尝尝这种奶酪,看你喜欢不喜欢。

tasteful /'teɪstfl/ *adjective* 形容词
attractive and of good quality, and showing that you can choose nice things 有品位的;高雅的;雅致的: *tasteful furniture* 雅致的家具 ⊃ OPPOSITE **tasteless** 反义词为 tasteless

▸ **tastefully** /'teɪstfəli/ *adverb* 副词: *The room was tastefully decorated.* 房间装饰得很雅致。

tasteless /'teɪstləs/ *adjective* 形容词
1 having little or no flavour 无味的: *a bowl of tasteless soup* 一碗淡而无味的汤 ⊃ OPPOSITE **tasty** 反义词为 tasty
2 of bad quality and not attractive, showing that you cannot choose nice things 没有品位的;俗气的: *tasteless furniture* 俗气的家具 ⊃ OPPOSITE **tasteful** 反义词为 tasteful

tasty /'teɪsti/ *adjective* 形容词 (tastier, tastiest)
good to eat 美味的；可口的；好吃的：
The soup was very tasty. 这汤非常美味。

tattoo¹ /tə'tuː/ *noun* 名词 (*plural* 复数形式 tattoos)
a picture on somebody's skin, made with a needle and coloured liquid 文身：*She has a tattoo of a tiger on her shoulder.* 她肩膀上刺着一只老虎。

tattoo² /tə'tuː/ *verb* 动词 (tattoos, tattooing, tattooed /tə'tuːd/)
to mark somebody's skin with a picture, made with a needle and coloured ink 给⋯文身；在⋯上刺花纹：*He had a snake tattooed on his arm.* 他胳膊上刺了一条蛇。

taught *form of* TEACH * teach 的不同形式

tax¹ 0—ᴡ /tæks/ *noun* 名词 (*plural* 复数形式 taxes)
money that you have to pay to the government. You pay **tax** from the money you earn or when you buy things. 税；税款：*There is a tax on cigarettes in this country.* 在这个国家香烟要上税。

tax² /tæks/ *verb* 动词 (taxes, taxing, taxed /tækst/)
to make somebody pay TAX 对⋯征税

taxi 0—ᴡ /'tæksi/ (*also* 亦作 **cab**) *noun* 名词
a car that you can travel in if you pay the driver 出租车；计程车；的士：*I took a taxi to the airport.* 我乘出租车去机场了。
◇ *I came by taxi.* 我是坐计程车来的。
つ Look at Picture Dictionary page **P1**. 见彩页 P1。

tea 0—ᴡ /tiː/ *noun* 名词
1 (*no plural* 不用复数形式) the dry leaves of a special plant that you use to make **tea** to drink 茶叶
2 (*no plural* 不用复数形式) a brown drink that you make with hot water and the dry leaves of a special plant 茶；茶水：*Would you like a cup of tea?* 你想喝杯茶吗?
つ Look at Picture Dictionary page **P6**. 见彩页 P6。
3 (*plural* 复数形式 teas) a cup of this drink 一杯茶：*Two teas, please.* 请来两杯茶。
4 (*plural* 复数形式 teas) (*British* 英式英语) a small afternoon meal of SANDWICHES (= two slices of bread with food between them), cakes and cups of tea 下午茶；茶点

♪ CULTURE 文化资料补充
Some people call their evening meal **tea**, especially when it is eaten early in the evening. 有些人把晚点叫做 tea，特别是当这顿饭是在傍晚吃的时候。
つ Look at the note at **meal**. 见 meal 条的注释。

tea bag /'tiː bæg/ *noun* 名词
a small paper bag with tea leaves inside. You use it to make tea. 袋泡茶；茶包

teach 0—ᴡ /tiːtʃ/ *verb* 动词 (teaches, teaching, taught /tɔːt/, has taught)
1 to give lessons to students, for example in a school or college 教；教授：*He teaches English as a foreign language.* 他教作为外语的英语。
2 to show somebody how to do something 教；教导：*My mother taught me how to drive.* 我母亲教我开车。
▶ **teaching** /'tiːtʃɪŋ/ *noun* 名词 (*no plural* 不用复数形式): *modern teaching methods* 现代教学方法

teacher 0—ᴡ /'tiːtʃə(r)/ *noun* 名词
a person whose job is to teach 教师；老师：*He's my English teacher.* 他是我的英语老师。つ Look at Picture Dictionary page **P12**. 见彩页 P12。

team 0—ᴡ /tiːm/ *noun* 名词
1 a group of people who play a sport or a game together against another group （体育或游戏的）队：*Which team do you play for?* 你为哪个队效力?◇ *a football team* 足球队
2 a group of people who work together （一起工作的）团队，团体，组：*a team of doctors* 医疗小组

teapot 茶壶

spout 嘴

teapot /'tiːpɒt/ *noun* 名词
a container for making and pouring tea 茶壶

tear 撕

'Oh no! I just **tore** my shirt!'
不好了！我刚剐破了衬衫。

She **tore** the letter in half.
她把信撕成了两半。

tear¹ 0ᵆ /teə(r)/ *verb* 动词 (tears, tearing, tore /tɔː(r)/, has torn /tɔːn/)

🔎 PRONUNCIATION 读音说明

The verb and noun **tear¹** and **tear²** sound like **hair** or **care**. * tear 作动词和名词时读音像 hair 或 care。

1 to damage something by pulling it apart or making an untidy hole in it 撕裂；扯破；撕开（洞）： *She tore her dress on a nail.* 她的连衣裙被钉子剐破了。◇ *I tore the piece of paper in half.* 我把那张纸撕成了两半。◇ *I can't use this bag – it's torn.* 这个袋子我不能用，它已经破了。
2 to come apart; to break 裂开；破碎： *Paper tears easily.* 纸很容易撕破。
3 to take something from somebody or something in a quick and violent way 扯下；撕掉；夺走： *He tore the bag out of her hands.* 他从她手中一把抢走了包。
4 to move somewhere very fast 飞跑；狂奔；疾驰： *He tore down the street.* 他沿大街飞奔。

tear something up to destroy something by pulling it into small pieces 撕毁；撕碎： *I tore the letter up and threw it away.* 我把信撕碎扔了。

tear² 0ᵆ /teə(r)/ *noun* 名词
an untidy hole in something like paper or material 破洞；裂口： *You've got a tear in your jeans.* 你的牛仔裤上有个破洞。

tear³ 0ᵆ /tɪə(r)/ *noun* 名词

🔎 PRONUNCIATION 读音说明

With this meaning, **tear** sounds like **near** or **cheer**. 作此义时 tear 读音像 near 或 cheer。

a drop of water that comes from your eye when you cry 眼泪；泪水；泪珠： *I was in tears* (= crying) *at the end of the film.* 电影结尾时我哭了。◇ *She read the letter and burst into tears* (= suddenly started to cry). 她读着信突然哭了起来。

tease /tiːz/ *verb* 动词 (teases, teasing, teased /tiːzd/)
to laugh at somebody in a friendly way or in order to upset them 取笑；戏弄；揶揄；寻开心： *Don't take any notice of him – he's only teasing you.* 别理会他，他只是在拿你开心。

teaspoon /ˈtiːspuːn/ *noun* 名词
a small spoon that you use for putting sugar into tea or coffee 茶匙；小匙
➔ Look at the picture at **spoon**. 见 spoon 的插图。

tea towel /ˈtiː taʊəl/ *noun* 名词
a small cloth that you use for drying things like plates and cups after you wash them（擦干已洗茶具的）茶巾，抹布

technical 0ᵆ /ˈteknɪkl/ *adjective* 形容词
connected with the machines and materials used in science and in making things 技术的： *The train was delayed due to a technical problem.* 由于技术故障火车延误了。

technician /tekˈnɪʃn/ *noun* 名词
a person who works with machines or instruments 技术员；技师： *a laboratory technician* 实验室技术员

technique /tekˈniːk/ *noun* 名词
a special way of doing something 技巧；技艺： *new techniques for learning languages* 学习语言的新技巧

technology 0ᵆ /tekˈnɒlədʒi/ *noun* 名词 (no plural 不用复数形式)
knowing about science and about how things work, and using this to build and make things 科技；技术： *science and technology* 科学技术 ◇ *developments in computer technology* 电脑技术的发展

teddy bear 玩具熊

teddy bear /'tedi beə(r)/ (plural 复数
形式 teddy bears) (also 亦作 teddy /'tedi/,
plural 复数形式 teddies) noun 名词
a toy for children that looks like a BEAR
(= a big wild animal with thick fur)
泰迪熊；玩具熊

tedious /'ti:diəs/ adjective 形容词
very long and not interesting 冗长乏味的
◯ SAME MEANING **boring** 同义词为 boring:
a tedious journey 枯燥乏味的旅程

teenager /'ti:neɪdʒə(r)/ noun 名词
a person who is between 13 and 19 years
old （13 至 19 岁的）青少年
▸ **teenage** /'ti:neɪdʒ/ adjective 形容词:
comic books for teenage boys 以青少年
男孩为对象的连环画杂志

teens /ti:nz/ noun 名词 (plural 用复数形式)
the time when you are between the ages
of 13 and 19 青少年时期（13 至 19 岁）:
She is in her teens. 她十多岁。

teeth plural of TOOTH * tooth 的复数形式

telephone¹ ◯ /'telɪfəʊn/ (also 亦作
phone) noun 名词
a piece of equipment that you use for
talking to somebody who is in another
place 电话；电话机: What's your
telephone number? 你的电话号码是什么?
◇ Can I make a telephone call? 我能打个
电话吗? ◇ The telephone's ringing – can
you answer it? 电话铃在响，你能接一下
吗?
on the telephone using a telephone to
speak to somebody 在打电话；在通电话:
He's on the telephone to his wife. 他正与
妻子通电话。◯ Look at Study Page S11.
见研习专页 S11。

telephone² ◯ /'telɪfəʊn/ verb 动词
(telephones, telephoning, telephoned
/'telɪfəʊnd/) (British 英式英语) (formal 正式)
to use a telephone to speak to somebody
给…打电话 ◯ SAME MEANING **call, phone**
同义词为 call 和 phone: I must telephone
my parents. 我得给我父母打电话。◯ Look
at Study Page S11. 见研习专页 S11。

telephone box /'telɪfəʊn bɒks/ noun
名词 (plural 复数形式 telephone boxes)
another word for PHONE BOX * phone box
的另一种说法

telephone directory /'telɪfəʊn
dɪrektəri/ noun 名词 (plural 复数形式
telephone directories)
a book of people's names, addresses
and telephone numbers 电话号码簿;
电话簿

telescope 望远镜

telescope /'telɪskəʊp/ noun 名词
a long round piece of equipment with
special glass inside it. You look through it
to make things that are far away appear
bigger. 望远镜

television ◯ /'telɪvɪʒn/ noun 名词
(abbr. 缩略式 TV)
1 (plural 复数形式 televisions) (also 亦作
television set) (British informal also 英式
英语非正式亦作 telly) a piece of electrical
equipment with a screen that shows
moving pictures with sound 电视机:
to turn the television on 打开电视机
◯ Look at Picture Dictionary page P10.
见彩页 P10。
2 (no plural 不用复数形式) things that
you watch on a television 电视（节目）:
I watched television last night. 我昨天晚上
看电视了。◇ What's on television? 电视上
有什么节目? ◇ a television programme
电视节目
3 a way of sending pictures and sounds
so that people can watch them on
television 电视播送: satellite television
卫星电视

tell ◯ /tel/ verb 动词 (tells, telling, told
/təʊld/, has told)
1 to give information to somebody by
speaking or writing 告诉；告知: I told
her my new address. 我把我的新地址告诉
了她。◇ This book tells you how to make
bread. 这本书教人如何做面包。◇ He
told me that he was tired. 他跟我说他
累了。
2 to say what somebody must do 吩咐:
Our teacher told us to read this book.
老师叫我们看这本书。
3 to know, guess or understand
something 知道；猜出；理解: I can tell
that she's been crying because her eyes are
red. 我看得出她哭过，因为她的眼睛红红
的。◇ I can't tell the difference between
James and his brother. They look exactly
the same! 我分辨不出詹姆斯和他的弟弟,

他们俩看上去一模一样！ ⊃ Look at the note at **say**¹. 见 **say**¹ 条的注释。

tell somebody off to speak to somebody in an angry way because they have done something wrong 责备; 斥责; 责骂: *I told the children off for making so much noise.* 孩子们太吵了，我把他们骂了一顿。

telly /'teli/ *noun* 名词 (*plural* 复数形式 **tellies**) (*British* 英式英语) (*informal* 非正式) another word for TELEVISION * television 的另一种说法

temper /'tempə(r)/ *noun* 名词
1 If you have a **temper**, you get angry very easily. 脾气; 易怒的性情: *She must learn to control her temper.* 她得学会控制性子。
2 the way you are feeling at a certain time 情绪; 心情 ⊃ SAME MEANING **mood** 同义词为 mood: *Why are you in a bad temper?* 你为什么心情不好呢?

in a temper angry 发脾气; 发火: *She's in a temper because she's tired.* 她发脾气是因为她累了。

lose your temper to suddenly become angry 发脾气: *She lost her temper with a customer and shouted at him.* 她对一名顾客发脾气，冲着人家大喊大叫。

temperature 0= /'temprətʃə(r)/ *noun* 名词
how hot or cold a thing or a place is 温度; 气温: *On a hot day, the temperature can reach 35° C.* 在炎热的日子，气温能达到 35 摄氏度。 ◇ *a high temperature* 高温

have a temperature to feel very hot because you are ill 发烧; 发热

take somebody's temperature to see how hot somebody is, using a special instrument (called a **thermometer**) 给某人量体温

temple /'templ/ *noun* 名词
a building where people go to say prayers to a god or gods 庙宇; 寺院

temporarily /'temprərəli/ ,tempə'rerəli/ *adverb* 副词
for a short time only 暂时; 临时: *The road is temporarily closed for repairs.* 这条路因维修而暂时封闭。 ⊃ OPPOSITE **permanently** 反义词为 permanently

temporary 0= /'temprəri/ *adjective* 形容词
Something that is **temporary** lasts for a short time. 暂时的; 临时的; 短暂的: *I had a temporary job in the summer holidays.* 我暑假时做过临时工。

⊃ OPPOSITE **permanent** 反义词为 permanent

tempt /tempt/ *verb* 动词 (**tempts, tempting, tempted**)
to make somebody want to do or have something, especially something that is wrong 引诱; 诱惑: *He saw the money on the table, and he was tempted to take it.* 他看见桌上放着钱就动了心，想把它拿走。

temptation /temp'teɪʃn/ *noun* 名词
1 (*no plural* 不用复数形式) a feeling that you want to do something that you know is wrong 引诱; 诱惑: *I couldn't resist the temptation to open the letter.* 我受不住诱惑，把信打开了。
2 (*plural* 复数形式 **temptations**) a thing that makes you want to do something wrong 引诱人的事物: *Don't leave the money on your desk – it's a temptation to thieves.* 别把钱放在桌上，这对窃贼是个诱惑。

tempting /'temptɪŋ/ *adjective* 形容词
Something that is **tempting** makes you want to do or have it. 诱人的; 吸引人的: *That cake looks very tempting!* 那个蛋糕看上去非常诱人!

ten 0= /ten/ *number* 数词
10 十

tenant /'tenənt/ *noun* 名词
a person who pays money (called **rent**) to live in or use a place 房客; 租户; 佃户

tend 0= /tend/ *verb* 动词 (**tends, tending, tended**)
to usually do or be something 往往会; 通常是: *Men tend to be taller than women.* 男子通常比女子长得高。

tendency /'tendənsi/ *noun* 名词 (*plural* 复数形式 **tendencies**)
something that a person or thing usually does 倾向; 偏好: *He has a tendency to be late.* 他总爱迟到。

tender /'tendə(r)/ *adjective* 形容词
1 kind, gentle and loving 亲切的; 温柔的: *a tender look* 温柔的表情
2 **Tender** meat is soft and easy to cut or bite. (肉) 嫩的 ⊃ OPPOSITE **tough** 反义词为 tough
3 If a part of your body is **tender**, it hurts when you touch it. (身体部位) 疼痛的，一触即痛的 ⊃ SAME MEANING **sore** 同义词为 sore

▶ **tenderly** /'tendəli/ *adverb* 副词 in a kind and gentle way 温柔地: *He touched her arm tenderly.* 他温柔地抚摸她的胳膊。
▶ **tenderness** /'tendənəs/ *noun* 名词

(*no plural* 不用复数形式): *a feeling of tenderness* 柔情

tennis/'tenɪs/ *noun* 名词 (*no plural* 不用复数形式)
a game for two or four players who hit a ball to each other over a net using a piece of equipment (called a racket) 网球: *Let's play tennis.* 咱们打网球吧。◇ *a tennis court* (= a place where you play tennis) 网球场 ⊃ Look at Picture Dictionary page **P14**. 见彩页 P14。

tense¹/tens/ *adjective* 形容词
1 worried or nervous and not able to relax 神经紧张的；不安的；焦虑的: *I always feel very tense before exams.* 我考试前总是很紧张。⊃ OPPOSITE **relaxed** 反义词为 relaxed
2 pulled tightly, not relaxed 绷紧的: *tense muscles* 绷紧的肌肉

tense²/tens/ *noun* 名词
(*grammar* 语法) the form of a verb that shows if something happens in the past, present or future （动词的）时，时态

tension/'tenʃn/ *noun* 名词 (*no plural* 不用复数形式)
being worried or nervous and not able to relax 紧张不安: *Tension can give you headaches.* 神经紧张会引起头痛。

tent 帐篷

tent /tent/ *noun* 名词
a kind of small house made of cloth. You sleep in a **tent** when you go camping. 帐篷: *We put up our tent.* 我们把帐篷搭起来了。

tentacle/'tentəkl/ *noun* 名词
one of the long thin parts like legs on the body of some sea animals （某些海洋生物的）触角，触手，触须: *An octopus has eight tentacles.* 章鱼有八只触手。 ⊃ Look

at the picture at **octopus**. 见 octopus 的插图。

tenth /tenθ/ *pronoun, adjective, adverb* 代词，形容词，副词
1 10th 第十
2 one of ten equal parts of something; ¹⁄₁₀ 十分之一

term/tɜːm/ *noun* 名词
1 a word or group of words connected with a special subject 术语；专门用语: *a computing term* 电脑术语
2 (*British* 英式英语) (*American* 美式英语 **trimester**) one of the three periods that the school or college year is divided into 学期: *The summer term is from April to July.* 夏季学期从四月开始，七月结束。

terminal/'tɜːmɪnl/ *noun* 名词
a building where people begin and end their journeys by bus, train, plane or ship （公共汽车、火车或船的）终点站；航空站: *All remaining passengers for Nairobi should go to Terminal 2.* 所有前往内罗毕的余下乘客请到第二航站楼。

terms/tɜːmz/ *noun* 名词 (*plural* 用复数形式)
the things that people must agree to when they make an arrangement or an agreement （协议的）条件，条款: *Under the terms of the contract you must complete all work by the end of the year.* 根据合同条款，你必须在年底前完成所有的工作。

terrace/'terəs/ *noun* 名词
1 (*British* 英式英语) a line of houses that are joined together 排房，排屋（连成一排的房屋）
2 a flat place outside a house or restaurant （房屋或餐馆外的）露天平台，阳台: *We had our lunch on the terrace.* 我们在阳台上吃午饭。

terraced house /ˌterəst 'haʊs/ *noun* 名词 (*British* 英式英语)
a house that is part of a line of houses that are all joined together 排房（成排相连房屋的其中一栋） ⊃ Look at the picture at **house**. 见 house 的插图。

terrible /'terəbl/ *adjective* 形容词
very bad 极坏的；糟糕的: *She had a terrible accident.* 她出了严重事故。◇ *The food in that restaurant is terrible!* 那家餐馆的食物糟透了！

terribly/'terəbli/ *adverb* 副词
1 very 非常；极其: *I'm terribly sorry!* 我非常抱歉！
2 very badly 非常坏；很糟糕: *He played terribly.* 他打得很糟糕。

A
B
C
D
E
F
G
H
I
J
K
L
M
N
O
P
Q
R
S
T
U
V
W
X
Y
Z

terrific /təˈrɪfɪk/ *adjective* 形容词
(*informal* 非正式)
very good; excellent 极好的；绝妙的；
了不起的：*What a terrific idea!* 多么妙的
主意啊！

terrified /ˈterɪfaɪd/ *adjective* 形容词
very frightened 很害怕；很恐惧：*He is
terrified of dogs.* 他很怕狗。

terrify /ˈterɪfaɪ/ *verb* 动词 (**terrifies**,
terrifying, **terrified** /ˈterɪfaɪd/, **has
terrified**)
to make somebody feel very frightened
使非常害怕；使惊恐：*Spiders terrify me!*
我非常怕蜘蛛！

territory /ˈterətri/ *noun* 名词 (*plural*
复数形式 **territories**)
the land that belongs to one country
领土；领地；版图：*This island was once
French territory.* 这个岛一度是法国的
领地。

terror /ˈterə(r)/ *noun* 名词 (*no plural* 不用
复数形式)
very great fear 恐惧；惊恐：*He screamed
in terror as the rats came towards him.*
老鼠朝他跑过来的时候，他吓得尖叫起来。

terrorism /ˈterərɪzəm/ *noun* 名词
(*no plural* 不用复数形式)
when a group of people hurt or kill other
people, for example by putting a bomb
in a public place, in order to try to make
a government do what they want 恐怖
主义：*the fight against terrorism* 对抗恐怖
主义的斗争

terrorist /ˈterərɪst/ *noun* 名词
a person who hurts or kills people, for
example by putting a bomb in a public
place, in order to try to make the
government do what they want 恐怖主义
者；恐怖分子：*a terrorist attack* 恐怖袭击

test¹ 0➡ /test/ *noun* 名词
an exam that you do in order to show
what you know or what you can do
测验；考试：*We have a spelling test every
Friday.* 我们每周五有拼写测验。◇ *Did you
pass your driving test?* 你通过驾驶考试
了吗？

test² 0➡ /test/ *verb* 动词 (**tests**, **testing**,
tested)
1 to ask somebody questions to find out
what they know or what they can do
测验；考查：*The teacher tested us on our
spelling.* 老师要我们做拼写测验。
2 to use or look at something carefully to
find out how good it is or if it works well
测试；检查：*I don't think drugs should be
tested on animals.* 我认为不应该在动物

身上做药物试验。◇ *The doctor tested my
eyes.* 医生检查了我的眼睛。

test tube /ˈtest tjuːb/ *noun* 名词
a long thin glass tube that you use in
chemical experiments 试管

text¹ 0➡ /tekst/ *noun* 名词
1 (*no plural* 不用复数形式) the words in
a book, newspaper or magazine（书、
报纸或杂志的）正文：*This book has a lot
of pictures but not much text.* 这本书有
很多插图，但文字不多。
2 (*plural* 复数形式 **texts**) another word for
TEXT MESSAGE * text message 的另一种说法
3 (*plural* 复数形式 **texts**) a book or a short
piece of writing that you study 课本；
课文：*Read the text and answer the
questions.* 阅读这篇文章，然后回答问题。

text² /tekst/ *verb* 动词 (**texts**, **texting**,
texted)
to send someone a message on a mobile
phone（用手机）发短信：*He texted me
to say he'd arrived in Prague.* 他发短信
告诉我他已经到了布拉格。

textbook /ˈtekstbʊk/ *noun* 名词
a book that teaches you about something
课本；教材；教科书：*a biology textbook*
生物学教科书 ➡ Look at Picture Dictionary
page **P11**. 见彩页 P11。

text message /ˈtekst mesɪdʒ/ (*also* 亦作
text) *noun* 名词
a message that you send in writing from
one mobile phone to another（手机）
短信，简讯

texture /ˈtekstʃə(r)/ *noun* 名词
the way that something feels when you
touch it 质感；质地；手感：*Silk has a
smooth texture.* 丝绸摸起来很光滑。

than 0➡ /ðən; ðæn/ *conjunction*,
preposition 连词，介词
You use 'than' when you compare people
or things.（用于比较）比，较：*I'm older
than him.* 我比他大。◇ *You speak Spanish
much better than she does.* 你西班牙语
说得比她好很多。◇ *We live less than a
kilometre from the beach.* 我们住的地方
离海滩不到一公里。

thank 0➡ /θæŋk/ *verb* 动词 (**thanks**,
thanking, **thanked** /θæŋkt/)
to tell somebody that you are pleased
because they gave you something or
helped you 谢谢；感谢：*I thanked her
for my birthday present.* 我感谢她送我
生日礼物。◇ Look at **thanks** and **thank
you**. 见 thanks 和 thank you。

thankful /'θæŋkfl/ *adjective* 形容词
happy that something good has
happened or that something bad has not
happened 感激；欣慰：*I was **thankful for**
a rest after the long walk.* 走了很长的路之
后能休息一下，我感到欣慰。

▶ **thankfully** /'θæŋkfəli/ *adverb* 副词：
*There was an accident, but thankfully
nobody was hurt.* 出了事故，幸而没人
受伤。

thanks ⊶ /θæŋks/ *noun* 名词 (*plural*
用复数形式)
a word that shows you are pleased
because somebody gave you something
or helped you 感谢；感激；谢意：*Please
give my **thanks** to your sister **for** her help.*
请转达我对你姐姐的谢意，感谢她的
帮助。

thanks to somebody or 或 **something**
because of somebody or something
幸亏；由于：*We're late, thanks to you!*
我们迟到了，都是因为你！⊃ Look at
thank and **thank you**. 见 thank 和
thank you。

Thanksgiving /,θæŋks'gɪvɪŋ/ (*also* 亦作
Thanksgiving Day /,θæŋks'gɪvɪŋ deɪ/) *noun*
名词 (*no plural* 不用复数形式)
a public holiday in November in the US
or October in Canada. In the past, people
thanked God on this day for their food.
感恩节（美国和加拿大的公休日，美国的在
十一月，加拿大的在十月）

thank you ⊶ /'θæŋk ju/ *noun* 名词
words that show you are pleased because
somebody gave you something or helped
you 谢谢你；感谢；致谢 ⊃ SAME MEANING
thanks 同义词为 thanks：*Thank you for
your letter.* 谢谢你的来信。◇ *'How are
you?' 'I'm fine, thank you.'* "你好吗？"
"我很好，谢谢。"

no, thank you , **no, thanks** You use
these words to say that you do not want
something.（用于婉谢）不用了，谢谢：
*'Would you like some more tea?' 'No, thank
you.'* "你要添点茶吗？" "不用了，
谢谢。"

that¹ ⊶ /ðæt/ *adjective, pronoun*
形容词，代词 (*plural* 复数形式 **those**)
a word that you use to talk about a
person or thing that is there or then 那；
那个：*'Who is that boy in the garden?'
'That's my brother.'* "花园里的那个男孩是
谁？" "那是我弟弟。" ◇ *She got married
two years ago. At that time, she was a
teacher.* 她两年前结了婚。那时她是个
老师。⊃ Look at the picture at **this¹**.
见 this¹ 的插图。

that² ⊶ /ðət/ *pronoun* 代词
which, who or whom（用作关系代词，
引导从句）：*A lion is an animal that lives
in Africa.* 狮子是生活在非洲的一种动物。
◇ *The people (that) I met were very nice.*
我遇到的人都非常好。◇ *I'm reading the
book (that) you gave me.* 我正在读你给我
的那本书。

that³ ⊶ /ðət; ðæt/ *conjunction* 连词
a word that you use to join two parts of
a sentence（用于引导从句）：*Jo said
(that) she was unhappy.* 乔说她不开心。◇
I'm sure (that) he will come. 我确信他一定
会来。◇ *I was so hungry (that) I ate all the
food.* 我饿得把所有食物都吃光了。

that⁴ /ðæt/ *adverb* 副词
as much as that 那么；如此 ⊃ SAME
MEANING **so** 同义词为 so：*The next village
is ten kilometres from here. I can't walk
that far.* 邻近的村子离这儿十公里。我可
走不了那么远。

thaw /θɔː/ *verb* 动词 (**thaws** , **thawing**
/'θɔːɪŋ/ , **thawed** /θɔːd/)
to warm something that is frozen so that
it becomes soft or liquid; to get warmer
so that it becomes soft or liquid（使）
融化，消融，解冻：*The ice is thawing.*
冰正在融化。⊃ OPPOSITE **freeze** 反义词为
freeze

the ⊶ /ðə; ði; ðiː/ *article* 冠词
1 a word that you use before the name of
somebody or something when it is clear
what person or thing you mean（表示
确指的人或事物）：*I bought a shirt and
some trousers. The shirt is blue.* 我买了
一件衬衫和一条裤子。衬衫是蓝色的。◇
The sun is shining. 太阳照耀着。
2 a word that you use before numbers
and dates（用于数词或日期之前）：
Monday the sixth of May 五月六日星期一
3 a word that you use to talk about a
group of people or things of the same
kind（表示泛指的一类人或事物）：*the
French* (= all French people) 法国人 ◇
Do you play the piano? 你会弹钢琴吗？
4 a word that you use before the names
of rivers, seas, etc. and some countries
（用于河流、海洋或某些国家的名称
之前）：*the Seine* 塞纳河 ◇ *the Atlantic*
大西洋 ◇ *the United States of America*
美利坚合众国

> 🖋 GRAMMAR 语法说明
> Before the names of most countries,
> we do not use **the**: *I went to France.*
> (NOT *I went to the France*). 大多数国名

前不用 **the**: **I went to France**. （不说 I went to the France）。

the ... , **the** ... words that you use to talk about two things happening together because of each other 越…越…: *The more you eat, the fatter you get.* 吃得越多就会越胖。

theatre ⊶ (*British* 英式英语) (*American* 美式英语 **theater**) /ˈθɪətə(r)/ *noun* 名词
a building where you go to see plays 剧场；剧院: *I'm going to the theatre this evening.* 我今天晚上去看戏。

theft /θeft/ *noun* 名词
the crime of stealing something from a person or a place 偷窃；盗窃: *She was sent to prison for theft.* 她因盗窃而入狱。 ◇ *I told the police about the theft of my car.* 我向警方报案我的汽车被盗了。 ⊃ Look at **thief**. 见 thief.

their ⊶ /ðeə(r)/ *adjective* 形容词

🔊 PRONUNCIATION 读音说明
The word **their** sounds just like **there** and **they're**. * their 读音同 there 和 they're。

of or belonging to them 他们的；她们的；它们的: *What is their address?* 他们的地址是什么？

theirs ⊶ /ðeəz/ *pronoun* 代词
something that belongs to them 他们的；她们的；它们的: *Our house is smaller than theirs.* 我们的房子比他们的小。

them ⊶ /ðəm; ðem/ *pronoun* 代词 (*plural* 用复数形式)
1 a word that shows more than one person, animal or thing （用作宾语）他们，她们，它们: *I wrote them a letter and then I phoned them.* 我给他们写信，然后又打了电话。 ◇ *I'm looking for my keys. Have you seen them?* 我在找我的钥匙，你有没有看到？
2 him or her （用作宾语）他，她: *If anybody phones, tell them I'm busy.* 要是有人来电话，就说我很忙。

theme /θiːm/ *noun* 名词
something that you talk or write about （谈话或写作的）主题，主旨: *The theme of his speech was 'the future of our planet'.* 他演讲的主题是"我们星球的未来"。

themselves ⊶ /ðəmˈselvz/ *pronoun* 代词 (*plural* 用复数形式)
1 a word that shows the same people, animals or things that you have just talked about（指前述的人、动物或事物）

他们自己，她们自己，它们自己: *They bought themselves a new car.* 他们给自己买了一辆新车。
2 a word that makes 'they' stronger （表示强调）他们自己，她们自己，它们自己: *Did they build the house themselves?* 房子是他们自己盖的吗？
by themselves
1 alone; without other people （他们）独自，单独: *The children went out by themselves.* 孩子们自己出去了。
2 without help （他们）独立地: *They cooked dinner by themselves.* 他们自己做饭。

then ⊶ /ðen/ *adverb* 副词
1 at that time 当时；那时: *I became a teacher in 1999. I lived in London then, but now I live in Paris.* 我 1999 年当了教师。那时我住在伦敦，现在我住在巴黎。 ◇ *I'm going tomorrow. Can you wait until then?* 我明天走。你能等到那个时候吗？
2 next; after that 然后；接着；后来: *We had dinner and then watched a movie.* 我们吃了饭，然后看了场电影。
3 if that is true 既然如此；那么: *If you miss that train then you'll have to get a bus.* 你要是没赶上那趟火车，就得乘公共汽车。

theory /ˈθɪəri/ *noun* 名词 (*plural* 复数形式 **theories**)
an idea that tries to explain something 理论；学说: *There are a lot of different theories about how life began.* 关于生命的起源有多种不同的说法。

therapy /ˈθerəpi/ *noun* 名词 (*no plural* 不用复数形式)
a way of helping people who are ill in their body or mind, usually without drugs （通常不用药物的）治疗，疗法: *speech therapy* 语言治疗

there ⊶ /ðeə(r)/ *adverb, pronoun* 副词，代词

🔊 PRONUNCIATION 读音说明
The word **there** sounds just like **their** and **they're**. * there 读音同 their 和 they're。

1 a word that you use with verbs like 'be', 'seem' and 'appear' to show that something is true or that something is happening （与 be、seem、appear 等动词连用，表示存在或发生）: *There is a man at the door.* 门口有个男人。 ◇ *Is there a film on TV tonight?* 今晚电视上会播电影吗？ ◇ *There aren't any shops in this village.* 这个村子没有商店。

2 in, at or to that place 在那里；往那里：
Don't put the box there – put it here. 别把
箱子放在那里，放这儿吧。◇ *Have you
been to Bonn? I'm going there next week.*
你去过波恩吗？我下星期会去那里。
3 a word that makes people look or listen
（用以引起注意）：*Oh look, there's Kate.*
瞧，是凯特。

there you are words that you say when
you give something to somebody（用于
给人东西时）给你，拿去吧：*'There you
are,' she said, giving me a cake.* "给你。"
她边说边给我一块蛋糕。

therefore 0➔ /'ðeəfɔ:(r)/ *adverb* 副词
for that reason 因此；所以；因而：*Simon
was busy and therefore could not come to
the meeting.* 西蒙很忙，所以不能来开会。

thermometer /θə'mɒmɪtə(r)/ *noun* 名词
an instrument that shows how hot or cold
something is 温度计；体温计；寒暑表

thesaurus /θɪ'sɔ:rəs/ *noun* 名词 (*plural*
复数形式 **thesauruses**)
a book that has lists of words and phrases
with similar meanings 同义词词典

these 0➔ /ði:z/ *adjective*, *pronoun*
形容词，代词 (*plural* 用复数形式)

> 🔎 GRAMMAR 语法说明
> **These** is the plural form of **this**. * these
> 是 this 的复数形式。

a word that you use to talk about people
or things that are here or now 这些（人
或事物）：*These books are mine.* 这些书
是我的。◇ *Do you want these?* 你要这些
吗？ ➋ Look at the picture at **this¹**.
见 this¹ 的插图。

they 0➔ /ðeɪ/ *pronoun* 代词 (*plural*
用复数形式)
1 the people, animals or things that the
sentence is about（用作主语）他们，
她们，它们：*Jo and David came at two
o'clock and they left at six o'clock.* 乔和
戴维两点钟来的，六点钟走了。◇ *'Where
are my keys?' 'They're (= they are) on the
table.'* "我的钥匙在哪儿？" "在桌子
上。"
2 a word that you use instead of 'he' or
'she'（用作主语）他，她：*Someone
phoned for you – they said they would
phone again later.* 有人给你打过电话，
说稍后会再打给你。
3 people（泛指）人们：*They say it will
be cold this winter.* 大家都说今年冬天会
很冷。

they'd /ðeɪd/ *short for* THEY HAD; THEY
WOULD * they had 和 they would 的缩略式

they'll /ðeɪl/ *short for* THEY WILL * they
will 的缩略式

they're /ðeə(r)/ *short for* THEY ARE * they
are 的缩略式

they've /ðeɪv/ *short for* THEY HAVE * they
have 的缩略式

thick 0➔ /θɪk/ *adjective* 形容词 (**thicker**,
thickest)
1 far from one side to the other 厚的；
粗的：*The walls are very thick.* 这些墙
非常厚。◇ *It's cold outside, so wear a thick
coat.* 外面很冷，穿件厚大衣吧。
➋ OPPOSITE **thin** 反义词为 thin
2 You use **thick** to say or ask how far
something is from one side to the other.
有…厚：*The ice is six centimetres thick.*
冰厚六厘米。
3 with a lot of people or things close
together 密集的；浓密的；稠密的：*thick
dark hair* 浓密的黑发
4 If a liquid is **thick**, it does not flow
easily.（液体）浓的，粘稠的：*This paint
is too thick.* 这涂料太稠了。➋ OPPOSITE
thin 反义词为 thin
5 difficult to see through 能见度低的；
浑浊的；浓的：*thick smoke* 浓烟
▸ **thickness** /'θɪknəs/ *noun* 名词
(*no plural* 不用复数形式)：*The wood is
3 cm in thickness.* 这块木料 3 厘米厚。

thief 0➔ /θi:f/ *noun* 名词 (*plural* 复数形式
thieves /θi:vz/)
a person who steals something 小偷；
贼：*A thief stole my car.* 窃贼偷走了我
的车。

> 🔎 WORD BUILDING 词汇扩充
> A **thief** is a general word for a person
> who steals things, usually secretly and
> without violence. The name of the
> crime is **theft**. * thief 是窃贼的通称，
> 通常是暗中偷盗而不使用暴力。盗窃罪
> 叫做 theft。
> A **robber** steals from a bank, shop, etc.
> and often uses violence or threats.
> * robber 指劫匪，经常采用暴力或威吓
> 去抢劫银行或商店等。
> A **burglar** takes things from your house
> when you are out or asleep. * burglar
> 指入屋偷盗的窃贼：*We had burglars
> while we were on holiday and all my
> jewellery was stolen.* 我们度假时家里
> 遭窃，我所有的首饰都给偷了。

thigh /θaɪ/ *noun* 名词
the part of your leg above your knee
大腿；股 ➋ Look at Picture Dictionary
page **P4**. 见彩页 P4。

A B C D E F G H I J K L M N O P Q R S **T** U V W X Y Z

A
B
C
D
E
F
G
H
I
J
K
L
M
N
O
P
Q
R
S
T
U
V
W
X
Y
Z

thin ⟨◦⟩ /θɪn/ *adjective* 形容词 (thinner, thinnest)

1 not far from one side to the other 薄的: *The walls in this house are very thin.* 这所房子的墙很薄。◇ *I cut the bread into thin slices.* 我把面包切成了薄片。 ⊃ OPPOSITE **thick** 反义词为 thick

2 not fat 瘦的: *He's tall and thin.* 他又高又瘦。 ⊃ OPPOSITE **fat** 反义词为 fat

> 🔍 WORD BUILDING 词汇扩充
> We say **slim** to talk about people who are **thin** in an attractive way.
> * slim 表示苗条好看: *How do you manage to stay so slim?* 你是怎样保持体态这么苗条的?
> If you say somebody is **skinny**, you mean that he or she is too thin.
> * skinny 表示骨瘦如柴。

3 not close together 稀疏的; 稀疏的: *My father's hair is getting thin.* 我父亲的头发越来越稀疏了。 ⊃ OPPOSITE **thick** 反义词为 thick

4 If a liquid is **thin**, it flows easily like water. (液体) 稀的 ⊃ SAME MEANING **runny** 同义词为 runny: *The soup was very thin.* 这汤很稀。 ⊃ OPPOSITE **thick** 反义词为 thick

thing ⟨◦⟩ /θɪŋ/ *noun* 名词

1 an object 物; 东西: *What's that red thing?* 那个红色的东西是什么?

2 things (*plural* 用复数形式) objects, clothes or tools that belong to you or that you use for something (个人的) 用品, 物品: *Have you packed your things for the journey?* 你旅行用的东西都收拾好了吗?

3 what happens or what you do 事; 事情: *A strange thing happened to me yesterday.* 昨天我遇到了件怪事。◇ *That was a difficult thing to do.* 那件事很难办。

4 an idea or a subject 想法; 话题: *We talked about a lot of things.* 我们谈了很多事情。

think ⟨◦⟩ /θɪŋk/ *verb* 动词 (thinks, thinking, thought /θɔːt/, has thought)

1 to have an opinion about something; to believe something 认为; 觉得: *I think it's going to rain.* 我看要下雨了。◇ *'Do you think Sara will come tomorrow?' 'Yes, I think so.'* (= I think that she will come) "你觉得萨拉明天会来吗?" "我想会的。" ◇ *I think they live in Rome but I'm not sure.* 我想他们住在罗马吧, 可是我不确定。◇ *What do you think of this music?* 你觉得这音乐怎么样?

2 to use your mind 想; 思考; 思索: *Think before you answer the question.* 回答问题前先想一下。◇ *I often think about that day.* 我常常想起那一天。

think about doing something to consider doing something 考虑, 打算 (做某事): *He's thinking about leaving his job.* 他在考虑辞职。

think of something, think of doing something

1 to have something in your mind 记得; 想起: *I can't think of her name.* 我想不起她的名字来。

2 to try to decide whether to do something 考虑做某事: *We're thinking of going to America.* 我们正在考虑去美国。

thinly /ˈθɪnli/ *adverb* 副词 in a way that makes a thin piece of something 薄薄地: *Slice the potatoes thinly.* 把土豆切成薄片。

third ⟨◦⟩ /θɜːd/ *pronoun, adjective, adverb* 代词, 形容词, 副词

1 3rd 第三

2 one of three equal parts of something; ⅓ 三分之一

thirst /θɜːst/ *noun* 名词 (no plural 不用复数形式) the feeling you have when you want to drink something 渴; 口渴

> 🔍 GRAMMAR 语法说明
> Be careful! We say **I am thirsty** not I have thirst. 注意: 表示口渴要说 I am thirsty, 不说 I have thirst.

thirsty ⟨◦⟩ /ˈθɜːsti/ *adjective* 形容词 (thirstier, thirstiest) If you are **thirsty**, you want to drink something. 渴的; 口渴的: *I'm thirsty. Can I have a drink of water, please?* 我很渴, 请给我一杯水好吗? ⊃ Look at **hungry**. 见 hungry。

thirteen ⟨◦⟩ /ˌθɜːˈtiːn/ *number* 数词 13 十三

▸ **thirteenth** /ˌθɜːˈtiːnθ/ *pronoun, adjective, adverb* 代词, 形容词, 副词 13th 第十三

thirtieth ⟨◦⟩ /ˈθɜːtiəθ/ *pronoun, adjective, adverb* 代词, 形容词, 副词 30th 第三十

thirty ⟨◦⟩ /ˈθɜːti/ *number* 数词

1 30 三十

2 the thirties (*plural* 用复数形式) the numbers, years or temperature between 30 and 39 三十几; 三十年代 **in your thirties** between the ages of 30 and 39 * 30 多岁

this 这个

THIS
THESE
THAT
THOSE

this **these** **that** **those**
这个 这些 那个 那些

He caught **this fish**.
他钓到了这条鱼。
He didn't catch **that fish**.
他没有钓到那条鱼。
THAT

this[1] 0‒ /ðɪs/ ***adjective, pronoun*** 形容词，代词 (*plural* 复数形式 **these**)
1 a word that you use to talk about a person or thing that is close to you in time or space 这；这个： *Come and look at this photo.* 来看看这张照片。 ◇ *This is my sister.* 这是我妹妹。 ◇ *These boots are really comfortable.* 这双靴子真的很舒服。 ◇ *How much does this cost?* 这个多少钱？
2 a word that you use with periods of time that are connected to the present time（用于时间）今，本，这个： *I am on holiday this week.* 我这个星期放假。 ◇ *What are you doing **this evening*** (= today in the evening)*?* 你今晚做什么？

this[2] /ðɪs/ ***adverb*** 副词
so 这样；这么： *The road is not usually this busy* (= not as busy as it is now)*.* 这条路平常没这么繁忙。

thistle /ˈθɪsl/ ***noun*** 名词
a plant with sharp pointed leaves and purple flowers 蓟（叶有刺，花呈紫色）

thong /θɒŋ/ ***noun*** 名词 *American English for* FLIP-FLOP 美式英语，即 flip-flop

thorn /θɔːn/ ***noun*** 名词
a sharp point that grows on a plant（植物的）刺，棘刺： *Rose bushes have thorns.* 玫瑰丛有刺。 ➲ Look at the picture at **plant**[1]. 见 plant[1] 的插图。

thorough /ˈθʌrə/ ***adjective*** 形容词
careful and complete 彻底的；全面的；细致的： *We gave the room a thorough clean.* 我们彻底打扫了房间。

thoroughly /ˈθʌrəli/ ***adverb*** 副词
1 carefully and completely 彻底地；仔细地： *He cleaned the room thoroughly.* 他把房间彻底打扫干净了。
2 completely; very or very much 完全；很；非常： *I thoroughly enjoyed the film.* 我非常喜欢这部电影。

those 0‒ /ðəʊz/ ***adjective, pronoun*** 形容词，代词 (*plural* 用复数形式)

> **GRAMMAR** 语法说明
> **Those** is the plural form of **that**.
> * those 是 that 的复数形式。

a word that you use to talk about people or things that are there or then 那些（人或事物）： *I don't know those boys.* 我不认识那些男孩。 ◇ *Her grandfather was born in 1850. In those days, there were no cars.* 她祖父生于 1850 年。那时还没有汽车。 ◇ *Can I have those?* 我可以要那些吗？ ➲ Look at the picture at **this**[1]. 见 this[1] 的插图。

though[1] 0‒ /ðəʊ/ ***conjunction*** 连词

> **PRONUNCIATION** 读音说明
> The word **though** sounds like **go**.
> * though 读音像 go。

1 in spite of something 虽然；尽管 ➲ SAME MEANING **although** 同义词为 although： *I was very cold, though I was wearing my coat.* 虽然我穿着大衣，可还是很冷。 ◇ *Though she was in a hurry, she stopped to talk.* 尽管她赶时间，她还是停了下来说话。 ◇ *I went to the party, **even though** I was tired.* 尽管我很累，我还是参加聚会去了。
2 but 但是；可是： *I thought it was right, though I wasn't sure.* 我认为那是对的，不过我并没有把握。
as though in a way that makes you think something 似乎；好像；仿佛： *The house looks as though nobody lives there.* 房子看起来好像没人住。 ◇ *I'm so hungry – I feel as though I haven't eaten for days!* 我饿极了，觉得就像好几天没吃东西似的！

though[2] 0‒ /ðəʊ/ ***adverb*** 副词
however 然而；可是： *I like him very much. I don't like his wife, though.* 我非常喜欢他，可是我不喜欢他的妻子。

thought[1] *form of* THINK * think 的不同形式

thought[2] 0‒ /θɔːt/ ***noun*** 名词
1 (*no plural* 不用复数形式) thinking 思考；思索；思维： *After a lot of thought, I decided not to take the job.* 再三考虑之后，我决定不接受那份工作。

A B C D E F G H I J K L M N O P Q R S **T** U V W X Y Z

2 (*plural* 复数形式 **thoughts**) an idea 想法；看法；主意： *Have you had any* ***thoughts about*** *what you want to do when you leave school?* 你想过离开学校以后要干什么吗？

thoughtful /ˈθɔːtfl/ *adjective* 形容词
1 thinking carefully 沉思的；深思的： *She listened with a thoughtful look on her face.* 她听着，一脸沉思的样子。
2 thinking about other people 关心别人的；体贴的 ⊃ SAME MEANING **kind, considerate** 同义词为 **kind** 和 **considerate**： *It was very thoughtful of you to cook us dinner.* 你给我们做了饭，想得真周到。

thoughtless /ˈθɔːtləs/ *adjective* 形容词
not thinking about other people 欠考虑的；不为他人着想的 ⊃ SAME MEANING **inconsiderate** 同义词为 **inconsiderate**： *It was very thoughtless of them to leave the room in such a mess.* 他们太不顾及别人了，走的时候把房间弄得乱糟糟的。

thousand 0━ /ˈθaʊznd/ *number* 数词
1 000 一千： *a thousand people* 一千人 ◇ *two thousand and fifteen* 两千零十五 ◇ *There were* ***thousands of*** *birds on the lake.* 湖上有成千上万只鸟。
▶ **thousandth** /ˈθaʊznθ/ *pronoun, adjective, adverb* 代词，形容词，副词
1 000th 第一千

thread¹ 0━ /θred/ *noun* 名词

> 𝒫 PRONUNCIATION 读音说明
> The word **thread** sounds like **red**.
> * thread 读音像 red。

a long thin piece of cotton, wool, etc. 线： *I need a* ***needle and thread***. 我需要针线。 ⊃ Look at the picture at **sew**. 见 **sew** 的插图。

thread² /θred/ *verb* 动词 (**threads, threading, threaded**)
to put THREAD through the hole in a needle 穿，纫（针）；将线穿过： *to thread a needle* 穿针

threat 0━ /θret/ *noun* 名词
1 a promise that you will hurt somebody if they do not do what you want 威胁；恐吓
2 a person or thing that may damage or hurt somebody or something 构成威胁的人（或事物）： *Pollution is a* ***threat to*** *the lives of animals and people.* 污染威胁着动物和人类的生命。

threaten 0━ /ˈθretn/ *verb* 动词
(**threatens, threatening, threatened** /ˈθretnd/)

1 to say that you will hurt somebody if they do not do what you want 威胁；恐吓： *They* ***threatened to*** *kill everyone on the plane.* 他们扬言要杀死飞机上所有的人。 ◇ *She* ***threatened*** *him* ***with*** *a knife.* 她拿刀威胁他。
2 to seem ready to do something bad 预示不好的事： *The dark clouds* ***threatened*** *rain.* 乌云密布预示着要下雨。

three 0━ /θriː/ *number* 数词
3 三

threw *form of* THROW * throw 的不同形式

thrill¹ /θrɪl/ *noun* 名词
a sudden strong feeling of excitement 兴奋；激动： *It gave me a big* ***thrill*** *to meet my favourite footballer in person.* 能和我最喜欢的足球运动员见面让我兴奋不已。

thrill² /θrɪl/ *verb* 动词 (**thrills, thrilling, thrilled** /θrɪld/)
to make somebody feel very excited or pleased 使非常兴奋；使非常激动： *This band has thrilled audiences all over the world.* 这支乐队使全世界的观众狂热痴迷。

thrilled /θrɪld/ *adjective* 形容词
very happy and excited 非常兴奋的；极为激动的： *We are all thrilled that you have won the prize.* 你获奖我们都欣喜若狂。

thriller /ˈθrɪlə(r)/ *noun* 名词
an exciting book, film or play about a crime （以罪案为题材的）惊险小说（或电影、戏剧）

thrilling /ˈθrɪlɪŋ/ *adjective* 形容词
very exciting 使人兴奋不已的；扣人心弦的；紧张刺激的： *a thrilling adventure* 紧张刺激的冒险经历

throat 0━ /θrəʊt/ *noun* 名词
1 the front part of your neck 颈前部
2 the part inside your neck that takes food and air down from your mouth into your body 咽喉；喉咙： *I've got a* ***sore throat***. 我喉咙痛。

throb /θrɒb/ *verb* 动词 (**throbs, throbbing, throbbed** /θrɒbd/)
to make strong regular movements or noises; to beat strongly 律动；搏动： *His heart was throbbing with excitement.* 他兴奋得心怦怦直跳。

throne /θrəʊn/ *noun* 名词
a special chair where a king or queen sits （国王或女王的）御座，宝座

through 0━ /θruː/ *preposition, adverb* 介词，副词

🔍 **PRONUNCIATION** 读音说明

The word **through** sounds like **who**, because we don't say the letters **-gh** in this word. ✱ through 读音像 who，因为 -gh 在这里不发音。

1 from one side or end of something to the other side or end 穿过；贯穿；通过: *We drove through the tunnel.* 我们开车穿过了隧道。 ◇ *What can you see through the window?* 你透过窗户能看见什么？ ◇ *She opened the gate and we walked through.* 她打开大门，我们从中走了过去。
2 from the beginning to the end of something 自始至终；从头到尾: *We travelled through the night.* 我们走了一夜。
3 connected by telephone 接通（电话）: *Can you* **put me through** *to Jill Knight, please?* 请把电话接给吉尔·奈特好吗？ ◇ *I tried to phone you but I couldn't* **get through**. 我给你打电话，可是打不通。
4 (*American* 美式英语) (*also informal* 非正式亦作 **thru**) until, and including 直至，一直到（所指时间包括在内）: *We'll be in New York Tuesday through Friday.* 我们星期二到星期五都在纽约。
5 because of somebody or something 由于；因为: *She got the job through her father.* 她因为父亲而得到这份工作。

throughout /θruːˈaʊt/ *preposition, adverb* 介词，副词
1 in every part of something 在各处；遍及: *We painted the house throughout.* 我们把整个房子都粉刷了。 ◇ *She is famous throughout the world.* 她举世闻名。
2 from the beginning to the end of something 自始至终；从头到尾: *They talked throughout the film.* 他们从电影开始到结束一直说个没完。

throw 0ーw /θrəʊ/ *verb* 动词 (throws, throwing, threw /θruː/, has thrown /θrəʊn/)

🔍 **PRONUNCIATION** 读音说明

The word **throw** sounds like **go**. ✱ throw 读音像 go。

1 to move your arm quickly to send something through the air 扔；投；掷；抛: ***Throw the ball to Alex.*** 把球扔给亚历克斯。 ◇ *The boys were* **throwing** *stones at people.* 那些男孩子向人扔石块。
2 to do something quickly and without care 匆匆做；随意地做: *She threw on her coat* (= put it on quickly) *and ran out of*

the house. 她匆匆套上大衣就从房子里跑了出去。
3 to move your body or part of it quickly 迅速移动（身体或身体部位）: *He threw his arms up.* 他猛地举起双臂。
throw something away or 或 **out** to get rid of rubbish or something that you do not want 扔掉；丢弃: *Don't throw that box away.* 别把那个箱子扔掉。
▶ **throw** *noun* 名词: *What a good throw!* 扔得好！

thru /θruː/ (*informal* 非正式) *American English* for THROUGH (4) 美式英语，即 through 第 4 义

thrust /θrʌst/ *verb* 动词 (thrusts, thrusting, thrust, has thrust) to push somebody or something suddenly and strongly 猛推；挤；塞: *She* **thrust** *the money* **into** *my hand.* 她把钱硬塞进我手里。
▶ **thrust** *noun* 名词: *He killed her with a thrust of the knife.* 他一刀刺死了她。

thud /θʌd/ *noun* 名词 the sound that a heavy thing makes when it hits something 砰的一声；扑通一声: *The book hit the floor* **with a thud**. 书砰的一声掉到地上了。

thug /θʌɡ/ *noun* 名词 a violent person 暴徒；恶棍

thumb 0ーw /θʌm/ *noun* 名词

🔍 **PRONUNCIATION** 读音说明

The word **thumb** sounds like **come**, because we don't say the letter **b** in this word. ✱ thumb 读音像 come，因为 b 在这里不发音。

the short thick finger at the side of your hand 拇指 ⊃ Look at the picture at **hand¹**. 见 hand¹ 的插图。

thumbtack /ˈθʌmtæk/ *American English* for DRAWING PIN 美式英语，即 drawing pin

thump /θʌmp/ *verb* 动词 (thumps, thumping, thumped /θʌmpt/)
1 to hit somebody or something hard with your hand or a heavy thing （用手或重物）重击，猛打: *He* **thumped** *on the door.* 他使劲捶门。
2 to make a loud sound by hitting or beating hard （重击或敲打时）砰砰地响: *Her heart was thumping with fear.* 她害怕得心怦怦直跳。

thunder¹ /ˈθʌndə(r)/ *noun* 名词 (*no plural* 不用复数形式) a loud noise in the sky when there is a storm 雷；雷声: *There was thunder and*

A B C D E F G H I J K L M N O P Q R S **T** U V W X Y Z

lightning. 雷电交加。 ➲Look at the note at **storm**¹. 见 storm¹ 条的注释。

thunder² /ˈθʌndə(r)/ ***verb*** 动词 (**thunders**, **thundering**, **thundered** /ˈθʌndəd/)

1 When it **thunders**, there is a loud noise in the sky during a storm. 打雷： *It thundered all night.* 整晚都在打雷。

2 to make a very loud deep noise 发出雷鸣般响声： *The lorries thundered along the road.* 卡车隆隆驶过公路。

thunderstorm /ˈθʌndəstɔːm/ ***noun*** 名词
a storm with a lot of rain, THUNDER and flashes of light (called **lightning**) in the sky 雷雨；雷暴 ➲Look at the note at **storm**¹. 见 storm¹ 条的注释。

Thursday 🗝 /ˈθɜːzdeɪ/ ***noun*** 名词
the day of the week after Wednesday and before Friday 星期四 ➲Look at the note at **day**. 见 day 条的注释。

thus /ðʌs/ ***adverb*** 副词 (*formal* 正式)

1 in this way 依此方式；如此： *Hold the wheel in both hands, thus.* 双手握住方向盘，就如这样。

2 because of this 因此；从而： *He was very busy and was thus unable to come to the meeting.* 他很忙，所以不能来开会。

tick¹ /tɪk/ ***verb*** 动词 (**ticks**, **ticking**, **ticked** /tɪkt/)

1 (used about a clock) to make short repeated sounds（钟表）滴答响： *I could hear a clock ticking.* 我可以听到时钟滴答作响。

2 (*British* 英式英语) (*American* 美式英语 **check**) to make a mark like this ✓ by something 在…上打钩；在…上打对号： *Tick the right answer.* 在正确答案旁边打钩。

tick² /tɪk/ ***noun*** 名词

1 (*British* 英式英语) (*American* 美式英语 **check mark**, **check**) a small mark like this ✓ 对钩；对号： ***Put a tick** by the correct answer.* 在正确答案旁边打钩。

2 one of the short repeated sounds that a clock makes（钟表的）滴答声

ticket 票

Oxford – London
ADULT RETURN
0813 030400

ticket 🗝 /ˈtɪkɪt/ ***noun*** 名词
a piece of paper or card that you buy to travel, or to go into a cinema, theatre, etc. 票；入场券： *Do you want a single or a return ticket?* 你要单程票还是往返票？ ◇ *a theatre ticket* 戏票

ticket office /ˈtɪkɪt ɒfɪs/ ***noun*** 名词
a place where you buy tickets 售票处

tickle /ˈtɪkl/ ***verb*** 动词 (**tickles**, **tickling**, **tickled** /ˈtɪkld/)

1 to touch somebody lightly with your fingers to make them laugh 呵痒；胳肢： *She tickled the baby's feet.* 她胳肢宝宝的脚。

2 to have the feeling that something is touching you lightly 觉得痒；发痒： *My nose tickles.* 我鼻子发痒。

tide /taɪd/ ***noun*** 名词
the movement of the sea towards the land and away from the land 潮；潮汐： *The tide is **coming in**.* 涨潮了。◇ *The tide **is going out**.* 退潮了。

> 🔍 **WORD BUILDING** 词汇扩充
> **High tide** is when the sea is nearest the land, and **low tide** is when the sea is furthest from the land. * high tide 指高潮，low tide 指低潮。

tidy¹ 🗝 /ˈtaɪdi/ ***adjective*** 形容词 (**tidier**, **tidiest**)

1 with everything in the right place 整齐的；井井有条的： *Her room is very tidy.* 她的房间很整洁。

2 liking to have everything in the right place 爱整洁的；爱整齐的： *a tidy boy* 爱整洁的男孩 ➲ OPPOSITE **untidy** 反义词为 untidy

▸ **tidily** /ˈtaɪdɪli/ ***adverb*** 副词： *Put the books back tidily when you've finished with them.* 书用完后要整齐地放回原处。

▸ **tidiness** /ˈtaɪdinəs/ ***noun*** 名词 (*no plural* 不用复数形式)

tidy² 🗝 /ˈtaɪdi/ (*also* 亦作 **tidy up**) ***verb*** 动词 (**tidies**, **tidying**, **tidied** /ˈtaɪdid/, **has tidied**)
to make something tidy 使整洁；使整齐： *I tidied the house before my parents arrived.* 我在父母来之前把房子收拾整齐。 ◇ *Can you help me to tidy up?* 你能帮我收拾一下吗？

tie¹ 🗝 /taɪ/ ***verb*** 动词 (**ties**, **tying**, **tied** /taɪd/, **has tied**)

1 to fasten or fix something using rope, string, etc. 捆；绑；系： *I tied my hair back with a ribbon.* 我用丝带把头发束在脑后了。 ◇ *I tied a scarf round my neck.* 我在脖子上围上了围巾。◇ *The prisoner was tied to a chair.* 囚犯被绑在椅子上。

2 to end a game or competition with the same number of points for both teams or players（比赛）得分相同，打成平局：*France **tied with** Spain for second place.* 法国队和西班牙队并列第二。

tie somebody up to put a piece of rope around somebody so that they cannot move 捆绑某人：*The robbers tied up the owner of the shop.* 劫匪把店主捆了起来。

tie something up to put a piece of string or rope around something to hold it in place 捆牢；系紧；拴住：*I tied up the parcel with string.* 我用绳子把包裹绑好了。◇ *The dog was tied up in the garden.* 狗被拴在花园里了。

tie² 🔑 /taɪ/ ***noun*** 名词

1 a long thin piece of cloth that you wear round your neck with a shirt 领带 ➲ Look at Picture Dictionary page **P5**. 见彩页 P5。

2 when two teams or players have the same number of points at the end of a game or competition（比赛）平局，不相上下：*The match ended in a tie.* 比赛以平局告终。

3 ties (*plural* 用复数形式) a connection between people or organizations 联系；关系：*Our school has **ties with** a school in France.* 我们学校跟法国的一所学校有联系。

tiger /ˈtaɪɡə(r)/ ***noun*** 名词

a wild animal like a big cat, with yellow fur and black stripes. **Tigers** live in Asia. 虎；老虎 ➲ Look at Picture Dictionary page **P3**. 见彩页 P3。

tight 🔑 /taɪt/ ***adjective*** 形容词 (**tighter**, **tightest**)

> **PRONUNCIATION 读音说明**
> The word **tight** sounds like **white**.
> * tight 读音像 white。

1 fixed firmly so that you cannot move it easily 牢固的；紧的：*a tight knot* 系紧的结 ◇ *I can't open this jar of jam – the lid is too tight.* 我打不开这罐果酱，盖子太紧了。 ➲ OPPOSITE **loose** 反义词为 loose

2 Tight clothes fit very closely in a way that is often uncomfortable.（衣服等）紧身的，过紧的：*These shoes are too tight.* 这双鞋太紧了。◇ *tight trousers* 紧身裤

▸ **tight** (*also* 亦作 **tightly** /ˈtaɪtli/) ***adverb*** 副词：*Hold tight!* 握紧！◇ *I tied the string tightly around the box.* 我用绳把盒子捆紧了。

tighten /ˈtaɪtn/ ***verb*** 动词 (**tightens**, **tightening**, **tightened** /ˈtaɪtnd/)

to become tighter or to make something tighter（使）变紧：*Can you tighten this screw?* 你能把这枚螺丝拧紧吗？

➲ OPPOSITE **loosen** 反义词为 loosen

tightrope /ˈtaɪtrəʊp/ ***noun*** 名词

a rope or wire high above the ground. People (called **acrobats**) walk along **tightropes** as a form of entertainment.（高空杂技表演用的）钢丝，绳索

tights /taɪts/ ***noun*** 名词 (*plural* 用复数形式)

a thin piece of clothing that a woman or girl wears over her feet and legs（女式）裤袜，紧身裤：*a pair of tights* 一条裤袜

➲ Look at Picture Dictionary page **P5**. 见彩页 P5。

tile /taɪl/ ***noun*** 名词

a flat square object. We use **tiles** for covering roofs, walls and floors. 瓷砖；（铺设屋顶、墙壁和地板用的）瓦，地砖

➲ Look at Picture Dictionary page **P10**. 见彩页 P10。

▸ **tile** ***verb*** 动词 (**tiles**, **tiling**, **tiled**): *Dad is tiling the bathroom.* 爸爸正在浴室铺地砖。

till¹ 🔑 /tɪl/ ***conjunction***, ***preposition*** 连词，介词 (*informal* 非正式) = UNTIL: *Let's wait till the rain stops.* 咱们等雨停吧。◇ *I'll be here till Monday.* 我会待在这儿直到星期一。◇ *They didn't arrive till six o'clock.* 他们六点钟才到。

till² /tɪl/ ***noun*** 名词

a drawer or machine for money in a shop（商店）放钱的抽屉，收款机

tilt /tɪlt/ ***verb*** 动词 (**tilts**, **tilting**, **tilted**)

to have one side higher than the other; to move something so that it has one side higher than the other（使）倾斜，倾侧：*She tilted the tray and all the glasses fell off.* 她把托盘一歪，玻璃杯全倒了。

timber /ˈtɪmbə(r)/ ***noun*** 名词 (*no plural* 不用复数形式)

wood that we use for building and making things 木材；木料

time¹ 🔑 /taɪm/ ***noun*** 名词

1 (*no plural* 不用复数形式) a period of seconds, minutes, hours, days, weeks, months or years 时间：***Time passes*** *quickly when you're busy.* 忙碌的时候时间过得很快。◇ *They have lived here **for some time*** (= for quite a long time). 他们在这儿住了颇长时间。◇ *I haven't got **time to** help you now – I'm late for school.* 我现在没时间帮你 —— 我上学要迟到了。

◊ *It takes a long time to learn a language.* 学会一门语言要花很长时间。

2 (*plural* 复数形式 **times**) a certain point in the day or night, that you say in hours and minutes 时间；钟点；时候：*'What time is it?' 'It's twenty past six.'* "几点了？""六点二十分。" ◊ *What's the time?* 几点了？ ◊ *Can you tell me the times of trains to Brighton, please?* 请告诉我到布赖顿每趟火车时刻好吗？ ◊ *It's time to go home.* 该回家了。◊ *By the time* (= when) *we arrived they had eaten all the food.* 我们到达时，他们已经把食物都吃光了。

3 (*plural* 复数形式 **times**) a certain moment or occasion 次；回：*I've seen this film four times.* 我已经看过这部电影四遍。◊ *Come and visit us next time you're in England.* 你下次到英格兰的时候，来我们这儿玩玩。

4 (*plural* 复数形式 **times**) an experience; something that you do（有某种经历或做某事）时刻，时光：*We had a great time on holiday.* 我们假期过得很愉快。

5 (*plural* 复数形式 **times**) certain years in history 时期；时代：*In Shakespeare's time, not many people could read.* 在莎士比亚的时代，识字的人不多。

at a time together; on one occasion 同时；每次：*The lift can carry six people at a time.* 这部电梯每次能载六人。

at one time in the past, but not now 从前；曾经；一度：*We were in the same class at one time.* 我们以前是同班同学。

at the time then 那时；当时：*My family moved to London in 1986 – I was four at the time.* 我家在 1986 年搬到了伦敦，当时我四岁。

at times sometimes 有时；间或：*A teacher's job can be very difficult at times.* 教书这一工作有时可以很困难。

for the time being now, but not for long 暂时；目前：*You can stay here for the time being, until you find a flat.* 你可以暂时住在这儿，直到你找到房子为止。

from time to time sometimes; not often 有时；偶尔：*I see my cousin from time to time.* 我有时会看望我的表妹。

have a good time enjoy yourself 玩得开心：*Have a good time at the party!* 聚会上玩得开心点！

in a week's, two months', a year's, etc. time after a week, two months, a year etc. 一个星期（或两个月、一年等）之后：*I'll see you in two weeks' time.* 我们两周后再见。

in good time at the right time or early 在适当的时候；及早：*I want to get to the station in good time.* 我想早点到火车站。

in time not late 来得及；及时：*If you hurry, you'll arrive in time for the film.* 你要是抓紧时间就能赶得及看这场电影。

it's about time (*informal* 非正式) words that you use to say that something should be done now 该是…的时候了：*It's about time you started studying if you want to pass the exam.* 如果你想通过考试，该开始温习了。

on time not late or early 准时；按时：*My train was on time.* 我搭的火车准点。

spare time, free time time when you do not have to work or study 空闲时间：*What do you do in your spare time?* 你空余时间干什么？

spend time to use time to do something 花时间（做某事）：*I spend a lot of time playing tennis.* 我很多时间打网球。

take your time to do something slowly 从容不迫；慢慢来

tell the time to read the time from a clock or watch（看钟表）说出时间：*Can your children tell the time?* 你的孩子会看表了吗？

time after time, time and time again many times 屡次；一再

time² /taɪm/ *verb* 动词 (**times, timing, timed** /taɪmd/)

1 to plan something so that it will happen when you want 设定…的时间：*The bomb was timed to explode at six o'clock.* 炸弹设定在六点钟爆炸。

2 to measure how much time it takes to do something 计时：*We timed the journey – it took half an hour.* 我们计算了旅程的时间，要半个小时。

times¹ /taɪmz/ *preposition* 介词 (**symbol** 符号 **x**)

multiplied by 乘以：*Three times four is twelve* (3 x 4 = 12). 三乘以四等于十二。

times² /taɪmz/ *noun* 名词 (*plural* 用复数形式)

a word that you use to show how much bigger, smaller, more expensive, etc. one thing is than another（用于比较）倍：*Edinburgh is five times bigger than Oxford.* 爱丁堡比牛津大四倍。

timetable /'taɪmteɪbl/ (*British* 英式英语) (*American* 美式英语 **schedule**) *noun* 名词

a list of times when something happens 时间表；时刻表：*a train timetable* 火车时刻表 ◊ *a school timetable* (= showing when lessons start and finish) 学校课程表

timid /'tɪmɪd/ *adjective* 形容词

shy and easily frightened 胆怯的；羞怯的

▶ **timidly** /'tɪmɪdli/ *adverb* 副词: *She opened the door timidly and came in.* 她小心翼翼地开门进来了。

tin ⌐○/tɪn/ *noun* 名词
1 (*no plural* 不用复数形式) (*symbol* 符号 Sn) a soft white metal 锡
2 (*plural* 复数形式 **tins**) (*British* 英式英语) (*American* 美式英语 **can**) a metal container for food and drink that keeps it fresh（装食物或饮料的）罐，罐头: *I opened a tin of beans.* 我开了一罐青豆。
▶ **tinned** /tɪnd/ *adjective* 形容词: *tinned peaches* 罐头桃 ⊃ Look at the picture at **container**. 见 container 的插图。

tin-opener 开罐器

tin-opener /'tɪn əʊpnə(r)/ *noun* 名词
a tool for opening tins 开罐器；罐头起子

tiny /'taɪni/ *adjective* 形容词 (**tinier, tiniest**)
very small 极小的；微小的: *Ants are tiny insects.* 蚂蚁是很小的昆虫。

tip¹ /tɪp/ *noun* 名词
1 the pointed or thin end of something 尖端；末端: *the tips of your fingers* 手指尖
2 a small, extra amount of money that you give to somebody who has done a job for you 小费；小账: *I left a tip on the table.* 我留了小费在桌上。
3 a small piece of advice 窍门；提示: *She gave me some useful tips on how to pass the exam.* 她给了我一些如何通过考试的有用提示。

tip² /tɪp/ *verb* 动词 (**tips, tipping, tipped** /tɪpt/)
1 to move so that one side goes up or down; to move something so that one side goes up or down（使）倾斜，翘起: *Don't tip your chair back.* 不要把椅子往后仰。
2 to turn something so that the things inside fall out 倾倒；倒出: *She opened a tin of beans and tipped them into a bowl.* 她打开了罐头，把里面的豆倒出碗里。
3 to give somebody an extra amount of money to thank them for something they have done for you as part of their job 给小费；给小账: *Do you tip taxi drivers*

in your country? 在你们国家，会给出租车司机小费吗？

tip over, tip something over to turn over; to make something turn over（使）倾复，翻倒: *The boat tipped over and we all fell in the water.* 船翻了，我们都掉进了水里。◇ *Don't tip your drink over!* 别把你的饮料弄翻！

tiptoe /'tɪptəʊ/ *verb* 动词 (**tiptoes, tiptoeing, tiptoed** /'tɪptəʊd/)
to walk quietly on your toes 踮着脚走；蹑手蹑脚地走: *He tiptoed into the bedroom.* 他蹑手蹑脚地走进了卧室。

on tiptoe standing or walking on your toes with the rest of your feet off the ground 踮着脚；蹑手蹑脚: *She stood on tiptoe.* 她踮着脚。

tire *American English for* TYRE 美式英语，即 tyre

tired ⌐○/'taɪəd/ *adjective* 形容词
needing to rest or sleep 疲倦的；疲劳的: *I've been working all day and I'm tired out* (= extremely tired). 我工作了一整天，真的累坏了。◇ *He's feeling tired.* 他感到疲倦。

be tired of something to have had or done too much of something, so that you do not want it any longer 厌倦；厌烦: *I'm tired of watching TV – let's go out.* 电视我看腻了，咱们出去吧。

tiring ⌐○/'taɪərɪŋ/ *adjective* 形容词
making you feel tired 使人疲劳的；令人疲惫的: *a tiring journey* 使人疲倦的旅程

tissue /'tɪʃuː/ *noun* 名词
1 (*plural* 复数形式 **tissues**) a thin piece of soft paper that you use to clean your nose 纸巾: *a box of tissues* 一盒纸巾
2 (*no plural* 不用复数形式) all the cells that form the bodies of humans, animals and plants（人、动植物细胞的）组织

tissue paper /'tɪʃuː peɪpə(r)/ *noun* 名词 (*no plural* 不用复数形式)
thin paper that you use for wrapping things（包装用的）薄纸，绵纸

title ⌐○/'taɪtl/ *noun* 名词
1 the name of something, for example a book, film or picture（书籍、电影、图画等的）标题，题目，名称: *What is the title of this poem?* 这首诗的题目是什么？
2 a word like 'Mr', 'Mrs' or 'Doctor' that you put in front of a person's name 称号；头衔；称谓

to ⌐○/tə; tu; tuː/ *preposition* 介词
1 a word that shows direction 向；朝；往；到: *She went to Italy.* 她去了意大利。◇ *James has gone to school.* 詹姆斯上学

去了。◇ *This bus goes to the city centre.* 这路公共汽车开往市中心。
2 a word that shows the person or thing that receives something（引出接受者）给，予： *I gave the book to Paula.* 我把书给葆拉了。◇ *He sent a letter to his parents.* 他给父母寄了一封信。◇ *Be kind to animals.* 要善待动物。
3 a word that shows the end or limit of something（表示终点或极限）到，至： *The museum is open **from** 9.30 **to** 5.30.* 博物馆开放时间为 9 点 30 分至 5 点 30 分。◇ *Jeans cost **from** £20 **to** £45.* 牛仔裤的价格从 20 到 45 英镑不等。
4 on or against something 对着；靠着： *He put his hands to his ears.* 他双手捂住耳朵。◇ *They were sitting back to back.* 他们背靠背坐着。
5 a word that shows how something changes（表示变化）： *The sky changed **from** blue **to** grey.* 天空由蓝色变成了灰色。
6 a word that shows why（表示原因）： *I came to help.* 我是来帮忙的。
7 a word that you use for comparing things（用于比较）： *I prefer football to tennis.* 我喜欢足球甚于网球。
8 a word that shows how many minutes it is before the hour（表示时间）在…之前，差，离： *It's two minutes to six.* 差两分钟就六点了。
9 a word that you use before verbs to make the INFINITIVE (= the simple form of a verb)（用于动词之前，构成不定式）： *I want to go home.* 我想回家。◇ *Don't forget to write.* 别忘了写信。◇ *She asked me to go but I didn't want to* (= to go). 她叫我去，但我不想去。

toad 蟾蜍

toad /təʊd/ ***noun*** 名词
a small animal with rough skin that lives in or near water 蟾蜍；癞蛤蟆 ➲ Look at **frog**. 见 frog。

toast /təʊst/ ***noun*** 名词 (*no plural* 不用复数形式)
1 a thin piece of bread that you have cooked so that it is brown 烤面包片；吐司： *I had a **slice of toast** and jam for breakfast.* 我早餐吃了一片果酱吐司。
2 the act of holding up a glass of wine and wishing somebody happiness or success before you drink 祝酒；敬酒；干杯： *They **drank a toast to** the Queen.* 他们为女王干杯。
▸ **toast** ***verb*** 动词 (**toasts, toasting, toasted**)： *toasted sandwiches* 烤过的三明治 ◇ *We all toasted the bride and groom* (= at a wedding). 我们全体向新郎新娘祝酒。

toast 烤面包片

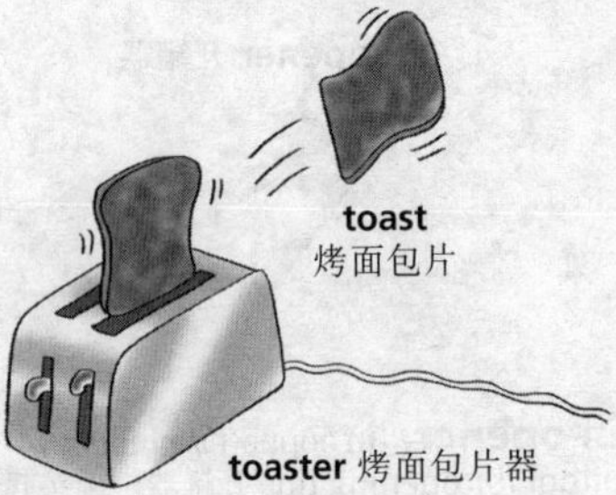

toaster /ˈtəʊstə(r)/ ***noun*** 名词
a machine for making TOAST (1) 烤面包片器；吐司炉

tobacco /təˈbækəʊ/ ***noun*** 名词 (*no plural* 不用复数形式)
special dried leaves that people smoke in cigarettes and pipes 烟草；烟叶

toboggan /təˈbɒɡən/ ***noun*** 名词
a type of flat board that people use for travelling down hills on snow for fun 长雪橇；平底雪橇 ➲ Look also at **sledge**. 亦见 sledge。

today 0┳ /təˈdeɪ/ ***adverb, noun*** 副词，名词 (*no plural* 不用复数形式)
1 this day; on this day 今天；在今天： *What shall we do today?* 我们今天做什么？◇ *Today is Friday.* 今天是星期五。
2 the present time; at the present time 当今；现今；如今 ➲ SAME MEANING **nowadays** 同义词为 nowadays： *Most families in Britain today have a car.* 如今英国的大多数家庭都有汽车。

toddler /ˈtɒdlə(r)/ ***noun*** 名词
a young child who has just started to walk 学步的幼儿；刚学会走路的小孩

toe 0┳ /təʊ/ ***noun*** 名词
1 one of the five parts at the end of your

foot 脚趾 ➔ Look at the picture at **foot**. 见 foot 的插图。

2 the part of a shoe or sock that covers the end of your foot （鞋或袜的）脚尖部

toenail /'təʊneɪl/ *noun* 名词
the hard part at the end of your toe 趾甲 ➔ Look at the picture at **foot**. 见 foot 的插图。

toffee /'tɒfi/ *noun* 名词
a hard brown sweet made from sugar and butter 太妃糖；乳脂糖

together 0̄ /tə'geðə(r)/ *adverb* 副词
1 with each other or close to each other 一起；共同：*John and Lisa usually walk home together.* 约翰和莉萨通常一起走回家。◇ *Stand with your feet together.* 双脚并拢站立。◇ *They live together.* 他们住在一起。
2 so that two or more things are joined to or mixed with each other （连接或混合到）一起：*Tie the ends of the rope together.* 把绳子两端系在一起。◇ *Add these numbers together.* 把这些数字加起来。◇ *Mix the eggs and sugar together.* 把鸡蛋和糖混合在一起。

toilet 0̄ /'tɔɪlət/ *noun* 名词
1 a large bowl with a seat, that you use when you need to empty waste from your body 坐便器；抽水马桶
2 (*British* 英式英语) (*American* 美式英语 **bathroom**) a room that contains a **toilet** （带抽水马桶的）卫生间，厕所：*I'm going to the toilet.* 我去上厕所。➔ Look at Picture Dictionary page **P10**. 见彩页 P10。

🔍 WORD BUILDING 词汇扩充
In their houses, British people usually say **the toilet** or, informally, **the loo**. **Lavatory** and **WC** are formal and old-fashioned words. 英国人通常用 the toilet 或非正式的 the loo 来指家中的卫生间。lavatory 和 WC 是正式用语，现已过时。
In public places in Britain, the toilets are called **the Ladies** or **the Gents**. 英国的公共场所用 the Ladies 表示女厕，the Gents 表示男厕。
In American English, people say **the bathroom** in their homes and **the restroom**, **ladies' room** or **men's room** in public places. 美国人家里的卫生间为 the bathroom，公共厕所称 the restroom，女厕称 ladies' room，男厕称 men's room。

toilet paper /'tɔɪlət peɪpə(r)/ *noun* 名词 (*no plural* 不用复数形式)
paper that you use in the toilet 卫生纸；手纸

toilet roll /'tɔɪlət rəʊl/ *noun* 名词
a roll of paper that you use in the toilet 卫生纸卷；手纸卷

token /'təʊkən/ *noun* 名词
1 a piece of paper, plastic or metal that you use instead of money to pay for something 代币；代币券：*a book token* 书券
2 a small thing that you use to show something else 象征物；标志：*This gift is a token of our friendship.* 这份礼物是我们友谊的象征。

told *form of* TELL * tell 的不同形式

tolerant /'tɒlərənt/ *adjective* 形容词
letting people do things even though you do not like or understand them 容忍的；宽容的：*We must be tolerant of other people's beliefs.* 对他人的信仰我们得抱宽容的态度。
▶ **tolerance** /'tɒlərəns/ *noun* 名词 (*no plural* 不用复数形式)：*tolerance of other religions* 对其他宗教的宽容

tolerate /'tɒləreɪt/ *verb* 动词 (**tolerates**, **tolerating**, **tolerated**)
to let people do something even though you do not like or understand it 容忍；包容：*He won't tolerate rudeness.* 他不会容忍粗鲁的行为。

tomato 0̄ /tə'mɑːtəʊ/ *noun* 名词 (*plural* 复数形式 **tomatoes**)
a soft red fruit that you cook or eat cold in salads 西红柿；番茄：*tomato soup* 番茄汤 ➔ Look at Picture Dictionary page **P9**. 见彩页 P9。

tomb /tuːm/ *noun* 名词
a thing made of stone where a dead person's body is buried 坟墓

tombstone /'tuːmstəʊn/ *noun* 名词
a large flat stone on the place where a person is buried (their **grave**) showing their name and the dates when they lived 墓碑

tomorrow 0̄ /tə'mɒrəʊ/ *adverb*, *noun* 副词，名词 (*no plural* 不用复数形式)
the day after today; on the day after today 明天；在明天：*Let's go swimming tomorrow.* 咱们明天去游泳吧。◇ *I'll see you tomorrow morning.* 我会明天上午见你。◇ *We are going home the day after tomorrow.* 我们将于后天回家。

ton /tʌn/ *noun* 名词
1 a unit for measuring weight. There are 2 240 pounds (= 1 016 kilos) in a British **ton**. In the US, a **ton** is 2 000 pounds. 吨（在英国等于 2 240 磅；在美国等于 2 000 磅）
2 tons (*plural* 用复数形式) (*informal* 非正式) a lot 大量；许多：*He's got **tons** of money.* 他有很多钱。

tone /təʊn/ *noun* 名词
the way that something sounds 语气；语调；口吻：*I knew he was angry by the **tone** of his voice.* 我从他的语气中听出他生气了。

tongs 夹钳

tongs /tɒŋz/ *noun* 名词 (*plural* 用复数形式)
a tool with two parts that you use for holding things or picking things up 夹钳；夹具

tongue 0→ /tʌŋ/ *noun* 名词

> *Ω* **PRONUNCIATION** 读音说明
> The word **tongue** sounds like **young**. * tongue 读音像 young。

the soft part inside your mouth that moves when you talk or eat 舌；舌头

tongue-twister /'tʌŋ twɪstə(r)/ *noun* 名词
words that are difficult to say together quickly 绕口令：*'Red lorry, yellow lorry' is a tongue-twister.* * red lorry, yellow lorry 是绕口令。

tonight 0→ /tə'naɪt/ *adverb*, *noun* 副词，名词 (*no plural* 不用复数形式)
the evening or night of today; on the evening or night of today 今天晚上；在今天晚上：*I'm going to a party tonight.* 我今晚要去参加聚会。◇ *Tonight is the last night of our holiday.* 今晚是我们假期的最后一个晚上。

tonne /tʌn/ *noun* 名词
a measure of weight. There are 1 000 kilograms in a **tonne**. 公吨（重量单位；1 公吨等于 1 000 公斤）

too 0→ /tu:/ *adverb* 副词
1 more than you want or need 太；过于：*These shoes are too big.* 这双鞋太大了。◇ *She put too much milk in my coffee.* 她在我的咖啡里放了太多牛奶。

2 also 也；还 *ↄ* SAME MEANING **as well**
同义词为 as well：*Green is my favourite colour but I like blue too.* 我最喜欢绿色，但也喜欢蓝色。

too 过于

Tom's sweater is **not** big **enough**.
汤姆的毛衣不够大。

Kevin's sweater is **too** big.
凯文的毛衣太大了。

took *form of* TAKE * take 的不同形式

tool 0→ /tu:l/ *noun* 名词
a thing that you hold in your hand and use to do a special job 工具：*Hammers and saws are tools.* 锤子和锯子是工具。

> *Ω* WORD BUILDING 词汇扩充
> There are many different types of **tool**. Here are some of them: **drill, hammer, knife, saw, screwdriver**. Do you know any others? * tool 的种类很多，如：drill（钻）、hammer（锤子）、knife（刀）、saw（锯）、screwdriver（螺丝刀）。你还知道别的吗？

tooth 0→ /tu:θ/ *noun* 名词 (*plural* 复数形式 teeth /ti:θ/)
1 one of the hard white things in your mouth that you use for eating 牙；牙齿：*I brush my teeth after every meal.* 我每餐后都刷牙。 *ↄ* Look at Picture Dictionary page P4. 见彩页 P4。

> *Ω* WORD BUILDING 词汇扩充
> A **dentist** is a person whose job is to look after teeth. 牙医是 dentist。
> If a tooth is bad, the dentist may **fill** it (= put a substance in the hole) or **take it out**. 牙齿要是蛀了，牙医可能会补（fill）牙或把它拔掉（take out）。
> People who have lost their own teeth

can wear **false teeth**. 失去牙齿的人可以戴假牙（false teeth）。

2 one of the long narrow pointed parts of an object such as a COMB (= an object that you use for making your hair tidy) （梳子等的）齿，齿状部分

toothache /'tuːθeɪk/ *noun* 名词 (*no plural* 不用复数形式)
a pain in your tooth 牙痛：*I've got toothache.* 我牙疼。

toothbrush /'tuːθbrʌʃ/ *noun* 名词 (*plural* 复数形式 **toothbrushes**)
a small brush for cleaning your teeth 牙刷 ➋ Look at the picture at **brush¹**. 见 brush¹ 的插图。

toothpaste /'tuːθpeɪst/ *noun* 名词 (*no plural* 不用复数形式)
a substance that you put on your TOOTHBRUSH and use for cleaning your teeth 牙膏

top¹ ⊶ /tɒp/ *noun* 名词
1 the highest part of something 顶；顶部；顶端：*There's a church at the top of the hill.* 山顶上有座教堂。 ➋ OPPOSITE **bottom** 反义词为 bottom
2 a cover that you put on something to close it 盖子；塞子：*Where's the top of this jar?* 这个罐的盖子在哪儿？
3 a piece of clothing that you wear on the top part of your body 上衣：*I like your top – is it new?* 我喜欢你的上衣，是新的吗？
on top on its highest part 在顶部；在顶端：*The cake had cream on top.* 蛋糕顶部有奶油。
on top of something on or over something 在…上面；在…上方：*A tree fell on top of my car.* 一棵树倒在我的汽车上了。

top² ⊶ /tɒp/ *adjective* 形容词
highest or best 最高的；最好的：*Put this book on the top shelf.* 把这本书放在书架的最上层。 ◇ *She's one of the country's top athletes.* 她是该国的顶尖运动员之一。

topic /'tɒpɪk/ *noun* 名词
something that you talk, learn or write about 话题；题目 ➋ SAME MEANING **subject** 同义词为 subject：*The topic of the discussion was war.* 讨论的话题是战争。

torch /tɔːtʃ/ *noun* 名词 (*plural* 复数形式 **torches**) (*British* 英式英语) (*American* 美式英语 **flashlight**)
a small electric light that you can carry 手电筒 ➋ Look at the picture at **light¹**. 见 light¹ 的插图。

tore, torn *forms of* TEAR¹ * tear¹ 的不同形式

tornado /tɔːˈneɪdəʊ/ *noun* 名词 (*plural* 复数形式 **tornadoes**)
a violent storm with a very strong wind that blows in a circle 龙卷风

torpedo /tɔːˈpiːdəʊ/ *noun* 名词 (*plural* 复数形式 **torpedoes**)
a type of bomb in the shape of a long tube that is fired from a ship that travels under the water (a **submarine**) 鱼雷

torrent /'tɒrənt/ *noun* 名词
a strong fast flow of water 急流；激流；湍流：*The rain was coming down in torrents.* 大雨倾泻而下。
▶ **torrential** /təˈrenʃl/ *adjective* 形容词：*torrential rain* 倾盆大雨

tortoise 龟

shell 壳

tortoise /'tɔːtəs/ *noun* 名词 (*American also* 美式英语亦作 **turtle**)
an animal with a hard shell on its back, that moves very slowly 龟；陆龟

torture /'tɔːtʃə(r)/ *noun* 名词 (*no plural* 不用复数形式)
the act of making somebody feel great pain, often to make them give information 酷刑；（常指）拷打，拷问：*His confession was obtained under torture.* 他的供词是在拷问之下逼出来的。
▶ **torture** *verb* 动词 (**tortures, torturing, tortured** /'tɔːtʃəd/)：*Many of the prisoners had been tortured.* 许多囚犯都受过严刑拷打。

the Tory Party /ðə 'tɔːri pɑːti/ *another word for* THE CONSERVATIVE PARTY * the Conservative Party 的另一种说法

toss /tɒs/ *verb* 动词 (**tosses, tossing, tossed** /tɒst/)
1 to throw something quickly and without care （随手）扔，抛，掷：*I tossed the paper into the bin.* 我随手把纸扔进了垃圾箱。
2 to move quickly up and down or from side to side; to make something do this

A B C D E F G H I J K L M N O P Q R S T U V W X Y Z

A B C D E F G H I J K L M N O P Q R S T U V W X Y Z

（使）摇摆，颠簸: *The boat was being tossed by the huge waves.* 船在巨浪里颠簸。

3 to decide something by throwing a coin in the air and seeing which side shows when it falls 掷（硬币）决定: *We tossed a coin to see who would pay for the meal.* 我们掷硬币决定这顿饭谁来结账。

total¹ 0⃗ /'təʊtl/ *adjective* 形容词
complete; if you count everything or everybody 完全的；总共的；总计的: *There was total silence in the classroom.* 教室里一片寂静。◇ *What was the total number of people at the meeting?* 会议上一共有多少人?

total² 0⃗ /'təʊtl/ *noun* 名词
the number you have when you add everything together 总数；总额；共计: *Enter the total at the bottom of the page.* 在页面的末端输入总数。

totally 0⃗ /'təʊtəli/ *adverb* 副词
completely 完全；彻底；全部地: *I totally agree.* 我完全同意。

touch¹ 0⃗ /tʌtʃ/ *verb* 动词 (touches, touching, touched /tʌtʃt/)

🔍 **PRONUNCIATION** 读音说明
The word **touch** sounds like **much**.
* touch 读音像 much。

1 to put your hand or finger on somebody or something 触摸；碰: *Don't touch the paint – it's still wet.* 别碰油漆，它还没干。◇ *He touched me on the arm.* 他碰了碰我的胳膊。
2 to be so close to another thing or person that there is no space in between 接触；触及: *The two wires were touching.* 两根电线搭在了一起。◇ *Her coat was so long that it touched the ground.* 她的大衣长得都拖到地面了。

touch² 0⃗ /tʌtʃ/ *noun* 名词
1 (*plural* 复数形式 touches) the action of putting a hand or finger on somebody or something 触摸；碰: *I felt the touch of his hand on my arm.* 我感觉到他的手碰了一下我的胳膊。
2 (*no plural* 不用复数形式) the feeling in your hands and skin that tells you about something 触觉: *We had to feel our way by touch.* 我们只能靠摸索走下去。
be or 或 **keep in touch with somebody** to meet, telephone or write to somebody often 与某人保持联系: *Are you still in touch with Kevin?* 你跟凯文还有联系吗? ◇ *Let's keep in touch.* 咱们保持联系吧。

get in touch with somebody to write to, or telephone somebody 与某人联系: *I'm trying to get in touch with my cousin.* 我正设法联系我的表妹。
lose touch with somebody to stop meeting, telephoning or writing to somebody 与某人失去联系: *I've lost touch with all my old friends from school.* 我跟学校所有的老朋友都失去联系了。

tough 0⃗ /tʌf/ *adjective* 形容词 (tougher, toughest)
1 difficult 困难的；艰难的；棘手的 ⊃ SAME MEANING **hard** 同义词为 hard: *This is a tough job.* 这是一项很难的工作。
2 strict or firm 严格的；严厉的；强硬的 ⊃ SAME MEANING **hard** 同义词为 hard: *He's very tough on his children.* 他对子女管得很严。◇ OPPOSITE **soft** 反义词为 soft
3 very strong 健壮的；强健的: *You need to be tough to go climbing in winter.* 冬天爬山需要有强健的体魄。
4 Tough meat is difficult to cut and eat. （肉）难切开的，嚼不烂的 ⊃ OPPOSITE **tender** 反义词为 tender
5 difficult to break or tear 坚固的；结实的: *a tough pair of boots* 一双结实的靴子

tour 0⃗ /tʊə(r)/ *noun* 名词
1 a journey to see a lot of different places 旅游；旅行: *We went on a tour of Scotland.* 我们去苏格兰旅行了。
2 a short visit to see a building or city 游览；参观: *They gave us a tour of the house.* 他们带我们参观了房子。
▶ **tour** *verb* 动词 (tours, touring, toured /tʊəd/): *We toured France for three weeks.* 我们在法国旅游了三个星期。

tourism /'tʊərɪzəm/ *noun* 名词 (*no plural* 不用复数形式)
the business of arranging holidays for people 旅游业: *The country earns a lot of money from tourism.* 这个国家靠旅游业赚到不少钱。

tourist 0⃗ /'tʊərɪst/ *noun* 名词
a person who visits a place on holiday 游客；旅客

tournament /'tʊənəmənt; 'tɔːnəmənt/ *noun* 名词
a sports competition with a lot of players or teams 锦标赛；联赛: *a tennis tournament* 网球锦标赛

tow /təʊ/ *verb* 动词 (tows, towing, towed /təʊd/)
to pull a vehicle using a rope or chain （用绳索或链）拖，拉，拽: *My car was towed to a garage.* 我的汽车被拖到了修车厂。

A

towards 0➔ /təˈwɔːdz/ *(also* 亦作
toward /təˈwɔːd/) *preposition* 介词
1 in the direction of somebody or
something 向；朝；对着：*We walked
towards the river.* 我们朝那条河走去了。
◇ *I couldn't see her face – she had her
back towards me.* 我看不见她的脸，
她背对着我。
2 near a time or a date 接近，临近（某一
时间或日期）：*Let's meet towards the end
of the week.* 咱们接近周末时见面吧。◇
It gets cooler towards evening. 临近傍晚的
时候，天气变得更凉了。
3 to somebody or something 对；对于：
*The people in the village are always very
friendly towards tourists.* 村民对游客一向
很友善。
4 to help pay for something 用作（付款
的）一部分：*Tom gave me £10 towards
Sam's birthday present.* 汤姆给了我 10
英镑，用作凑钱给萨姆买生日礼物。

towel 0➔ /ˈtaʊəl/ *noun* 名词
a piece of cloth that you use for drying
yourself 毛巾；抹布：*I washed my hands
and dried them on a towel.* 我洗完手后用
毛巾擦干了。

tower 0➔ /ˈtaʊə(r)/ *noun* 名词
a tall narrow building or a tall part of
a building 塔；塔楼：*the Eiffel Tower*
埃菲尔铁塔 ◇ *a church tower* 教堂塔楼

tower block /ˈtaʊə(r) blɒk/ *noun* 名词
(*British* 英式英语)
a very tall building with a lot of flats or
offices inside 高层建筑；公寓大楼；办公
大楼

town 0➔ /taʊn/ *noun* 名词
a place where there are a lot of houses,
shops and other buildings 城镇；市镇：
Banbury is a town near Oxford. 班伯里是
牛津附近的一个镇。◇ *I'm going into town
to do some shopping.* 我进城去买些东西。

🔎 WORD BUILDING 词汇扩充
A **town** is bigger than a **village** but
smaller than a **city**. * town 比 village
（村庄）大，比 city（城市）小。

town hall /ˌtaʊn ˈhɔːl/ *noun* 名词
a large building that contains the local
government offices of a town or city
市政厅；镇公所

toxic /ˈtɒksɪk/ *adjective* 形容词
containing poison 有毒的 ➔ SAME
MEANING **poisonous** 同义词为 poisonous：
Toxic waste had been dumped on the site.
有毒废料被倾倒在工地上。

toys 玩具
propeller 螺旋桨
toy aeroplane   **toy soldier**
玩具飞机   玩具士兵

toy 0➔ /tɔɪ/ *noun* 名词
a thing for a child to play with 玩具

trace¹ /treɪs/ *verb* 动词 (**traces, tracing,
traced** /treɪst/)
1 to look for and find somebody or
something 追查；查找；追踪：*The police
traced the gang to a house in Manchester.*
警方追查到那帮歹徒在曼彻斯特的一所
房子里。
2 to put thin paper over a picture and
draw over the lines to make a copy
（用薄纸覆盖在图画上）描摹，复制 描绘.

trace² /treɪs/ *noun* 名词
a mark or sign that shows that a person
or thing has been in a place 痕迹；踪迹：
*The police could not find any trace of the
missing child.* 警方找不到那名失踪孩子的
任何踪迹。

track¹ 0➔ /træk/ *noun* 名词
1 a rough path or road 小路；小径：
We drove along a track through the woods.
我们开车沿着林间小道穿行。
2 tracks (*plural* 用复数形式) a line of
marks that an animal, a person or a
vehicle makes on the ground（动物或人
的）足迹，踪迹；车辙：*We saw tracks in
the snow.* 我们在雪地上看到足迹。
3 the metal lines that a train runs on
火车轨道：*The train had left the tracks.*
火车已经脱轨了。➔ Look at the picture
at **train¹**. 见 train¹ 的插图。
4 a special road for races 跑道；赛道：
a racing track 赛车道
5 one song or piece of music on a tape,
CD or record（磁带、CD 或唱片的）一首
歌曲，一首乐曲：*Which is your favourite
track?* 你最喜欢里面哪首歌曲？
lose track of somebody or 或
something to not have information
about what is happening or where

B
C
D
E
F
G
H
I
J
K
L
M
N
O
P
Q
R
S
T
U
V
W
X
Y
Z

somebody or something is 与…失去
联系；不了解…的动态：*I lost all track
of time* (= forgot what time it was).
我当时完全不知道时间。

track² /træk/ *verb* 动词 (tracks, tracking,
tracked /trækt/)
to follow signs or marks to find somebody
or something 跟踪；追踪
track somebody or 或 **something
down** to find somebody or something
after looking in several different places
搜寻到；追踪到：*The police have so far
failed to track down the attacker.* 警方至今
未能追捕到袭击者。

tracksuit /'træksuːt/ *noun* 名词
a special jacket and trousers that you
wear for sport 运动服；运动套装

tractor 拖拉机

tractor /'træktə(r)/ *noun* 名词
a big strong vehicle that people use on
farms to pull heavy things 拖拉机

trade¹ /treɪd/ *noun* 名词
1 (*no plural* 不用复数形式) the buying and
selling of things 贸易；交易；买卖：*trade
between Britain and the US* 英美两国之间
的贸易
2 (*plural* 复数形式 **trades**) a particular
type of business 行业：*the building trade*
建筑业
3 (*plural* 复数形式 **trades**) a job for which
you need special skills, especially with
your hands （尤指手工）职业；手艺：
Dave is a plumber by trade. 戴夫的职业是
水暖工。◇ *to learn a trade* 学一门手艺

trade² /treɪd/ *verb* 动词 (trades, trading,
traded)
to buy and sell things 做买卖；做生意；
从事贸易活动：*Japan trades with many
different countries.* 日本与很多不同的国家
有贸易往来。

trademark /'treɪdmɑːk/ *noun* 名词 (*abbr.*
缩略式 **TM**)
a special mark or name that a company

puts on the things it makes and that
other companies must not use 商标

tradesman /'treɪdzmən/ *noun* 名词
(*plural* 复数形式 **tradesmen** /'treɪdzmən/)
(*British* 英式英语)
a person who sells things, especially in
a small shop （尤指小商店的）售货员，
店主：*Local tradesmen are opposed to the
new supermarket.* 当地的小商户抵制那家
新超市。

trade union /ˌtreɪd 'juːniən/ (*also* 亦作
union) *noun* 名词
a group of workers who have joined
together to try to get better pay and
working conditions 工会

tradition Oₘ /trə'dɪʃn/ *noun* 名词
something that people in a certain place
have done or believed for a long time
传统；习俗：*In Britain it's a tradition to
give chocolate eggs at Easter.* 在英国，
复活节时赠送巧克力蛋是传统风俗。
▸ **traditional** /trə'dɪʃənl/ *adjective*
形容词：*traditional English food* 传统的
英国食物
▸ **traditionally** /trə'dɪʃənəli/ *adverb*
副词：*Driving trains was traditionally
a man's job.* 开火车传统上是男性的工作。

traffic Oₘ /'træfɪk/ *noun* 名词 (*no plural*
不用复数形式)
all the cars and other vehicles that are on
a road 交通；车流；路上的车辆：*There
was a lot of traffic on the way to work this
morning.* 今天早上上班路上车辆很多。

traffic circle /'træfɪk sɜːkl/ *American
English for* ROUNDABOUT (1) 美式英语，
即 roundabout 第 1 义

traffic jam /'træfɪk dʒæm/ *noun* 名词
a long line of cars and other vehicles that
cannot move or can only move slowly
塞车；交通堵塞

traffic lights /'træfɪk laɪts/ *noun* 名词
(*plural* 用复数形式)
lights that change from red to orange
to green, to tell cars and other vehicles
when to stop and start 交通信号灯

traffic warden /'træfɪk wɔːdn/ *noun*
名词 (*British* 英式英语)
a person whose job is to check that cars
park in the right places and for the right
time （处理违章停车的）交通管理员

tragedy /'trædʒədi/ *noun* 名词 (*plural*
复数形式 **tragedies**)
1 a very sad thing that happens 悲惨的
事；不幸：*The child's death was a
tragedy.* 那个孩子的死是一大不幸。

2 a serious and sad play 悲剧；悲剧作品: *Shakespeare's 'King Lear' is a tragedy.* 莎士比亚的《李尔王》是一出悲剧。 ⊃ Look at **comedy**. 见 comedy。

tragic /'trædʒɪk/ *adjective* 形容词
very sad 悲惨的；可悲的: *a tragic accident* 悲惨的事故
▸ **tragically** /'trædʒɪkli/ *adverb* 副词:
He died tragically at the age of 25.
他 25 岁时不幸去世。

trail¹ /treɪl/ *noun* 名词
1 a line of marks that show which way a person or thing has gone （显示行踪的）踪迹，足迹，痕迹: *There was a trail of blood across the floor.* 地板上有一行血迹。
2 a path in the country （乡间）小径:
We followed the trail through the forest.
我们顺着小路穿过森林。

trail² /treɪl/ *verb* 动词 (trails, trailing, trailed /treɪld/)
to pull something along behind you; to be pulled along behind somebody or something （被）拖，拉: *Her skirt was too long and it trailed along the ground.* 她的裙子太长，都拖到了地上。

trailer /'treɪlə(r)/ *noun* 名词
1 a container with wheels that a vehicle pulls along 拖车；挂车: *The car was towing a boat on a trailer.* 汽车后面拖着载有小船的拖车。
2 (*American* 美式英语) a vehicle without an engine, that can be pulled by a car or truck or used as a home when it is parked 旅行拖车（无发动机，由其他车拖动，可供住宿用）
3 a short piece from a film that shows you what it is like （电影）预告片

train¹ 🔊 /treɪn/ *noun* 名词
a vehicle that is pulled by an engine along a railway line 火车；列车: *I'm going to Bristol by train.* 我正坐火车去布里斯托尔。 ◇ *We caught the 7.15 train to Leeds.* 我们赶上了 7 点 15 分去利兹的火车。 ◇ *You have to change trains at Reading.* 你得在雷丁换车。

⌕ WORD BUILDING 词汇扩充
You get **on** and **off** trains at a **station**.
上火车说 get on，下火车说 get off，火车站说 station。
A **goods train** or a **freight train** carries things and a **passenger train** carries people. 货运列车是 goods train 或 freight train，客运列车是 passenger train。

train 火车

carriage (*British* 英式英语)
car (*American* 美式英语) 客车厢
engine 火车头
track 铁轨

train² 🔊 /treɪn/ *verb* 动词 (trains, training, trained /treɪnd/)
1 to teach a person or an animal to do something 训练；培训: *He was trained as a pilot.* 他受过飞行员训练。
2 to make yourself ready for something by studying or doing something a lot 接受培训；进行训练: *Ann is training to be a doctor.* 安正在接受医生培训。 ◇ *She's training for the Olympics.* 她正在为参加奥运会进行训练。

trainer /'treɪnə(r)/ *noun* 名词
1 trainers (*plural* 用复数形式) (*British* 英语) (*American* 美式英语 **sneakers**) soft shoes that you wear for doing sport or with informal clothes 运动鞋；便鞋 ⊃ Look at Picture Dictionary page **P5**. 见彩页 P5。
2 a person who teaches people or animals to do something 教员；教练；驯兽师: *teacher trainers* 培训师资的教员

training /'treɪnɪŋ/ *noun* 名词
(*no plural* 不用复数形式)
the process of getting ready for a sport or job 训练；培训: *She is in training for the Olympic Games.* 她正在为参加奥运会进行训练。

traitor /'treɪtə(r)/ *noun* 名词
a person who harms their own country in order to help another country 叛徒；卖国贼

tram /træm/ (*British* 英式英语) (*American* 美式英语 **streetcar**) *noun* 名词
an electric bus that runs along metal tracks (called **rails**) in the road 有轨电车

A B C D E F G H I J K L M N O P Q R S **T** U V W X Y Z

A B C D E F G H I J K L M N O P Q R S T U V W X Y Z

tramp /træmp/ ***noun*** 名词
a person with no home or job, who goes from place to place 流浪汉；流浪者

trample /'træmpl/ ***verb*** 动词 (**tramples, trampling, trampled** /'træmpld/)
to walk on something and damage it with your feet 践踏；踩坏： *Don't* ***trample on*** *the flowers!* 别踩坏那些花！

trampoline /'træmpəliːn/ ***noun*** 名词
a piece of equipment for jumping up and down on 蹦床，跳床，弹床（运动器械）

transfer /træns'fɜː(r)/ ***verb*** 动词 (**transfers, transferring, transferred** /træns'fɜːd/)
to move somebody or something to a different place （使）转移，搬迁，调动： *I want to* ***transfer*** *£500* ***to*** *my savings account.* 我想把 500 英镑转到我的储蓄账户。
▸ **transfer** /'trænsfɜː(r)/ ***noun*** 名词： *Barnes has asked for* ***a transfer to*** *a different team.* 巴恩斯已经提出要转会到另一个队伍。

transform /træns'fɔːm/ ***verb*** 动词 (**transforms, transforming, transformed** /træns'fɔːmd/)
to change a person or thing completely 使彻底改变： *Electricity has transformed people's lives.* 电力彻底改变了人的生活。
▸ **transformation** /ˌtrænsfə'meɪʃn/ ***noun*** 名词： *The city's transformation has been amazing.* 这个城市的变化非常惊人。

transistor /træn'zɪstə(r)/ ***noun*** 名词
a small electronic part inside something such as a radio, a television or a computer 晶体管

transitive /'trænsətɪv/ ***adjective*** 形容词
(*grammar* 语法) A **transitive** verb has an object. （动词）及物的： *In the sentence 'Jane opened the door', 'opened' is a transitive verb.* 在 Jane opened the door 一句中，opened 是及物动词。 ➲ Look at **intransitive**. 见 intransitive。

translate 🔑 /træns'leɪt/ ***verb*** 动词 (**translates, translating, translated**)
to change what somebody has said or written in one language to another language 翻译；译： *Can you* ***translate*** *this letter* ***into*** *English for me?* 你能帮我把这封信翻译成英文吗？
▸ **translation** /træns'leɪʃn/ ***noun*** 名词： *a translation* ***from*** *English* ***into*** *French* 从英语到法语的翻译 ◇ *I've only read his books* ***in translation***. 我只读过他作品的译本。
▸ **translator** /træns'leɪtə(r)/ ***noun*** 名词： *She works as a translator.* 她是做翻译的。

transparent 🔑 /træns'pærənt/ ***adjective*** 形容词
If something is **transparent**, you can see through it. 透明的；清澈的： *Glass is transparent.* 玻璃是透明的。

transport 🔑 /'trænspɔːt/ ***noun*** 名词 (*no plural* 不用复数形式)
a way of carrying people or things from one place to another 交通运输： *road transport* 公路运输 ◇ *I travel to school by* ***public transport*** (= bus or train). 我乘坐公共交通工具上学。
▸ **transport** /træn'spɔːt/ ***verb*** 动词 (**transports, transporting, transported**): *The goods were transported by air.* 货物是空运的。

trap[1] /træp/ ***noun*** 名词
1 a thing that you use for catching animals 捕兽器；捕捉器；罗网： *The rabbit's leg was caught in a trap.* 兔子的腿给捕捉器夹住了。
2 a plan to trick somebody （骗人的）圈套，陷阱： *I knew the question was a trap, so I didn't answer it.* 我知道那个问题是个圈套，所以没有回答。

trap[2] /træp/ ***verb*** 动词 (**traps, trapping, trapped** /træpt/)
1 to keep somebody in a place that they cannot escape from 使陷入困境；困住： *They were trapped in the burning building.* 他们被困在燃烧着的大楼里。
2 to catch or trick somebody or something 捕捉；使上当： *Police are hoping this new evidence could help trap the killer.* 警方希望这一新证据可以助他们抓住杀人凶手。

trash /træʃ/ *American English for* RUBBISH 美式英语，即 rubbish

trash can /'træʃ kæn/ *American English for* DUSTBIN, LITTER BIN 美式英语，即 dustbin 和 litter bin

travel 🔑 /'trævl/ ***verb*** 动词 (*British* 英式英语 **travels, travelling, travelled** /'trævld/) (*American* 美式英语 **traveling, traveled**)
1 to go from one place to another 旅行；出行： *I would like to travel round the world.* 我想环游世界。 ◇ *I travel to school by bus.* 我坐公共汽车上学。
2 to make a journey of a particular distance 行驶，走过（一定距离）： *She travelled 800 km in one day.* 她一天走了 800 公里的路。

▶ **travel** *noun* 名词 (*no plural* 不用复数形式)：*My hobbies are music and travel.* 我的爱好是音乐和旅游。

> 🔎 **WHICH WORD?** 词语辨析
>
> **Journey, trip** or **travel?** 用 journey、trip 还是 travel?
>
> You say **journey** to talk about going from one particular place to another. A journey can be long or short. 从某个地方到另一地方用 journey。journey 可以指长途或短途的旅程：*the journey across Canada* 横跨加拿大之旅 ◇ *the journey to work* 上班的路程
>
> You often use **trip** when you are thinking about the whole visit, including your stay in a place. * trip 常用于表示整个旅程，包括在某地的逗留：*We're just back from a trip to Japan. We had a wonderful time.* 我们刚从日本旅行回来，玩得很开心。A trip can be short. * trip 可以是短途：*a school trip* 学校旅行 ◇ *a shopping trip* 逛商店
>
> You say **travel** to talk about the general activity of moving from place to place. * travel 泛指从一地到另一地的活动：*Foreign travel is very popular these days.* 如今出国旅行非常盛行。**Travel** has no plural, so you cannot say 'go on a travel'. You **go on a journey** or **a trip**. * travel 没有复数形式，所以不说 go on a travel，要说 go on a journey 或 go on a trip。

travel agency /'trævl eɪdʒənsi/ *noun* 名词 (*plural* 复数形式 **travel agencies**)
a company that plans holidays and journeys for people 旅行社

travel agent /'trævl eɪdʒənt/ *noun* 名词
a person who works in a TRAVEL AGENCY 旅行代办人；旅游代理商

traveller (*British* 英式英语) (*American* 美式英语 **traveler**) /'trævələ(r)/ *noun* 名词
a person who is travelling 旅行者；旅游者；旅客

traveller's cheque (*British* 英式英语) (*American* 美式英语 **traveler's check**) /'trævələz tʃek/ *noun* 名词
a special cheque that you can use when you go to other countries 旅行支票

trawler /'trɔːlə(r)/ *noun* 名词
a large fishing boat 拖网渔船

tray /treɪ/ *noun* 名词
a flat object that you use for carrying food or drinks（放食物或饮料的）托盘，盘

tray 托盘

treacle /'triːkl/ *noun* 名词 (*no plural* 不用复数形式)
a thick, dark, sticky liquid that is made from sugar 糖浆

tread /tred/ *verb* 动词 (**treads, treading, trod** /trɒd/, **has trodden** /'trɒdn/)
to put your foot down while you are walking 踩；踏：*He **trod** on my foot.* 他踩了我的脚。

treason /'triːzn/ *noun* 名词 (*no plural* 不用复数形式)
the crime of harming your country by helping its enemies 叛国罪

treasure /'treʒə(r)/ *noun* 名词 (*no plural* 不用复数形式)
a collection of gold, silver, jewellery or other things that are worth a lot of money 金银财宝；宝藏：*They were searching for **buried treasure**.* 他们在寻找埋藏的宝物。

treasurer /'treʒərə(r)/ *noun* 名词
a person who looks after the money of a club or an organization（社团或组织的）司库，出纳，会计，财务主管

treat¹ ⭕ /triːt/ *verb* 动词 (**treats, treating, treated**)
1 to behave in a certain way towards somebody or something（以…方式）对待：*How does your boss treat you?* 你的老板待你如何? ◇ ***Treat** these glasses **with** care.* 这些玻璃杯要轻拿轻放。
2 to think about something in a certain way 看待；把…看作：*They **treated** my idea **as** a joke.* 他们把我的想法当做笑话。
3 to try to make a sick person well again 治疗；医治：*Several people are being **treated for** burns.* 有几个人因烧伤而在接受治疗。
4 to give yourself or another person something special or enjoyable 请（客）；款待：*I **treated** the children **to** an ice cream.* 我请孩子们吃了冰激凌。

A B C D E F G H I J K L M N O P Q R S T U V W X Y Z

A B C D E F G H I J K L M N O P Q R S **T** U V W X Y Z

treat² /triːt/ *noun* 名词
something special or enjoyable that makes somebody happy 乐事；款待： *My parents took me to the theatre as a treat for my birthday.* 我父母带我去看戏来庆祝我的生日。

treatment 0ᴖ /'triːtmənt/ *noun* 名词
1 (*plural* 复数形式 **treatments**) the things that a doctor does to try to make a sick person well again 治疗；疗法： *a new treatment for cancer* 癌症的新疗法
2 (*no plural* 不用复数形式) the way that you behave towards somebody or something 对待： *Their treatment of the animals was very cruel.* 他们对待动物的手法非常残忍。

treaty /'triːti/ *noun* 名词 (*plural* 复数形式 **treaties**)
a written agreement between countries（国家之间的）协定，条约： *The two countries signed a peace treaty.* 两国签署了和平协定。

tree 0ᴖ /triː/ *noun* 名词
a big plant that can live for a long time. Trees have a central part (called a **trunk**) and many smaller parts (called **branches**). 树；树木： *an oak tree* 橡树 ◇ *Apples grow on trees.* 苹果长在树上。

🔎 WORD BUILDING 词汇扩充
There are many different types of **tree**. Here are some of them: **fir**, **oak**, **palm**, **pine**. Do you know any others? * tree 的种类很多，如：fir（冷杉）、oak（橡树）、palm（棕榈树）、pine（松树）。你还知道别的吗？

tremble /'trembl/ *verb* 动词 (**trembles**, **trembling**, **trembled** /'trembld/)
to shake, for example because you are cold, afraid or ill（因寒冷、恐惧或生病）颤抖，哆嗦： *She was trembling with fear.* 她吓得直发抖。

tremendous /trə'mendəs/ *adjective* 形容词
1 very big or very great 极大的；巨大的： *The new trains travel at a tremendous speed.* 新列车以极快的速度行驶。
2 very good 极好的；精彩的： *The match was tremendous.* 比赛精彩极了。
▸ **tremendously** /trə'mendəsli/ *adverb* 副词： *The film was tremendously exciting.* 这部电影非常刺激。

trench /trentʃ/ *noun* 名词 (*plural* 复数形式 **trenches**)
a long narrow hole that is dug in the ground, for example to put pipes or wires in 沟；渠

trend /trend/ *noun* 名词
a change to something different 趋势；趋向；动态： *new trends in science* 科学的新趋势

trendy /'trendi/ *adjective* 形容词 (**trendier**, **trendiest**) (*informal* 非正式式)
fashionable 时髦的；流行的： *a trendy new bar* 时髦的新酒吧

trespass /'trespəs/ *verb* 动词 (**trespasses**, **trespassing**, **trespassed** /'trespəst/)
to go on somebody's land without asking them if you can 擅自进入；擅闯
▸ **trespasser** /'trespəsə(r)/ *noun* 名词： *A sign on the gate said 'No Trespassers'.* 大门上的告示写着"严禁擅进"。

trial 0ᴖ /'traɪəl/ *noun* 名词
1 the process in a court of law when people (called the **judge** and the **jury**) can decide if a person has done something wrong and what the punishment will be 审判；审讯；审理： *He was on trial for murder.* 他因涉嫌谋杀而受审。
2 the process of testing something to see if it is good or bad 试验；试用： *They are conducting trials of a new drug.* 他们在对一种新药进行试验。

triangle 0ᴖ /'traɪæŋgl/ *noun* 名词
a shape with three straight sides 三角形 ◐ Look at the picture at **shape¹**. 见 **shape¹** 的插图。
▸ **triangular** /traɪ'æŋgjələ(r)/ *adjective* 形容词： *triangular shapes* 三角形状

tribe /traɪb/ *noun* 名词
a small group of people who have the same language and customs 部落： *the Zulu tribes of Africa* 非洲祖鲁人的部落
▸ **tribal** /'traɪbl/ *adjective* 形容词： *tribal dances* 部族的舞蹈

tribute /'trɪbjuːt/ *noun* 名词
something that you do, say or give to show that you respect or admire somebody 致敬；致意；颂辞： *They built a statue in London as a tribute to Nelson Mandela.* 他们在伦敦竖起一座雕像，向纳尔逊•曼德拉致敬。

trick¹ 0ᴖ /trɪk/ *noun* 名词
1 a clever plan that makes somebody believe something that is not true 花招；诡计；骗局： *They used a trick to get past the guards.* 他们用诡计骗过了门卫。
2 something clever that you have learned to do 戏法；把戏： *Do you know any card tricks?* 你会纸牌戏法吗？

play a trick on somebody to do something that makes somebody look silly, in order to make other people laugh 捉弄某人；戏弄某人: *The children played a trick on their teacher by hiding her books.* 孩子们捉弄老师，把她的书藏了起来。

trick² 0ᴍ /trɪk/ *verb* 动词 (tricks, tricking, tricked /trɪkt/)
to do something that is not honest to get what you want from somebody 欺骗；欺诈: *He **tricked** the old lady **into** giving him all her money.* 他骗走了那个老太太所有的钱。

trickle /ˈtrɪkl/ *verb* 动词 (trickles, trickling, trickled /ˈtrɪkld/)
to move slowly like a thin line of water （液体）慢慢流淌: *Tears trickled down her cheeks.* 泪水顺着她的脸颊流下来了。
▶ **trickle** *noun* 名词: *a trickle of blood* 一股血的细流

tricky /ˈtrɪki/ *adjective* 形容词 (trickier, trickiest)
difficult; hard to do 难办的；棘手的: *a tricky question* 难以回答的问题

tricycle 三轮车

tricycle /ˈtraɪsɪkl/ *noun* 名词
a type of bicycle with three wheels 三轮车

tried *form of* TRY * try 的不同形式

tries
1 *form of* TRY * try 的不同形式
2 *plural of* TRY * try 的复数形式

trigger /ˈtrɪɡə(r)/ *noun* 名词
the part of a gun that you pull with your finger to fire it （枪的）扳机

trim /trɪm/ *verb* 动词 (trims, trimming, trimmed /trɪmd/)
to cut a small amount off something to make it tidy 修剪；修整: *He trimmed my hair.* 他给我修剪了头发。

▶ **trim** *noun* 名词: *My hair needs a trim.* 我得理发了。

trimester /traɪˈmestə(r)/ *noun* 名词
American English for TERM (2) 美式英语，即 term 第 2 义

trip¹ 0ᴍ /trɪp/ *noun* 名词
a journey to a place and back again 旅行；旅游: *We **went on a trip** to the mountains.* 我们去了山区旅行。
↪ Look at the note at **travel**. 见 travel 条的注释。

trip² 0ᴍ /trɪp/ *verb* 动词 (trips, tripping, tripped /trɪpt/)
to hit your foot against something so that you fall or nearly fall 绊；绊倒: *She **tripped over** the step.* 她在台阶上绊倒了。

trip somebody up to make somebody fall or nearly fall 将某人绊倒: *Gary put out his foot and tripped me up.* 加里伸出脚把我绊倒。

triple /ˈtrɪpl/ *adjective* 形容词
with three parts, happening three times or containing three times as much as usual 三部分的；三次的；三倍的: *a triple murder (= in which three people were killed)* 三人死亡的谋杀案
▶ **triple** *verb* 动词 (triples, tripling, tripled /ˈtrɪpld/) to become or to make something three times bigger （使）增至三倍: *Sales have tripled this year.* 今年的销售额增加了两倍。

triumph /ˈtraɪʌmf/ *noun* 名词
great success 巨大成功；伟大胜利: *The race ended **in triumph** for the German team.* 比赛随着德国队大胜结束了。

triumphant /traɪˈʌmfənt/ *adjective* 形容词
very happy because you have won or succeeded at something 欢欣鼓舞的；凯歌高奏的
▶ **triumphantly** /traɪˈʌmfəntli/ *adverb* 副词: *The winning team ran triumphantly round the stadium.* 获胜队欣喜雀跃地在体育场内绕场奔跑。

trivial /ˈtrɪviəl/ *adjective* 形容词
not important 不重要的；琐碎的；微不足道的: *She gets angry about trivial things.* 她常为鸡毛蒜皮的事生气。

trod, trodden *forms of* TREAD * tread 的不同形式

trolley /ˈtrɒli/ *noun* 名词 (plural 复数形式 trolleys) (British 英式英语) (American 美式英语 cart)
a thing on wheels that you use for

A
B
C
D
E
F
G
H
I
J
K
L
M
N
O
P
Q
R
S
T
U
V
W
X
Y
Z

carrying things 手推车: *a supermarket trolley* 超市手推车

trolleys 手推车

supermarket trolley
超市手推车

luggage trolley
行李手推车

trombone /trɒmˈbəʊn/ *noun* 名词
a large musical instrument. You play it by blowing and moving a long tube up and down. 长号

trombone 长号

troops /truːps/ *noun* 名词 (*plural* 用复数形式)
soldiers 士兵；军队；部队

trophy /ˈtrəʊfi/ *noun* 名词 (*plural* 复数形式 **trophies**)
a thing, for example a silver cup, that you get when you win a competition（竞赛的）奖杯，奖座: *a tennis trophy* 网球赛奖杯

the tropics /ðə ˈtrɒpɪks/ *noun* 名词 (*plural* 用复数形式)
the part of the world where it is very hot and wet 热带；热带地区

▶ **tropical** /ˈtrɒpɪkl/ *adjective* 形容词: *tropical fruit* 热带水果

trot /trɒt/ *verb* 动词 (**trots**, **trotting**, **trotted**)
to run with short quick steps 快步；疾走；小跑: *The horse trotted along the road.* 马沿路小跑。

trouble¹ 0─ /ˈtrʌbl/ *noun* 名词
1 (*plural* 复数形式 **troubles**) difficulty, problems or worry 困难；问题；烦恼: *We had a lot of **trouble** finding the book you wanted.* 我们费尽周折才找到你要的书。
2 (*no plural* 不用复数形式) extra work 额外的工作；麻烦: *'Thanks for your help!' 'Oh, it was no trouble.'* "谢谢你的帮助！""噢，没什么。"
3 (*plural* 复数形式 **troubles**) a situation in which people are fighting or arguing 纷争；骚乱；闹事: *There was trouble after the football match last Saturday.* 上星期六足球比赛后发生了骚乱。
4 (*no plural* 不用复数形式) pain or illness 疼痛；疾病: *He's got heart trouble.* 他有心脏病。

be in trouble to have problems, for example because you have done something wrong 有麻烦: *I'll be in trouble if I'm late home again.* 我要是再晚回家就麻烦了。
get into trouble to get into a situation which is dangerous or in which you may be punished 惹上麻烦: *He got into trouble with the police.* 他闯了祸落到警方手里了。
go to a lot of trouble to do extra work 付出额外的努力；不辞劳苦: *They went to a lot of trouble to help me.* 他们不辞劳苦地帮助我。

trouble² /ˈtrʌbl/ *verb* 动词 (**troubles**, **troubling**, **troubled** /ˈtrʌbld/)
1 to worry somebody 使忧虑；使烦恼: *I was troubled by the news.* 我听到那条消息后很烦恼。
2 (*formal* 正式) a word that you use when you need to disturb somebody by asking them something（用于请求）打扰，麻烦 ⊃ SAME MEANING **bother** 同义词为 bother: *I'm sorry to trouble you, but you're sitting in my seat.* 很抱歉，打扰一下，你坐的是我的座位。

troublemaker /ˈtrʌblmeɪkə(r)/ *noun* 名词
a person who deliberately causes trouble 制造麻烦的人；捣乱者

trough /trɒf/ *noun* 名词
a long open container that holds food or water for animals（供动物吃饲料或饮水的）槽

trousers ⊶ /'traʊzəz/ (*British* 英式英语) (*American* 美式英语 **pants**) *noun* 名词 (*plural* 用复数形式)
a piece of clothing for your legs and the lower part of your body 裤子：*Your trousers are on the chair.* 你的裤子在椅子上。 ⊃ Look at Picture Dictionary page **P5**. 见彩页 P5。

> 🔍 GRAMMAR 语法说明
> Be careful! You cannot say 'a trousers'. You can say **a pair of trousers**. 注意：不说 a trousers，说 a pair of trousers：*I bought a new pair of trousers.* 我买了一条新裤子。 You can also say '*I bought some new trousers*'. 也说 I bought some new trousers。

trout /traʊt/ *noun* 名词 (*plural* 复数形式 **trout**)
a fish that lives in rivers and that you can eat 鳟鱼

truant /'truːənt/ *noun* 名词
a child who stays away from school when they should be there 旷课的小学生
play truant to stay away from school when you should be there 旷课；逃学

truce /truːs/ *noun* 名词
an agreement to stop fighting for a short time 休战协定

truck ⊶ /trʌk/ *noun* 名词 (*American* 美式英语) (*British* 英式英语 **lorry**)
a big vehicle for carrying heavy things 卡车；货车：*a truck driver* 卡车司机

true ⊶ /truː/ *adjective* 形容词
1 right or correct 对的；正确的：*Is it true that you are leaving?* 你要走是真的吗？
◇ *Glasgow is in England: true or false?* 格拉斯哥在英格兰，对还是错？ ⊃ OPPOSITE **untrue, false** 反义词为 untrue 和 false
2 real 真正的；真实的：*A true friend will always help you.* 真正的朋友会随时相助。
◇ *It's a true story* (= it really happened). 这是真事。 ⊃ The noun is **truth**. 名词为 truth。
come true to happen in the way that you hoped or imagined 实现；成为现实：*Her dream came true.* 她梦想成真了。

truly /'truːli/ *adverb* 副词
really 真正；确实：*I'm truly sorry.* 我真的很抱歉。
Yours truly (*American* 美式英语) (*formal* 正式) words that you can use at the end of a formal letter before you write your name（正式信函末署名前的套语）谨启

trumpet 小号

trumpet /'trʌmpɪt/ *noun* 名词
a musical instrument that is made of metal and that you blow 小号；喇叭

truncheon /'trʌntʃən/ *noun* 名词 (*British* 英式英语)
a short thick stick that a police officer carries as a weapon 警棍

trunk /trʌŋk/ *noun* 名词
1 the thick part of a tree, that grows up from the ground 树干
2 *American English for* BOOT (2) 美式英语，即 boot 第 2 义
3 the long nose of an ELEPHANT (= a very large grey animal) 象鼻
4 trunks (*plural* 用复数形式) = SWIMMING TRUNKS
5 a big strong box for carrying things when you travel 大行李箱
⊃ Look at the picture on the next page. 见下页的插图。

trust¹ ⊶ /trʌst/ *noun* 名词 (*no plural* 不用复数形式)
the belief that somebody is honest and good and will not hurt you in any way 信任；信赖

trust² ⊶ /trʌst/ *verb* 动词 (**trusts, trusting, trusted**)
to believe that somebody is honest and good and will not hurt you in any way 信任；信赖：*I just don't trust him.* 我就是不信任他。 ◇ *You can trust Penny to do the job well.* 你可以放心，彭尼能做好这份工作。

A B C D E F G H I J K L M N O P Q R S T U V W X Y Z

trustworthy /ˈtrʌstwɜːði/ *adjective* 形容词
A **trustworthy** person is somebody that you can trust. 值得信赖的；可靠的

truth ⁒ /truːθ/ *noun* 名词 (*no plural* 不用复数形式)
being true; what is true 真实；真相；实情：*There is **no truth in** these rumours.* 这些谣言完全失实。◇ *We need to find out the **truth about** what happened.* 我们需要查找事情的真相。◇ *Are you **telling me the truth**?* 你跟我说的是实话吗？

truthful /ˈtruːθfl/ *adjective* 形容词
1 true 真实的；确实的：*a truthful answer* 如实的回答
2 A person who is **truthful** tells the truth. (人）讲真话的，诚实的
▶ **truthfully** /ˈtruːθfəli/ *adverb* 副词：*You must answer me truthfully.* 你必须如实回答我的问题。
▶ **truthfulness** /ˈtruːθfəlnəs/ *noun* 名词 (*no plural* 不用复数形式)：*I have doubts about the truthfulness of her story.* 我对她所讲的事是否真实感到怀疑。

trunks 树干；象鼻；大箱子

— trunk 树干

— trunk 象鼻

trunk 大行李箱

try ⁒ /traɪ/ *verb* 动词 (tries, trying, tried /traɪd/, has tried)
1 to make an effort to do something 试图；设法；努力；想要：*I **tried to** remember her name but I couldn't.* 我努力想她的名字，却想不起来。◇ *I'm not sure if I can help you, but I'll try.* 我说不准是否能帮你，但我试试看吧。
2 to use or do something to find out if you like it 尝试；试用；试做：*Have you ever tried Japanese food?* 你尝过日本菜吗？
3 to ask somebody questions in a court of law to decide if they have done something wrong 审讯；审判：*He was **tried for** murder.* 他因涉嫌谋杀而受审。
try and do something (*informal* 非正式) to try to do something 设法做；尽力做：*I'll try and come early tomorrow.* 我明天尽可能早点来。
try something on to put on a piece of clothing to see if you like it and if it is big enough 试穿（衣服）：*I tried the jeans on but they were too small.* 我试了一下牛仔裤，可是太小了。
▶ **try** *noun* 名词 (*plural* 复数形式 tries)：*I can't open this door – will you **have a try**?* 我打不开这扇门，你来试一下好吗？

T-shirt /ˈtiː ʃɜːt/ *noun* 名词
a kind of shirt with short sleeves and no COLLAR (= the folded part round the neck) * T 恤衫；短袖汗衫

tsunami /tsuːˈnɑːmi/ *noun* 名词 (*plural* 复数形式 tsunamis)
a very large wave in the sea, usually caused by the sudden strong shaking of the ground (called an earthquake) 海啸

tub /tʌb/ *noun* 名词
a round container 盆；桶：*a tub of ice cream* 一桶冰激凌

tube ⁒ /tjuːb/ *noun* 名词
1 (*plural* 复数形式 tubes) a long thin pipe for liquid or gas（输送液体或气体的）管，管子
2 (*plural* 复数形式 tubes) a long thin soft container with a hole and a lid at one end 软管；管状物：*a tube of toothpaste* 一管牙膏 ⊃ Look at the picture at **container**. 见 container 的插图。
3 (*no plural* 不用复数形式) (*British* 英式英语) (*informal* 非正式) the underground railway in London（伦敦）地铁：*Shall we go by bus or by tube?* 我们坐公共汽车还是坐地铁？

tuck /tʌk/ *verb* 动词 (tucks, tucking, tucked /tʌkt/)
to put or push the edges of something inside or under something else 塞进；

披进：*He **tucked** his shirt **into** his trousers.*
他把衬衫的下摆塞进裤子里了。
**tuck somebody in, tuck somebody
up** to make somebody feel comfortable
in bed by pulling the covers around them
给某人掖好被子：*I'll come up later and
tuck you in.* 我等会儿来给你掖好被子。

Tuesday ⊶ /'tjuːzdeɪ/ *noun* 名词
the day of the week after Monday and
before Wednesday 星期二 ⊃ Look at the
note at **day**. 见 day 条的注释。

tuft /tʌft/ *noun* 名词
a small amount of something such as hair
or grass growing together 一绺，一丛
（毛发、草等）

tug¹ /tʌg/ *verb* 动词 (tugs, tugging, tugged
/tʌgd/)
to pull something hard and quickly（猛地
用力）拉，拖，拽：*I tugged at the rope
and it broke.* 我猛地一拉，绳子就断了。

tug² /tʌg/ *noun* 名词
1 a sudden hard pull 猛拉；猛拽：*The
little girl gave my hand a tug.* 小女孩猛地
拉了一下我的手。
2 (*also* 亦作 **tugboat** /'tʌgbəʊt/) a small
strong boat that pulls big ships 拖船

tuition /tju'ɪʃn/ *noun* 名词 (*no plural*
不用复数形式)
teaching, especially to a small group
（尤指以小组形式）教学，讲授：*A lot of
students have extra tuition before their
exams.* 很多学生在考试前都上补习班。

tulip 郁金香

tulip /'tjuːlɪp/ *noun* 名词
a brightly coloured flower that comes in
spring and is shaped like a cup 郁金香

tumble /'tʌmbl/ *verb* 动词 (tumbles,
tumbling, tumbled /'tʌmbld/)
to fall suddenly（突然）跌倒，摔倒，
滚落：*He tumbled down the steps.* 他从
台阶上摔了下来。

tummy /'tʌmi/ *noun* 名词 (*plural* 复数
形式 tummies) (*informal* 非正式)
the part of your body between your chest
and your legs 肚子；腹部 ⊃ SAME MEANING
stomach 同义词为 stomach

tuna /'tjuːnə/ *noun* 名词 (*plural* 复数形式
tuna)
a large fish that lives in the sea and that
you can eat 金枪鱼；吞拿鱼

tune¹ ⊶ /tjuːn/ *noun* 名词
a group of musical notes that make a
nice sound when you play or sing them
together 曲调；曲子：*I know the tune but
I don't know the words.* 我知道这曲调，
但不晓得歌词。

tune² /tjuːn/ *verb* 动词 (tunes, tuning,
tuned /tjuːnd/)
to make small changes to a musical
instrument so that it makes the right
sounds（给乐器）调音，校音：*She
tuned her guitar.* 她给吉他调了弦。

tunnel 隧道

tunnel ⊶ /'tʌnl/ *noun* 名词
a long hole under the ground or sea for
a road or railway 地下通道；地道；隧道

turban /'tɜːbən/ *noun* 名词
a covering that some men wear on their
heads. You make a **turban** by folding a
long piece of material round and round.
（某些男人用的）包头巾

turkey /'tɜːki/ *noun* 名词 (*plural* 复数形式
turkeys)
a big bird that people keep on farms and
that you can eat. People eat **turkeys**
especially at Christmas in Britain, and at
Thanksgiving in the US. 火鸡 ⊃ Look at
Picture Dictionary page **P2**. 见彩页 P2。

turn¹ ⊶ /tɜːn/ *verb* 动词 (turns, turning,
turned /tɜːnd/)
1 to move round, or to move something
round（使）转动，旋转：*The wheels are
turning.* 轮子在转动。◇ *Turn the key.* 转动
钥匙。◇ *She turned round and walked
towards the door.* 她转身朝门口走去。
2 to move in a different direction 转向；
转弯：*Turn left at the traffic lights.*
在红绿灯处向左转。

A B C D E F G H I J K L M N O P Q R S **T** U V W X Y Z

A B C D E F G H I J K L M N O P Q R S **T** U V W X Y Z

3 to become different 变成；变得： *The weather has turned cold.* 天气已经转冷。

4 to make somebody or something change 使改变： *The sun turned her hair blond.* 太阳把她的头发晒成金黄色。

5 to find a certain page in a book 翻，翻动（书页）： *Turn to page 97.* 翻到第 97 页。

turn something down
1 to say no to what somebody wants to do or to give you 拒绝；回绝： *They offered me the job but I turned it down.* 他们给我那份工作，可我没接受。

2 to make something produce less sound or heat by moving a switch 调低（音量或暖气）： *I'm too hot – can you turn the heating down?* 我太热了，你可以把暖气调低点吗？

turn into something to become different; to change somebody or something into something different（使）变成： *Water turns into ice when it gets very cold.* 水在非常冷的时候会结成冰。

turn something off to move the handle or switch that controls something, so that it stops 关掉（开关）： *Turn the tap off.* 把水龙头关上。 ◊ *She turned off the television.* 她关掉了电视。

turn something on to move the handle or switch that controls something, so that it starts 打开（开关）： *Could you turn the light on?* 你开灯好吗？

turn out to be something in the end 结果是： *It has turned out to be a lovely day.* 结果天气非常好。

turn something out to switch off a light, etc. 关掉（灯等）： *Can you turn the lights out before you leave?* 你走之前能把那些灯关掉吗？

turn over to move so that the other side is on top 翻身；翻转： *She turned over and went back to sleep.* 她翻了个身，又睡着了。

turn something over to move something so that the other side is on top 使翻转： *If you turn over the page you'll find the answers on the other side.* 把这一页翻过来，答案就在后面。

turn up (used about a person) to arrive（人）来到，到达： *Has David turned up yet?* 戴维来了没有？

turn something up to make something produce more sound or heat by moving a switch 开大，调高（音量或暖气）： *Turn up the TV – I can't hear it properly.* 把电视声音开大些，我听不清楚。

turn² 0ー /tɜːn/ *noun* 名词
1 the action of turning something round 转动；旋转： *Give the screw a few turns.* 把螺丝拧几下。

2 a change of direction 转向；转弯： *Take a left turn at the end of this road.* 在这条路的尽头向左拐。

3 the time when you can or should do something（依次轮到的）机会： *It's your turn to do the washing-up!* 轮到你洗碗了！
in turn one after the other 依次；轮流；逐个： *I spoke to each of the students in turn.* 我依次和每个学生谈话。

take turns at something, take it in turns to do something to do something one after the other 依次，轮流（做某事）： *You can't both use the computer at the same time. Why don't you take it in turns?* 你们俩不可能同时用这台电脑，为什么不轮流用呢？

turning /'tɜːnɪŋ/ (*British* 英式英语) *noun* 名词
a place where one road joins another road 拐弯处；岔道口： *Take the first turning on the right.* 在第一个路口向右转。

turnip /'tɜːnɪp/ *noun* 名词
a round white vegetable that grows under the ground 芜菁；蔓菁

turquoise /'tɜːkwɔɪz/ *adjective* 形容词
with a bright colour between blue and green 青绿色的

turtle 海龟

turtle /'tɜːtl/ *noun* 名词
1 an animal that lives in the sea and has a hard shell on its back 海龟
2 (*informal* 非正式) *American English for* TORTOISE 美式英语，即 tortoise

tusk /tʌsk/ *noun* 名词
a long pointed tooth that grows beside the mouth of an ELEPHANT (= a very big grey animal that lives in Africa and Asia), etc.（象等的）长牙 ➲ Look at the picture at **elephant**. 见 elephant 的插图。

tutor /'tjuːtə(r)/ *noun* 名词
a teacher who teaches one person or a small group 家庭教师；私人教师

TV 0→ /,tiː 'viː/ *abbreviation* 缩略式 short for TELEVISION * television 的缩略式：*All rooms have a bathroom and colour TV.* 所有房间都有浴室和彩电。

tweezers /'twiːzəz/ *noun* 名词 (*plural* 用复数形式)
a small tool made of two pieces of metal joined at one end. You use **tweezers** for holding or pulling out very small things. 镊子；小夹钳：*She pulled the splinter out of her finger with a pair of tweezers.* 她用镊子把手指上的刺拔了出来。

twelfth 0→ /twelfθ/ *adjective, adverb, pronoun* 形容词，副词，代词
12th 第十二

twelve 0→ /twelv/ *number* 数词
12 十二

twentieth 0→ /'twentiəθ/ *adjective, adverb, pronoun* 形容词，副词，代词
20th 第二十

twenty 0→ /'twenti/ *number* 数词
1 20 二十
2 the twenties (*plural* 用复数形式) the numbers, years or temperature between 20 and 29 二十几；二十年代
in your twenties between the ages of 20 and 29 * 20 多岁

twice 0→ /twaɪs/ *adverb* 副词
two times 两次；两倍：*I have been to Japan twice.* 我去过两次日本。◇ *He ate twice as much as I did.* 他吃的是我的两倍。

twig /twɪg/ *noun* 名词
a small thin branch of a tree 细枝；小树枝

twilight /'twaɪlaɪt/ *noun* 名词 (*no plural* 不用复数形式)
the time after the sun has gone down and before it gets completely dark 暮色；黄昏 ⊃ Look at **dusk**. 见 dusk.

twin /twɪn/ *noun* 名词
1 one of two people who have the same mother and were born at the same time 双胞胎之一；孪生儿之一：*David and John are twins.* 戴维和约翰是双胞胎。◇ *I have a twin sister.* 我有个孪生妹妹。
2 one of two things that are the same 两个相同事物之一：*a room with twin beds* 有两张单人床的房间

twinkle /'twɪŋkl/ *verb* 动词 (twinkles, twinkling, twinkled /'twɪŋkld/)
to shine with a small bright light that comes and goes 闪烁；闪耀：*Stars twinkled in the night sky.* 星星在夜空中闪烁。

twist 0→ /twɪst/ *verb* 动词 (twists, twisting, twisted)
1 to change the shape of something by turning it in different directions; to turn in many directions （使）扭曲，弯曲：*She twisted the metal into strange shapes.* 她把那金属扭曲成奇形怪状。◇ *The path twists and turns through the forest.* 小路弯弯曲曲穿过森林。
2 to turn something with your hand （用手）转动，旋转：*Twist the lid off the jar.* 把罐子的盖拧开。
3 to turn something round another object many times 捻；绞；缠绕：*They twisted the sheets into a rope and escaped through the window.* 他们把床单绞成绳子，然后从窗口逃走了。
4 to hurt part of your body by suddenly turning it in a way that is not natural 扭伤；崴伤：*She fell and twisted her ankle.* 她摔了一跤，扭伤了脚踝。
▶ **twist** *noun* 名词：*the twists and turns of the river* 这条河的蜿蜒曲折 ◇ *She gave the handle a hard twist.* 她用力转动了一下把手。

twitch /twɪtʃ/ *verb* 动词 (twitches, twitching, twitched /twɪtʃt/)
to make a sudden quick movement with a part of your body 抽搐；抽动：*Rabbits twitch their noses.* 兔子常抽动鼻子。

two 0→ /tuː/ *number* 数词
2 二
in two into two pieces 一分为二；分成两半：*The cup fell on the floor and broke in two.* 杯子掉到地上摔成了两半。

tying *form of* TIE¹ * tie¹ 的不同形式

type¹ 0→ /taɪp/ *noun* 名词
1 (*plural* 复数形式 types) a group of things that are the same in some way 类型；种类 ⊃ SAME MEANING **kind, sort** 同义词为 kind 和 sort：*An almond is a type of nut.* 杏仁是一种坚果。◇ *What type of music do you like?* 你喜欢什么类型的音乐？
2 (*no plural* 不用复数形式) the letters that a machine makes on paper （机器印出的）文字，字体，字型：*The type was so small I couldn't read it.* 这种印刷文字太小了，我看不清楚。

type² 0→ /taɪp/ *verb* 动词 (types, typing, typed /taɪpt/)
to write something using a machine that has keys, such as a computer or a TYPEWRITER （用电脑或打字机）打字：

A
B
C
D
E
F
G
H
I
J
K
L
M
N
O
P
Q
R
S
T
U
V
W
X
Y
Z

Her secretary types all her letters. 她所有的信都是她的秘书打的。◇ *Can you type?* 你会打字吗?

typewriter /'taɪpraɪtə(r)/ *noun* 名词
a machine with keys that you use for writing 打字机: *an electric typewriter* 电动打字机

typhoon /taɪ'fuːn/ *noun* 名词
a violent storm with strong winds in a hot country 台风 ⊃ Look at the note at **storm**[1]. 见 storm[1] 条的注释。

typical ০━ /'tɪpɪkl/ *adjective* 形容词
Something that is **typical** is a good example of its kind. 典型的; 有代表性的: *We had a typical English breakfast – bacon, eggs, toast and tea.* 我们吃了一顿典型的英式早餐, 有熏猪肉、鸡蛋、吐司和茶。

▸ **typically** /'tɪpɪkli/ *adverb* 副词: *She is typically British.* 她是典型的英国人。

typist /'taɪpɪst/ *noun* 名词
a person who works in an office typing letters and documents 打字员

tyrant /'taɪrənt/ *noun* 名词
a person with a lot of power who uses it in a cruel way 暴君; 暴虐的统治者
▸ **tyrannical** /tɪ'rænɪkl/ *adjective* 形容词: *a tyrannical ruler* 残暴的统治者

tyre ০━ (*British* 英式英语) (*American* 美式英语 tire) /'taɪə(r)/ *noun* 名词
a circle of rubber around the outside of a wheel, for example on a car or bicycle 轮胎: *I think we've got a flat tyre* (= a tyre with not enough air inside). 我想我们的车胎瘪了。 ⊃ Look at the picture at **bicycle**. 见 bicycle 的插图。

U u

U, u /juː/ *noun* 名词 (*plural* 复数形式 U's, u's /juːz/)
the twenty-first letter of the English alphabet 英语字母表的第 21 个字母: *'Ugly' begins with a 'U'.* * ugly 一词以字母 u 开头。

UFO /ˌjuː ef ˈəʊ/ *abbreviation* 缩略式 (*plural* 复数形式 UFOs)
a strange object that some people think they have seen in the sky and that may come from another planet. UFO is short for 'unidentified flying object'. 不明飞行物，飞碟，幽浮（UFO 是 unidentified flying object 的缩略式）

ugly 🔑 /ˈʌgli/ *adjective* 形容词 (uglier, ugliest)
not pleasant to look at 丑陋的；难看的: *an ugly face* 丑陋的脸 ◇ *The house was really ugly.* 那所房子难看极了。 ⊃ OPPOSITE **beautiful** 反义词为 beautiful

> 🔎 SPEAKING 表达方式说明
> It is not polite to say somebody is **ugly**. It is better to say **unattractive**. 用 ugly 形容人不礼貌，宜说 unattractive。

ulcer /ˈʌlsə(r)/ *noun* 名词
a painful area on your skin or inside your body 溃疡: *a mouth ulcer* 口腔溃疡

ultimate /ˈʌltɪmət/ *adjective* 形容词
happening at the end of a long process 最后的；最终的: *Our ultimate goal is independence.* 我们最终的目标是争取独立。

umbrella 雨伞

ultraviolet /ˌʌltrəˈvaɪələt/ *adjective* 形容词
Ultraviolet light cannot be seen and makes your skin go darker. （光）紫外线的: *You must protect your skin from harmful ultraviolet rays.* 要远离有害的紫外线以保护皮肤。

umbrella /ʌmˈbrelə/ *noun* 名词
a thing that you hold over your head to keep you dry when it rains 伞；雨伞: *It started to rain, so I put my umbrella up.* 开始下雨了，我便撑开了伞。

umpire /ˈʌmpaɪə(r)/ *noun* 名词
a person who watches a game such as TENNIS or CRICKET to make sure the players obey the rules （网球、板球等的）裁判
▶ **umpire** *verb* 动词 (umpires, umpiring, umpired /ˈʌmpaɪəd/): *The match was umpired by an Italian.* 这场比赛由一名意大利人当裁判。 ⊃ Look at **referee**. 见 referee。

the UN /ðə ˌjuː ˈen/ *abbreviation* 缩略式
short for THE UNITED NATIONS * the United Nations 的缩略式

un- /ʌn/ *prefix* 前缀
You can add **un-** to the beginning of some words to give them the opposite meaning, for example （用在某些词前构成反义）: *unhappy* (= not happy) 不高兴的 ◇ *untrue* (= not true) 不真实的 ◇ *undress* (= to take clothes off) 脱衣服

unable 🔑 /ʌnˈeɪbl/ *adjective* 形容词
not able to do something 不能；无法: *John is unable to come to the meeting because he is ill.* 约翰因病不能来开会。 ⊃ The noun is **inability**. 名词为 inability。

unacceptable /ˌʌnəkˈseptəbl/ *adjective* 形容词
If something is **unacceptable**, you cannot accept or allow it. 不能接受（或允许）的: *This behaviour is completely unacceptable.* 这种行为完全不能接受。 ⊃ OPPOSITE **acceptable** 反义词为 acceptable

unanimous /juˈnænɪməs/ *adjective* 形容词
with the agreement of every person （决定等）一致的，一致同意的: *The*

A
B
C
D
E
F
G
H
I
J
K
L
M
N
O
P
Q
R
S
T
U
V
W
X
Y
Z

decision was unanimous. 这项决定获得了一致通过。

unarmed /ˌʌnˈɑːmd/ *adjective* 形容词
not carrying a gun or any weapon 不带武器的；非武装的：*an unarmed police officer* 没有武装的警察 ➋ OPPOSITE **armed** 反义词为 armed

unattractive /ˌʌnəˈtræktɪv/ *adjective* 形容词
not nice to look at 不好看的；不漂亮的 ➋ OPPOSITE **attractive** 反义词为 attractive ➋ Look at the note at **ugly**. 见 ugly 条的注释。

unavoidable /ˌʌnəˈvɔɪdəbl/ *adjective* 形容词
If something is **unavoidable**, you cannot stop it or get away from it. 无法阻止的；不可避免的：*This tragic accident was unavoidable.* 这起悲惨的事故无法避免。

unaware /ˌʌnəˈweə(r)/ *adjective* 形容词
not knowing about or not noticing somebody or something 不知道；未察觉：*I was unaware of the danger.* 我没有意识到有危险。 ➋ OPPOSITE **aware** 反义词为 aware

unbearable /ʌnˈbeərəbl/ *adjective* 形容词
If something is **unbearable**, you cannot accept it because it is so bad. 无法接受的；难以容忍的：*Everyone left the room because the noise was unbearable.* 大家都离开了那个房间，因为噪音教人难以忍受。
▸ **unbearably** /ʌnˈbeərəbli/ *adverb* 副词：*It was unbearably hot.* 天气热得让人受不了。

unbelievable /ˌʌnbɪˈliːvəbl/ *adjective* 形容词
very surprising or difficult to believe 惊人的；难以置信的 ➋ SAME MEANING **incredible** 同义词为 incredible

unborn /ˌʌnˈbɔːn/ *adjective* 形容词
not yet born 未出生的：*an unborn child* 未出生的孩子

uncertain /ʌnˈsɜːtn/ *adjective* 形容词
not sure; not decided 不确定的；拿不准的；未决定的 ➋ SAME MEANING **unsure** 同义词为 unsure：*I'm uncertain about what to do.* 我在犹豫该怎么办。 ◇ *an uncertain future* 渺茫的前景 ➋ OPPOSITE **certain** 反义词为 certain
▸ **uncertainty** /ʌnˈsɜːtnti/ *noun* 名词 (*plural* 复数形式 **uncertainties**)：*This decision should put an end to all the uncertainty.* 这一决定应该会消除所有的不确定性。

uncle ०ᴄ /ˈʌŋkl/ *noun* 名词
the brother of your mother or father, or the husband of your aunt 舅父；叔父；伯父；姑父；姨父：*Uncle Paul* 保罗叔叔

uncomfortable ०ᴄ /ʌnˈkʌmftəbl/ *adjective* 形容词
not pleasant to wear, sit on, lie on, etc. 使人不舒服的；令人不舒适的：*The chair was hard and uncomfortable.* 椅子很硬，坐上去不舒服。 ➋ OPPOSITE **comfortable** 反义词为 comfortable
▸ **uncomfortably** /ʌnˈkʌmftəbli/ *adverb* 副词：*The room was uncomfortably hot.* 房间里热得让人很不舒服。

uncommon /ʌnˈkɒmən/ *adjective* 形容词
not usual 不常有的；罕见的 ➋ SAME MEANING **rare** 同义词为 rare：*This tree is uncommon in Britain.* 这种树在英国很少见。 ➋ OPPOSITE **common** 反义词为 common

unconscious ०ᴄ /ʌnˈkɒnʃəs/ *adjective* 形容词
1 If you are **unconscious**, you are in a kind of sleep and you do not know what is happening. 无知觉的；昏迷的：*She hit her head and was unconscious for three days.* 她撞到头部，昏迷了三天。
2 If you are **unconscious** of something, you do not know about it. 不知道；未察觉：*Mike seemed unconscious that I was watching him.* 迈克好像没察觉我在看他。 ➋ OPPOSITE **conscious** 反义词为 conscious
▸ **unconsciousness** /ʌnˈkɒnʃəsnəs/ *noun* 名词 (*no plural* 不用复数形式)：*She slipped into unconsciousness.* 她陷入了昏迷状态。

uncontrollable /ˌʌnkənˈtrəʊləbl/ *adjective* 形容词
If a feeling is **uncontrollable**, you cannot control or stop it. 无法控制的；抑制不住的：*I suddenly got an uncontrollable urge to sneeze.* 我突然忍不住要打喷嚏。
▸ **uncontrollably** /ˌʌnkənˈtrəʊləbli/ *adverb* 副词：*He started laughing uncontrollably.* 他忍不住笑了起来。

uncountable /ʌnˈkaʊntəbl/ *adjective* 形容词
(*grammar* 语法) **Uncountable** nouns are ones that have no plural and cannot be used with 'a' or 'an', for example *advice* or *furniture*. （名词）不可数的 ➋ OPPOSITE **countable** 反义词为 countable

uncover /ʌnˈkʌvə(r)/ *verb* 动词 (**uncovers**, uncovering, uncovered /ʌnˈkʌvəd/)
1 to take something from on top of

another thing 揭开…的盖子: *Uncover the pan and cook the soup for 30 minutes.* 揭开锅盖，让汤煮 30 分钟。 ⊃ OPPOSITE **cover** 反义词为 cover

2 to find out something that was secret 发现；揭露: *Police uncovered a plot to steal the painting.* 警方侦破了一起企图偷画的阴谋。

undeniable /ˌʌndɪˈnaɪəbl/ *adjective* 形容词
clear, true or certain 明确的；不可否认的: *It is undeniable that girls mature faster than boys.* 女孩比男孩发育得快是不容争辩的。

under 0▬ /ˈʌndə(r)/ *preposition, adverb* 介词，副词
1 in or to a place that is lower than or below something 在…下面；到…下面: *The cat is under the table.* 猫在桌子底下。 ◇ *We sailed under the bridge.* 我们驾船从桥下驶过。 ◇ *The boat filled with water, then went under.* 船入了水，然后沉下去了。
2 less than something 少于；小于；不足: *If you are under 17 you are not allowed to drive a car.* 未满 17 岁不准开车。
3 covered by something 由…覆盖 ⊃ SAME MEANING **underneath** 同义词为 underneath: *I'm wearing a vest under my shirt.* 我衬衫里面穿着一件背心。
4 controlled by somebody or something 由…控制: *The team are playing well under their new captain.* 这个队在新队长的带领下表现很好。

under- /ˈʌndə(r)/ *prefix* 前缀
1 You can add **under-** to the beginning of some words to show that something is under another thing. 在…下面: *underwater* (= below the surface of water) 在水下 ◇ *underwear* (= clothes that you wear under your other clothes) 内衣
2 You can add **under-** to the beginning of some words to show that something is not enough. 不足；未: *undercooked* (= not cooked enough) 未煮熟的 ◇ *underpaid* (= not paid enough) 报酬过低的

underage /ˌʌndəreɪdʒ/ *adjective* 形容词
too young to be allowed by law to do something 未到法定年龄的；未成年的: *underage drinking* 未成年饮酒

undergo /ˌʌndəˈɡəʊ/ *verb* 动词
(undergoes, undergoing, underwent /ˌʌndəˈwent/, has undergone /ˌʌndəˈɡɒn/)
to have a difficult or unpleasant experience 经历，经受（苦难或不快的

事）: *Laura is in hospital undergoing an operation.* 劳拉现正在医院做手术。

undergraduate /ˌʌndəˈɡrædʒuət/ *noun* 名词
a student at a university who is studying for his or her first degree 大学生；本科生 ⊃ Look at **graduate**[1] (1). 见 graduate[1] 第 1 义。

underground[1] 0▬ /ˈʌndəɡraʊnd/ *adjective, adverb* 形容词，副词
under the ground 地下的；在地下: *an underground car park* 地下停车场 ◇ *Moles spend much of their time underground.* 鼹鼠大多数时间都在地下生活。

underground[2] /ˈʌndəɡraʊnd/ (*also* 亦作 the Underground) (*British* 英式英语) (*American* 美式英语 **subway**) *noun* 名词
(*no plural* 不用复数形式)
an underground railway system in a city 地铁；地下铁路系统: *I go to work by underground.* 我坐地铁上班。 ◇ *We took the Underground to Piccadilly Circus.* 我们坐地铁到了皮卡迪利广场。 ⊃ Look at Picture Dictionary page **P1**. 见彩图 P1。

undergrowth /ˈʌndəɡrəʊθ/ *noun* 名词
(*no plural* 不用复数形式)
bushes and other plants that grow under trees 下层灌木丛: *There was a path through the undergrowth.* 灌木丛中有一条小径。

underline /ˌʌndəˈlaɪn/ *verb* 动词
(underlines, underlining, underlined /ˌʌndəˈlaɪnd/)
to draw a line under a word or words. 在（文字下面）画线: *This sentence is underlined.* 这个句子画了底线。

underneath 0▬ /ˌʌndəˈniːθ/ *preposition, adverb* 介词，副词
under or below something 在…下面（或底下）；在下面（或底下）: *The dog sat underneath the table.* 狗趴在桌子底下。 ◇ *She wore a black jacket with a red jumper underneath.* 她穿了黑色的夹克，里面有件红色的套头毛衣。

underpants /ˈʌndəpænts/ *noun* 名词
(*plural* 用复数形式)
1 (*British* 英式英语) (*British informal also* 英式英语非正式亦作 **pants**) a piece of clothing that a man or boy wears under his trousers（男用）内裤，衬裤: *a pair of underpants* 一条内裤
2 (*American* 美式英语) a piece of clothing that men or women wear under trousers, a skirt, etc.（男、女）内裤，衬裤

undershirt /ˈʌndəʃɜːt/ *American English for* VEST (1) 美式英语，即 vest 第 1 义

A B C D E F G H I J K L M N O P Q R S T **U** V W X Y Z

understand 0̶ₘ /ˌʌndəˈstænd/ *verb*
动词 (understands, understanding,
understood /ˌʌndəˈstʊd/, has understood)
1 to know what something means or why
something happens 懂得；理解；领会；
明白：*I didn't understand what the
teacher said.* 我不理解老师说的话。◇
He doesn't understand Spanish. 他不懂
西班牙语。◇ *I don't understand why you're
so angry.* 我不明白你为什么这么生气。
2 to know something because somebody
has told you about it 得知；据悉 ⊃ SAME
MEANING **believe** 同义词为 believe：
*I understand that the plane from Geneva
will be late.* 我听说从日内瓦来的飞机会
晚点。
make yourself understood to make
people understand you 把自己的意思
说清楚：*My German isn't very good but
I can usually make myself understood.*
我的德语不太好，但通常还能把事情说
清楚。

understanding¹ /ˌʌndəˈstændɪŋ/ *noun*
名词 (no plural 不用复数形式)
knowing about something 理解；掌握；
了解：*He's got a good **understanding** of
computers.* 他很懂电脑。

understanding² /ˌʌndəˈstændɪŋ/
adjective 形容词
ready to listen to other people's problems
and try to understand them 善解人意的；
体谅人的 ⊃ SAME MEANING **sympathetic**
同义词为 sympathetic：*My parents are
very understanding.* 我父母亲很通情达理。

understood *form of* UNDERSTAND
* understand 的不同形式

undertaker /ˈʌndəteɪkə(r)/ *noun* 名词
a person whose job is to organize
FUNERALS (= the time when dead people
are buried or burned) 殡葬承办人；殡仪
服务员

underwater 0̶ₘ /ˌʌndəˈwɔːtə(r)/
adjective, adverb 形容词，副词
below the surface of water 水下的；在水
下：*Can you swim underwater?* 你会潜泳
吗？◇ *an underwater camera* 水下摄影机

underwear 0̶ₘ /ˈʌndəweə(r)/ *noun*
名词 (no plural 不用复数形式)
clothes that you wear next to your body,
under your other clothes 内衣

underwent *form of* UNDERGO * undergo
的不同形式

undo /ʌnˈduː/ *verb* 动词 (undoes /ʌnˈdʌz/,
undoing, undid /ʌnˈdɪd/, has undone
/ʌnˈdʌn/)
to open something that was tied or fixed

打开；解开；拆开：*I can't undo this zip.*
这个拉链我拉不开。◇ *to undo a jacket*
解开夹克衫 ⊃ OPPOSITE **do something up**
反义词为 do something up

undone /ʌnˈdʌn/ *adjective* 形容词
not tied or fixed 未扣；未系；松开：*Your
shoelaces are undone.* 你的鞋带松了。

undoubtedly /ʌnˈdaʊtɪdli/ *adverb* 副词
certainly; without doubt 肯定；毫无
疑问：*She is undoubtedly very intelligent.*
毫无疑问她非常聪明。

undress /ʌnˈdres/ *verb* 动词 (undresses,
undressing, undressed /ʌnˈdrest/)
to take clothes off yourself or another
person（给…）脱衣服：*He undressed
and got into bed.* 他脱衣上床了。◇ *She
undressed her baby.* 她给宝宝脱了衣服。
⊃ OPPOSITE **dress** 反义词为 dress
▶ **undressed** /ʌnˈdrest/ *adjective*
形容词：*I got undressed and had a
shower.* 我脱了衣服，冲了个澡。

uneasy /ʌnˈiːzi/ *adjective* 形容词
worried that something is wrong 担心的；
忧虑的；不安的：*I started to feel uneasy
when the children were late coming home.*
孩子们回家晚了，我不由得担心起来。
▶ **uneasily** /ʌnˈiːzɪli/ *adverb* 副词：*She
looked uneasily around the room.* 她忐忑
不安地环顾房间四周。

unemployed /ˌʌnɪmˈplɔɪd/ *adjective*
形容词
If you are **unemployed**, you can work but
you do not have a job. 失业的；待业的；
下岗的：*She has been unemployed for
over a year.* 她已经失业一年多了。
⊃ OPPOSITE **employed** 反义词为 employed

unemployment 0̶ₘ /ˌʌnɪmˈplɔɪmənt/
noun 名词 (no plural 不用复数形式)
when there are not enough jobs for the
people who want to work 失业；失业
人数：*If the factory closes, unemployment
in the town will increase.* 这家工厂要是
倒闭，镇上的失业人数就会增加。
⊃ OPPOSITE **employment** 反义词为
employment

uneven /ʌnˈiːvn/ *adjective* 形容词
not smooth or flat 凹凸不平的；不平坦
的：*We had to drive slowly because the
road was so uneven.* 由于道路凹凸不平，
我们只好缓慢行驶。⊃ OPPOSITE **even**
反义词为 even

unexpected 0̶ₘ /ˌʌnɪkˈspektɪd/
adjective 形容词
surprising because you did not expect it
出乎意料的；始料不及的：*an unexpected
visit* 意外的到访

▶ **unexpectedly** /ˌʌnɪk'spektɪdli/ *adverb*
副词: *She arrived unexpectedly.* 没料到
她来了。

unfair 0━ /ˌʌn'feə(r)/ *adjective* 形容词
Something that is **unfair** does not treat
people in the same way or in the right
way. 不公正的; 不公平的: *It was unfair
to give chocolates to some of the children
and not to the others.* 把巧克力给一些孩子
而不给另一些孩子是不公平的。 ➲ OPPOSITE
fair 反义词为 fair
▶ **unfairly** /ˌʌn'feəli/ *adverb* 副词: *He
left his job because the boss was treating
him unfairly.* 他辞职了, 因为老板对他
不公正。

unfamiliar /ˌʌnfə'mɪliə(r)/ *adjective*
形容词
that you do not know; strange 不熟悉的;
陌生的: *I woke up in an unfamiliar room.*
我醒来的时候在一个陌生的房间里。
➲ OPPOSITE **familiar** 反义词为 familiar

unfashionable /ʌn'fæʃnəbl/ *adjective*
形容词
not popular at a particular time 不流行
的; 不时髦的: *unfashionable clothes*
过时的衣服 ➲ OPPOSITE **fashionable**
反义词为 fashionable

unfasten /ʌn'fɑːsn/ *verb* 动词 (unfastens,
unfastening, unfastened /ʌn'fɑːsnd/)
to open something that was tied or fixed
解开; 松开: *to unfasten your seat belt*
解开安全带 ➲ OPPOSITE **fasten** 反义为
fasten

unfit /ʌn'fɪt/ *adjective* 形容词
1 not good enough or not right for
something 不合格的; 不适合的; 不适宜
的: *This house is unfit for people to live
in.* 这所房子不适合住人。
2 not healthy or strong 不健康的; 不健壮
的: *She never takes any exercise – that's
why she's so unfit.* 她从来不锻炼, 难怪
身体那么差。 ➲ OPPOSITE **fit** 反义词为 fit

unfold /ʌn'fəʊld/ *verb* 动词 (unfolds,
unfolding, unfolded)
to open something to make it flat; to
open out and become flat (使) 展开;
打开 (折叠的东西): *Marie unfolded the
newspaper and started to read.* 玛丽打开
报纸阅读起来。 ◇ *The sofa unfolds to
make a bed.* 这个沙发打开可当床用。
➲ OPPOSITE **fold** 反义词为 fold

unfortunate /ʌn'fɔːtʃənət/ *adjective*
形容词
not lucky 不幸的; 倒霉的: *It's
unfortunate that you were ill on your*
birthday. 你生日那天病了, 真不走运。
➲ OPPOSITE **fortunate** 反义词为 fortunate

unfortunately 0━ /ʌn'fɔːtʃənətli/
adverb 副词
a word that you use to show that you
are not happy about a situation or fact
不幸地; 遗憾地: *I'd like to give you some
money, but unfortunately I haven't got
any.* 我想给你些钱, 可惜我身无分文。
➲ OPPOSITE **fortunately** 反义词为
fortunately

unfriendly 0━ /ʌn'frendli/ *adjective*
形容词
not friendly; not kind or helpful to
other people 不友好的; 不和蔼可亲的
➲ OPPOSITE **friendly** 反义词为 friendly

ungrateful /ʌn'greɪtfl/ *adjective* 形容词
If you are **ungrateful**, you do not show
thanks when somebody helps you or
gives you something. 不感激的; 不领情
的: *Don't be so ungrateful! I spent all
morning looking for this present.* 别那么
不领情! 我花了整整一上午为选中这份
礼物。 ➲ OPPOSITE **grateful** 反义词为
grateful

unhappy 0━ /ʌn'hæpi/ *adjective*
形容词 (unhappier, unhappiest)
not happy 不快乐的; 不高兴的 ➲ SAME
MEANING **sad** 同义词为 sad: *He was very
unhappy when his wife left him.* 妻子离开
他时, 他很难过。 ➲ OPPOSITE **happy**
反义词为 happy
▶ **unhappily** /ʌn'hæpɪli/ *adverb* 副词:
'I failed the exam,' she said unhappily.
"我考试没及格。" 她沮丧地说。
▶ **unhappiness** /ʌn'hæpinəs/ *noun* 名词
(*no plural* 不用复数形式): *John has had a
lot of unhappiness in his life.* 约翰一生中
经历过很多不如意的事情。

unhealthy /ʌn'helθi/ *adjective* 形容词
(unhealthier, unhealthiest)
1 not well; often ill 不健康的; 常生病的:
an unhealthy child 身体虚弱的孩子
2 that can make you ill 会致病的; 不利于
健康的: *unhealthy food* 不健康的食品
➲ OPPOSITE **healthy** 反义词为 healthy

unhelpful /ʌn'helpfl/ *adjective* 形容词
not wanting to help somebody; not useful
不愿帮忙的; 无用的; 无益的: *I'm afraid
the shop assistant was rather unhelpful.*
恐怕那个售货员不肯帮忙。 ➲ OPPOSITE
helpful 反义词为 helpful

uniform 0━ /'juːnɪfɔːm/ *noun* 名词
the special clothes that everybody in the
same job, school, etc. wears 制服; 校服:

A
B
C
D
E
F
G
H
I
J
K
L
M
N
O
P
Q
R
S
T
U
V
W
X
Y
Z

Police officers wear blue uniforms. 警察穿蓝色的制服。

unimportant /ˌʌnɪmˈpɔːtnt/ *adjective* 形容词
not important 不重要的；无足轻重的
つ OPPOSITE **important** 反义词为 important

uninhabited /ˌʌnɪnˈhæbɪtɪd/ *adjective* 形容词
where nobody lives 无人居住的：
an uninhabited island 荒岛

union 0ᵐ /ˈjuːniən/ *noun* 名词
1 (*plural* 复数形式 unions) (*also* 亦作 trade union) a group of workers who have joined together to talk to their managers about things like pay and the way they work 工会： *the National Union of Teachers* 全国教师工会
2 (*plural* 复数形式 unions) a group of people or countries that have joined together 协会；联合会；联邦；联盟：
the European Union 欧洲联盟
3 (*no plural* 不用复数形式) coming together 联合；结合；合并： *The union of England and Scotland was in 1707.* 英格兰和苏格兰于 1707 年合并。

the Union Jack /ðə ˌjuːniən ˈdʒæk/ *noun* 名词
the flag of the United Kingdom 联合王国国旗；英国国旗

unique /juˈniːk/ *adjective* 形容词
not like anybody or anything else 唯一的；独一无二的；独特的： *Everybody in the world is unique.* 世界上每个人都是独一无二的。

unit 0ᵐ /ˈjuːnɪt/ *noun* 名词
1 one complete thing or group that may be part of something larger 单位；单元：
The book has twelve units. 这本书有十二个单元。
2 a measurement （计量）单位： *A metre is a unit of length and a kilogram is a unit of weight.* 米是长度单位，千克是重量单位。

unite 0ᵐ /juˈnaɪt/ *verb* 动词 (unites, uniting, united)
to join together to do something together; to put two things together 联合；联手；团结： *We must unite to defeat our enemies.* 我们必须联合起来打败敌人。
▶ **united** /juˈnaɪtɪd/ *adjective* 形容词：
the United States of America 美利坚合众国

the United Nations /ðə juˌnaɪtɪd ˈneɪʃnz/ *noun* 名词 (*no plural* 不用复数形式) (*abbr.* 缩略式 UN)
the organization that tries to stop world problems and to give help to countries that need it 联合国

universal /ˌjuːnɪˈvɜːsl/ *adjective* 形容词
connected with, done by or for everybody 普遍的；全体的；共同的： *The environment is a universal issue.* 环境是关乎所有人的问题。
▶ **universally** /ˌjuːnɪˈvɜːsəli/ *adverb* 副词： *to be universally accepted* (= accepted everywhere and by everybody) 得到普遍接受

the universe 0ᵐ /ðə ˈjuːnɪvɜːs/ *noun* 名词 (*no plural* 不用复数形式)
the earth and all the stars, planets and everything else in space 宇宙；天地万物

university 0ᵐ /ˌjuːnɪˈvɜːsəti/ *noun* 名词 (*plural* 复数形式 universities)
a place where people go to study more difficult subjects after they have left school 大学；高等学府： *I'm hoping to go to university next year.* 我希望明年能上大学。 ◇ *My sister is at university studying Chemistry.* 我姐姐在大学攻读化学。

> 🔎 WORD BUILDING 词汇扩充
> If you pass all your exams at a university, you get a **degree**. 要是通过大学的所有考试，就可以得到学位（degree）。

unjust /ˌʌnˈdʒʌst/ *adjective* 形容词
not fair or right 不公平的；不公正的
つ SAME MEANING **unfair** 同义词为 unfair：
This tax is unjust because poor people pay as much as rich people. 这项税不合理，因为穷人与富人缴的一样多。

unkind 0ᵐ /ˌʌnˈkaɪnd/ *adjective* 形容词
unpleasant and not friendly 不亲切的；不友善的： *It was unkind of you to laugh at her.* 你嘲笑她，未免有点刻薄。
つ OPPOSITE **kind** 反义词为 kind

unknown 0ᵐ /ˌʌnˈnəʊn/ *adjective* 形容词
1 that you do not know 未知的；不知道的
つ SAME MEANING **unfamiliar** 同义词为 unfamiliar： *an unknown face* 陌生的脸
2 not famous 不出名的；无名的： *an unknown actor* 不出名的演员 つ OPPOSITE **famous, well known** 反义词为 famous 和 well known

unleaded /ˌʌnˈledɪd/ *adjective* 形容词
Unleaded petrol is less harmful to the environment because it does not contain any LEAD (= a soft heavy grey metal). 无铅的；不含铅的

unless 🔑 /ən'les/ ***conjunction*** 连词
if not; except if 除非；如果不：*You will be late unless you leave now.* 除非现在离开，否则你会迟到。◇ *Unless you work harder you'll fail the exam.* 除非你用功一些，否则考试就不会及格。

unlike /ˌʌn'laɪk/ ***preposition*** 介词
different from 与…不同；不像：*She is unlike anyone I've ever met.* 她跟我见过的所有人都不同。➲ OPPOSITE **like** 反义词为 like

unlikely 🔑 /ʌn'laɪkli/ ***adjective*** 形容词 (**unlikelier**, **unlikeliest**)
If something is **unlikely**, it will probably not happen. 不大可能发生的：*It is **unlikely that** it will rain.* 下雨的机会不大。◇ *He is **unlikely to** pass the exam.* 他不太可能通过考试。➲ OPPOSITE **likely** 反义词为 likely

unload /ˌʌn'ləʊd/ ***verb*** 动词 (**unloads**, **unloading**, **unloaded**)
to take things that have been carried somewhere off or out of a car, lorry, ship or plane（从交通工具上）卸下，取下：*I unloaded the shopping from the car.* 我把买来的东西从车上卸了下来。◇ *They unloaded the ship at the dock.* 他们在码头卸货。

unlock /ˌʌn'lɒk/ ***verb*** 动词 (**unlocks**, **unlocking**, **unlocked** /ˌʌn'lɒkt/)
to open something with a key 用钥匙打开：*I unlocked the door and went in.* 我打开门锁进去了。

unlucky /ʌn'lʌki/ ***adjective*** 形容词 (**unluckier**, **unluckiest**)
having or bringing bad luck 不幸的；倒霉的；不吉利的：*They were unlucky to lose because they played very well.* 他们打得非常出色，却不幸输了。◇ *Some people think the number 13 is unlucky.* 有些人认为 13 这个数字不吉利。➲ OPPOSITE **lucky** 反义词为 lucky
▶ **unluckily** /ʌn'lʌkɪli/ ***adverb*** 副词：*Unluckily, I missed the bus.* 可惜我没赶上公共汽车。

unmarried /ˌʌn'mærid/ ***adjective*** 形容词
not married; without a husband or wife 未婚的；单身的 ➲ SAME MEANING **single** 同义词为 single

unmistakable /ˌʌnmɪ'steɪkəbl/ ***adjective*** 形容词
If something is **unmistakable**, it is easy to recognize and will not be confused with anything else. 容易辨认的；不会弄错的；确定无疑的：*Her Australian accent was unmistakable.* 她的澳大利亚口音清晰可辨。

unnatural /ʌn'nætʃrəl/ ***adjective*** 形容词
different from what is normal or expected 不自然的；反常的：*There was an unnatural silence.* 一阵异乎寻常的寂静。➲ OPPOSITE **natural** 反义词为 natural

unnecessary /ʌn'nesəsəri/ ***adjective*** 形容词

> **SPELLING 拼写说明**
> Remember! You spell **unnecessary** with **NN**, one **C** and **SS**. 记住：unnecessary 拼写中有 nn、一个 c 和 ss。

not needed, or more than is needed 不需要的；不必要的；多余的：*All this fuss is **totally unnecessary**.* 这一切的大惊小怪是毫无必要的。

unofficial /ˌʌnə'fɪʃl/ ***adjective*** 形容词
not accepted or approved by a person in authority 非官方的；非正式的；未经正式批准的：*Unofficial reports say that four people died in the explosion.* 非官方的报道说，爆炸中有四人死亡。

unpack /ˌʌn'pæk/ ***verb*** 动词 (**unpacks**, **unpacking**, **unpacked** /ˌʌn'pækt/)
to take all the things out of a bag, suitcase, etc. 从（包、箱等中）取出：*Have you unpacked your suitcase?* 你把行李箱中的东西拿出来了吗？◇ *We arrived at the hotel, unpacked, and then went to the beach.* 我们到旅馆后取出箱子里的行李，然后去了海滩。

unpaid /ˌʌn'peɪd/ ***adjective*** 形容词
not yet paid 未付的；未偿付的：*unpaid bills* 未付的账单

unpleasant 🔑 /ʌn'pleznt/ ***adjective*** 形容词
not pleasant; not nice 令人不快的；不好的：*There was an unpleasant smell of bad fish.* 有一股难闻的烂鱼味。
▶ **unpleasantly** /ʌn'plezntli/ ***adverb*** 副词：*It was unpleasantly hot in that room.* 那个房间里热得难受。

unplug /ˌʌn'plʌg/ ***verb*** 动词 (**unplugs**, **unplugging**, **unplugged** /ˌʌn'plʌgd/)
to take out a piece of electrical equipment (called a **plug**) from the electricity supply 拔掉…的插头：*Could you unplug the TV?* 你把电视机的插头拔下来好吗？➲ OPPOSITE **plug something in** 反义词为 plug something in

unpopular /ʌn'pɒpjələ(r)/ ***adjective*** 形容词

A B C D E F G H I J K L M N O P Q R S T U V W X Y Z

A
B
C
D
E
F
G
H
I
J
K
L
M
N
O
P
Q
R
S
T
U
V
W
X
Y
Z

not liked by many people; not popular 不受欢迎的；不得人心的： *He's unpopular at work because he's lazy.* 他工作上人缘不好，因为他很懒。

unpredictable /ˌʌnprɪ'dɪktəbl/ *adjective* 形容词
If something is **unpredictable**, you cannot say how it will change in the future. 不可预测的；难以预料的： *The weather is very unpredictable at this time of year.* 一年中的这个时候天气总是变幻莫测。

unreasonable /ʌn'riːznəbl/ *adjective* 形容词
expecting too much 不合理的；期望过高的： *an unreasonable request* 不合理的要求

unreliable /ˌʌnrɪ'laɪəbl/ *adjective* 形容词
If something or somebody is **unreliable**, you cannot trust it or them. 不可靠的；不能信赖的： *Don't lend her any money – she's very unreliable.* 别借钱给她，她这人很不可靠。◇ *an unreliable car* 不牢靠的汽车

unruly /ʌn'ruːli/ *adjective* 形容词
difficult to control 难以控制的： *an unruly crowd* 难以控制的人群

unsafe /ʌn'seɪf/ *adjective* 形容词
dangerous; not safe 危险的；不安全的： *Don't climb on that wall – it's unsafe.* 别爬那堵墙，会有危险。

unsatisfactory /ˌʌnˌsætɪs'fæktəri/ *adjective* 形容词
not good enough; not acceptable 不够好的；不能令人满意的： *Your work is unsatisfactory. Please do it again.* 你的作业做得不好，请重做。

unstable /ʌn'steɪbl/ *adjective* 形容词
Something that is **unstable** may fall, move or change. 不稳定的；易变的： *This bridge is unstable.* 这座桥不稳。◇ *an unstable government* 不稳固的政府

unsuccessful /ˌʌnsək'sesfl/ *adjective* 形容词
If you are **unsuccessful**, you have not done what you wanted and tried to do. 不成功的；失败的；落空的： *I tried to repair the bike but I was unsuccessful.* 我试图修理自行车，可没修好。
▸ **unsuccessfully** /ˌʌnsək'sesfəli/ *adverb* 副词： *He tried unsuccessfully to lift the box.* 他想抬起箱子却抬不动。

unsuitable /ʌn'suːtəbl/ *adjective* 形容词
not suitable; not right for somebody or something 不合适的；不适宜的；不恰当

的： *This film is unsuitable for children.* 这部影片儿童不宜。

unsure /ˌʌn'ʃʊə(r)/ *adjective* 形容词
not sure about something 不确定；无把握；犹豫： *We were unsure what to do.* 我们拿不准要做些什么。

unsympathetic /ˌʌnˌsɪmpə'θetɪk/ *adjective* 形容词
If you are **unsympathetic**, you are not kind to somebody who is hurt or sad, and you show that you do not understand their feelings and problems. 无同情心的；不表示同情的；冷漠的

untidy ⚡ /ʌn'taɪdi/ *adjective* 形容词 (untidier, untidiest)
not tidy; not with everything in the right place 不整洁的；凌乱的 ⊃ SAME MEANING **messy** 同义词为 messy： *Your room is always so untidy!* 你的房间总是那么乱七八糟！
▸ **untidiness** /ʌn'taɪdinəs/ *noun* 名词 (no plural 不用复数形式)： *I hate untidiness!* 我讨厌不整洁！

untie /ʌn'taɪ/ *verb* 动词 (unties, untying, untied /ʌn'taɪd/, has untied)
to remove a knot; to take off the string or rope that is holding something 解开…的结；松开（绳子）： *Can you untie this knot?* 你能解开这个结吗？◇ *I untied the parcel.* 我拆开了包裹。

until ⚡ /ən'tɪl/ (*also informal* 非正式亦作 till) *conjunction, preposition* 连词，介词

> 🔍 SPELLING 拼写说明
> Remember! You spell **until** with one **L** (but you spell **till** with LL). 记住：until 拼写中有一个 l（但 till 有 ll）。

up to a certain time or event 直到…为止；直到…才： *The shop is open until 6.30.* 这家店开到 6 点 30 分。◇ *Stay in bed until you feel better.* 你要卧床休息，等到好一些再起来。◇ *I can't come until tomorrow.* 我要到明天才能来。

untrue /ʌn'truː/ *adjective* 形容词
not true or correct 不真实的；不正确的： *What you said was completely untrue.* 你所说的完全不对。

unusual ⚡ /ʌn'juːʒuəl/ *adjective* 形容词
If something is **unusual**, it does not often happen or you do not often see it. 不寻常的；罕见的： *It's unusual to see a cat without a tail.* 很少看到没有尾巴的猫。◇ *What an unusual name!* 多么罕见的名字啊！

▶ **unusually** /ʌnˈjuːʒuəli/ *adverb* 副词:
It was an unusually hot summer. 那是个异常炎热的夏天。

unwanted /ˌʌnˈwɒntɪd/ *adjective* 形容词
not wanted 不想要的；没人要的:
an unwanted gift 没人要的礼物

unwelcome /ʌnˈwelkəm/ *adjective* 形容词
If somebody or something is **unwelcome**, you are not happy to have or see them. 不受欢迎的；没人想要的: *an unwelcome visitor* 不受欢迎的访客

unwell /ʌnˈwel/ *adjective* 形容词
not well; ill 不适；有病；不舒服

unwilling /ʌnˈwɪlɪŋ/ *adjective* 形容词
If you are **unwilling** to do something, you are not ready or happy to do it. 不情愿；不愿意: *He was unwilling to lend me any money.* 他一分钱都不愿借给我。

unwind /ˌʌnˈwaɪnd/ *verb* 动词 (unwinds, unwinding, unwound /ˌʌnˈwaʊnd/, has unwound)
1 to open out something that has been wrapped into a ball or around something else 解开，打开，松开（缠绕之物）: *to unwind a ball of string* 解开一团绳子
2 to start to relax, after working hard or worrying about something 放松；松弛: *Watching television helps me unwind after a busy day.* 忙碌一天后，看电视让我放松下来。

unwise /ˌʌnˈwaɪz/ *adjective* 形容词
showing that you do not make good decisions 不明智的；愚蠢的 ⊃ SAME MEANING **foolish** 同义词为 foolish:
It would be unwise to tell anybody about our plan yet. 现在告诉别人我们的计划并不明智。

▶ **unwisely** /ˌʌnˈwaɪzli/ *adverb* 副词:
Perhaps unwisely, I agreed to help her. 也许是太轻率了，我答应了帮她。

unwrap /ʌnˈræp/ *verb* 动词 (unwraps, unwrapping, unwrapped /ʌnˈræpt/)
to take off the paper or cloth that is around something 打开（或解开、拆开）…的包装: *I unwrapped the parcel.* 我拆开了包裹。 ⊃ OPPOSITE **wrap something up** 反义词为 wrap something up

up 0ᴍ /ʌp/ *preposition, adverb* 介词，副词
1 in or to a higher place 在（或向）较高的位置；在上面；向上: *We climbed up the mountain.* 我们爬上了山。 ◇ *Put your hand up if you know the answer.* 知道答案的就举手。 ⊃ OPPOSITE **down** 反义词为 down

2 from sitting or lying to standing 起立；起身: *Stand up, please.* 请站起来。 ◇ *What time do you get up (= out of bed)?* 你什么时候起床？ ◇ *'Is Joe up (= out of bed)?' 'No, he's still asleep.'* "乔起来了吗？" "没有，他还在睡呢。"
3 to the place where somebody or something is 朝（某人或某物）的方向；向…的地方: *She came up to me and asked me the time.* 她走到我跟前问我时间。
4 a word we use to show an increase in something 增加；增长；增高: *Prices are going up.* 物价在上涨。 ◇ *Please turn the radio up – I can't hear it.* 请把收音机音量调高，我听不见。 ⊃ OPPOSITE **down** 反义词为 down
5 into pieces 成碎片: *Cut the meat up.* 把肉切碎。
6 so that it is finished 完全；彻底: *Eat up, I want you to finish this food.* 把它吃光，我想你把这食物吃完。
7 in a certain direction 朝，向（某个方向）: *We walked up the road.* 我们沿着路走。 ⊃ OPPOSITE **down** 反义词为 down
8 (*informal* 非正式) a word that you use to show that something unusual or unpleasant is happening（异常或不快的事）发生，出现: *I could tell something was up by the looks on their faces.* 从他们的脸色我可以看出有事发生了。 ◇ *What's up (= What's the matter)?* 怎么回事？

be up to somebody to be the person who should do or decide something 是某人的责任；由某人决定: *'What shall we do this evening?' 'I don't mind. It's up to you.'* "我们今天晚上做什么？" "我无所谓，你决定吧。"

up to
1 as far as; until 直到: *Up to now, she has worked very hard.* 到目前为止，她工作都很努力。
2 as much or as many as 多达；多至: *Up to 300 people came to the meeting.* 多达 300 人参加会议。
3 doing something, especially something bad 在捣鬼；在做坏事: *What is that man up to?* 那个男的在捣什么鬼？

update /ˌʌpˈdeɪt/ *verb* 动词 (updates, updating, updated)
to make something more modern or add new things to it 使现代化；更新: *The information on our website is updated every week.* 我们网站上的信息每周都会更新。

upgrade /ˌʌpˈɡreɪd/ *verb* 动词 (upgrades, upgrading, upgraded)

A B C D E F G H I J K L M N O P Q R S T **U** V W X Y Z

to change something so that it is better
升级；改进： *I've just upgraded my PC.*
我刚给电脑升了级。
▶ **upgrade** /'ʌpgreɪd/ *noun* 名词:
to install an upgrade 安装更新软件

uphill /ˌʌp'hɪl/ *adverb* 副词
going up, towards the top of a hill
向山上；朝上坡方向： *It's difficult to ride
a bicycle uphill.* 骑自行车上坡很费劲。
➲ OPPOSITE **downhill** 反义词为 downhill

upon /ə'pɒn/ *preposition* 介词 (*formal* 正式)
on （与 on 同义）: *The decision was
based upon the doctor's evidence.* 这个
决定是基于医生提供的证据作出的。

🔎 SPEAKING 表达方式说明
On is the word that we usually use.
* on 是常用词。

upper 0🖝 /'ʌpə(r)/ *adjective* 形容词
in a higher place than something else
上边的；上面的；上层的： *the upper lip*
上唇 ➲ OPPOSITE **lower** 反义词为 lower

upper case /ˌʌpə 'keɪs/ *noun* 名词
(*no plural* 不用复数形式)
the large form of letters, for example A,
B, C (not a, b, c) 大写字母： *'BBC' is
written in upper case.* * BBC 用大写。
➲ OPPOSITE **lower case** 反义词为 lower
case

upright /'ʌpraɪt/ *adjective*, *adverb*
形容词，副词
standing straight up, not lying down
直立（的）；挺直（的）： *Put the ladder
upright against the wall.* 把梯子靠墙竖
起来。

upset¹ 0🖝 /ʌp'set/ *verb* 动词 (upsets,
upsetting, upset, has upset)
1 to make somebody feel unhappy or
worried 使不快；使烦恼： *You upset Tom
when you said he was fat.* 你说汤姆胖，
他很不开心。
2 to make something go wrong 打乱；
搅乱： *The bad weather upset our plans
for the weekend.* 恶劣的天气打乱了我们的
周末计划。
3 to knock something so that it turns over
and things fall out 打翻；碰倒： *I upset
a glass of wine all over the table.* 我碰倒了
一杯酒，洒了一桌子。

upset² 0🖝 /ʌp'set/ *adjective* 形容词
1 unhappy or worried 不高兴；忧愁；
难过： *The children were very upset when
their dog died.* 孩子们的狗死了，他们都
非常伤心。
2 ill 不适的；不舒服的： *I've got an upset
stomach.* 我肠胃不适。

▶ **upset** /'ʌpset/ *noun* 名词 an illness in
your stomach 肠胃病： *Sara has got a
stomach upset.* 萨拉肠胃不舒服。

upsetting /ʌp'setɪŋ/ *adjective* 形容词
making you feel unhappy or worried
令人不快的；使人烦恼的： *The experience
was very upsetting for all of us.* 这次经历
让我们所有人都感到很不开心。

upside down 上下颠倒

The painting is **upside down**.
这幅画上下颠倒了。

upside down /ˌʌpsaɪd 'daʊn/ *adverb*
副词
with the top part at the bottom 上下颠
倒；倒转： *The picture is upside down.*
这幅画上下颠倒了。

upstairs 0🖝 /ˌʌp'steəz/ *adverb* 副词
to or on a higher floor of a building
往楼上；在楼上： *I went upstairs to bed.*
我上楼去睡觉了。
▶ **upstairs** /'ʌpsteəz/ *adjective* 形容词:
An upstairs window was open. 楼上有扇窗
开着。 ➲ OPPOSITE **downstairs** 反义词为
downstairs

up to date /ˌʌp tə 'deɪt/ *adjective* 形容词
modern; using new information 现代的；
最新的： *Is this information up to date?*
这信息是最新的吗？

upwards 0🖝 /'ʌpwədz/ (*also* 亦作
upward /'ʌpwəd/) *adverb* 副词
up; towards a higher place 向上；向高
处： *We climbed upwards, towards the
top of the mountain.* 我们向山顶爬上去。
➲ OPPOSITE **downwards** 反义词为
downwards

urban /'ɜːbən/ *adjective* 形容词
connected with a town or city 城镇的；
城市的；都市的： *urban areas* 市区

urge¹ /ɜːdʒ/ *verb* 动词 (urges, urging,
urged /ɜːdʒd/)

to try to make somebody do something
敦促；催促；力劝: *I urged him to stay for dinner.* 我力劝他留下来吃晚饭。

urge² /ɜːdʒ/ *noun* 名词
a strong feeling that you want to do something 强烈的欲望；冲动: *I had a sudden urge to laugh.* 我突然想笑出来。

urgency /'ɜːdʒənsi/ *noun* 名词 (*no plural* 不用复数形式)
the need to do something quickly because it is very important 紧急（情况）

urgent ⊶ /'ɜːdʒənt/ *adjective* 形容词
so important that you must do it or answer it quickly 紧急的；紧迫的；迫切的: *The doctor received an urgent telephone call.* 医生接到了紧急电话。
▶ **urgently** /'ɜːdʒəntli/ *adverb* 副词:
I must see you urgently. 我有急事必须马上见你。

us ⊶ /əs; ʌs/ *pronoun* 代词 (*plural* 用复数形式)
me and another person or other people; me and you 我们；咱们: *We were pleased when she invited us to dinner.* 她邀请我们吃饭，我们都很高兴。◇ *Come with us.* 跟我们来。

use¹ ⊶ /juːz/ *verb* 动词 (uses, using, used /juːzd/)

> 🔊 PRONUNCIATION 读音说明
> When the word **use** is a verb, it sounds like **shoes** or **choose**. * use 作动词时，读音像 shoes 或 choose。
> When the word **use** is a noun, it sounds like **juice** or **loose**. * use 作名词时，读音像 juice 或 loose。

1 to do a job with something 使用；利用；运用: *Could I use your telephone?* 我可以用一下你的电话吗？◇ *Do you know how to use this machine?* 你会操作这台机器吗？◇ *Wood is used to make paper.* 木材可用来造纸。
2 to take something 消耗: *Don't use all the milk.* 不要把牛奶都用光。
use something up to use something until you have no more 用光；耗尽: *I've used up all the coffee, so I need to buy some more.* 我把咖啡都喝完了，需要再买点。

use² ⊶ /juːs/ *noun* 名词
1 (*no plural* 不用复数形式) using something or being used 使用；利用；运用: *This pool is for the use of hotel guests only.* 这个游泳池仅供旅馆宾客使用。

2 (*plural* 复数形式 uses) what you can do with something 用途；功能: *This machine has many uses.* 这台机器用途广泛。
3 (*no plural* 不用复数形式) the opportunity to use something, for example something that belongs to somebody else 使用的机会: *I've got the use of Jim's car while he's on holiday.* 吉姆去度假的时候，我可以用他的汽车。
it's no use doing something it will not help to do something 没有帮助；没有用处: *It's no use telling her anything – she never listens.* 跟她说什么都没用，她总当耳边风。
make use of something to find a way of using something 使用；利用: *If you don't want that box, I can make use of it.* 你如果不要那个箱子，我倒用得上。

used¹ ⊶ /juːst/ *adjective* 形容词
be used to something to know something well because you have seen, heard, tasted, done, etc. it a lot 习惯于；适应: *I'm used to walking because I don't have a car.* 我惯于走路，因为我没有汽车。
get used to something to begin to know something well after a time 开始适应: *I'm getting used to my new job.* 我正逐渐适应我的新工作。

used² ⊶ /juːzd/ *adjective* 形容词
that had another owner before; not new 用过的；旧的；二手的 ⊃ SAME MEANING **second-hand** 同义词为 second-hand: *The garage sells used cars.* 那修车厂出售二手汽车。⊃ OPPOSITE **new** 反义词为 new

used to ⊶ /'juːst tə; 'juːst tu/ *modal verb* 情态动词
words that tell us about something that happened often or that was true in the past 过去常常；过去曾经: *She used to smoke when she was young.* 她年轻的时候抽烟。◇ *I used to be afraid of dogs, but now I like them.* 我以前怕狗，现在倒很喜欢。

> 🔊 GRAMMAR 语法说明
> To form questions we use **did** with **use to**. 构成疑问句用 did 和 use to: *Did she use to smoke when she was young?* 她年轻时抽烟吗？
> We form negatives with **didn't use to**. 构成否定句用 didn't use to: *I didn't use to like fish, but I do now.* 我以前不喜欢吃鱼，现在可喜欢了。

useful ⊶ /'juːsfl/ *adjective* 形容词
good and helpful for doing something

A
B
C
D
E
F
G
H
I
J
K
L
M
N
O
P
Q
R
S
T
U
V
W
X
Y
Z

有用的；有帮助的；有益的： *This bag will be useful for carrying my books.* 这个包给我带书很有用。

useless 0━ /'juːsləs/ *adjective* 形容词
1 not good for anything 无用的；无价值的： *A car is useless without petrol.* 汽车没有汽油就毫无用处。
2 that does not do what you hoped 无效的；无济于事的： *It was useless asking my brother for money – he didn't have any.* 问我哥哥要钱也没用，他根本没有。

user 0━ /'juːzə(r)/ *noun* 名词
a person who uses something 使用者；用户： *computer users* 电脑用户

user-friendly /juːzə 'frendli/ *adjective* 形容词
easy to understand and use 易懂的；便于使用的： *Computers are much more user-friendly now than they used to be.* 现在的电脑比以前的容易操作得多。

usual 0━ /'juːʒuəl/ *adjective* 形容词
that happens most often 通常的；惯常的
⊃ SAME MEANING **normal** 同义词为

normal： *He arrived home later than usual.* 他回家比平时晚了一些。
as usual in the way that happens most often 照例；照旧；像往常一样： *Julie was late, as usual.* 朱莉照例又迟到了。

usually 0━ /'juːʒuəli/ *adverb* 副词
in the way that is usual; most often 通常；一般： *I'm usually home by six o'clock.* 我一般六点前到家。

utensil /juː'tensl/ *noun* 名词
a tool that is used in the home （家庭）用具，器皿： *cooking utensils* 炊具

utter¹ /'ʌtə(r)/ *adjective* 形容词
complete 完全的；彻底的： *He felt an utter fool.* 他觉得自己是个十足的笨蛋。

utter² /'ʌtə(r)/ *verb* 动词 (utters, uttering, uttered /'ʌtəd/) (*formal* 正式)
to say something or make a sound with your mouth 说；讲；出声： *She did not utter a word.* 她一句话也没说。

utterly /'ʌtəli/ *adverb* 副词
completely or very 完全；非常： *That's utterly impossible!* 那是绝对不可能的！

V v

V, v /viː/ *noun* 名词
1 (*plural* 复数形式 **V's, v's** /viːz/) the twenty-second letter of the English alphabet 英语字母表的第 22 个字母: *'Voice' begins with a 'V'.* * voice 一词以字母 v 开头。
2 V *short for* VOLT * volt 的缩略式
3 v (*British* 英式英语) (*American* 美式英语 vs) *short for* VERSUS * versus 的缩略式: *Liverpool v Manchester United* 利物浦队对曼彻斯特联队

vacancy /'veɪkənsi/ *noun* 名词 (*plural* 复数形式 **vacancies**)
1 a job that nobody is doing 职位空缺: *We have a vacancy for a secretary in our office.* 我们办公室有个秘书的职位空缺。
2 a room in a hotel that nobody is using 旅馆空房: *The sign outside the hotel says 'no vacancies'* (= the hotel is full). 旅馆外面的牌子上写着"客满"。

vacant /'veɪkənt/ *adjective* 形容词
1 empty or not being used 空着的; 闲置的; 未占用的: *a vacant room* 空房
2 If a job in a company is **vacant**, nobody is doing it and it is available for somebody to do. (职位)空缺的

vacation 0= /və'keɪʃn/ *noun* 名词 (*American* 美式英语) (*British* 英式英语 **holiday**)
a period of time when you are not working or studying 假期: *They're on vacation in Hawaii.* 他们正在夏威夷度假。

vaccinate /'væksɪmeɪt/ *verb* 动词 (**vaccinates, vaccinating, vaccinated**)
to put a substance into a person's or an animal's blood using a needle, to stop them getting a disease 给…种疫苗; 给…打防疫针: *Have you been vaccinated against measles?* 你接种过麻疹疫苗吗?

vaccination /,væksɪ'neɪʃn/ *noun* 名词
when a substance is put into a person's or an animal's blood with a needle, to stop them getting a disease 疫苗接种: *a vaccination against measles* 麻疹疫苗的接种

vaccine /'væksiːn/ *noun* 名词
a substance that is put into a person's or an animal's blood using a needle, to stop them getting a disease 疫苗

vacuum /'vækjuəm/ *noun* 名词
a space with no air, gas or anything else in it 真空

vacuum cleaner 真空吸尘器

vacuum cleaner /'vækjuəm kliːnə(r)/ *noun* 名词
a machine that cleans carpets by sucking up dirt 真空吸尘器

vagina /və'dʒaɪnə/ *noun* 名词
the part of a woman's or a female animal's body that leads to the place where a baby grows (called the womb) 阴道

vague /veɪɡ/ *adjective* 形容词 (**vaguer, vaguest**)
not clear or not exact 模糊的; 含糊的; 不确切的: *I couldn't find the house because he gave me very vague directions.* 我找不到那所房子, 因为他给我的指示很含糊。
▶ **vaguely** /'veɪɡli/ *adverb* 副词: *I vaguely remember what happened.* 我隐约记得发生的事情。

vain /veɪn/ *adjective* 形容词 (**vainer, vainest**)
1 too proud of what you can do or how you look 虚荣的; 自负的 ⊃ The noun is **vanity**. 名词为 vanity。
2 useless; without success 无用的; 徒劳的; 枉然的: *They made a vain attempt to save his life.* 他们努力拯救, 但未能保住他的命。

in vain without success 徒劳；枉然:
I tried in vain to sleep. 我试着睡觉，
却怎么也睡不着。

valid /'vælɪd/ *adjective* 形容词
able to be used; acceptable 有效的；
认可的: *Your bus ticket is valid for one week.* 你的公共汽车票有效期为一个星期。
✪ OPPOSITE **invalid** 反义词为 invalid

valley 0̱ /'væli/ *noun* 名词 (plural 复数
形式 valleys)
the low land between mountains; the
land that a river flows through 谷；
山谷；溪谷

valuable 0̱ /'væljuəbl/ *adjective*
形容词
1 worth a lot of money 值钱的；贵重的:
Is this ring valuable? 这枚戒指很值钱吗?
2 very useful 十分有用的；宝贵的: *The
book contains some valuable information.*
这本书有一些很有用的信息。

value¹ 0̱ /'vælju:/ *noun* 名词
1 (plural 复数形式 values) how much
money you can sell something for（物品
的）价值: *The thieves stole goods with
a total value of $100 000.* 窃贼偷走了共值
10 万元的物品。
2 (no plural 不用复数形式) (British 英式
英语) how much something is worth
compared with its price（相对于价格
的）划算程度，值: *The meal was good
value at only €8.50.* 这一餐只花了 8.5
欧元，很划算。
3 (no plural 不用复数形式) how useful or
important something is 好处；重要性:
Their help was of great value. 他们的帮助
极为重要。

value² /'vælju:/ *verb* 动词 (values, valuing,
valued /'vælju:d/)
1 to think that something is very
important 珍视；珍爱: *I value my
freedom.* 我珍视自己的自由。
2 to say how much money something is
worth 给…估价；给…定价: *The house
was valued at $800 000.* 这所房子估价为
80 万元。

valve /vælv/ *noun* 名词
a part in a pipe or tube which lets air,
liquid or gas flow in one direction only
阀；阀门；气门

vampire /'væmpaɪə(r)/ *noun* 名词
a person in stories who drinks people's
blood（传说中的）吸血鬼

van /væn/ *noun* 名词
a kind of big car or small lorry for
carrying things 厢式小货车；客货车

van 客货车

vandal /'vændl/ *noun* 名词
a person who deliberately damages
public property 故意破坏公物者:
*Vandals have damaged the benches in the
park.* 有人故意毁坏了公园里的长凳。

vandalism /'vændəlɪzəm/ *noun* 名词
(no plural 不用复数形式)
the crime of destroying or damaging
public property deliberately and for
no good reason 故意破坏公物（罪）:
*Vandalism is a problem in this part of the
city.* 城中的这一带常有公物遭蓄意破坏的
问题。

vandalize /'vændəlaɪz/ *verb* 动词
(vandalizes, vandalizing, vandalized
/'vændəlaɪzd/)
to damage public property deliberately
故意破坏（公物）

vanilla /və'nɪlə/ *noun* 名词 (no plural
不用复数形式)
a substance from a plant that gives a
taste to some sweet foods 香草香精（用于
甜食调味）: *vanilla ice cream* 香草冰激凌

vanish /'vænɪʃ/ *verb* 动词 (vanishes,
vanishing, vanished /'vænɪʃt/)
to go away; to stop being seen 消失；
不见踪影 ✪ SAME MEANING **disappear**
同义词为 disappear: *The thief ran into
the crowd and vanished.* 小偷跑进人群后
就失去踪影了。

vanity /'vænəti/ *noun* 名词 (no plural
不用复数形式)
being too proud of what you can do or
how you look 虚荣；自负 ✪ The adjective
is **vain.** 形容词为 vain。

vapour (British 英式英语) (American 美式
英语 vapor) /'veɪpə(r)/ *noun* 名词
very small drops of liquid that look like
a gas 蒸气；雾气: *water vapour* 水蒸气

varied¹ 0̱ /'veərid/ *adjective* 形容词
including a lot of different things 各种
各样的；形形色色的: *I try to make my
lessons as varied as possible.* 我尽力让我的
课内容多样。

varied² *form of* VARY * vary 的不同形式

varies *form of* VARY * vary 的不同形式

variety ⚬┐ /vəˈraɪəti/ *noun* 名词
1 (*no plural* 不用复数形式) a lot of different things 多种多样；多种式样: *There's a wide variety of dishes on the menu.* 菜单上有各种各样的菜肴。
2 (*no plural* 不用复数形式) the fact that you are not always doing the same things 多样化；多变性: *There's a lot of variety in my new job.* 我的新工作内容五花八门。
3 (*plural* 复数形式 varieties) a type of something 种类；品种: *This variety of apple is very sweet.* 这个品种的苹果很甜。

various ⚬┐ /ˈveəriəs/ *adjective* 形容词
several different 不同的；各种各样的: *We sell this shirt in various colours and sizes.* 我们出售的这款衬衫有多种颜色和尺码。

varnish /ˈvɑːnɪʃ/ *noun* 名词 (*no plural* 不用复数形式)
a clear paint with no colour, that you put on something to make it shine 清漆；罩光漆
▸ **varnish** *verb* 动词 (varnishes, varnishing, varnished /ˈvɑːnɪʃt/): *The doors are then stained and varnished.* 然后这些门要染色并涂上清漆。

vary ⚬┐ /ˈveəri/ *verb* 动词 (varies, varying, varied /ˈveərid/, has varied)
1 to be different from each other or to change according to the situation 有差别；（根据情况）变化，改变: *Class sizes vary from 8 to 15.* 班级人数由 8 人至 15 人不等。◇ *The price varies according to the quality.* 价格因质量不同而有所变化。
2 to make something different by changing it often in some way（不时）改变，变更: *We try to vary the course to suit students' needs.* 我们尝试调整课程以适应学生的需求。

vase 花瓶

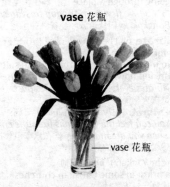

——— vase 花瓶

vase /vɑːz/ *noun* 名词
a pot that you put cut flowers in 花瓶

vast /vɑːst/ *adjective* 形容词
very big 庞大的；巨大的；浩大的 ⊃ SAME MEANING **enormous**, **huge** 同义词为 enormous 和 huge: *Australia is a vast country.* 澳大利亚是个幅员辽阔的国家。

VCR /ˌviː siː ˈɑː(r)/ *noun* 名词
a machine connected to a television, that you use for recording or showing programmes. **VCR** is short for 'video cassette recorder'. （盒式）录像机（VCR 是 video cassette recorder 的缩略式）

VDU /ˌviː diː ˈjuː/ *noun* 名词
a computer screen. **VDU** is short for 'visual display unit'. 视频显示器（VDU 是 visual display unit 的缩略式）

veal /viːl/ *noun* 名词 (*no plural* 不用复数形式)
meat from a young cow (a calf) 小牛肉 ⊃ Look at the note at **cow**. 见 cow 条的注释。

vegan /ˈviːɡən/ *noun* 名词
a person who does not eat meat or any other foods that come from animals, such as eggs or milk 纯素食主义者（不吃肉类和蛋、奶等任何产自动物的食物）

vegetable ⚬┐ /ˈvedʒtəbl/ *noun* 名词
a plant or part of a plant that we eat 蔬菜: *The students grow vegetables such as cabbages, beans and carrots.* 学生种植卷心菜、豆荚、胡萝卜等蔬菜。 ⊃ Look at Picture Dictionary page **P9**. 见彩页 P9。

vegetarian /ˌvedʒəˈteəriən/ *noun* 名词
a person who does not eat meat or fish 素食者；吃素的人
▸ **vegetarian** *adjective* 形容词: *a vegetarian restaurant* 素菜馆

vehicle ⚬┐ /ˈviːəkl/ *noun* 名词 (*formal* 正式)
a car, bus, lorry, bicycle, etc.; a thing that takes people or things from place to place 交通工具；车辆: *Are you the owner of this vehicle?* 你是这辆车的车主吗?

veil /veɪl/ *noun* 名词
a piece of material that a woman puts over her head and face （女用）面纱

vein /veɪn/ *noun* 名词
one of the small tubes in your body that carry blood to the heart 静脉

Velcro™ /ˈvelkrəʊ/ *noun* 名词 (*no plural* 不用复数形式)
two bands of special material that stick together to fasten clothes, shoes, etc. 维可牢搭扣；魔术贴；尼龙搭扣

A
B
C
D
E
F
G
H
I
J
K
L
M
N
O
P
Q
R
S
T
U
V
W
X
Y
Z

velvet /'velvɪt/ **noun** 名词 (*no plural* 不用复数形式)

cloth that is soft and thick on one side 丝绒；天鹅绒：*red velvet curtains* 红色的丝绒窗帘

ventilate /'ventɪleɪt/ **verb** 动词 (**ventilates, ventilating, ventilated**)

to allow air to move through a building 使（建筑物）通风；使空气流通

▶ **ventilation** /ˌventɪ'leɪʃn/ **noun** 名词 (*no plural* 不用复数形式)：*The only ventilation was one tiny window.* 唯一的通风口是一扇小窗。

veranda (*also* 亦作 **verandah**) /və'rændə/ (*British* 英式英语) (*American* 美式英语 **porch**) **noun** 名词

a covered area with an open front, which is joined to a house on the ground floor （房屋底层有顶半敞的）走廊，游廊

verb /vɜːb/ **noun** 名词

(*grammar* 语法) a word that tells you what somebody does or what happens. 'Go', 'sing', 'do' and 'be' are all **verbs**. 动词

verdict /'vɜːdɪkt/ **noun** 名词

a decision in a court of law about whether somebody is guilty or not （法庭的）裁定，裁决：*The jury returned a verdict of 'not guilty'.* 陪审团作了无罪的裁决。

verse /vɜːs/ **noun** 名词

1 (*no plural* 不用复数形式) words arranged in lines with a definite beat, often with sounds repeated at the ends of lines 诗；韵文 ⊃ SAME MEANING **poetry** 同义词为 poetry：*The play is written in verse.* 这个剧本是用韵文写的。
2 (*plural* 复数形式 **verses**) a group of lines in a song or poem （歌曲或诗的）节，段落：*This song has five verses.* 这首歌有五段。

version /'vɜːʃn/ **noun** 名词

1 a form of something that is different in some way 版本；变体：*the latest version of the software* 这个软件的最新版本
2 what one person says or writes about something that happened （对所发生事件的）说法，描述：*His version of the accident is different from mine.* 他对这一事故的叙述和我说的不同。

versus /'vɜːsəs/ (*abbr.* 缩略式 **v, vs**) **preposition** 介词

on the other side in a sport （表示体育运动中双方对阵）对 ⊃ SAME MEANING **against** 同义词为 against：*There's a good football match on TV tonight – England*

versus Brazil. 今晚电视上有场精彩的足球比赛——英格兰对巴西。

vertical /'vɜːtɪkl/ **adjective** 形容词

going straight up or down at an angle of 90° from the ground 竖的；垂直的；直立的：*a vertical line* 垂直线 ⊃ Look at **horizontal**. 见 horizontal。⊃ Look at the picture at **line¹**. 见 line¹ 的插图。

very¹ 0- /'veri/ **adverb** 副词

You use 'very' before another word to make it stronger. 很；非常；十分：*Very few people know that.* 很少人知道那件事。◇ *She speaks very quietly.* 她说话声音非常轻。◇ *I like chocolate very much.* 我非常喜欢吃巧克力。◇ *I'm not very hungry.* 我不太饿。

very² /'veri/ **adjective** 形容词

exact; same 正是的；恰好的；同一的：*You are the very person I wanted to see!* 你正是我想见的人！◇ *We climbed to the very top of the mountain.* 我们登上了山的最高处。

vest /vest/ **noun** 名词

1 (*British* 英式英语) (*American* 美式英语 **undershirt**) a piece of clothing that you wear under your other clothes on the top part of your body （衣服里面贴身穿的）背心，汗衫 ⊃ Look at Picture Dictionary page **P5**. 见彩页 P5。
2 *American English for* WAISTCOAT 美式英语，即 waistcoat

vet /vet/ (*British* 英式英语) (*American* 美式英语 **veterinarian** /ˌvetərɪ'neəriən/) (*British formal also* 英式英语正式亦作 **veterinary surgeon** /'vetrənri sɜːdʒən/) **noun** 名词

a doctor for animals 兽医 ⊃ Look at Picture Dictionary page **P12**. 见彩页 P12。

via /'vaɪə/ **preposition** 介词

going through a place 经，经由（某地方）：*We flew from London to Sydney via Bangkok.* 我们从伦敦经曼谷飞往悉尼。

vibrate /vaɪ'breɪt/ **verb** 动词 (**vibrates, vibrating, vibrated**)

to move very quickly from side to side or up and down 震动；颤动：*The house vibrates every time a train goes past.* 每次火车经过，房子就震动。

▶ **vibration** /vaɪ'breɪʃn/ **noun** 名词：*You can feel the vibrations from the engine when you are in the car.* 坐在汽车里你能感受到发动机的震动。

vicar /'vɪkə(r)/ **noun** 名词

a priest in some Christian churches 代牧；教区牧师

vice /vaɪs/ *noun* 名词
1 (*no plural* 不用复数形式) criminal activities involving sex or drugs（与性或毒品有关的）罪恶活动，罪行：*detectives from the vice squad* 扫黄缉毒队的警探
2 (*plural* 复数形式 vices) a moral weakness or bad habit 不道德行为；恶行；恶习

vice- /vaɪs/ *prefix* 前缀
next to the leader in importance; able to represent the leader 副；代理：*He's vice-captain of the team.* 他是该队的副队长。◇ *the vice-president* 副总统

vicinity /və'sɪnəti/ *noun* 名词
in the vicinity (*formal* 正式) in an area; near a place 在周围地区；附近：*There are three parks in the vicinity of the school.* 学校周围有三个公园。

vicious /'vɪʃəs/ *adjective* 形容词
violent and cruel 残暴的；残酷的：*a vicious attack* 凶残的袭击

victim /'vɪktɪm/ *noun* 名词
a person or thing that is hurt, damaged or killed by somebody or something 受害者；罹难者；牺牲品：*the innocent victims of crime* 罪案的无辜受害者

victorious /vɪk'tɔːriəs/ *adjective* 形容词
successful in a fight, game or war 胜利的；获胜的：*the victorious team* 获胜队

victory /'vɪktəri/ *noun* 名词 (*plural* 复数形式 victories)
success in a fight, game or war 胜利：*the team's 3–2 victory against Poland* 该队以 3 比 2 战胜波兰队

video 0━ /'vɪdiəʊ/ *noun* 名词 (*plural* 复数形式 videos)
1 (*also* 亦作 videotape) tape in a plastic box (called a cassette) on which a film, TV programme or real event is recorded（盒式）录像带：*You can get this film on video or on DVD.* 你可以买到这部电影的录像带或 DVD。◇ *We stayed at home and watched a video.* 我们待在家里看录像了。◇ *They made a video of the wedding.* 他们给婚礼拍了录像。
2 (*British* 英式英语) (*also* 亦作 video recorder) a machine connected to a television, that you use for recording or showing programmes 录像机：*Have you set the video?* 你设定好录像机了吗？

video game /'vɪdiəʊ ɡeɪm/ *noun* 名词
a game that you play using a TV or computer screen 电子游戏

view 0━ /vjuː/ *noun* 名词
1 what you believe or think about something 观点；看法；见解 ⊃ SAME MEANING **opinion** 同义词为 opinion：*He has strong views on marriage.* 对于婚姻，他有坚定的主张。◇ *In my view, she has done nothing wrong.* 依我看来，她做得没有一点错。
2 what you can see from a place 景观；视野：*There were beautiful views of the mountains all around.* 四周都能看到群山的美景。◇ *At the top of the hill, the lake came into view* (= could be seen). 从山顶上望去，这个湖映入眼帘。

in view of something because of something 由于；鉴于：*In view of the bad weather we decided to cancel the match.* 由于天气欠佳，我们决定取消比赛。

on view in a place for people to see 在展出：*Her paintings are on view at the museum.* 她的画正在博物馆展出。

viewer /'vjuːə(r)/ *noun* 名词
a person who watches a television programme 电视观众

vigorous /'vɪɡərəs/ *adjective* 形容词
strong and active 强壮的；充满活力的：*vigorous exercise* 剧烈运动
▶ **vigorously** /'vɪɡərəsli/ *adverb* 副词：*She shook my hand vigorously.* 她用力地和我握手。

vile /vaɪl/ *adjective* 形容词 (viler, vilest)
extremely unpleasant 糟糕透顶的；极坏的 ⊃ SAME MEANING **horrible** 同义词为 horrible：*What a vile smell!* 多恶心的气味！

villa /'vɪlə/ *noun* 名词
a house with a garden in the countryside, especially in southern Europe（尤指南欧的）乡间庄园，别墅

village 0━ /'vɪlɪdʒ/ *noun* 名词
a very small town in the countryside 村；乡村；村庄 ⊃ Look at the note at **town**. 见 town 条的注释。

villager /'vɪlɪdʒə(r)/ *noun* 名词
a person who lives in a village 村民

villain /'vɪlən/ *noun* 名词
a bad person, usually in a book, play or film（书、戏剧或电影中的）坏人，坏蛋

vine /vaɪn/ *noun* 名词
the plant that produces GRAPES (= small fruits that we eat or use to make wine) 葡萄藤；葡萄蔓

vinegar /'vɪnɪɡə(r)/ *noun* 名词 (*no plural* 不用复数形式)
a liquid with a strong sharp taste that is used in cooking 醋：*I mixed some oil and*

A
B
C
D
E
F
G
H
I
J
K
L
M
N
O
P
Q
R
S
T
U
V
W
X
Y
Z

A
B
C
D
E
F
G
H
I
J
K
L
M
N
O
P
Q
R
S
T
U
V
W
X
Y
Z

vinegar to put on the salad. 我调了些油和醋加在沙拉上。 ⊃ Look at Picture Dictionary page **P6**. 见彩页 P6。

vineyard /'vɪnjəd/ *noun* 名词
a piece of land where GRAPES are grown to make wine（种植酿酒葡萄的）葡萄园

viola /vi'əʊlə/ *noun* 名词
a musical instrument like a large VIOLIN 中提琴

violence ⚬ /'vaɪələns/ *noun* 名词 (*no plural* 不用复数形式)
1 violent behaviour 暴力；暴行: *There's too much violence on TV.* 电视上的暴力画面太多了。
2 force or power 激烈的力量: *the violence of the storm* 暴风雨的威力

violent ⚬ /'vaɪələnt/ *adjective* 形容词
strong and dangerous; causing physical harm 暴力的；狂暴的: *Her husband was a violent man.* 她丈夫是个粗暴的人。◇ *The protest march started peacefully but later turned violent.* 抗议游行一开始以和平的方式进行，但后来转变成暴力。
▸ **violently** /'vaɪələntli/ *adverb* 副词:
Did she behave violently towards you? 她有对你暴力相向吗？

violet /'vaɪələt/ *noun* 名词
1 a small purple flower 紫罗兰
2 a colour that is between dark blue and purple 蓝紫色；紫罗兰色
▸ **violet** *adjective* 形容词: *violet eyes* 蓝紫色的眼睛

violin 小提琴

bow 琴弓

violin /ˌvaɪə'lɪn/ *noun* 名词
a musical instrument that you hold under your chin and play by moving a stick (called a **bow**) across the strings 小提琴

VIP /ˌviː aɪ 'piː/ *noun* 名词
a person who is famous or important. **VIP** is short for 'very important person'. 要人，贵宾（VIP 是 very important person 的缩略式）

virtual /'vɜːtʃuəl/ *adjective* 形容词
1 being almost or very nearly something 几乎⋯的；事实上的；实际上的: *He married a virtual stranger.* 他娶了一个几乎素不相识的女子。
2 made to appear to exist by a computer（电脑）虚拟的

virtually /'vɜːtʃuəli/ *adverb* 副词
almost 几乎；差不多: *The two boys look virtually the same.* 两个男孩长得几乎一模一样。

virtual reality /ˌvɜːtʃuəl ri'æləti/ *noun* 名词 (*no plural* 不用复数形式)
computer images that seem to be all around you and seem almost real（电脑）虚拟现实，拟境，虚拟时空

virtue /'vɜːtʃuː/ *noun* 名词
behaviour that shows high moral standards; a good quality or habit 高尚的道德；美德: *a life of virtue* 品行高尚的生活 ◇ *He has many virtues.* 他有很多美德。

virus /'vaɪrəs/ *noun* 名词 (*plural* 复数形式 viruses)
1 a living thing that is too small to see but that can make you ill 病毒；滤过性病毒: *a flu virus* 流感病毒
2 (*computing* 电脑) a program that enters your computer and stops it from working properly 电脑病毒

visa /'viːzə/ *noun* 名词
an official piece of paper or mark in your passport to show that you can go into a country 签证

visible /'vɪzəbl/ *adjective* 形容词
If something is **visible**, you can see it. 看得见的；可见的: *Stars are only visible at night.* 星星只有在夜晚才看得见。
⊃ OPPOSITE **invisible** 反义词为 invisible

vision /'vɪʒn/ *noun* 名词
1 (*no plural* 不用复数形式) the power to see 视力；视觉 ⊃ SAME MEANING **sight** 同义词为 sight: *He wears glasses because he has poor vision.* 他因视力差而戴眼镜。
2 (*plural* 复数形式 visions) a picture in your mind; a dream 幻象；想象；梦幻: *They have a vision of a world without war.* 他们幻想一个没有战争的世界。

visit ⚬ /'vɪzɪt/ *verb* 动词 (visits, visiting, visited)

to go to see a person or place for a short time 访问；拜访；看望；参观：*When you go to London you must visit the Science Museum.* 你去伦敦的时候，可得参观一下科学博物馆。◇ *She visited me in hospital.* 她到医院看望了我。
▶ **visit** *noun* 名词：*This is my first visit to New York.* 这是我第一次到访纽约。◇ *He promised to pay us a visit next year.* 他答应了明年来看望我们。

visitor 0➡ /ˈvɪzɪtə(r)/ *noun* 名词
a person who goes to see another person or a place for a short time 访问者；来访者；参观者；游客：*The old lady never has any visitors.* 这个老太太从来没有人来看她。◇ *Millions of visitors come to Rome every year.* 每年数以百万计的游客来到罗马。

visual /ˈvɪʒuəl/ *adjective* 形容词
connected with seeing 视觉的：*Painting and cinema are visual arts.* 绘画和电影是视觉艺术。

visual aid /ˌvɪʒuəl ˈeɪd/ *noun* 名词
an object that a teacher shows you in lessons to help you learn something 直观教具；视觉辅助教具

vital /ˈvaɪtl/ *adjective* 形容词
very important 极其重要的；必不可少的：*It's vital that she sees a doctor – she's very ill.* 她一定要去看医生，她病得很重。

vitamin /ˈvɪtəmɪn/ *noun* 名词
one of the things in food that you need to be healthy 维生素；维他命：*Oranges are full of vitamin C.* 橙子含有丰富的维生素 C。

vivid /ˈvɪvɪd/ *adjective* 形容词
1 making a very clear picture in your mind 生动的；清晰的；逼真的：*I had a very vivid dream last night.* 我昨晚做了一个非常逼真的梦。
2 having a strong bright colour（颜色）鲜明的，鲜艳的：*vivid yellow* 鲜艳的黄色
▶ **vividly** /ˈvɪvɪdli/ *adverb* 副词：*I remember my first day at school vividly.* 我对第一天上学的情景记忆犹新。

vocabulary /vəˈkæbjələri/ *noun* 名词
1 (*plural* 复数形式 vocabularies) all the words that somebody knows or that are used in a particular book or subject（个人掌握的或某书籍、学科的）词汇，词汇量：*He has an amazing vocabulary for a five-year-old.* 他才五岁，掌握的词汇却多得惊人。
2 (*no plural* 不用复数形式) all the words in a language（某一语言的）词汇：*New*

words are always entering the vocabulary. 不断有新词成为词汇的一部分。

vodka /ˈvɒdkə/ *noun* 名词
1 (*no plural* 不用复数形式) a strong alcoholic drink 伏特加（烈性酒）
2 (*plural* 复数形式 vodkas) a glass of vodka 一杯伏特加

voice 0➡ /vɔɪs/ *noun* 名词
the sounds that you make when you speak or sing 说话声；嗓音：*Steve has a very deep voice.* 史蒂夫的嗓音很低沉。
at the top of your voice very loudly 最大声地；非常响亮地：*'Come here!' she shouted at the top of her voice.* "到这儿来！"她扯着嗓子大喊。
raise your voice to speak more loudly 提高嗓门

voicemail /ˈvɔɪsmeɪl/ *noun* 名词
(*no plural* 不用复数形式)
an electronic system that lets you leave or listen to telephone messages 语音信箱；电话留言：*Have you checked your voicemail?* 你查过你的语音信箱了吗？

volcano /vɒlˈkeɪnəʊ/ *noun* 名词 (*plural* 复数形式 volcanoes)
a mountain with a hole in the top where fire, gas and hot liquid rock (called lava) sometimes come out 火山
▶ **volcanic** /vɒlˈkænɪk/ *adjective* 形容词：*volcanic rocks* 火山岩

volleyball /ˈvɒlibɔːl/ *noun* 名词
(*no plural* 不用复数形式)
a game where two teams try to hit a ball over a high net with their hands 排球运动：*We played volleyball on the beach.* 我们在沙滩上打排球。

volt /vəʊlt/ *noun* 名词 (*abbr.* 缩略式 V)
a measure of electricity 伏，伏特（电压单位）

volume /ˈvɒljuːm/ *noun* 名词
1 (*no plural* 不用复数形式) the amount of space that something fills, or the amount of space inside something 体积；容积；容量：*What is the volume of this box?* 这个箱子的容积是多少？
2 (*no plural* 不用复数形式) the amount of sound that something makes 音量：*I can't hear the radio. Can you turn the volume up?* 我听不见收音机的声音。你能把音量调大些吗？
3 (*plural* 复数形式 volumes) a book, especially one of a set（尤指一套书的）卷，册：*The dictionary is in two volumes.* 这部词典有两卷。

voluntarily /ˈvɒləntrəli/ *adverb* 副词
because you want to, not because you

A B C D E F G H I J K L M N O P Q R S T U **V** W X Y Z

must 自愿地；主动地: *She left the job voluntarily.* 她自愿离职。

voluntary /ˈvɒləntri/ *adjective* 形容词
1 If something is **voluntary**, you do it because you want to, not because you must. 自愿的；主动的: *She made a voluntary decision to leave the job.* 她决定自动离职。
2 without payment 义务的；无偿的: *He does voluntary work at a children's hospital.* 他在一家儿童医院做义工。

volunteer[1] /ˌvɒlənˈtɪə(r)/ *noun* 名词
a person who says that they will do a job without being forced or without being paid 志愿者；义务工作者: *They're asking for volunteers to help at the Christmas party.* 他们征求在圣诞派对上帮忙的义工。

volunteer[2] /ˌvɒlənˈtɪə(r)/ *verb* 动词
(volunteers, volunteering, volunteered /ˌvɒlənˈtɪəd/)
to say that you will do a job without being forced or without being paid 自愿，志愿，主动（做某事）: *I volunteered to do the washing-up.* 我主动提出由我来洗碗。

vomit /ˈvɒmɪt/ *verb* 动词 (vomits, vomiting, vomited)
When you **vomit**, food comes up from your stomach and out of your mouth. 呕吐 ➲ SAME MEANING **be sick** 同义词为 be sick
▶ **vomit** *noun* 名词 (*no plural* 不用复数形式) the food that comes up from your stomach when you VOMIT 呕吐物

vote 0── /vəʊt/ *noun* 名词
when you choose somebody or something by writing on a piece of paper or by putting up your hand 投票；表决: *There were 96 votes for the plan, and 25 against.* 这个计划有 96 票赞成，25 票反对。
▶ **vote** *verb* 动词 (votes, voting, voted): *Who did you vote for in the election?* 选举中你投票支持谁？

voter /ˈvəʊtə(r)/ *noun* 名词
a person who votes in a political election 投票人；选民

voucher /ˈvaʊtʃə(r)/ *noun* 名词 (*British* 英式英语)
a piece of paper that you can use instead of money to pay for something 代币券；票券

vowel /ˈvaʊəl/ *noun* 名词
1 one of the letters *a, e, i, o* or *u* 元音字母
2 a sound represented by one of the letters *a, e, i, o, u* or *y*, or by a set of letters such as *ea, ow* or *oy* 元音；母音 ➲ Look at **consonant**. 见 consonant。

voyage /ˈvɔɪɪdʒ/ *noun* 名词
a long journey by boat or in space 航行；航海；航天: *a voyage from London to New York* 从伦敦到纽约的海上航行

vs *short way of writing* VERSUS * versus 的缩写形式

vulgar /ˈvʌlgə(r)/ *adjective* 形容词
not showing good judgement about what is attractive or appropriate; not polite or well behaved 庸俗的；粗俗的；不雅的: *She found their behaviour rather vulgar.* 她觉得他们的行为相当粗野。

vulnerable /ˈvʌlnərəbl/ *adjective* 形容词
likely to be hurt or damaged 易受伤害的；脆弱的: *The soldiers' position meant that they were vulnerable to attack.* 士兵所处的位置意味着他们易受攻击。

vulture 秃鹫

vulture /ˈvʌltʃə(r)/ *noun* 名词
a type of bird that eats dead animals 秃鹫

W w

W, w /ˈdʌblju:/ *noun* 名词
1 (*plural* 复数形式 W's, w's /ˈdʌblju:z/) the twenty-third letter of the English alphabet 英语字母表的第 23 个字母: *'Water' begins with a 'W'.* * water 一词以字母 w 开头。
2 W *short for* WATT * watt 的缩略式

wade /weɪd/ *verb* 动词 (wades, wading, waded)
to walk through water 涉水；蹚水: *Can we wade across the river, or is it too deep?* 咱们能蹚水过河吗，还是水太深了？

wag /wæg/ *verb* 动词 (wags, wagging, wagged /wægd/)
to move or make something move from side to side or up and down （使）摇摆，摆动: *The dog wagged its tail.* 狗摇了摇尾巴。

wages /ˈweɪdʒɪz/ *noun* 名词 (*plural* 用复数形式)
the money that you receive every week for the work that you do （按周领的）工资: *Our wages are paid every Friday.* 我们每周五发工钱。◇ *low wages* 低薪

wagon /ˈwægən/ *noun* 名词
1 a vehicle with four wheels that a horse pulls 四轮马车
2 (*British* 英式英语) (*American* 美式英语 freight car) a part of a train where things like coal are carried （火车的）货车车厢

wail /weɪl/ *verb* 动词 (wails, wailing, wailed /weɪld/)
to make a long sad noise 号哭；恸哭: *The little boy started wailing for his mother.* 小男孩大哭起来，要找妈妈。

waistcoat 西服背心

waist /weɪst/ *noun* 名词
the narrow part around the middle of your body 腰；腰部 ⊃ Look at Picture Dictionary page **P4**. 见彩页 **P4**。

waistcoat /ˈweɪskəʊt/ (*British* 英式英语) (*American* 美式英语 vest) *noun* 名词
a piece of clothing like a jacket with no sleeves 西服背心

wait¹ 0━ /weɪt/ *verb* 动词 (waits, waiting, waited)
to stay in one place until something happens or until somebody or something comes 等候；等待: *If I'm late, please wait for me.* 我要是迟了，请等我一下。◇ *Have you been waiting long?* 你等了很长时间吗？◇ *The doctor kept me waiting* (= made me wait) *for half an hour.* 医生让我等了半个小时。
can't wait used when somebody is very excited about something that is going to happen 迫不及待: *I can't wait to see you again!* 我迫不及待想再见到你!
wait and see to be patient and find out later 等着瞧；走着瞧: *'What are we having for dinner?' 'Wait and see!'* "我们晚饭吃什么?" "等着瞧吧!"
wait up to not go to bed until somebody comes home 熬夜等某人回家；等门: *I'll be home late tonight so don't wait up for me.* 我今晚回家晚，所以不用熬夜等我了。

wait² /weɪt/ *noun* 名词
a time when you wait 等候；等待: *We had a long wait for the bus.* 我们等公共汽车等了很长时间。

waiter /ˈweɪtə(r)/ *noun* 名词
a man who brings food and drink to your table in a restaurant （餐馆）服务员 ⊃ Look at Picture Dictionary page **P12**. 见彩页 **P12**。

waiting room /ˈweɪtɪŋ ru:m/ *noun* 名词
a room where people can sit and wait, for example to see a doctor or to catch a train 等候室；候诊室；候车室

waitress /ˈweɪtrəs/ *noun* 名词 (*plural* 复数形式 waitresses)
a woman who brings food and drink to your table in a restaurant （餐馆）女服务员

A
B
C
D
E
F
G
H
I
J
K
L
M
N
O
P
Q
R
S
T
U
V
W
X
Y
Z

A

B

C

D

E

F

G

H

I

J

K

L

M

N

O

P

Q

R

S

T

U

V

W

X

Y

Z

wake ✎ /weɪk/ (*also* 亦作 wake up) *verb* 动词 (wakes, waking, woke /wəʊk/, has woken /'wəʊkən/)

1 to stop sleeping 睡醒；醒来: *What time did you wake up this morning?* 你今天早上什么时候醒的？

2 to make somebody stop sleeping 唤醒；弄醒: *The noise woke me up.* 噪声把我吵醒了。◇ *Don't wake the baby.* 不要把宝宝弄醒。

> ✎ SPEAKING 表达方式说明
> It is more usual to say **wake up** than **wake**. * wake up 较 wake 常用。

walk¹ ✎ /wɔːk/ *verb* 动词 (walks, walking, walked /wɔːkt/)

to move on your legs, but not run 走路；行走；步行: *I usually walk to work.* 我通常步行上班。◇ *We walked 20 kilometres today.* 我们今天走了 20 公里。

walk out to leave suddenly because you are angry 愤然离开: *He walked out of the meeting.* 他愤然退出了会议。

walk² ✎ /wɔːk/ *noun* 名词

a journey on foot 步行；散步: *The beach is a short walk from our house.* 我们家到海滩走几步就到了。◇ *I took the dog for a walk.* 我带狗去散步了。◇ *It was a lovely day so we went for a walk in the park.* 那天天气很好，所以我们到公园散步去了。

walker /'wɔːkə(r)/ *noun* 名词

a person who is walking 步行者；散步的人

walking stick /'wɔːkɪŋ stɪk/ *noun* 名词

a stick that you use to help you walk 拐杖；拐棍

wall ✎ /wɔːl/ *noun* 名词

1 a side of a building or room 墙壁: *There's a picture on the wall.* 墙上挂着一幅画。

2 a thing made of stones or bricks that is built around an area 围墙；城墙: *He went through a gate in the wall.* 他穿过一道围墙门。◇ *Tom sat on the garden wall.* 汤姆坐在花园的墙头上。◇ Look at the picture at **fence**. 见 fence 的插图。

wallet /'wɒlɪt/ *noun* 名词 (*British* 英式英语) (*American* 美式英语 billfold, pocketbook)

a small flat case for money and bank cards 钱包: *A pickpocket stole my wallet.* 有个扒手把我的钱包偷了。

wallpaper /'wɔːlpeɪpə(r)/ *noun* 名词 (*no plural* 不用复数形式)

special paper that you use for covering the walls of a room 壁纸；墙纸

▸ **wallpaper** *verb* 动词 (wallpapers, wallpapering, wallpapered /'wɔːlpeɪpəd/)

to put WALLPAPER onto the walls of a room 贴壁纸: *We wallpapered the living room ourselves.* 我们自己给客厅贴了壁纸。

walnut /'wɔːlnʌt/ *noun* 名词

a type of nut that we eat 核桃；胡桃 ◇ Look at the picture at **nut**. 见 nut 的插图。

wander /'wɒndə(r)/ *verb* 动词 (wanders, wandering, wandered /'wɒndəd/)

to walk slowly with no special plan 漫游；闲逛；游荡: *We wandered around the town until the shops opened.* 我们在镇上闲逛，直至商店开门。

want ✎ /wɒnt/ *verb* 动词 (wants, wanting, wanted)

1 to wish to have or do something 想要；要: *Do you want a chocolate?* 你想吃块巧克力吗？◇ *I want to go out tonight.* 我今晚想出去。◇ *She wanted me to give her some money.* 她想我给她一点钱。

> ✎ SPEAKING 表达方式说明
> **Would like** is more polite than **want**. 用 would like 较 want 更有礼貌: *Would you like a cup of tea?* 给你来杯茶好吗？

2 (*informal* 非正式) to need something 需要: *Your car wants a wash!* 你的汽车该洗一下了！◇ *You want to be careful of that dog.* 你得当心那条狗。

war ✎ /wɔː(r)/ *noun* 名词

fighting between countries or between groups of people 战争: *War had broken out* (= started). 战争爆发了。◇ *The two countries have been at war* (= fighting) *for five years.* 两个国家已经打了五年的仗。◇ *Britain declared war on Germany.* 英国向德国宣战了。

ward /wɔːd/ *noun* 名词

a room in a hospital that has beds for the patients 病房: *He worked as a nurse on the children's ward.* 他在儿科病房当过护士。

warden /'wɔːdn/ *noun* 名词

a person whose job is to look after a place and the people in it 看守人；管理人: *the warden of a youth hostel* 青年旅舍的管理人 ◇ Look also at **traffic warden**. 亦见 traffic warden。

wardrobe /'wɔːdrəʊb/ *noun* 名词

a cupboard where you hang your clothes 衣柜；衣橱 ◇ Look at Picture Dictionary page P10. 见彩页 P10。

warehouse /'weəhaʊs/ *noun* 名词 (*plural* 复数形式 warehouses /'weəhaʊzɪz/)

a big building where people keep things before they sell them 仓库；货仓：
a furniture warehouse 家具仓库

warfare /ˈwɔːfeə(r)/ *noun* 名词 (*no plural* 不用复数形式)
the activity of fighting a war 战事： *naval warfare* 海战

warm¹ ᴏ⃗ /wɔːm/ *adjective* 形容词 (**warmer, warmest**)

> 🔍 **PRONUNCIATION** 读音说明
> The word **warm** sounds like **storm**.
> * warm 读音像 storm。

1 having a pleasant temperature that is fairly high, between cool and hot 温暖的；暖和的： *It's warm by the fire.* 火炉边很暖和。 ⊃ Look at the note at **hot**. 见 hot 条的注释。
2 Warm clothes are clothes that stop you feeling cold. （衣服）保暖的，保温的：
It's cold in the mountains, so take some warm clothes with you. 山区很冷，你带些保暖的衣服吧。
3 friendly and kind 友好的；热情的：
Martha is a very warm person. 玛莎待人很热情。 ⊃ OPPOSITE **cold** 反义词为 cold
▸ **warmly** /ˈwɔːmli/ *adverb* 副词： *The children were warmly dressed.* 孩子们穿得很暖和。 ◇ *He thanked me warmly.* 他热情地谢了我。

warm² ᴏ⃗ /wɔːm/ *verb* 动词 (**warms, warming, warmed** /wɔːmd/)
warm up, warm somebody or 或 **something up** to become warmer, or to make somebody or something warmer （使）变暖，暖和： *I warmed up some soup for lunch.* 我午饭热了些汤喝。 ◇ *It was cold this morning, but it's warming up now.* 今天早上很冷，现在暖和些了。

warmth /wɔːmθ/ *noun* 名词 (*no plural* 不用复数形式)
1 a pleasant temperature that is not too hot 温暖；暖和： *the warmth of the sun* 阳光的温暖
2 the quality of being kind and friendly 热情；友善： *the warmth of his smile* 他微笑中表现的热情

warn ᴏ⃗ /wɔːn/ *verb* 动词 (**warns, warning, warned** /wɔːnd/)
to tell somebody about danger or about something bad that may happen 提醒注意；警告： *I warned him not to go too close to the fire.* 我提醒了他不要离火炉边太近。

warning ᴏ⃗ /ˈwɔːnɪŋ/ *noun* 名词
something that tells you about danger or

about something bad that may happen 警告；警示： *There is a warning on every packet of cigarettes.* 每包香烟上都有健康忠告。 ◇ *The storm came without warning.* 暴风雨毫无先兆地袭来。

warrant /ˈwɒrənt/ *noun* 名词
an official document giving somebody permission to do something 执行令；授权令： *Police have issued a warrant for his arrest.* 警方发出了逮捕他的执行令。

was *form of* BE * be 的不同形式

wash¹ ᴏ⃗ /wɒʃ/ *verb* 动词 (**washes, washing, washed** /wɒʃt/)
1 to clean somebody, something or yourself with water 清洗；洗涤： *Have you washed the car?* 你把车子洗了吗？ ◇ *Wash your hands before you eat.* 饭前洗手。 ◇ *I washed and dressed quickly.* 我很快洗了澡，穿上了衣服。
2 (used about water) to flow somewhere （水）流向，冲向： *The waves washed over my feet.* 海浪冲刷着我的脚。
wash somebody or 或 **something away** (used about water) to move or carry somebody or something to another place （水）冲走： *The house was washed away by the river.* 房子给河水冲走了。
wash up
1 (*British* 英式英语) to clean the plates, knives, forks, and pans after a meal 洗餐具；洗碗： *I washed up after dinner.* 饭后我洗了碗。
2 (*American* 美式英语) to wash your face and hands 洗脸和手

wash² /wɒʃ/ *noun* 名词 (*no plural* 不用复数形式)
cleaning something with water 洗涤；清洗： *She gave the car a wash.* 她清洗了汽车。 ◇ *I had a quick wash before dinner.* 我在吃饭前匆匆洗了个澡。
in the wash (used about clothes) being washed （衣物）正在洗： *All my socks are in the wash!* 我的袜子都正在洗呢！

washbasin /ˈwɒʃbeɪsn/ (*also* 亦作 **basin**) *noun* 名词
the place in a bathroom where you wash your hands and face 洗脸盆 ⊃ Look at Picture Dictionary page **P10**. 见彩页 P10。

washing ᴏ⃗ /ˈwɒʃɪŋ/ *noun* 名词 (*no plural* 不用复数形式)
clothes that you need to wash or that you have washed 待洗（或洗好）的衣服：
I've done the washing. 我已经把衣服洗了。 ◇ *Shall I hang the washing outside to dry?* 我把洗好的衣服晾在外面吗？

A
B
C
D
E
F
G
H
I
J
K
L
M
N
O
P
Q
R
S
T
U
V
W
X
Y
Z

washing machine /'wɒʃɪŋ məʃiːn/ *noun* 名词
a machine that washes clothes 洗衣机 ⊃ Look at Picture Dictionary page **P10**. 见彩页 P10。

washing powder /'wɒʃɪŋ paʊdə(r)/ *noun* 名词 (no plural 不用复数形式)
soap powder for washing clothes 洗衣粉

washing-up /ˌwɒʃɪŋ 'ʌp/ *noun* 名词 (no plural 不用复数形式) (British 英式英语)
the work of washing the plates, knives, forks, and pans after a meal（饭后）洗餐具，洗碗: *I'll do the washing-up if you cook the meal.* 你烧饭，我就洗碗。

washing-up liquid /ˌwɒʃɪŋ 'ʌp lɪkwɪd/ *noun* 名词 (no plural 不用复数形式) (British 英式英语)
liquid soap that you use for washing dishes 洗涤液

washroom /'wɒʃruːm/ *noun* 名词 (American 美式英语)
a room with a toilet in it 厕所；洗手间

wasn't /'wɒznt/ *short for* WAS NOT * was not 的缩略式

wasp /wɒsp/ *noun* 名词
a yellow and black insect that flies and can sting people 黄蜂

waste¹ ⊶ /weɪst/ *verb* 动词 (wastes, wasting, wasted)
to use too much of something or not use something in a good way 浪费；滥用: *She wastes a lot of money on sweets.* 她买糖果浪费很多钱。 ◇ *He wasted his time at university – he didn't do any work.* 他上大学时虚度光阴，根本没有用功。

waste² ⊶ /weɪst/ *noun* 名词 (no plural 不用复数形式)
1 not using something in a useful way 浪费；滥用: *It's a waste to throw away all this food!* 把这些食物都扔掉，真是浪费！ ◇ *This watch was a waste of money – it's broken already!* 这手表纯粹是糟蹋钱，它已经坏了！
2 things that people throw away because they are not useful 废物；垃圾: *A lot of waste from the factories goes into this river.* 工厂很多废料都排入这条河里。

waste³ ⊶ /weɪst/ *adjective* 形容词
not useful or needed 无用的；废弃的: *There's an area of waste ground outside the town where people dump their rubbish.* 镇子外面有块荒地，人们在那儿倾倒垃圾。 ◇ *waste paper* 废纸

waste-paper basket /ˌweɪst 'peɪpə bɑːskɪt/ *noun* 名词 (British 英式英语)

(American 美式英语 wastebasket /'weɪstbɑːskɪt/)
a container where you put things like paper that you do not want 废纸篓；废纸筐 ⊃ Look at Picture Dictionary page **P11**. 见彩页 P11。

watch¹ ⊶ /wɒtʃ/ *verb* 动词 (watches, watching, watched /wɒtʃt/)
1 to look at somebody or something for some time 注视；观看: *We watched television all evening.* 我们整晚都在看电视。 ◇ *Watch how I do this.* 看我这个怎么做吧。 ⊃ Look at the note at **see**. 见 see 条的注释。
2 to look after something or somebody 照看；照管: *Could you watch my bags while I buy a ticket?* 我去买票，你给我看一下包好吗？

watch out to be careful because of somebody or something dangerous 当心；小心 ⊃ SAME MEANING **look out** 同义词为 look out: *Watch out! There's a car coming.* 小心！有辆车要过来了。

watch out for somebody or 或 **something** to look carefully and be ready for somebody or something dangerous 小心；当心；密切注意；留意 ⊃ SAME MEANING **look out for somebody or something** 同义词为 look out for somebody 或 something: *Watch out for ice on the roads.* 当心路上有冰。

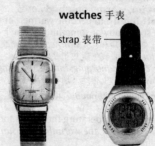

watches 手表
strap 表带
watch 手表 **digital watch** 数字表

watch² ⊶ /wɒtʃ/ *noun* 名词
1 (plural 复数形式 watches) a thing that you wear on your wrist so you know what time it is 手表: *She kept looking at her watch nervously.* 她一直紧张不安地看手表。 ⊃ Look at the note at **clock**. 见 clock 条的注释。
2 (no plural 不用复数形式) the action of watching something in case of danger or

problems 监视；观察： *The soldier was keeping watch at the gate.* 士兵在大门口放哨。

water¹ 0= /'wɔ:tə(r)/ *noun* 名词 (*no plural* 不用复数形式)
the liquid that is in rivers, lakes and seas 水： *I'd like a glass of water.* 我想要一杯水。◇ *After the heavy rain a lot of the fields were **under water**.* 大雨过后，很多田被水淹了。

water² /'wɔ:tə(r)/ *verb* 动词 (waters, watering, watered /'wɔ:təd/)
1 to give water to plants 给…浇水；灌溉： *Have you watered the plants?* 你给这些植物浇过水吗？
2 When your eyes **water**, they fill with tears. 充满眼泪： *The smoke made my eyes water.* 烟熏得我眼睛直流泪。

watercolour /'wɔ:təkʌlə(r)/ *noun* 名词
1 watercolours (*plural* 用复数形式) paints that you mix with water 水彩（颜料）
2 a picture that you paint with **watercolours** 水彩画

waterfall 瀑布

waterfall /'wɔ:təfɔ:l/ *noun* 名词
a place where water falls from a high place to a low place 瀑布

watering can /'wɔ:tərɪŋ kæn/ *noun* 名词
a container that you use for watering plants （浇花草用）洒水壶，喷壶

watermelon /'wɔ:təmelən/ *noun* 名词
a big round fruit with a thick green skin. It is pink inside with a lot of black seeds. 西瓜

waterproof /'wɔ:təpru:f/ *adjective* 形容词
If something is **waterproof**, it does not let

water go through it. 不透水的；防水的： *a waterproof jacket* 防水夹克

waterskiing /'wɔ:təski:ɪŋ/ *noun* 名词 (*no plural* 不用复数形式)
the sport of moving fast over water on long boards (called waterskis), pulled by a boat 水橇滑水运动 ↪ Look at Picture Dictionary page P14. 见彩页 P14。

watt /wɒt/ *noun* 名词 (*abbr.* 缩略式 W)
a unit of electrical power 瓦，瓦特（电功率单位）： *a 60-watt light bulb* * 60 瓦的电灯泡

wave 挥手

wave¹ 0= /weɪv/ *noun* 名词
1 one of the lines of water that moves across the top of the sea 海浪；波浪： *Waves crashed against the cliffs.* 海浪拍打着悬崖。
2 a movement of your hand from side to side in the air, to say hello or goodbye, or to make a sign to somebody 挥手；招手；摆手： *As she turned the corner, she gave me a wave.* 她转过街角的时候向我挥了挥手。
3 a gentle curve in hair （头发）拳曲，波浪形
4 the form that some types of energy such as heat, light and sound take （热、光、声音等的）波： *radio waves* 无线电波

wave² 0= /weɪv/ *verb* 动词 (waves, waving, waved /weɪvd/)
1 to move your hand from side to side in the air to say hello or goodbye, or to make a sign to somebody 挥手；招手；摆手： *She waved to me as the train left the station.* 火车离站时她向我挥手告别。◇ *Who are you waving at?* 你在跟谁招手？
2 to move something quickly from side to side in the air 挥动；挥舞： *The children waved flags as the President's car drove past.* 总统的汽车驶过时，孩子们挥舞着旗子。
3 to move up and down or from side to side 飘动；起伏： *The flags were waving in the wind.* 旗子随风飘扬。

wavelength /'weɪvlenθ/ *noun* 名词
the size of a radio wave that a particular radio station uses to send out its programmes（广播电台的）波长
be on the same wavelength (*informal* 非正式) to have the same way of thinking as another person 具有相同的思路；合拍: *We get on OK, but we're not really on the same wavelength.* 我们相处得还好，但不是特别的合拍。

wavy 波浪似的

a wavy line 波浪线

a straight line 直线

a dotted line 虚线

wavy /'weɪvi/ *adjective* 形容词 (wavier, waviest)
having curves; not straight 波浪似的；拳曲的: *a wavy line* 波浪线 ◇ *She has wavy black hair.* 她长了一头鬈曲的黑发。⊃ Look at the picture at **hair**. 见 hair 的插图。

wax /wæks/ *noun* 名词 (no plural 不用复数形式)
the substance that is used for making CANDLES (= tall sticks that you burn to give light) or for making things shine 蜡: *wax floor polish* 地板上光蜡

way ⊶ /weɪ/ *noun* 名词
1 (*plural* 复数形式 ways) a method or style of doing something 方法；方式；手段；途径: *What is the best way to learn a language?* 学习语言用什么方法最好? ◇ *He smiled in a friendly way.* 他友善地笑了笑。
2 (*plural* 复数形式 ways) a road or path that you must follow to go to a place 路线；路径；通路: *Can you tell me the way to the station, please?* 请问到车站怎么走? ◇ *I lost my way and I had to look at the map.* 我迷了路，只得查看地图。◇ *We stopped for a meal on the way to Bristol.* 我们在去布里斯托尔的路上停下来吃了顿饭。◇ *Here's the museum. Where's the way in?* 博物馆就在这里，入口在哪里呢? ◇ *I can't find the way out.* 我找不到出口。
3 (*plural* 复数形式 ways) a direction; where somebody or something is going

or looking 方向: *Come this way.* 这边走。◇ *She was looking the other way.* 她正往另一边看。◇ *Is this picture the right way up?* 这幅画上下放正了吗? ◇ *Those two words are the wrong way round.* 那两个词颠倒了。
4 (no plural 不用复数形式) distance 距离: *It's a long way from Glasgow to London.* 格拉斯哥距离伦敦很远。
by the way words that you say when you are going to talk about something different（转换话题时说）顺便提一下，附带说一句: *By the way, I had a letter from Ann yesterday.* 顺便说一句，我昨天收到了一封安寄来的信。
give way
1 to stop and let somebody or something go before you 让路: *You must give way to traffic coming from the right.* 必须让右方驶来的车辆先行。
2 to agree with somebody when you did not agree before 让步；妥协: *My parents finally gave way and said I could go on holiday with my friends.* 父母终于松了口，答应我可以跟朋友一起去度假。
3 to break 断裂: *The ladder gave way and Ben fell to the ground.* 梯子断了，本摔到地上。
in the way in front of somebody so that you stop them from seeing something or moving 挡住: *I can't see – you're in the way.* 我看不见，你挡着我了。
no way (*informal* 非正式) a way of saying 'no' more strongly 不行；没门儿: *'Can I borrow your bike?' 'No way!'* "我能借你的自行车吗?" "不行!"
out of the way no longer stopping somebody from moving or doing something 不再挡住；不再碍事: *Get out of the way! There's a car coming!* 走开! 有辆汽车正驶来!
way of life how people live 生活方式: *Is the way of life in Europe different from America?* 欧洲人的生活方式跟美国人的不一样吗?

WC /,dʌblju: 'si:/ *noun* 名词 (*British* 英式英语) (*formal* 正式)
(often written on signs and doors in public places) a toilet 洗手间，厕所（常见于公众场所的指示牌和门上）⊃ Look at the note at **toilet**. 见 toilet 条的注释。

we ⊶ /wi:/ *pronoun* 代词 (*plural* 用复数形式)
I and another person or other people; you and I 我们; 咱们: *Mick and I went out last night – we went to the theatre.*

我和米克昨晚出去了 —— 我们到剧院
看戏。◇ *Are we late?* 我们迟到吗?

weak 0ー /wiːk/ *adjective* 形容词
(weaker, weakest)

> 🔑 PRONUNCIATION 读音说明
> The word **weak** sounds just like **week**.
> * weak 读音同 week。

1 not powerful or strong 虚弱的;无力
的;软弱的: *She felt very weak after her
long illness.* 她久病之后身体很虚弱。◇ *He
is too weak to be a good leader.* 他太软弱,
当不了一个好领导。 ⊃ OPPOSITE **strong**
反义词为 strong
2 Something that is **weak** can break
easily. 不牢固的;易破的: *The bridge is
too weak to carry heavy traffic.* 这座桥
不够结实,无法承受繁重的交通流量。
3 (used about a drink) containing a lot of
water; not strong in taste (饮料)稀的、
淡的: *I like my tea quite weak.* 我喜欢喝
相当淡的茶。 ⊃ OPPOSITE **strong** 反义词为
strong

▶ **weakly** /'wiːkli/ *adverb* 副词: *She
smiled weakly at them.* 她勉强地朝他们笑
了笑。

weaken /'wiːkən/ *verb* 动词 (weakens,
weakening, weakened /'wiːkənd/)
to become less strong or to make
somebody or something less strong
(使)虚弱、减弱: *He was weakened by
the illness.* 他因病变得虚弱。

weakness 0ー /'wiːknəs/ *noun* 名词
1 (*no plural* 不用复数形式) the state of not
being strong 虚弱;软弱;懦弱: *He
thought that crying was a sign of weakness.*
他觉得哭是懦弱的表现。
2 (*plural* 复数形式 weaknesses)
something that is wrong or bad in a
person or thing 弱点;缺点;不足
⊃ OPPOSITE **strength** 反义词为 strength

wealth /welθ/ *noun* 名词 (*no plural* 不用
复数形式)
a lot of money, land, or property 财富;
财产: *He is a man of great wealth.*
他家财万贯。

▶ **wealthy** /'welθi/ *adjective* 形容词
(wealthier, wealthiest) ⊃ SAME MEANING
rich 同义词为 rich: *a wealthy family*
富有的家庭

weapon 0ー /'wepən/ *noun* 名词
something such as a gun that is used for
fighting or killing people 武器;兵器;
凶器: *nuclear weapons* 核武器 ◇ *The
police still haven't found the murder
weapon.* 警方仍未找到杀人凶器。

wear¹ 0ー /weə(r)/ *verb* 动词 (wears,
wearing, wore /wɔː(r)/, has worn /wɔːn/)

> 🔑 PRONUNCIATION 读音说明
> The word **wear** sounds just like **where**.
> * wear 读音同 where。

to have clothes, jewellery, etc. on your
body 穿;戴;佩戴: *She was wearing a
red dress.* 她穿着红色的连衣裙。◇ *I wear
glasses.* 我戴眼镜。

wear off to become less strong 变弱;
减弱: *The pain is wearing off.* 疼痛渐渐
减轻了。

wear out to become thin or damaged
because you have used it a lot; to make
something do this (使)磨破、磨坏、
磨损: *Children's shoes usually wear out
very quickly.* 小孩的鞋子通常很快磨坏。

wear somebody out to make
somebody very tired 使疲乏;使筋疲
力尽: *She wore herself out by working too
hard.* 她太拼命工作,搞得自己疲惫不堪。

wear² /weə(r)/ *noun* 名词 (*no plural* 不用
复数形式)
1 clothes 衣着;服装: *sportswear* 运动装
2 long use which damages something
磨损;耗损: *This carpet is showing signs
of wear.* 这块地毯有磨损的迹象。

weary /'wɪəri/ *adjective* 形容词 (wearier,
weariest)
very tired 疲劳的;疲倦的;疲惫的:
a weary traveller 疲惫不堪的旅客

▶ **wearily** /'wɪərəli/ *adverb* 副词: *She
sank wearily into a chair.* 她疲惫地坐到
椅子上。

weather 0ー /'weðə(r)/ *noun* 名词 (*no
plural* 不用复数形式)
how much sun, rain or wind there is at
a certain time, or how hot or cold it is
天气;气象: ***What's the weather like
where you are?*** 你那边天气如何? ◇ *We
had bad weather last week.* 上周天气很
恶劣。 ⊃ Look at Picture Dictionary page
P16. 见彩页 P16。

weather forecast /'weðə fɔːkɑːst/ *noun*
名词
words on television, radio or in a
newspaper that tell you what the weather
will be like 天气预报: *The weather
forecast says it will be sunny and dry
tomorrow.* 天气预报说明天晴朗干燥。

weave /wiːv/ *verb* 动词 (weaves, weaving,
wove /wəʊv/, has woven /'wəʊvn/)
to make cloth by putting threads over and
under one other 编织: *These scarves are
woven by hand.* 这些围巾是手工编织的。

A
B
C
D
E
F
G
H
I
J
K
L
M
N
O
P
Q
R
S
T
U
V
W
X
Y
Z

web /web/ *noun* 名词
1 (*plural* 复数形式 webs) a thin net that a spider makes to catch flies 蜘蛛网 ⮧ Look at the picture at **spider**. 见 spider 的插图。
2 the Web (*no plural* 不用复数形式) (*computing* 电脑) the system that makes it possible for you to see information from all over the world on your computer 万维网；环球信息网 ⮧ SAME MEANING **the World Wide Web** 同义词为 the World Wide Web

webcam (*British* 英式英语) (*American* 美式英语 Webcam™) /'webkæm/ *noun* 名词
a video camera that is connected to a computer so that you can watch what it records on a website as it is happening 网络摄像机；网络摄影机；网络摄像头

web page /'web peɪdʒ/ *noun* 名词
a part of a website that you can see on your computer screen 网页： *We learned how to create and register a new web page.* 我们学会了如何制作和注册新网页。

website 0➔ /'websaɪt/ *noun* 名词
a place on the Internet that you can look at to find out information about something 网站： *I found this information on their website.* 我在他们的网站上找到这条信息。 ◇ *Visit our website to learn more.* 欲知详情，请访问我们的网站。

we'd /wiːd/ *short for* WE HAD; WE WOULD
* we had 和 we would 的缩略式

wedding 0➔ /'wedɪŋ/ *noun* 名词
a time when a man and a woman get married 婚礼： *Billy and Elena invited me to their wedding.* 比利和埃琳娜邀请了我参加他们的婚礼。 ◇ *She wore a long white wedding dress.* 她穿了一件白色的长婚纱。

🔎 WORD BUILDING 词汇扩充
At a **wedding**, two people **get married**. 在婚礼（wedding）上，两个人结婚（get married）。
On their **wedding day**, the woman is called the **bride** and the man is the **groom** (or **bridegroom**). They are helped during the **wedding ceremony** by the **best man** and the **bridesmaids**. 在结婚日（wedding day），新娘叫做 bride，新郎叫做 groom 或 bridegroom。在结婚典礼（wedding ceremony）上帮忙的伴郎叫做 best man，伴娘叫做 bridesmaid。
After the ceremony, there is usually a **wedding reception** (= a formal party).

Many **couples** go on a **honeymoon** (= a holiday) after getting married. 婚礼后通常有婚宴（wedding reception）。不少夫妇（couple）婚后会去度蜜月（honeymoon）。
Marriage is the relationship between a **husband** and a **wife**. 婚姻（marriage）表示丈夫（husband）和妻子（wife）之间的关系： *They had a long and happy marriage.* 他们的婚姻长久而幸福。

Wednesday 0➔ /'wenzdeɪ/ *noun* 名词
the day of the week after Tuesday and before Thursday 星期三 ⮧ Look at the note at **day**. 见 day 条的注释。

weed¹ /wiːd/ *noun* 名词
a wild plant that grows where you do not want it 杂草；野草： *The garden of the old house was full of weeds.* 旧房子的花园里杂草丛生。

weed² /wiːd/ *verb* 动词 (weeds, weeding, weeded)
to pull WEEDS out of the ground 除草

week 0➔ /wiːk/ *noun* 名词
1 a time of seven days, usually from Sunday to the next Saturday 星期；周；礼拜： *I'm going on holiday next week.* 我下周会去度假。 ◇ *I play tennis twice a week.* 我一星期打两次网球。 ◇ *I saw him two weeks ago.* 我两周前见过他。

🔎 WORD BUILDING 词汇扩充
In British English, a period of two weeks is called a **fortnight**. 在英式英语中，表示两星期用 fortnight。

2 the part of the week when people go to work, especially Monday to Friday 工作周（尤指周一至周五）： *I work during the week but not at weekends.* 我周一至周五上班，周末休息。

weekday /'wiːkdeɪ/ *noun* 名词
any day except Saturday or Sunday 工作日（周一至周五任何一天）： *I only work on weekdays.* 我只在星期一到星期五上班。

weekend 0➔ /ˌwiːk'end/ *noun* 名词
Saturday and Sunday 周末（星期六和星期日）： *What are you doing at the weekend?* 你周末干什么？

weekly /'wiːkli/ *adjective, adverb* 形容词，副词
happening or coming every week or once a week 每周（的）；每周一次（的）： *a weekly magazine* 周刊 ◇ *I am paid weekly.* 我每周领一次工资。

weep /wi:p/ *verb* 动词 (weeps, weeping, wept /wept/, has wept) (*formal* 正式)
to cry, usually because you are sad （通常因悲伤）哭泣

> 🔎 SPEAKING 表达方式说明
> **Cry** is the word that we usually use.
> * cry 是常用词。

weigh ○╼ /weɪ/ *verb* 动词 (weighs, weighing, weighed /weɪd/)

> 🔎 PRONUNCIATION 读音说明
> The word **weigh** sounds just like **way**.
> * weigh 读音同 way。

1 to measure how heavy somebody or something is using a machine (called scales) （用磅秤）称重量: *The shop assistant weighed the tomatoes.* 售货员称了番茄的重量。
2 to have or show a certain weight 重量为; 有…重: *'How much do you weigh?' 'I weigh 55 kilos.'* "你有多重？""我有 55 公斤重。"

weight ○╼ /weɪt/ *noun* 名词
1 (*no plural* 不用复数形式) how heavy somebody or something is 重量: *Do you know the weight of the parcel?* 你知道包裹的重量吗？ ◇ *I'm getting fat – I need to lose weight* (= get thinner)! 我越来越胖，我要减肥！ ◇ *He's put on weight* (= got fatter) *lately.* 他最近体重增加了。
2 (*plural* 复数形式 weights) a piece of metal that weighs a particular amount and is used to measure the weight of something, or which people lift in order to improve their strength and as a sport 砝码; 哑铃; 杠铃: *She lifts weights as part of her training.* 她锻炼的其中一环是举杠铃。

weightlifting /ˈweɪtlɪftɪŋ/ *noun* 名词 (*no plural* 不用复数形式)
a sport in which people lift heavy metal weights 举重

weird /wɪəd/ *adjective* 形容词 (weirder, weirdest)
very strange 奇怪的; 怪异的: *I had a weird dream.* 我做了个离奇的梦。

welcome¹ ○╼ /ˈwelkəm/ *verb* 动词 (welcomes, welcoming, welcomed /ˈwelkəmd/)
to show that you are happy to have or see somebody or something 欢迎; 迎接: *He came to the door to welcome us.* 他到了门口来迎接我们。
▶ **welcome** *noun* 名词: *They gave us*

a great welcome. 我们受到了他们隆重的欢迎。

welcome² ○╼ /ˈwelkəm/ *adjective* 形容词
1 If somebody or something is **welcome**, you are happy to see them or it. 受欢迎的; 受人喜欢的: *The cool drinks were welcome on such a hot day.* 大热天里，这些冷饮很受欢迎。 ◇ *Welcome to Oxford!* 欢迎来到牛津！
2 (*informal* 非正式) used to say that you are happy for somebody to do something if they want to （表示乐于让某人做某事）可随意: *If you come to England again, you're welcome to stay with us.* 你要是再来英格兰，我们欢迎你住我们这里。
make somebody welcome to show a visitor that you are happy to see them 使（来访者）感到受欢迎
you're welcome polite words that you say when somebody has said 'thank you' 别客气; 不用谢: *'Thank you.' 'You're welcome.'* "谢谢你。""别客气。"

welfare /ˈwelfeə(r)/ *noun* 名词 (*no plural* 不用复数形式)
the health and happiness of a person 福祉; 健康与幸福: *The school looks after the welfare of its students.* 学校照顾学生的身心健康。

well¹ ○╼ /wel/ *adverb* 副词 (better, best)
1 in a good or right way 好; 对: *You speak English very well.* 你英语说得很好。 ◇ *These shoes are very well made.* 这双鞋做工精致。 ⊃ OPPOSITE **badly** 反义词为 badly
2 completely or very much 完全; 彻底; 相当: *I don't know Cathy very well.* 我不怎么认识凯茜。 ◇ *Shake the bottle well before you open it.* 先把瓶子摇匀再打开。
as well also 也; 还 ⊃ SAME MEANING **too** 同义词为 too: *'I'm going out.' 'Can I come as well?'* "我要出去。""我也去行吗？" ⊃ Look at the note at **also**. 见 also 条的注释。
as well as and also 除…之外: *She has a flat in London as well as a house in Edinburgh.* 她在伦敦有套公寓，在爱丁堡还有一所房子。
do well to be successful 成功; 做得好: *He did well in his exams.* 他考得很好。
may or 或 **might as well** words that you use to say that you will do something, often because there is nothing else to do 不妨: *If you've finished your work, you may as well go home.* 你要是完成了工作，就不妨回家吧。

well done! words that you say to somebody who has done something good （表示赞赏）干得好: *'I got the job!' 'Well done!'* "我得到那份工作了！" "干得好！"

well² 0— /wel/ *adjective* 形容词 (**better**, **best**)
healthy 健康: *'How are you?' 'I'm very well, thanks.'* "你好吗？" "我很好，谢谢。" ⊃ OPPOSITE **ill** 反义词为 **ill**

well³ 0— /wel/ *exclamation* 感叹词
1 a word that you often say when you are starting to speak （用于开始说话时）嗯，噢: *'Do you like it?' 'Well, I'm not really sure.'* "你喜欢它吗？" "嗯，我不太肯定。"
2 a word that you use to show surprise （表示惊讶）哎呀，哟: *Well, that's strange!* 哎呀，那真奇怪！

well⁴ /wel/ *noun* 名词
a deep hole for getting water or oil from under the ground 井；水井；油井: *an oil well* 油井

we'll /wiːl/ *short for* WE WILL; WE SHALL * we will 和 we shall 的缩略式

well behaved /ˌwel bɪˈheɪvd/ *adjective* 形容词
behaving in a way that most people think is good 行为端正的；彬彬有礼的: *Their children are very well behaved.* 他们的孩子都彬彬有礼。

well dressed /ˌwel ˈdrest/ *adjective* 形容词
wearing attractive or expensive clothes 穿着讲究的

wellingtons /ˈwelɪŋtənz/ (*also* 亦作 **wellington boots** /ˌwelɪŋtən ˈbuːts/) (*British* 英式英语) (*British informal also* 英式英语非正式亦作 **wellies** /ˈweliz/) (*American* 美式英语 **rubber boots**) *noun* 名词 (*plural* 用复数形式)
long rubber boots that you wear to keep your feet and part of your legs dry 威灵顿长筒靴；长筒橡胶雨靴 ⊃ Look at the picture at **shoe**. 见 shoe 的插图。

well known /ˌwel ˈnəʊn/ *adjective* 形容词
famous 著名的；知名的: *a well-known writer* 著名的作家 ⊃ OPPOSITE **unknown** 反义词为 unknown

well off /ˌwel ˈɒf/ *adjective* 形容词
rich 有钱的；富裕的 ⊃ SAME MEANING **wealthy** 同义词为 wealthy: *They must be very well off – their house is huge.* 他们一定很有钱，房子那么大。

went *form of* GO¹ * go¹ 的不同形式

wept *form of* WEEP * weep 的不同形式

were *form of* BE * be 的不同形式

we're /wɪə(r)/ *short for* WE ARE * we are 的缩略式

weren't /wɜːnt/ *short for* WERE NOT * were not 的缩略式

west 0— /west/ *noun* 名词 (*no plural* 不用复数形式)
1 (*abbr.* 缩略式 W) the direction you look towards to see the sun go down 西；西方: *Which way is west?* 哪边是西？ ◇ *They live in the west of England.* 他们住在英格兰西部。 ⊃ Look at the picture at **compass**. 见 compass 的插图。
2 the West the countries of North America and Western Europe 西方国家 （指北美和西欧诸国）
▶ **west** *adjective, adverb* 形容词，副词: *I live in west London.* 我住在伦敦西部。 ◇ *The town is five miles west of here.* 那个镇在这里向西五英里处。

western¹ 0— /ˈwestən/ *adjective* 形容词
in or of the west of a place 西方的；西部的: *Western parts of the country will be very cold.* 该国的西部地区将会很冷。

western² /ˈwestən/ *noun* 名词
a film or book about life in the west of the US in the past （美国）西部电影，西部小说

wet 0— /wet/ *adjective* 形容词 (**wetter**, **wettest**)
1 covered in water or another liquid 湿的: *This towel is wet – can I have a dry one?* 这条毛巾湿了，可不可以给我一条干的？
2 with a lot of rain 多雨的: *a wet day* 下雨天 ⊃ OPPOSITE **dry** 反义词为 dry

we've /wiːv/ /wiv/ *short for* WE HAVE * we have 的缩略式

whale 鲸

whale /weɪl/ *noun* 名词
a very big animal that lives in the sea and looks like a very big fish 鲸

what ⟲ /wɒt/ *pronoun, adjective* 代词，形容词
1 a word that you use when you ask about somebody or something（疑问词）什么: *What's your name?* 你叫什么名字? ◇ *What are you reading?* 你在读什么? ◇ *What time is it?* 几点了? ◇ *What kind of music do you like?* 你喜欢什么类型的音乐?
2 the thing that（指事物）什么: *I don't know what this word means.* 我不知道这个词的意思是什么。 ◇ *Tell me what to do.* 告诉我该做什么。
3 a word that you use to show surprise or other strong feelings 多么: *What a terrible day!* 多么糟糕的一天! ◇ *What beautiful flowers!* 多漂亮的花啊!
what about … ? words that you use when you suggest something（用于提议）…怎么样 ⊃ SAME MEANING **how about … ?** 同义词为 how about … ?: *What about going to the cinema tonight?* 今天晚上去看电影怎么样?
what … for? for what purpose or reason? 为何目的; 为何理由; 有何用途: *What did you say that for?* 你说那些干什么? ◇ *What's this machine for?* 这台机器有什么用?
what is … like? words that you use when you want to know more about somebody or something …是什么样的: *'What's her brother like?' 'He's very nice.'* "她弟弟人怎么样?" "他人挺不错的。"
what's on? words that you use when you want to know what television programmes or films are being shown 播放什么节目; 上映什么电影: *What's on TV tonight?* 今晚电视上有什么节目?
what's up? what is wrong? 怎么了 ⊃ SAME MEANING **what's the matter?** 同义词为 what's the matter?: *You look sad. What's up?* 你看起来很伤心。怎么了?

whatever ⟲ /wɒtˈevə(r)/ *adjective, pronoun, adverb* 形容词，代词，副词
1 any or every; anything or everything 任何; 每一; 任何事物; 一切事物: *These animals eat whatever food they can find.* 这些动物找到什么食物就吃什么。 ◇ *I'll do whatever I can to help you.* 我会尽我所能帮助你。
2 it does not matter what 无论什么; 不管什么: *Whatever you do, don't be late.* 你无论如何也不要迟到。

3 (*informal* 非正式) a word that you say to show that you do not mind what you do or have 无所谓; 什么都可以: *'What shall we do tomorrow?' 'Whatever.'* "我们明天干什么?" "随便。"

what's /wɒts/ *short for* WHAT IS; WHAT HAS * what is 和 what has 的缩略式

wheat /wiːt/ *noun* 名词 (*no plural* 不用复数形式)
a type of grain that can be made into flour 小麦; 麦子

wheel¹ ⟲ /wiːl/ *noun* 名词
a thing like a circle that turns round to move something such as a car or a bicycle 轮子; 车轮: *His favourite toy is a dog on wheels.* 他最喜欢的玩具是一只带轮子的狗。 ⊃ Look at the picture at **bicycle**. 见 bicycle 的插图。

wheel² /wiːl/ *verb* 动词 (wheels, wheeling, wheeled /wiːld/)
to push along something that has wheels 推（有轮之物）: *I wheeled my bicycle up the hill.* 我推了自行车上山。

wheelbarrow 独轮手推车

wheelbarrow /ˈwiːlbærəʊ/ *noun* 名词
a container with one wheel and two handles that you use outside for carrying things 独轮手推车

wheelchair /ˈwiːltʃeə(r)/ *noun* 名词
a chair with wheels for somebody who cannot walk 轮椅 ⊃ Look at the picture on the next page. 见下页的插图。

when ⟲ /wen/ *adverb, conjunction* 副词，连词
1 at what time 什么时候; 何时: *When did she arrive?* 她什么时候到的? ◇ *I don't know when his birthday is.* 我不知道他的生日是哪一天。
2 at the time that 在…时候; 当…时: *It was raining when we left school.* 我们离开学校的时候正下着雨。 ◇ *I saw her in May, when she was in London.* 我在五月见到

A
B
C
D
E
F
G
H
I
J
K
L
M
N
O
P
Q
R
S
T
U
V
W
X
Y
Z

她，当时她在伦敦。◇ *He came when I called him.* 我叫他，他就来了。

whenever ⊶ /wen'evə(r)/ *conjunction* 连词
1 at any time that 在任何时候；无论何时：*Come and see us whenever you want.* 随时来看看我们。
2 every time that 每当；每次：*Whenever I see her, she talks about her boyfriend.* 我每次见到她，她都谈她的男朋友。

where ⊶ /weə(r)/ *adverb, conjunction* 副词，连词
1 in or to what place 在哪里；到哪里：*Where do you live?* 你住在哪里？◇ *I asked her where she lived.* 我问她住在什么地方。◇ *Where is she going?* 她要去什么地方？
2 in which; at which …的那个地方（或情况）：*This is the street where I live.* 这是我居住的街道。

whereas ⊶ /ˌweər'æz/ *conjunction* 连词
a word that you use between two different ideas（表示对比）而，可是：*John likes travelling, whereas I don't.* 约翰喜欢旅行，而我却不喜欢。

wherever ⊶ /weər'evə(r)/ *adverb, conjunction* 副词，连词
1 at, in or to any place 在任何地方；到任何地方：*Sit wherever you like.* 你喜欢坐哪儿就坐哪儿吧。
2 a way of saying 'where' more strongly（加强语气）究竟在哪里：*Wherever did I put my keys?* 我到底把钥匙放在哪里了？

whether ⊶ /'weðə(r)/ *conjunction* 连词
1 a word that we use to talk about choosing between two things（表示选择）…还是…：*I don't know whether to go or not.* 我不知道去还是不去好。
2 if 是否：*She asked me whether I was Spanish.* 她问我是不是西班牙人。

wheelchair 轮椅

which ⊶ /wɪtʃ/ *pronoun, adjective* 代词，形容词

> 🔊 PRONUNCIATION 读音说明
> The word **which** sounds just like **witch**.
> * which 读音同 witch。

1 what person or thing 哪一个：*Which colour do you like best – blue or green?* 你最喜欢哪种颜色，蓝色还是绿色？◇ *Which flat do you live in?* 你住在哪个公寓？
2 a word that shows exactly what thing or things you are talking about（用以指明谈及的事物）…的那个：*Did you read the poem (which) Louise wrote?* 你读过路易丝写的那首诗吗？
3 a word that you use before you say more about something（用以补充信息）…的那个：*Her new dress, which she bought in London, is beautiful.* 她在伦敦买的那条新连衣裙非常漂亮。

whichever /wɪtʃ'evə(r)/ *adjective, pronoun* 形容词，代词
any person or thing 无论哪个：*Here are two books – take whichever you want.* 这儿有两本书，你挑一本你想要的吧。

while¹ ⊶ /waɪl/ (*also formal* 正式亦作 whilst /waɪlst/) *conjunction* 连词
1 during the time that; when 在…期间；当…的时候：*The telephone rang while I was having a shower.* 我在淋浴的时候电话铃响了。
2 at the same time as 与…同时：*I listen to the radio while I'm eating my breakfast.* 我边吃早饭边听收音机。

while² ⊶ /waɪl/ *noun* 名词 (*no plural* 不用复数形式)
a period of time 一段时间；一会儿：*Let's sit here for a while.* 咱们在这儿坐一会儿吧。◇ *I'm going home in a while* (= soon). 我待会儿就回家。

whilst /waɪlst/ (*formal* 正式) = WHILE¹：*He waited whilst I looked for my keys.* 我找钥匙的时候他等着我。

whimper /'wɪmpə(r)/ *verb* 动词 (whimpers, whimpering, whimpered /'wɪmpəd/)
to make a soft crying noise, because you are hurt or afraid（因受伤或害怕）抽泣，呜咽，啜泣：*'Don't leave me alone,' he whimpered.* "不要把我一个人留下。"他呜咽着说。
▶ **whimper** *noun* 名词：*The dog gave a whimper.* 狗发出了呜咽声。

whine /waɪn/ *verb* 动词 (whines, whining, whined /waɪnd/)
to make a long high sad sound 哀鸣；惨叫：*The dog was whining outside the door.* 狗在门外嗷嗷地叫。

whinge /wɪndʒ/ *verb* 动词 (whinges, whingeing, whinged /wɪndʒd/) (*British* 英式英语) (*informal* 非正式)
to complain about things in an annoying way 絮絮叨叨地抱怨：*She's always whingeing about how much homework she has to do.* 她总是啰啰唆唆地抱怨自己的家庭作业太多。
▸ **whinge** *noun* 名词

whip¹ /wɪp/ *noun* 名词
a long piece of leather or rope with a handle, used for making animals move or for hitting people 鞭子

whip² /wɪp/ *verb* 动词 (whips, whipping, whipped /wɪpt/)
1 to hit an animal or a person with a WHIP 鞭打：*The rider whipped the horse to make it go faster.* 骑手鞭打着马让它跑快点。
2 to mix food very quickly with a fork, for example, until it is light and thick 搅打：*whipped cream* 搅打过的奶油

whirl /wɜːl/ *verb* 动词 (whirls, whirling, whirled /wɜːld/)
to move round and round very quickly 旋转；打转：*The dancers whirled around the room.* 舞蹈演员在房间里飘然旋转。

whisk¹ /wɪsk/ *verb* 动词 (whisks, whisking, whisked /wɪskt/)
1 to mix eggs or cream very quickly with a fork or a WHISK 搅打（鸡蛋或奶油）
2 to take somebody or something somewhere very quickly 匆匆带走；迅速送走：*The President was whisked away in a helicopter.* 总统被直升机迅速送走。

whisk² /wɪsk/ *noun* 名词
a tool that you use for mixing eggs or cream very quickly 打蛋器；搅拌器

whisker /ˈwɪskə(r)/ *noun* 名词
one of the long hairs that grow near the mouth of cats, mice and some other animals（猫、鼠等的）须 ➭ Look at the picture at **cat**. 见 cat 的插图。

whisky /ˈwɪski/ *noun* 名词 (*British* 英式英语)

🔎 SPELLING 拼写说明
In the US and in Ireland the spelling is **whiskey**. 在美国和爱尔兰拼作 whiskey。

1 (*no plural* 不用复数形式) a strong alcoholic drink 威士忌
2 (*plural* 复数形式 whiskies) a glass of **whisky** 一杯威士忌

whisper /ˈwɪspə(r)/ *verb* 动词 (whispers, whispering, whispered /ˈwɪspəd/)
to speak very quietly to somebody, so that other people cannot hear what you are saying 耳语；窃窃私语；小声说：*He whispered so that he would not wake the baby up.* 他低声说话以免把宝宝吵醒。
▸ **whisper** *noun* 名词：*She spoke in a whisper.* 她低声地说话。

whistle¹ /ˈwɪsl/ *noun* 名词
1 a small musical instrument that makes a long high sound when you blow it 哨子：*The referee blew his whistle to end the match.* 裁判吹哨结束了比赛。
2 the long high sound that you make when you blow air out between your lips or when you blow a **whistle** 口哨；哨声

whistle² /ˈwɪsl/ *verb* 动词 (whistles, whistling, whistled /ˈwɪsld/)
to make a long high sound by blowing air out between your lips or through a WHISTLE 吹口哨；打呼哨：*He whistled a tune to himself.* 他自个儿哼吹着曲子。

white¹ 0➔ /waɪt/ *adjective* 形容词 (whiter, whitest)
1 with the colour of snow or milk 白的；白色的：*He wore a white shirt and a blue tie.* 他穿了一件白色的衬衫，系了条蓝色的领带。
2 with pale skin 白种人的；白人的
3 (*British* 英式英语) **White** coffee is made with milk.（咖啡）加牛奶的：*I'd like a white coffee.* 我想要一杯加奶的咖啡。
4 White wine is wine with a light colour.（葡萄酒）白的

white² 0➔ /waɪt/ *noun* 名词
1 (*no plural* 不用复数形式) the colour of snow or milk 白色：*She was dressed in white.* 她一身白色衣服。
2 (*plural* 复数形式 whites) a person with pale skin 白种人；白人
3 (*plural* 复数形式 whites) the part inside an egg that is around the yellow middle part 蛋白；蛋清：*Add the whites of two eggs.* 加上两个鸡蛋的蛋白。 ➭ Look at the picture at **egg**. 见 egg 的插图。

A B C D E F G H I J K L M N O P Q R S T U V W X Y Z

A B C D E F G H I J K L M N O P Q R S T U V **W** X Y Z

whizz (*British* 英式英语) (*American* 美式英语 whiz) /wɪz/ *verb* 动词 (whizzes, whizzing, whizzed /wɪzd/) (*informal* 非正式)
to move very quickly 快速移动: *The bullet whizzed past his head.* 子弹从他的头边飞过。

who ⚓ /hu:/ *pronoun* 代词
1 a word we use in questions to ask about the name, position, etc. of one or more people（询问姓名、职务等）谁，什么人: *Who is that girl?* 那个女孩是谁? ◇ *I don't know who did it.* 我不知道是谁干的。
2 a word that shows which person or people you are talking about（表示谈及的人）: *I like people who say what they think.* 我喜欢直言不讳的人。◇ *The woman (who) I work for is very nice.* 我的老板是个很友善的女人。

who'd /hu:d/ *short for* WHO HAD; WHO WOULD * who had 和 who would 的缩略式

whoever ⚓ /hu:'evə(r)/ *pronoun* 代词
1 the person who; any person who …的那个人; …的任何人: *Whoever broke the glass must pay for it.* 打破这块玻璃的人一定要赔。
2 a way of saying 'who' more strongly（加强语气）究竟是谁，到底是谁: *Whoever could have done that?* 究竟会是谁干的呢?

whole¹ ⚓ /həʊl/ *adjective* 形容词

🔊 PRONUNCIATION 读音说明
The word **whole** sounds just like **hole**, because we don't say the w in this word. * whole 读音同 hole，因为 w 在这里不发音。

complete; with no parts missing 全部的; 完全的; 完整的: *He ate the whole cake!* 他把整个蛋糕都吃了! ◇ *We are going to Australia for a whole month.* 我们会去澳大利亚整整一个月。

whole² ⚓ /həʊl/ *noun* 名词 (*no plural* 不用复数形式)
1 a thing that is complete 整个; 整体: *Two halves make a whole.* 两个一半构成一个整体。
2 all of something 所有; 全部; 全体: *I spent the whole of the weekend in bed.* 我整个周末都赖在床上。
on the whole generally, but not always completely true 总的说来; 大体上: *On the whole, I think it's a good idea.* 大体说来，我觉得这是个好主意。

who'll /hu:l/ *short for* WHO WILL * who will 的缩略式

wholly /'həʊlli/ *adverb* 副词 (*formal* 正式)
completely 完全地; 全面地 ⊃ SAME MEANING **totally** 同义词为 totally: *He is not wholly to blame for the situation.* 造成这样的局面不能全怪他。

whom ⚓ /hu:m/ *pronoun* 代词 (*formal* 正式)
a word we use instead of 'who' as the object of a verb or PREPOSITION（代替 who，用作动词或介词宾语）: *To whom did you give the money?* 你把钱给了谁? ◇ *She's the woman (whom) I met in Greece.* 她就是我在希腊遇到的那个女人。

🔊 SPEAKING 表达方式说明
Whom is very formal. **Who** is the word that we usually use. * whom 非常正式。who 是常用词。

who's /hu:z/ *short for* WHO IS; WHO HAS * who is 和 who has 的缩略式

whose ⚓ /hu:z/ *adjective, pronoun* 形容词，代词
1 used to ask who something belongs to（询问物品的所属）谁的: *Whose car is this?* 这是谁的汽车?
2 used to say exactly which person or thing you mean, or to give extra information about a person or thing（特指或提供额外信息时）那个人的，那一个的，其: *That's the boy whose sister is a singer.* 那就是姐姐是个歌手的男孩。

who've /hu:v/ *short for* WHO HAVE * who have 的缩略式

why ⚓ /waɪ/ *adverb* 副词
for what reason 为什么; 为何: *Why are you late?* 你为什么迟到了? ◇ *I don't know why she's angry.* 我不知道她为什么会生气。
why not? words that you use to make or agree to a suggestion（表示提出或赞同建议）干吗不呢，何不，好哇: *Why not ask Kate to go with you?* 何不叫凯特跟你一起去呢?

wicked /'wɪkɪd/ *adjective* 形容词
1 very bad 很坏的; 邪恶的 ⊃ SAME MEANING **evil** 同义词为 evil: *a story about a wicked witch* 一个关于恶毒女巫的故事
2 (*informal* 非正式) very good 极好的; 很棒的: *This song is wicked!* 这首歌棒极了!

wide¹ ⚓ /waɪd/ *adjective* 形容词 (wider, widest)
1 far from one side to the other 宽的;

宽阔的： *We drove down a wide road.* 我们顺着一条宽阔的路行驶。 ➲ OPPOSITE **narrow** 反义词为 narrow

2 You use **wide** to say or ask how far something is from one side to the other. 宽度为；有…宽： *The table was 2 m wide.* 桌子宽 2 米。 ◇ *How wide is the river?* 这条河有多宽？

3 completely open 睁大的；敞开的： *The children's eyes were wide with excitement.* 孩子们兴奋得睁大了眼睛。 ➲ The noun is **width**. 名词为 width。

wide[2] /waɪd/ ***adverb*** 副词

completely; as far or as much as possible 完全；充分；尽可能： *Open your mouth wide.* 把嘴张大。 ◇ *I'm **wide awake**!* 我清醒得很！ ◇ *She stood with her feet **wide apart**.* 她双腿叉开站在那里。

widely /ˈwaɪdli/ ***adverb*** 副词

by a lot of people; in or to a lot of places 普遍地；广泛地；范围广地： *He has travelled widely in Asia.* 他去过亚洲很多地方。

widen /ˈwaɪdn/ ***verb*** 动词 (**widens, widening, widened** /ˈwaɪdnd/)

to become wider; to make something wider（使）变宽；加宽；拓宽： *They are widening the road.* 他们在拓宽道路。

widespread /ˈwaɪdspred/ ***adjective*** 形容词

If something is **widespread**, it is happening in many places. 普遍的；广泛的： *The disease is becoming more widespread.* 这种病传播得越来越广了。

widow /ˈwɪdəʊ/ ***noun*** 名词

a woman whose husband is dead 寡妇；孀妇

widower /ˈwɪdəʊə(r)/ ***noun*** 名词

a man whose wife is dead 鳏夫

width /wɪdθ/ ***noun*** 名词

how far it is from one side of something to the other; how wide something is 宽度；广度： *The room is five metres **in width**.* 房间宽五米。 ➲ The adjective is **wide**. 形容词为 wide。

wife 🔑 /waɪf/ ***noun*** 名词 (*plural* 复数形式 **wives** /waɪvz/)

the woman that a man is married to 妻子；太太；夫人

wig /wɪg/ ***noun*** 名词

a covering for your head made of hair that is not your own 假发

wild 🔑 /waɪld/ ***adjective*** 形容词 (**wilder, wildest**)

1 Wild plants and animals live or grow in nature, not with people. 自然生长的；野生的： *We picked some wild flowers.* 我们采了些野花。

2 excited; not controlled 激动的；失控的： *She was wild with anger.* 她大发雷霆。 ◇ *The crowd **went wild** with excitement.* 群众兴奋若狂。

wildlife /ˈwaɪldlaɪf/ ***noun*** 名词 (*no plural* 不用复数形式)

animals and plants in nature 野生动植物；野生生物

will[1] 🔑 /wɪl/ ***modal verb*** 情态动词

> 🔎 **GRAMMAR** 语法说明
>
> The negative form of **will** is **will not** or the short form **won't** /wəʊnt/. * will 的否定式为 will not 或缩写为 won't /wəʊnt/： *They won't be there.* 他们不会在那里的。
>
> The short form of **will** is **'ll**. We often use this. * will 的缩略式为 'll，十分常用： *You'll* (= you will) *be late.* 你要迟到了。 ◇ *He'll* (= he will) *drive you to the station.* 他会开车送你去车站。

1 a word that shows the future（表示将来）将： *Do you think she will come tomorrow?* 你认为她明天会来吗？

2 a word that you use when you agree or promise to do something（表示同意或承诺做某事）愿，会，要： *I'll carry your bag.* 我来给你拿包吧。

3 a word that you use when you ask somebody to do something（表示请求）： *Will you open the window, please?* 请开一下窗好吗？ ➲ Look at the note at **modal verb**. 见 modal verb 条的注释。

will[2] 🔑 /wɪl/ ***noun*** 名词

1 (*no plural* 不用复数形式) the power of your mind that makes you choose, decide and do things 意志；毅力： *She has a very strong will and nobody can stop her doing what she wants.* 她意志坚定，想做的事谁也拦不住。

2 (*no plural* 不用复数形式) what somebody wants to happen 意愿；心愿： *The man made him get into the car **against his will*** (= when he did not want to). 那个男子逼他上了车。

3 (*plural* 复数形式 **wills**) a piece of paper that says who will have your money, house, etc. when you die 遗嘱： *My grandmother left me £2 000 in her will.* 祖母在遗嘱里留给了我 2 000 英镑。

willing /ˈwɪlɪŋ/ ***adjective*** 形容词

ready and happy to do something 愿意；乐意： *I'm **willing to** work at weekends.*

A B C D E F G H I J K L M N O P Q R S T U V W X Y Z

A
B
C
D
E
F
G
H
I
J
K
L
M
N
O
P
Q
R
S
T
U
V
W
X
Y
Z

我乐意在周末上班。 ⊃ OPPOSITE **unwilling**
反义词为 unwilling

▶ **willingly** /'wɪlɪŋli/ *adverb* 副词： *I'll willingly help you.* 我愿意帮助你。

▶ **willingness** /'wɪlɪŋnəs/ *noun* 名词
(*no plural* 不用复数形式)： *He showed no willingness to help.* 他全然无意帮忙。

win ⃝ /wɪn/ *verb* 动词 (wins, winning, won /wʌn/, has won)
1 to be the best or the first in a game, race or competition 获胜；赢： *Who won the race?* 谁赢了赛跑？ ◇ *Tom won and I was second.* 汤姆胜出，我第二。
⊃ OPPOSITE **lose** 反义词为 lose
2 to receive something because you did well or tried hard 赢得；获得： *I won a prize in the competition.* 我在比赛中获了奖。 ◇ *Who won the gold medal?* 谁得了金牌？

> 🔎 **WHICH WORD?** 词语辨析
>
> Be careful! You **earn** (not **win**) money by working. 注意：工作挣钱用 earn，不用 win。

▶ **win** *noun* 名词： *Our team has had five wins this year.* 我们队今年取得了五场胜利。

wind¹ ⃝ /wɪnd/ *noun* 名词
air that moves 风： *The wind blew his hat off.* 风把他的帽子吹掉了。 ◇ *Strong winds caused a lot of damage to buildings.* 强风对楼房造成了很大的破坏。

wind² /waɪnd/ *verb* 动词 (winds, winding, wound /waʊnd/, has wound)

> 🔎 **PRONUNCIATION** 读音说明
>
> The verb **wind** sounds like **find** and the past forms sound like **found**.
> * wind 作动词时读音像 find，过去式和过去分词读音像 found。

1 A road or river that **winds** has a lot of bends and turns. （道路或河流）蜿蜒，曲折： *The path winds through the forest.* 这条小路弯弯曲曲地穿过森林。
2 to make something long go round and round another thing 缠绕；把…绕成团： *The nurse wound the bandage around my knee.* 护士用绷带把我的膝盖包扎起来。
3 to turn a key or handle to make something work or move 转动，扭动（钥匙或把手）： *The clock will stop if you don't wind it up.* 这个钟不上发条就会停。 ◇ *The driver wound her car window down.* 司机把她的车窗摇下来。
wind somebody up (*British* 英式英语) (*informal* 非正式) to deliberately say

things that make somebody angry 惹某人生气；激怒： *You're just trying to wind me up!* 你就是在故意气我！

windmill 风车

windmill /'wɪndmɪl/ *noun* 名词
a tall building with long flat parts that turn in the wind 风车

window ⃝ /'wɪndəʊ/ *noun* 名词
an opening in a building or in a car door, for example, with glass in it 窗；窗户；窗口： *It was cold, so I closed the window.* 天气很冷，我把窗户关上了。 ◇ *She looked out of the window.* 她从窗口向外看。
⊃ Look at Picture Dictionary page **P10**. 见彩页 P10。

windowpane /'wɪndəʊpeɪn/ *noun* 名词
a piece of glass in a window （一块）窗玻璃

windowsill /'wɪndəʊsɪl/ (*also* 亦作 **window ledge** /'wɪndəʊ ledʒ/) *noun* 名词
a shelf under a window 窗台；窗沿
⊃ Look at Picture Dictionary page **P10**. 见彩页 P10。

windscreen /'wɪndskriːn/ (*British* 英式英语) (*American* 美式英语 **windshield**) *noun* 名词
the big window at the front of a car （车辆前面的）挡风玻璃，风挡 ⊃ Look at Picture Dictionary page **P1**. 见彩页 P1。

windscreen wiper /'wɪndskriːn waɪpə(r)/ (*British* 英式英语) (*American* 美式英语 **windshield wiper** /'wɪndʃiːld waɪpə(r)/) *noun* 名词
a thing that cleans rain and dirt off the WINDSCREEN while you are driving 挡风玻璃刮水器；风挡雨雪刷

windshield /'wɪndʃiːld/ *American English for* WINDSCREEN 美式英语，即 windscreen

windsurfer /'wɪndsɜːfə(r)/ *noun* 名词
1 a special board with a sail. You stand on it as it moves over the water. 帆板

2 a person who rides on a board like this 帆板运动员

windsurfing /'wɪndsɜːfɪŋ/ *noun* 名词 (*no plural* 不用复数形式)
the sport of moving over water on a special board with a sail 帆板运动：
We like to go windsurfing at the weekend. 我们周末喜欢去玩帆板。 ⊃ Look at Picture Dictionary page **P14**. 见彩页 P14。

windy /'wɪndi/ *adjective* 形容词 (windier, windiest)
with a lot of wind 多风的；风大的： *It's very windy today!* 今天风很大！ ⊃ Look at Picture Dictionary page **P16**. 见彩页 P16。

wine ⊶ /waɪn/ *noun* 名词
an alcoholic drink made from small green or purple fruit (called grapes) 葡萄酒：
Would you like red or white wine? 你要红葡萄酒还是白葡萄酒？ ◇ *She ordered a glass of wine.* 她点了一杯葡萄酒。

wing ⊶ /wɪŋ/ *noun* 名词
1 one of the two parts that a bird or an insect uses to fly （鸟或昆虫的）翅膀，翼： *The chicken ran around flapping its wings.* 鸡拍打着翅膀跑来跑去。 ⊃ Look at the picture at **bird**. 见 bird 的插图。
2 one of the two long parts at the sides of a plane that support it in the air 机翼 ⊃ Look at Picture Dictionary page **P1**. 见彩页 P1。

wink /wɪŋk/ *verb* 动词 (winks, winking, winked /wɪŋkt/)
to close and open one eye quickly as a friendly or secret sign to somebody 眨一只眼；眨眼示意： *She winked at me.* 她朝我眨了眨眼。
▸ **wink** *noun* 名词： *He gave me a wink.* 他向我眨了一下眼。 ⊃ Look also at **blink**. 亦见 blink。

winner ⊶ /'wɪnə(r)/ *noun* 名词
a person or an animal that wins a game, race or competition 获胜者；胜出者：
The winner was given a prize. 胜出者获得了奖品。 ⊃ OPPOSITE **loser** 反义词为 loser

winning /'wɪnɪŋ/ *adjective* 形容词
The **winning** person or team is the one that wins a game, race or competition. 获胜的；赢的： *the winning team* 获胜队

winter ⊶ /'wɪntə(r)/ *noun* 名词
the coldest part of the year 冬天；冬季： *It often snows in winter.* 冬天经常下雪。 ⊃ Look at Picture Dictionary page **P16**. 见彩页 P16。

wipe¹ /waɪp/ *verb* 动词 (wipes, wiping, wiped /waɪpt/)
1 to make something clean or dry with a cloth 擦；拭；抹： *The waitress wiped the table.* 女服务员把桌子擦干净。 ◇ *I washed my hands and wiped them on a towel.* 我洗完手用毛巾擦干。
2 to take away something by rubbing it 擦掉；抹掉： *She wiped the writing off the blackboard.* 她把黑板上的字擦掉。 ◇ *I wiped up the milk on the floor.* 我把地板上的牛奶抹掉。
wipe something out to destroy a place completely 彻底消灭；摧毁： *The bombs wiped out whole towns.* 炸弹把一个个的城镇摧毁了。

wipe² /waɪp/ *noun* 名词
1 the action of wiping something 擦；拭；抹： *He gave the table a quick wipe.* 他很快地擦了擦桌子。
2 a piece of paper or thin cloth with a special liquid on it that you use for cleaning things （湿）纸巾，抹布： *a box of face wipes* (= for cleaning your face) 一盒洁面巾

wire ⊶ /'waɪə(r)/ *noun* 名词
a long piece of very thin metal 金属丝；金属线： *The box was fastened with a piece of wire.* 箱子用一根铁丝捆紧了。 ◇ *The telephone wires had been cut.* 电话线已经切断了。

wisdom /'wɪzdəm/ *noun* 名词 (*no plural* 不用复数形式)
knowing and understanding a lot about many things 智慧；才智： *Some people think that old age brings wisdom.* 有些人认为人老见识广。 ⊃ The adjective is **wise**. 形容词为 wise。

wise /waɪz/ *adjective* 形容词 (wiser, wisest)
knowing and understanding a lot about many things 智慧的；明智的；英明的： *a wise old man* 智叟 ◇ *Do you think this is wise?* 你认为这样做明智吗？
▸ **wisely** /'waɪzli/ *adverb* 副词： *Many people wisely stayed at home in the bad weather.* 天气恶劣，很多人明智地待在家里。

wish¹ ⊶ /wɪʃ/ *verb* 动词 (wishes, wishing, wished /wɪʃt/)
1 to want something that is not possible or that will probably not happen 希望（不太可能的事发生）： *I wish I could fly!* 要是我能飞就好了！ ◇ *I wish I had passed the exam!* 我要是考试及格就好了！ ◇ *I wish we were rich.* 我们要是有钱就好了。
2 to say to yourself that you want something and hope that it will happen

A
B
C
D
E
F
G
H
I
J
K
L
M
N
O
P
Q
R
S
T
U
V
W
X
Y
Z

盼望；期盼：*You can't have everything you wish for.* 你不可能想要什么就有什么。
3 (*formal* 正式) to want to do or have something 希望（做某事）；想要：*I wish to see the manager.* 我想见经理。

> 🔊 SPEAKING 表达方式说明
> This is very formal. It is more usual to say **want** or **would like**. 此用法非常正式。较常用 want 或 would like。

4 to say that you hope somebody will have something 祝；祝愿：*I wished her a happy birthday.* 我祝她生日快乐。

wish² 0━ /wɪʃ/ *noun* 名词 (*plural* 复数形式 wishes)
1 a feeling that you want to do or have something 愿望；希望：*I have **no wish** to go.* 我不愿意离开。
2 an act of trying to make something happen by saying you want it to happen or hoping that it will happen 愿；心愿：*Close your eyes and **make a wish**!* 闭上眼睛许个愿吧！
best wishes words that you write at the end of a letter, before your name, to show that you hope somebody is well and happy（书信结束语）祝福，祝愿：*See you soon. Best wishes, Lucy.* 再见。祝好，露西。

wit /wɪt/ *noun* 名词 (*no plural* 不用复数形式)
speaking or writing in a clever and funny way 机智；才思；风趣

witch /wɪtʃ/ *noun* 名词 (*plural* 复数形式 witches)

> 🔊 PRONUNCIATION 读音说明
> The word **witch** sounds just like **which**. * witch 读音同 which。

a woman in stories who uses magic to do bad things（故事中的）女巫，巫婆 ⊃ Look also at **wizard**. 亦见 wizard。

with 0━ /wɪð/ *preposition* 介词
1 a word that shows people or things are together 和⋯⋯一起；跟；同：*I live with my parents.* 我和父母住在一起。◇ *Mix the flour with milk.* 把面粉和牛奶掺在一起。◇ *I agree with you.* 我和你的意见一致。
2 having or carrying 有；具备；携带：*He's an old man with grey hair.* 他是个头发花白的老人。◇ *I want to live in a house with a garden.* 我想住在一个带花园的房子里。◇ *I passed a woman with an enormous suitcase.* 我跟一个提着极大的行李箱的妇人擦肩而过。

3 using 用；使用：*I cut it with a knife.* 我用刀把它切开了。◇ *Fill the bottle with water.* 把瓶子装满水。
4 against 与⋯⋯对立：*I played tennis with my sister.* 我和妹妹打网球。
5 because of 因为；由于：*Her hands were blue with cold.* 她的手冻得发青。

withdraw /wɪðˈdrɔː/ *verb* 动词 (withdraws, withdrawing, withdrew /wɪðˈdruː/, has withdrawn /wɪðˈdrɔːn/)
1 to move back or away 撤回；撤离：*The army withdrew from the town.* 军队从镇上撤走了。
2 to say that you will not take part in something 退出：*Rob has withdrawn from the race.* 罗布退出了赛跑。
3 to take something out or away 提取；收回：*I withdrew $100 from my bank account.* 我从银行账户提取了 100 元。

wither /ˈwɪðə(r)/ *verb* 动词 (withers, withering, withered /ˈwɪðəd/)
If a plant **withers**, it becomes dry and dies. 枯萎；凋谢：*The plants withered in the hot sun.* 这些植物在烈日下枯萎了。

within 0━ /wɪˈðɪn/ *preposition* 介词
1 before the end of 在⋯⋯之内：*I'll be back within an hour.* 我一小时以内回来。
2 not further than 不出（某段距离）：*We live within a mile of the station.* 我们住的地方离车站不到一英里。
3 (*formal* 正式) inside 在⋯⋯里：*There are 400 prisoners within the prison walls.* 这座监狱里有 400 名囚犯。

without 0━ /wɪˈðaʊt/ *preposition, adverb* 介词，副词
1 not having, showing or using something 没有；缺乏：*It's cold – don't go out without your coat.* 天气很冷，不要没穿大衣就出去。◇ *I drink coffee without sugar.* 我喝咖啡不加糖。
2 not being with somebody or something 不和⋯⋯在一起：*He left without me.* 他甩下我走了。
do without to manage when something is not there 将就；凑合着应付：*There isn't any tea so we will have to do without.* 没有茶叶了，我们只得将就了。
without doing something not doing something 没有做某事：*They left without saying goodbye.* 他们不辞而别。

witness /ˈwɪtnəs/ *noun* 名词 (*plural* 复数形式 witnesses)
1 a person who sees something happen and can tell other people about it later 目击者；见证人：*There were two witnesses to the accident.* 这起事故有两个目击者。

2 a person who goes to a court of law to tell people what they saw（出庭作证的）证人: *a witness for the defence* 辩方证人
▶ **witness** *verb* 动词 (witnesses, witnessing, witnessed /'wɪtnəst/): *She witnessed a murder.* 她目击了一起谋杀案。

witty /'wɪti/ *adjective* 形容词 (wittier, wittiest)
clever and funny 机智的；诙谐的: *a witty answer* 巧妙的回答

wives *plural of* WIFE * wife 的复数形式

wizard /'wɪzəd/ *noun* 名词
a man in stories who has magic powers（故事中的）巫师，术士 ⊃ Look at **witch**. 见 witch。

wobble /'wɒbl/ *verb* 动词 (wobbles, wobbling, wobbled /'wɒbld/)
to move a little from side to side 摇摆；摇晃: *That chair wobbles when you sit on it.* 那把椅子坐上去会摇晃。
▶ **wobbly** /'wɒbli/ *adjective* 形容词: *a wobbly table* 摇摇晃晃的桌子

woke, woken *forms of* WAKE * wake 的不同形式

wolf /wʊlf/ *noun* 名词 (plural 复数形式 wolves /wʊlvz/)
a wild animal like a big dog 狼 ⊃ Look at Picture Dictionary page **P3**. 见彩页 P3。

woman 0➔ /'wʊmən/ *noun* 名词 (plural 复数形式 women /'wɪmɪn/)
an adult female person 成年女子；妇女: *men, women and children* 男人、女人和儿童 ◇ *Would you prefer to see a woman doctor?* 你希望让女医生给你看病吗？

womb /wuːm/ *noun* 名词
the part of a woman's body where a baby grows 子宫

won *form of* WIN * win 的不同形式

wonder¹ 0➔ /'wʌndə(r)/ *verb* 动词 (wonders, wondering, wondered /'wʌndəd/)
to ask yourself something; to want to know something 想知道；想弄明白: *I wonder what that noise is.* 我心里想那是什么声音呢。 ◇ *I wonder why he didn't come.* 我想知道他为什么没来。
I wonder if … words that you use to ask a question politely（用于礼貌地提问）: *I wonder if I could use your phone.* 请问可不可以用您的电话？

wonder² /'wʌndə(r)/ *noun* 名词
1 (no plural 不用复数形式) a feeling that you have when you see or hear something very strange, surprising or beautiful 惊奇；惊异；惊叹: *The children stared* in wonder at the elephants. 孩子们惊奇地盯着大象看。
2 (plural 复数形式 wonders) something that gives you this feeling 奇迹；奇观；奇事: *the wonders of modern medicine* 现代医学的奇迹
it's a wonder … it is surprising that … 令人惊奇的是；…真是奇迹: *It's a wonder you weren't killed in the accident.* 你在事故中大难不死真是奇迹。
no wonder it is not surprising 不足为奇；难怪: *She didn't sleep last night, so no wonder she's tired.* 她昨天晚上没有睡，难怪这么累。

wonderful 0➔ /'wʌndəfl/ *adjective* 形容词
very good 极好的；绝妙的；精彩的 ⊃ SAME MEANING **fantastic** 同义词为 fantastic: *What a wonderful present!* 多么棒的礼物啊！ ◇ *This food is wonderful.* 这食物太好吃了。

won't /wəʊnt/ *short for* WILL NOT * will not 的缩略式

wood 0➔ /wʊd/ *noun* 名词
1 (no plural 不用复数形式) the hard substance that trees are made of 木；木头；木材: *Put some more wood on the fire.* 往火里再加点柴。 ◇ *The table is made of wood.* 这张桌子是木制的。
2 (also 亦作 woods) a big group of trees, smaller than a forest 树林；林子: *a large wood* 一大片树林 ◇ *a walk in the woods* 在树林中散步

wooden 0➔ /'wʊdn/ *adjective* 形容词
made of wood 木制的；木头的: *The toys are kept in a wooden box.* 玩具放在木盒里。

wool 0➔ /wʊl/ *noun* 名词 (no plural 不用复数形式)
1 the soft thick hair of sheep 羊毛
2 thread or cloth that is made from the hair of sheep 毛线；毛料；毛织物: *The cat was playing with a ball of wool.* 猫在玩一团毛线。 ◇ *This jumper is made of pure wool.* 这件套头毛衣是纯羊毛的。 ⊃ Look at the picture at **knit**. 见 knit 的插图。

woollen (British 英式英语) (American 美式英语 woolen) /'wʊlən/ *adjective* 形容词
made of wool 毛纺的；羊毛制的: *woollen socks* 羊毛袜子

woolly (British 英式英语) (American 美式英语 wooly) /'wʊli/ *adjective* 形容词
made of wool, or like wool 羊毛制的；羊毛似的: *a woolly hat* 毛质的帽子

word ⚬➐ /wɜːd/ *noun* 名词
1 (*plural* 复数形式 **words**) a sound that you make, or a letter or group of letters that you write, which has a meaning 单词; 词; 字: *What's the Italian word for 'dog'?* * dog 这个词用意大利语怎么说? ◇ *Do you know the words of this song?* 你知道这首歌的歌词吗?
2 something that you say 说的话; 话语; 言语: *Can I have a word with you?* 我能跟你谈一谈吗? ◇ *Don't say a word about this to anybody.* 这件事别对任何人吐露半句。
3 (*no plural* 不用复数形式) a promise 诺言; 许诺: *She gave me her word that she wouldn't tell anyone.* 她向我保证她不会告诉任何人。 ◇ *Claire said she would come, and she kept her word* (= did what she had promised). 克莱尔说她会来, 她果真守信。
in other words saying the same thing in a different way 换句话说; 也就是说: *Joe doesn't like hard work – in other words, he's lazy!* 乔不喜欢辛苦工作。换句话说, 他很懒!
take somebody's word for it to believe what somebody says 相信某人的话
word for word using exactly the same words 一字不差地; 逐字地: *Ian repeated word for word what you told him.* 伊恩把你告诉他的话一字不差地重复了一遍。

word processor /ˈwɜːd ˌprəʊsesə(r)/ *noun* 名词
a small computer that you can use for writing 文字处理机

wore *form of* WEAR[1] * wear[1] 的不同形式

work[1] ⚬➐ /wɜːk/ *verb* 动词 (**works, working, worked** /wɜːkt/)
1 to be busy doing or making something 做; 劳动; 干活: *You will need to work hard if you want to pass the exam.* 你想通过考试就得用功。 ◇ *I'm going to work on my essay this evening.* 我今天晚上打算写我的作文。
2 to do something as a job and get money for it 受雇于; 从事…工作: *Susy works for the BBC.* 苏茜在英国广播公司工作。 ◇ *I work at the car factory.* 我在汽车制造厂上班。
3 to go correctly or to do something correctly 运转; 运行: *We can't watch TV – it isn't working.* 我们无法看电视, 电视机坏了。 ◇ *How does this camera work?* 这台照相机是怎么运作的?
4 to make something do something 开动; 操作; 使运作: *Can you show me*

how to work the coffee machine? 你能教我这台咖啡机怎么用吗?
5 to have the result you wanted 产生预期的效果; 奏效: *I don't think your plan will work.* 我认为你的计划行不通。

work out
1 to have the result you wanted 达到预期的效果: *I hope things work out for you.* 我希望你一切顺利。
2 to do exercises to keep your body strong and well 锻炼身体; 做运动: *She works out every day.* 她每天都锻炼身体。 ⊃ Look at Picture Dictionary page **P15**. 见彩页 P15。
work something out to find the answer to something; to calculate something 找到…的答案; 解决; 计算出: *We worked out the cost of the holiday.* 我们把度假的费用算了出来。 ◇ *Why did she do it? I can't work it out.* 她为什么这么做? 我想不通。

work[2] ⚬➐ /wɜːk/ *noun* 名词
1 (*no plural* 不用复数形式) the job that you do to earn money 工作; 职业: *I'm looking for work.* 我正在找工作。 ◇ *What time do you start work?* 你几点钟开始上班? ◇ *How long have you been out of work* (= without a job)? 你失业多长时间了?

> 🔍 **WHICH WORD?** 词语辨析
>
> **Work or job?** 用 work 还是 job?
> **Work** has no plural, so you cannot say 'a work' or 'works'. * work 没有复数形式, 所以不说 a work 或 works。You can say 可以说: *I'm looking for work.* 我在找工作。Or you have to say **a job** or **jobs**. 或者用 a job 或 jobs: *I'm looking for a job.* 我在找工作。

2 (*no plural* 不用复数形式) the place where you have a job 工作地点; 工作场所: *I phoned him at work.* 我上班时给他打的电话。 ◇ *I'm not going to work today.* 我今天不去上班。
3 (*no plural* 不用复数形式) doing or making something 工作; 活计: *Digging the garden is hard work.* 给花园松土是件苦差。 ◇ *She's so lazy – she never does any work.* 她真的很懒, 什么活儿都不干。 ◇ *The group are at work on* (= making) *a new album.* 乐队正在录制新唱片。
4 (*no plural* 不用复数形式) something that you make or do 工作成果; 作品; 作业: *The teacher marked our work.* 老师批改了我们的作业。 ◇ *The artist only sells her work to friends.* 这个艺术家只把作品卖给朋友。

5 (*plural* 复数形式 **works**) a book, painting or piece of music 著作；画作；（音乐）作品： *He's read the complete works of Shakespeare.* 他读过莎士比亚全集。◇ *A number of priceless **works of art** were stolen from the gallery.* 好几件价值连城的艺术品从美术馆中被盗了。
6 works (*plural* 用复数形式) a place where people make things with machines 工厂： *My grandfather worked at the steelworks.* 我祖父曾在炼钢厂工作。
get to work to start doing something 开始，着手（工作）： *Let's get to work on this washing-up.* 咱们开始洗碗吧！

workbook /'wɜːkbʊk/ *noun* 名词
a book where you write answers to questions, that you use when you are studying something 练习册；作业本

worker 0➔ /'wɜːkə(r)/ *noun* 名词
a person who works 工作者；工作人员： *an office worker* 办公室职员

workman /'wɜːkmən/ *noun* 名词 (*plural* 复数形式 **workmen** /'wɜːkmən/)
a man who works with his hands to build or repair something 工人；工匠

worksheet /'wɜːkʃiːt/ *noun* 名词
a piece of paper where you write answers to questions, which you use when you are studying something 活页练习题

workshop /'wɜːkʃɒp/ *noun* 名词
1 a place where people make or repair things 车间；工场；作坊
2 a time when people meet and work together to learn about something 研讨会；研习班： *We went to a drama workshop.* 我们参加了一个戏剧研习班。

world 0➔ /wɜːld/ *noun* 名词
1 (*no plural* 不用复数形式) the earth with all its countries and people 世界；地球；天下： *There was a map of the world on the classroom wall.* 教室墙上有一张世界地图。◇ *Which is the biggest city in the world?* 世界上最大的城市是哪个？
2 (*plural* 复数形式 **worlds**) all the people who do the same kind of thing 界： *the world of politics* 政界
think the world of somebody or 或 **something** to like somebody or something very much 对⋯非常喜爱： *She thinks the world of her grandchildren.* 她非常疼爱孙子孙女。

world-famous /ˌwɜːld 'feɪməs/ *adjective* 形容词
known everywhere in the world 举世闻名的；世界著名的： *a world-famous writer* 世界著名的作家

worldwide *adjective* 形容词 /'wɜːldwaɪd/, *adverb* 副词 /ˌwɜːld'waɪd/
existing or happening everywhere in the world 全世界的；在全世界： *Pollution is a worldwide problem.* 污染是全球问题。◇ *They sell their computers worldwide.* 他们的电脑出售到世界各地。

the World Wide Web /ðə ˌwɜːld waɪd 'web/ (*also* 亦作 **the Web**) *noun* 名词 (*no plural* 不用复数形式) (*abbr.* 缩略式 WWW)
the system of computers that makes it possible to see information from all over the world on your computer 万维网；环球信息网 ➋ Look at **Internet**. 见 Internet。

worm 蠕虫

worm /wɜːm/ *noun* 名词
a small animal with a long thin body and no legs 蠕虫

worn *form of* WEAR[1] * wear[1] 的不同形式

worn out /ˌwɔːn 'aʊt/ *adjective* 形容词
1 old and completely finished because you have used it a lot 用旧的；用坏的： *These shoes are completely worn out.* 这双鞋子破得不能再穿了。◇ *worn-out carpets* 破旧的地毯
2 very tired 筋疲力尽的；疲惫不堪的 ➋ SAME MEANING **exhausted** 同义词为 exhausted： *He's worn out after his long journey.* 他在长途旅行后已经疲惫不堪了。

worried 0➔ /'wʌrid/ *adjective* 形容词
unhappy because you think that something bad will happen or has happened 担心的；担忧的；忧虑的： *Fiona is worried that she's going to fail the exam.* 菲奥娜担心自己考试会不及格。◇ *I'm worried about my brother – he looks ill.* 我担心我的弟弟 — 他气色不好。

worry[1] 0➔ /'wʌri/ *verb* 动词 (**worries**, **worrying**, **worried** /'wʌrid/, has **worried**)
to feel that something bad will happen or has happened; to make somebody feel this （使）担心，担忧，发愁： *I always worry when Mark doesn't come home at*

A B C D E F G H I J K L M N O P Q R S T U V W X Y Z

the usual time. 每次马克没按时回家，我就很担心。◇ **Don't worry** if you don't know the answer. 你要是不知道答案也不必担心。◇ There's nothing to worry about. 没什么可担心的。◇ What worries me is how we are going to get home. 教我发愁的是我们将怎么回家。

worry² 0➔ /'wʌri/ noun 名词
1 (no plural 不用复数形式) a feeling that something bad will happen or has happened 担心；忧虑；发愁：Her face showed signs of worry. 她脸上露出忧愁的神情。
2 (plural 复数形式 worries) something that makes you feel worried 令人担忧的事；让人发愁的事：I have a lot of worries. 我有很多烦恼。

worse 0➔ /wɜːs/ adjective, adverb 形容词，副词 (bad, worse, worst)
1 not as good or as well as something else 更差（的）；差一些（的）：The weather today is **worse than** yesterday. 今天的天气比昨天的还糟。◇ Her Spanish is bad but her Italian is **even worse**. 她的西班牙语很差，意大利语则更差。
2 more ill 病得更重；更不舒服：If you get worse, you must go to the doctor's. 你要是病情恶化，就得去看医生。
⊃ OPPOSITE **better** 反义词为 better

worship /'wɜːʃɪp/ verb 动词 (worships, worshipping, worshipped /'wɜːʃɪpt/)
1 to show that you believe in God or a god by saying prayers 崇拜，敬仰（上帝或神）；做礼拜：Christians usually worship in churches. 基督徒通常在教堂做礼拜。
2 to love somebody very much or think that somebody is wonderful 热爱；爱慕；崇拜：She worships her grandchildren. 她十分疼爱孙子孙女。
▶ **worship** noun 名词 (no plural 不用复数形式)：A mosque is a place of worship. 清真寺是礼拜场所。

worst¹ 0➔ /wɜːst/ adjective, adverb 形容词，副词 (bad, worse, worst)
the least pleasant or suitable; the least well 最差（的）；最糟糕（的）：He's the worst player in the team! 他是队中最差的球员！◇ That was the worst day of my life. 那是我一生中最糟糕的一天。◇ Everyone played badly, but I played worst of all. 大家都表现得很差，而我是表现最差的。
⊃ OPPOSITE **best** 反义词为 best

worst² 0➔ /wɜːst/ noun 名词 (no plural 不用复数形式)
something or somebody that is as bad as it or they can be 最糟糕的人（或事物）：

I'm **the worst** in the class **at** grammar. 我是班里语法最差的。◇ OPPOSITE **best** 反义词为 best
if the worst comes to the worst if something very bad happens 如果最坏的情况发生；万不得已的时候：If the worst comes to the worst and I fail the exam, I'll take it again next year. 要是最坏的情况发生，考试不及格的话，我明年再考一次。

worth¹ 0➔ /wɜːθ/ adjective 形容词
1 having a particular value 有…价值；值（…钱）：This house is worth $700 000. 这座房子值 70 万元。
2 good or useful enough to do or have 值得：Is this film worth seeing? 这部电影值得看吗？◇ It's not worth asking Lyn for money – she never has any. 找琳恩要钱没有用——她从来都没钱。

worth² /wɜːθ/ noun 名词 (no plural 不用复数形式)
1 value 价值：The painting is of little worth. 这幅画价值不高。
2 how much or how many of something an amount of money will buy 价值…的东西：I'd like twenty pounds' worth of petrol, please. 请给我加二十英镑的汽油。

worthless /'wɜːθləs/ adjective 形容词
having no value or use 毫无价值的；无用的：A cheque is worthless if you don't sign it. 支票上面不签字就毫无价值。

worthwhile /ˌwɜːθ'waɪl/ adjective 形容词
good or useful enough for the time that you spend or the work that you do 值得花时间（或努力）的：Passing the exam made all my hard work worthwhile. 考试及格了，我所有的努力没有白费。

worthy /'wɜːði/ adjective 形容词 (worthier, worthiest)
good enough for something or to have something 值得的；配得的：He always felt he was not **worthy of** her. 他总是觉得自己配不上她。

would 0➔ /wʊd/ modal verb 情态动词

> 🔍 GRAMMAR 语法说明
> The negative form of **would** is **would not** or the short form **wouldn't** /'wʊdnt/. * would 的否定式为 would not 或缩写为 wouldn't /'wʊdnt/：He **wouldn't** help me. 他不会帮我。
> The short form of **would** is **'d**. We often use this. * would 的缩略式为 'd，十分常用：I'd (= I would) like to meet her. 我想见见她。◇ They'd (= they

would) *help if they had the time.* 他们要是有时间就会帮忙。

1 a word that you use to talk about a situation that is not real（表示想象）会：*If I had a million pounds, I would buy a big house.* 我要是有一百万英镑，就会买所大房子。

2 a word that you use to ask something in a polite way（用于礼貌地请求）：*Would you close the door, please?* 请关上门好吗？

3 a word that you use with 'like' or 'love' to ask or say what somebody wants（与 like 或 love 连用，表示询问或表达意愿）：*Would you like a cup of tea?* 你想喝杯茶吗？ ◇ *I'd love to go to Africa.* 我想去非洲。

4 the past form of 'will'（will 的过去式）将，将会：*He said he would come.* 他说他会来。◇ *They wouldn't tell us where she was.* 他们不肯告诉我们她在哪儿。

5 a word that you use to talk about something that happened many times in the past（表示过去经常发生的情况）总是，老是：*When I was young, my grandparents would visit us every Sunday.* 我小时候，祖父母每个星期天都来看我们。 ⊃ Look at the note at **modal verb**. 见 modal verb 条的注释。

would've /ˈwʊdəv/ *short for* WOULD HAVE * would have 的缩略式

wound¹ /wuːnd/ *noun* 名词
a hurt place in your body made by something like a gun or a knife（身体上的）伤，伤口：*He had knife wounds in his chest.* 他胸部有刀伤。

wound² /wuːnd/ *verb* 动词 (wounds, wounding, wounded)
to hurt somebody with a weapon 使受伤；（用武器）伤害：*The bullet wounded him in the leg.* 子弹伤了他的腿。
▶ **wounded** /ˈwuːndɪd/ *adjective* 形容词：*She nursed the wounded soldier.* 她照料那个受伤的士兵。

wound³ *form of* WIND² * wind² 的不同形式

wove, woven *forms of* WEAVE * weave 的不同形式

wow /waʊ/ *exclamation* 感叹词 (informal 非正式)
a word that shows surprise and pleasure（表示惊奇和高兴）哇，呀：*Wow! What a lovely car!* 哇！多么漂亮的车子啊！

wrap /ræp/ *verb* 动词 (wraps, wrapping, wrapped /ræpt/)
to put paper or cloth around somebody or something 包；裹：*The baby was wrapped in a blanket.* 小宝宝用毯子包着。◇ *She wrapped the glasses up in paper.* 她用纸把玻璃杯包了起来。⊃ OPPOSITE **unwrap** 反义词为 unwrap

wrapper /ˈræpə(r)/ *noun* 名词
a piece of paper or plastic that covers something like a sweet or a packet of cigarettes 包装纸；包装塑料：*Don't throw your wrappers on the floor!* 不要把包装纸扔在地上！

wrapping /ˈræpɪŋ/ *noun* 名词
a piece of paper or plastic that covers a present or something that you buy 包装纸；包装塑料：*I took the shirt out of its wrapping.* 我拆开包装，取出衬衫。

wrapping paper /ˈræpɪŋ peɪpə(r)/ *noun* 名词 (no plural 不用复数形式)
special paper that you use to wrap presents（礼品的）包装纸 ⊃ Look at the picture at **present²**. 见 present² 的插图。

wreath /riːθ/ *noun* 名词 (plural 复数形式 wreaths /riːðz/)
a circle of flowers or leaves 花环；花圈：*She put a wreath on the grave.* 她把花圈放在坟墓上了。

wreck¹ /rek/ *noun* 名词
a ship, car or plane that has been very badly damaged in an accident（事故中）严重损毁的船（或汽车、飞机）：*a shipwreck* 沉船 ◇ *The car was a wreck, but no one was hurt.* 汽车在事故中严重损坏，但是没人受伤。

wreck² /rek/ *verb* 动词 (wrecks, wrecking, wrecked /rekt/)
to break or destroy something completely 毁坏；破坏；损坏：*The fire had completely wrecked the hotel.* 大火已经把旅馆彻底烧毁了。◇ *Our holiday was wrecked by the strike.* 我们的假期因为罢工而弄砸了。

wreckage /ˈrekɪdʒ/ *noun* 名词 (no plural 不用复数形式)
the broken parts of something that has been badly damaged 残骸；废墟：*A few survivors were pulled from the wreckage of the train.* 一些幸存者从火车残骸中给拉了出来。

wrench /rentʃ/ *American English for* SPANNER 美式英语，即 spanner

wrestle /ˈresl/ *verb* 动词 (wrestles, wrestling, wrestled /ˈresld/)

to fight by trying to throw somebody to the ground, especially as a sport 摔跤

▶ **wrestler** /'reslə(r)/ *noun* 名词: *He used to be a professional wrestler.* 他曾经是职业摔跤运动员。

▶ **wrestling** /'reslɪŋ/ *noun* 名词 (*no plural* 不用复数形式): *a wrestling match* 摔跤比赛

wriggle /'rɪgl/ *verb* 动词 (wriggles, wriggling, wriggled /'rɪgld/)
to turn your body quickly from side to side 扭动身体；扭来扭去: *The teacher told the children to stop wriggling.* 老师叫学生不要再动来动去。

wring 绞

wring /rɪŋ/ *verb* 动词 (wrings, wringing, wrung /rʌŋ/, has wrung)
to press and twist something with your hands to make water come out 绞，拧（以挤出水）: *He **wrung** the towel **out** and put it outside to dry.* 他把毛巾拧干后晾在外面。

wrinkle 皱纹

wrinkle /'rɪŋkl/ *noun* 名词
a small line in something, for example in the skin of your face （脸上的）皱纹: *My grandmother has a lot of wrinkles.* 我祖母满脸皱纹。

▶ **wrinkled** /'rɪŋkld/ *adjective* 形容词: *His face is very wrinkled.* 他一脸皱纹。

wrist /rɪst/ *noun* 名词
the part of your body where your arm joins your hand 手腕 ⊃ Look at Picture Dictionary page P4. 见彩页 P4。

write 0━ /raɪt/ *verb* 动词 (writes, writing, wrote /rəʊt/, has written /'rɪtn/)

🔊 **PRONUNCIATION** 读音说明
The word **write** sounds just like **right**.
* write 读音同 right。

1 to make letters or words on paper using a pen or pencil 写字；书写: *Write your name at the top of the page.* 把你的名字写在这一页的上方。◇ *He can't read or write.* 他不识字。

2 to create a story, book, song, piece of music, etc. 写作；作曲；编写: *Shakespeare wrote plays.* 莎士比亚写过剧本。◇ *I've written a poem for you.* 我给你写了首诗。

3 to write and send a letter to somebody 写信: *My mother **writes to** me every week.* 母亲每星期给我写信。◇ *I wrote her a postcard.* 我给她写了张明信片。

write something down to write something on paper, so that you can remember it 写下；记下: *I wrote down his telephone number.* 我把他的电话号码写了下来。

writer 0━ /'raɪtə(r)/ *noun* 名词
a person who writes books, stories, etc. 作家；作者；著者: *Charles Dickens was a famous writer.* 查尔斯·狄更斯是著名的作家。

writing 0━ /'raɪtɪŋ/ *noun* 名词
(*no plural* 不用复数形式)
1 the activity or skill of putting words on paper 书写；写作: *Today we're going to practise our writing.* 今天我们要练习一下写作。
2 words that somebody puts on paper; the way a person writes （书写的）文字；字迹；笔迹: *I can't read your writing – it's so small.* 我看不清你写的字——太小了。
in writing written on paper 以书面形式: *They have offered me the job on the telephone but not in writing.* 他们打电话说给我这份工作，但没有书面通知。

writing paper /'raɪtɪŋ peɪpə(r)/ *noun* 名词 (*no plural* 不用复数形式)
paper for writing letters on 信纸；信笺

written *form of* WRITE * write 的不同形式

wrong[1] 0━ /rɒŋ/ *adjective* 形容词
1 not true or not correct 错误的；不对的；不正确的: *She gave me the wrong key, so I couldn't open the door.* 她给我的

钥匙不对，所以我开不了门。◇ *This clock is wrong.* 这钟不准。 ➲ OPPOSITE **right** 反义词为 right

2 not the best 不是最好的；不合适的: *We took the wrong road and got lost.* 我们走错方向迷路了。➲ OPPOSITE **right** 反义词为 right

3 not as it should be, or not working well 有毛病；不正常: *There's something **wrong with** my car – it won't start.* 我的汽车出了故障，发动不起来。◇ *'What's wrong with Judith?' 'She's got a cold.'* "朱迪丝怎么了？" "她感冒了。"

4 bad, or not what the law allows 坏的；不正当的: *Stealing is wrong.* 盗窃是不对的。 ◇ *I haven't **done** anything wrong.* 我没做过坏事。 ➲ OPPOSITE **right** 反义词为 right

wrong² ०➞ /rɒŋ/ *adverb* 副词
not correctly; not right 错误地；不正确；不对: *You've spelt my name wrong.* 你把我的名字拼错了。➲ OPPOSITE **right** 反义词为 right

go wrong

1 to not happen as you hoped or wanted 出问题；遇到困难: *All our plans went wrong.* 我们所有的计划都出了问题。

2 to stop working well 发生故障；出毛病: *My watch keeps going wrong.* 我的手表老是出毛病。

wrong³ /rɒŋ/ *noun* 名词 (*no plural* 不用复数形式)
what is bad or not right 坏事；错误: *Babies don't know the difference between right and wrong.* 婴儿不懂分辨是非。

wrongly /ˈrɒŋli/ *adverb* 副词
not correctly 错误地；不正确地: *He was wrongly accused of stealing the money.* 有人冤枉他偷了钱。

wrote *form of* WRITE * write 的不同形式

wrung *form of* WRING * wring 的不同形式

WWW /ˌdʌbljuː dʌbljuː ˈdʌbljuː/ *short for* THE WORLD WIDE WEB * the World Wide Web 的缩略式

X x

X, x /eks/ *noun* 名词 (*plural* 复数形式 X's, x's /'eksɪz/)
the twenty-fourth letter of the English alphabet 英语字母表的第 24 个字母:
'X-ray' begins with an 'X'. * X-ray 一词以字母 x 开头。

Xmas /'krɪsməs; 'eksməs/ (*informal* 非正式*) short way of writing* CHRISTMAS * Christmas 的缩写形式

> 🔎 SPEAKING 表达方式说明
>
> **Xmas** is used mainly in writing. * Xmas 主要用于书写: *Happy Xmas and New Year!* 圣诞快乐! 新年快乐!

X-ray /'eks reɪ/ *noun* 名词
a photograph of the inside of your body that is made by using a special light that you cannot see * X 光照片:
*The doctor **took an X-ray of** my shoulder.* 医生给我的肩部拍了 X 光照片。

▶ **X-ray** *verb* 动词 (X-rays, X-raying, X-rayed /'eksreɪd/): *She had her leg X-rayed.* 她的腿做了 X 光检查。

xylophone /'zaɪləfəʊn/ *noun* 名词
a musical instrument with metal or wooden bars that you hit with small hammers 木琴

Y y

Y, y /waɪ/ *noun* 名词 (*plural* 复数形式 Y's, y's /waɪz/)
the twenty-fifth letter of the English alphabet 英语字母表的第 25 个字母: *'Yawn' begins with a 'Y'.* * yawn 一词以字母 y 开头。

yacht /jɒt/ *noun* 名词

> 🔎 **PRONUNCIATION** 读音说明
> The word **yacht** sounds like **hot**.
> * yacht 读音像 hot。

1 a boat with sails that people go on for pleasure 帆船: *a yacht race* 帆船比赛
2 a big boat with an engine that people go on for pleasure 摩托艇；游艇: *a millionaire's yacht* 百万富翁的游艇
➲ Look at the picture at **boat**. 见 boat 的插图。

yard /jɑːd/ *noun* 名词
1 an area next to a building, usually with a fence or wall around it 院子: *The children were playing in the school yard.* 孩子们在学校院子里玩耍。◇ *a farmyard* 农家庭院
2 *American English for* GARDEN 美式英语，即 garden
3 (*abbr.* 缩略式 yd) a measure of length (= 91 centimetres). There are three feet in a **yard**. 码（长度单位；1 码等于 91 厘米或 3 英尺）➲ Look at the note at **foot**. 见 foot 条的注释。

yawn /jɔːn/ *verb* 动词 (yawns, yawning, yawned /jɔːnd/)
to open your mouth wide and breathe in deeply because you are tired 打哈欠
▶ **yawn** *noun* 名词: *'I'm going to bed now,' she said with a yawn.* "我现在要去睡觉。" 她打着哈欠说道。

yd *short way of writing* YARD (3) * yard 第 3 义的缩写形式

yeah /jeə/ *exclamation* 感叹词 (*informal* 非正式)
yes 是；对；好

year 0➞ /jɪə(r)/ *noun* 名词
1 a period of 365 or 366 days from 1 January to 31 December. A year has twelve months and 52 weeks. 年；日历年: *Where are you going on holiday **this year**?* 你今年要去哪里度假？◇ *'What year*

were you born?' '1973.' "你是哪一年出生的？" "1973 年。" ◇ *I left school last year.* 我去年离开学校了。
2 any period of twelve months 一年时间: *I've known Chris for three years.* 我认识克里斯三年了。◇ *My son is five years old.* 我儿子五岁。◇ *I have a five-year-old son.* 我有个五岁的儿子。◇ *I've got a two-year-old.* 我有个两岁的孩子。

> 🔎 **GRAMMAR** 语法说明
> Be careful! You can say **She's ten** or **She's ten years old** (BUT NOT *'She's ten years'*). 注意：可以说 She's ten 或 She's ten years old（但不说 She's ten years）。

3 (*British* 英式英语) the level that a student is at school or university 年级: *I'm in year nine.* 我上九年级。◇ *They're third-year students.* 他们是三年级学生。
all year round for the whole year 全年；一年到头: *The swimming pool is open all year round.* 游泳池全年开放。
➲ Look also at **leap year** and **new year**. 亦见 leap year 和 new year。

yearly /ˈjɪəli/ *adjective, adverb* 形容词，副词
happening or coming every year or once a year 每年（的）；一年一次（的）: *a yearly visit* 一年一度的访问 ◇ *We meet twice yearly.* 我们一年见两次面。

yeast /jiːst/ *noun* 名词 (*no plural* 不用复数形式)
a substance that you use for making bread rise 酵母；酵母菌

yell /jel/ *verb* 动词 (yells, yelling, yelled /jeld/)
to shout loudly 大喊；叫喊: *Stop yelling at me!* 别冲我大喊大叫！
▶ **yell** *noun* 名词: *He gave a yell of pain.* 他疼得大叫一声。

yellow 0➞ /ˈjeləʊ/ *adjective* 形容词
with the colour of a lemon or of butter 黄的；黄色的: *She was wearing a yellow shirt.* 她穿着黄衬衫。
▶ **yellow** *noun* 名词: *Yellow is my favourite colour.* 黄色是我最喜爱的颜色。

A B C D E F G H I J K L M N O P Q R S T U V W X Y Z

A
B
C
D
E
F
G
H
I
J
K
L
M
N
O
P
Q
R
S
T
U
V
W
X
Y
Z

yes 0️⃣ /jes/ *exclamation* 感叹词
a word that you use for answering a question. You use 'yes' to agree, to say that something is true, or to say that you would like something. 是；对；好：
'Have you got the key?' 'Yes, here it is.'
"你有钥匙吗？" "有，在这儿。" ◇
'Would you like some coffee?' 'Yes, please.'
"你想喝点咖啡吗？" "好的，谢谢。"

yesterday 0️⃣ /ˈjestədeɪ/ *adverb, noun*
副词，名词 (*no plural* 不用复数形式)
(on) the day before today 昨天；在昨天：
Did you see Tom yesterday? 你昨天见到汤姆了吗？ ◇ I phoned you yesterday afternoon but you were out. 我昨天下午给你打过电话，可是你出去了。 ◇ I sent the letter **the day before yesterday**. 我前天把信寄出了。 ➜ Look at **tomorrow**. 见 tomorrow。

yet 0️⃣ /jet/ *adverb, conjunction* 副词，连词
1 a word that you use for talking about something that has not happened but that you expect to happen（表示预期发生的事尚未发生）还，尚：I haven't finished the book yet. 我还没看完这本书。◇ Have you seen that film yet? 你看过那部电影吗？➜ Look at the note at **already**. 见 already 条的注释。
2 now; as early as this 现在；即刻：You don't need to go yet – it's only seven o'clock. 你不必马上走，现在才七点钟。
3 in the future 早晚；迟早：They may win yet. 他们日后可能会赢。
4 but; in spite of that 但是；然而：We arrived home tired yet happy. 我们到家时很累，但很开心。
yet again once more 再一次；又一次：John is late yet again! 约翰又迟到了！

yield /jiːld/ *verb* 动词 (yields, yielding, yielded)
1 to produce something such as crops or results 生产，出产（作物）；产生（结果）：The survey yielded some interesting information. 调查得出一些耐人寻味的信息。
2 to allow somebody to have power or control 屈服；让步 ➜ SAME MEANING **give in** 同义词为 give in：The government eventually yielded to the rebels. 政府最终向叛军屈服了。

yob /jɒb/ *noun* 名词 (British 英式英语) (informal 非正式)
a young man who is rude and sometimes violent 粗俗横蛮的青年男子

yoga /ˈjəʊɡə/ *noun* 名词 (no plural 不用复数形式)
a system of exercises that helps you relax both your body and your mind 瑜伽 ➜ Look at Picture Dictionary page **P15**. 见彩页 P15。

yogurt (also 亦作 yoghurt) /ˈjɒɡət/ *noun* 名词
a thick liquid food made from milk 酸奶；优格：strawberry yogurt 草莓酸奶 ◇ Do you want a yogurt? 你想来份酸奶吗？

yolk /jəʊk/ *noun* 名词
the yellow part in an egg 蛋黄 ➜ Look at the picture at **egg**. 见 egg 的插图。

you /juː; ju/ *pronoun* 代词
1 the person or people that I am speaking to 你；您；你们：You are late. 你迟到了。◇ I phoned you yesterday. 我昨天给你打过电话。
2 any person; a person 任何人；一个人：You can buy stamps at a post office. 在邮局可以买到邮票。

you'd /juːd/ *short for* YOU HAD; YOU WOULD * you had 和 you would 的缩略式

you'll /juːl/ *short for* YOU WILL * you will 的缩略式

young¹ 0️⃣ /jʌŋ/ *adjective* 形容词 (younger /ˈjʌŋɡə(r)/, youngest /ˈjʌŋɡɪst/)
in the early part of life; not old 幼小的；年轻的：They have two young children. 他们有两个年幼的孩子。◇ You're younger than me. 你比我年轻。➜ OPPOSITE **old** 反义词为 old

young² /jʌŋ/ *noun* 名词 (plural 用复数形式)
1 baby animals 幼崽；幼兽；幼鸟：Birds build nests for their young. 鸟为幼鸟筑巢。
2 the young children and young people（统称）年轻人，青年人：a television programme for the young 针对年轻人的电视节目

youngster /ˈjʌŋstə(r)/ *noun* 名词
a young person 年轻人：There isn't much for youngsters to do here. 年轻人在这儿没什么可做的。

your 0️⃣ /jɔː(r)/ *adjective* 形容词
1 of or belonging to the person or people you are talking to 你的；您的；你们的：Where's your car? 你的汽车在哪儿？◇ Do you all have your books? 你们都有书了吗？◇ Show me your hands. 把你的手给我看看。
2 belonging to or connected with people in general（泛指）大家的，人们的：You should have your teeth checked every six months. 应该每六个月检查一次牙齿。

you're /jɔː(r)/ *short for* YOU ARE * you are 的缩略式

yours 0━ /jɔːz/ *pronoun* 代词
1 something that belongs to you 你的；您的；你们的： *Is this pen yours or mine?* 这支笔是你的还是我的？
2 Yours a word that you write at the end of a letter（用于书信结尾）： *Yours sincerely …* …敬启 ◇ *Yours faithfully …* …谨启

yourself 0━ /jɔː'self/ *pronoun* 代词 (*plural* 复数形式 yourselves /jɔː'selvz/)
1 a word that shows 'you' when I have just talked about you 你自己；您自己： *Did you hurt yourself?* 你伤着自己了吗？ ◇ *Buy yourselves a drink.* 给你们自己买份饮料吧。
2 a word that makes 'you' stronger（表示强调）你自己，您自己： *Did you make this cake yourself?* 这个蛋糕是你自己做的吗？ ◇ *'Who told you?' 'You told me yourself!'* "是谁告诉你的？" "是你自己告诉我的！"
by yourself, by yourselves
1 alone; without other people（你或你们）独自，单独： *Do you live by yourself?* 你一个人住吗？
2 without help（你或你们）独立地： *You can't carry all those bags by yourself.* 你一个人是拿不了所有那些袋子的。

youth 0━ /juːθ/ *noun* 名词
1 (*no plural* 不用复数形式) the part of your life when you are young 青年时期： *She regrets that she spent her youth travelling and not studying.* 她遗憾自己年轻时把时间花在旅游上，没有好好读书。 ◇ *He was a fine musician in his youth.* 他年轻时是个杰出的音乐家。 ◒ OPPOSITE **old age** 反义词为 old age

2 (*plural* 复数形式 youths /juːðz/) a boy or young man 男孩；小伙子： *The fight was started by a gang of youths.* 打斗是一帮小伙子挑起的。
3 the youth (*no plural* 不用复数形式) young people（统称）青年，年轻人： *We must do more for the youth of this country.* 我们必须为这个国家的年轻人多做些事情。

youth club /juːθ klʌb/ *noun* 名词
a club for young people 青年俱乐部

youth hostel /juːθ hɒstl/ *noun* 名词
a cheap place where people can stay when they are travelling 青年旅舍（为旅行的青年人提供廉价的住宿）

you've /juːv/ *short for* YOU HAVE * you have 的缩略式

yo-yo /'jəʊ jəʊ/ *noun* 名词 (*plural* 复数形式 yo-yos)
a toy which is a round piece of wood or plastic with a string round the middle. You put the string on your finger and make the yo-yo go up and down. 溜溜球，摇摇（拉线使圆盘沿着线上下来回旋转的玩具）

yuck /jʌk/ *exclamation* 感叹词 (*informal* 非正式)
a word that you say when you think something looks or tastes disgusting（表示恶心）讨厌，可恶： *Yuck! I hate cabbage!* 可恶！我讨厌卷心菜！

yummy /'jʌmi/ *adjective* 形容词 (*informal* 非正式)
tasting very good 很好吃的；美味的 ◒ SAME MEANING **delicious** 同义词为 delicious： *This cake is yummy.* 这个蛋糕很好吃。

A
B
C
D
E
F
G
H
I
J
K
L
M
N
O
P
Q
R
S
T
U
V
W
X
Y
Z

Z z

Z, z /zed/ *noun* 名词 (*plural* 复数形式 Z's, z's /zedz/)

🔍 **PRONUNCIATION** 读音说明
In American English, the letter 'Z' is pronounced /ziː/. 在美式英语中，字母 Z 发 /ziː/ 音。

the twenty-sixth and last letter of the English alphabet 英语字母表的第 26 个字母: *'Zoo' begins with a 'Z'*. * zoo 一词以字母 z 开头。

zebra 斑马

zebra /ˈzebrə/ *noun* 名词 (*plural* 复数形式 **zebras** or 或 **zebra**)
an African wild animal like a horse, with black and white lines on its body 斑马

zebra crossing /ˌzebrə ˈkrɒsɪŋ/ *noun* 名词 (*British* 英式英语)
a black and white path across a road. Cars must stop there to let people cross the road safely. 斑马线；人行横道线

zero 🔑 /ˈzɪərəʊ/ *noun* 名词 (*plural* 复数形式 **zeros** or 或 **zeroes**)
1 the number 0 零
2 freezing point; 0°C 冰点；零摄氏度: *The temperature is five degrees below zero.* 气温是零下五摄氏度。

zigzag 之字形

zigzag /ˈzɪɡzæɡ/ *noun* 名词
a line that goes up and down, like a lot of letter W's, one after the other 之字形；锯齿状

zinc /zɪŋk/ *noun* 名词 (*no plural* 不用复数形式) (*symbol* 符号 Zn)
a blue-white metal 锌

zip 拉链

zip /zɪp/ (*British* 英式英语) (*American* 美式英语 **zipper**) *noun* 名词
a long metal or plastic thing with a small part that you pull to close and open things like clothes and bags 拉链；拉锁
▶ **zip** *verb* 动词 (**zips**, **zipping**, **zipped** /zɪpt/)

zip something up to fasten something together with a ZIP 拉上…的拉链: *She zipped up her dress.* 她拉上了连衣裙的拉链。

zip code (*also* 亦作 **ZIP code**) /ˈzɪp kəʊd/ *American English for* POSTCODE 美式英语，即 postcode

zipper /ˈzɪpə(r)/ *American English for* ZIP 美式英语，即 zip

zone /zəʊn/ *noun* 名词
a place where something special happens（特别的）地区，地带: *Do not enter the danger zone!* 切勿进入危险区！

zoo /zuː/ *noun* 名词 (*plural* 复数形式 **zoos**)
a place where wild animals are kept and people can go and look at them 动物园

zoom /zuːm/ *verb* 动词 (**zooms**, **zooming**, **zoomed** /zuːmd/)
to move very fast 快速移动: *The traffic zoomed past us.* 车辆从我们身边急驶而过。

zucchini /zuˈkiːni/ (*plural* 复数形式 **zucchini** or 或 **zucchinis**) *American English for* COURGETTE 美式英语，即 courgette

Geographical names 地名

If there are different words for the adjective and the person who comes from a particular place, we also give the word for the person, for example **Finland; Finnish;** (*person*) **Finn.**
若地名的形容词与来自该地的人用不同的词表示，本词典也将表示人的词语列出，如 Finland 芬兰；Finnish 芬兰的；（人）Finn 芬兰人。

Geographical name 地名	Adjective 形容词
Afghanistan /æfˈɡænɪstæn/ 阿富汗	Afghan /ˈæfɡæn/ 阿富汗的
Africa /ˈæfrɪkə/ 非洲	African /ˈæfrɪkən/ 非洲的
Albania /ælˈbeɪniə/ 阿尔巴尼亚	Albanian /ælˈbeɪniən/ 阿尔巴尼亚的
Algeria /ælˈdʒɪəriə/ 阿尔及利亚	Algerian /ælˈdʒɪəriən/ 阿尔及利亚的
America /əˈmerɪkə/ 美洲；美国	American /əˈmerɪkən/ 美洲的；美国的
Angola /æŋˈɡəʊlə/ 安哥拉	Angolan /æŋˈɡəʊlən/ 安哥拉的
Antarctica /ænˈtɑːktɪkə/ 南极洲	Antarctic /ænˈtɑːktɪk/ 南极洲的
Antigua and Barbuda /ænˌtiːɡə ən bɑːˈbjuːdə/ 安提瓜和巴布达	Antiguan /ænˈtiːɡən/ 安提瓜的 Barbudan /bɑːˈbjuːdən/ 巴布达的
the Arctic /ði ˈɑːktɪk/ 北极	Arctic /ˈɑːktɪk/ 北极的
Argentina /ˌɑːdʒənˈtiːnə/ 阿根廷	Argentinian /ˌɑːdʒənˈtɪniən/ 阿根廷的 (*person* 人) Argentine /ˈɑːdʒəntaɪn/ 阿根廷人
Armenia /ɑːˈmiːniə/ 亚美尼亚	Armenian /ɑːˈmiːniən/ 亚美尼亚的
Asia /ˈeɪʃə, ˈeɪʒə/ 亚洲	Asian /ˈeɪʃn, ˈeɪʒn/ 亚洲的
the Atlantic /ði ətˈlæntɪk/ 大西洋	Atlantic /ətˈlæntɪk/ 大西洋的
Australia /ɒˈstreɪliə/ 澳大利亚	Australian /ɒˈstreɪliən/ 澳大利亚的
Austria /ˈɒstriə/ 奥地利	Austrian /ˈɒstriən/ 奥地利的
Azerbaijan /ˌæzəbaɪˈdʒɑːn/ 阿塞拜疆	Azerbaijani /ˌæzəbaɪˈdʒɑːni/ Azeri /əˈzeəri/ 阿塞拜疆的
the Bahamas /ðə bəˈhɑːməz/ 巴哈马	Bahamian /bəˈheɪmiən/ 巴哈马的
Bahrain, Bahrein /bɑːˈreɪn/ 巴林	Bahraini, Bahreini /bɑːˈreɪni/ 巴林的
Bangladesh /ˌbæŋɡləˈdeʃ/ 孟加拉国	Bangladeshi /ˌbæŋɡləˈdeʃi/ 孟加拉国的
Barbados /bɑːˈbeɪdɒs/ 巴巴多斯	Barbadian /bɑːˈbeɪdiən/ 巴巴多斯的
Belarus /ˌbeləˈruːs/ 白俄罗斯	Belorussian /ˌbeləˈrʌʃn/ 白俄罗斯的
Belgium /ˈbeldʒəm/ 比利时	Belgian /ˈbeldʒən/ 比利时的
Belize /bəˈliːz/ 伯利兹	Belizean /bəˈliːziən/ 伯利兹的
Benin /beˈniːn/ 贝宁	Beninese /ˌbenɪˈniːz/ 贝宁的
Bhutan /buːˈtɑːn/ 不丹	Bhutanese /ˌbuːtəˈniːz/ 不丹的
Bolivia /bəˈlɪviə/ 玻利维亚	Bolivian /bəˈlɪviən/ 玻利维亚的
Bosnia-Herzegovina /ˌbɒzniə ˌhɜːtsəɡəˈviːnə/ 波斯尼亚－黑塞哥维那	Bosnian /ˈbɒzniən/ 波斯尼亚的
Botswana /bɒtˈswɑːnə/ 博茨瓦纳	Botswanan /bɒtˈswɑːnən/ 博茨瓦纳的 (*person* 人，单数) Motswana /mɒtˈswɑːnə/ 博茨瓦纳人 (*people* 人，复数) Batswana /bætˈswɑːnə/ 博茨瓦纳人
Brazil /brəˈzɪl/ 巴西	Brazilian /brəˈzɪliən/ 巴西的
Britain /ˈbrɪtn/ 不列颠 → the United Kingdom	
Bulgaria /bʌlˈɡeəriə/ 保加利亚	Bulgarian /bʌlˈɡeəriən/ 保加利亚的
Burkina /bɜːˈkiːnə/ 布基纳	Burkinese /ˌbɜːkɪˈniːz/ 布基纳的
Burma /ˈbɜːmə/ 缅甸 (now officially 现在官方名称 **MYANMAR**)	Burmese /bɜːˈmiːz/ 缅甸的
Burundi /bʊˈrʊndi/ 布隆迪	Burundian /bʊˈrʊndiən/ 布隆迪的
Cambodia /kæmˈbəʊdiə/ 柬埔寨	Cambodian /kæmˈbəʊdiən/ 柬埔寨的

Geographical name 地名	Adjective 形容词
Cameroon /ˌkæmə'ruːn/ 喀麦隆	Cameroonian /ˌkæmə'ruːniən/ 喀麦隆的
Canada /'kænədə/ 加拿大	Canadian /kə'neɪdiən/ 加拿大的
the Caribbean /ðə ˌkærə'biːən/ 加勒比海地区	Caribbean /ˌkærə'biːən/ 加勒比海地区的
Central African Republic (CAR) /ˌsentrəl ˌæfrɪkən rɪ'pʌblɪk/ 中非共和国	Central African /ˌsentrəl 'æfrɪkən/ 中非的
Chad /tʃæd/ 乍得	Chadian /'tʃædiən/ 乍得的
Chile /'tʃɪli/ 智利	Chilean /'tʃɪliən/ 智利的
China /'tʃaɪnə/ 中国	Chinese /tʃaɪ'niːz/ 中国的
Colombia /kə'lɒmbiə/ 哥伦比亚	Colombian /kə'lɒmbiən/ 哥伦比亚的
Congo /'kɒŋgəʊ/ 刚果	Congolese /ˌkɒŋgə'liːz/ 刚果的
the Democratic Republic of the Congo (DROC) /ðə ˌdeməˌkrætɪk rɪ'pʌblɪk əv ðə 'kɒŋgəʊ/ 刚果民主共和国	Congolese /ˌkɒŋgə'liːz/ 刚果的
Costa Rica /ˌkɒstə 'riːkə/ 哥斯达黎加	Costa Rican /ˌkɒstə 'riːkən/ 哥斯达黎加的
Côte d'Ivoire /ˌkəʊt diː'vwɑː/ 科特迪瓦	Ivorian /aɪ'vɔːriən/ 科特迪瓦的
Croatia /krəʊ'eɪʃə/ 克罗地亚	Croatian /krəʊ'eɪʃn/ 克罗地亚的
Cuba /'kjuːbə/ 古巴	Cuban /'kjuːbən/ 古巴的
Cyprus /'saɪprəs/ 塞浦路斯	Cypriot /'sɪpriət/ 塞浦路斯的
the Czech Republic /ðə ˌtʃek rɪ'pʌblɪk/ 捷克共和国	Czech /tʃek/ 捷克的
Denmark /'denmɑːk/ 丹麦	Danish /'deɪnɪʃ/ 丹麦的 (person 人) a Dane /deɪn/ 丹麦人
Djibouti /dʒɪ'buːti/ 吉布提	Djiboutian /dʒɪ'buːtiən/ 吉布提的
East Timor /ˌiːst 'tiːmɔː(r)/ 东帝汶	East Timorese /ˌiːst tɪmə'riːz/ 东帝汶的
Ecuador /'ekwədɔː(r)/ 厄瓜多尔	Ecuadorian /ˌekwə'dɔːriən/ 厄瓜多尔的
Egypt /'iːdʒɪpt/ 埃及	Egyptian /i'dʒɪpʃn/ 埃及的
El Salvador /el 'sælvədɔː(r)/ 萨尔瓦多	Salvadorean /ˌsælvə'dɔːriən/ 萨尔瓦多的
England /'ɪŋglənd/ 英格兰	English /'ɪŋglɪʃ/ 英格兰的 (person 人) an Englishman /'ɪŋglɪʃmən/ 英格兰男人 an Englishwoman /'ɪŋglɪʃwʊmən/ 英格兰女人
Equatorial Guinea /ˌekwətɔːriəl 'gɪni/ 赤道几内亚	Equatorial Guinean /ˌekwətɔːriəl 'gɪniən/ 赤道几内亚的
Eritrea /ˌerɪ'treɪə/ 厄立特里亚	Eritrean /ˌerɪ'treɪən/ 厄立特里亚的
Estonia /e'stəʊniə/ 爱沙尼亚	Estonian /e'stəʊniən/ 爱沙尼亚的
Ethiopia /ˌiːθi'əʊpiə/ 埃塞俄比亚	Ethiopian /ˌiːθi'əʊpiən/ 埃塞俄比亚的
Europe /'jʊərəp/ 欧洲	European /ˌjʊərə'piːən/ 欧洲的
Fiji /'fiːdʒiː/ 斐济	Fijian /fiː'dʒiːən/ 斐济的
Finland /'fɪnlənd/ 芬兰	Finnish /'fɪnɪʃ/ 芬兰的 (person 人) a Finn /fɪn/ 芬兰人
France /frɑːns/ 法国	French /frentʃ/ 法国的 (person 人) a Frenchman /'frentʃmən/ 法国男人 a Frenchwoman /'frentʃwʊmən/ 法国女人
FYROM /'faɪrɒm/ 前南斯拉夫马其顿共和国 → (the) Former Yugoslav Republic of Macedonia	
Gabon /gæ'bɒn/ 加蓬	Gabonese /ˌgæbə'niːz/ 加蓬的
the Gambia /ðə 'gæmbiə/ 冈比亚	Gambian /'gæmbiən/ 冈比亚的
Georgia /'dʒɔːdʒə/ 格鲁吉亚	Georgian /'dʒɔːdʒən/ 格鲁吉亚的
Germany /'dʒɜːməni/ 德国	German /'dʒɜːmən/ 德国的
Ghana /'gɑːnə/ 加纳	Ghanaian /gɑː'neɪən/ 加纳的
Great Britain /ˌgreɪt 'brɪtn/ 大不列颠	British /'brɪtɪʃ/ 英国的 (person 人) a Briton /'brɪtn/ 英国人
Greece /griːs/ 希腊	Greek /griːk/ 希腊的
Grenada /grə'neɪdə/ 格林纳达	Grenadian /grə'neɪdiən/ 格林纳达的

Geographical name 地名	Adjective 形容词
Guatemala /ˌgwɑːtəˈmɑːlə/ 危地马拉	Guatemalan /ˌgwɑːtəˈmɑːlən/ 危地马拉的
Guinea /ˈgɪni/ 几内亚	Guinean /ˈgɪniən/ 几内亚的
Guinea-Bissau /ˌgɪni bɪˈsaʊ/ 几内亚比绍	Guinean /ˈgɪniən/ 几内亚的
Guyana /gaɪˈænə/ 圭亚那	Guyanese /ˌgaɪəˈniːz/ 圭亚那的
Haiti /ˈheɪti/ 海地	Haitian /ˈheɪʃn/ 海地的
Holland /ˈhɒlənd/ 荷兰 → the Netherlands	
Honduras /hɒnˈdjʊərəs/ 洪都拉斯	Honduran /hɒnˈdjʊərən/ 洪都拉斯的
Hungary /ˈhʌŋɡəri/ 匈牙利	Hungarian /hʌnˈgeəriən/ 匈牙利的
Iceland /ˈaɪslənd/ 冰岛	Icelandic /aɪsˈlændɪk/ 冰岛的 (person 人) an Icelander /ˈaɪsləndə(r)/ 冰岛人
India /ˈɪndiə/ 印度	Indian /ˈɪndiən/ 印度的
Indonesia /ˌɪndəˈniːʒə/ 印度尼西亚	Indonesian /ˌɪndəˈniːʒn/ 印度尼西亚的
Iran /ɪˈrɑːn/ 伊朗	Iranian /ɪˈreɪniən/ 伊朗的
Iraq /ɪˈrɑːk/ 伊拉克	Iraqi /ɪˈrɑːki/ 伊拉克的
the Republic of Ireland /ðə rɪˌpʌblɪk əv ˈaɪələnd/ 爱尔兰共和国	Irish /ˈaɪrɪʃ/ 爱尔兰的 (person 人) an Irishman /ˈaɪrɪʃmən/ 爱尔兰男人 an Irishwoman /ˈaɪrɪʃwʊmən/ 爱尔兰女人
Israel /ˈɪzreɪl/ 以色列	Israeli /ɪzˈreɪli/ 以色列的
Italy /ˈɪtəli/ 意大利	Italian /ɪˈtæliən/ 意大利的
the Ivory Coast /ðiː ˌaɪvəri ˈkəʊst/ 象牙海岸 → Côte d'Ivoire （现称）科特迪瓦	
Jamaica /dʒəˈmeɪkə/ 牙买加	Jamaican /dʒəˈmeɪkən/ 牙买加的
Japan /dʒəˈpæn/ 日本	Japanese /ˌdʒæpəˈniːz/ 日本的
Jordan /ˈdʒɔːdn/ 约旦	Jordanian /dʒɔːˈdeɪniən/ 约旦的
Kazakhstan /ˌkæzækˈstæn/ 哈萨克斯坦	Kazakh /ˈkæzæk/ 哈萨克的
Kenya /ˈkenjə/ 肯尼亚	Kenyan /ˈkenjən/ 肯尼亚的
Korea, North /ˌnɔːθ kəˈrɪə/ 朝鲜	North Korean /ˌnɔːθ kəˈrɪən/ 朝鲜的
Korea, South /ˌsaʊθ kəˈrɪə/ 韩国	South Korean /ˌsaʊθ kəˈrɪən/ 韩国的
Kuwait /kʊˈweɪt/ 科威特	Kuwaiti /kʊˈweɪti/ 科威特的
Kyrgyzstan /ˌkɜːgɪˈstæn/ 吉尔吉斯坦	Kyrgyz /ˈkɜːgɪz/ 吉尔吉斯的
Laos /laʊs/ 老挝	Laotian /ˈlaʊʃn/ 老挝的
Latvia /ˈlætviə/ 拉脱维亚	Latvian /ˈlætviən/ 拉脱维亚的
Lebanon /ˈlebənən/ 黎巴嫩	Lebanese /ˌlebəˈniːz/ 黎巴嫩的
Lesotho /ləˈsuːtuː/ 莱索托	Sotho /ˈsuːtuː/ 索托的 (person 人，单数) Mosotho /məˈsuːtuː/ 索托人 (people 人，复数) Basotho /bəˈsuːtuː/ 索托人
Liberia /laɪˈbɪəriə/ 利比里亚	Liberian /laɪˈbɪəriən/ 利比里亚的
Libya /ˈlɪbiə/ 利比亚	Libyan /ˈlɪbiən/ 利比亚的
Lithuania /ˌlɪθjuˈeɪniə/ 立陶宛	Lithuanian /ˌlɪθjuˈeɪniən/ 立陶宛的
Luxembourg /ˈlʌksəmbɜːg/ 卢森堡	Luxembourg 卢森堡的 (people 人) a Luxembourger /ˈlʌksəmbɜːgə(r)/ 卢森堡人
the Former Yugoslav Repulic of Macedonia /ðə ˌfɔːmə ˌjuːgəʊslɑːv rɪˌpʌblɪk əv ˌmæsəˈdəʊniə/ 前南斯拉夫马其顿共和国	Macedonian /ˌmæsəˈdəʊniən/ 马其顿的
Madagascar /ˌmædəˈgæskə/ 马达加斯加	Madagascan /ˌmædəˈgæskən/ Malagasy /ˌmæləˈgæsi/ 马达加斯加的
Malawi /məˈlɑːwi/ 马拉维	Malawian /məˈlɑːwiən/ 马拉维的
Malaysia /məˈleɪʒə/ 马来西亚	Malaysian /məˈleɪʒn/ 马来西亚的
Mali /ˈmɑːli/ 马里	Malian /ˈmɑːliən/ 马里的
Mauritania /ˌmɒrɪˈteɪniə/ 毛里塔尼亚	Mauritanian /ˌmɒrɪˈteɪniən/ 毛里塔尼亚的
the Mediterranean /ðə ˌmedɪtəˈreɪniən/ 地中海	Mediterranean /ˌmedɪtəˈreɪniən/ 地中海的

Geographical name 地名	Adjective 形容词
Mexico /'meksɪkəʊ/ 墨西哥	Mexican /'meksɪkən/ 墨西哥的
Moldova /mɒl'dəʊvə/ 摩尔多瓦	Moldovan /mɒl'dəʊvən/ 摩尔多瓦的
Mongolia /mɒŋ'gəʊliə/ 蒙古	Mongolian /mɒŋ'gəʊliən/ Mongol /'mɒŋgl/ 蒙古的
Montenegro /ˌmɒntɪ'ni:grəʊ/ 黑山	Montenegrin /ˌmɒntɪ'ni:grm/ 黑山的
Morocco /mə'rɒkəʊ/ 摩洛哥	Moroccan /mə'rɒkən/ 摩洛哥的
Mozambique /ˌməʊzæm'bi:k/ 莫桑比克	Mozambican /ˌməʊzæm'bi:kən/ 莫桑比克的
Myanmar /miˌæn'mɑ:(r)/ 缅甸 (*see also* 亦见 BURMA)	
Namibia /nə'mɪbiə/ 纳米比亚	Namibian /nə'mɪbiən/ 纳米比亚的
Nepal /nə'pɔ:l/ 尼泊尔	Nepalese /ˌnepə'li:z/ 尼泊尔的
the Netherlands /ðə 'neðələndz/ 荷兰	Dutch /dʌtʃ/ 荷兰的 (*person* 人) a Dutchman /'dʌtʃmən/ 荷兰男人 a Dutchwoman /'dʌtʃwʊmən/ 荷兰女人
New Zealand /ˌnju: 'zi:lənd/ 新西兰	New Zealand 新西兰的 (*person* 人) a New Zealander /ˌnju: 'zi:ləndə(r)/ 新西兰人
Nicaragua /ˌnɪkə'rægjuə/ 尼加拉瓜	Nicaraguan /ˌnɪkə'rægjuən/ 尼加拉瓜的
Niger /ni:'ʒeə(r)/ 尼日尔	Nigerien /ni:'ʒeəriən/ 尼日尔的
Nigeria /naɪ'dʒɪəriə/ 尼日利亚	Nigerian /naɪ'dʒɪəriən/ 尼日利亚的
Northern Ireland /ˌnɔ:ðən 'aɪələnd/ 北爱尔兰	Northern Irish /ˌnɔ:ðən 'aɪrɪʃ/ 北爱尔兰的
Norway /'nɔ:weɪ/ 挪威	Norwegian /nɔ:'wi:dʒən/ 挪威的
Oman /əʊ'mɑ:n/ 阿曼	Omani /əʊ'mɑ:ni/ 阿曼的
the Pacific /ðə pə'sɪfɪk/ 太平洋	Pacific /pə'sɪfɪk/ 太平洋的
Pakistan /ˌpækɪ'stæn/ 巴基斯坦	Pakistani /ˌpækɪ'stæni/ 巴基斯坦的
Panama /'pænəmɑ:/ 巴拿马	Panamanian /ˌpænə'memiən/ 巴拿马的
Papua New Guinea /ˌpæpjuə ˌnju: 'gmi:/ 巴布亚新几内亚	Papuan /'pæpjuən/ 巴布亚的
Paraguay /'pærəgwaɪ/ 巴拉圭	Paraguayan /ˌpærə'gwaɪən/ 巴拉圭的
Peru /pə'ru:/ 秘鲁	Peruvian /pə'ru:viən/ 秘鲁的
the Philippines /ðə 'fɪlɪpi:nz/ 菲律宾	Philippine /'fɪlɪpi:n/ Filipino /ˌfɪlɪ'pi:nəʊ/ 菲律宾的
Poland /'pəʊlənd/ 波兰	Polish /'pəʊlɪʃ/ 波兰的 (*person* 人) a Pole /pəʊl/ 波兰人
Portugal /'pɔ:tʃʊgl/ 葡萄牙	Portuguese /ˌpɔ:tʃʊ'gi:z/ 葡萄牙的
Puerto Rico /ˌpwɜ:təʊ 'ri:kəʊ/ 波多黎各	Puerto Rican /ˌpwɜ:təʊ 'ri:kən/ 波多黎各的
Qatar /'kʌtɑ:(r), kæ'tɑ:(r)/ 卡塔尔	Qatari /'kʌtɑ:ri, kæ'tɑ:ri/ 卡塔尔的
Romania /ru'memiə/ 罗马尼亚	Romanian /ru'memiən/ 罗马尼亚的
Russia /'rʌʃə/ 俄罗斯	Russian /'rʌʃn/ 俄罗斯的
Rwanda /ru'ændə/ 卢旺达	Rwandan /ru'ændən/ 卢旺达的
Samoa /sə'məʊə/ 萨摩亚	Samoan /sə'məʊən/ 萨摩亚的
Saudi Arabia /ˌsaʊdi ə'reɪbiə/ 沙特阿拉伯	Saudi /'saʊdi/ Saudi Arabian /ˌsaʊdi ə'reɪbiən/ 沙特阿拉伯的
Scotland /'skɒtlənd/ 苏格兰	Scottish /'skɒtɪʃ/ Scots /skɒts/ 苏格兰的 (*person* 人) a Scot /skɒt/ 苏格兰人 a Scotsman /'skɒtsmən/ 苏格兰男人 a Scotswoman /'skɒtswʊmən/ 苏格兰女人
Senegal /ˌsenɪ'gɔ:l/ 塞内加尔	Senegalese /ˌsenɪgə'li:z/ 塞内加尔的
Serbia /'sɜ:biə/ 塞尔维亚	Serbian /'sɜ:biən/ 塞尔维亚的 (*person* 人) a Serb /sɜ:b/ 塞尔维亚人
Sierra Leone /siˌerə li'əʊn/ 塞拉利昂	Sierra Leonean /siˌerə li'əʊniən/ 塞拉利昂的
Singapore /ˌsɪŋə'pɔ:(r)/ 新加坡	Singaporean /ˌsɪŋə'pɔ:riən/ 新加坡的

Geographical name 地名	Adjective 形容词
Slovakia /sləˈvækiə/ 斯洛伐克	Slovak /ˈsləʊvæk/ 斯洛伐克的
Slovenia /sləˈviːniə/ 斯洛文尼亚	Slovene /ˈsləʊviːn/ Slovenian /sləˈviːniən/ 斯洛文尼亚的
Somalia /səˈmɑːliə/ 索马里	Somali /səˈmɑːli/ 索马里的
South Africa /ˌsaʊθ ˈæfrɪkə/ 南非	South African /ˌsaʊθ ˈæfrɪkən/ 南非的
Spain /speɪn/ 西班牙	Spanish /ˈspænɪʃ/ 西班牙的 (person 人)a Spaniard /ˈspæniəd/ 西班牙人
Sri Lanka /ˌsri ˈlæŋkə/ 斯里兰卡	Sri Lankan /ˌsri ˈlæŋkən/ 斯里兰卡的
Sudan /suˈdɑːn/ 苏丹	Sudanese /ˌsuːdəˈniːz/ 苏丹的
Suriname /ˌsʊərɪˈnɑːm/ 苏里南	Surinamese /ˌsʊərəˈmiːz/ 苏里南的
Swaziland /ˈswɑːzilænd/ 斯威士兰	Swazi /ˈswɑːzi/ 斯威士兰的
Sweden /ˈswiːdn/ 瑞典	Swedish /ˈswiːdɪʃ/ 瑞典的 (person 人)a Swede /swiːd/ 瑞典人
Switzerland /ˈswɪtsələnd/ 瑞士	Swiss /swɪs/ 瑞士的
Syria /ˈsɪriə/ 叙利亚	Syrian /ˈsɪriən/ 叙利亚的
Tajikistan /tæˌdʒiːkɪˈstæn/ 塔吉克斯坦	Tajik /tæˈdʒiːk/ 塔吉克的
Tanzania /ˌtænzəˈniːə/ 坦桑尼亚	Tanzanian /ˌtænzəˈniːən/ 坦桑尼亚的
Thailand /ˈtaɪlænd/ 泰国	Thai /taɪ/ 泰国的
Togo /ˈtəʊgəʊ/ 多哥	Togolese /ˌtəʊgəˈliːz/ 多哥的
Trinidad and Tobago /ˌtrɪnɪdæd ən təˈbeɪgəʊ/ 特立尼达和多巴哥	Trinidadian /ˌtrɪnɪˈdædiən/ 特立尼达的 Tobagan /təˈbeɪgən/ 多巴哥的
Tunisia /tjuˈnɪziə/ 突尼斯	Tunisian /tjuˈnɪziən/ 突尼斯的
Turkey /ˈtɜːki/ 土耳其	Turkish /ˈtɜːkɪʃ/ 土耳其的 (person 人)a Turk /tɜːk/ 土耳其人
Turkmenistan /tɜːkˌmenɪˈstæn/ 土库曼斯坦	Turkmen /ˈtɜːkmen/ 土库曼的
Uganda /juˈgændə/ 乌干达	Ugandan /juˈgændən/ 乌干达的
Ukraine /juˈkreɪn/ 乌克兰	Ukrainian /juˈkreɪniən/ 乌克兰的
the United Arab Emirates /ðə juˌnaɪtɪd ˌærəb ˈemɪrəts/ 阿拉伯联合酋长国	Emirati /emɪˈrɑːti/ 阿联酋的
the United Kingdom /ðə juˌnaɪtɪd ˈkɪŋdəm/ 联合王国；英国	British /ˈbrɪtɪʃ/ 英国的 (person 人)a Briton /ˈbrɪtn/ 英国人
the United States of America /ðə juˌnaɪtɪd ˌsteɪts əv əˈmerɪkə/ 美利坚合众国； 美国 (also 亦作 the USA and 和 the US)	American /əˈmerɪkən/ 美国的
Uruguay /ˈjʊərəgwaɪ/ 乌拉圭	Uruguayan /ˌjʊərəˈgwaɪən/ 乌拉圭的
Uzbekistan /ʊzˌbekɪˈstæn/ 乌兹别克斯坦	Uzbek /ˈʊzbek/ 乌兹别克的
Venezuela /ˌvenəˈzweɪlə/ 委内瑞拉	Venezuelan /ˌvenəˈzweɪlən/ 委内瑞拉的
Vietnam /ˌvjetˈnæm/ 越南	Vietnamese /ˌvjetnəˈmiːz/ 越南的
Wales /weɪlz/ 威尔士	Welsh /welʃ/ 威尔士的 (person 人)a Welshman /ˈwelʃmən/ 威尔士男人 a Welshwoman /ˈwelʃwʊmən/ 威尔士女人
Yemen Republic /ˌjemən rɪˈpʌblɪk/ 也门共和国	Yemeni /ˈjemən i/ 也门的
Zambia /ˈzæmbiə/ 赞比亚	Zambian /ˈzæmbiən/ 赞比亚的
Zimbabwe /zɪmˈbɑːbwi/ 津巴布韦	Zimbabwean /zɪmˈbɑːbwiən/ 津巴布韦的

2 000 keywords 2 000 个核心词

This is a list of the 2000 most important words to learn at this stage in your language learning. If you know these words, then you will be able to understand all the definitions in this dictionary, as well as most of the words you will come across in your listening and reading. 以下所列的是在此英语学习阶段必须掌握最重要的 2000 个词。掌握了这些词，不仅可以理解本词典所有的义项，还能理解在听、读中遇到的大多数词语。

Keywords which are marked in the dictionary, but not included in this list are numbers, days of the week and the months of the year. For more information about how to use those important words, look at Study Pages **S6–10**. 在本词典中已标示但未列入此表的核心词包括数字和表示星期几和月份的词语。有关那些词的更多信息，可参见研习专页 S6–10。

A

a, an *indefinite article*
ability *n.*
able *adj.*
about *prep., adv.*
above *prep., adv.*
abroad *adv.*
absolutely *adv.*
accept *v.*
acceptable *adj.*
accident *n.*
  by accident
account *n.*
achieve *v.*
acid *n.*
according to *prep.*
accuse *v.*
across *adv., prep.*
act *n., v.*
action *n.*
active *adj.*
activity *n.*
actor, actress *n.*
actual *adj.*
  actually *adv.*
add *v.*
address *n.*
admire *v.*
admit *v.*
adult *n., adj.*
advantage *n.*
adventure *n.*
advertisement *n.*
advice *n.*
advise *v.*
affect *v.*
afford *v.*
afraid *adj.*
after *prep., conj., adv.*
afternoon *n.*
afterwards *adv.*

again *adv.*
against *prep.*
age *n.*
aged *adj.*
ago *adv.*
agree *v.*
agreement *n.*
ahead *adv.*
aim *n., v.*
air *n.*
aircraft *n.*
airport *n.*
alcohol *n.*
alcoholic *adj.*
alive *adj.*
all *adj., pron., adv.*
all right *adj., adv., exclamation*
allow *v.*
almost *adv.*
alone *adj., adv.*
along *prep., adv.*
alphabet *n.*
already *adv.*
also *adv.*
although *conj.*
always *adv.*
among *prep.*
amount *n.*
amuse *v.*
  amusing *adj.*
ancient *adj.*
and *conj.*
anger *n.*
angle *n.*
angry *adj.*
  angrily *adv.*
animal *n.*
announce *v.*
annoy *v.*
  annoyed *adj.*
  annoying *adj.*
another *adj., pron.*
answer *n., v.*
any *adj., pron., adv.*

anyone *pron.*
anything *pron.*
anyway *adv.*
anywhere *adv.*
apart *adv.*
  apart from
apparently *adv.*
appear *v.*
appearance *n.*
apple *n.*
apply *v.*
appropriate *adj.*
approval *n.*
approve *v.*
area *n.*
argue *v.*
argument *n.*
arm *n.*
army *n.*
around *prep., adv.*
arrange *v.*
arrangement *n.*
arrest *v.*
arrive *v.*
arrow *n.*
art *n.*
article *n.*
artificial *adj.*
artist *n.*
artistic *adj.*
as *conj. prep.,*
ashamed *adj.*
ask *v.*
asleep *adj.*
at *prep.*
atmosphere *n.*
attack *n., v.*
attention *n.*
attract *v.*
attractive *adj.*
aunt *n.*
autumn *n.*
available *adj.*
avoid *v.*
awake *adj.*

aware *adj.*
away *adv.*

B

baby *n.*
back *n., adj., adv.*
backwards *adv.*
bad *adj.*
  go bad
badly *adv.*
bad-tempered *adj.*
bag *n.*
balance *n.*
ball *n.*
band *n.*
bank *n.*
bar *n.*
base *n., v.*
basic *adj.*
basis *n.*
bath *n.*
bathroom *n.*
be *v.*
beach *n.*
bear *v.*
beard *n.*
beat *v.*
beautiful *adj.*
beauty *n.*
because *conj.*
become *v.*
bed *n.*
bedroom *n.*
been *v.*
beer *n.*
before *prep., conj.*
begin *v.*
beginning *n.*
behave *v.*
behaviour *n.*
behind *prep., adv.*
belief *n.*
believe *v.*
bell *n.*
belong *v.*

below *prep., adv.*
belt *n.*
bend *v.*
beneath *prep., adv.*
benefit *n.*
beside *prep.*
between *prep., adv.*
beyond *prep., adv.*
bicycle *n.*
big *adj.*
bill *n.*
biology *n.*
bird *n.*
birth *n.*
birthday *n.*
biscuit *n.*
bit *n.*
bite *v.*
bitter *adj.*
black *adj.*
blame *v., n.*
block *n.*
blood *n.*
blow *v.*
blue *adj., n.*
board *n.*
boat *n.*
body *n.*
boil *v.*
bomb *n.*
bone *n.*
book *n.*
boot *n.*
border *n.*
bored *adj.*
boring *adj.*
born: be born *v.*
borrow *v.*
both *adj., pron.*
bottle *n.*
bottom *n.*
bowl *n.*
box *n.*

boy n.
boyfriend n.
brain n.
branch n.
brave adj.
bread n.
break v.
breakfast n.
breath n.
breathe v.
brick n.
bridge n.
brief adj.
bright adj.
  brightly adv.
bring v.
broken adj.
brother n.
brown adj., n.
brush n., v.
bubble n.
build v.
building n.
bullet n.
burn v.
burst v.
bury v.
bus n.
bush n.
business n.
busy adj.
but conj.
butter n.
button n.
buy v.
by prep.
bye exclamation

C

cake n.
calculate v.
call v., n.
  be called
calm adj.
camera n.
camp n., v.
camping n.
can modal v., n.
  cannot
  could modal v.
capable adj.
capital n.
car n.
card n.
cardboard n.
care n., v.
  take care
  care for
career n.

careful adj.
  carefully adv.
careless adj.
carelessly adv.
carpet n.
carry v.
case n.
  in case of
cash n.
castle n.
cat n.
catch v.
cause n., v.
CD n.
ceiling n.
celebrate v.
celebration n.
cell n.
cent n. (abbr. c, ct)
centimetre
  (BrE) (AmE
  centimeter) n.
  (abbr. cm)
central adj.
centre (BrE)
  (AmE center) n.
century n.
ceremony n.
certain adj.
certainly adv.
certificate n.
chain n.
chair n.
challenge n.
chance n.
change v., n.
character n.
characteristic n.
charge n., v.
  in charge of
charity n.
chase v., n.
cheap adj.
cheat v., n.
check v., n.
cheek n.
cheese n.
chemical adj., n.
chemistry n.
cheque n.
chest n.
chicken n.
chief adj., n.
child n.
chin n.
chocolate n.
choice n.
choose v.
church n.

cigarette n.
cinema n.
circle n.
city n.
class n.
clean adj., v.
clear adj., v.
clearly adv.
clever adj.
climate n.
climb v.
clock n.
close /kləʊz/ v.
close /kləʊs / adj.
closed adj.
closely adv.
cloth n.
clothes n.
clothing n.
cloud n.
club n.
coal n.
coast n.
coat n.
coffee n.
coin n.
cold adj., n.
collect v.
collection n.
college n.
colour (BrE)
  (AmE color) n.
coloured (BrE)
  (AmE colored)
  adj.
column n.
combination n.
combine v.
come v.
comfortable adj.
command n.
comment n., v.
common adj.
communicate v.
communication n.
community n.
company n.
compare v.
comparison n.
competition n.
complain v.
complaint n.
complete adj., v.
completely adv.
complicated adj.
computer n.
concentrate v.
concert n.
conclusion n.

condition n.
confidence n.
confident adj.
confuse v.
  confusing adj.
confused adj.
connect v.
connection n.
conscious adj.
consider v.
consist v.
contact n., v.
contain v.
container n.
continue v.
continuous adj.
contract n.
contrast n., v.
contribute v.
control n., v.
  in control
  under control
conversation n.
convince v.
cook v.
cooker n.
  (AmE stove)
cookie n.
cooking n.
cool adj.
copy n., v.
corner n.
correct adj., v.
  correctly adv.
cost n. v.
cotton n.
cough v., n.
count v.
country n.
countryside n.
couple n.
course n.
  of course
court n.
cousin n.
cover v., n.
covering n.
cow n.
crash n., v.
crazy adj.
cream n., adj.
create v.
credit card n.
crime n.
criminal adj., n.
crisis n.
criticism n.
cross n.
crowd n.

crowded adj.
cruel adj.
crush v.
cry v., n.
culture n.
cup n.
cupboard n.
curly adj.
curtain n.
curve n.
custom n.
customer n.
cut v., n.

D

damage n., v.
dance n., v.
  dancing n.
dancer n.
danger n.
dangerous adj.
dark adj., n.
date n.
daughter n.
day n.
dead adj.
deal v.
dear adj.
death n.
debt n.
decide v.
decision n.
declare v.
decorate v.
deep adj.
deeply adv.
defeat v., n.
definite adj.
definitely adv.
degree n.
deliberately adv.
deliver v.
demand n., v.
dentist n.
department n.
depend v.
describe v.
description n.
desert n.
design n., v.
desire n.
desk n.
destroy v.
detail n.
  in detail
determination n.
determined adj.

develop v.
development n.
diagram n.
diamond n.
dictionary n.
die v.
difference n.
different adj.
difficult adj.
difficulty n.
dig v.
dinner n.
direct adj., adv., v.
direction n.
directly adv.
dirt n.
dirty adj.
disadvantage n.
disagree v.
disagreement n.
disappear v.
disappoint v.
disappointed adj.
disappointing adj.
disappointment n.
disaster n.
discover v.
discuss v.
discussion n.
disease n.
disgust n., v.
disgusted adj.
disgusting adj.
dish n.
dishonest adj.
disk n.
distance n.
disturb v.
divide v.
division n.
do v.
doctor n.(abbr. Dr)
document n.
dog n.
dollar n.
door n.
double adj.
doubt n.
down adv., prep.
downstairs adv.
downwards adv.
draw v.
drawer n.
drawing n.
dream n.,v.
dress n., v.
drink v., n.

drive v., n.
driver n.
drop v., n.
drug n.
drunk adj.
dry adj., v.
during prep.
dust n.
duty n.
DVD n.

E

each adj., pron.
each other pron.
ear n.
early adj., adv.
earn v.
earth n.
easily adv.
east n., adj., adv.
eastern adj.
easy adj.
eat v.
edge n.
educate v.
education n.
effect n.
effort n.
egg n.
either adj., pron.,
    adv.
election n.
electric adj.
electrical adj.
electricity n.
electronic adj.
else adv.
email n., v.
embarrass v.
embarrassed adj.
embarrassing adj.
embarrassment n.
emergency n.
emotion n.
employ v.
empty adj., v.
encourage v.
end n., v.
   in the end
enemy n.
energy n.
engine n.
enjoy v.
enjoyable adj.
enjoyment n.
enough adj.,
    pron., adv.
enter v.
entertain v.

entertainment n.
enthusiasm n.
enthusiastic adj.
entrance n.
environment n.
equal adj., v.
equally adv.
equipment n.
error n.
escape v.
especially adv.
etc. abbr.
euro n.
even adv.
evening n.
event n.
eventually adv.
ever adv.
every adj.
everybody pron.
everyone pron.
everything pron.
everywhere adv.
evidence n.
evil adj.
exact adj.
exactly adv.
exaggerate v.
exam n.
examination n.
examine v.
example n.
excellent adj.
except prep.
exchange n., v.
   in exchange
excited adj.
excitement n.
exciting adj.
excluding prep.
excuse n., v.
exercise n.
exhibition n.
exist v.
expect v.
expensive adj.
experience n., v.
experiment n., v.
expert n.
explain v.
explanation n.
explode v.
explore v.
explosion n.
expression n.
extra adj., adv.
extreme adj.
extremely adv.
eye n.

F

face n., v.
fact n.
factory n.
fail v.
failure n.
fair adj.
fairly adv.
fall v., n.
familiar adj.
family n.
famous adj.
far adv., adj.
farm n.
farmer n.
farming n.
fashion n.
fashionable adj.
fast adj., adv.
fasten v.
fat adj., n.
father n.
fault n.
favour n.
   in favour
favourite adj., n.
fear n.
feather n.
feature n.
feed v.
feel v.
feeling n.
female adj., n.
fence n.
festival n.
few adj., pron.
   a few
field n.
fight v., n.
figure n.
file n.
fill v.
film n., v.
final adj., n.
finally adv.
financial adj.
find v.
   find sth out
fine adj.
finger n.
finish v.
fire n., v.
firm n., adj.
firmly adv.
first adj., adv., n.
   at first
fish n., v.
fit v., adj.
fix v.

fixed adj.
flag n.
flame n.
flash v., n.
flat adj., n.
flavour n.
flight n.
float v.
flood n.
floor n.
flour n.
flow n., v.
flower n.
fly v., n.
flying adj.
fold v., n.
follow v.
following adj.
food n.
foot n.
football n.
for prep.
force n., v.
foreign adj.
forest n.
forget v.
forgive v.
fork n.
form n., v.
formal adj.
forward adv.
frame n.
free adj., adv., v.
freedom n.
freeze v.
fresh adj.
friend n.
friendly adj.
friendship n.
frighten v.
frightened adj.
frightening adj.
from prep.
front n., adj.
   in front
frozen adj.
fruit n.
fry v.
fuel n.
full adj.
fully adv.
fun n.
funny adj.
fur n.
furniture n.
further adj., adv.
future n., adj.

G

gain *v.*
game *n.*
garden *n.*
gas *n.*
gate *n.*
general *adj.*
  in general
generally *adv.*
generous *adj.*
gentle *adj.*
  gently *adv.*
get *v.*
  get on
  get off
gift *n.*
girl *n.*
girlfriend *n.*
give *v.*
  give sth away
  give (sth) up
glass *n.*
glasses *n.*
glove *n.*
go *v.*
  be going to
goal *n.*
god *n.*
gold *n., adj.*
good *adj., n.*
  good at
  good for
goodbye
  exclamation
goods *n.*
government *n.*
grade *n.*
grain *n.*
gram *n.*
grammar *n.*
granddaughter *n.*
grandfather *n.*
grandmother *n.*
grandson *n.*
grass *n.*
grateful *adj.*
great *adj.*
green *adj.*
grey *adj., n.*
ground *n.*
group *n.*
grow *v.*
  grow up
growth *n.*
guard *n., v.*
guess *v., n.*
guest *n.*
guide *n., v.*
guilty *adj.*

gun *n.*

H

habit *n.*
hair *n.*
half *n., adj., pron.,*
  adv.
hall *n.*
hammer *n.*
hand *n.*
handle *n., v.*
hang *v.*
happen *v.*
happiness *n.*
happy *adj.*
hard *adj., adv.*
hardly *adv.*
harm *n., v.*
harmful *adj.*
hat *n.*
hate *v., n.*
have *v.*
  have to *modal v.*
he *pron.*
head *n.*
health *n.*
healthy *adj.*
hear *v.*
heart *n.*
heat *n., v.*
heaven *n.*
heavy *adj.*
height *n.*
hello *exclamation*
help *v., n.*
helpful *adj.*
her *pron.*
here *adv.*
hers *pron.*
herself *pron.*
hide *v.*
high *adj.*
highly *adv.*
hill *n.*
him *pron.*
himself *pron.*
his *adj., pron.*
history *n.*
hit *v., n.*
hobby *n.*
hold *v., n.*
hole *n.*
holiday *n.*
home *n., adv.*
honest *adj.*
hook *n.*
hope *v., n.*
horn *n.*
horse *n.*

hospital *n.*
hot *adj.*
hotel *n.*
hour *n.*
house *n.*
how *adv.*
however *adv.*
huge *adj.*
human *adj., n.*
humour *n.*
hungry *adj.*
hunt *v., n.*
hurry *v., n.*
hurt *v.*
husband *n.*

I

I *pron.*
ice *n.*
ice cream *n.*
idea *n.*
identify *v.*
if *conj.*
ignore *v.*
ill *adj.*
illegal *adj.*
  illegally *adv.*
illness *n.*
image *n.*
imagination *n.*
imagine *v.*
immediate *adj.*
immediately *adv.*
impatient *adj.*
importance *n.*
important *adj.*
impossible *adj.*
impression *n.*
impressive *adj.*
improve *v.*
improvement *n.*
in *prep., adv.*
include *v.*
including *prep.*
increase *v., n.*
indeed *adv.*
independent *adj.*
individual *adj.*
industry *n.*
infection *n.*
influence *n.*
inform *v.*
informal *adj.*
information *n.*
injury *n.*
insect *n.*
inside *prep., adv.,*
  adj., n.
instead *adv., prep.*

instruction *n.*
instrument *n.*
insult *v., n.*
intelligent *adj.*
intend *v.*
intention *n.*
interest *n., v.*
interested *adj.*
interesting *adj.*
international *adj.*
Internet *n.*
interrupt *v.*
interview *n.*
into *prep.*
introduce *v.*
introduction *n.*
invent *v.*
investigate *v.*
invitation *n.*
invite *v.*
involve *v.*
iron *n., v.*
island *n.*
issue *n.*
it *pron.*
item *n.*
its *adj.*
itself *pron.*

J

jacket *n.*
jam *n.*
jeans *n.*
jewellery *n.*
job *n.*
join *v.*
joke *n., v.*
journalist *n.*
journey *n.*
judge *n., v.*
judgement *n.*
juice *n.*
jump *v., n.*
just *adv.*

K

keep *v.*
key *n.*
kick *v., n.*
kill *v.*
kilogram *n.*
  (abbr. kg)
kilometre (*BrE*)
  (*AmE* kilometer)
  n. (abbr. k, km)
kind *n., adj.*
kindness *n.*
king *n.*
kiss *v., n.*

kitchen *n.*
knee *n.*
knife *n.*
knock *v., n.*
knot *n.*
know *v.*
knowledge *n.*

L

lack *n.*
lady *n.*
lake *n.*
lamp *n.*
land *n., v.*
language *n.*
large *adj.*
last *adj., adv.,*
  n., v.
late *adj., adv.*
later *adv., adj.*
laugh *v., n.*
law *n.*
lawyer *n.*
lay *v.*
layer *n.*
lazy *adj.*
lead /liːd/ *v.*
leader *n.*
leaf *n.*
lean *v.*
learn *v.*
least *adj., pron.,*
  adv.
  at least
leather *n.*
leave *v.*
left *adj., adv., n.*
leg *n.*
legal *adj.*
  legally *adv.*
lemon *n.*
lend *v.*
length *n.*
less *adj., pron.,*
  adv.
lesson *n.*
let *v.*
letter *n.*
level *n., adj.*
library *n.*
lid *n.*
lie *v., n.*
life *n.*
lift *v., n.*
light *n., adj., v.*
  lightly *adv.*
like *v., prep., conj.*
likely *adj.*
limit *n., v.*

line *n.*
lip *n.*
liquid *n., adj.*
list *n., v.*
listen *v.*
literature *n.*
litre (*BrE*) (*AmE*
  liter) *n.* (*abbr.* l)
little *adj., pron.,*
  adv.
  a little
live /lɪv/ *v.*
living *adj.*
load *n., v.*
loan *n.*
local *adj.*
lock *v., n.*
lonely *adj.*
long *adj., adv.*
look *v., n.*
  look after
  look for
  look forward to
loose *adj.*
lorry *n.*
lose *v.*
loss *n.*
lost *adj.*
lot *pron., adv.*
  a lot (of)
loud *adj., adv.*
  loudly *adv.*
love *n., v.*
low *adj., adv.*
luck *n.*
lucky *adj.*
luggage *n.*
lump *n.*
lunch *n.*

M

machine *n.*
mad *adj.*
magazine *n.*
magic *n., adj.*
mail *n., v.*
main *adj.*
mainly *adv.*
make *v., n.*
male *adj., n.*
man *n.*
manage *v.*
manager *n.*
many *adj., pron.*
map *n.*
march *v., n.*
mark *v., n.*

market *n.*
marriage *n.*
married *adj.*
marry *v.*
match *n., v.*
material *n.*
mathematics *n.*
matter *n., v.*
may *modal v.*
maybe *adv.*
me *pron.*
meal *n.*
mean *v.*
meaning *n.*
measure *v., n.*
measurement *n.*
meat *n.*
medical *adj.*
medicine *n.*
medium *adj.*
meet *v.*
meeting *n.*
melt *n.*
member *n.*
memory *n.*
mental *adj.*
mention *v.*
message *n.*
metal *n.*
method *n.*
metre (*BrE*)
  (*AmE* meter) *n.*
midday *n.*
middle *n., adj.*
midnight *n.*
might *modal v.*
mile *n.*
milk *n.*
mind *n., v.*
mine *pron., n.*
minute *n.*
mirror *n.*
Miss *n.*
miss *v.*
missing *adj.*
mistake *n., v.*
mix *v.*
mixed *adj.*
mixture *n.*
mobile phone *n.*
model *n.*
modern *adj.*
moment *n.*
money *n.*
month *n.*
mood *n.*
moon *n.*
moral *adj.*
  morally *adv.*

more *adj., pron.,*
  adv.
morning *n.*
most *adj., pron.,*
  adv.
mostly *adv.*
mother *n.*
motorbike *n.*
mountain *n.*
mouse *n.*
mouth *n.*
move *v., n.*
movement *n.*
movie *n.*
Mr *n.*
Mrs *n.*
much *adj., pron.,*
  adv.
mud *n.*
multiply *v.*
murder *n., v.*
muscle *n.*
museum *n.*
music *n.*
musical *adj.*
musician *n.*
must *modal v.*
my *adj.*
myself *pron.*
mysterious *adj.*

N

nail *n.*
name *n., v.*
narrow *adj.*
national *adj.*
natural *adj.*
nature *n.*
navy *n.*
near *adj., adv.,*
  prep.
nearby *adj.*
nearly *adv.*
necessary *adj.*
neck *n.*
need *v., n.*
needle *n.*
negative *adj.*
neighbour *n.*
neither *adj.,*
  pron., adv.
nerve *n.*
nervous *adj.*
net *n.*
never *adv.*
new *adj.*
news *n.*
newspaper *n.*
next *adj., adv., n.*

nice *adj.*
night *n.*
no *exclamation,*
  adj.
nobody *pron.*
noise *n.*
noisy *adj.*
  noisily *adv.*
none *pron.*
nonsense *n.*
no one *pron.*
nor *conj.*
normal *adj.*
normally *adv.*
north *n., adj., adv.*
northern *adj.*
nose *n.*
not *adv.*
note *n., v.*
nothing *pron.*
notice *n., v.*
novel *n.*
now *adv.*
nowhere *adv.*
nuclear *adj.*
number *n.* (*abbr.*
  No., no.)
nurse *n.*
nut *n.*

O

object *n.*
obtain *v.*
obvious *adj.*
occasion *n.*
occur *v.*
ocean *n.*
o'clock *adv.*
odd *adj.*
of *prep.*
off *prep., adv., adj.*
offence (*AmE*
  offense) *n.*
offer *v., n.*
office *n.*
officer *n.*
official *adj.*
  officially *adv.*
often *adv.*
oh *exclamation*
oil *n.*
OK *exclamation,*
  adj.
old *adj.*
old-fashioned *adj.*
on *prep., adv.*
once *adv.*
one *number, adj.,*
  pron.

one another *pron.*
onion *n.*
only *adj., adv.*
onto *prep.*
open *adj., v.*
operate *v.*
operation *n.*
opinion *n.*
opportunity *n.*
opposite *adj.,*
  adv., prep., n.
or *conj.*
orange *n., adj.*
order *n., v.*
ordinary *adj.*
organization *n.*
organize *v.*
organized *adj.*
original *adj., n.*
other *adj., pron.*
otherwise *adv.*
ought to *modal v.*
our *n.*
ours *pron.*
ourselves *pron.*
out *adv., adj.*
outdoors *adv.*
out of *prep.*
outside *n., adj.,*
  prep., adv.
oven *n.*
over *adv., prep.*
owe *v.*
own *adj., pron., v.*
owner *n.*

P

pack *n., v.*
package *n.*
packet *n.*
page *n.*
pain *n.*
painful *adj.*
paint *n., v.*
painter *n.*
painting *n.*
pair *n.*
pale *adj.*
pan *n.*
paper *n.*
parent *n.*
park *n., v.*
part *n.*
  take part (in)
particular *adj.*
particularly *adv.*
partly *adv.*
partner *n.*
party *n.*

pass v.
passage n.
passenger n.
passport n.
past adj., n.,
   prep., adv.
path n.
patient adj., n.
pattern n.
pay v., n.
payment n.
peace n.
peaceful adj.
pen n.
pencil n.
penny n. (abbr. p)
people n.
perfect adj.
perform v.
performance n.
perhaps adv.
period n.
permanent adj.
permission n.
person n.
personal adj.
persuade v.
pet n.
petrol n.
phone n., v.
photograph n., v.
photographer n.
phrase n.
physical adj.
  physically adv.
piano n.
pick v.
  pick sth up
picture n.
piece n.
pig n.
pile n., v.
pilot n.
pin n.
pink adj., n.
pipe n.
pity n.
place n., v.
  take place
plain adj.
plan n., v.
plane n.
planet n.
plant n., v.
plastic n.
plate n.
platform n.
play v., n.
player n.

pleasant adj.
please
  exclamation, v.
pleased adj.
pleasure n.
plenty pron.
plural adj., n.
pocket n.
poem n.
poetry n.
point n., v.
pointed adj.
poison n., v.
poisonous adj.
police n.
polite adj.
  politely adv.
political adj.
politician n.
politics n.
pool n.
poor adj.
popular adj.
port n.
position n.
positive adj.
possibility n.
possible adj.
possibly adv.
post n., v.
post office n.
pot n.
potato n.
pound n.
pour v.
powder n.
power n.
powerful adj.
practical adj.
practice n. (BrE,
  AmE), v. (AmE)
practise v. (BrE)
prayer n.
prefer v.
pregnant adj.
preparation n.
prepare v.
prepared adj.
present adj., n., v.
president n.
press n., v.
pressure n.
pretend v.
pretty adv., adj.
prevent v.
previous adj.
price n.
priest n.
prime minister n.

print v.
priority n.
prison n.
prisoner n.
private adj.
prize n.
probable adj.
probably adv.
problem n.
process n.
produce v.
product n.
production n.
profession n.
professional adj.
profit n.
program n., v.
programme n.
progress v., n.
project n.
promise v., n.
pronounce v.
proof n.
proper adj.
properly adv.
property n.
protect v.
protection n.
protest n., v.
proud adj.
prove v.
provide v.
pub n.
public adj., n.
  in public
  publicly adv.
publish v.
pull v., n.
punish v.
punishment n.
pupil n.
pure adj.
purple adj., n.
purpose n.
  on purpose
push v., n.
put v.
  put sth on

Q

quality n.
quantity n.
quarter n.
queen n.
question n., v.
quick adj., adv.
  quickly adv.
quiet adj.
  quietly adv.

quite adv.

R

race n., v.
radio n.
railway n.
rain n., v.
raise v.
rare adj.
rarely adv.
rather adv.
reach v.
reaction n.
read v.
ready adj.
real adj.
reality n.
realize v.
really adv.
reason n.
reasonable adj.
receive v.
recent adj.
recently adv.
recognize v.
recommend v.
record n., v.
recover v.
red adj., n.
reduce v.
refer to v.
refuse v.
region n.
regular adj.
  regularly adv.
relation n.
relationship n.
relative n.
relax v.
relaxed adj.
release v.
relevant adj.
relief n.
religion n.
religious adj.
rely v.
remain v.
remark n.
remember v.
remind v.
remove v.
rent n., v.
repair v.
repeat v., n.
replace v.
reply v., n.
report v., n.
represent v.
request n., v.

require v.
rescue v., n.
research n., v.
reserve v.
respect n., v.
responsibility n.
responsible adj.
rest n., v.
restaurant n.
result n., v.
return v., n.
rice n.
rich adj.
rid: get rid of adj.
ride v., n.
right adj., adv., n.,
  exclamation
ring n., v.
rise n., v.
risk n., v.
river n.
road n.
rob v.
rock n.
role n.
roll n., v.
romantic adj.
roof n.
room n.
root n.
rope n.
rough adj.
round adj., adv.,
  prep.
route n.
row /rəʊ/ n.
royal adj.
rub v.
rubber n.
rubbish n.
rude adj.
  rudely adv.
ruin v.
rule n., v.
run v., n.
rush v., n.

S

sad adj.
  sadness n.
safe adj.
  safely adv.
safety n.
sail v., n.
sailor n.
salad n.
sale n.
salt n.

same *adj., pron.*
sand *n.*
satisfaction *n.*
satisfied *adj.*
sauce *n.*
save *v.*
say *v.*
scale *n.*
scene *n.*
school *n.*
science *n.*
scientific *adj.*
scientist *n.*
scissors *n.*
score *n., v.*
scratch *v.*
screen *n.*
sea *n.*
search *v., n.*
season *n.*
seat *n.*
second *adj., adv., n.*
secret *n., adj.*
secretary *n.*
secretly *adv.*
section *n.*
see *v.*
seed *n.*
seem *v.*
sell *v.*
send *v.*
senior *adj.*
sense *n.*
sensible *adj.*
sensitive *adj.*
sentence *n.*
separate *adj., v.*
  separately *adv.*
series *n.*
serious *adj.*
seriously *adv.*
serve *v.*
service *n.*
set *v., n.*
settle *v.*
several *adj., pron.*
sew *v.*
sewing *n.*
sex *n.*
sexual *adj.*
shade *n.*
shadow *n.*
shake *v.*
shall *modal v.*
shame *n.*
shape *n., v.*
shaped *adj.*

share *v., n.*
sharp *adj.*
she *pron.*
sheep *n.*
sheet *n.*
shelf *n.*
shell *n.*
shine *v.*
shiny *adj.*
ship *n.*
shirt *n.*
shock *n., v.*
  shocked *adj.*
  shocking *adj.*
shoe *n.*
shoot *v.*
shop *n., v.*
shopping *n.*
short *adj.*
shot *n.*
should *modal v.*
shoulder *n.*
shout *v., n.*
show *v., n.*
shower *n.*
shut *v., adj.*
shy *adj.*
sick *adj.*
  be sick
  feel sick
side *n.*
sight *n.*
sign *n., v.*
signal *n., v.*
silence *n.*
silly *adj.*
silver *n.*
similar *adj.*
simple *adj.*
since *adv., prep.,*
  conj.
sing *v.*
singer *n.*
single *adj.*
sink *v.*
sir *n.*
sister *n.*
sit *v.*
  sit down
situation *n.*
size *n.*
skill *n.*
skin *n.*
skirt *n.*
sky *n.*
sleep *v., n.*
sleeve *n.*
slice *n. v.*
slide *v.*

slightly *adv.*
slip *v.*
slow *adj.*
  slowly *adv.*
small *adj.*
smell *v., n.*
smile *v., n.*
smoke *n., v.*
smooth *adj.*
  smoothly *adv.*
snake *n.*
snow *n., v.*
so *adv., conj.*
soap *n.*
social *adj.*
society *n.*
sock *n.*
soft *adj.*
soil *n.*
soldier *n.*
solid *adj., n.*
solution *n.*
solve *v.*
some *adj., pron.*
somebody *pron.*
somehow *adv.*
someone *pron.*
something *pron.*
sometimes *adv.*
somewhere *adv.*
son *n.*
song *n.*
soon *adv.*
  as soon as
sore *adj.*
sorry *adj.*
sort *n., v.*
sound *n., v.*
soup *n.*
south *n., adj., adv.*
southern *adj.*
space *n.*
speak *v.*
speaker *n.*
special *adj.*
speech *n.*
speed *n.*
spend *v.*
spice *n.*
spider *n.*
spirit *n.*
spite: in spite of *n.*
spoil *v.*
spoon *n.*
sport *n.*
spot *n.*
spread *v.*
spring *n.*
square *adj., n.*

stage *n.*
stair *n.*
stamp *n.*
stand *v., n.*
  stand up
standard *n.*
star *n., v.*
stare *v.*
start *v., n.*
state *n., v.*
statement *n.*
station *n.*
stay *v., n.*
steady *adj.*
steal *v.*
steam *n.*
step *n., v*
stick *v., n.*
sticky *adj.*
still *adv., adj.*
stomach *n.*
stone *n.*
stop *v., n.*
store *n., v.*
storm *n.*
story *n.*
straight *adv., adj.*
strange *adj.*
street *n.*
strength *n.*
stretch *v.*
strict *adj.*
string *n.*
strong *adj.*
  strongly *adv.*
structure *n.*
student *n.*
study *n., v.*
stuff *n.*
stupid *adj.*
style *n.*
subject *n.*
substance *n.*
succeed *v.*
success *n.*
successful *adj.*
successfully *adv.*
such *adj.*
  such as
suck *v.*
sudden *adj.*
suddenly *adv.*
suffer *v.*
sugar *n.*
suggest *v.*
suggestion *n.*
suit *n., v.*
suitable *adj.*
suitcase *n.*

sum *n.*
summer *n.*
sun *n.*
supply *n.*
support *v.*
suppose *v.*
sure *adj., adv.*
  make sure
surface *n.*
surprise *n., v.*
surprised *adj.*
surprising *adj.*
surround *v.*
survive *v.*
swallow *v.*
swear *v.*
sweat *v., n.*
sweet *adj., n.*
swim *v.*
swimming pool *n.*
switch *n., v.*
  switch sth off
  switch sth on
symbol *n.*
system *n.*

T

table *n.*
tail *n.*
take *v.*
  take sth off
talk *v., n.*
tall *adj.*
tap *v., n.*
tape *n.*
task *n.*
taste *n., v.*
tax *n.*
taxi *n.*
tea *n.*
teach *v.*
teacher *n.*
team *n.*
tear /teə(r)/ *v., n.*
tear /tɪə(r)/ *n.*
technical *adj.*
technology *n.*
telephone *n., v.*
television *n.*
tell *v.*
temperature *n.*
temporary *adj.*
tend *v.*
tent *n.*
terrible *adj.*
test *n., v.*
text *n.*
than *conj., prep.*
thank *v.*

thanks n.
thank you n.
that adj., pron., conj.
the definite article
theatre (BrE) (AmE theater) n.
their adj.
theirs pron.
them pron.
themselves pron.
then adv.
there adv., pron.
therefore adv.
these adj., pron.
they pron.
thick adj.
thief n.
thin adj.
thing n.
think v.
thirsty adj.
this adj., pron.
those adj., pron.
though conj., adv.
thought n.
thread n.
threat n.
threaten v.
throat n.
through prep., adv.
throw v.
   throw sth away
thumb n.
ticket n.
tidy adj., v.
tie v., n.
tight adj., adv.
till conj., prep.
time n.
tin n.
tired adj.
tiring adj.
title n.
to prep.
today adv., n.
toe n.
together adv.
toilet n.
tomato n.
tomorrow adv., n.
tongue n.
tonight adv., n.
too adv.
tool n.
tooth n.
top n., adj.
total adj., n.
totally adv.

touch v., n.
tour n.
tourist n.
towards prep.
towel n.
tower n.
town n.
toy n.
track n.
tradition n.
traffic n.
train n., v.
training n.
translate v.
transparent adj.
transport n., v.
travel v., n.
treat v.
treatment n.
tree n.
trial n.
triangle n.
trick n., v.
trip n., v.
trouble n.
trousers n.
truck n.
true adj.
trust n., v.
truth n.
try v.
tube n.
tune n.
tunnel n.
turn v., n.
twice adv.
twist v.
type n., v.
typical adj.
tyre n.

U
ugly adj.
unable adj.
uncle n.
uncomfortable adj.
unconscious adj.
under prep., adv.
underground adj., adv.
underneath prep., adv.
understand v.
underwater adj., adv.
underwear n.
unemployment n.

unexpected adj.
   unexpectedly adv.
unfair adj.
unfortunately adv.
unfriendly adj.
unhappy adj.
   unhappiness n.
uniform n.
union n.
unit n.
unite v.
universe n.
university n.
unkind adj.
unknown adj.
unless conj.
unlikely adj.
unpleasant adj.
untidy adj.
until conj., prep.
unusual adj.
up prep., adv.
upper adj.
upset v., adj.
upstairs adv., adj.
upwards adv.
urgent adj.
us pron.
use v., n.
used adj.
   be/get used to sth
used to modal v.
useful adj.
useless adj.
user n.
usual adj.
usually adv.

V
vacation n.
valley n.
valuable adj.
value n.
varied adj.
variety n.
various adj.
vary v.
vegetable n.
vehicle n.
very adv.
video n.
view n.
village n.
violence n.
violent adj.
visit v., n.
visitor n.

voice n.
vote n., v.

W
wait v.
wake (up) v.
walk v., n.
wall n.
want v.
war n.
warm adj., v.
warn v.
warning n.
wash v.
washing n.
waste v., n., adj.
watch v., n.
water n.
wave n., v.
way n.
we pron.
weak adj.
weakness n.
weapon n.
wear v.
weather n.
website n.
wedding n.
week n.
weekend n.
weigh v.
weight n.
welcome v., adj., n.
well adv., adj., exclamation
   as well (as)
west n., adj., adv.
western adj.
wet adj.
what pron., adj.
whatever adj., pron., adv.
wheel n.
when adv., conj.
whenever conj.
where adv., conj.
whereas conj.
wherever adv., conj.
whether conj.
which pron., adj.
while conj., n.
white adj., n.
who pron.
whoever pron.
whole adj., n.
whom pron.
whose adj., pron.

why adv.
wide adj.
wife n.
wild adj.
will modal v., n.
win v.
wind /wɪnd/ n.
window n.
wine n.
wing n.
winner n.
winter n.
wire n.
wish v., n.
with prep.
within prep.
without prep., adv.
woman n.
wonder v.
wonderful adj.
wood n.
wooden adj.
wool n.
word n.
work v., n.
worker n.
world n.
worried adj.
worry v., n.
worse adj., adv.
worst adj., adv., n.
worth adj.
would modal v.
wrap v.
write v.
writer n.
writing n.
wrong adj., adv.
   go wrong

Y
year n.
yellow adj., n.
yes exclamation
yesterday adv., n.
yet adv., conj.
you pron.
young adj.
your adj.
yours pron.
yourself pron.
youth n.

Irregular verbs 不规则动词

Infinitive 不定式	Past tense 过去式	Past participle 过去分词	Infinitive 不定式	Past tense 过去式	Past participle 过去分词
arise	arose	arisen	flee	fled	fled
babysit	babysat	babysat	fling	flung	flung
be	was/were	been	fly	flew	flown
bear	bore	borne	forbid	forbade	forbidden
beat	beat	beaten	forecast	forecast	forecast
become	became	become	foresee	foresaw	foreseen
begin	began	begun	forget	forgot	forgotten
bend	bent	bent	forgive	forgave	forgiven
bet	bet	bet	freeze	froze	frozen
bid	bid	bid	get	got	got; (American 美式英语) gotten
bind	bound	bound			
bite	bit	bitten			
bleed	bled	bled			
blow	blew	blown	give	gave	given
break	broke	broken	go	went	gone
breed	bred	bred	grind	ground	ground
bring	brought	brought	grow	grew	grown
broadcast	broadcast	broadcast	hang	hung, hanged	hung, hanged
build	built	built			
burn	burnt, burned	burnt, burned	have	had	had
			hear	heard	heard
burst	burst	burst	hide	hid	hidden
buy	bought	bought	hit	hit	hit
catch	caught	caught	hold	held	held
choose	chose	chosen	hurt	hurt	hurt
cling	clung	clung	keep	kept	kept
come	came	come	kneel	knelt, kneeled	knelt, kneeled
cost	cost	cost			
creep	crept	crept	know	knew	known
cut	cut	cut	lay	laid	laid
deal	dealt	dealt	lead	led	led
dig	dug	dug	lean	leant, leaned	leant, leaned
do	did	done			
draw	drew	drawn	leap	leapt, leaped	leapt, leaped
dream	dreamt, dreamed	dreamt, dreamed	learn	learnt, learned	learnt, learned
drink	drank	drunk	leave	left	left
drive	drove	driven	lend	lent	lent
eat	ate	eaten	let	let	let
fall	fell	fallen	lie	lay	lain
feed	fed	fed	light	lit, lighted	lit, lighted
feel	felt	felt	lose	lost	lost
fight	fought	fought	make	made	made
find	found	found	mean	meant	meant
			meet	met	met

Infinitive 不定式	Past tense 过去式	Past participle 过去分词	Infinitive 不定式	Past tense 过去式	Past participle 过去分词
mislead	misled	misled	speed	sped, speeded	sped, speeded
mistake	mistook	mistaken	spell	spelt, spelled	spelt, spelled
misunderstand	misunderstood	misunderstood	spend	spent	spent
mow	mowed	mown	spill	spilt, spilled	spilt, spilled
outgrow	outgrew	outgrown	spin	spun	spun
overcome	overcame	overcome	spit	spat	spat
overhear	overheard	overheard	split	split	split
oversleep	overslept	overslept	spoil	spoilt, spoiled	spoilt, spoiled
overtake	overtook	overtaken	spread	spread	spread
pay	paid	paid	spring	sprang	sprung
prove	proved	proved, proven	stand	stood	stood
put	put	put	steal	stole	stolen
quit	quit	quit	stick	stuck	stuck
read	read	read	sting	stung	stung
repay	repaid	repaid	stink	stank	stunk
rewind	rewound	rewound	stride	strode	—
ride	rode	ridden	strike	struck	struck
ring	rang	rung	swear	swore	sworn
rise	rose	risen	sweep	swept	swept
run	ran	run	swell	swelled	swollen, swelled
saw	sawed	sawn	swim	swam	swum
say	said	said	swing	swung	swung
see	saw	seen	take	took	taken
seek	sought	sought	teach	taught	taught
sell	sold	sold	tear	tore	torn
send	sent	sent	tell	told	told
set	set	set	think	thought	thought
sew	sewed	sewed, sewn	throw	threw	thrown
shake	shook	shaken	thrust	thrust	thrust
shed	shed	shed	tread	trod	trodden
shine	shone	shone	undergo	underwent	undergone
shoot	shot	shot	understand	understood	understood
show	showed	shown, showed	undo	undid	undone
shrink	shrank, shrunk	shrunk	unwind	unwound	unwound
shut	shut	shut	upset	upset	upset
sing	sang	sung	wake	woke	woken
sink	sank	sunk	wear	wore	worn
sit	sat	sat	weave	wove	woven
sleep	slept	slept	weep	wept	wept
slide	slid	slid	win	won	won
sling	slung	slung	wind	wound	wound
slit	slit	slit	withdraw	withdrew	withdrawn
smell	smelt, smelled	smelt, smelled	wring	wrung	wrung
sow	sowed	sown, sowed	write	wrote	written
speak	spoke	spoken			

Key to study pages 研习专页答案

Prepositions of place
方位介词 [S2]

1 Who's who? 谁是谁?

1 Tom   4 James
2 Sarah   5 Jack
3 Diana   6 Jill

2 Describing pictures 描述图画

A	B
1 in	1 below
2 on top of	2 against
3 above	3 under
4 below	4 among
5 between	5 opposite

Prepositions of movement
移动方向介词 [S3]

1 Where are they going? 他们去哪里?

1 up   6 out of
2 along   7 through
3 down   8 over
4 into   9 round
5 across   10 towards

**2 Giving and following directions
指示和辨别方向**

1 right   4 down this road
2 turn left   5 take the second turning
3 left again   6 on the right

Exam practice 考试练习 [S4–5]

Part 1 第一部分

1 C   2 D   3 F   4 I   5 H   6 B

Part 2 第二部分

1 igloo   4 palace
2 tent   5 nest
3 bungalow   6 caves

Part 3 第三部分

1 B   4 B
2 C   5 C
3 A   6 A

Part 4 第四部分

1 are
2 there
3 is
4 in
5 am
6 sleep/stay/camp
7 breakfast/lunch/dinner/supper/tea
8 will

Numbers 数字 [S6–8]

1 One or first? 用 one 还是 first?

A				
1	one		1st	first
2	two		2nd	second
3	three		3rd	third
4	four		4th	fourth
5	five		5th	fifth
6	six		6th	sixth
7	seven		7th	seventh
8	eight		8th	eighth
9	nine		9th	ninth
10	ten		10th	tenth
11	eleven		11th	eleventh
12	twelve		12th	twelfth
13	thirteen		13th	thirteenth
14	fourteen		14th	fourteenth
15	fifteen		15th	fifteenth
16	sixteen		16th	sixteenth
17	seventeen		17th	seventeenth
18	eighteen		18th	eighteenth
19	nineteen		19th	nineteenth
20	twenty		20th	twentieth
21	twenty-one		21st	twenty-first
30	thirty		30th	thirtieth
40	forty		40th	fortieth
50	fifty		50th	fiftieth
60	sixty		60th	sixtieth
70	seventy		70th	seventieth
80	eighty		80th	eightieth
90	ninety		90th	ninetieth
100	a/one hundred		100th	hundredth
101	a/one hundred and one		101st	hundred and first
200	two hundred		200th	two hundredth
1 000	a/one thousand		1 000th	thousandth
1 000 000	a/one million		1 000 000th	millionth

B	1 third	4 sixtieth	7 seven
	2 twelve	5 forty-nine	8 second
	3 fifth	6 hundredth	

2 Large numbers 大数目

1 three hundred and sixty-five (365)
2 one hundred and eighty (180)
3 nine thousand eight hundred and fifty (9850)

4 Fractions and mathematical expressions 分数和数学表达法

A 1 $^1/_2$ a half
   4 $^1/_8$ an/one eighth
   2 $^1/_3$ a/one third
   5 $^1/_{16}$ a/one sixteenth
   3 $^1/_4$ a/one quarter
   7 $^3/_4$ three quarters
   6 $1^2/_5$ one and two fifths

B 1 four
   2 eighty-five
   3 one hundred and fifty
   4 seven point eight
   5 fifty-four
   6 three quarters

Time and dates
时间和日期 [S9–10]

1 What time is it? 几点了?

3 six **thirty**
4 (a) **quarter** to four
5 ten **past** eleven
6 twenty **to** twelve or eleven **forty**

2 What's the date? 今天几号?

B 1 Man landed on the moon on 20 July, 1969.
   2 William Shakespeare was born on 23rd April, 1564.
   3 The first ever website appeared on August 6, 1991.
   4 Queen Elizabeth II became Queen of the United Kingdom on 2 June, 1953.

We say 读作
1 the twentieth of July, nineteen sixty-nine
2 the twenty-third of April, fifteen sixty-four
3 August the sixth, nineteen ninety one
4 the second of June, nineteen fifty-three

Telephoning 打电话 [S11]

1 Asking for and saying telephone numbers 询问和读出电话号码

What's your number?
What's your phone number?
What's your mobile number?

2 Using the telephone 打电话

1 make a phone call   6 on the phone
2 pick up   7 engaged
3 dial   8 leave a message
4 rings   9 call you back
5 hang up

3 Talking on the telephone 通电话

A 1 Hello. 56767.
   2 Hello. Is Sally there, please?
   3 Sally speaking.
   4 Oh hello, Sally. It's John.

B 1 Good morning, Dr Lee's surgery.
   2 Hello. Can I speak to Dr Lee, please?
   3 Who's calling?
   4 It's Mr White.
   5 I'm sorry — he's out. Can I take a message?
   6 No, thank you. I'll call back later.

Words that go together
词语搭配 [S12–13]

1 Prepositions 介词

A Adjectives with prepositions 形容词接介词

1 at   4 about   7 of
2 of   5 of   8 about
3 in   6 with

B Verbs with prepositions 动词接介词

1 with   4 for   7 about
2 for   5 on   8 in
3 at   6 for

2 Verb + noun 动词 + 名词

A take a photo   say goodbye
   give somebody a call   tell a lie
   make a mess   pass your exams
   do your homework   catch a cold

B
1 give you a call
2 pass your exams
3 take a photo
4 saying goodbye
5 making a mess
6 told a lie
7 done my homework
8 caught a cold

3 Finding information in the dictionary
在本词典查找信息

A Bed: go to bed, in bed, make the bed, single bed, double bed, bunk beds
Bread: loaf of bread
Computer: by computer, on the computer, computer program, computer games
Diet: go on a diet
Hardly: could hardly, hardly any, hardly ever
Holiday: summer holiday, on holiday, public holiday, bank holiday
Morning: this morning, tomorrow morning, on Tuesday morning, all morning, in the morning

B
1 no answer   5 go on a diet
2 go to bed   6 hardly ever
3 a loaf of bread 7 on holiday
4 on the computer 8 in the morning

Education 教育 [S14–15]

1 School subjects 学校科目

A

2 The Education System 教育制度

A **In Britain ...**   **In the US ...**
在英国   在美国

1 nursery school   1 nursery school
2 primary school   2 elementary school
3 secondary school 3 high school
4 college/university 4 college/university

B
1 attend   7 university
2 private school   8 graduate
3 terms   9 degree
4 pupils   10 public schools
5 GCSE   11 grades
6 A level   12 semesters

Health 健康 [S16–17]

1 How are you? 你好吗?

A How are you?
How are you feeling?
How do you feel?

B ☺   😐   🙁
Very well,   I'm not too   I'm sick.
thank you.   bad, thanks. I feel awful.
I feel great. I'm ok.   I'm not very well.
I'm fine.   I'm ill.

2 What's the matter? 你怎么了?

B
1 headache   3 earache
2 backache   4 stomach ache

3 Going to the doctor's 看医生

1 make an appointment
2 symptoms
3 examine
4 temperature
5 write a prescription
6 medicine
7 get better

Writing letters and emails
写信和写电邮 [S18–19]

3 Formal beginnings and endings
正式的开头和结尾

A
✓ Dear Sir   ✓ Yours faithfully
✓ Dear Madam   ✓ Yours sincerely
✓ Dear Sir or Madam ✗ Your faithful
✗ Dear Miss   ✗ Yours hopefully
✓ Dear Ms Jackson   ✓ Yours truly

B   I   Lots of love, Vicky
     F   Yours faithfully, Victoria Dawson

     F   Dear Mr Khan
     I   Dear Ali

     F   I enclose a cheque for …
     I   Here's some money for …

     I   I'm writing to you …
     F   I am writing to you …

     I   Could you …?
     F   I would be grateful if you could …

     I   Write back soon!
     F   I look forward to hearing from you.

4   Emails 电邮

   1   Hi Carlos   4   Must go
   2   to hear from you   5   keep in touch
   3   what's more   6   Bye for now

Filling in forms 填写表格 [S20]

1   Different types of form 不同的表格

A   1 C   2 A   3 B

B   1   application
     2   order
     3   membership

2   Understanding forms 理解表格的内容
     1   last name, initials
     2   nationality
     3   in capitals
     4   password
     5   tick
     6   sign, signature

3   Filling in a form 填写表格

Language Exchange Application
(example answer 范例)

First name   *Sara*   Last name   *Esposito*

Nationality   *Mexican*   Age   *19*

Daytime telephone number   *80610 415353*

Email address   *sesposito5@newmail.com*

What is your first language?   *Spanish*

How long have you been learning English?
5 years

What are your reasons for learning English?
(Write in 10–20 words.)
I would like to visit the UK. I like watching
English and American films.

What area of English would you most like
to practise? Please tick the one(s) that are
important for you.

✓ speaking   listening   ✓ reading
   grammar   writing   pronunciation

Signature   *SMEsposito*

Date   *8th March, 2009*

图书在版编目(CIP)数据

牛津初阶英汉双解词典/(英)沃特斯(Waters, A.),
(英)布尔(Bull, V.)著;高永伟译.—3版.—北京:商务
印书馆,2011 (2013.3 重印)
ISBN 978-7-100-07582-4

Ⅰ.①牛... Ⅱ.①沃...②布...③高... Ⅲ.①英语—
双解词典 ②双解词典—英、汉 Ⅳ.①H316

中国版本图书馆 CIP 数据核字(2010)第 250235 号

NIÚJĪN CHŪJIĒ YĪNGHÀN SHUĀNGJIĔ CÍDIĂN
牛津初阶英汉双解词典(第 3 版)

出版:商务印书馆
(北京王府井大街 36 号 邮政编码 100710)
牛津大学出版社(中国)有限公司
(香港英皇道 979 号太古坊和域大厦东翼十八楼)
国内总发行:商务印书馆
国外以及香港、澳门、台湾地区总发行:
牛津大学出版社(中国)有限公司
印刷:北京中科印刷有限公司
ISBN 978-7-100-07582-4

1999 年 6 月第 1 版　　　　开本 880×1230　1/32
2011 年 7 月第 2 版　　　　印张 23¼
2013 年 3 月北京第 42 次印刷　印数 150 000 册
定价:45.00 元